Multinational Pharmaceutical Companies

Principles and Practices

Second Edition

OTHER BOOKS BY BERT SPILKER

Guide to Clinical Studies and Developing Protocols
  (Raven Press, 1984)

Guide to Clinical Interpretation of Data
  (Raven Press, 1986)

Guide to Planning and Managing Multiple Clinical Studies
  (Raven Press, 1987)

Multinational Drug Companies: Issues in Drug Discovery and Development*
  (Raven Press, 1989)

Inside the Drug Industry
  (with Pedro Cuatrecasas, Prous Science Publishers, 1990)

Quality of Life Assessments in Clinical Trials
  (Edited, Raven Press, 1990)

Presentation of Clinical Data
  (with John Schoenfelder, Raven Press, 1990)

Patient Compliance in Medical Practice and Clinical Trials
  (Edited with Joyce Cramer, Raven Press, 1991)

Data Collection Forms in Clinical Trials
  (with John Schoenfelder, Raven Press, 1991)

Guide to Clinical Trials
  (Raven Press, 1991)

Patient Recruitment in Clinical Trials
  (with Joyce A. Cramer, Raven Press, 1992)

*The first edition of this book

Multinational Pharmaceutical Companies

Principles and Practices

Second Edition

Bert Spilker, Ph.D., M.D.

Executive Director
Orphan Medical
Minnetonka, Minnesota

Adjunct Professor of Pharmacology, Adjunct Professor of Medicine and
*   Clinical Professor of Pharmacy*
University of North Carolina Schools of Medicine and Pharmacy
Chapel Hill, North Carolina

Clinical Professor of Pharmacy Practice
University of Minnesota Medical School
Minneapolis, Minnesota

Raven Press 🔖 *New York*

Raven Press, Ltd., 1185 Avenue of the Americas, New York, New York 10036

Made in the United States of America

Library of Congress Cataloging-in-Publication Data

Spilker, Bert.
  Multinational pharmaceutical companies : principles and practices/
Bert Spilker.—2nd ed.
    p.   cm.
  Rev. ed. of: Multinational drug companies. © 1989
  Includes bibliographical references and index.
  ISBN 0-7817-0100-7
    1. Pharmaceutical industry.   2. Pharmaceutical industry—Technological
  innovations.   3. Drugs—Research—Management.   4. International business
  enterprises.   I. Spilker, Bert.
    Multinational Drug Companies.   II. Title.
    HD9665.5.S68   1994
    338.8' 8716151—dc20

                                                                    94-5876
                                                                    CIP

9 8 7 6 5 4 3 2 1

*To everyone in the pharmaceutical industry
who helps discover, develop, produce, and market
new medicines of medical value.*

Contents

List of Figures xi

List of Tables xxi

Terminology xxix

Foreword xxxi

Preface to the First Edition xxxiii

Preface xxxv

Acknowledgments for the First Edition xxxvii

Acknowledgments xxxix

About the Author xli

1 Introduction 1

Section I: Overview of a Pharmaceutical Company and the Industry

2 Pharmaceutical Industry: Definitions 7

3 The Big Picture 15

4 Standards 35

5 Mergers, Joint Ventures, and Alliances 47

6 Pharmacopolitics 59

7 Institutional Memory 69

8 Keys for Pharmaceutical Success 73

Section II: Corporate Organization and Management Issues

9 Models of International Operations 85

10 Organization at the Corporate Level 95

11 Corporate Management 107

12 Enhancing Communication 127

13 Personnel Issues 139

14 Golden Rules of Staffing 149

15 Conflicts of Interest 153

16 Crisis Management 167

17 Differences Between Pharmaceutical Companies 173

18 Future Environments for Medicine Discovery and Development 187

Section III: Medicine Discovery and Development

19 Overview of Factors Affecting Medicine Discovery 199

20 The Medicine Discovery Process 207

21 Golden Rules of Medicine Discovery 235

22 The Medicine Development Process 243

23 Golden Rules of Medicine Development 251

24 Biotechnology 257

25 Extrapolating Animal Safety Data to Humans 267

26 Evaluating and Interpreting Data 273

27 Stimulating Innovation and Increasing Efficiency 283

28 The Future of Medicine Discovery 299

Section IV: Research and Development Organization and Management Issues

29 Organizing Research and Development 307

30 Managing Research and Development 317

31 Personnel Issues in Medicine Discovery and Development 329

32 Balancing Line Function and Matrix Approaches 337

33 Choosing the Number of Medicines to Develop 351

34 Criteria for Developing Medicines 357

35 Evaluating a Portfolio of Investigational Medicine Projects 365

36 Productivity, Innovation, and Project Success 401

Section V: The Medical-Marketing Interface

37 Corporate Issues Regarding the Medical-Marketing Interface 421

38 Organizational and Staffing Issues Regarding the Medical-Marketing Interface 429

39 Medical and Marketing Needs, Wants, Possibilities, and Problems in Developing

    New Medicines 439

40 Joint Medical and Marketing Activities 447

Section VI: Technical and Functional Issues and Activities

41 Information Technology 461

42 Providing Product Information 475

43 Data Management and Statistics 485

44 Toxicology Issues 493

45 Clinical Trials 499

46 Issues of Technical Development 521

47 Marketing Issues 539

48 Licensing Issues 567

49 Regulatory Affairs 585

50 Production Issues 595

51 Patent Issues 613

52 Legal Activities and Issues 623

53 Financial Issues 637

Section VII: Major Corporate Issues and Challenges

54 Animal Testing and Animal Welfare 657

55 Patient Package Inserts 665

56 Patent Expiration 673

57 Switching Prescription Medicines to Over-the-Counter Status 679

58 Interaction with Legislators and the Public 687

59 Costs and Pricing 697

60 International Development 711

Section VIII: External Interactions and Relationships

61 Interactions and Relationships with Academic Institutions 721

62 Technology Transfer from Academia 731

63 Interactions and Relationships with Government Agencies 735

64 Interactions and Relationships between Pharmaceutical Companies: Competition

and Collaboration 747

65 Interactions and Relationships with Trade Associations 753

66 Interactions and Relationships with Health Professionals 757

67 Interactions and Relationships with Patients and the Public 761

68 Interactions and Relationships with the Media 769

Selected Books About Medicine Development or of Particular Interest to the

Pharmaceutical Industry 775

References 779

First Author Index 783

Subject Index 785

List of Figures

FIG. 2.1. Schematic illustration of groups that are progressively further from the core pharmaceutical companies. 10

FIG. 2.2. Schematic illustration of types of medicines and chemicals that are progressively further from those that prevent disease. 12

FIG. 2.3. Types of medicines, devices, and other modalities used in human health care. 13

FIG. 3.1. How the perception of a medical innovation changes over time. 19

FIG. 3.2. Major stages of medicine discovery, development, and marketing. 21

FIG. 3.3. Selected metaphors of medicine discovery and development. 22

FIG. 3.4. Pipeline concept of medicine development. 23

FIG. 3.5. Selected types of subpipelines in medicine development. 24

FIG. 3.6. "Seat-of-the-pants" medicine development. 28

FIG. 3.7. Safety and efficacy standards viewed as a pair of high jumps for the medicine to exceed. 29

FIG. 3.8. Various means for a medicine to improve on the standards of previous therapy. 30

FIG. 3.9. Examples of medicines where there is great room for improvement in both safety and efficacy. 31

FIG. 4.1. The regulatory cascade and selected examples. 36

FIG. 4.2. Steps involved in the implementation of laws, regulations, and guidelines, and the assessment of compliance. 37

FIG. 4.3. Schematic presentation of metaphors of several types of standards and other terms (e.g., regulations, guidelines, and standard operating procedures) using the high jump. 38

FIG. 4.4. Relationship between principles and the achievement of company goals and objectives. 39

FIG. 4.5. Relationship between different types of standards. 40

FIG. 4.6. Major factors that influence a company to modify its standard operating procedures (SOPs). 43

FIG. 5.1. Schematics showing two companies that form a third company and assign it specific products to market. 49

FIG. 5.2. Several potential types of partners for pharmaceutical company to form an alliance with. 55

xi

FIG. 6.1. Examples of external group interactions (i.e., people and groups outside the double-line circle) between a pharmaceutical company and its external world. 61

FIG. 6.2. The primary driving forces behind many pharmaceutical companies for the decades from 1900 to the present, plus a prediction of the forces that will influence and drive companies in the 21st century. 64

FIG. 8.1. An overall calendar of all potential product launches scheduled by quarter. 77

FIG. 8.2. A schedule of monthly project status prepared on each project. 79

FIG. 8.3. A general schedule of meetings to be held each year. 80

FIG. 9.1. Schematic of the distinction between organizational structure and international operations. 86

FIG. 9.2. Spectrum of the five models that are described in the text. 88

FIG. 9.3. Models of a central headquarters and subsidiaries. 90

FIG. 9.4. Schematic illustrating uses of the terms national, international, global, worldwide, and confederation. 93

FIG. 10.1. Functional model of an organization. 97

FIG. 10.2. Product-oriented model of an organization. 97

FIG. 10.3. Matrix model of an organization. 98

FIG. 10.4. Business- and function-oriented model of an organization. 99

FIG. 10.5. Business- and matrix-oriented model of an organization. 100

FIG. 10.6. Patterns of corporate development. 101

FIG. 10.7. Organizational processes that support development patterns in FIG. 10.6. 102

FIG. 11.1. A scale to measure leadership practices. 110

FIG. 11.2. Characteristics of leaders and managers. 113

FIG. 11.3. A leader's relationship to his or her group. 114

FIG. 11.4. Steps that are often involved in making major corporate changes. 121

FIG. 11.5. A strategic planning model. 123

FIG. 11.6. Selected businesses related to ethical pharmaceuticals. 124

FIG. 12.1. Two pyramids that represent the hierarchical medical and marketing organization of a company at its headquarters or at a major subsidiary. 130

FIG. 12.2. Four models illustrating basic communications problems. 130

FIG. 12.3. Some of the many pyramids that exist in multinational pharmaceutical companies. 131

FIG. 12.4. The communication cross. 133

FIG. 12.5. Four examples of communication problems. 134

FIG. 12.6. Different types of monologues and dialogues. 135

FIG. 12.7. The many rays of communication indicating representative groups and also methods of communication. 136

FIG. 12.8. The communication alphabet. 137

FIG. 15.1. Spectra that illustrate the range of conflict of interest. 154

FIG. 15.2. Selected institutions, groups, or individuals that may be involved in conflict-of-interest issues related to medicines. 155

FIG. 15.3. Possible outcomes or responses of a person who has an actual conflict of interest. 157

FIG. 15.4. Four models of various types of influences on a person and how these influences may modify one's behavior. 158

FIG. 15.5. Models of how someone inside the pharmaceutical industry may be indirectly (models I, II, IV) or directly and indirectly (model III) influenced by conflict of interest. 159

FIG. 15.6. Illustrating possible relationships of conflict of interest, scientific misconduct, and fraud. 161

FIG. 15.7. Four spectra that illustrate the nature and importance of the work done by outside scientists for a pharmaceutical company. 162

FIG. 15.8. Conflict of interest statement prepared by the National Institute of Drug Abuse for reviewers of concept proposals. 163

FIG. 16.1. The ripple effect of a crisis on groups and individuals affected differently over time. 171

FIG. 17.1. Characterizing the marketing position of a specific company. 175

FIG. 17.2. Susceptibility of various pharmaceutical companies to generic substitution. 176

FIG. 17.3. Susceptibility of a particular company to generic substitution over a period of years. 176

FIG. 17.4. Visual models of medicine development illustrating different types of plans or approaches followed. 177

FIG. 17.5. Illustration of the three types of target dates that may be established for any specific activity 179

FIG. 17.6. Illustration of a fat versus lean development plan with aspects of each shown. 183

FIG. 17.7. Illustration of fat versus lean plans for a clinical trial in terms of the amount of data collected. 184

FIG. 19.1. Matrix of factors affecting innovation based on types of organization, organizational levels, and types of influence or pressure. 200

FIG. 19.2. Positive factors enhancing a scientists' innovation and promoting the discovery of new medicines. 203

FIG. 19.3. Spectrum of methods used to discover new medicines. 204

FIG. 19.4. Discovering new biomedical activities on compounds or medicines through serendipity or intentional testing. 204

FIG. 20.1. Major processes used to discover a new chemical lead. 208

FIG. 20.2. Major sources of a new medicine. 209

FIG. 20.3. Four levels considered in conducting research seeking to discover a new medicine. 213

FIG. 20.4. Selected therapeutic opportunities in cardiology for new medicine development. 214

FIG. 20.5. The competition for resources in discovery activities. 216

FIG. 20.6. Metabolic degradation of diazepam leads to nordiazepam, which in turn is converted to oxazepam, each of which is a useful medicine. 221

FIG. 20.7. Successful molecular manipulations leading to useful medicines. 222

FIG. 20.8. Selected chemical groups that could be placed on a chemical backbone. 223

FIG. 20.9. Types of alterations in biological activity that may be observed in a series of closely related compounds with a single chemical modification. 224

FIG. 20.10. Types of alterations in biological activity observed in a series of compounds with two chemical modifications. 225

FIG. 20.11. Scope of biological activity in compounds with modified structures. 226

FIG. 20.12. Progressive improvements in histamine type-2 receptor antagonists. 227

FIG. 20.13. Histamine receptor type-2 antagonists developed after cimetidine, which were able to be patented. 228

FIG. 20.14. Progressive improvements in the early development of beta-receptor antagonists. 229

FIG. 20.15. Spectrum of research activities in a pharmaceutical company ranging from purely targeted to purely exploratory. 230

FIG. 20.16. Hypothetical formats for organizing multiple animal models and tests 232

FIG. 20.17 Example of a series of screens used to evaluate compounds for inotropic activity 233

FIG. 21.1. Four of the major factors that influence and motivate scientists. 238

FIG. 22.1. Stages of medicine discovery and development. 244

FIG. 23.1. The quantity of effort spent on planning compared with that spent on conducting activities. 252

FIG. 23.2. The consequences of good or poor quality of effort spent on planning activities. 253

FIG. 24.1. Schematic illustration of the process of recombinant DNA engineering. 260

FIG. 24.2. A few of the complexities and options that sometimes arise in the manufacture of biotechnology products. 265

FIG. 26.1. Hierarchies (i.e., different levels) in the therapeutic process. 275

FIG. 26.2. Hierarchies in the actions of cardiac glycosides. 276

FIG. 27.1. Outputs of innovation and processes followed to improve on a chemical's activity. 284

FIG. 27.2. Examples of negative tangents in a medicine's development. 288

FIG. 27.3. Medicines in search of a disease. 289

FIG. 28.1. Interactions of various influences and factors that create the megatrends which will influence/affect our future world. 301

FIG. 29.1. Traditional discipline-oriented organization of research and development activities in a pharmaceutical company. 309

FIG. 29.2. Therapeutically based organization of research and development activities in a pharmaceutical company. 310

FIG. 29.3. Matrix (horizontal) organization of medicine development project activities in a pharmaceutical company. 311

FIG. 29.4. Types and levels of support for medicine development activities. 312

FIG. 29.5. Organizational relationships and interactions between chemists and biologists in medicine discovery activities. 314

FIG. 30.1. Extrapolating management information and beliefs through various levels of research and development (R&D). 318

FIG. 30.2. Different approaches to assigning staff to projects. 323

FIG. 30.3. Assigning staff to projects, showing that a specific person may be assigned to one or more projects. 324

FIG. 30.4. Assigning tasks to specific staff and indicating their degree and nature of involvement with the task. 324

FIG. 30.5. Evaluating how research and development resources are being applied to areas of company strengths and weaknesses. 326

FIG. 30.6. Evaluating how research and development resources are being moved to areas of particular interest. 327

FIG. 31.1. Interactions among clinicians and statisticians at different sites of a single company. 333

FIG. 31.2. Support and services required when a MD joins the staff of a pharmaceutical company. 334

FIG. 32.1. Elements in the project-driven matrix management philosophy. 338

FIG. 32.2. Leadership of a project team as it changes from a preclinical scientist to clinical scientist and to a marketer. 340

FIG. 32.3. Illustrating the different orientation of a line manager and project manager for conducting work on an individual project. 341

FIG. 32.4. A possible basis for establishing project coordinators within selected functions or disciplines to interact with the central project coordination function. 346

FIG. 32.5. A model for the interaction between the central project coordination staff and technical development coordinators. 347

FIG. 32.6. A model for the interaction between the central project coordination staff and technical development coordinators. 348

FIG. 34.1. General process of establishing, monitoring, and reviewing criteria and dates (i.e., deadlines) for project milestones. 362

FIG. 35.1. Illustrates the four levels of viewing projects in a portfolio analysis and the key issues associated with each level. 367

FIG. 35.2. A. Number of new projects initiated per year. B. Head count currently applied to a project and its commercial attractiveness. 372

FIG. 35.3. Presentation of all projects in a portfolio over time with the outcome of each project shown. 373

FIG. 35.4. Cost of development (i.e., research and development) and commercial value of individual projects. 374

FIG. 35.5. "Thermometer" model used to illustrate the proportion of money already spent on a project. 375

FIG. 35.6. Comparison of staff allocated to a project and expected sales of that project. 376

FIG. 35.7. Average cost of work effort on a project. 377

FIG. 35.8. Illustration of total head count across all projects. 377

FIG. 35.9. Illustrating a portfolio of new medicines on the basis of risk. 378

FIG. 35.10. The probability of technical success versus the commercial value of individual projects. 379

FIG. 35.11. The probability of technical success versus the commercial value of individual projects. 380

FIG. 35.12. Illustrating a change in a project portfolio over a period of time (e.g., year). 380

FIG. 35.13. A comparison of the relative market share with relative company sales in several therapeutic areas. 381

FIG. 35.14. A presentation of expected patent life remaining for projects in the portfolio at various stages of development. 381

FIG. 35.15. A presentation of projects at different stages of development and what their strength is expected to be in the market. 382

FIG. 35.16. Illustrating a portfolio of new medicines on the basis of the technology's maturity. 382

FIG. 35.17. Illustrating the number of regulatory submissions made per year. 383

FIG. 35.18. Illustrating the time taken for a large number of projects (i.e., A to AA) to be approved after submission. 384

FIG. 35.19. Illustration of the number of IND submissions made per year for NCEs and other medicines. 385

FIG. 35.20. Presenting the time for filing an IND after project formation. 385

FIG. 35.21. The number of regulatory staff assigned to high-priority projects over the period between 1972 and 1985. 386

FIG. 35.22. Illustration of a series of projections and actual results of regulatory submissions made over a few years. 387

FIG. 35.23. Presentation of a series of projected dates for three separate activities and how those dates changed over time. 388

FIG. 35.24. Return on investment in a portfolio versus the probability of exceeding the return on investment. 388

FIG. 35.25. Percent of total sales and profits derived from new products in each of several years. 389

FIG. 35.26. Sales and profits of new medicines per year. 390

FIG. 35.27. Percent of a company's total sales and profits derived from new products. 391

FIG. 35.28. Research expenditures on medicine discovery activities required to generate a NCE project. 392

FIG. 35.29. Grid of market size versus level of medical need. 393

FIG. 35.30. Growth share matrix illustrating four basic types of medicines or businesses. 393

FIG. 35.31. Product market evolution matrix. 394

FIG. 35.32. General Electric's Nine-Cell Planning grid of business strength versus industry (product market) attractiveness. 394

FIG. 35.33. Company position versus industry attractiveness figure. 395

FIG. 36.1. Tracking the time required for regulatory review and approval of new medicines. 406

FIG. 36.2. Illustration of the cumulative phase success rate for compounds reaching a milestone and individual phase success rate for compounds entering each specific phase of development. 412

FIG. 36.3. Example of determining the success of projects based on the individual phase success rate. 414

FIG. 36.4. Time taken for 27 companies to file specific NDAs from the time of patent filing. 415

FIG. 36.5. Illustration of a large project with many regulatory submissions and approvals shown on a time versus cumulative spend on the project. 415

FIG. 36.6. Cumulative sales of a single product over time with superimposed time of introduction of various dosage forms and dosage strengths of that product. 416

FIG. 37.1. Illustration of interrelationships between medical and marketing functions in terms of internal and external company groups that interact with each other. 422

FIG. 37.2. Schematic to show the predominant forces influencing the pharmaceutical industry and its decision making during the 20th century. 424

FIG. 37.3. Four models of medical-marketing relationships. 424

FIG. 38.1. Organizational chart for the marketing function based on line management structure and focusing on therapeutic area products. 430

FIG. 38.2. Organizational chart for the marketing function based on a matrix management structure of separate business units. 431

FIG. 38.3. Organizational chart for the marketing function based on a line management structure focusing on the customer's facilities, type of customer (i.e., national accounts) and type of product (i.e., hospital products or consumer products). 432

FIG. 38.4. Organizational chart for the marketing function based on a matrix management structure. 432

FIG. 38.5. Selected areas and activities at which medical and marketing staff interact on a formal and informal basis. 436

FIG. 39.1. A hypothetical comparison of project needs versus allocated resources in terms of both money and head count in medical and marketing departments. 442

FIG. 39.2. A comparison of medical and marketing training and orientation along three spectra. 445

FIG. 40.1. A method to illustrate marketing opportunity to develop a new medicine in terms of moral obligation versus the potential (or likelihood) of profit. 450

FIG. 40.2. One means of conceptualizing the medical-marketing profile using three dimensions to illustrate dosage form, indication, and the aspect of the profile. 453

FIG. 40.3. A method to illustrate the spectra of physician needs and the importance of different factors in choosing a medicine to use in their patients. 456

FIG. 40.4. Three examples of one-dimensional spectra shown as visual analog scales for pain. 457

FIG. 40.5. A hatched area superimposed on a one-dimensional spectrum to illustrate the segment of a market being targeted with a new medicine. 457

FIG. 40.6. Two examples of two-dimensional spectra to illustrate different characteristics. 457

FIG. 41.1. Prototype pattern of how information usually flows from the time it is obtained. 463

FIG. 41.2. The relative amount of information transfer is increasingly occurring between people and machines (panel B) and also between machines (panel C). 464

FIG. 41.3. Showing the cyclical nature of computer systems. 466

FIG. 41.4. Example of how electronic publishing facilitates submission of documents to regulatory authorities by using a computer to help in regulatory dossier preparation. 467

FIG. 41.5. Creation of information and data, plus its progressive enhancement and use by various groups. 468

FIG. 41.6. Showing that information underlies essential questions and issues decided in a medicine's discovery, development, and marketing. 469

FIG. 41.7. Three models by which documents arrive at a central repository or archive. 471

FIG. 42.1. Flow of questions from health professionals into a pharmaceutical company and routing to various departments for a response. 477

FIG. 42.2. Processing a question by a company's external information department when additional help from the company's staff is needed. 478

FIG. 42.3. Possible groups that interact with a company's external information department. 479

FIG. 42.4. Processing a question by a company's external information department when the answer can be determined within the department. 480

FIG. 42.5. Illustration of the message side of a folded postcard sent to health professionals by the Upjohn Co. to request an evaluation of their medical and drug information service. 483

FIG. 45.1. Levels and sublevels of clinical trials. 501

FIG. 45.2. Selected approaches to clinical medicine development. 504

FIG. 45.3. Planning and tracking the indications and dosage forms studied. 506

FIG. 45.4. Patient participation in clinical trials. 507

FIG. 45.5. "Lasagna's Law." 508

FIG. 45.6. Identifying the adverse reaction. 510

FIG. 45.7. Hypothetical types of reporting patterns of adverse reactions over time. 514

FIG. 46.1. Selected types of apparatus used to evaluate medicine dissolution. 529

FIG. 47.1. Three models of how medical groups can be organized to conduct marketing studies. 546

FIG. 47.2. Illustration of the concept of potency where Medicine A is ten times as potent as Medicine B. 557

FIG. 47.3. Interactions of physicians, pharmacists, patients, and pharmaceutical companies. 559

FIG. 47.4. A patient's steps in obtaining and following medical treatment with medicines. 560

FIG. 47.5. Market share for seven medicines over a period of years illustrating a stable total market size. 562

FIG. 47.6. Market share for antiarthritic medicines over 1976 to 1981, illustrating an expanding market. 563

FIG. 48.1. The upper diagram describes a complex licensing situation that was successfully solved using the approach in the lower panel. 581

FIG. 49.1. Two schematics of the hierarchies within the U.S. Food and Drug Administration and a pharmaceutical company. 590

FIG. 49.2. Regulatory affairs organizational chart for a group organized primarily by functional discipline. 592

FIG. 49.3. Regulatory affairs organizational chart for a group organized primarily by therapeutic area. 592

FIG. 50.1. Procedures of quality assurance and quality control. 601

FIG. 51.1. Five stages of a patent. 614

FIG. 51.2. Series of major events in the patenting of a new compound. 615

FIG. 51.3. Illustration of how differences between first-to-invent and first-to-file patent systems may lead to different results. 616

FIG. 53.1. Financial projection for a company over a number of years with different assumptions shown in the figure. 639

FIG. 53.2. Illustrating the staff assigned to a select group of projects (i.e., first quartile) for a specific period. 640

FIG. 53.3. Illustrating the hierarchical levels in a company at which actual budgets exists, from the overall company to individual sections within a department. 643

FIG. 53.4. Research and development expenditures by function. 646

FIG. 53.5. Selected methods of illustrating overall expenditures within research and development (*R&D*). 648

FIG. 53.6. Selected methods of illustrating expenditures within research and development (*R&D*) according to function. 649

FIG. 53.7. Illustrating expenditures in various therapeutic areas over a period of years. 651

FIG. 53.8. Graphing projected versus actual expenditures over a period of time (e.g., days, weeks, months, years). 652

FIG. 54.1. Three models of conceptualizing the animal world, based on the qualitative distinctions one makes between different species or groups of species. 658

FIG. 58.1. Different approaches to viewing prices of medicines. 690

FIG. 58.2. A realistic model to view factors leading to higher prices and the balance achieved by savings in the health care system. 694

FIG. 58.3. An indirect model of how pharmaceutical companies can attempt to influence patients and the public about the industry's view concerning prices. 695

FIG. 59.1. Diagnostic representation of a spectrum of European government policies on pricing pharmaceuticals. 704

FIG. 60.1. Two models for marketing groups to consider in obtaining the data they need to market their medicines. 712

FIG. 60.2. Two models of medicine discovery and development that provide data needed by marketing. 713

FIG. 60.3. Models of project teams that may be used for international medicine development. 715

FIG. 61.1. Levels within the pharmaceutical industry and academia that may directly interact. 723

FIG. 61.2. Selected areas where indirect interactions occur between academia and the pharmaceutical industry. 724

FIG. 63.1. Flow of regulatory dossiers between countries. 738

List of Tables

TABLE 1.1. Values for selected medical and scientific discoveries or developments: examples of marked differences in values 2

TABLE 1.2. Selected differences in interpretation of phrases or gestures between an American and English company 4

TABLE 2.1. Types of companies and groups that directly provide professional services to pharmaceutical companies 9

TABLE 2.2. Types of companies and groups that indirectly provide services to pharmaceutical companies 9

TABLE 3.1. Typical periods of time required to develop new medicines 26

TABLE 3.2. Resources available for use by a company 32

TABLE 3.3. General comparison of multinational pharmaceutical companies in the 1950s and 1960s versus the 1990s 32

TABLE 3.4. Impact of various factors on the overall speed and quality of a medicine's development 33

TABLE 4.1. Operational definitions of various terms 37

TABLE 4.2. Types of standards relating to various aspects of the pharmaceutical industry 38

TABLE 5.1. Selected reasons for pharmaceutical companies to enter a joint venture or alliance 50

TABLE 5.2. Factors to consider before entering a joint venture or alliance 50

TABLE 5.3. Factors to evaluate for each partner and the proposed new entity 51

TABLE 6.1. External groups that interact with pharmaceutical companies 60

TABLE 6.2. Internal groups that interact with pharmaceutical companies 60

TABLE 6.3. Representative pharmacopolitical issues 63

TABLE 8.1. To encourage a sense of urgency within the company 78

TABLE 10.1. Selected factors that tend to increase pharmaceutical company growth 104

TABLE 10.2. Selected factors that tend to diminish pharmaceutical company growth 105

TABLE 11.1. Some major functions of management 116

TABLE 12.1. Selected signs of subtle and mild problems in communication 133

TABLE 12.2. Selected signs of moderate and severe problems in communication 133

TABLE 12.3. Examples of marked communication problems within a company 133

TABLE 12.4.   Methods of rapid communication 137

TABLE 13.1.   Selected examples of internally taught professional development courses that could be offered to company staff 143

TABLE 13.2.   Selected characteristics of each training course that should be given to potential enrollees prior to requiring them to register 144

TABLE 13.3.   Characteristics of high scientific performers 144

TABLE 13.4.   Factors influencing motivation of employees 145

TABLE 13.5.   Possible reasons for low employee productivity 145

TABLE 14.1.   Considerations in assessing the number of staff required for a general area and for specific projects 150

TABLE 15.1.   Selected examples of financial relationships between an individual outside a company and the company itself that may create a conflict of interest 156

TABLE 16.1.   Selected product crises classified by cause 168

TABLE 16.2.   Selected corporate crises classified by cause 168

TABLE 16.3.   Specific examples of product crises 168

TABLE 16.4   External groups that are involved or interested in many pharmaceutical company crises 169

TABLE 17.1.   Selected differences in management philosophy between companies or between individuals within companies 174

TABLE 17.2.   Selected differences in medicine development philosophy between companies or between individuals within companies 175

TABLE 17.3.   Types of important project milestones 179

TABLE 20.1.   Selected medicines that are prepared from natural plants 210

TABLE 20.2.   Selected examples of clinical serendipity 211

TABLE 20.3.   Basic combinations of approaches to the three levels of therapeutic areas 213

TABLE 20.4.   Uses of extrapolating in vivo pharmacological data from animals 220

TABLE 22.1.   Research and development criteria to evaluate a new compound for potential development as a medicine 245

TABLE 22.2.   Activities performed on marketed medicines in research departments 247

TABLE 22.3.   Activities performed on marketed medicines in medical departments 248

TABLE 22.4.   Activities performed on marketed medicines in technical development and regulatory affairs departments 249

TABLE 24.1.   Selected products of biotechnology 258

TABLE 24.2.   Three general categories of biotechnology-derived medicines 258

TABLE 24.3.   Biotechnology company data 259

TABLE 24.4.   Selected techniques of biotechnology 261

TABLE 24.5.   Selected areas and goals for biotechnology research and medicine development: present and future 262

TABLE 24.6.   Comparison of typical pharmaceutical and biotechnology companies 264

TABLE 25.1. Types of extrapolations between species 268

TABLE 25.2. Selected reasons for false-positive results in toxicology 269

TABLE 25.3. Selected reasons for false-negative responses in toxicology studies 270

TABLE 25.4. Major medicine-induced adverse reactions since 1961 270

TABLE 26.1. Characteristics of an ideal clinical method for evaluating topical antipruritics 281

TABLE 26.2. Characteristics of an ideal antiepileptic medicine for treating partial seizures 282

TABLE 27.1. Standard approach used by many consultants prior to receiving a contract 286

TABLE 27.2. Selected myths of innovation 290

TABLE 27.3. Advantages in waiting until a generally complete profile is obtained about a
chemical series before a lead compound is chosen for testing in humans, plus counterarguments 296

TABLE 27.4 Advantages in taking early chemical leads rapidly into humans for testing, plus
counterarguments 296

TABLE 28.1. New medicines and techniques predicted to be "right around the corner" for over
25 years that have not yet achieved their predicted degree of success 299

TABLE 28.2. Trends in the medical field that are reasonably likely to occur in the distant
future (or sooner) 300

TABLE 28.3. Major influences to consider when predicting the future 300

TABLE 28.4. Steps to follow after distant future megatrends are identified 302

TABLE 30.1. Basic issues frequently considered in the management of research and development 319

TABLE 32.1. Sample project meeting agenda 344

TABLE 34.1. Relationship of criteria, characteristics, and standards 358

TABLE 34.2. Advantages and disadvantages of using the ideal set of criteria for medicine
discovery 359

TABLE 34.3. Advantages and disadvantages of using the realistic set of criteria for medicine
discovery 359

TABLE 34.4. Selected scientific/medical characteristics that could be used to establish
specific standards 361

TABLE 34.5. Examples of ideal, realistic, and minimally acceptable criteria for a hypothetical
antiepileptic medicine during its clinical development 363

TABLE 35.1. Possible data to determine for projects in a portfolio 375

TABLE 35.2. Selected questions to consider in interpreting a portfolio analysis 395

TABLE 35.3. Aspects to identify for each project relating to its priority 397

TABLE 36.1. Parameters for measuring productivity of research and development activities 405

TABLE 36.2. Points designed to increase productivity and quality 410

TABLE 36.3. Considerations of how to improve productivity in pharmaceutical research and
development 411

TABLE 36.4. Analyses used to calculate success rates of compounds developed as medicines 412

TABLE 36.5. Calculating the success rates for compounds and medicines shown in Fig. 36.2 413

TABLE 38.1. Marketing services that are often provided within a marketing division 433

TABLE 39.1. Selected examples of standards used to define minimally acceptable or desirable criteria for a medicine 440

TABLE 39.2. Headings to consider for tables presenting marketing priorities 443

TABLE 39.3. Marketing data required by medical groups 443

TABLE 39.4. Selected headings for a form to track the progress of projects 443

TABLE 39.5. Selected headings to use for a table summarizing medical trials for a marketing group(s) 444

TABLE 40.1. Marketing criteria to consider for a new project 452

TABLE 40.2. Relative importance of marketing input in research and development activities 454

TABLE 41.1. Issues to address in developing a data base management system 465

TABLE 41.2. Issues in validating computer systems 466

TABLE 42.1. Standard goals of medicine information groups 475

TABLE 42.2. Types of functions that may be assigned to a product information group 476

TABLE 42.3. Representative areas in which questions are asked by health professionals 476

TABLE 42.4. Categories of information provided to health professionals by a company 481

TABLE 42.5. Formats of information provided 481

TABLE 42.6. Table heading for a form to evaluate the progress of the information staff in responding to questions from health professionals outside the company 482

TABLE 42.7. Representative complaints from outside health professionals about pharmaceutical company information departments 482

TABLE 42.8. Characteristics of a state-of-the-art medicine information group 482

TABLE 43.1. Selected medicine development areas that may be automated 486

TABLE 43.2. Selected clinical areas of medicine development that may be automated 487

TABLE 43.3. Primary factors used to select systems and equipment to store information 487

TABLE 45.1. Selected means to increase the rate of clinical medicine development 505

TABLE 45.2. Considerations for a formulary committee to weigh in evaluating a new medicine 518

TABLE 46.1. Activities of technical development departments during the medicine discovery period 522

TABLE 46.2. Selected roles of technical development departments during Phases I to III 522

TABLE 46.3. Activities of technical development departments after a medicine is marketed 523

TABLE 46.4. Typical scale factors for chemical syntheses 523

TABLE 46.5. Typical quantities of a compound required by various groups for conducting development activities 524

TABLE 46.6. Requirements of an environmental assessment in the United States 525

TABLE 46.7. Activities conducted by a pharmaceutical development department 526

TABLE 46.8. Selected issues in the development of a medicine formulation 530

TABLE 46.9. Selected uses of laboratory robotics 531

TABLE 46.10. Selected responsibilities of a person (or group) who plans and coordinates activities among technical development departments 531

TABLE 46.11. Selected functions of the analytical development department 533

TABLE 47.1. Assessment of new products by marketing 540

TABLE 47.2. General types of marketing-related activities in the pharmaceutical industry 541

TABLE 47.3. Reasons for termination of medicine projects by Hoechst-Roussel Pharmaceuticals Inc. between 1972 and 1978 541

TABLE 47.4. Reasons for termination of new chemical entities under development by seven United Kingdom-owned companies between 1964 and 1980 541

TABLE 47.5. Top medicines in sales of leading manufacturing companies in the United States in 1985 542

TABLE 47.6. Number of medicines constituting 50 percent of a company's sales 545

TABLE 47.7. Selected methods used to assess customer needs and satisfaction 550

TABLE 47.8. Potential methods to select trademarks 553

TABLE 47.9 Costs of three medicines of the same type (e.g., beta receptor antagonists) expressed in three ways 554

TABLE 47.10. Profile of traditional and professional types of over-the-counter medicines 558

TABLE 47.11. Factors that may lead to an inaccurate marketing forecast 558

TABLE 47.12. Possible reasons used to explain poor sales performance 564

TABLE 48.1. Prototype table of contents for a licensing-out proposal 568

TABLE 48.2. Standard steps in processing a typical licensing opportunity 574

TABLE 48.3. Representative types of information to track on licensing opportunities 574

TABLE 48.4. Competitive analysis table that compares medicines that work by different mechanisms to treat a single disease 575

TABLE 48.5. Factors for a company that is licensing-in a medicine to consider in evaluating opportunities 576

TABLE 48.6. Range of positions on major licensing issues 578

TABLE 48.7. Selected points to settle during negotiations and to clarify in contracts 579

TABLE 48.8. Considerations in evaluating the desirability of manufacturing a licensed-in medicine 580

TABLE 48.9. General types of agreements made 580

TABLE 48.10. Contents of a typical license agreement 580

TABLE 48.11. Examples of major types of product trades 581

TABLE 48.12. Topics to include in forms that are used to track compliance with agreements 582

TABLE 49.1. Selected functions of regulatory affairs professionals 586

TABLE 49.2. Selected steps in preparing documents for regulatory submission 586

TABLE 49.3. Selected topics that are discussed between a regulatory affairs department and regulatory authorities on an investigational medicine's development or dossier 587

TABLE 49.4. Selected topics that are discussed between a regulatory affairs department and regulatory authorities on marketed medicines 587

TABLE 49.5. Selected types of documents submitted to regulatory authorities 587

TABLE 50.1. Selected production activities to support various projects 596

TABLE 50.2. Production and other groups that are often on a production project team 597

TABLE 50.3. Major quality assurance functions on investigational medicines prior to marketing 600

TABLE 50.4. Measurement of tablet weight 604

TABLE 50.5. Selected production issues relating to a physical plant and its equipment 608

TABLE 50.6. Selected production issues relating to the processes conducted 608

TABLE 50.7. Selected production issues relating to people involved 608

TABLE 50.8. Selected production issues relating to products made 609

TABLE 50.9. Items to include in a synopsis of production status for individual medicines 609

TABLE 51.1. Contents of a patent application 615

TABLE 51.2. Types of data that are truly confidential 620

TABLE 52.1 Types of contracts and legal agreements 624

TABLE 53.1. Selected categories to use in comparing the financial status of pharmaceutical companies 638

TABLE 53.2. Research and development expenditures by function in West Germany and the United States 647

TABLE 53.3. Parameters evaluated for each product included in a financial analysis model 647

TABLE 54.1. Suggested contents of a protocol for experimenting on animals 660

TABLE 54.2. Principles of the humane use of animals 662

TABLE 54.3. Selected veterinary principles used in animal care 662

TABLE 54.4. Selected physical characteristics of animal housing facilities that must be considered in designing and regulating such facilities 662

TABLE 55.1. Selected issues and questions to consider in preparing patient package inserts 667

TABLE 55.2. Categories of professional labeling in the United States 668

TABLE 55.3. Selected categories of information that should be considered for inclusion in a patient package insert 669

TABLE 55.4. Selected categories for inclusion in a patient package insert 669

TABLE 55.5. Selected topics that could be discussed in a patient-oriented disease brochure 670

TABLE 55.6. Selected topics that could be discussed in a patient-oriented brochure about a specific medicine 670

TABLE 56.1. Approaches to extend the commercial life of a medicine whose patent is expiring 674

TABLE 57.1. Reasons to consider switching a medicine from prescription to over-the-counter status 680

TABLE 57.2. Safety issues to consider 684

TABLE 59.1. Costs associated with discovering, developing, and selling a medicine 698

TABLE 59.2. Properties of beta-blockers important in choosing an oral agent for an individual patient or in adjusting dosage following substitution 709

TABLE 59.3. Selected advantages of the marketed oral beta-blockers 709

TABLE 60.1. Selected causes of differences in technical regulations and general practices among countries 718

TABLE 61.1. Types of interactions between pharmaceutical companies and academic institutions 722

TABLE 61.2. Selected biomedical relationships between universities and pharmaceutical companies 722

TABLE 63.1. Approaches for a subsidiary that receives a New Drug Application submission from their headquarters 740

TABLE 65.1. Selected activities conducted by trade associations 754

TABLE 66.1. Selected roles of pharmacists who are external to a pharmaceutical company 758

Terminology

AIDS Acquired Immune Deficiency Syndrome.

FDA Food and Drug Administration. Regulatory agency in the United States that must approve new medicines for marketing. Oversees many postmarketing practices of the pharmaceutical industry.

GCP Good Clinical Practice. Unofficial term in the United States used to include proposed regulations governing conduct of sponsors and investigators during clinical trials. Also refers to approved United States regulations governing IRBs, INDs, and informed consents. Official term in many countries for regulations or guidelines governing the conduct of clinical trials.

GMP Good Manufacturing Practice. United States regulations governing quality assurance procedures in medicine manufacturing. Approved in 1963. Comparable standards exist in most developed countries.

HMO Health Maintenance Organization. A prepaid health group.

IND Investigational New Drug Application. FDA regulatory document allowing clinical trials to proceed on an investigational medicine or investigational use of an approved marketed medicine.

IRB Institutional Review Board. An ethics committee that must approve protocols for human studies at the institution where they are to be done.

NCE New Chemical Entity. A novel chemical compound that may be tested as a medicine.

NDA New Drug Application. An application to the FDA for approval of a new medicine in the United States.

OTC Over-the-counter. Medicines sold without prescription.

Phase I Initial safety trials on a new medicine, usually conducted in normal male volunteers. An attempt is made to establish the dose range tolerated by volunteers for single and for multiple doses. Phase I trials are sometimes conducted in severely ill patients (e.g., in the field of cancer) or in less ill patients when pharmacokinetic issues are addressed (e.g., metabolism of a new antiepileptic medicine in stable epileptic patients whose microsomal liver enzymes have been induced by other antiepileptic medicines). Pharmacokinetic trials are usually considered Phase I trials regardless of when they are conducted during a medicine's development.

Phase IIa Pilot clinical trials to evaluate efficacy (and safety) in selected populations of patients with the disease or condition to be treated, diagnosed, or prevented. Objectives may focus on dose-response, type of patient, frequency of dosing, or numerous other characteristics of safety and efficacy.

Phase IIb Well-controlled trials to evaluate efficacy (and safety) in patients with the disease or condition to be treated, diagnosed, or prevented. These clinical trials usually represent the most rigorous demonstration of a medicine's efficacy. Sometimes referred to as pivotal trials.

Phase IIIa Trials conducted after efficacy of the medicine is demonstrated, but prior to regulatory submission of a New Drug Application (NDA) or other dossier. These clinical trials are conducted in patient populations for which the medicine is eventually intended. Phase IIIa clinical trials generate additional data on both safety and efficacy in relatively large numbers of patients in both controlled and uncontrolled trials. Clinical trials are also conducted in special groups of patients (e.g., renal failure patients), or under special conditions dictated by the nature of the medicine and disease. These trials often provide much of the information needed for the package insert and labeling of the medicine.

Phase IIIb Clinical trials conducted after regulatory submission of an NDA or other dossier, but prior to the medicine's approval and launch. These trials may supplement earlier trials, complete earlier trials, or may be directed toward new types of trials (e.g., quality of life, marketing) or Phase IV evaluations. This is the period between submission and approval of a regulatory dossier for marketing authorization.

Phase IV Studies or trials conducted after a medicine is marketed to provide additional details about the medicine's efficacy or safety profile. Different formulations, dosages, durations of treatment, medicine interactions, and other medicine comparisons may be evaluated. New age groups, races, and other types of patients can be studied. Detection and definition of previously unknown or inadequately quantified adverse reactions and related risk factors are an important aspect of many Phase IV studies. If a marketed medicine is to be evaluated for another (i.e., new) indication, then those clinical trials are considered Phase II clinical trials. The term postmarketing surveillance is frequently used to describe those clinical studies in Phase IV (i.e., the period following marketing) that are primarily observations or nonexperimental in nature, to distinguish them from well-controlled Phase IV clinical trials or marketing studies.

PLA Product License Application. A regulatory application for any NCE outside the United States or for a biological medicine in the United States.

QA Quality Assurance. Process of validating individual steps in a toxicology study, manufacturing process, or other area.

QC Quality Control. Process of validating the final step in manufacturing or another area.

R & D Research and development.

USP United States Pharmacopeia.

WHO World Health Organization.

Foreword

This is a valuable book for anyone, within or without the pharmaceutical industry, who would like to understand the complexities involved in discovering and developing new drugs — what *Newsweek* magazine has called the "enchanted substances" that prolong and improve the quality of life.

This is the first time, as far as I know, in which all of the many elements of pharmaceutical research and development are discussed in one book — medical, scientific, production, marketing, financial, legislative, and public affairs. The result is a unique overview of the various factors that must be considered in the quest to develop new and more effective medicines.

The book is *not* a dry and technical treatise, although the technical aspects of drug discovery and development are fully covered. Rather, it is written in an interesting manner that reflects the author's wide knowledge of literature, philosophy, history, and management. It nicely mixes the practical and the theoretical.

The book clearly shows that, while pharmaceutical companies are similar in many ways to other businesses, they are also unique. A research-based pharmaceutical company is in the innovation business, involved in the long, expensive, highly risky, and highly regulated activity of finding new ways to cure and treat age-old diseases, such as cancer, and new plagues, such as AIDS. It is a business literally of life and death — in which we all have a stake.

This book, by a physician/pharmacologist who has spent more than 22 years in research and development with four different pharmaceutical companies, provides a real insight into the critical pharmaceutic R&D process.

Gerald J. Mossinghoff
President
Pharmaceutical Manufacturers Association

Preface to the First Edition

People who want to identify possible solutions to problems in drug discovery and development, to learn about current standards, and to improve their efficiency have a difficult task in finding published sources of help. Those who desire to understand the processes and issues involved in multinational drug discovery and development also have a hard time finding useful references. This book provides information that addresses those needs. The specific approaches this book uses to achieve these goals and the specific audiences targeted are described more fully at the start of Chapter 1.

The book focuses on five broad topics, each dealt with in a separate section of the book. The first section covers the central issue of discovering and developing drugs. Processes are discussed along with means of enhancing the success of these activities. Section two focuses on the corporate level and describes organizational, personnel, and future-oriented issues. It also identifies many ways in which companies differ from each other. The third section concentrates on research and development. Research and development activities are discussed from various perspectives. The discussions focus on organization, management, personnel, productivity, and efficiency issues. The fourth section presents more detailed descriptions of many technical functions and departments, including information management, toxicology, clinical, marketing, and production. Lastly, the fifth section discusses interactions and relationships between pharmaceutical companies and external groups or organizations such as government agencies, academic institutions, trade associations, the press, and the public. It is hoped that this book will be useful to both experienced managers and other individuals who wish to learn more about the pharmaceutical industry.

Bert Spilker

Preface

The style and organization of this book is similar to that of the first edition with two major changes. The first is that 35 new chapters discuss issues and disciplines either not covered or not covered in detail in the original volume. The second change is that new material has been added to the currently existing chapters, and a few chapters from the original volume have been divided into two independent ones. New chapters have been integrated into the five original sections of the book, and three new sections (numbers one, five and seven) have been added. Section one is titled "Overview of a Pharmaceutical Company and the Industry." Section five is titled "The Medical-Marketing Interface" and focuses on issues in this critically important relationship within a company. Section seven is titled "Major Corporate Issues and Challenges." The seven chapters in this section discuss some of the most important questions and problems facing pharmaceutical companies today.

This enlarged book describes most of the principles and practices operating in multinational pharmaceutical companies. Although many examples are drawn from North American experiences, it is believed that they are generally applicable to multinational companies that operate anywhere in the world. It is important to stress that this book focuses on pharmaceutical companies, and not on the pharmaceutical industry. This important distinction is discussed in the introduction.

Acknowledgments for the First Edition

It is a great pleasure to thank Mr. Doug Henderson-James, Dr. John Kelsey, and Dr. John Schoenfelder who reviewed the manuscript and made many valuable suggestions.

The author appreciates helpful discussions with the following people, most of whom also reviewed portions of this book. Mr. Glenn Andrews, Mr. J.M. Arnold, Ms. Kathy S. Bartlett, Mr. Michael T. Burke, Dr. Donald Clive, Ms. Karen Collins, Mr. Jerry D. Crandall, Dr. Joann Data, Mr. N. Ranthi Dev, Dr. Gertrude B.Elion, Ms. Janyth Fredrickson, Dr. Charles W. Gorodetsky, Mr. Robin K. Henning, Dr. David W. Henry, Dr. Steven Jacobs, Mr. Tim Kvanvig, Mr. Al MacKinnon, Dr.Warren McAllister, Dr. Lloyd G. Millstein, Mr. David A. Moyer, Dr. Donald H.Namm, Dr. Lawrence A. Nielsen, Dr. Joel E. Sutton, Dr. Roy Swaringen, Dr.George Szczech, Dr. Hugh Tilson, Ms. Ildiko Trombitas, Mr. Glenn K.Weingarth, Dr. Thomas L. Wenger, and Mr. J.R. Whitehead.

Excellent editorial help of Mr. Allen Jones, assistance with literature searches by Mr. Rolly Simpson, and illustrations by Ms. Jacqueline Jenks are appreciated. A very special thanks is due Mrs. Joyce B. Carpunky, who cheerfully typed each of the drafts and revisions as this book took shape.

Acknowledgments

The author sincerely thanks the following people for their help in reviewing the contents of the chapters and material added to this edition: Ms. Beverly F. Atwood, Mr. William H. Barnett, Mr. Thomas K. Beckett, Dr. Robert M. Bell, Mr. G. Edward Collins, Mr. Jerry D. Crandall, Dr. Michael J. Dalton, Mr. Jonas B. Daugherty, Mr. N. Ranthi Dev, Dr. Mark D. Dibner, Ms. Irish Howsam Dunlap, Mr.. Wayne R. Eberhardt, Dr. Henry G. Grabowski, Mr. William F. Hall, Mr. Robin K. Henning, Mr. Paul A. Holcombe, Jr., Dr. Steven J. Jacobs, Mr. Laurence D. Jenkins, Ms. Laura Mansberg, Ms. Anne F. McKay, Dr. Stephen R. Mosier, Dr. Donald H. Namm, Dr. Lawrence A. Nielsen, Ms. Gail L. Pilgrim, Mr. David C. Pressel, Dr. John Schoenfelder, Mr. Marc H. Shapiro, Dr. Robert D. Small, Dr. Mickey C. Smith, Dr. George Szczech, Mr. Richard P. Teske, Dr. Hugh H. Tilson, Ms. Ildiko D. Trombitas, and Ms. Carol F. Winkelman. They provided many ideas that enhanced the value of this work and their contributions are greatly appreciated. The views expressed in this book are solely those of the author and do not reflect opinions or practices of any specific company, unless clearly identified.

The author also thanks the following people for providing critical technical assistance during the preparation of this book: Ms. Caryn L. Cassidy, Ms. Thomasine M. Cozart, Mr. Rolly L. Simpson, Ms. Lynne M. Spencer, and Ms. Janice L. Wilson.

The following table lists the new chapters included in this edition that were originally published elsewhere. The author appreciates permission of the publishers to reprint the material intact or in a modified form in this book. These references are not listed in the bibliography.

TABLE A. *Published materials used as the basis of selected chapters*[a]

Chapter number in this volume	Original title of article or book chapter	Original publisher and city	Reference
2	Defining the Pharmaceutical Industry	Prous Science Publishers, Barcelona	*Drug News and Perspectives*, 1992; 5: 139-144
4	Standards of Medicine Development	Prous Science Publishers, Barcelona	*Drug News and Perspectives*, 1992; 5:595–603
5	Mergers, Joint Ventures, and Alliances	Prous Science Publishers, Barcelona	*Drug News and Perspectives*, 1993; 6:169–176
6	Pharmacopolitics	Prous Science Publishers, Barcelona	*Drug News and Perspectives*, 1992; 5: 69-77
7	Institutional Memory	Prous Science Publishers, Barcelona	*Drug News and Perspectives*, 1991; 4: 25-27
9	Models of International Operations	Prous Science Publishers, Barcelona	*Drug News and Perspectives*, 1992; 4: 142-149
12	Enhancing Communication	Prous Science Publishers, Barcelona	*Drug News and Perspectives*, 1992; 5: 236-246
14	Golden Rules of Staffing	Prous Science Publishers, Barcelona	*Drug News and Perspectives*, 1991; 4: 358-361
15	Conflicts of Interest in Pharmaceutical Companies	Prous Science Publishers, Barcelona	*Drug News and Perspectives*, 1992; 5:561–571
16	Crisis Management	Prous Science Publishers, Barcelona	*Drug News and Perspectives*, 1992; 5:422–426
19	Overview of Factors Affecting Medicine	Quay Publishing, Lancaster, UK	In: *Creating the Right Environment for Drug Discovery*, Ed., S.R. Walker, Discovery 11-23, 1991
23	Golden Rules of Medicine Discovery	Prous Science Publishers, Barcelona	*Drug News and Perspectives*, 1989; 2: 26-30
24	Extrapolating Animal Safety Data to Humans	Prous Science Publishers, Barcelona	*Drug News and Perspectives*, 1991; 4: 211-216
27	The Future of Medicine Discovery	Prous Science Publishers, Barcelona	*Drug News and Perspectives*, 1991; 4: 389-393
33	Criteria to Develop Medicines	Prous Science Publishers, Barcelona	*Drug News and Perspectives*, 1991; 4: 453-458
37	Providing Product Information to Health Professionals	Prous Science Publishers, Barcelona	*Drug News and Perspectives*, 1993; 6:114–122
42	Licensing Issues	Prous Science Publishers, Barcelona	*Drug News and Perspectives*, 1992; 5:6-19
48	Patient Package Inserts	Prous Science Publishers, Barcelona	*Drug News and Perspectives*, 1993; 6:42–48
49	Strategies for Dealing with Patent Expiration	Prous Science Publishers, Barcelona	*Drug News and Perspectives*, 1992; 5: 370-374
50	Switching Prescription Medicines to Over-the-Counter Status	Prous Science Publishers, Barcelona	*Drug News and Perspectives*, 1992; 5:494–500
51	Interaction with Legislators and the Public	Aster Publishing Co., Eugene, Oregon	*Pharm. Exec.*, May 1992, 58-66
55	Technology Transfer From Academia to Pharmaceutical Companies	Prous Science Publishers, Barcelona	*Drug News and Perspectives*, 1991; 4: 597-600

[a]Each of these articles or chapters was written by Dr. Spilker.

About The Author

Bert Spilker, Ph.D., M.D., F.C.P., F.F.P.M. is the Executive Director of Orphan Medical and Chairman of the Board of the Society for Chronic Diseases, a recently formed charity that provides medicines free to people who are uninsured. He holds faculty appointments as Adjunct Professor at the University of North Carolina in the Schools of Medicine (Departments of Medicine and Pharmacology) and as Clinical Professor of Pharmacy. He is also Clinical Professor of Pharmacy Practice at the University of Minnesota. Dr. Spilker has over 22 years experience in the pharmaceutical industry, having worked for Pfizer Ltd. (United Kingdom), Philips-Duphar B.V. (The Netherlands), Sterling Drug Inc. (Rensselaer, New York), and the Burroughs Wellcome Co. (Research Triangle Park, North Carolina). He has experience with a private consulting company in the Washington, DC area and has worked in the private practice of general medicine.

Bert Spilker received his Ph.D. in pharmacology from the State University of New York, Downstate Medical Center, and did post-doctoral research at the University of California Medical School in San Francisco. He received his M.D. from the University of Miami Ph.D. to M.D. Program and did a residency in internal medicine at Brown University Medical School. Bert Spilker is the author of over 100 publications plus thirteen books in a wide area of pharmacology, clinical medicine, and medicine development. He is the recipient of numerous honors including the FDA Commissioner's Special Citation for work on orphan medicines.

Dr. Spilker is married and has two grown children.

1 / Introduction

Three Conceptual Levels for Viewing
    Pharmaceutical Activities.................. 1
Four Values of a Medicine: Commercial,
    Medical, Scientific, and Image.............. 1
The Role of Common Sense in Developing
    Medicines................................ 2
Reading This Book 3

Purpose 3
Approaches Used in This Book 3
Intended Audience 3
The Importance of Emphasis and Tone in
    Reading a Text........................... 3
Perspectives About Time...................... 4

The only way to keep your health is to eat what you don't want, drink what you don't like, and do what you'd rather not. Mark Twain

THREE CONCEPTUAL LEVELS FOR VIEWING PHARMACEUTICAL ACTIVITIES

Mark Twain's words reflect a common and long-held notion—that achieving and maintaining optimal health is difficult and unpleasant. Notwithstanding recent health claims for the benefits of drinking red wine, most people still view the attainment of good health as an arduous task. This book focuses on the industry that discovers, develops, manufactures, and markets medicines designed to improve health and prevent or cure disease.

The many issues involving individual pharmaceutical companies and the overall pharmaceutical industry may be conceptualized and written about in many ways. This brief introduction describes the frame of reference used in this book, but it could also be applied to a number of other books and articles about medicines and their discovery, development, production, and marketing.

Most issues and activities relating to pharmaceuticals fall into one of three categories:

1. *The Industry*—when the issues discussed or the data presented relate to a group of pharmaceutical companies.
2. *The Company*—concerning the activities and issues of a single company, either as a single corporate entity or as one or more departments or functions within the company.
3. *The Medicine*—relating to one or more medicines; these issues are usually discussed in terms of a specific activity or discipline (e.g., clinical, marketing, regulatory). This category could be viewed as having various sublevels, such as the number of medicines in the therapeutic area(s) involved.

This book focuses on the second of these categories or levels (the company). The industry-wide (macro) level is written about in many newsletters and journals on a weekly basis, as well as in many articles and books. Information on the third level is primarily found in the scientific and medical literature. The individual disciplines (e.g., discovery research, regulatory affairs, marketing, patents, production) that deal with various pharmaceutical issues may readily be discussed at each of the three levels described. It is for this reason that the three-level concept is used as the underlying organizational basis of this book, even though little information is presented or discussed at the first and third levels.

FOUR VALUES OF A MEDICINE: COMMERCIAL, MEDICAL, SCIENTIFIC, AND IMAGE

A concept underlying many of the ideas presented in this book is that a medicine has several different types of values. Four major ones are discussed in numerous chapters: commercial, medical, scientific, and image.

The *commercial value* is primarily a financially based determination concerned with sales, cost of goods, profits, and related fiscal parameters. Other commercial factors include the ability of sales representatives to promote a new medicine, and the ability of a medicine to obtain competitive advantage.

The *medical value* is a clinically based determination concerned with therapeutic benefits, risks, medical need, and similar clinical parameters.

The *scientific value* is based on the scientific interest in the medicine's mechanism of action and the importance

1

TABLE 1.1. *Values for selected medical and scientific discoveries or developments: examples of marked differences in values*[a]

Event	Commercial value	Medical value	Scientific value	Image value
Discovery of mannitol for cerebral edema	+, ++	++++	0 to +[b]	+++
Improvements in sanitation (19th century)	Variable	++++	+	+++
Use of enkephalins for treating diarrhea	0 to +	+	++++	++
Medicines found unsuitable for treating humans, but useful as research tools[c]	0	0[d]	++++	++
Status of many useful medicines shortly prior to their patent expiration	+ to ++++	++++	+[e]	+++
Status of new "me-too" medicines	+ to ++++	+ to +++	0 to +	0 to +

[a] 0 = very low, ++++ = very high; other symbols lie between these extremes.
[b] The mechanism of action of mannitol (i.e., osmotic diuretic) was well known when the discovery was made.
[c] Examples include SKF 525-A (Proadifen), MER-29 (Triparanol), and MK-801 (Dizocilpine).
[d] Indirect medical value could occur from discoveries made using one of these research tools.
[e] It is assumed that the scientific value decreases over time, but there are noteworthy exceptions to this rule.

of the medicine to scientific theory; it is used as a basis for studying compounds, medicines, and diseases.

The *image value* refers to the nontangible benefits in terms of good will, publicity, and related public relations concepts that are associated with a medicine and with the sponsor or others (e.g., licensee) that develop and/or market it.

Most new medicines have similar degrees of medical and scientific value, although their commercial values may be vastly different. The image value of a new medicine is usually correlated with its medical value. A number of marked exceptions to these principles are shown in Table 1.1. Sometimes different values exist and a company must determine whether or not a medicine (e.g., orphan medicine) will be developed and marketed.

THE ROLE OF COMMON SENSE IN DEVELOPING MEDICINES

It is common to claim that the myriad of activities associated with the development of a medicine require the application of common sense. This attitude assumes that the correct choices may be made by asking oneself which approach or choice makes the most sense. While most people do not say that using common sense prevents one from considering the complex pros and cons of an issue or the implications of various choices based on extensive experience and detailed knowledge, that is exactly what they are stating.

The fallacy of using common sense as a guide becomes more obvious when one examines the process more closely. What is considered common sense in one country is not considered common sense in another. A simple example illustrates this point. If a self-employed person lives in a country with relatively low taxes that are not steeply graded with rising income, then it makes sense for most people to work longer hours if they will earn more money by doing so. A self-employed person (in the

same field of work) in a country where taxes are higher and the tax rate is steeper will find that common sense indicates that he or she should not work more than a fixed number of hours per week.

If ten people are discussing an issue, there could and probably will be ten different opinions on any specific question. Each person could easily claim they are using "common sense" to support their position. If one accepts the view that common sense is based on the total sum or integral of an individual's biases and opinions over his or her life, then it is quite possible for all ten opinions to be based on common sense. Does common sense have any real meaning in medicine development? The general answer is that it cannot be relied on to help reach the correct decision. It provides little or no help in addressing such basic questions as should a specific clinical trial be contracted out, or should three indications (or dosage forms) for one medicine be developed sequentially or simultaneously. A large amount of information must be gathered to enable the company to decide correctly the answers to these (or many other) development issues.

If common sense is not helpful, then what tools are? A logical approach that identifies and considers all possible alternatives in terms of achieving goals and maximizing one's chances of attaining them is important. Asking basic questions (e.g., who, what, where, when, how, why, and how much?) about the topic also helps obtain the information that results in the best decisions. It is also useful to apply lateral thinking—clearly not a method reliant upon common sense.

When someone states that his or her approach to a medicine development issue is common sense, it is really a statement of his or her position. If the person's position is modified after hearing other people's views, does this mean that their original view was not really common sense? No, it means that the original view was modified and presumably improved after hearing another view—in other words, the person's common sense made more sense or was more logical. Alternatively, the person may receive more information that stimulates a change in opinion. This example also illustrates that common sense is not particularly useful in arriving at the best, or even a good, solution. Rather, experience, intelligence, a logical mind, and knowledge of the subject are essential tools that will lead to finding the best solution to a problem.

A final description of how common sense can be highly misleading is given in Chapter 75 of *Guide to Clinical Trials* (Spilker, 1991) in the discussion of Simpson's Paradox.

READING THIS BOOK

Purpose

This book has one major objective—to present both specific and general information on issues faced within a company during medicine discovery and development. The specific information is intended to help both experienced and inexperienced individuals in the pharmaceutical industry perform their work more effectively and better understand other areas of the industry or company with which they interact. The general information is intended to help individuals within as well as outside the pharmaceutical industry better understand and appreciate the operations and issues faced by the entire company or by a specific part of that company. A discussion of various means of addressing issues and problems is also presented. Both specific and general standards used in medicine discovery and development are mentioned and discussed.

Approaches Used in This Book

Most issues are not covered in great depth here for two reasons. First, the book would expand to many times its present length, and second, each situation that arises regarding medicine discovery, development, and marketing differs in some aspects from those that have preceded it. One advantage of the broad approach of this book is that it allows the reader to view a wide range of medicine discovery, development, and marketing issues from a single perspective. Both practical and theoretical information is presented as a guide to both understanding and improving the inner workings of a pharmaceutical company. The specific approach used in this book is to present and discuss a mixture of concepts, problems, state-of-the-art procedures, and considerations that may influence decisions. Numerous examples, tips, approaches, suggestions, options, and opinions are offered to help the reader select those pieces of information of greatest value.

Intended Audience

Many senior and junior positions in a pharmaceutical company's hierarchy are held by executives who have little formal scientific training. The fundamental ways in which the pharmaceutical industry differs from other industries (e.g., long time required to develop medicines, uncertainty of a medicine's future, impossibility of making many decisions on a quantitative basis, and the necessity of making decisions with incomplete information) are not fully understood by many of them. Some of these individuals, however, often must make decisions involving research, development, or marketing issues. This book is intended to provide knowledge and indicate factors that those individuals should consider when making informed decisions. It presents a broad overview of the medicine discovery, development, production, and marketing process using a practical approach to help these nonscientists and others within the industry gain a better understanding of many scientific and nonscientific issues.

This book is also directed to scientists, clinicians, and marketing specialists directly involved in medicine discovery and development. These people may be located in industry, government, or academia, or they may function as independent consultants or contractors. Most of these individuals work in one discipline and do not deal with the broad spectrum of issues found in discovery and development. By placing most of the issues that they deal with in a broader perspective, this book will allow them to see how their work fits into the overall process.

The issues discussed are also addressed to professionals and health care workers in government agencies, trade associations, academic centers, hospitals, and other places who interact with the pharmaceutical industry. Many interactions are described in this book in separate chapters devoted to government agencies, trade associations, and academic institutions. This book should help these individuals who are not employed in the pharmaceutical industry to understand better the nature and complexity of many issues faced during medicine discovery, development, production, and marketing.

The chapters of this book are self-contained and may be read in any order. Entire books have been written on the subjects of many of the individual chapters. The information in this book is based on the author's experiences at four pharmaceutical companies, the literature, and communications with individuals employed at many companies; it is not a reflection of any single company.

The Importance of Emphasis and Tone in Reading a Text

At a deposition defending another pharmaceutical company the plaintiff's attorney asked me "Do you

TABLE 1.2. *Selected differences in interpretation of phrases or gestures between an American and English company*

Phrase	American interpretation	English interpretation
We do not support X	We do not agree with X	We do not pay for X
I'll do it presently	I'll do it at once	I'll do it later
Let's table it	Let's discuss it later	Let's discuss it now
(Person nods head)	I agree with what you said	I hear you and understand what you have said

agree with the statement that *everything* of importance should be learned about a new medicine?" When I said that I'd like to qualify the statement he immediately jumped up and shouted, "But that is what you have written as a golden rule of medicine development, and you do not agree with it?" It immediately became apparent that the tone and emphasis he used for the word "everything" differed from my own, and that in my own mind I had emphasized the word "importance" when I had written the sentence. The meaning of the principle I described changed dramatically in his reading of it. Thus, dear reader, I find myself now at your mercy whenever you pick up this book to read a passage. I have tried to avoid vague sentences that seem particularly susceptible to this type of altered emphasis, but realize that it is possible in almost any passage to read a sentence in different ways. If any sentence in this book does not seem to make sense to you, please try to read it with a different emphasis. In addition to the problem of emphasis and tone, definitions may vary greatly between seemingly similar languages. For example, a few of the many important differences between American and English are listed in Table 1.2.

PERSPECTIVES ABOUT TIME

Time is generally viewed, at least in medium- and large-sized companies, as the single most precious resource. A few of the basic reasons for this are discussed in the text. This book tries to present the underlying mind set that it is essential to get tasks completed on time, regardless of attempting to achieve every last minute detail. The regulatory authority's mind set is usually that every last detail must be right regardless of the time it takes to achieve that goal. Time pressures rarely have the same impact on regulatory authorities as they do on the pharmaceutical industry, and the numerous ramifications of this difference influence much of the behavior and attitudes of the two groups.

SECTION I

Overview of a Pharmaceutical Company and the Industry

2 / Pharmaceutical Industry: Definitions

How Is a National Pharmaceutical Industry
  Defined? 7
Inclusion of Non-Company Organizations Within
  the Definition and Scope of the
  Pharmaceutical Industry.................... 8
  Trade Associations 8
  Professional Societies, Associations, or
    Foundations 8
  Individuals and Groups Hired by the Industry
    to Represent Them........................ 9
  Companies, Individuals, and Groups That
    Directly Provide Services to the Core
    Companies................................ 9

Overview of the Industry........................ 9
  Viewing the Pharmaceutical Industry: The
    Fable of Six Blind Men and the Elephant ... 9
  The Pharmaceutical Industry as Viewed by
    External Groups 9
  The Pharmaceutical Industry as Viewed by
    Internal Groups.......................... 11
Perspectives From Which to View the
  Pharmaceutical Industry and
  Pharmaceutical Companies 11
  Understanding the Macro Level.............. 11
  Understanding the Micro Level 13

Many persons have an idea that one cannot be in business and lead an upright life, whereas the truth is that no one succeeds in business to any great extent, who misleads or misrepresents. John Wanamaker

It is possible to define the pharmaceutical industry as the collection of companies that discover, develop, manufacture, and market medicines for human use, but this definition is insufficient for several purposes. Although there is a core group of companies that are research based and fulfill all four of these criteria, many others only meet one, two, or three of the four criteria. For example, some generic pharmaceutical companies only manufacture medicines, whereas others market them as well. In addition, there are many companies that do not directly carry out any of the four functions, but facilitate medicine development by interacting with companies and providing important services.

There are many examples of this kind of activity. Contract research organizations provide medical, statistical, and other help to pharmaceutical companies. Consultants provide an even wider variety of services to the pharmaceutical industry. Market research firms, advertising agencies, and a large number of other organizations also provide services under contracts or other agreements. All of these service organizations, individuals, and groups can be considered part of a national pharmaceutical industry.

Governments that wish to stimulate growth within their national pharmaceutical industry or, alternatively, to tax certain companies want to understand the various categories of companies within this industry. Whether a government legislature decides to define the national pharmaceutical industry in a narrow restricted way or in a broad inclusive way depends on the viewpoint of the legislators and those who influence them.

HOW IS A NATIONAL PHARMACEUTICAL INDUSTRY DEFINED?

A country trying to protect or stimulate growth in its industry will find that defining its national pharmaceutical industry is a complex process. To illustrate this point, six different categories of companies are described from the perspective of a developed country.

1. Uninational pharmaceutical companies with sales activities that only occur within the country.
2. Multinational pharmaceutical companies with a single corporate headquarters that is located within the country.
3. Multinational pharmaceutical companies with corporate headquarters located in another country, but with relatively large research and development and sales activities within the country.

4. Multinational pharmaceutical companies with corporate headquarters in another country, and with a relatively large manufacturing plant or technical development laboratory and sales activity within the country; however, no major research and development group exists within the country.

5. Multinational pharmaceutical companies with corporate headquarters in another country, and only relatively small operations for technical development, research, or manufacturing, in addition to sales activity, within the country.

6. Multinational pharmaceutical companies with only sales activities within the country. Sales activities could be extremely large or small.

From an economic perspective, companies in categories 1 through 4 should be included as part of the nation's industry; they contribute in a significant manner to that country's tax base and employment. From a strict ownership perspective, however, only companies in categories one and two would qualify as part of the nation's industry. Several other factors further complicate this analysis. Any company with headquarters in a foreign country could be partially, or even more than 50%, owned by citizens or corporations in the country of interest. For example, from the U.S. perspective, an American multinational pharmaceutical company could be owned by a Swiss, German, or French multinational company (e.g., a bank or holding company) that operates a different business. The opposite situation, in which an American (nonpharmaceutical) company owns a foreign multinational pharmaceutical company, is of particular interest to the definitional issue from the U.S. perspective. If the foreign company (owned by Americans) is a category 3 to 6 pharmaceutical organization in the United States, it could be considered as part of the American pharmaceutical industry.

The definition of a national pharmaceutical industry is affected by issues of *control* and *time,* in addition to ownership. Control relates to whether the foreign-based company controls most important decisions within the American subsidiary, or whether the subsidiary has at least a semiautonomous position to influence its own direction. Examples of both situations are common in the United States. A subsidiary with more autonomy could play an active role in advancing causes and interests of the American pharmaceutical industry. A tightly controlled U.S. subsidiary (from its parent headquarters) might not have this opportunity. The length of time a company has been operating in the United States and the degree to which it is integrated into the American pharmaceutical industry (i.e., has it joined some or all major trade associations, and does it participate in pharmacopolitics as an active partner with other American companies?) help determine that company's status and position in the U.S. pharmaceutical industry.

A nation's pharmaceutical industry is defined according to the perspective(s) of the group making the definition, and this depends on the purpose(s) for which the definition is used. For example, the United States International Trade Commission (1991) issued a document in which it defined the U.S. pharmaceutical industry in a relatively narrow way. "The U.S. industry is defined as all *producers* in the United States, including subsidiaries of foreign-based firms" (italics added). Their restrictive definition was most likely chosen because the International Trade Commission's study on international competitiveness was based on a request from the U.S. Senate Finance Committee to study three advanced technology *manufacturing* industries in the United States.

INCLUSION OF NON-COMPANY ORGANIZATIONS WITHIN THE DEFINITION AND SCOPE OF THE PHARMACEUTICAL INDUSTRY

Trade Associations

The definition of an industry should not, in the author's opinion, be strictly limited to those companies within it, but should also include groups, companies, and individuals hired to represent the overall collection of companies. Given this definition, all pharmaceutical trade associations with only pharmaceutical companies as members (i.e., companies that discover, develop, market, or manufacture medicines) are part of the pharmaceutical industry. But, what of trade associations that have members from other industries (e.g., chemical or cosmetics) as well? Should they be considered part of the industry? It is reasonable to believe that associations are part of the pharmaceutical industry if a *majority* of their members are pharmaceutical companies. If trade associations even have as part of their mission the promotion, protection, or representation of the interests of the pharmaceutical company members, they should generally be considered part of the industry. The major functions of trade associations and their interactions with the pharmaceutical industry have been described in Chapter 65.

Professional Societies, Associations, or Foundations

The same principle applies to these groups as for trade associations, i.e., if a group's members are solely from individual pharmaceutical companies, or the majority are, and the group's mission is to support the pharmaceutical industry and its interests, even in a philanthropic way, then it should be considered as part of the industry.

Individuals and Groups Hired by the Industry to Represent Them

There can be little doubt that groups or individuals hired by the industry as their representatives must be considered as part of the industry. After those individuals' contracts expire, they would no longer be considered as part of the industry. A gray area is occupied by individuals who simultaneously maintain contracts inside and outside of the industry. If at least 50% (or another percent) of their time or salary is involved with pharmaceutical companies, they should be considered as part of the industry.

It is important to define the term "hire" in this context of who is part of the industry. Does it include an honorarium given for a talk? While the answer to this question is generally "no," it does represent a gray area and these people are often viewed as industry representatives (or at least spokesmen if not actual representatives). The touchstone is to determine whether these individuals are expressing their own views or whether they were asked to present a specific (or general) industry view. In the former case they would not literally represent the industry; in the latter case they would.

Companies, Individuals, and Groups That Directly Provide Services to the Core Companies

None of the companies, groups, or individuals that directly (or indirectly) provide services to the core companies (i.e., pharmaceutical companies) or to the industry overall are considered part of the industry. In many important and even critical ways they advance the programs and causes of the industry, but they are still considered support groups. Examples of types of companies, groups, and individuals that provide direct services to core companies are listed in Table 2.1; those that provide indirect services are listed in Table 2.2. This is schematically illustrated in Fig. 2.1. Groups and individuals who provide services to the industry or to companies are not considered as part of the industry.

TABLE 2.1. *Types of companies and groups that directly provide professional services to pharmaceutical companies*

1. Medical contractors and data processors
2. Market research organizations
3. Advertising companies
4. Brand-name consultants
5. Academic experts in specific areas
6. Computer hardware and software groups
7. Information technology specialists
8. Consultants in finance, production, human resources, marketing, and other areas
9. Attorneys who prepare and try legal cases
10. Patent attorneys
11. Publishers of materials prepared directly for companies
12. Statistical contractors

TABLE 2.2. *Types of companies and groups that indirectly provide services to pharmaceutical companies*

1. Subcontractors or consultants for any of the companies or groups mentioned in Table 2.1
2. Publishers of materials (e.g., brochures, books, or journals) used by companies but not specifically requested by them
3. Consumer advocates that espouse causes supported by or in support of individual companies

Service companies, groups, or individuals may represent specific companies rather than merely providing services. In this particular case the group or individual is considered part of the industry. This means that the total sum of companies, groups, and individuals that constitute the pharmaceutical industry is a dynamic group and varies over time depending on those who represent it, provide services, or function as its individual member companies.

OVERVIEW OF THE INDUSTRY

The pharmaceutical industry is much more than a collection of individual companies. As stated above, it includes trade associations and groups hired to represent the industry. Nonetheless, those inside the industry often form a view of it through their experiences and knowledge gained primarily through work in their own company. This information is assimilated from many sources, including professional and other literature readings, informal discussions, popular media reports, and formal talks at meetings. These images and assessments are often generalized to other companies and then generalized to the industry as a whole.

Viewing the Pharmaceutical Industry: The Fable of Six Blind Men and the Elephant

Unfortunately, many individuals' image of the pharmaceutical industry is a stereotyped one. This stereotype is present sometimes in a sophisticated form even inside the industry. The well-known Indian fable of six blind men and the elephant reminds one of the way various groups tend to view the industry. In this fable six blind men are asked to describe an elephant to a maharaja who has never seen one. Each feels a different part of the elephant (i.e., tusk, trunk, ear, body, tail, or leg) and provides a totally different description of what the elephant looks like.

The Pharmaceutical Industry as Viewed by External Groups

External groups who watch the industry include (1) regulators, (2) academicians, (3) physicians in practice,

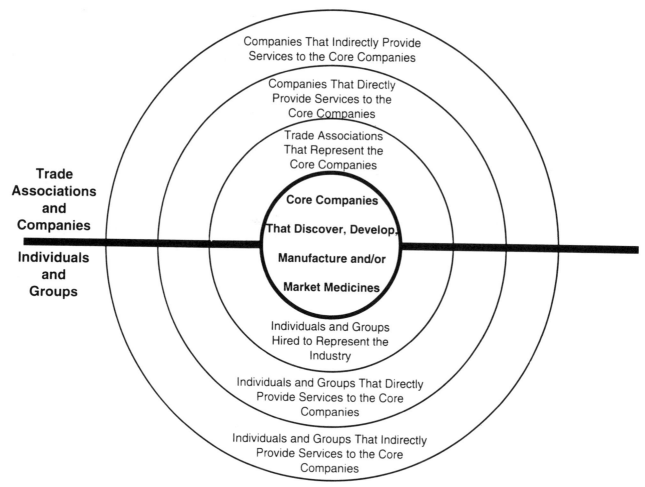

FIG. 2.1. Schematic illustration of groups that are progressively further from the core pharmaceutical companies (i.e., those that discover, develop, manufacture, or market medicines).

(4) consumer advocates, (5) patients/public, (6) legislators, and (7) others (e.g., contractors, consultants, and vendors). While marked differences exist among individuals within each group, there are certain stereotyped views of the industry held by many members of each group.

1. *Regulators.* Regulators usually view the pharmaceutical industry as an adversary. They see the industry as extremely strong and powerful. Regulators believe that many industrial companies and representatives try to get away with as much as possible in preparing dossiers for new medicines, in promoting marketed medicines, and in other activities. The general attitude of regulators is that the industry must be carefully monitored and controlled to prevent unethical and perhaps illegal behavior. A few examples of exceptional cooperation and collaboration in developing new medicines (e.g., Retrovir) have not convinced the Food and Drug Administration to seek improved relationships with industry on a broad scale.

2. *Academicians.* Academicians who actually (or potentially) interact with the industry often view it as a source of new compounds or medicines that they may study scientifically or clinically. Many other attitudes exist, both positive and negative, but these usually focus on a particular type of business relationship the academician has with one or more companies.

3. *Physicians in practice.* Most practicing physicians do not know many (or often, any) pharmaceutical professionals and view the company's sales representatives they meet as the embodiment of the company. The promotional practices of the sales people are viewed as representing the essence of the company, in terms of both ethics and quality. Physicians also form opinions about a specific company based on its journal advertisements, media reports, and comments of their peers at various meetings.

4. *Consumer advocates.* These groups usually have clear directions and goals and view all external groups according to how they either enhance or hinder the advocates' program. Such groups usually see pharma-

ceutical companies in black-and-white terms. Not all consumer advocate groups are anti-industry, but their views are usually quite focused and clear.

5. *Patients/public.* Patients and the public primarily view the pharmaceutical industry in terms of problems they hear via the media and in terms of costs for medicines. The industry is viewed as extremely profitable and the costs for medicines are viewed as excessive. Media reports that present negative stories about the pharmaceutical industry influence and flavor the attitudes of patients and the public. From the public's perspective, there is usually no distinction between the pharmaceutical industry and a single pharmaceutical company. This means that a negative report about a single company is usually extrapolated to include all companies as an indication of industry-wide behavior. This pattern is understandable in that the public has no means of determining whether a specific charge is likely to be true or false, and whether a real problem at one company is likely to be a widespread practice or an isolated case.

6. *Legislators.* Legislators are influenced by and respond to constituents, their political party's leadership, and to various other groups and pressures. Their constituents have little reason to praise the industry to their legislators, and have little or no real knowledge of the issues and facts underlying medicine discovery, development, and marketing. Most people who make the effort to contact their legislators about the industry are usually strong critics. The major area they criticize is what they perceive as excessive prices of medicines coupled with the industry's profitability. Legislators themselves are dependent on young and often inexperienced staff to provide them with information and views, and these people generally do not understand the nature of the industry any more than the lay public. Furthermore, lobbyists who talk with them appropriately focus on one or a few points, rather than trying to provide a broad education.

7. *Others.* This category includes vendors, contractors, and consultants who interact with companies on a business level. Their views are influenced by many of the factors that have been described.

The Pharmaceutical Industry as Viewed by Internal Groups

Junior and mid-level individuals working inside the industry view their own company and the industry with numerous biases. Such groups include (1) scientists attempting to discover important new medicines and who resent almost any control imposed on their scientific freedom; (2) medical personnel developing a new medicine who often want to impose their own views on how a medicine's development should be structured; (3) mar-

keting personnel who desire wide latitude to promote a new medicine to the health care community; (4) production personnel who manufacture the medicine and are dependent on orders furnished by marketers; (5) financial personnel who study and track various aspects of the business and may not be convinced that all marketing, research, and development expenses are fully justified; (6) attorneys who become involved in contracts, litigation, and legal issues concerning problems that arise; and (7) personnel staff who are usually praised when salary growth is tightly controlled and all government requirements (e.g., Equal Employment Opportunity) are met. The various perspectives of these groups are generally well known and are not described here. Many stereotypes held by each group greatly impede effective communications. Many professionals within a company do not make a sufficient distinction between the activities, behavior, and financial health of their company and the overall industry.

How enlightened are the senior managers of these (and other) groups? Have they been educated about major company-level issues, the specific functions and processes of their company, and the major issues that exist at the industry level? The answers to these questions vary greatly among companies. Senior managers, however, teach their subordinates about these issues and the company's beliefs, in addition to directing their activities, and managers should have appropriate knowledge and resources to do this effectively.

PERSPECTIVES FROM WHICH TO VIEW THE PHARMACEUTICAL INDUSTRY AND PHARMACEUTICAL COMPANIES

At least three different perspectives, analogous to different scientific instruments, are needed to observe and understand the industry and its individual companies. To understand the global, industry-wide (i.e., macro) level, it may be best to be positioned outside, or for insiders intellectually to step outside the industry and to use a telescope. To study an individual pharmaceutical company (i.e., the micro level) and to understand its detail, it is necessary to use a microscope. To understand the individuals' behavior and management practices within a company, it is important to use a stethoscope. This instrument allows one to study the individual's and company's vital organs. The proper understanding of pharmacopolitics as practiced by pharmaceutical groups requires use of all three of these tools.

Understanding the Macro Level

The telescope approach can be described in several ways. Using one lesson of the six blind men and the elephant, to get an overall picture, one must be at a sufficient distance to view the *entire* elephant, not focus only on one part, or even one part at a time. This overall view may be achieved by any objective individual or group, with an interest, but evaluations and reports about this macro level are most credible when they are written by groups who do not benefit from reaching either positive or negative outcomes and conclusions. Independent committees or commissions established by a national academy of sciences are one means of achieving the necessary level of credibility for convincing or influencing both those within and those outside the industry. Independent committees or commissions appointed by government agencies sometimes have the required credibility as well, even though their findings and recommendations are often ignored. The challenge for government legislators or the executive branch is far greater than just examining the pharmaceutical industry as a whole; the value of all new medicines should be evaluated in the context of the nation's entire health care budget. A government should view the value of the pharmaceutical industry to its society in the context of all of its national industries. To do this appropriately, the industry's contribution to the nation's balance of payments as well as other economic indicators should be assessed.

Even the most objective group in the world, however, could view the industry in the context of its being primarily (1) a *manufacturing industry* and apply various targets and measures to evaluate it, (2) an *innovation-based, high technology research-based industry* seeking new discoveries in a high-risk environment, or (3) a *health care industry* providing medicines used by patients to cure disease and improve health. Not only external groups, but internal industry professionals as well often view the industry in one of these three ways and make important decisions and seek allies based on their perceptions. The research-based pharmaceutical industry has never presented itself as solely one of the three and has tended to emphasize that side of its image that it felt to be most appropriate at the time.

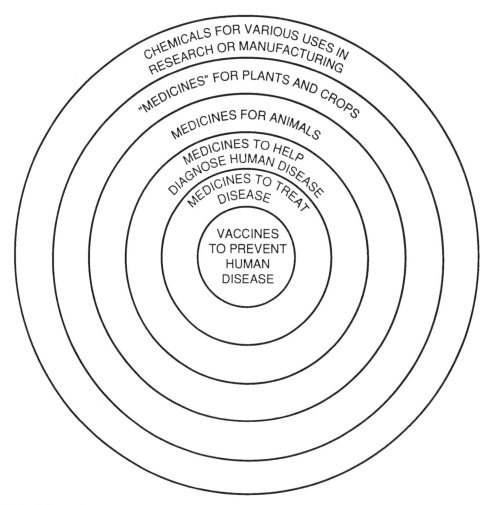

FIG. 2.2. Schematic illustration of types of medicines and chemicals that are progressively further from those that prevent disease. The diagnostics industry and those industries focusing on the outer three rings are not specifically discussed in this chapter.

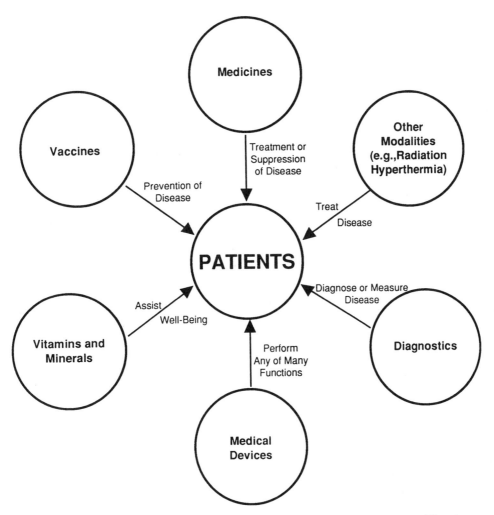

FIG. 2.3. Types of medicines, devices, and other modalities used in human health care. The pharmaceutical industry is involved with medicines and vaccines. Vitamins and minerals may or may not be considered as part of the pharmaceutical industry.

Understanding the Micro Level

The micro level is used to designate a specific company, as opposed to the entire industry. This level and many of its issues can be understood by examination of its many parts using a microscope. This approach initially dissects the company into its various functions (e.g., marketing, research, production). The "Big Picture" of a company as well as its dissection into many components is presented in Chapter 3. Figures 2.2 and 2.3 are two schematics that help identify which types of medicines and health care products the company is involved in. These categories allow one to view a company with a low-power lens on the microscope. Higher resolution examinations of these and other areas are not discussed here.

A third scientific tool, the stethoscope is used not only to evaluate behavior, attitudes, morale, and the milieu of individuals within a company, but also the management styles and performance of the people who operate a company. If listened to with knowledge and objectivity, the stethoscope provides valuable information on the company's current health and provides information of what treatments to prescribe for improving the company's health.

Although each of the three instruments described was discussed as the sole method to evaluate a specific area, all three instruments are sometimes actually used for each of the purposes described. Their proper use enables the user to understand better the industry, its companies, and employees.

In conclusion the pharmaceutical industry may be defined in many ways depending on the purpose(s) of the definition. The most appropriate one for any situation requires consideration of the various approaches and factors discussed in this chapter.

3 / The Big Picture

The Crucial Issue Facing Pharmaceutical Companies Today	**15**
Functions of Medicines	**16**
Overall Perspective of Pharmaceutical Companies	**16**
Uniqueness of the Pharmaceutical Industry ...	16
Attributes of Pharmaceutical Companies......	17
Pharmaceutical Costs and Profits	18
Competition Within the Pharmaceutical Industry	18
Perspectives of Different Groups About New Pharmaceuticals..........................	18
Synopsis of Medicine Discovery and Development.....................	**20**
Medicine Discovery	20
Medicine Development.....................	20
Influence of Regulations on Medicine Discovery and Development...............	22
Metaphors of Medicine Discovery and Development...........................	**25**

Pipeline of Medicine Discovery, Development, and Marketing	25
Horse Race.................................	26
Poker Game................................	27
Orchestra..................................	27
Hurdles Race...............................	27
Ocean Liner................................	27
Maze......................................	28
Connect-the-Dots, Lottery, and Other Metaphors	28
High Jump.................................	29
How Do People View Metaphors?	31
Interfaces in a Company Between Major Functions	**31**
Resource Allocation...........................	**32**
Allocation of Resources: Pitfalls to Avoid	32
Major Changes in the Pharmaceutical Industry Since 1962................................	**33**

To survive and succeed in a hot market, a company must be willing to change everything about itself except its basic beliefs. . . . Give the individual full consideration, spend a lot of time making customers happy, go the last mile to do a thing right. Thomas J. Watson, Jr., former chief executive of IBM. From *Fortune* (August 31, 1987).

THE CRUCIAL ISSUE FACING PHARMACEUTICAL COMPANIES TODAY

For research-based pharmaceutical companies the most critical issue today is maintaining a flow of new, innovative medicines that ensure the company's growth and even survival. Most pharmaceutical companies are fully committed to this challenge because the alternative of having a dry period without new products is unattractive and its consequences clear. To meet the challenge, companies are adopting strategies of developing their medicines on a global basis utilizing state-of-the-art technologies and attempting to improve their efficiency of medicine discovery and development. Companies primarily obtain their new medicines from in-house research discoveries, licensing from other companies or groups, and joint ventures with other companies. This book describes the state-of-the-art standards that exist in many aspects of medicine discovery and development.

Another response to the challenge of preventing dry periods without new products is to conduct a detailed analysis of the entire research and development process and seek ways of improving current systems, organizational structures, and approaches. These internal evaluations used to occur approximately once in a five- to ten-year period and often involved an outside consulting firm. At the present time, this process tends to occur on a more frequent or even on a continual basis. This book provides specific techniques to help managers judge a company's strengths and weaknesses and many detailed methods used to analyze a pharmaceutical company or its research and development activities are presented.

The world of medicine discovery and development is rapidly changing, and there is a need for companies to take a broad view to develop useful strategies and take advantage of opportunities. The information explosion in the published literature provides details of technical aspects of medicine discovery and development on a daily basis. The press, trade associations, and numerous other sources provide information about the pharmaceutical industry as a whole (or selected parts) to the public and to health professionals. There are no sources, however, that provide a broad view of the issues of medicine discovery and development from a specific company's perspective. That is the intention of this book.

FUNCTIONS OF MEDICINES

When Sir Walter Raleigh was facing the headman's ax in his final moments, he reportedly said, "It's a sharp medicine, but it cures all ills." Many people believe that medicines are intended to "cure all ills," but relatively few medicines actually cure a disease. Most have other functions. They are briefly described because, during the medicine discovery process, scientists are consciously seeking to find a compound with specific properties or functions. During clinical development one or more of these functions are specifically studied. The various uses or functions of medicines can be arbitrarily divided into six categories.

1. *Prevention* Some medicines are used prophylactically to prevent disease. Medicines such as vaccines or fluoride may be given to normal individuals to prevent the initial occurrence of a disease (e.g., polio, smallpox, or dental carries) or may be given to patients at high risk of contracting a certain disease or problem to reduce the chance of its occurrence. Another form of disease prevention is sometimes called suppression (see category 4).
2. *Cure* The ideal form of treatment occurs when medicines are used to cure a disease (e.g., antibiotics are used to cure certain bacterial infections or anthelmintics are used to cure certain worm infections). A cure represents a complete eradication of the disease.
3. *Treatment* Medicines are often used to alleviate symptoms for patients who have many chronic diseases. These medicines do not cure a disease and usually do not affect the underlying pathophysiology (e.g., antiasthmatics or antianginals), but the medicines improve the patient's signs and/or symptoms and lead to clinical improvement. Medicines that reduce the risk of disease progression illustrate a type of treatment.
4. *Suppression* Medicines are often used to suppress the signs and/or symptoms of a disease and prevent them from occurring, or to prevent the disease process from progressing. Suppression is often a continuation of maintenance therapy after the acute episode or problem has improved. Suppression is a type of prevention, but is used in patients who have a disease as opposed to normal persons who want to prevent getting a disease.
5. *Diagnosis* Some medicines are used to help physicians establish the diagnosis of a patient's disease or problem (e.g., radiocontrast dyes). It would be desirable if there were many medicines available for this purpose, but relatively few such medicines exist.

Medicines are sometimes used for a short time as a therapeutic trial to help prove a diagnosis. It is assumed that if a patient improves after a therapeutic trial with a medicine that the diagnosis is proven. If the patient does not improve, the conclusion is reached that the diagnosis is incorrect. This practice is considered to be an undesirable way of practicing medicine in many situations (e.g., to use antibiotics without obtaining cultures) because physicians should assiduously attempt to diagnose medical problems before initiating treatment.
6. *Enhancement of health* People desire the best state of health possible. Many try and achieve this state through medicines (e.g., vitamins and minerals) as well as through other means (e.g., diet and exercise). These medicines cannot be said to be replacing a deficiency and may only offer a psychological sense of well-being.

Many medicines fit into two or more of these categories. Such medicines may be used for either one or two functions at the same time. One example of this latter situation is illustrated with the Fab antibody fragment of digoxin. This medicine (Digibind) simultaneously diagnoses and treats life-threatening digoxin toxicity by binding molecules of digoxin in the blood making them unavailable for binding at their site of action on cells in the body. If the patient has toxicity resulting from a digoxin overdose, then he or she will usually be helped with the medicine. If the patient does not have a digoxin-induced toxicity, then the medicine will be ineffective. Some medicines that usually fit in one category may also be used for other purposes. One example is when antibiotics are used prophylactically in high-risk patients to prevent development of a bacterial infection as well as therapeutically in others to cure many specific infections.

OVERALL PERSPECTIVE OF PHARMACEUTICAL COMPANIES

Uniqueness of the Pharmaceutical Industry

It is critically important for senior executives to have a detailed understanding of their industry. This helps them reach more informed and sometimes better decisions about many important issues, policies, and questions that frequently arise. Yet, one often reads speeches of a pharmaceutical company's chief executive or senior company officers who may be top lawyers, financiers, or marketing experts, but do not understand the basic concepts and processes of how medicines are discovered and developed. The various factors that influence medicine discovery and development may also not be well understood. Although most companies may be operated and managed as if they make "widgets," a pharmaceutical company must not.

Major factors that differentiate pharmaceutical companies from other companies are listed below. Some of these factors are only a matter of degree (1) the long period of time required to develop and market a newly discovered medicine; (2) the high degree of financial risk and uncertainty of a medicine's future, even after it is launched; (3) the large number of highly restrictive regulations that govern all aspects of a medicine's development, production, and marketing; (4) the inability to predict when the next important medicine discovery will occur; and (5) the large number of variables and factors that are involved in biological experiments, technical development, and especially clinical trials. This last point means that a large number of interpretations are possible in many situations. Each of these critical aspects requires an understanding of the medicine discovery and development process. It is also important to understand the factors that relate to creating and maintaining an appropriate environment in which medicine discovery may occur.

The pharmaceutical industry shares some characteristics with many other industries, including other high technology industries, as follows:

1. A rapidly changing environment in which products are sold. Many of these changes are highly unpredictable, both in the nature and rate of change.
2. Competition in many areas including product discovery, development, and marketing.

Many aspects of the corporate environment in which these activities take place are nuances of the corporate culture. Corporate culture shapes the strategies used by a company to develop medicines and is discussed in several other chapters of this book. This culture-strategy interaction is also discussed by Shrivastava and Guth (1985).

Attributes of Pharmaceutical Companies

Many individuals, especially those who have limited time to devote to an issue or question, want to understand "the big picture." In some circles this cliché is as common as "the bottom line" (i.e., the overall impression or amount). The big picture obtained after looking at a pharmaceutical company includes consideration of its (1) core and other businesses, (2) overall size, (3) current and planned activities, (4) profitability, (5) approaches to medicine discovery and development, and (6) current portfolio of marketed and investigational medicines.

Core and Other Businesses

Is the company strictly a pharmaceutical company, a health care company, or a company engaged in a wide variety of businesses? If the latter, how does the medicine business fit into the company's overall mission?

Overall Size

This aspect may be described in terms of sales per year, numbers of workers, assets, or other factors. Size does not necessarily correlate with profit or number of medicines marketed. This topic is described more in Chapter 10.

Current and Planned Activities

This aspect primarily relates to whether the company is research based or generic, is development oriented (i.e., licenses-in most or all of its medicines), or is a biotechnology company. This topic is described throughout this book.

Profitability

The relative profitability of a pharmaceutical company may be based on a comparison with other pharmaceutical companies, or a between-industry comparison with other companies of the same size. A few means of illustrating a company's profitability are illustrated in Chapter 35 and establishing prices in Chapter 59.

Approaches to Medicine Discovery and Development

Companies vary from those that utilize highly formal approaches to medicine development to those that emphasize flexibility. This aspect is described throughout this book. Organizational structures are primarily described in Chapters 10 and 29.

Current Portfolio of Marketed and Investigational Medicines

The portfolio of marketed medicines may include both multisource (i.e., medicines susceptible to generic competition), patent-protected, or otherwise protected (e.g., with exclusivity under the Orphan Drug Act) medicines. Medicines under development (i.e., investigational medicines) are assessed by the medical and commercial value of the company's portfolio of potential new products (see Chapter 35).

Pharmaceutical Costs and Profits

A significant part of the "big picture" relates to profits. Food and Drug Administration (FDA) regulations and guidelines since 1962 have required many more premarketing studies to be conducted than previously. Good Laboratory Practices and Good Manufacturing Practices regulations have also increased the costs of bringing a new medicine to market. Regulations, however, are only one of many factors that have resulted in the higher prices charged for medicines. Other factors include the steadily mounting costs for laboratory equipment, clinical trials, staff salaries, and other components of medicine discovery and development. As a result of increased health care expenditures during the 1960s and 1970s, the government reacted. It has taken various steps (e.g., encouraging generic competition, passing maximum allowable cost regulations, and providing bonuses to pharmacists who dispense generic medicines) to force medicine prices down. Food and clothing prices, however, have been kept artificially high by government price support programs for agriculture and tariffs and import quotas on foreign textiles.

The major reason why pharmaceutical companies are willing to invest hundreds of millions in high-risk research is that the rates of return for the few commercially successful medicines are also high. If the rates of return are markedly diminished, as is already occurring in some countries, pharmaceutical companies will be much less willing in the future to invest their money in research. Economic analyses clearly show that, if regulations diminish profits for pharmaceutical companies on their few successful medicines below a certain minimum, the companies will reduce the investments they are willing to make in research. Without sufficient research, medicine discovery will be slowed and this will decrease the rate at which new medicines will reach the market.

Competition Within the Pharmaceutical Industry

An additional piece of the "big picture" is the risk from competition. Competition within the pharmaceutical industry exists on several levels. These include (1) being first to enter new therapeutic markets, (2) price and other types of competition (e.g., perceived benefits) on similar products within a single therapeutic market, and (3) manufacturing generic versions of the same medicine. The evidence that supports the view that there is significant competition in the pharmaceutical industry includes (1) price flexibility on specific products; (2) instability of market share over a period of a few years; (3)

high rate of corporate mergers, buyouts, and bankruptcies; and (4) licensing arrangements. The pharmaceutical industry has the second highest rate of market share instability of all industries in the United States (Schnee and Caglarcan, 1978).

Perspectives of Different Groups About New Pharmaceuticals

When medicine discovery and development issues are being presented and discussed, numerous perspectives could be used. These include those of various groups both within and outside the pharmaceutical industry. Representative groups within the industry would include people in marketing, production, science, medical, and technical development functions. Representative groups outside the industry include patients, physicians, and regulatory agencies. Most of this book presents the perspectives of those within the industry. Nonetheless, it is useful to review briefly the overall perspective of some groups from both within and outside the industry.

Perspectives About New Medicines by Groups Within the Pharmaceutical Industry

The perspectives of pharmaceutical company employees about new medicines are somewhat influenced by their background and discipline within their company. Informed and knowledgeable people view medicines in terms of a combination of medical, scientific, and commercial parameters. Others focus more on one of these (or other) aspects of a new medicine.

Many groups within and outside the pharmaceutical industry often ascribe a logic to a medicine's discovery or its development that is actually a convenient teleological explanation (i.e., they work backward to derive an explanation that fits the observed events). Events usually seem more clear in hindsight when numerous activities are rearranged in people's minds, rough edges are smoothed out, and loose threads (e.g., false leads and approaches) are conveniently forgotten or ignored. As a result, the story of many medicines' discovery and development appears logical and orderly, whereas many false turns, accidents, and mistakes, as well as luck were involved. Lucky errors may have directed the medicine along the right path to its success. Many medicine discoveries have occurred and paths of development were correctly followed despite some people's attempts to proceed in a different direction. There are a few noteworthy exceptions to this somewhat cynical view that truly illustrate a logical and stepwise approach to medicine discovery and development.

People in each company often talk about new upcoming medicines much as company stocks are described.

The perceived value of a medicine to a company often has precipitous changes based on casual or formal comments from the FDA, investigators, or company scientists. These changes are often more related to emotional reactions to the medicine's characteristics, uninformed judgments, or other reactions that do not reflect the medicine's true value. The perceived value of a medicine to stockbrokers and to stockholders in terms of eventual profit also rises and falls precipitously based on news, which may or may not be accurate or relevant to the medicine's true value. These changes in perceived value are illustrated in Fig. 3.1.

Perspectives About New Medicines by Groups Outside the Pharmaceutical Industry

The perspective about new medicines under development in groups outside the pharmaceutical industry varies widely depending on the medicine and the specific audience. A number of generalizations, however, can be made because different groups have differing frames of reference for looking at new medicines.

1. *Patients* Patients view new medicines in terms of hopes for improvement of symptoms, underlying disease, or risk factors. Cost of new therapy may also be a major consideration. More sophisticated patients will have at least some awareness of risks and the benefit-to-risk ratio present with the new therapy.
2. *Regulatory Authorities* Regulatory authorities view new medicines from the nation's health perspective in terms of potential health problems resulting from adverse reactions as well as potential benefits. Regulatory agencies often focus on worst-case scenarios.
3. *Competitors* Competitors within the pharmaceutical industry view a new medicine as a minor to major threat to their own marketed medicines and/or new investigational medicines. In some cases a company's own development strategies will be markedly in-

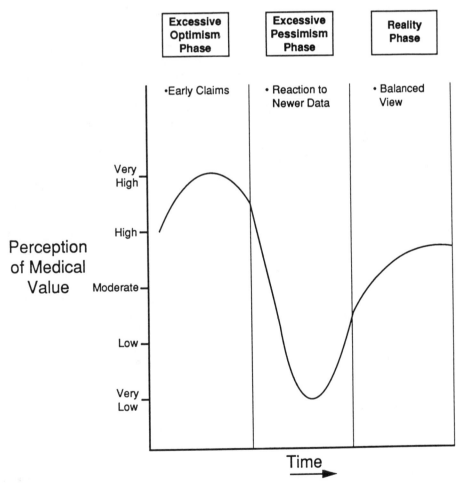

FIG. 3.1. How the perception of a medical innovation changes over time from an exaggerated phase to an overly pessimistic phase and then to a balanced view. This latter phase may lead to rejection or enthusiastic acceptance as well as the in-between conclusion shown.

fluenced by competitors, and in other cases the potential competitors will be ignored.

Some perspectives of consumer advocates, trade associations, physicians, academicians, legislators, and other groups are discussed in the last section of this book.

SYNOPSIS OF MEDICINE DISCOVERY AND DEVELOPMENT

Medicine Discovery

When asked for a definition of Hinduism one religious scholar said, "It's simple; anyone who says he is a Hindu is one." The reason for this statement is that Hinduism has not rejected or cast out beliefs of the past but has continued to build on them and to add new beliefs. Likewise, the processes of medicine discovery are multifaceted and new ways of finding medicines are continually being added without discarding methods of the past. Thus, some people view medicine discovery primarily in terms of the new methods of biotechnology, whereas others emphasize the importance of computer-assisted methods of medicine discovery. Neither of these relatively new approaches is the major means of discovering novel medicines, nor are the oldest methods of random screening or haphazard trial and error that have been used for over 100 years.

The major methods of discovering new medicines today are those used during the past 50 years. The most important method is the trial-and-error empirical approach. Novel compounds called analogues are made that are similar to marketed or known medicines. Other compounds are also made that are distantly related or totally unrelated to marketed or known medicines. These compounds are hypothesized to have biological activity and are then tested by empirical methods using relevant animal models. Some animal models are related to human disease. If the compound is found to have biological activity of interest it is called a chemical lead or a *lead compound*. If the lead is highly active it will stimulate chemists to make many new compounds that are chemically related to the lead compound. Eventually, a compound is hopefully found that has sufficient positive qualities and few negative qualities compared to existing therapy to justify additional animal studies. It is usually hoped that this compound will become a medicine. *This marks the end of the medicine discovery period and the start of medicine development*. The compound is now considered as a *candidate compound* for medicine development.

The processes of medicine discovery are not straightforward. There is a certain amount of disorder in the system. Too much order and control are usually considered detrimental, although there should be a sound rationale underlying the activities conducted.

Many factors must be considered by scientists when choosing specific compounds to make and test. These issues as well as other methods of discovering medicines are discussed in Chapter 20. The one final method of medicine discovery that must be mentioned is serendipity or accident. Mark Twain once aptly said that the greatest inventor of all was accident.

Medicine Development

Medicine development is a highly complex process involving thousands of different activities. For the most part these activities are not described in this book, but may be found in references (see Bibliography). Figures 124.1 and 124.2 in the book *Guide to Clinical Trials* (Spilker, 1991) illustrate how many of these activities are interconnected. As opposed to medicine discovery, where a certain degree and type of disorder is encouraged, medicine development has order, organization, and discipline as goals. Too much disorder can be highly detrimental to the process of bringing a medicine to market.

After a candidate compound to be studied further as a potential medicine is identified, we enter the world of medicine development. Figure 3.2 illustrates the different stages of medicine discovery (i.e., stages A to C), development (i.e., stages D and E), and marketing (i.e., stage F). Early activities of medicine development involve an in-depth analysis of the candidate compound's profile in additional animal studies. This period usually lasts from six to 18 months. If both the positive and negative attributes are acceptable, it means that the compound has a benefit-to-risk ratio adequate to pursue development. At that point the candidate compound is elevated to become a *project compound,* which means that it will be tested in humans if it can pass other preclinical requirements. Project compounds are developed by a project team whose members represent different departments within the company.

The project compound progresses through technical development, toxicology, metabolism, and other animal studies until it receives a green light to be tested in humans. At the time of initial testing in humans a project compound becomes a *project medicine*. There are three phases of clinical trials (see terminology page) that a medicine passes through before it receives regulatory approval and may be sold as a *marketed medicine*. In a few situations (e.g., medicine for a life-threatening disease without adequate treatment or medicine for a rare disease) Phase III may be omitted.

The attrition rate from stage to stage is usually high. It

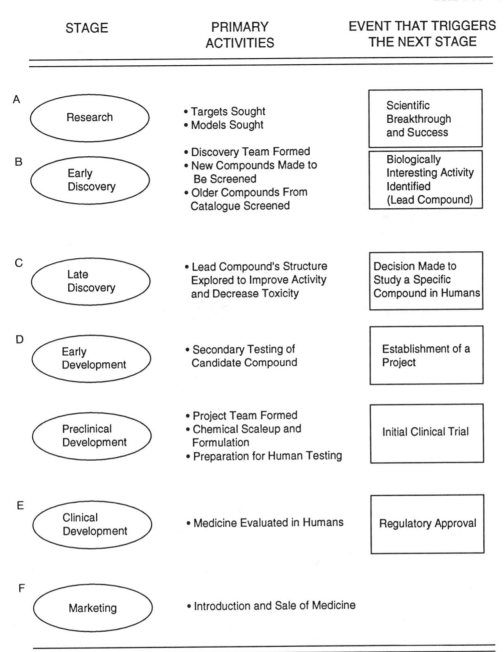

STAGE	PRIMARY ACTIVITIES	EVENT THAT TRIGGERS THE NEXT STAGE
A Research	• Targets Sought • Models Sought	Scientific Breakthrough and Success
B Early Discovery	• Discovery Team Formed • New Compounds Made to Be Screened • Older Compounds From Catalogue Screened	Biologically Interesting Activity Identified (Lead Compound)
C Late Discovery	• Lead Compound's Structure Explored to Improve Activity and Decrease Toxicity	Decision Made to Study a Specific Compound in Humans
D Early Development	• Secondary Testing of Candidate Compound	Establishment of a Project
Preclinical Development	• Project Team Formed • Chemical Scaleup and Formulation • Preparation for Human Testing	Initial Clinical Trial
E Clinical Development	• Medicine Evaluated in Humans	Regulatory Approval
F Marketing	• Introduction and Sale of Medicine	

FIG. 3.2. Major stages of medicine discovery, development, and marketing indicating some of the primary activities conducted during each period and the event that triggers or initiates the next stage.

is estimated that as many as 10,000 compounds are synthesized for every ten that reach the stage of human testing. Of these ten compounds only one eventually reaches the market. The success rate of new compounds and projects is discussed further in Chapter 36.

The terms used to describe the various stages a medicine passes through (lead compound, candidate compound, project compound, project medicine, and marketed medicine) are presented to clarify the various stages of discovery and development. These terms are not all in current use throughout the industry.

Medicine development involves a feedback loop to help future medicine discoveries. Information on a project compound in preclinical studies may indicate a beneficial attribute or toxicological effect that may be hopefully accentuated in the former case or eliminated in the latter case. This information helps chemists design new (and hopefully better) compounds to make and test for their activity. A feedback loop also exists between the clinic and laboratory. Human data enables chemists to design and make better compounds that may eventually be tested as new medicines.

Influence of Regulations on Medicine Discovery and Development

Advances in science and changes in government regulations are the two most important factors to influence the discovery and development of medicines since the Second World War. Specific advances in science will not be discussed here, except to note that many breakthroughs in basic science have eventually led to discoveries of important new medicines.

Many regulations have affected medicine development but two of the most important are the 1938 Food, Drug, and Cosmetic Act, which mandated that medicines must be safe, and the 1962 Kefauver-Harris amendments to the 1938 Act. The latter amendments raised the standards for approval of new medicines, especially in terms of their efficacy. This has provided benefits to many patients who buy and take medicines. Because of these amendments, certain ineffective and partially effective medicines were removed from the market. On the other hand, there is a price paid for these

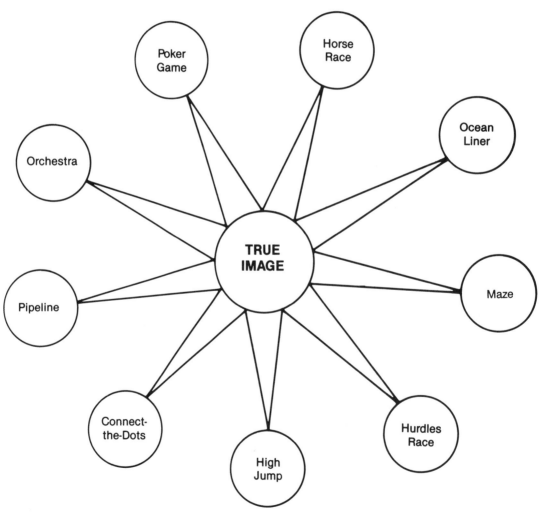

SELECTED METAPHORS OF DRUG DISCOVERY AND DEVELOPMENT

FIG. 3.3. Selected metaphors of medicine discovery and development. The true image for a particular medicine is a combination of some or all of these metaphors.

PIPELINE CONCEPT OF MEDICINE DEVELOPMENT

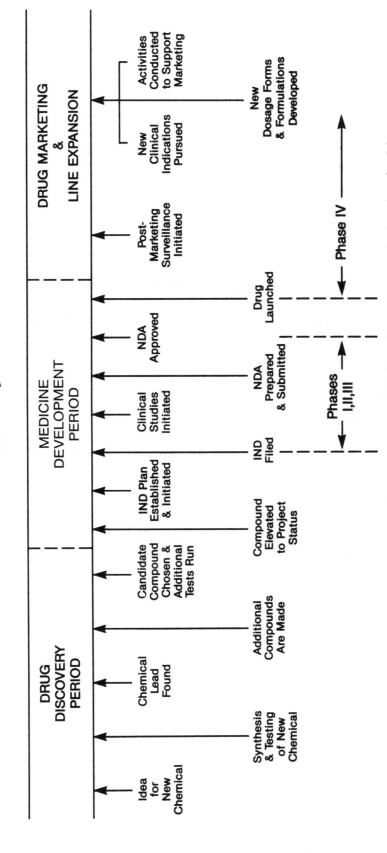

FIG. 3.4. Pipeline concept of medicine development. This figure illustrates general categories of activities that take place during the three main periods of medicine discovery, medicine development, and medicine marketing, shown within the pipeline. IND, Investigational New Drug Application; NDA, New Drug Application.

SELECTED TYPES OF SUBPIPELINES
IN MEDICINE DEVELOPMENT

A. Data from a clinical trial after its completion:

B. Toxicology data:

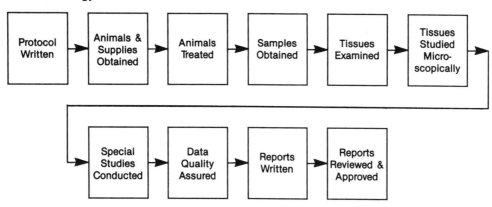

C. Drug prepared for use in clinical studies:

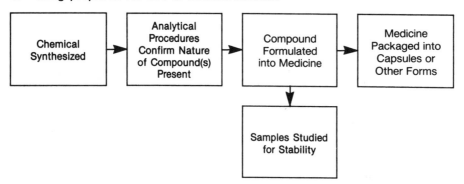

FIG. 3.5. Selected types of subpipelines in medicine development. Five representative subpipelines are presented that occur during medicine development. Each is usually modified for the development of specific medicines. In panel B, many steps are performed in the United States according to Good Laboratory Practices regulations. In panel E, samples refer to blood, urine, or other biological samples. DCF, data collection form.

gains: (1) fewer medicines are brought to market each year, (2) the time after a company submits a New Drug Application (NDA) to the FDA until its approval has grown significantly longer, (3) the higher standards have raised the costs of medicine development, (4) the FDA has decreased the physician's ability (according to some) to choose a medicine to prescribe for patients as freely as in the past, and (5) a medicine lag developed (i.e., there was a greater delay for introducing most medicines in the United States than in certain European countries).

D. Drug packaged for clinical studies:

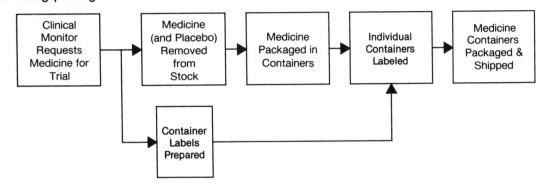

E. Drug levels measured in animal or human samples:

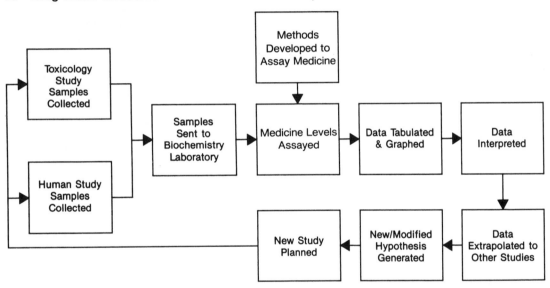

FIG. 3.5. *Continued.*

METAPHORS OF MEDICINE DISCOVERY AND DEVELOPMENT

Because the processes of medicine discovery and development are so complex there are often times when it is useful to describe them using metaphors or analogies. These metaphors are described because they are an easy way to conceptualize many of the processes of medicine discovery or development. There is no single metaphor or analogy that is entirely appropriate or best and many have been used (Fig. 3.3). The metaphors described are (1) pipeline, (2) horse race, (3) poker game, (4) orchestra, (5) hurdles race, (6) ocean liner, (7) connect-the-dots, (8) maze, and (9) high jump.

The pipeline metaphor refers to both discovery and development; the maze refers only to discovery and the orchestra and connect-the-dots, only to development. The others may refer to either discovery or development. Managers often have one or two that they particularly favor. In some situations one metaphor may stand out and capture its essence.

Pipeline of Medicine Discovery, Development, and Marketing

The overall picture of medicine discovery and development has sometimes been described as a pipeline with three main parts: medicine discovery, medicine development, and medicine marketing (Fig. 3.4). Medicine discovery originates with ideas and new chemicals and includes biological testing in various animal models.

Eventually, one or more chemicals emerge as a significant lead (i.e., an important compound to evaluate further and to use as a model to make other related compounds). These leads advance through many stages of preclinical biological testing, and if they do not falter they are evaluated in humans. Clinical evaluation, toxicology, and preclinical studies continue up to the point of the regulatory submission of a NDA. A myriad of interactions, feedback loops, and other activities continue throughout this process. Thus, medicine development should be viewed as a dynamic system that has various bulges of activities and bottlenecks, and not as a rigid pipeline.

As a simple exercise, try to imagine the development activities of a single medicine (i.e., a single project) as it travels through the pipeline. The first stage is the discovery of the compound that will proceed through the pipeline. This may take any number of years because there is no way to predict when (or if) a discovery will be made. The usual range would be from one to 12 years for most medicines. Once the compound is identified, activities are initially begun in some preclinical science departments to evaluate the compound's profile and safety in detail. Eventually, more departments become involved (e.g., chemical scaleup, formulations, statistics, and regulatory affairs) as the compound progresses along the pipeline. Some departments remain active throughout a project's life, while others may be active for only a limited period. This major pipeline is really composed of many smaller pipelines or subpipelines, within a single department or single function. A few of these are shown in Fig. 3.5. The typical time period required to take a medicine through the pipeline after it has been identified and chosen for development is six to 12 years (Table 3.1).

The single project described may be major in terms of resources required and it may stretch the capacity of the company's resources as it travels along the pipeline. When a major project is being developed, the pipeline is sometimes viewed like a snake that has swallowed a huge ball. A "visible" bulge passes progressively through its body. The resolution of temporary bottlenecks (i.e., areas that have insufficient personnel or other resources and have created a large backlog of work) often may be expedited with temporary staff or novel solutions.

TABLE 3.1. *Typical periods of time required to develop new medicines*

Stage of development: usual range of required approximate mean time (in years)
1. Project formation to IND:[a] filing 0.5 to 2.5
2. Phase I clinical trials: 0.5 to 1.5
3. Phase II clinical trials: 1.0 to 5.0
4. Phase III clinical trials and preparation of NDA:[a] 1.0 to 5.0
5. FDA:[a] review of NDA, 1.0 to 5.0 total, 4.0 to 19.0

[a] FDA, Food and Drug Administration; IND, Investigational New Drug Application; NDA, New Drug Application.

In practice, the overall pipeline within a company involves more than a single medicine because many projects are pursued simultaneously. Imagine a long snake that has swallowed not one project, but 40 or more. Some are small and others, far greater in magnitude. In addition to adding new projects to the system, other projects are expanding, and still others are being terminated. New regulations also have a marked influence on many of the activities within this pipeline by influencing which areas of the snake must expand or change.

To address many of these issues, a company must monitor what is occurring at each part of the pipeline (i.e., within various departments) and ensure that each department is prepared for the projects that are heading toward it. Sometimes it is necessary to add more staff because of markedly increased work loads, but there are many other solutions that may also be tried in attempting to maintain the balance among the work load of groups active in medicine development. These solutions include reassigning personnel, hiring temporary staff, contracting work to outside groups, and delaying some projects. Other factors to consider include building new facilities, purchasing new equipment, and licensing medicine in (or out). As a result of this dynamic environment the balance between research and development activities in the pipeline must be periodically, if not continually, observed and readjusted.

The third stage of the pipeline occurs after a medicine is launched on the market. It includes development of new formulations, routes of administration, dosage forms, and new indications. These activities are often critical in the ability of a company to improve the medicine's market share and viable life.

Horse Race

Some companies occasionally put a lot of their resources on one of their horses entered in a commercially minor race. The company works hard to win that race while allowing its horses, competing in more important races, to finish back in the pack. It is clearly better from a commercial viewpoint to come in second or even third in an important horse race than to win a minor race. The difficult part for companies to know is whether each of the races they enter is an important race or not. Many seemingly important races turn into minor ones after the horses are halfway around the track.

For example, interferon had so much media and scientific hype in the late 1970s that it appeared to be an incredibly important race. As a result, many companies invested enormous resources, despite the fact that most of the ultimate clinical uses of interferon were purely speculative. Little hard data were available and no clinical uses were documented. As the data were received and a sound judgment made, it became apparent that the true market size during the 1980s was minuscule compared to the original expectations. The two major companies in this area continued to invest enormous resources, and apparently did not markedly scale back their efforts. The opposite situation in which a commonly accepted minor race turns into a major one (e.g., the development of antiulcer medicines) can also occur. It is interesting to note that after a decade of use the interferon market is now expanding rapidly in hepatitis B and hepatitis C indications.

Poker Game

The poker game describes medicine research as a game where numerous competitors are at the same table. The table usually refers to a specific disease or therapeutic area. A certain investment is required to enter and to play the game. Before each card is taken, players must either ante up more money or withdraw from the game. As in stud poker, a few cards of each player are on the table for all to see, but what is not seen is usually of critical importance. Decisions on whether to fold or to continue playing are based on how one's own cards are evaluated and on guesses of what cards are held by the other players. If the game is in a new therapeutic area, it is possible for beginners to win and players usually continue until one or more do win. Nonetheless, most games are won by professionals. The stakes in a game may be small or high depending on how each player sees the commercial importance of what is in the pot. If the game is to see who can first develop a new medicine that is available to several players (e.g., interferons, interleukins, or tissue plasminogen activator), then most players will quickly drop out of the game or develop a new game plan. Some players will be using more of their chips in that game, whereas others may be using them at another table. The strategy of two or more players may be tc combine their hands and play their best cards (i.e., form a joint venture). Another strategy is to start a new game in a new therapeutic or disease area where no one else or few others are involved. Each company is involved in a different number and choice of games, all of which are being played simultaneously.

Orchestra

Each major function in a pharmaceutical company working on medicine development may be viewed as one of the sections of an orchestra. Preclinical groups may be viewed as the string section; marketing, as the brass section; technical development, as the woodwinds; and so forth. Within each orchestra section are individual instruments (i.e., departments) and there are individual musicians (i.e., professionals) who play them. Unless the entire group plays together and in harmony the piece will not sound correct. The better the musicians in the orchestra are, the faster they will learn the score and create a better sound.

The conductor is usually the head of research and development, and the musical score he or she follows is the medicine development plan. Sometimes, the musical score must be rearranged to sound better or to suit the musicians playing it. Sometimes, the tempo may have to be adjusted. There are a small group of music teachers (i.e., regulators) who are listening to the practices and dress rehearsal. These teachers must approve the performance before it is played for the audience of physicians and patients on opening night (i.e., product launch). If the performance gets rave reviews from the critics, then it will usually have a long and commercially successful run. Of course, performances by other orchestras may draw the crowds away, and problems with the quality of the performance may always arise that can close the show.

Hurdles Race

Developing a medicine may be imagined as a race with a series of both high and low hurdles that the medicine must jump over while racing around the track. Each company in this race occupies one or more lanes. Each lane is occupied by a separate indication or dosage form for the medicine to compete in. Medicines may start in one lane and transfer to another lane or run in multiple lanes at the same time. It is important to prevent the medicine's development from going off on tangents, such as off the track. Most tangents are along paths that never return to the main track nor reach the finish line of the race.

The hurdles for a new medicine to clear before it can be approved are an adequate efficacy, safety, and manufacturing quality. In some countries (e.g., Norway) the regulatory authorities add another hurdle to those used by other nation's regulatory authorities. This hurdle is social need. Social need means that a company must demonstrate a need for the medicine to ensure it is not purely a "me-too" medicine.

While every company desires medicines that soar over the minimally acceptable standards this seldom happens. Instead, a medicine often is fully safe and partially effective or partially safe and fully effective. The Japanese would generally prefer to have the former; American companies prefer the latter.

Ocean Liner

Large pharmaceutical companies, as well as the individual events of medicine development, have been described as a huge ocean liner steering a course through calm or stormy seas. This metaphor is mainly used to describe the situation that occurs when the captain decides to turn the boat sharply (or gradually) in a different direction. It takes both time and distance for any effect on the boat's course to occur and to be seen. The captain's command must be relayed to the people controlling the steering wheel and then sheer inertia takes the boat many miles further before any difference in direction is noted. Most medicine development projects start out as small motorboats darting in and out amongst larger boats, but over time they generally increase in size and slow in their ability to maneuver rapidly toward their goals.

Maze

The image of a maze probably originated because there are usually many choices of paths to follow in medicine discovery. Many of these paths lead to dead ends, and it is rarely certain that the goal of discovering a new medicine will be achieved. This metaphor should not be used to describe medicine development because it would imply that medicine development is either haphazard, lost, or nonfocused (Fig. 3.6).

Connect-the-Dots, Lottery, and Other Metaphors

A simple metaphor of medicine development often used as a slur by some managers who are outside the complexity of research and development activities is connect-the-dots. This simplistic image is an attempt by nonscientific people to provide a frame of reference for themselves to tie together many activities that they know occur, but do not understand. This book attempts to demystify many of those activities and also to indicate why this metaphor is not correct.

The lottery image has nothing to recommend it, except that there is usually a certain amount of luck involved in discovering a new medicine, but in almost all cases there is much more to discovery than just luck. The concept of medicine development being a lottery is to-

SEAT-OF-THE-PANTS MEDICINE DEVELOPMENT

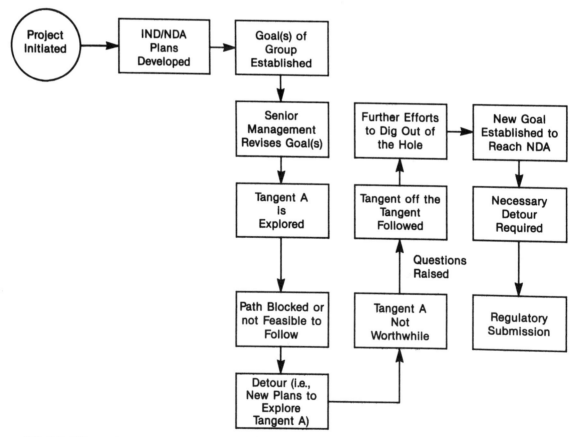

FIG. 3.6. "Seat-of-the-pants" medicine development. An example of a haphazard approach to developing medicines.

tally inaccurate. Chess is also considered as an inappropriate metaphor for many reasons, but the major one is that it is played by individuals and not teams. Other reasons include fixed rules and a war mentality in all games.

Two metaphors were used by Weisblat and Stucki (1974) to describe the differences between two types of research and development organizations. They described the traditional discipline-oriented approach to medicine discovery and development as resembling a relay team where the baton is passed from one solo performer to another. The therapeutic area team approach used at The Upjohn Company was described as being similar to a football team where the ball is moved forward under a quarterback's direction.

High Jump

One final metaphor of medicine development is that of the high jump. Safety and efficacy standards for treating a particular disease are established when a novel medicine is introduced for a previously untreatable disease. All new medicines to be discovered and developed in the future must meet or surpass those levels to be acceptable to regulatory authorities and to physicians. As more effective and safe treatments become available, the standards are progressively raised (by the medicines themselves). Medicines that would have been approved a short period before can no longer get over the regulatory bar (standards) required for approval.

Types of High Jumps

The standards that must be achieved in developing new medicines are equivalent to the bars on a high jump. A variety of high jumps for a new medicine to surpass may be described as follows, although safety and efficacy are the most important.

1. Safety.
2. Efficacy: objective measures.
3. Efficacy: subjective measures.
4. Pharmacokinetic characteristics.
5. Economic factors.
6. Image, social, and political issues.
7. Competitive environment.
8. Ease or convenience of using the treatment.
9. Technical specifications.
10. Production issues (e.g., environmental waste).

It is important to be aware of all the high jumps in a competition and not misjudge either the number or their height. Some inexperienced companies see certain bars to clear and attempt to pole vault over them rather than to just clear the bar or to clear it with a small amount of space. For example, if a therapeutic ratio of 5 is desirable, they may decide that 10 is the minimally acceptable value. If an improvement of 20% in the major parameter of efficacy is required to show clinical benefit, they may decide that a much higher value is necessary, even if the competition cannot surpass 20%. The concepts of high jump standards are figuratively shown in Figs. 3.7 to 3.9.

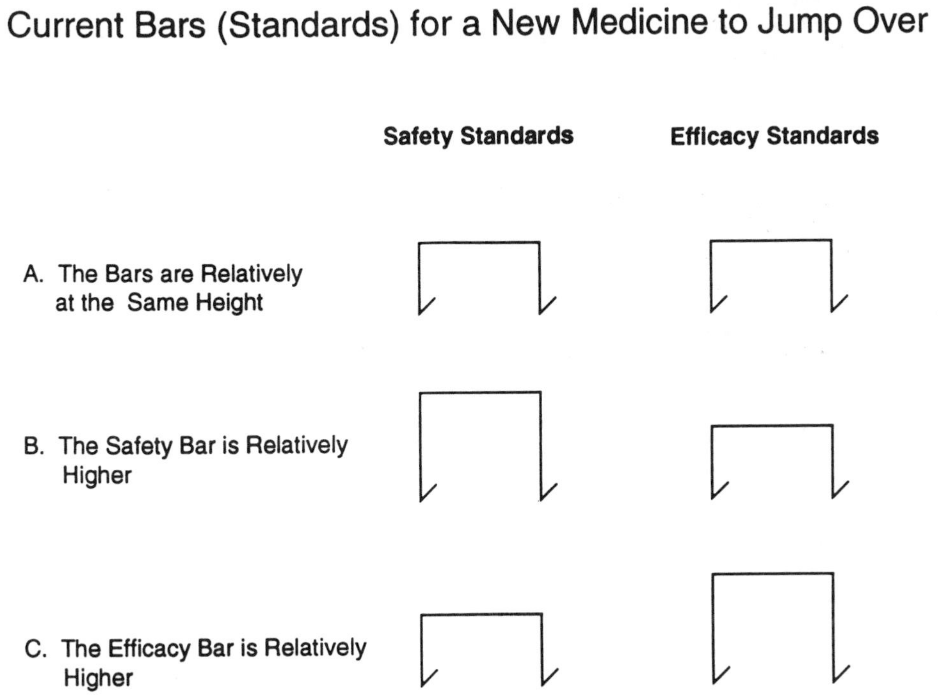

Current Bars (Standards) for a New Medicine to Jump Over

FIG. 3.7. Safety and efficacy standards viewed as a pair of high jumps for the medicine to exceed.

Raising the Standards Of a New Medicine

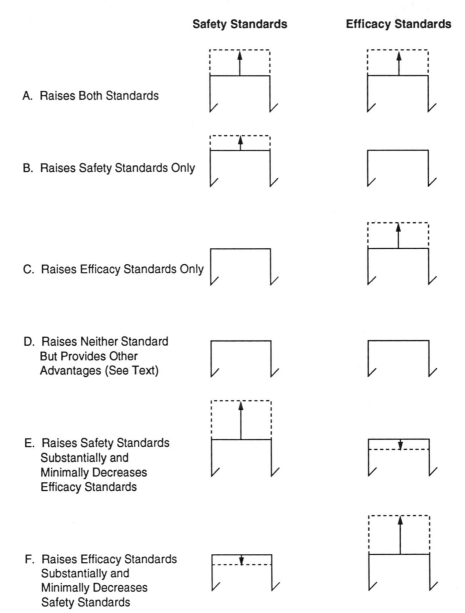

FIG. 3.8. Various means for a medicine to improve on the standards of previous therapy. Caution must be used in evaluating whether the risk-to-benefit ratio is improved or not in panels E and F.

Current Standards for Selected Types of Medicines

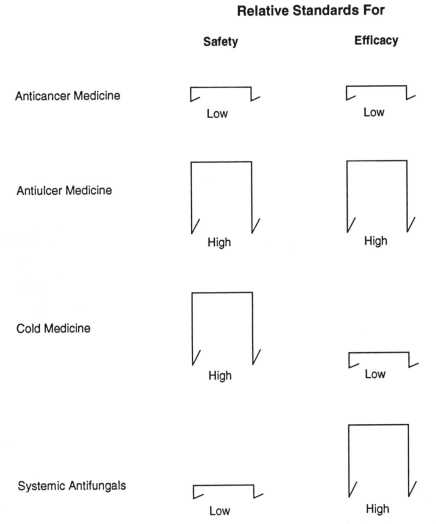

FIG. 3.9. Examples of medicines where there is great room for improvement in both safety and efficacy (i.e., anticancer medicine), in one or the other, or where both safety and efficacy standards are high.

How Do People View Metaphors?

Do you, the reader, think of medicine discovery or development in terms of metaphors? It would be interesting for some people to learn if scientists usually use different metaphors than nonscientists, if Americans use different metaphors than Europeans, and if managers use different than workers, or actually how many people even think about medicine discovery or development in this way. This information would indicate whether the basic concept of medicine discovery or development is viewed in generally similar or different terms. A company might decide to promote one particular metaphor as a means of encouraging their employees to utilize the same concept about their activities.

INTERFACES IN A COMPANY BETWEEN MAJOR FUNCTIONS

Numerous interfaces exist between major functions (i.e., research and development, marketing, and production in all pharmaceutical companies, unless they are unifunctional companies, e.g., small biotechnology companies that only conduct basic research). The most important interfaces are those between marketing and production and those between marketing and research and development. Marketing and production groups are sometimes 180° apart in needs and orientation and yet managing this interface appropriately is critical to a company's success. One of the reasons for this difference is that marketing staff need to wait until the last minute to place a production order, and production staff need the most time possible to prepare a medicine. Special attention must be given to ensure this interface runs smoothly. One means of doing this is to establish or to use already established committees to discuss relevant issues and problems. This action must occur at multiple levels of the company to be effective.

The interface between research and development with production is also important but few major differences exist in the philosophy, goal, and orientation of these two groups. This means that fewer basic conflicts arise than in the other two cases. Likewise, the interface between discovery research and medicine development used to be more of an issue in the past, but this has been improved. Most large companies handle this interface quite well. If problems exist, they are primarily management issues to address. Many other interfaces exist between departments (e.g., statistics and clinical or advertising and product managers) and smaller groups that often raise problems of philosophical differences must be addressed. A number of these situations are discussed in the text. Some of the interfaces between support groups or between support groups and the major functions are also discussed in the text.

The interface between marketing and research and development is quite variable in different companies and depends on many factors. It may be characterized best by any one of the following (or other) terms: close cooperation and teamwork, independence of each, dominance of one group, competition, distrust, disdain, and so forth. This area is so important that four chapters are devoted to it in the text (Chapters 37 to 40).

One of the keys to improving the interactions between groups is to focus on the education of each staff member who interacts across functional lines. This education should focus on the perspectives of the other group. This requires an ongoing series of talks and multiple-day orientations to enhance teamwork and communications. Other basic techniques are to have people work together, focusing on issues to solve jointly rather than creating we–them relationships. This approach requires frequent communication, in addition to openness and honesty.

RESOURCE ALLOCATION

Many of the issues and problems that arise between different functions within a company relate to identifying who has the responsibility for what activities and who has the resources to carry out those activities. Resources involve much more than people and money (Table 3.2), but those two are usually the most important to consider. While the heads of production, marketing, finance, legal, personnel, and research and development (and others) usually can move people and other re-

TABLE 3.2. *Resources available for use by a company[a]*

1. Time
2. Money
3. People
4. Experience and knowledge
5. Personal contacts
6. Equipment and facilities (e.g., state of the art and time to work on activities needed)
7. Image and reputation of company (e.g., credibility)
8. Human interactions and networks
9. Agreements with other companies, institutions, and individuals
10. Patents
11. Marketed products
12. Investigational products

[a] These categories are quite disparate and some categories only apply to specific cases or situations.

sources within their jurisdiction to achieve their goals, resources are seldom moved between functions. Dividing new resources among functions may involve more political infighting than application of logic. This issue is one of the underlying problems at some companies as they attempt to achieve their various goals.

Allocation of Resources: Pitfalls to Avoid

A common pitfall is that projects that consume a small head count and little money are generally considered as a minor project consuming few resources. While this may be true, many seemingly minor projects consume a disproportionate amount of (1) a senior manager's time to sort out and settle minor (or major) issues, (2) regulatory affairs department's time to deal with many regulatory issues, (3) patent attorney's time maintaining patents, and (4) administrative activities conducted throughout the company. Thus terminating some apparently minor

TABLE 3.3. *General comparison of multinational pharmaceutical companies in the 1950s and 1960s versus the 1990s*

	1950s to early 1960s	1990s
No. of pharmaceutical companies	Many	Fewer and larger
No. of biotechnology companies	None	Many
Costs of preclinical research	Modest	Much higher
Competition	Modest	More intense
Regulatory requirements	Modest	More sophisticated
Time to develop medicines	Two or three years	Eight to twelve years
Communication between regulatory agencies	Little	Much more

TABLE 3.4. *Impact of various factors on the overall speed and quality of a medicine's development[a]*

Facilities and equipment	Procedures and systems	Resulting efficiency of the development process	Quality of the staff	Standards and sense of urgency	Resulting quality and speed of medicine development
Poor	Poor	Low	Low	Low	Poor
Poor	Poor	Low	High	High	Fair/Good
Fair/Good	Fair/Good	Good	Low	Low	Poor
Fair/Good	Fair/Good	Good	High	High	Excellent
Excellent	Excellent	Excellent	Low	Low	Fair
Excellent	Excellent	Excellent	High	High	Highest

[a] Even excellent quality and speed do not relate to the quality of the specific medicine that is being developed. Commercial success depends on that quality, marketing factors, and the timing of the launch. This last factor is related to the issues presented in this table. Other combinations of the factors than those shown in this table could be presented.

projects may result in a relatively major savings of staff and managerial time, even though on paper the resources gained through termination appear to be minor or even unchanged.

MAJOR CHANGES IN THE PHARMACEUTICAL INDUSTRY SINCE 1962

In looking at the international pharmaceutical industry since 1945, the year 1962 is extremely important. That year was the year that the Kefauver-Harris amendments to the 1938 Food, Drug, and Cosmetic Act passed Congress and mandated that efficacy as well as safety be demonstrated for all new medicines. Since 1962 the industry has grown in many different directions.

Some of the major developments over the last 35 years are briefly listed below and summarized in Table 3.3 (and most are described elsewhere in this book).

Research
1. Laboratory instruments connected to computers.
2. Closer connection between basic research and business ventures, particularly in biotechnology.
3. Increased importance of interdisciplinary discovery teams.

Data Management and Projects
1. Computer searchable data bases.
2. Global planning and management.
3. Integrated systems to manage information.
4. National and international project teams.

Clinical Research
1. Higher standards for all aspects of clinical trials.
2. Increased role of statistics.
3. Ultra-large clinical trials sponsored by companies.
4. Explosive growth of contract research organizations.
5. Explosive growth of postmarketing surveillance.

Technical Development
1. Ability to detect smaller quantities of materials and other technical improvements has led to markedly increased standards.
2. Quality assurance groups have developed as a specialty.

Regulatory Authorities
1. Increased harmonization of regulations.
2. Increased communications among authorities.
3. Increasing acceptance of computer assisted NDAs.
4. Higher standards and increased scrutiny of all areas of medicine development, production, and marketing.

Business-Related Activities
1. Increased licensing of medicines and ideas from other companies, individuals, and institutions.
2. Increased competition among companies.
3. Increased spending on research and development.

Marketing
1. Extremely rapid loss of a market on patent expiration to generic medicines.
2. Tighter regulatory control on promotional and advertising practice.

A general overview of the relative importance of facilities, systems, equipment, standards, and staff is given in Table 3.4. This table emphasizes the importance of the staff in the successful development of medicines.

4 / Standards

The Regulatory Cascade	35
Standards: What, Why, and How?	36
What Are Standards?	36
Why Create Standards?	36
How Are Standards for Medicine Development Created?	36
Why Has Controversy Developed About Standards in Recent Years?................	39
How Do Standards Differ From Principles and Golden Rules?	40
Relationships Among Different Types of Standards...................................	40
Minimally Acceptable Standards..............	41
How Are Higher Standards Achieved?	41
Influence of Regulatory Authorities	41
Influence of Pharmaceutical Companies.......	41
Influence of Academic and Government Scientists..................................	41
Who Should Lead the Movement Toward Adopting the Most Appropriate Standards................................	42

Standards of Quality..........................	42
Using the Concept of Quality to Judge the Pharmaceutical Industry......................	42
Clinical Trials	42
Manufacturing of Medicines..................	42
Safety Studies in Animals.....................	43
Modifying Company Procedures to Adhere to New Standards.............................	43
Technical and Production Standards: Regulatory Issues.....................................	44
Standards That Spiral Upward................	44
Impurities and Degradation Products	44
Stability Tests	44
Environmental Impact Analyses	44
Validation of Analytical Methods	44
Auditing Adherence to Standards................	45
Conclusion....................................	45

Health is a complete state of physical, mental, and social well-being and not merely absence of disease.
World Health Organization, 1947.

For the development of a medicine to proceed smoothly, it is important to differentiate among the following terms: standards, regulations, guidelines, policies, principles, recommendations, and golden rules. Clear definitions facilitate and enhance communications. Nevertheless, many of these terms overlap and distinctions among them are generally unclear. As a result, the terms are often misused (e.g., principles are often called guidelines). This chapter discusses the definitions of multiple terms and explores the relationship between them. Its primary focus, however, is to describe the various types of standards used in medicine development and to discuss the relationships among them.

THE REGULATORY CASCADE

Legislators and regulatory authorities use specific definitions for the terms laws, regulations, and guidelines.

The relationship among these terms is described as a "regulatory cascade." This relationship is shown in Fig. 4.1. The term cascade is used because the initial activity of government legislators passing laws often necessitates the development of specific regulations that interpret the law. Those regulations in turn often require the publication of specific guidelines to help people follow the regulations. This cascade continues in progressively less formal steps via points to consider, recommendations, and finally informal comments. Figure 4.2 shows that the ways in which compliance with laws, regulations, and guidelines are assessed follow generally similar procedures.

Regulatory terms described as part of the regulatory cascade are used with the same definitions by pharmaceutical companies. Other terms that are used in almost all regulatory and industrial institutions and organizations are standard operating procedures, policies, and standards. Each of these terms is briefly defined in Table 4.1.

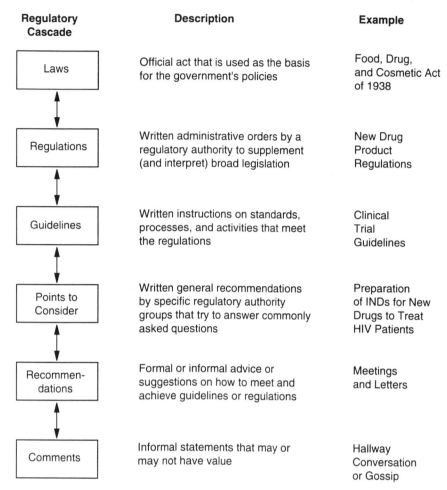

Regulatory Cascade	Description	Example
Laws	Official act that is used as the basis for the government's policies	Food, Drug, and Cosmetic Act of 1938
Regulations	Written administrative orders by a regulatory authority to supplement (and interpret) broad legislation	New Drug Product Regulations
Guidelines	Written instructions on standards, processes, and activities that meet the regulations	Clinical Trial Guidelines
Points to Consider	Written general recommendations by specific regulatory authority groups that try to answer commonly asked questions	Preparation of INDs for New Drugs to Treat HIV Patients
Recommendations	Formal or informal advice or suggestions on how to meet and achieve guidelines or regulations	Meetings and Letters
Comments	Informal statements that may or may not have value	Hallway Conversation or Gossip

FIG. 4.1. The regulatory cascade and selected examples.

STANDARDS: WHAT, WHY, AND HOW?

What Are Standards?

Standards may be thought of as bars on a high jump that an athlete must clear to be successful in a particular endeavor (Fig. 4.3). Figure 4.3 also illustrates related metaphors for a few other terms discussed in this chapter. Numerous types of standards exist for the development of new medicines (Table 4.2). These include (1) ethical standards, (2) regulatory standards, (3) state-of-the-art technical standards, (4) practical standards, and (5) commonly used industry standards. In some cases all of these standards are nearly identical, but in most situations there are great differences among them. Adherence to one set of standards often leads to failure to meet others. Moreover, meeting or even surpassing one set of standards (e.g., regulatory) in a particular country (e.g., Sri Lanka) does not mean that (regulatory) standards for the same issue will be met in all countries. Great differences from country to country often exist for all types of standards, except for technical state-of-the-art standards, which are universal.

Why Create Standards?

Ethical standards, practical standards, state-of-the-art technical standards, and commonly used industry standards all exist for many particular aspects of medicine development. Regulatory standards are the only type that do not *a priori* (i.e., necessarily) exist. Regulatory standards are established by a government to protect the health of a nation's patients when taking medicines. Prior to the 20th century, few regulatory standards existed and the overall control of medicine composition, manufacture, and sale was often grossly inadequate to protect people's health. Many dangerous medicines were widely promoted and sold for use in totally unethical ways (e.g., morphine was given as a pacifier to quiet "noisy" babies).

How Are Standards for Medicine Development Created?

Each of the five general types of standards described below is often applied to specific issues in toxicology, clinical trials, manufacturing, or any other aspect of the

Implementation of Laws, Regulations and Guidelines

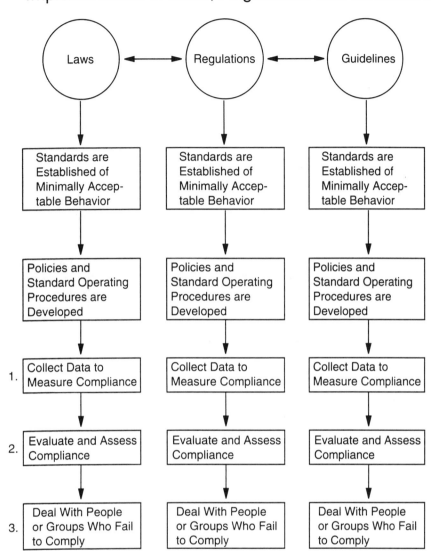

FIG. 4.2. Steps involved in the implementation of laws, regulations, and guidelines, and the assessment of compliance.

TABLE 4.1. *Operational definitions of various terms*

Term	Definition
Law	Principles and official codes established by an authority and applied to the people in a given area. In science, the description of thoroughly tested and accepted phenomena
Rule	A principle, regulation, or guideline that is generally based on an accumulation of observations and tests. Prescribed or suggested guide for conduct or action
Regulation	The specification of rules by a government or other official organization and issued by government departments to carry out the intent of the law
Standard	An approved reference of a specific type or magnitude that is considered by an authority or by general agreement to be the accepted reference for comparison, control, or for securing uniformity
Guideline	A statement or rule to guide conduct according to an accepted policy to carry out a regulation, achieve a standard, or follow a rule
Policy	General principles by which an organization manages its activities and makes its decisions
Standard operating procedures	Methods and instructions of how various activities are to be performed to carry out policies of specific organizations, in order to achieve the group's goals and objectives. These are usually written documents and change over time to adhere to new regulations, company policies, or new technologies

High Jump Metaphor for Selected Types of Standards

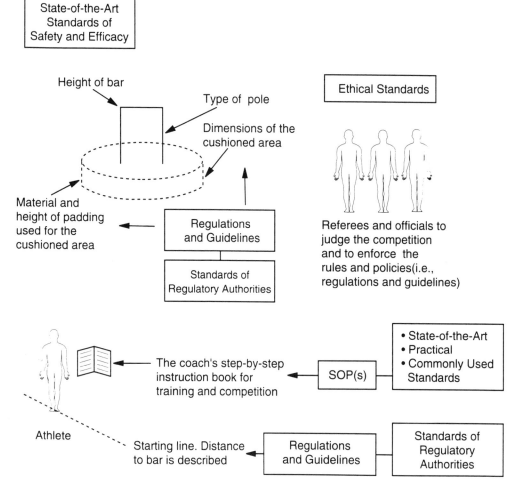

FIG. 4.3. Schematic presentation of metaphors of several types of standards and other terms (e.g., regulations, guidelines, and standard operating procedures) using the high jump.

TABLE 4.2. *Types of standards relating to various aspects of the pharmaceutical industry*

Commonly used pharmaceutical industry standards	Those followed by most research and development-based companies
Pharmaceutical company standards[a]	Standards of various types are reflected in the company's standard operating procedures, and are reflected in the ways in which a company conducts its business
Regulatory standards	Sometimes approach the state of the art, but usually are at or near the level of the most advanced companies
Clinical methodology standards	Golden rules and principles followed in clinical trials
Legal standards	Laws of each country regarding the pharmaceutical industry
Ethical standards	Medical practice (community standards) and professional societies often establish these
Professional standards	Various medical, scientific, and other professional societies create or describe standards
Technical standards	Specification that must be met by the company in producing a medicine

[a] Many of these (or others in this table) may be considered as practical standards.

discovery, development, production, or marketing of medicines. This chapter cannot explore those detailed applications. Rather, a brief description is given of how each of the types of standards is created.

Regulatory standards are created as laws by governments (Congress in the United States) and interpreted through regulations, guidelines, and comments by the national regulatory authority that is charged with approving and reviewing the safety of medicines.

State-of-the-art technical standards are created by innovative scientists and clinicians in the forefront of their fields, and by those who influence thinking in the disciplines in which they work. Some of this latter group of people are methodologists who are concerned with refining established approaches and methods within their own discipline.

Practical standards are created by the companies developing medicines. They determine what level of effort is feasible and cost effective to achieve the specific goals they set. Practical standards are often below state-of-the-art standards. Nonetheless, practical standards can be appropriate when studying certain topics.

Ethical standards are created informally by common usage (i.e., community standards) and formally by professional societies and other professionals groups (e.g., boards of medicine) that specifically develop such standards. Various international organizations (e.g., World Health Organization or World Medical Assembly) also develop and refine various sets of ethical standards.

Commonly used industry standards are based on current practices within the pharmaceutical industry. There is probably greater variation among countries in this set of standards than in any other set. Even within a small group of professionals in a single area there may be strong disagreements about what practices meet "commonly used standards."

Why Has Controversy Developed About Standards in Recent Years?

Standards have become a major issue of debate in recent years because there is a growing difference between certain sets of standards (e.g., between state-of-the-art technical standards and practical standards); furthermore various groups within industry and also some governments are sometimes unsure about which set to adopt and use. Several decades ago the commonly used standards and ethical standards that were followed during evaluation of medicines in clinical trials were found to be inadequate to allow scientists to reach reliable conclusions about a medicine's efficacy and safety. It made sense at that time for regulators to raise the standards markedly. This had a major beneficial effect both on medical practice and on the development of new medicines that were effective and safe. Now, with the rapid

rise in state-of-the-art standards in toxicology, data analysis, data transmission, technical assays, formulation, and quality assurance, it is likely, in some areas, that at least state-of-the-art standards have progressed beyond what is practical or necessary to ensure patient safety. If the state-of-the-art standards are higher than the regulatory standards, it is probable that this gap is acceptable and should not be closed, as long as the public's safety is maintained.

There have been few public debates over whether regulatory standards are adhering too closely to state-of-the-art standards in certain technical areas and over whether the higher regulatory standards are worth the additional costs in terms of money and time required of a company. These additional costs delay new medicines from reaching the patients who need them and contribute, often in a major way, to the higher prices charged for new medicines. Resolution of this debate often can be reached by

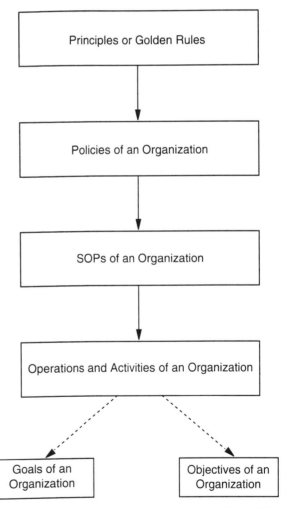

FIG. 4.4. Relationship between principles and the achievement of company goals and objectives. The solid arrow means that points in the category shown above the arrow are used to help create and drive the category shown below it. The dotted arrows means that the category above helps achieve the category below.

determining at what point further increases in standards for new medicines do not achieve commensurate benefits for the ultimate user—the patient.

How Do Standards Differ From Principles and Golden Rules?

Principles are the foundation on which most standards are based. On the other hand, commonly used industry standards are based on practices. Certain standards are universally accepted and followed because the principles supporting them are believed. Other standards, such as some enacted by regulators, may be widely ignored or challenged if the most important principles underlying them are not accepted by those who are being regulated. It is appropriate to conceptualize that a single set of principles underlies most standards within a specific area. Golden rules are the same as important principles and have been proposed by Spilker (1991) in a number of different areas of medicine development, including:

- Overall medicine development
- Clinical development
- Data management
- Monitoring of trials

One framework for conceptualizing how principles or golden rules potentially enable a company to achieve its goals and objectives is shown in Fig. 4.4.

RELATIONSHIPS AMONG DIFFERENT TYPES OF STANDARDS

A hierarchy of standards is illustrated in Fig. 4.5. The figure illustrates that, in areas where multiple types of standards exist, each set influences the others and is influenced by others. The magnitude of the distances labeled A, B, C, and D in this figure vary from case to case, and in many situations two or more of these distances may be identical or nearly so. It is also possible that there is no difference between two (or more) sets of standards. The type and degree of influence of ethical and regulatory standards on the others is also variable: precise influences vary from situation to situation and from country to country.

When one compares sets of standards between two disciplines other differences may be noted. For example,

Relationship Between Different Types of Standards

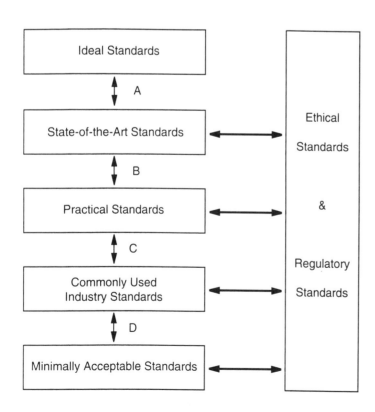

FIG. 4.5. Relationship between different types of standards. The magnitude of A, B, C, and D (1) may vary from zero to a large amount, (2) could be equal or unequal, and (3) usually differs for standards in any scientific or nonscientific discipline.

standards in technical areas (e.g., assay procedures) are usually more quantitative than are standards in nontechnical areas, such as clinical medicine. Clinical standards are usually more general and rely on such factors as clinical judgment and the benefit-to-risk ratio in deciding whether they are being met or not.

Minimally Acceptable Standards

Minimally acceptable standards may be created that apply to regulatory, ethical, or commonly accepted standards. The question arises as to whether there can be multiple types or a broad range of minimally acceptable standards for developing new medicines. The answer is "yes," because these standards of medicine development involve the application of some judgment (e.g., the minimally acceptable regulatory standard for a new oncologic medicine is lower than the corresponding standard for an antiallergy medicine) and are not fixed requirements. Regulatory, ethical, or commonly accepted standards may be discussed and applied to medicine development either in a broad manner or quite specifically.

Some of the groups concerned with determining minimally acceptable standards for a medicine or medical practice are (1) journal editors, (2) ethics committees/institutional review boards, (3) industrial sponsors, (4) regulators, and (5) physicians in practice. Minimally acceptable standards frequently change, and what is acceptable at one time (or in one country) may no longer be so at a later date or in another country.

HOW ARE HIGHER STANDARDS ACHIEVED?

The major use of standards in clinical trials is as a guide for sponsors, investigators, and others about (1) how protocols should be designed and written, (2) how trials should be conducted, and (3) how the collected data should be analyzed and reported. In other areas of medicine development standards have a comparable role in influencing the goals for work and any outputs (e.g., reports or samples). If one or more standards are lower than desired by the public or the medical community, the standard(s) may be forced to a higher level. If the requirements for meeting regulatory standards are deemed excessive, vague, or conflicting, a variety of forums should be established in which the standards can be discussed or debated.

Influence of Regulatory Authorities

Regulatory authorities, primarily in the United States, have been responsible for the dramatic increase in standards used to develop and manufacture medicines this century. One of the current debates about standards is over whether the Food and Drug Administration (FDA) has pulled the pharmaceutical industry beyond a reasonable standard and nearly up to the state-of-the-art in certain areas. The fact that analytical techniques and other technical methods are continually improving is not necessarily a valid reason for expecting or requiring that pharmaceutical companies meet each of those standards. Yet this is exactly what is happening in many cases. State-of-the-art standards for many of these techniques will undoubtedly continue to improve and eventually will exceed any reasonable level as regulatory standards. Regulatory authorities should consider using standards that in some cases may be significantly below the state-of-the-art possibilities yet adequate to ensure safe and reliable medicine products.

Influence of Pharmaceutical Companies

Increasing competition among pharmaceutical companies is pressuring many to raise their standards of clinical development voluntarily. A strategy of some companies is to inform regulatory authorities indirectly about the possibility of adhering to higher clinical standards and thus encourage the authority to require all companies (i.e., particularly the competition) to adhere to the higher standards. Another strategy is for a company to obtain particular types of data (e.g., quality of life or pharmacoeconomic) at a higher standard to ensure that its medicine is placed on a formulary by a committee that reviews the data. This approach may then encourage formulary committees or other groups to raise their standards. Promotional benefits may also be achieved through conducting clinical trials at a higher standard than required. For example, if regulatory authorities require the company to demonstrate a specific effect on a surrogate end point for a new medicine, the company may also (or alternatively) conduct trials on the real end point (e.g., mortality). These results may have major promotional value far exceeding the cost of the trial.

Influence of Academic and Government Scientists

Academic and government-sponsored (e.g., National Institutes of Health in the United States) clinical trials may establish a new standard in a disease area and may influence pharmaceutical sponsors to increase their clinical trial standards. This is more likely to occur in disease areas where major state-of-the-art academic and government trials are common (e.g., oncology or epilepsy). Although high standards used in certain nonindustry-sponsored trials do not necessarily have to be adopted by pharmaceutical companies, important advances made by academic or government clinicians or others are often widely adopted by companies within a short period.

Academic trials, like industry-sponsored trials, are designed and conducted using a wide spectrum of standards. Academic, government, and industrial professionals pay particular attention to, and often criticize, poorly designed trials sponsored by others. Academicians often criticize many marketing studies sponsored by the pharmaceutical industry that are designed and conducted at a lower standard than well-controlled Phase II or III trials. Some of the same academicians appear unaware that many of the Phase II, III, and IV clinical trials, including those that set new standards of excellence, are designed by industry physicians and medical staff. On the other side of the fence, it is common for many pharmaceutical company medical staff to read one underpowered academic-sponsored trial after another in the medical literature and form a poor opinion of academic trials. In both instances poorly designed clinical trials are only part of the complete profile of all trials conducted.

Who Should Lead the Movement Toward Adopting the Most Appropriate Standards?

It is this author's opinion that the pharmaceutical industry rather than regulatory authorities should take the lead in establishing appropriate technical and clinical standards for all aspects of medicine development. In some cases this would result in the use of higher standards, while in others, current standards may be relaxed to a more appropriate level. The industry should approach the regulatory authorities to recommend that a joint approach to this exercise be conducted, possibly with involvement of government and academic scientists. If regulatory authorities are unwilling to engage in this type of dialogue, then industry could take the initiative to conduct this exercise itself and then take appropriate steps to ensure that its standards are acceptable to and accepted by regulatory authorities. For example, meetings could be arranged with regulatory authorities to discuss any recommendations or proposals that are developed by the pharmaceutical industry.

STANDARDS OF QUALITY

Using the Concept of Quality to Judge the Pharmaceutical Industry

Many aspects of the pharmaceutical industry are evaluated in terms of quality. The quality of a medicine relates to the levels it achieves for many specific standards (both technical and clinical). The word quality has been used more in recent years, and the concept has taken on

importance through the universal concern that money spent on health care should yield the greatest benefits attainable. In most countries concern is mounting over whether (1) the money spent on medicines is either too much or too little, (2) money is spent in the most appropriate therapeutic areas, and (3) money is spent on the most appropriate medical technologies. Frustration exists among legislators, health policy administrators, academicians, and others because there is a lack of accurate and adequate data to address these three questions. Also, evidence continues to accumulate about growing problems with the quality of health care in most nations. People can more readily agree on identifying the problem than they can on the best solution. Each group seems to have its own solution or solutions to propose. It is always easier to write about problems than to propose solutions that are generally viewed as appropriate, affordable, and practical (i.e., realistic).

The term quality is applied to a broad spectrum of activities in medicine development and manufacture including those in the three areas discussed.

Clinical Trials

Quality in a clinical trial relates to the degree that (1) the trial design meets current standards, (2) the trial adheres to the protocol, (3) the level of care provided patients during the trial's conduct adheres to current standards, and (4) the data analysis and interpretation adhere to current state-of-the-art standards. The quality of a clinical trial could be extremely high even if the medicine tested was not better than a placebo against which the medicine is tested. The value of a medicine and the impact of a particular clinical trial on medical practice are related to the importance of the specific trial, not its quality. Nonetheless, it is unlikely that an important clinical trial will be of poor quality. Clinical trials often are audited to ensure adherence to good clinical practice (GCP) standards. GCPs represent the most appropriate and accepted clinical standards in the country(ies) involved.

Manufacturing of Medicines

Quality in manufacturing relates to the degree to which the actual processes and activities used meet the standards and specifications established. Special groups (Quality Assurance Departments) ensure the company's adherence to these standards, by following the company's standard operating procedures. These procedures are designed to ensure that the company adheres to Good Manufacturing Practice regulations. If such regulations do not exist, then the standard operating procedures must ensure that a company meets its own standards, those of all relevant regulatory authorities, and those of the purchasers of its products.

Safety Studies in Animals

Quality relates to the standards adhered to in the care of animals, the design and conduct of preclinical studies, collection of data, processing of data, and interpretation of the data. A special group or department exists in some companies to ensure adherence to the company's standard operating procedures and Good Laboratory Practice regulations. In some countries, auditing these standards requires that the same or another group review the results of assays used to measure the levels of medicines in biological samples from these animals (i.e., the field of toxicokinetics).

The motivation of a company to increase quality in one or more areas is to improve morale, improve productivity, and improve the chances of its own survival. Many years ago the question often raised about quality was "Is it worth the cost?," i.e., it became an economic issue. The success of the Japanese automobile and electronics manufacturers who stressed quality markedly changed this thinking. Today people believe quality is something that must be continually worked at.

Modifying Company Procedures to Adhere to New Standards

As standards change in any area that a company wishes to meet, it modifies its standard operating procedures to adhere to the new standards. Some of the different reasons for a company to modify its standard operating procedures are shown in Fig. 4.6. One circle in this figure indicates regulation changes. This may occur either where the regulations themselves change, or where they stay the same but their interpretation changes.

Basis for Modifying SOP(s)

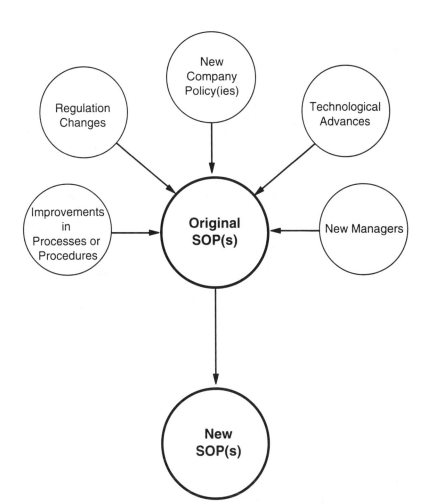

FIG. 4.6. Major factors that influence a company to modify its standard operating procedures (SOPs).

TECHNICAL AND PRODUCTION STANDARDS: REGULATORY ISSUES

Specific examples are given below that illustrate the ways in which standards and regulations affect the pharmaceutical industry.

Standards That Spiral Upward

Various government inspectors that tour manufacturing plants impose their own subjective interpretation of the regulations on the company they are inspecting. This is almost unavoidable because regulations are often vague. Regulations must be interpreted because they cannot cover or anticipate every situation. As a result, the inspector may decide that a company is out of compliance with a regulation. The company may be requested to purchase new equipment or somehow modify their manufacturing process. Alternatively, the company may decide on their own to upgrade their systems to take care of a situation described by the inspector. When the inspector returns, he or she notices that standards are raised, even though up to this time, no other company may have followed or implemented the new standards. This inspector and others may now confidently tell other companies that they too must raise their standards to meet those achieved by the original company. Thus, a new state of the art has been created. This cycle may continue in many different ways, and the result is that production costs escalate for the companies affected. These costs are eventually passed on to the consumer in most situations.

Impurities and Degradation Products

Many impurities occur in any final active compound as a result of the various steps and procedures during its chemical synthesis. For example, some reactions may not be 100% complete. Impurities also arise when chemists use less than pure starting materials. Degradation (i.e., breakdown) products of a compound occur as a result of its breakdown after synthesis, which can occur for any of many reasons. The existence of either type of product (i.e., impurity or degradation) will be unknown if it is present in extremely small amounts that are below the level of detection. During the 1980s there were numerous technological advances that enabled the detection of much smaller quantities of compounds, often down to femtogram levels (10^{-15} g). The ability to detect ultrasmall amounts of impurities led regulators to consider requiring analysis for minute levels of impurities or degradation products. Regulatory authorities have generally required that amounts of impurities or degradation products as small as 0.1% be identified chemically in the submission requesting marketing approval.

In addition to requiring that smaller quantities of impurities be identified chemically, some regulatory authorities have demanded that this take place earlier in the medicine development process. Some regulatory authorities are now requesting these data when the initial request to conduct human trials is submitted.

Stability Tests

The process of conducting accelerated stability tests was quite common in the early 1980s. This meant that any breakdown or instability of a compound that occurred within a specific time period of testing under relatively extreme conditions of temperature, humidity, and light was extrapolated to a longer period at more normal conditions. This practice generally has been replaced worldwide by real-time stability tests and extrapolation to longer periods is no longer accepted. In the past, accelerated stability studies were always confirmed by real-time tests, which were often conducted while the medicine was on the market.

In the past, stability tests were performed on development-size batches of material made in a pilot scale plant or elsewhere. This generally meant that the final scale-up development to production-size batches had not been completed. Problems could arise during this procedure that would affect the compound's stability (and thus its shelf life) or its impurity profile. The FDA now requires that stability tests be conducted on full production-size batches for New Drug Applications (NDA). This change has had a major impact within the pharmaceutical industry and has forced companies to conduct earlier scaleup and manufacture of production-size batches.

Environmental Impact Analyses

During the 1970s, the FDA began requiring an environmental analysis as part of the NDA. In the last few years the requirements (i.e., standards) for this document have greatly escalated. This has added an enormous amount of work that previously was not required. Nonetheless, it is important to recycle waste materials whenever possible and to maintain, if not improve, the status of the air, water, and land quality of the environment. The cost for a company of compliance with regulatory guidelines is ultimately passed on to the consumer in the price of medicines. This topic is discussed in Chapters 46 and 50.

Validation of Analytical Methods

It is important for a pharmaceutical company and the regulatory authorities to know that the analytical methods used to measure the active and inactive compounds present in raw chemicals as well as in the formulated medicine are accurate and reliable. The tests to prove this are understandably rigorous and time consuming. These tests must now be performed earlier in the development process than previously. This means additional time and expense for studies that will be wasted for medicines that never reach the market and a slowdown of all development projects, unless additional staff are hired and equipment purchased. This is an expensive process.

These examples illustrate that some technical standards used by regulatory authorities have increased in both total requirements and the times when they must be met. This has meant increased costs, staff, and time for pharmaceutical companies to comply with steadily increasing standards.

AUDITING ADHERENCE TO STANDARDS

To influence and increase the quality of a company's work, it is necessary to establish standards and then to audit or otherwise measure adherence to these standards. While this is a reasonably straightforward activity in the three areas mentioned above, it is more difficult in other areas. For example, it would be extremely difficult to audit and assess the effectiveness of the physician–patient relationship in the clinical trial setting. Moreover, before this could be done it would be necessary to establish standards of care for many practical aspects of this relationship (e.g., the time needed to spend together and transfer of information about medicines). Current society, professional, and government guidelines in this area are often vague, ambiguous, and difficult to measure. Guidelines of practical aspects of physician–patient relationships are often based on consensus views that minimize differences of opinion and do not enable many variations on standard interactions to be readily judged.

CONCLUSION

In conclusion, the standards used in medicine development, production, and marketing activities are of many types and many different applications depending primarily on the technical discipline involved. Attention to details in this area by a pharmaceutical company is essential to ensure that its medicines are developed as rapidly and efficiently as possible.

5 / Mergers, Joint Ventures, and Alliances

Mergers and Acquisitions 47
  Definitions 47
  General Industry Concepts That Promote
    Mergers 47
  Specific Company Factors That Promote
    Mergers or Acquisitions 48
  Evaluating Partners for a Possible Merger or
    Acquisition 49
  Alternatives to a Merger or Acquisition 49
  Definition of Strategic Alliance 49
Joint Ventures 50
  Research and Development Joint Venture 50
  Marketing Joint Venture.................... 51
  Production Joint Venture................... 51
Alliances Between Companies and Academic
  Institutions.............................. 51
  Advantages of a Company–Academic
    Alliance................................. 51
  Issues to Discuss Prior to Formalizing
    Alliances Between Companies and
    Academic Institutions 52
  Transferring Discoveries From Academia to
    Industry 52
  Other University Concerns 53
Comarketing and Copromotion 53

Comarketing 53
Comarketing Advantages and
  Disadvantages............................. 53
Copromotion.................................. 54
Copromotion Advantages..................... 54
When Should a Company Seek a Copromotion
  Partner?.................................. 54
Who Should a Company Seek as a Partner for
  Copromotion? 54
Coordinating Copromotional Activities
  Between the Two Partners.................. 55
Issues to Clarify Between the Two Partners.... 55
Worldwide Copromotions 56
Process for Choosing Partners for a
  Collaboration 56
Financial Evaluations........................ 56
The Agreement............................. 56
Societal Forces and Pressures That May Affect
  Future Mergers, Acquisitions, and
  Alliances................................. 57
Money Spent by a Country on Health Care ... 57
Patent Protection........................... 57
Technology................................. 57
Worldwide Regulations...................... 57
Pricing Initiatives........................... 57

It is industries, not nations, that compete globally. Gail D. Fosler, Chief Economist, The Conference Board

Many pressures on pharmaceutical companies over recent decades have increased the number of mergers and acquisitions between two large pharmaceutical companies. Development of novel technologies by many small companies has also led to acquisitions of such companies by large pharmaceutical companies. This article explores the types of mergers, acquisitions, joint ventures, and alliances often observed and several of the issues involved.

MERGERS AND ACQUISITIONS

Definitions

A merger is a "combination of two or more companies, either through a pooling of interests, where the accounts are combined; a purchase, where the amount paid over and above the acquired company's book value is carried on the books of the purchaser as goodwill; or a consolidation, where a new company is formed to acquire the net assets of the combining companies." An acquisition is "one company taking over controlling interest in another company" (United States Congress, Office of Technology Assessment, 1991).

A pharmaceutical company may consider merging with another company for any of a number of reasons. These reasons can be classified into two groups: (1) general industry-wide concepts and (2) company-specific reasons.

General Industry Concepts That Promote Mergers

Two general concepts that encourage pharmaceutical companies to merge are independent of the specific companies involved. These are the "bigger is better" concept and the "only the large will survive" concept.

Many professionals accept the common belief that "bigger is better" when it comes to pharmaceutical companies. Implicit in this belief is the notion that economies of scale and greater efficiencies are present in very large companies. The advocates of this belief reject the concept that companies have an optimal size that they should not grow beyond. A related corollary is the idea that stockholders reject the concept of limiting growth and wish companies to grow as large as possible in terms of their profits because any cap on growth eventually places a cap on profits.

Many people both within and outside the pharmaceutical industry have the attitude that only extremely large pharmaceutical companies will survive current and future pressures and, ultimately, prosper as research-based companies. These pressures come from many sources, including regulatory authorities, legislators, other companies, and consumer advocates. A merger helps ensure that the new larger company will be a survivor in this hostile environment—even though the new company may survive in an altered form and in an industry that is itself greatly altered.

Specific Company Factors That Promote Mergers or Acquisitions

Some or all of the following more specific reasons may operate for a company considering a merger. Each reason should be evaluated in terms of the strengths and weaknesses of the two independent companies and also of the single, combined group that will result. This analysis will facilitate a judgment on the quality of the proposed match and the degree of fit.

Many of the following specific goals might be achieved through a merger. These goals may be summarized as searches for (1) increased productivity in research, development, and marketing; (2) greater efficiencies in conducting business (overlapping programs and unneeded positions are eliminated or reassigned); and (3) improved company strengths that increase the likelihood of surviving a hostile regulatory and commercial environment.

1. To improve the company's cash flow situation. One of the companies may have chronic (or just acute) cash flow problems and is seeking a partner who has sufficient money to invest in worthwhile projects. The cash-rich company may need something the poorer company has. This may be (1) research staff, (2) manufacturing facilities, (3) well-trained sales force, (4) valuable portfolio of marketed medicines, (5) valuable portfolio of investigational medicines, (6) experienced management team, (7) tax incentives, or (8) something else. Alternatively, the earnings of a pharmaceutical company may fluctuate from year to year more than is desirable and a merger with a wealthy partner is viewed as a means of preventing or at least reducing this fluctuation.

2. To improve the size of the company's sales force. A merger is a rapid means of increasing the size of a company's sales force, particularly when the company that seeks to gain the larger sales force has something of value to the other to bring to the negotiations. Various pressures may exist in other areas of marketing that encourage the merger (e.g., long history of successful marketing and launches of projects).

3. To improve the quality of the company's portfolio of medicines. This may be with regard to marketed or investigational medicines, or with regard to prescription or over-the-counter medicines. Given the escalating costs of conducting research and development, a merger may help bring this aspect under greater control through the development of only those projects of highest medical and commercial value.

4. To improve technical expertise or to increase the number of professional staff in important areas. A common example of this type of acquisition is for a large pharmaceutical company to acquire a biotechnology firm. This has colloquially been referred to as "achieving critical mass," a popular term for having sufficient capability to conduct a defined set of activities. Each company has a different idea about what quantity of staff is necessary to achieve a critical mass, and also what activities one should be able to handle within the organization. Given the increasing complexity of innovation in discovery research, it is progressively more difficult to attract and retain top-class creative researchers in all disease areas being investigated.

5. To increase the number of therapeutic or disease areas the company can research. A merger with a company that is actively conducting research in different therapeutic areas is a rapid means of expanding into new areas and increasing the chances of making a new discovery.

6. To expand the geographic scope of the company. A company may desire to expand its operations into new territories but has not done so for various reasons. The merger may be a straightforward means to achieve this goal.

7. To expand the number of businesses that the company is engaged in. The company may seek diversification into new business areas and see the merger as a means of accomplishing this goal.

8. To form a whole pharmaceutical company. Two companies focused on different activities that complement each other could merge and thus be capable of more than was possible as single separate entities. For example, a well-established company that licenses in and develops medicines could merge with a company that focuses on research and discovery activities.

9. To acquire an important technology. A company may adopt the merger approach to acquire an important technology (e.g., medicine delivery system, sustained-release formulation, or soft gelatin capsule formulation) rather than license it. The acquisition of a unique technology could provide an important competitive advantage.

Evaluating Partners for a Possible Merger or Acquisition

The initial stage is for a company to have a clear objective or goal in mind that it wishes to achieve through a merger or acquisition, and also a focused strategy of how it is seeking to address that objective. While a company can "fall" into a perfect match by chance the likelihood of that happening is small. The second stage is to evaluate each organization's strengths and weaknesses and compare these to the strengths and weaknesses with the combined "parent" company. The major areas to assess are finances, patents, product portfolio of marketed and investigational medicines, market positions in important disease and therapeutic areas in important markets, and the nature of the research and development groups. Although this may be interpreted as an evaluation of the pharmaceutical business, all other businesses owned by the proposed partner must be considered as well. If there are redundant assets can they be disposed of readily? The cultures of the two organizations must be carefully considered, whether the merger is friendly or represents a hostile takeover. Surprisingly, there have been recent mergers between French and United States companies that have worked out better than mergers between two American companies where there was a major clash in corporate cultures (i.e., one company was more regimented and the other extremely informal).

Alternatives to a Merger or Acquisition

Even when a merger is a suitable option for a company, other alternatives should be considered and evaluated. Five alternatives are:

1. *Strategic Alliances.* The term strategic alliance is a general one and includes alternatives 3 and 5 below. Formal alliances with other companies or institutions can provide a company with some of the benefits of a merger without many of the risks. This approach is discussed later.
2. *Form a Separate Company.* A company that wants to preserve its identity, size, and culture, may expand boldly using this approach as modeled in Fig. 5.1. The parent company could "divest" itself of one or more of its ancillary business activities that might flourish in this new relationship. Alternatively, the

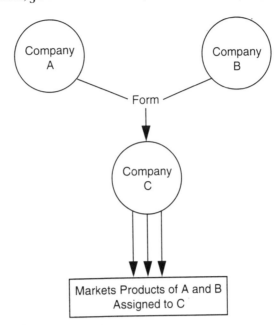

FIG. 5.1. Schematic showing two companies that form a third company and assign it specific products to market.

new company could remain in the pharmaceutical business along with one or both parents.
3. *Comarket an Important Product.* Joint marketing activities can greatly enhance sales and commercial benefits for appropriate products. This subject is also discussed later.
4. *Purchase a Subsidiary.* This could be done to achieve the type of experience or technology (e.g., biotechnology) sought in the merger. A biotechnology company could be purchased and retained as a subsidiary. One advantage of this approach is that it retains the scientific expertise within the company for consulting, biological manufacturing, or other needs.
5. *Loose or Tight Alliance.* This alternative is really a joint venture. A valuable advantage could be gained by two companies from different cultures (e.g., France and the United States or Japan and England) agreeing to work together on many joint projects, but not to exchange any capital. Each company would preserve its cash flow in the major markets, but would be able to (or would be committed to) enter more and more projects as partners.

Definition of Strategic Alliance

Strategic alliances are "associations between separate business entities that fall short of a formal merger but that unite certain agreed on resources of each entity for a limited purpose. Examples are equity purchase, licensing and marketing agreements, research contracts, and joint ventures" (United States Congress, Office of Technology Assessment, 1991).

JOINT VENTURES

Joint venture agreements are designed to cover a specific area or topic for two (or more) companies. Joint ventures may be developed that focus on research, development, marketing, or on production activities. Selected reasons for companies to consider a joint venture are listed in Table 5.1. Considerations for a company to review before entering a joint venture or alliance of any type are listed in Tables 5.2 and 5.3. While not every item is critical in each proposed agreement, the majority should be carefully considered to ensure that important issues are not overlooked.

In the development area, a joint venture allows a small organization or company with a valuable property (i.e., medicine) to join forces with a much larger company on a relatively equal basis for the purpose of developing the medicine. The two companies may do this through a contract or by forming a separate company in which each of the two groups are equal partners (i.e., each owns 50% [or less] of the stock). Using this approach the small company does not lose control over the medicine's development (and may actually guide it). A small company would tend to have less control over a medicine's development if it licensed the product. In the type of joint venture described the small company provides basic research expertise in addition to the product, while the large company provides capital and development expertise. The small company also learns from the marketing, production, and technical expertise of the larger company. The larger company benefits because it obtains rights to a potentially important new medicine for possibly a small (or moderate) expenditure. The new company formed to develop the medicine may license the medicine to the larger partner or to an outside company.

Advantages for both members of the joint venture are that they share the risk in a high-risk and high-cost project. If both groups are substantial in size, the joint ven-

TABLE 5.1. *Selected reasons for pharmaceutical companies to enter a joint venture or alliance*

1. Increase the speed of development and therefore reach the market faster with a new product
2. Obtain management expertise currently unavailable in the company
3. Obtain research and development expertise and skills currently unavailable in the company
4. Obtain funds to pursue a medicine's development
5. Share the risks of developing a product in development or a concept in research
6. Obtain access to an important new technology
7. Achieve a competitive advantage in a specific area
8. Increase the chances of making an important discovery
9. Join with a partner who has a large development and marketing staff
10. Pool resources to achieve a larger "critical mass" in an important area

TABLE 5.2. *Factors to consider before entering a joint venture or alliance[a]*

1. What percent of the research and development budget is needed to fund the alliance?
2. What new investments will be required? How major are they?
3. Are the new investments ones that will enhance the company's strength?
4. What are your motivations and those of your partner for entering an alliance? Do your goals clash?
5. Who benefits the most from the alliance?
6. Does the alliance change the basic direction or goals of the organization?
7. Are the philosophies or cultures of the partners different, and if so, is that a problem?
8. How well do you trust your future partner? What is the basis for this statement and is it sufficient?
9. Do you believe the level of commitment is appropriate on both sides?
10. Does the alliance seem like a win–win idea?
11. What is the projected rate of growth of the market in the specific disease or therapeutic area(s) involved?
12. What is the number of competitors currently in the area and estimated over a multiyear future period?
13. Is there stability of the technology(ies) involved?
14. What is the estimated duration of the life cycle of the product(s) involved?
15. What is the amount of current and future customer demand and how well will it be met?
16. What is the ease for new competitors to enter the market now and in the future?
17. Do both groups agree on the goals for the alliance?
18. Can any aspects of the contract be interpreted in more than one way?
19. Have the implications of each aspect of the contract been identified?

[a] In assessing each of these factors it will be important to consider (1) the response today versus what is expected at a relevant point in the future and (2) the degree of certainty about each of the responses.

ture may achieve a critical mass of expertise and both groups also may share the costs. Some countries do not allow foreign companies to own more than 49% of a pharmaceutical company in their country. In those situations a joint venture satisfies the laws for joint ownership of certain businesses; this invariably involves a company based in that country. Other benefits of a joint venture may come from utilizing tax laws and accepted accounting practices that financial experts may recommend to improve company profits.

Research and Development Joint Venture

The way that two groups combine their research and development efforts in a joint venture is extremely important. It is not possible simply to combine two groups and achieve a synergistic result, and that type of approach often leads to a negative outcome if sufficient

TABLE 5.3. *Factors to evaluate for each partner and the proposed new entity*

1. Reputation of existing products
2. Size of the market pursued
3. Amount of current research and development effort
4. Quality and quantity of innovations under development
5. Financial sales and profits
6. The importance of this disease or therapeutic area to the company
7. Production capacity and state of equipment (e.g., age, quality, or condition)
8. Marketing expertise and promotional activities
9. Sales representatives and their successes
10. Position in the industry and market share
11. Trend in market share and position within the industry
12. Degree of vertical integration
13. Percent of company sales that come from products in this area
14. Reputation of the organization

care is not taken. For example, if one attempts to combine a group of small strength with one of great strength the combined program is unlikely to be enhanced beyond the better program and the combination could be worse. Successful joint ventures require a lot of thought; for instance, if the large program is to be expanded, in what direction should this expansion take place? One must determine whether the smaller group could help achieve one of these directions, even through redefining (within acceptable limits of staff expertise) the smaller group's current role. Synergies must be quantifiable to make sense to both groups, whether the joint venture involves research and development or marketing. A gain of 50% or more is typically sought by the joint venture partners before they are willing to sign a formal contract.

Marketing Joint Venture

A company with an inadequate sales force to promote the company's products may create a joint venture with a larger sales force. This should improve the entry of a new product into the market and assist the marketing of existing products. The joint venture may be limited to a specific therapeutic area, or even to a specific disease area. Joint marketing ventures include comarketing and copromotion arrangements, which are described in the next section.

Production Joint Venture

One version of production joint venture is to agree to manufacture medicines of the other company under certain circumstances. This could be an important and valuable arrangement in certain countries that are far from the manufacturing facilities, particularly if they are operating at or near full capacity. This approach is also important to consider so that the company has a viable means to manufacture medicines in case of a disaster at one of its plants. It is usually too late to transfer know-how and obtain regulatory approval for a new manufacturing site after a crisis occurs. This is clearly an area where forethought is necessary.

ALLIANCES BETWEEN COMPANIES AND ACADEMIC INSTITUTIONS

The primary motivation for a company to seek an alliance with an academic department or an entire institution is to expand the company's internal research capacity, particularly in areas where expertise is lacking. Such an arrangement may enable the company to enter a new therapeutic/scientific area or to probe an existing area in new ways. This type of alliance, as opposed to those between companies almost always involves a financial grant.

Advantages of a Company–Academic Alliance

The academic institution receives several benefits from a financial grant from a pharmaceutical company. Typically, such a grant is large and represents a long-term provision of funds for the institution's staff. Additional benefits for the academic group include:

1. Ability to recruit additional faculty and to expand the scientific base of the institution.
2. Ability to develop a new area of research or to expand an existing area that was not previously attempted because of lack of funds. This additional money may enable the institution to develop a critical mass of staff in one or more scientific areas of particular interest. That, in turn, may be parlayed into important publicity about the growth of the institution and, possibly, additional grants from foundations and government agencies.
3. Possibility of having new or improved facilities paid for by the industrial partner.

Potential benefits for a company entering into an alliance with a competent academic group include:

1. Increased research capacity in existing scientific areas of importance to the company. This occurs more rapidly than if the growth were solely internal.
2. Development of research capacity in new scientific areas of importance to the company.
3. Increased professional interaction for the company's senior scientists with leading academic scientists at the frontiers of research of major importance to the company.

Issues to Discuss Prior to Formalizing Alliances Between Companies and Academic Institutions

Several issues must be discussed and satisfactorily resolved between companies and academic institutions before research agreements may be formally signed. Representative issues are briefly described and other considerations are presented in Tables 5.2 and 5.3.

Academic Freedom

Preserving the freedom of academic scientists is a *sine qua non* of all arrangements between academic institutions and industrial companies, but what exactly is "academic freedom"? This term can be summarized in a few concepts.

- To conduct research in an area of the scientist's choosing.
- To conduct research using methods and approaches of the scientist's choosing.
- To modify the research program in a manner and direction that the scientist chooses.
- To publish papers on topics and in journals that the author(s) chooses and containing the information and interpretation that the author(s) decides.

Clearly, there are numerous pressures on scientists that influence how they actually pursue each of these activities. These pressures include department requirements, need for obtaining funds to support the research, agreements made with companies or other groups to focus major efforts in one or more specific areas, and continuing the research program initiated by the scientist and for which he or she is most well known. The subject of academic freedom usually does not lead to problems with a pharmaceutical company that is considering (or is actively) investing large amounts of money in an academic institution, although the potential for such problems is great (e.g., if a well-established scientist suddenly decides to change his or her research area).

Confidentiality of Data

Confidentiality of data is probably the one issue that most commonly leads to difficult relationships between companies and institutions. This has most often become manifested in regard to the research that is conducted by graduate students as part of their theses or publications. If the research work included evaluation of company compounds, the company may fear that disclosure of the results could be premature and could easily jeopardize the company's ability to obtain a patent, or alternatively, it might alert competitors to information that the company wanted to keep private for a period. In some cases

this issue is easily avoided by having graduate students work on a carefully designed research program that does not require any company compounds or investigational medicines that the company is not willing to disclose publicly. The golden rule in this area is to consider the issue in advance of providing compounds if graduate students will be involved. If no graduate students are involved, the topic must still be discussed, particularly because the academic scientists must know the company's policy and thoughts in advance of initiating the research.

Intellectual Property Rights

Intellectual property rights to compounds created or discoveries made as a result of the agreement are usually retained by the academic institution, but the company would be given the right of first refusal to license those compounds. In some contracts and agreements it is possible to describe the broad, or even specific, terms of any future licensing agreements, but in other contracts this possibility is precluded by particular laws or policies. This issue will operate for a considerable period because compounds derived after the agreement has terminated may have resulted from scientific research conducted while the project was still active. Ownership and the rights to license those compounds may have to be separately negotiated before the contract is signed. If this has not been done, then a supplemental agreement should be reached before the period of joint activities is completed.

General Issues

Academic institutions usually wish to retain freedom of choice in the specific topics to be researched as well as the direction to be followed, although the general subject (e.g., inflammation) or disease (e.g., pancreatitis) chosen may be identified in advance and agreed to by both parties. Other requirements for a fruitful relationship are the free exchange of information and collaboration among scientists, control of publications by scientists, and a decision at the outset on which group will take out an Investigational New Drug or other regulatory application to conduct human trials and which will conduct Phase I, II, and III trials. The academic group may be able to conduct Phase I and early Phase II trials within their academic institutions, but this may not be acceptable to the corporate sponsor who may wish to sponsor the trial themselves at another institution.

Transferring Discoveries From Academia to Industry

Many academic scientists have limited expertise in licensing products to other groups. In some cases the problem is not one of expertise, but of time available to pursue a generally time-intensive activity. Sometimes it makes sense to hire a person or group who can provide this service; this could be a venture capital group, technology transfer group, patent (or other) attorney, or most commonly, an office within the academic institution. The subjects of transferring discoveries from academia to industry and licensing are discussed in Chapters 48 and 62.

The company's perspective is that it wishes to influence the direction of some or all research activities covered by the contract. Its most critical need is to ensure that patents on new compounds or technology resulting from the contract are applied for at the appropriate time, whether by the institution or the company. This must occur before any data or ideas are published or disclosed to the public in any way. The other requirement of companies is to have exclusive rights to license patents that are held by the university.

Overall, it must be recognized that success in many alliances is difficult to predict in advance. Some will work smoothly but bear no fruit. Those alliances that will actually benefit both partners financially are impossible to predict. Nonetheless, a company must judge which relationships are most likely to offer the best opportunities for success.

Other University Concerns

Academic groups generally have other concerns about alliances with pharmaceutical companies. These include:

1. The stability of long-term corporate funding.
2. Restriction of the faculty's freedom in consulting with other companies and start-up ventures.
3. Whether the agreement will diminish research that would be otherwise pursued (but will not because it does not have commercial interest).
4. Ownership of buildings funded by the company.

COMARKETING AND COPROMOTION

Comarketing

Comarketing involves the sale of one product (e.g., medicine) by two companies, each using its own trade name. This is a type of licensing whereby one company allows the rights to their product in exchange for royalties, and possibly in exchange for up-front payments or other benefits. Comarketing may involve a worldwide agreement or it may be limited to a specific geographic region. Alternatively, the agreement may be limited to certain dosage forms or to specific indications of the medicine.

Some examples of comarketing include:

1. Inderal was licensed by ICI to American Home Products.
2. Nifedipine was licensed by Bayer (Miles) to Pfizer.
3. Isoptin was licensed by BASF (Knolle) to Searle (Calan).
4. Ibuprofen (Rufen) was licensed by Boots to Upjohn (Motrin).
5. Lisinopril (Prinivil) was licensed by Merck to ICI (Zestril).

Comarketing Advantages and Disadvantages

A company that allows another company to sell its product receives a number of benefits, the most obvious being the additional royalties. Another potential advantage is the competition generated among sales representatives in the field. This can be a friendly and productive type of competition or a nasty, destructive, and counterproductive situation. The latter situation should trigger major changes to the agreement or the scrapping of it altogether.

When two companies try to sell the same product under different brand names the market is disrupted. Comarketing of an important product has many of the advantages and disadvantages of win–lose, or win big–win small relationships. Each partner is taking certain risks in entering the relationship; these are generally less substantial than those experienced under copromotion. The disadvantages of comarketing that are more predictable are the additional costs incurred by the original owner to promote the medicine and the large total expenditure necessary.

If the original owner does not spend more money than it would as the sole marketer of the product, then it is likely to lose sales to its partner. In fact, depending on the exact conditions of the market, the agreement, and the product, it is likely that the original company may achieve less sales than it would have with solo marketing. The opposite situation would be more likely to occur if the product achieved commercial success as a result of the larger sales force achieving a critical mass that affected medical practice. A final problem that could arise is each group developing a different promotional message and marketing strategy which results in confusion for physicians, pharmacists, and other customers and audiences (e.g., compendia).

Cases are known in which the company that received the license discounted the product substantially compared to the original and promoted it intensively (anonymous, 1991). This forced the original company to match the price and also the money and efforts spent on promotion.

Copromotion

Copromotion involves the sale of a single product (e.g., medicine) by two companies using a single trade name. This could be viewed as a merger arrangement for a particular product: one company provides the medicine and the other provides a large sales force.

Some examples of copromotion include:

1. Zantac was promoted by both Glaxo and Roche.
2. Capoten was promoted by both Squibb and McNeil.
3. Hytrin was promoted by both Abbott and Burroughs Wellcome.

In each case the first company listed was the original developer.

Copromotion Advantages

Copromotion achieves several benefits for the two partners in addition to the possibility of making money. The partners should aim for a win–win situation in working out the details of their agreement. Four possible advantages are briefly described.

Single marketing message. This is one of the most essential aspects of any marketing strategy. Clarity of focus in this regard helps the medicine achieve a better market penetration throughout the country(ies) involved.

Economies of scale. This relates to manufacturing larger amounts of the medicine, as well as utilizing the services of a larger sales force to present the companies' message to physicians, pharmacists, and other professionals. The effectiveness of both sales forces acting together should be greater than the sum of its parts.

Sales partnership. The activities of copromotion involve less competition between the two sales forces than occurs with comarketing. Both partners should benefit financially from what should be viewed as a sales partnership. Interactions between marketing and sales professionals usually result in educational benefits as well as stimulation for the people involved.

Fill detailing time. During a slow period for the partner company this approach may help fill the time of its sales representatives. The time spent by sales representatives could be paid for by the product's originator, which could also pay a certain percent of royalties to the partner for sales obtained.

When Should a Company Seek a Copromotion Partner?

A few of the factors that are of paramount significance include:

1. The medicine should have significant sales potential, probably greater than 75 million dollars per year in the United States or an equivalent amount in Europe.
2. The medicine should be sensitive to detailing by sales representatives. Some medicines such as over-the-counter medicines and medicines for rare diseases do not meet this criterion.
3. The medicine should be in a highly competitive market. There may be situations when this criterion is not necessary.
4. The time in the marketing history must be appropriate; for instance, the medicine was recently launched or will soon be launched.
5. Adequate incentives (e.g., commissions) must be available to encourage the sales force and elicit their enthusiastic participation in this activity.

Who Should a Company Seek as a Partner for Copromotion?

The ideal partner (or, at the minimum, an appropriate partner) for a company to seek should meet the following criteria.

1. The organizational culture of the partner must fit that of the medicine's owner, or at least must be acceptable to the medicine's owner. Any discomfort about the proposed partner that is felt at the outset of the arrangement would probably be magnified greatly as time progressed. Organizational culture relates to company's internal values, style of operations, and internal atmosphere or milieu.
2. The image of the partner must be positive and provide value to the agreement and promotional campaign.
3. The sales force of the partner should ideally detail a different group of physicians. For instance, one group of representatives might target hospitals while the other group targets physicians in private practice. If this approach is not possible, then other means of complementing the sales forces' activities should be sought in order to prevent them from calling on the same physicians. The partner should have adequate experience in detailing to its customers.
4. The sales representatives from the partner must have detail time available for the copromotion and also must be able to coordinate the message with their own detailing. This means, in part, that the partner cannot have their own medicine for the disease that the copromoted product targets. Two exceptions would be (1) an extremely old and unpromoted medicine of the partner and (2) the partner's medicine is for a different form of the disease (e.g., a different type of epilepsy), a different severity of the disease, or is differentiated in another meaningful way.

Coordinating Copromotional Activities Between the Two Partners

The two marketing groups will have to meet frequently at the outset of the product's launch, or at the onset of copromotional activities, to plan and coordinate their activities. The frequency of such meetings will certainly decrease over time. Generally, once a maintenance phase of the copromotional activities is reached, meetings to review sales figures and sales strategies can occur every four to six months, unless problems arise. It is essential that the two groups not compete with each other even after the copromotional contract expires. The contract must include terms that ensure this.

Issues to Clarify Between the Two Partners

One of the most essential issues to resolve is to decide which partner will interact with the regulatory authority. While it is most common for the partner that owns the rights to the medicine to assume this role, there could be numerous reasons for the new partner to take over this responsibility. For example, the original partner could be a small company or a large foreign-based company with a small company in the country of interest, or the new partner could be a national-based company with closer relations with the regulatory authority. National laws or regulations may influence company decisions on this issue.

Another potential issue could be deciding how to obtain additional data of importance on the medicine. This could involve conducting new marketing studies, quality of life trials, or pharmacoeconomic trials, or developing additional indications. However, these aspects are usually not part of a copromotion. The two partners should seek to identify the best arrangement for addressing these and any other issues they can anticipate prior to signing the copromotion agreement formally. Other factors to consider in a copromotion are mentioned in Tables 5.1 and 5.2 and a general view of identifying potential corporate partners is shown in Fig. 5.2.

Types of Corporate Alliances: Source of Partner

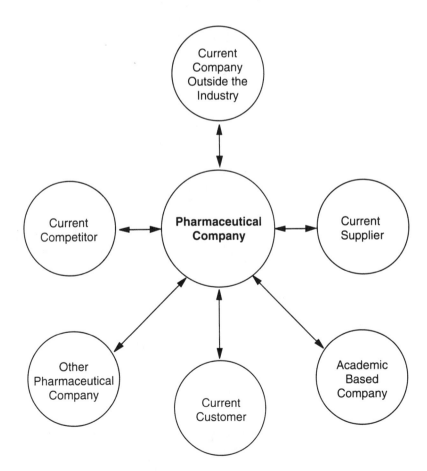

FIG. 5.2. Several potential types of partners for pharmaceutical company to form an alliance with.

Worldwide Copromotions

A new type of copromotional arrangement that could be formed would be for two companies to agree to copromote each other's product line or for one company to copromote the entire line of the other. This approach could be used by a Japanese company (or one from another country) that desired to enter the United States market in a comfortable manner. The arrangement would enable the non-American company to develop a sales forces while its products became better known in the United States as a result of its partner's efforts. The partner would have a larger portfolio of marketed products to promote and both partners should benefit financially.

PROCESS FOR CHOOSING PARTNERS FOR A COLLABORATION

A company choosing a partner for a collaboration may follow these basic steps:

1. Create a list of all possible companies or institutions that are involved in the technology or area of interest. A few companies or institutions might be added to this list that are not currently pursuing the topic of interest, but which might do so.
2. Determine the criteria of greatest importance that the ideal partner should possess. It is possible that the criteria could focus more on specific products than on the group.
3. Profile each company or institution according to each criterion of importance.
4. Determine the top two to four groups, and then conduct a more intensive evaluation of each to determine which one is best suited to become a partner.
5. Approach the top candidate through the most appropriate contact.

This straightforward systematic approach helps ensure that the best partner is found rather than a partner being close friends with a senior manager.

Financial Evaluations

It is usually necessary to use more than a single method to value a company that may be acquired. The values obtained with different methods should be compared. Four methods that can be used are:

1. *Market value.* Estimate the company's value based on selling prices for other similar companies sold within the last few years.
2. *Stock value.* Calculate the value of the company based on the total stock value.
3. *Liquidation value.* Estimate the company's value based on selling all company assets over a reasonable period of time.
4. *Net present value of the dividend stream.* Calculate expected cash flows after discounting for risk and time.

It is essential to consider all costs that are to be involved. Costs may be calculated in four categories.

Direct Costs. This category includes costs for personnel (e.g., hiring costs, and salaries and benefits), supplies, equipment, and others (e.g., new buildings).

Indirect Costs. This category includes costs for consultants, travel, and other items.

Overhead Costs. This category includes costs for management as well as building maintenance and operations.

Fees and Royalty Costs. This category includes milestone fees and royalties on sales. Royalties may be calculated in various ways.

The Agreement

It is obvious that the identification of the perfect partner is only one step in reaching an agreement on a merger, joint venture, or alliance. The two (or more) groups involved must be able to reach a satisfactory agreement on all essential terms. Many of the essential points to describe in an agreement have been discussed above; a few others are briefly mentioned below.

1. Basic area covered by the agreement. Is it for a single compound, therapeutic area, or multiple areas?
2. Geographical area. Is it for a single country, region, or is it worldwide?
3. Royalties. Is a fixed percent identified or is it a variable percent, depending on the magnitude of sales?
4. Fees. Are up-front fees to be paid and are milestone fees to be paid? What are the milestones used?
5. Management. Is board of directors membership an issue and are board members voting members?
6. Change of ownership. If one company is sold or has new owners how will the agreement be affected?
7. Patent life. What changes will occur to the agreement after the patent(s) expire?
8. Manufacturing. Is manufacturing to be shared or exclusive to one partner?
9. Marketing. Is marketing to be shared or exclusive to one partner?
10. Equity. Is one partner purchasing equity in the other? If two (or more) groups establish a new venture, how is ownership determined?
11. Who owns what and when?

Before an agreement is finalized it is important to gain the assurance that no pertinent information is being withheld. Such assurance is in large part based on the trust of the new partner, but it also requires a certain amount of interrogation of the new partner. It is often difficult, if not impossible, to ascertain that all relevant information is being shared. An escape clause could be inserted in a contract to cover this contingency, but that is often too late for divorce to occur without pain and financial hardship.

SOCIETAL FORCES AND PRESSURES THAT MAY AFFECT FUTURE MERGERS, ACQUISITIONS, AND ALLIANCES

This chapter concludes by briefly viewing five forces and pressures that are likely to affect future mergers, acquisitions, and alliances.

Money Spent by a Country on Health Care

As the percent of a country's gross national product that is spent on health care increases, political pressures to control prices more tightly are increased. Because the cost of medicines are an easily targeted focus, many countries attempt to institute or tighten controls on medicine prices. This could easily be the single most important pharmaceutical issue over the next decade(s). Many industry experts are convinced that this is the greatest threat to the industry's profitability and the very existence of many companies.

Patent Protection

Patents on all medicines are like clocks ticking away and all medicines will eventually lose their protection. Inevitably this will lead to the marketing of more generic medicines. Companies should have strategies in place to deal with this issue for each marketed medicine. It is also important to develop an overall strategy (e.g., to review the patent expiration strategy on every medicine on an annual basis).

Technology

Given the large number of possible therapeutic areas and research tools, companies must make choices about where and how to allocate their limited research resources. This usually is interpreted to mean that a company must identify a specific number of therapeutic areas that it wishes to focus on; these areas are developed and others are deemphasized or eliminated.

Worldwide Regulations

The increasing harmonization of regulations worldwide represents both great opportunities and great challenges for all pharmaceutical companies. Larger companies as well as smaller, efficient companies could take advantage of the improved climate to achieve marketing of their medicines more rapidly. Smaller companies as well as less efficient companies will lose commercial advantages to those who start later but are more efficient, aggressive, and/or opportunistic.

Pricing Initiatives

Companies will probably use pricing more and more as a competitive tool. This will particularly occur where companies are allowed to set their own prices for medicine, as long as their total profits are limited to a predetermined level (e.g., 20% profit). This occurs in the United Kingdom today.

In conclusion, mergers, joint ventures, acquisitions, and alliances offer pharmaceutical companies incredible opportunities to improve their strength and profits, but the risks in many ventures may be enormous. It is hoped that these ventures are entered to achieve win–win situations, but the steadily increasing pressures on companies are likely to force more ventures that are not beneficial to both parties.

6 / Pharmacopolitics

Narrow Versus Broad Definitions 59
Major Pressures at the Industry Level That
    Create Pharmacopolitical Issues 60
Major Pressures at the Company Level That
    Create Pharmacopolitical Issues 62
Selected Pharmacopolitical Issues 62
Why Pharmacopolitical Issues Develop for the
    Pharmaceutical Industry and Individual
    Companies 63
    True Images and Perceptions 64
How Should a Company Examine and Organize
    Its Pharmacopolitical Activities? 65
Informing Staff About Company Positions 65

Interaction Among Companies 66
General Steps for Dealing with Most
    Pharmacopolitical Issues 66
Future Megatrends That Will Affect the
    Industry's Political Environment 67
    Attitudinal Changes of Patients and the Public 67
    Regulatory Changes Worldwide 67
    Third-Party Reimbursement of Investigational
      Treatments 67
    Spread of Existing and New Diseases 67
    Need for Innovation Within the Industry 67
    Need for Education of Outside Groups by the
      Industry 67

Interferon is a substance you rub on stockbrokers. A scientist quoted in *Forbes,* September 1980.

Over the centuries pharmacopolitics (i.e., interactions between people concerning medicines) has taken many forms. Pharmacopolitics probably originated with primitive medicine men interacting with their patients and with the apportioning of the primitive society's herbal supply. Today at a national or "macro" level, pharmacopolitics encompasses the allocation of each society's resources to medicines, equipment, and hospitals and the implementation of health care policies that control or influence most aspects of a nation's medical system and patient health.

At a "micro" level are the politics regarding medicine discovery, development, and marketing at the individual pharmaceutical or biotechnology company. The micro level is represented by the interactions of a pharmaceutical company with many external groups, including those listed in Table 6.1. Interactions within a company are also part of this micro level.

Pharmacopolitics is particularly relevant to three major groups—government regulators, the public, and the medical profession. First, the scope and influence of government regulations on the pharmaceutical industry's activities are increasing in many countries. Industry's responses have sometimes been organized and effective, but a great deal of progress could be achieved if the industry presented a unified message. Second, the extent of the public's interest and involvement in pharmaceutical issues is increasing and many more interactions are occurring at the international, national, and company lev-

els. Responses by the industry and by individual companies to these opportunities must be appropriate and effective. In fact, the survival of the research-based industry depends, in large part, on how effectively it responds to external challenges. Third, the extent of the medical profession's interest and involvement in pharmaceutical issues is increasing. Formulary committees have a steadily growing voice over which medicines may be prescribed by physicians in their jurisdiction, and cost-containment issues are significantly influencing physician prescribing habits as well as the ways in which medicines are promoted.

NARROW VERSUS BROAD DEFINITIONS

At the company level, the most narrow definition of pharmacopolitics considers only government interactions. Although the definition could exclude interactions with regulatory authorities and solely consider interactions with legislative and judicial groups, that would be overly restrictive. Progressively wider definitions would include more and more of the external groups with which a company interacts, until all of its external group interactions were included. This broad definition is favored by the author.

Even broader definitions of pharmacopolitics, to include internal company interactions, which are often described as political (see Table 6.2), are inappropriate be-

TABLE 6.1. *External groups that interact with pharmaceutical companies*

1. Government regulatory authorities that evaluate and approve new medicines and regulate marketed ones
2. Government legislative authorities (e.g., national, province, state, or local)
3. Government judicial authorities that rule on patent, liability, and other issues
4. International organizations (e.g., World Health Organization)
5. Health care provider organizations (e.g., health maintenance organizations and hospitals) who purchase medicines
6. Formulary committees who act as gatekeepers
7. Third-party payers and insurance companies
8. Trade associations that represent their members
9. Physicians who treat patients
10. Pharmacists who serve as medicine distributors and patient advisers
11. Patients as individual consumers who receive prescriptions and also purchase medicines
12. Patients as members of therapeutic-oriented groups that attempt to influence other groups
13. Consumer activist groups that attempt to influence other groups
14. Media that broadcast and write about medicines and the industry's image
15. Media that focus their health activities either within the industry or on other nonpublic groups in this list
16. Other pharmaceutical companies (e.g., competitors or collaborators)
17. Professional societies, associations, and other groups who adopt both proactive and reactive positions to influence other groups
18. Universities and researchers who are involved in grant writing

cause the concept of politics has long been rooted in external interactions. Internal company interactions are excluded from the definition of pharmacopolitics used here. Comparable considerations also exist at the industry level, i.e., a narrow definition would consider only government interactions and a broad definition would include all external group interactions.

The author's preferred definition of pharmacopolitics from the industry's perspective is "interactions of the pharmaceutical industry, one of its companies, or one of its representatives with external individuals or groups" (see Fig. 6.1). An alternative definition is "the interac-

TABLE 6.2. *Internal groups that interact with pharmaceutical companies*

1. Unions
2. Individual employees
3. Task forces assigned to investigate or evaluate an issue
4. Committees or teams that make specific recommendations to senior management
5. Departments or divisions within the company
6. Subsidiaries (see Spilker, 1991)

tion between two or more individuals or groups attempting to influence decisions or opinions of the other regarding medicine discovery, development, production, marketing, sales, policy, or other related pharmaceutical areas, where one group (or person) is within the industry and the other is not." The remainder of this article uses these definitions. The central group in Fig. 6.1 could also be a regulatory agency, legislators, consumer activists, third-party payers, physicians, patients, or other groups. If one of the other groups is considered at the center, then the definition of pharmacopolitics would involve interactions of that group with each of its external groups. Thus, the most general definition is simply interactions of two separate groups concerning medicines.

MAJOR PRESSURES AT THE INDUSTRY LEVEL THAT CREATE PHARMACOPOLITICAL ISSUES

A few of the major pressures exerted on the pharmaceutical industry from external sources are listed below. The basis of many pressures is the strain between the pharmaceutical industry being viewed as a commercial for-profit business and as a provider of medicines as part of the health care profession. It has not helped the industry's position that it sometimes emphasizes one side of this Janus head to one group and another side to different groups.

During the 19th century, the many problems of patent medicines and charlatans led to the need and eventual passage of laws in the United States to control vaccines (i.e., the 1813 Vaccine Act), imported medicines (i.e., the 1848 Import Drug Act), adulterated and mislabeled medicines (i.e., the 1906 Pure Food and Drugs Act), followed by the well-known 1938 Food, Drug, and Cosmetic Act that focused on safety, and its 1962 Amendments (i.e., the Kefauver-Harris Amendments) that focused on efficacy.

Pressures on the industry from external groups should elicit a broadly defined political response that is coordinated among many, if not most, companies. This response could be expressed through either trade associations or independent organizations. More specifically, political attacks should receive a political response and economic issues and questions raised should receive an economic response. There are numerous occasions where the industry's response to a political attack has been with an economic response (e.g., discussion of the high costs of research and development).

Increasing regulatory standards are pressuring companies to discover highly profitable medicines to support their large research and development budgets. Other pressures (e.g., increasing competition among companies, stockholders, and cost-containment practices) are also contributing to this result.

EXAMPLES OF
EXTERNAL GROUP INTERACTIONS

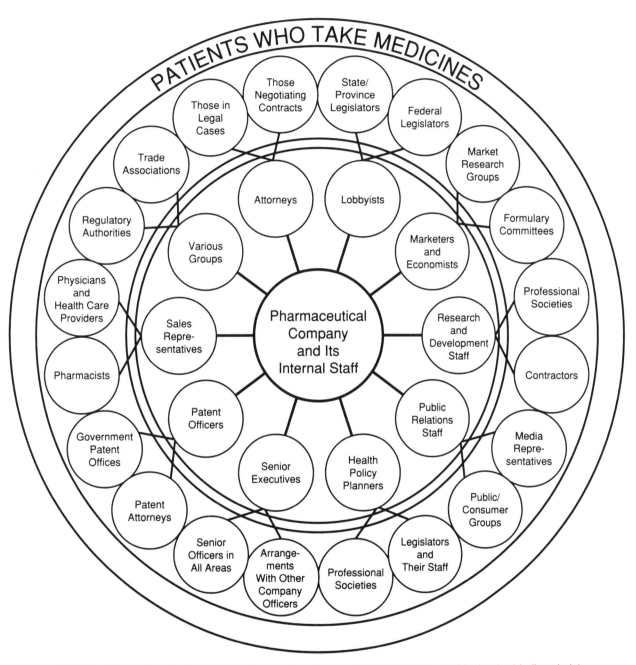

FIG. 6.1. Examples of external group interactions (i.e., people and groups outside the double-line circle) between a pharmaceutical company and its external world. These are pharmacopolitical interactions. Internal groups with whom the external groups interact are shown within the double-line circle. Other constituencies (e.g., physicians or regulatory agencies) could be substituted for the company in the center and an entirely new set of external group interactions described.

Many different groups are increasing their pressures on the industry to lower prices for older pharmaceuticals and to keep newer ones at relatively low prices. This is not a purely economic attack on prices; it is the tip of the political iceberg questioning whether a reasonable price for a pharmaceutical is based on free market economics (as exists for most industries) or is based on what the country can afford (i.e., more of a socialized health care concept).

Delays, unnecessary duplications, and inefficiencies in their view of regulatory submissions worldwide create pressures of several types on the industry to develop their medicines more rapidly, efficiently, and to charge higher prices for them once they reach the market.

MAJOR PRESSURES AT THE COMPANY LEVEL THAT CREATE PHARMACOPOLITICAL ISSUES

Some of the major pressures exerted on individual companies that generally elicit a political response are

- Pressures to maintain a full pipeline of medically and commercially promising new medicines at each phase of development.
- Pressures to join other companies in mutually beneficial relationships to discover, develop, cross-license, or comarket medicines jointly or otherwise to create mutually beneficial relationships.
- Pressures to respond to external crises (e.g., product tampering or organized demonstrations) or internal crises (e.g., fires or sabotage) in a prompt, ethical, and appropriate manner. Astute senior managers of some companies have created a number of contingency plans to deal with these and other crises.
- Pressures on some individuals to compromise their high ethical standards (1) in designing clinical trials, (2) to omit conducting clinical and nonclinical studies believed necessary or appropriate, or (3) to submit regulatory applications prematurely so that a list of deficiencies to remedy is received at an early date.
- Pressures on the company to provide patients with package inserts for each of the company's products. Many perspectives exist on this particular topic.
- Pressures from shareholders and financial analysts to provide a high rate of financial return on a continual basis to stockholders, recognizing the innately high-risk nature of the industry.

SELECTED PHARMACOPOLITICAL ISSUES

Historically, pharmacopolitical issues have arisen out of concerns expressed by groups external to the pharmaceutical industry. A number of issues are mentioned for several of the most important groups after indicating one or more of each group's primary goals.

1. Legislators
    Goal: To provide patients with the lowest cost health care programs that do not harm quality or restrict access (i.e., cost containment).
    Issues: Initiation and direction of political and legislative change. Generic substitution of medicines. Imposing a maximum price at which a medicine could be sold. Imposing sales caps on some or all orphan medicines. Use of essential medicine lists created by the World Health Organization. Population control.

2. Regulators
    Goal: To ensure that government programs do not harm the public.
    Issues: Speed of approval of new medicines and supplemental applications. Approvals of patents and duration of the patent. Imposing a medical needs clause for all new medicines as part of their requirements for regulatory approval.

3. Physicians
    Goal: To provide health care as they have been trained.
    Issues: Roles of physicians regarding therapeutic substitution. Pharmaceutical industry's practices in promoting medicines to physicians. Decreased ability of marketing representatives to detail directly to physicians.

4. Pharmacists
    Goal: To create a profession based on counseling patients and providing information to other health care professionals, rather than mechanically filling prescriptions.
    Issues: Ability of pharmacists to make sound medical decisions regarding both generic substitution and therapeutic substitution. Providing information to patients about medicines, and also counseling patients about medicines.

5. Patients
    Goals: Receive adequate health care as a basic right and challenge any obstacles that question this right or, alternatively, receive the best health care they can afford to purchase.
    Issues: Direct promotion of prescription medicines to patients. Patient package inserts appear to be coming in Europe and this will pressure companies to do the same in the United States.

6. Consumer Activists
    Goals: Protect their perceived rights, obtain their common goals, and defend their constituency.
    Issues: Special interest groups have often focused on emotionally charged issues involving the

pharmaceutical industry. These include (1) animal rights, (2) abortion rights, (3) environmental issues, (4) radioactive waste disposal, (5) limited availability of investigational medicines, (6) high prices of new medicines, and (7) withholding of important information from government regulators.

7. Media

Goal: To obtain a good story in which sick patients are pitted against a highly profitable corporation and industry.

Issues: The media influence and to a great degree control the image of the industry perceived by the public. The industry is strongly affected if excessive profits and unethical behavior are stressed by media reports rather than the value of research and the importance of the industry to the country's balance of payments and its future. Media reports have triggered government investigations. Distribution of medicines to underdeveloped countries is sometimes focused on by reporters.

8. Formulary Committees

Goal: To reduce expenses and save money for their organization.

Issues: Requirements placed on the industry by formulary committees to add new medicines to a formulary are increasing, primarily in terms of cost effectiveness or quality of life. An increasing number of formularies restrict the pharmaceutical companies from promoting their products directly to prescribing physicians.

9. Third-Party Payers

Goal: To reduce expenses and save money for their organization.

Issues: Insurance companies usually do not pay for investigational medicines, even if one medicine of a multiple medicine combination in cancer chemotherapy is marketed, but not for that type of cancer. This impedes research advances.

10. Employers

Goal: To bring premiums for health care insurance under control.

Issues: Insurance rates are rapidly rising while employees are requesting broader coverage in all areas of health (e.g., dental, vision care, and day care).

Some important pharmacopolitical issues currently being debated are given in Table 6.3.

WHY PHARMACOPOLITICAL ISSUES DEVELOP FOR THE PHARMACEUTICAL INDUSTRY AND INDIVIDUAL COMPANIES

The pharmaceutical industry and its various audiences (i.e., external groups shown in Fig. 6.1) often have conflicting perspectives, outlooks, and goals. The industry is often viewed as outliers in the world of commerce because pharmaceuticals provide health benefits and are not merely manufactured commodities. Moreover, many medicines are nonsubstitutable by other medicines, whereas a television, iron, hose, socks, or washing machine can be substituted by a different manufacturer's product. In the world of medicine and health care the pharmaceutical industry is viewed as making high profits from people's illnesses and also as being uncaring about the high prices they charge. These problems have sometimes been compounded by arrogance and/or naiveté in public relations and legislative relations when answering such charges. These episodes have compromised some credibility and have also earned distrust for the industry by many members of the external groups with which companies interact.

1. The industry is sometimes portrayed as "crying wolf" too often about falling profits when the opposite has occurred (profits have improved). Often this is the result of confusing overall industry results with those of some specific companies. Some companies have serious financial troubles, whereas others are quite prosperous today.

2. Some members of the industry have complained about the rising costs of developing new medicines. This complaint has not impressed many people, who say, "but look at the profits of the few medicines that do do well."

3. It is common for industry representatives to be misquoted by the press. The practice of "pseudo quotes" enables reporters to create stories that are designed to sell newspapers or magazines, not to inform readers. No one should forget that most television networks,

---

TABLE 6.3. *Representative pharmacopolitical issues*[a]

1. Telling industry's story to external groups
2. Lobbying issues
3. Influencing formulary committees
4. Influencing health care policy
5. Interacting with regulatory authorities
6. Establishing prices for medicines
7. Adhering to appropriate and ethical promotional practices
8. Countering unfounded accusations by various activists (e.g., animal rights or disease-specific activists)
9. Responding to product tampering and other crises
10. Interaction between headquarters and subsidiaries

[a] For each of these and other issues, a company could develop information on pitfalls and effective approaches. At that point, an effective strategy, or at least an agreed-on approach, could be created.

radio stations, newspapers, and magazines are private businesses, particularly in the United States. These media say and print the stories they believe will enhance the value and sales of their own companies. Part of the reason for this problem is mentioned in the following point.

4. Reactions to crises within the industry have not always been handled by professionals who understood the full scope of the problems. Some managers in the limelight have responded in naive and inexperienced ways to charges from external groups of mishandling a crisis.

5. When a group is accused of either ethical or criminal misdeeds, it is forced to respond from a defensive posture. Individual companies as well as the entire industry have been in this situation. The public sees and hears the charges made in newspapers, on television, and in other media on a frequent basis and people tend to believe that a group would not be accused if the charges were not at least partially true. Even if a group is later found to be innocent of all charges, the taint or stigma of the accusations usually persists for a long time because accusation is often considered equivalent to conviction. Moreover, a finding of innocence is rarely presented in the media to the same degree and with the same fanfare as the accusation of guilt. A more effective response is to accuse your accusers by exposing their true motivations (i.e., "the best defense is a good offense").

True Images and Perceptions

It is important for the pharmaceutical industry to consider the following question. Are external groups relating to an image of the pharmaceutical industry that they have created out of their perceptions, beliefs, values, and interpretations or are they relating to an accurate image of the industry that could be described and documented with a large number of objective measures? The real world for an individual is the one he or she creates out of his or her perceptions and interpretations; likewise, society's collective vision of reality is created out of its collective perceptions and interpretations. Therefore, even if some believe the pharmaceutical industry is not truly the

way it is depicted, it makes little difference. The depiction or image of the industry is the same as the true industry for most people, regardless of whether the image can be objectively substantiated.

Even periods of history are given labels that at best only reflect some highlights of the period. The 1960s were labeled by many as the "love" and "civil rights" period and many events were interpreted in that context. The 1980s were widely described as the "me" period. Every decade receives labels that are supposed to characterize one or more of their dominant traits. The dominant forces that appear to drive many pharmaceutical companies may also be identified and associated with different decades (Fig. 6.2).

There are examples from every century and every group of society where perceptions did not mirror objective reality. Decisions and behaviors of society have often been based on misperceptions (e.g., devils and witches) and not on objective reality. This includes the use of medicines and medical treatments in good faith that actually made patients worse (e.g., the use of medicines containing arsenic, mercury, or strychnine). This does not even consider the problems that arise when individuals with hidden motives attempt to distort others' perceptions to achieve their own goals. Various individuals and groups describe the pharmaceutical industry in a way that many others (both within and outside the industry) claim is false or distorted. If one assumes that the defenders of the industry are correct (and I believe they are), one next must ponder whether the negative perceptions and distortions of the industry also are in a sense true (or valid) simply because they exist and are believed by some people! Unfortunately for the industry, the inaccurate and false beliefs and perceptions must be treated as true because they are believed by many important and influential people. The industry cannot be complacent because its detractors' perceptions are partially inaccurate and because various objective evaluations can "prove" that fact. The industry must work hard to do whatever is necessary to educate people as to what it considers to be more appropriate perceptions and what it views as appropriate approaches to evaluate the industry.

A medicine that has a high perceived risk (e.g., the risk of fetal malformations caused by Bendectin) will be dealt

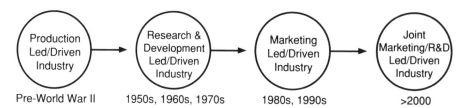

FIG. 6.2. The primary driving forces behind many pharmaceutical companies for the decades from 1900 to the present, plus a prediction of the forces that will influence and drive companies in the 21st century.

with by various groups as if that risk were true, despite numerous objective assessments by independent groups that the medicine poses no additional risks. Another example was evident during the mid-1960s when the risks of developing lung cancer were shown to be high for cigarette smokers, but many individual smokers rejected the evidence and believed that their personal risk was low.

This example points out a major problem in medicine. Physicians have been trained for centuries to pass on their individual knowledge to the next generation of physicians based on their own knowledge and experience. Not only do physicians "lay their hands" on patients, but they also do the same on their medical students, residents, and colleagues. It is not surprising that physicians are influenced and develop clinical judgment based more on the experiences of the few patients they have treated with a particular medicine than by large well-controlled clinical and epidemiological (i.e., population) trials.

The 1990s are a period when this personal-based orientation of new knowledge is being radically challenged and changed to personal knowledge based on the results of population-based trials and evaluations. Thus, medical decision making by individuals will in the future be based more on health outcomes research and aggregated data (e.g., from meta-analyses) rather than on personal experiences. When a new generation of physicians is trained to think epidemiologically with this new approach it will increase the scientific and clinical level of the practice of medicine.

HOW SHOULD A COMPANY EXAMINE AND ORGANIZE ITS PHARMACOPOLITICAL ACTIVITIES?

The initial step in this process is for the company to recognize that pharmacopolitics is an important (some would say critical) area that must be thoughtfully and appropriately dealt with. Even if some senior managers accept this view it will probably be insufficient for the company to approach this area adequately until the chief executive officer agrees with this view and desires to influence the company's response.

A company that is considering how to organize its pharmacopolitical activities should appoint an internal task force to examine this subject. It is essential that this activity not be assigned to external consultants. Although they could be extremely useful adjuncts to the activities of the task force, on their own, however, those individuals would be unable to assess directly and accurately how the company operates and could not sufficiently understand the corporate culture and traditions. These are vital aspects of pharmacopolitics, particularly at the micro level.

Representatives from all major areas of the company (e.g., marketing, production, finance, legal, discovery research, technical development, medical, human resources, public relations, and government affairs) should be on the task force to obtain necessary input as well as commitment to any recommendations developed.

This task force should identify the specific issues previously mentioned for the external groups it wishes to examine and then determine how to explore each. The issues would be explored to identify (in regard to any decisions made of altering company behavior): (1) what types of decisions are made, (2) who is involved in making each type of decision, (3) what is the process used to make the decision, and (4) what is the quality of the decisions made? This task force would also examine the process and efficiency with which decisions are executed, addressing similar questions to those above. Finally, the outcomes of the decisions should be addressed in terms of whether the desired results were obtained. It is often important to determine if other approaches would have been more fruitful. The task force then can derive lessons from their analysis and determine whether any change(s) in company procedures or organization would facilitate the future process of decision making.

Because there is a wide variety of pharmacopolitical issues, it is impossible for any company to centralize its response to all of those issues. Virtually all areas of a company's work are subject to political issues, many of which arise on a daily basis. Nonetheless, a centralized committee or task force could coordinate company responses to political issues.

Companies must expend more effort and resources to make their major trade association(s) stronger and more effective. Trade associations must ensure that their activities are always focused on the most essential targets, and that they are presenting the most cogent arguments to convince legislators, regulators, the public, and other groups of the industry's message. A company or trade association that decides to focus attention on pharmacopolitical issues may decide to have a staff review of their current practices. This could lead the group to alter its operating procedures or organization in specific areas. The message that everyone in a company is affected by pharmacopolitical issues should be widely disseminated to all employees. In turn, the help of employees should be sought whenever needed (e.g., to write letters to legislators).

INFORMING STAFF ABOUT COMPANY POSITIONS

Each company has different views about how much information about pharmacopolitical issues to share with employees. To some companies, describing the activities of a political action committee is sufficient to discharge this responsibility, while other companies attempt to educate their staff more broadly.

Staff members who represent their companies at pharmacopolitical functions or meetings should be informed ahead of time about the employers' positions. This is rarely done at most companies, not primarily because those who have the information are too busy to discuss company positions with relevant staff, but because few companies have articulated clear positions on most pharmacopolitical issues.

The result of this situation is that when staff attend trade association or other meetings, they speak for themselves rather than for their company. While this does not create problems in most situations, there are occasions when it does. Any company wants its members to know and promote its position when relevant, rather than arbitrarily espousing what may be inadequately considered views. One solution to this potential problem is to develop a coordination system within a company to provide the company's view whenever appropriate, and serve as a catalyst to form company positions when they do not exist.

INTERACTION AMONG COMPANIES

Movement toward greater openness between companies has been occurring over the last decade in:

- Licensing opportunities.
- Cross-licensing of products.
- Joint research seeking to discover new medicines.
- Joint development of new compounds or medicines.
- Comarketing of one company's medicine.
- Cooperation at trade associations.
- Sharing of information on adverse reaction reporting, information science, and other subjects.

This trend is based on the realization that many arrangements are mutually beneficial and will enhance the ability of the companies involved to remain viable. Dry spells (i.e., periods during which no new medicines are brought to market) are no longer acceptable in most research-based companies because these periods tend to lead to commercial atrophy and make the company vulnerable to an acquisition. Nonetheless, any company interacting with another must recognize that there are legal limits to the cooperation possible that are based on a consideration of restraint of trade, and the possibility of collusion.

At the same time that this greater collaboration is occurring among companies, there is also a greater degree of competition. Seeds of competition lie in generic substitutions, as well as in growth of cost-containment policies around the world. Competition among companies is a major factor fueling the need for increased efficiency in medicine development. Most research-and-development-based companies are focusing discovery activities in a few selected therapeutic areas. This virtually ensures strong competition in medicine discovery research and in the development of compounds that are discovered. This competition among companies will probably intensify even further in the future.

GENERAL STEPS FOR DEALING WITH MOST PHARMACOPOLITICAL ISSUES

Many (but not all) long-term pharmacopolitical issues can be dealt with in six separate steps or stages. On the other hand, these steps are not sufficient to address political attacks that require a response within hours or the next day. Political experts within a company must be present to deal effectively with such attacks, because it is these sudden attacks that often create negative images of the industry.

Step 1. *Identify that a problem/issue exists.* Feelings of vague discomfort can exist for a long time before one may say definitively what is the cause of that unease. People also are often unsure as to whether or not a problem truly exists.

Step 2. *Clarify and focus on the problem/issue.* It is necessary to go beyond the general identification of a problem/issue; clarification and focus on the underlying issue(s) is needed.

Step 3. *Consult with the appropriate group(s).* When the person or group that has conducted steps 1 and 2 is not the appropriate person or group to address the issue, obtain additional assistance and expertise.

Step 4. *Address the problem/issue.* This may require a long and complex evaluation and analysis phase. Many interviews or other types of research may be required. Step 4 is a fact-finding, information-gathering period.

Step 5. *Solve the problem, reach agreement, or propose alternatives.* It is often impossible to determine at Steps 2, 3, or 4 whether the problem is solvable. In some cases, determining a number of possible solutions is all that can be accomplished. In other cases, a compromise may be suggested.

Step 6. *Communicate the agreement or decision reached to relevant people.* Within a company, certain attitudes can control how widely information is disseminated, even on important issues. Attitudes range from (1) only telling those who need to know, (2) telling all relevant people both above and below the central individual (and at the same level), or (3) only telling those who must be told—because guarding information is perceived as a way of enhancing one's power and importance.

FUTURE MEGATRENDS THAT WILL AFFECT THE INDUSTRY'S POLITICAL ENVIRONMENT

There are several major ongoing and projected trends in health care that will influence the political climate in which the pharmaceutical industry operates.

Attitudinal Changes of Patients and the Public

Changing demographics (e.g., more people are entering older age groups and thus are having more medical problems) will result in an increased emphasis on medicines that enhance the quality of life relative to other treatments. The political power of patients is steadily growing because of increasing activism. Individuals often exert this power via elected officials.

Medicines currently are used to prevent complications of hypertension, myocardial infarction or reinfarction, osteoporosis, episodes of herpes genitalis, and many other medical problems. Vaccines are used to prevent many infectious diseases. Future attention will focus even more strongly on discovering medicines and vaccines that can be used to prevent diseases and complications of diseases.

Unfortunately, many physicians and patients have not yet been properly educated about the level of risk associated with most medicines. Patients still believe that most modern medicines have little risk. Because perceptions like these have such a major influence on patient and physician reaction to adverse reactions and subsequent patient compliance, educational efforts must be increased in this area.

Regulatory Changes Worldwide

Increased harmonization of regulatory requirements within the European Economic Community (EEC) is resulting in the gradual simplification throughout Europe of the procedures for approving new medicines. This should occur within a few years. It is hoped that the time for medicine approval will be shortened. Depending on how these changes occur, there should be a move for regulatory harmonization between the EEC and North America, although this could take a long time to accomplish. Increased standards for regulatory dossiers in Europe mean that more data collected for EEC submissions will be submitted to and accepted by the Food and Drug Administration.

Industry should encourage a greater role for regulatory authority advisory committees and outside reviewers of applications, and other measures to streamline and speed the medicine approval process. Pressures from many groups for earlier approval of novel medicines of great medical value coupled with increased postmarket-ing evaluations should also be strongly encouraged. Another major issue relates to the requirement in some countries (e.g., Norway and Australia) for sponsors to demonstrate medical value or need for their new medicine as a requirement for approval above the demonstration of efficacy and safety.

Third-Party Reimbursement of Investigational Treatments

Sponsors often require that investigational therapies be paid for by third-party payers to support the sponsor's development activities. This is particularly relevant for some orphan medicines, as well as most medicines from small companies. Investigator-sponsored medicine trials cannot be done in some situations when there is no insurance coverage.

Spread of Existing and New Diseases

All diseases have natural histories, and their virulence, spread, and symptomatology (nature and intensity) change over the years. New diseases periodically appear and sometimes have devastating consequences. Companies closely track these events and attempt to discover and develop new medicines and therapies to influence or alter disease patterns.

Need for Innovation Within the Industry

Pharmaceutical companies experience great pressure in the form of the need to be continually innovative and the increased competition in the face of more and more generic medicines. It is ironic that the more successful the industry is in discovering and developing new, improved medicines, the greater will be the pressures in the future to do the same thing all over again when those patents expire. This cycle to continually higher standards almost guarantees that many research-based pharmaceutical companies of today will not be around in ten to 50 years.

Need for Education of Outside Groups by the Industry

Education about the roles of the industry and the upward spiral of pressures must be provided to the external groups with which the industry interacts. Education of health care professionals on the correct use of therapies is a critical and continual challenge to the industry. Information about a medicine is a basic right of patients who are advised to take that medicine. The methods and the standards used to provide this information (e.g., patient package inserts and interactive televisions in pharmacies) are being developed. It is anticipated that competition among companies for over-the-counter medicines will lead to more widespread use of interactive televisions in pharmacies. New regulations in Europe regarding patient package inserts should eventually lead to increased use of this important method in North America as well.

It is essential for the pharmaceutical industry and individual companies to learn what people think about the industry and the products it produces. It also is essential to learn why people think what they do. This latter information about public perceptions will provide the basis for mounting a campaign to address the issues most effectively. It is also essential to recognize that our industry plays a relatively minor role within the entire health care debate, despite the fact that we often seem to be at center stage. This perspective will help us to build relationships, to relate better to many of our natural allies within this arena, and to achieve our goals better.

This discussion has sought to tie many disparate issues together under the heading of pharmacopolitics—political issues between a company or the entire industry and external groups or individuals. Describing these issues as part of pharmacopolitics will focus attention on them and ensure that the company, industry, or individual addresses them as efficiently as possible.

7 / Institutional Memory

Components of Institutional Memory **69**	Providing Practical and Theoretical Lessons on Medicine Discovery, Development, and
Experience 69	Marketing. 71
Lessons 70	**How Is Institutional Memory Created and**
Information 70	**Used?** **71**
Tangible Items 70	How May the Institutional Memory be
Why Is Institutional Memory Valuable? **71**	Consulted or Promoted? 71
Recruiting New Employees 71	Who Should Be Involved? 72
Interactions Among Current Employees....... 71	

Make three correct guesses consecutively and you will establish a reputation as an expert. Laurence J. Peter

The term institutional memory refers to the nature of the pharmaceutical company in terms of its traditions, values, myths, and information that have value and should be preserved and handed on to future employees. Institutional memory is really the wisdom of a company, which is a distillation of the people's experiences. Each company should have both formal and informal methods for collecting, storing, and passing on information, knowledge, and data obtained by company employees. These data, which are important for historical purposes, future evaluations, and future analyses, enable the company to preserve its individual and collective wisdom and the company's identity.

The assumption underlying this chapter is that both an institutional memory and its traditions offer benefits and significant value that far outweighs the efforts and money that must be spent by the company to create and maintain them.

COMPONENTS OF INSTITUTIONAL MEMORY

Every company has at least the rudiments of an institutional memory. This may exist only in the minds of a few employees in a large company or in the mind of the single member of the company. At the other extreme is a large organization that has accumulated a large number of experiences, lessons, information, and tangible items, and actively works to provide these to their current staff. Most companies are in the large middle area where little attention is paid to the concept and no systematic efforts are focused on it.

A company's institutional memory includes (1) old equipment, relics, photographs, and souvenirs of past events and buildings; (2) reports and analyses, especially those which present a broad overview of the company and may be useful to managers who are able to utilize the data; (3) specific analyses and reports created for the purpose of developing an institutional memory, such as lessons gained from terminated projects and important measures and trends in productivity; and (4) professional know-how that is often lost when scientists, clinicians, or marketing or other professionals leave the company. The latter may be captured by carefully structured interviews and through other means, such as retaining certain individuals as consultants after they retire or leave.

Experiences

People who have participated in important activities within an organization have valuable experiences that should become part of the institutional memory. These experiences may be collected on audio tape or on video tape using structured interviews conducted by professional interviewers. Topics that should be discussed include (1) the problems faced by these individuals, (2) how those problems were addressed, (3) how the organizational structure and company operations assisted or hindered their efforts, (4) what lessons they learned at the time of the event(s), and (5) what lessons they currently see as emanating from their experiences. They should be asked what they would have done at the time that is different from what they did and, also, how they would approach the same or similar problem today.

In some cases a professional writer may be asked to conduct various interviews and to prepare a written document on a subject of particular interest, such as the discovery and development of an important medicine. It must be stressed that honesty in reporting is mandatory if this information is to have any lasting value. Attempting to gloss over problems or to present a more polished view of events than what really occurred does not provide the institutional memory with real value and benefit. Moreover, the information may easily be counterproductive if people are led to draw the wrong conclusions and lessons from the information, and then possibly use the "lessons" inappropriately.

Experiences of employees, their families, and others who participate in company-sponsored events also become part of the institutional memory. Traditions carried on for numerous years, such as picnics, retreats, and staff meetings, are particularly valuable events in this regard.

Lessons

Employees who have been at a company for a long time often serve as a repository for various types of information and as internal consultants as well as mentors for newer and also for younger employees. A company with rapid turnover risks losing important people who retain part of the company's identity and can help train new employees in many cultural, as well as methodological, aspects of the company.

Although there are several components of an institution's memory, the most important is probably the lessons learned that can help current employees perform their jobs more effectively. These lessons may come from the experiences collected, items collected, and other information, but to extract and identify important lessons a company should pursue one or more steps beyond simply gathering these items. The first step in this process is to have one or more people review the information gathered in an attempt to elicit the lessons of current or potentially future value. A second step is to ask those people interviewed to discuss the lessons they learned from their experiences. A third step is to contact important individuals at the company, such as project leaders and product managers, to identify both specific and general lessons learned from their projects, and to write those down in a suitable format for future use. These could be collected from project leaders after a project is terminated as a result of success or failure to achieve its goals. Product managers also could be interviewed at important product milestones. Alternatively, the lessons they learned could be solicited from both groups on a periodic basis (e.g., every two years).

A description of the lessons collected could be placed in a loose-leaf binder for use. The information should be categorized as well as cross-indexed by all relevant terms (e.g., regulatory affairs, Phase I, medicine X, and chemical scaleup).

Information

Companies generate, as well as collect, a great amount of information every day. This information varies in its relevance for a company's institutional memory, primarily depending on the breadth of the company's definition of this term, as well as its interest in creating and preserving its institutional memory. Part or all of the material published by company employees may be chosen to be part of the institutional memory. The company may be interested in all company-produced brochures, package inserts, newsletters, and magazines. Examples of out-of-date regulatory applications, adverse experience reports, plus letters to and from regulatory authorities about the company's products may also be of interest. Some or all published information about a company's products may also be of interest. Relevant published information may be saved, based on the specific product, the author(s) of the article, the year of publication, or other factors. The information would be collected, coded, and stored in a facility with ability for rapid retrieval. This historical data base could also be stored on hard copy (i.e., paper) or in a deep-freeze facility (i.e., warehouse), where it would be less accessible for rapid retrieval.

Tangible Items

Every company generates and collects many tangible items that relate to its own activities over the years. Most of those items are eventually discarded but some become collector's items and increase in value. All companies would be wise to set apart and store some of these items. Even a small company can place some of the more interesting items in a small cabinet or case in their lobby for their employees and visitors to view.

If the company has been in business for a long period or is fairly large, it may have sufficient material to justify dedicating an entire room for this purpose. If the number and nature of the items collected warrant, an entire museum may be created.

The types of items that should be saved include

1. Medicine bottles and containers made by the company, plus their original boxes, when possible.
2. Catalogs of the company's products.
3. Brochures prepared for physicians, patients, sales representatives, employees, and others.
4. Issues of the company's newsletters and magazines.
5. Special awards given by the company to various employees.
6. Photographs and paintings of well-known people or events associated with the company.
7. Items of interest given to or by the company for special occasions.

8. Newspapers with stories about the company or its products.
9. Press kits and press releases used for the launch of the company's products.
10. Video tapes of news programs describing the company's products in a positive manner.
11. Video tapes of people from the company receiving awards or making presentations on behalf of the company.
12. Any other items of scientific, medical, marketing, or production interest, including old scientific equipment used by the company.

Companies that have not systematically collected these items may allocate a certain sum to purchase them from former employees, specialized antique stores, or at auction.

WHY IS INSTITUTIONAL MEMORY VALUABLE?

Institutional memory should primarily be viewed as a viable, dynamic part of a company that serves many purposes. A company that has developed a comprehensive institutional memory can use it in several ways.

Recruiting New Employees

A prospective employee who sees some of the tangible items from the company's past, as well as information disseminated in the form of newsletters and magazines, realizes that the company has traditions that it values and a culture that brings an institutional identity to the employees. These factors generally make a positive impression on potential employees, no matter how young or small the company.

Interactions Among Current Employees

All employees feel positive about a company that has traditions and a positive cultural identity and heritage. The techniques described in this article help define, create, and maintain some of those traditions. Whether employees read all newsletters they are sent or whether they actually visit a room of exhibits, they are still aware of the values the company represents and promotes.

Providing Practical and Theoretical Lessons on Medicine Discovery, Development, and Marketing

Of all the reasons for establishing and maintaining an institutional memory, this may be the most important. A group that does not learn from its past experiences is forced to repeat many of its errors. If this were a perfect world, then everyone would retain knowledge of all lessons they had learned and would be able to determine the appropriate conditions for which they apply. Even in a perfect world, however, some lessons are lost through turnover of staff. In this far from perfect world, companies with significant turnover may lose part of their institutional memory if the lessons learned are not captured in some way for the benefit of current and future staff. Even a low rate of turnover of important staff may cause a large loss of institutional memory. When one considers the enormous financial investment made by a company in the ongoing training of staff, it makes little sense for a company not to obtain the full benefits of its investment through the relatively inexpensive means of collecting employee ideas that are of high caliber.

HOW IS INSTITUTIONAL MEMORY CREATED AND USED?

Every organization that desires to create an institutional memory should use as many methods as possible to achieve that goal. Generally, the only limitations to creating institutional memory are generally lack of perceived value and lack of resources. The understanding of this concept's value by one or more senior managers should be sufficient to initiate at least some activities toward creation of institutional memory.

One particular issue is how to separate the lessons that have real value from the dross. A group of senior staff could review this information periodically. Material could be categorized as (1) important lessons that were obtained under specific circumstances and are not generalizable, (2) important lessons that are generalizable, and (3) material to be deleted.

How May the Institutional Memory Be Consulted or Promoted?

The company must decide to what degree they wish to be proactive and promote various aspects of the institutional memory to their employees, and to what degree they wish to adopt a more passive stance and allow employees to initiate their own personal approaches. The correct decision for a company probably solves both active and passive approaches, depending on the particular aspect of the institutional memory that is considered.

Various aspects of the institutional memory may be discussed at a periodic (e.g., annual) meeting open to all company employees, or merely made available on request to all employees above a certain level. This could be in the form of a loose-leaf binder. Another approach is to have an annual lecture series at the company that honors a former manager, scientist, or an otherwise well-known individual. The holding of this lecture, plus an accompanying reception or dinner, would generate yet another company tradition.

A company's newsletter about its affairs and people that is published (for example) monthly could be placed at convenient locations throughout the company for interested employees to take. Alternatively, the newsletter could be sent to all employees, either through the internal mail or to their homes. Although the postage paid could be a significant expense in the latter case, using the mail would serve to provide a larger number of family members of employees with the company's message.

The lessons of medicine discovery, development, and marketing could be assembled on paper, computer disk, or audio cassette. These should be updated on a periodic (e.g., annual or biannual) basis and provided to all relevant personnel. If this information was considered confidential, the company could employ appropriate measures to ensure that distribution of copies was controlled. The more tailored the lessons are to the vagaries or operating procedures of the specific company, the less value they would have for other companies.

Certain materials on audio cassette and video cassette could be checked out of the library or training offices. Relevant video cassettes could be shown to new employ-ees to help orient and indoctrinate them in the company's philosophy. Others might be relevant to play in a public area, perhaps in the lobby outside the company's cafeteria.

Who Should Be Involved?

A specific individual should be charged with responsibilities for organizing and maintaining activities relating to the institution's memory. That person could be previously (or simultaneously) involved with work in technical information, marketing promotional activities, corporate public relations, library work, or another area. The individual could spend anywhere from 1% to 100% of his or her time on these activities. The amount of effort spent could be modified based on the interest shown by employees and also based on the perceived benefit to the company.

In conclusion, the concept of institutional memory offers potential benefits to both employees and employer and is one example of a win–win situation. The major issue is how extensive the procedures and processes should be to achieve the greatest benefits with reasonable or limited efforts.

8 / Keys for Pharmaceutical Success

Areas on Which to Focus	**73**	Addressing the Key Focus Areas	76
Focus Your Businesses	73	**Key Success Factors**	**76**
Focus Your Management Message and		**Key Characteristics of the Research and**	
Style	74	**Development Director**	**76**
Focus Your Standards	74	Establishing Deadlines and Target Dates	77
Focus Your Strategies	74	**Basic Management Issues**	**78**
Focus Your Organization	74	Finding the Right Balance in Judging	
Focus Your Portfolio	74	Important Issues	78
Focus Your Approaches to People and Groups		Basic Differences in Priorities	80
Outside the Company	75	Required Knowledge for Officers of a	
Focus Your Markets..........................	75	Pharmaceutical Company	81
Focus Your Growth Plans and Goals	75	**The Negative Spiral of Success**..................	**81**
Focus Your Company's Image	75	**Key Golden Rules**...............................	**81**

The intensity of a conviction that a hypothesis is true has no bearing over whether it is true or not. Peter Medawar

The author is often asked why, in the first edition of this book, he did not directly state his own personal views about the optimal way to organize and operate a pharmaceutical company. This book (and others written by the author) generally avoids personal opinions or stating what solution is best, and attempts to present options and considerations to use in arriving at a decision because there is no single approach to problem solving that is optimal for all companies in all situations. Nonetheless, there are some principles and practices that I do consider to be better than others, and I have tried to bring many of these together in this chapter. For those who object to some (or many) of the statements in this chapter—I agree that there are exceptions to any principle and various ways to approach any problem or issue.

Ten keys for success in the pharmaceutical industry are described below. They relate to areas of a company's business activities that should be evaluated and then focused. Devoting thought and effort to these key areas should prevent many problems from occurring, enable more rapid and appropriate responses to those that do arise, and lead to improved efficiency, productivity, and profit for the organization. This chapter also includes a number of other issues that should be considered in a successful company. Because each topic discussed is also presented in other chapters, specific cross references are generally not included here.

AREAS ON WHICH TO FOCUS

Focus Your Businesses

There is a spectrum of whether a company is extensively diversified into other businesses (e.g., chemicals or agricultural products) or whether it is 100% focused on discovering, developing, and marketing ethical pharmaceuticals. The position of a company on this spectrum and also the direction of a company should be determined along this spectrum. This information should be communicated widely within the organization. During the 1970s many pharmaceutical companies diversified into various other businesses. Some of these businesses were unrelated to pharmaceuticals. During the late 1980s it was apparent that many companies were divesting some (or all) of these other nonpharmaceutical businesses and had decided to focus primarily or solely on discovering, developing, and marketing medicines.

The correct position on this spectrum of being highly focused to being highly diversified for a specific company depends primarily on its history, financial status, pipeline of new products, and management philosophy. Despite these caveats there are many reasons to believe that most companies should become more focused rather than more diversified in the future.

Another spectrum along which companies vary is the amount of risk-taking behavior. The degree of risk taking that the senior managers are comfortable with will undoubtedly influence which specific businesses to enter. A common mistake made by some large nonpharmaceutical companies (e.g., chemical companies) that enter this industry is to acquire a pharmaceutical company and to manage it as if it was similar to any other high technology company. This error led to a wide variety of problems including demotivating staff, turnover of staff, decreased productivity, and decreased profits.

Focus Your Management Message and Style

If senior managers strongly try to pull the company in different directions, they make it more difficult for the company to move forward. The staff receive different messages about important topics and find it difficult (or almost impossible) to work cooperatively with other company staff.

One manager who delegates work and responsibilities appropriately and another manager who acts as a dictator not only have problems working together, but many of their staff also have the same problem. Senior managers should not micromanage their areas of responsibility, but should delegate as much as is reasonable, based on the competence and trustworthiness of their staff.

The degree to which the company is centralized or decentralized and the ways in which decisions are made should be clear to the most senior managers and communicated to others in a variety of ways. Changes in the management style that are close to being implemented along the centralized–decentralized spectrum should be communicated clearly to all senior managers. The subject of this spectrum is discussed further in Chapter 9. Of the various organizational models described in that chapter the author believes that the centralized collaborative model is the best one to use in almost all companies.

Focus Your Standards

There are many types of standards used in medicine discovery, development, manufacturing, and marketing. Even for a single type of standard (e.g., clinical trial standards) a company uses different types at different times (e.g., the standards for a pivotal trial of a major new medicine differ from standards used in Phase IV marketing studies). It is important for a company to know when it is appropriate and important to use each type of standard.

Focus Your Strategies

Just as with standards, there are many types of strategies. It is imperative to create and review periodically such strategies at all company levels (e.g., board of directors and departments) if medicines are to be discovered, developed, and marketed successfully. Many fads and fashions in management are always being trumpeted by consultants and others as the best way to achieve one's goals. Two examples include Theory Q and management by walking around. Most of these popular fashions should be avoided, unless it directly fits what you are doing or are planning to do. There are also management fashions that are prevalent during most of one or more decades. For example, operations research was developed in the 1940s, systems analysis in the 1950s, strategic planning in the 1960s and 1970s, and Japanese management quality control in the 1980s.

Marketing strategies must focus on achieving effective communication with physicians who generate prescriptions for the company's products, and not merely on conducting a broad promotional approach to all physicians. Research strategies must focus on achieving information that provides competitive advantages in a variety of different ways and allocates the company's resources in numerous important areas.

Focus Your Organization

This concept has been interpreted in recent years as having as flat an organizational structure as possible. This approach eliminates unnecessary layers of management and improves the access of staff to more senior managers. Also eliminate as many peripheral service groups as possible that are not truly needed. Increasing the number of ancillary staff facilitates medicine development and the efficiency of professionals only up to a certain size.

Focus Your Portfolio

There is a balance for a company to seek between focusing on too few and too many projects. If termination of any single project would raise a major problem for the company, then there are probably too few projects in the portfolio. If there are insufficient resources to advance each project at a satisfactory rate, then there are probably too many in the portfolio. Portfolio focus must be present in the number of therapeutic areas studied, as well as in the number of projects. The most critical factor, however, is to focus on projects of moderate and high commercial and medical value.

A focused (and balanced) portfolio means that:

1. New projects enter the portfolio when they meet certain criteria.
2. Existing projects within the portfolio are broadly prioritized into two to four categories.
3. Projects receive resources based on their priority and need.
4. Resources are sufficient to develop all of the highest priority projects at full speed.
5. Minimally acceptable criteria are established that must be met at each scientific, regulatory, and operational milestone (e.g., Phase II) for any project to remain in the portfolio.
6. Various types of gaps in the portfolio are identified and plans are created to close them.
7. Analyses of the portfolio are conducted on a periodic basis.
8. The results of an annual portfolio review are presented to senior managers and to senior staff, along with strategies and recommendations for enhancing productivity and innovation.
9. General information about the company's portfolio and its future is relayed to all relevant employees via talks and printed reports.

Focus Your Approaches to People and Groups Outside the Company

Presentations about the company, its products, and its plans must be made to stockholders, stock analysts, physicians, academic scientists, community civic leaders, politicians, business leaders, and lay medical groups to maintain a positive relationship with all constituencies that interact with the company. These are generally valuable opportunities to promote the company. Before such presentations are made, communicate with all speakers representing the company as to what points should be emphasized.

Another type of approach to people and groups outside the company is the way in which business is conducted. Appropriate standard operating principles should be followed strictly (e.g., medicine should not be shipped to other companies for further formulation or testing until a contract is signed). Shipping medicine based on the anticipation that a contract will be signed may lead to various complex and unnecessary problems arising.

Focus Your Markets

Companies must be clear about which markets they are in and which ones are outside their comfort zone. Areas of strength and weakness should be identified. Within the group of strengths the company must decide on the importance of each market to the organization and the efforts that the company should exert to retain their position or to establish a stronger one. Within the group of weaknesses the company must decide whether they want to build a specific weakness into an area of strength, maintain it at current intensity, or diminish its importance. If the decision is made to build the area of weakness into one of strength, a plan of how to achieve this goal should be developed.

Focus Your Growth Plans and Goals

Identify an existing, or new, corporate group whose responsibility is to create a one-, three-, and five-year plan to ensure appropriate company growth. Have this group present the results of progress each year against the preceding year's plans, and update these plans annually. Plans are dynamic and must be reviewed and changed over time. There is a balance that must be found between creating rigid plans and totally flexible plans. Creation of plans at either extreme is counterproductive for developing medicines. Determine the people or committee to which this group reports and what formats (e.g., verbal presentation, slide show, written report, all three, or others) it should use. Seek to improve communications within the company and also the input of groups, such as marketing, into the research and development (R & D) process.

Focus Your Company's Image

Although an image is difficult and time consuming to build, it is an easy thing to tear down. A company's image is important both internally and externally because:

- Many physicians prescribe certain medicines based (at least in part) on the specific company that makes them.
- The company's symbol may project a positive image and promote positive values (e.g., promoting health).
- People may work for the company based on its history and tradition of emphasizing basic research or of developing important orphan medicines designed to treat patients with rare diseases.
- People at the company take pride in a company that pursues humanitarian goals and maintains high ethical standards.
- Regulatory authorities may form positive opinions of a company based on its willingness to develop a portfolio of medically important but commercially unattractive medicines.
- Legislators' attacks against the pharmaceutical industry could be parried in part by how they or others view the company.

An external group of consultants can determine strengths and weaknesses of a company's image by interviewing important thought leaders and policy makers across the nation. Based on the results, the company could create a plan to improve or retain those traits that they believe are of particular importance.

Addressing The Key Focus Areas

A company that wishes to assess its status on the numerous keys discussed in this chapter could form one or more professional groups to conduct this exercise. The more experienced the in-house staff in applying the methodologies and approaches to be used in the evaluation, the less need they have to enlist external help. If they need supplemental help, then one or two experienced consultants from a business school might be suitable to act as facilitators for the evaluation process. Hiring a large outside organization to perform this entire evaluation is usually an extremely poor idea because evaluating these areas requires an intimate and detailed knowledge of the company, and it would require an inordinate amount of education by company staff to have outside consultants correctly understand the issues, the organization, and the people. Moreover, having company people run the exercise increases the likelihood of their acceptance of the results and increases the chance that others will as well.

Overall, for a company to focus its efforts means that it is prepared to work in selected therapeutic areas and on specific certain diseases to develop those medicines with high commercial or medical value. The company's resources should be placed on developing the most appropriate opportunities, even though different managers in a company will interpret that directive differently.

Ensure that the company does not evaluate opportunities and make decisions by only considering the extremes (e.g., a very lean or very fat development plan for a new medicine). There is a large area between these extremes, and it is important to recognize and consider not only the extremes but also the pros and cons of each method between. Using the metaphor of vehicles one can get from point A to point B with an ox cart or with a Ferrari, but there are many other possibilities as well. For example, a lean clinical plan may be accompanied by a fat manufacturing and controls plan.

KEY SUCCESS FACTORS

For a pharmaceutical company to be successful it should create strategies to achieve each of the following:

1. Initiate research in a few therapeutic areas first. As the company expands do not spread its resources too thinly across therapeutic areas. Choosing the optimal areas to focus on is an important decision requiring marketing input as well as input from R & D managers.

2. Capture as many important innovations as possible through licensing. Develop a licensing strategy to do this efficiently. A company without good products and a promising pipeline will find it increasingly difficult to remain in business.

3. Communicate effectively within and between groups and disciplines throughout the company.

4. Create efficient systems for the rapid international development of new medicines. Efficient international development requires constant attention to keep activities coordinated. A corporate culture that breeds the creation and endorsement of efficient systems and successful marketing of new products is invaluable because those companies who have it achieve one success after the other, whereas others fail and do not achieve success.

5. Focus attention on political and social challenges that have an impact on the company and on the pharmaceutical industry. Do not adopt a purely reactive posture, but plan proactive steps and activities. These should emanate from the company as well as from trade associations.

6. Hire the best staff possible and support them fully. The people in your company are even more important than your patents and technology. Good people with high motivation and imagination who are right for the organization (i.e., fit well) make greater successes of mediocre ideas and medicines than poor people do with great ideas and medicines.

The great ice hockey star Wayne Gretsky was asked what quality enabled him to score so many goals and outscore other fine players. Gretsky reportedly answered that his success came because he skated to where he thought the puck would be. Having a sense of where the future targets for medicines and treatments will be in future years should enable perceptive companies to "skate" to the right places and be in position to score important pharmaceutical goals.

KEY CHARACTERISTICS OF THE RESEARCH AND DEVELOPMENT DIRECTOR

The following characteristics are a starting point for discussion.

1. A clear vision of the company's future and an ability to communicate this vision to all employees in the organization.

2. An understanding of the relevant disciplines of science and medicine.

3. An adherence to appropriately high ethical and scientific standards in discovering and developing medicines.

4. The ability to ask the right questions and take some risks to achieve major successes rapidly (i.e., not always choosing the most conservative approach to discovering and to developing medicines).

5. A desire to encourage staff to create clear goals for each investigational medicine and standards (e.g., minimally acceptable criteria) for their development.

6. A commitment to do whatever it takes to achieve company goals in the most rapid time possible and a no-excuses attitude.

7. A warm personal approach with his or her staff that provides appropriate rewards and recognition. A certain degree of charisma is an important means of motivating staff. Be polite, but politeness should never interfere with pursuing activities that assist the company's progress.

8. A delegational managerial style is used for medicine discovery where the control placed on scientists is extremely loose. Use of more planning and control for developing medicines. Utilization of appropriate organizational systems to achieve these goals.

9. Attempt to simplify responsibilities and activities within the company. Do not make them more complex. Provide clear instructions to all staff of how to conduct activities.

10. A minimal personal ego. Realize that giving credit to another rebounds to one's own credit.

Establishing Deadlines and Target Dates

Three examples are given of how projected dates for completing milestones in developing medicines were used by three different R & D directors.

1. The first R & D director delegated all major activities, and as long as he was convinced people were working hard—he did not fuss with his staff about achieving dates. He created a general calendar of potential launches (Fig. 8.1) and although he said dates were

CALENDAR OF POTENTIAL LAUNCHES

	Jan./March	April/June	July/Sept.	Oct./Dec.
1994				
1995				
1996				
1997				
1998				
1999				

FIG. 8.1. An overall calendar of all potential product launches scheduled by quarter (i.e., three-month period) for four years and by half-year for the fifth and sixth year. Relevant products and projects are listed in appropriate cells. A similar calendar for regulatory submissions is also often made.

TABLE 8.1. *To encourage a sense of urgency within the company*

1. Have all people identify their most important objectives for the year
2. Encourage people to ask themselves if their work each day is directed to meeting their objectives
3. Encourage people to challenge the status quo
4. Request a commitment to reach each milestone but challenge them to ensure they are stretched ones
5. Have early drafts of important reports reviewed to prevent the staff from polishing lumps of coal rather than diamonds
6. Have systems that check up on commitments

important, he kept moving deadlines backward. One problem was that many unapproved tangents were being pursued by medical staff, and most people did not have any sense of urgency or of being accountable for not meeting deadlines. The dates were rarely realistic, and for a period of time, ideal dates were requested from project team members. Table 8.1 indicates some methods that enhance the sense of urgency.

2. Another R & D director followed the same approach, except that to increase the speed of development he tracked dates on each project milestone more carefully and on a monthly basis (Fig. 8.2). Whenever dates slipped by two or more months he required an explanation from the project leader. Fewer unapproved tangents were followed and the R & D director created a greater sense of urgency than did the first manager. The director requested realistic dates for establishing the project plans, although no one was held accountable when deadlines were not met.

3. The third R & D director substantially increased pressure on all project leaders to shorten dates continually to achieve milestones. In this director's approach a strong sense of urgency prevailed, nonapproved tangents were totally eliminated and for the first time in the company, people were held accountable for the dates they provided. Staff were rewarded more (and punished more) when important dates were made (or missed). The R & D group in cooperation with other groups developed an integrated calendar of important meetings so that each was scheduled appropriately to provide relevant information to others. Calendars were used at various hierarchical levels (Fig. 8.3) within the company.

BASIC MANAGEMENT ISSUES

Asking the right question may be more important for managers than spending their efforts and those of their staff addressing inappropriate ones. A few selected questions that should frequently be raised are listed below.

1. What are we really trying to accomplish? Will this activity truly help us accomplish our goals, and who will benefit from the activity?
2. How large should our group (or company) be? Is unlimited growth our goal?
3. Do we know why all of the activities on this list (or in this document) are being conducted or are being proposed? Is it clear what the goals are, or could it be that the proposal is just to gather more data or to give some people new or increased responsibilities or power?
4. It is often easy to say why something will not work, but more difficult to say what can be done to ensure it does work. Are the staff and managers figuring out how to make something work or are they making excuses for why something does not work without addressing the problem?
5. How important is it for the company to obtain high quality in the science and the data they create versus just meeting minimum standards in conducting its activities?
6. How does the company encourage creativity and evaluate it in their scientists? Has the company identified its most creative scientists and rewarded them appropriately to minimize the chance of their leaving?
7. Are backlogs of work at the company a result of excessive loading of activities and assignments on a group or do they represent inefficiency or a deliberate attempt to allow the backlog to grow?
8. Are people focusing too much on what was said and done in the past rather than dealing with the current situation and how to achieve future goals?
9. What will the effect be if I make a certain decision? Will it be good, bad, or neutral?

Finding the Right Balance in Judging Important Issues

It is important to know when to:

1. Jump on the latest bandwagon versus stick to older approaches. Neither extreme usually works well. The difficulty is to know which newer ideas will eventually turn out to be the best for the company. A certain degree of risk in making these decisions is inevitable.
2. Use the computer software you know if it meets your needs. This may be past the point when computer experts claim that learning new software is necessary. Some companies jettison their software too quickly and their staff have to learn new systems an excessive number of times.
3. Allow each local company to decide whether to market a new medicine instead of having the central headquarters make this decision for them.
4. Develop at least some high-risk medicines, in terms of the likelihood of achieving an adequate efficacy

MONTHLY PROJECT STATUS

Date: _____

Project No. & Name: _____ Project Leader: _____

Indication 1: _____

Milestones	Planned/Actual Dates	Current Plan (Check if Unchanged)	Is Slippage Potential or Actual?
IND Submission			
Phase I-Completion			
Phase II-Start			
Phase II-End			
Data Cutoff			
NDA Submission			
Other:			

Comment on slippage in any department of two months or longer, even if it will **not** affect the dates above. If relevant, include suggestions on means to prevent the slippage from occurring.

Indication 2: _____

Milestones	Planned/Actual Dates	Current Plan (Check if Unchanged)	Is Slippage Potential or Actual?
IND Submission			
Phase I-Completion			
Phase II-Start			
Phase II-End			
Data Cutoff			
NDA Submission			
Other:			

Comment on slippage in any department of two months or longer, even if it will **not** affect the dates above. If relevant, include suggestions on means to prevent the slippage from occurring.

FIG. 8.2. A schedule of monthly project status prepared on each project. The project leader, project manager, or project planner can be assigned the responsibility of preparing this document. It could be modified for various types of projects as necessary.

CALENDAR OF MEETINGS OF INTEREST
TO _____ STAFF, 199 ___

	Staff Meeting	Sr. Mgr Meeting	QA	Patents	Res. Comm.	Bus. Dev.	Board of Dir.				
JAN.											
FEB.											
MARCH											
APRIL											
MAY											
JUNE											
JULY											
AUG.											
SEPT.											
OCT.											
NOV.											
DEC.											

The site of meetings, nature of projects reviewed, or other information can be indicated by a code or abbreviation in the boxes.

FIG. 8.3. A general schedule of meetings to be held each year. Dates would be added for all relevant meetings to facilitate an overview, particularly when meetings have to be rescheduled.

profile or therapeutic ratio (particularly if the commercial potential is large) instead of following a more conservative style.

5. Allow senior managers in R & D or marketing to establish many support functions under their control (e.g., finance, regulatory affairs, legal, human resources, technical development, and medical) instead of keeping these functions centralized. Groups that are allowed to acquire these functions tend to operate almost as independent companies. This can either be good or bad for the overall company, depending on its goals and organizational structure.

Basic Differences in Priorities

It is essential to learn how various groups outside the company think, establish priorities, and are motivated. Overall, this means understanding their perspectives.

The same principle occurs for groups other than one's own but inside the company. It may be important or even critical for a company to have a supplemental or original New Drug Application approved rapidly, but it may not be high in the regulatory agency's interest or priorities. This timing issue is part of the continual conflict between private and public priorities or interests.

Businesses like to be out of the public limelight, and public interest groups like to be in it. Businesses in general tend to minimize hazards, whereas public interest groups tend to exaggerate them. Although businesses are legally liable for dangerous products, public interest groups are not legally at risk for information they provide that is incorrect. This allows them more freedom in promulgating their views, even those that are not fully thought through or documented.

Trade associations serve a valuable function, but they do not always function as efficiently as possible. All companies should support their activities and also work hard to make them more productive and also responsive to company needs.

Required Knowledge for Officers of a Pharmaceutical Company

Should a chief executive officer and members of the board of directors know anything about the science and technology of how medicines are discovered and developed? The answer is yes because this important knowledge will help teach them:

- Who they can trust as their advisors.
- What their options are in making decisions as well as the pros and cons of each option.
- How their company compares with the competition.
- How to identify the strengths and weaknesses of their company.
- Whether the company's activities are consistent with its goals.

They should also understand the golden rules of discovering and developing new medicines described in Chapters 21 and 23 even if they do not have the technical background to appreciate all of the nuances of these principles.

THE NEGATIVE SPIRAL OF SUCCESS

A company that has a major financial success with a new breakthrough medicine receives a large amount of money. This "windfall" must be handled intelligently or it can adversely affect the company. One scenario where that problem could occur is described as a series of ten events that flow one from the other. This scenario or a related one has occurred at several companies over the last 40 years, and most companies are now sensitized to its danger.

A decision is made that the money will primarily be used to expand research and development activities. Part of this money is used for physical expansion and the company builds a large (and expensive) new research building. New staff are employed rapidly over a short period and because of the rush and number of new positions the best people are not hired. The company also starts looking for medicine discoveries in several new therapeutic areas. The culture of the company begins to change, in that money starts being spent much more freely for many luxuries (e.g., corporate airplanes, suites in hotels, and more elaborate meals). To keep the expanded staff fully occupied an inappropriate portfolio of investigational medicines is created. Eventually the patent expires on the company's major medicine and its sales fall dramatically. High development costs required for the larger portfolio of new investigational compounds and medicines raise major financial issues for the company. As a consequence, a low-risk portfolio develops. During this period frequent organizational changes in R & D occur through forced resignations trying to "get the formula right." The scientific image of the company declines and the company has a difficult time hiring outstanding scientists and managers.

KEY GOLDEN RULES

A few golden rules are taken from elsewhere in this book and repeated because of their enormous importance to a company's success.

1. An idea's value equals its intrinsic worth multiplied by the administrative level of the idea's proponent to the third power (sic). While this is unfortunate and should not be the case it indicates that the chance of a concept being accepted and implemented is greater if one's boss can be persuaded to promote the idea. This practice leads to the company adopting better ideas.
2. The value of a licensing opportunity equals its intrinsic worth multiplied by its length along the development pipeline to the fifth power (sic).
3. Truly great scientists do not generally make truly great managers. Creative scientists must be encouraged, stimulated, and rewarded to remain creative scientists.
4. Attempting to exert strong managerial control on basic research is counterproductive and will rarely lead to important discoveries of new medicines.
5. Treat people with respect in an open and honest manner.

Following all of the keys in this chapter guarantees a company nothing, but a company that adheres to these principles is in a better position to be successful and increases the likelihood of that occurring.

SECTION II

Corporate Organization and Management Issues

9 / Models of International Operations

Types of Subsidiaries and Medicine Development
    Sites...................................... 86
    Type One Subsidiary: A Fully Functional
        Research and Development Site 87
    Type Two Subsidiary: A Group That
        Functions at a Lower Level Overall or Less
        Broadly Than a Type One Subsidiary 87
    Type Three Subsidiary: A Group That
        Functions at a Limited or Less Complete
        Level Than Type One or Two
        Subsidiaries 87
    Major Versus Minor Subsidiaries 87
Models of International Operations and Styles of
    Decision Making 88
    Model 1: Centralized International Operations
        With a Dictatorial Decision Making Style... 88
    Model 2: Centralized International Operations
        With a Collaborative Decision Making
        Style 88
    Model 3: Balanced International Operations
        With an Egalitarian Style of Decision
        Making 89
    Model 4: Decentralized International
        Operations With a Semi-Autonomous Style
        of Decision Making 89

Model 5: Decentralized International
    Operations and an Independent Style of
    Decision Making 89
Generalized Models 90
Major Questions and Issues Regarding the Five
    Models of International Operations 90
Managing Subsidiaries From the
    Headquarters 90
Changing From One Model to Another 91
How to Determine if the Model of
    International Operations and Style Used Are
    Appropriate 91
Measuring Productivity...................... 91
Staff Morale 92
How to Choose a Model to Use 92
May a Subsidiary–Parent Relationship Utilize
    Two or More International Operations
    Models Simultaneously?.................... 93
Who Determines the Models Chosen?......... 93
Alternative Spectra For Describing
    International Operations 93
Conclusion................................. 93

A method developed on one continent has difficulty being accepted on another. Fritz Beller

The term international operations is used in this chapter to describe how a multinational pharmaceutical company functions when it has sites in two or more countries that are actively involved in discovering and developing new medicines. Another way of viewing this concept is to examine how the organizational structure actually works. Although this question is important to consider at all levels of a company (e.g., individual scientist, department, large division such as marketing, overall), this chapter focuses particularly on the overall company level. The major distinctions between organizational structure and international operations are shown in Fig. 9.1.

Numerous models exist of how a multinational pharmaceutical company is organized or structured (Chapter 10). The overall organizational structure of a company may or may not reflect the nature of its international operations. A company's organizational chart describes reporting relationships but does not necessarily indicate how decisions are made. For example, it is important for subsidiary companies to know whether they have any input into major decisions reached at headquarters that affect them, and whether the subsidiaries may make decisions independent of the parent group. This chapter discusses operations at the overall company level and is not concerned with organizational structure. While it

How Does The Organizational Structure Operate Internationally ?

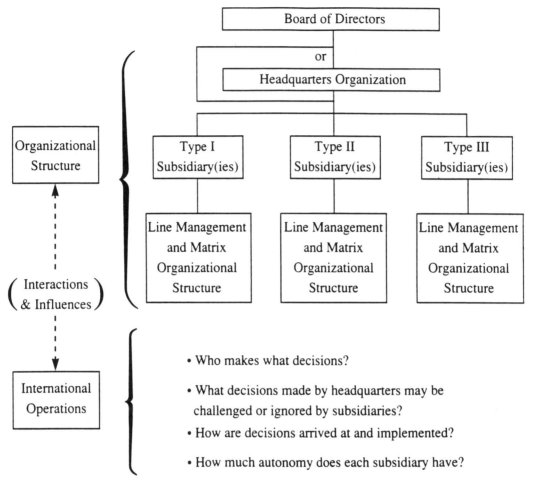

FIG. 9.1. Schematic of the distinction between organizational structure and international operations. A simple organizational structure model is presented above and considerations relevant to operations are listed below.

may initially appear that the operations and the styles of an organization are more or less fixed, most organizations operate in a state of flux. Many move in a narrow area around a fixed concept or anchor, others appear to wander aimlessly from one style or approach to another, and still others move in a predetermined direction toward a goal.

This chapter does not discuss reporting relationships, matrix versus line management concepts, or whether to organize a group by functions and responsibilities or according to the skills and personalities of the senior managers. Those concepts are discussed in Chapter 10 and in *Guide to Clinical Trials* (Spilker, 1991). This chapter describes the manner and style by which the overall company functions.

TYPES OF SUBSIDIARIES AND MEDICINE DEVELOPMENT SITES

Before describing five basic models of international pharmaceutical operations, it is important to describe the concept and range of subsidiaries. A headquarters is defined as the place where the multinational company has its major or parent offices. Subsidiaries are defined as those company sites that are wholly, primarily, or partly owned by the parent organization. Only one subsidiary of a single company is said to exist within a single country. If a company owns a manufacturing plant in one city and a research facility in another city within the same country, and a sales office in a third city, all three together are considered a single subsidiary. Joint ventures, comarketing activities, and licensed activities are not specifically described.

This particular discussion is limited to human pharmaceutical products (i.e., medicines), to simplify the points to be made, although the descriptions may apply to other products made by pharmaceutical companies (e.g., agricultural products, veterinary products). Three different types of subsidiaries are described, based on the scope of their functions.

Type One Subsidiary: A Fully Functional Research and Development Site

The most complete pharmaceutical subsidiary is one that conducts all three basic functions of industrial research and development, i.e., discovers new medicines, develops new medicines, and expands the medicines' characteristics or product line after initial marketing. This site also markets the company's medicines, and may or may not be involved in their manufacture. It is not necessary that a site at this level be 100% able fully to conduct every step in the discovery–development-marketing chain, although many multinational pharmaceutical companies have at least one subsidiary that is able to achieve this scope of activities. This type of subsidiary is referred to as a major subsidiary throughout this chapter.

Type Two Subsidiary: A Group That Functions at a Lower Level Overall or Less Broadly Than a Type One Subsidiary

This type of a pharmaceutical subsidiary has somewhat limited functions. The subsidiary may solely conduct discovery research, technical development, or clinical activities, in addition to the critically important function of marketing the company's products. This subsidiary may even conduct all of these activities, but is not considered a Type One subsidiary because of its small size, limited expertise, or limited range of activities. It may be highly specialized in a single therapeutic area. The subsidiary is generally viewed by headquarters as an important subsidiary that contributes in a substantial way to the development of a specific type of medicine, or in a specific technical area (e.g., the subsidiary represents the core of a certain expertise within the company).

Type Three Subsidiary: A Group That Functions at a Limited or Less Complete Level Than Type One or Two Subsidiaries

The third type of subsidiary primarily markets the company's products, and in addition may conduct a clinical trial on an investigational or marketed medicine within a single country. The clinical trials conducted by the subsidiary may be proposed by the medical director or staff within the subsidiary or by the headquarters staff. The trial is approved either (1) solely by the headquarters, (2) jointly by the headquarters and subsidiary, or (3) solely within the subsidiary. The choice among these approaches is generally, but not necessarily, based on the operational model used by the specific company. This type of subsidiary rarely, if ever, participates in developing the overall clinical plan on a new investigational medicine. Many subsidiaries of this type are solely sales organizations and never conduct any clinical trials.

Regulatory affairs personnel within this type of subsidiary may take the headquarters' dossier on a new medicine, add on any nationally conducted clinical trials or studies, and rework the dossier for submission to their national regulatory authorities. On the other hand, the regulatory affairs group within this subsidiary are sometimes instructed to submit the dossier prepared for them by the headquarters staff. In that situation the local regulatory affairs personnel are still often responsible for interacting with their regulatory affairs personnel when questions arise.

Major Versus Minor Subsidiaries

The most common distinction made between major (i.e., Type One) and minor (i.e., Type Three) subsidiaries are those that are conducting research and medicine development and those that are not. This distinction may be adequate for some pharmaceutical companies, but for others greater clarity is desired, particularly for considering Type Two subsidiaries. Type Two subsidiaries are not purely major or minor subsidiaries but fit somewhere between those extremes. Finer distinctions between major and minor subsidiaries for Type Two could include consideration of the following two questions.

1. Does the subsidiary conduct research directed toward discovery of new medicines? Companies usually limit the number of countries in which significant discovery activities occur. There is currently some controversy whether multinational pharmaceutical companies should seek to centralize this function or divide it into two or more distinct parts. This issue is not discussed in this chapter, although it is clear that there is no consensus on this question and different companies are moving in different directions.

2. Does the subsidiary conduct development activities on investigational medicines that are intended to help achieve regulatory authority approval to launch the medicine in major territories? This consideration may be used to distinguish between those subsidiaries that conduct marketing-oriented studies (on investi-

gational medicines) primarily or solely intended for their own market. These studies are usually included in a regulatory dossier to provide the regulatory authorities of that country with an enhanced "comfort level" that patients within their own country have been treated with a new medicine and respond similarly to the medicines as do patients from other countries.

MODELS OF INTERNATIONAL OPERATIONS AND STYLES OF DECISION MAKING

A single spectrum of international pharmaceutical company operations and styles is described, ranging from highly centralized to highly decentralized operations. Five models along that spectrum are illustrated and discussed (see Fig. 9.2).

1. A centralized international operation with a dictatorial one-way style of decision making that flows from headquarters to all subsidiaries.
2. A centralized international operation with a collaborative style of decision making involving headquarters and the major subsidiary(ies).
3. A balanced international operation with a style emphasizing equality in decision making between headquarters and the major subsidiary(ies).
4. A decentralized international operation with a semi-autonomous style of decision making for the headquarters and major subsidiary(ies).
5. A decentralized international operation with an independent style of decision making for the major subsidiary(ies).

Major pharmaceutical companies may be identified that match or approximate each of these five styles, but this information is not presented in this chapter.

Model 1: Centralized International Operations With a Dictatorial Decision Making Style

In many ways this model is the easiest one for a company to establish and maintain. This model is implemented so that a single site controls all of the major decisions and subsidiaries are provided (hopefully) with clear directions to follow. Assuming that each of the five models has been sensibly established and is being efficiently run, fewer questions or issues generally arise with this model as compared with the others.

The major disadvantage of this model is that the managers of the major subsidiaries are removed from the major decision making process. This is often demotivating for highly competent managers, even if all decisions made by the parent organization are correct and appropriate. Any mistakes by the parent group will be magnified because of lack of "buy-in" and shared decision making by the subsidiaries. This should be avoided as much as possible by the parent group that uses this model, and may be accomplished through informal discussions with subsidiary managers prior to announcing and implementing decisions. Nonetheless, the subsidiary managers recognize their lack of decision making ability at the highest levels and must be content with their power within limits established by the headquarters.

Model 2: Centralized International Operations With a Collaborative Decision Making Style

The major difference between this model and the preceding one is that this model includes formal consultations and involvement with major subsidiary managers before decisions are made. This usually takes the form where major subsidiary managers are members of im-

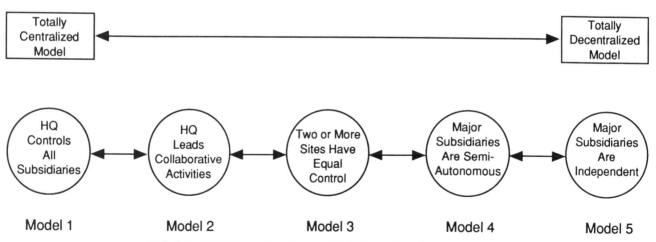

FIG. 9.2. Spectrum of the five models that are described in the text.

portant decision making committees, possibly including the Board of Directors of the parent company.

In every model discussed here, the role of senior managers in major Type One subsidiaries differs from that of senior managers in less significant Types Two and Three subsidiaries. The precise distinctions are not discussed, because each company has its own systems and rules. A single multinational company may utilize different methods of decision making in each subsidiary. The differences in decision making may be small or large and complex between the subsidiaries. For example, in Models 2 through 5, all subsidiaries of Type Three (i.e., those that are not involved in the development of investigational medicines) may receive all major decisions from the headquarters as would be expected in Model 1. Moreover, the medical directors of Type Three subsidiaries of any model may either be encouraged or discouraged to propose clinical trials for their own region.

Model 3: Balanced International Operations With an Egalitarian Style of Decision Making

Some large multinational companies have found that major stresses are created when an imbalance in power exists between their headquarters and major subsidiaries. This is particularly apt to occur when the headquarters is not located within the major commercial market for the company's products, or when the standards used within the headquarters country are lower than those used by one or more of its major subsidiaries. One approach to correcting this situation is to create an organization where important decisions are made by a small group or committee whose members are representatives of each major subsidiary plus the headquarters. Another approach toward establishing balanced operations is to have joint approval and sign-off of major decisions without the need for formal meetings.

This model is probably the most difficult one to establish and maintain because there are usually strong internal tensions and pressures within any company that would destroy the balance, if it were delicate. These pressures are created by groups and individuals who have strong opinions and desires for certain decisions to be made. Whenever compromises cannot be achieved and there are clear winners and losers on an important issue, thought must be given to how resulting stresses and negative reactions within the company may be minimized.

Model 3 requires extraordinarily careful attention to the needs of all decision makers. The standards used by all senior managers must be uniform. For example, the company may decide that any medicine, no matter where it is developed, should meet Food and Drug Administration standards. In addition, for this process to

succeed, it is important for there to be a collective desire for it to succeed. Any lack of commitment by senior managers to this collective will may be devastating and could undermine the organization's success and certainly the success of the particular issue. The author considers it particularly noteworthy that one major pharmaceutical company that utilized this model switched to another model after only one to two years.

Model 4: Decentralized International Operations With a Semi-Autonomous Style of Decision Making

The hallmark of this model is that senior managers at each major site make their own decisions. Decisions are reached after discussion and attempts to collaborate with the other major subsidiaries. Each major subsidiary and the headquarters attempts to coordinate their activities so that a unified medicine discovery and development approach may be designed and followed. Differences in market considerations, development approaches, standards, and plans generally exist among major research and development sites, and each major site that uses this model reserves the right to pursue its own course independently of the other major sites or headquarters. Each site may "for good reasons" opt out of an overall decision, although minor subsidiaries usually do not have this "luxury." This system works best when a major site does not opt out of any coordinated plan without the agreement of the other major site(s).

The advantage of this approach is the flexibility it offers the overall organization to design efficient medicine development and marketing plans specifically for each medicine. There is no necessity to have or follow a centralized approach or to fear that unpopular views and plans will be imposed by a central headquarters on a major subsidiary.

Model 5: Decentralized International Operations and an Independent Style of Decision Making

In many ways it is easiest to create and maintain an organization that is positioned at one extreme of a spectrum. This model is an extreme in itself—a system where different major subsidiaries or sites discuss plans with each other, but do not insist on following the same approach. The opportunities for efficient medicine development are theoretically no less for a company that uses Model 5 than for companies that use the other models. But in the real world, communication problems among people are greater when differences exist in the cultures and goals of those communicating. These factors usually mean that a model where people may easily opt out of a

MODELS OF A HEADQUARTERS AND ITS SUBSIDIARIES

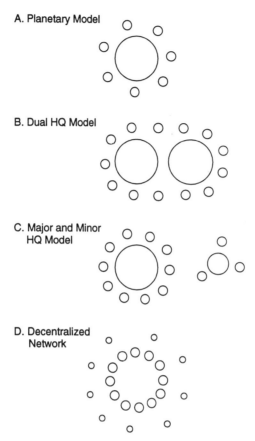

FIG. 9.3. Models of a central headquarters and subsidiaries where diameter equals relative importance. In reality all subsidiaries (i.e., the smaller circles) would have different diameters, based on one or multiple factors (e.g., sales volume, size of staff, development activities).

unifying decision and pursue their own paths is less efficient from a global perspective than a model where there are greater forces on the senior managers to arrive at a joint decision and to stick with it. Thus, Model 5 is the least efficient path to follow for developing new medicines efficiently worldwide. In this model, each major subsidiary may even be viewed as functioning as a separate pharmaceutical organization.

Generalized Models

The above concept may be generalized and illustrated somewhat differently (Fig. 9.3). In this figure the planetary model is the centralized concept and panel D shows the decentralized concept. The balanced version is shown in panel D and panel C shows an alternative presentation that could be either centralized or decentralized, but most commonly would be the latter.

MAJOR QUESTIONS AND ISSUES REGARDING THE FIVE MODELS OF INTERNATIONAL OPERATIONS

Managing Subsidiaries From the Headquarters

Managers at the headquarters who make decisions for the subsidiaries must both understand and be sensitive to the culture of their subsidiaries. This can be accomplished by several methods, including (1) hiring managers who are natives of the countries of the major subsidiaries, (2) sending managers to live and work for a period of time in the subsidiary countries of interest, (3) consulting informally with managers in the subsidiary country before announcing any major decisions or changes, and (4) having all decisions and major statements reviewed by suitable personnel within the headquarters who are both knowledgeable and sensitive to the culture, customs, and situation within the subsidiary. Approaches such as these enable the headquarters to retain its credibility within the major subsidiaries when major points are announced that affect the subsidiary. The alternative of proposing or insisting on inherently unreasonable or unpalatable actions even in relatively minor areas may seriously affect or even destroy the respect and credibility of the parent organization. This is particularly true when the headquarters is forced to retract or significantly change an announced decision.

Changing From One Model to Another

All five models lie on a continuum and are dynamic rather than static concepts. It is possible for a company to move its international operations and style from one model to another over time (evolutionary change). It is also possible for a company to change their operational approach and style suddenly (revolutionary change).

Professionals and managers who work within any one style of operations often complain about the weaknesses they perceive within their organization. These people often state that they would like to see certain changes occur and may be initially pleased if these certain changes do in fact occur. Because there are both clear advantages and disadvantages of each operational system, the movement of a company from one model to another usually represents a change from one mix of advantages and disadvantages to a different mix. Changes from one model to another cannot be viewed as simply leaving a bad model and acquiring a good one. Still, the optimal model that enables a specific company to be most efficient will change over time, and it is essential for senior management to recognize this factor and the need for occasional change. Refinements within a model should always be considered by senior managers and represent a different approach to improving efficiency than attempting to change the model used.

The decision to change the model of international operations should be dictated by need and perceived benefits rather than by a desire to "stir things up" or "try a different approach" because of boredom or inadequately thought-through suggestions. Although these comments may appear to be obvious to all readers, the author is aware of at least two large pharmaceutical companies that instituted major operational changes for precisely those reasons.

Many managers are tempted to institute a revolutionary change (e.g., a sudden change of at least two model jumps along the spectrum) that is most in line with their own personal views. Even if their choice of a new operational model represents the one that would be most suited to their company at that moment, it may be preferable to take an evolutionary approach and proceed stepwise over a period of time to introduce the model. The

reason for using an evolutionary approach is that most staff professionals and managers are used to the current system and know how to operate within that system, even if most agree that it is not the most ideal system for the company to use. Sudden drastic changes to the model places these people in a far different mode of operation than they are accustomed to. Many managers will resent and resist the new system and it may either not be used or may be used incorrectly. The degree of success managers achieve in adopting a new model depends on their personalities, their desires for the new system, their roles in the new model, and their previous roles and responsibility.

These cautions apply most to a research group trying to discover new medicines, less to a technical development group, and least to a production group where new types of operations may be imposed with the least disruption in productivity. These cautions also apply to a marketing group because of the stakes involved for the entire company in making major changes.

How to Determine if the Model of International Operations and Style Used Are Appropriate

A major blunder in the area of international operations is to modify the company's structure or style without sufficient forethought so that the company becomes weaker or less productive. This may occur for numerous reasons, including an inaccurate assessment of whether the current organization is operating effectively. In addressing the issue of whether the company is operating effectively it must be assumed that no organizational structure or model of operations works perfectly. Not only are the people who operate within any general structure imperfect, but also the ideal type of operations for each person differs. While some senior managers operate most effectively in a decentralized model where they retain the rights and power to make important decisions, other managers operate best when they are receiving commands.

Measuring Productivity

Measures of productivity should be used to judge an overall organization's progress from year to year. Similar or different measures should also be developed and used to measure individual groups (e.g., research and development, marketing, production) within an organization. Furthermore, this process should be followed at all levels, down to that of the individual. Details of specific measures of productivity are discussed in Chapter 36.

If the trend of productivity at any level is negative, then steps should be taken to address the problem. If this issue occurs at the individual or small group level, then it is rarely if ever necessary to alter the organizational structure or operations. The transfer of one or more people within the institution, however, may be required. If the problem in trend is observed at the overall group level (e.g., marketing, research, and development), it may then be relevant to consider changes in the company's approach to international operations. It must be stressed, however, that most problems that occur at the level of an individual or small group do not require, nor even suggest, the need for organizational changes.

Changes in productivity must be examined and assessed to determine their cause. The cause could be identified as inefficiency in the organizational structure. For example, the structure could be so rigid that people are unable to do their job efficiently or there may be an enormous bureaucracy that depresses most professionals who are enthusiastic. Another possibility is that the organization may have so many steps to process requests for activities or to review work that is done that delays occur that have a major effect on slowing the development process.

It is possible to address these issues by modifying the process and procedures used to conduct certain activities and to leave the organizational structure and international operations alone. In fact, it is usually preferable to modify procedures rather than the organizational structure or the international operations. On the other hand, the existing procedures may be viewed as adequate and appropriate and the structure, itself, may be identified as the cause of the problem. If this event occurs, the major decision makers for the company or groups concerned should meet to discuss the issue. The type of company problem to be addressed and not the hidden agendas of senior managers should dictate whether the organization moves toward a more centralized or decentralized manner of operating.

Staff Morale

To determine if the model of international operations is appropriate, it is also important to assess staff morale. It is possible that serious problems of staff morale may appear to be problems of productivity (or vice versa). The distinction between these two types of problems, and the identification of which is the true cause of the other are important because problems that primarily relate to morale should not be addressed (at least not in the first instance) by organizational changes aimed at improving productivity. It is essential to determine the underlying causes of morale problems and to address those issues as specifically as possible. Staff morale may be seriously affected by events such as the quality of cafeteria food, parking, or company policy on almost anything. Addressing these issues directly is the obvious and

only sensible approach to improving staff morale. In addition, there may be serious problems of the company itself (e.g., decreasing revenues, lack of interesting medicines in the pipeline).

How to Choose a Model to Use

There are only a few opportunities when an organization may choose with complete freedom which organizational structure or type of international operations they will use. Those opportunities often arise when a group of people or companies decide to start a new organization, or when a small group decides to establish a major subsidiary site in another country. Choosing a new model is always possible, however, because a new model is merely a modification of an existing system. The following discussion focuses on how to match the best model to a particular situation.

In the simple case where a single group of people is involved, they must determine the relationship that is most comfortable to them and then they must utilize that model. It may not be possible to implement their decision, however, if the person or people who will head the group or subsidiary formed are uncomfortable with or actively dislike the model proposed. The major people involved both at the headquarters and at the subsidiary must be willing to accept the proposed model as the basis of the organization's operations. If they are not in agreement, then either the model or the people must be changed.

The decision makers at the headquarters must be willing to share power with senior managers in at least one subsidiary in Models 2, 3, 4, and 5. Clearly, Model 2 involves a minimum degree of sharing power and in actuality little power may be shared. A company may state that they are following Model 2, but in actuality they may use Model 1. In Models 4 and 5 a company's decision makers at headquarters not only give up more power than in Models 2 or 3, but they also lose control of many decisions. While the headquarters may still influence or control certain aspects of their subsidiaries the headquarters may be powerless when Model 5 (for example) is being used.

Models 1 to 3 are more effective than Models 4 and 5 for companies that operate (or wish to operate) globally, i.e., as one company worldwide. Models 4 and 5 are used by companies that wish to operate as two or more separate groups, i.e., enabling each major subsidiary to function independently when appropriate. Project teams and review committees tend to be better coordinated and may even be integrated (i.e., a single international project team per medicine) in companies that use Models 1 to 3. Coordination between major sites is much looser in Models 4 and 5 than in the other models.

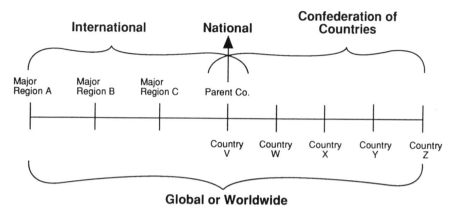

FIG. 9.4. Schematic illustrating uses of the terms national, international, global, worldwide, and confederation.

May a Subsidiary–Parent Relationship Utilize Two or More International Operations Models Simultaneously?

This question is an important one to consider, and the answer is clearly "yes" for independently operating groups. For example, the research and development function at headquarters may operate using any of the models described, while the marketing and production functions at headquarters may utilize other models. At the interface between these groups there will be a variety of issues to address. Those issues are not necessarily greater than the issues that would arise if both groups used the same model. Smooth interactions may be best accomplished with a series of standard operating procedures and open discussions at all levels of the two groups with their counterparts. Any problems created by using different models simultaneously within an organization can be overcome if both groups desire a harmonious and productive relationship.

When one considers a lower level than overall research and development (e.g., discovery research, technical development, clinical development) different models may be used by two or more groups operating at the same site. On the other hand, far more problems are created using multiple models at this level than would occur at the overall research and development or marketing level, because the frequency of interactions and dependence of these lower level groups on each other are much greater. When one considers using different organizational models simultaneously at a still lower level, such as the individual department (e.g., pharmacology, biochemistry, virology, organic chemistry), the number of problems would become so great that it is highly doubtful that the possibility exists for this approach to be seriously considered.

Who Determines the Models Chosen?

It is necessary to involve the chief executive officer of a company in addition to the heads of the function(s) af-

fected at all major sites in any decision regarding the international operations model. The company's main board of directors and those at major subsidiaries (if the boards exist) must also be involved. Apart from this core group of individuals various managers and professionals throughout the organization may be involved on a formal (e.g., task force) or informal basis. Consultants may also be approached for their assessment of which model would best suit the company or specific group.

Alternative Spectra For Describing International Operations

Many terms that describe international operations are found in the literature. Some of these terms are used rather loosely. Formal, albeit simple, definitions are given below and are illustrated in Fig. 9.4.

Global or Worldwide. The entire world is considered.

International. The company focuses on selected regions or areas.

National. The company conducts all development activities in one country.

Confederation of Countries. Countries of specific importance to the parent country.

The term multinational is a general one that is used to denote any of the above definitions except for national.

Conclusion

Five models of international pharmaceutical company operations and decision making styles are described, and distinctions between these models and models of organizational structure are discussed. It is important for any company to understand where it exists on the spectrum of models described and where it believes it wants to be. These decisions will enable a company to develop and sell its new medicines more efficiently and, it is hoped, will facilitate the medicine discovery process.

10 / Organization at the Corporate Level

Viewing an Overall Corporate Organization **95**
Various Perspectives of a Company's Structure 95
Issues to Address in Deciding How to Organize
a Company or a Subunit 96
Models of a Company's Overall Organization.... **96**
Functional Model 96
Product-Oriented Model..................... 98
Matrix Model 98
Other Models 99
Placing Departments and Groups in the
Correct Position in the Organizational
Model Chosen 100
Corporate Organizational Issues **101**
Hierarchical Versus Flat Management 101
Types of Subsidiaries of Pharmaceutical
Companies............................... 102

Pros and Cons of International Centralization . 103
Pros and Cons of International
Decentralization 103
Distribution of Services Within a Country—
Centralization Versus Decentralization 103
Appropriate Size of a Pharmaceutical Company . **104**
How Large Is Large?........................ 104
Is Larger Better?........................... 104
Benefits of Being Smaller 105
Methods to Achieve Company Growth in
Head Count............................. 105
Methods to Decrease Head Count............. 105
Critiquing the Organizational Structure Chosen.. **106**
Important Questions........................ 106
Developing Standard Operating Procedures ... 106

A staff of four hundred represents the critical number in a firm taken over. It is the number which separates the personal boss from the high-level manager. A man (person) may run a firm of four hundred or fewer people extremely well, but that is the maximum he can run personally, knowing all their names, without too much delegated authority. If you expand that firm to, say, 1,100, you may destroy him: Instead of all being people he knows by name, they become pegs on a board; instead of just doing and deciding he has to do a lot of explaining and educating; instead of checking up on everything himself, he has to institute a system and establish procedures. All this demands skills quite different from those he built his success on, and ones which he may well lack. Antony Jay. From *Management and Machiavelli*.

VIEWING AN OVERALL CORPORATE ORGANIZATION

Various Perspectives of a Company's Structure

Before discussing models that are frequently used to organize a pharmaceutical company, it is important to identify how a company is viewed by managers who must establish and operate the organization. Two basic ways of viewing a company as an outside observer are in terms of either (1) current organizational structures and reporting relationships that have grown up over the years or (2) activities that are carried out by groups that make up the company. The former view takes cognizance of the contradictions and conflicts, plus other warts and blemishes

in the way a company is structured and operates. Titles and even arbitrarily imposed reporting relationships are viewed as relevant and important. The other viewpoint is functionally oriented and sees a company in terms of flow charts. Relevant groups are considered in terms of their activities, procedures, and interactions. According to this functional view, a company should be organized to facilitate these activities and relationships.

A company may also be viewed from the outside as an allocation of resources from senior managers to more junior managers and then to even more junior managers and finally to the staff who use those resources. Resources are primarily staff and money, but also include information and other categories (see Chapter 3). Each level in a company has different needs and wants in terms of resources required to fulfill their function. When an organization is structured to facilitate communications amongst and between its employees and managers, it is better able to allocate its resources.

Finally, a company may also be viewed from the perspective of an insider in terms of one's own discipline and department. This view stresses the relationship between one's area and the overall organization in terms of structure and function. On this more personal level, employees may perceive benefits and drawbacks of their positions relative to the way that the company is organized. They may also assess the structure insofar as it facilitates or hinders various work activities, and facilitates or hinders progress in medicine development. Other criteria used from an insider's personal perspective may be expressed in terms of company culture, image, traditions, personnel, political issues, and the way in which work actually is accomplished.

These different views present a challenge. How may a single organizational structure and set of operating procedures be established to fit all of the dissimilar and conflicting aspects of the perspectives described while maintaining balance and cooperation in developing medicines and running a company?

Issues to Address in Deciding How to Organize a Company or a Subunit

The two most important issues to focus on in deciding how to organize a company (or another group) in the pharmaceutical industry are (1) personnel—specific individuals present who will be involved (or could be involved) in the organization and (2) functions that must be accomplished through the organization. Either of these considerations (or a blend of both) could be the major influence on the particular organizational structure that is established.

A company may be people oriented and want to use that factor as the basis for their organizational structure, but the company may not have a sufficient number of suitable staff around whom to structure their company, division, or department. In that situation, the most senior position should be filled first and that individual would then help recruit and hire the rest of the staff. For example, Glaxo Inc. hired Dr. Pedro Cuatrecasas to establish a research group in the United States. He then began to hire senior managers, and the research organization rapidly took shape. If a company believes that structure itself is more important to define than to identify the people who will fill each slot, then relevant individuals may proceed to organize their company on paper. The most appropriate people to fill each position are considered and chosen after the agreed-on organizational structure is in place. One of the justifications for this latter

approach is that people come and go, but a company's structure should have a greater permanence. This is especially true for larger companies.

When building an organization based on function, it is especially important that the logic underlying the new structure make sense to employees. The logic used should mimic present routes of work that are efficient whenever it is realistic to do so. If work patterns and procedures are to change because of a new or modified structure, a great deal of education may be needed to convince people that the new organizational structure will improve efficiency.

Building a large organizational structure solely around people or around work functions is generally inappropriate. An organizational structure based on an ideal or theoretical set of functions is sterile, because it does not consider specific people present in the company who will be asked to fill most if not all positions. Building a structure solely around people may lead to serious problems when an important person leaves the company or changes positions within the company. This is a dilemma that is faced by many companies and there is no easy answer except to aim for a system that best fits the company.

When a company's organizational structure is to be modified, it is important that the changes made are in concert with other parts of the organization that are intended to remain stable. It is clearly necessary to plan carefully the integration of established and newly modified (or added) areas.

MODELS OF A COMPANY'S OVERALL ORGANIZATION

It is said by some theoretical business school academicians that all businesses are organized according to one of three basic models. These models are to organize (1) by function, (2) by division or product (profit center), or (3) using a matrix approach. These three models are illustrated in Figs. 10.1 to 10.3.

Functional Model

The functional model (Fig. 10.1) is the structure present in most pharmaceutical companies. The departments in each function report to a central person (e.g., department head), who governs the group's activities. The major advantage of organizing a company according to the functional model is that individuals deal most often with people who have similar backgrounds and training. The major disadvantages are that there tends to be little communication with groups in other functional areas, and fewer people have an overall or broad corporate view.

FUNCTIONAL ORGANIZATION

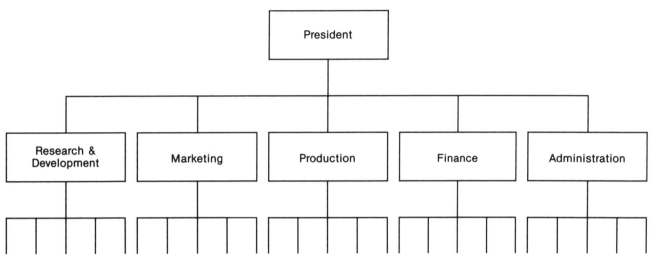

FIG. 10.1. Functional model of an organization.

PRODUCT ORIENTED ORGANIZATION

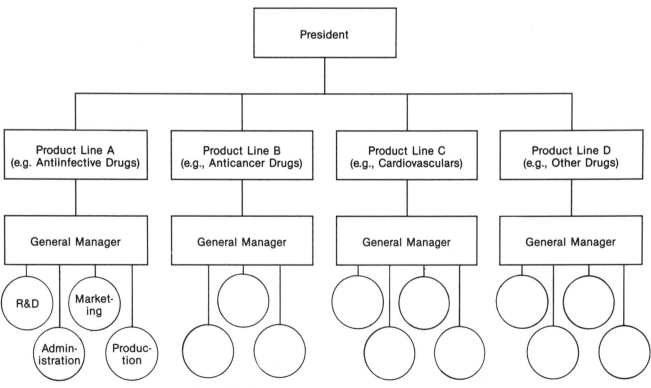

FIG. 10.2. Product-oriented model of an organization.

MATRIX ORGANIZATION

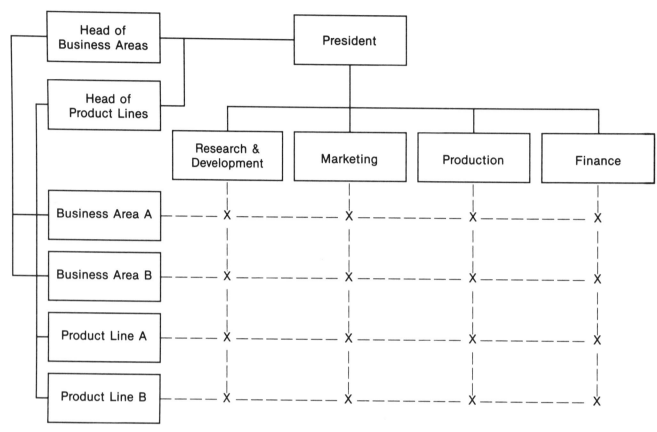

FIG. 10.3. Matrix model of an organization. The "X"s are coordination relationships. The business areas and product lines shown could be replaced by projects, each led by a project manager who would report to a single head of projects.

Product-Oriented Model

Figure 10.2 illustrates a product-oriented (i.e., division-oriented) organization. The prototype company that used the divisional approach is General Motors. Each car division was at one time organized like a stand-alone business and had its own marketing, research and development, and other functions. Some pharmaceutical companies have organized themselves around self-contained business units such as consumer products, diagnostics, hospital supplies, and ethical medicines. In theory, at least, each of these business units could be almost totally independent. A major advantage of this approach is to encourage the General Manager of each division to be as successful as possible. The major disadvantage is a duplication of many functions that otherwise would be centralized. One variation on this theme is for only one of the functions in Fig. 10.1 to organize itself using this model.

Matrix Model

Figure 10.3 illustrates a matrix structure. The matrix approach recognizes the importance of both functional and product-oriented models. None of the business managers control the resources they need, but must negotiate with line managers to get resources. Businesses may therefore compete among themselves for resources. Separate teams are established to run each business. This model has advantages over the divisional model in Fig. 10.2 because there is less duplication, waste, and inefficiency. Resources are shared between businesses in the matrix model. The matrix model recognizes business interdependence and in theory offers greater flexibility than the other models.

Advantages of a matrix organization are that it is client oriented, promotes teamwork, minimizes intergroup conflict, is more responsive to change, provides greater visibility for lower level employees, and offers multiple career paths. Major disadvantages of a matrix organization are that it (1) dilutes authority of line function managers, (2) requires greater interpersonal skills on the part of numerous managers to succeed, (3) requires cooperation of line function managers, and (4) leads to a greater erosion of detailed technical skills.

An organization's matrix should not solely be viewed in two dimensions as shown in Figs. 10.3 to 10.5. It is really necessary to think along three axes. The major axes for a multinational pharmaceutical company are (1) business areas, (2) function or discipline, and (3) geographical location. A particular company may be balanced or dominated by one or more of these dimensions. For example, the over-the-counter (OTC) business may be dominant (dimension one), the marketing function may be dominant (dimension two), or the United States operation may be dominant (dimension three).

Although the model in Fig. 10.3 illustrates integration of an entire company, it is possible for one group of a functional model (Fig. 10.1) to use some methods of this matrix model; however, the head of the functional group who uses a matrix cannot give as much autonomy to a matrix group as in the pure matrix model shown in Fig. 10.3 where all functional groups are involved. In the matrix model it is possible to organize a company around types or groups of products (e.g., diagnostics, OTCs) or customers (e.g., hospitals, health maintenance organizations, private doctors).

Other Models

In addition to the traditional models shown in Figs. 10.1 to 10.3, there are numerous hybrid type organizations that are possible (e.g., Figs. 10.4 and 10.5).

Of the many approaches that describe how to organize a company, the author prefers that of Futterman (1985). She boils the discussion down to three key issues or dimensions which, once addressed, give shape to a structure that will best meet a company's needs. These key issues are to identify where the company places itself along three scales:

1. *Scope of business activities:* From undiversified or narrow (e.g., a pharmaceutical company that makes

BUSINESS ORIENTED—FUNCTIONAL ORGANIZATION

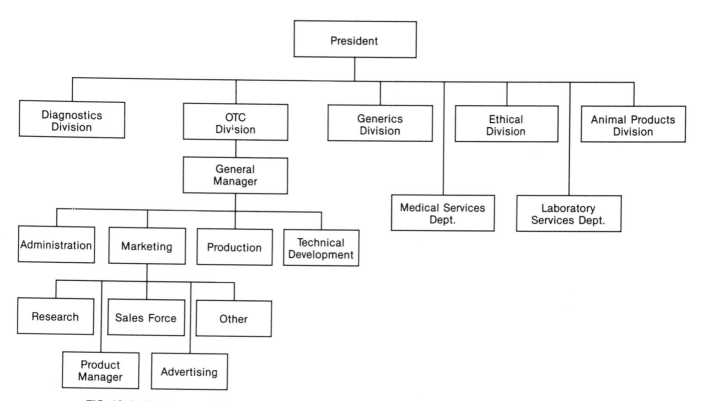

FIG. 10.4. Business- and function-oriented model of an organization. OTC, over-the-counter medicines.

BUSINESS ORIENTED—MATRIX ORGANIZATION

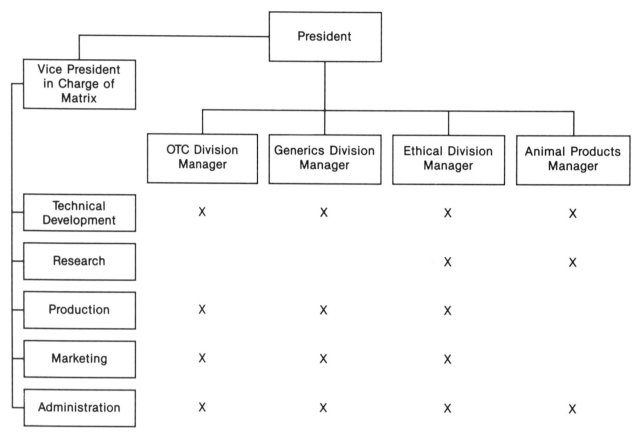

X=Contracts are negotiated with each of the groups on the left for services and support.

FIG. 10.5. Business- and matrix-oriented model of an organization. The ''X''s are coordination relationships.

and sells only prescription medicines) to fully diversified (e.g., a company that makes and sells medical supplies, chemicals, veterinary products, OTC medicines, and prescription medicines).

2. *Domain of the company's business:* From stable to changing. Research-based pharmaceutical companies are engaged in a changing market. Some of their other businesses may be more stable.

3. *Search for growth opportunities:* From purely internal (i.e., within the company's businesses) to external (i.e., to seek other opportunities, usually acquisition of new products, companies, or licensed products).

Based on a company's responses to these fundamental choices, which include considerations of current businesses and future plans, Futterman proposes eight organizational models (Figs. 10.6 and 10.7). She describes these as an indication of important organizational issues

to consider rather than as a blueprint to follow. Utilizing this approach would lead a company toward developing a hybrid organizational structure in terms of the previously described models.

Placing Departments and Groups in the Correct Position in the Organizational Model Chosen

Many factors influence how a company places numerous groups and departments in the organizational chart. Placement usually depends primarily on the personalities of the managers involved and their relative power. Logic usually comes in a poor second in this decision-making exercise. Different companies place departments such as licensing, patents, and regulatory affairs in totally different functional areas. Service groups such as the library, computer support, and graphics services are

PATTERNS OF CORPORATE DEVELOPMENT

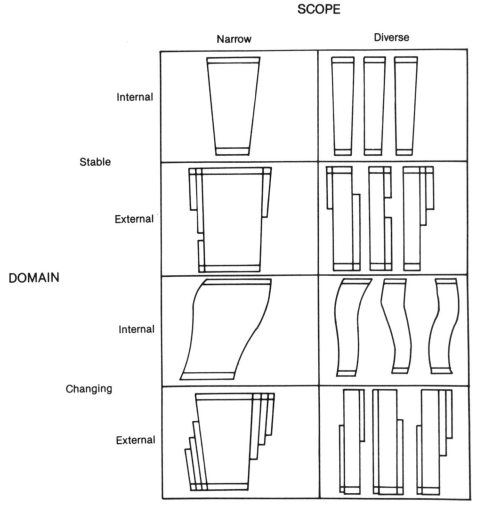

FIG. 10.6. Patterns of corporate development. From Futterman (1985) with permission of Warren, Gorham & Lamont, Inc. The parameters are defined and described in the text.

examples of technical groups that are administratively located in widely different functional areas of different companies.

CORPORATE ORGANIZATIONAL ISSUES

Hierarchical Versus Flat Management

Some pharmaceutical companies of approximately equal size have many more managerial levels than others. Those with many levels may be said to be hierarchically oriented, whereas those with relatively few levels are often said to have a broad or flat management. This latter type of company utilizes greater delegation of responsibility, has easier access to superiors, and usually has more flexibility than a more vertically structured company. Too many hierarchical levels tend to choke a company in forms, procedures, and sign-offs, and usually result in decreased efficiency. The numerous advantages of a broad management and organization are only achieved if authority is delegated downward. If this is not done then too many people compete for their bosses' attention to make decisions, sign forms, and so on. Another requirement is a cadre of senior managers who want this approach to work and can manage relatively large numbers of other managers (e.g., ten to 20) reporting to them.

ORGANIZATIONAL PROCESSES THAT SUPPORT IDENTIFIED DEVELOPMENT PATTERNS

		Scope	
	Search	Narrow	Diverse
Stable — Internal	Internal	• Integrated operations • Decentralized • Middle management initiative Model I	• Autonomous operations • Decentralized • Middle management initiative Model III
Stable — External	External	• Integrated operations • Decentralized • Top management initiative Model II	• Autonomous operations • Decentralized • Top management initiative Model IV
Changing — Internal	Internal	• Integrated operations • Centralized • Middle management initiative Model V	• Autonomous operations • Centralized • Middle management initiative Model VII
Changing — External	External	• Integrated operations • Centralized • Top management initiative Model VI	• Autonomous operations • Centralized • Top management initiative Model VIII

FIG. 10.7. Organizational processes that support development patterns in Fig. 10.6. From Futterman (1985) with permission of Warren, Gorham & Lamont, Inc.

Types of Subsidiaries of Pharmaceutical Companies

Multinational pharmaceutical companies often have several different types of subsidiaries around the world. Each subsidiary includes groups that are active in one or more of the following activities:

1. Conduct research and development.
2. Market medicines.
3. Manufacture medicines.
4. Conduct limited technical development activities for local use only.
5. Conduct clinical trials.
6. Conduct highly focused research.
7. Obtain regulatory approval of specific medicines.
8. Obtain medicine-related information for the central company.

These groups may be autonomous and totally independent, or they may lie anywhere along the "independence spectrum" from total autonomy to total dependence on central headquarters. Multinational pharmaceutical companies usually adopt a strategy of either marketing their medicines in almost all countries or limiting their activities to specific countries or regions.

Specific countries chosen for research and development, manufacturing, or other facilities are selected for different reasons. These include:

1. Country A may have a strong science tradition.
2. Country B may have a local company that was recently acquired.
3. Country C may have favorable tax laws or incentives.
4. Country D may have a suitable labor market.
5. Country E may have a government requiring many on-site activities of the company (i.e., political pressures may be exerted on the company). Many countries prevent multinational companies from owning more than 49% of a subsidiary. Types of subsidiaries are also discussed in Chapter 9.

Pros and Cons of International Centralization

Some of the major issues a company deals with that relate to its organizational structure are an outgrowth of whether the overall multinational structure is centralized or decentralized.

Pharmaceutical companies that develop medicines at two or more sites may be organized internationally to emphasize centralized or decentralized features. The value of centralization in a multinational company is that it provides standardization and conformity across all business units or across all similar units (e.g., production, research) in policies, procedures, and practices. Centralization decreases unnecessary duplication of effort and allows for cost savings, while ensuring that good business practices are adhered to by all parts of the worldwide company. A team of highly skilled and competent experts may be assembled at the central site who are also available to subsidiaries that could not ordinarily afford their services. Apart from the many administrative and personnel services that may be centralized (e.g., purchasing, training), systems analysts, industrial engineers, and other types of experts may also be assembled at a central site.

Other advantages of centralization include decision making by senior managers who (1) generally have the most experience in the company, (2) generally have the broadest perspective of what is occurring in the company, and (3) are best able to balance the resources and power amongst the various functional groups. The decision about which products are to be sold in which countries is usually either a central or local one, although a certain amount of negotiation must occur. There are numerous advantages to either approach.

Disadvantages of centralization include a potentially excessive bureaucracy, slow response time because many decisions must be passed higher in an organization, and lack of sensitivity to local issues. Decision making becomes more personalized, based on the judgments of a few senior executives who wield a great deal of power. Most other managers have less of a sense of participation and the most creative ones will tend not to stay.

Pros and Cons of International Decentralization

Decentralization involves a division or a delegation of authority, power, and responsibility from a central group to other managers, possibly to some lower level managers. This tends to decrease the work load on the senior managers and motivates the lower level managers to work harder and be more productive. More rapid decisions may be made at each facility in a decentralized organization because decisions do not have to be passed as high in an organization. Because the local manager is usually more familiar with the conditions concerning the issue, better decisions are often reached. See Chapter 29 for an additional discussion.

A decentralized site or facility may encounter problems if its decisions conflict with those of the headquarters, or if its decisions cause regulatory, legal, or other problems because the headquarters was unaware of the local decision. Coordinating a decentralized system is much more difficult than coordinating a centralized one, and there are many more opportunities for problems to arise. Not only can the overall company's efficiency be compromised, but the speed of developing medicines is also likely to be slowed down.

Distribution of Services Within a Country— Centralization Versus Decentralization

The major issue in organizing a company relating to many services is whether to centralize them as a department or decentralize them into the functional areas where they are most needed and used. The answer for several services is clearly one of centralization. This applies to groups such as patents, mail room, toxicology, printing, photography, and so on. Decentralization is generally used for other services such as secretarial support and intragroup coordination. Most services fall into a gray zone that may be handled in many different ways, including various combinations of both centralization and decentralization.

Library and Computer Services

Most medium and large libraries usually have the bulk of their materials centralized, but have decentralized satellite libraries in various departments as well. Libraries also exist in individual offices that are tied to a central library. Books purchased for individuals to keep on an extended loan basis are often subject to recall for use by others.

Computer services are handled differently in many companies, as well as within companies over time. The actual services provided are evolving and companies are continually exploring the optimal means of utilizing groups of computer experts to provide services. They may be centralized at either a corporate or functional level (e.g., production, marketing, research and development) and/or decentralized within specific departments.

Coordination of Medicine Development

Coordination of medicine development activities across departments and functions is discussed in Chapter 32 on the matrix approach. Most companies have established a separate department within the last decade to coordinate project activities. There are also coordinators who work within the line function of each separate division at the divisional, department, and/or section level. These vertically oriented coordinators usually interact with horizontally oriented coordinators who work in the central matrix group.

APPROPRIATE SIZE OF A PHARMACEUTICAL COMPANY

How Large Is Large?

Organizations usually grow in size as their products are commercially successful and profitable. Large pharmaceutical companies are arbitrarily defined as those with annual sales of over one billion dollars. Medium-sized pharmaceutical companies are defined as those with sales varying from 100 million to one billion dollars per year. Small pharmaceutical companies are defined as those with smaller annual sales.

Small companies that are successful often have a well-defined corporate culture that is credited with bringing them success. They usually try to retain this culture as they grow in size. Nonetheless, compromises are forced on all growing companies, and their atmosphere and culture almost always change as their size increases.

The issue sometimes arises as to how large a company wishes to become. This may seem to be a bizarre question to those who view unlimited growth as a desirable goal. Some people believe, however, that each pharmaceutical company has an optimal size and to surpass that size has an adverse affect on efficiency of developing medicines, in addition to adversely influencing company values and atmosphere. Many pharmaceutical companies are highly successful financially and must decide how to deal with their profits. When profits mount, they may be put back into the company to strengthen and build the core business to an even greater size. Profits may also be invested in many other ways, such as to purchase-related (or unrelated) businesses. The vision of a company's future objectives and goals should have a major bearing on the specific ways that profits are dispersed. When a company faces strong threats to its core business, its profits must be spent in a defensive manner (e.g., to buy outstanding stock, emphasize work on line-extensions).

Is Larger Better?

Many executives believe that "larger" is not necessarily "better" for a pharmaceutical company. The efficiency with which a company is able to operate is usually compromised as its size increases beyond a certain point. This will undoubtedly slow the company's ability to complete clinical trials and register new medicines in a timely manner. If certain functions such as research are divided and two heads rather than one are appointed, it may lead both to competition between them and decreased efficiency. Of course, two or more separate research and development groups may be established if there is an appropriate way of dividing the group. A number of types of research and development groups that could logically be established as separate entities are (1) human research and development, (2) animal research and development, (3) pesticides, (4) biologicals, (5) diagnostics, and (6) market-support activities in technical development. These and/or other categories could be organized as two (or more) separate research and development groups, as long as each of their heads reported to a single research and development head. The purpose of having a single overall head would be to (1) encourage cooperation, (2) minimize competition, (3) improve communications, (4) improve coordination, and (5) provide a scientific arbiter when necessary between the groups.

Scaling up the size of a company not only requires new buildings, but also demands new departments to provide services where a single person or small group was previously able to handle the work load. Adding new levels of supervisory personnel is usually unavoidable, but this step should be kept to a minimum. Nonetheless, the ways of conducting work that were effective when performed by a certain size group may be impossible when the group's size increases. Totally new approaches to maintaining efficiency often have to be found. Factors that tend to increase or decrease the rate or extent of pharmaceutical company growth are listed in Tables 10.1 and 10.2.

Over the last decade, newer approaches to this issue have been initiated by Merck and Co. One approach they adopted was to form a new company with Dupont,

TABLE 10.1. *Selected factors that tend to increase pharmaceutical company growth*

1. Larger number of patients use medicines as the demographic profile of industrialized countries changes toward an older age distribution
2. Additional life-span of patients with chronic diseases
3. Increasing demand for medicines in less-developed countries
4. New innovations and technology (e.g., medicine delivery systems)
5. Greater number and availability of effective OTC[a] medicines
6. Highly attractive commercial returns from major breakthrough medicines
7. Development of new diagnostic tests that can detect biochemical changes indicative of early stages of disease. This will then provide a target for medicines that reverse or suppress the progression of these changes

[a] OTC, over-the-counter medicines.

TABLE 10.2. *Selected factors that tend to diminish pharmaceutical company growth*

1. Increased costs of research and development
2. Increased risks of research and development
3. Reduced length of effective patent life
4. Increased regulatory requirements
5. Increased controls on prices that companies are able to charge for products
6. Customers becoming more cost conscious and making decisions based purely on economic grounds
7. Fewer independent doctors, pharmacies, and hospitals as customers
8. Greater constraints on sales promotion activities
9. Negative attitudes about the pharmaceutical industry created by consumer groups
10. Fewer significant new medicine discoveries[a]

[a] Points one to nine affect most research-based pharmaceutical companies in a country where these primarily external factors occur. The last point is primarily internal and depends on the success of specific companies.

called Dupont-Merck. This company was given several Merck products to promote and sell while it developed other new medicines to add to its marketed portfolio. Another Merck approach was to form a major joint venture with Astra that, at this time, appears to be doing well. A third approach was to form an alliance with Johnson and Johnson to sell OTC medicines. The point is that Merck, the world's largest pharmaceutical company, sought growth through innovative alliances with other pharmaceutical partners, rather than merely attempting to enlarge their own internal core business.

Benefits of Being Smaller

Benefits of smallness are obviously desired by most companies that decentralize their management, whereas those which consolidate and centralize usually desire the benefits of larger size. A major issue for each company is to find the size that balances advantages obtained from being both large and small and minimizes disadvantages. People often join a company when it is relatively small. Marked company growth often changes their personal interactions with other staff and their work in a major way that some staff perceive as undesirable (e.g., separation into different buildings, lack of being involved with as many different activities).

Advantages of a smaller size include (1) being able to respond rapidly to new opportunities, (2) having greater flexibility in modifying operating procedures and organizational structures, (3) having fewer managerial levels, which often translates into less bureaucracy, (4) having a greater chance of an intimate work environment, and (5) enhancing communications and cooperation through personal contacts. As a company grows, many critical factors that contributed to its original success will change

or disappear. Many of these factors (e.g., knowing everyone by name, interacting with many or all company functions on a daily basis) are impossible to achieve in larger companies. Significant growth in overall size does not necessarily correlate with growth in profits. Some larger companies divide into smaller autonomous (or semiautonomous) companies to achieve increased efficiencies, a greater esprit de corps, and competitive advantages present in many smaller companies.

Methods to Achieve Company Growth in Head Count

Growth in head count at a company is appropriate when it is based on greater profits and leads to a competitive advantage for the company. The probability of achieving greater head count and/or profits should be carefully assessed prior to a decision to initiate steps for expansion and growth. The two most important competitive advantages a company may attain for their medicines are product differentiation (i.e., a unique feature of a medicine that serves a medical need not served by other competing medicines) and cost advantage.

An important question in the pharmaceutical industry is how growth in the number of employees is best achieved and managed. One desirable method is to add people when a new medicine is discovered that brings "megabucks" into a company. Growth in head count funded by sales of an increased number of medicine units because of a new promotional campaign is also desirable. Increased production of medicine units achieved by cutting wholesale medicine prices may not increase profits sufficiently or at all. This method may become an inefficient and costly approach for a company to stimulate growth. Growth that is based on one or two major medicines leads to a potentially vulnerable position for a company. When those medicines go off patent and generic substitution occurs, the sales will usually drop. For example, Roche Laboratories laid off approximately 1,000 workers at about the time when Valium's patent expired. If an unexpected and serious human adverse reaction or animal toxicity is reported for a major medicine, that company may be placed in a precarious financial position.

Methods to Decrease Head Count

Many successful pharmaceutical companies, in addition to all unsuccessful ones, experience times when the number of employees must be decreased. This may occur in a particular business or group of a company for any of many reasons, or it may occur across the entire organization. Depending on the number of people involved, the urgency of change required, and levels of people within an organization affected, a number of approaches may be followed. Staff may be decreased by (1) firing them directly, (2) allowing them to resign, (3) allowing them to transfer within the company, (4) encouraging some to retire early, (5) finding alternative work, (6) allowing some to work part-time, (7) eliminating unfilled positions, or (8) not replacing employees who leave. The exact method(s) chosen depends on many factors, but the culture of the company often predominates in the choice made.

CRITIQUING THE ORGANIZATIONAL STRUCTURE CHOSEN

Important Questions

A few questions should be considered in evaluating a company's organizational structure.

1. Does the structure reflect the ways in which people operate to conduct work and the ways in which they see themselves (e.g., as a member of group X or Y)?
2. Is the structure most suitable for carrying out the mission of the company (division, department)?
3. Do conflicting structures in different parts of the company lead to problems?
4. What are the real problems or issues with the present structure?
5. What problems may be anticipated with the structure and how may they be addressed?
6. Have all relevant managers had an opportunity for input into the structure and a chance to critique it?
7. What are the plans to disseminate information on the organizational structure plus receive feedback and to review suggestions?
8. How will changes in the organization's structure be implemented?

Once these questions are considered, ways to address each issue should be determined.

Developing Standard Operating Procedures

An organization's structure is in some senses a static picture of where people and functions are placed. What breathes life and activity into this picture are the operational guidelines that inform people of how they are to behave to get work accomplished and goals achieved. Standard Operating Procedures (SOPs) differ greatly for all companies, and within a single company, they differ greatly over a period of time. All companies attempt to balance flexibility and rigidity in developing SOPs that will enhance activities and efficiency, rather than inhibit and squelch them. Pharmaceutical companies have experience in developing policies, guidelines, and SOPs that attempt to achieve their goals.

11 / Corporate Management

Communicating With and Influencing Others **108**
  Introduction.................................. 108
  Why Do Nonscientists Sometimes (or Often)
    Have Difficulty Communicating with
    Scientists About Scientific Issues?.......... 108
  How Can Nonscientists Evaluate Medical
    Claims?.................................... 108
  Dividing Work Between Two Sites in an
    Organization.............................. 109
  Techniques Used by Managers to Influence
    Others 109
  Improving Communication.................. 109
Management Models and Styles................. **111**
  The Spectrum from Autocratic to Committee
    Styles 111
  Four-Dimensional Model.................... 111
  Social Style................................. 112
  Other Styles 112
  Measuring One's Leadership Skills........... 112
  Boards of Directors........................ 112
  Entrepreneurship in the Pharmaceutical
    Industry 112
  Individualists in the Pharmaceutical Industry.. 115
Approaches to Management.................... **115**
  Are the Right Questions Being Asked? 115
  Quality of Management 115
  Functions of Management.................. 116
  Management of Subsidiaries 116
  Duplication of Efforts Within a Company..... 117
  Ideal Pharmaceutical Company Environment . 117
  Level of Technical and Administrative Support
    Services to Provide Employees............. 118
  Management That Follows the Latest Fad or
    Fashion................................... 118
  Who Is in Charge?.......................... 118

Observers, Experts, and Managers............. 119
Awareness of Activities One Manages 119
Time Management 119
Minimizing Risk to a Pharmaceutical
  Company 119
Approach to Making Major Changes in a
  Company................................. **120**
  Approach to Making Major Company Changes 120
  Observation of a Problem or Issue 120
  Desire for Change 120
  Consensus That a General (or Specific) Change
    Is Worthwhile............................ 120
  Agreement on the Specific Change That
    Should Occur 120
  Proposals on How to Achieve the Agreed-On
    Change 120
  Agreement on a Set of Mechanisms and
    Systems to Achieve the Desired Change..... 120
  Implementation of Mechanisms and Systems
    to Achieve Goals......................... 121
  Evaluation of Change Made 121
  Fine-Tuning the Mechanisms and Systems
    Underlying the Change.................... 122
Developing and Implementing Strategies **122**
  Defining a Company's Objectives 122
  Which Businesses Should a Pharmaceutical
    Company Be in? 122
  Determining Strategies...................... 122
  Communicating Strategies 125
  Implementing Strategies 125
Establishing Priorities **125**
Long-Range Company Planning **125**
  Functions of a Planning Staff 125
  Procedures of Strategic Planning 126
  Assessing the Value of Strategic Planning 126

The key element in developing a shared purpose is mutual trust. Without trust, people will engage in all kinds of self-centered behavior to assert their own identities and influence coworkers to their own ends. Under these circumstances, they just won't hear others, and efforts to develop a shared vision are doomed. Nothing destroys trust faster than hard box attitudes toward problems that don't require such treatment. David K. Hurst. From *Harvard Business Review* (May–June, 1984, p. 85).

Good ideas and good products are a dime a dozen. Good execution and good management—in a word, good people—are rare. Arthur Rock. From *Harvard Business Review* (November–December, 1987, p. 63).

COMMUNICATING WITH AND INFLUENCING OTHERS

Introduction

Nonscientists are usually unable to understand the details of work of most technical specialists (e.g., computer programmers, scientists). Some specialists therefore claim that nonscientists cannot really appreciate the significance or meaning of their work. This statement should not be accepted by nonscientists, regardless of whether they are managers or have other positions. Every scientist should be able to explain the nature of his or her projects, goals, strategies, and other issues in simple and clear terms that any educated individual can understand. When a scientist retreats into jargon it is a statement that the speaker does not truly want to communicate with the listener, or that the speaker is unable to do so. Many scientists who are unable to communicate effectively with nonscientists are also unable to communicate with other scientists. In dealing with such scientists, managers must adhere to good manners, which means that they should not give offense unintentionally.

Why Do Nonscientists Sometimes (or Often) Have Difficulty Communicating with Scientists About Scientific Issues?

A wide gulf often appears to exist between the thinking of scientists and nonscientists. There is much more to explain about the gap between scientists and nonscientists than to state merely that their training is different and nonscientists are not trained in the scientific method. One important difference between these groups may be illustrated with an example.

Cause and Effect Exercise

Assume that a particular disease is either present or absent in people. The disease appears to be associated with a particular symptom. The question to consider is whether the symptom and disease are truly related. Experimental data obtained from an investigation of this association will fit four categories.

These four categories are:

1. Patients in whom both the disease and symptom are present.
2. Patients in whom the disease is present but the symptom is absent.
3. Patients in whom the disease is absent but the symptom is present.
4. Patients in whom both the disease and symptom are

absent. This example is also referred to as a two by two contingency table.

It is common for nonscientists to rely primarily on information in the first category when reaching a decision as to whether there is a relationship between the disease and symptom, especially if the numbers in the first category are much larger than in other categories. This approach is incorrect. People who only pay attention to two (or even three) of these categories may also be misled in their conclusion. For example, if more people with the disease lack the symptom than have it, nonscientists may conclude that there is no association between the two. Scientists are taught that a valid conclusion may only be reached by considering all four of these categories. Statistical techniques can readily compare relative proportions in all four categories to arrive at a conclusion of whether there is an association and how strong it is.

Another important reason why scientists and nonscientists may interpret information differently is that scientists are taught to be skeptical because of the many types of bias that may enter an experiment or clinical trial. Many subtle (or obvious) types of bias may greatly affect the design, conduct, analysis, and interpretation of an experiment or clinical trial. We have all heard many examples of data that suggest one interpretation, only to be told later about a previously unsuspected bias or problem that greatly affected that interpretation. As an example, "In 1978, a Los Angeles study was released that showed that persons living in areas where jet plane noise was greater than 90 decibels had a significantly increased death rate." The popular press got some mileage out of this: *Time* magazine headed its article "Sonic Doom— Can Jet Noise Kill?" Shortly thereafter, the study was published in a scientific journal, where its merits could be more closely examined. The strong possibility of a secondary association was raised by the fact that people who live in the devalued housing close to airports are often poorer, older, or otherwise different from the general population. A subsequent study reanalyzed the data from Los Angeles and controlled for the confounding effects of age, race, and sex. When those differences were taken into account, jet noise was found to have no effect on mortality. (Michael et al., 1984). A more detailed discussion of biases is given in *Guide to Clinical Trials* (Spilker, 1991).

How Can Nonscientists Evaluate Medical Claims?

The most widely accepted answer to this common issue is that nonscientists must consult trusted scientists or clinicians who are knowledgeable in therapeutic areas of interest. If the professional evaluation received is not satisfactory to the nonscientist, then it is useful to obtain a second opinion. This second opinion may be obtained from an individual, committee, or task force from inside the company. If the question has major implications for a company, then it may also be useful to involve outside consultants.

Dividing Work Between Two Sites in an Organization

Two (or more) semi-independent research and development sites of a company may each (1) duplicate work of the other group, (2) have totally separate functions or areas to study and work on, or (3) have some overlap in their assigned areas and functions. Although there is not a single best approach for all companies to use in dividing work between two (or more) sites, it is necessary that the missions of each group be clearly established and known by all relevant people. For example, medicine discovery research could be handled in several ways. This research could be conducted at only one site. Research in certain therapeutic areas (e.g., on parasites and bacteria) could be conducted at one site and all other research conducted at a second site. Another possibility is that some or all research could be contracted to universities. In deciding how to divide the total research and development effort between two sites of one company, it is important to consider that certain groups of people may perform specific activities better than other groups, and that people are generally much happier doing what they do best. A related issue is deciding which activities should not be conducted in-house and which activities should be contracted to universities, consultants, or independent contract houses.

Techniques Used by Managers to Influence Others

Basic approaches to exerting influence on others include using the following techniques: (1) authority, (2) bargaining, (3) persuasion, and (4) intellectualizing.

In choosing one or more of these approaches there are several factors that a manager should weigh. As one moves from techniques utilizing pure authority (point 1) to pure intellectualizing (point 4):

1. It takes more time to use the procedures.
2. The vulnerability of the manager increases.
3. The impact on subsequent behavior increases.
4. The flexibility of how the approach is used tends to increase.
5. Resentment in the listener tends to decrease.
6. The quality of the other's performance after the discussion tends to increase.

In using one (or more) of these approaches to influence someone, it is important to understand and use the sources of one's power or ability to influence. These can be summarized as:

1. *Rewards* This category is not meant primarily as monetary or material rewards, but includes such benefits as (1) sharing information, (2) introducing the other person to "important" individuals, (3) praising the person to others, and (4) writing positive comments and statements about the individual in reports.
2. *Punishment* Similar concepts apply as for rewards, although with the opposite approach.
3. *Expertise* This includes not only technical knowledge, but also the knowledge of how to accomplish tasks in the organization and knowledge of the proper sequence of activities to follow.
4. *Legitimacy* This derives from one's position of being higher in an organization compared to another person.
5. *Interpersonal Skills* The power of one's personality may be the only means available to influence others.

Improving Communication

It is important for relevant people to have the most complete and accurate information possible. One alternative to accurate information that unfortunately occurs is that people create their own stories, fleshing out areas where information is skimpy or absent. During periods of early discussions, it is important to either keep the topic 100% secret or keep all relevant people fully abreast of the current status. While plans are being developed it is likely that gossiping and rumors will occur. This leads to people hearing incorrect or distorted information, which in turn may lead them to become upset and to criticize negatively other people in the company. Sometimes it is worth initiating a rumor of a planned decision or action to determine what reactions it engenders. This practice is commonly used by senior managers.

One easy means of improving communication within a company is to send important memos and reports to all people that should have the information. Spreading information not only builds good will, but prevents others from having to try and obtain the same information for themselves. In addition, it often leads to greater efficiency and helps prevent misunderstandings.

Another easy means of improving communication is to keep a list of action points and points of agreement at meetings. Formal minutes of most meetings are rarely referred to or used. Action points state what is to be done and who has the responsibility for doing it or leading the effort. Follow-up of these points at future meetings can usually be handled easily and efficiently. At the end of any meeting, the chairperson or another person should review major points of consensus and major items to be dealt with in the future. Other means of enhancing communication are discussed in Chapter 12.

LEADERSHIP EFFECTIVENESS SCALE

Instructions: This rating form describes 30 practices that are commonly demonstrated by acknowledged leaders. Please read each statement carefully. Then decide the extent to which the person being rated demonstrates that practice. Indicate your decision by checking the appropriate box to the right of each practice. (To score the results, see next page.)

The person being rated:	Usually If Not Always	Fairly Often	Occasionally	Rarely If Ever
1. Keeps group members informed.				
2. Expresses thoughts clearly and forcefully.				
3. Speaks well from a platform.				
4. Is a good listener.				
5. Attracts others to want to hear what he/she has to say.				
6. Communicates a sense of "being in charge."				
7. Encourages upward communication from followers.				
8. Demonstrates compassion for others.				
9. Provides rewards that are important to followers.				
10. Is sensitive to the needs of others.				
11. Attracts others to want to join his/her group.				
12. Has the full backing of all those who work under him/her.				
13. Provides enough structure to create a cohesive feeling among his/her subordinates.				
14. Establishes an authority line that is clear, consistent, and appropriate for the situation.				
15. Strives to win by allowing subordinates to also win.				
16. Gets tough when necessary.				
17. Is respected by subordinates when authority is used.				
18. Uses the power that he/she has with firmness, but also with sensitivity.				
19. Consults with others before making important decisions.				
20. Has a strong track record for making solid decisions.				
21. Follows a logical pattern in making decisions.				
22. Communicates decisions with pride and decisiveness.				
23. Is able to admit mistakes when he/she makes them.				
24. Faces up to and makes hard decisions.				
25. Gets others caught up in his/her positive force.				
26. Creates an active tempo that others emulate.				
27. Communicates a positive attitude during difficult or tough times.				
28. Always puts his/her best foot forward.				
29. Articulates an inspiring mission for the group.				
30. Generates a feeling of pride and accomplishment in his/her followers.				

A

FIG. 11.1. A scale to measure leadership practices. From Martin (1985) with permission of Penton Publishing Co.

HOW TO RATE

To calculate your score on the Leadership Effectiveness Scale, give yourself 4 points for every U/A, 3 points for every FO, 2 points for every OC, and 1 point for every R/E. Record the subtotal of each category in the corresponding section below.

SUBSCALES

Communicator (Questions 1-6)   Subtotal _____

Mutual Rewarder (Questions 7-12)   Subtotal _____

Power Figure (Questions 13-18)   Subtotal _____

Decision-Maker (Questions 19-24)   Subtotal _____

Positive Force (Questions 25-30)   Subtotal _____

LEADERSHIP EFFECTIVENESS   TOTAL _____

INTERPRETATION

105-120   Strong Leader

90-104   Good Leader

75-89   Fair Leader

B **Under 75** Improvement needed

FIG. 11.1. *Continued.*

MANAGEMENT MODELS AND STYLES

Before discussing management styles that are particularly appropriate for the pharmaceutical industry, it is worth mentioning some of the basic approaches and models of management presented in recent years. A few representative systems are mentioned to show the variety in styles that may be conceptualized and to illustrate that several authors have tried to boil down a great deal of information to a few simple concepts. These systems have the advantage of being easily understood, although that understanding does not on its own enable managers to change their beliefs or basic approach easily. In fact, it is amazing how many managers are unable to recognize their own style after reading one of these books, even when their style is transparent to many others.

The Spectrum from Autocratic to Committee Styles

Many managers' styles may be viewed as lying at one or more places along a continuum from autocratic/dictatorial at one end to a democratic committee approach at the other end. Some of the other styles that may be described along this spectrum are:

Passive Consultation Where a manager passively listens to colleagues' and others' views, if offered, before reaching a decision.

Active Consultation Where a manager actively seeks ideas and input from others before reaching a decision.

Consensus Management Where a manager actively seeks ideas and input from others and also ensures that discussions continue until a general consensus is reached about the most appropriate decision.

A single manager or committee may function along the lines of two or more of the five styles mentioned.

When a manager is promoted to a new position it is important for that person to take the necessary time to learn about the style and desires of those who interact with and are influenced by that person. Failure to do this has led many new managers into serious difficulties, regardless of their personal style. Additional issues arise when a manager's style differs markedly from that of a predecessor. This may be an advantage, but often raises more caution signals for the manager to heed.

Four-Dimensional Model

The book *Improving Productivity Through People Skills* by Lefton et al. (1980) describes four styles of management. These are autocratic, unassertive, easygoing, and collaborative styles and are based on two scales: warmth to hostility, and submission to dominance. This system describes management styles in terms of "Q's," a short-cut system used to describe complex concepts.

Social Style

Four social styles (analytical, driver, amiable, expressive) are described in the book *Social Style/Management Style: Developing Productive Work Relationships* by Bolton and Bolton (1984).

Other Styles

Other styles, approaches, and models focus on a "hard" rationale using elements such as structure, people, tasks, strategies, and decision processes, or on a "soft" intuitive model using elements such as roles, groups, networks, rewards, shared vision, and common purpose. Hurst (1984) describes each and shows that both hard and soft approaches are necessary in a company and may be combined to work more effectively.

A large amount of material has been written about advantages of the Japanese approach to management. Their approach is briefly and succinctly presented by Tsurumi (1982). He stresses the "human side of labor" and stresses that American managers have focused on the wrong methods of improving productivity. The correct approach according to Tsurumi is an easy one to utilize, and his brief article is highly recommended.

Measuring One's Leadership Skills

There are many books and articles about differences between leadership and management (Geneen, 1984; Bennis and Nanus, 1985) and how an individual can easily measure his or her own leadership skills (Martin, 1985). One example is shown in Fig. 11.1. This simple test may be taken by individuals who wish to rate either themselves or the effectiveness of others. A summary of characteristics of leaders and managers is given in Fig. 11.2. Commonly encountered relationships of leaders to their group is shown in Fig. 11.3. The potential scenarios shown in Fig. 11.3 become much more complex when multiple leaders are involved, as well as consideration of other factors that influence a group and its leader.

Boards of Directors

Boards of directors of pharmaceutical companies primarily deal with large business issues and allocation of resources. Their members are often chosen because of their knowledge about such matters; however, they should also be instructed in the methods, concepts, and issues of medicine discovery and development. In addition, these groups must reach important decisions about many scientific and medical issues. Therefore, representatives of both science and medicine should be present on the board. It is not sufficient to have only scientists on the board of directors, since most scientists do not adequately understand medical aspects of medicine development or the thinking processes of physicians. Chapter 26 describes how scientists and clinicians are trained to think differently. The management styles of boards of directors vary along the spectrum described earlier in this section of autocratic rule to democratic committee.

Entrepreneurship in the Pharmaceutical Industry

The term "entrepreneurship" has become a widely used buzzword in all industries. It is difficult to find a current journal on management techniques that does not discuss entrepreneurship. Two representative articles are by Stevenson and Gumpert (1985) and Shays and de Chambeau (1984). Within the pharmaceutical industry some departments tend to form and develop around successful scientists. This is clearly an example of entrepreneurship, especially when a department's function partly or completely overlaps with that of an already existing department.

Burroughs Wellcome Co. is a large pharmaceutical company, which evolved to the point approximately 20 years ago, where it had a small research group within the larger research division that actually duplicated several functions (e.g., synthetic chemistry, biological testing, metabolism, pharmacology, and even toxicology). This group, headed by Dr. Gertrude Elion, was remarkably productive and successful as an entrepreneurial activity. This approach probably would not work at all pharmaceutical companies. If this approach is utilized today it could most easily either focus on one scientific discipline (e.g., biochemistry) or on one therapeutic area (e.g., psychiatry) where several disciplines are represented.

It takes a special talent to function as an entrepreneur in a pharmaceutical company. Whereas artists are often characterized as dreamers and workers as doers, entrepreneurs may be thought of as people who are both dreamers and doers. They want their ideas to be tested and to succeed in the real world of patient care. They are not the types of scientists who are always saying "let's study it further."

Most pharmaceutical companies that believe the entrepreneur concept has value understand that there can only be a small number of entrepreneurs. The entrepreneur primarily functions either as an individual or as leader of a small group, whereas to get medicines developed efficiently it is necessary to have mostly "***team players***" working in synchrony.

LEADERS' BOLDNESS CONTRASTED WITH MANAGERS' CAUTIOUSNESS

LEADERS	MANAGERS

Who They Are

Leaders are heroes. Their strong sense of personal mastery compels them to direct affairs. Leaders use power to influence others' thoughts and actions. They are driven by a grand design and have intuitive flashes of insight that lead to dramatic breakthroughs.

Managers are problem solvers. They achieve results through persistence, tolerance, and good will — three useful traits in large, conservative organizations. They achieve their goals through a cautious process of trial and error.

How They View Themselves

Leaders seek to profoundly alter human, economic, and political relationships. Their sense of who they are does not depend upon their job titles or other social indicators of identity.

Managers strive to protect the existing order of affairs. They identify with the status quo. Strengthening existing institutions heightens their self-worth.

How They View Their Work

Leaders seek risk and danger, especially where opportunity and reward appear high. They question established procedures and create new concepts. Leaders create excitement and inspire co-workers. They want results.

Managers fear uncertainty. They prefer to manipulate co-workers and to use established policies to reach organizational goals. Managers are more concerned with the processes that achieve results than with the results themselves.

How They View Their Goals

Leaders are driven by their personal goals. They are innovators who strive to alter established policies that they feel uncomfortable with. Leaders alter expectations and change the way people think. They create ideas instead of merely reacting to them.

Managers focus on the organization's goals. They are driven by a need to conform rather than a desire to change existing systems. They are passive individuals whose goals are shaped by their organization's history and culture.

How They View Others

Leaders arouse intense feelings of admiration and devotion. They care about people and their needs.

Managers relate to people according to their job titles and social status. They are more concerned with people's roles in a process than with their needs.

How They Achieve Respect

Leaders' authority derives from their personal relationships.

Managers' authority stems from their positions.

Where They Are Found

Leaders may be found anywhere in an organization — from the loading dock to the CEO's office.

Managers are supervisors, department heads, and administrators.

FIG. 11.2. Characteristics of leaders and managers. From *Business Week Quarterly* with permission.

A LEADER'S RELATIONSHIP TO HIS OR HER GROUP

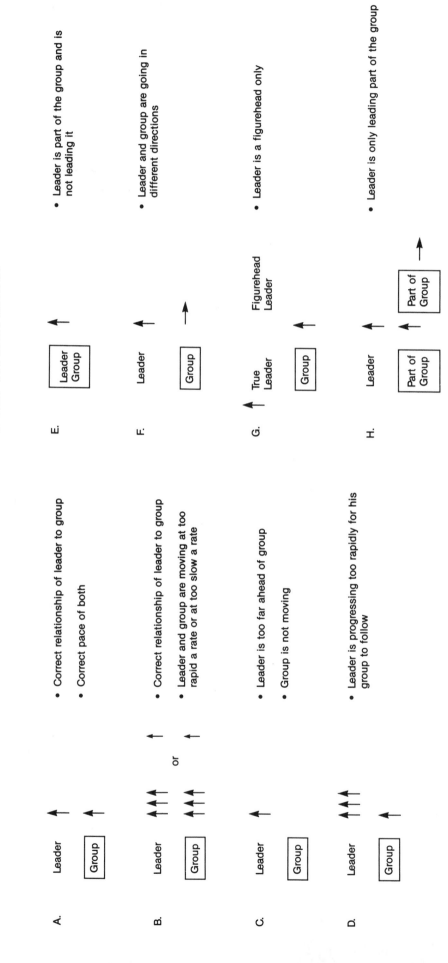

FIG. 11.3. A leader's relationship to his or her group. The reasons for problems in B through H may be that the leader is out of touch with his or her group, is unable to control it, has lost interest in some or all of the group, or another reason. The arrows are the direction of movement. Three arrows are used to show rapid movement and a short arrow is used to depict slow movement.

Individualists in the Pharmaceutical Industry

Some individualists in pharmaceutical companies are not entrepreneurs and create problems within a pharmaceutical company. Each company desires to have individualists who have a positive influence within the organization, as well as have team players. Individualistic scientists who vigorously attempt to opt out of the medicine discovery process, refuse to screen medicines, and/or are unwilling to participate in medicine development are often counterproductive. These scientists usually define their role in industry solely in terms of their own freedom, professional career, and reputation. Many people believe that this group of scientists do not belong in the pharmaceutical industry and would function more effectively in an academic environment where being a team player is usually less important.

Different types of project teams exist in medicine discovery and development, depending on the nature of the task and the professional discipline or department of the members. Keidel and Umen (1984) describe different teams in terms of analogies to baseball, football, and basketball. They point out various management issues relating to the team's function.

APPROACHES TO MANAGEMENT

A number of basic characteristics and issues relating to management are described.

Are the Right Questions Being Asked?

An important issue to consider is whether managers are asking the most appropriate questions to help meet a company's needs and goals. If only partially correct questions are asked or the questions asked are not phrased properly, then even the best obtainable answers may be irrelevant to answer the most pertinent questions. Thus, it is essential to ensure that the questions asked are the correct ones and to discuss relevant assumptions and definitions before embarking on the quest for the answer. If assumptions and definitions underlying a question are not clear, and especially if the question is not explicitly stated, then the exercise may be destined for failure from the outset. The ability to (1) pose the best questions, (2) have the right timing, (3) interpret data appropriately, (4) not procrastinate, and (5) reach the best decisions, all depend on the quality of pharmaceutical company personnel. One reason why the specific questions asked are so important is because a great deal of time and effort are spent by many employees on analyses, reports, memoranda, meetings, and information gathering that are all designed to answer questions posed by managers and senior executives.

The problems a company tackles may be real, potential, or imagined. Potential problems have a greater or lesser probability of occurring. Some of them are important for a company to deal with, but many others waste valuable resources and time. Real problems must be assessed for their importance and urgency, while potential and imagined problems must be identified as such and carefully discussed before allocating resources to their solution.

It is important and often essential to ask whether or not a question need even be asked. Alternative means to obtaining answers sometimes exist. For example, if a clinical group is intending to initiate a study to answer a well-phrased specific objective, it must be determined whether the data already exist in a company's archives or elsewhere (e.g., a government archive). In verbal communication, the tone in which a question is asked is also important to determining the answer obtained.

The Multiplier Effect

All managers and committees throughout an entire company from the board of directors down pose appropriate questions. One difference between a question posed by a chief executive officer (CEO) and a manager of a small group at a low level in the company is that there is a large multiplication effect when the question is posed by the CEO. This is analogous to a model of moving gears. If the largest gear on top of a pyramid of gears (i.e., CEO) moves one notch (i.e., raises a minor point or question), his lieutenants' gears move several notches in the amount of activity they conduct to review the question, in the decisions they make on how to delegate work to answer the question, and then in the process of actually delegating the work. Each of their movements of several notches is sufficient to move the gears of several or numerous workers below them through a complete rotation and so on, until many levels lower in the organization, the people, who are doing most of the actual work to address an important (or idle) question, are scurrying around, sometimes frantically. Moreover, people often temporarily stop work on important issues to work on the senior manager's question that is of far less importance to the company. The managers at a lower level in a company do not generally create a large multiplier effect, except in a limited way with their subordinates.

Quality of Management

In situations where managerial competence is good at senior levels and poor at lower levels, much of a company's work is often not implemented or conducted properly and many problems are not appropriately solved. There are also situations where the quality of management and decision making is poor at upper levels and excellent at lower levels. If leaders do not impose bad decisions and directions on their subordinates, this situation may be compensated for by having an excellent staff. If leaders take a company in an undesirable direction, however, then even the best staff in the world may be unable to correct this error. Two examples of bad directions include:

1. Diverting a company's resources too widely away from the core business, especially to areas where little expertise is present and where the company may become too widely dispersed either geographically or in the number of businesses pursued.
2. Concentrating a company's resources too heavily in a narrow area of medicine discovery and development, which makes the company vulnerable to unexpected changes in the marketplace and to changes in medical practice.

These relatively extreme, but opposite, approaches to management are reminiscent of the Japanese board game of "Go." In this game, either too strong a defensive or offensive posture usually leads to weaknesses in one's position and to eventual defeat by one's opponent.

Functions of Management

Many functions served by management vary between different levels in a corporation. While individuals on several levels deal with generally similar or identical issues, conflicts often arise when a group attempts to deal with the functions of another group. Some major functions of management are shown in Table 11.1, with a focus on research activities. The major group(s) usually responsible is (are) also indicated.

Management of Subsidiaries

Ideally, each subsidiary should be managed according to a plan or strategy that is tailored to that subsidiary. Adopting a single approach to all subsidiaries will force some of them into uncomfortable and ineffective ways of conducting business, not to mention creating strains between the groups involved. Nonetheless, this latter approach is often desirable.

The management plan developed must consider central headquarters' objectives, importance of the subsidiary, and various conditions within the industry and country (e.g., economic, social, political, cultural). Past performance of the subsidiary plus future expectations will help shape this plan, which focuses on budget, growth, profitability, return on investment, and specific goals to be achieved.

One alternative to the approach of using a single management strategy for all subsidiaries is to allow each subsidiary to be an autonomous entity and establish its own plans. A second alternative is to govern all subsidiaries in the same manner. A third approach is the "management by crisis" philosophy. Only subsidiaries with current crises become actively involved with the central corporation. A fourth approach would be to invest money in those subsidiaries that submit proposals for using money in ways consistent with the corporation's goals.

Subsidiaries have a resemblance to children in that they are often born through the parent company's efforts to start a new group. This group may consist of one person or only a few people. The group usually begins to grow in size and soon demands more and more independence from the parent company. Offspring may develop

---

TABLE 11.1. *Some major functions of management*

Function of management	Committee and/or individual usually responsible
1. Establish overall corporate mission, objectives, goals, and strategies. Provide leadership and direction	Board of directors or chairman of the board
2. Determine allocation of resources for various functions of the company	Board of directors or chairman of the board
3. Determine overall research policies[b]	Research policy committee, head of R and D[a] and/or head of research
4. Determine research approaches to be used and allocate resources[b]	Research and development management committee, head of R and D, and/or individual heads of research and development departments
5. Monitor and review progress of medicine development strategies[b]	Project steering committee, various individuals, or committees
6. Implementation of strategies	International project team, project team leader or manager

[a] R and D, research and development.
[b] Comparable functions exist for all areas of a company (e.g., marketing, production).

in ways that are unexpected or undesired by the parent company. Eventually, some subsidiaries may become bigger than their parent and a few may attain independence. A subsidiary that has grown up and is then purchased by another company, according to this metaphor, could be viewed by the new parent as an adopted child. The parent company hopefully knows both their bad traits as well as their good ones.

Another means for multinational pharmaceutical companies to obtain a wholly owned subsidiary is to acquire an existing domestic or foreign company. This method is a more rapid means of establishing a viable company than building one *de novo*. Other advantages of this approach include the contacts, market information, and roots in the community that are likely to be present in the acquired company.

Duplication of Efforts Within a Company

In examining activities conducted at separate research and development sites of a large pharmaceutical company, it is clear that a certain amount of duplication will occur. Duplication is of several types:

1. *Worthwhile duplication* that is synergistic and contributes to progress on medicine discovery and/or development.
2. *Unnecessary duplication* that may not be valuable, but does not delay progress on medicine discovery or development.
3. *Unnecessary duplication* that is not valuable, but delays progress on medicine discovery or development.
4. *Counterproductive duplication* that is competitive in a negative sense and may actually be detrimental for a company.

Several variations of these possibilities occur. The challenge is to foster an appropriate amount of the first type and to eliminate the last two types of duplication. One of the reasons for the third type of duplication is poor organization and/or poor planning. Poor organization would be responsible if duplication were a part of a company's operations, whereas poor planning might be responsible if a duplication occurred primarily on one or a small number of medicines, projects, programs, or activities.

Counterproductive duplication arises from many causes. One cause is different philosophical approaches to an issue that orients the sites in different directions. Each site may use a different template to view and interpret the same data and thus reach conflicting interpretations. Another philosophical difference might relate to a highly conservative individual who supports the status quo ("If it ain't broke, don't fix it") versus a person (or group) who seeks change and appears to thrive on it, regardless of its real value.

Ideal Pharmaceutical Company Environment

Each individual has their own idea of what constitutes an ideal pharmaceutical company environment. Three aspects of an ideal environment are presented, along with possible means of moving toward those goals.

Mutual Respect and Trust

The first aspect is that there should be mutual respect and trust between professionals and between employees and their managers, including senior managers. There are many ways to achieve this state. On a general level this includes being honest at all times and using a policy of openness in dealing with people, where problems and issues are frankly discussed. Specifically, there are many forums and methods that may be used to increase and maintain the type of communications where this atmosphere will develop and flourish. These include: (1) holding periodic seminars for an entire company where current status of the company and/or a specific function (e.g., marketing, research and development) are presented, (2) holding periodic seminars for senior managers with the same purpose, (3) providing training programs of various types, (4) promoting employees from within the company, and (5) encouraging formal and informal presentations about (and by) staff at meetings, in company magazines, in newsletters, and on bulletin boards.

Positive Values and Goals

The second aspect of an ideal environment is where the corporate mission, objectives, and goals emphasize positive values that employees believe in and will work hard to support. The corporate mission should serve as a unifying mechanism that makes employees feel positive about working for that company. Discovering, developing, producing, and marketing new medicines to treat human disease and relieve suffering is a valuable goal and is a strong motivating factor for most employees of a pharmaceutical company.

Positive Company Culture

The last aspect of an ideal environment to be discussed is that of maintaining a positive company culture. This is more controversial than the former two characteristics and certainly is not viewed the same way by all pharmaceutical companies. A positive culture may be defined as one where (1) employees are guaranteed employment as long as the company is financially stable, (2) benefits provided are at least at a reasonable (if not better) level in comparison with the pharmaceutical industry and with local industry, and (3) the company shows in many ways that it cares about its employees. This culture and outlook must emanate from the most senior managers. If they believe in and promulgate these principles, then these principles will become the established culture of the company.

Level of Technical and Administrative Support Services to Provide Employees

The issue is how to determine the appropriate balance for a company, between providing the minimal level of technical services (e.g., photography, graphics, laboratory assistants) to professionals who are discovering, developing, manufacturing, and marketing new medicines and providing so many services that corporate profitability is seriously eroded. Clearly, if internal staff support is too lean the professionals must either do without important services, obtain them through other means, or perform the tasks themselves. In any of these cases their productivity will suffer. One clearly does not want PhD chemists spending their time washing glassware. A comparable issue relates to hiring administrative assistants, secretaries, and clerks for each group of professionals.

A lean professional staff that is well motivated and working hard is often more productive than one where a larger number of ancillary services are available. So many people may be hired to provide services that what was once a single service job becomes divided into multiple jobs and many people are underutilized and underemployed. This is the so-called "fat organization" with duplication of services and activities. The excessive levels of bureaucracy that are created usually lead to inefficiency and disgruntlement.

Management That Follows the Latest Fad or Fashion

Every year or two new books appear in the field of management that are extremely widely read. These are often hailed as a major step forward in one or more aspects of business. These books apparently have had a significant impact in the management of many pharmaceutical companies. Usually, the glow starts to fade after a few years and a new wave of ideas (often from newer books) appear that, if followed, would take the company in a different direction. If each of the ideas proposed were looked at clearly and calmly and senior managers were not pushing hard to implement the latest fads in management, then fewer faddish ideas would be imposed on many companies. Some of these ideas do have value, but usually they must be thoughtfully processed through the company's culture and current conditions to determine the best way to incorporate the concept. Some of the many faddish concepts include:

1. *Sloganeering* The negative rebound is usually substantial when companies decide that "We Stand for the Best" or some other slogan is ideal for the company. The company often extensively promotes the phrase. Few professionals in the pharmaceutical industry are truly motivated by slogans, which at best are viewed in a neutral context and at worst as highly counterproductive forces.

2. *Use of management by objectives techniques* This concept was fairly widely explored a decade and more ago. Its value for the pharmaceutical industry, especially within research and development, was not found to be positive. This resulted in large measure from the high degree of uncertainty and frequent changes in plans and strategies required for efficient medicine development.

3. *Formally identifying and grooming candidates for many senior positions* The many drawbacks of identifying "high potential candidates" make it difficult to understand why this concept was ever seriously considered. Although the identity of candidates should remain secret, this information has a way of leaking out. This knowledge demotivates those who are not chosen and creates expectations of rapid promotions in those who are. This is an example of a lose–lose situation (i.e., where everybody loses). Creating a list of succession is a different matter and does have value for a company.

Whatever the theme of the book of the year (e.g., *Theory Q, The One Minute Manager, Megatrends, In Pursuit of Excellence, The Changemasters*) it is essential to evaluate thoroughly and clearly whether any aspects have relevance for a specific company before a concept is endorsed and implemented.

Who Is in Charge?

If someone outside your company viewed the company's activities as a whole, would he or she say that senior managers were appropriately making the major decisions and delegating others? Or, would that person say that senior managers were watching and not directing what is going on, apart from providing minimal input and review. Who determines whether medicine development on each medicine should proceed along broad or narrow lines? Are management decisions on resource allocations and other issues followed efficiently, or is better focus and control needed?

Some line function groups try to control as much decision-making responsibility as possible, even in areas in which they are not directly involved. When these line managers are asked about whether they can handle another project or a different responsibility with their current staff, their answer is always "yes." Several months later senior managers usually receive an urgent request from these line managers for additional head count positions. These managers are usually empire builders. One cure for this problem is to insist on well thought-out estimates of personnel requirements at or near the outset of each project, another is to reassign staff according to current priorities, and a third is to avoid the multiple tangents that some managers are always proposing to follow. Still another approach is to insist on the group doing all the work without any increases in head count. This usually forces the manager-in-charge to look for more efficiencies in his or her group.

Observers, Experts, and Managers

People in leadership positions may behave as observers, experts, or managers. Ideally, they behave as all three at the appropriate time.

Observers

Observers are individuals who usually have some experience in the area they are observing or describing. They often view activities outside themselves based on literature, observations, interviews, opinions, and their experience. They generally comment in greater breadth than the expert. These people may create policies or documents that do not help the organization's progress, or they may understand the big picture and generate policies that enable their company to improve its flow of development, production, or marketing activities.

Experts

Experts are individuals who have large amounts of experience within their particular area of expertise. These people have done the work they are commenting about many times. They are aware of the variations, and subtleties of their specific area, but they may or may not understand its relationship with other disciplines and activities.

Managers

Managers may fit anywhere along the spectrum from being a pure expert to a pure observer. The ideal manager possesses both skills. He or she has the experience and knowledge of the expert, plus the vision and overview of the observer, and understands when to use one set of skills and approaches and when to use the other. When a needed skill is missing, the manager takes appropriate action (e.g., consults others, hires a consultant, delegates responsibility).

Awareness of Activities One Manages

Only some activities of a department, division, or unit are known to senior managers. Their information comes through reports and other forms of communication. Although it is not important for senior managers to know details about most activities that would not affect their decisions, there is invariably some information that should be known but is not. One issue to consider is which system will minimize this category of unknown (but important) information. An ideal system would probably include a combination of both formal and informal methods. Formal methods should avoid placing strong pressure on people, while still auditing relevant activities. It is important that all or almost all work being conducted in departments is conducted with the knowledge of the relevant department heads.

Time Management

Five major problems relating to how managers spend their time were stated by Humble (1980) to be (in order of importance):

1. *Telephone interruptions*—Both in the number of calls and the length of time spent on many calls.
2. *Meetings*—Managers often attend too many meetings that last too long, often are unnecessary, and often are poorly run. Everyone could add an Amen here.
3. *Unexpected visitors*—Too many people drop in without an appointment or any notice.
4. *Poor delegation*—Work that could be and should be delegated is often done by the manager.
5. *Crises*—Unexpected problems often upset one's work plans.

Managers who are efficient usually attempt to minimize the time that they spend or waste on these (and other) activities.

Minimizing Risk to a Pharmaceutical Company

Senior executives at pharmaceutical companies that are spending up to hundreds of millions of dollars on research and development wish to develop medicines that are both commercially and medically rewarding. Although many companies can afford to develop a small number of medically but not commercially important medicines, this potential (or desire) must be balanced by the need to minimize risks to the company of not developing profitable medicines. There is a popular belief in the pharmaceutical industry that by only developing medicines that are within established clinical classes (e.g., beta-receptor antagonists) or are likely to reach the market, a company minimizes the chance that it will have a huge commercial success. Another way of expressing this view is that conservative companies that do not take risks will not reap a major commercial success and that big rewards go to big risk takers. Although this axiom is true in some cases, there is no reason why it should be true for any particular company or situation. In fact, some companies have achieved enormous financial success and strength by being second to reach the market with a new type of medicine (e.g., Glaxo Inc. with ranitidine for treating patients with duodenal ulcers). In addition, a methodical, conservative, low risk-taking company may discover an ideal artificial sweetener or a safe medicine for weight reduction. This one medicine may catapult the company into a strong financial position. The point is that major new medicines do not necessarily involve more commercial or scientific risk in their development than medicines of lesser importance.

Most of a company's risk in terms of investing money occurs during the medicine discovery period. A highly conservative posture is usually noted in those companies that primarily or solely develop licensed-in medicines and also concentrate on line-extensions of their current products. If the latter approach is used as a major strategy, it generally represents a short-term effort to improve the company's financial health, but will probably not reap the greatest profits over the long term.

APPROACH TO MAKING MAJOR CHANGES IN A COMPANY

Approach to Making Major Company Changes

An approach that may be considered when major (or even some minor) company changes are considered is shown in Fig. 11.4. This approach usually requires that each step be considered in the order shown, although modifications may be appropriate for specific situations. Each step in the figure may be proposed or evaluated by external consultants in addition to (or in lieu of) in-house experts and managers.

Some individuals may progress in their thinking rapidly and in a stepwise order through each of these phases. That process is rarely adequate, however, to achieve a major company change, because most or all relevant executives must be brought through this process. It is often best to bring them along as a group. If this attempt is rushed it usually leads to a counterreaction, and the proposed changes are likely to be turned down. What many people refer to as "timing" is in reality having all key people in agreement about one stage so that they may proceed toward the next stage together. The nine stages shown are really part of three larger processes. These three processes are (1) consensus that a specific change is desirable, (2) agreement on which mechanisms will be used to achieve the change, and (3) implementation of the mechanisms required to achieve the change. A few additional comments on each of the steps are given below.

Observation of a Problem or Issue

The initial observation is made either by a person or group, but usually the same observation must be made by a number of people before additional steps are taken. A relatively long period of time may elapse between successive attempts to bring about a major change.

Desire for Change

The concept of the desired change will vary along several spectra. These include the spectrum of (1) general to specific ideas about what change is needed, (2) vague off-the-cuff to well-thought-through ideas about the change, and (3) short-term to long-term changes desired.

Consensus That a General (or Specific) Change Is Worthwhile

It is necessary to build a consensus among relevant people to ensure the success of changes made. Changes have a better chance of being accepted and lasting if they are not forced on people. As many people as practical should be allowed and encouraged to participate in developing the proposed change.

Agreement on the Specific Change That Should Occur

General goals must be established relating to the specific change desired. Relevant analyses should be conducted to obtain as much information as possible to help in the decision-making process.

Proposals on How to Achieve the Agreed-On Change

Each available option is described. The data are presented and the pros and cons of each option are discussed.

Agreement on a Set of Mechanisms and Systems to Achieve the Desired Change

Once a specific proposal is accepted, plans must be established to implement it. All hierarchical levels in a company must be considered in terms of whether they will be affected, if so, how, and what influence that will have on the proposed mechanisms and systems.

THE PROCESS OF MAKING A MAJOR CORPORATE CHANGE

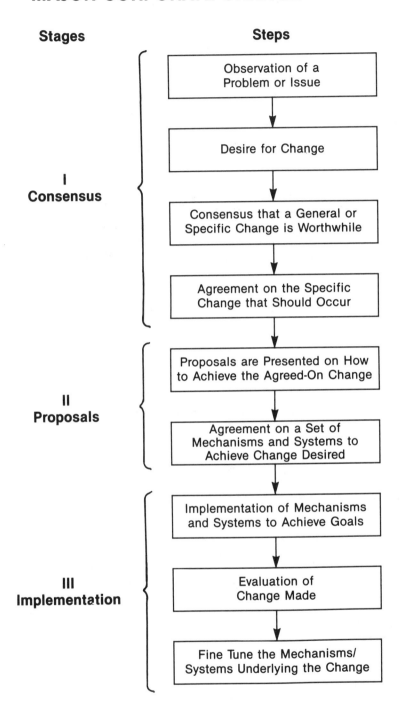

Stages   **Steps**

Observation of a Problem or Issue

Desire for Change

Consensus that a General or Specific Change is Worthwhile

Agreement on the Specific Change that Should Occur

Proposals are Presented on How to Achieve the Agreed-On Change

Agreement on a Set of Mechanisms and Systems to Achieve Change Desired

Implementation of Mechanisms and Systems to Achieve Goals

Evaluation of Change Made

Fine Tune the Mechanisms/Systems Underlying the Change

I Consensus

II Proposals

III Implementation

FIG. 11.4. Steps that are often involved in making major corporate changes.

Implementation of Mechanisms and Systems to Achieve Goals

The implementation phase may begin with a pilot project. This is especially worth considering if resources and time constraints allow this approach. The time lost in conducting a pilot study is often more than made up for in improvements incorporated into the fully implemented plan.

Evaluation of Change Made

Evaluations of the change made may occur at periodic intervals, preset intervals, on an ad hoc basis, or on a crisis basis. In some situations it is important to plan evaluations when the mechanisms and systems are being implemented. It is almost always relevant to question and assess whether the goals of the change are being met. But, this aspect is often ignored after a change is implemented. The importance of these postchange evaluations is to modify changes made to bring them more in keeping with the original goals. If the change was mandated by an executive pronouncement rather than the process described, it is even more critical to follow up and evaluate whether the change was enacted.

Fine-Tuning the Mechanisms and Systems Underlying the Change

Fine-tuning usually occurs as a result of the evaluation conducted. Some important and basic differences exist between companies or between two subsidiaries of the same company that may influence the approach taken to bring about change. Nonetheless, differences between pharmaceutical companies are sometimes exaggerated. It reminds one of the differences between capitalism and communism. Some people state that in capitalism, man exploits man, and in communism it is the opposite.

DEVELOPING AND IMPLEMENTING STRATEGIES

Companies have overall missions, whether stated or not, as well as goals and/or objectives. In addition they have strategies or plans of how they will achieve those goals. These concepts are discussed in greater detail in *Guide to Clinical Trials* (Spilker, 1991). The rest of this section primarily discusses a company's objectives and strategies for achieving them.

Defining a Company's Objectives

Pharmaceutical companies should have an overall strategy or direction to follow. It is amazing to learn that some pharmaceutical companies do not have one. A strategy refers to a company plan that is used as the company travels toward a specific objective or goal. If that goal is to become a highly diversified health care company, of which pharmaceuticals are a small part, the path will be quite different from that of a company that has decided to focus entirely on prescription pharmaceuticals. Goals of another pharmaceutical company might be to focus on (1) over-the-counter and prescription medicines equally, (2) to diversify so that approximately 50% of revenues come from nonhealth care businesses, or (3) to enlarge the medical device and diagnostic part of their business until it contributes 20% of total sales. Many

pharmaceutical companies are owned by a nonmedicine business and their goals may be phrased differently.

Once the overall corporate objective is established, it is easier to consider and respond to many issues that a board of directors often have to deal with. Typical issues include deciding how much money can be allocated to (1) buying a new business and diversifying the company, (2) expanding present manufacturing capacity and facilities, (3) expanding basic research in hopes of finding a novel medicine, or (4) investing in new opportunities of various types.

Developing the overall company strategy may be done by (1) the CEO dictating which direction the company will take, (2) the CEO and board of directors debating this issue and reaching consensus, or (3) having a specific group (e.g., task force, planning committee) develop recommendations and present them to the board of directors for discussion. Other alternatives such as hiring management consultants may also be followed. A strategic planning model is shown in Fig. 11.5.

Which Businesses Should a Pharmaceutical Company Be in?

Every company will answer this question differently, which is appropriate. Furthermore, the most appropriate answer for any company will change over the years. It is essential for senior management to pay close attention to new opportunities and the changing health care environment so that the company is appropriately positioned. Most large research-based pharmaceutical companies are primarily focused on discovering and developing medicines, even though they may own numerous other businesses. Some of the businesses that are relatively close to the core business of ethical pharmaceuticals are shown closest to the center of Fig. 11.6. Other businesses that are somewhat less related to ethical medicines are farther from the center. This does not imply that those businesses closest to the center are preferable, or that those further away are to be eschewed. The right blend for each company differs and must be determined by its own senior managers and/or owners.

A company's core business is one that (1) is an essential part of the company's image and reputation, (2) generates a large portion of the company's sales and profits, and (3) utilizes the knowledge and expertise of the company.

Determining Strategies

The company's strategy determines where the company should be in X years and what type of company it wants to be. Once that decision is made, each group within the company, whether an independent business

A STRATEGIC PLANNING MODEL

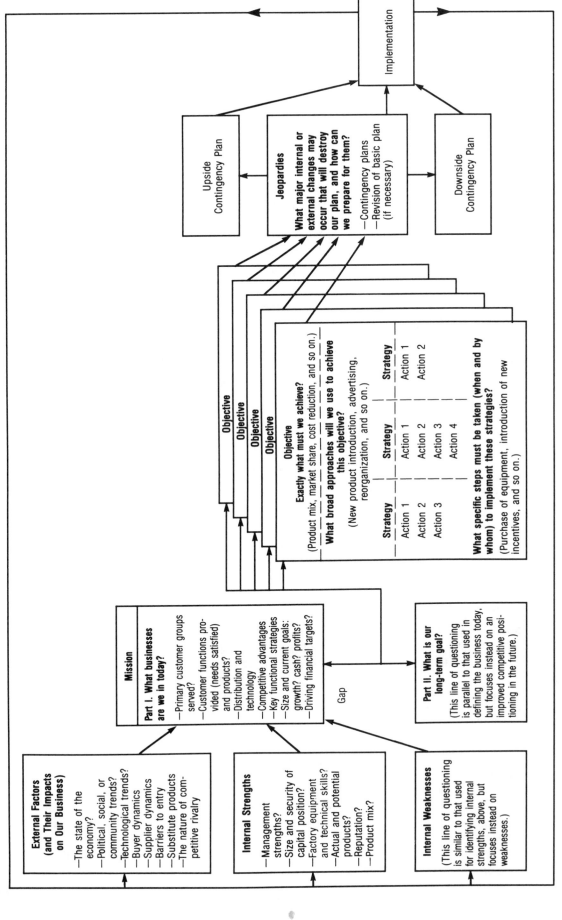

FIG. 11.5. A strategic planning model. From Stringer and Uchenick (1986) with permission of Lexington Books.

POTENTIAL BUSINESSES RELATED
TO ETHICAL PHARMACEUTICALS

FIG. 11.6. Selected businesses related to ethical pharmaceuticals.

unit, function (e.g., research, production), department, or matrix group can determine their own strategies, which will further the attainment of the overall company strategy.

Companies without an overall strategy have additional difficulties when important opportunities present themselves. Company officials must decide which opportunities to exploit and which ones to reject. If there are a variety of potentially conflicting goals amongst people who determine the company's response, then it will be quite difficult for a series of important decisions to be made using the same criteria. Major company decisions should attempt to (1) lead to change that is constructive, (2) build on previous decisions, and (3) help move the company toward its objectives.

As an exercise on how to choose strategies, consider the following situation. Assume that there is approximately a 5% chance that a new project on an experimen-

tal medicine in early Phase II studies will be a breakthrough medicine and an overwhelming success. The chance of it being a small or moderate success is approximately 60%, and the chance of its failing and not showing activity is assessed as 35%. How should one prioritize this medicine's development and set company objectives?

The answer certainly depends on (1) other medicines in the company's portfolio, (2) their stage of development, and (3) the specific resources needed to develop this medicine. The need for resources could potentially put the medicine in conflict with other projects. In the example given, to purchase expensive raw materials and make a large amount of medicine stock based on a 5% chance of the medicine's being a breakthrough medicine is usually too high a risk for most companies to take. In fact, unlike some old wine, the profiles of most medicines do not improve with age, rather they usually tarnish and become spotted with adverse reactions and stories of patients and populations in whom the medicine does not satisfactorily work.

Communicating Strategies

In communicating the company's strategies to staff and workers, management must ensure that the strategies are clear to everyone. The first group to consider are the senior managers and others who will be promulgating the strategy. Unless the entire concept and purposes it serves are totally clear in their minds, they will be unable to communicate effectively this information to others. Differences in presentation or hearing someone give different messages on different occasions must be avoided. Sufficient detail must be presented to allow relevant individuals to understand the overall strategy. The information must be presented so that employees have an opportunity to discuss and question the ideas. People want to know what the strategy is, why the strategy points were chosen, what difference it will make for the company, and what the strategy means for them. Hopefully, when all of this is complete the employees will agree with and support the strategies presented.

In addition to providing a written document, a company's strategy may be communicated via large conferences and/or a series of smaller meetings where relevant issues are discussed and questions answered. This is a critical step in having the strategy adopted by employees. If this is not done, the strategy may remain the manager's strategy without sufficient acceptance by employees.

Implementing Strategies

The major activities that lead strategies from paper to reality should be clear. Goals and objectives that strategies are designed to accomplish should also be clear. Some of the steps to conduct are:

1. The people who are responsible for conducting each of the activities should be identified.
2. A plan to communicate the strategy should be in place.
3. Potential problems that are inherent in the plan should be known prior to its dissemination. Counterarguments should be prepared and some of these should be presented, even if the anticipated criticisms are not raised.
4. Potential sources of employee resistance to the plan should be anticipated and counterarguments prepared.
5. A follow-up monitoring plan should be developed and agreed on before the strategy is widely disseminated.

6. Future meetings to review progress made on the strategy should be scheduled.
7. Methods for updating the strategy should be outlined.

The contents of a corporate strategy may sometimes turn out to be less important than the processes used to generate and communicate it and the reactions it engenders in employees.

ESTABLISHING PRIORITIES

Once decisions are made on important medicine development priorities, the information must flow both upward and downward through a company. Systems should be used to disseminate this information that ensures all relevant people are informed in a timely manner about decisions that affect their work. Regardless of the system used to establish priorities (i.e., formal or informal) and to disseminate information in a company, the methods used to reach decisions on priorities should be consistent for all medicines.

Every professional in a pharmaceutical company has some of their priorities (1) established entirely by themselves, (2) set in conjunction with others (primarily supervisors), and (3) imposed by others. Decisions on priorities are therefore made at multiple levels and requests for decisions on priorities flow both upward and downward in the company. An individual who is uncomfortable with making a decision about a priority, or is comfortable but desires agreement from others, will generally either refer the decision upward or make the decision in conjunction with others. Some decisions rise all the way up to the chief executive officer before a final decision is made. Some companies like to push decision-making responsibility down to lower levels in the organization. This correctly suggests that the appropriate level for making the identical type of decision varies in different companies. The actual situation is far more complex because even a single type of decision is often made at different levels within each pharmaceutical company. One of the reasons for this additional complexity is that certain individuals at all companies attempt to avoid making decisions, whereas others make many decisions that are not strictly within their prerogative or purview. Thus, it is usually too simplistic to say that company A makes its decisions at a higher organizational level than company B.

LONG-RANGE COMPANY PLANNING

Functions of a Planning Staff

What a variety of tasks are put under this title! Every company that has a long-range planning office defines it differently and places it in different parts of the organization. To some companies, long-range corporate planning is a strictly financial position staffed by one individual or by an entire department. The primary function is to prepare corporate budgets and/or forecasts of sales and profits. The time limit or horizon of these forecasts may be one year or may extend to approximately seven years. Although there is no limit on how many years may be forecasted, the benefits of extending forecasts in the pharmaceutical industry past five to ten years should be seriously questioned. A financially oriented corporate planning group may also examine the previous year's performance or that of several previous years each time the budget is prepared. This allows a better view of past trends to be coupled with future directions (or at least projections).

Other companies define long-range planning in a broader manner. For example, the planning group could focus on defining, critiquing, and reevaluating the company's mission, objectives, goals, and strategies. The person or group who has this function acts in some ways as the company's soul. It is their responsibility to ensure that senior company managers have appropriate templates against which they make decisions and chart the company's course. Junior managers and workers should be given a sense of corporate direction, as well as company values and strategies that are utilized to achieve the goals. Some of these corporate attributes (e.g., mission, values, objectives) may only have to be reevaluated every several years. But, specific goals and strategies should be reevaluated on an annual or semiannual basis, utilizing an agreed-on set of procedures.

A third role for a long-range planning group would be to analyze business opportunities. They would evaluate current businesses and propose (1) new business opportunities that should be sought and (2) businesses that should be divested. Opportunities that the company has in terms of business acquisitions, mergers, or divestitures could be evaluated by this group. It is also possible for them to evaluate licensing opportunities, joint venture possibilities, and other product-related issues. In fulfill-ing this role they may produce explanatory material and/or analyses. These could be highly detailed and comprehensive, or summarize materials prepared by other groups.

Procedures of Strategic Planning

Numerous references describe the process of strategic planning for a company to use. It is interesting that the methods presented are remarkably similar in various references (Stringer and Uchenick, 1986; Porter, 1980, 1985; Waddell, 1986; Guth, 1985). The reader is referred to these or other references for details, but the basic approach is shown in the model illustrated in Fig. 11.5. This approach may readily be fitted to a pharmaceutical company. There are many viewpoints to consider, either before strategic planning is started or when it is reviewed (e.g., see Gray, 1986; Hayes, 1985). Strategic planning is one area where the basic methods do not have to be modified because of differences between the pharmaceutical industry and other industries.

Assessing the Value of Strategic Planning

No matter which of the above roles (or others) is served by a corporate planning group, it is essential to ask periodically, "What is the value of the group's outputs?" Planning groups sometimes grow with a company and their size may become large and their operations geared toward producing reports for others. The materials they generate may become voluminous, giving the appearance of a worthwhile activity. But, the real value of thick reports must be carefully assessed. Sometimes, totally eliminating periodic or other types of reports causes a sigh of relief and no complaints about a loss of important information. These people may be free to do their work rather than being obligated to document and write about work they have already done or are planning to do.

12 / Enhancing Communication

Barriers to Communication...................... 127
  Barriers Among Professionals in a Single Group 127
  Barriers Among Professionals in Two or More
    Separate Groups 128
  Barrier I: Cultural Separation of Professionals . 128
  Barrier II: Inappropriate Separation of
    Professionals into Departments or Divisions 129
  Barrier III: Hierarchical Separation of
    Professionals 129
  Barrier IV: Information Separation of
    Professionals in Different Areas............ 130
  Barrier V: Bureaucratic Separation........... 131
  How to Assess Communication Barriers....... 131
Methods of Communication Between
  Professionals in Different Disciplines 131

Written Communication 132
Communication Skills of an Effective Manager 132
Communications Styles and Effectiveness
  Based on Individual and Company
  Concerns and Orientation 132
Communicating the Conclusions of a
  Committee............................... 132
Directions of Communication Flow........... 133
Types of Communication Problems............. 133
  Signs of Poor Communication 133
Enhancing Communication 135
  Pointers for Dialogue with Individuals 135
  Pointers for Dialogue with Organizations...... 135
  Written Versus Spoken Words 136

Having served on various committees, I have drawn up a list of rules: Never arrive on time; this stamps you as a beginner. Don't say anything until the meeting is half over; this stamps you as wise. Be as vague as possible; this avoids irritating the others. When in doubt, suggest a subcommittee be appointed. Be the first to move for adjournment; this will make you popular; it's what everyone is waiting for. Harry Chapman

Many books describe theoretical problems of communication and have proposed and discussed methods to overcome them. While most general issues relate to all organizations some are particular to specific groups. This chapter focuses on viewing communication within the pharmaceutical industry.

Communication is an essential skill that is used during most of our waking hours, and certainly during most of one's time at work. The four parts of communication are (1) communicator, (2) message, (3) vehicle of communication, and (4) audience. The major tools used to communicate are listening, speaking, reading, writing, and body movement. The first four tools are used most often in descending order (i.e., we listen more than we speak, we speak more than we read, and we read more than we write). The great irony is that our formal education devoted to these four skills focuses on them in the opposite order (i.e., the most time is spent on developing writing skills and the least on developing listening skills).

One of the major means of enhancing communication is to teach people how to listen better, and how to retain more of what they have heard. One process to do this is termed active listening (i.e., recapitulating what you have just heard in terms of the message delivered rather than the words spoken). It is a valuable tool that enhances communication by improving the likelihood that both speaker and listener have the same understanding of what has been said.

Barriers to effective communication and approaches that should improve the quality of communication are the first major issue discussed.

BARRIERS TO COMMUNICATION

Barriers Among Professionals in a Single Group

One of the most important barriers to effective communication involves a person's hidden agenda. This term means that a person's apparent goals are not their true ones. A person may purposely deceive or lie to another to hide the fact that they have a hidden agenda. Alternatively, the person may simply focus on selected aspects and not mention their true intentions. This problem can occur at all levels of a company and in any department. A simple example is an individual who pretends to have the company's interest in mind but acts primarily on his or her own behalf. Although it is generally difficult to alter someone's hidden agenda, understanding its existence may enable people to work together more effectively.

Another barrier to communication is poor listening skills. Few people are taught how to listen to others, and most people are so busy phrasing or constructing their response that they forget to listen to what is being said. A third barrier is individual accent; this becomes a barrier when people pay more attention to the way the other person speaks than they do to what the other person is saying.

Barriers Among Professionals in Two or More Separate Groups

In some pharmaceutical companies, it often seems that a marketing group prepares the specifications of what they want manufactured and then throws the report over a wall to the production group. The production people look at the document and take the contents apart, reassemble it in their own terms, and then throw their response back over the wall to marketing. This process is usually repeated a number of times. Unfortunately, marketing and medical groups often also work in this out-of-date and grossly inefficient way. It is no surprise that significant delays and problems generally result from this approach. Obviously, it would be preferable for both groups to sit down together and work jointly on solving or at least addressing the issues. Improved communication is not achieved, however, by merely having the relevant groups sit at the same table to work together. They must share a common outlook about their company and the style of medicine development that is most appropriate. In addition, they must have a positive success-oriented vision of achieving goals in as rapid a time period as possible. Often, this does not happen because of the multiple barriers that exist between medical and marketing groups, or between any two entirely different groups.

Five categories of barriers are discussed below: cultural, functional, hierarchical, informational, and bureaucratic. While these barriers are described as existing between people in different groups (e.g., financial, medical, marketing, legal) they could generally be applied as well to professionals within a single group. There is no particular importance to the order in which these categories are discussed.

Barrier I: Cultural Separation of Professionals

In this chapter, culture is used to mean the way that professionals think based on their training and experiences. This type of barrier is more heterogeneous than the other four and is further broken down. The categories or factors that make up cultural separation include (1) type of professional training, (2) long-range versus short-range orientation, (3) focus on bottom line financial results or patient improvement, and (4) the different influences of money and professional recognition on personal motivation.

Professional Training

Training and orientation of various professional groups creates some strong differences in outlook that may raise barriers to communication. For example, a scientist who wishes to withhold judgment until he or she has completed all necessary research will have difficulties communicating with a marketer who wants to see decisions made immediately to help a project move more rapidly toward clinical trials.

Some of the basis for the different approaches of scientists and physicians, and the source of tensions between them, become apparent when one looks at the respective training of each. A scientist's training focuses on using a logical approach to either induce or deduce certain facts and conclusions. A scientist then challenges, modifies, and strengthens the truthfulness of those conclusions. On the other hand a physician's training focuses on developing clinical judgment skills with the goal of becoming fast, accurate, and skillful at diagnosing and in treating patients. A practicing physician often reaches a decision with data that are available; withholding judgment until a diagnosis is made is not always possible (e.g., in an emergency situation). It is usually possible for a scientist to wait until sufficient data are available. A marketing professional's training focuses on achieving desired results (i.e., improving the bottom line) in the most rapid time and in the most efficient manner. This type of training focuses on the importance of expediency and of clearly differentiating between good or bad approaches to solving a problem or addressing a goal.

Long-Range Versus Short-Range Orientation

Pharmaceutical company scientists working on long-range projects may not expect a potential medicine to evolve from their work for up to ten to 20 years. The work of other scientists; in the same company is much closer in time to an important discovery; their hope is to identify a specific compound for development within a one- to three-year period. Even at that stage, another five to ten or more years is often required to bring the discovery to the market.

In most other industries, marketers plan in terms of months for the development of new products. Their training promotes this short-term horizon as a reasonable period to see sales results of changes they institute in a product or its promotion. In the pharmaceutical industry, over-the-counter medicines and many line-extensions of marketed products have a much shorter time horizon than that of prescription medicines. Nonetheless, there is a tension between marketing and medical personnel created by the impatience of many marketers with what they perceive as a slow development pace within research and development groups, which often is coupled with a failure of some people to possess a "sense of urgency" in expediting the development process.

Focus on Financial Versus Clinical Results

Marketers tend to be oriented, more than medical staff, toward financial outcomes of a new medicine, and medical personnel tend to be more oriented toward clinical outcomes. The company must assess whether these orientations create barriers to effective communication between the two groups. The personalities of the specific people involved will determine the strength of these barriers, as will the steps the company has taken to minimize or eliminate them. Any company that identifies such problems should address them by uniting the groups with common company-oriented goals and a better understanding of the orientation and thinking of other groups within the organization.

Motivating Factors

To understand another person, it is usually vital to perceive the major factor(s) that motivate that individual. This is particularly true if one wishes to improve or alter that person's performance. The motivating factors that influence medical and marketing staff generally differ. Knowing whether a hidden agenda exists is often difficult, but one should try to understand the true motivations of a person one is negotiating with.

Medical personnel derive enormous satisfaction from being part of or leading a team that is developing an important new medicine that will help many patients. The more important the medicine is in terms of its breakthrough qualities and medical benefits, the greater this positive feeling. In addition, many medical personnel have various opportunities to achieve professional recognition, not only within their company, but at outside professional meetings where they are asked to present papers, chair sessions, sit on panels, serve as officers of societies, receive prizes, and so forth. Writing articles, editorials, chapters in books, and reviewing manuscripts are common publication activities of many scientists and clinicians.

Marketing professionals have far fewer opportunities than their medical colleagues to become involved in professional societies and to receive comparable professional recognition. Their major rewards are financial, in terms of salary, bonus, commissions, and other monetary benefits. This fits well with their orientation to financial results in judging the success of most products from the company's perspective. The recognition they receive for their marketing efforts usually relates directly to the company's financial achievements rather than to personal intellectual achievements as is the case for many medical professionals.

Barrier II: Inappropriate Separation of Professionals into Departments or Divisions

Each discipline conducts its own functional activities at multiple hierarchical levels (e.g., divisions, departments, sections). The separation of some (or many) activities between marketing and medical (or other disciplines) is necessary and important. But, an additional inappropriate type of separation may occur because the company has not placed both medical and marketing representatives on the same project teams, committees, task forces, and other groups. This makes communication among professionals more difficult in important arenas where (1) decisions are made, (2) teamwork is fostered, and (3) understanding develops. This is a relatively easy problem to remedy or improve, as long as the senior managers understand the importance of lowering barriers and encouraging interactions between groups representing different disciplines.

Barrier III: Hierarchical Separation of Professionals

The medical and marketing functions may be conceptualized as pyramids (Fig. 12.1). Communication within and between the pyramids must be organized to some degree or it would be random and gross inefficiency would generally result. If one listened with a stethoscope to the medical (or marketing) pulse within the pyramid in many companies, great differences would be apparent. In some companies, very little would be said because managers were holding onto information and not discussing it with relevant staff either above or below them in the pyramid, nor with others who are at the same level. In other companies, there would be a large amount of important communication, but on closer listening it would be noted that it was all flowing in one direction, toward the top of the organization. In yet other companies, effective communication would be flowing both upward and downward within each pyramid, but little or none would be flowing between the pyramids. In other companies there would be a large volume of communication, but the quality of information conveyed would be inadequate. Other patterns could be described that indi-

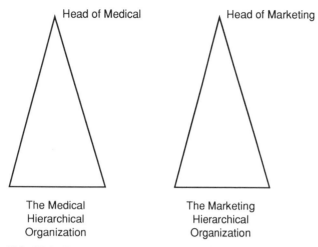

FIG. 12.1. Two pyramids that represent the hierarchical medical and marketing organization of a company at its headquarters or at a major subsidiary. A more complete illustration might show a separate pyramid for prescription marketing and over-the-counter marketing, plus other pyramids for different functions (e.g., production, legal, finance).

cate specific types of problems (Fig. 12.2), particularly when multiple groups and multiple sites are considered.

A pharmaceutical company must ensure that adequate communication flows both within each pyramid and among all relevant pyramids. It is obviously inadequate if the heads of medical and marketing communicate adequately but their subordinates do not (or vice versa). Each level within the hierarchy must communicate effectively for the entire process to operate efficiently.

The actual situation is far more complex in pharmaceutical companies that have more than the typical two large pyramids and several smaller ones (e.g., finance, production, legal, personnel); these international companies can have several large pyramids in different countries (Fig. 12.3). Many of these pyramids speak different languages, have different cultures, and appear to think and behave differently. Some of these pyramids create communication problems for the other major pyramids. The principles for ensuring effective communication with foreign pyramids are no different than those for communicating with any other single group or groups. The first step is a desire by both parties to improve and maintain appropriate communications. This obvious and apparently straightforward goal sometimes takes many years and major efforts to achieve in many pharmaceutical companies, particularly in certain countries or cultures or with certain managerial styles (e.g., dictatorial).

Barrier IV: Information Separation of Professionals in Different Areas

Unless professionals are interested in sharing information, effective communication cannot occur. Relying solely on the interest or desire of most professionals to communicate effectively is insufficient for a pharmaceutical company. There will always be some people in a company who can unilaterally disrupt the flow of information and effectively short circuit important activities. Unfortunately, many of these people apparently enjoy this role.

What is needed within each organization are both a clearly stated policy and a tradition of following open and full communications. Enforcement of that policy is needed when it is not adhered to. The policy should be established that all relevant information is always shared among those who "need to know." Second, people in other groups (medical to marketing or vice versa) who would benefit from the information, even though it is only "nice to know," should also receive it. Third, people within one's own group who would benefit from the information generally should receive it.

This policy or any policy on communication (i.e., dissemination) of information is difficult to implement fairly and consistently. It depends on many interpreta-

Model A

Little Communication
Flow in Volume

Model B

Primarily Upward
Flow of
Communication

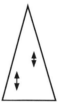

Model C

Poor Content Quality
of Information
Communicated

Model D

Good Communication
Flow Within a
Group But Not to
External Groups

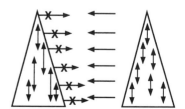

FIG. 12.2. Four models illustrating basic communications problems. Models A to C are problems within a group and Model D is a problem between groups.

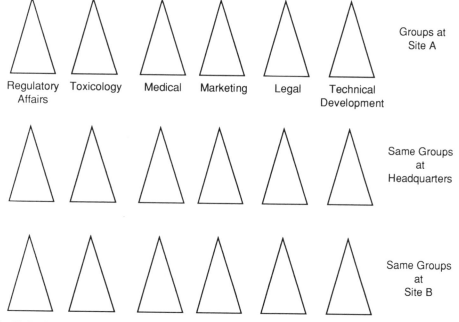

FIG. 12.3. Some of the many pyramids that exist in multinational pharmaceutical companies.

tions that are made daily. Some people believe the policy described is incorrect because it results in too wide a dissemination of information within the company. Because having information is a type of power, many people believe the myth that telling others about various findings is inappropriate. Clearly there is a balance, but overly restricting information can lead to decreased motivation, efficiency, creativity and productivity; it will lead to poor decisions by managers who do not have sufficient information.

Barrier V: Bureaucratic Separation

Another aspect of this barrier is the many bureaucratic systems that may be enacted within and between groups. Standard operating procedures may seem to create problems for accomplishing one's objectives rather than helping to facilitate one's work.

How To Assess Communication Barriers

When people do not desire to communicate with other groups, many reasons can be found to justify their behavior and many barriers can be created by these individuals. This problem may occur even if an individual is communicating to a higher organizational level. It is the responsibility of the company to ensure that this problem is either nonexistent or minimal. For example, individuals who continually refuse or simply do not follow the organization's policy on communicating information must be instructed about acceptable standards and behavior. The author knows some perennial offenders of this principle who act like small children in the apparent belief that receiving negative attention is better than receiving none.

While a series of interviews or a thorough review could be conducted by external consultants to assess communication barriers within a company, a well-designed and critiqued questionnaire could be constructed (and used) by the company. It could be given to most employees in the relevant group(s) every two or three years to observe trends in communication styles and effectiveness. This process could also evaluate the impact of specific efforts implemented to remedy problems identified in previous questionnaires. Statisticians and other professionals should be involved in (1) designing the questionnaire, (2) assessing its validity, (3) determining its timing, (4) determining the size of the group to receive it, (5) assessing the issue of anonymity of responders, (6) deciding who will conduct the analysis, and (7) deciding who has access to the data generated by the questionnaire.

One or more of the steps could be conducted by outside contractors hired by the company. The emphasis must be on developing as high a quality instrument as possible to benefit both the company and its employees. Any approach to this project that does not adhere to the highest scientific and ethical standards will make the project one of ridicule by the employees and will not obtain valid data on which to base decisions.

METHODS OF COMMUNICATION BETWEEN PROFESSIONALS IN DIFFERENT DISCIPLINES

It is difficult to communicate accurately, even between professionals working at the same position in the same company. When those professionals do not share the same training and professional experiences, communication can be more difficult. If each uses different jargon, and particularly when they are motivated by different values, interests, and types of accomplishments, then communication becomes still more difficult.

Written Communication

One way to enhance the quality of communication is to have professionals use more than just verbal dialogue. Information transmittal tends to be more accurate and effective when it takes place through written memoranda and responses to requests. Formal documentation increases the likelihood that statements are understood and are remembered (and recorded) accurately, both by the writer as well as by the receiver. On the other hand, excessively long documents or an excessive use of written records is often counterproductive.

Some individuals take documentation to the point that they ignore verbal requests. The rationale behind this is the theory that it is easy for anyone to deny that they made a request or to say that they were misunderstood. A policy of requiring formal requests to be written makes sense when one realizes that many verbal requests are often modified, canceled, or otherwise changed after they are made and the current status of an issue may be unclear if no documentation trail exists.

Communication Skills of an Effective Manager

Some of the principal communication skills of an effective manager are the ability to:

1. Talk with team members between meetings. This is an important, if not essential, means of staying abreast of all current issues and problems.
2. Anticipate potential or future issues or problems and communicate them to appropriate staff, at the same level (i.e., colleagues), at a higher level (i.e., bosses, superiors), and at a lower level (i.e., more junior staff).
3. Accumulate multiple types of information rapidly and accurately. Great skill is required to request, collect, and assimilate useful data and to avoid information of little or no usefulness.
4. Extract information from individuals who are reluctant to share the information or do not share it willingly.
5. Use intuition appropriately when reaching judgments on choosing which communication methods to use and how to use them.
6. Match the efforts expended on communication with the priority of the topic. It is fruitless to spend a significant portion of one's time communicating about topics that have a low priority. While there will never be an ideal match between how a senior manager appor-

tions his or her time and the priority assigned task, these should, on average, be effectively balanced.
7. Be open and honest. It is far better to say "I am not at liberty to discuss that topic" than to make up a story.

Communication Styles and Effectiveness Based on Individual and Company Concerns and Orientation

Four extremes of communication style can be identified based on the nature and degree of an individual or team's concern and orientation for other people in the company and/or for their company. The implications of each model within an organization depend on which managers follow which approach, particularly the most senior managers. This scheme is complicated by the degree to which individuals are concerned with their own future career and how their ambitions affect their concerns for others and for their company.

1. *Low concern for "all" individuals and for the company.* This leads to a lack of effective communication and delays progress on some or many activities. If not addressed, this problem may lead to serious consequences (e.g., failure to demonstrate the positive activity that is inherent in a medicine). This model is characterized by disinterest.
2. *Low concern for "all" individuals and high concern for the company.* This model leads to communication that is based on obedience to an authority and following a mandate. People obey orders because they have to, but there are severe underlying problems in any organization where blind obedience is required, particularly if this attitude is allowed to continue for an extended period. This model is characterized by loyalty only to the company.
3. *High concern for oneself and low concern for the company.* This model leads to poor communication in most instances. People use communication based on their own selfish motives and not those of advancing the company's goals. When individual goals change it is clear that communication channels will as well. This model is characterized by selfishness.
4. *High concern for "all" individuals and for the company.* This leads to the most effective form of communication. It is based on the project team concept of respect for both individual and company goals. This model is characterized by teamwork.

Communicating the Conclusions of a Committee

The degree to which a committee's decisions or conclusions are communicated to others depends in part on the degree to which the members of a committee agree with the decision(s), as well as the degree to which the superiors of the committee members endorse or agree with the decisions. Various methods of communicating

The Communication Cross

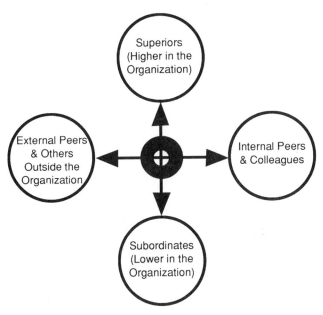

FIG. 12.4. The communication cross. Each person may visualize himself or herself at the center of the cross in conceptualizing four basic directions.

a committee's conclusions are illustrated in Fig. 125.1 of *Guide to Clinical Trials* (Spilker, 1991).

If a group has collectively adopted a decision that does not reflect an individual's perspective, that person may be less willing to endorse, disseminate, and support the decision(s). The degree to which this occurs is influenced by the culture of the organization (e.g., authoritarian, democratic) as well as by the culture of the geographical area(s) involved (e.g., pressure to follow the group or team's decision, as in Japan; ability to place individual rights above company interests as sometimes occurs in the United Kingdom).

Directions of Communication Flow

The major paths or direction of communication flow are shown in the communication cross (Fig. 12.4). This

TABLE 12.1. *Selected signs of subtle and mild problems in communication*

1. Important memoranda are circulated to few individuals and others suffer by not having information that would enable them to perform their job more effectively
2. People have to repeat a request to have it implemented, when the importance of the request should have led to its more rapid implementation
3. Deadlines are often not met, but major activities do not suffer by significant delays
4. Discussions at meetings reveal that different interpretations exist on one or more points where the same interpretation would have been expected

TABLE 12.2. *Selected signs of moderate and severe problems in communication*

1. People do not attend meetings because they are unaware of their occurrence
2. People do not receive letters, memoranda, or other materials reportedly sent to them, and this results in a domino effect of their not informing others about decisions, information, or requests
3. People do not attend important meetings prepared to discuss relevant issues and state they were unaware or unconvinced of the need for such discussions to take place
4. People indicate that they are not being informed about important information they need to have to conduct their job, and thus did not conduct important activities or make specific decisions
5. Senior managers observed that their orders are not being implemented despite repeated requests, and no feedback about the reasons for the failure is given to them

illustrates the four basic paths of communication, upward, downward, to other internal staff, and to external individuals. This simplistic figure may serve as a useful reminder about the need to consider communication in all four directions.

TYPES OF COMMUNICATION PROBLEMS

Signs of Poor Communication

Many obvious signs of poor communication are apparent in the later stages of deteriorating communication. Obviously, progression to this stage should be prevented.

TABLE 12.3. *Examples of marked communication problems within a company*

1. Decisions of a product manager or project leader are frequently overruled
2. Within project or product committees, individuals raise major surprise issues (e.g., unexpected problems that were not told to the committee chair) that disrupt the meeting and are then debated at great length
3. Projects for line-extensions are requested for implementation by senior marketing managers without prior communication with the relevant brand manager. The latter person is then unprepared to respond to medical requests for additional information
4. Marketing decisions on dosage forms, dose sizes, tablet shapes, and tablet colors often are reversed by marketing staff at the last moment. This necessitates a great deal of additional technical development work
5. Sales forecasts on one (or more) medicine(s) vacillate widely without an obvious external (or internal) event causing the change
6. Policies or reasons for conducting certain activities are unclear in the minds of many professionals who are responsible for implementing them
7. Guidelines as to who may or should attend some or many important company meetings are unclear
8. Messages received from one group by the other do not appear to be consistent

Instead, subtle signs occurring early in the downward spiral of poor communication should be detected and steps should be taken to prevent communication from deteriorating further. Signs that may occur and should be looked for at early and late stages of communication problems are listed in Tables 12.1, 12.2, and 12.3.

A number of basic types of communication problems are listed below and diagrammed in Fig. 12.5.

1. An insufficient amount of information is being communicated.
2. The wrong information is being inadvertently communicated.
3. Inaccurate information is purposely being communicated.
4. The information being communicated is unclear or confusing. This may result from an excessive use of jargon, a superficial presentation, an overly complex presentation, or a document that is poorly written.
5. An excessive amount of information is being communicated. The information may or may not be relevant to the topic, but it is inappropriate (in quantity) for the recipient.
6. The wrong media or approach is used to communicate the information. This may decrease its value in any of many ways.
7. The wrong format is used to present data (e.g., tables rather than graphs).
8. The wrong audience is being targeted.
9. The information is communicated either prematurely or too late.

Many of these problems can be avoided by asking appropriate people (e.g., the target group or others) to re-

A. Direction of Communication Flow (i.e. Transmission)

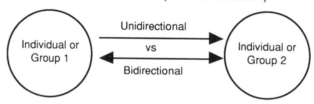

B. Reception of Communication (i.e. Receiving)

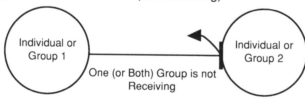

C. Quality of Communication

D. Result of Communication (i.e., Followup)

FIG. 12.5. Four examples of communication problems.

view a draft document prior to issuing the final one. Another approach is to discuss one's plans with a number of appropriate people within and/or outside the organization.

ENHANCING COMMUNICATION

It is a true cliché that both sides must want to communicate and must be able to listen for effective communication to occur. If both parties speak "simultaneously," neither can truly hear the other. Barriers to communication should be identified and a plan developed for how to deal most appropriately with these problems.

Pointers for Dialogue with Individuals

A few basic pointers for dialogue with individuals (Fig. 12.6) are mentioned below.

1. Ask people to repeat their statements when you do not hear them.
2. Ask people to explain what they meant when you do not understand the meaning of their statement.
3. Ask people to explain the reasons for their statement(s) when you do not agree with their point.
4. Show the other person that you clearly understand their views when you differ with him or her.

Pointers for Dialogue with Organizations

Some of the many types of organizations engaged in dialogue with the pharmaceutical industry are shown in Fig. 12.7. Collectively, these relationships are like the many rays of communication emanating to and from the individual or group at the center. The advantages and disadvantages of numerous methods (vehicles) of communication are listed in Table 12.4. If one wishes to

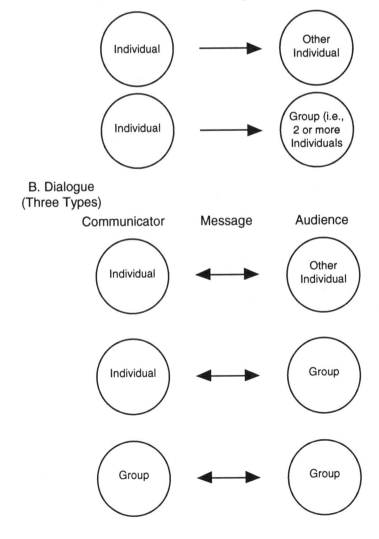

A. Monologue (Two Types)

Communicator — Message — Audience

Individual → Other Individual

Individual → Group (i.e., 2 or more Individuals

B. Dialogue (Three Types)

Communicator — Message — Audience

Individual ↔ Other Individual

Individual ↔ Group

Group ↔ Group

FIG. 12.6. Different types of monologues and dialogues. The fourth communication element (vehicle) is not presented.

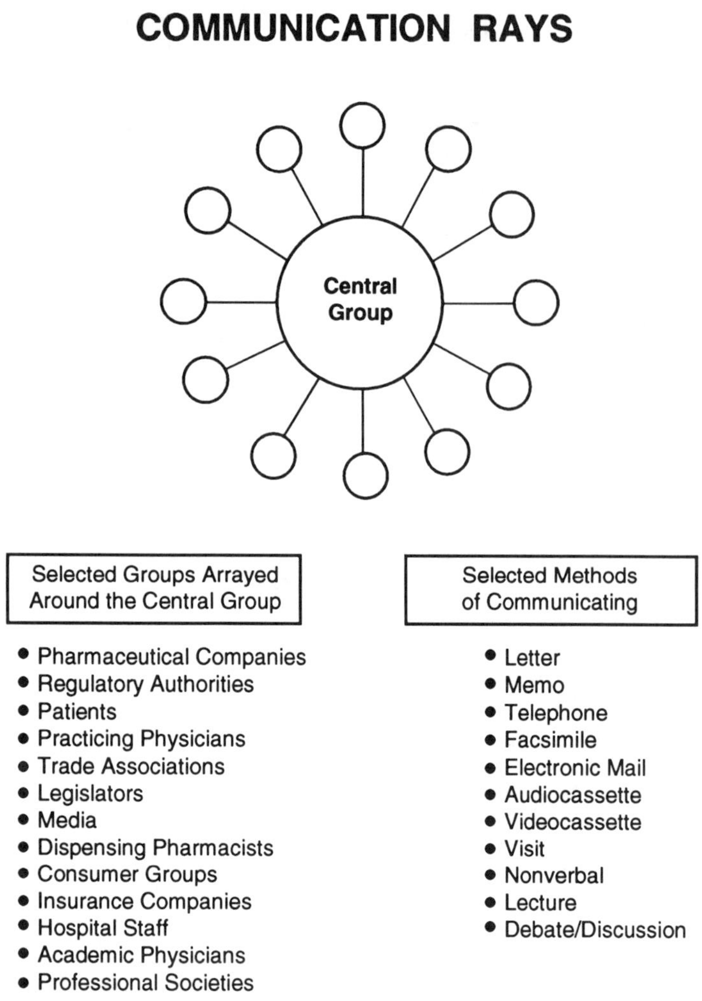

COMMUNICATION RAYS

Selected Groups Arrayed Around the Central Group	Selected Methods of Communicating
• Pharmaceutical Companies • Regulatory Authorities • Patients • Practicing Physicians • Trade Associations • Legislators • Media • Dispensing Pharmacists • Consumer Groups • Insurance Companies • Hospital Staff • Academic Physicians • Professional Societies	• Letter • Memo • Telephone • Facsimile • Electronic Mail • Audiocassette • Videocassette • Visit • Nonverbal • Lecture • Debate/Discussion

FIG. 12.7. The many rays of communication indicating representative groups and also methods of communication.

analyze one's own methods of communication, it is desirable to

1. Identify specific group(s) that one communicates with both inside and external to the organization.
2. Describe and analyze how you presently communicate with them.
3. Evaluate the success of your communications.
4. Propose how you could improve communication with those groups with whom inadequate communication exists.
5. Implement the plans to achieve these goals.
6. Review and evaluate the success of your modified communication techniques at a later date.

Written Versus Spoken Words

Many critical comments made to others are harmless in conversation where tone is important and can convey a balance or enable one to explain how the comments are meant. This allows people to laugh off comments such as "you really messed up this project." Even though there is usually truth in the statement, the person who is guilty can often accept blame and move on to other issues. The same sentence in a written memorandum is not easy for an individual to laugh off and will usually create a hostile reaction. This occurs because of the nature (and permanency) of the written record—not because someone else has received a copy—although that would make a bad situation even worse.

A few simple methods or rules should be followed to enhance the likelihood that memoranda and other written documents will be received and interpreted the way you desire.

Consider the amount of emotion shown. Any document written in anger should be placed aside for at least 24 hours to allow a "cooling-off period." It is often desirable to discuss the issue with one or more people or to show them the document. Remember that it's best not to give offense unintentionally. Add emotion to a document when you decide to do so dispassionately.

Consider who the reader(s) is(are). Read your writing from the viewpoint of the other person. If the recipient is from a different culture, consider having someone in your office or someone else you know from that culture read the letter. If that is impossible or inappropriate, you

TABLE 12.4. *Methods of rapid communication*

Method	Advantages	Disadvantages
1. Telephone	1. Helps build bonds 2. Can solve issues rapidly	1. People often are not there and the game of "telephone tag" starts 2. Many people do not return calls
2. Facsimile ("fax")	1. Rapid 2. Clearly see what the other person has to communicate	1. Some lines seem to always be busy 2. Some machines produce difficult to read copy
3. Electronic mail (E-mail)	1. Can confirm telephone calls 2. Rapid	1. Person may not have computers or E-mail system 2. Person may not search E-mail for messages
4. Voice mail	1. Convenient when person is out of town or often out of his or her office	1. Some people have an aversion to this system
5. Visits	1. Personal 2. Builds bonds 3. Facilitates real communication	1. Often impractical 2. Takes more time for each interaction
6. Memos and letters	1. Can identify details 2. The length is rarely limited	1. Slow for foreign mail 2. Delivery is often unreliable
7. Sending delegates	1. One's message can be delivered by an individual	1. The messenger may be unable to answer some questions adequately
8. Videocassette	1. Can transmit a great deal of information needing visual impact	1. Recipient must have video player and television 2. Different national systems exist
9. Audiocassette	1. Highly portable	1. May be erased by magnets
10. Telex	1. Rapid	1. Not required given other systems
11. Couriers	1. Send original documents rapidly 2. Reliable	1. Expensive

could ask how people from X country or culture generally respond to receiving a letter that contains certain characteristics (specify relevant points).

Consider the hierarchical level of your reader(s). The style of memoranda and documents should be modified based on the level of the recipient(s) within an organization. One may generally be direct and to the point when writing to superiors. Your subservience is assumed because of your lower position. Do not gingerly lead up to the issue you are discussing. Writing to peers or subordinates should not be done in that style because it is likely to be interpreted by peers as you exceeding your authority and by subordinates as your criticizing them.

Consider how you can request cooperation. In writing a document where you seek cooperation of the readers(s) to (1) follow a rule you are setting or changing, (2) provide you with information, or (3) perform a certain task, it is desirable to provide at least one reason for the re-

A Speaker's Communication Alphabet

A	Attitude	Speakers should show a desire to communicate their message.
B	Background	Briefly set the stage for the main message.
C	Central Theme	Present the message's theme and the major points.
D	Details	Describe all details of importance and relevance.
E	Enough is Enough	Do not bore listeners with excessive information or repetition.
F	Finish	Finish the talk or informal comments with a brief summary.
G	Give Listeners a Chance	Listeners should be given a chance to comment or to ask questions.
H	Here's How	Determine the approach to be used and practice the presentation.

FIG. 12.8. The communication alphabet.

quest. Even a chief executive officer who is writing or speaking to junior staff should follow this approach and not adopt the tone that communicates the statement: "You shall."

Consider how your comments and requests are qualified. It is important to use words such as "should" instead of "must," and generally to say "it is desirable" rather than "it is critical." Expressing understanding of the other person's view is always well received even though the recipient may know or believe you are angry and are only being "diplomatic." An example of diplomacy is to write: "I understand that the large number of demands on your time have caused you to miss the deadline that was set," rather than directly criticizing the reader for missing the deadline.

Consider the "communication alphabet" mnemonic in preparing talks or documents. The mnemonic shown in Fig. 12.8 is a simple means of organizing or presenting a talk of 60 seconds to an hour. It also is useful in preparing written documents.

Take a course in writing to improve your communication skills. Many courses in writing show the participants how simple formats and approaches may be used to improve communication.

Avoid the use of jargon that is unfamiliar to your audience. A simple means of ensuring that your comments are received poorly, are misinterpreted, and generally do not achieve their results is to use an excessive amount of jargon. While there is a place for its use, jargon should be assiduously avoided in all communication with those who do not understand or use it. Slang should be avoided in most instances.

13 / Personnel Issues

Personnel Issues at the Corporate Level **139**
   Basic Characteristics of a Wise Chief Executive
     Officer 139
   Should Academicians and Government
     Officials Be Hired as Senior Managers in the
     Pharmaceutical Industry? 139
   Determining an Appropriate Staffing Level, or
     How to Avoid Over- and Understaffing 140
   Changes in Work Load Over Time 141
   Countering Employee Burnout 141
   Jargon 141
   Trade-offs Between Quality and Quantity of
     Staff 141
   Critical Mass 142
   Hiring the Best Staff into a Company 142
   Orientation and Training of New Employees .. 143
Motivation and Productivity **144**
   Motivating Factors 144

Improving Productivity 145
Attitudes of Workers Toward Medicine
   Development—Negative, Overly Optimistic,
   and Realistic **146**
   General Attitudes 146
   Negative Disease 146
   Foxhole Mentality 146
   Overly Optimistic Disease 146
   Difficult Individuals Who Either Create
     Problems or Prevent Their Resolution 146
   Using a Balanced Perspective 147
Liaison Between Different Functions **147**
   Examples of One Division Doing Work for
     Another 147
   Reconciling Problems When Work Done by
     Another Division Is Not Satisfactory 147
   Case Studies in Marketing and
     Pharmacokinetics 147

You can issue directives and policy statements and messages to staff until the wastepaper baskets burst, but they are nothing compared with promotions. Promotions are the one visible, unmistakable sign of the corporation's standard of values, an irrevocable declaration of the qualities it prizes in its staff, a simultaneous warning and example to everyone who knows the nature of the job and the qualities of its new incumbent. Men who have worked diligently and successfully and then see those who have worked less diligently and less successfully promoted above them start to read the management want ads in the paper the following morning. Antony Jay. From Management and Machiavelli.

PERSONNEL ISSUES AT THE CORPORATE LEVEL

Basic Characteristics of a Wise Chief Executive Officer

Pharmaceutical companies are potentially faced with many problems when the chief executive officer does not understand basic issues of medicine development, marketing, or production and yet insists on being actively involved in decision making in these areas. A wise chief executive officer who does not have a background in these areas (and even if he or she does) will delegate responsibility to his or her most senior managers. By doing this the chief executive officer usually enhances his or her own image within the company and enables it to be run more efficiently. If the chief executive officer does not have adequate confidence in his or her senior managers' ability to make sound decisions or does not trust

them in other ways, then those managers should be given different tasks, transferred, or encouraged to resign.

Should Academicians and Government Officials Be Hired as Senior Managers in the Pharmaceutical Industry?

To become a truly effective senior manager in the pharmaceutical industry, it is essential to understand how medicines are developed and how the industry operates. Even the heads of personnel and human resource departments require this knowledge. Clearly, many companies either do not believe this principle or believe that it only takes a short while to learn about the pharmaceutical industry. For example, some companies hire academicians with (1) impressive reputations, (2) solid understanding of science, and (3) important contacts, for senior managerial positions within research and development (R and D). These people often have little or no industry experience, and have only interacted with a company as a consultant. Another comparable example occurs when government executives are brought to a company because of their contacts and knowledge about the Food and Drug Administration (FDA). It is ironic that a company's board of directors sometimes turn over important senior R and D responsibilities to people with little or no knowledge about medicine discovery, medicine development, and the pharmaceutical industry. Nonetheless, both scientifically sophisticated academicians and knowledgeable government employees often add important characteristics and input to a company, but not as new senior managers of a highly complex system they know little about.

Companies should primarily promote experienced managers or leaders from within the pharmaceutical industry to their most senior positions, even if their scientific reputation is not as illustrious as that of some academicians, or their connections are not as impressive as those of some government employees. The mistake of hiring inexperienced senior managers from outside the industry is often so dramatic in its impact on the productivity of a company that it is surprising that it occurs on so many occasions. The author's observations are that it usually takes new managers from outside the industry several years to learn fully the basics of industrial medicine discovery, medicine development, and marketing activities. During this period their company's research effort may stagnate, go off on tangents, make many mistakes, or at the least, not move forward aggressively in a desired direction. In addition, many outside scientists who are hired to head R and D groups overly emphasize the research function they are usually most familiar with and pay insufficient attention to maintaining a balance with other functions that they are usually less familiar and comfortable with. Moreover, medicine discovery activities in industry are quite different than medicine research in academia, and many academic scientists never learn the basics of industrial medicine discovery research.

Who should a company want to hire as a director of research in charge of new medicine discovery? This person could be a top administrator, a top scientist, a top leader, or someone with other qualifications and characteristics. If so, which characteristics are most important? These questions are answered differently in different companies because each company's needs differ, the people making the selection have their own biases, and the characteristics of potential candidates will also differ.

Determining an Appropriate Staffing Level, or How to Avoid Over- and Understaffing

A major personnel issue concerns whether to staff an organization based on peak periods of activity, lean periods of activity, or some middle position. In groups, departments, or companies where staffing is based on meeting anticipated (or actual) demands experienced during peak periods, there is almost invariably a problem encountered during slack periods. The problem is that a significant amount of staff time is underutilized and unproductive. Employees may be fired or forced to take early retirement in organizations that are less concerned about employee well-being and are not "paternal." In other organizations, personnel may be reassigned or allowed to "weather mild storms." When an organization expands its staff during good times and trims back during lean periods, the process is sometimes referred to as an "accordion effect." This phenomenon is often observed in small consulting companies. After they win a large contract they rapidly hire new staff to help conduct the work. When the contract is over, many staff members are let go or fired if a sufficient number of new contracts have not been obtained to provide adequate employment. In extreme cases, companies are forced to go out of business. This latter phenomenon is relatively common for small consulting companies.

Chronically understaffing a company is usually an unsatisfactory approach because it creates a large backlog of work and places heavy pressures on the staff. One alternative to avoid undue pressure is to contract work that cannot be conducted in a timely manner in-house to outside groups. Contracting work to outside groups is often more expensive for a company than if the work were done in-house. Nonetheless, if additional work occurs sporadically and may be satisfactorily performed by contractors, then the contracting approach makes good business sense.

The advantages of understaffing are that people generally (1) work hard because they have a large workload, (2) become more efficient in performing their work, and (3) put aside less important work (this may also be a disadvantage). This type of lean and efficient organization often (4) develops a positive esprit de corps, and (5) almost everyone cooperates with each other, because they feel that they are playing an important part in a group effort. On the other hand, the staff may be overburdened for a long period with an excessive amount of work, or employees may believe that their employer is cheap, purposely keeping the group understaffed, and is profiting unfairly from their difficult conditions. Workers often become burned-out or disgruntled in this situation and their efficiency markedly decreases. To achieve the desired balance between under- and overstaffing, one should analyze staffing issues in the context of a cost–benefit analysis.

The cost side of the cost–benefit analysis includes both actual direct costs (e.g., low unemployment keeps the unemployment tax rate low) and less indirect costs (e.g., training of staff). The benefits of understaffing include steady employment. But, if a company understaffs by too many people, it can lead to situations where important errors are made by overworked staff or inexperienced temporaries. A major problem with overstaffing is that it threatens steady employment over a long period. One rough measure of whether a firm is over- or understaffed is to examine the ratio of total company revenues per employee for several companies. This figure does not indicate whether the staff are deployed appropriately, and these numbers are also influenced by the nature of the marketed medicine portfolio. Nonetheless, there may be valuable information in a comparison with competitors to indicate the degree of over- or understaffing.

Changes in Work Load Over Time

The level of medicine development activities (i.e., work load) in a specific department or group varies as a single major medicine travels through the development pipeline. The work load of a group also varies over time as more or fewer medicines are being developed simultaneously. The numbers of permanent staff may be adjusted to account for long-term changes in the total work load. It is more difficult, however, and it makes little sense to adjust a department's staff continually based on temporary changes in their level of activities. Two major types of changes occur over time. First, there are changes in work load that are of long duration and may be viewed as relatively permanent. Second, there are transitional changes which fluctuate over a shorter time span, on the order of weeks or months.

The staffing options for fluctuating changes usually require a different approach than for long-term changes. Some possible solutions to meeting short-term staffing needs involve temporary adjustments, such as (1) adding temporary help, (2) contracting work to outsiders, (3) allowing backlogs to develop temporarily, (4) reassigning personnel, or (5) using special deployment teams.

Countering Employee Burnout

Employees who have been overworked for a period of time may reach a stage at which they are unable to function effectively (i.e., partial burnout) or at all (i.e., complete burnout). Managers should be aware of this problem and learn to recognize early signs of burnout and then to counteract it.

The signs of burnout may include nervousness, irritability, depression, unusual and atypical behavior, and decreased productivity. These are often observed after a period of particularly long hours and weekends. Burnout is not the same as stress, although stress may contribute to burnout.

The best procedure to counter burnout is to prevent it from occurring, and the worst step is to replace people who experience burnout. If burnout is observed, the staff should be strongly encouraged to take a short vacation or to attend a professional meeting. A more long lasting solution is to increase their resources that helps the individual perform his or her work more efficiently. Another step to prevent burnout is to hold managers responsible for preventing it. Managers could rotate work assignments among staff, change the work environment, or send people on various courses to add stimulation to their work.

Jargon

Every few years there seems to be an entirely new vocabulary that is popular in the management literature. Terms enter common usage that seem to present new concepts, but are generally new jargon for older concepts.

Some recent terms and concepts that have intrinsic value, but should be dejargonized for effective communication are:

Organizational delayering
People empowerment
Quality
Time-based competition

All professionals should strive to eschew jargon from their vocabulary when they are speaking with individuals from outside their discipline. Even within their discipline jargon may easily be misinterpreted or given a different "spin" (sic). The use of jargon is often exaggerated by management consultants.

There are few disciplines outside of management itself with more jargon per sentence than management consultants talking about production and productivity. When it comes to making major improvements in R and D or marketing these people show less enthusiasm than they do in tackling production problems. This enthusiasm for production may result from the mechanistic nature of much of the manufacturing operations and its ability to be described conceptually in terms of logically applied systems. These comments should not be interpreted as anti-consultants or proposing new procedures. Rather, these comments focus on the importance of consultants substituting sound ideas for jargon and empty phrases.

Trade-offs between Quality and Quantity of Staff

In the long term, no pharmaceutical company can combine overstaffing and overpaying its employees. To do so would put the firm's cost structure out of line with competitive firms. The company should carefully analyze which positions are most critical to its success and set its pay levels high enough to attract and retain individuals with sufficient skills to create and maintain competitive advantages for the firm. Conversely, the firm should be careful not to overpay positions where high skill levels are not critical to the success of the enterprise. In such areas, the quantity of staff may be more important than quality.

Companies can purchase many ingredients of medicine development (e.g., rights to a medicine, services of contractors to develop a medicine, consultants, people to design and monitor studies). One key ingredient that companies cannot easily purchase is a talented and loyal senior management group that understands the subtleties of medicine development, knows the professional people within the company, and works together as a team. On the other hand, it is often easier to replace a senior manager than a middle level manager who has specific skills and experience necessary for medicine discovery or development.

Critical Mass

The term critical mass is widely used today. Critical mass is a concept that is applied to many areas within a company. Everyone at a medium or large pharmaceutical company appears to want to achieve it, but what exactly does it mean?

Critical mass may be narrowly defined as: a sufficient number of professional and nonprofessional staff with appropriate skills and talents to achieve specifically defined tasks or activities within a specified time period. This definition indicates several factors that must be described in some detail, including the (1) number of staff, (2) skills of staff, (3) experience and training of staff, (4) management levels of staff in the organization, (5) time available to complete the assigned task, and (6) nature of the assignment.

A broader definition of critical mass is: a sufficient number or amount of resources to achieve specific defined tasks or activities within a specified time period. This definition would include all of the resources needed to complete the activities on schedule. These resources would include funds for specific activities (e.g., promotional expenses), equipment (e.g., in technical development laboratories), as well as staff in all relevant areas.

Critical mass also may be applied to successful completion of a general activity requiring many staff and a large number of activities, such as (1) a medicine's development or (2) a medicine's launch. It could be applied globally in terms of the total number of staff and money to conduct discovery research or much more narrowly to a specific function such as the staff needed to discover (hopefully) a compound to inhibit a specific enzyme.

In deriving an estimate of the critical mass for an activity, different people will derive highly different values depending on:

1. The amount of money the organization has to spend.
2. The personality of the estimator.
3. Whether the concept of critical mass is interpreted as

the barest minimum number of staff to do a job, or as a number to do the job easily and comfortably.

These comments indicate that critical mass should be clarified before anyone attempts to provide a specific value or series of values for this concept in terms of staff, money, or other resource quantities.

Hiring the Best Staff into a Company

Important characteristics to seek in new staff and to help foster and develop in current staff are briefly mentioned. Each of these characteristics and their description clearly reflect the author's biases. Few people (unfortunately) possess all traits listed.

1. *Honesty* Unless a person has this quality it will be impossible to trust him or her. Once a person's honesty is seriously questioned (or lost) it is extremely difficult for someone to rebuild confidence and trust in that individual.
2. *Openness* Interacting with people in a frank, productive way facilitates business decisions and efficiency. However, the capacity for openness depends, to a large degree, on one's background and culture. For example, it is uncommon to observe a significant degree of openness in Japanese businessmen.
3. *Self-confidence* To operate effectively in modern business it is important to have a strong sense of self-identity and self-worth without being arrogant. A self-confident person will be proactive in setting priorities and accepting responsibility for his or her actions.
4. *Well organized* Staff who are highly organized in their thinking are more logical, efficient, and generally more productive as well.
5. *Goal oriented* People who understand their goals and keep them in mind while they work have a better chance of achieving them. These people are more likely to prioritize their activities and follow them in the best order, rationing their efforts according to the importance of the work.
6. *Respect for others* A person who truly respects others will generally earn their respect in return. A respectful person listens carefully and empathetically and seeks win–win solutions to problems and negotiations. A person with a high degree of respect for others tries to make other people feel good about themselves by offering praise for things that the other person does well.
7. *Ability to split and/or lump* This refers to an analytical personality or an amalgamator of disparate information. Although these are two separate skills most people who excel are outstanding at only one of these characteristics.
8. *Creativity* This characteristic would take several chapters or books to describe fully. A person who is

inquisitive, asks a lot of probing questions, and raises unique points to consider is more likely to be creative and to make many novel suggestions.

9. *Risk taker* A person who has the other traits described is generally more willing to put his or her reputation on the line and to take chances. A certain amount of risk-taking behavior is highly desirable. Risk-taking behavior is usually less common inside a large pharmaceutical company than in a smaller biotechnology one.

10. *Sense of humor* People who are funny and make others laugh are not only fun to be with but often bring out the best characteristics in others. While few people have this talent many more appreciate humor and show this in their interactions with others.

11. *Ability to work on many projects simultaneously* A person who likes having many activities conducted simultaneously usually accomplishes much more than those who pursue one or two activities at a time.

Orientation and Training of New Employees

Orientation

Each pharmaceutical company has its own corporate culture, which is largely influenced by the company's mission, values, objectives, beliefs, and goals. The aspects of corporate culture that vary most between pharmaceutical companies are generally each company's myths and traditions. The orientation of new employees is an ideal opportunity to present that culture and to initiate a specific type of corporate thinking.

Orientation programs should also include various other relevant aspects of the company and new employee's division (e.g., research, marketing, production). This includes a review of the company's history and its contributions to medicine and science, plus personnel issues, information about the company's products, and other appropriate information. It is also important to discuss procedures that are used to derive the philosophy and approaches that a company uses in reaching decisions. These objectives are usually addressed using a combination of talks, tours, brochures, videos, and slide presentations. Factors that have a positive or negative effect on employees' motivation should be considered not only in creating the initial orientation program, but in other interactions between a company and its employees such as training programs.

Training

Current staff may be offered or required to have training in new areas of responsibility, as well as to improve skills in various aspects of their current position. Courses focus on manual, technical, managerial, personal, psychological, and/or communication and decision-making skills. (Tables 13.1 and 13.2).

When new staff are hired to meet a crisis, replace staff, or enlarge a group, it takes time for them to develop sufficient experience to contribute fully to the company. It is important to consider the rate of growth in staff size, so that new employees may be assimilated well into the company. One means of expediting their learning curve and minimizing the orientation time is with well-thought-out training programs.

Training programs should be as well tailored to the individual as is consistent with efficient use of time and the efforts of others. There are so many options available that are both cost and time effective that to allow only on-the-job training makes little sense and may be largely counterproductive for many employees. Scientific, clinical, marketing, finance, and production staff usually have a wide variety of both internal company and external training opportunities. The staff's problem is mainly one of choosing the right formats and finding the time to take courses or attend meetings. Courses sponsored by the company may be either on- or off-site. There are many obvious advantages to run a course off-site, when it is practical to do so. This issue is discussed in greater

TABLE 13.1. *Selected examples of internally taught professional development courses that could be offered to company staff*

1. Accessing internal company information
2. Assertiveness skills
3. Corporate organization and culture
4. Policies and procedures for staff levels A to F or for levels G and higher
5. Pharmaceutical industry overview
6. Career development for staff levels A to F or for levels G and higher
7. Decision making
8. Scientific writing
9. Business writing
10. Performance evaluation
11. Financial management
12. Developing ideas
13. Personal interactions with others
14. Introduction to management
15. Developing a team
16. Leadership
17. Laboratory practices
18. Sexual harassment
19. Meeting dynamics and leadership
20. Public and company presentations
21. Project management
22. Selling your ideas
23. Interviewing process
24. Computer training[a]

[a] A large number of courses may be created for different uses of computers as well as for different software and hardware.

TABLE 13.2. *Selected characteristics of each training course that should be given to potential enrollees prior to requiring them to register*

1. Prerequisites
2. Overview
3. Objectives
4. Methods used
5. Major topics covered
6. Duration of course
7. Preparation required
8. Work required during the course
9. Staff who should consider the course
10. Benefits expected to be gained from taking the course

length relating to project leader training in *Guide to Clinical Trials* (Spilker, 1991). Courses have the best chance of being successful when they are developed or modified to suit the specific participants and also are evaluated in a pilot program.

MOTIVATION AND PRODUCTIVITY

Motivating Factors

The motives of professional staff vary in different areas of a pharmaceutical company. Obviously, money is an extremely important motivator, but its importance varies for different people. For those in marketing it is usually relatively more important than for scientists in R and D. Scientific achievement and professional recognition are also extremely important motivators for scientists and clinicians in pharmaceutical companies. For business staff, power and authority are often extremely important motivators. One of the corollaries of these differences is that mechanisms to improve productivity and morale vary greatly in different professional areas within a pharmaceutical company. For example, the characteristics of high scientific performers are listed in Table 13.3. The points designed to increase productivity and quality in a company are discussed elsewhere in this text.

Recognizing differences between groups, in terms of their interests, training, perspective, and manner of working as well as the motivational factors discussed, allows a company to derive more effective use of employees' abilities and skills.

Some people believe that the motivators described in the paragraph above (e.g., money, recognition, power) only relate to senior managers. Although these motivators are most obvious in terms of their use for senior management, they also exist at lower levels within a company. The degree to which they are present at lower levels depends primarily on whether managers throughout a company desire to pass such benefits down through the company and also on whether they are allowed to do so. Even when certain managers are prevented from providing additional money to lower levels as salaries or as a

bonus they may be allowed to provide additional responsibilities. If this too is prevented, they may always provide additional recognition to staff below them in the form of public thanks, notices on bulletin boards, articles in company publications, dinners where the employee's spouse is also invited, or various other mechanisms that are known to be meaningful. Trinkets, certificates, or other approaches should only be used when they are known to be valued by the recipient, because recognition in a form that is distasteful to the recipient may be counterproductive. A few factors that have a positive or negative effect on employee motivation are listed in Table 13.4.

What Do Workers Really Want?

Surveys of managers and workers usually turn up highly different views of what each thinks that the workers really want. Although specific details of each survey differ, the most important points generally reported by workers (in order of importance) are:

TABLE 13.3. *Characteristics of high scientific performers*[a]

1. Freedom: Is coordination compatible with freedom? Best performance occurred when both were present
2. Communication: Effective scientists both sought and received more contact with colleagues
3. Diversity: In both research and development, the more effective scientists undertook several specialties or technical functions
4. Dedication: Several simple questions showed that high-performing scientists and engineers were deeply involved in their work
5. Motivations: Among various motives characterizing high performers, an outstanding trait was self-reliance
6. Satisfaction: Effective scientists reported good opportunities for professional growth and higher status, but were not necessarily more satisfied
7. Similarity: Colleagues of high performers disagreed with them on strategy and approach but drew stimulation from similar sources
8. Creativity: Creative ability enhanced performance on new projects with free communication but seemed to impair performance in less flexible situations
9. Age: Performance peaked at midcareer then dropped —but less among inner-motivated scientists and those in development labs
10. Age and Climate: As age increased, performance was sustained with periodic change in project, self-reliance, and interest both in breadth and depth
11. Coordination: In loosely coordinated settings, the most autonomous individuals did poorly, perhaps because they were isolated from stimulation
12. Groups: Groups declined in performance after several years, but less if the members became cohesive and intellectually competitive

[a] These are the chapter headings from the book *Scientists in Organizations* by Pelz and Andrews (1976). Reprinted with permission of the Institute for Social Research of the University of Michigan.

TABLE 13.4. *Factors influencing motivation of employees[a]*

A. Positive motivating factors
1. Flexibility in work schedules
2. Flexibility in vacation schedules
3. Ability to discuss issues with people at all levels in the company
4. Recognition for contributions
5. Ability to attend professional meetings
6. Ability to help plan in-house scientific meetings
7. Awareness of how one's work fits into the "big picture"

B. Demotivating factors
1. Unethical approach to medicine development and/or marketing
2. Insufficient staff to conduct relevant activities
3. Overstaffing and resultant idle time
4. Lack of any decision making
5. Promotion of individuals considered to be unqualified
6. General lack of information about the relevance of one's work

[a] An excellent article on motivation (Herzberg, 1987), originally published by the *Harvard Business Review* in 1968, has sold more reprints (1.2 million) than any other article published by that journal.

1. Appreciation for work done. Employee attitude surveys consistently show that managers neglect to meet workers' needs for psychological recognition. Most people have an almost unlimited capacity for being recognized when they have done a good job. Managers too often fail to take advantage of this no-cost means of improving worker morale.
2. A feeling of being "in" on things, i.e., being "part of the action" or at least aware of the major activities going on in their group. This involves both downward communication to workers from management and upward communication from workers to management.
3. Job security.
4. Good wages.

When surveys are made about workers' attitudes, or other personnel issues, it is important to propose recommendations or solutions as well as describing the results.

Improving Productivity

Many personnel issues are directed toward increasing productivity. A few additional comments are made here of points not discussed elsewhere. These are not presented in any particular order. Additional ideas for increasing the productivity of technical professionals are presented by Griggs and Manring (1986). The characteristics of high scientific performers are listed in Table 13.3, and a number of reasons for low employee productivity are given in Table 13.5.

1. The number of people who work together in a single office is usually inversely related to their productivity.

At both junior and senior levels, each professional should have their own office space with privacy. Putting two people in the same office markedly diminishes productivity, unless they are working in a laboratory or in an environment where their work does not require privacy. When people find it difficult to hold meetings or even telephone calls in their room and must spend time going elsewhere to conduct business, it creates problems. It may become a major problem of decreased productivity if many people have to conduct their business under crowded conditions.

2. When professionals spend a significant portion of their time handling routine matters that could be dealt with by a clerk it compromises their productivity. If many people in a company operate in this manner, the efficiency of medicine development may be significantly compromised. One assistant may handle time-consuming activities of several professionals, allowing the professionals to utilize their time on more important and/or complex issues. The question is to determine how many assistants to hire. Hiring too many assistants may be counterproductive and adversely affect a group's efficiency.

3. Encouraging professionals to ride to work in car pools and company-owned vans is a means of facilitating intellectual sparks and original ideas. This is one type of the intellectual turbulence described in Chapter 47, where imaginative people help each other solve problems or define new approaches to issues.

4. A few of the more recently developed tools to help individuals improve their productivity include: (1) electronic mail, (2) electronic conferencing, (3) voice mail, (4) calendar management, (5) calendar scheduling, (6) computer filing system, and (7) numerous other computer software packages.

TABLE 13.5. *Possible reasons for low employee productivity[a]*

1. Boredom
2. Lack of clear responsibilities
3. Individuals never see a finished product of their work
4. Bureaucratic rules, excessive paper work, and red tape
5. Supervisors who do not encourage and support employees
6. Lack of adequate physical comforts in the environment
7. Frequent transfers of personnel
8. A new supervisor
9. Incompatibility between the supervisor and his or her employees
10. Poor communication between staff or between managers and employees
11. Lack of openness and honesty in the environment
12. Benefits that have not kept pace with those of other companies
13. Political maneuvering of senior managers, which creates stress and pressures on employees

[a] These may also be applied to an individual employee. These are not listed in any particular order.

Many other issues relating to productivity are discussed in Chapters 27 and 36.

ATTITUDES OF WORKERS TOWARD MEDICINE DEVELOPMENT—NEGATIVE, OVERLY OPTIMISTIC, AND REALISTIC

General Attitudes

When someone is discussing a particular aspect of medicine development, listen closely. Is he or she saying, "What if all of these negative things happen with a medicine?" in a way that says he or she does not want to take a chance and develop a medicine, even though others believe it to have a reasonable chance of success? Is the person always saying, "Let's try this. I know it'll work," after many previous trials have failed? Is this optimistic person always wanting to try one more thing before a dead medicine is finally buried? On the other hand there are realistic people who say, "Why not try such and such to overcome the problems we face or the potential problems that may occur?" Attitudes differ, but at some companies (and perhaps in some countries) there is a preponderance of people who have a generalized form of "negative disease."

Negative Disease

It is important to be objective and to evaluate carefully and critically new ideas. Being skeptical of many new claims is prudent (see, for example, the section on advertising claims in Chapter 47). The pertinent question is whether this attitude is manifested as objectivity or as negativity. The author has met relatively few people in the pharmaceutical industry who are overly optimistic and positive about most new medicines under development. Many do develop myopia, however, about one or two particular medicines for a variety of reasons. But, numerous individuals in the pharmaceutical industry have "negative disease" and have usually found it safer to raise objections than to agree or take a realistic approach. Companies are fortunate if they are dominated by a realistic group of senior managers.

Other aspects of "negative disease" are where people are (1) more comfortable repeating old work than starting new work, (2) more comfortable starting one clinical trial after another without having a clear regulatory endpoint in focus, (3) always attempting to answer basic questions about how a medicine works rather than initiating studies to move the medicine forward toward regulatory approval in the most straightforward manner possible, (4) certain that if they have not done all relevant work themselves they must repeat the work before it can be believed, and (5) certain that their country is the true center of the world for medicine development.

Foxhole Mentality

A foxhole is a trench dug in the ground as a shelter to protect one or more people from the enemy during a war. Foxhole mentality is another cause of negative disease in staff members. This refers to people who are afraid to stick their heads out of their foxhole, because they have been "shot at" in the past. Once someone is shot at they usually become gun shy, or they stock up on ammunition and plan their next assault more carefully. Some people operate entirely in a foxhole. They listen to the "big guns" blasting overhead and occasionally (or often) see flares and lights in the nighttime sky that indicate a battle occurring some distance away. People who operate in isolation in individual foxholes probably have a higher incidence of negative disease (a form of trench fever) than do other workers.

Overly Optimistic Disease

The author has met fewer people with this condition than those with negative disease. Optimistic disease folks are prone to make comments such as:

"Our data look great, let's write up the New Drug Application now."
"The FDA will *have* to approve this promptly."
"Let's use all European data. After all, the FDA accepts it now."
"Let's take the Product License Application from England and send it to the FDA."

These comments are often naive, but those who make such statements with force and have positions of power may be viewed as strong, forceful leaders. These traits are really counterproductive in a senior manager who believes he or she is inspiring and leading his or her troops.

Difficult Individuals Who Either Create Problems or Prevent Their Resolution

Unfortunately, many individuals who personally hamper solutions to problems desire to be the center of attention, even of negative attention. Some of the people who either place themselves or are placed in a central position where a problem or issue exists have been in a company for many years. Some may have positions of authority but have been bypassed for more senior positions. They obviously derive a great sense of enjoyment and/or importance from creating bottlenecks and difficulties for other people in the company. Alternatively, the obstreperous people may simply be used to doing their job in the "old way" and may be unable or unwilling to change and adapt to new situations.

If this type of individual is found to be responsible for an important problem, then spending a significant amount of time to resolve one situation will usually not lead to a long-lasting solution. Related situations will often arise within a number of months, if not sooner. In such cases it is generally desirable to replace the person. This individual may be moved to a position outside the mainstream of the company's activities. Alternatively, a mechanism may be developed which would force the person to accept a system which he or she could not (or at least, not easily) alter, block, or delay.

Using a Balanced Perspective

In dealing with many medicine discovery, development, and marketing problems, it is usually wise to remember that there are more than a dozen ways to do almost anything. There are also many perspectives on most issues. Thus, when hearing that someone has done something "outrageous," it is best to avoid accepting that conclusion easily. It usually turns out that their perspective is also valid. This is especially true for people who are generally considered to be reliable.

Companies would do well to have a few basic rules and policies to help guide their behavior and reactions to various situations. This is similar to the concept of adopting some principles of living, such as: (1) never eat in a restaurant called "Mom's," (2) never eat in a restaurant with more than four calendars on the wall, (3) never play cards with a man named "Doc," and (4) never shoot pool with a man named after a city.

LIAISON BETWEEN DIFFERENT FUNCTIONS

All companies require different groups to cooperate and to function well together. One factor that differs between companies is how well different functions cooperate and conduct work for each other.

Examples of One Division Doing Work for Another

There is often a desire or need in one group to have someone in another group perform work for them. A few examples of this are listed.

1. R and D wants someone in marketing to evaluate the current status of competitive medicine projects and medicines already in the market.
2. Marketing wants someone in R and D to develop planning charts and flow diagrams to assist them in scheduling the launch of a new product.
3. Production wants technical assistance from chemical and analytical development units to assist with problems of a recently transferred process.
4. R and D wants production to manufacture clinical trial medicine supplies for a large upcoming clinical trial.

5. Marketing wants specific medical studies conducted on soon-to-be-marketed and currently marketed medicines to support promotional claims.
6. R and D wants marketing research data to assist in reaching various decisions.

Many other cases could be listed. These examples require coordination and cooperation between different functions in a company. When the quality and rapidity of service provided by one group on major priority items are not acceptable, strains develop and alternative solutions are often sought. Some of these are described below.

Reconciling Problems When Work Done by Another Division Is Not Satisfactory

Alternative solutions usually exist for a group or unit that is displeased with the quality, quantity, or timeliness of services received from another group or unit within the same company. These may involve (1) discussing the issues involved and agreeing on what work will be able to be handled over a given period, plus identifying necessary conditions for its completion, (2) contracting the work to outside groups, and (3) developing the capability within the group that is displeased to handle the necessary work themselves.

Developing the capability of conducting work usually performed by others solves problems in some situations. The value of this approach varies from a positive duplication of effort to an unnecessary if not a counterproductive duplication. The decision of whether the duplication is positive depends on many factors that are not enumerated here because each situation is quite different. A few specific cases are discussed below.

Another approach that is sometimes followed is for the group that is providing the service to hire one or more additional people who are dedicated to helping the other function. This approach sounds reasonable, is logical, and may be a satisfactory solution. Nonetheless, the author has observed that in several situations where it has been tried, the people hired to do work for another group spend less and less time on that work. This has occurred even when their salary comes from the group that desires the work. These people become involved in work directed by their administrative superiors, rather than their "clients."

Case Studies in Marketing and Pharmacokinetics

Case I

The marketing division desires to have some clinical trials performed which will help them support advertising claims they would like to make on both new and old medicines. In addition, there are several line-extensions to existing products that they want to have developed, as well as obtaining an increased shelf life for other products. Each of these items is requested of R and D through appropriate channels. Much of the work, however, never seems to get done, and other work gets done much more slowly than marketing believes reasonable. In an extreme case, marketing's highest priorities are not completed by R and D. Marketing executives are now thinking about how to deal with this situation.

Case II

The department of pharmacokinetics and metabolism conducts various studies on animals to determine the profile of new medicines. The priorities within that department are set by the head of that department, who believes that medicines at a later phase of clinical development should receive much higher priority than medicines currently in an early phase.

The medical department relies on the department of pharmacokinetics and metabolism to help plan the pharmacokinetic aspects of medicine protocols and also to assay biological samples (e.g., blood) for determination of medicine levels. The particular problem is that the medical department wants certain assays performed as soon as possible on a completed Phase I trial. These data are necessary to help design the next Phase I clinical trial for that medicine. Nonetheless, this work is given a low priority by the department of pharmacokinetics and the work does not seem to get done.

Discussion of the Two Cases

The particular cases cited are representative of innumerable examples that could be described where staff in one reporting group are requesting work or service from another group. They illustrate division-to-division differences (case I) and department-to-department differences (case II). These types of problems also exist at both higher and lower levels within a corporation.

The easiest way to solve many such problems is for relevant individuals to communicate (by telephone, meeting, or memo) and to reach an amicable solution.

Unfortunately, this approach is not always used or may not be sufficient to solve a problem. Other methods must often be sought. Another common solution is for the aggrieved parties to take their case to an arbiter, usually an individual who is above them in the company's hierarchy. This person may resolve the issue, either amicably or by imposing a solution. But, this more senior individual may not be willing to settle the issue or may not settle it so that both parties are pleased. In such situations, the problem(s) generally continues to brew and may boil over again in the future. In thinking about differences between one's approaches and those of others one is reminded of Mark Twain's line from *Pudd'nhead Wilson*, "Nothing so needs reforming as other people's habits."

Another approach to resolving differences is to establish formal and/or informal mechanisms to deal expressly with problems. A mechanism that might be proposed in case I would be for the marketing division to establish its top priorities on an annual (or semiannual) basis. These would then be communicated to R and D via an established route. This would avoid having numerous individuals within marketing each attempt to have their own plans carried out by individuals within R and D. This standardized approach would allow R and D groups to deal more uniformly and effectively with medicine development requests from marketing.

Marketing may make reasonable requests that are within the capabilities of R and D, but cannot be accomplished because of insufficient resources. One means of solving this problem is for R and D to increase its resources so that it may adequately provide all reasonable services requested. Another alternative is for the marketing division to establish their own medical department, whose priorities would be determined solely by marketing interests. A third alternative would be for the marketing division to place some or all of their studies with outside contractors who would either conduct the studies themselves or act as middlemen and place them with investigators. A fourth alternative is for the marketing division to contract with the R and D group and to pay for such studies. A combination of these or other alternatives is possible. Many of these approaches have analogous solutions for case II. There will always be many complex or difficult issues between departments and between divisions, but most can be resolved if there is genuine interest in doing so.

14 / Golden Rules of Staffing

Evaluating Staff Ratios 149
Why the Optimal Number of Staff Per Project
    Changes Over Time 150
Head Count Quality Versus Numbers 151
Determining the Number of Staff Necessary for a
    Given Project 151

Phase IV Clinical Studies 152
Influence of a Company's Affluence on Golden
    Rules of Staffing 152
Conclusion....................................... 152

I am wondering what would have happened to me if some fluent talker had converted me to the theory of the eight-hour day and convinced me that it was not fair to my fellow workers to put forth my best efforts in my work. I am glad that the eight-hour day had not been invented when I was a young man. If my life had been made up of eight-hour days I do not believe I could have accomplished a great deal. Thomas A. Edison

All managers who allocate staff to different activities desire golden rules or principles that would help them determine the number and type of staff they need to conduct their work. Such rules would also help managers to predict future resource needs more accurately. Many professionals within the pharmaceutical industry believe that golden rules exist for calculating the total head count (i.e., staff) that is most appropriate to assign per activity—i.e., per clinical trial, per formulation, per toxicology study, or per any other medicine development activity. This chapter strongly challenges that view and advances the position that such golden rules of staffing are illogically devised and that the use of such rules is counterproductive.

The major example used in this chapter is that of assigning staff to initiate and monitor clinical trials. Typically, a company would like to know how many clinical trial sites a single monitor could adequately handle. (One major company believes the answer is 15.) A company would also want to know how many clinical trial sites a data processor can handle and how many protocols a statistician can analyze. (The same company's answers to these questions are 30 sites and three protocols.) With these simple answers the company may easily determine their staffing needs in these three areas and readily determine if they are currently under- or overstaffed. Although the optimal numbers of clinical sites or trials for company monitors, data processors, and statisticians to handle do exist, these numbers exist only for a specific point in time and for a specific medicine. These numbers and ratios differ for other medicines and will differ at other points in time for a single medicine. Therefore, the golden rule numbers must be determined by each group for each of their medicines at a specific time.

EVALUATING STAFF RATIOS

It can be demonstrated that a given number of staff above the golden rule number (or range) is still too low for the particular situation, and also that a number below the golden rule number (or range) is still too high. For example, if the golden rule number is determined to lie between four and eight clinical sites per professional staff member, then one can show that three sites per professional is still too many to allocate to some work, and that nine sites per staff member is still too few for other trials.

One must assume that the golden rule numbers are determined for a mid-range of projects, in terms of complexity and demands on time. Thus, three clinical sites per staff member could be too many for large and complex projects with difficult to measure endpoints that require large amounts of resources. Such projects could require more than one staff monitor per three clinical sites to deal with its many aspects and to advance the medicine expeditiously through the clinical development subpipeline. Each site could also have an extremely large number of patients enrolled. Moreover, if the company's future is closely tied to the success of one or two specific investigational medicines, then all necessary staff should be assigned to its development to ensure that maximum speed is achieved.

A counterargument might be that the golden rule of four to eight trial sites per monitor was based on developing only new chemical entities as medicines and not on developing line-extensions. (The counter-counterargument is that new chemical entity medicines also have widely differing staff requirements in terms of time and effort required to monitor each clinical trial site.) A broad golden rule range would be necessary if one wished to include most new chemical entity projects. If a range is established that includes every new chemical entity, then the rule ceases to have any meaning or usefulness, because an extremely broad range must be narrowed down individually for each new project. Moreover, as the project development continued, the range would have to be reassessed on a frequent basis. A broad range cannot be used to determine a company's total staff needs—which is the main reason for constructing a golden rule. In summary, a golden rule has less use if it is not a specific number, and if it is a range, the broader its range, the less useful the rule becomes.

The same logic can be applied to extremely straightforward projects such as developing line-extensions that require only a few simple clinical trials in small numbers of readily available patients. There always are going to be outliers for even a broad range of hypothetical staff needs.

The optimal number of clinical trial sites per staff member exists for a company at a specific point in time. This number is a bench mark, however, and it varies to a small or large degree among different medicine projects, as described above. This number also varies over time within a company for the same medicine. Because the optimal head count requirements vary so greatly among large and small projects; important and less important projects; and complex, time-consuming, and easy to

monitor clinical trial sites, it makes little sense to focus attention on determining the average project's requirements (or average clinical site's requirements), except possibly for long-term planning purposes. In the short-term, it is far more important to allocate the existing and expected (or projected) head count appropriately based on several factors (see Table 14.1).

WHY THE OPTIMAL NUMBER OF STAFF PER PROJECT CHANGES OVER TIME

The number of staff needed for each specific project and each specific indication or dosage form within the project to progress changes over time because:

1. The priority given any specific project often changes; the company may decide to place either fewer or greater resources on the project's progression. Although this may result from changes in a medicine's medical or commercial value, it may also result from changes in the value of other projects in the portfolio.
2. The medical value of a medical project may change. Because most new compounds begin their "life" in a pristine state, the changes observed in medical value during the course of development are usually negative. This may mean that a project's priority will also decrease, and correspondingly the appropriate amount of resources (including staff) to assign to the project will also decrease.
3. The commercial value of a project may change. This may occur independently of the intrinsic medical value of the specific medicine being developed. For example, competitive medicines may be introduced, standard medicines may be removed from the market, or medical practice may change.
4. The systems and standard operating procedures used within an organization to process the data and to monitor the clinical trials may change. This may occur with the purchase of more sophisticated equipment or the creation of a larger number of national dossiers for registering a medicine. This often means that fewer (or potentially more) personnel are required to conduct the same operation.
5. Regulatory requirements are in a continual state of change and, over the years, the changes have generally resulted in an increase in the amount of data required for approval. The number of people at a company who are required to conduct and complete additional studies to meet new requirements also increases. This results from increased requirements for documentation of existing procedures, increased numbers of procedures to be followed, additional studies to be conducted, or from other changes.
6. The amount of resources necessary to develop a medicine is related to the phase of the medicine's

---

TABLE 14.1. *Considerations in assessing the number of staff required for a general area and for specific projects*[a]

1. What are the medical, commercial, scientific, and public relations values of each project in the portfolio?
2. What is the priority for developing each project and of each of its separate indications and dosage formulations?
3. What are the special needs of each project that affect head count which are required to pursue its development? For example, do staff have to monitor each site at double the usual frequency?
4. Is existing staff currently apportioned based on all of the above considerations? If not, should this be done prior to determining the needs for additional staff?
5. How close to or far from regulatory approval and marketing is each of the projects in the portfolio?
6. What is the certainty that each project in the portfolio will be marketed?
7. What additional projects are anticipated to enter the portfolio over the next 6, 12, and 18 months and what are each of their projected staffing needs?
8. What areas of expertise are insufficiently present within the company and which are present in excess? Are licensed-in opportunities likely that would utilize staff expertise that is currently present in excess?
9. Consider each of the above questions in terms of both junior and senior level staff.

[a] For the considerations in this table to be most useful, they should not only focus on a specific medicine, but should be indication-specific, route of administration-specific, and possibly formulation-specific.

development. More resources are usually needed during Phase II than during Phase I, and the greatest amount is usually needed during Phase III. As more projects move from Phase I to II and from Phase II to III, the head count required per project tends to increase in clinical areas. The clinical trials are also more complex in Phase II than in Phase I and a single professional cannot monitor the same number of sites. On the other hand, a monitor may need to spend much more time at a Phase I site than at a Phase II site to ensure everything goes well. The amount of staff required for a project in Phase IV varies enormously among projects.

7. The types and complexity of clinical trials often change in unanticipated ways. Additional detailed "troubleshooting" protocols that are labor intensive may be mandated. Alternatively, simply designed and easily monitored clinical trials may be sufficient in Phase III. It is not always possible to know long in advance how complex future trials will have to be.

8. The amount of clinical data collected per patient may greatly increase or decrease for a specific medicine over time in a series of protocols. While this change is often related to the phase of the medicine's development, it may also relate to other aspects of the medicine such as unanticipated problems, or to changes in the development plans.

9. The number of patients enrolled per clinical trial may unexpectedly increase or decrease, based on the specific objectives of the trial, power considerations, competitive medicines, problems with the medicine (or class of medicines), or new regulatory requirements. This may greatly influence the total resources required, particularly if patient recruitment is a major issue.

10. Each specific disease varies in its needs for labor-intensive clinical trials. Anti-infective and dermatological trials tend to be less complex and less labor intensive than clinical trials of antipsychotic and antiepileptic medicines. The major factors affecting the need for labor relate to the complexity and quantity of measurements of efficacy and safety parameters.

11. The quality, expertise, and experience of staff all influence allocation of resources. New employees require a significant period of training before they can be as productive as seasoned employees. Attempting to apply golden rules of staffing to all employees in any department independent of their skills and experience can lead to major problems.

12. Staff do not usually perform just one job or activity, but most have multiple functions. Thus, to state that one needs X number of staff in a department for one job and Y number of staff for another job, based on golden rules, makes no sense when some staff fulfill both functions or their roles change over time.

One assumption underlying the use of the golden rule concept for planning future resource needs is that the total amount of personnel resources required to develop a larger company's entire portfolio of projects of a fixed size does not change much over time. This belief is readily challenged by noting that, within any portfolio of fixed size, each project's resources differ substantially, depending on the factors described above. For example, projects with extremely high commercial value are assigned a disproportionate number of staff in most cases. Even if the additional head count applied to important projects come from temporary staff or from medical contractors, the golden rules of staffing would still be violated.

HEAD COUNT QUALITY VERSUS NUMBERS

A crucial issue relating to head count concerns the staff members' experience, degree of effectiveness, and ability to move their project forward. The actual number of staff assigned to an activity is sometimes secondary; a few extremely efficient and motivated people can often accomplish more productive work than a large group that is not efficiently working together. It is essential for all managers to utilize their existing staff as productively as possible. It is the responsibility of research managers to assure senior management that their staff meet appropriate criteria and are being appropriately deployed. Managers who focus solely or primarily on numbers of staff may be using the numbers as a smoke screen to justify one or more poor performers. Nonetheless, there are many examples in all organizations when additional staff improve productivity.

One of the major justifications for hiring additional clinical staff is to reduce or eliminate bottlenecks. However, bottlenecks can be lessened by means other than hiring more staff. Important methods are to (1) improve the efficiency of systems used to develop, review, and approve protocols; (2) improve the efficiency of systems used to schedule and visit sites, edit and process data; (3) purchase better hardware; (4) hire temporary staff; (5) contract work out; or (6) transfer staff.

DETERMINING THE NUMBER OF STAFF NECESSARY FOR A GIVEN PROJECT

It is essential to judge each medicine's staffing requirements individually rather than to rely on average ratios of head count, which can lead to excessive or insufficient requests for resources. A general assessment of the work loads of individuals and the level of individual efficiency provide the necessary information (assuming that the projects they are working on are the most relevant activities for them to pursue). It is also important to judge the performance of each individual against their previous performance, against a plan, and in comparison to other staff.

In determining the appropriate number of staff, it is necessary to begin with a clinical development plan, a technical development plan, and a preclinical development plan for each project. These plans must then be integrated to ensure that all activities fit together both in time and in the amount of effort expended in each area. The amount of effort expended is in turn based on the priority given each project. The plans should include the appropriate level of detail in each department involved in development. Resource needs are estimated for completing each activity in the plan. Based on the activities that are approved, one calculates for each department the resources necessary to carry out the program over a specified number of years. Ideal head count needs for moving the project forward at maximal speed are totaled and compared with the number of staff available in each area. The difference between the number of staff available and needed is the excess or short fall. In the case of a short fall, these staff must either be found (e.g., new hires, contractors, staff transfers) or the activities scheduled must be delayed or decreased.

If two or more activities can use the same resources, then certain efficiencies or economies in the plan may be found. Contracting some activities to outside groups may also save head count or time.

Historical company data may be used to improve the accuracy of assigning staff to projects. These data should only be used if they are known to be accurate and collected from company staff over a period of years.

PHASE IV CLINICAL STUDIES

The usefulness of golden rules of staffing also breaks down when one considers Phase IV clinical studies. Marketing studies are often easier to design and perform than Phase II and III efficacy trials, so that fewer people can monitor more marketing studies. But postmarketing surveillance studies, also conducted during Phase IV, have quite different needs for head count than do marketing studies. Quality of life and economic studies also vary greatly in their staff needs. Does this mean that a separate staffing rule should be created for each type of clinical study or trial? Of course not! It does mean, however, that a rule for one type of clinical study or trial may be inappropriate for others.

INFLUENCE OF A COMPANY'S AFFLUENCE ON GOLDEN RULES OF STAFFING

The discussion so far has focused on whether golden rules for staffing should be created, and if created, how they would differ under a variety of conditions. The assumption behind the golden rule concept is that a single number or range can be found for each type of activity. Although this clearly is not the case, assume for a moment that an ideal golden rule number could be developed. This number might be based on the assumption that the company has unlimited resources to hire staff to place on each of its investigational medicines. A company that is financially troubled might desire to know the "minimal staff golden rule," i.e., a lower number of staff per activity. Less affluent companies would have fewer staff to implement the same number of clinical trials or other activities. Between these extremes of a minimal and maximal staff golden rule lie the resources other companies might allow for the creation and use of an intermediate golden rule number. This "spectrum of affordability" provides yet another reason to reject the usefulness of a golden rule concept to the activity of staff allocation.

CONCLUSION

Because of the many factors involved in determining golden rules for staff allocation, and their changing values over time, it makes virtually no sense for a company to expend its efforts in this activity. There are much simpler and straightforward approaches for judging whether a company requires additional or fewer staff for any specific activity. The more desirable approaches allow greater flexibility and yield greater efficiencies than does using a so-called golden staffing rule.

15 / Conflicts of Interest

Definitions....................................	153
Factors That Create Conflicts of Interest	155
Types of Conflicts of Interest Involving Pharmaceutical Companies	156
Direct Conflict of Interest Involving Pharmaceutical Companies................	156
Indirect Conflict of Interest Involving Pharmaceutical Companies.................	156
How Should a Company Deal with Conflict of Interest?	157
Examples of Conflict of Interest Involving a Pharmaceutical Company...................	157
Examples of Conflict of Interest Within a Pharmaceutical Company	157
Examples of Conflict of Interest Between a Pharmaceutical Company and External Individuals Who Provide or Seek to Provide Services to the Company	158
Examples of Conflict of Interest Between a	
Pharmaceutical Company and External Groups	160
How Do Conflicts of Interest Relate to Misconduct and Fraud?	160
Industry–University Relationships	160
Other Types of Conflict of Interest Faced by Health Care Professionals..................	162
Journal Article Publication	162
Consulting Relationships	162
Physician Referral to Other Professionals......	164
Judging Work of a Friend, Relative, or Colleague	164
Informing Prospective Patients for a Clinical Trial About the Investigator's Financial Involvement in the Trial	164
Responses to Conflict of Interest Issues by Government and the Industry..............	164
Golden Rules That Help to Avoid or Prevent Conflict of Interest	164

The trouble with always trying to preserve the health of the body is that it is so difficult to do without destroying the health of the mind. G. K. Chesterton

This chapter discusses conflicts of interest from a pharmaceutical company perspective. It describes many of the situations in which conflict of interest can arise and suggests principles that should be used to guide corporate behavior in response to these situations. Additional conflict-of-interest situations that often affect health care professionals outside of the industry also are briefly described.

DEFINITIONS

A conflict of interest can be defined as a situation in which one's self-interests are in conflict with the interests of others one has responsibilities to, i.e., one's loyalties are divided. Alternatively, one's responsibilities to two (or more) external groups are in conflict. From the perspective of a pharmaceutical company, conflict of interest arises when an individual's ability to fulfill his or her professional responsibilities in an unbiased and objective way is impaired or could be impaired by that person's involvement or interest in the outcome of the activity. A

conflict of interest may arise through financial activities, ethical beliefs, religious beliefs, a relationship through blood, or on another basis. A conflict of interest often occurs when a person could create an unfair competitive advantage for himself or herself, others, or an organization (e.g., company). The conflict may actually exist, or it may only have the potential to exist. Even when an actual conflict of interest clearly exists, that person's behavior will not necessarily be influenced. Moreover, situations that appear to one person to be a definite conflict of interest may not appear to be a conflict to another. For example, an academic investigator who establishes a professional relationship with a company may be viewed as having a conflict of interest by some, but this relationship might be a mutually beneficial working one.

Conflicts of interest can be found in so many situations that if one actually looked for them, they would cease to have any significance. For example, a physician who wants to earn money, avoid committing malpractice, and spend time on personal activities while being available to treat his or her patients could do almost nothing that would be 100% free of possible accusations of conflict of interest. But there are standards of behavior for professionals within each culture that are widely accepted. Some of these are codified as principles of medical ethics or principles of specific societies. Certain behaviors are agreed to be below universally accepted ethical standards in all developed countries (e.g., accepting bribes, providing secret kickbacks of money for services provided), although one hears frequent reports of their occurrence.

Conflicts of interest may be categorized into four groups.

1. Real but unknown to the individuals involved (e.g., a person may be studying or testing a product from a company that licensed it from another company in which that person owns stock). This raises the question of whether someone must be aware of a situation for it to be a conflict of interest.
2. Real and known to the individuals involved (e.g., a person owns a major amount of stock in a company whose product he or she is testing or studying).
3. Potential, but would become real if certain events occurred. For example:

- A person purchases stock in a company whose product he or she is testing after their involvement in a project is initiated.
- A person or their child marries someone who is an officer in the company that owns the product they are testing.
- A person is offered stock or other financial incentives by a company after that person becomes involved in a project to test the company's product.
- A person engages in certain activities. For example, when Merck and Co. allowed a senior scientist, Dr. William Abrams, to go to the Food and Drug Administration (FDA) in Washington, DC, on a part-time basis to help establish the FDA's training and education program, people in government and at Merck realized that some of his activities could potentially lead to a conflict of interest (Dr. William Abrams, personal communication). This was avoided by a memo of understanding drawn up in advance by attorneys for the FDA and Merck. This agreement specified areas of work and other activities that he would avoid,

A. Perceived Conflict of Interest (By Others)

Extremely
Minor

Extremely
Major

B. Actual Conflict of Interest

Extremely
Weak

Extremely
Strong

C. Awareness of Conflict of Interest (By Involved Person)

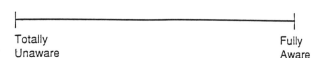

Totally
Unaware

Fully
Aware

D. Response/Reaction to Conflict of Interest (By Involved Person)

None

Major
Influence

FIG. 15.1. Spectra that illustrate the range of conflict of interest as (1) it is perceived by others (panel **A**), (2) it actually occurs (panel **B**), (3) people involved are aware of it (panel **C**), and (4) people respond to the conflict of interest (panel **D**).

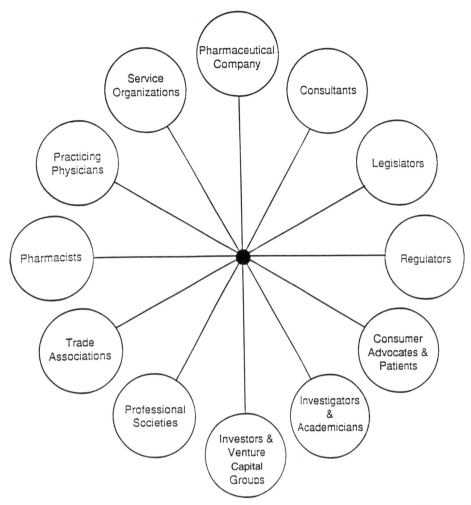

FIG. 15.2. Selected institutions, groups, or individuals that may be involved in conflict-of-interest issues related to medicines. Conflicts of interest may reside solely within a group or may exist between any two (or more) groups.

both at Merck and the FDA, during his period at the FDA. Thus, conflict of interest was avoided.

4. Perceived by others but not currently perceived as a conflict by the person "involved." Perceptions of conflict of interest by others often make a conflict real, even though it may not be true.

A summary of the definitions used in this article are given below and the spectra described in this section are summarized in Fig. 15.1.

Potential Conflict of Interest. A conflict of interest does not exist at the start of a relationship, but the possibility exists that one or more conflict-of-interest situations may develop before the relationship is ended.

Perceived Conflict of Interest. Conflict of interest is believed to be present, but it is not. The perception can be that the conflict of interest is extremely minor or may vary all the way to being extremely major or strong.

Actual Conflict of Interest But Without Consequence. An actual conflict of interest can be demonstrated, but the individual has not been influenced by it. In some

cases the person is unaware of the conflict of interest. The degree of the conflict of interest may vary from extremely weak to extremely strong. In other cases the person is aware of the conflict, but even his or her awareness varies along a spectra.

Actual Conflict of Interest With Consequence. A person has been influenced by a conflict of interest; this influence is manifested as a a slight, extreme, or moderate response.

The major groups involved in conflicts of interest in the pharmaceutical industry are indicated in Fig. 15.2. Any two groups potentially could be involved, although this article primarily focuses on situations in which one group is a pharmaceutical company.

FACTORS THAT CREATE CONFLICTS OF INTEREST

The most common factor that creates conflicts of interest is financial gain. Financial gain may be in the form of

TABLE 15.1. *Selected examples of financial relationships between an individual outside a company and the company itself that may create a conflict of interest*[a]

1. Stock ownership in a company that would benefit from the individual's research or public statements
2. Stock options, profit sharing, royalties, or other financial relationships with a company
3. Consulting arrangements with a company
4. Lectures, talks, or tours conducted on behalf of a company, and for which the person receives pay or honoraria
5. Contract with a company to provide a service

[a] These financial relationships may exist between a company and the individual in question, his or her spouse or immediate family, or a company or group associated with or owned by the primary person.

money, stocks, stock options, royalties, or other economic benefits (Table 15.1). The gain may be immediate or delayed, but the possibility of financial benefit is the factor that has influenced the person affected.

Money is not the only major influence that often leads to or creates conflicts of interest. Other factors include the desire of the person influenced for (1) career growth, (2) recognition and prestige, (3) increased power within a group or organization, (4) maintaining (i.e., not losing) one's current job or position, and (5) obtaining sexual favors. While these factors are nonfinancial, a few (e.g., career growth, increasing power) may lead to improved economic status. Nonetheless, money is not the primary reason that the specific factor has created a conflict of interest.

Conflicts of interest arise for either passive or active reasons. Passive reasons are those that the person has little or no control over (e.g., blood relationships) prior to becoming involved in a specific situation in which conflict of interest arises. Active reasons are those created by the person himself or herself (e.g., purchases stock), either prior to or subsequent to the situation or event in which the conflict of interest arises.

TYPES OF CONFLICTS OF INTEREST INVOLVING PHARMACEUTICAL COMPANIES

Direct Conflict of Interest Involving Pharmaceutical Companies

If all investigators who have ever worked on an investigational medicine or were associated with it in any way are kept off advisory groups or were unable to consult for regulatory authorities (e.g., FDA), some panels and committees would eliminate the majority of the most competent workers from participation, and the regulatory authority might not be able to seek advice from the most important and relevant consultants. This would indirectly hurt the pharmaceutical industry because addi-

tional time would be needed for the government to find qualified and "pure" scientists to enlist on the panels or to serve as consultants. Delays in finding appropriate members for advisory committees or consultants would directly lead to delays in approving new medicines. In some therapeutic areas the number of highly qualified professionals is not as great as in other areas.

If a scientist or clinical investigator owned 100 shares of a large pharmaceutical company, would that truly represent a significant conflict of interest that should prevent him or her from joining a panel or consulting to a regulatory authority? Most people would probably say that this minor investment would not create a true conflict of interest, but many regulators seek to make prominent distinctions and therefore state that no stock in a company may be owned by a scientist or clinician in any situation where a conflict of interest could arise. Other people say that the financial temptation must be "substantial" to create a true conflict of interest, but defining substantial is difficult because people are influenced differently. Ideally, each case must be judged individually and not solely by applying rigid definitions. However, it is clearly much easier to apply a guideline stating that no stock may be owned in cases where conflict of interest is a possibility.

Indirect Conflict of Interest Involving Pharmaceutical Companies

In addition to the many conflicts of interest that may directly affect people within the pharmaceutical industry, there are other conflicts that may indirectly affect the same (or other) people within the industry. Whenever a company allows a government group (e.g., National Institutes of Health (NIH), National Institute of Neurological Diseases and Stroke (NINDS), National Institute of Drug Abuse (NIDA)) to participate in the development of an investigational medicine, the company takes a number of risks. One of those risks is that the public may perceive a conflict of interest by interpreting the relationship as one of the government using taxpayers' money to help a company increase its own profit. This perception can create a backlash and hurt a company more than the time or money saved as a result of the government's assistance with the medicine's development.

If the government chooses investigators who have a conflict of interest to help study a new medicine, it could inadvertently compromise the commercial sponsor who either was unaware of the investigator's potential conflict or was unaware that the specific investigator would be chosen. The commercial sponsor would be tarnished indirectly (guilt by association) if a major issue arose, although it would be through no fault of its own. This could pose major problems for the company at a later date when it seeks to have the investigational medicine approved for marketing and the regulatory authority spends extra time examining the situation in detail, searching for any improprieties and assessing the government-sponsor relationship.

HOW SHOULD A COMPANY DEAL WITH CONFLICT OF INTEREST?

Two basic approaches exist for dealing with the myriad of conflict-of-interest issues. The first approach is to prevent these situations from arising, and the second is to determine how they should be dealt with when they do arise.

Prevention of conflict of interest is usually achieved through the establishment of various policies, rules, and guidelines. Many academic institutions have adopted guidelines that attempt to prevent financial conflict of interest in clinical trials and also in the publication of scientific and clinical data. Journals increasingly are asking authors for more complete disclosure of potential (or actual) conflicts of interest for all articles and documents submitted for publication.

An investigator who passes all conflict-of-interest tests before a clinical trial is initiated cannot be considered totally free of potential conflicts of interest until he or she is reevaluated after the trial is completed. This is rarely done. The data may be audited by an independent group to confirm that major biases did not influence the investigator. A formal audit and peer review may be a necessary step if one wishes to demonstrate that the data are free of biases and the staff free of conflicts of interest. Of course one cannot assume that an investigator who has many conflicts of interest will necessarily generate invalid data or biased conclusions (Fig. 15.3).

Before discussing examples of conflict of interest and some strategies to deal with them, it is relevant to review a number of models of how individuals are influenced (Fig. 15.4) and to consider whether influences are primarily on people within or outside the industry (Fig. 15.5). Figure 15.4 stresses the point that everyone is exposed to many influences that affect behavior; some influences raise conflicts of interest, and if a person, group, or institution desires, they can create barriers to minimize or eliminate certain conflicts of interest (e.g., spouses not having to report to each other or not being in the same line of command in a company, or even stronger, some companies state that spouses may not be employed in the company).

EXAMPLES OF CONFLICT OF INTEREST INVOLVING A PHARMACEUTICAL COMPANY

Examples of Conflict of Interest Within a Pharmaceutical Company

1. A company sells two medicines for the same (or nearly the same) indication. One product is owned 100% by the company and the other product was developed jointly with a small company (or alternatively, was licensed in with a large royalty payment). The conflict arises in deciding how heavily the company should promote each product. A company should be careful about licensing a product to another

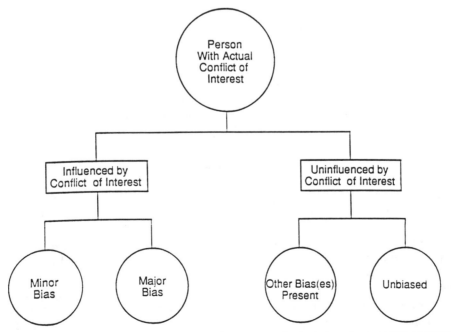

FIG. 15.3. Possible outcomes or responses of a person who has an actual conflict of interest.

Models of Influences on Individuals

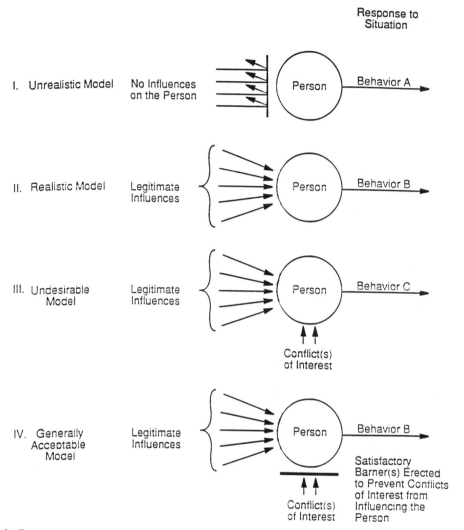

FIG. 15.4. Four models of various types of influences on a person and how these influences may modify one's behavior. Note that the behavior (B) in models two and four are the same.

company that has other products that will compete with the licensee's product.

2. A clinical auditor is asked to audit ongoing clinical trials that the medical department wants completed as rapidly as possible. Major problems are found at the clinical site but the auditor knows that his or her supervisor (who is in the medical department) does not want them reported because it would delay the trial's completion. This conflict would generally be avoided if the auditor reported to a different department or division, as is mandatory for Good Manufacturing Practices and Good Laboratory Practices.

3. The person chosen by a company to write an expert report on a company's medicine for the marketing authorization dossier may have a conflict of interest regarding how he or she presents a controversial subject and discusses the relevant evidence.

Examples of Conflict of Interest Between a Pharmaceutical Company and External Individuals Who Provide or Seek to Provide Services to the Company

1. A company invites clinical experts to visit the company and to discuss (individually or as a panel) the strategy for developing a new medicine. Invariably the panel or most individuals on the panel suggest initiating the types of clinical trials that they are best suited to conduct. These consultants are often rewarded for their advice by receiving the right to conduct those trials by an appreciative company. If the recommendation is to suggest a strategy, then the experts usually recommend a strategy that they are in the best position to help implement. A more objective view would be obtained by the company if the experts

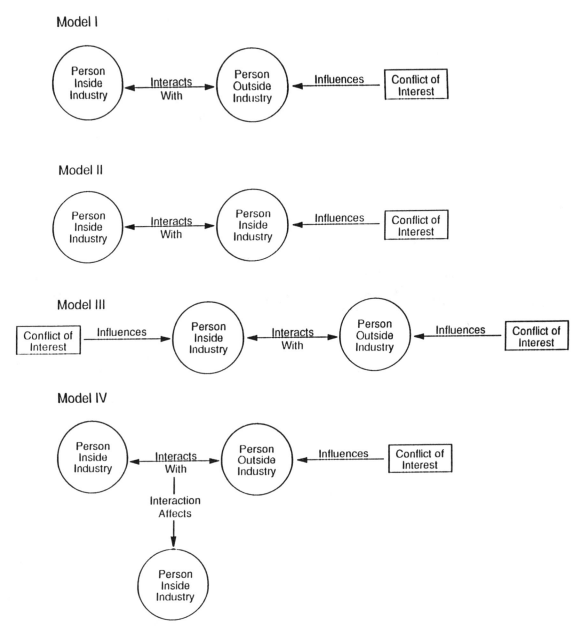

FIG. 15.5. Models of how someone inside the pharmaceutical industry may be indirectly (models I, II, IV) or directly and indirectly (model III) influenced by conflict of interest. It is assumed that the industry representative is aware of the conflict of interest. Comparable models could be shown where the industry representative is unaware of some or all of the conflicts of interest. A variation of model IV is where there is also a conflict of interest influencing the person in industry.

had less conflict of interest. This goal could be achieved by informing the experts when they are invited to the company that, regardless of the strategy or clinical trials they propose, they will not be asked to conduct any trials on that medicine. If this proposal is unacceptable to them, then other experts should be asked to help formulate the strategy, and the original experts would preserve their ability to conduct trials. This approach cannot always be used, however, because in some therapeutic areas there are very few experts.

2. A company asks a clinical investigator to conduct a trial for the company. Unbeknown to the company, the investigator has been a large investor in the company.

3. Companies commonly invite experts to speak at foreign scientific meetings and pay for the individuals' transportation, hotels, meals, and provide them with an honorarium. This practice has been seriously questioned in recent years, both by some regulatory authorities as well as by certain physicians. New codes of practice in the United States place certain restrictions on this practice.

An even more serious conflict of interest would arise if the expert was asked to speak at a scientific meeting prior to completing his or her part of a clinical trial. Although the conflict of interest is real, it would not necessarily influence the investigator's behavior.

4. A small biotechnology company's product is being studied by an academic investigator who owns substantial stock in the company. Because the outcome of a single clinical trial often has a major influence on the company's stock, and sometimes its very survival, this type of conflict of interest must be made public in any announcement of results or in any publications that result.

5. A company asks a consultant to review a problem and to suggest a solution. Part of the solution usually is to hire the consultant to address the problem rather than to use company staff. A related conflict of interest is when the consultant knows the conclusion that a senior manager within the company hopes will result from the study; this places a great deal of pressure on the consultant to propose a preordained solution.

6. A company's customer or supplier of services or materials seeks to influence company employees to favor them in some way by providing gifts or entertainment that goes beyond commonly acceptable standards. Payment of any type is unethical.

Examples of Conflict of Interest Between a Pharmaceutical Company and External Groups

1. A consumer activist group contacts a company and demands that it expedite development of an investigational medicine and also initiate open-label compassionate protocols for all patients with the disease. At the same time, the activists accuse the company of delaying the release of important data (to protect the company's publications) rather than making the information available and to treat and care for patients who need the medicine. The company must avoid snubbing the activists, yet it must also avoid compromising its medicine development program. The company may indirectly place more pressure on a regulatory agency to speed a medicine's approval by acceding to the consumer advocates' demands; at the same time, the company may know that the quality of data obtained in a compassionate plea protocol will be less than those obtained by pursuing the company's original design. Ironically, these data may raise questions and slow the medicine's development.

2. A pharmaceutical executive is asked to advise the government's regulatory authority about policies that could directly affect the industry. This is an obvious conflict of interest, regardless of how ethical the company executive is. Alternatively, the expert could be asked about helping to organize the regulatory authority's operations in a new area or to reorganize an older area. This is a less serious (or nonexistent) conflict of interest.

3. An Institutional Review Board (IRB) that operates for profit knows that if it is too demanding or does not approve protocols submitted by companies, it will likely lose the company's repeat business. A company-sponsored ethics committee/IRB has a similar conflict of interest, and if any company personnel serve on the ethics committee then they have additional conflicts of interest. The problem can be decreased if no one from the company is on the IRB. Ideally, the company's IRB should be run completely independently of the company.

4. The author offered free copies of some of his books to the FDA library. Although the head librarian initially accepted, she was informed that acceptance would raise a potential conflict of interest and that the books had to be returned.

An excellent discussion on the guidelines used in a multicenter clinical trial was given by Healy et al. (1989).

How Do Conflicts of Interest Relate to Misconduct and Fraud?

Conflicts of interest arise when there is an influence or pressure on an individual (or group) to behave in a certain way. If that individual (or group) knowingly follows through with that behavior, that is an example of misconduct. If a person lies or knowingly deceives another person or a group, that is fraud. Thus, conflicts of interest are pressures on a person or group to act in a certain way, and misconduct and fraud are behaviors committed by an individual or group, possibly as a result of conflicts of interest. Figure 15.6 attempts to present this schematically. Approaches and outcomes of investigations of these behaviors also are shown.

Industry–University Relationships

Because many pharmaceutical company conflicts of interest arise in company relationships with academic institutions, those interactions must be examined. A number of spectra regarding these relationships are shown in Fig. 15.7. These relationships include:

1. Industrial support of scientific research conducted in academic institutions.

2. Industrial support of graduate-level educational activities in academic institutions.

3. Industrial support of education of students within industry (e.g., postdoctoral fellowships, residency programs).

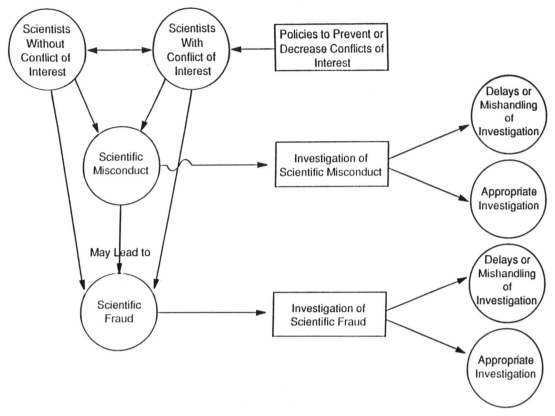

FIG. 15.6. Illustrating possible relationships of conflict of interest, scientific misconduct, and fraud. Scientists without and with conflicts of interest do not usually proceed to misconduct or fraud, although the path of acceptable behavior is not illustrated.

4. Major research programs and collaborations between entire departments or institutes and an industrial company.

Each of these, as well as other relationships, raises potential problems of conflicts of interest.

Policies adopted by many universities to deal with conflicts of interest include guidelines about:

1. The time permitted for academic faculty to consult outside the institution.
2. The time permitted for academic faculty to devote to entrepreneurial activities.
3. The amount of time that university equipment, facilities, and staff may be used for commercial activities and other nonacademic work.
4. The degree to which the university is willing to become involved in technology transfer activities and in start-up ventures.
5. The ownership of intellectual property rights, and the licensing of such rights or patents.
6. Acceptable delays of scientific publications to enable patents to be secured or for manuscripts to be reviewed by sponsors.
7. Guidelines and standards for the ethical interac-

tion of academicians and the institution with corporations.

The sponsor itself should also establish guidelines to prevent or minimize conflicts of interest. Some of the principles and points to consider in such a document include clear statements of:

1. The relationship that the sponsor has with the external individual, group, or organization.
2. The nature of the work to be conducted.
3. Assurances that the sponsor will respect the independence of the investigator, scientist, academician, or other professional.
4. A schedule of payments and milestones when the person is to be paid and the basis on which payments are to be calculated (e.g., completed patients versus patients lost to follow-up).
5. The methods to be used for arbitrating any disputes that arise.
6. Conditions relating to publication or dissemination of the results.

Additional discussions on this topic are presented by Gluck et al. (1987), DeForest et al. (1988), Louis et al.

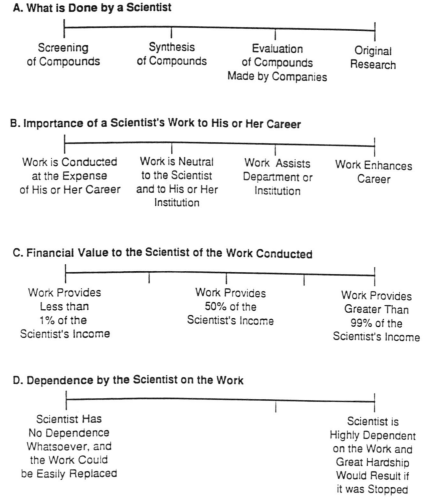

FIG. 15.7. Four spectra that illustrate the nature and importance of the work done by outside scientists for a pharmaceutical company.

(1989), Council on Scientific Affairs and Council on Ethical and Judicial Affairs (1990), AHC Task Force on Science Policy (1990), Institute of Medicine Committee on Potential Conflicts of Interest in Patient Outcomes Research Teams (1991), Cuatrecasas (1992), and Porter and Malone (1992).

OTHER TYPES OF CONFLICT OF INTEREST FACED BY HEALTH CARE PROFESSIONALS

All health care professionals face the potential for experiencing conflict of interest at some time in their careers, whether they are in academia, government, private practice, industry, consulting, or elsewhere. The topic has become widely discussed over the last decade, appearing in media presentations, legislative committee discussions, and policy debates at a large number of government and academic institutions. Some of the more frequently discussed conflicts of interest are indicated below.

Journal Article Publication

A conflict of interest arises when the author of an article fails to indicate the existence of a financial or other important connection to the specific group, product, or organization that is being discussed. An increasing number of journals are adopting more stringent reporting requirements, including (1) information on all sources that financially supported the work, (2) institutional and corporate affiliations of each author, (3) any commercial or other associations (e.g., family relationships) that might pose a conflict of interest, and (4) the signature of all authors stating that their statements are correct and that they do not have any conflicts of interest that have not been disclosed. Detailed editorials and discussions on these topics are often published (Rennie et al., 1991).

Consulting Relationships

Various groups that hire consultants (e.g., government agencies) now require consultants to sign statements

NATIONAL INSTITUTE ON DRUG ABUSE
OFFICE OF EXTRAMURAL PROGRAM REVIEW
CONTRACTS REVIEW BRANCH

CERTIFICATION ON SPECIAL RELATIONSHIPS FOR CONCEPT REVIEWERS

For purposes of this certification, and to the best of my knowledge and belief I certify that: (Check only one line below)

I am _____   I am not _____

aware of any of the following types of special relationships or similar relationships which, from the viewpoint of a reasonable person, could be or appear to be a potential conflict of interest; give the appearance of favoritism or preferential treatment; or result in loss of independence or impartiality concerning review of concepts submitted under RFC NO. 271-92-9401 sponsored by the National Institute on Drug Abuse (NIDA).

Examples of Special Relationships Include:

1. Kinship or relationship by marriage between yourself and a) an individual offeror, or an officer or employee (*) of an offeror; or, b) an employee of NIDA;

2. A current or former (within last two years) employer-employee relationship between yourself (or a member of your immediate family) and a) an individual offeror or an officer or employee of an offeror (or a member of his/her immediate family); or, b) an employee of NIDA (or a member of his/her immediate family);

3. A financial relationship or interest, including prospective employment between yourself (or a member of your family or other persons with whom you have a close personal relationship, and a) an offeror; or, b) an employee of NIDA;

4. A close professional or personal relationship between yourself and a) an individual offeror, or an officer or employee of an offeror; or, b) an employee of NIDA;

5. Any other circumstances that could appear to provide the potential for favoritism or loss of objectivity.

If you checked the "am" line above certifying that you are aware of any of these special relationships, describe each to the best of your knowledge (on the reverse side), including the number of the relevant project, the name(s) and titles(s) of individuals involved, organizational affiliation(s), and the nature of the special relationship. **Contact your NIDA Review Manager at once (301) 443-1644 to discuss a perceived or potential conflict of interest, and whether you should be excused as a concept reviewer.**

_____   _____
Signature   Date

_____
Please Print/Type Name

The phrase "officer or employee" is intended to cover only those individuals in organizational divisions, sub-divisions, and offices responsible for or directly involved in either the preparation of the specific concept and/or the work to result from acceptance of the concept, plus the general executive officers of the divisions, sub-divisions, and offices.

FIG. 15.8. Conflict of interest statement prepared by the National Institute of Drug Abuse for reviewers of concept proposals.

about conflicts of interest. Figure 15.8 is a sample of one such form.

Physician Referral to Other Professionals

Many physicians benefit financially when they recommend that a patient have specific tests (e.g., X-rays, electrocardiograms, sonograms) or obtain specific services (e.g., dietary counseling, psychological counseling). In some cases patients are aware of this fact, but in most cases they are not informed that the physician benefits financially from the referral or the test conducted. In an era of defensive medicine there is enormous pressure on health professionals not to overlook tests that might provide important results, even though the likelihood of that happening is low. The uncertainty of the need for many tests and conflict of interest (i.e., a referral fee or profit from the use of specific equipment) may influence whether a recommendation is made. How strongly a physician promotes a specific location or facility as the site where a patient should have a test performed can lead to suspicions of conflict of interest. The legal aspects of these and other referrals are discussed by Rodwin (1989).

The Council on Ethical and Judicial Affairs of the American Medical Association has recently (1992) reviewed physician ownership of medical facilities in relation to conflict of interest and proposed several recommendations.

Judging Work of a Friend, Relative, or Colleague

A conflict of interest exists when a professional is asked to judge a grant, publication, or other work of a friend, relative, or colleague. Such a review may be acceptable and even desirable in very informal settings, particularly if it is done in an open manner, and both parties are aware of what is requested. In most situations, however, it is unacceptable and many organizations have attempted to prevent such practices through regulations and rules. It is clear, for example, that judging a friend's work as the basis of offering tenure raises an unacceptable conflict of interest. The peer review system is used to avoid such problems. Nonetheless, the peer review system has numerous problems. For example, Cantekin et al. (1990) discuss the difficulties of having dissenting views on a paper presented to peer reviewers.

Informing Prospective Patients for a Clinical Trial About the Investigator's Financial Involvement in the Trial

Investigators who benefit financially from patients who enroll in a clinical trial have a clear conflict of interest when they speak with prospective enrollees. It is extremely rare for prospective patients who are learning about a clinical trial to be informed about the investigator's personal financial involvement in the trial. This involvement is often substantial in sponsored trials, particularly if the investigator rather than the department receives the money. Personal financial involvement may also be substantial if the investigator owns stock in a small company whose product he or she is testing. Shimm and Spece (1991) discuss this issue and propose that the informed consent should contain this type of information.

If patients are recruited to an investigator's own trial although they do not meet all the entry criteria, the money received for the patients' enrollment creates a conflict of interest. In a nonsponsored trial, an investigator's enrollment of a patient who should be disqualified, but is enrolled because of haste to complete the trial also creates a similar conflict of interest.

RESPONSES TO CONFLICT OF INTEREST ISSUES BY GOVERNMENT AND THE INDUSTRY

The United States Congress has reacted to the numerous conflict-of-interest issues in medical sciences by holding hearings on the topic (Human Resources and Intergovernmental Relations Subcommittee of the Committee on Government Operations House of Representatives, 1989a,b). Other United States government groups (e.g., National Institutes of Health) have developed guidelines for behavior of their scientists, as have many academic and other institutions. Most of these guidelines focus on prior disclosure of relevant information or the elimination of specific types of financial relationships. Most guidelines also recognize that other influences such as career growth, publicity, and recognition by peers affect a professional's decisions and behavior. Conflict-of-interest guidelines are sometimes created separately from guidelines that are designed to prevent fraud. The latter guidelines focus on the responsibility of scientific managers for (1) auditing the data of their staff, (2) including as authors only those people who have made a major contribution to the work, and (3) requiring that all authors accept responsibility for the accuracy of all the published data.

GOLDEN RULES THAT HELP TO AVOID OR PREVENT CONFLICT OF INTEREST

The following principles are based on the premise that it makes good business sense for a company to avoid conflict of interest.

1. Academic (as well as industry) scientists must not be paid based on the outcome of their experiments. In exceptional cases, a bonus may be given for a specific (or general) accomplishment, but not based on the result of the experiment.

2. Investigators must not be paid based on the outcome of a clinical trial they are conducting. Those who complete a trial ahead of schedule may sometimes be given a bonus.

3. Patients must not be paid based on the outcome of a clinical trial in which they are participating.

4. Data monitoring boards that are established to review ongoing data for a clinical trial should be paid a single fee to review the data regardless of the number of times they meet. If the trial is terminated early, the fee should not be changed. Charges (i.e., reimbursement) for transportation, food, hotels, and other travel expenses are paid separately and are calculated on a per-meeting basis.

5. Clinical trial results will be seriously questioned if it is shown that one or more investigators have a serious conflict of interest. It therefore makes good business sense for the industry not to include in trials investigators who have known conflicts of interest.

6. Designing well-controlled clinical trials and conducting careful monitoring are two of the best ways to ensure honesty and to avoid problems in most clinical trials. The pharmaceutical industry benefits from well-designed and well-conducted clinical trials. The data obtained are more credible and convincing to scientists, physicians, and regulators than are data from less well-designed trials. Ensuring that the investigator does not own a significant amount of stock in the sponsor company, or has no relatives working there, will do little to ensure that the results are reliable if the trial is poorly designed or inadequately monitored. A clinical audit is an important step that may be used to assure various groups that adequate standards are maintained and followed in all aspects of a clinical trial. As part of an audit, scientists/investigators must be questioned about potential conflicts of interest.

Nonetheless, it is insufficient to assume that the scientific or clinical data obtained are acceptable because scientists/investigators have been shown to be free of conflict of interest.

7. Do not have auditors report to the line management of the groups they are auditing. This rule is codified in regulations (in the United States) for auditors in Good Manufacturing Practices and Good Laboratory Practices, and should also be used as a principle for Good Clinical Trials Practice worldwide.

8. Remove the source of a conflict whenever reasonable. For example, an investigator who owns stock in a company whose medicine he or she is evaluating can be asked to sell their stock.

9. Disclose the potential or actual conflict to the people involved in the trial and in its publication, and discuss equitable ways to address it.

Conflicts of interest that influence data submitted to a company will be minimized if the company follows these principles.

16 / Crisis Management

The Types of Crises 167
Managing a Crisis 168
    Form a Team or Task Force to Direct
        Activities................................. 168
    Develop a Focused Approach and Message.... 168
    Keep Target Audiences in Mind While
        Developing and Implementing Plans........ 169
    Identify Company Spokespeople 169
    Consult with External Experts 169
Train Senior Executives in Dealing with the
    Media...................................... 170
Be Proactive and Not Reactive Whenever
    Possible................................... 170
Consider Wider Implications of the Crisis 170
A Proactive Approach to Crisis Management 170
    Steps to Prevent Crises...................... 170
    Developing a Plan to Manage Crises
        Proactively................................ 171

The Arms industry's image improved greatly when they switched their name to the defense industry—perhaps the drug industry would do well to rename itself as the health defense industry. Sir Christopher Booth

Pharmaceutical companies have experienced a wide range of crises in recent years, from product tampering to environmental disasters. Some of these crises have led to decreased sales, loss of market share, regulatory constraints, decreased confidence within the investment community, diminished image of a product, and diminished reputation of the company. In some cases these problems were unavoidable. In others the companies handled the crises well and recovered both commercially and in terms of reputation (e.g., McNeil Consumer Group and the Tylenol tampering). A number of principles and lessons emerged from these experiences, and this chapter discusses some of them.

Other types of crises—such as those that arise when animal or human toxicity is detected for a marketed product or when a patent expires—are not discussed here. Financial problems for a company and the effects of price controls are additional types of crises but also are not discussed in this chapter.

THE TYPES OF CRISES

Two categories of crises are discussed—corporate crises and product crises. Corporate crises include those primarily affecting the company and its ability to manufacture and ship medicines. These may be caused by a strike; a major fire, flood, earthquake, tornado, or other natural disaster; sabotage or other human-instigated disaster; a threat or an attempt at a hostile takeover; and the death of one or more valuable corporate officers (e.g., in an airplane accident).

Product crises include those primarily affecting one or more products, including tampering with a product, recall of a product, major lawsuits, boycott against one or more of the company's products, and quality control problems in which the product is found to be defective in any of many ways. Production crises relating to an inability to manufacture a commercially important product may arise for many reasons (e.g., lack of starting materials and equipment problems).

Both types of crises may be caused by problems either internal to the product (or company) or external to the product (or company). Tables 16.1 and 16.2 illustrate these distinctions, and examples of product crises are listed in Table 16.3. Clearly, both types of crises overlap to a significant degree. It is also important to note that, whereas a particular corporate crisis may affect some products more than others, all product crises affect the company.

The occurrence of a crisis may or may not come as a surprise to a company. Some crises brew for a period of time before they occur (e.g., problems with certain manufacturing equipment, threatened boycotts), whereas others occur without warning (e.g., tornado, sabotage, tampering). A company often feels a partial loss of control when a sudden crisis occurs and may lack enough information, initially, to deal adequately with many crises.

TABLE 16.1. *Selected product crises classified by cause*

A. Cause of the crisis is *internal* to the product or to the company
  1. Toxicity in animals
  2. Toxicity in humans
  3. Patent expiration
  4. Production problems
B. Cause of the crisis is *external* to the product or to the company
  1. Tampering by outsiders
  2. Regulatory constraints or actions
  3. Recall of product
  4. Major lawsuits
  5. Boycott or demonstration

MANAGING A CRISIS

Described below are a series of procedures for dealing with a crisis effectively. Because crises vary greatly in characteristics, intensity, and importance, the approaches taken to address crises vary greatly as well. The most important principles are to (1) make an effort to identify potential crises before they occur, (2) take steps to prevent crises for which effective countermeasures exist, and (3) establish procedures to deal with crises before they occur.

Form a Team or Task Force to Direct Activities

At the first report of an actual crisis, impending crisis, or possible crisis, the most senior manager (i.e., usually the chief executive officer) should be informed. This person must decide whether to ask an already existing task force to deal with the crisis (assuming one exists), to appoint a group *de novo,* or to follow another course (e.g., wait for further developments). Even if the decision is to wait for further developments, this senior manager should initiate the establishment of procedures to deal with a worst-case scenario. The most unfortunate scenario is waiting until the "tidal wave" breaks and then having insufficient time to develop a strategy to diffuse

TABLE 16.2. *Selected corporate crises classified by cause*

A. Cause of the crisis is *internal* to the company, its physical plant, and its employees
  1. Financial problems
  2. Strike
  3. Fire
  4. Sabotage
  5. Death of important employees
  6. Production problems
B. Cause of the crisis is *external* to the company, its physical plant, and its employees
  1. Natural disaster (e.g., flood, earthquake)
  2. Price controls
  3. Threatened takeover
  4. Boycott/demonstration

TABLE 16.3. *Specific examples of product crises*

1. Data from clinical studies are extremely unfavorable to a product (e.g., severe adverse reactions are reported).
2. The benefit-to-risk ratio of a product falls because a new competitive product is introduced that is safer, is more effective, or provides improved benefits in other areas (e.g., packaging that is more convenient to use, fewer doses per day).
3. Product tampering of capsules (or other dosage forms) leads to poisonings and possibly patient deaths.
4. Allegations of severe problems caused by a product are made by consumer groups.
5. Major legal suits are initiated against the product and receive media attention.
6. Highly negative reports about a product appear in the media.
7. A regulatory authority asks for a black box warning or some other highly negative change to be placed in the labeling.
8. Another government group strongly criticizes the medicine.
9. The product is unable to meet production specifications.
10. A major recall is initiated by a regulatory authority.
11. Toxicology studies report findings of carcinogenicity or another severe toxicity in animals.
12. The product is starting to be abused by those in the drug culture.
13. Starting materials to manufacture the product are unavailable at all suppliers.
14. Equipment to manufacture the product breaks down.

the crisis. To use an analogy from battle strategy, we can say that plans should be mapped and relevant people should be trained, told to report to their battle stations, and placed on alert. If the appropriate troops have already been trained and procedures established, then the warning sound of alert should be rung at this time.

The crisis management task force should include senior managers in legal, marketing, regulatory, production, medical, public communications, and other relevant areas (e.g., administration). One manager should be appointed as leader of the group. If the crisis is severe, then this individual should delegate his or her normal duties for a period of time and assume full-time charge of the task force. It is important that this task force be a decision-making body that is not required to refer its recommendations to another group for ratification. That approach would hamper the ability to move expeditiously when needed. In cases when a "minor" crisis is being handled and speed is not as urgent, it is quite reasonable for the task force to ask for review of its recommendations.

Develop a Focused Approach and Message

Most outside groups will view negatively the company that appears to be vacillating or flip-flopping on important issues relating to the crisis (e.g., should the product be withdrawn from the market?). The media will rise to the scent as sharks are attracted by blood and will castigate the company for indecision and poor management. The task force should determine the company's position, the company's course of action, and the steps to take to achieve the company's goals. The group should prepare or supervise the preparation of necessary documents to communicate with the press (a press release); the company's workers (a "dear employee" letter); practicing physicians (a "dear doctor" letter); pharmacists (a "dear pharmacist" letter), and editors of medical newspapers, newsletters, and journals (a "dear editor" letter). For this to be done most expeditiously, a current mailing list of relevant individuals and groups must be maintained or readily obtainable. This approach overlaps with the next step.

Keep Target Audiences in Mind While Developing and Implementing Plans

Each of the external groups that the company should communicate with directly should be identified in advance. Generally, for each type of crisis it will be relevant to contact only a few of these groups (see Table 16.4). For example, a fire that destroys a part of a production facility would not be of great interest to wholesalers, distributors, pharmacists, or practicing physicians if the company's production was not affected, but

TABLE 16.4. *External groups that are involved or interested in many pharmaceutical company crises*

1. Regulatory authorities who are concerned with public health implications
2. Dispensing pharmacists in hospitals or retail stores who are concerned with various implications
3. Congressional legislators who may question whether legislation is required
4. Newspaper reporters and newscasters who are interested in immediate news
5. Journal and newsletter editors who are interested in long-term news
6. Unions who represent employees or other groups that interact with a company
7. Suppliers of various items to a company who are concerned about orders
8. Local community leaders who are concerned about employment, safety, and image issues
9. Medical practitioners who use the product(s) affected
10. Academic scientists who are conducting preclinical or clinical research on the product or are interacting in other ways with the company
11. Inventors who want to design something to prevent future problems
12. Financial investors who are considering investing in a company
13. Financial analysts and stockbrokers who assess the damage and financial implications
14. Consultants who are specialists in crisis management
15. Contractors who are actively studying (or are hoping to study) the product (e.g., conducting marketing research)

this would be of interest to regulatory authorities. A fire, flood, or tornado might require that more materials be ordered from suppliers, or it might require that production be switched to another facility. An internal company crisis that affected its ability to supply distributors adequately with life-saving medicines could be a major one, and the crisis would generally involve or influence the financial community, regulatory authorities, and other companies.

In addition, a company must be assiduous in communicating appropriately with its own staff. Employees' interest in all crises is strong, and the company must be totally honest in everything that it tells them. The company may, however, not be able to release all of the details about a crisis or the company's plans to address it while those plans are being developed or implemented. Internal staff includes the company's sales force.

Identify Company Spokespeople

One or more people on the company's staff should be appointed to represent the company with outside groups. For major tampering cases, this person has generally been the chief executive officer. The person chosen should not have an issue of credibility with the press and public. This problem developed after the Exxon Valdez spilled oil off Alaska's coast, partly because Exxon appointed one of their vice presidents instead of the president or chairman of the board to deal with the issue. Because the person chosen as a spokesperson personifies the company to external groups, his or her appearance, demeanor, style, and tone of voice are all important from the company's perspective. This individual must be familiar and comfortable interacting with the media.

If the chief executive officer interacts with the press, one or more additional company officers also should be present to support him or her with information and to answer questions, if necessary. Various other audiences external to the company (e.g., regulatory authorities) are likely to interact with other company representatives.

Consult with External Experts

Companies often utilize the services of external experts to discuss options and to obtain advice. In some cases these people may act as spokespeople for the company, at least with certain audiences. These experts must be credible with the audiences that they interact with and must also be seen as independent of the company in rendering opinions.

Prior to major press briefings or to television appearances, it may be useful to have a rehearsal for all relevant people. This provides an opportunity to polish each presentation and to identify weak areas that should be bolstered. Although chief executive officers and external experts are not actors, they are usually scrutinized on television as if they are. This emphasizes the importance of developing a polished presentation that is both understandable and convincing to the audience. Polish that seems too smooth, unrealistic, or dishonest will be counterproductive to the firm; the most appropriate balance must be sought. The following section presents a method for proactively addressing this issue.

Train Senior Executives in Dealing with the Media

Selected senior executives should undergo training with an experienced media expert (e.g., a current or former newscaster who understands the techniques of the media) to learn how to give an interview and also how not to give an interview. Other aspects of the training should include information on (1) appropriate dress, (2) how to speak at the proper cadence and in the right tone, (3) how to formulate responses to questions, (4) how to hold one's body and hands, (5) how much to move, and so forth. All of these (and other) mannerisms are essential for executives to master if the few words usually aired on television are to be believed by the viewers. A sincere and honest chief executive may not be believed if constantly fidgeting and may not be heard if appearing extremely stiff or moving his or her eyes frequently.

It is important to present positive statements about the company and its products regardless of the question asked. Although a small number of television viewers may feel that a question is inadequately addressed, most people will be impressed about the positive contributions of the company. Denying false accusations requires the use of some negative terms and is usually less productive than focusing on positive statements (e.g., we are developing new medicines for babies as well as older patients).

Be Proactive and Not Reactive Whenever Possible

A company that is perceived as merely reacting to an unfolding crisis (e.g., a series of tamperings occurring over time) will be viewed negatively as weak and uncaring. It is important that the company be perceived as being open and having nothing to hide and as trying to do everything possible to resolve the issue appropriately. To do this a company should issue information bulletins to the public that clearly show a proactive "take charge" approach and establish credibility for the company.

This effort is more likely to be successful if the company staff understand what the media they interact with are trying to achieve. The media want to present a good story that is interesting to their audience; this often involves a search for cause or blame of a crisis. As a result,

the media want to know what a company has learned about the cause(s) and effects of a crisis and what they are going to do. Trying to enlist media representatives as allies in the investigation and resolution of the crisis is an important goal (though one that is not always possible to achieve).

Consider Wider Implications of the Crisis

The identity of the people and groups immediately affected by the crisis is generally obvious. Those people and groups who are more indirectly affected or who will be directly affected at a later time may be identified or guessed after some discussion (Fig. 16.1). A final, less obvious group is the people/groups who may be indirectly affected at a later time; these also should be identified. This information will enable appropriate steps to be taken in regard to all three categories of people and groups.

A few questions will help identify any wider implications of the crisis.

1. How will all groups directly or indirectly influenced by the crisis be affected in turn? Who in turn will be influenced by those groups, and how will they be influenced?

2. What are the international implications of the crisis for the company, other regulatory agencies, and other groups external to the company?

3. How will the company's partners in various types of alliances (e.g., licensing agreements, joint ventures, comarketing) be affected, both nationally and internationally?

4. Which groups or people are likely to be influenced by and react to the media reports, and how are they likely to react?

A PROACTIVE APPROACH TO CRISIS MANAGEMENT

Steps to Prevent Crises

Two broad approaches should be considered by a company that wishes to take proactive steps to prevent crises and to deal effectively with those that occur. The first approach is to develop a strategy that could be implemented any time a crisis develops. The procedures could be implemented for a limited time or to a limited degree, depending on the nature of the crisis. Although a fire or tornado would elicit a different response than would sabotage and those would each elicit a different response than would product tampering, many of the general procedures to implement and the people who would be involved are the same. The procedures that a company should have in place were discussed earlier.

FIG. 16.1. The ripple effect of a crisis on groups and individuals affected differently over time.

These primarily involve identifying people to place on a task force, identifying their roles, and having them meet a few times to prepare themselves mentally to initiate action as soon as an alarm sounds. A single annual meeting to review relevant topics could be viewed as a "fire drill" to ensure their preparedness and to train any new members assigned to the group.

The second approach is to determine specific potential crises and to develop detailed plans for approaching each one of them. One crisis eventually faced by all companies is the patent expiration of one or more major medicines that the company sells. Another crisis that will affect almost all companies is the threat of price controls in the United States. A proactive approach to this latter issue is discussed in Chapter 58.

Steps to prevent the occurrence of product crises involve the development, approval, and initiation of specific plans. Commonly occurring product crises involve serious problems with the production of an important medicine. If the crisis is expected to last for only a short time (e.g., new equipment or raw materials should arrive), then moving stocks (i.e., inventories) from one place to another until production is renewed may be sufficient. If longer term (e.g., three or more months) disruption of a medicine's production is likely to occur, then an alternate production site should be determined

in advance. This could be within the company's overall organization, at a contract facility, or at another company. Formal arrangements for any of these facilities to take over the production of a medicine must be made in advance and appropriate submissions approved by regulatory authorities. Plans to deal with production or other product crises (e.g., tampering, recall, sabotage) should also be made.

Developing a Plan to Manage Crises Proactively

A proactive plan to prepare for potential crises should consider the following five elements, as well as other relevant issues pertinent to the specific crisis.

Education

A plan to educate all relevant groups should be developed. While the education may primarily be internal to the company, individuals and groups in government and academia that require education should also be identified. The nature and type of education and preparation will vary for each type of crisis, as well as for the groups involved.

Conducting Studies

Studies that will obtain data on a medicine's safety or efficacy or that survey people's views and behavior should be implemented. In this way a company gains information on a medicine's metabolism, toxicology, and effects in large patient populations or in specific populations (e.g., pregnant women).

Monitoring Activities

A systematic plan should be developed to monitor a product's performance in the marketplace. Companies also should monitor other activities that would help identify potential crises or that would help the company deal with such a crisis should it arise. It is possible that the task force could delegate this activity to the company's project team or product team currently in charge of the medicine.

Develop Personal Relationships

Relationships should be forged and maintained by company managers with all appropriate groups, includ-ing media, disease-oriented societies, legislators, regulators, the medical community, academicians, scientists, and so forth. It may be relevant to identify specific groups that should be enlisted as allies and to develop plans of how to elicit their cooperation. This is particularly relevant if the company wishes to concern itself with reacting to issues of price control.

Create an International Strategy

Few crises are totally localized to a single country, particularly because the large majority of the world's 50 largest pharmaceutical companies are multinational. For instance, a plant in one country usually affects sales and other activities in many other countries. The proactive plan should be international in scope.

No company can be assured of preventing all problems and that it will not face a crisis; in fact, the opposite is more often correct. But a company should be prepared when a crisis occurs. To meet a crisis appropriately, a company should have considered the preventive actions described above. These procedures should help a company address any crisis with appropriate methods and approaches and minimize the financial and reputation damage incurred.

17 / Differences Between Pharmaceutical Companies

Institutional Culture **173**
   Background 173
   Company Culture 174
Institutional Management **174**
Attitudes and Approaches Toward Medicine
   Discovery and Development **174**
   Factors Influencing Attitudes Toward
     Medicine Development................... 174
   Strengths and Weaknesses of a Company in
     Different Therapeutic Areas 175
   Approaches to Medicine Discovery and
     Development at Various Companies........ 177
   Internal Company Hype and the "Emperor's
     New Clothes" Syndrome 179
   Reasons for Internal Company Hype......... 180
   The Importance of Minimizing Internal
     Company Hype 180

Holding Open and Honest Discussions of
   Issues on New Medicines 180
The "Not Invented Here" Syndrome.......... 181
Philosophical Issues That Vary Between
   Companies **181**
Studying Medicines That Will Never Be
   Marketed 181
Studying Multiple Related Compounds in
   Humans 181
Determining How High a Dose Should Be
   Evaluated in Phase I Studies............... 182
Fat Versus Lean Development Programs...... 182
Problem Situations and Danger Signs 183
Achieving High Standards 185

The best person to decide what research work shall be done is the man who is doing the research, and the next best person is the head of the department, who knows all about the subject and the work; after that you leave the field of the best people and start on increasingly worse groups, the first of these being the research director, who is probably wrong more than half the time; then a committee, which is wrong most of the time; and, finally a committee of vice-presidents, which is wrong all the time. C.E.K. Mees. Former head of research at Eastman Kodak Co. Quoted by Pelz and Andrews (1976, p. 322).

My way of doing business was never entirely scientific, but I think the emotional, dramatic kind of manager can hold his own with a scientific manager. Thomas Watson, Jr., former chief executive of IBM. From *Fortune* (August 31, 1987).

INSTITUTIONAL CULTURE

Background

Within any company there are many philosophical and other differences concerning the methods that are the most efficient, most ethical, most practical, and most cost-effective for developing medicines. It is a happy but unusual occasion when there is total agreement among all managers about how to develop even a single medicine.

This issue becomes more complex when a company is simultaneously developing a particular medicine in two or more countries. This is especially relevant if the company is not run as a centralized "dictatorship," and each company site running a development program for the medicine has a voice in the decision-making process. There are a number of issues that are generally addressed differently in various countries, and these differences often place strains on any unified development plan. Differences within a company are usually a reflection of the types of differences that also exist between companies.

Although many of these differences are discussed throughout the book, some overall areas where differences exist are reviewed in this chapter.

Company Culture

The culture of a pharmaceutical company influences the approaches used in medicine development. A highly conservative approach in medicine development is where each major question that could be raised by a regulatory agency has been studied and discussed. A less conservative approach could be to conduct a minimal number of studies and to assemble a lean New Drug Application (NDA) in terms of quantity of data. Proponents of the lean approach hope that various potential issues about the medicine are not raised and that the quantity of data submitted will be sufficient to obtain regulatory approval. Other aspects of the impact of a company's culture on medicine development relate to whether a company is prone to challenge Food and Drug Administration (FDA) requests for additional data or whether the company accepts FDA requests without comments. Some companies attempt to achieve a close "alliance" with the FDA on a medicine's development from the time the initial plan is formulated through each stage of its development.

Culture may be viewed on at least three separate levels. The *first level is the overall company level,* where one may focus on aspects that distinguish each company. These include the internal company environments, traditions, values, image, and reputation, plus the personalities and style of the most senior leaders. Cultures might differ in the relative roles of marketing and research and development in major decisions made about identifying therapeutic areas to research and specific medicines to develop and prioritize. Either marketing or research and development might have a major role in establishing company goals and objectives.

The *second level is that of the entire function* (e.g., research and development, marketing, or production). This level of culture depends on the same aspects as the corporate level plus the nature of the present staff and the most senior manager or leader and the characteristics of the specific function. The *third level relates to the specific people with whom each worker directly interacts in his or her daily activities.* This level of culture depends on all of the above-noted factors plus the specific attributes and environment of the person or group involved and those with whom they interact.

Knowledge of a company's culture is essential. It allows people to know (1) who to go to when you want things done, (2) where the real power lies, (3) who to avoid, and (4) how to build a consensus in achieving one's objectives. It allows people to function more effectively in their various roles.

INSTITUTIONAL MANAGEMENT

Major differences between pharmaceutical companies exist at all levels and in all disciplines in terms of company management. The subject areas in which significant differences between companies occur are discussed in almost every chapter of this book, particularly those focusing on management styles, concepts, golden rules, and keys for success. No further elucidation is deemed necessary here, except to summarize a few differences in management philosophy (Table 17.1) and a few differences in general development philosophy (Table 17.2).

ATTITUDES AND APPROACHES TOWARD MEDICINE DISCOVERY AND DEVELOPMENT

Factors Influencing Attitudes Toward Medicine Development

Widely differing attitudes toward medicine development exist both within and between companies. One scale along which attitudes vary is from optimistic, positive, and enthusiastic at one end of the spectrum to pessimistic, negative, and discouraged at the opposite pole. Factors that affect attitudes of managers and employees include the (1) number of medically and commercially exciting medicines in the development pipeline, (2) opportunities for career advancement and enhancement, (3) working conditions, (4) attitudes of superiors, (5) attitudes of top management, (6) financial health of the company, (7) personalities of the people involved, and (8) overall trends of the company's performance.

The style that is generally used to develop medicines differs between different companies. The choice of a company's style is usually a reflection of the personality of the most senior manager or group of managers. Some may emphasize pharmacokinetic studies or mechanism of action studies or have a desire to explore many different indications for each medicine. Other aspects of style relate to the degree of caution or risk usually taken. Dif-

TABLE 17.1. *Selected differences in management philosophy between companies or between individuals within companies*

1. The company may be driven by research and development or by marketing.
2. Managers may use a dictatorial style or a consensus style.
3. Fairly rigid or loose standard operating procedures may be present.
4. Fixed hurdle rates (i.e., forecasted sales above a magic number) may be used as part of the decision process to develop a new medicine.
5. Staff may follow rigid rules and checklists assiduously, or they may be encouraged to think and act creatively and not to accept requests they believe are wrong.

TABLE 17.2. *Selected differences in medicine development philosophy between companies or between individuals within companies*

1. Whether volunteers should be dosed to toxicity in Phase I clinical trials
2. Whether efficacy data should be carefully sought in Phase I clinical trials
3. Whether fat or lean development plans should be created
4. Whether a large amount of clinical data should be collected in each trial
5. Whether staff are allowed to bring up major surprises at large meetings or must contact relevant people ahead of time
6. Whether staff are entitled to agree with a request for an action at a meeting and then not follow through
7. Whether metabolism studies in humans should be done extremely early or much later in a medicine's development

ferences may exist in different businesses or divisions of a company because of differences between the managers that direct each. In large companies the chief executive officer needs a strong personality to influence the entire company. This may be accomplished in many different ways from group meetings with hoopla to quiet sessions with one or a few individuals.

Strengths and Weaknesses of a Company in Different Therapeutic Areas

Many approaches to developing medicines within a company depend on how the company perceives its own strengths and weaknesses. Marked differences between companies are often based on the relative strengths in different therapeutic areas and whether the therapeutic areas represent growing, mature, or dying areas for future medicine development (Fig. 17.1). A method to illustrate the susceptibility of companies to competition from generic substitution is shown in Fig. 17.2 and the susceptibility of a single company over a period of years is shown in Fig. 17.3. In Fig. 17.2 each company's position is indicated by a single point on a grid of estimated future sales of new products over an arbitrarily chosen number of years versus estimated future sales losses of current products over the same period because of competition from generic medicines.

There are proponents in each company who strongly espouse the view of building on the company's strengths. A great deal of common sense underlies this proposal, and this approach is often essential for companies to follow if they wish to remain viable. Nonetheless, there is a danger that if a company concentrates all of its efforts and resources on building its strengths, the company may become too narrow in its focus. This in turn could make it more vulnerable to competitive forces. Building up highly selected areas of weakness is also important if those areas have been targeted as future areas of strength. This pendulum must be continually balanced because a company that becomes too diversified also becomes vulnerable to its competitors. The most appropriate balance between building on strengths versus developing weaknesses changes over the years and must be continually reassessed.

CHARACTERIZING A COMPANY'S MARKETING POSITION

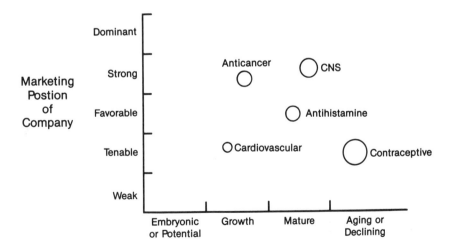

FIG. 17.1. Characterizing the marketing position of a specific company. The size of the *circle* is proportional to the relative size of sales. *CNS*, central nervous system.

SUSCEPTIBILITY OF MULTIPLE DRUG COMPANIES TO GENERIC SUBSTITUTION

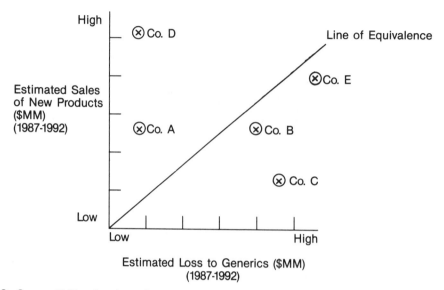

FIG. 17.2. Susceptibility of various pharmaceutical companies to generic substitution. This factor varies for different companies at a specific point in time. Those below the line are more susceptible than those above the line.

SUSCEPTIBILITY OF A SINGLE DRUG COMPANY TO GENERIC SUBSTITUTION

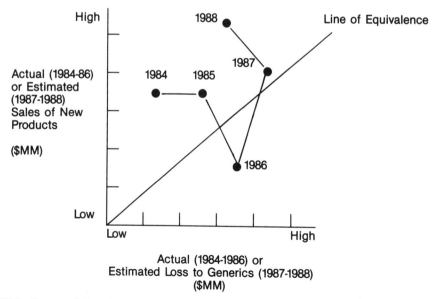

FIG. 17.3. Susceptibility of a particular company to generic substitution over a period of years.

Approaches to Medicine Discovery and Development at Various Companies

Using Visual Models to Develop an Overall Concept of Medicine Development

If several companies each discovered or licensed the same medicine, they would each develop it in a somewhat different manner. The basic approaches to development would differ as to the number of indications to pursue, whether to conduct them simultaneously or sequentially, how to prioritize each of them, and how much resource to assign to each. The same would be true for determining the number of dosage forms and routes of administration to pursue and whether to pursue them simultaneously or sequentially. Differences between companies might emanate from sources within research and development, marketing, or both groups.

It is desirable for a company to choose an overall concept for a medicine's development before development is actually initiated. One method to do this is to discuss a medicine's development in terms of a visual model. This would enable each manager to have the same mental image of how the medicine's strategy will be applied to its development. Figure 17.4 illustrates general types of approaches that may be followed to develop a new medicine. The width of each figure is proportional to the total number of dosage forms, indications, routes of administration, and dosage regimens. These figures may serve as a frame of reference when planning the development of a new medicine and are described in more detail in Chapter 115 of *Guide to Clinical Trials* (Spilker, 1991). Most pharmaceutical companies focus on reviewing and refining the plan that is proposed for a medicine's development. This is appropriate to consider *after* a general concept is adopted.

Allocation of Resources

In terms of how each specific indication of a medicine would be developed, the greatest difference between companies would probably be based on the amount of re-

VISUAL MODELS OF MEDICINE DEVELOPMENT PLANS

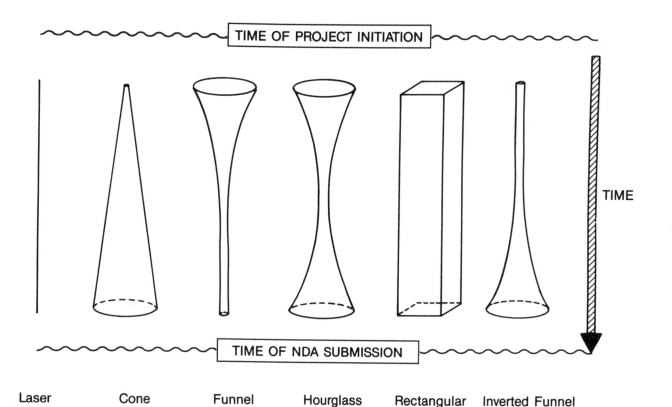

FIG. 17.4. Visual models of medicine development illustrating different types of plans or approaches followed. The width of each figure equals the total number of dosage forms, indications, routes of administration, and dosage regimens. *NDA,* New Drug Application. From Spilker (1991) with permission of Raven Press.

sources applied. Some companies have adopted the strategy of applying many resources to a few medicine development projects; in recent years, however, more companies have tended to apply fewer resources to more projects. At least one large company attempts to fully resource all projects in their portfolio. The general procedures used to plan, monitor, and manage the development process have become rather standardized and are generally similar among companies. Nonetheless, some companies are more efficient than others in how well they conduct their development activities.

Another consideration concerning the allocation of resources relates to the amount of risk that a company is willing to take. High-risk projects usually take more time and require more resources to be expended than do low-risk projects, before a decision point is reached that a medicine has an acceptable profile and will be marketed.

Setting and Using Target Dates

Attitudes toward target dates for completion of defined medicine development activities are generally viewed similarly in production plants at most companies where schedules are adhered to as closely as possible. The same approach occurs in most technical development laboratories. Attitudes about target dates, however, differ at various companies in research, medical, or marketing departments. At some companies, dates are used in some of these departments as a means of establishing work schedules and assigning responsibilities. At other companies, dates are considered as convenient targets and as a guide to help plan work. Dates may be established for completing project activities using knowledge of other conflicting project work going on or to be conducted in the same department. Alternatively, dates may be set independently of any other project work. It makes most sense to use the former method (i.e., consider other projects) as the other approach of setting dates independently represents an ideal case and will make dates of little practical use. A few companies place so much stress on achieving target dates that the quality of work produced or reports written is often compromised. There are many advantages to gain by allowing some slippage in dates if a better output from the responsible department is attained. Figure 17.5 illustrates three types of target dates that may be established for achieving a milestone, and Table 17.3 lists the various types of milestones that are used in medicine development.

Business Sources of New Medicines

Companies place a different emphasis on various methods used to obtain new medicines. Companies may emphasize any combination of proactive in-house medicine research programs, licensing, purchase of products, or joint ventures. These topics are dealt with below and also in more detail in various other chapters. Most companies sell medicines that come from multiple types of business sources. These sources include the following.

1. *Internal research and development*—This may be entirely conducted at a single pharmaceutical company based in one location. When a company is able to develop a full and adequate portfolio of investigational and marketed medicines from their own research, less need and emphasis is placed on points 2 to 4.

Internal research and development may be conducted at two or more independently functioning sites of a single pharmaceutical company. Many possibilities exist of how two sites work together, even within the same company. For example, a medicine may have been discovered at one site and developed at the other, the medicine may have been synthesized at one site and originally tested at the other, or there may be joint development. Chapter 60 (International Development) discusses global medicine development in more detail.

2. *Licensing*—Medicines may be licensed-in at any stage of development. This ranges from licensing a general concept or idea for a new medicine where specific molecules may not have been designed to licensing a compound that is in an early, middle, or late preclinical stage. A medicine could be licensed that is in any stage of clinical investigation or have achieved regulatory approval and be marketed in one or more countries (see Chapter 48, Licensing Issues).

Companies may adopt a reactive or proactive stance to licensing. In the former mode, the company responds to offers made from external sources and, in the latter case, they actively seek to license medicines into the company.

3. *Purchase*—The ownership of marketed or investigational medicines may be bought and sold. This is common for over-the-counter (OTC) nonprescription medicines as well as for prescription medicines.

4. *Joint venture*—Two or more companies may jointly develop medicines that either has discovered. They may also establish a third company or identify an existing third company, which is then asked to develop a medicine. The joint venture mechanism is especially useful when the companies each bring something unique to the agreement. This should lead to a complementary relationship in terms of expertise, capital, resources, patents, and/or ideas. This mechanism allows a very large and a very small company to participate on an equal, or nearly equal, basis in developing and marketing a medicine (see Chapter 5, Mergers, Joint Ventures, and Alliances). Certain medicines may be developed by a joint venture that could not otherwise be developed by the separate partners.

Marketed medicines may come from the same company, other companies, private entrepreneurs, academi-

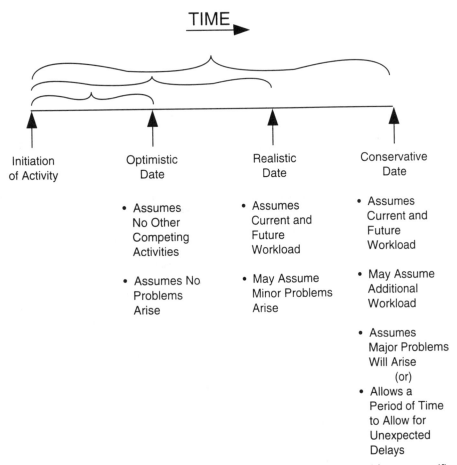

FIG. 17.5. Illustration of the three types of target dates that may be established for any specific activity or milestone. A number of caveats are indicated below each type.

TABLE 17.3. *Types of important project milestones*

1. Scientific milestones relating to demonstrating specific product characteristics
2. Legal and patent milestones relating to specific events (e.g., contract signed, patent approved)
3. Regulatory milestones (e.g., IND submitted, NDA approved)[a]
4. Marketing milestones (e.g., product launched, sales forecast achieved)
5. Medical milestones (e.g., investigator's brochure completed, Phase I completed, Phase III initiated)
6. Licensing milestones (e.g., expiration of option, time for each payment)
7. Production milestones (e.g., equipment ordered, equipment and processes validated)
8. Operational milestones not described above (e.g., project formed)

[a] IND, Investigational New Drug Application; NDA, New Drug Application.

cians, government laboratories, or other sources. Nonetheless, numerous studies show that approximately 90% of medicines come from the pharmaceutical industry. This topic is reviewed by Kahn et al. (1982; see p. 109, 110).

Internal Company Hype and the "Emperor's New Clothes" Syndrome

One of the greatest dangers faced by all pharmaceutical companies is that the hype of new investigational medicines inside a company will affect decisions made about its development so that nonobjective and incorrect decisions are made. A description of hype includes perceiving a medicine in a nonobjective way and believing, or at least expressing, unrealistic expectations for the speed of a medicine's regulatory approval and the magnitude of its commercial success. On the other hand, a medicine can rarely be described by a single image that is totally objective and universal. This is because a medicine's characteristics are complex and may be viewed from many perspectives. Even though an objective view of a medicine's profile and expectations should be sought, there is obvious value to a company when its employees are enthusiastic about all medicines currently being investigated.

Individuals who present data about a medicine to senior managers often promote and extol the medicine far more than can be supported by current data and results. This may lead those managers to repeat the praises and high expectations of the medicine to others, even though some may have serious unexpressed doubts about the medicine's qualities. This is what is referred to as the "Emperor's New Clothes" Syndrome. This is the story where the emperor is sold a set of clothes that do not exist. He puts on the imaginary garments and the emperor's closest advisors, staff, and townspeople are afraid to tell him the truth. Only a small boy has the courage to express it.

Reasons for Internal Company Hype

A common reason for hype about a new medicine is because one or more individuals in a central position relative to a medicine (e.g., the project leader) are ambitious and desire additional recognition or power within their company. These individuals may also believe that senior managers want to hear only good news. These reasons lead them to "accentuate the positive and de-emphasize the negative." The desired outcome is to make their medicine (and indirectly, themselves) the center of attention. They continually request more resources and personnel to develop the medicine. They attempt to investigate as many additional indications, dosage forms, routes of administration, and dosing regimens as possible. Their recommendations may appear to be sound and clearly planned. The most questionable aspects of their behavior often are inappropriate acceleration and expansion of plans, plus failure to present potential (and actual) drawbacks of the medicine. Most competent managers in reviewing these recommendations can determine when wrong answers are given, but it takes a creative manager to identify when the wrong questions are being asked.

Another reason for internal hype is that some senior managers believe strongly in the value of their own pet project and discourage criticism of its efficacy or safety profile. They generate an inflated profile of their project to keep resources allocated to it at a high level and to prevent (or at least minimize) either criticism or a careful appraisal of the project's true value. Whatever the reason for internal company hype, it is an indication of prob-

lems within a company. This problem reflects (at least in part) an inability of senior managers to be honest and open about the quality of their projects.

The Importance of Minimizing Internal Company Hype

It is rarely in a company's interest for individuals to accept positive statements about a medicine without asking questions, requesting data, and, when relevant, expressing doubts. If people are not willing to do this, and usually few are, a company may unnecessarily spend a lot of money and resources. The ensuing major discouragement and disappointment might have been avoided. Resources expended could have been better spent on other medicines and projects. If scientists and clinicians believe that management is pushing a dead horse around the track, then this view may also lead to serious problems in employee morale and to decreased productivity. This in turn can have an even more widespread negative impact on a company.

All companies should strive for an open dialogue on the attributes of a medicine and the best way to develop each medicine, so that all views may be heard and judged. It is sad when no one is willing or feels able to express his or her views. Fear of retribution often inhibits open and appropriate critical comments. In extreme situations a company may delude itself for years. The FDA sometimes has to play the role of the young boy in the "Emperor's New Clothes" who states that the emperor is not wearing any clothes.

Another form of this syndrome of internal hype concerns the true market value of a medicine. Marketing estimates may have been inflated for various reasons, and the eventual sales picture may turn out to be a major disappointment. Alternatively, the marketing estimates may be unrealistic because of assumptions made. Individuals who claim that the emperor is being sold a suit of exaggerated figures are usually brave. The project being touted may be the "pet idea" of a senior manager. The lack of objectivity may be concentrated on the medicine's efficacy, safety, technical problems, manufacturing, market potential, or a combination of these. It is hoped that the types of problems described are rare occurrences, but discussions with many industry professionals convince me that they are relatively common.

Holding Open and Honest Discussions of Issues on New Medicines

Companies should encourage open and continuous discussions of relevant issues on investigational medicines. Most, if not all, senior managers believe that they do this. The issue is whether most middle and lower level managers believe that this is being done. Many individuals may have mixed or even negative feelings as to one or more medicines' value to the company. The question is whether that individual is openly discussing his or her concern. If a medicine has inherent problems it is better to identify them sooner rather than later. On the other hand, encouraging an objective approach does not mean that a company should seek to evaluate various types of *potential* problems or allow a medicine to be tested in nonessential studies where a negative outcome is likely.

When minimally accepted criteria of a medicine's profile or commercial potential cannot be achieved, it is usual to terminate the medicine's development. Some individuals appear to require absolute certainty that criteria cannot be achieved before they are willing to terminate a project, whereas others reach this decision more rapidly. Many dollars, resources, and time may be saved when this decision is reached expeditiously, before every minute point or remote possibility is explored in detail.

Politics (i.e., personal interactions and relationships) have the same role in the pharmaceutical industry as in other industries or settings. The political strength of people depends on their real or perceived power in a company. One way to discuss this topic is in terms of gaining or losing influence. A good book on this subject is *Power! How to Get it, How to Use it* (Korda, 1987).

The "Not Invented Here" Syndrome

The usual abbreviation for the National Institutes of Health is NIH, but NIH is also used for another widely known term, "Not Invented Here." In this context, the NIH syndrome refers to the lack of enthusiasm, commitment, and even activity on a project that did not originally come from the group currently responsible for working on it. For example, an original concept or medicine may be licensed-in from another company, or it may have been originally developed by another branch of the same company. The department or group responsible for performing certain work is saying, in effect, "We do not want any ideas or projects in our department that are not ours." One can recognize this syndrome when referring to new ideas by comments like: "That's not the way we do things here," or "We've tried it once that way and it didn't work," and "Don't let Mr. X know you're working on that approach." When referring to new medicines, various disparaging comments are made or else the project is virtually ignored. It is clear that insecurity and jealousy are two key ingredients that often lead to the NIH syndrome.

Whatever the origin, it is management's responsibility to minimize and eliminate this type of thinking and behavior. If not eradicated it can compromise a group's performance or a medicine's entire development program. This problem is best prevented in advance by fostering a spirit of cooperation between different parts of a company and by stressing advantages gained through co-operation. To do this it is often valuable to invite participation of all professionals associated with a new project at an early stage in decision making to discuss how to create or modify the development plan. This should enhance the commitment of all people to the plans reached.

PHILOSOPHICAL ISSUES THAT VARY BETWEEN COMPANIES

Studying Medicines That Will Never Be Marketed

The attitude with which companies take new medicines into humans for testing differs among companies and often between different locations of the same company. At some companies, there is a clear understanding, usually unwritten and often unstated, that all compounds taken into humans will be pursued as far as possible toward regulatory submission and marketing. In other companies, this attitude may apply only to some medicines, while other compounds are taken to humans on an experimental or research basis. This concept usually means that a medicine will be studied in humans to determine whether it has activity or to answer a specific question. In this experimental situation it is known that the compound tested in humans will never be marketed. If the experimental medicine possesses sufficient efficacy, the company may feel more secure about committing additional resources to synthesize and evaluate related chemicals that would be expected to be more active, more potent, or less toxic or to have other properties that are not considered adequate in the original compound. A few of the reasons why the original compound tested in humans may be inadequate for marketing are that it may (1) not be absorbed orally, (2) have a short duration of action, (3) be too weak, or (4) have toxic metabolites. One reason why this approach rarely works as planned is that evaluating the hypothesis in humans requires so much time and money that it usually makes more sense to devote those resources to preclinical efforts attempting to discover a medicine with the desired characteristics.

Studying Multiple Related Compounds in Humans

One variation on the theme described above is to take several related compounds to the clinic simultaneously. This practice is not as common today as it was 20 or more years ago. When several compounds are studied side by side, a choice as to which specific compound should be pursued further is made after Phase I and/or some Phase II data are collected. Government regulations have increased so dramatically over the last few decades that the time, effort, and cost needed to evaluate compounds in this manner is so great that the approach is no longer feasible or productive in the United States. If costs of developing new compounds through part (or all) of Phase II were less and regulations were less stringent, there is little doubt that many companies would utilize this approach more often. The approach has a major advantage in that similar compounds differing in only one or a few vital respects (e.g., effect on an enzyme of potential significance) could be evaluated and the clinical importance of that aspect evaluated.

Determining How High a Dose Should Be Evaluated in Phase I Studies

Companies vary in how they determine the point at which to stop a Phase I safety trial where the dose is progressively increased. Some conservative companies only evaluate doses that they believe will be studied for efficacy in Phase II trials. Other companies increase dosage to the point at which some patients experience mild to moderate adverse reactions. Although the term *patients* is used throughout this book, it also refers to normal volunteers who enroll in most Phase I trials. If a trial is stopped at the first signs of an adverse reaction, then the maximal dose that patients can tolerate will not be learned. This is because initial adverse reactions observed in a gradual dose escalation study are probably mild and may not even occur at higher doses. Moreover, adverse reactions may have been (1) observed in the most sensitive volunteers or patients, (2) really an artifact or a placebo response, or (3) confounded by other factors that may or may not be understood.

If Phase I trials are continued after mild adverse reactions occur, it is possible that the medicine's higher doses may cause severe adverse reactions. In this situation patients given those doses may be exposed to unnecessary risks, which is both unacceptable and unethical. The balance between prematurely stopping a dose escalation study or unacceptably pushing a dose higher is to establish, prior to initiating the study, the criteria on which dose escalation will be stopped. This usually relates to seeking the dose at which adverse reactions occur that would not be tolerated by patients who are given the medicine during actual treatment. For anticancer medicines this endpoint will differ greatly than for mild analgesics (pain killers), because there are already safe medicines available in the latter case. Of course, all of this preparation may be jettisoned when the first patient has a clinically important problem that lies in the gray zone and a rapid (or even slow) decision must be made about whether to expose other patients to a higher dose or even to continue dosing patients with the medicine.

Phase I Trials in the United Kingdom Versus the United States

There is a striking difference between requirements that must be satisfied prior to studying a new medicine in humans for the first time in the United Kingdom and the United States. At present, a medicine may be studied in the equivalent to Phase I in normal volunteers in the United Kingdom without obtaining regulatory approval or even informing government authorities. In addition, the medicine may be studied without obtaining any approval from or even informing any ethics committee. British pharmaceutical companies obtain permission from an ethics committee, even though they are not currently required to do so in all situations.

In the United States, the FDA's awareness of all trials of investigational medicines in humans is assured through regulations. A sponsor is obligated to submit a large quantity of preclinical and manufacturing data, as well as detailed plans for clinical evaluation, information provided to the investigator, and the curricula vitae (resumes) of all investigators, prior to initiating a trial. Additional details of information presented in an initial regulatory submission are given in *Guide to Clinical Trials* (Spilker, 1991). All trials must also be reviewed by an Ethics Committee (Institutional Review Board) at each site where the study will be conducted.

Most initial Phase I trials in the United States are considered as dose-ranging tolerance studies and adhere to the policy of progressively increasing the dose until moderate adverse reactions are observed. This policy is much less often used in the United Kingdom, where initial studies are considered as primarily pharmacokinetic trials. British scientists study doses of a medicine expected to yield efficacy in Phase II trials. This difference in approach sometimes leads to different doses of a medicine being evaluated in Phase II and helps explain why different doses may eventually be recommended for patients and marketed in various countries.

It is an interesting side note that scientists in the pharmaceutical industry must obtain formal licenses to operate on or use animals in the United Kingdom, whereas no such formal requirements exist in the United States.

Fat Versus Lean Development Programs

Some pharmaceutical companies traditionally design their master development plan to be extremely lean and include only those studies and the number of patients believed absolutely required to obtain regulatory approval. Other companies design a full (i.e., fat) development program that includes numerous studies (e.g., metabolic, toxicological, clinical) that are nice to have but presumably will not be required for regulatory approval

(Fig. 17.6). It is not clear how many companies distinguish between these two types of development programs and make a conscious decision to include or reject most or all studies that are nice to have but are not required. The same concept may be applied to the amount of data collected in any study (e.g., a clinical trial as shown in Fig. 17.7).

Problem Situations and Danger Signs

A few situations that represent potentially serious problems for a pharmaceutical company are briefly mentioned. Each of these issues would be handled differently within different companies. Great variations also exist in how these situations are handled within a company, depending both on the perceived importance of the problem and on the personality of the people involved. When any of the situations described are spotted, senior managers should initiate plans to address the issue.

1. *Insufficient communications between different levels or functions of a company*—This problem is noticed when senior managers observe that two or more groups are not working well together, are not holding necessary meetings to resolve issues, or are not appropriately transferring information and reports upward, downward, and across functions.

2. *Inaccurate communications between different levels or functions of a company*—This problem is noted through similar methods as those mentioned above.

3. *Deteriorating or poor staff morale*—One sign of this problem may be an increase in staff turnover, but the problem may be recognized in many different ways (e.g., increases in absenteeism, complaints about a wide variety of issues, requests for transfer). The reasons for this problem must be determined and addressed.

4. *Poor cooperation between different departments or functions*—This is often part of another problem such as those mentioned above. This issue should not be approached in isolation. Poor cooperation may result from high walls being erected between departments (see Chapter 27, Stimulating Innovation and Increasing Efficiency), from a manager's attempts at empire building, or for other reasons.

5. *Negative disease*—(see Chapter 13, Personnel Issues).

6. *NIH syndrome*—(see description in this chapter).

7. *Creating problems*—There is value in anticipating problems that may arise in moving a project forward or in attempting to carry out any plan. Alternative strategies may then be thought through and evaluated prior to

A Fat Versus Lean Development Plan for a Single Indication and Single Dosage Form

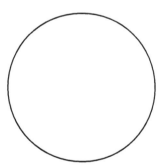

Excessive Number of Studies (i.e., Fat Plan)

Insufficient Number of Studies (i.e., Lean Plan)

- Many clinical trials
- Many technical studies to address potential regulatory questions
- Large amount of supportive data may be present

- Few clinical trials
- No technical studies that are not required for a regulatory submission
- No additional supportive data beyond those required

FIG. 17.6. Illustration of a fat versus lean development plan with aspects of each shown. A single medicine could have a whole spectrum of fat and/or lean plans for individual indications and routes of administration.

A Fat Versus Lean Amount of Data Collected in a Single Clinical Trial

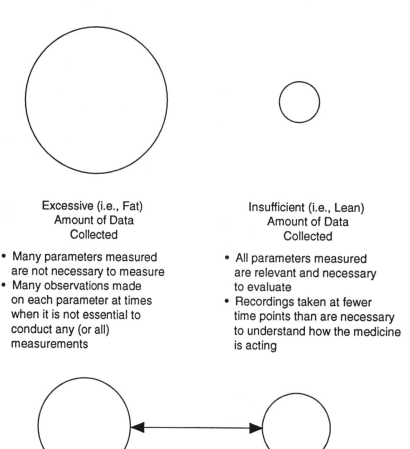

Excessive (i.e., Fat)
Amount of Data
Collected

- Many parameters measured
  are not necessary to measure
- Many observations made
  on each parameter at times
  when it is not essential to
  conduct any (or all)
  measurements

Insufficient (i.e., Lean)
Amount of Data
Collected

- All parameters measured
  are relevant and necessary
  to evaluate
- Recordings taken at fewer
  time points than are necessary
  to understand how the medicine
  is acting

Appropriate Amount of Data Collected

FIG. 17.7. Illustration of fat versus lean plans for a clinical trial in terms of the amount of data collected.

the need for such contingencies. This is a positive example of "what if" exercises. On the other hand, this approach can be taken to extremes when too many potential problems are imagined or a few *potential* problems are thought of as *actual* problems. In either situation, a group may become paralyzed or move in one or multiple tangents. This may be a part of the "woe is me" or "woe is us" syndrome and usually reflects an ineffective leader.

8. *False belief syndrome*— Many companies fall into the trap of believing a medicine to be effective, primarily based on their faith in one or more positive reports by outside scientists or the company's own scientists. Sometimes this belief persists for several years and costs the company many millions of dollars in fruitless research, clinical trials, and technical development. What many of these companies lack is an individual or group who is asked to look at the evidence objectively. This issue is

discussed in the sections in this chapter that discuss "hype."

9. *Judging people by their activity level and not by their results*—In most situations in a pharmaceutical company (except for aspects of medicine discovery), individuals should be judged by the results they achieve and not by how busy they appear to be. This refers to analyzing the quality and not merely the quantity of work attained. Professionals in the personnel office, for example, should be judged by whether the right people are hired and not by the number of applicants screened and interviewed. Professionals in training departments should be judged by the education and benefits that course participants achieve, not by the number of classes held.

10. *Systems that become ends in themselves*—As the size of a company increases, it is necessary to develop and institute more systems for senior managers to know

what is occurring and also to allow line managers to handle more activities efficiently. In some departments and even companies, the importance of systems becomes too great. Instead of their being used as tools to assist medicine discovery and development, they become ends in themselves. Reports are written that are unnecessary, and excessive time is spent on activities with little meaning and that could be readily eliminated.

Many other differences exist among companies in the ways in which they go about discovering and developing medicines, in their marketing activities, and in their relationships with the public, press, and other external groups. Many of these differences are described throughout this book.

Achieving High Standards

It is worth remembering the principle that "excellence exists" when medicines are being developed. Excellence can be found in (1) the quality and abilities of people the company hires, (2) the principles and values these people espouse, and (3) the standards used in developing medicines. Companies differ in how they value and how close they come to achieving these three standards of excellence. Unfortunately, not every company aims at achieving the highest standards possible. Some try to cut corners whenever possible. It is suggested that, by adhering to high standards, companies will actually increase their chances of making major commercial profits. For example, "me-too" medicines usually do not generate great profits, and sloppily conducted and analyzed studies usually delay regulatory submissions much longer than the additional time that would have been spent conducting a study the proper way. It is important at all levels of a company to carefully and thoroughly review plans proposed and work conducted, rather than superficially approving whatever information and data are proposed.

18 / Future Environments for Medicine Discovery and Development

Will Change in the Pharmaceutical Industry Be Revolutionary or Evolutionary? **188**
Introduction................................. 188
What Future Are We Talking About? 188
What Will Medicines Be Like in the Year 2020?.................................... 188
Revolutionary Answer...................... 188
Evolutionary Answer 189
Future Environments Affecting Medicine Discovery................................. 189
Future Environments Affecting Medicine Development 189
Internal Company Environment **189**
Commercial and Business Environment.......... **189**
Competition Between Companies............. 189
Number of Disease Areas in Which Pharmaceutical Companies Are Seeking New Medicines............................ 189
Number of Independent Research-Based Pharmaceutical Companies................. 190
Increasing Pressures on Research and Development 190
Regulatory Environment **190**
Requirements for Postmarketing Studies 190
Standardization of New Medicine Dossiers Worldwide................................ 191
Standards for Medicine Approval 191

Social and Political Environment **191**
Current Trends Toward Increased Patient Responsibility for Their Own Care.......... 191
Current Trends in Characteristics of the Population................................. 192
Public Pressures for New Regulations 192
Industry Pressures for New Regulations and an Improved Relationship with the Food and Drug Administration....................... 192
Academic Environment **192**
Competition for Funds and Grants............ 192
Medical and Health Care Environment **193**
The Changing Concept of Health Care 193
The Changing Nature of Medical Practice..... 193
Sales of Future Medicines.................... 194
Major Factors Influencing Health Care Over the Next 3 to 30 Years 194
Putting the Factors Together That Will Influence Future Health Care.............. 195
Factors Underlying Environmental Changes **195**
Communication............................. 195
Information 195
Cooperation................................ 195
Political and Social Pressures 196
Scientific Discoveries 196
Fads/Fashions.............................. 196

The only solid piece of scientific truth about which I feel totally confident is that we are profoundly ignorant about nature. Indeed, I regard this as the major discovery of the past hundred years of biology. It is, in its way, an illuminating piece of news. It would have amazed the brightest minds of the eighteenth-century Enlightenment to be told by any of us how little we know, and how bewildering seems the way ahead. It is this sudden confrontation with the depth and scope of ignorance that represents the most significant contribution of twentieth-century science to the human intellect. We are, at last, facing up to it. In earlier times, we either pretended to understand how things worked or ignored the problem or simply made up stories to fill the gaps. Now that we have begun exploring in earnest, doing serious science, we are getting glimpses of how huge the questions are, and how far from being answered . . . It is not so bad being ignorant if you are totally ignorant; the hard thing is knowing in detail the reality of ignorance. Lewis Thomas, American physician and essayist. From *The Medusa and the Snail.*

May you live in interesting times. Chinese Proverb.

WILL CHANGE IN THE PHARMACEUTICAL INDUSTRY BE REVOLUTIONARY OR EVOLUTIONARY?

Introduction

It is important to look at future environments for medicine discovery and development in a broad section on corporate issues relating to medicine discovery and development. Decisions made about where to allocate resources, which businesses to enter or leave, and what strategies to use are in large part based on the corporate perception of future environments. Each of us views the future with a somewhat different perspective and reaches different conclusions about the relative importance of various factors that will influence it. This chapter identifies many factors that will undoubtedly play a significant role in shaping the future environment. Some important questions to consider about these factors will also be discussed.

What Future Are We Talking About?

The *near-term future* (i.e., over the next 1 to 2 years) is not discussed in this chapter. The *midterm future* (i.e., from 2 to 12 or so years, which is the time necessary to develop medicines that have already been discovered) may be assessed with some assurances, and several aspects of this period are discussed. The more distant *long-term future* cannot be visualized and predicted with as much clarity, but this is the major period described in this chapter. No conclusions will be reached about what distant future environments will be like (e.g., in the year 2020). A number of trends that will influence the distant future world of medicine discovery and development are already under way and will be discussed.

What Will Medicines Be Like in the Year 2020?

Two general types of answers are usually given to this question, revolutionary and evolutionary. The type of future forecast that any particular scientist, clinician, or marketer favors undoubtedly says more about their own personality and beliefs than about the likelihood of one of these scenarios being closer to the truth. The revolutionary view is most often held by optimistic upbeat managers and the evolutionary view by conservative and more pragmatic managers. As an aside, the author believes the future will be closer to the evolutionary answer.

Revolutionary Answer

Numerous individuals and groups are predicting a new revolution in medicine discovery and treatment of many diseases (Wells, 1983; Faust, 1984a,b; Taylor and Voivodas, 1987; Unger, 1987). A representative quote of the revolutionary style answer is taken from Unger (1987): "Sometime in the early part of the next century, it is generally felt that we will be relatively free of disease and that the new medicine development research will focus more on cures and on the correction of deficiencies . . . Medicines will be 'engineered' rather than 'discovered,' and therefore the process will be more efficient . . . It seems likely that virtually any receptor or enzyme will be able to be characterized (both functionally and structurally) by the year 2000."

The temptation to predict widespread changes in the future is based on a few assumptions:

1. The rate of medicine discovery in the past can be extrapolated into the future.
2. New techniques of biotechnology (see Table 2.9) plus sophisticated computer modeling techniques of molecular structures will lead to a large number of new medicines.
3. Most new medicine discoveries that may potentially occur will actually occur.

The problem with the first assumption is that great discoveries do not occur according to a time schedule. Just because one can usually know with reasonable certainty that the next generation of an electronic device or computer hardware or software is possible to design and build, it does not mean that truly novel medicines are going to be found at a predetermined rate. This lack of predictability, however, means that changes and discoveries may occur either faster or slower than anticipated. The ability to extrapolate from past successes (and failures) in medicine discovery to major long-term future discoveries is obviously unknown. Almost any scenario could be vigorously defended with many facts and figures. Nonetheless, such extrapolations are made using personal judgment and guesswork.

The problem about the potential of recombinant and other methods of biotechnology to supply new medicines (second assumption) is that, at present, this potential cannot yet be evaluated accurately. For one thing, these techniques are primarily applied to protein medicines, which must be used parenterally (primarily intravenously). Most proteins will only be therapeutically useful until smaller molecules are discovered that are clinically equivalent and may be taken orally.

The third assumption is difficult to assess, except that there is little reason to believe that the current intensity of competition between pharmaceutical companies will diminish, unless the pharmaceutical industry in certain countries is nationalized or prices are controlled in the United States. Therefore, every attempt will be made by companies to exploit both potential and actual opportunities for medicine discovery, development, and marketing advantages.

If it is possible to combine biotechnology with electronics and create a new hybrid, then a new revolution would be at hand. The marriage of microchips and biochips would have potential that is difficult to fully imagine. At this time we must consider this possibility as remote and only unfettered speculation.

Evolutionary Answer

The evolutionary answer to predicting the future is based on the belief that the rate of discovery of important new "miracle" medicines will remain about the same as that over the last decade or will decline slightly. Medicines with small but real improvements will gradually replace some older medicines. Although new types of medicine delivery forms (e.g., edible whips, transdermal patches) will be found useful for some medicines, they will not be used for most medicines. Capsules, tablets, and intravenous solutions will still remain the most common types of medicines.

Future Environments Affecting Medicine Discovery

The single aspect that will probably have the greatest influence on medicine discovery from today through the year 2020 is the additional scientific and medical knowledge gained about health, disease, and functions of cells and organs. Research scientists in academic, industrial, and government laboratories seek this knowledge every day. This information is critical to the future success of the research-based pharmaceutical industry because scientific breakthroughs are often converted into new approaches for medicine discovery.

Future Environments Affecting Medicine Development

There are multiple environments in which medicines are developed and which in turn influence medicine development. These environments include the (1) internal environment or milieu within a company; (2) commercial and business environment outside a company in which medicines are manufactured, distributed, and sold; (3) regulatory environment in which medicines must be approved and in which their progress is monitored; (4) social and political environments in which medicines are developed and sold; (5) academic environment in which medicines are clinically evaluated; and (6) medical and health care environments in which medicines are used. Each of these six environments is discussed below. Several factors that will influence future environments are then discussed. Additional information and perspectives on the future of medicine development may be obtained in *Pharmaceuticals in the Year 2000* (Bezold, 1983), *The Second Pharmacological Revolution* (Wells, 1983), and other books listed in the references about the pharmaceutical industry at the end of the text.

INTERNAL COMPANY ENVIRONMENT

There are major differences in the environments within pharmaceutical companies today. Future changes will be based primarily on the same factors that affect the current environment. These factors include (1) size of a company, (2) nature of a company and its organization, (3) personalities of key individuals who control and manage a company, (4) current success of a company's products and the company's degree of financial solvency, (5) expectations for major new products in the therapeutic areas being studied, and (6) traditions and heritage. These factors will change to a different degree and in different ways over time within each company. Numerous interactions occur among these factors. For example, there is usually a strong correlation between the current success of a company's products and the size of the research and development budget.

COMMERCIAL AND BUSINESS ENVIRONMENT

Competition Between Companies

Competition between companies is intense in many disease areas. This competition results from many factors such as generics and multiple brands available in some medicine classes. Profits are being squeezed by cost containment measures and increased research budgets. These and other reasons are raising pressures on pharmaceutical companies to succeed or possibly face buyout or extinction. This pressure is most squarely placed on research and development units in research-based companies.

Most research-based companies are working at the frontiers of knowledge and are competing with each other. When medicines are discovered and are undergoing development, the competitive intensity heats up. The intensity of competition that has always been strong in the marketing area is becoming stronger during the medicine development period. One reason is that the first medicine to reach the market usually is able to retain the greatest market share, even after other medicines are approved and marketed. Threats of therapeutic substitution and actual generic substitution add fuel to this fire of competition. See Chapter 64 (Interactions and Relationships Between Pharmaceutical Companies: Competition and Collaboration) for an additional discussion of competition between companies.

Number of Disease Areas in Which Pharmaceutical Companies Are Seeking New Medicines

There is an extremely large number of disease areas where new medicines may be discovered and developed. Nonetheless, most companies are searching for new medicines in a relatively small number of disease areas.

There are several reasons why most companies are concentrating on a limited number of therapeutic areas. First, there is a lack of suitable animal models in many areas and also a lack of sufficient scientific information about cellular problems and the causes of many diseases. A third reason that reduces the number of areas in which most pharmaceutical companies are active is that the potential for profit is limited in most therapeutic areas. Few companies are willing to invest (i.e., risk) millions of dollars, pounds, or marks looking for beneficial medicines unless there is a reasonable expectation of profit.

Number of Independent Research-Based Pharmaceutical Companies

There has been a long-term trend toward decreasing numbers of research-based pharmaceutical companies. This trend has been more apparent in some countries than others but has been fairly universal in industrialized countries for more than 25 years. The trend toward decreasing numbers of manufacturers of medicines has not been as consistent. The former trend will probably continue despite the fact that a number of bulk chemical companies new to medicine discovery have moved into this area (e.g., Eastman Kodak, E.I. du Pont de Nemours & Co.), and also a number of companies have started from scratch in the last decade (e.g., many biotechnology companies). Mergers and buyouts of biotechnology companies by major pharmaceutical companies will reduce the number of independent biotechnology companies. This trend is already apparent, as is their relatively high failure rate. Japanese pharmaceutical companies are expected to become more active in international markets in the future.

The impact of fewer research-based pharmaceutical companies on medicine discovery and development is not clear. A smaller number of companies may employ the same number of professionals employed currently, although it is more likely that the total number will be reduced. It is impossible to know how successful these companies will be at discovering new medicines. Many different scenarios could be hypothesized.

Increasing Pressures on Research and Development

The factors that are primarily responsible for the overall trend toward fewer research-based pharmaceutical companies include (1) increased costs of discovering and developing a medicine, (2) decreasing life of patent protection for most medicines, and (3) decreasing economic return from sales because of generic manufacturers, cost containment, and price controls. These latter issues force pharmaceutical companies to deal more with health maintenance organizations (HMOs), preferred provider organizations (PPOs), and mail-order companies to sell their medicines, rather than with physicians who prescribe them. The erosion of a medicine's sales to generic competition is occurring more rapidly today than in the past. One to two decades ago it took about ten years for a brand name medicine to lose most of its market. Today, because of more rapid entry by generics onto the market and more substitution within pharmacies, markets are being lost within a few years. This trend may even accelerate in the future. Other factors include progressively restrictive government regulations of those agencies that approve and control medicines used. These factors also place a greater emphasis on the need for pharmaceutical companies to discover new chemical entities (NCEs) with commercial value to remain in business. This tends to pressure most research-based companies to explore the same therapeutic areas, many times using the same animal models and biological endpoints.

REGULATORY ENVIRONMENT

Regulations affect medicine development much more than they do medicine discovery. Only a few of the many areas influenced by regulations are mentioned. Examples are chosen to illustrate that costs of meeting regulatory standards are increasing, even though initial movements toward international harmonization of regulatory requirements are occurring. Accurately predicting the regulatory environment that will be present in the year 2020 for any country or group of countries is simply impossible.

Requirements for Postmarketing Studies

Adverse reaction reporting requirements for marketed medicines currently differ in many countries. Over the last decade, there have been steadily increasing requirements for companies to conduct more postmarketing studies to measure the incidence of adverse reactions of newly approved medicines. At least a dozen countries already require information on adverse reactions that occur in other countries. This has led to a virtual explosion of new requirements for companies to supply such data to regulatory agencies in many countries. This type of information must be supplied using different forms and definitions of important terms. In addition, the amount of data required as well as the frequency of reporting also differ between countries. Although this recent trend toward increased complexity is quite alarming, there are encouraging signs that the situation is improving. One such sign is that a group of regulatory agencies and companies have met and derived common definitions, forms, and approaches that would simplify this issue. A pilot study utilizing these standardized forms was successful, and the forms are being used in several countries.

The future world of 2020 will probably involve reporting of all serious adverse reactions to a central source that will communicate with national regulatory agencies. Alternatively, companies will utilize a standard form to provide this information to national regulatory agencies on a single agreed-on frequency with standard definitions of terms and standard methods. Most companies will have centralized these operations.

Standardization of New Medicine Dossiers Worldwide

There is a growing trend for national regulatory agencies to communicate more with each other and to share more information than ever before. This is taking place both prior to and subsequent to the time of medicine approval. A trend toward increasing uniformity among regulatory agencies is noted in the efforts of the European Economic Community (EEC) to standardize applications for medicine approval in their member countries. This procedure has been implemented, but its success or failure will take a number of years to assess. The trend toward greater harmonization of regulatory requirements and possibly a single regulatory dossier for most countries seems inevitable. Nonetheless, this trend is currently moving at a rather slow rate.

Standards for Medicine Approval

Perhaps the greatest influence of regulations on medicine development will result from the standards used to approve medicines in terms of efficacy, safety, or quality of life. It is conceivable that regulatory authorities may require data that demonstrate the superiority of a new medicine over existing therapy before the medicine may be approved for marketing. This type of change would be vigorously protested by the pharmaceutical industry.

Advantages of a new medicine may be demonstrated not only in terms of efficacy and/or safety, but also in terms of quality of life, compliance, pharmacokinetics, cost effectiveness, or in another area. Standards for having a new medicine added to the formulary of many hospitals, HMOs, and PPOs already require this type of data to be presented. Pharmaceutical companies vigorously attack such requirements in most situations for numerous reasons. These reasons include the impossibility of knowing for many years whether or not a medicine in development will actually be demonstrated to be superior to existing therapy. New areas of clinical usefulness or superiority over existing therapy have sometimes been found for newly introduced medicines that were originally considered to be "me too" medicines.

The standards for medicine approval resemble a high jump where the bar is constantly raised as improved medicines are approved. The standards are actually set by the medicines themselves that are available, not by an arbitrary ruling of a regulatory authority. Nonetheless, at some point the bar will be so high for many disease areas that it will cease to be profitable for pharmaceutical companies to develop new medicines that are not greatly superior to existing therapy.

SOCIAL AND POLITICAL ENVIRONMENT

The social and political environment in which medicines are developed overlaps to a large degree with both regulatory and medical environments.

Current Trends Toward Increased Patient Responsibility for Their Own Care

The current trend toward increased patient responsibility for their own care is expected to continue and become even more widespread in the future. One aspect of this trend is that patients want more medical information than they are receiving on medicines that are prescribed or available over the counter (OTC). Medicine manufacturers may decide to provide patient package inserts for their medicines. This type of information sheet could present (1) useful suggestions for taking medicines, (2) information about recognizing adverse reactions, and (3) answers to commonly asked questions. These sheets could be dispensed at the time the prescription is written or at the time it is filled (see Chapter 47, Marketing Issues, for additional discussion on this topic).

Other potential directions are for more medicines to be marketed over the counter. Over-the-counter medicines usually bypass the physician's influence in that other sources influence a patient's choice about which medicine(s) to purchase. Future OTC medicines will come from currently available (and future) prescription medicines. It is unlikely in the United States that NCE medicines will initially be granted OTC status. An additional offshoot may be for more diagnostic kits to be developed and marketed directly to patients, similar to the current marketing of pregnancy kits, occult blood detectors, ovulation predictors, urine glucose tests, and blood glucose tests. Future diagnostic kits will probably include tests to diagnose strep throat and urinary tract infections. Kits to monitor treatment may be marketed to enable patients to ensure that their blood levels remain within the therapeutic range.

Medicine tampering (i.e., poisoning of capsules) should be less prevalent in the future because of tamper-resistant capsules, gelatin-banded capsules, caplets, and the elimination of all capsules by some manufacturers. This issue is discussed further in both the marketing and production chapters of this book (Chapters 47, Marketing Issues, and 50, Production Issues).

Current Trends in Characteristics of the Population

There is a trend in the population of developed countries for a steadily larger number and percentage of their population to be older. The increased number of older people will undoubtedly focus increased attention on (1) the number of medicines prescribed for older patients, (2) the appropriate doses to prescribe, and (3) the duration of medicine treatment. These considerations in turn will raise other issues of patient compliance, medicine interactions, and adverse reactions. One likely result of this overall issue is for physicians to prescribe medicines more carefully for older patients. From both an economic and a medical viewpoint this is highly desirable and should reduce the number of hospitalizations resulting from medicine interactions and other medicine-related causes. From a company's commercial viewpoint, any decrease in sales that results from more careful medical treatment will be more than compensated for by the increased number of patients expected to use the medicine.

Public Pressures for New Regulations

Politically, it is difficult to predict whether future events will trigger major changes in medicine legislation as occurred in 1906, 1938, and 1962. The regulatory pendulum has swung toward ensuring state-of-the-art purity, safety, and efficacy of medicines. The chances are therefore diminished for a national tragedy occurring through human callousness or ignorance on the scale of those that triggered the passage of the Pure Food and Drug Act of 1906, the Food, Drug and Cosmetic Act of 1938, or the Kefauver-Harris Amendments of 1962 (to the 1938 Act). Nonetheless, a major medicine tragedy may still occur. If one does occur it is vital that political reactions be rational and balanced. If standards for medicine approval are increased further, they could easily go beyond realistic levels and prevent or markedly delay many medically valuable medicines from being approved. Risks of further withholding of valuable new medicines from patients would probably not be worth any small medical benefits to society achieved in terms of increased safety requirements for new medicines.

The medicine approval process could undergo a large change if the United States Congress mandated that the Food and Drug Administration (FDA) rapidly approve all new medicines that have demonstrated therapeutic value and an acceptable benefit-to-risk ratio. The FDA has no current mandate to *approve* medicines. Finally, *Congress should provide the FDA with sufficient resources to allow them to review New Drug Applications (NDAs) expeditiously. Alternatively, Congress could enact a new system to approve medicines* (see Chapter 63,

Interactions and Relationships with Government Agencies, for a discussion on this point and a proposal).

The situation in every other developed country is different. The major points are that (1) public pressures are important in influencing new regulations and (2) strong pressures for regulatory changes often arise from regulatory changes in other developed countries.

Industry Pressures for New Regulations and an Improved Relationship with the Food and Drug Administration

A movement toward partial pharmaceutical industry deregulation in the United States may occur in the future, although at the moment this possibility appears remote. Certain aspects have already been proposed, such as allowing companies to use some or all Institutional Review Boards (IRBs) to approve Phase I trials without first submitting an Investigational New Drug Application (IND) to the FDA.

The relationship between the FDA and the pharmaceutical industry is primarily adversarial. Nonetheless, for some medicines development was marked by a spirit of cooperation (e.g., Retrovir). It is hoped that the number of cases of collaborative medicine development between the American government and the pharmaceutical industry will increase. There is a great amount of progress that could be made in this area. Improved relationships between national regulatory agencies and the pharmaceutical industry should be encouraged in every way possible. This issue is further discussed in Chapter 63, Interactions and Relationships with Government Agencies.

ACADEMIC ENVIRONMENT

Competition for Funds and Grants

A major trend that will probably continue in the academic environment within the United States is increased competition for grants and financial support. In recent years this had led to increased requests from academicians for financial support by the pharmaceutical industry. The pharmaceutical industry has generally responded, although much more so in some areas than others. It is only natural that pharmaceutical companies support work that is of primary interest to them. This has occurred through a variety of programs and mechanisms that are discussed in Chapter 61, Interactions and Relationships with Academic Institutions. A major cutback of government support for academic research in the future would probably intensify the same trends present today. Any major increase in government funds for academic scientists and clinicians would probably have a relatively small effect on academic interest in collaborating in medicine development. This is because many studies sponsored by pharmaceutical companies are of great interest to academicians in terms of career enhancement or as a relatively secure source of funds. On the other hand, many new medicines of minor clinical importance might have a more difficult time being developed if fewer clinicians need financial support.

MEDICAL AND HEALTH CARE ENVIRONMENT

The Changing Concept of Health Care

At the beginning of this century, medicine was limited in the range of effective treatments it could offer patients, and the term *health care* was primarily used to describe caring for the sick. As a result of the antibiotic revolution and the development of many other medicines, by the 1960s the term *health care* had come to include the concept of treatment, plus some cures for many bacterial diseases. Current research and medical emphasis have been shifting the pendulum of health care toward earlier diagnosis and prevention of disease. This change is being accompanied, and in part caused, by greater interest in self-care by patients. People are accepting a greater responsibility for their own health. Fitness, exercise, use of vitamins, and other practices associated with healthy lives have all become part of many people's desire to optimize their health and prevent disease. Thus, health care in the 1990s will place a heavy emphasis on fitness and prevention of disease. The pharmaceutical industry has responded to this trend in many ways (e.g., providing methods to stop smoking, developing various combinations of vitamins and minerals). Future trends in this direction will be fascinating to observe.

The public is learning much more about health care and is more oriented toward evaluating medicine and medical care as a commodity. As a result, there will probably be (1) more advertising directed to the public, (2) greater choice of health care providers, and (3) greater demands made of health care providers. How each of these relates to a specific pharmaceutical company will differ and must primarily be addressed by marketing and public relations groups.

The Changing Nature of Medical Practice

The nature of medical practice and the types of patient treatments influence which medicines and dosage forms are developed. The opposite is also true (i.e., medicines and dosage forms developed influence medical practice). For example, inpatient treatment for some diseases encourages parenteral dosage forms to be developed, and new technologies, including transdermal patches, influence the ways physicians treat their patients.

The way in which medicine is practiced has constantly changed since 1900, and the rate of change has clearly accelerated over the last decade. Present differences in the practice of medicine between countries are likely to remain, although these differences may become somewhat less.

United States

In the United States the number of physicians practicing by themselves has decreased as the trend toward group practice has accelerated. More physicians are also joining HMOs, PPOs, and other prepaid groups that provide health care to a growing percentage of the United States population. The impact of these groups on the practice of medicine is being felt at a national level and has encouraged several large companies, such as General Motors, to enter the health care market themselves to provide services for their employees. There is no doubt that, if this trend toward managed health care continues, the practice of medicine will be entirely different in another decade or two than that of just a few years ago.

Many models of HMOs exist (e.g., staff model HMO, open access HMO, individual practice association HMO). Other models of health care include PPOs, exclusive provider organizations, managed fee for service, and unmanaged fee for service. Over the next ten or so years, many models will probably persist and the field will not be reduced to a few winners. Some large hospital chains and HMOs are now offering many health plans instead of the one or few plans that they used to offer.

Health maintenance organizations and large hospital chains are oriented to cost containment and are able to purchase the medicines they need in more economic ways than can a single hospital or group of physicians. One reason that medicine costs are closely examined by many groups is that costs for other hospital services such as nursing care, pharmacy services, and many other aspects of running a hospital must be present and available 24 hours a day. It is not as easy to cut back and control these costs even though the extent of their utilization may vary widely from day to day. Potential savings in these areas would probably be much greater than for medicines, because medicines constitute a much smaller percentage of a hospital's expenses. It has been calculated that only approximately 6% to 8% of total medical costs within the United States are for medicines.

Because HMOs and other prepaid groups currently utilize more generic medicines than do non-HMO groups, the trend toward greater use of generic medicines will also increase. Goldsmith (1986) has described various aspects of the future health care system in more detail.

Europe

The practice of medicine is changing as rapidly within Europe as within the United States. In the past, many countries had vastly different orientations to practicing medicine (Payer, 1988), but these differences are progressively narrowing. The reasons for this are regulatory as well as cultural. Nonetheless, medical practice differences among countries will probably persist for a long period, although the differences in how clinical trials are conducted in various countries are constantly narrowing because of multinational trials that follow a single protocol.

Sales of Future Medicines

Hospitals, large department stores, and professional associations are starting to enter the mail-order pharmaceutical business. These groups are specializing in selling medicines to patients who require long-term chronic use or periodic use. This practice will undoubtedly have a growing impact on the business of small pharmacies. Pharmaceutical companies will probably have more national purchasers and fewer small stores to sell to. This will further increase price competition, especially on multisource (i.e., generic) products and on products where therapeutic equivalents (i.e., different medicines that act the same way) exist. There is even a trend in some areas for physicians to dispense the medicines they prescribe. Although this is the current practice in Japan, it has elicited a major debate in the United States. This event has pitted pharmacists against physicians in extremely acrimonious legislative battles.

Major Factors Influencing Health Care Over the Next 3 to 30 Years

The most important factor that has brought about the changes in health care over the last decade is probably the switch from the concept of "quality care for everyone" to "cost containment." The driving force behind this switch was the rising percentage of the Gross National Product spent on health. Interestingly, the amount of money spent on medicines as a percentage of the health budget of the United States has fallen over this same period. For example, the percentage was 14% in 1960 and had decreased to 7% by 1984.

A list of important factors expected to influence health care and its delivery over the next two decades includes the following. A brief comment addressing a likely way in which medicine discovery or development will be affected is included. Although a number of possibilities are given, current trends in health care delivery may have a minimal influence on future fruits of the medicine discovery process.

1. *Rapid growth in expenditures on health*—The rate of increase in national health expenditures is slowing, but in 1987 it reached over 500 billion dollars, or 11% of the Gross National Product (GNP). Health expenditures are estimated to reach 15% of the GNP by the year 2000, primarily because the United States' population is aging. These sums demonstrate a growing market for useful medicines.

2. *Additional cost containment measures*—This factor could make it more difficult for expensive new medicines to be widely used, unless the medicine provides a major benefit in terms of financial savings, efficacy, safety, or quality of life.

3. *Increasing age of the population*—This factor should provide continued stimulation for companies to invest heavily in research and development. The total market for medicines will undoubtedly increase in terms of the number of units sold.

4. *Reduced demand for institutional care*—This factor is not expected to have a major impact on research and development.

5. *Increase in health care companies (e.g., HMOs)*—This factor is discussed elsewhere in this chapter.

6. *Decrease in number of independent hospitals*—This factor is discussed below.

7. *Increase in self-care by patients*—This factor will affect some therapeutic areas and types of medicines (e.g., OTCs) more than others. This is also related to an increased emphasis on health and fitness.

8. *Increase in organizations focusing on health*—More groups are forming with specialized purposes. They are already attempting to influence how research funds are spent by government, academia, and industry in looking for new medicines and other types of cures for diseases.

9. *Oversupply of physicians in some specialties and locations*—This factor is not expected to have a major impact on research and development, except possibly to stimulate more physicians to consider careers in the pharmaceutical industry.

10. *Increasing government regulations*—This factor could easily become a major one in decreasing company incentives to invest heavily in research and development. The specific influence will result from interactions among many aspects of the regulations and may vary from medicine to medicine.

11. *Increasing number of multisourced medicines (i.e., generics)*—This factor will lead to increased competition and is discussed elsewhere in this chapter.

12. *Improved packaging and product development*—This factor (e.g., better needles for patient use, unit-of-use packages, time-release medicines) will encourage

public acceptance of greater medicine use than is medically appropriate.

13. *Increase in government price-setting policies*—This factor is already squeezing company profits in many cases and may negatively influence a company's ability to invest in research and development.

14. *Improved technology*—The ramifications of improved technology are difficult to predict but should allow many processes of today to be done more easily.

15. *Changes in values*—This factor is possibly the most difficult one to predict. Although many values go through historical cycles, they usually return in altered forms and have different influences on society.

Putting the Factors Together That Will Influence Future Health Care

In attempting to decipher how this mix of real and possible influences will affect a company, it is useful to determine both a best-case and a worst-case scenario. Based on those assessments, some steps may become apparent that should improve chances of achieving a positive outcome. It is important for managers who are charting the company's course to pose many difficult questions, even though the answers cannot be known with great assurance. The best guesses as to future trends will enable various decisions to be made. In fact, some of these trends may not occur or may be reversed, which will greatly alter the predicted outcomes. Thus, overall strategies developed must be flexible if they are to deal effectively with a rapidly changing environment.

If the theme of cost containment continues, and most indications are that it will, there will be further competition between pharmaceutical companies based on price and increasing numbers of generic medicines. At the present time, most of the 200 most widely used medicines are not protected by patents. Shortly after the turn of the 21st century, none of the presently patented medicines will remain covered. This means that only medicines yet to be discovered will still be covered by patents in the year 2020. If that group of medicines is to be prescribed, the medicines will have to offer improved benefits over current therapy, which by then will be available in less expensive generic versions.

Future trends toward consolidation of medical care providers will continue, possibly at an increased rate. There will probably be fewer owners of hospitals, pharmacies, nursing homes, physician offices, and pharmaceutical manufacturers. This trend may extend to HMOs and PPOs as well. This will tend to increase pressures on pharmaceutical companies to demonstrate advantages of their medicines over their competitors. This in turn will influence the clinical trials conducted and tests used in the future. Areas that will become more important in this regard are quality of life, compliance, and cost effectiveness.

FACTORS UNDERLYING ENVIRONMENTAL CHANGES

Each environment discussed will change over the next 30 years based on a number of underlying factors. To better understand the likelihood of each potential change described for these environments, it is necessary to understand how each of the underlying factors may itself change. These factors will be major influences on medicine discovery and medicine development in the future.

Communication

The recent and still ongoing revolution in communications has been largely triggered by developments in computer hardware and software. There is no reason to expect that this movement will not continue. This will influence all environments, but the potential impact on the regulatory environment may be particularly noteworthy. This is because computers are underutilized in respect to regulatory review of submissions, as well as in their communications with the pharmaceutical industry.

Information

It is difficult to predict if future directions will change qualitatively from those that are apparent today. One change will probably be an increased accuracy of data and reports, given the enormous room for improvement in these areas. See *Guide to Clinical Trials* (Spilker, 1991) for a more detailed discussion on this topic.

Cooperation

Future improvements in cooperation between national regulatory agencies will most likely lead toward a single regulatory dossier. Increased pressures for research-based companies to discover novel medicines may lead toward more collaborations between pharmaceutical companies in the areas of licensing and joint ventures. Whether cooperation between pharmaceutical companies and regulatory authorities will improve in the future is uncertain, but this is clearly desirable. Many industries presently have positive relationships with government agencies in the United States. Why not the pharmaceutical industry?

Political and Social Pressures

There is little doubt that strong social pressures lead to relatively rapid political responses. One need only look at the reasons why major regulations have been passed. An early regulatory law in the United States was the Biologics Control Act. This was passed after diphtheria toxin accidentally contaminated with tetanus was given to protect children, and ten children died as a result. This regulation established standards for the preparation of serum and vaccines. The Pure Food and Drug Act was passed in 1906 as a result of public outrage over adulterated products described in *The Jungle* (by Upton Sinclair) and other books. The Food, Drug, and Cosmetic Act was passed in 1938 as a result of public horror over approximately 100 deaths of Americans from a toxic solvent used to prepare a liquid form of the antibiotic sulfanilamide. The Kefauver-Harris Amendments to the 1938 Act were passed in 1962 because of public reaction to the thalidomide tragedy.

Although each of those examples of public opinion led to stronger regulations, there is no reason to believe that social and political pressures could not be exerted in different directions regarding medicine development. For example, if the plight of the pharmaceutical industry became more strained and this story became widely known, political pressures might mount to provide the FDA with a mandate to approve medicines, to require the FDA to review NDAs and NDA supplements more rapidly, or to develop a new system to have medicines approved.

It is incumbent on the pharmaceutical industry to place far greater emphasis on influencing the political system than it has done in the past. These actions should be made through legislators at the local, state, and federal levels; through regulatory agencies; and perhaps most importantly through the many public audiences with which they interact (see Chapter 67, Interactions and Relationships with Patients and the Public).

Scientific Discoveries

Future scientific breakthroughs will influence each of the six environments. The magnitude of this influence is impossible to gauge accurately. Experimentation with new life forms may lead to important changes in social and political environments. The major influence on medicine discovery will be in the internal company environment. Future discussions about human disease, animal models, physiological processes, biochemical mechanisms underlying medicine effects, and other areas will all direct the search for new medicines in directions that cannot be accurately known today.

Fads/Fashions

There is no limit to the number of fads or their pervasiveness in influencing each of the various environments. This is not a totally negative influence, because it often targets public and political attention and resources toward important areas, although often for the wrong reasons. A number of fads in management are described in Chapter 11, Corporate Management.

SECTION III

Medicine Discovery and Development

19 / Overview of Factors Affecting Medicine Discovery

The Matrix Approach as a Frame of Reference .. **199**
National Level **200**
  Economic Policies 200
  Regulatory Policies 201
  Social Policies 201
  Medical Practice 201
  Scientific Status 201
Institutional Level **202**

Departmental Level **202**
  Cultivating the Innovative Process Leading to
    the Discovery of New Medicines 202
Individual Scientist Level **202**
  Basic Methods of Discovering New Medicines. 203
  The Five Categories of Factors and Their
    Impact on Individual Scientists 205
  Freedom and Creativity 205

Laws of Project Management

1. *Murphy's Law*
   If anything can go wrong, it will.
2. *O'Toole's Commentary on Murphy's Law*
   Murphy was an optimist.
3. *Nonreciprocal Laws of Expectations*
   Negative expectations yield negative results.
   Positive expectations yield negative results.
4. *Howe's Law*
   Every man has a scheme that will not work.
5. *Zymurgy's First Law of Evolving System Dynamics*
   Once you open a can of worms, the only way to recan them is to use a larger can, giving you a bigger can of worms.
6. *Gordon's First Law*
   If a research project is not worth doing at all, it is not worth doing well.
7. *Maler's Law*
   If the facts do not confirm the theory, they must be disposed of.
8. *Boren's First Law of Communication*
   When in doubt, mumble.
9. *Ninety-ninety Rule of Project Scheduling*
   The first 90% of the job takes 90% of the time, and the last 10% takes the other 90%.
10. *Law of Project Arithmetic*
    Some of it plus the rest of it equals all of it.

THE MATRIX APPROACH AS A FRAME OF REFERENCE

The numerous factors that influence innovation may be viewed from many perspectives. The perspective described in this chapter focuses on a matrix model composed of levels of organization, categories of influence, and types of organization, as depicted in Fig. 19.1.

The matrix approach is a useful frame of reference to view both major and minor factors that affect and influence innovation. Major categories of influence include economic, social, regulatory, medical practice, and scientific factors. The discussion focuses on how these five major categories operate within the four major levels of organization in the matrix: national/international, institutional, departmental, and individual. The major types

Matrix of Factors Affecting Innovation

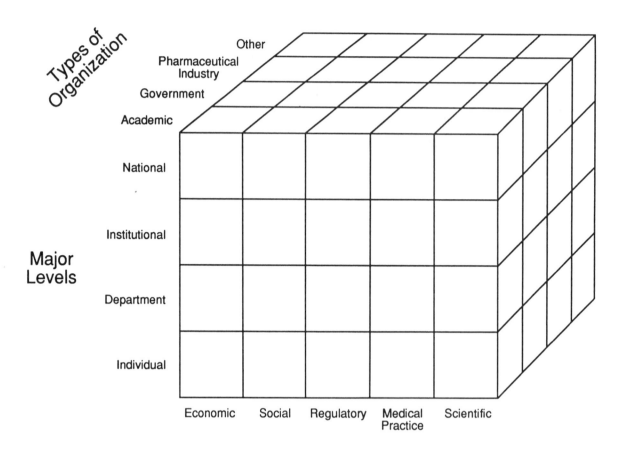

FIG. 19.1. Matrix of factors affecting innovation based on types of organization, organizational levels, and types of influence or pressure.

of organizations at which innovation occurs form the third arm of this matrix: academic, government, pharmaceutical industry, and others, such as professional societies or professional associations.

This matrix has 80 individual cubes that could be discussed, although not every one would be worth investigating and describing; some are much more interesting than others. The 80 individual cubes should be thought of as encompassing both the macro- and the micro-levels of factors that affect innovation.

The remainder of this discussion focuses on how the major categories of influence operate within each of the four major levels of organization—national, institutional, departmental, and individual.

NATIONAL LEVEL

At the national (macro) level, there is clearly an overlap among the five major categories that influence medi-

cine discoveries: economics, regulatory policy, social policy, medical practice, and the state of the art in science.

Economic Policies

The economic policies of a country influence innovation through many practices, but only three are mentioned: tax laws, patent laws, and pricing policies. Tax laws provide incentives (or disincentives) for various groups to invest in medicine discovery. If tax write-offs for research activities were made looser or tighter, it is certain that this would have a stimulating or inhibiting effect on innovation. Patents are probably the single most important factor that influences innovation on the national level, as well as on the institutional and departmental levels. Over the previous two decades a lot of attention has been paid, at least in the United States and more and more elsewhere, to patent laws. It has been said that during the late 1970s and early 1980s the Pharmaceutical Manufacturers Association (PMA) focused most of its efforts on attempts to revise the patent laws. The PMA helped achieve the Patent-Term Restoration Act of 1984 in the United States.

National governmental authorities control prices for new medicines in most countries. The policies these agencies adopt and use have a major influence on the willingness of some groups to invest in innovation and discovery. The pricing of medicines has not had a great impact on innovation in the past but probably will have increased impact in the future. Patent laws and pricing policies may be viewed from both an economic and a regulatory perspective.

Regulatory Policies

Other regulatory influences on innovation (apart from patent laws and pricing policies) come from certain national authorities, such as the Department of Health in the United Kingdom and the Food and Drug Administration (FDA) in the United States, that must approve new medicines for marketing. Companies have been known to avoid the search for new medicines in specific disease areas because of a belief that an important regulatory agency was unlikely to approve for marketing any such medicines that the company might discover. For example, several years ago, a medicine to treat cocaine abuse would usually not have been pursued by a pharmaceutical company because of the regulatory concern about the potential for abusing the new medicine. Part of the reasoning for this belief is based on the personalities of important decision-making regulators and their opinions.

Social Policies

Social policies are dependent on the type of organization that people work in, the ethical standards followed by the organization, and the public image and reputation of scientists, physicians, and others who are engaged in medicine discovery. This image is primarily influenced by the media, as well as by the scientists' own efforts, contacts, and achievements. A positive image encourages the most creative people in society to choose scientific careers.

Fewer students in recent years have been choosing careers in the sciences. This may be partly a result of the many stories of fraud, deception, and misconduct that have somewhat tarnished the public image of scientists. The issue of fraud in science is being addressed in numerous positive ways by journal editors and university committees. Universities and other groups are establishing standards and guidelines designed to self-police the integrity of research and reduce the likelihood of fraud. Scientists must accept responsibility for the work that they publish and must include as authors only colleagues who

have made a substantial contribution to the project. In many ways the whole issue of fraud is being dealt with better than the issue of deception. Deception is not spoken about as much as fraud, but it exists in many forms (e.g., in clinical trials where patients are deceived by not being told that they may receive a placebo or by being told that they will receive a placebo when they are being given an active medicine).

Medical Practice

The diagnosis of many medical problems as specific diseases or syndromes is highly variable among countries. As a result the diseases that "exist" differ from country to country. Some of these differences are real, others are artificial, and a third group is hard to characterize. There are numerous diseases that are relatively common in some countries but which are not believed to exist in others. In Germany, for example, low blood pressure is frequently diagnosed as the disease hypotension, yet this disease is not believed to exist in many other countries. German physicians treat hypotensive patients with medicines to raise their blood pressure. On the other hand, German physicians do not diagnose irritable bowel syndrome, which is a relatively common diagnosis in many other countries. Few German researchers and pharmaceutical companies would try to discover treatments for irritable bowel syndrome, although a new compound for this disease could be sought for eventual testing in another country. It is less likely that original research would be conducted on a disease that physicians do not believe exists.

The culture of a country and diseases that are considered particularly important influence the allocation of funds for innovation research. In general, French physicians emphasize the liver to a larger extent than do physicians in other countries and diagnose and treat many medical problems as caused by liver abnormalities (Payer, 1988). The French also discuss many diseases that are said to influence the liver. In Germany, the heart is often considered to be of paramount importance, and many diseases are looked at quite differently from the way they are viewed in other countries (Payer, 1988). Hyperkinetic children are seen to be more of a problem in the United States than in the United Kingdom, where many professionals believe Americans are spoiling their children and overdiagnosing this problem. Few companies in the United Kingdom would be expected to invest significant funds to look for new medicines in that particular disease area.

Scientific Status

The level of sophistication of scientific practice and the political importance of a disease or therapeutic area are important factors that influence a country's efforts toward medicine innovation and discovery. A major scientific breakthrough that enables new treatments to be discovered in an important disease area would be a stimulus to increase spending for research in that area. Professional societies and government granting agencies are two groups that are influenced by the scientific state of the art.

INSTITUTIONAL LEVEL

Institutions include academic organizations (e.g., medical centers and their individual departments), pharmaceutical companies, and government agencies and offices (e.g., National Institutes of Health and Centers for Disease Control in the United States and Medical Research Council in the United Kingdom). Other groups include independent institutes, professional associations, and consumer groups. The same five categories of influence described above (i.e., economics, regulatory policy, social policy, medical practice, and scientific status) may be analyzed at the institutional level to assess their impact on innovation. Economic factors, such as the potential commercial return of a new medicine, are strong driving forces for pharmaceutical companies, which also respond strongly to regulatory policies at all levels of their organization. It would be ideal if the humanitarian motivations within the social and medical practice realms were in balance with economic and regulatory forces, but there are few companies, if any, that have achieved an overall balance that is acceptable to all of their members.

Pressures from institutional groups, particularly consumer and professional societies and associations, over the last decade, have led to a wider search for medicines to treat rare diseases. This has occurred in both academic and government laboratories, as well as within the pharmaceutical industry, whose members have conscientiously developed many orphan medicines. The Orphan Drug Act in the United States has tended to focus pharmaceutical companies' attention on this topic. When a medicine with potential to treat a rare disease is identified, a company will recognize the possibility of economic benefits in terms of marketing exclusivity. In addition to the medical value, other potential benefits exist in terms of publicity, corporate image, and other noncommercial factors.

DEPARTMENTAL LEVEL

At the departmental level within an institution, one of the most important influences on innovation is the management of scientists and the innovative process. The medicine discovery process should be managed differently from the medicine development process. This difference can be characterized by the word *control*. One cannot control basic innovation and medicine discovery the way one can plan and control a medicine's development. In each area, however, the basic management of people is generally the same. Plans and time lines may be created and utilized for medicine development activities, but this approach is not useful for planning the innovation and discovery process. The time when the next discovery will occur is usually impossible to predict and schedule.

The separation of activities into discovery and development is not the same as the separation of preclinical and clinical activities. Many preclinical activities are part of development. The period of medicine discovery is defined as the time until one identifies the specific compound to be developed—when one has sufficient information to say, "This is the compound that is going to become a medicine." When a compound is first given to humans, it becomes a medicine. When the compound to be pursued is identified, development activities begin. Development includes all the subsequent preclinical activities, as well as all clinical activities.

Cultivating the Innovative Process Leading to the Discovery of New Medicines

The process of discovery is like the cultivation of a very rare plant whose blossoms will ripen into an economically valuable fruit. Senior managers plant many seeds and note that numerous small, fragile plants emerge. Too much fertilizer, water, or sun will kill a plant, just as too little fertilizer, water, or sun will also kill it. One must nurture a few plants very carefully; others will have to wither and die. The success of this management can be measured by how many buds form. At that point the plants are generally more hardy and mature and can be handled in a more rigorous manner. Although it is primarily the scientists who monitor and encourage the new blooms, it is the managers who must maintain the proper environment in which the scientist operates to help the plants to grow and blossom. Eventually, the plants, flowers, and fruits are transplanted and placed under the care of other individuals.

INDIVIDUAL SCIENTIST LEVEL

The major factors that positively influence innovative activities of an individual scientist are shown in Fig. 19.2. These factors can best be achieved by having the right people, the right management, the right attitudes, and the right environment within an organization. Individual scientists must have a strong desire to succeed and to be creative if they are to be successful.

Factors that inhibit the process of innovation and medicine discovery on the individual level are implied by Fig. 19.2. If the positive factors are used or manipulated

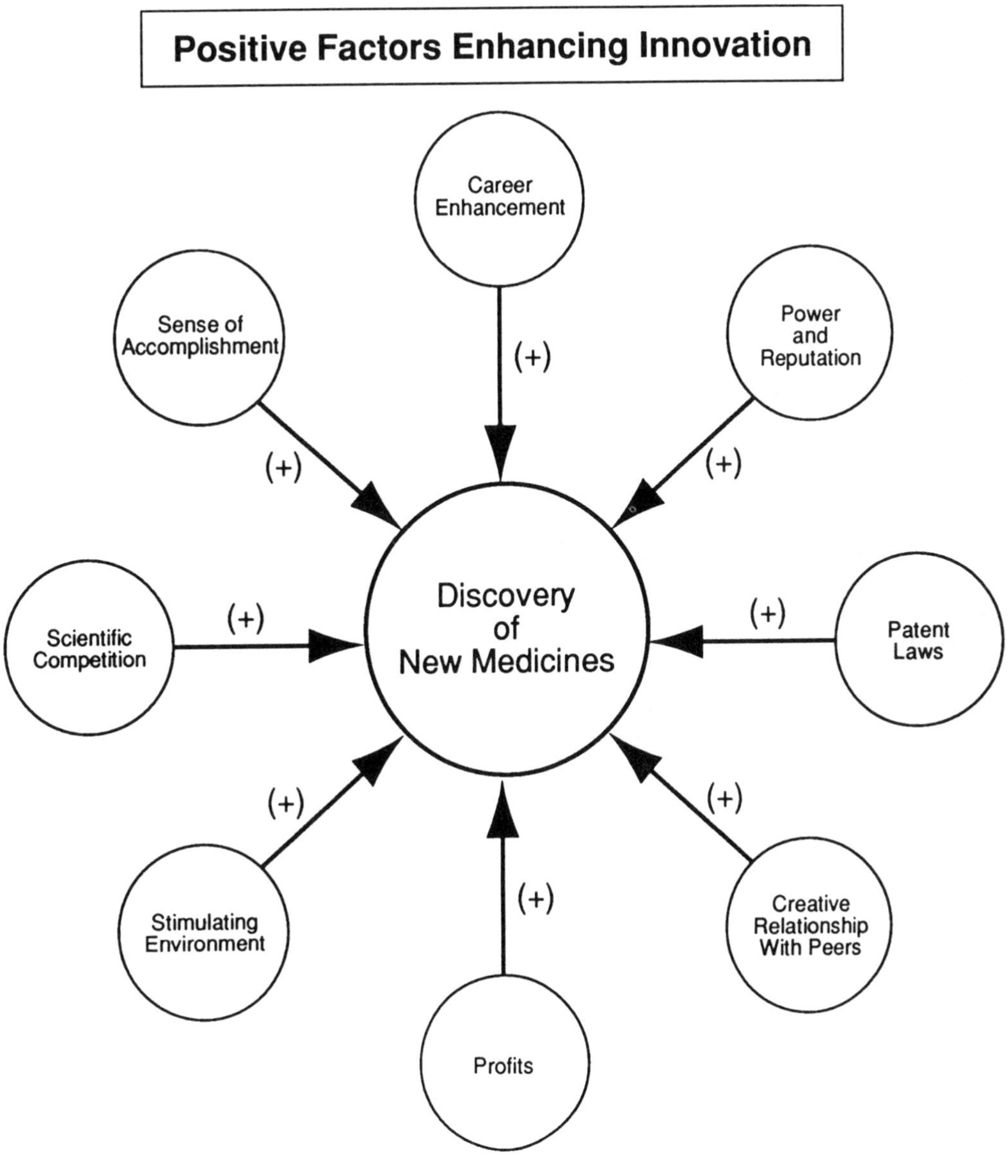

Positive Factors Enhancing Innovation

FIG. 19.2. Positive factors enhancing a scientist's innovation and promoting the discovery of new medicines.

in a negative or controlling way, they will be counterproductive. Some additional factors that may negatively affect an individual's innovation are (1) strong pressure to produce results, (2) tight management control of acceptable targets and experiments, and (3) uncertainty in an organization about its leadership, its future direction, and the scientist's own security.

Basic Methods of Discovering New Medicines

Four basic methods are used to discover new medicines. The methods used lie within two spectra. Three of these methods lie within the spectrum of "rationality of innovation" (Fig. 19.3). At the two poles of the spectrum are pure random screening and pure rational discovery.

No pharmaceutical company could survive if it depended on either of these approaches. Few companies conduct random screening, except for some companies that use it for specialized substances (e.g., natural products). In the past, numerous companies used this method to screen soil samples from all corners of the globe for antibiotics.

At the opposite extreme, scientists design molecules that they believe (or hope) will reach receptor binding sites on molecules that are usually complex or large. It is believed that the medicine-receptor binding will yield desired biological and clinical responses. Although great progress has been made toward the goal of this rational method—whereby the chemical structure of the single perfect compound for a specific receptor could be predicted in advance, synthesized, and then found to be-

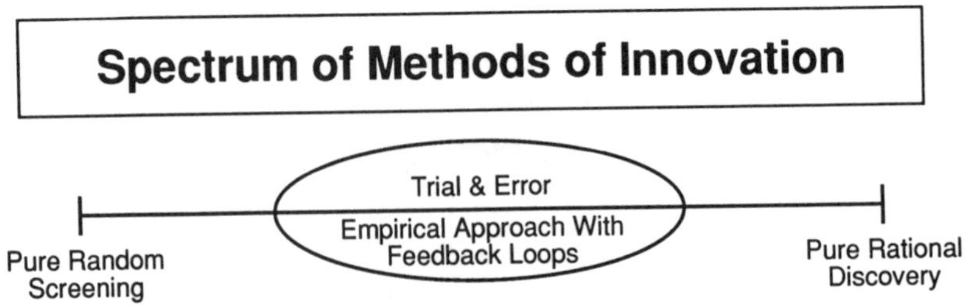

Spectrum of Methods of Innovation

Trial & Error
Empirical Approach With
Feedback Loops

Pure Random
Screening

Pure Rational
Discovery

FIG. 19.3. Spectrum of methods used to discover new medicines. The three methods indicated overlap along this spectrum.

have as predicted—the age of rational medicine discovery is not yet here. Many anecdotes written about this approach are written as if this state is currently operational. In fact, however, no medicine has been discovered in this manner. Chemists and other scientists will continue to strive toward this goal and, undoubtedly, will make important progress.

The scientific state of the art in each specific disease or therapeutic area determines where on the methodological spectrum (Fig. 19.3) scientists operate to discover medicines. Most discovery efforts have been and will continue to be in the large empirical area in the middle of the spectrum rather than at the purely rational or random ends. The empirical trial-and-error approach consists of a core team comprising a chemist and a biologist, usually a pharmacologist, finding a lead compound with some degree of desired activity. The team then attempts to improve on the activity, such as the magnitude of effect or potency, of the compound while also improving its safety. In other words, they attempt to accentuate the positive and eliminate the negative. This indicates a willingness, and often a necessity, to accept trade-offs in

order to achieve the optimal balance between safety and efficacy.

A great deal of logic and scientific rationale is used in the empirical approach to discovering medicines. One must determine the proper problem(s) to study and the proper target(s) to use, and all of these decisions require sophisticated scientific thinking and perspective. To label and discuss one extreme end of the spectrum as the pure rational approach does not imply that other methods are irrational or unscientific.

A second spectrum (Fig. 19.4) considers another method of new medicine discovery—serendipity. This spectrum extends over time, from early during the preclinical and prediscovery experimental period until after a new medicine has been on the market for a period of years. The emphasis of the figure is that serendipity occurs all along this spectrum. Although serendipity is usually discussed as a clinical event, it also operates during preclinical studies. Figure 19.4 also illustrates that the discovery of new useful activities may either be unintentional—true serendipity—or intentional, based on a theory or hunch.

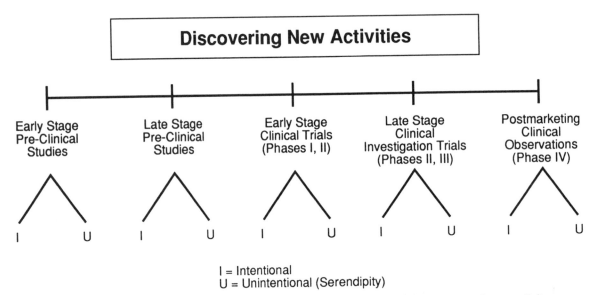

FIG. 19.4. Discovering new biomedical activities on compounds or medicines through serendipity or intentional testing. This diagram illustrates that both processes occur throughout the discovery, development, and marketing periods.

The Five Categories of Factors and Their Impact on Individual Scientists

The major factors that influence individual scientists who attempt to discover new medicines may also be viewed in terms of the economic, social, and medical practice and scientific state-of-the-art concepts. Regulatory issues are less important for medicine discovery at the micro-level. Economics refers to the financial support needed to obtain equipment, assistance, students, and facilities to work on research problems. The disease areas investigated by scientists in industry depend to some degree on what is of commercial interest to the company. In academia, the area depends primarily on what is of personal importance to the scientist. Commercial interest and academic freedom are strongly influenced by the view of managers and the availability of funds. The specific approaches used to discover medicines are usually chosen by the individual scientist working on the problem, even within the industrial environment.

Freedom and Creativity

Academic freedom is a frequently used term, but it is usually perceived to be greater than it actually is. How much freedom does an academic have if his or her grant proposals must be slanted to a popular approach to obtain funding? The freedom of a scientist in a pharmaceutical company or government laboratory is generally quite different in concept from that of the scientist within academia. Pharmaceutical scientists rarely have to apply for grants to be approved, although their ideas must have value. Teaching responsibilities are minimal or nonexistent, and committee assignments are also generally minimal. The influences of freedom on a scientist's innovation are clear. This discussion cannot take the space to describe these concepts in detail, but scientists will find that each concept and the way that a particular group or organization utilizes it will have a different appeal.

Numerous senior research and development directors have stated that most discoveries of new medicines and the most creative ideas within each pharmaceutical company come from about 1% of the company's scientists. Most scientists and managers in an organization know who these people are and can readily identify them. Management should do whatever it takes to keep these people happy and productive.

In many areas of government, academia, and industry, the most creative scientists are converted into managers in the belief that they will instill in others what they have achieved themselves. This rarely comes to pass. Many, if not most, brilliant and extremely creative scientists have turned out to be poor managers. Many do not understand that management of the discovery process is totally different from management of the development process. Moreover, it is highly uncertain that these fine scientists can instill in others the creativity, drive, enthusiasm, and sparks of genius that characterized their own scientific careers. Transforming competent scientists into managers is one of the cardinal sins that often occurs in managing the discovery process.

Meaningful and important rewards, in addition to money, must be given to these scientists. These rewards can and should include nonprofessional recognition, such as a private parking place, a place in the executive dining room, articles about the individual in company publications, and plaques, such as "scientist of the year," in public places within the company. Professional recognition includes asking these people's opinion on relevant issues and asking them to chair research-oriented task forces or therapeutic area committees. Stature must be given to these people so that they will want to continue discovering new medicines of significant value and not feel that moving into management is the only career development path open to them.

20 / The Medicine Discovery Process

Sources of New Medicines 208
   What Is Meant by "Sources"?................. 208
   Sources of Ideas for New Medicines.......... 208
   Sources of Materials for New Medicines....... 210
   Medicines Originally Used in Animals 210
   Old Medicines Developed for New Uses....... 210
   Who Discovers Medicines? 210
   When Is a Medicine Discovered?............. 211
Choosing Therapeutic Areas to Research 211
   Where Does One Look to Find a New
      Medicine?................................... 211
   Description and Definitions of Therapeutic
      Areas 212
   Who Has Input and Who Decides About
      Therapeutic Areas to Explore?............. 212
   Marketing Input into Choosing Therapeutic
      Areas to Explore 212
   How Many Different Therapeutic Areas
      Should Be Explored Simultaneously? 213
   What Are the Criteria to Use in Determining
      Which Therapeutic Areas to Explore?....... 214
   Competition of Medicine Discovery Ideas for
      Resources................................. 215
   Initiating Activities in a New Therapeutic Area
      of Research 216
   Should Pharmaceutical Companies Be
      Engaged in Basic Research?................ 216
   Research Programs 217

Methods of Medicine Discovery................. 218
   Which Comes First—The Biological
      Mechanism or the New Chemical
      Compound?................................ 218
   Establishing Criteria for a Compound's
      Performance During the Discovery Period .. 218
   Basic Approaches and Methods of Medicine
      Discovery 218
   Improving the Biological Profile of an Active
      Compound................................. 221
   Looking for Chemical Analogues When a New
      Activity Is Found for a Marketed
      Medicine.................................. 221
   Choosing the Specific Compounds to
      Synthesize 223
   Identifying Backup Candidates................ 226
   Examples of Success Stories.................. 228
Selected Research Issues Presented in Greater
   Depth..................................... 228
   Molecular Modeling Tools to Help Design
      Better Medicines 228
   Is Medicine Discovery a Rational Process? 229
   Gradient from Targeted to Exploratory
      Research.................................. 229
   Is There a Long-Term Future for the Empirical
      Approach to Medicine Discovery? 230
   Use of Animal Models in Medicine Discovery
      and Development 231

The discovery of adrenaline came about through a mistaken impression. A certain Dr. Oliver had developed a gadget which he thought measured the diameter of that artery at the wrist which is used for feeling the pulse. He measured the diameter of this artery in his son under a variety of conditions. One of the conditions involved the injection of an extract of calves' adrenal glands. He thought he detected that this injection decreased the size of the artery. We now know that the effect of adrenaline on the diameter of a large artery would be undetectable. Dr. Oliver rushed off to let the world know of his discovery. The world, as represented by Professor Schafer, a renowned physiologist, was disbelieving. But Dr. Oliver's enthusiasm eventually persuaded the professor to inject some of the extract into a dog whose blood pressure was being measured. To his amazement the blood pressure rose in an extraordinary fashion. Adrenaline had been discovered.

It is possible to point out many other instances where an effective discovery came at the end of a line of reasoning which was certainly not correct at every stage. It is like walking over a rocky beach. One way is to move slowly and cautiously; making sure that at each step you are firmly balanced on the rock on which you are standing before you take another step. The other way is to move swiftly over the rocks pausing so briefly on each that a precise balance at every step is no longer required. When you have got somewhere interesting, that is the time to look back and pick out the surest way of getting there again. Sometimes it is very much easier to see the surest route to a place only after you have arrived. You may have to be at the top of a mountain to find the easiest way up. Edward de Bono, English physician and writer. From *The Use of Lateral Thinking.*

SOURCES OF NEW MEDICINES

What Is Meant by "Sources"?

From a company's perspective there are several different usages of the term *sources of new medicines.* They include (1) the source of the intellectual idea that led to the medicine's discovery, (2) the source of the material that is the medicine, (3) the business source from which the company obtained the medicine, and (4) the type of institution in which the medicine was discovered.

The first usage refers to the discovery of the medicine. If the medicine was synthesized, what was the source of the idea that led to the compound? Was it a close analogue or metabolite of a known compound, was it a pro-medicine (i.e., a chemical that is converted inside the body into the active medicine), or did the idea come from another direction? Figure 20.1 shows a number of processes or sources used to discover a chemical with an interesting biological activity (i.e., a chemical lead). The second usage refers to whether the molecule's origins came from a natural source (i.e., plant, mineral, or animal), or whether it was artificially synthesized.

The third group of sources refers to business sources. These include licensing arrangements, joint ventures, in-house research, purchases, or other types of business arrangements. The fourth type of source refers to the nature of the institution that developed the idea. Marketed medicines may come from pharmaceutical companies, private entrepreneurs, academicians, government laboratories, or other types of businesses. Nonetheless, approximately 90% of new medicines come from the pharmaceutical industry (Schwartzman, 1976). This subject is reviewed by Kahn et al. (1982, p. 109, 110).

Sources of Ideas for New Medicines

There is no limit to the intellectual sources of ideas for new medicines. Four common sources are shown in Fig. 20.2.

Adverse Reactions

Ideas may also result from problems (i.e., adverse reactions) with existing medicines. Adverse reactions for one

MAJOR PROCESSES USED TO DISCOVER A NEW CHEMICAL LEAD

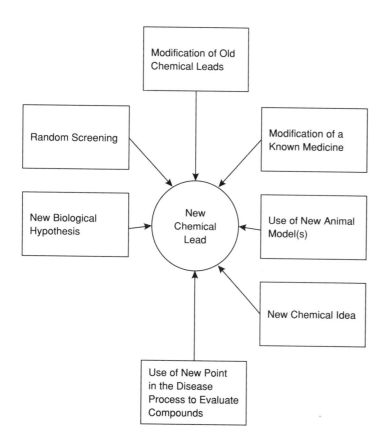

FIG. 20.1. Major processes used to discover a new chemical lead.

MAJOR SOURCES OF A NEW MEDICINE

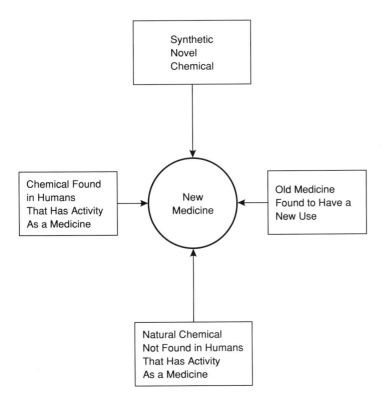

FIG. 20.2. Major sources of a new medicine.

use of a medicine may serve as a new indication for the same medicine. For example, a medicine that is found to cause constipation as an adverse reaction (e.g., morphine) may be used as an active antidiarrheal. A medicine that causes sedation (e.g., certain antihistamines) may be used as a sleep-promoting agent. Adverse reactions also stimulate companies to search for chemically related compounds that have more potent actions of the desired type. A well-known example of this situation relates to the sulfonamide antibacterial medicines. It was noticed that "sulfa" medicines lowered blood sugar and caused diuresis (excessive urination) as adverse reactions. Many new compounds were synthesized over many years in an attempt to exploit these adverse reactions. Eventually, the oral antidiabetic medicines (sulfonylureas) were discovered. Thiazide diuretics are also a descendant of many years of molecular modifications, searching for a sulfonamide diuretic.

Improving on Activity

Benefits observed with some medicines have provided the impetus to companies to try to improve on this activity and develop a new therapeutic agent. In some cases the original benefit either is a weak effect or is not observed in all patients. Therefore, there is need to improve the magnitude of the effect. For example, 6-mercaptopurine (6MP) is an antileukemic medicine. It was found by Dr. Robert Schwartz at Tufts Medical Center in Boston to influence the immune response. Dr. Schwartz convinced Dr. G. Hitchings and Dr. G. Elion at the Burroughs Wellcome Co. that it was important to search for other immunosuppressive compounds that might have less toxicity. They screened numerous compounds in the laboratory and found that azathioprine (Imuran) was highly active and had a much better therapeutic index in mice. During this time Dr. Roy Calne in London read Dr. Schwartz's paper on 6MP and tested it in dogs who had received kidney transplants. He found that the medicine had some activity in preventing the body's rejection of the kidney. He came to the United States to do a fellowship and on his way to Boston stopped by the laboratories of Burroughs Wellcome Co., just outside New York City. In discussions about a better medicine than 6MP, Drs. Hitchings and Elion gave Dr. Calne azathioprine to test as an immunosuppressive medicine. He did. This medicine had better activity than 6MP and eventually opened up the whole field of renal transplantation.

Sources of Materials for New Medicines

Medicines Found in Natural Plants

Plants have been a source of medicines for many millennia, and some of the most important medicines still come from plants (Table 20.1). Additional information on this topic is plentiful (e.g., Balandrin et al., 1985; Steiner, 1986). Nonetheless, proportionally fewer and fewer medicines are derived from plants, and the science of pharmacognosy is less frequently taught in pharmacy schools. There are some strong believers who think that there are many effective medicines in the folk medicine of China, Africa, and other societies that are unknown or underutilized in Western countries. On the other hand, several pharmaceutical companies have screened many thousands of folk remedies (seeking active medicines) with limited success.

Medicines Found in Animals and Humans

Medicines have been obtained from human and animal glands for several decades (e.g., insulin, vitamin B_{12}, adrenaline, thyroid hormone, growth hormone). The advent of biotechnology brought a virtual explosion in the type and number of biologicals that are being developed as medicines (e.g., tissue plasminogen activator, interferons, various growth factors, factor 8, and numerous others). Chapter 24 has a more detailed discussion on biotechnology.

Medicines Originally Used in Animals

There are many examples where medicines used in humans were subsequently tested and eventually marketed for use in animals. There are few examples, however, of the opposite situation, where medicines used in animals were eventually used in humans. One example of this situation occurred with permethrin. Permethrin is applied as an ear tag to cattle and helps keep flies away. This is important because certain types of flies interfere with normal grazing of these animals. This medicine has been found to kill lice and to treat scabies in humans.

Old Medicines Developed for New Uses

The discovery that an already marketed medicine could be useful for treating a new disease is usually made in the clinic. This discovery may have been logically conceived prior to evaluation, or it may result from serendipity. A number of examples are given in Table 20.2.

Who Discovers Medicines?

A medicine's discovery is rarely the sudden achievement of one person's sole idea. Many people's ideas and brainpower invariably contribute to the discovery. Sometimes there are several people who have made a major contribution. Because of human nature and many people's desire to simplify the truth, one person usually receives credit for the discovery of a newly synthesized compound with important biological activity. This individual is often a chemist, although other people may provide intellectual input into the compound's design. With some well-known medicines, however, other individuals (e.g., pharmacologists, research managers) have been given credit for a medicine's discovery. In some situations this is clearly an example of power and glory going to the powerful. On the other hand, these people are often critically important as promoters of a medicine. Many medicines would never reach the market if they were not pushed and promoted within a company,

TABLE 20.1. *Selected medicines that are prepared from natural plants*

Names of medicines	Plant source	Therapeutic use
General classes of medicines		
Digitalis glycosides (e.g., digoxin, digitoxin)	Foxglove	Cardiac stimulant
Opium alkaloids (e.g., morphine, codeine)	Opium poppy	Analgesics (pain killers)
(Belladonna alkaloids (e.g., atropine, scopolamine)	Belladonna, stramonium	Parasympathomimetic blocking medicines
Catharanthus alkaloids (e.g., vincristine, vinblastine)	Madagascar periwinkle	Anticancer agents
Specific medicines		
Quinidine	Bark of *Cinchona* tree	Antiarrhythmic
Quinine	Bark of *Cinchona* tree	Antimalarial
Cocaine	Coca plant	Local anesthetic
Curare	South American plants	Skeletal muscle relaxant
Reserpine	Root of plant—*Rauwolfia serpentina*	Antipsychotic
Pilocarpine	Leaf of *Pilocarpus microphyllus*	Antiglaucoma agent
Colchicine	Autumn crocus	Antigout

TABLE 20.2. *Selected examples of clinical serendipity*

Medicine(s)	Original use(s) or intended use(s)	Uses discovered serendipitously in clinical practice[a]
Chlorpromazine	Antimotion sickness	Antipsychotic
Tricyclics	Major tranquilizers	Antidepressants
Meprobamate	Muscle relaxant	Tranquilizer
Iproniazid	Antituberculous agent	Antidepressant
Procaine	Local anesthetic	Antiarrhythmic
Amantadine	Antiviral	Parkinson's disease
Propranolol	Antiarrhythmic	Antimigraine
	Antianginal	Prevention of myocardial reinfarction
Allopurinol	Adjunct in cancer chemotherapy[b]	Antigout
Corticosteroids	Adrenal steroid replacement	Anti-inflammatory

[a] While most of these medicines' uses were found purely by serendipity, a few also involved hypothesis testing (e.g., allopurinol for gout, propranolol for prevention of myocardial reinfarction).

[b] Allopurinol was originally used in conjunction with 6-mercaptopurine (6MP) to prevent its oxidation and therefore potentiate 6MP's anticancer effect.

because of the strong competition that usually exists for attention and resources.

When Is a Medicine Discovered?

The discovery of a medicine may be defined as occurring at the time when a new biological or clinical use of a compound or medicine is identified. Using this broad definition a number of discoveries may occur for a single medicine after the original discovery of its biological activity. Numerous processes are used to discover a medicine during its life—from the initial synthesis or extraction to the end of its marketing. These processes include the following.

1. An idea for a new medicine stimulates a chemist to synthesize a compound that is found to have the hypothesized activity and is designated as a lead compound. Alternatively, a biologically active substance may be distilled or extracted from naturally occurring products or may be produced by cells and isolated. This is an important discovery, even if it is not the discovery of the specific compound or material that eventually becomes the medicine.

2. A biologist (e.g., pharmacologist) provides feedback of information to a chemist that leads to synthesis of a new compound that eventually becomes a medicine.

3. Biological activity of an unanticipated type is discovered during preclinical testing. This use is eventually developed as an indication (or as the indication) for the medicine.

4. A novel clinical activity of a medicine is discovered serendipitously during investigational studies in humans. This use becomes a major, or possibly the only, use of the medicine (e.g., the antihypertensive effect of propranolol was discovered during antianginal studies in humans).

5. A theory is tested in humans for a new use of an investigational medicine and found to be correct.

6. Processes described in items 4 or 5 above may occur for a medicine that is already marketed.

Table 20.2 lists some examples where marketed medicines were found to have new activities that became their major use.

CHOOSING THERAPEUTIC AREAS TO RESEARCH

Where Does One Look to Find a New Medicine?

There is a well-known story that captures the essence of the answer to this question. An adult man was down on all fours late at night, obviously looking for something under a street lamp. Another man walked up and told the first man that he would be happy to help, but where did the man lose the object? The first man answered, "Oh, about 20 yards away." "Then why look here?" the other asked. "Because, this is where the light is," the first man replied.

In pharmaceutical research, companies are focusing most of their efforts in areas where the light is, not in many of the dark areas, where they believe many important medicines are. This is unfortunate, but researchers are generally limited to looking for new medicines where biological tests exist to evaluate compounds. Also, the data from those tests must be sufficiently predictive of human activity to justify spending the large sums of money necessary to develop a medicine to the point where activity in humans can be assessed. In many situations, such as looking for new medicines for schizophrenia or Alzheimer's disease, we know that we would like to look in different areas using better glasses. Another way of expressing this concept is that we would like to have better tests to aid our search for new medicines, but those improved glasses (animal test models) do not yet exist in many disease areas.

Description and Definitions of Therapeutic Areas

One of the most sensitive and important issues in research-based pharmaceutical companies concerns the decision of which therapeutic areas to explore in a search for new medicines. Although this issue may superficially appear to have a simple answer (e.g., those areas of greatest medical and commercial need), it is actually a complex issue at many companies, with many tensions and pressures from both within and outside the research groups. Identifying new therapeutic areas to explore is an infrequent but important decision at most companies.

A therapeutic area is defined as a major area of medicine in which medicines are presently or could potentially be used. These areas include basic specialties of internal medicine (e.g., cardiology, gastroenterology, rheumatology, nephrology) plus psychiatry, neurology, anesthesiology, and numerous other fields of medicine. These categories may be viewed as a *primary level.* Specific diseases, syndromes, or conditions within each of those medical areas represent a *secondary level* of the therapeutic areas.

A *tertiary level* relating to therapeutic areas may be defined as the approaches and methods followed to discover new medicines within each of the secondary areas (i.e., diseases) being researched. More specifically, this tertiary level refers to the number of different places in biochemical pathways, pharmacological systems, physiological processes, and/or pathological stages of a disease that are being explored (often simultaneously) in looking for a new medicine. Decisions about therapeutic areas to explore are made on at least the three different levels described. These may be summarized as (1) broad therapeutic areas, (2) specific diseases, and (3) approaches to be used. More decisions relate to the latter two levels than to the first.

Who Has Input and Who Decides About Therapeutic Areas to Explore?

Within the research and development group, the major individuals who have input into decisions about therapeutic areas to explore (primary level) are the (1) director of research and development, (2) head of research, (3) department heads of relevant preclinical departments (e.g., organic chemistry, pharmacology, biochemistry, molecular biology), and (4) senior scientists within the relevant preclinical departments. The actual decision may be made at one or more of these administrative levels and usually depends primarily on whether the proposal contains good ideas scientifically. In addition, the decision makers will usually consider company objectives, marketing goals, and the company's comfort zone. If the decision is not made by the director of research and development, then each of the relevant individuals must

usually review decisions made with those people above them in the research and development hierarchy. Depending on the training and personality of the company's president and chief executive officer, he or she may also desire to review and approve these decisions.

Decisions on secondary areas to explore and the tertiary level of approaches are usually made at lower levels in the organization. Research scientists often propose the tertiary level approaches they believe offer the best opportunities for discovering a new medicine.

The above discussion assumes that a company has a single site at which research to discover medicines is conducted. This is often untrue, because multinational companies usually have two or more research centers. In those instances, each site may explore and also develop different therapeutic areas, or another means of dividing their research activities may be used.

Marketing Input into Choosing Therapeutic Areas to Explore

Outside the research and development environment, there are a number of groups (primarily in marketing) that often seek to influence the areas in which research is conducted. Marketing personnel are usually primarily interested in the second level of therapeutic areas (i.e., specific diseases). Research scientists are generally aware of which medical areas have unmet therapeutic needs and usually understand whether there is or is not commercial value for such potential medicines. It is often important to identify therapeutic areas that a company does not wish to explore.

Commercial information from marketing personnel provides valuable input to research scientists in assisting them to make decisions about the first two levels. One of the difficulties with accepting a marketing assessment of which therapeutic or disease areas to research is that a group attempting to find a medicine for Disease X may uncover a medicine for Disease Y or Z. Medicines for Diseases Y or Z may be much less attractive to marketing than a medicine for Disease X. Also, the commercial value of a medicine depends to a large degree on how closely its activity profile compares with that of an ideal or the best available medicine for the specific disease. The answer to that question cannot be known until the medicine has been in clinical trials for a number of years. A "slight" change in efficacy or safety often determines whether a medicine is a large moneymaker or an "also ran" that never repays its cost of development. Finally, medicines developed for one disease are sometimes found to be useful for others. In addition to this happening for a number of common medicines, many and possibly most medicines used to treat rare diseases (i.e., orphan medicines) are found in this manner.

TABLE 20.3. *Basic combinations of approaches to the three levels of therapeutic areas*

	Number of general therapeutic areas (primary level)	Number of diseases within each therapeutic area (secondary level)	Number of approaches used to study each disease (tertiary level)
1.	Few	Few	Few
2.	Few	Many	Few
3.	Few	Many	Many
4.	Few	Few	Many
5.	Many	Few	Few
6.	Many	Many	Few
7.	Many	Many	Many
8.	Many	Few	Many

How Many Different Therapeutic Areas Should Be Explored Simultaneously?

This question stimulates endless debate between those who wish to explore a small area intensively and those who believe that spreading research resources thinly over a broad area increases the chances of success (i.e., discovering a medicine). There are no simple answers to this debate.

The decision of how broadly to explore each therapeutic area being researched is usually made by the director of research and development in conjunction with the head of research. Other individuals may also be involved in this decision. The personalities, philosophies, and interests of the individuals involved will determine the decisions reached. One aspect of their philosophy would involve their general concept of research. If they have an image analogous to looking for a few diamonds lying on

Choosing Therapeutic and Disease Areas to Research for Medicine Discoveries

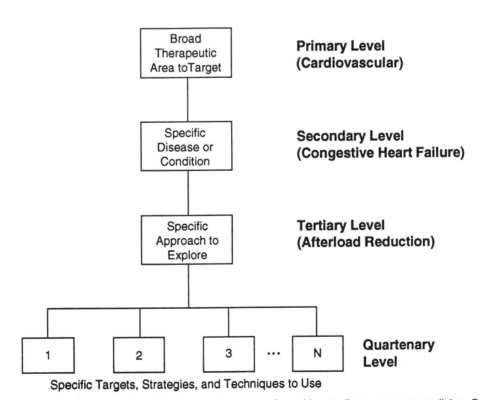

FIG. 20.3. Four levels considered in conducting research seeking to discover a new medicine. Specific examples of the first three are given. Multiple or a single target, strategy, and technique may be used to explore the tertiary level. A company may explore many (or few) approaches at each level.

the surface of a large endless landscape, they might tend to deploy their staff over a broad area. If their image is analogous to looking for a diamond amidst tons of coal and rubble in a deep mine, they may choose to focus activities on a smaller number of areas to search more intensively. One of these basic approaches is usually followed at a pharmaceutical company, although it probably makes sense for most companies to use both approaches but in different therapeutic areas.

To illustrate possible approaches to the three levels of therapeutic areas, basic combinations are listed below. The therapeutic areas and diseases being researched may represent any of the combinations found in Table 20.3 and in Fig. 20.3.

It is unlikely that any company's research group approaches this issue as systematically as described here, but their philosophy will tend to lead them toward using a few of these eight general directions. The actual situation followed at many research-based pharmaceutical companies is that within some therapeutic areas many diseases are pursued and within other therapeutic areas few diseases are pursued.

What Are the Criteria to Use in Determining Which Therapeutic Areas to Explore?

There are numerous broad or general criteria, as well as many specific criteria that should be considered in determining which general therapeutic areas to explore. Once these criteria are used, the decision about each of the potential therapeutic areas to explore should be more straightforward. Broad criteria include:

1. medical value in terms of therapeutic need in each of the areas being considered (e.g., Fig. 20.4);
2. commercial value of each market area in terms of both present and anticipated future size;

SELECTED THERAPEUTIC OPPORTUNITIES IN CARDIOLOGY

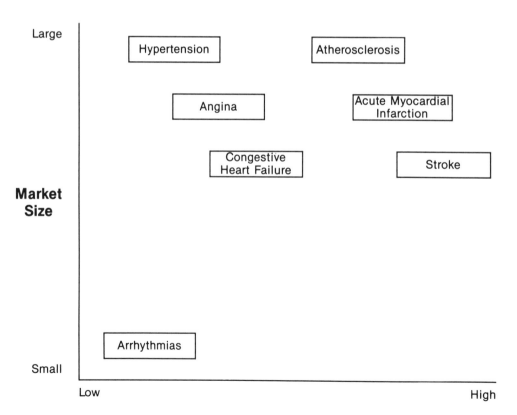

FIG. 20.4. Selected therapeutic opportunities in cardiology for new medicine development.

3. skills of the scientific staff presently employed and those available to be hired or consulted;
4. interests of the scientific staff and managers;
5. other medicines (both marketed and investigational) in the area from the same company;
6. availability of suitable animal models to predict efficacy in humans; and
7. traditions of the company in emphasizing certain therapeutic areas.

A more specific criterion is the presence of worthwhile chemical leads or novel scientific ideas for developing medicines.

Choosing the Number of New Compounds of One Type to Develop

There may be sound medical reasons (e.g., greater convenience and compliance, improved tolerance, efficacy for patients not helped by others) to develop several medicines of one therapeutic or chemical class such as beta-blockers or nonsteroidal anti-inflammatory medicines. But, after 10 or 15 medicines of the same type are marketed, it is difficult to justify the development of additional ones. Some research and marketing directors believe that most markets can only support two to four medicines of any one type. Incentives to develop additional medicines of the same type generally decrease as regulatory agencies become more resistant to approving newer versions where many similar medicines exist. This trend is already occurring in North America where many nonsteroidal anti-inflammatory medicines, beta-receptor antagonists, and other examples exist. Another factor that will diminish "me-too" medicines is the fact that hospitals, health maintenance organizations (HMOs), provinces with national health, and other medical provider organizations that have formularies are becoming resistant to including new medicines that have no demonstrated benefits over existing therapy. Such benefits may, however, be defined in terms of quality of life, cost effectiveness, compliance, and other categories in addition to just efficacy and safety.

Competition of Medicine Discovery Ideas for Resources

Within most medicine discovery groups of research-based pharmaceutical companies, literally hundreds if not thousands of novel ideas surface each year. Many of these require resources in terms of staff effort and time to evaluate their feasibility or quality. Because of commitments to ongoing projects, only a small number of these ideas can be evaluated, and usually only a tiny number are fully evaluated. One critical question is which ideas are evaluated and to what degree? In an ideal situation ideas with the greatest scientific merit would be the ones evaluated. But, in this imperfect world, there are two other major factors that influence the decision.

First, it is often impossible to determine the true scientific value of an idea until after the idea is actually tested. Some of the most outlandish ideas are found to be correct after the experiments have been done, and other ideas that seem both true and valuable are shown to be false. Therefore, there is a degree of guesswork at an early stage in ranking ideas according to their ultimate value.

Second, there is the issue of company politics. Everyone knows (or should know) that the value of an idea equals its intrinsic value times the position of the idea's proponent to the third power. Therefore, if someone wants to have an idea receive a more sympathetic hearing from management, that person might wish to seek a superior in the company to sponsor the idea. Alternatively, the innovator might turn the idea over to a superior in the hope that that would enhance its chance of being approved for evaluation. If a committee is to evaluate the idea, it might be advisable for the idea's proponent to meet each of the members in advance to review and lobby for the idea before it is actually proposed. Many ideas are turned down because they were never properly understood by the group that discussed them. This situation could often be avoided by having the idea's sponsor conduct preliminary discussions with committee members. This is especially important when the idea's sponsor is not present at the major meeting where the idea's ultimate fate is determined.

Pertinent questions for a company to assess are whether the best ideas are being proposed or being suppressed? Do scientists believe their ideas are being given a fair hearing? Also, is there a formal system to air new ideas of medicine discovery? For example, a written document could be presented every half year in which new ideas could be presented. In addition, a scientific forum could be held periodically where ideas would be presented and critiqued. Ultimately, ideas that require major resources must be evaluated by senior research managers, and those that require little time or resources may be reviewed by scientists who would perform the experiments. Figure 20.5 illustrates some of these issues.

A few other suggestions for scientists or others who wish to have their research (or other) ideas adopted are to (1) attempt to integrate the proposed idea into existing work or into a part of the company (as opposed to proposing that a totally new group or department be formed), (2) identify each of the steps that will be necessary to propose the idea, (3) plan each of those steps in a logical sequence, (4) initiate the process but do not rush any of the individual steps, (5) show how others will benefit from the proposal, (6) include a clear rationale in the proposal, (7) conduct a few preliminary tests to demonstrate the likely value of the concept, (8) support the concept with published information, and (9) include other scientists in the proposal.

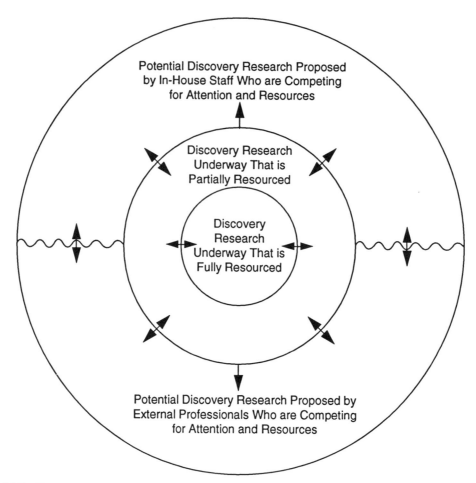

FIG. 20.5. The competition for resources in discovery activities. Activities closest to the center are best financed and intellectually supported, and those at the perimeter are least well supported.

Initiating Activities in a New Therapeutic Area of Research

After a decision is reached to conduct research in a new therapeutic area (primary level), it may be quite convenient and straightforward to reassign scientists to the new therapeutic area within their own discipline (e.g., biochemistry). If the new area of research requires the same general skills and methods, then reassigning personnel is usually possible. The ability to reassign people successfully to a new therapeutic area depends on the individuals, their interests, and how well their knowledge and experience enable them to make the transition. If a totally new therapeutic area is to be explored, then many scientists would balk at being reassigned from an area in which they are trained, are experienced, and are building their careers. This is generally the case for pharmacologists and physiologists who are asked to take on totally new types of methods and approaches. On the other hand, many biochemists and chemists would not have to alter their technical skills and approaches in

switching from one therapeutic field to another, and it is much easier to make a switch in those disciplines.

Because of limitations in moving personnel in many biological sciences, it is often necessary to hire a number of new scientific staff when a decision is made to enter a new therapeutic area. When a relatively large group of five or more professional staff is needed within a single discipline, it is usually desirable to hire initially a single experienced individual to head the group. That person is then given the task of hiring the additional staff needed. This approach helps assure that the group assembled will work well together and have skills that are appropriate to deal with their newly assigned tasks.

Should Pharmaceutical Companies Be Engaged in Basic Research?

Many scientists talk about basic and applied research as if they were easily separated categories. The fact is that many definitions are used for each term, and sometimes there is a great deal of overlap between the two terms.

Numerous scientists deny that any meaningful distinction can be made. For example, Bartholini (1983, p. 143) wrote that "basic and applied research, by my approach, are unified; the same investigator has to screen—which is a fundamental part of pharmacological research—and has to investigate biological mechanisms." The mechanisms referred to are usually considered as part of basic research, and screening is considered as applied research. Nonetheless, these views depend on to whom one speaks. The author believes there are different types of research conducted within a pharmaceutical company and that they may be visualized as a spectrum that includes both basic and applied research. One such spectrum is shown in Fig. 20.15. Toward the basic research end of the spectrum, the connection to medicine discovery or development becomes progressively weaker. Research-based pharmaceutical companies must be engaged in both basic and applied types of research. One major issue is to decide how much of each activity should be conducted, although certain research has both applied and basic characteristics.

Some people use the term "basic research" to apply to speculative, fundamental, nondirected, nontargeted, or exploratory research that is curiosity-driven and without any clearly identifiable usefulness. This type of research is most often conducted in academic institutions. Using this definition, many research-based pharmaceutical companies desire to conduct a limited amount of basic research. This is often justified by the belief that this type of work is far removed from medicine discovery. It is accepted that basic research has the potential for leading to a major breakthrough in scientific understanding, which *may* be able to be converted into (1) a new animal test model, (2) a new chemical series, or (3) a new approach to discovering medicines. One of these three tools *may* eventually in turn lead to discovery of a breakthrough medicine. For example, if a little-studied or previously unknown enzyme is found to be important for a specific disease (scientific breakthrough), then animal tests can be established to look for compounds that act as inhibitors, stimulators, or mimics of the enzyme. If an active lead compound is found, it would encourage chemists to make many analogues.

In the scenario described, it is clear that a scientific breakthrough is not adequate on its own to discover a new medicine. It is for this reason (and others) that many research-based companies rely on scientific breakthroughs achieved in the academic community, rather than trying to compete with the small staff that the company could assign to exploratory research. All research-based pharmaceutical companies carefully read important scientific journals looking for information that could trigger a new approach to discover worthwhile and important medicines. Some research directors claim that *exploratory research* (i.e., toward the basic research end of the spectrum) conducted within the pharmaceutical

company is the "seed corn" of future medicine discoveries for their company. But a little reflection will reveal several weaknesses of this rationale (e.g., the small staff size of a single company is competing with much larger numbers of academicians, the connection between a successful scientific breakthrough and the discovery of a medicine that exploits the breakthrough may never be made, many major scientific discoveries are available to be exploited for medicine discoveries by anyone who reads the literature).

Comroe and Dripps (1976) described six types of basic research:

1. basic research unrelated to the solution of a clinical problem (e.g., Landsteiner's discovery of human blood groups, found as he was investigating an immunological problem);
2. basic research related to the solution of a clinical problem (e.g., Landsteiner's discovery that a virus caused poliomyelitis in monkeys);
3. studies not concerned with basic biological, chemical, or physical mechanisms (e.g., purely descriptive studies of a new disease or clinical observations that did not initially require research, such as the observation that inhalation of ether causes anesthesia);
4. review and critical analysis of published work and synthesis of new concepts (without new experimental data);
5. developmental work to create, improve, or perfect apparatus or a technique for research use; and
6. developmental work to create, improve, or perfect apparatus or a technique for use in diagnosis or care of patients.

Research Programs

Research programs may be defined in many ways. One typical definition is that it is a research project that involves two or more scientists from two or more departments. Programs may be coordinated and led by formally appointed leaders or managed through informal reporting and communication lines. If the appointed leader coordinates activities in two or more departments, then this is an example of the matrix approach. The coordinator may also be responsible for the scientific and technical direction of the program as well as for conduct of the research within his or her discipline.

Each research program may be initiated informally or only after a written proposal for the new program has been prepared and adopted. This proposal could include minimum criteria for a new candidate medicine to achieve. Progress on each program may be monitored through reports and periodic reviews. Criteria for a new compound to achieve before it is advanced toward human studies may be theoretical (i.e., ideal), may be realistic, or may represent the minimal acceptable criteria (see Chapter 34, Criteria for Developing Medicines).

METHODS OF MEDICINE DISCOVERY

Scientists seek to identify a sensitive locus (target for a medicine to act at) that has importance in a biological system (e.g., an important enzyme, a receptor, a physiological system) and then to look for compounds that affect this locus.

Which Comes First—the Biological Mechanism or the New Chemical Compound?

A biological mechanism of action is an explanation of how a compound or medicine elicits a biological (or clinical) activity. Biological mechanisms exist at many levels, such as subcellular, cellular, tissue, organ, entire animal or human organism, and population of animal or human organisms. Therefore, a medicine does not have a single mechanism of action. The term often refers to a biochemical description at the subcellular or cellular level or to a physiological description at the tissue or organ level.

The answer to the question of which comes first is—either or both. Some compounds or medicines are found empirically to have a biological activity, and a search is then mounted to determine their mechanism of action. In other situations, biological mechanisms are used as targets in animal test models (e.g., enzyme stimulation, receptor inhibition, ion movements, biochemical changes). Newly made chemicals are evaluated in these tests for their activity. In those cases, knowledge of a compound's mechanism precedes the discovery of a chemical compound that has an acceptable profile. A test may be established to measure a compound's ability to stimulate a particular enzyme, which is believed to be responsible for eliciting a physiological effect that leads to clinical improvement. The mechanisms of action of most medicines are unknown. Even when a biological mechanism is known at one level, activities at other biological levels are often not known with certainty and must be investigated after an active compound is found. The usual situation involves a variety of theories and hypotheses about each of the multiple mechanisms for a single medicine and different amounts of evidence that exist in support of each.

Establishing Criteria for a Compound's Performance During the Discovery Period

Three major types of criteria may be established for a compound to meet during the discovery period: ideal, realistic/desirable, and minimally acceptable. A company may have some or all research programs or projects that use one (or more) of these criteria. It should be clear to both scientists and managers whether the criteria are of the first, second, or third type. The criteria would describe the nature and magnitude of activities, potencies, toxicities, and other relevant compound characteristics. These should be reviewed by all departments participating in the discovery phase of the particular program or project. This approach would ensure that successful compounds would be advanced by consensus and also that compounds that did not achieve at least minimal criteria would not be advanced. An example of ideal criteria is given in Table 26.2. The pros and cons of using realistic versus ideal versus minimal criteria are not discussed here.

In addition to these three types of prospective criteria for a compound to meet, it is also important to determine which criteria are *musts* and which are *shoulds*. The latter criteria are desirable but not essential. In some circumstances a range of activity may be used in describing a criterion (see Chapter 34, Criteria for Developing Medicines).

There is some overlap between criteria used for a compound's performance during the discovery and development periods. Criteria for a medicine's development are discussed later in this chapter. If a new indication is identified at any stage during the discovery or development period, the relevant criteria may be entirely or partially established retrospectively, instead of prospectively, as described.

Basic Approaches and Methods of Medicine Discovery

A specific chemist who is synthesizing novel compounds to be evaluated as medicines and the biologists testing those compounds may or may not have a systematic and logical approach to their work. Even if their approach is not totally systematic, they usually do have a sound underlying concept or rationale. It is possible that their hypothesis is totally flawed, but their approach may still be sound and logical. This latter situation is known as being on a "wild goose chase," because there is almost no chance of success. The general approaches of medicine discovery utilize *empirical* (i.e., trial and error), *rational* (i.e., totally planned), *random* (i.e., testing any compounds), and *serendipitous* (i.e., pure chance) methods. These four approaches are described below. Most often two or more of these methods are involved in the discovery of any single medicine (see Chapter 19, Overview of Factors Affecting Medicine Discovery).

Random Screening

The approach of screening compounds with little preselection is not being currently used at most companies, although some companies use this method to screen natural products or compounds. This method is a minor one even in those companies that use it. Prior to 1950 it was used to a greater extent.

Serendipity

Serendipity may occur at any stage of discovery, development, or marketing by scientists or clinicians outside as well as inside the company. This method cannot be planned for in the sense that serendipity is not used as a formal tool to discover new medicines. "Intentional serendipity" is an approach to evaluate low-probability ideas. True serendipity occurs more frequently to those people intellectually capable of understanding the point and who are also sensitized to receiving or looking for it. This type of serendipity is more successful in companies with more creative scientists and clinicians.

Rational Medicine Discovery

There is a great deal of variation in the scope of activities referred to as rational medicine discovery. At one extreme, any concept or approach that involves a scientific rationale may be considered as rational discovery. This is a far too open-ended and liberal definition because it would include almost anything that is not purely random screening of materials for biological activity. This definition also would include the empirical trial-and-error approach as being part of rational discovery. At the other end of the spectrum is pure rational discovery, in which a computer model of an active site enables a chemist to design the single molecule that will bind to the receptor. This is followed by its synthesis and testing, wherein the compound is found to be active. The preferred definition is one that focuses on this end of the spectrum, i.e., where a known chemical that is hypothesized to have a specific activity based on computer modeling techniques is designed based on a theoretical model. Thus, there is an enormous gap between a sound scientific rationale and rational medicine development.

Rational medicine discovery means that a person or group has designed (often using computers) a specific molecule that will have a desired biological effect. This process occurs prior to making the compound or testing in animals. The molecule is then synthesized, and it is found to cause the predicted biological effect. Rational medicine discovery is often discussed in the press as if it is a current reality, instead of an ultrarudimentary tool that we hope will someday be able to design medicines that help treat patients.

No single medicine has ever been found using a purely rational method. British anti-Lewisite (BAL), which perhaps comes closest to this ideal, was based on a scientifically rational concept, but over 100 different compounds were made before BAL was discovered. This discovery occurred as a result of the trial-and-error approach and not as a result of rational techniques. Thus, rational medicine discovery may trigger the search and provide a starting point for the search, but it has not yet provided the structure of a compound that has become a useful medicine.

Perhaps later in the 21st century our improved knowledge of biology plus enhanced computer modeling capabilities may enable scientists to approach this desired state (i.e., rational medicine design). But that goal is unlikely to be achieved. While we may conceptualize the structure of a compound that reaches the active site on an enzyme and causes the receptor to be blocked or inhibited, it is pure science fiction (at least today) to imagine that the safety of the molecule in humans may be assured in advance of clinical testing.

In some fields where the structure of the active site is known and active medicines or compounds are available, improved medicines that have enhanced activity or potency can sometimes be designed. Nonetheless, pure rational methods will never totally replace the empirical trial-and-error approach to the testing of compounds. For example, even a change as small as changing the salt used for a medicine may have a major impact on safety that could not be known or predicted prior to synthesis and testing of the new compound.

Biotechnology

Biotechnology is often mentioned as the answer to the desire to achieve rational medicine discovery. Biotechnology products, however, usually involve proteins or polypeptides, which are pieces of proteins. Almost all of these molecules are simply too large to be absorbed orally or are rapidly destroyed in the stomach and intestine by digestive enzymes. These compounds must be administered parenterally to patients, usually by the intravenous route. Although new active molecules will be found through biotechnology methods, their effects on most diseases in medicine will generally be limited until smaller molecules are made that can be taken orally or improved methods are discovered to get large-molecular-weight compounds absorbed. Biotechnology techniques are becoming more widely used with sugars, lipids, and nucleic acids of relatively small molecular weights. An example of a smaller molecule causing the same clinical response as a large one is noted with meperidine (Demerol) versus large-molecular-weight endorphins to relieve pain. Other potential problems caused by using the larger protein or polypeptide molecules are (1) the development of antibodies within the body and (2) the contamination by foreign protein during manufacture. These problems, however, are usually soluble.

The question sometimes arises as to whether using biotechnology techniques to prepare molecules is an example of rational medicine discovery. When an extract of biological material or a mixture of natural products is found to cause an important physiological response, scientists attempt to isolate the active substance. The active substance may be able to be prepared in large scale by biotechnology techniques to test it further. This process is not an example of rational medicine discovery. Also, preparing monoclonal antibodies is not an example of rational medicine discovery because scientists make whole series of antibodies and can make numerous manipulations for each. All of these products are tested for their activity, and the best products pursued. Interestingly, the specific targeted disease cannot usually be identified in advance of finding activity in specific biological tests.

The methods used to discover medicines focus on the following topics.

Animal Models of Human Diseases

It is desirable when an animal model that yields valid data is available to use for testing compounds. Extrapolations of data obtained in *in vivo* animal tests to human patients is usually better than extrapolating *in vitro* data. Unfortunately, data obtained in most animal models often extrapolate poorly to human patients. Table 20.4 lists ways that *in vivo* pharmacological data obtained in animals may be extrapolated to humans or animals.

Most medicines elicit many pharmacological and biochemical effects. In many situations it is uncertain which specific properties of a medicine play an essential role in providing clinical benefits. This information is important if scientists are to design and develop the most appropriate animal models to test new compounds. Issues relating to animal models are described in more detail later in this chapter.

TABLE 20.4. *Uses of extrapolating* in vivo *pharmacological data from animals*

A. To understand and explain the following (in animals):
  1. Effects at a physiological, biochemical, or molecular level
  2. Effects of other *in vivo* pharmacological tests
  3. Effects of *in vitro* pharmacological tests
  4. Results in toxicology tests
  5. Results in the same test under different experimental conditions (e.g., different dosages, routes of administration, test parameters, dosing regimens)
B. To understand and explain the following (in humans):
  1. Efficacy in one or more diseases
  2. Toxicity
  3. Absorption
  4. Duration of action

Biological Mechanisms of Human Diseases

It may be desired to find new compounds that act similarly to a particular known medicine. A specific biological mechanism may be identified that is responsible for a desired therapeutic effect. In other cases, however, the biological mechanism of a known medicine may be uncertain. For example, a known antidepressant may interact with an important chemical transmitter in the brain (e.g., dopamine, norepinephrine, serotonin). Even though it is uncertain that this mechanism is the basis for the medicine's action, it is hypothesized to be important. Thus, new compounds are tested to determine if they possess the same effect. If they do, then consideration of advancing them toward clinical trials is made.

Hypothetical Systems to Evaluate Compound Activity

A specific biochemical reaction in a metabolic pathway or an enzyme's activity may be hypothesized to be important in a particular disease. Even though no medicines may currently exist that act specifically on the biochemical reaction or enzyme, new chemicals are made that are directed at one of these two targets. Preclinical trials are conducted to test for the desired activity.

Targeting Compounds to Interact with Receptors

A receptor may be thought of as whatever the medicine attaches to in order to cause its effect. The chemist wants to know how the receptor "sees" the potential medicine molecule and where the key points are for the medicine to attach to the receptor (e.g., enzyme, cell). In this manner, when a chemist makes a small compound that is a piece of an enzyme, hormone, or other large chemical, the chemist hopes that it will preserve the activity of the much larger molecule. This has occurred in many situations (e.g., with enkephalins).

Evaluation of Metabolites

Metabolic aspects of medicines may also serve as a source of ideas for medicine discovery. Most medicines, like food, are chemically changed or metabolized inside our bodies. Although this process primarily occurs in the liver, it also takes place in the kidneys, lungs, and other organs. Although medicines are usually converted to less toxic and less effective compounds, a number of metabolites are actually more toxic or more active than the parent medicine. Some metabolites may have unexpected activities. It is these unexpected activities that may make the metabolite a model for further chemical manipulation. The metabolite thus serves as a chemical lead that stimulates the chemist to synthesize new compounds.

A metabolite may have more desirable properties than the parent medicine. In such situations the metabolite may also be developed as a medicine (e.g., desmethylimipramine is a metabolite of imipramine, and both are marketed for treatment of depression). Alternatively, the metabolite may replace the parent medicine in medical therapy (e.g., acetaminophen is a metabolite of phenacetin), or the parent medicine may be viewed as a promedicine that delivers the more active metabolite to the body (e.g., the promedicine 6-mercaptopurine is converted to the active metabolite 6-mercaptopurine ribonucleotide, the promedicine acyclovir is converted to the active metabolite acyclovir triphosphate). Some metabolites possess sufficient biological activity to be used as medicines. An example of this is shown in Fig. 20.6. Diazepam is metabolized to nordiazepam, which in turn is metabolized to oxazepam. Each of these metabolites was developed and marketed as a separate medicine.

Using a Combination of Approaches

Two or more of the above approaches may be combined, either in the same test for a new medicine or as part of multiple biological (e.g., pharmacological) tests performed to evaluate a single medicine. This topic is described in greater detail in Chapter 89 of *Guide to Clinical Trials* (Spilker, 1991).

Improving the Biological Profile of an Active Compound

Once a compound with a desired biological activity is found, others are made to try to optimize the beneficial activities while eliminating as many of the potentially toxic effects as possible (i.e., the chemists attempt to accentuate the positive and eliminate the negative). Although there is no relationship between the difficulty of making compounds and their biological activity, many chemists believe one of Nature's laws dictates that the most difficult compounds to make are the most active and interesting ones biologically. Another point of view is that the first compound made in a series often turns out to be the best.

One approach to designing chemicals is to create a hybrid compound that is based on two (or more) different structures that are each known to have activity. For example, if two medicines used to treat a disease act by different mechanisms, it may be possible to "marry" those two chemical structures into one molecule. It might also be possible to marry the *active* parts of those two molecules and achieve a medicine that works by both mechanisms. This approach is usually unsuccessful, but there are enough successes to make it an attractive proposition to try in numerous situations.

Looking for Chemical Analogues When a New Activity Is Found for a Marketed Medicine

What happens when a marketed medicine is found to have activity in a different disease than the one for which it is sold? Assume that the new disease was previously either untreatable or poorly treatable. Assume further that there are no adequate and widely accepted animal models that can predict activity in the new disease. What usually happens in this situation is as follows: the company whose medicine this is, as well as some (or many) academicians, will attempt to discern the medicine's mechanism of action (i.e., how and why the medicine elicited a beneficial response in the new disease). The chances of success are small, because the actual molecular mechanism of action of most medicines is unknown. Nonetheless, theories and hypotheses are proposed to explain the activity of all medicines. There are often many theories to explain how a single medicine works. Preclinical and clinical evidence is put forth in the medical literature to support or challenge each hypothesis.

If a particular hypothesis becomes widely accepted, and sometimes even if it does not, companies will establish biological tests to search for the same biological activity in other compounds. The assumption is that because the active medicine has a specific biological effect, which

METABOLIC DEGRADATION LEADING TO USEFUL NOVEL AGENTS

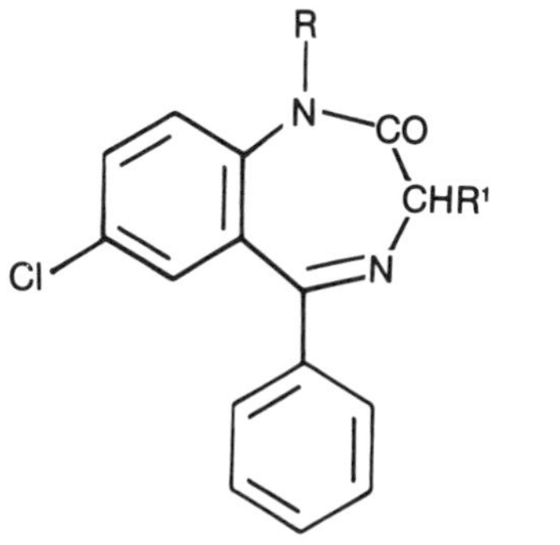

	R	R^1
Diazepam	CH$_3$	H
Nordiazepam	H	H
Oxazepam	H	OH

FIG. 20.6. Metabolic degradation of diazepam leads to nordiazepam, which in turn is converted to oxazepam, each of which is a useful medicine.

is hypothesized to be responsible for its clinical activity, other compounds that have the same biological activity will have the same clinical effect. This scientific approach to medicine discovery can be described as looking for analogues of the active medicine. It was also previously described as the biological mechanism approach, but in this situation the connection between the mechanism and the clinical effect is often highly uncertain.

Companies are motivated to begin this search when an active medicine has significant drawbacks. Therefore, close chemical analogues are often sought that may be more potent, be less toxic, have a greater therapeutic index, or have some other desired characteristic. Once an analogue is found with the desired characteristic(s), that analogue is developed further and, if appropriate, it is studied in humans. If this analogue also possesses clinical activity and especially if the desired characteristics are found in humans (e.g., greater potency, less toxicity), it tends to strongly support, and to a degree validate, the model(s) that demonstrated better activity or less toxicity than the original medicine.

Figure 20.7 illustrates a number of successful molecular manipulations that have been made in this way. Some of these required many compounds and years of

SUCCESSFUL MOLECULAR MANIPULATIONS

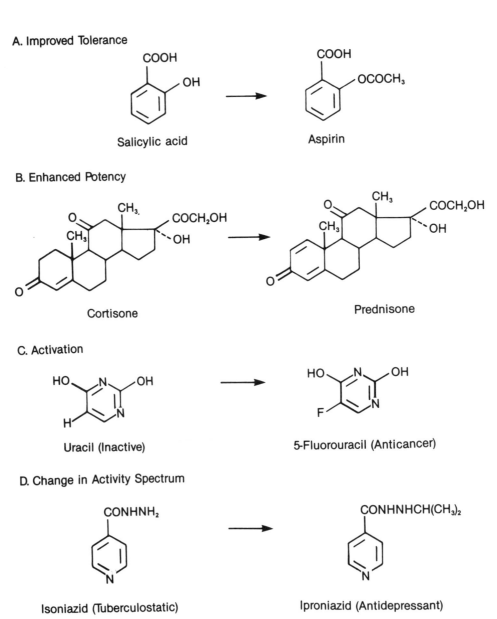

FIG. 20.7. Successful molecular manipulations leading to useful medicines. From Pletscher (1983) with permission of Raven Press.

effort before the improved medicine was identified. The characteristics of the original medicine that were improved are indicated in the figure.

Choosing the Specific Compounds to Synthesize

Figure 20.8 illustrates a sample of the enormously large number of different chemical substituents that can be placed on a simple or complex skeletal backbone. Realizing that the total number of possible changes is really the multiple of all possible changes at each point in the molecule (i.e., W possible changes at Point 1 times X possible changes at Point 2 times Y possible changes at Point 3 times Z possible changes at Point 4, etc.), it is clear that the number of different chemicals that could be synthesized based on a single, even simple, chemical structure could easily run into the hundreds of millions or billions. The basic structure shown in Fig. 20.8 is a natural product of the anthracycline group. Members of this chemical family are used as antitumor agents and antibiotics. Activities of related compounds vary by several orders of magnitude. In this particular example, substituents have been made at every possible position on the molecule.

The staggering numbers of possible compounds emphasize the need for scientific judgment in choosing which ones to synthesize. Fortunately, chemists usually have bits of information that help guide their choices so that they are not usually blindly choosing compounds to make. For example, they may know that adding certain types of chemical groups to the basic structure will raise or lower the compound's acidity or alkalinity, make the compound more (or less) soluble in water, mimic other compounds with known activity, enable the compound to resist metabolic breakdown in the body, assist in the compound's absorption, allow (or block) the compound's ability to penetrate the brain, or possess any one of numerous other physical, chemical, or biological properties. Certain parts of a chemical molecule are found to be more important than others for modifying a medicine's activity or toxicity. All of this information is used when a chemist decides which compounds to synthesize.

Several chemical and physical properties can be predicted in advance by analyzing structure-activity relationships or through using sophisticated computer modeling and electronic techniques. Nonetheless, it is virtually always necessary to make each compound to determine accurately whether the theory is in fact correct. Many surprises do arise.

When two or more chemists are given the task of modifying the same medicine or basic molecule, they are apt to approach the problem from different directions. Alternatively, they may proceed in the same direction but synthesize different specific compounds. Given the almost limitless number of possible variations to try, this is not surprising. On the other hand, certain chemical substituents seem to capture the attention of chemists as useful pieces to attach to a basic chemical backbone. Some chemists excel at designing new compounds to make, whereas others are more skillful in solving technical problems that occur in actually making new compounds.

POSSIBLE CHEMICAL MODIFICATIONS TO A CHEMICAL STRUCTURE

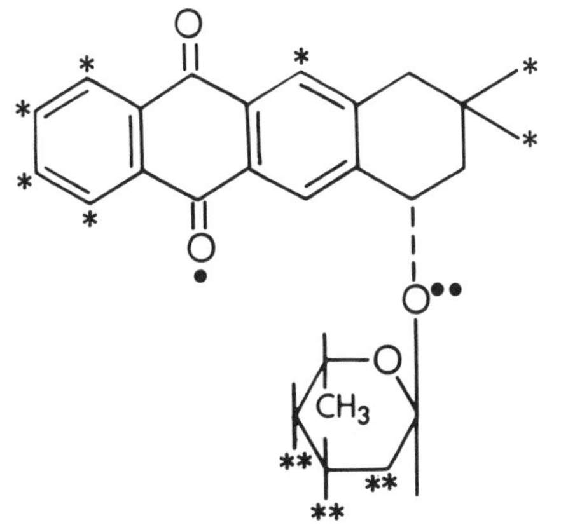

Site on Chemical	Representative Chemical Substituents to Add
*	H, OH, OCH_3, Cl, Br, I, F, NO_2 CN, OR, CH_2CH_3, $CH_2CH_2CH_3$, CF_3, CH_3, CH=CHR, $COCH_3$, $COCH_2OH$, $CO(CH_2)_nCH_3$, $CO(CH_2)_nOH$
**	H, NH_2, OH, Cl, Br, I, F, CF_3, $NHCOCH_3$, 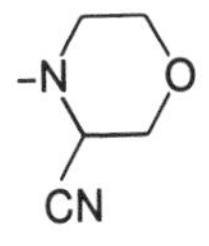 (morpholine ring)
●	NH, CN
●●	S, CH_2

R=Any of various other chemical groups

FIG. 20.8. Selected chemical groups that could be placed on a chemical backbone. The letter *R* stands for any chemical group.

Structure-Activity Relationships

A minor chemical change on a molecule sometimes leads to major changes in biological activity, while at other times a major chemical change has little or no effect on biological activity. The relationship between chemical structure and the biological activity that the chemicals elicit is called a structure-activity relationship (SAR). If minor chemical changes lead to major differences in pharmacological activity, it usually means that a lot of chemical work is necessary to fully characterize the SAR.

Figure 20.9 illustrates a series of structure-activity relationships for a hypothetical series of compounds. The vertical axis of biological activity refers to any pharmacological or other biological endpoint measured. The horizontal axis illustrates a property of the chemical compounds in the particular series being evaluated. Figure 20.9A illustrates ten compounds from any chemical series where the structures differ only in the length of one particular chain of atoms. Six of many possible SARs are illustrated in Panels A to F. Figure 20.10 illustrates an SAR pattern when the situation illustrated in Fig. 20.9A is modified so that changes are now occurring at different places on the chemical molecule. Individual chemicals are illustrated as dots in Figs. 20.9 and 20.10. Struc-

STRUCTURE-ACTIVITY RELATIONSHIPS

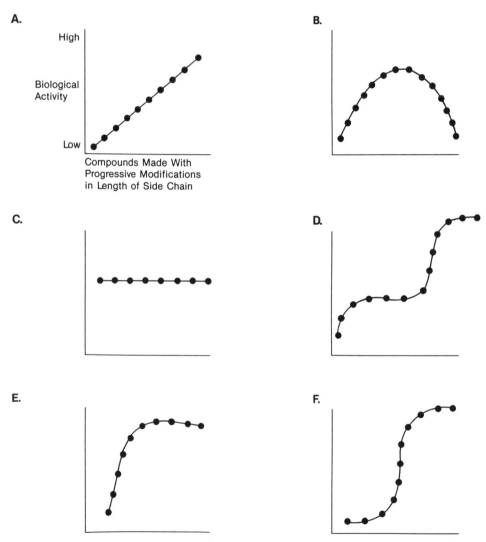

FIG. 20.9. Types of alterations in biological activity that may be observed in a series of closely related compounds with a single chemical modification. Each *dot* represents a single successive change (e.g., increasing the length of a side chain on the molecule).

STRUCTURE-ACTIVITY RELATIONSHIPS

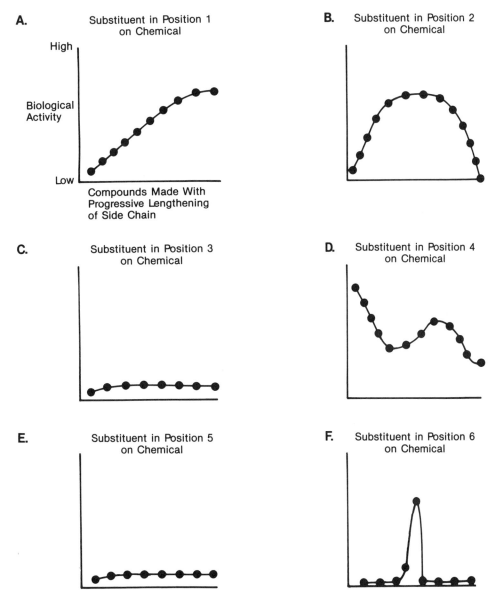

FIG. 20.10. Types of alterations in biological activity observed in a series of compounds with two chemical modifications (e.g., changing the position of one of the constituents and modifying the length of a side chain).

ture-activity relationships usually demonstrate more discontinuity than is shown in either Fig. 20.9 or Fig. 20.10.

Many other chemical parameters beside chain length could be evaluated for their influence on a specific biological activity. These parameters include basicity, acidity, lipophilicity, size of molecule, shape of molecule, and ability of the molecule to bind or dissociate. Chemists often do not change only one parameter at a time. Actual SARs are more complex when multiple parameters

differ between chemically related compounds, which makes the interpretation of SARs more difficult.

When a patent application is submitted for a chemically related group of compounds, it is desirable to have identified the most active compounds. Figure 20.11 illustrates four of many possible situations that refer to this issue. Each symbol represents the overall biological activity of a different chemical. This figure is drawn in two dimensions but is a schematic of a three-dimensional axis where three of the most important

STRUCTURE-ACTIVITY RELATIONSHIPS

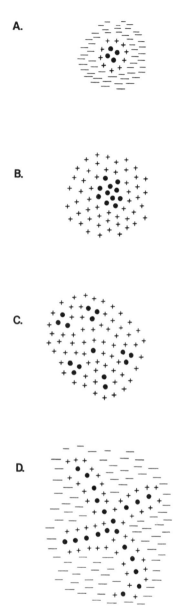

FIG. 20.11. Scope of biological activity in compounds with modified structures. Each *circle, plus,* or *minus* symbol represents the overall biological activity of a single chemical in a related series. **Panel A** illustrates high activity in four closely related compounds (●), lesser activity (i.e., fair to good) (+) in a group resembling them, and no activity (−) in all other variations made. Patent protection is relatively easy for this group. **Panel B** illustrates a situation where a wide variety of compounds are active, though the best activity resides in a single group of closely related compounds. **Panel C** shows excellent activity in several groups of compounds with different structures. It will generally be more difficult to patent these compounds unless all groups are known. **Panel D** represents a series of highly active compounds that, once defined, may be patented. The compound in the center represents the index compound. Those further away have progressively more modifications. It is important to synthesize many compounds to determine which model is pertinent to a specific case.

chemical parameters influencing biological activity are plotted. Panel A illustrates the best patentable situation from a chemical perspective because there is a clear delineation between active and inactive compounds. Panels B and C provide a good patentable situation to make a broad claim, but it is important to know where inactive compounds begin. Panel D illustrates a situation where it would be difficult to make a good patent claim unless one had made all of the compounds where activity resided. Otherwise, competitors could make and patent related compounds with the likelihood of detecting good biological activity. An example of this situation is illustrated later in this chapter for antihistamines (see "Examples of Success Stories").

Basic Questions to Ask About New Compounds

There are numerous pertinent questions that chemists (and biologists) often ask about new compounds.

1. How reproducible are the biological data obtained?
2. What is the physiological significance of the specific biological activity measured in animals?
3. What is the projected clinical significance of the biological effects measured in animals? Some biologists may not have already asked and answered this question.
4. If predicted biological effects are not observed, how can that information be interpreted and used to best advantage?
5. Is there a correlation between observed biological effects and the structures of the chemicals made (i.e., is there a structure-activity relationship)? This is a crucial issue in the medicine discovery process.

I hope that the information in this chapter points out that medicine discovery is not a process of someone suddenly shouting "eureka." Instead, it is a gradual, step-by-step improvement in activity and decrease of toxicity, involving the commitment of many people. Progress often seems to be a question of three steps forward and two steps backward. Eventually it is hoped that a compound with an acceptable biological profile will be found that may be developed into a medicine.

Identifying Backup Candidates

A backup candidate is a compound that may replace the medicine currently being developed (or one that is on the market) if it encounters serious problems (e.g., toxicity, lack of effect) and work must be terminated (or the medicine must be withdrawn from the market). Backup compounds should have one or more clinically important advantages over the initial medicine, which could be used by marketing people to position and sell the medicine.

It is almost always important for a company to search for one or more backup compounds for several reasons.

1. The first medicine may fail for reasons that might not cause the backup compound to fail.
2. The backup may have desirable characteristics not found in the first and could thus be marketed as an improvement or a second-generation medicine.
3. The backup might have a better patent life than the original medicine.
4. The backup could compete with the first medicine and possibly enlarge the total market or at the minimum make it difficult for other competitors to enter the market.
5. The backup could be licensed to another company.

MAJOR STEPS IN THE DEVELOPMENT OF CIMETIDINE

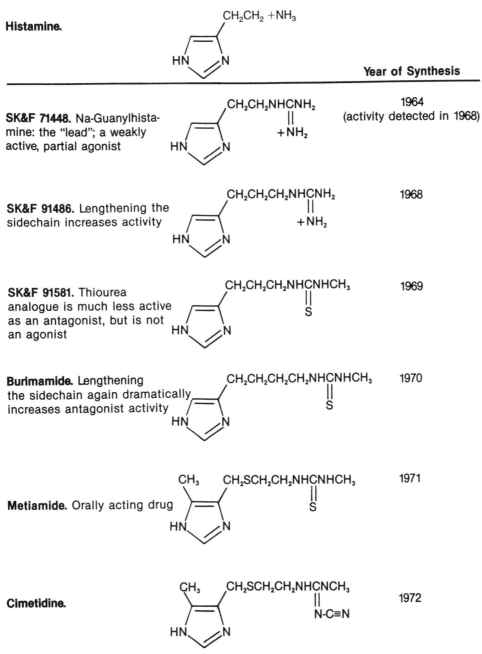

FIG. 20.12. Progressive improvements in histamine type-2 receptor antagonists. Compounds were all made by Smith Kline & French Laboratories and were modeled after histamine. Data were obtained primarily from Duncan and Parsons (1980). The year of cimetidine's original synthesis was kindly supplied by Dr. Anthony Flind of Smith Kline & French Laboratories (United Kingdom).

Examples of Success Stories

Smith Kline & French Laboratories developed bur-imamide for duodenal ulcers but terminated its development because of insufficient potency and a relative lack of oral activity. They then developed a backup compound, metiamide, but this medicine was terminated because of some cases of agranulocytosis. They developed a third compound, cimetidine (Tagamet), which was launched and became the most commercially successful medicine in the world for a number of years. The chemical differences between these three medicines and their predecessors are shown in Fig. 20.12. Other companies started developing antihistamine type-2 medicines and found that similar chemical structures still retained biological activity (Fig. 20.13) but allowed new patents to be obtained. Whereas Smith Kline & French Laboratories used an imidazole ring structure, which they considered important for activity, other companies found that different chemical ring systems could also be used.

A similar case can be described for the beta-receptor blocking medicines of ICI Holdings Ltd. (Imperial Chemical Industries). Their first medicine, dichloroiso-proterenol, was followed by pronethalol and finally by propranolol (Fig. 20.14). The chemical differences between the medicines in each series described are not great, but the medical and commercial differences between them are astronomical.

SELECTED RESEARCH ISSUES PRESENTED IN GREATER DEPTH

Molecular Modeling Tools to Help Design Better Medicines

Molecular modeling techniques utilize computers to help design chemical structures of compounds that should be able to bind to their target (i.e., receptor). Sometimes these tools are also able to predict whether the compound will bind or attach to the target and how well it will bind. A great deal of knowledge about the structure of an enzyme is needed to use this sophisticated approach, and in most therapeutic areas this approach

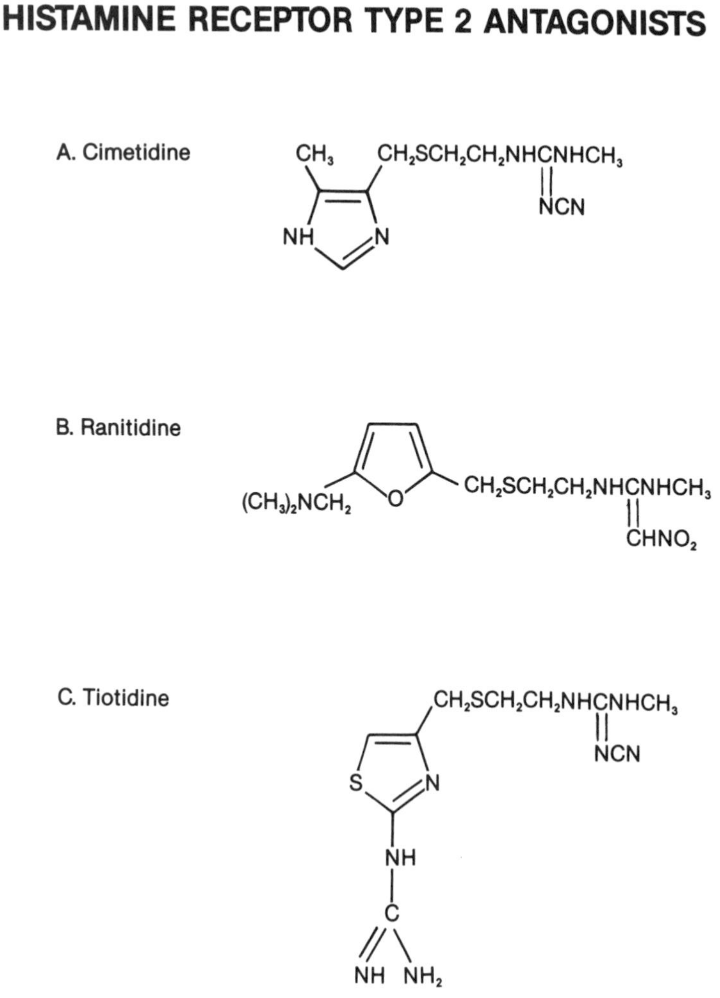

HISTAMINE RECEPTOR TYPE 2 ANTAGONISTS

FIG. 20.13. Histamine receptor type-2 antagonists developed after cimetidine, which were able to be patented. Ranitidine is made by Glaxo Inc., and tiotidine by ICI Holdings.

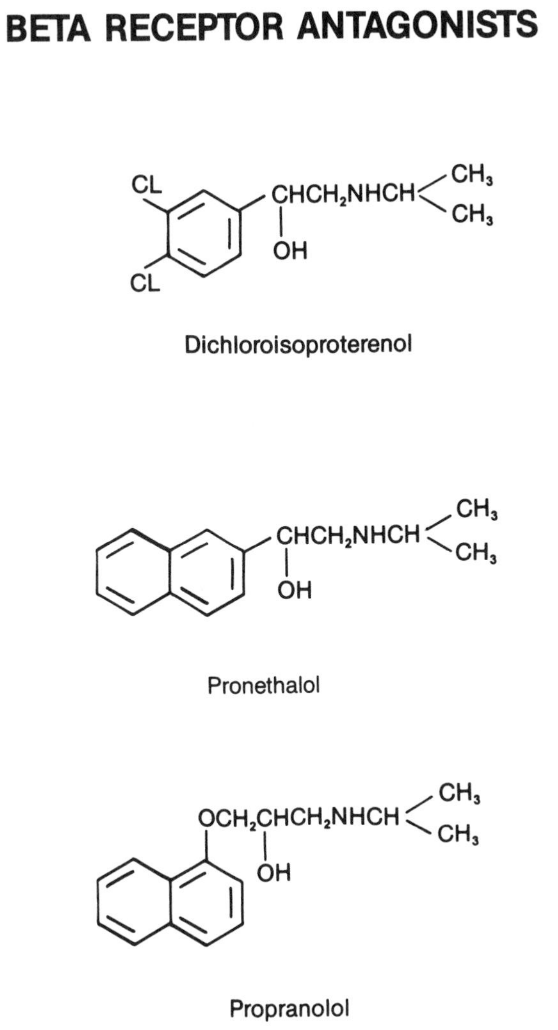

BETA RECEPTOR ANTAGONISTS

Dichloroisoproterenol

Pronethalol

Propranolol

FIG. 20.14. Progressive improvements in the early development of beta-receptor antagonists.

cannot currently be used because of a lack of this knowledge. It has been stated informally that these techniques were used to aid in the medicine design process for certain angiotensin-converting enzyme inhibitors. The situation regarding molecular modeling is changing rapidly, and a future hope is that predictions of biological events may be made based on changes in a compound's molecular structure.

Molecular modeling techniques involve determining x-ray structures of an enzyme and using computer graphics to convert this to a molecular image. This process stimulates chemists to design or modify a molecule by adding side chains or altering the constituents in a theoretical way. Quantitative structure-activity relationships have become an important tool that is used in molecular modeling (Schein et al., 1970; Kubinyi, 1990). A computer is then used to predict how those changes will affect the compound's physical and chemical properties. The compound may then be synthesized and its binding to receptors measured in different systems to evaluate

the accuracy of the original predictions. Even accurate predictions do not guarantee positive results in humans, because the wrong target may have been chosen or the actual target may be a combination of several enzymes or it may consist of other structures. It is usually not possible to determine the influence of a particular enzyme in affecting the course of a particular disease. These considerations indicate why imagination, creativity, and a certain degree of luck are necessary to achieve major advances in discovering medicines.

Is Medicine Discovery a Rational Process?

Well, partly. It is currently fashionable to claim that medicine discovery is evolving or, according to some, has evolved to a rational state. This latter statement is untrue, and the former possibility ("is evolving") is partly true. Even when important biological activity is uncovered as a result of rational concepts, it is still the old empirical trial-and-error approach that is used to evaluate additional compounds and to select the best compound to test in humans.

The more pertinent issue is really how can medicine discovery become a more rational process? The answer to this question must depend on development of newer technologies and experimental tools. With currently available methods the possibilities of utilizing a rational approach to discover new medicines are quite limited. Rational concepts may provide a starting point, but on their own they cannot lead to discovery of a satisfactory new medicine. In addition to the process of trial and error, serendipity is still an important element in discovering a new medicine or a new use for a marketed medicine.

The way a research question is posed is essential to how experiments are designed and conducted. For example, if one asks, "Why do platelets sometimes stick to the wall of a patient's diseased arteries?," it will lead scientists in a different direction when designing experiments than

if one asks, "Why do platelets not stick to the walls of healthy people's arteries?." This point is to indicate that creative scientists may approach a standard problem in a nonstandard way and attain a solution that has eluded others. Many aspects of such novel approaches are described in de Bono's book *The Use of Lateral Thinking* (1967) and in his other excellent books.

Gradient from Targeted to Exploratory Research

Almost all research in pharmaceutical companies may be called targeted because, with few exceptions, research may be associated with a particular disease or medical problem. Nonetheless, there is a gradient of research from that which is oriented toward discovering a new medicine to that which is exploratory and far from the paths of traditional medicine discovery (Fig. 20.15). In the more targeted discovery areas are those experiments and studies where new or known compounds are being screened for a biological activity or improved animal testing methods are being developed. Research into a specific activity attempting to find a target that can be used to discover medicines is an intermediate stage, as are studies evaluating a hypothesis that, if proven, could be used as a basis for medicine discovery. Toward the more exploratory end of this spectrum are studies evaluating a hypothesis that will not directly relate to medicine discovery. The connection of this type of exploratory research to new medicine discovery is usually remote and is generally viewed as having more long-term potential benefits to a company.

There is a widespread belief both inside and outside pharmaceutical companies that most new breakthrough medicines will come from more exploratory types of research. The truth of this view is debatable, because there are also examples of major breakthrough medicines coming from evaluating hypotheses much closer to the targeted end of the spectrum (e.g., inhibition of histamine receptors in the stomach to decrease gastric acid and improve the clinical status of patients with peptic ulcers). This topic is often discussed using the terms *basic research* and *applied research* discussed earlier in this chapter.

Is There a Long-Term Future for the Empirical Approach to Medicine Discovery?

There is no doubt that the empirical approach will always play a major role in discovering new medicines. The empirical approach, as differentiated from the rational, random, and serendipitous approaches to medicine discovery, involves taking a theory or a chemical lead compound and going back and forth between the chemist and biologist in a feedback loop to explore and develop means of improving the compound's beneficial effects and decreasing the toxic effects. This is primarily done by making new compounds to test.

Many, if not most, chemicals that are part of our body are presently either unknown or poorly characterized. After the chemical identity and biological function of additional compounds become known, they are likely to provide a model for chemists to use when synthesizing mimics and antagonists. Biologists in various disciplines (e.g., pharmacology, biochemistry, virology) will develop new screens to test these compounds for appropriate activities. This empirical approach to medicine discovery is the major approach currently used to discover new medicines at research-based pharmaceutical companies.

Empirical testing will always remain an important cornerstone in medicine discovery for a number of rea-

SPECTRUM OF RESEARCH ACTIVITIES IN A PHARMACEUTICAL COMPANY

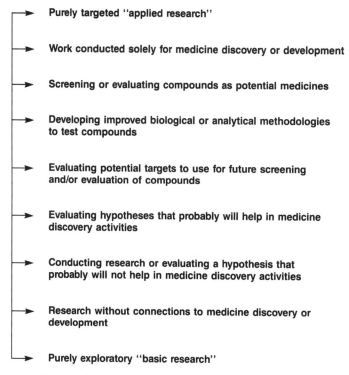

→ Purely targeted "applied research"

→ Work conducted solely for medicine discovery or development

→ Screening or evaluating compounds as potential medicines

→ Developing improved biological or analytical methodologies to test compounds

→ Evaluating potential targets to use for future screening and/or evaluation of compounds

→ Evaluating hypotheses that probably will help in medicine discovery activities

→ Conducting research or evaluating a hypothesis that probably will not help in medicine discovery activities

→ Research without connections to medicine discovery or development

→ Purely exploratory "basic research"

FIG. 20.15. Spectrum of research activities in a pharmaceutical company ranging from purely targeted to purely exploratory.

sons. First, new scientific breakthroughs in many areas will indicate (1) certain chemical series that should be explored, (2) new biological processes to exploit, (3) new metabolic routes to influence, (4) new viruses to attack, and so forth, in attempts to discover new medicines. It is naive to think that human knowledge will ever be so thorough that humans can *a priori* derive the most appropriate molecule from computer-generated information and that this molecule will turn out to be the best compound of a series to develop as a medicine. Second, new chemicals are constantly being synthesized for a specific test of a particular type of biological activity. It is certain that companies will always desire to maximize their potential for medicine discovery from each compound made. This means empirically testing it in a number of other test systems where there is a reasonable chance that it could demonstrate activity. This latter approach would therefore be an empirical and not a random test of the medicine.

Use of Animal Models in Medicine Discovery and Development

Purposes and Types of Animal Models

Animal models are used to evaluate compounds for potential efficacy and safety in humans. In some therapeutic areas models generally have great predictability for efficacy in humans (e.g., anti-infectives), whereas the predictability in other therapeutic areas is weak (e.g., compounds affecting the central nervous system). The predictability for safety also varies. In addition to providing data that may be extrapolated to humans, animal models help scientists investigate the etiology, progression, and prevention of the disease process. Animal models may use normal cells, tissues, organs, or entire organisms. Some animal models evaluate one time point in the progression of a disease (e.g., many *in vitro* tests in which a tissue is removed at a specific time after the animal is pretreated or affected in a desired manner). Other models mimic the entire progression of the disease (e.g., Japanese quail model of atherosclerosis, which progresses to a fatal myocardial infarction in 60% to 80% of the animals at approximately nine months).

Animal models used to evaluate medicines may be described as belonging to one of three categories.

1. *Spontaneous models*—An animal model has a natural or spontaneously developed characteristic of interest to study or evaluate (e.g., Syrian hamsters with spontaneous congestive heart failure).
2. *Experimental models*—An animal model has an experimentally induced change to create characteristics of interest to study or evaluate (e.g., anesthetized dogs treated with propranolol to create heart failure).
3. *Normal models*—An animal model is a normal counterpart of the disease state in humans (e.g., normal

papillary muscles are used to measure contractions of heart tissue).

Few animal models, if any, are exact duplicates of human disease. Scientists usually attempt to create models that are as close as possible to the clinical situation. There are many reasons for the inability to create exact models, including incomplete knowledge of most diseases, the highly complex nature of many diseases, and technical difficulties in creating complex models. Animal models must be compared with the human situation in regard to the lesion or condition that is created and the predictability of the data that the model yields. It is clearly the latter consideration that is of primary importance, because a pathologically lesioned animal that exactly mimics human disease but provides spurious or inconsistent results is of little predictive value. Reasons for poorly predictive models of this type may relate to differences in absorption, distribution, metabolism, or excretion between species, or different receptors.

Although most animal tests are imperfect models of human disease, some models mimic human disease more closely than do others. For example, spontaneously hypertensive rats are a better model of hypertension than is the mere injection into a normotensive animal of a medicine to raise its blood pressure acutely. Animals that are normotensive yield relatively poor data about antihypertensive effects of medicines compared with data obtained in hypertensive animals. It is preferable to select compounds for initial testing in humans based on the most predictive models available.

Establishing and Validating a New Animal Model

It is important to develop a list of both required and desired characteristics for a new model. Required characteristics should include both aspects that must be present and those that must be absent.

Characteristics that are often required of new animal models are the ability to (1) yield predictive data for humans; (2) obtain statistically treatable data; (3) conduct a certain number of tests that can be performed each day, week, or month; (4) demonstrate activity of treatments that work in humans with an acceptable rate of false-positive and -negative responses; (5) utilize a given (i.e., minimum) amount of compound per test; and (6) cost no more than a specified amount per test. Desirable characteristics include the ability to obtain (1) objective data that may be tested statistically, (2) a dose-response relationship, (3) a preliminary estimate of toxicity, (4) reproducible results from experiment to experiment, (5) an indication of the duration of effect, (6) data that are relevant to study both cause and treatment of a specific disease, (7) a similarity of symptoms in the model and humans, and (8) underlying pathology, physiology, and biochemistry that are similar in animals and humans.

The model should be able to be reproduced by other investigators. Required characteristics for some models would only be desirable characteristics for other models (and vice versa).

There are several ways in which a new animal model can be validated. These potentially include utilizing techniques from all biological disciplines, including histology, pathology, physiology, pharmacology, biochemistry, immunology, virology, and microbiology. In most cases, utilizing techniques of multiple disciplines will more firmly establish the model as valid. Within each discipline, numerous techniques may be applied. The use of multiple techniques will generally yield more convincing data than will a single test and will help validate the model. One specific method to validate animal models as predictors of human efficacy data is to evaluate a series of different medicines in an animal test and to compare the relative potencies with data derived in human studies.

In some diseases such as Alzheimer's, it is virtually impossible to validate animal models until at least one medicine is clearly shown to be active. If an animal test showed that specific medicine to be active, but all others to be inactive, then that result would be an important step toward validation of the model.

Developing a Battery of Animal Models and Tests to Evaluate Compounds

There are no perfect animal models that provide all of the data required to determine if a given compound will be effective in humans. In addition to providing efficacy data, animal models must be used to derive safety and other types of data. Thus, a wide variety of animal models must be used. The pros and cons for each must be understood to interpret the data in a meaningful way.

In developing multiple tests, it is possible to use them

REPRESENTATIVE TYPES OF BATTERIES OF ANIMAL TESTS

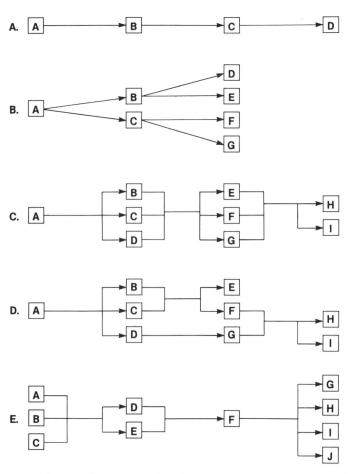

FIG. 20.16. Hypothetical formats for organizing multiple animal models and tests to screen for and study medicine activity. Each *letter* represents a separate model or test. See text for explanation.

in different ways, depending on the purpose(s) of the models and the nature of the scientific or therapeutic area being studied. Figure 20.16 illustrates five common patterns. In this figure, each box represents a separate test and may yield different types of data. Each test may also be conducted with techniques of multiple scientific disciplines. Boxes may represent different animal models or the same model with different conditions or objectives (e.g., to obtain effects of a single dose or a dose-response relationship). A illustrates a simple sequential ordering of models, whereas B illustrates a pyramid type of ordering. C–E illustrate more complex patterns and are the more usual systems used by pharmacology departments in the pharmaceutical industry. Each system is used to screen and/or evaluate properties of medicines in a given therapeutic area or with a specific targeted objective.

An actual series of multiple animal tests used to screen and progress compounds for their inotropic activity is shown in Fig. 20.17. Clearly, a great deal of additional information would have to be provided for the screening tests as to conditions, dosages to test, and interpretative guides.

When multiple animal models are used, there is a tendency in some therapeutic areas to initially use more broad screens and to progress to those that evaluate more specific biological questions (e.g., evaluating antibacterials). In other therapeutic areas or for other reasons, specific biological activity is screened for initially (e.g., when a specific biochemical activity is desired). Some animal models are highly selective for determining activity of compounds that act via a single specific mechanism, and others will show activity for compounds acting via any one of many mechanisms.

A. Evaluate the compound (10^{-8} to 10^{-4} M) on electrically-driven guinea-pig atria *in vitro* under specific experimental conditions of temperature, salt bath ingredients, rate of electric stimulation, resting muscle tension, etc.

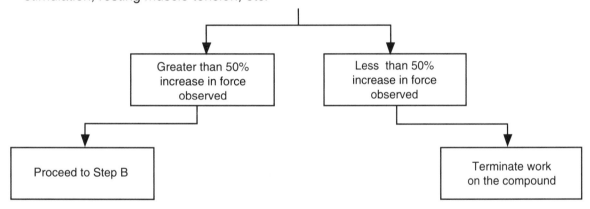

B. Evaluate the compound at the same doses on electrically-driven cat papillary muscle under specific experimental conditions.

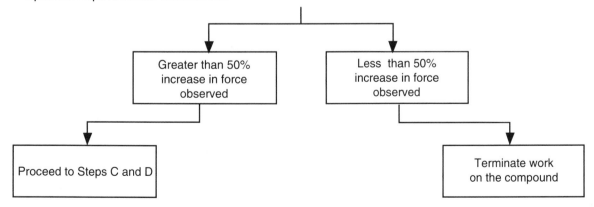

FIG. 20.17. Example of a series of screens used to evaluate compounds for inotropic activity (i.e., those that increase the force of cardiac contraction) in animal test systems. This is an example of a test battery shown in Fig. 20.16.

C. Evaluate the compound on spontaneously beating guinea-pig atria *in vitro* under specific experimental conditions.

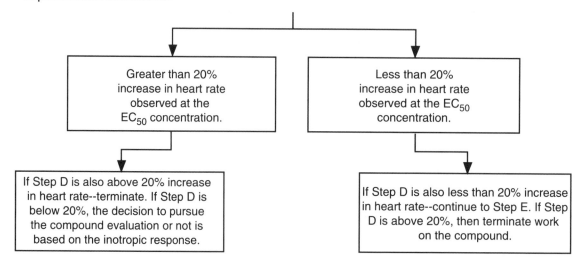

D. Evaluate the compound in anesthetized dogs (*in vivo*) measuring the differential of left ventricular end diastolic pressure (i.e.,dp/dt) to provide a measure of inotropism. Also measure several other cardiovascular parameters.

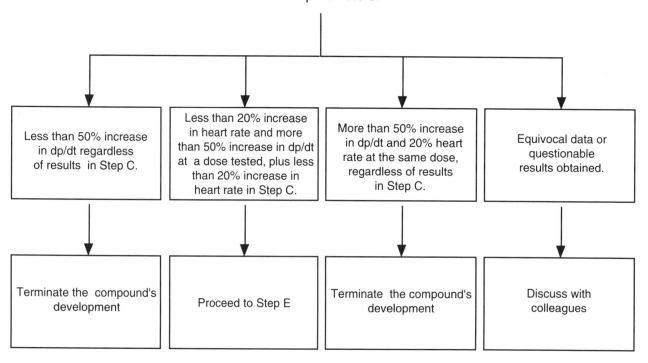

E. Evaluate the compound in conscious dogs (*in vivo*) who have a surgically implanted strain gauge to measure the force of left ventricular contraction. Depending on the results (specified in advanced) proceed to evaluations in other inotropic tests as well as in other pharmacological tests in animals.

FIG. 20.17. *Continued.*

21 / Golden Rules of Medicine Discovery

Choosing Appropriate Disease and Therapeutic
    Areas to Research and the Methods and
    Strategies to Use........................... 236
Creating a Suitable Research Environment and
    Appropriate Attitudes 237

Reviewing Research Activities and Allocating
    Resources.................................. 238
Stimulating Innovation, Both Within and Outside
    the Company.............................. 239
Advancing Compounds into Development........ 240

One must learn by doing the thing, for although you think you know it you may have no certainty until you try. Sophocles

The three major functions of research and development groups in pharmaceutical companies are to discover medicines, develop medicines to reach the market, and protect and extend the scope of medicines that are marketed. This last function includes development of new indications, formulations, dosage strengths, routes of administration, and packages. Important principles (i.e., golden rules) of medicine development are presented in Chapter 23, Golden Rules of Medicine Development. These golden rules differ from the mission, objectives, goals, strategies, or tactics of a research and development group (defined and described by Spilker, 1991).

Medicine discovery should be differentiated from medicine development for this discussion. The preferred definition of medicine discovery is that it includes preclinical activities leading to the identification of a specific compound that possesses a desirable profile of biological activity. At that time, a decision is made to undertake additional animal studies to ensure that the compound has adequate safety to be tested in humans.

It is not always possible to determine the precise point at which the medicine discovery phase is completed and the medicine development phase begins. In general, that point occurs when preclinical activities change from a search for an agent with a desired biological profile to the focused evaluation of a specific compound. The safety and efficacy profile is determined in greater depth to assure that the compound is acceptable for testing in humans. There is usually a period of time during which the medicine discovery process for a particular compound is ending and its development period is building. Even though a compound enters the development stage, there

may be no commitment to evaluate it in humans. For example, the compound may be developed as a prototype to acquire information that will be applied to other, future compounds.

Safety testing in animals includes both toxicological evaluation and pharmacological studies. There is often no toxicological evaluation of a compound during the discovery period. However, there is a tendency for more toxicological testing to occur earlier so that the results may be considered before a decision is made on whether to have the compound enter development.

The total amount of pharmacological testing conducted on a specific disease using a specific target during the discovery period (as opposed to the development period) is highly variable and depends on the amount of research necessary to determine which particular compound is a lead compound. A lead compound is one with sufficient activity in a single screen to encourage structural modification to improve the activity or to decrease the toxicity. Studies that further refine the biological profile and activity of a specific compound are conducted during early stages of medicine development. At an appropriate stage during this development period, the compound is usually proposed for evaluation in humans. This may not be done if a compound with greater biological activity or less toxicity is available or strongly desired or if additional compounds are being made. Typically, 12 to 36 months of preclinical and associated tests (e.g., formulation, stability) are required before a compound entering the development phase can be tested in humans. Medicine discovery may also occur in the clinic when a new use for a known medicine is found. This type

235

of medicine discovery, usually resulting from serendipity, is not discussed in this chapter.

Most general principles of medicine development are relevant (with some modification) to activities conducted during the medicine discovery phase. Major differences exist, however, between the ways in which medicine development and discovery are managed. Whereas medicine development may be planned and controlled with a certain degree of assurance, attempts to plan and control medicine discovery often stifle and destroy the creative process.

Golden rules of medicine discovery have been grouped into five broad categories for ease of discussion.

CHOOSING APPROPRIATE DISEASE AND THERAPEUTIC AREAS TO RESEARCH AND THE METHODS AND STRATEGIES TO USE

1. Determine the specific therapeutic and disease areas to explore. Most companies should focus discovery activities in a relatively limited number of therapeutic areas. There are few companies, if any, that can successfully conduct research and discovery activity in all therapeutic areas. By focusing efforts, companies can develop areas of strength that should enhance their medicine discovery activities.

2. Identify the therapeutic areas to explore at four levels: (1) general therapeutic area (e.g., central nervous system, cardiovascular, gastrointestinal), (2) specific diseases, (3) targets (e.g., physiological and/or biochemical mechanisms) within each therapeutic area, and (4) specific approaches and methods to follow to seek compounds that have the mechanism for each target identified.

3. Determine whether the company should seek to discover medicines that are chemically or functionally similar to existing medicines. The second or third medicine marketed of a new class often attains significant sales. Clarify the type and number of "me-too" medicines that are desirable or acceptable to seek. This may be determined by establishing the minimally acceptable criteria that each research project must meet to be judged successful.

4. Establish the types of criteria for each potential medicine to meet. Three types of criteria that may be used for this purpose are ideal, realistic/desirable, and minimally acceptable criteria. For each characteristic of a compound for which criteria are established, determine which specific criteria the compound must achieve and which criteria the compound should achieve. Criteria should be written to facilitate management review and so that characteristics of compounds proposed for study in humans may be compared with this list.

5. Use the most highly validated animal models and tests to search for and choose medicines to develop. Organize the various tests in a logical sequence to develop the profile of the compound. In some cases this involves progressing from broad to specific tests, while in other cases the opposite approach will be used. If some important test systems are unavailable in-house, then work should be contracted to scientists who have appropriate facilities or equipment.

6. Use rational approaches (e.g., molecular modeling) to medicine discovery whenever possible. Do not forgo or minimize the other major approaches of medicine discovery: empirical trial and error and the greatest method of all—serendipity. Be receptive to the unexpected. Carefully consider the role of random screening and targeted screening of selected types of compounds.

7. Use animals bred by reputable suppliers in all but unusual situations. Avoid using animals from pounds or shelters. Choose the lowest species on the evolutionary scale consistent with objectives of the research. All protocols involving animals should be reviewed to ensure that acceptable ethical standards are followed. Treat all animals with respect and appropriate care.

8. Develop one-, three-, and five-year plans to implement research projects and achieve realistic goals. For example, a goal could be to explore the anti-X activity of chemical series A and B. Review these plans at least annually. Terminate nonviable research projects as soon as possible.

9. Create an international research plan for each site that is attempting to discover medicines. Minimize any unnecessary duplication of effort between sites, but maintain supplementary programs. Develop programs and systems that facilitate cooperation among researchers at all discovery sites. These goals are best met through periodic meetings to develop and implement an effective international discovery strategy in each disease area.

10. Create and use systems and standard operating procedures that assist the discovery process. Do not allow systems to become bureaucracies, restrain creativity, or compromise efficiency. This is often a difficult goal to achieve because systems that improve efficiency (e.g., through standardization) may do so at the expense of scientific creativity. Utilize computer systems that are either identical or compatible among all major sites of a company that are seeking to discover medicines.

11. Develop a portfolio of research projects that balances high- and low-risk projects. Include projects that will probably require long-term as well as short-term completion cycles. Attempt to include some projects that have a chance of becoming breakthrough medicines. If there is a paucity of such ideas or an insufficient number of such compounds to develop, then hire more scientists who are known to be creative or license in more exciting compounds or technologies.

12. Develop a clear licensing policy and strategy that

allows all research or technological opportunities to be reviewed and assessed rapidly for possible benefit to the company. Establish alliances with other companies (e.g., joint ventures) that enhance research activities of great interest. Caution must be used to avoid antitrust conflicts in establishing business relationships. Many ideas for compounds that have never been made, or the compounds themselves, are available for licensing. These compounds often require a significant amount of additional work in the medicine discovery phase before it is known whether they are candidates for medicine development.

13. Solicit ideas from the staff as well as consultants for new research compounds or approaches to discover medicines that could be explored. Many novel ideas and suggestions within a company are forgotten or are not implemented for many reasons. Try to capture these ideas on paper so that they can be followed up at the appropriate time. An idea's value to the company usually equals its intrinsic worth multiplied by the administrative level (or position) of the idea's proponent to the third power. Therefore, it often helps to have one's ideas accepted if you have your boss serve as the spokesperson for the idea. An even better approach is to turn your idea over to your boss so that it becomes his or her idea.

CREATING A SUITABLE RESEARCH ENVIRONMENT AND APPROPRIATE ATTITUDES

1. Create a positive environment in which to discover medicines. Although the ideal environment would theoretically differ somewhat for each scientist, there are numerous aspects of a desirable work environment that most people prefer. These include freedom to express one's scientific creativity in medicine discovery activities and flexibility in the reviews of research by management.

2. Develop a sound patent strategy. This will protect the company's future medicines and encourage people to believe that the fruits of their creative efforts have value and are being appropriately protected.

3. Hire the best people possible for all positions in research, even at the most junior level. Appropriately train and orient staff in the methods, traditions, and ethos of the company. Educate them also in the goals and concepts of the pharmaceutical industry.

4. Develop a core team (e.g., chemist and biologist) to approach research projects. For some larger projects a larger team may be assembled. In some situations a therapeutic area team or committee may also be formed to pursue or to oversee discovery activities.

5. Do not appoint academic or government scientists or administrators as heads of a pharmaceutical company's research division unless these individuals are highly experienced in industrial medicine discovery activities, thinking, and management approaches. There are great conceptual differences in methodology, perspective, management, and orientation between basic research conducted in academia and medicine discovery activities conducted in the pharmaceutical industry. Many distinguished academicians and government officials and scientists have not successfully made this transition.

6. Do whatever is necessary to encourage openness, honesty, cooperation, teamwork, and shared goals among different scientific disciplines that work together (e.g., chemistry and pharmacology). Achievement of these goals depends on trust, accurate communication, acceptance of unorthodox ideas, and the creation of a positive working environment. Disseminate appropriate information both upward and downward throughout the company. Stress the concept of sharing information and avoiding surprises whenever possible.

7. Adhere to the highest standards of ethics in the planning and conduct of scientific studies. This practice will provide numerous benefits to the company in terms of rapid regulatory reviews of preclinical documents and improved ability to respond to questions, criticisms, and accusations from external sources; furthermore, it is a strong and positive motivating factor for the staff.

8. Obtain strong corporate backing for the medicine discovery effort. This must be a long-term commitment of an appropriate funding level. Without this commitment, there is a danger that serious morale problems will develop, important studies will be slowed or even stopped, and some of the most creative staff will depart.

9. Do not turn the company's most creative and productive scientists into administrators and managers. Most companies promote their successful scientists to managerial positions. These companies seem to believe that great scientists make great managers, but generally this is not true. Imagination is needed to break this tradition. A company must find ways to retain these extremely valuable people in roles that are most important and provide the most value for the company. Solutions may involve providing the most creative scientists with public recognition, nonmanagement leadership roles (e.g., of committees, task forces, therapeutic review groups, planning groups), tangible benefits (e.g., salary, bonuses, parking places, awards), and support for their scientific efforts (e.g., staff, equipment). A company will have achieved success in this area when its creative scientists are motivated to continue their scientific careers and the company is able to retain this extremely valuable staff.

10. Understand the major motivations of the discovery scientists (Fig. 21.1) and seek to influence them through support of their goals.

FACTORS THAT MOTIVATE SCIENTISTS

1. All are Equal

A = Altruism
B = Fame
C = Fortune
D = Scientific Interest

2. All are Unequal

3. One Predominates

4. Two Predominate
and No Overlap
Exists

FIG. 21.1. Four of the major factors that influence and motivate scientists. These factors (or others) have a variety of effects on different scientists and also on a single scientist over time. The degree of overlap in **Panels 1** to **3** may vary widely.

REVIEWING RESEARCH ACTIVITIES AND ALLOCATING RESOURCES

1. Determine who has the authority to propose changes in the overall therapeutic areas being explored, the specific diseases and targets studied within each therapeutic area, and the specific approaches and methods used. Who has the authority to approve such proposals at each of these four levels? Does this process occur informally or formally? Are changes in direction initiated after open discussion in a "large" forum or by a few people who decide in private?

2. Focus management review on (1) the research questions asked, (2) the directions followed, (3) the quality of the effort, and (4) the results obtained. Do not focus too strongly on quantitative aspects of the program (e.g., number of compounds made or tested). Senior research managers should strive to maintain an appropriate balance between a lack of control and tight control over scientists. Although most managers undoubtedly believe that they personally understand this concept and actually implement the proper balance overall, it might be valuable for an independent consultant to assess the scientists' view of this issue. It is also necessary for a single manager to apply a different degree of control when dealing with different scientists. Senior managers should

avoid the temptation to micromanage research programs that are nominally under their control.

3. Ensure that the basic questions regarding research results and direction are posed during appropriate research reviews. This can happen in periodic reports written by scientists as well as by specific questions from scientific managers at review meetings. These questions include the following: (1) What are your next steps? (2) What is the patent situation? (3) What other compounds are you going to make and what are the reasons for these choices? (4) What do standard medicines do in this system? (5) What else can be done to speed up progress on this compound? (6) Are there reasons why we cannot go into humans with this compound? (7) What other biological targets could be used to affect the target disease? and (8) Which disease(s) could be affected if we inhibit (or stimulate) this specific biological target system?

4. Determine how to apportion research efforts (e.g., resources) along the spectrum from basic or exploratory (nontargeted) research to applied (targeted) research (see Fig. 20.15). Targeted research is defined as research directed toward a specific disease or objective. This is not an all-or-none situation and a wide spectrum exists.

5. Balance the resources applied to medicine discovery between chemistry, pharmacology, and other research departments (e.g., biochemistry, molecular biology). This comment assumes that the medicine

discovery function is organized into departments according to scientific discipline. Medicine discovery activities also may be organized according to therapeutic area. In this latter situation, all disciplines involved in medicine discovery in the same therapeutic area work together as a single group. It is, nonetheless, always possible to place more resources in one scientific discipline than another or to modify current apportionments.

6. Identify areas of strengths and weaknesses in the research departments and also in therapeutic areas being explored. Identify the weak areas that need building up and develop a plan to do so. Develop another plan to ensure that areas of strength remain strong in the future. Tracking the allocation of resources to therapeutic areas over time is a valuable means to assure that specific goals for buildup are achieved.

7. Assign personnel and other resources according to the importance of each series of compounds being made and tested and according to the value of each idea being tested or explored. Scientific, medical, and commercial values must be considered, although they are rarely of equal importance for any one compound. A balance must be achieved between placing resources on a few research projects and spreading resources too thinly across many projects. This balance is usually established by the head of research alone or in conjunction with the head of development.

8. Reevaluate each project and the overall portfolio of research projects on a relatively frequent basis (e.g., every 6 to 12 months). Reviews must be objective and use agreed-on methods. Reviewers must always distinguish between the strong desire that some people have for a compound to be effective and safe and the actual demonstration, with a sufficient amount of appropriate scientific data, that a compound is, or is likely to be, effective and safe. Ensure that all appropriate managers and workers understand current priorities of the research division as well as the priorities of their specific department, insofar as the two may differ.

9. Identify the rate-limiting step of each research project. Ensure that appropriate and adequate resources and attention are focused on these areas, at least in the most important research projects.

10. Do not eschew reasonable risks, especially if potential results would be important to the company.

STIMULATING INNOVATION, BOTH WITHIN AND OUTSIDE THE COMPANY

1. Develop general guidelines that assist senior scientists who are attempting to expedite the discovery or early development process of lead compounds. These guidelines would contain information on the criteria to use for obtaining patents, the initial toxicology evalua-

tion, a pharmacology screen profile, as well as on when and how to hold a meeting to choose among active compounds.

2. Develop a matrix system for research projects to expedite their efficient progression. A small group or even a single individual could handle this role at most pharmaceutical companies. This individual could also (1) conduct various analyses of the research discovery system (e.g., analyze the number of different primary biological screens that compounds are tested in and how this has changed over the years), (2) maintain a list of current lead compounds that are in early or late stages of preclinical work and that are approaching development (i.e., project) status, (3) serve as a troubleshooter to identify interdepartmental issues that should be addressed, and (4) fulfill any additional roles desired. This person or group would act in an analogous capacity in the research discovery system to the project coordinator/planner in the project development system.

3. Utilize a "sunset rule" for most or all research projects. This means that every research project (with few or no exceptions) will terminate after a certain period unless continuation of the work can be justified. The usual period for funding a research discovery project would be two to four years, depending on its nature and importance. At that time progress would be assessed (in addition to more frequent reviews) and the projects' renewal or termination determined. A single appeal might be part of this process.

4. Develop a strategy for licensing-in early-stage research compounds that meet preestablished criteria. Because the value of research compounds is much less than that of more advanced investigational medicines being evaluated in the clinic, it is important to utilize high standards.

5. Conduct brainstorming sessions among relevant scientists and possibly others (e.g., marketers). This enables numerous people to be involved and to provide input. It also helps to stimulate and motivate a research group and usually generates positive growth of the concept or the actual work being discussed.

6. Conduct retreats for individual research departments as well as retreats just for senior managers from all research departments. These are valuable opportunities to build relationships and team spirit, solve specific problems, revitalize spirits of overworked staff, and accomplish other general or specific goals. Develop either a loose or a structured agenda that is designed to achieve the retreat's objectives.

7. Opportunities should exist for scientists to present their work to their peers for scientific review and comment. This should occur both within the company and at professional meetings outside the company. Within the company, meetings should occur at the department level, within therapeutic area groups, and in other appro-

priate forums. An emphasis should generally be placed at in-house meetings on presenting ongoing research and problems encountered, rather than on presenting a polished presentation of completed work.

8. Encourage company scientists to be connected to and integrated with the outside world of science and scientists. Company scientists should be encouraged to publish important papers and reviews, attend scientific meetings, and participate in professional societies. Maintaining a network with prominent scientists outside the company is in its interests. To do this correctly requires some in-house scientists to be at the frontiers of research in their field.

9. Utilize consultants to assist projects and to help solve problems. Consultants should always be viewed as providing positive value for enhancing medicine discovery activities. If they are not viewed this way, then either the system for choosing consultants or the specific consultant whose value is questioned should be evaluated thoroughly. Alternatively, the attitude of the scientific staff needs to be reviewed and possibly modified.

10. Establish ties with university groups and other pharmaceutical companies via joint ventures and other arrangements. Many situations exist where both groups benefit from joint efforts, and it is common for 5% to 20% of the research discovery budget to be devoted to activities conducted by external groups of scientists.

11. Encourage scientists to follow tangents that depart from chosen or traditional paths of medicine discovery, except when (1) the tangent has been tried several times, (2) the tangent is carefully reviewed before it is implemented and is considered unworthy of pursuit, or (3) it will require an excessive amount of resources.

12. Attempt to learn everything important that is relevant about compounds of interest, even what may be considered as "bad news." Terminating work on compounds at an early stage will save many months or years of staff work and a large amount of money that could be better used on other research projects, provided that termination is clearly appropriate.

13. Encourage the creative scientists to spend approximately 10% to 15% of their time on pet ideas or hypotheses they want to test or explore in appropriate general areas of research. A small core group of scientists may be encouraged to spend most of their time on personal projects that have been reviewed.

14. Ensure that scientific literature is carefully read for ideas that may assist the medicine discovery process. These ideas may identify new targets, new animal models, or new approaches or may provide other important information.

15. Placing marked pressure, deadlines, and tight control on scientists is usually counterproductive for discovering an important new medicine. A sense of urgency is nonetheless a stimulating factor and is usually extremely important in the 1990s. This sense may arise from competition with groups at other companies who are attempting to discover a similar medicine or solve a similar problem. Alternatively, it may be fostered by the company that wishes to increase its chances of success and, possibly, of survival itself.

16. If a research group has not demonstrated innovativeness over a long period, the reason(s) must be determined. Managers who stifle their scientists, mismanage excellent compounds, or otherwise are not capitalizing on worthwhile ideas and opportunities can be the cause of this problem. If the problem lies primarily in management, then it will usually be difficult for this information to come to the attention of managers who are senior enough to rectify the issue. It is often easy for senior managers to cover up management problems or to blame others. If suspicions exist that this problem may be present, then an independent group of outside consultants may be asked to evaluate this issue. On the other hand, the problem may be that there are too few creative scientists in a company. If the pool of innovative scientific talent is deemed insufficient, then specific scientists should be hired who have a proven record of innovation and discovery. These people should continue to work in scientific research and not be promoted to management roles.

ADVANCING COMPOUNDS INTO DEVELOPMENT

1. Ensure that activities to implement and carry out each of the principles discussed in this chapter follow an appropriate pace. If any of these principles is pushed too rapidly then it becomes more likely that the right compounds will not be developed, the quality of the results will suffer, problems will arise, mistakes will be made, and waste will occur. The pace of research activities should not be too rapid, nor should too many pressures be applied, so that professionals are encouraged to cut corners or make unwarranted assumptions about a compound's efficacy or safety. Progressing a poor compound is extremely wasteful of limited resources.

2. Ensure that new compounds are not being kept in research departments too long before being proposed for evaluation in humans. Sometimes this happens because of the possessiveness of one or a few scientists who have championed the compound's discovery and early development. Another reason might relate to the conservativeness of scientist(s) who want to learn an excessive amount of information about each compound before proposing it for human testing. A third problem may be the inability of the most senior scientists to determine which compound from one (or more) chemical series to propose for development. In this situation, attempts must be made to differentiate between the compounds or to progress two or three compounds simultaneously.

3. As a compound approaches the development stage and a project is being considered, determine which characteristics would be desirable in a backup compound. Attempt to find a backup compound that could either be a second-generation medicine or replace the leading compound should it falter during its development.

Other important principles could be included in this list of golden rules. Their omission does not signify they are any less important than those included. Golden rules may also be developed for specific disciplines within medicine discovery or medicine development. One such set of principles relating to clinical medicine development is included in *Guide to Clinical Trials* (Spilker, 1991). Others are listed in that book as well as in this one.

Merely understanding the golden rules and believing in their general validity are not sufficient to realize them in practice. It is also necessary to have a competent group of managers who are able to put these rules into practice. There is yet one final step required to implement the golden rules. That step is the attainment of a collective will and desire within the organization to follow these principles and use them (and others) as the basis of an ethos of medicine discovery.

22 / The Medicine Development Process

Approaches to Medicine Development........... 243
  Nature of Medicine Development............. 243
  How Does a Company Decide Which
    Compounds to Develop as Medicines?...... 243
  Master Development Plan 245
  Establishing Criteria for a Medicine's
    Performance during its Development 246
  Transfer of a Project from Preclinical to

Clinical Development and from Clinical
  Development to Marketing and
  Production................................. 246
Should Medicine A, Which Is Being Studied in
  Disease W, Also Be Tested in Diseases X,
  Y, or Z?.................................. 248
How Is Medicine Labeling Developed?........ 250

The stumbling way in which even the ablest of the scientists in every generation have had to fight through thickets of erroneous observations, misleading generalizations, inadequate formulations, and unconscious prejudice is rarely appreciated by those who obtain their scientific knowledge from textbooks. James Bryant Conant, *Science and Common Sense*

APPROACHES TO MEDICINE DEVELOPMENT

Nature of Medicine Development

Medicine development is the second major function of research and development groups. Medicine discovery is the first function and marketing support, the third. Development is defined differently in different situations. It may specifically refer to technical aspects of chemical scaleup, analytical analysis of material, and pharmaceutical development of a dosage form and formulation. Alternatively, or in addition, the term development may refer to the entire process of taking a newly discovered compound through regulatory approval and to the point of marketing (Fig. 22.1). This broad definition is used in this book. Many aspects of medicine development are described in other chapters (e.g., technical development, clinical trials, and matrix concepts). A few additional points are presented below.

The importance of adhering to high standards in the conduct, analysis, and interpretation of all preclinical and clinical trials must be stressed. Poorly planned or conceived studies will often raise questions that will be difficult to explain. Such studies are shortsighted, as it may take many months or years plus valuable resources to sort out the details and explain problems that did not have to arise in the first place. In addition, the data they generate will generally delay important regulatory submissions.

How Does a Company Decide Which Compounds to Develop as Medicines?

The simplest answer to this question, and also one that has a lot of truth, is that written or unwritten criteria are established (or should be established) for all research efforts directed at discovering a new medicine. When a chemical compound is found that meets these criteria, then it is (usually) developed as a medicine. The compound continues to be developed until events demonstrate that some of the criteria (primarily of safety and efficacy) cannot be met and that a medically and commercially viable medicine is no longer likely or possible to achieve.

Because research programs in one therapeutic area may lead to a compound that has activity in another area, carefully developed criteria are not always present when a new direction in a medicine's development is debated. Considerations include determining how the compound fits into the company's strategies and portfolio for current and future medicine development. This includes evaluation of old product line-extensions, entrance into new product lines, perceived medical need, perceived commercial gains, plus the patent situation on the new compound.

In addition to the company's basic strategies, there are issues about resources necessary to test and develop a new medicine. Will it be relatively straightforward to evaluate the medicine's efficacy, as with a diuretic or

STAGES OF MEDICINE DISCOVERY AND DEVELOPMENT

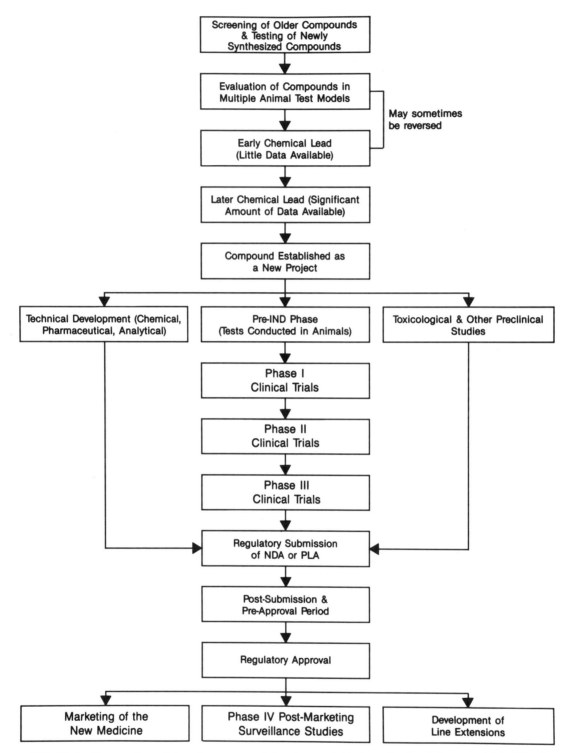

FIG. 22.1. Stages of medicine discovery and development. Various feedback loops exist in this diagram, especially during the initial stages of medicine discovery.

neuromuscular blocking agent, or will it be much more complex and expensive, as with an antipsychotic. Is the path to regulatory approval different than that with an "average" medicine? For instance, chemical classes of medicines with toxicity known to be greater than that of others in the same therapeutic class are not looked on favorably by regulatory authorities. In addition, each regulatory agency may require different types and degrees of proof of efficacy. This will tend to make a medicine's development far more complex and costly for one country than for another.

Depending on the answers to these (and other) questions and criteria (Table 22.1), the company may decide to go all out, to go ahead with a limited program, to develop the medicine only for certain countries, to license the medicine to another company, or to take a different course of action.

Master Development Plan

Some companies prepare a comprehensive plan for a medicine's development at the outset of the project formation. This usually occurs from one to two years before the medicine is evaluated in humans for totally new medicines and approximately six months to one year for medicines that have already been evaluated in patients in other countries. The same times generally apply for medicines licensed-in from other companies. This master plan is put together by the project leader or manager and becomes a "Bible" for many companies to follow. This document may be organized in any way a company desires or the format may be left to the author's discretion.

One approach is to present the plan in three separate parts. The first part includes preclinical activities from project initiation until early Phase I studies. This con-tains the background information nominating the compound for project status and discusses the pharmacology and toxicology programs. Alternatively, the compound may be proposed for project status in a prior document that focuses on the scientific, medical, and marketing rationales. A clinical feasibility section is included either in this part or as a separate document. Tables 111.1 to 111.3 in *Guide to Clinical Trials* (Spilker, 1991) illustrate three examples of tables of contents of a clinical feasibility report.

Part two covers the period from initial regulatory submission (e.g., Investigational New Drug Application) to the end of Phase II. This part contains the plan for metabolic studies, toxicology, regulatory affairs, chemical scaleup, supply sources, formulation, and clinical plan. The development of a product profile is considered, as are the target dates for any end-of-Phase II meeting within the company or at the Food and Drug Administration (FDA) or other regulatory authority. This part of the master plan may not be able to be written as soon as the first part, but should be completed prior to the initial regulatory submission. The clinical development plan may include consideration of alternative paths, depending on the results of pilot studies. For example, if one study shows the medicine to be effective and also toxic, plans may be developed to study lower doses. If the medicine is found ineffective and safe, plans may be proposed to study different patient populations with the same disease who may be more sensitive to the medicine, or to initiate new pilot studies in different diseases.

A go–no go decision point occurs in the development of many medicines toward the end of Phase II. At that point a sufficient amount of clinical efficacy and safety data are available to evaluate the medicine and the likelihood of its going to a New Drug Application (NDA) is assessed. If this probability is relatively high, it provides the impetus to commit company resources necessary for large-scale Phase III studies. There are certainly a few instances when such funds and an all-out development effort are appropriate to initiate before proof of efficacy is obtained, but this decision should be made with full cognizance of the financial risks involved, as well as the awareness of which other medicine development activities may be slowed or not pursued at all.

Part three covers the period from mid- or late-Phase II to registration filings or preferably to marketing. This part often contains a draft of the package insert, dosage forms to be developed, other aspects of technical development, details of manufacturing (including location, data processing, registration plans, and support functions), required clinical trials by country, specialized studies, and discussion of which expert opinions are required. Input on this section is required from all clinical and technical groups. This part may not be possible to write in detail until after the medicine has entered or even completed Phase II studies.

TABLE 22.1. *Research and development criteria to evaluate a new compound for potential development as a medicine[a]*

1. Likelihood of technical success
2. Estimated time to develop the medicine to NDA[b]
3. Time to reach a go–no go decision[c]
4. Anticipated technical development problems (e.g., stability of the product)
5. Availability in desired dosage forms
6. Presence of skills to develop the medicine
7. Degree of medical need for the type of medicine
8. Medical advantages of the medicine compared with alternative therapies
9. Actual or potential restrictions on the medicine's use
10. Cost to develop in comparison to anticipated third-year sales or profits. May be calculated in terms of time to pay back the investment
11. Number of potential indications
12. Any known limitations or problems not covered above

[a] A number of additional criteria are described in the text.
[b] NDA, New Drug Application.
[c] This point usually occurs during Phase II.

Determining the Appropriate Scope of a Medicine Development Plan: Lean Versus Fat

A preclinical and clinical program of appropriate and well-designed studies may be planned to address all appropriate issues. A company may attempt to do this by developing a plan that emphasizes any desired approach varying from a *lean* one that eliminates all studies that are not absolutely essential to a *fat* approach that includes all possible considerations and studies. If the approach chosen is too lean and incomplete, it may not achieve regulatory approval in some or all of the target countries. A plan that is far in excess of what is regulatorily necessary would not only take extra years to complete, but would generate excessive data that would require additional time for processing, analysis, and interpretation.

How may a company know that it has an appropriate balance between these extremes? In many cases the answer is difficult, but there are some principles to follow. First, determine if it would be reasonable to conduct any of the clinical trials after the medicine is marketed. Second, determine what would be lost if each study on the list were deleted. Which studies are mandatory to conduct? Third, review the size of each study with a statistician. Could any be abbreviated? Fourth, discuss the clinical plan in detail with the FDA and/or other regulatory authorities. Additional steps might be (1) to evaluate the number and nature of studies conducted on recently approved medicines of the same type, (2) to discuss the issue with knowledgeable consultants, or (3) to develop alternative stepwise plans.

The master plan must distinguish between studies that are nice or desirable to conduct and those that are necessary to conduct. This principle applies to clinical, toxicological, metabolic, pharmacokinetic, and other categories of studies. The distinction between these two types of studies often changes during a medicine's development. Even though the master plan represents the blueprint of a medicine's development, the plans must frequently be reassessed and necessary changes made.

Establishing Criteria for a Medicine's Performance during its Development

Compounds that have achieved the criteria established during the medicine discovery period are advanced into medicine development. Even if clear criteria have not been established preclinically during the discovery period, it is important to set criteria during medicine development. This is primarily to know when the medicine's development should be terminated.

Criteria established at an early stage of development to judge each medicine's future performance should include medical, technical, and commercial considerations. If the medicine falls below or otherwise fails to meet these standards, then its termination should be considered. This does not mean that a company would not develop one or more orphan medicines where there is little hope of ever repaying their development costs. However, it does mean that appropriate standards should be established for orphan medicines, just as for other medicines. Thus, the company's management would agree to accept lower minimal medical and/or commercial standards for some medicines. If medical and/or commercial criteria are established, a project's termination would be expedited if the medicine's characteristics demonstrated that the minimally acceptable criteria could not be met.

The criteria used to determine whether a medicine passes the go–no go decision point in Phase II may be set to a particularly high or low standard. This is often desirable from a marketing viewpoint. For example, the marketing group may believe they do not want to sell a medicine unless it is sensational medically, or they may believe that it is desirable to have the medicine available for sale, even if it is not as effective or safe as the medical staff and managers hope it will be.

An important new medicine with great medical value is of limited commercial benefit to a company if actual sales are small or modest, but this type of medicine often provides numerous other benefits to a company (e.g., enhanced reputation and improved access to physicians by sales representatives). The company's overall reactions to this type of medicine as well as others depends to a large degree on their original expectations. These expectations relate in many ways to the criteria established for the medicine's development.

Transfer of a Project from Preclinical to Clinical Development and from Clinical Development to Marketing and Production

The project team that oversees development activities during preclinical and clinical periods is usually similar, although representatives are usually added during the clinical period from departments that become more involved in development activities (e.g., data processing and statistics). Representatives of some preclinical departments (e.g., organic chemistry or pharmacology) may be dropped from the team. The leadership of the project often changes from a scientist to a clinician when the project compound enters Phase I or at some time during this period. Some companies have a bridge department manage a project during the transition from preclinical to clinical activities. This step should not be necessary, and the author believes that such a department would complicate rather than expedite efficient transfer and continuity.

Marketing representatives may form their own team or group during Phase III, but they often take over the management of the project after the medicine is marketed. Production departments usually form an independent group to manage manufacturing issues. Even after medicines are marketed there still are many activities conducted in research departments (Table 22.2), medical departments (Table 22.3), and in technical development and regulatory affairs departments (Table 22.4).

TABLE 22.2. *Activities performed on marketed medicines in research departments*[a]

A. Any research department
 1. Additional evaluation of the medicine's mechanism of action
 2. Training of sales representatives
 3. Support marketing, medical, legal, production, and other departments with information
 4. Participate in writing and reviewing promotional materials
 5. Participate in writing and reviewing technical materials for compendia (e.g., *United States Pharmacopeia*)
 6. Answer telephone calls and written requests for relevant information
B. Organic chemistry
 1. Synthesis of additional compounds for patent protection of marketed medicines. Important structural relatives of marketed medicines must be made to protect them from the inevitable intense research conducted in the same chemical areas by competitors as well as to seek successor medicines
C. Medicinal biochemistry
 1. Measure medicine concentrations in samples obtained in clinical studies that are evaluating new indications
 2. Conduct biochemical or metabolic studies to evaluate the basis for adverse reactions
 3. Monitor medicine concentrations in life-threatening situations
 4. Refine and report on assay methodologies that may be used by outside laboratories
 5. Participate in interlaboratory validation of methods
 6. Expand data base in specific patient populations, (e.g., neonates)
 7. Conduct studies to help develop new formulations
D. Pharmacology
 1. Investigation of medicine–medicine interactions that are reported in the literature or to the company
 2. Investigation of a newly found therapeutic indication
E. Toxicology
 1. Carcinogenicity or other toxicological studies dictated by clinical effects observed before or after marketing
 2. Limited toxicology on new formulations
F. Other departments
 1. Assay of clinical samples of patients participating in clinical studies, especially in pursuit of added indications
 2. Assay of samples from nonstudy patients treated with the medicine
 3. Assistance to outside laboratories in setting up assays
 4. Pharmacokinetic studies in special patient groups (e.g., dialysis patients)
 5. Computer assistance for analysis of assay data collected by other laboratories
 6. Resistance studies

[a] Defined as preclinical departments not primarily concerned with technical development.

The term "technology transfer" is generally avoided in this book. It is currently in vogue and widely used by many people in science as well as business. Nonetheless, this term often has a number of connotations that the author considers inappropriate. These include the implication that the initial group may not or does not adequately understand the implications of their work for the group that will continue the medicine's development, or that the initial group is unable to transfer the project effectively to the next group without a third party to facilitate the transfer. This latter concept is promulgated by individuals and companies who promote themselves as experts at technology transfer.

It is the author's belief that most preclinical scientists who are engaged in either the search for new medicine or the evaluation of compound activity understand both the clinical and marketing relevance of their work. Also, these scientists can effectively transfer the project to clinical staff at the appropriate time. Likewise, most clinical scientists understand the commercial value of the medicines they are developing and are also able to transfer their project effectively to both marketing and production individuals or groups at the appropriate time.

The Number of People Who "Control" and Transfer a Medicine during its Development

An important principle is that a minimum number of major transfers (e.g., preclinical to clinical) should be made as a medicine proceeds along the development pipeline. Each time a medicine project is transferred from one function to another, it creates the opportunity for a person (or department) to hold onto it too long and thereby delay its development. The opposite problem, in which the compound is transferred too soon, is also a serious problem that could complicate its development. The person (or team) taking over at the next stage may or may not be ready and prepared to act expeditiously and appropriately to develop the medicine. It is possible that the person who is taking over a project may view the added work of leading the team as an imposition. Whatever his or her personal view, it requires a period of time for that person to become sufficiently familiar with the details of the medicine to ensure that full development speed is established and maintained. Thus, the more transfers that occur during development, the longer will be the nonproductive time.

It is theoretically possible to have transfers occur when the project is formed and when the medicine enters each clinical phase (Phases I to IV). This process would create a total of five development leaders, plus those in production and marketing. This is clearly an excessive number of transfers and would be highly inefficient. A more efficient system is for a single project manager to lead the project from its initiation to market launch when it is turned over to someone within the marketing function.

TABLE 22.3. *Activities performed on marketed medicines in medical departments*[a]

A. Developing new indications:
  1. Develop plans for new indications for marketed products
  2. Conduct clinical trials relative to new indications
  3. Process and analyze data collected into statistical and clinical reports
  4. Prepare regulatory submissions for new indications
B. Developing new product formulations and changes in product labeling:
  1. Improve product delivery systems or dosing of marketed products
  2. Conduct clinical trials
  3. Conduct postmarketing surveillance studies
C. Providing assistance to marketing:
  1. Conduct clinical studies requested for marketing purposes
  2. Answer telephone calls and written requests for information from physicians, pharmacists, health care personnel, and sales representatives
  3. Answer telephone calls about medical emergencies and adverse experiences; generate written correspondence relative to the documentation of these
  4. Approve advertisements; occasionally assist in the preparation of such advertisements with advertising agency personnel
  5. Approve marketing copy for other purposes, particularly sales promotion
  6. Aid marketing personnel in recommending/producing product plans and analyses of marketing data (such as IMS[b] data)
  7. Address pertinent issues relative to marketed products, such as adverse reactions reports and formulation problems. Plan and conduct clinical trials as appropriate to avert potential problems
  8. Assist in handling product complaints
  9. Participate in training of sales representatives at the company or at outside meetings
  10. Participate in meetings or symposia sponsored by marketing
  11. Monitor the published literature for relevant materials for promotional activity
  12. Provide medicine to physicians for special needs, such as the conduct of clinical studies, at the recommendation of sales representatives
  13. Handle requests for compounds for use by clinical or research laboratories
  14. Participate in writing compendia for marketed products and their updates
  15. Assist in preparation of display materials, as well as manning exhibit booths at major medical meetings at the request of marketing
  16. Recommend and approach investigators for a speakers' program
  17. Prepare annual reports or other documents for submission to regulatory agencies
  18. Aid in preparation of materials for submission to state formularies, including occasional travel to present data at meetings of state formularies
  19. Help plan and implement postmarketing studies
  20. Aid the marketing divisions of subsidiary companies in other countries
D. Providing assistance in legal activities:
  1. Review and analyze case documents
  2. Meet with attorneys and provide affidavits
  3. Give depositions or courtroom testimony

[a] Most of these activities may be coordinated loosely between individuals involved or they may be handled more formally between departments or between entire divisions. Payment in terms of internal company credit may be utilized, if desired, with several different mechanisms.
[b] IMS, Intercontinental Medical Statistics.

If additional research and development work is necessary, then the original project (and team) should not be terminated—even though a separate team may be assembled within marketing, as well as in production, to expedite the medicine's progress in those functional areas.

Should Medicine A, Which Is Being Studied in Disease W, Also Be Tested in Diseases X, Y, or Z?

It is assumed that medicine A is available in the appropriate dosage form(s) to treat patients with these diseases and that the medicine's formulation is appropriate in terms of stability, bioavailability, and other technical considerations. Questions to ask include:

1. What clinical evidence already exists that medicine A is also effective in patients with these other diseases? How strong (i.e., convincing) is this evidence?
2. What animal data already exist that medicine A will be effective in patients with these other diseases? How strong is this evidence?
3. What clinical and animal data suggest that medicine A will *not* be effective in patients with these other diseases? How strong is this evidence?

TABLE 22.4. *Activities performed on marketed medicines in technical development and regulatory affairs departments*

A. Library and information services[a]
   1. Monitor published literature for product papers
   2. Index published product papers
   3. Perform ad hoc searches on published product literature
   4. Prepare bibliographies for the FDA[b] and/or other regulatory agencies
B. Pharmaceutical research and development laboratories
   1. Provide technical support for production
   2. Improve various processes
   3. Develop improved formulations or additional dosage forms
   4. Conduct stability studies
   5. Evaluate new packaging components and prepare submissions
   6. Prepare medicine materials for clinical trials
   7. Validate equipment and processes
   8. Prepare documents on formulation/manufacturing procedures/stability data for annual reports to FDA and other regulatory authorities
   9. Evaluate new equipment
   10. Evaluate materials from alternate suppliers
   11. Participate in establishing release guidelines and revised specifications for marketed products
C. Chemical development laboratories
   1. Provide technical support for chemical production (e.g., troubleshoot problem batches or process steps, optimization/fine-tuning of processes, and reuse or recover waste)
   2. Search for and develop improved synthetic route
   3. Transfer the synthesis to the United States of a foreign-synthesized product
   4. Provide regulatory affairs with documents supporting manufacturing changes
   5. Develop alternate source of key raw materials or intermediates
D. Analytical development laboratories
   1. Maintain and update development standards and analytical standards for reports to regulatory authorities
   2. Convert development standards to analytical standards where applicable
   3. Validate the file modifications to assays and other tests procedures with the FDA
   4. Validate and file modifications to analytical procedures found necessary as the result of improved formulations
   5. Validate and file modifications to the testing methods for raw materials, intermediates, and bulk medicine
   6. Prepare USP[b] style monographs for medicine and dosage forms
   7. Troubleshoot products to minimize back orders
E. Regulatory affairs department
   1. Submit annual reports to the FDA on each product, describing serious adverse reactions and ongoing clinical trials
   2. Compile, submit, and track all submissions on marketed medicines to the FDA for new indications, formulations, new routes of synthesis, labeling changes, and manufacturing control supplements
   3. Provide support for state formulary activities
   4. Submit adverse reactions reports to the FDA and other regulatory agencies as required by law
   5. Assist the legal department in relevant activities including recalls and liability actions
   6. Maintain official records on all marketed medicines

[a] This group is usually situated organizationally in research and development, but is considered a company resource.
[b] FDA, Food and Drug Administration; USP, United States Pharmacopeia.

4. What is the medical need for a new medicine to treat patients with other diseases?
5. What is the potential commercial value for a new medicine to treat patients with other diseases?
6. What is the status of the original work on medicine A to treat the disease for which the medicine was originally developed?
7. Does treating one or more additional diseases represent a tangent or part of the anticipated development plan? See Fig. 17.4 on models of medicine development and the discussion on tangents in Chapter 27.
8. How will studies on other diseases affect resources allocated to the original project goals and the dates of achieving the original milestones?
9. What is the opinion of the marketing function on pursuing these other indications?
10. How easy or difficult will it be to obtain regulatory approval for the proposed indications?

11. How expensive will it be in terms of money, time, and resources to complete a regulatory submission for each disease?

Situations Where Evidence of Efficacy Is Weak

In many situations the animal and clinical evidence will be weak that medicine A will be active in diseases X, Y, and Z. In those situations it is important to evaluate the hypotheses about how the medicine works and also what causes the disease and how the disease process may be affected to help patients. These hypotheses may be speculative for a medicine but known with a high degree of certainty for the disease (or vice versa). In this situation it often makes sense to conduct a pilot study to evaluate a medicine's activity. However, if the mechanism of both the medicine and the disease are speculative, and there is no evidence that the medicine will have activity in treating patients with the disease, it should be strongly questioned whether the company's interests are best served by conducting a pilot study. It is hoped that the company will have more worthwhile hypotheses to test with a higher likelihood of success.

How Is Medicine Labeling Developed?

Pharmaceutical companies often develop a standard worldwide labeling for a medicine. This helps preserve consistency from country to country because regulatory authorities and local medical and regulatory directors of the company both usually desire to make various modifications. The most important point for a company to insist on is that various aspects of medicine labeling (e.g., contraindications, maximum dose per day or course, minimum age allowable, and approved indications) must remain uniform throughout the world. To prevent safety warnings from being diluted, the precise wording of various key sentences should be as uniform as possible in every country in which the medicine is registered.

Different approaches to the labeling issue are followed by pharmaceutical companies. One approach is to develop a prototype of the label that the company expects eventually to have approved. Many companies initially write and approve the label at the outset of a project, even before the compound has usually been given to humans. As additional data are collected the labeling becomes more and more refined, until the NDA is eventually submitted and approved. One of the motivations for using this approach is to establish minimally acceptable criteria for moving the medicine forward in development. If the medicine does not meet these criteria, the project is terminated.

An alternative approach is to wait until the NDA is nearly completed by the sponsor. At that time a specific person or group is requested to prepare the first draft of the labeling. This is then revised and included in the regulatory submission. Drafts of the labeling are often based on existing labeling for other medicines. The FDA utilizes class labeling for certain groups of medicines, which means that many sections of the labeling are identical for all medicines of the group. Additional details about labeling were published by Millstein (1987).

Because pharmaceutical companies and regulatory agencies want to be cautious about a medicine's labeling, almost all adverse reactions observed with a medicine tend to be listed. This occurs even if the association between the medicine and adverse reaction is weak. No incidence figures of adverse reactions are routinely given in labeling or standard references used by most physicians. Prescribing physicians cannot usually get an adequate perspective from the medicine's labeling of which adverse reactions are most important or most frequent for their patients.

This situation is changing, however, as more package inserts in the United States contain a table of adverse reactions incidence rates observed in a group of clinical trials. There is often a column of the results obtained with placebo in the same trials so that a better interpretation of the results may be made.

23 / Golden Rules of Medicine Development

Principles and Golden Rules as Starting Points
for Thinking About Problems and Not as
Solutions.................................... 251
Plans, Strategies, and Systems 252
Staff... 254
Portfolio..................................... 254

Values, Attitudes, and Behavior 254
Regulatory Submissions......................... 255
Golden Rules for Vendors and Consultants 255
Additional Golden Rules 255
Implementing These Golden Rules 256

How to win people to your way of thinking:

The only way to get the best of an argument is to avoid it.
Show respect for the other person's opinions. Never say, "You're wrong."
If you are wrong, admit it quickly and emphatically.
Begin in a friendly way.
Get the other person saying "Yes, yes" immediately.
Let the other person do a great deal of the talking.
Let the other person feel that the idea is his or hers.
Try honestly to see things from the other person's point of view.
Be sympathetic with the other person's ideas and desires.
Appeal to the nobler motives.
Dramatize your ideas.
Throw down a challenge. Dale Carnegie

PRINCIPLES AND GOLDEN RULES AS STARTING POINTS FOR THINKING ABOUT PROBLEMS AND NOT AS SOLUTIONS

Many presentations at professional meetings as well as articles in the literature describe principles of medicine development. These generalizations are useful places to begin thinking about a problem, but they do not necessarily provide answers to problems. Clearly it is important to have experienced and intelligent staff who can evaluate whether or not the current situation represents an exception to the principles and, if so, who know how to choose the best path for resolving the problem.

A number of principles of medicine development have been written by management consultants and could have been written by pharmaceutical company staff. Typically, such principles describe methods to reduce the time of medicine development and to get products to the market faster. Although the principles appear reasonable at first glance they are often impossible to fulfill for many valid reasons. A few examples are listed:

1. Write all clinical protocols in a few weeks and do not stretch this out to months. Approval inside a company should be completed within three days.
2. Develop all medicines using a simultaneous plan and not a sequential plan.
3. Stick to development plans and target dates. Do not waiver or change dates.

There are so many exceptions to each of these statements that it would be foolish to call them "golden rules"; they are simplistic generalizations.

Golden rules of medicine discovery are discussed in Chapter 21; this chapter discusses golden rules for medicine development. Golden rules may be thought of as the most important principles in a specific area. Most of these are well known but are inconsistently followed for a variety of reasons.

Each of the golden rules described has exceptions, sometimes many, but the rules still provide an important measurement with which to guide behavior. Adherence often saves years of unnecessary or inefficient work and large amounts of resources. Because all of these principles are described in detail elsewhere in this book and in *Guide to Clinical Trials* (Spilker, 1991), specific cross-references are not given in this chapter.

The underlying principle of medicine development is that activities must be planned, coordinated, and to some degree controlled using appropriate systems and methods—after the specific compound to be developed has been identified. The processes of medicine discovery, on the other hand, are much less conducive to planning or control. Attempts to control medicine discovery often stifle and destroy the creative process.

The golden rules are described under several headings. Other important principles that overlap with the golden rules in this chapter are discussed in Chapter 8.

PLANS, STRATEGIES, AND SYSTEMS

1. Formulate an overall concept and strategy of how each medicine, indication, and formulation will be

BALANCING THE EFFORT SPENT ON PLANNING AND CONDUCTING ACTIVITIES

A. More Effort Spent on Planning Than Conducting Activities ⟶ Overplanning

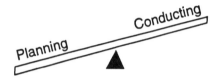

B. Equal Effort Spent on Planning and Conducting Activities ⟶ Overplanning

C. More Effort Spent on Conducting Than Planning Activities ⟶ Correct Balance

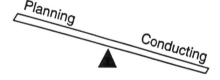

D. Almost All Effort Spent on Conducting Activities ⟶ Underplanning

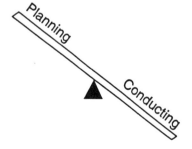

FIG. 23.1. The quantity of effort spent on planning compared with that spent on conducting activities. Planning includes developing, reviewing, and revising plans. The optimal balance is shown in panel **C**.

developed. Seek input from marketing to help formulate various goals and strategies. Establish minimally acceptable criteria that a medicine must achieve to continue its development. Detailed strategies must be developed in several functional areas (e.g., marketing or research and development) and at several levels (e.g., individual sections and departments). Ensure that effort is appropriately divided between planning and carrying out of plans. This principle is schematically represented in Fig. 23.1. This figure shows that equal efforts on planning and conducting activities are not desirable.

2. Create an international development plan that minimizes duplication and stresses efficiency. An unsound development plan may actually hamper development of a medicine (Fig. 23.2). Determine the appropriate balance between a "lean plan" that will generate the absolute minimal amount of data required for regulatory approval and a "fat plan" that goes far beyond what is required.

3. Use a team approach to manage the project through product launch and beyond (e.g., to develop new indications and dosage forms). The ultimate target should be market launch and not New Drug Application submissions.

4. Avoid tangents that depart from the chosen path of development, except when (a) the tangent is to become the new path (i.e., a new strategy is adopted) or (b) the tangent is carefully reviewed before it is implemented and is considered worthy of pursuit. The tangent is then incorporated into the existing strategy.

5. Focus on a parallel and not sequential development plan insofar as possible. This goal has to be modified if compound supplies are limited, or for other agreed-to reasons (e.g., low priority).

6. Protect and extend the medicine's indications and formulations after initial marketing. Protection may include conducting additional clinical trials, synthesizing additional compounds, or conducting postmarketing studies. Extension of a product's available formulations, approved indications, and current packaging usually enhances appropriate medical uses of a medicine and improves its commercial returns.

7. Attempt to learn everything of relevance about a medicine—even that which may be considered bad news. Although it is unnecessary to learn everything of relevance prior to regulatory approval, it is vital for a company to continue trials postmarketing to know as much important and relevant information as possible about their medicines. This enables the company to deal most effectively with questions, criticisms, and accusations.

8. Ensure that activities to implement and carry out

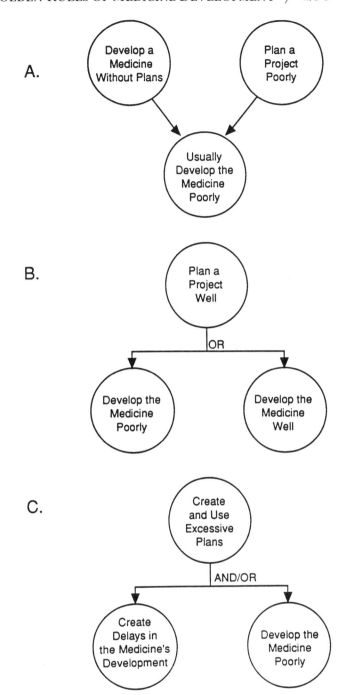

FIG. 23.2. The consequences of good or poor quality of effort spent on planning activities. Even proper planning (panel **B**) does not guarantee a positive outcome, but it improves the chances that it will occur. The concepts of "well" and "poorly" in developing medicines are complex and include an evaluation of the efficiency and the outcome of the development.

each of these principles follow an appropriate pace. If any of these principles is pushed too rapidly, then the quality of the results will suffer, problems will arise, mistakes will be made, and waste will occur. If the pace of development is too slow, then valuable patent life will be lost and competitive medicines may overtake one's own medicine. Appropriate activities should be conducted simultaneously at a rapid pace that may be followed in an efficient manner. The pace should not be so rapid that professionals feel pressured to cut corners or make unwarranted assumptions about a medicine's efficacy or safety.

9. Create and use systems and standard operating procedures that assist the development processes. *Do not allow systems to become bureaucracies, restrain development, or compromise efficiency.* Utilize computer systems that are either identical or compatible between each major site of a company developing medicines. Avoid systems that appear to be fair but really create more problems.

10. Develop a clear licensing policy and strategy that allows all product, technology, and other opportunities (e.g., acquisitions) to be reviewed rapidly and assessed for possible benefit to the company. This includes both licensing-in and licensing-out opportunities. Establish alliances with other companies (e.g., joint ventures) that enhance medicine development activities.

11. Focus development activities in a relatively limited number of therapeutic areas. There are few companies, if any, that can adequately develop medicines in all therapeutic areas. By focusing efforts, companies can develop areas of strength, which will expedite medicine development as well as medicine discovery and pharmaceutical marketing activities.

12. Develop a long-term (e.g., five- to ten-year) direction (and possibly goal), and then create a strategy that will achieve it. Cut programs that are dragging on and on with little likelihood of success. Justify all exceptions to this principle.

STAFF

1. Hire the best people possible for all positions in a company, even at the most junior level. Appropriately train and orient staff in both the methods and ethos of the company. Do not appoint academic scientists or government administrators to head a pharmaceutical company's research and development division, unless they are highly experienced in medicine discovery and development.

2. Assign personnel and other resources according to both the value and the importance of each indication and formulation being developed. Scientific, medical, and commercial values must be considered, although each are not of equal importance. Consideration must also be given to other medicines in the portfolio. A balance must be achieved between placing almost all resources on a few projects and spreading resources thinly across many projects.

3. Move staff to those projects and activities where their help is most needed to develop medicines expeditiously. Staff must be flexible and willing to help the company. On the other hand, no one should be moved too often or without full consideration of all relevant factors.

4. Senior managers should seek to build people's careers through delegating responsibilities. This occurs when managers trust their subordinates. Do not act as a dictator.

5. Hire sufficient staff for the midpoint of expected work, not for the peak work load. Supplement the staff with flexible resources (e.g., contract groups or temporary help) when peaks occur.

PORTFOLIO

1. Develop a portfolio of investigational medicines that balances high- and low-risk projects, and include medicines that will be developed in both a long-term and short-term time period. Attempt to have some projects with a chance of becoming breakthrough medicines.

2. Reevaluate each project and the overall portfolio on a relatively frequent, periodic basis. Reviews must be objective. Reviewers must not be misled by a strong desire of some or many people for a medicine to be effective and safe; they must expect a sufficient amount of hard data of appropriate magnitude that demonstrates effectiveness and safety. Ensure that all appropriate managers and workers understand current priorities of the research and development division as well as the priorities of their specified department, insofar as the two differ.

3. Identify the rate-limiting steps of each medicine's development. Ensure that appropriate and adequate resources and attention are focused on these areas.

4. The most valuable investigational medicines for a company are usually those that are close to the market. The likelihood of a medicine being marketed increases as it progresses through development. A smaller sales forecast for a medicine in late Phase III generally makes that medicine more valuable than a highly exciting compound with a large sales forecast just entering the preclinical development phase.

5. Develop milestone targets and minimally acceptable criteria for all projects. Identify the path to a negative answer (i.e., to terminate the project) in the shortest time.

VALUES, ATTITUDES, AND BEHAVIOR

1. Do whatever is necessary to encourage openness, honesty, cooperation, teamwork, and shared goals between functions (e.g., research and development, mar-

keting, and production). Achievement of these goals depends on trust, accurate communication, and the creation of a positive working environment. Disseminate appropriate information upward, horizontally, and downward throughout the company. Stress the concept of sharing information and avoiding surprises whenever possible.

2. Adhere to the highest standards of ethics in scientific, medical, marketing, and other activities. In addition to providing a strong motivating factor to staff, this behavior will provide numerous benefits to the company in terms of regulatory reviews and ability to respond to questions, criticisms, and accusations from external sources.

3. The correct attitude toward medicine development includes a positive view that may be expressed as "We will do whatever is necessary to ensure that we meet realistic plans and targets."

This attitude requires a commitment on the part of staff to:

1. Identify the most pertinent issues and problems to address; discuss these issues and problems appropriately before initiating action.

2. Make active decisions and not allow decisions to be made by avoiding issues.

3. Cooperate as fully as possible with all relevant individuals who are members of a medicine development team.

Attitudes that are most conducive to efficient medicine development must be present throughout the organization. It may be possible for a company to develop medicines efficiently if there are one or two senior research and development managers who do not share the attitudes described or who do not believe in the golden rules. But if more than a small number of senior managers or if senior managers in critical positions do not share these beliefs, the entire development process will be threatened and adversely affected. A company operating with one or more albatrosses about its collective neck must shed them or risk the undesirable consequences of inefficient medicine development in industry.

It is important for all professional staff to understand why they do the work they do. It is also essential for professional staff to understand the impact that their work has on others.

REGULATORY SUBMISSIONS

1. Attempt to create and maintain a cooperative relationship with the Food and Drug Administration and other regulatory authorities.

2. Regulatory guidelines must be viewed as guidelines and not requirements. In discussions with regulatory authorities it is necessary to differentiate between real demands or requirements, imagined demands, suggestions, and hearsay.

3. Prepare logical and straightforward regulatory submissions. Lead the regulatory reviewer step by step through each aspect of the application. Do not make reviewers work hard to understand the content of the application and the company's logic in proceeding in a specific direction. Be up-front with any problems in the application and do not attempt to hide bad data. When it is reasonable to perform multiple analyses of data, conduct most, if not all. Include complete details of the most relevant ones (one) and summaries of less important ones in regulatory applications. Indicate the reasons why a particular analysis is preferred (if that is the case).

4. Include information on dose–response relationships for investigational medicines. Dose–response relationships are obtained for safety in Phase I clinical trials, in most other clinical trials, and in toxicology studies. Dose–response relationships are obtained for efficacy in selected Phase II or III trials.

5. Always be as realistic as possible in predicting dates for approvals or reviews. Develop contingency plans for dealing with undesired outcomes. Be open with marketing staff about the type of labeling that is likely to be approved.

6. Adhere to five "C"s in preparing submissions, i.e., clearly written, consistently organized, correct information, complete, and a concise submission.

GOLDEN RULES FOR VENDORS AND CONSULTANTS

1. Provide realistic costs, dates, and number estimates to the client or potential client.

2. Do whatever is possible to establish and maintain a positive, open, and honest relationship with each client.

3. Be proactive about providing information and suggestions to help a client enhance the quality or speed of their work.

4. Appoint a primary contact person to interact with each client.

5. Do whatever is necessary to meet one's time and cost commitments.

6. Provide the highest quality product possible given the time and cost constraints.

7. Provide all services required and be willing to go beyond the strict limits of the contract to ensure the client is pleased with the services.

ADDITIONAL GOLDEN RULES

Other important principles could be included here. Their omission does not signify that their importance is any less than those listed above, especially in specific situations. Each individual department or function involved in medicine development could also create its own list of general or more specific golden rules.

Decisions that influence a medicine's development should be based on logical, practical, and other rational considerations that consider the company's past, present, and future. It is hoped that progressively fewer decisions will be based on emotions, whims, political considerations, or other personal reasons.

IMPLEMENTING THESE GOLDEN RULES

Merely understanding and believing in the golden rules described is not sufficient to realize them. It is also necessary to have a competent group of managers who are able to put these rules into practice. There is a final step required beyond understanding, acceptance, and having competent staff. That step is the collective will and desire to have these principles followed and incorporated as part of the ethos of medicine development within the company.

24 / Biotechnology

Introduction 257
Types of Biotechnology Companies in
     Pharmaceuticals........................... 258
  Maturity of Biotechnology Companies 258
Methodologies Used by Biotechnology
     Companies 259
  Cells as Factories 259
  Cells as Products 261
  Altered Cells Inside Organisms............... 261
  Plants as Sources of Products 261
  Are Biotechnology Methods Examples of
    Rational Discovery?...................... 261
Trends in Biotechnology Research.............. 261
  Genetic Therapy 261
  Medicine Delivery Issues 262
  Other Trends, Targets, and Goals 262

Patent Issues 262
International Competition 263
Biotechnology and Pharmaceutical Companies ... 263
  Differences and Similarities Between
    Biotechnology and Pharmaceutical
    Companies............................... 263
  Alliances of Biotechnology and
    Pharmaceutical Companies................ 263
  Lessons of the Biotechnology Revolution for
    Pharmaceutical Companies................ 264
Selected Issues 264
  Technical Issues 264
  Manufacturing Issues 264
  Regulatory Issues........................... 266
  Clinical Issues 266
  Ethical Issues.............................. 266

It has now been more than fifteen years since Robert Swanson, a young man who understood both finance and science, invited Herbert Boyer, a shy molecular biologist at the University of California, San Francisco, out for a beer. Swanson described his vision to Boyer: that the techniques and ideas that Boyer had devised for manipulating DNA could be translated into products at a private company yet to be established. As a result of that meeting, Genentech, the first well-known biotechnology corporation, was founded; Swanson and Boyer made their fortunes; and profound changes ensued in academic biomedical research. Robert Bazell, *The New Republic*, April 1991

As we move through the next millennium, biotechnology will be as important as the computer. John Naisbitt and Patricia Aburdene, *Megatrends 2000*

INTRODUCTION

Biotechnology is the term used to denote the production of commercially useful and/or scientifically interesting products by living cells. The United States Congress Office of Technology Assessment (1991) proposed two definitions in 1984, one broad and one narrow. The broad definition states that biotechnology is "any technique that uses living organisms (or parts of organisms) to make or modify products, to improve plants or animals, or to develop micro-organisms for specific uses." The more narrow definition refers to "the industrial use of rDNA, cell fusion, and novel bioprocessing techniques." A reference to synthetic peptides is also included in some definitions.

Biotechnology is a set of novel biological techniques applied to both basic research and to developing products. Through the techniques of biotechnology, it is possible to produce large quantities of specific products

(usually proteins) that are almost totally pure. Purity depends on bioseparation methods. While some methods of biotechnology have been known for millennia (e.g., fermentation to make beer and wine), the start of the modern biotechnology industry can be dated to the discovery of genetic engineering methods (cell line fusion and cloning) and hybridoma production in 1973 (Weatherall, 1991), although some use the time decades earlier when the structure of DNA was identified. Over the 20 years since 1973 approximately 1,500 companies have been founded worldwide (approximately 900 in the United States) to focus on biotechnology techniques and methods. More than half of these companies have focused on health care. Other areas of activity include the development of diagnostics, reagents, fine chemicals, and modified plant products. Some of the types of products made are shown in Table 24.1.

In the early 1980s, many biotechnology companies in

TABLE 24.1. *Selected products of biotechnology*

Product	Produced in/by (among other sources)
Vaccines (e.g., polio, rabies, or measles). Many vaccines are antigens	Animal cells
Antibodies (e.g., immunoglobulins or antitetanus serum)	Animals
Lymphokines (e.g., interferons or interleukins)	White blood cells
Blood products (e.g., factor VIII or factor IX)	Human blood and endothelial tissues
Monoclonal antibodies	Lymphocytes, myelomas, and hybridoma cell lines
Enzymes	Fermentation
Antibiotics (e.g., penicillin)	Fermentation
Synthetic peptides (e.g., enkephalins)	Synthetic chemistry

the pharmaceutical area appeared ignorant of regulatory requirements for developing new medicines and believed that the Food and Drug Administration (FDA), for example, would "just have to approve our new medicine within a few months, after they see how important our data are." This naiveté evaporated during the 1980s following some notable rejections and delays by the FDA. Most biotechnology companies in operation today have obtained or are seeking investment capital to fund the many years of development needed to obtain a sufficient amount of high quality data to meet modern regulatory requirements.

Biotechnology and genetic engineering techniques are generally applied to developing natural or modified human protein as medicines (e.g., interferons, tissue plasminogen activator, growth hormone, and urokinase). This has stimulated a search for potential medicines among the many natural human proteins. Many proteins are currently being investigated in a wide variety of diseases (e.g., erythropoietin, colony-stimulating factors, superoxide dismutase, interleukins, tumor necrosis factor, and epidermal growth factor). There are also many proteins "looking for a disease." The types of medicines created by biotechnology may be classified into three groups (Table 24.2).

TYPES OF BIOTECHNOLOGY COMPANIES IN PHARMACEUTICALS

There is no single accepted classification of biotechnology companies, and a broad description is given below.

In the most common usage, the biotechnology industry is based on the new technologies described in this chapter, although each company may have a unique orientation and approach. In the particular system shown below, any company could fit into one, two, or even more categories, i.e., the categories are not mutually exclusive.

Research Companies. Companies without a specific product in development. These companies may focus on a niche or broad therapeutic area.

Single-Product Companies. Companies that have a single product they are developing. Their product may be either in preclinical or clinical stage.

Multiple-Product Companies. Companies with multiple products in development.

Enabling-Technology Companies. Companies with patents on a scientifically important technology that they hope can be applied to create multiple products. These companies have important research tools that may play a major role in medicine discovery.

A summary of the size, age, budget, and revenues of various types of biotechnology companies is given in Table 24.3. It shows that therapeutic oriented companies are generally more research oriented, prevalent, and some are more commercially successful.

Maturity of Biotechnology Companies

One spectrum for viewing biotechnology companies is based on their stage of development and maturity. In that consideration, five stages may be defined. In addi-

TABLE 24.2. *Three general categories of biotechnology-derived medicines[a]*

Type	Mechanism of action	Molecular size	Diseases where active	Examples
Medicine type I	Well known	Large, usually a protein	Generally well established	Human insulin, tPA[b], and human growth hormone
Medicine type II	Not well known	Large, usually a protein	Must be found by trial and error	Interleukin-2 and tumor necrosis factor
Medicine type III	Variable	Relatively small size	Variable	Penicillins and most antibiotics

[a] This category includes pharmaceuticals made using biotechnology methods in at least one step of the synthesis.
[b] tPA, tissue plasminogen activator.

TABLE 24.3. *Biotechnology company data[a]*

Items	All companies	Therapeutics	Diagnostics	Agriculture	Equipment–reagents	Diagnostics
Numbers of firms	742	206	162	127	88	29
Year founded	1982 (1912–1991)	1984 (1925–1990)	1982 (1939–1990)	1978 (1912–1990)	1984 (1978–1990)	1984 (1967–1991)
Employees	98 (1–2020)	135 (2–2020)	97 (2–1550)	124 (2–2000)	66 (1–1300)	43 (2–180)
R&D[b] budget ($ millions)	4.9 (0.003–173)	12.3 (0.1–173)	1.9 (0.02–17)	4.2 (0.003–269)	1.3 (0.15–14)	1.7 (0.05–15)
Revenues ($ millions)	16.3 (0.002–476)	32.2 (0.105–476)	6.6 (0.07–73)	25.8 (0.002–213)	11.5 (0.003–152)	19.3 (0.6–120)

[a] Based on data from 431 surveys in 1991, the average data for year founded, total employee number, R&D budget for the current fiscal year, and expected revenues for the current fiscal year are shown. Beneath each value is the range of values in that category. The first row of data shows the number of firms in each category. The agriculture category includes animal agriculture, plant agriculture, and veterinary medicine. Reprinted from Dibner (1991) with permission.

[b] R&D, research and development.

tion, a prestage exists when scientists and venture capitalists are thinking about starting a company. In some cases it is possible for a company to be in two stages at the same time.

Stage I: New private company being formed or formed within the last year.

Stage II: Existing private company conducting research and possibly development activities.

Stage III: Mature private company that has products in development past the go–no go decision point.

Stage IV: New public company that is conducting research and possibly development activities.

Stage V: Mature public company that has products in development past the go–no go decision point.

METHODOLOGIES USED BY BIOTECHNOLOGY COMPANIES

Biotechnology can be viewed as a manufacturing process or as a research and development process to produce certain products with biological activity. In this aspect of biotechnology, it is useful to have an overview of the usual process used (Fig. 24.1). This figure illustrates that bacteria, yeast, or other cells are prepared so that they are able to produce a protein of interest. The production cycle should be as short as possible, usually in terms of days. This time indicates the number of cycles per month. The yield of product at the time of harvest is expressed as the number of micrograms per milliliter of cell culture. Purification is expressed as the percent average.

The major methodologies (i.e., genetic engineering) that are used to produce biotechnology derived products (e.g., recombinant products or monoclonal antibodies) are briefly described below.

Cells as Factories

Gene splicing is used to obtain a unique cell that manufactures a desired product. A portion of the genetic material (i.e., DNA) that includes a gene from one species (usually mammalian and often human) is removed from the chromosome or reverse transcribed from messenger RNA (complementary DNA) and spliced into the DNA of a second species. The DNA pieces are thus recombined (thus explaining the term recombinant DNA) and the properties of DNA from the first species are expressed by the total DNA of the second. Thus, if the gene from the first species (e.g., human) coded for a specific protein that could be used as a medicine (e.g., tissue plasminogen activator, insulin, or human growth hormone), then the bacteria or yeast that received this human gene is able to produce the desired human protein. As the cell with recombined DNA continues to divide and redivide, all of its progeny contain the genetic ability to manufacture the same protein. A company allows many cell divisions to occur usually in a deep cell fermentation tank or in a culture vat. After the original cell has divided into billions of cells (amplification) and production of the desired protein is stimulated, the protein product is harvested by separation from the cells. The product then undergoes a series of purification steps. Medicines *produced* in this way include alpha interferon, tissue plasminogen activator, erythropoietin, and human growth hormone. The second species is usually a bacterium (e.g., *Escherichia coli*) or yeast acting as a factory to make the protein of interest. In addition to genes coding for a specific protein, some genes also contain information that regulates the production of proteins.

A related methodology using an *in vitro* cultured hybridoma cell line enables one to prepare a monoclonal antibody that has a therapeutic (e.g., antirejection), pre-

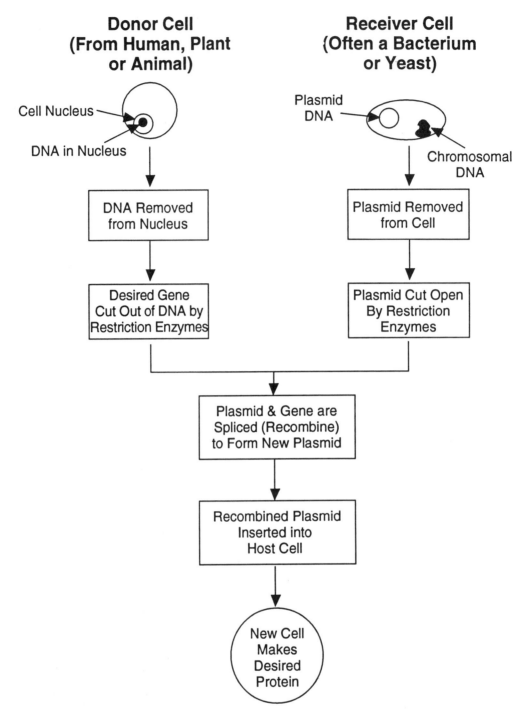

FIG. 24.1. Schematic illustration of the process of recombinant DNA engineering. In the situation where the messenger RNA is used from the cytoplasm outside the nucleus, it reassembles to form a new plasmid containing the DNA of interest. The host cell may be yeast. The recombination of the plasmid and gene is accomplished by splicing. The final step occurs as a result of amplification processes.

ventive (e.g. vaccination), or diagnostic (e.g., assay kit) use. All copies of an antibody produced by these means are identical.

Cells as Products

This is gene splicing to obtain an altered cell as a product. The method described above is used to introduce a foreign or modified gene into a cell. This confers new properties on the cell which in turn divides and is then harvested. This method differs from the first method in that the cell itself is the desired product, rather than a protein made by the cell. This use of biotechnology has been studied for various environmental purposes (e.g., cleaning oil spills) and agricultural purposes, and it may be applied for pharmaceutical effects in the future.

Altered Cells Inside Organisms

Gene splicing is used to obtain altered cells in an intact organism. In this method, a gene of interest is removed from one species as above and recombined with a cell from the same or another species. The recombined cell is introduced into a host animal. Providing a normal cell and gene to manufacture something the body is unable to make could lead to creation of transgenic animals. For example, humans with adenosine deaminase deficiency have been given the gene to make this enzyme. Humans with various metabolic deficiencies could theoretically be cured using human gene treatment. This is one of the most exciting possible uses of gene therapy. If the recombinant cell is a germ cell or a pluripotential embryonic stem cell, this process could lead to the creation of transgenic animals. If the recombinant gene is a somatic cell, the inserted gene cannot be inherited. For this ethical reason only somatic cells are targets for human gene therapy.

The main techniques used in these methods are listed in Table 24.4.

TABLE 24.4. *Selected techniques of biotechnology*

1. Recombinant DNA and expression cloning
2. Human gene mapping
3. Large fragment DNA separation
4. Gene amplification
5. Automated DNA sequencing
6. Microprotein sequencing
7. Human hybridoma formation
8. Mammalian cell cultures
9. Receptor isolation and identification
10. Protein structure analysis
11. Transgenic combinations
12. Bioseparations
13. Protein engineering

Plants as Sources of Products

Some plants have their DNA altered so that they are useful to produce a medicine. An example is the production of taxol in genetically modified yews. Potatoes and tobacco have been engineered to produce human albumin and interferon. A modified form of DNA from the bacterium *Agrobacterium tumefaciens* (the bacteria that naturally infects plant cells) has been made into a vector to carry new genes into plants.

Are Biotechnology Methods Examples of Rational Discovery?

The press often describes biotechnology as a scientific example of rational medicine discovery, but it is not. Of course, scientists using biotechnology techniques often have a strong scientific rationale for what they do, but a valid scientific rationale is different than using rational medicine discovery techniques (see Chapter 20). For example, scientists using biotechnology techniques cannot determine in advance exactly what specific proteins or polypeptides will have what specific biological effect—a requirement of rational discovery. If a protein with a known action is cut into two (or more) pieces, it is not known *a priori* which piece will retain all (or most) of the biological activity. A trial-and-error approach to testing the pieces is needed to assess the activity. Likewise, if a polypeptide is synthesized, it is not known (without testing) whether the biologically active part of the molecule has been captured in the amino acid sequence that is made.

TRENDS IN BIOTECHNOLOGY RESEARCH

Current trends and specific related details can best be found in the biotechnology, scientific, and medical literature. A few general observations are offered about broad directions being pursued and expected to be pursued over the next decade.

Genetic Therapy

In addition to acting as a factory to make medicines (proteins), cells may be used for a specific task (e.g., to digest and inactivate toxins). A potential future use is to introduce a gene into the body to make an enzyme that is congenitally absent. For example, children with Lesch-Nyhan syndrome are born without the enzyme hypoxanthine guanine phosphoribosyltransferase (HGPRT) and thus a buildup of uric acid occurs, leading to mental retardation and a syndrome that includes profound self-mutilation. Cells could theoretically be removed from these children's bone marrow and the gene from normal cells that make the enzyme, inserted. The product then could be returned into the child's bone marrow to produce HGPRT. If this is done at an early age, then mental retardation and other disease-related symptoms should be avoided. Another target for enzyme replacement is in children who are deficient in adenosine deaminase, which is currently being tested.

Medicine Delivery Issues

The major new direction in the 1990s is based on the realization that small peptides and compounds that mimic peptides can often be ingested and absorbed orally. This enables the technology to move far ahead of the limitations for only parenteral treatments of biotechnology products developed in the 1980s. Of course, the science and technology to achieve orally absorbed large molecules is extremely challenging and the major problems are not yet completely solved. Another possibility for biotechnology is to design small molecular weight molecules that have the ability only to combine with specific receptors. Biotechnology companies that follow this approach become more similar to traditional pharmaceutical companies.

Many other ideas are being explored for the delivery of medicines (e.g., inhalation, liposomes, and transdermal).

Other Trends, Targets, and Goals

Other trends and innovations include "subunit vaccines, anti-idiotype technology, and the application of genetic engineering to produce peptides or glycoproteins" (Weatherall, 1991). Weatherall also speculates on other advances that might be achieved in the future. The general target areas and goals used in biotechnology research are listed in Table 24.5. Other targets include triple strands and anti-sense.

While most biotechnology companies produced medicines from proteins, polypeptides, and pieces of proteins

TABLE 24.5. *Selected areas and goals for biotechnology research and medicine development: present and future*

1. Using proteins as targets for selective actions of potential medicines
2. Using endogenous proteins as medicines
3. Using pieces of endogenous proteins as medicines
4. Modifying pieces of endogenous proteins as medicines
5. Creating modified pieces of proteins as medicines
6. Combining parts of antibodies from different species
7. Using human genes as medicines
8. Using human genes as targets for selective actions of potential medicines
9. Use carbohydrates, lipids, nucleic acids, or other chemicals derived through biotechnology techniques as medicines
10. Medicines produced in goat's milk
11. Medicines obtained from plants

through the 1980s, the industry has broadened its approaches and is now producing medicines and biologically active molecules from sugars, nucleic acids, and fats. Not only does this change represent an expansion of the potential horizons for the industry, it also represents a step beyond seeking to mimic naturally occurring hormones by creating new biological entities. Some companies are focusing on one or more nonprotein types of molecules, attempting to exploit a wide range of hypotheses. These involve blocking specific receptors on the cell's surface, interfering with the cell's signaling pathway inside the cell, or a host of other mechanisms.

PATENT ISSUES

The ability to obtain a patent to a known protein derived by biotechnology techniques has been controversial, but many patents have been granted. Some patents have been issued regarding procedures used for expressing the gene, purifying the product, and otherwise producing the product. This has meant that having a patent on a biotechnology product is sometimes insufficient to simply allow the patent holder to make their patented product because of other blocking patents that exist (e.g., for a purification step). Licensing the rights to those patents from the patent holders has often been possible in exchange for a royalty fee.

Many ethical issues surrounding the creation of new animals and the possibility of altering humans has been one reason why the United States Patent and Trademark Office has moved slowly to issue new patents in this area. Other important issues in this area are (1) whether proteins with slight chemical differences from patented proteins are also patentable and (2) whether the same proteins made in two different organisms are each patentable.

The Office of Orphan Products Development of the FDA deals with this issue of distinguishing between similar molecules for the designation of orphan medicines. This office has stated that, for a chemical difference between two molecules to be sufficient to qualify for the designation of an orphan medicine, there had to be a demonstrable clinical difference between them (Marlene Haffner, personal communication).

Many of the patent-related issues (e.g., is a protein expressed by yeast the same as the "same" protein expressed by *Escherichia coli* bacteria?) will take a number of years to be resolved. In the meantime many companies will have to take additional risks in developing biotechnology products. There is no guarantee that the European Community (EC) countries will reach the same conclusions as the United States. No one expects all other countries to accept the opinions of either the United States or the EC countries in this matter. In fact, given the complexity of many patent issues, one could almost anticipate the exact opposite result, i.e., countries will reach different conclusions. A universal conference on this issue is one means of attempting to reach a resolution of this dilemma.

One of the major brakes on the biotechnology industry (which may be good or bad depending on one's perspective) is the extremely large backlog of patent applications internationally. There is a much longer waiting time for patents to be issued than for other technologies. Until some basic issues (e.g., what can be patented) are answered it is unlikely that a more rapid answer will be found. This issue and related ones are reviewed in the book *Biotechnology in a Global Economy* (United States Congress Office of Technology Assessment, 1991).

INTERNATIONAL COMPETITION

Several governments (e.g., Japan, Germany, and the United Kingdom) have attempted to stimulate the biotechnology industry within their countries through creation of various programs (Dibner, 1990). These programs include (1) targeting specific research areas to explore, (2) assisting technology transfer to industry, (3) assisting growth of the industry, (4) developing fermentation processes, and (5) developing other manufacturing procedures.

Biotechnology companies in some countries are able to obtain help through a variety of technical and financial assistance from their national government. In the United States, governmental help is not as readily available, but a number of other alternatives exist. One example involves biotechnology centers that are supported by more than 30 states. These centers are nonprofit organizations either associated with a state university or a geographic region that help develop the local biotechnology industry. The goals of these centers involve one or more of the following: (1) provide grants to researchers, (2) help university departments obtain staff and equipment, (3) educate high school students about biotechnology, (4) help new firms with economic advice, (5) study the biotechnology industry, (6) provide information, and (7) act as a focal point for a variety of biotechnology-related activities.

BIOTECHNOLOGY AND PHARMACEUTICAL COMPANIES

Differences and Similarities Between Biotechnology and Pharmaceutical Companies

There are important differences in the research techniques leading to discovery of a potentially valuable medicine and in the nature of scaleup and production between biotechnology and pharmaceutical companies. One of the most important differences is the need for biotechnology companies to have completed their scaleup and process development work at an earlier stage in

order to conduct clinical trials on the final product that is being manufactured. However, the principles, practices, and activities of biotechnology companies and pharmaceutical companies are almost identical in most areas of medicine development. Because this book is written at the company level, almost all chapters relate to both types of companies. Important differences between the two groups of companies exist, however, at the industry level. This relates to government funding, competition among companies, and many financial, social, and ethical issues that are omitted or are only touched on in this chapter. Patent issues also differ and have been briefly mentioned in this chapter.

Because of the difference in size between most biotechnology and pharmaceutical companies, an often-described image used to compare them is that of a large ocean traveling vessel and a small high-powered speedboat. Although the differences in size, power, and resources are obvious, the smaller vessel can move ahead more rapidly, change directions more easily, and is often more fun for those aboard. Of course, the larger vessel could be described as being anywhere along the spectrum of luxury liner to tramp steamer. A comparison of the two types of companies is given in Table 24.6, and indicates some of the strengths and weaknesses of many companies within each of the two categories.

Alliances of Biotechnology and Pharmaceutical Companies

Most of the 50 largest pharmaceutical companies worldwide engage in biotechnology programs, either through biotechnology groups working within their organization, through products licensed-in from biotechnology companies, or through research contracts or other alliances established with biotechnology companies. In addition, pharmaceutical companies often use biotechnology methods to help them synthesize small molecules, antibodies, and peptides.

Alliances between biotechnology companies and pharmaceutical companies will become more numerous in the future, as will outright acquisitions of biotechnology companies by pharmaceutical companies. Alliances include joint development ventures, licensing, contract research, marketing, comarketing, and equity purchase of part of the company. In addition to the capital that is sometimes critical to their survival, advantages for the biotechnology companies in these arrangements include the likelihood of gaining experience in medicine development, marketing, and other disciplines.

Numerous pharmaceutical companies have purchased stock (often in the range of 5% to 30%) in one or more biotechnology companies. The formation of multiple alliances with pharmaceutical companies by a single biotechnology company has also been relatively common.

TABLE 24.6. *Comparison of typical pharmaceutical and biotechnology companies*[a]

Characteristic	Biotechnology company	Pharmaceutical company
Size	Small	Large
Sales per year	5 to 20 MM$[b]	2000 to 4000 MM$
Number of marketed products	0 to 1	25 to 100
Years in operation	Up to 15	50 to 150
Major influence	Research	Marketing
Number of employees	20 to 300	10,000 to 30,000
Ownership	Stock or private	Stock
Subsidiaries	None	Many
Alliances	Several to many	Many
Sales representatives	None to few	Many
Ability to make rapid decisions	Varies, generally yes	Varies, often no
Percent of staff in science	±50%	±10%

[a] Exceptions exist for each characteristic. This table is meant to be illustrative only.
[b] Few biotechnology companies currently have sales of their biotechnology products or are profitable.
MM, millions of dollars (U.S.).

Lessons of the Biotechnology Revolution for Pharmaceutical Companies

Like the Indian fable of the blind men and the elephant (see Chapter 2), the biotechnology industry appears extremely different to various individuals and groups. Nonetheless, there are a few clear lessons that should be apparent to large pharmaceutical companies.

The first lesson is that the biotechnology revolution cannot be ignored. Biotechnology techniques must be used by all companies to produce small molecules and possibly peptides when advantages are gained. Biotechnology offers important opportunities to discover and develop therapeutically important medicines. To take maximum advantage of the possibilities to discover new medicines, it is important for large companies to diversify their strategies and approaches by including biotechnology opportunities or techniques in their portfolio. This includes the possibility of obtaining an equity position (i.e., purchasing stock) in some companies, forming strategic alliances of various types with some, and possibly acquiring a company. Other important approaches for large companies to consider include adopting an aggressive licensing policy, supporting research or projects at selected universities and companies, in addition to incorporating biotechnology methods into their own research operations.

All of the above approaches will enlarge the scientific base in which important medical discoveries can be made.

SELECTED ISSUES

Technical Issues

A number of technical issues are briefly indicated.

Contaminants

There are some significant differences between biological and common synthetic medicines. Contaminants from the host, virus, yeast, or bacteria may get through the manufacturing process and be present in the final product. These could have deleterious consequences for patients and must be eliminated with process controls. It is much more difficult to ensure the quality of the final biological product with present physical physicochemical control methods than for most synthetic medicines.

Absorption

There is a need for improved delivery systems to make most potentially available proteins as practical as medicines. Proteins cannot usually be absorbed orally without being digested into smaller pieces in the stomach and intestines because their molecular weight is too high. This implies that parenteral absorption, usually by intravenous injection, will be necessary to give these medicine to patients. This is often impractical. Many companies are devoting their primary activities to improving delivery of medicines by various approaches. These include: liposomes, coupling to molecules to enhance absorption, and a variety of other approaches.

Manufacturing Issues

Validations

When a company desires to manufacture a biological product at a new facility, more extensive validations must be done than for other medicines. In addition, clinical validation studies such as comparability studies may be required to ensure that the new product yields the same clinical responses as the original product. It is also necessary to confirm that the same product is being made from batch to batch at a single site.

Cell Production

A group of genetically engineered cells that are being used as the core for growth are referred to as a cell bank. They are cultured in tanks in a growth phase that eventually enters a production cycle or phase, a purification phase, and a formulation phase prior to the filling and labeling of vials, ampules, or other dosage forms.

Each of these phases may require several separate steps (e.g., fermentation, ultrafiltration, removing cells from the supernatant, and separating products on affinity columns). Almost any seemingly minor change in manufacture may lead to an altered product, so that it is essential to establish the optimal procedures as early in

the development process as possible. The manufacture of biotechnology products may occur at multiple sites in one or more countries (Fig. 24.2). This raises a new series of issues regarding import and export laws plus other regulations (e.g., quarantine, stability, and acceptable excipients).

Scaleup and Bioseparation

As the fermentation or other culture steps are scaled up to larger size tanks, many issues may arise such as (1) the stability of cells in the larger tanks, (2) the viability of cells throughout the production phase, (3) ultrafiltration of the crude product, (4) blockage of affinity columns with pieces of cells, and (5) the stability of the formulation. The major part of the manufacturing costs of biotechnology are often the bioseparation processes. A company that achieves greater efficiency in these steps may

VARIATIONS IN THE MANUFACTURE OF BIOLOGICAL PRODUCTS

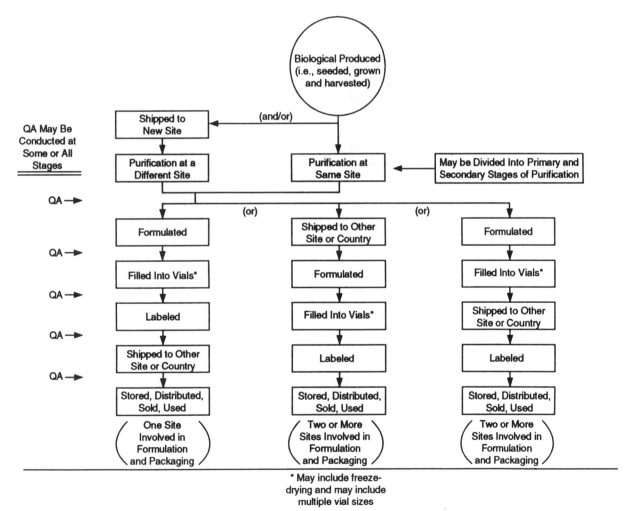

Fig. 24.2. A few of the complexities and options that sometimes arise in the manufacture of biotechnology products.

achieve a more cost-effective means of producing one (or more) medicines.

Regulatory Factors

It is important to maintain a close dialogue with regulatory authorities over many issues relating to submission and approval of the New Drug Application. In particular, it is essential to maintain a close dialogue with regulatory authorities about their reactions to manufacturing changes. If the changes are considered to be routine they usually only require a demonstration that technical specifications of the product remain unchanged. If the change is not considered routine, new clinical trials may be required to demonstrate the comparability of the new and original biological products.

Some regulatory agencies focus on the processes used for manufacturing, whereas others emphasize the characteristics of the finished products. There is a gradual increase in the standards used to evaluate the product's specifications. The following changes in the production of biologicals are often not considered routine by regulatory authorities: (1) moving the purification site to a new building, (2) moving the cell culture to a new scaleup tank, (3) contracting out the filling of vials with the product, and (4) contracting out the cell culture production to a company that is provided with part of the original sample. This means that it is necessary to show that these changes did not cause the finished product to change in a significant way.

Many of the above issues occur because many biological products are proteins and not because of the process (i.e., biotechnology) that produces them. It is usually no more difficult to purify or perform quality control on a protein produced by biotechnology than on one extracted from natural sources. In fact, it is often easier to obtain biotechnology-derived proteins.

Clinical Issues

Antigenic Responses

Foreign proteins create an antigenic response. Numerous factors play a role in affecting the formation of antibodies to biotechnology-derived proteins and products. These factors include the (1) immunological status of the patient, (2) the nature of the protein and its characteristics (e.g., size and purity), the dosing regimen, and the

route of administration. The clinical relevance of antibody formation is unknown despite years of study. For example, interferon induces antigen formation in some patients, with variable clinical effects.

Ethical Issues

Biotechnology companies and pharmaceutical companies using biotechnology must educate the public about many of the important ethical and social issues. Failure to do this may lead to a backlash from a public that poorly understands the safety aspects of biotechnology and develops fears that may be poorly founded.

Some of the major ethical issues surrounding the biotechnology industry include:

1. Should transgenic animals be developed and what restrictions should be placed, if any, on their development and use?
2. Should genetically manipulated microorganisms or cells be allowed to be released into the environment without approval, and if not, what controls should be placed on them? This issue is unlikely to affect pharmaceutical company development of new medicines.
3. Should pieces of the human genome be patentable? What restrictions and regulations, if any, should be developed to ensure the public safety and benefit?
4. Should genetically engineered cells and animals be patentable? If so, how much novelty is required before a patent is issued?
5. To what degree should the United States government assist the biotechnology industry? In particular, should the National Institutes of Health continue the cooperative research and development agreements with industry, and if so, should the current terms be modified?
6. If information about people's potential for disease can be measured, should these data be kept from insurance companies? If not, then issues of privacy must be considered for the data that have potential for great misuse.

In conclusion, the biotechnology revolution is a true revolution in science, medicine, and society. There are important lessons for all pharmaceutical companies in experiences of the industry. Even though many, if not most, current biotechnology companies will not survive as independent entities in the future their messages and creativity must become part of the large pharmaceutical companies.

25 / Extrapolating Animal Safety Data to Humans

Types of Extrapolations........................ 267
Four Issues/Questions Regarding Extrapolations
   of Safety Data 268
   Issue/Question 1: How Does One Evaluate
      Whether Data Obtained in Animals Are
      Extrapolatable to Humans?................ 268
   Issue/Question 2: How Reliable Are the
      Animal Toxicity Data Collected? 268
   Issue/Question 3: What Do Literature Data
      Show about Extrapolating Animal Safety
      Data? 269
   Could Toxicology Studies Designed in
      Hindsight Predict Actual Human Adverse
      Reactions? 269

Selected Factors Affecting Toxicological
   Effects Observed Within Species 270
Issue/Question 4: Are Useful Medicines Being
   Lost Because When Toxic Effects Observed
   in Laboratory Animals Are Extrapolated to
   Humans False Positives Result? 270
What Principles Can Be Extracted from the
   Published Data on Extrapolation of Animal
   Safety Data to Humans? 271

Some of the drugs popular in (country X) and not elsewhere fall into the category of good ideas that lack good data to support their efficacy. Lynn Payer, *Medicine and Culture*

This chapter describes various types of extrapolation, then raises four issues (in the form of questions) about extrapolation of preclinical safety data. General principles of extrapolation of data obtained from animals to humans are also described.

TYPES OF EXTRAPOLATIONS

Extrapolation of data can be categorized in several ways. One approach is to focus on three dimensions: the type of organism or species from which the data are obtained, the type of organism or species to which the data are extrapolated, and the type of data involved. Thus, there are six major types of extrapolation (Table 25.1).

This presentation focuses on the third and fourth types of extrapolation given in Table 25.1, i.e., animal safety data being extrapolated to other animal species and to humans. The four other types of extrapolation are discussed in Chapters 89 and 90 of *Guide to Clinical Trials* (Spilker, 1991).

Other types of extrapolation using toxicology data to predict safety may be made. These include extrapolations of results from:

1. Higher doses to lower doses (e.g., using high-dose findings in animals to comment on the effects that may be observed in humans using much lower doses).
2. Acute treatment to chronic treatment (e.g., using the lethal dose for 50% of animals value to comment on the relative safety of a chronic medicine).
3. *In vitro* to *in vivo* results (e.g., using *in vitro* mutagenicity tests to draw conclusions or inferences about carcinogenicity).
4. One type of animal exposed to a medicine to a different type of animal from another species (e.g., a healthy rat to a sick patient).

Each of these aspects are separate types of extrapolation. If each of these types is defined as a dimension, then the more dimensions one extrapolates across, the less certain the extrapolation is. Numerous results are frequently extrapolated across several of these dimensions

TABLE 25.1. *Types of extrapolations between species*

Type of data	From	To
1. Efficacy	Animals	Other animal species
2. Efficacy	Animals	Humans
3. Safety	Animals	Other animal species
4. Safety	Animals	Humans
5. Efficacy	Humans	Other humans
6. Safety	Humans	Other humans

(e.g., teratogens studied in an animal species using high doses of a medicine given subacutely in healthy animals yield data that are extrapolated to different species, doses, duration of treatment, and type of animal).

FOUR ISSUES/QUESTIONS REGARDING EXTRAPOLATIONS OF SAFETY DATA

If the extrapolation of preclinical safety data could perfectly predict human responses, then most issues concerning extrapolation would not exist. Likewise, if there was absolutely no utility of extrapolating animal data to humans, there would also be little need for detailed preclinical investigations. The actual situation lies in the gray area between these two extremes. The major discussion in this article is organized around the following four issues/questions. Based on the information presented in addressing these questions and also based on data in the literature, a number of principles are then described.

1. How does one evaluate whether data obtained in animals are extrapolatable to humans? This question is addressed differently for efficacy and for safety data.
2. How reliable are the animal toxicity data collected?
3. What do literature data show about extrapolating animal safety data?
4. Are useful medicines being lost because when toxic effects observed in laboratory animals are extrapolated to humans false positives result?

ISSUE/QUESTION 1: How Does One Evaluate Whether Data Obtained in Animals Are Extrapolatable to Humans?

The most direct approach for determining the extrapolatability of toxicological effects for humans is to measure retrospectively the correlation between results obtained in animals and humans. Even the most accurate data, however, do not enable one to predict whether extrapolation for the next compound tested will yield false-negative, false-positive, or correct data about the effects that will be observed in humans.

One of the reasons why it is difficult to make a direct comparison of animal and human data is that most medicines that are highly toxic in animals are never tested in humans. Thus, it is never known if these medicines

would be equally toxic in humans and have the same profile of toxicity. This problem makes it extremely difficult to study accurately the predictive value of preclinical toxicology studies.

ISSUE/QUESTION 2: How Reliable Are the Animal Toxicity Data Collected?

This issue/question does not focus on the quality of the data obtained in specific laboratories (although that is sometimes an important consideration). If Good Laboratory Practice regulations are in force, the staff is able and experienced, the facilities are appropriate, and the equipment is up to date, then the quality of the data collected should be acceptable and not be an issue. The questions raised by Issue 2 are (1) how consistent are the data obtained? (2) are the numbers of animals used in protocols sufficient to detect uncommon adverse reactions? and (3) are differences in interpretation of toxicity results among laboratories relatively common, and are such differences important?

If the rate of false positives and false negatives for extrapolating safety data were less than 5%, one might take the position that toxicological data should be accepted as valid, but the larger percentage of false positives and negatives reported in the literature means that responses to all potential medicines must be evaluated in humans whenever possible. Nonetheless, only compounds with toxicity profiles that are judged as appropriate may be ethically tested in humans. This means that some potentially valuable medicines are lost because their toxicity in animals is judged greater than what would be acceptable for humans, even though it is not known that those medicines would be as toxic in humans.

In addition, if one assumes that rare adverse reactions in humans are also rare in animals, then many, if not most, uncommon adverse reactions in humans will not be observed in animals. This is noteworthy because few animals are evaluated in toxicology studies, in comparison with the numbers of humans exposed to most medicines.

Innumerable issues are related to Issue/Question 2. I will limit my discussion to a brief mention of only one representative issue. A number of other issues relating to the extrapolation of safety data to humans are discussed in Chapter 88 of *Guide to Clinical Trials* (Spilker, 1991).

There is an old joke among pathologists that if you get five pathologists together, you get eight separate opinions on interpreting a histological slide. No consensus exists among pathologists as to whether pathologists should read tissue slides and interpret specimens blinded or unblinded. The argument for reading slides unblinded states, in part, that knowledge of the clinical diagnosis helps the pathologist better interpret the data, since numerous types of interpretations could usually be made.

An extremely defensive editorial in support of unblinded slide reading (Society of Toxicologic Pathology, 1983) does not present objective evidence to support its actual position, but ironically presents reasons to support blinding (e.g., "The long-standing practice of open or nonblinded slide reading is based on the fact that morphologic diagnostic pathology is a highly subjective and complex discipline.") and even fails to consider various methods for blinding slides (e.g., blinding only to treatment group). The argument for blinded reading is based on the notion that the biases that readily enter data analysis and interpretation are minimized. The author agrees with this latter approach of blinding in almost all situations.

ISSUE/QUESTION 3: What Do Literature Data Show about Extrapolating Animal Safety Data?

Ralph Heywood (1990) summarized a correlation of adverse reactions in humans and animal toxicology data and stated that it was in the range of 5% to 25%. One reason for such poor correlations is that many toxicology studies are conducted using standard study designs without full consideration of how they should be modified to consider human pharmacokinetics, metabolism, and methods of use (e.g., manner of administering the medicine or the frequency of administration). Heywood quoted other studies (Heywood, 1981; Falahee et al., 1983) showing that the correlation between toxicological results in rats and a nonrodent species is about 30%. Fletcher (1978) predicted, based on 45 medicines studied, that 25% of the toxic effects in animals would occur in humans.

Heywood (1990) states that only four of 22 major adverse reactions observed in humans since 1960 were predictable from animal studies, and another two adverse reactions were questionable. It is therefore apparent that most of this group of adverse reactions could not be predicted using animal studies.

Litchfield (1962) evaluated six compounds studied in humans, rats, and dogs and calculated the likelihood that (1) adverse reactions would be found in humans if they were found in both rats and dogs and (2) adverse reactions would not be found in humans if they were only found in one animal species. He found that 68% of the toxic effects observed in both rats and dogs were found in humans and only 21% of toxic effects found in a single animal species were found in humans. He found that for the specific medicines tested, the dog yielded better data than did the rat for predicting human responses (Litchfield, 1961). The best correlations between animal and human data were reported for gastrointestinal complaints, especially vomiting. Schein et al. (1970) reported that Litchfield's analysis overstated the results by not accounting for the large number of false negatives

in animals, which accounted for 68% of the toxicity observed in humans. Selected reasons for false-positive and false-negative observations in toxicology studies are listed in Tables 25.2 and 25.3. Additional discussions on this topic are presented in a recent book, *Animal Toxicity Studies: Their Relevance for Man* (Lumley and Walker, 1990).

Three reasons were given by Johnsson et al. (1984) to explain why it is difficult to relate human adverse reactions to animal data: (1) subjective adverse reactions are not detectable in animals (e.g., dizziness, headache, and nausea), (2) medicine doses (and plasma levels) are often excessive in animal studies, and (3) immunological effects are difficult to detect in animals. A detailed discussion of this topic for a single hepatotoxic medicine is given by Clarke et al. (1985).

Could Toxicology Studies Designed in Hindsight Predict Actual Human Adverse Reactions?

Heywood (1984) evaluated many of the major clinical adverse reactions reported in the literature since 1961 and determined whether designing animal toxicological tests (in hindsight) would have been predictive of the clinical problem. These data are shown in Table 25.4. Fourteen specific medicines or types of medicines are listed as causing 13 adverse reactions in humans. Of the seven cases in which confirmatory animal results were observed in hindsight (after the human toxicity was known), several involved either uncommon testing procedures (e.g., experimental lactic acidosis induced in dogs) or the use of uncommon species for routine toxicological studies (e.g., Syrian hamsters were used to demonstrate a lethal enterocolitis from clindamycin or lincomycin). Issues relating to the predictive utility of preclinical toxicological testing for various medicines (e.g., bethanidine, bromocriptine, cimetidine, and tamoxifen) are explored by Laurence et al. (1984).

TABLE 25.2. *Selected reasons for false-positive results in toxicology*[a]

1. Excessive dosage
2. Creation of metabolites in animals (but not in humans) that lead to toxicity
3. Environmental factors favor the lesion, but these factors would not occur in humans
4. Species-specific effect unexplained by any of the other factors
5. Physiological or anatomical differences
6. Differences in metabolism, distribution, or elimination
7. Microbial status of the animals differ
8. Animal housing inappropriate
9. Diet of animals (e.g., sterile distilled water versus tap water or autoclaved food versus normal animal food)
10. Technician errors

[a] Many other reasons discussed in this article also apply.

TABLE 25.3. *Selected reasons for false-negative responses in toxicology studies*

1. Species difference (e.g., genetic factors)
2. Poor absorption
3. Differences in metabolism or elimination[a]
4. Physiological or anatomical differences
5. Enzyme induction
6. Failure to observe subjective symptoms
7. Failure to observe most skin reactions
8. Failure to observe hypersensitivity reactions
9. Absence of the disease and its pathological effects
10. Failure to measure the effect later found to occur in humans
11. Differences in microbial status
12. Underlying pathology of disease in humans exacerbated by medicines in humans, but not observed in animals

[a] Target organ may not have received sufficient exposure.

Selected Factors Affecting Toxicological Effects Observed Within Species

Toxicological effects observed with a specific medicine may differ within a single species depending on the strain or other species-related factors. Numerous environmental factors may also influence toxicological effects in a single species. These two types of effects are defined as Type I and Type II intraspecies effects.

Type I Intraspecies Effects. These depend on factors relating to the species, such as strain, sex, metabolism, genetic breeding, weight, age, or other factors.

Type II Intraspecies Effects. These depend on factors relating to the environment, such as temperature, housing conditions, humidity, type of diet, amount of food, number and proximity of animals, amount of light, and amount of handling.

All of these factors, plus others (e.g., protocol-related factors, such as whether medicine is placed in drinking water or given by gavage) should be considered when interpreting animal data to determine its implications for humans.

ISSUE/QUESTION 4: Are Useful Medicines Being Lost Because When Toxic Effects Observed in Laboratory Animals Are Extrapolated to Humans False Positives Result?

There is little doubt that some valuable medicines have been lost because (1) their clinical development was terminated prematurely, (2) they were never tested in humans because of toxicity observed in animals that would not be present in humans, or (3) they were withdrawn from the market because of toxic effects found in animals. The exact number of these lost medicines can never be determined. There are several reasons why these medicines may not have been toxic in humans. These reasons include (1) large multiples of the doses used in humans are tested in animals, (2) differences in metabolism often occur between species, and (3) saturation of the animals' metabolic capacity with high doses may lead to the creation of new and toxic molecules or toxicological effects that would never occur in humans. Another reason relates to the nature of the toxicity observed in animals. Certain types of toxicity (e.g., carcinogenicity) ethically prevent testing of those compounds in humans. Although some anticancer and anti-acquired immune deficiency syndrome medicines are known to also cause cancer in laboratory animals, the vast majority of medicines do not cause cancer in laboratory animals. Nonetheless, a finding in animals that a medicine causes cancer would not ethically permit initiation or continuation of human testing of most compounds.

Although some potentially useful medicines are lost because of society's conservative approach, preclinical safety testing of compounds is essential. No universally accepted substitute for chronic toxicology studies exists, and it is ethically as well as regulatorily mandated that a sufficient number of various types of toxicological studies be conducted before a new medicine is released to the market. Case histories have been presented by numerous authors (Thiede et al., 1964; Fraumeni and Miller, 1972;

TABLE 25.4. *Major medicine-induced adverse reactions since 1961[a]*

Medicine	Adverse reaction in humans	Animal toxicity
Practolol	Oculomucocutaneous syndrome	Not predictive
Oral contraceptives	Thromboembolism	Not predictive
Phenacetin (analgesics)	Nephropathy	Confirmatory in rat[b]
Phenformin	Lactic acidosis	Confirmatory in dog
Sympathomimetic aerosols	Asthmatic death	Not predictive
Clioquinol	Subacute myelooptic neuropathy	Confirmatory in dog
Diethylstilbestrol	Vaginal cancer in female offspring	Confirmatory in mice and cebus monkeys
Chloramphenicol	Aplastic anemia	Not predictive
Halothane	Jaundice	Predictable in rats, mice, dogs, and monkeys
Methysergide	Retroperitoneal fibrosis	Not predictive
Lincomycin and clindamycin	Pseudomembranous colitis	Confirmatory in hamster
Phenylbutazone	Aplastic anemia	Not predictive
Phenothiazines	Dyskinesia	Predictable in dogs and monkeys

[a] Reproduced by permission of Almqvist and Wiksell from Heywood (1984).
[b] High doses and physiological modification.

and Nester, 1975) of disastrous consequences that occurred when adequate safety studies on medicines were not conducted in animals.

WHAT PRINCIPLES CAN BE EXTRACTED FROM THE PUBLISHED DATA ON EXTRAPOLATION OF ANIMAL SAFETY DATA TO HUMANS?

Numerous principles may be derived based on reviewing the data regarding extrapolation of animal toxicity data to humans. Some of them are indicated below (the order is not significant).

1. The ability to extrapolate accurately the animal toxicological data to humans has been shown to be enhanced if the effect is observed at low multiples of the medicine's therapeutic dose. A fivefold multiple, for example, means that the dose of the medicine in animals is five times the therapeutic dose given (or anticipated to be given) to humans.

2. It is important for regulators, pharmaceutical sponsors, and others to take every toxicity finding seriously and to evaluate its potential to affect humans.

3. Many factors of the animal protocol relating to dosing as well as the methods used for sample collection, preparation, and analysis are often critical in determining whether or not animal toxicity is observed. These factors may also influence whether the toxic effects will also be observed in humans. For example, animals may be dosed once daily or a fixed number of times daily or animals may be dosed continuously by receiving the medicine in their food or drinking water. These factors may determine not only if toxicity is observed, but also its severity.

4. The impact on a medicine's future of finding a new and serious adverse reaction (e.g., cancer) depends to a large degree on whether the medicine is investigational or marketed and on whether it is considered an essential or secondary medicine.

5. The more animal species that demonstrate a toxic effect, the greater the likelihood that the effect will also be observed in humans. Nonetheless, the extrapolation of a specific toxic effect observed in multiple animal species to humans is never certain.

6. It is sometimes impossible to design animal studies, even in hindsight, to observe a well-characterized human adverse reaction. This inability may occur even if the metabolism of the medicine is similar in both animals and humans.

7. Data from the highest species studied from an evolutionary perspective do not always have a greater chance of predicting human responses than do data from lower species.

8. Dose–response relationships of toxic effects in animals usually have a better chance of identifying potential human problems than do effects observed at a single dose level.

9. Extremely large doses of a compound or medicine given to animals often elicit effects that are highly unlikely to occur in humans. Multiples of over 1,000 times the anticipated human dose should generally not be tested, unless there is a specific reason to do so. The metabolic capacity of an animal given excessive doses may be overwhelmed and yield uncharacteristic responses.

10. Public perception of human adverse reactions may force the removal of a medicine from the market, despite strong scientific data that challenges the veracity of the charge. This occurred with Bendectin (Sheffield and Batagol, 1985) where the causality between the adverse reaction and the medicine was never established.

11. The benefit-to-risk balance perceived by both regulators and pharmaceutical companies usually places more credence and importance on the risk part of the equation. This is in large part because of the regulator's need to protect society and the concern of the pharmaceutical company about product liability.

12. The question of establishing the appropriate duration of toxicology studies is unsettled to date. Nonetheless, there are data that suggest few effects are observed in a one-year study that are not observed in six months (Griffin, 1986).

13. The question of whether mutagenicity tests are worthwhile is still controversial. The initial enthusiasm for successful extrapolation was overly optimistic. Correlations between positive results for mutagenicity tests and the ability to test substances to produce cancer in rodents is only about 50%.

14. Carcinogenicity studies in animals often yield discordant results, depending on the species, strain, and sex of animals tested. Carcinogenicity tests, as well as mutagenicity tests, may yield false-positive results (in relation to humans) (e.g., chrysazin, Heywood, 1990).

15. Potential human carcinogens can best be detected through (1) comparison of chemical structure of the test compound with other tested agents, (2) bioassays of these potential carcinogens conducted in two species, and (3) mutagenicity tests.

16. The trend toward measuring plasma levels of medicines in toxicology studies will help enhance knowledge of the relationship between a medicine's dose and its toxic effects. Toxicokinetics is an exciting and important area of study that will contribute significantly to knowledge about the extrapolation of animal data to humans. It is necessary to measure blood levels to prove that compounds given to animals are actually absorbed. A relatively clean toxicological profile would result if a compound is not ab-

sorbed (e.g., this phenomenon was observed with clioquinol, Heywood, 1990).

17. Many adverse reactions that occur in humans cannot be predicted by animal studies. These include allergies, hypersensitivity, immunotoxicity, and subjective reactions. The ability of future toxicological methods to improve this situation is doubtful at present.

18. Toxic effects noted only in animal organs or tissues that are present in animals but not in humans can generally be disregarded.

19. Determining the metabolism of a medicine in various animal species and in humans may help select which species will yield data that correlates best with humans.

20. Any medicine or biological substance may be abused by humans (e.g., water overdose leading to toxicity and death and smoking cloves or other herbs or spices). This abuse may cause effects in humans that could not be expected or predicted to occur in animals (e.g., analgesic nephropathy resulting from phenacetin abuse).

21. The study and understanding of the mechanism(s) of toxicity in both animals and humans has great potential to enhance the predictive aspects of toxic results, and will improve our ability to extrapolate results from animals to humans.

Evaluating the extrapolation of animal toxicity data to humans, we learn that each situation is quite different, and a few generalizations or principles will never enable conscientious scientists to prevent some unfortunate experiences of human toxicity from occurring in the future. The fortunate part is that animal toxicology studies will ensure that this number of adverse reactions will be much smaller than it otherwise would be.

Accumulation of large amounts of animal and human data in the future is unlikely to affect most of these principles. However, the probability of being able to extrapolate the safety of certain chemicals more accurately (e.g., those with specific structures) will improve. The design of appropriate toxicological studies to obtain better quality data should also improve. It is hoped that these principles can be further refined, quantified, and expanded and that more data supporting them will be obtained. Thus, further credence would be added to the practice of extrapolation of safety data, and there would be relative degrees of assurance for making various types of extrapolations.

26 / Evaluating and Interpreting Data

Background Information about Medicines and Diseases	**273**
What Is a Drug and What Is a Medicine?......	273
Medicines Work at Multiple Levels	274
What Are Medical Facts?	274
How Much Do We Really Know?—Viewing the Cell as an Island	274
Why Do New Diseases Occur?	275
What Is the Natural History of a Disease?	277
Scientific Logic and Interpretations..............	**277**
Choosing a Puzzle to Work On	277
What Does a Scientist See?	277
Holding Contradictory Beliefs or Ideas	278
Traps and Pitfalls in Thinking	278
Why Scientists Often Require Conclusive Proof Before Reaching a Conclusion and Making Decisions	279
Post Hoc Ergo Propter Hoc Issues.............	279
Extrapolations of Data and Interpretations	**279**
Purposes of Extrapolations....................	280
Extrapolations from Animals to Animals......	280
Extrapolations from Animals to Humans	280
Establishing New Animal Models to Test Medicines and Establishing Criteria of an Ideal Medicine	281
Extrapolations from Humans to Humans	281
Forming a Concept of a Medicine's Risks and Benefits	282

Men love to wonder, and that is the seed of science. Ralph Waldo Emerson (1803–1882), American essayist and poet. From *Society and Solitude*, 1870.

He who understands nothing but chemistry does not truly understand chemistry either. Georg Lichtenberg, 18th century philosopher.

The aim of science is to seek the simplest explanation of complex facts. We are apt to fall into the error of thinking that the facts are simple because simplicity is the goal of our quest. The guiding motto in the life of every natural philosopher should be, "Seek simplicity and distrust it." Alfred North Whitehead. From *Concept of Nature*

BACKGROUND INFORMATION ABOUT MEDICINES AND DISEASES

This chapter provides some background on medicines and diseases. It also provides an orientation for nonscientists to better understand how scientists and clinicians think and utilize information.

What Is a Drug and What Is a Medicine?

No single definition of a drug is universally accepted. Instead, there are many definitions ranging from narrow and restricted ones to those that are extremely broad. The broadest definition is any chemical agent that affects living processes (*Goodman and Gilman's The Pharmacological Basis of Therapeutics*, seventh edition, Macmil-

lan Publishing Co., New York, 1985, page 1). An example of a narrower definition is any substance, other than food, used in the prevention, diagnosis, alleviation, treatment, or cure of disease in humans and animals (*Stedman's Medical Dictionary*, 22nd edition, Williams and Wilkins, Baltimore, 1972). Over the last several years the word "drug" has become increasingly associated with abused, usually illegal substances. The author believes (as do many others) that the time has come to differentiate between therapeutic and abused substances. In this book the word "drug" is reserved for a licit or illicit substance that is abused. The definition of a medicine in this book is a chemical substance that affects living tissue and is used to achieve a desired biological effect in a living organism. Some aspects of this definition are a little vague or may be debated (e.g., when are foods considered medicines and what medicines are present in foods). Nonetheless, this general definition allows for great latitude in discussing medicine development and uses.

A promedicine is defined as a substance that is converted inside the body into an active medicine, usually by metabolic processes in the liver or blood. A promedicine may be inactive on its own or it may have the same biological profile as the active medicine. Some people (including the author) believe that a chemical compound should first be referred to as a medicine when it is initially given to humans (i.e., in Phase I studies). Others prefer to make this distinction when the compound is first shown to be active in patients, which occurs in Phase II studies.

Medicines Work at Multiple Levels

A medicine works at a *clinical level* in addition to affecting organs and cells. A medicine improves a patient's symptoms and thereby enables the patient to feel better on a *physical level.* This leads to an improved sense of well-being on a *psychological level.* This in turn enables the patient to have improved interactions with others on a *social level.* The medicine acts to improve the patient's symptoms by affecting one or more processes on a physiological level (i.e., affecting [1] organs, such as the heart or stomach, [2] tissues, or [3] organ systems, such as cardiovascular or gastrointestinal). It does this in turn through actions at a *tissue level* and *cellular level,* that result from biochemical effects within and/or outside cells. Some scientific studies of how a medicine works investigate *subcellular* and *molecular levels.* For certain medicines, such as those with abuse potential, there is also a *population level* at which a medicine acts. This level involves interactions among groups of people. Figure 26.1 illustrates these levels.

Medicines may and do affect all of these levels so that there is really no single *pharmacological level.* On the other hand, pharmacological studies are usually conducted in animals at the cellular, tissue, and physiological levels, whereas in humans, pharmacological studies are often conducted at the level of organ systems and the whole organism.

Scientific understanding of how most medicines act is full of gaps. Sometimes these gaps are filled by hypotheses or ideas of how the medicine could work. Evidence is then gathered to support or refute the hypothesis. In some situations, multiple hypotheses are proposed to explain a single action of a medicine. Many scientific ideas may be viewed and explained simply as turning biologically active materials (e.g., enzymes) on or off. Other medicines work by blocking certain receptors or antagonizing certain chemicals.

Sometimes it is not the facts of how a medicine behaves at each level that are an issue, but how the effects at one level lead to the effects at another level (Fig. 26.1). Those bridges are as important to understand as how a medicine is acting at each specific level. An example is given in Fig. 26.2 that illustrates how cardiac glycosides work at multiple levels. Digitalis, digoxin, and ouabain are widely used medicines of this class.

What Are Medical Facts?

Are medical facts absolute and true for all time, or are they relative and dependent on the scientific, social, and political environment in which they are established? The answer is that all medical facts are relative and may be eventually replaced by more accepted or stronger facts. Most people understand that when facts are shown to be wrong, they are usually replaced by others. No one can say that we have the correct facts in any area of medicine. Most currently accepted medical facts will be replaced by others, and they in turn will eventually be replaced, and so on. The general modes of perception of the most influential scientists and clinicians are the bases of how facts are established.

How Much Do We Really Know?—Viewing the Cell as an Island

Many people have the perspective that medicine has made so much progress over the last century that we are getting to know most of what there is to know. The fallacy of this view can be commented on by describing an analogy.

Understanding the workings of a single cell has been described as analogous to viewing the island of Manhattan from above. Scientists are said to be in a helicopter high over the island. A few centuries ago, scientists were so far above the island that they did not know of its existence. As scientific and technical abilities improved, especially through invention of the microscope, the island (i.e., cell) was discovered.

Over the last 200 or so years our helicopter has moved steadily closer to the island and now we are able to identify not only Central Park (which was an early observation), but a number of specific buildings. We can often determine which buildings are bigger than others. Traffic patterns can also be observed and we can identify where most of the outdoor activities are occurring. The buildings, traffic, parks, and bodies of water we observe are analogous to the structural details of a cell that can now be identified with electron and scanning microscopes.

The interesting questions, however, are what the many managers are doing in each of the buildings and also what motivates them to make the decisions they reach. Trying to answer these questions based on the gross details of the buildings and vehicles we observe on the streets below is impossible. We do not know the iden-

HIERARCHIES IN THE THERAPEUTIC PROCESS

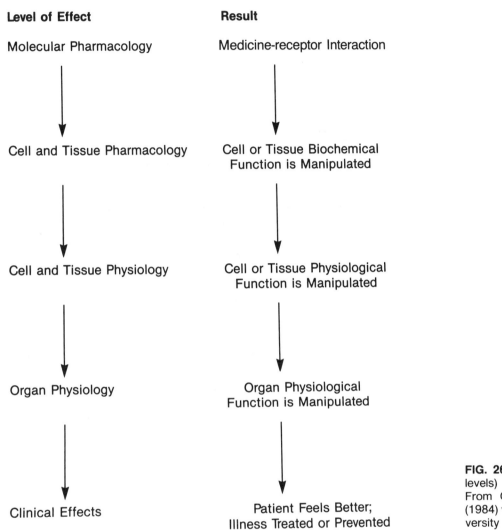

Level of Effect

Molecular Pharmacology

Cell and Tissue Pharmacology

Cell and Tissue Physiology

Organ Physiology

Clinical Effects

Result

Medicine-receptor Interaction

Cell or Tissue Biochemical Function is Manipulated

Cell or Tissue Physiological Function is Manipulated

Organ Physiological Function is Manipulated

Patient Feels Better; Illness Treated or Prevented

FIG. 26.1. Hierarchies (i.e., different levels) in the therapeutic process. From Grahame-Smith and Aronson (1984) with permission of Oxford University Press.

tity of most managers, let alone their actual activities. Nonetheless we make many hypotheses and develop theories. Inside our bodies and cells it is estimated that there are approximately 50,000 proteins, only one-tenth of which have been discovered. There is clearly a long way to go.

Why Do New Diseases Occur?

Diseases are usually a fixed concept in our minds that are all-or-none entities, even though we know we may get a mild or severe case of any disease. We may remember diseases that our parents or grandparents had and, in some cases, think how lucky we are to be vaccinated and therefore protected against them. In other cases, we know that we too may get the same disease as our parents. If so, there may or may not be effective treatments available.

Diseases are not fixed entities but have their own natural history and characteristics that evolve over time. A disease may change in such aspects as severity, after effects, frequency, types of symptoms, or rate of mortality. These changes may occur because people who get the disease change or because the cause of the disease changes. People may become better protected against the disease because of immunological resistance or improved nutritional status. Resistance may be acquired genetically over a long period of time or may be acquired artificially, as with vaccines. Some characteristics of a disease change because of altered environmental factors that affect health, such as sanitation, crowding, nutri-

DIGOXIN THERAPY IN PATIENTS WITH HEART FAILURE

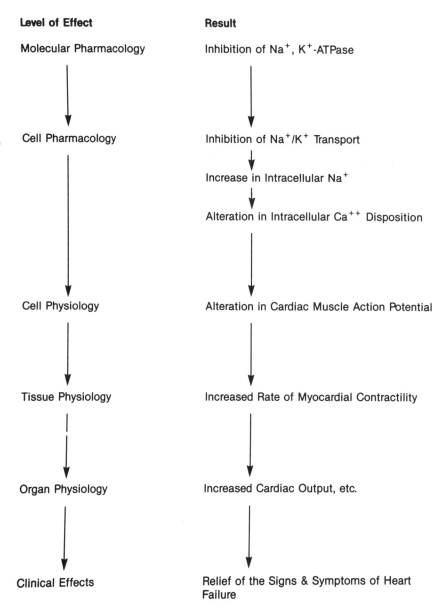

Level of Effect	Result
Molecular Pharmacology	Inhibition of Na$^+$, K$^+$-ATPase
Cell Pharmacology	Inhibition of Na$^+$/K$^+$ Transport
	Increase in Intracellular Na$^+$
	Alteration in Intracellular Ca^{++} Disposition
Cell Physiology	Alteration in Cardiac Muscle Action Potential
Tissue Physiology	Increased Rate of Myocardial Contractility
Organ Physiology	Increased Cardiac Output, etc.
Clinical Effects	Relief of the Signs & Symptoms of Heart Failure

Fig. 26.2. Hierarchies in the actions of cardiac glycosides. From Grahame-Smith and Aronson (1984) with permission of Oxford University Press.

tion, and personal hygiene. Also, as humans get to know more about each disease, ways of eradicating some diseases are found, as was done with the once-dreaded disease smallpox. The development of vaccines has allowed us to think in terms of eventually eradicating a number of other diseases as well (e.g., measles). Finally, a disease may change over decades, centuries, or millennia because of genetic changes within the viruses or bacteria that cause the disease (e.g., syphilis).

Trying to control or even effectively treat a number of diseases is a difficult battle when the cause of the disease is rapidly changing. A good example is the common influenza virus disease or "flu." This disease changes every couple of years as a new strain emerges and requires development of a new vaccine to prevent effectively the disease in those inoculated.

New diseases emerge for numerous reasons including mutations in the genetic makeup of viruses, bacteria, or other disease-causing agents. New diseases may emerge in a country because people, animals, or plants may carry diseases from one place to another. Diseases may move (or return to) a place where people have little natural resistance. In such a situation, the disease may not only spread rapidly but may occur in a more severe form than in the original population. An example of this reportedly occurred when syphilis was brought to Europe from either the New World or from Africa in the 15th century (Gottfried, 1983, pages 158 and 159). Interestingly, the Italians called syphilis the "French pox" and the French called it the "Italian pox." English called it the "Spanish pox," Poles called it the "German pox," and Russians called it the "Polish pox" (Gottfried, 1983).

New cultural practices, environmental factors, or almost any type of change may cause diseases to alter their natural history. Two examples within the last century are (1) increases in people smoking cigarettes has caused an enormous increase in lung cancer and (2) the high saturated fat diet in certain Western countries has led to increases in atherosclerosis and subsequently to an increased number of myocardial infarctions. Some diseases that were once limited to animal populations are now human diseases as well. The crossing of a disease from animals to humans may occur through close contact, eating part of the animal, or for unknown reasons. Some diseases may be transmitted from animals to humans (e.g., rabies, yellow fever, some types of food poisoning, and malaria), whereas others are not (e.g., feline leukemia). Other diseases are presumed to be transmitted both from animals to humans and vice versa (e.g., brucellosis) or are not transmitted from humans to animals (e.g., common cold).

What Is the Natural History of a Disease?

The changing natural history of disease can be readily appreciated from the changing mortality statistics for tuberculosis. In New York City the death rate from tuberculosis was 700 per 10,000 people in 1812. After some sanitation measures had been introduced, the rate fell to 400 per 10,000 about 1880. It further decreased to 180 (per 10,000 inhabitants) by 1910, and just before the age of antibiotic treatment of tuberculosis in 1945, the rate had decreased to 48 (per 10,000 inhabitants). The reasons for the changing nature of a disease over time vary from disease to disease. Sometimes, as with tuberculosis, the major reasons are primarily under human control (e.g., nutrition and sanitation). With other diseases the reasons for the changes are either unknown or are related to inherent changes in the cause(s) of disease (e.g., the viruses or bacteria) that are not under direct human control.

This chapter illustrates the dynamic nature of the medical environment in which medicines act. Changes in existing disease, emergence of new diseases (e.g., acquired immune deficiency syndrome), recognition of already existing diseases (e.g., Legionnaires' disease), and development of resistance or tolerance to medicines are all factors that have an impact directly on the quest for new medicines and the development of existing compounds and medicines.

SCIENTIFIC LOGIC AND INTERPRETATIONS

Choosing a Puzzle to Work On

Scientists are often driven by the challenge of solving puzzles. A creative scientist who solves a research problem uses many types of simple and complex concepts and often puts the pieces of a puzzle together in a novel way. Alternatively, a scientist may discover a new piece of a puzzle that eluded previous workers. The choice of a suitable problem to explore is an extremely important part of scientific research. Great scientists chose great problems to work on.

Many important scientific discoveries are made by people who are working in a field in which they were not trained. These people often view problems in a different way than those who are experts in the field. As a result, they approach problems differently and sometimes are able to solve them. For example, Dalton was a meteorologist who was studying the absorption of gases by water and the absorption of water by the atmosphere. To understand the physical processes involved better, he desired to learn the sizes and weights of the atomic particles involved in his mixtures. To condense a long story, Dalton invented the atomic theory of chemistry while trying to solve what was for him originally a meteorological problem.

What Does a Scientist See?

After a major scientific discovery has been made, the world is different! What people see is different. A lag period often exists between the discovery and the new way of seeing the world. There was a lag period before people saw what Copernicus discovered, i.e., that the earth revolves around the sun and not the other way around. Likewise, after Charles Darwin wrote *The Origin of the Species,* it took more than a generation for most people to see humans as descendants of animals and not as an almost instant creation of the Divine. In science, the Frenchman Lavoisier saw *oxygen,* whereas the Englishman Priestly saw "*dephlogisticated air.*" Lavoisier also saw *compounds* in the material Priestly called *earth.* These concepts represented real differences in how the world was perceived and were not merely semantic arguments. Many more examples of this phenomenon could be described. They show that major scientific advances change the way in which scientists and many others view the world.

A widespread belief in the world of both medicine and science views the clinical investigator or scientific experimenter as a detached observer of patients or scientific experiments. The concept of the totally independent observer, however, is a fiction. The observer is always part of the experiment or study and influences it, sometimes in subtle ways. The very act of measuring something often affects or changes what is being measured. This is a major reason for adding control groups to many investigations, in the belief that both (or all) groups will be similarly affected. Except for using clairvoyance or revelation, the major hope of arriving at or approaching an important scientific truth is to eliminate as many biases as possible and to design good experiments.

Most people have preconceived ideas about what relationship or outcome should be observed in a study or experiment. When the outcome is unexpected, some scientists or clinicians stretch or mold the data in a way that best fits the expected pattern. Other scientists interpret the data more objectively, find flimsy explanations, or decide that no useful interpretation is possible. Racial, ethnic, religious, national, geographical region, and occupational factors often play a large role in the expectations that individuals have about anticipated outcomes. Scientists are trained to minimize the impact of these factors on their judgments in reaching an interpretation of experimental data.

Some scientists and clinicians do not actually conduct experiments in which they test carefully constructed hypotheses about how a medicine acts in animals or patients. Rather, they choose a medicine to evaluate in a given test system under specified conditions to observe what results will be obtained. They may make many independent observations and collect a great deal of data, but the scientific weight of such observations is often weak. This is especially true if the studies are not carefully controlled. Many experiments are usually required to have enough weight and credibility to constitute scientific or medical proof.

Holding Contradictory Beliefs or Ideas

Creative and intelligent scientists (and nonscientists) often have beliefs and principles that appear to be contradictory. This may occur because people's views are vague, mixed up in their minds, or for other reasons. On the other hand, this may be a highly positive situation where intellectual flexibility allows people to hold contradictory beliefs. Apparent contradictions often result from scientific evidence that supports two or more conflicting theories or models. F. Scott Fitzgerald once wrote that "the test of a first-rate intelligence is the ability to hold two opposed ideas in the mind at the same time, and still retain the ability to function." In most situations one set of principles will eventually be found to be correct.

Traps and Pitfalls in Thinking

Some of the more common pitfalls that trap nonscientists as well as naive scientists are:

1. Too much confidence is placed in early trends or results. Most scientists and clinicians have experienced numerous situations where the first several experiments yielded a positive response, only to be followed by others that failed to demonstrate the same effect. The opposite situation also occurs where negative studies are followed by positive ones. Scientists with wisdom therefore express the view that initial results are encouraging or promising, but that additional studies must be conducted to confirm the results. Scientists with less experience are highly enthusiastic when their first few studies are positive. They may use the preliminary results to bolster their biases and become even less objective.

2. There is a tendency for many individuals to explain away unexpected results that do not confirm or support the views which are anticipated. One or more reasons may almost always be found that could have caused the undesired result. The undesired data are then often dismissed from the sample and if the experiment is published, the existence of these data may never be known to the readers. This practice, which may occur more commonly in animal and other preclinical studies than in clinical studies, is extremely uncommon in clinical trials sponsored by a pharmaceutical company. This is because all data from sponsored studies on new medicines that are included in regulatory submissions are subject to regulatory review and audit.

3. Expectations of being able to reproduce studies or experiments are extremely high. Even if a scientist or clinician is replicating his or her own work, there are various reasons why results often differ the second time around. This leads to the view that it is extremely important to obtain a second study that confirms the results of a first. Also, data that have been independently observed or confirmed in a second laboratory or clinic are much more convincing than those of studies reported from a single institution.

4. People overestimate or do not consider the "power" of a study. This is a statistical term that relates to the chance that a positive effect will be observed in an investigation if such an effect truly exists. This is critically important because it means that one may determine ahead of time that a particular study or experiment has little or almost no chance of finding a certain result *even if that result exists and is true!* This pitfall is often manifested through enrolling an insufficient number of patients in a clinical trial. This is an extremely common problem among academic clini-

cians, many of whom conduct studies where the chance of finding a positive response is unacceptably low. They may conduct such studies because they have insufficient funds to conduct studies in an appropriate number of patients or because they are unaware of the concept of power and are relying on the fact that many prior studies were also conducted in a comparable number of patients.

Why Scientists Often Require Conclusive Proof Before Reaching a Conclusion and Making Decisions

Nonscientists are sometimes upset and frustrated when scientists seem incapable of reaching conclusions without all possible information. One reason for scientific caution relates to the outcomes that often result when people reach rapid decisions. Every adult has had numerous experiences where their beliefs or conclusions had to be reversed or modified when additional information was obtained. Scientists are trained to withhold judgment until sufficient data are present. The real issue is to know how much data are necessary to reach a conclusion and not to delay decisions past a reasonable point. Scientists usually demand far more information than is demanded by nonscientists before reaching a conclusion.

Post Hoc Ergo Propter Hoc Issues

One of the best known issues that results from making rapid decisions is the *post hoc ergo propter hoc* problem. This refers to a cause-and-effect situation where it is concluded that if event B follows event A, then event B is caused by event A. This is generally more strongly believed when event B consistently follows event A. Although David Hume, an 18th century English philosopher, conclusively showed the fallacy of this type of thinking, it still survives and thrives today in many people's thinking. It is also related to the reasoning underlying many beliefs of primitive peoples. A few practical examples illustrate this issue. Although these examples may seem simple and lead people to smile, it is often extremely difficult to determine whether the relationship between two scientific or medical events (e.g., giving a medicine and measuring a response) is truly one of cause and effect.

Case 1

Certain green plants turn a light shade of green and then yellow during prolonged rain storms. Does this mean that an excessive amount of water causes the plants to turn yellow? No, careful studies have demon-

strated that it is the lack of sunshine during the rain that affects these plants and causes them to turn yellow (i.e., less green).

Case 2

A man drinking a well-known and widely used soft drink has a heart attack. Does this mean that the soft drink caused the man's heart attack? Probably not, but the details would have to be examined. The carbonation or caffeine may have contributed to the problem in this particular person, or possibly he drank it improperly, choked, and in the excitement that ensued, experienced a heart attack. Nonetheless, it would not be reasonable to conclude that drinking a certain brand of soda is likely to cause a heart attack.

Case 3

Primitive tribes have developed many customs because it once (or more than once) happened that one event followed another. They therefore associated the events and believe that to have a desired outcome (e.g., rain, good crops, or medical improvement) the initial event should be repeated. Therefore, they use an old ritual and utilize the medicines, dances, or chants that previously preceded the desired outcome. If that outcome does not occur, they create excuses for the exceptions, such as claiming that the gods were angry.

EXTRAPOLATIONS OF DATA AND INTERPRETATIONS

When scientists conduct experiments they seek to learn something from the specific results that will enable them to generalize the conclusion to another situation. The process of generalizing to a different situation is referred to as extrapolation. Data from scientific experiments or clinical trials are interpreted and these interpretations may be generalized (i.e., extrapolated). Pharmaceutical companies base many important decisions on extrapolations. Basic types of extrapolations in research and development are divided in three arbitrary categories: (1) animal to animal, (2) animal to human, and (3) human to human.

Another classification of extrapolations is based on scientific discipline (e.g., pharmacology, biochemistry, toxicology, and clinical medicine). In this classification, interpretations of data are extrapolated from the subcellular level to the cellular level and then to the tissue level and so on to the organ, organism, and society levels (Figs. 26.1 and 26.2). Data interpretations are also extrapolated in the other direction (i.e., from society toward the subcellular level). These extrapolations may be viewed as bridges in a hierarchical interpretation from one level to another. Clearly, most extrapolations do not involve all of these levels. Most involve a small number and may begin anywhere along the chain and move in either or both directions.

Examples of extrapolations include generalizing from effects observed with (1) one species to another, (2) a high dose of a medicine to a low dose, (3) acute treatment to chronic treatment, (4) *in vitro* to *in vivo* situations, or (5) one type of patient to another. All extrapolations of data involve some degree of judgment, especially when they are made across more than one of these five dimensions. It is much more difficult to extrapolate accurately across two or more of these dimensions.

A special case of extrapolation across three dimensions involves determining teratogenic (birth defect) risks. Data are often obtained in animals treated with extremely high doses of a medicine. The results of these studies are not only extrapolated to a different species, humans (the first dimension), but are also extrapolated to humans who are receiving relatively small doses of the medicine (second dimension) given over a prolonged period rather than a short time (third dimension).

Purposes of Extrapolations

One of the major purposes of extrapolating an interpretation of data is to develop a new hypothesis or model that may be tested in a future experiment or clinical trial. Another important purpose is to treat patients better with medicines. Extrapolations may also lead to further experiments or tests that allow new treatments to be confirmed under different conditions and/or in different types of patients.

Extrapolations from Animals to Animals

An interpretation being extrapolated usually relates to the safety, efficacy, or pharmacokinetic profile of a compound or medicine. Choosing the correct dose or dosage range to study in different animal tests involves extrapolation. This is necessary when data are extrapolated between *in vitro* and *in vivo* tests, or between two *in vitro* (or *in vivo*) tests. Extrapolations often involve two or more animal species, such as in toxicology or pharmacology studies. Experiments or clinical trials are often conducted to evaluate whether the extrapolations made are correct. If data demonstrate that an extrapolation is incorrect, then specific factors are evaluated to determine, whenever possible, the underlying reason(s) for the results observed.

Extrapolations from Animals to Humans

The most important extrapolation made during medicine development is the belief that data obtained in animal models suggest that a medicine will have benefits in treating patients with a specific disease or condition. A new compound may be tested in humans because it has an important biological action (such as stimulating or inhibiting an enzyme) that is not directly associated with a specific disease. It is possible that no particular activity was observed with the compound in any animal tests indicative of a specific human disease in which to test the medicine. In some of these cases it may still be thought worth evaluating the compound in one or a number of human diseases. The extrapolation made in this situation is that a medicine with the characteristics observed may have a beneficial effect in one of several diseases.

Conflicting conclusions often exist between the safety profile of a medicine tested in various species. It is usually impossible to predict in advance which species will best predict human results. Sometimes the reasons for differences between species are known or hypothesized. For example, species A may metabolize a medicine to a toxic product, whereas species B does not. This in turn may result from the presence of an enzyme in species A that is not present, is present to a lesser degree, or is present in a different form in species B.

Other extrapolations are based on the assumption that adverse reactions or lesions observed in toxicological studies conducted in animals also will be observed in humans; alternatively, the risk of these adverse reactions in humans is unacceptable and that human testing must stop. This usually occurs when problems are severe enough that no company, physician, or regulatory authority wishes to test whether the medicine will in fact cause the same toxicity in humans. This is one of the most common reasons why clinical trials (and all other work on a new medicine) are stopped. There may be one or many reasons why the problem observed in animals is unlikely to occur in humans, but risk-to-benefit considerations for patients usually suggest that termination of the medicine's development is advisable or necessary.

If an adverse reaction is found in animals and the medicine is already marketed, then a search will be made to determine the incidence of the problem in humans. If the incidence is acceptably low or if no cases have been reported, then there will probably not be a strong reason to remove the medicine from the market. One issue would relate to the question of what would be an "acceptably low" incidence. If the medicine caused cancer and was being used for a non-life-threatening disease, then no incidence rate in humans would be acceptably low. Even if no human cases of cancer were found or reported in humans associated with the medicine, sales of most medicines would stop, because the risks would be considered unacceptable, but if the medicine caused an adverse reaction that was reversible when the medicine was stopped and many patients were benefiting from treatment with the medicine, then it probably would be in most patients' interests to continue treatment, even if the problem were moderate or severe. The subgroups of patients who are at high risk of having the problem should be identified if possible. If this could be done, then special warnings would be given in the medicine labeling and possibly through direct letters or even advertisements to physicians.

Establishing New Animal Models to Test Medicines and Establishing Criteria of an Ideal Medicine

Animal models should be evaluated to see how predictive they are for human effects. When developing a new animal model, it is necessary to determine how close it comes to an ideal model. As an example, the characteristics of an ideal method for evaluating medicines on pruritus (itch) are presented in Table 26.1.

In addition to having criteria for an ideal model to test compounds or medicines, it is usually desirable to know the properties of an ideal medicine of the therapeutic class of interest. These properties allow one to construct tests and models to test compounds for these attributes. An example of requirements for an ideal medicine to treat epilepsy is shown in Table 26.2. These criteria may readily be used to judge new methods or new medicines.

The characteristics of an ideal medicine should not only list the positive attributes that are present, but should include negative attributes that must be absent. In addition to characteristics that pertain specifically to the therapeutic field, there are other characteristics of the medicine's activity that relate to virtually all medicines (e.g., onset of action, duration of action, cumulative effects, and reversibility). Additional characteristics of technical development (e.g., stability at room temperature, compressibility into tablets, and availability in multiple dosage forms) may be specified if desired. The test medicine may be readily compared in a table with standard medicines and other investigational medicines in terms of ideal characteristics.

Extrapolations from Humans to Humans

The general types of extrapolations of data made in clinical trials and treatment include extrapolations from:

1. One or a few patients to many patients.
2. Many patients (i.e., a patient population) to a particular patient.

TABLE 26.1. *Characteristics of an ideal clinical method for evaluating topical antipruritics[a]*

1. Rapid onset of experimentally induced pruritus: Pruritus should begin within a few minutes after administering the pruritic stimulus. This eliminates the need of requiring volunteers to wait for extended periods before the clinical trial begins or to return for testing at a specified time
2. Moderate intensity: If the pruritus is too intense it might not allow the medicines being tested to demonstrate efficacy. If the intensity is too weak, there might be an abnormally high placebo effect
3. Adequate duration: The duration produced must be long enough to allow the medicines being tested to demonstrate activity. The pruritus must disappear within a relatively short period of time to minimize the volunteers' discomfort. A duration of approximately 20 minutes is considered desirable if the presence of an antipruritic effect with rapid onset of activity is being evaluated. A longer duration would be required if the duration of a medicine's antipruritic effect was being studied
4. The pruritus produced is analogous to that observed in clinical conditions: The experimental method should produce an insult to the skin that mimics at least some symptomatic aspects of cutaneous disease
5. The pruritic effect must be reproducible within and between volunteers
6. The methodology should be simple to perform with readily available equipment, should not require excessive time for the volunteer or investigator, and should be relatively inexpensive to conduct
7. The methodology must be validated by testing standard topical antipruritic medicines versus placebo in a double-blind trial
8. No false-positive results should be obtained with medicines that are not antipruritics
9. The methodology must be suitable for use in double-blind trials and should be amenable for medicine evaluation and further clinical research
10. The data obtained must be quantifiable for statistical analysis

[a] From Spilker (1987b) with permission of S. Karger.

3. One physician's experience to another physician, who has different training, facilities, and so on.
4. One treatment setting to another (e.g., rural versus urban and primary versus tertiary care).
5. One historical time period to another (e.g., interpretations of patient care for a particular disease in the 1950s to the 1980s).
6. One level of organization to another (e.g., biochemical to physiological and single patient to population). This topic was discussed earlier.

Each of these general types of extrapolations may be influenced by many specific factors. These factors and extrapolations are described in more detail in Chapter 90 of *Guide to Clinical Trials* (Spilker, 1991).

TABLE 26.2. *Characteristics of an ideal antiepileptic medicine for treating partial seizures*[a]

1. Broad spectrum of activity: maximal electroshock, amygdala kindling, cortical kindling, and focal epilepsy models in various species
2. Lack of tolerance: test in 14-day maximal electroshock model
3. Selective pharmacological effect: devoid of effects on other organ systems
4. Long duration of action: half-life approximately 24 hours in humans and 8 to 12 hours in rodents
5. Water solubility: rapid and uniform dissolution in gastric juice
6. Lipophilicity: un-ionized form should penetrate the blood–brain barrier easily and distribute preferentially in the central nervous system
7. Lack of medicine interactions: low affinity to protein and lack of hepatic enzyme induction (P-450 microsomes)
8. Correlation should be high between blood level and antiepileptic activity

[a] From Cloutier et al. (1983) with permission.

Forming a Concept of a Medicine's Risks and Benefits

Patients as well as physicians should form a concept of a medicine's risk in a specific situation so that it may be compared with the concept of a medicine's benefit. This comparison is the well-known risk-to-benefit ratio and involves an extrapolation of previous data to a current clinical situation. Most patients do not know how to form an assessment of a medicine's risk or benefit and pharmaceutical companies may help educate physicians and, indirectly, patients through advertisements, brochures, and other educational tools, in addition to package inserts and the medical literature.

Major dimensions or spectra along which both risk and benefit may be judged include:

1. *Knowledge of the risks and benefits.* Unless a physician or patient is aware of each of the important risks and benefits, an informed risk-to-benefit comparison may not be made.
2. *Magnitude of the risks and benefits.* The degree or magnitude of risks in terms of severity should be assessed. Some adverse reactions are mild, while others are life threatening. Benefits may also be expressed along a similar but opposite scale.
3. *Probability of the risks and benefits occurring.* This dimension requires that the incidence of an adverse reaction's occurrence be generally known in the clinical situation. This may only be able to be expressed as unlikely, possible, probably, or certain. Benefits may be similarly expressed.
4. *Means to decrease risks and improve the chance of benefits occurring.* In some situations patients may diminish a risk by adhering to a specified behavior. For example, there is a risk of heart problems occurring if a beta-receptor antagonist is suddenly discontinued by a patient. This risk may be minimized, if not eliminated, if a patient remains compliant with his or her medicine schedule. Various ancillary behaviors may almost always be followed to improve the chances of benefits occurring (e.g., take the medicine as directed, do not drink alcohol, lose a few pounds of weight, reduce salt intake, and do not take other specific medicines).
5. *Risks and benefits of alternative medicine or nonmedicine therapy.* Comparison of risks should be made between each alternative therapy. The same type of comparison should be made for benefits. This is essentially stating that benefit-to-risk ratios should be compared between treatments, but the easiest means of doing this is to compare all risks separately from all benefits.
6. *Risk or benefits that may occur by not taking the medicine.* There is usually an option for patients not to take any medicine or to follow any prescribed therapy for a problem. The risks of adhering to the no-treatment option should be compared with those of taking the medicine. The same comparison should be made for benefits of the medicine versus those of no treatment.

An important factor relating to the no-treatment option is that some people prefer to accept larger risks if the risk is not under their control than a smaller risk in which they must make a positive decision to take an action. This was reportedly the reason why some mothers chose not to vaccinate their babies against pertussis.

27 / Stimulating Innovation and Increasing Efficiency

Introduction 284
Having the Right People and Groups 284
  Introduction to Personnel Issues 284
  The Core Team for Medicine Discovery 285
  Types of Consultants Who Interact with
    Pharmaceutical Companies in the Research
    and Development Area 285
  Management Consultant Companies 285
  Cautions about Hiring Consultants 285
  Choosing Consultants 286
  Task Forces 286
  Pitfalls and Potential Problems of Task
    Forces 286
  Special Deployment Teams 287
Creating the Right Milieu 287
Minimizing Nonproductive Tangents 288
  Recognizing Tangents 288
  Issues Relating to Tangents 290
  Minimizing Nonproductive Tangents 290
  Myths about Innovation, Medicine Discovery,
    and Medicine Development 290
Stimulating Innovation 291
  The Path of Innovation 291
  Stimulating Creativity 291
  Targeting Research 291
  Retreats and Off-Site Meetings 292
  Brainstorming 292
  Intellectual Turbulence 292
Developing Operating Procedures 292

Auditing Research, Development, and
  Manufacturing Activities (Quality Assurance
  and Quality Control Activities) 293
Clinical Audits Conducted by a
  Pharmaceutical Company 293
Communication between Functions 294
Adjusting Barriers between Departments: Are
  Walls Open, Flexible, Fixed, or
  Controlled? 294
Increasing Efficiency of Research and
  Development 294
  Methods to Increase Efficiency 294
  Efficiency, Efficacy, and Effectiveness 294
  Exploring a Few or Many Therapeutic Areas .. 295
  Improving Communication Between Scientists 295
  Providing Feedback to Scientists 295
  When Should a Compound Advance Toward
    Testing in Humans? 296
  Paralysis by Analysis 296
  When Should a Research Project Be
    Terminated? 296
  The Troubleshooter 297
  Extracting Lessons from a Medicine's
    History 297
Approaches to Difficult Situations 298
  Determining Whether a Medicine Should Be
    Withdrawn from the Market 298
  If It Ain't Broke, Don't Fix It 298

The first intimations of a new idea may be too nebulous to be captured and arranged for logical presentation. There is a natural inclination to pounce on such an idea and drag it out into full consciousness by giving it a definite form and shape. Before the idea has had a chance to grow in a haphazard (and original) fashion, it is organized and given shape. But the shape is one that has been chosen for the idea, not the one it might have grown into on its own. The free flight of the idea is curtailed, and it is as firmly fixed as a butterfly to the collector's board. Pouncing on an idea as soon as it appears kills the idea. Too early and too enthusiastic logical attention either freezes the idea or forces it into the old molds. Concentration on an idea isolates it from its surroundings and arrests its growth. The glare of attention inhibits the fertile semiconscious processes that go to develop an idea. Edward de Bono, English physician and writer. From *The Use of Lateral Thinking.*

Those who cannot remember the past are condemned to repeat it. George Santayana.

OUTPUTS OF INNOVATION

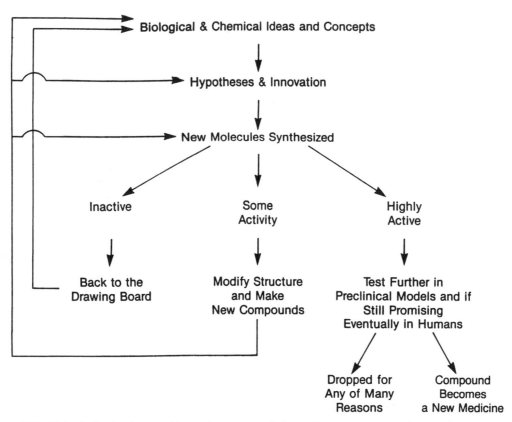

FIG. 27.1. Outputs of innovation and processes followed to improve on a chemical's activity.

INTRODUCTION

The magic formula to stimulate innovation and creativity in medicine discovery is as elusive as the fountain of youth. Given that no universal formula is currently known, is it possible to write a useful chapter on this topic? I believe the answer is yes. As one scans the history of creative endeavors, one notices certain periods (e.g., the Renaissance) and certain places (e.g., Florence, Italy) where creativity flourished. The question then arises as to whether there are certain aspects of an environment in which creativity is more likely to occur. If so, then it would be important to create and nurture this environment for scientists who are trying to discover novel medicines. One model of where innovation fits into the process of medicine discovery and development is shown in Fig. 27.1.

HAVING THE RIGHT PEOPLE AND GROUPS

Introduction to Personnel Issues

Stimulating innovation at a pharmaceutical company involves numerous personnel issues. The nature of the training and experience of certain scientists contributes to their innate characteristics and makes the scientists more innovative. When a reasonable state of harmony does not exist both within the scientist and within the company, the chance of discovering an important new medicine is diminished. This discussion assumes that the hypothetical company described has sufficient resources in terms of facilities, equipment, and money for efficient medicine development. Personnel issues include whether there is a sufficient degree of (1) inherent intellectual curiosity and creativity within the professional staff, (2) interest and involvement of the staff in their current work, (3) technical skills and abilities of the staff, and (4) cooperation between different groups.

Management must hire the best scientists they can find and then trust them to conduct their research appropriately. The old rule of respecting and listening to the staff's ideas is important. This requires a somewhat loose approach to management in which managers are willing to tolerate ambiguity in some results and often suspend judgment about others. These points are extremely important because judgment, unfortunately, often acts to kill creativity. It is usually difficult for managers to suspend judgment, however, because passing judgment is what most managers have been specifically trained to do, and the temptation to pass judgment on research results is great. The strong egos of both scientists and managers are often a roadblock to creativity and medicine discovery. The emphasis for both scientists and managers who wish to discover medicines must be to focus on the questions posed and not on the answers given. Being able to pose the correct questions will assist in deriving useful answers that will sometimes lead to a new medicine discovery.

The Core Team for Medicine Discovery

The core group involved in medicine discovery usually consists of a chemist and biologist. They must work closely together in trying to discover novel and useful medicines. To achieve this goal, however, it is necessary that they have a certain degree of autonomy. They must also have the support and trust of their supervisors. The best climate for innovation comes from their establishing an effective relationship based on openness, respect, cooperation, and corporate responsibility. A certain degree of conflict and confrontation in some relationships may have a positive influence on their productivity.

Types of Consultants Who Interact with Pharmaceutical Companies in the Research and Development Area

Consultants come in many shapes and sizes. In fact the only definition that seems to cover the field is that anyone who calls himself or herself a consultant is one. Consultants are people who provide services to others. Their services may be in the form of advice, evaluations, analyses, tangible work, or other nature. Common types of consultants to the pharmaceutical industry include:

1. Full-time university faculty who assist pharmaceutical companies on either an *ad hoc* or periodic basis. They often listen or participate in company presentations and then offer opinions relating to the major issues or questions raised. Alternatively, they may be asked to make presentations or respond to problems. Many academic institutions have adopted policies that govern the amount of time a faculty member may consult and also the disclosure required of faculty members to the university (Zinder and Winn, 1984).
2. Full-time consulting companies assist pharmaceutical companies, usually on a contract-by-contract basis, to place or conduct clinical trials, monitor studies, analyze biological samples, process data, analyze data, write medical or statistical reports, and prepare regulatory submissions. They may also assist compa-

nies by conducting audits of a small part of a department all the way to evaluating the overall corporation. These companies may be clinically, statistically, toxicologically, financially, management, or otherwise oriented.
3. Free-lance consultants assist companies in innumerable ways. These may be ex-company employees who are trying to develop a business of their own. It is often in a company's best interest to utilize the talents and experiences of these consultants in what can be an especially rewarding relationship.
4. Various other types of part-time and full-time consultants exist.

Management Consultant Companies

Some managers rely heavily on various types of consultants (e.g., academicians and management consultants) in charting the proper course to discover new medicines. Individual experts, consultants, and management firms may encourage the company's management to pursue activities in therapeutic areas or types of research that are incorrect for the company. Most management consultant companies lack adequate knowledge about the pharmaceutical industry, medicine development, and usually the particular company they are advising. Ironically, the consulting companies with some experience in advising the pharmaceutical industry are often the most dangerous to their clients. These management consultant companies tout their pharmaceutical industry experience, but their often slick presentations belie their superficial approaches and lack of true understanding about research and development in the pharmaceutical industry.

Cautions about Hiring Consultants

Numerous cautions must be considered before a consultant is hired. The situation described is where an in-depth analysis of a group or organization is required. If the most senior individual who hires a consultant(s) desires to maintain the status quo, then that is essentially what most consultants will recommend at the conclusion of their study. This occurs despite the fact that consultants are usually instructed to approach issues independently and without preconceived ideas. If consultants perceive that the person or group who hired them really wants to shake things up or provide an objective and impartial view, then there is a high likelihood that their report will reflect that approach. Careful instructions to consultants at the outset of their work are necessary if it is desired to avoid this problem.

Some consultants are hired as a personal favor to an executive in the company. Many of these consultants have a net negative effect because they require significant time of professional staff to educate them about current issues or problems. These consultants rarely make a real contribution toward reaching a solution or suggesting a desirable route to follow. Moreover, they may make suggestions of little value that "must" be followed because their personal contact in the company either gives the consultant unqualified support or does not wish to "insult" his or her friend or contact.

It is useful to have people who are (theoretically at least) using the services of consultants rate their usefulness on a periodic basis. That would help ensure that the company was benefitting from the relationship. The details of contractual arrangements should also be periodically evaluated. It is usually better to hire consultants on an hourly, daily, or even weekly fee basis than to provide them an annual retainer for services to be given as needed. In addition to saving money, this suggestion avoids having consultants present in a company when they are not needed (or desired).

Choosing Consultants

Competent consultants discuss the approach they will use to help the client (Table 27.1). In choosing between potential consultants it is important not only to critique carefully their presentation or proposal, but to evaluate their flexibility as well. A consultant's approach to various hypothetical problems that are raised "spontaneously" in a meeting may be used as a test of his or her potential usefulness. In addition, several references should be obtained and carefully checked to assess how well the consultants performed in previous assignments. It is essential to determine how well they understood their assignment, how efficient they were in conducting their work, and how closely their output matched their original plans. The impact and degree of interference the consultants had on daily operations of the company should be evaluated, as well as the quality of their experience in the pharmaceutical industry.

Many otherwise excellent consultants bring inappropriate advice and approaches from other industries to problems they are asked to address in pharmaceutical companies. Consultants without sufficient experience in a pharmaceutical company may drain significant senior staff time away from important company business in order to educate the consultant about the pharmaceutical industry. This may lead to highly educated consultants who are unable to provide useful advice to the company.

It is usually undesirable to use actual or potential investigators as consultants for a company. This practice introduces strong biases into their views on medicine development strategies, approaches, and other issues. This conflict of interest does not seem to concern many companies who adhere to the practice of using consultants as investigators. Despite the author's objections to this practice, in most situations there do not appear to be problems. Nonetheless, it is desirable not to use investigators as consultants (or vice versa) whenever possible.

Task Forces

A task force is a group of people from different functional areas who are brought together and asked to address a specific issue or issues and to prepare a report. A task force may participate in any or all of the following activities: (1) gather information, (2) analyze information, (3) make recommendations, (4) participate in the decision-making process, and (5) reach a decision on the topic they are addressing. Almost any issue relating to medicine discovery or development could be dealt with by a task force. Other functions may also be assigned to a task force (e.g., to help implement a new series of procedures). After the group completes its assignment it is generally disbanded.

Task forces can serve valuable functions by addressing specific issues that are not well suited to existing departments or groups, or where existing groups do not have adequate time to address the issue. Task forces often serve as internal consultants for a company, although outside consultants may also join or serve as advisors to the team.

Pitfalls and Potential Problems of Task Forces

There are a variety of issues relating to the use of task forces that should be considered before a decision is made to use such groups. One of the most important issues is that the appropriate professional level of people should be appointed to the task force. If the people appointed are too senior in the company, then they will not be using their time productively. If the members are at too junior a level, then they will either be unable to achieve the group's objectives satisfactorily, or possibly unable to convince others of the validity of their conclusions. In addition, the people appointed to "solve" a par-

TABLE 27.1. *Standard approach used by many consultants prior to receiving a contract*

1. Understand the assignment and what the client truly desires
2. State objective(s) of the assignment in verbal and written presentation
3. State approaches to be used
4. Describe the type(s) of results that will be obtained
5. Discuss any hypotheses to be used or tested
6. Discuss all relevant assumptions
7. Describe how plans and recommendations will be developed
8. Describe how the final output will be prepared and communicated

ticular problem should have had at least some experience with that problem prior to the formation of the task force.

Another point is that people should not be taken away on a full-time basis from their regular job to participate on a task force. There are several problems with doing this. The most important ones are that a task force made up of full-time members will have a major concern about what they will be doing when the work of their task force is completed. Their major priority will generally not be to examine their assignment objectively, but to make recommendations that provide future positions for themselves. This outcome will occur regardless of how relevant the proposed positions may be for the company's benefit and health. It is ironic that once this principle is perceived by senior managers, it will diminish the credibility of their report and make it unlikely that their recommendations will be accepted. One exception is for situations where the recommendations also meet the needs and/or desires of the manager(s) who appointed them.

A major problem that may affect any task force is the "swelled head syndrome." This refers to the fact that many people, especially at a junior level, who are placed on an important task force attribute this appointment to a recognition of their exceptional skills and talents. They believe that they have been anointed for an important future position in the company. If this public recognition fails to materialize (despite the fact that all individuals may have been told specifically that it would not happen), then some are likely to become disillusioned and even bitter when their "Cinderella" weekend is over. Their work may suffer and they will seek a transfer within the company or look for other employment. Being appointed to a task force may therefore be counterproductive for some people's careers. This is especially true when junior-level staff are appointed to a relatively important task force. The best workers at a certain level are often the ones chosen for task forces. It is ironic that it is these people who often develop "swelled heads" and become unhappy and less productive in their old positions after the task force is disbanded.

Special Deployment Teams

Special deployment teams are usually small groups of individuals who are trained in a specific scientific or technical area (e.g., chemistry, pharmacology, medical report writing, or medical monitoring) and can be assigned to help solve personnel shortages for a temporary period. The team is usually composed of junior- and senior-level professionals with experience in the area they are to work in temporarily. This means that a special deployment team for chemistry projects consists of chemists and remains in the chemistry department, and a team conducting medical monitoring is based in the medical department. A group of medical report writers, however, could free-lance from their homes if they had a sample report to use as a model or template and the data and references necessary to write the report.

After the deployment group has helped solve a personnel shortage, it may be difficult to terminate their role, because they could easily become "indispensable" to the people they were assigned to help. To avoid this problem, it is best, for the length of their assignment to be fixed and to terminate it on a certain date. Alternatively, their assignment could terminate after a certain function or activity is completed. Renewals to continue their work for another fixed time or until another specified function is completed could be negotiated. This would generally depend on the priorities of competing activities.

CREATING THE RIGHT MILIEU

The milieu in which scientists work may be modified to help stimulate the innovative process. Some of the factors that affect this milieu include (1) the scientific freedom to pursue ideas of personal interest, (2) the ability of company scientists to interact with other scientists within and outside the company, and (3) an accepting view of scientists' opinions by their managers. Management policies and behavior clearly play an essential role in creating and maintaining a suitable environment in which creativity and medicine discovery activities can flourish.

The nature and degree of cooperation between departments depends to a large degree on the personalities of the department heads and their desire to work together. If their relationships are not positive, it becomes difficult for their scientists to work together effectively. Solutions include creating guidelines (standard operating procedures), reorganizing departments, or transferring non-cooperative people.

A stimulating environment will be fostered by inviting outside speakers into the company to talk about scientific issues, by encouraging staff to accept adjunct faculty appointments at nearby universities, by conducting internal workshops on topical issues, and by inviting important outside scientists to participate as consultants in relevant company affairs. Conducting off-site retreats, symposia, and business meetings that are possibly limited to company scientists are other means of creating a stimulating environment. Speakers at various company meetings could also come from other pharmaceutical companies in addition to academia, government, and nonmedicine companies.

Even if an ideal milieu could be created at a pharmaceutical company, it will change over time. A positive environment, like marriage and many other things in life, must be continually worked at by all concerned. This approach will help ensure that the environment remains the way both management and scientists desire.

MINIMIZING NONPRODUCTIVE TANGENTS

Recognizing Tangents

Tangents are changes in the major direction or orientation of a project in terms of pursuing a new indication, new dosage form, new route of administration, or new patient population. It is best to recognize tangents when they are initially proposed. This is not always possible, and tangents are sometimes initially observed as a *fait accompli* or as an ongoing activity. The tangent is usually recognized because the proposed or actual activities do not adhere to the originally agreed-on plans and direction. Tangents vary greatly in the magnitude of time, effort, and resources expended and may use resources earmarked for the project's primary activities.

EXAMPLES OF NEGATIVE TANGENTS IN A MEDICINE'S DEVELOPMENT

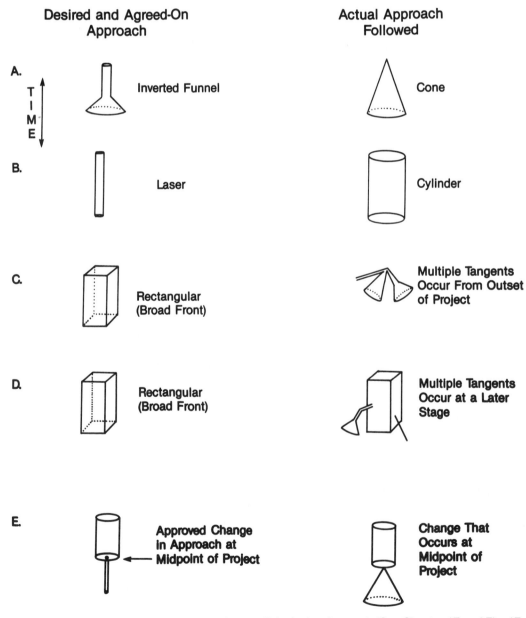

FIG. 27.2. Examples of negative tangents in a medicine's development. (See Chapter 17 and Fig. 17.4 for a description of the basic approaches.)

Many types of possible tangents exist (Figs. 27.2 and 27.3).

After the proposed or actual tangent is recognized, it is important to evaluate whether that tangent represents an improvement over the original plan or an unwanted direction. Some tangents may lead the project in more productive directions, but the majority are nonproductive. Groups who advocate going off on tangents often seem to have new ideas and "better" approaches to propose each time they present a report to a reviewing committee. Some people on such groups may have difficulty sticking to a plan that takes several years to complete. It is often more "fun" for them to try or explore new activities. These are people and groups that managers must keep under close observation.

Most tangents may be described as being positive or negative. Although it may appear that this may only be determined in hindsight, the value of pursuing a tangent may usually be determined in advance. Tangents are offshoots of the medicine's approved development plan. The group's intention may be to return to the original plan after the tangent is explored or to pursue both the original plan and tangent simultaneously. If the tangent is reviewed and approved by relevant senior managers or management committees, then the tangent is positive. For example, a few different types of cancers may be evaluated with an anticancer medicine during Phase II studies. A request to evaluate the medicine in several new types of cancers in other Phase II pilot studies would be a tangent. If this request is appropriately reviewed and approved, it would represent a positive tangent or a modification of the development plan, regardless of whether the results turn out to be positive.

Many early clinical explorations in different therapeutic directions could be viewed as positive tangents if they were agreed to as part of the original development plan. If these explorations were not approved then they would be undesirable tangents. One of the most wasteful and negative types of tangents is where new directions or activities are conducted in a haphazard way. These efforts either dilute or replace efforts on the main approach and waste company resources. Moreover, such tangents can create innumerable problems for a pharmaceutical company. These include clinical problems raised and the need to explain to regulatory agencies exactly what was done and why.

MEDICINES IN SEARCH OF A DISEASE

A. Tangents occur one at a time. The direction and focus of the project keep changing.

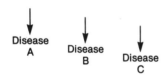

B. Multiple diseases targeted at the outset of a project to learn which approach is best.

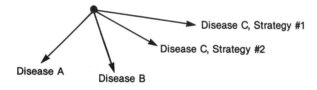

C. A combination of the above approaches is followed.

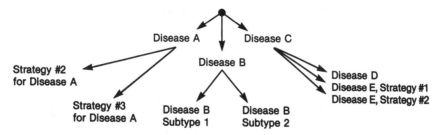

Each arrow differs in time, effort and resources expended. Strategies may differ in terms of route of administration, dosage form, dosing schedule, or other factors.

FIG. 27.3. Medicines in search of a disease. Each arrow differs in the amount of time, effort, and resources expended. Strategies may differ in terms of the route of administration, dosage form, dosing schedule, or other factors.

Issues Relating to Tangents

The major goals and issues relating to tangents that a review committee (or manager) should consider are:

1. To determine whether the idea or suggestion proposed is in fact a tangent to the agreed-on and approved project plans. For example, if the original clinical plan only covers Phases I and II, then plans for Phase III would not represent a tangent because this represents a completion and not a change of plans.
2. To evaluate whether the tangent is of scientific, medical, or commercial interest. This implies that various groups should review the value of the proposed change.
3. To evaluate how the tangent would affect current and future activities on the main project in terms of staff, other resources, time, priority, and other factors. This area, that is often superficially brushed aside, is of great importance to a company.
4. To compare scientific, medical, and commercial values of a tangent with those of the major effort.
5. To evaluate the impact that a tangent will have on staff motivation, morale, and other nontangible factors. Is the proposal a seriously considered one or does the group frequently propose tangents and seem to desire things to work on that are more fun?
6. To evaluate how the tangent will impact on other projects. This is primarily assessed in terms of competition for resources.
7. To evaluate the overall priority of the tangent compared with those of the major approach and other medicines under development.

Minimizing Nonproductive Tangents

Some of the ways to minimize nonproductive tangents are to:

1. Encourage all professionals to verbalize their opinions when new proposals are presented and discussed.
2. Utilize independent people to review controversial proposals. These people may be within or outside the company.
3. Develop an appropriate combination of formal and informal systems to handle new proposals.
4. Appoint groups to review all proposals and projects periodically.
5. Appoint groups to review and coordinate activities being conducted at multiple sites.
6. Encourage all relevant groups and committees to ascertain whether their present activities and plans are being directed toward their goals.
7. Encourage all relevant groups and committees to ascertain whether their own proposed activities will take them more rapidly or more directly toward their goals.
8. Aim for consistent medicine labeling between countries. Avoid conflicting information.
9. Utilize the fewest number of dosage shapes, tablet colors, and dosage forms consistent with sound business principles relating to marketing and regulatory responses.

Myths about Innovation, Medicine Discovery, and Medicine Development

The field of research is laden with myths about innovation and discovery. A number of general myths of innovation within research and development are listed in Table 27.2. Commonly perpetrated myths are one major reason why it is often dangerous to a company for scientific amateurs to become involved in decision making on technical issues.

In the world of medicine discovery and development, many myths exist about various issues. Some of these represent wishful thinking by knowledgeable experts and others emanate from news stories put together by reporters to create a good story. Most are based on a certain amount of truth. A few myths are listed. Each of these has numerous variations and overlaps with others to some degree.

Myths of Medicine Discovery

1. Empirical screening of compounds is being phased out as a means of discovering new medicines.

TABLE 27.2. *Selected myths of innovation[a]*

1. Complete technical specifications and a thoroughly researched market plan are invariant first steps to success
2. Substantial strategic/technological plans greatly increase the odds of a ''no surprises'' outcome
3. Big teams are necessary to rapidly blitz a project, especially a complex one
4. Time for reflection and thought built into the development process is essential to creative results
5. Big projects are inherently different from small projects and must be managed differently
6. Strong functions such as marketing, production, and finance (and, consequently, functional organizations) are imperative if the would-be innovators are to get a fair hearing
7. Product line/product family compatibility is the key to economic success
8. Customers tell you only about yesterday's needs
9. Technology push is the cornerstone of business sucess
10. Strive to optimize technical forecasting with 100,000-bubble PERT[b] charts and other methods, because perfectionism pays off

[a] From Peters (1983a, b) with permission of the Stanford Alumni Association.

[b] PERT, program evaluation and review technique.

2. Rational medicine discovery will be the major method used to discover medicines in the very near future.
3. Biotechnology methods are the most important tools for medicine discovery.
4. Molecular designing of medicines on computers will enable medicines to be designed to reach almost any desired target.

Myths of Medicine Development

1. The time planned to develop a medicine can be accurately determined at the outset of a project.
2. The master plan for medicine development can be followed without major alteration for most medicines.
3. A "quick and dirty" clinical trial is usually adequate to determine whether a medicine has activity in patients with a new disease.

STIMULATING INNOVATION

The Path of Innovation

The course of innovation is highly irregular and cannot be planned. Much of it appears to outsiders as sloppy and disorganized, and in many cases they are correct. Major breakthroughs in technological discoveries often come from unexpected sources (e.g., Kodachrome film was invented by musicians). Does this mean that managers should encourage chaos or wild and woolly off-the-wall ideas? Certainly not. What it does mean is that managers should concentrate on hiring the most innovative, imaginative, and creative people they can find, providing them with a stimulating environment and a challenging problem, and then letting them have some flexibility to explore ways of solving the problem. Managers should neither control every step taken by scientists, nor allow them carte blanche.

Nonetheless, scientists should be held accountable for demonstrating that they are making some progress on their project. If more than two or three years are spent on a problem without achieving significant results, it is important to assess whether the talents and money expended might be better spent on another project of interest. There are clearly more worthwhile topics to study than there are creative scientists to carry out the research.

Stimulating Creativity

The motivational state of an individual often has a direct effect on his or her creativity. Young adults in science are often motivated by intrinsic factors and the desire to accomplish something for its own sake, more than for an external goal that will be achieved. The environment that promotes this approach should not have (1) close supervision of all aspects of the work, (2) narrow choice in how to approach the problem, and (3) strong external evaluation and performance systems. Incentives play a role in some individuals, but this is generally a minor role. Non-monetary rewards have been reported (Griggs and Manring, 1986) to have little impact on a scientist's effectiveness.

Targeting Research

Each company wants its researchers to discover medicines in specific therapeutic areas. This may be viewed as exploring the land surface for new leads in some therapeutic areas and not in others. Each therapeutic area could be viewed as a separate province with both urban and rural areas. The urban areas are where medicine discoveries have been made or prior synthetic activities have pretty well combed the land surface looking for important leads. The rural areas are those relatively open and yet unexplored areas. The skill or trick (depending on one's viewpoint) is knowing (or guessing) where to look. Just as oil wells that are drilled usually come up empty, most compounds made either come up "empty" in terms of biological activity or they come up "full" in terms of serious toxicity problems.

The discovery of a potentially new medicine may lead the company into a new therapeutic area that it does not wish to pursue. In that situation, the company may change its attitude about the therapeutic area, or the compound/medicine may be licensed to another company. The decision about which path to follow is much easier to make if the company has identified its therapeutic comfort zone ahead of time.

Innovation flourishes in an environment of general scientific freedom, but too much scientific freedom in terms of undermanagement can lead to serious problems of declining innovation. Some scientists are apt to dabble in various areas without an adequate focus to their search for new medicines, and some may completely lose their orientation toward new medicine discovery. It is usually the department head and/or head of research who decide(s) how much research effort and other resources to place on each disease and therapeutic area. Scientists, however, should have a strong voice in the approaches chosen to explore targeted diseases.

Many, if not most, pharmaceutical companies tolerate some scientists working in nonconventional ways or on their own "pet" ideas for part of their time. Almost all companies, however, insist that scientists help with at least some screening of compounds when it is appropriate, and that their efforts are consistent with the objectives, goals, and strategies of the company.

Retreats and Off-Site Meetings

Retreats and other types of off-site meetings generally stimulate individuals' motivation, especially if the meeting is carefully planned. Meetings may encompass one or more departments, sections, or project teams. Managers from one or more functions or countries may be involved.

The retreat setting is often an ideal time and situation in which to deal with difficult issues. Issues and problems often seem more approachable for discussion when people have had a good meal, participated in vigorous sport competition, or have relaxed in a different environment. Openness of communication is often fostered along with a desire to resolve differences. If informality is desired, it may be encouraged by holding the meeting at a resort or under less formal conditions. If there is a serious problem to discuss, then spouses should generally not be invited. If social concerns are paramount and an informal atmosphere is desired, then invitations to spouses should be considered.

Brainstorming

Brainstorming sessions, whether at formal meetings or over drinks at a bar, may be focused through a few simple and well-known techniques. These include provoking discussion and responses focused around a number of key questions or propositions.

1. What if . . . ? This phrase is often followed by an event that is extremely negative, positive, or unlikely.
2. I wish. . . . People's strongest desires for a company. This may also be expressed as, "If I had the power to do anything in this company, I would. . . ." Participants may each be asked to complete this phrase.
3. Why not . . . ? This question is intended to initiate responses and discussion about new ideas or approaches.
4. If . . . then. . . . This approach may be used to work out contingency plans or to ensure that all relevant possibilities are considered (e.g., in a contract).

In discussing new concepts or interpreting data at brainstorming sessions, the interpretations reached must be accurate. If not, then incorrect conclusions will be drawn. For example, it was reported on English radio during a World War II air raid over England that the German bombs were all dropped at random. The next morning there were banner headlines in the German newspapers stating that the city of Random was completely destroyed.

Intellectual Turbulence

Bringing people with different backgrounds and experiences together in an environment where they can freely interact may lead to creative outputs. This situation may be achieved by physically placing certain departments in close proximity to each other within the company, having special spaces for socializing conveniently (and comfortably) placed in strategic areas, and arranging for meetings or other gatherings where personal interactions are likely to occur. These interactions should be planned to bring various groups together, including scientists with scientists, nonscientists with scientists, and marketing people with production people.

This approach is not easy to achieve if research and development is divided from the rest of a company and a separate research institute is established. It is one of the reasons why many research scientists in industry do not want to be separated from other scientists and nonscientists. Group meetings and social gatherings that precede or follow a talk or other event are particularly appropriate times for such interactions to occur. Any company that holds professional meetings without adequate time for social interaction (e.g., at long breaks) is missing an important opportunity for productive discussions and creativity. If time constraints become an issue at a particular meeting (as they often do), it is probably better to decrease the time for scientific presentations than to decrease the time allocated for breaks.

DEVELOPING OPERATING PROCEDURES

Having the right people and the right environment are the two most important aspects of creating the best situation in which a company may optimize its chances to discover and develop medicines. A lesser but also important aspect is to have operating procedures in place that facilitate rather than hinder the work of scientists, clinicians, and others who are discovering and developing medicines. Systems relate both to the bureaucracy that must be adhered to in any institution and to the facilities and equipment present to accomplish the work. Poor systems and facilities can easily lead to frustration and anger.

Examples of some of the pertinent questions that managers should ask about their systems and operating procedures are listed:

1. Are there 25 people in a company who must approve every request for an external grant?
2. Is there an excessive number of formal systems and standard operating procedures that are not really needed (or used)?
3. Are senior executives thinking and planning for the company's future health, or are they dealing with mundane issues created by systems that are either inefficient or do not work?
4. Is too much of a scientist's time and attention given to paper work and are too many highly polished plans and reports generated rather than doing the work itself?

Many managers believe that all of the beautiful plans a company may generate on early-stage medicines do not equal a single marketed medicine that is generating revenue. This reflects the philosophy that a medicine "in the hand" is worth the expectation of several that are currently "in the bush" at an early stage of development. Operating procedures used to bring a medicine to market must be designed to expedite each medicine's development.

Office automation is an area where great improvements in efficiency have been achieved over the last few decades. The number of new types of equipment and methods for speeding work output is truly staggering. The impact that this has had on improving business productivity, profitability, and competitive advantage is described in *The Information Edge* (Meyer and Boone, 1987).

Auditing Research, Development, and Manufacturing Activities (Quality Assurance and Quality Control Activities)

All pharmaceutical companies audit many of their ongoing activities. The extent of these internal audits varies widely from informal checks to highly formalized systems developed to evaluate specific activities. The research and development areas that are audited include some that are mandated by Good Manufacturing Practices (GMP) and Good Laboratory Practices (GLP). Specific areas audited include manufacturing of medicines used in clinical trials, conduct of toxicology studies, and metabolism studies. Manufacturing audits (e.g., quality assurance and quality control) include a description of all analytical tests and procedures used to control chemical synthesis and medicine manufacture. Also, each procedure and test used must be validated. Validation is the proof that each test actually does what it is supposed to do. This is further discussed in Chapter 50. Figure 50.1 illustrates various approaches to the issue of conducting quality assurance and quality control investigations.

Quality assurance in toxicology studies is governed by GLP regulations. The people who conduct the quality assurance are different than those who conduct the toxicology studies and do not report to the same supervisor. This is to prevent conflict-of-interest problems from arising. The most common pattern of conducting toxicology quality assurance is illustrated in panel A or panel E of Fig. 50.1 with the quality assurance steps shown in panel A. The final output is usually considered as a written final report of a toxicology study.

Clinical Audits Conducted by a Pharmaceutical Company

Good Clinical Practices (GCP) guidelines have been proposed by the European Community and govern the standards to be used in clinical trials. This is an important step toward the harmonization of international standards for clinical trial design and conduct.

Such guidelines have not yet officially been issued by the Food and Drug Administration (FDA) in final form and the term GCP has no official definition. It is used in this book to include five regulations covering the following subjects. The first three are final approved United States regulations, whereas the last two are proposed.

1. Investigational New Drug Application.
2. Institutional Review Boards (IRBs).
3. Informed Consents.
4. Obligations of Sponsors.
5. Obligations of Investigators.

The FDA takes no official position on whether pharmaceutical companies should conduct clinical audits of their own activities. The IRBs and clinical monitors conduct quality assurance activities. Theoretically, there should not be any reason why a separate clinical audit is necessary. On the other hand, one or two individuals working for a sponsor could provide a valuable service to monitors and/or investigators by reviewing files and records that would be checked during an FDA inspection to ensure that the files are accurate and complete.

A more thorough evaluation or audit of monitors' activities could be conducted, but this raises the possibility that the auditor would be viewed as a policeman and not as a helper. Some companies choose random clinical trials to audit, whereas other companies routinely audit all or only pivotal studies (i.e., generally the most well-controlled studies). The appropriate decision for a company regarding this issue is dependent on its traditions and culture as well as the nature of any problems that may exist. The author believes that clinical auditors should not be the same individuals who conduct GMP or GLP audits of data. The GMP or GLP auditors do not report to the same managers as the people in the groups being audited, and the auditors are also generally perceived in an adversarial role. This situation does not necessarily apply for GCP auditors. Companies that utilize GCP auditors have a wide variety of approaches to consider and this is a rapidly changing field.

Examples of quality assurance in clinical trials involve literally hundreds of separate checks that often must be made. These are described in *Guide to Clinical Trials* (Spilker, 1991), especially in the chapter on monitoring. A few examples include (1) comparing unexpected laboratory results observed in data collection forms with actual laboratory slips, (2) comparing numbers in tables of reports with summary statements elsewhere in reports, (3) determining whether patients were treated according to the protocol, and so on. Quality assurance evaluations are also made of data entered into computers to evaluate the accuracy of several steps in the processing.

Communication Between Functions

As pharmaceutical companies grow in size, their various functions (e.g., marketing, research and development, and production) usually grow further apart. Companies must put mechanisms in place to keep different functions close enough together in terms of their operations so that they work effectively and consider themselves as part of the same overall group. Common mechanisms to achieve this goal include forming committees, project teams, and task forces, plus holding joint retreats, seminars, and staff meetings. The difficulty that individuals have in crossing boundaries between departments or functions is usually greater in large companies. The best antidote to this problem is to promote managers who want to cooperate and be productive rather than those who want to promote their own views and build empires.

Adjusting Barriers Between Departments: Are Walls Open, Flexible, Fixed, or Controlled?

Every so often there is a flurry of articles or books stating that the functional and emotional walls between departments and groups should be broken down (and sometimes the physical walls as well) and that people should interact more and work as a single large group. At other times, there is a flurry of articles or books emphasizing that people often work most efficiently and productively when they have the security of knowing the limits of their position and knowing that their area of work will not be invaded or encroached upon by others. It is sometimes difficult to determine the optimal balance between these two approaches when establishing the optimal work environment.

Clearly, some individuals and disciplines generally function better when they are operating in a more open, flexible environment, and others function better in a more fixed and controlled environment. The financial, production, and legal groups of a pharmaceutical company tend (of necessity) to be more of the latter kind, while the marketing and research and development groups may be either. The particular style that suits a company at one point in its history may be less appropriate at another point. For example, during crisis periods it is not desirable for each person to be "doing their own thing," although this style may be more tolerated at other times. Also, the personalities of the chief executive officer, marketing head, and research and development director greatly influence the style of their group or company.

What should a company do about walls between groups? One approach is to think of them as movable. At appropriate times they should be higher and at other times they may be lowered. The trick is not to decide how high or low they should be, but to resolve how the decision will be reached of when to raise or lower them. More importantly, there is the question of who will coordinate the different groups' attitudes and activities so that one department head is not raising his or her barriers to cross-group interactions at a time when another department head is lowering his or hers.

INCREASING EFFICIENCY OF RESEARCH AND DEVELOPMENT

Research may be efficiently conducted in extremely small or large companies, in companies that have centralized or decentralized managements, and in companies with any organizational structure. On the other hand, research efficiency is often increased when there is (1) a positive attitude toward research and scientists from managers, (2) a sufficient number of peers for expert input and meaningful discussions, (3) adequate facilities and equipment, (4) adequate support staff and technical help, plus (5) various other factors that allow scientists to do their work effectively. A number of issues on increasing efficiency are discussed below; others are covered in Chapter 36.

Methods to Increase Efficiency

When a company desires to improve its efficiency, it has several areas to evaluate. One of the potential problems is that creating larger systems to streamline more activities may become so complex that it goes beyond the technical comfort level of the people who will use it (or design it). This is analogous to designing and building highly sophisticated military weapons systems that few soldiers are able to use appropriately and well. The systems involved are often so complex that airplanes are often in the hangar or repair shop being fixed. Given this caveat, it is relevant to:

1. Streamline processes and the portfolio.
2. Build strong support services without excess fat.
3. Integrate planning between more functions.
4. Develop more effective teams (e.g., praise good work).
5. Have management facilitate the process to keep it on track and on time rather than to control it.
6. Clarify decision criteria for all projects.
7. Hire the best possible staff and do what is needed to retain them.

Efficiency, Efficacy, and Effectiveness

Professional staff are often exposed to the terms "efficiency," "efficacy," and "effectiveness." The meaning of these terms is discussed in the context of the pharmaceutical industry because these terms are often used inappropriately.

Efficiency. An economic measure of performance that refers both to human and nonhuman activities and addresses the question of how well something is done in terms of energy, time, money, and other measures. This concept is often applied to the process of medicine development.

Efficacy. The ability of a medicine to elicit a beneficial clinical effect, often in a population of patients. Efficacy is measured or evaluated using objective or subjective parameters and is a characteristic of the medicine.

Effectiveness. A measure of the extent to which a medicine or therapeutic intervention is successful in treating one or more specific patients in a medical setting. For example, the effectiveness of aspirin used for treating a patient's headache is assessed by the degree to which his or her pain is alleviated.

A medicine may possess a high degree of efficacy, but if it does not work as desired in a given patient, its effectiveness would be low or none in that patient. Therefore, efficacy is an attribute of a medicine and effectiveness an outcome measure of the result produced by the medicine. Both efficacy and effectiveness are expected to vary in different patient populations based on many factors of the patient (e.g., demographic characteristics), his or her disease (e.g., forms of the disease), as well as the specific parameters used to assess efficacy or effectiveness.

Exploring a Few or Many Therapeutic Areas

Some research directors believe that many scientists working on a few programs have a better chance of discovering a medicine than having few scientists work on many programs. This is a controversial area. The former group of research and development heads place many resources on few projects. They believe that they are thereby able to achieve a critical mass and an adequate level of scientific expertise on each project. The appropriate number of these groups will depend on the size of the organization. Also, some research programs require much more scientific input and involvement than others. People who follow the opposite approach of placing few resources on many programs believe that a small number of dedicated, creative, and enthusiastic scientists unencumbered by bureaucratic restraints may make breakthroughs and discoveries as easily (or more easily) than larger groups.

When the size of research groups becomes too large, their productivity often decreases. Large groups usually develop a vertical hierarchical structure. A relatively flat or horizontal structure is viewed by many senior managers as a means of increasing efficiency. A horizontal structure implies that there are fewer hierarchical levels in the organization and more people report to each manager. Each manager is closer to the most senior and junior people in a horizontal structure than in one where many hierarchical levels exist.

Improving Communication Between Scientists

Scientists in different departments or sites of a research organization often are working on related research projects and could benefit from experiences and knowledge of others. Before dialogue can occur it is essential for them to know who has similar research interests. There is no single method that is best to facilitate these interactions, whether within a department, between departments, or across oceans.

One approach to this issue is to circulate a written synopsis of each scientist's research interests and active projects. Alternatively, this information could be entered in a computer, as a sort of bulletin board. One question that immediately arises is determining how much information is appropriate to circulate. The more information that is circulated about each scientist, the more precisely topics may be described. However, the information's security becomes a major concern and, also, if "too much" information is gathered, then fewer people will utilize it. If too little information is circulated, it may have less usefulness. A few lines about current research topics may be sufficient to allow scientists to identify whom they wish to contact.

Any system that is established, especially if utilizing computers, should be user friendly. This will allow scientists to operate the system themselves. To whatever degree a system like this operates it will provide benefits to the users who may collaborate on projects or help each other with scientific lessons about what approaches or techniques work in specific situations.

Providing Feedback to Scientists

Providing feedback to scientists from peers at staff conferences and in small group sessions are effective methods and forums for discussing and improving the quality of scientific ideas. Many scientists seek and obtain feedback from their peers without any prompting. Scientists who are more reticent about seeking feedback or are antagonistic to criticism should be encouraged by their managers to place themselves in situations where feedback will occur. Managers may foster this interchange through staff meetings where scientists receive feedback on their presentations. Staff conferences include both intra- and interdepartmental meetings. Scientists receive feedback at many other forums, including (1) scientific meetings of all types, (2) during casual or formal discussions with colleagues, and (3) through submitting articles for publication. Consultants may also be asked to evaluate the quality of a scientist's or department's research and to provide input that may lead to its being improved.

When Should a Compound Advance Toward Testing in Humans?

In deciding when a compound is ready to proceed to human testing, there are no rigid rules. This is a matter involving judgment, plus an assessment of the company's needs. Arguments can be made both for and against developing a complete preclinical profile prior to advancing a compound (Table 27.3) or going rapidly (Table 27.4) toward clinical tests.

Paralysis by Analysis

Paralysis by analysis refers to lack of action due to overanalyzing all the possibilities and planning for every contingency. It is preferable to plan only for the top-priority activities and functions. When something changes or problems arise, as one's expectations are not met, then additional planning is appropriate.

Some companies spend a far greater percent of the staff's time on planning activities than do others. Efficiency would be improved and more rapid progress made on important projects if the best balance between planning the work and doing the work is determined and maintained.

When Should a Research Program Be Terminated?

One of the most important decisions research managers make is which therapeutic, disease, or medicine areas to terminate. In some ways this is more important

TABLE 27.3. *Advantages in waiting until a generally complete profile is obtained about a chemical series before a lead compound is chosen for testing in humans, plus counterarguments*

Advantage	Counterargument
1. There is a better chance that the optimal compound in a series has been found	1. The best compound in a series is often one of the first made (Vane, 1967). If standards are set too high, potentially valuable medicines may never be tested in humans
2. Less money is spent on medicine development by being more certain about the potential of the compound that is advanced	2. It may take longer to get to this point than by deciding with less information. Time is usually more valuable than money in medicine development
3. More specific biological data will be obtained on the specific compound of interest	3. Same as 2

TABLE 27.4. *Advantages in taking early chemical leads rapidly into humans for testing, plus counterarguments*

Advantage	Counterargument
1. More rapid feedback is obtained about a medicine's efficacy and the value of developing a medicine further and pursuing backup candidates is assessed	1. Information obtained may only relate to the compound tested and may not be extrapolatable to others in the series
2. Possible problems with safety that could provide information about the entire series will be uncovered	2. A less toxic compound might be uncovered through additional synthetic work that would be a more rapid and less expensive way to learn the information
3. The entire series may be expanded in the laboratory to find the best backup candidate, while human work is underway	3. This is a costly approach and resources might be better applied to other projects while additional preclinical activities are carried out

than determining which areas or programs to initiate. Many research programs and projects appear to develop a life of their own after they are created, and it is often difficult to know how and when it is best to terminate them. The topic of terminating development projects is discussed in Chapter 131 of *Guide to Clinical Trials* (Spilker, 1991).

The decision to terminate work on a particular research program may be made at any one of several levels, depending on the type and magnitude of the work that is to be terminated, as well as the particular company. Specific approaches to evaluating a disease may often be terminated by a scientist, work on a specific disease may usually be terminated by a department head, and work on a therapeutic area may be terminated by the head of research. Each of these decisions should generally be discussed and reviewed by management and by others, if relevant. It is sometimes desirable to allow experienced scientists to use their intuition in reaching a decision to terminate work. It is also important to have a consensus of both managers and scientists on the appropriateness of terminating a research program or development project.

Another approach to terminating research programs is to adopt the philosophy that all programs are to be terminated every one, two, or three years unless a strong rationale can be advanced for their continuation. This approach recognizes that many research programs seem to take on a life of their own and acquire resources and momentum that are difficult to move in a different direction, let alone terminate. Requiring all research programs to be reassessed periodically and compete for resources in an objective manner would prevent the pitfall of continued momentum. Reassessment must be carefully conducted to prevent people from (1) spending an excessive amount of time justifying their program rather than doing the work, (2) competing for resources in a negative atmosphere, and (3) demoralizing the losers. If handled appropriately, it should serve to improve the efficiency of research.

A fascinating anecdote about temporarily suspending medicine development while safety questions are addressed concerns lovastatin, Merck & Co.'s new cholesterol-lowering medicine. After it was reported that a competitor (Sankyo Co. Ltd.) had stopped clinical trials on their medicine, reportedly because of cancerous tumors in dogs, Merck & Co. also stopped tests on their chemically related medicine and initiated more toxicology studies. Sankyo Co. Ltd. reportedly later said that the rumors were false and that they merely were replacing their medicine with a newer, more effective one (Byrne, 1987). According to the article in *Business Week,* Merck & Co. lost almost four years of their medicine development (and patent protection) from September 1980 to May 1984 when large-scale clinical trials were resumed. One moral of this episode is that the truth of important rumors must be established before allowing them to influence greatly the development of a valuable medicine. This may be done via regulatory agencies and possibly in other ways.

The Troubleshooter

Multinational companies usually have major differences between their subsidiaries and headquarters, as well as among various subsidiaries. Practical differences as well as philosophical differences and misunderstandings often exist and fester for long periods rather than being addressed promptly.

Solving some of these interregion and intercompany differences often requires the president or chairman of research and development to make a decision. In some cases the problems may be resolved by a troubleshooter appointed by the president. This person should report directly to the president in order to have the perceived and actual authority to help resolve issues. This individual could free the president to attend to more relevant issues.

Few companies have assigned someone to fulfill this role today, although the role is an important one. The background of the ideal troubleshooter would vary, but he or she should be intimately familiar with the company and the processes of medicine development. In addition, he or she should know how to solve problems, have a broad perspective, and have a fast thinking and logical mind.

Extracting Lessons from a Medicine's History

Lessons and experience are what one has remaining when a medicine fails. It is essential to learn from one's mistakes because, as Santayana wrote, "Those who cannot remember the past are condemned to repeat it." Although lessons should be learned as they occur, it is sometimes necessary to conduct a systematic evaluation of some medicines' histories to extract lessons. The lessons learned may then be widely disseminated within the company.

The history of a medicine's development to the time of marketing can be conveniently divided into four parts, although other divisions of activities could be used. The four are:

1. *Discovery.* How the compound was discovered.
2. *Preclinical evaluation.* How the compound was tested in animals.
3. *Clinical evaluation.* How the compound was tested in humans.
4. *Technical development.* How the compound was made into a medicine.

Postmarketing experiences may also be examined for valuable lessons with those medicines that have been marketed. Additional categories could be created that focus on marketing, production, or other aspects of medicine development.

Once an acceptable group of categories is chosen, it is necessary to choose the medicines to be examined. This examination exercise may be conducted because of general interest about a group of medicines and thus there would be no specific issue to evaluate. On the other hand, the exercise itself may have been suggested to address a particular question or issue specifically (e.g., have unsuccessful medicines been terminated more rapidly in the last three years than in a three-year period that occurred 12 years ago?). In choosing medicines to evaluate, it is essential to pick those with the highest likelihood of providing worthwhile lessons that may be extrapolated to other situations. This does not mean to avoid types of medicines that are not currently being studied, but to avoid medicines where experiences gained were generally unique to that medicine and are not likely to be repeated. Choose a variety of medicines to examine, not based on their therapeutic area, but on the plans followed for their development (e.g., laser, broad front, or cone). Evaluate both successful and unsuccessful medicines, especially if the unsuccessful medicines could have been developed successfully by other companies and the failure was not because of inherent problems in the molecule.

Develop a plan to identify the lessons utilizing all available sources. This may require some formal planning, but it could also be done rather casually and informally. Should certain people be interviewed? The most important part of this activity is determining how the lessons learned from the exercise will assist the future development of other medicines. This requires identifying how the lessons may be applied to medicine discovery and/or development activities, plus attaining management support for any recommendations that result from this exercise. Recommendations may be in the form of changes in the (1) organization, (2) responsibilities of individuals or groups within the organization, (3) sign-off procedures, (4) use of check lists at appropriate places and times, or (5) any of the various other means of preventing similar problems from occurring again.

APPROACHES TO DIFFICULT DECISIONS

Everyone has their own style of making difficult decisions, and many methods are used at pharmaceutical companies. A few of these techniques are briefly described. The assumption is made that all relevant information is available to assist in the decision-making process. The assumption is also made that the appropriate people are the ones who will deliberate about the decision. It is understood that these assumptions are often incorrect because the most appropriate people are not always the ones dealing with an issue, and not all information on any issue can ever be known.

Some of the formal methods and tools used to make decisions include decision trees, algorithms, and flow diagrams. These methods have the advantage of being able to illustrate and present the problem, relevant information, and alternatives in a clear manner. These techniques often expedite communications and allow one to identify where more information is needed, plus help in reaching a decision. The disadvantages are that not all decisions are amenable to these techniques, not everyone is comfortable with using them, and a rapid decision must sometimes be made before these tools could be used. These techniques utilize an extremely logical approach, although that in itself does not necessarily imply that they will lead to a correct answer. Many questions that do not lend themselves to black or white (i.e., yes or no) responses cannot be addressed in this way. These techniques should be learned by all people who make frequent or important decisions for those situations where these methods will be useful. These methods also help organize one's way of thinking about an issue.

Commonly used methods to arrive at difficult decisions are initially to (1) discuss issues with others, (2) think about the issue, (3) review the issue, (4) weigh the pros and cons of alternative solutions, and (5) consider if any of the alternatives could have negative outcomes, and finally (6) as an individual (or group), to reach a decision. The decision should be tentative, when possible, to allow time for reflection, new information, and other opinions to be heard. Critiquing one's own decisions is often done using the "devil's advocate" approach. Finally, the technique of lateral thinking is sometimes appropriate to use (de Bono, 1967).

Determining Whether a Medicine Should Be Withdrawn from the Market

Situations unfortunately arise when this question must be addressed. This discussion assumes that the question is posed within a pharmaceutical company and that no regulatory agency has mandated that the medicine must be withdrawn.

One of the most important considerations is that input is required from a variety of sources. These include legal, regulatory, commercial, medical, and possibly others. If a regulatory authority has not mandated a medicine's withdrawal then the decision may be primarily legal, such as when Bendectin was withdrawn by Parke-Davis. This medicine was unfairly persecuted and convicted in the press, which indirectly forced its removal from the market (Sheffield and Batagol, 1985).

The decision to withdraw a medicine may be primarily made on commercial grounds. This happens with many products each year that are not commercially viable. At a certain point it becomes uneconomic for a company to produce a medicine, and it is usually withdrawn from sale. Some of these medicines may not be readily or adequately replaced, and physicians may demand the medicine's reintroduction. A few case histories of this phenomenon have been described (Weintraub and Northington, 1986).

If It Ain't Broke, Don't Fix It

There are senior managers at all pharmaceutical companies who are frequently heard to use this or a similar phrase. In many cases it represents sound advice. On the other hand, this phrase is also a trap because it may lead some people to become complacent about the status of various issues and not actively to seek means of improving a company's performance and efficiency. Strategies and approaches that have led to past successes must continually be reappraised and updated if they will be used to achieve future successes.

When managers use the argument that there's no reason to change habits or rules, it is important to identify the reason for the statement. Are they seeking a reason to avoid facing either a problem or a change that would likely be beneficial (e.g., they are passive individuals) or are they providing sound advice?

28 / The Future of Medicine Discovery

Near-Term, Intermediate-Term, and Long-Term (i.e., Distant) Futures...................... 300
Three Approaches to Predicting the Distant Future: Science Fiction, Simple Extrapolation, and Analysis of Megatrends 301

Flaws in Making Predictions About the Distant Future 302
Failure to Consider Human Values in Making Predictions............................... 302

The future just ain't what it used to be. Attributed to Yogi Berra.

Like most people I have always been fascinated with forecasts of life in the future. I keenly remember as a teenager during the 1950s and as a young adult in the early 1960s reading as much as possible about the world we were going to live in during the 1970s and 1980s. Most people went to work in helicopters or drove in accident-free cars guided by electronic sensors placed in the roadbed. Africa would be relatively peaceful after the last of the colonial powers departed. Famine would be eradicated because of high-yield crops that were part of the green revolution, as well as through improved distribution systems. These improvements would lead to a higher standard of living in the Third World. On the negative side, nuclear bombs would be developed by about a dozen countries in the 1960s, about 25 in the 1970s, and by almost any country that wanted to in the 1980s. These and many other major predictions never came to pass. Traffic is worse than ever today, driving is not much safer, peace has not yet come to Africa, and famine still exists. On the other hand, a number of revolutionary changes barely conceived of in the 1950s are with us today, such as advanced supercomputers, a plethora of information on almost any subject available almost instantaneously, and the presence of computers in daily life.

In the field of medicine and pharmaceuticals, many predictions from the 1950s and 1960s have also been wrong. Table 28.1 lists some of these predictions. The state of medicine and pharmaceuticals in 1990 would be recognizable and comfortable to most people from 1960. I expect that the medical world of the next ten to 30 years

also will be very recognizable and comfortable to most people from today. Most of the guesses and predictions of future revolutionary changes in medicine currently discussed in both professional and lay literature will turn out to be wrong. Those predictions that come to fruition will be scattered among many wrong guesses made by the prophets of today.

Most predictions of revolutionary change in medicine are pure "hype." They are primarily fostered by reporters looking for stories and by scientists and clinicians seeking to promote their own work or to obtain publicity. True, there will be breakthroughs and unanticipated changes, but it is impossible to predict which ones will occur and when they will occur.

The following are valid questions about the future of medicine discovery: (1) in which therapeutic areas will medicines be discovered, (2) which scientific targets and

TABLE 28.1. *New medicines and techniques predicted to be "right around the corner" for over 25 years that have not yet achieved their predicted degree of success*

1. Liposomes as a common delivery vehicle for new and old medicines
2. Nonaddictive strong analgesics
3. Major breakthroughs in the use of medicines for treating patients with schizophrenia
4. Cognition-enhancing medicines
5. Medicines implanted under the skin to treat a large variety of diseases
6. Delivery systems to bring cytotoxic chemicals to only carcinogenic cells and tissues

TABLE 28.2. *Trends in the medical field*

1. The genetic code will be mapped.
2. Genetic therapy will become a reality with patients receiving genes that replace or supplement their iron-deficient or defective ones, i.e., primarily in inborn errors of metabolism.
3. Electrocardiograms from patients at risk will be telemonitored and sent to physicians' offices for analysis.
4. Patients will receive more elaborate treatment while in ambulances.
5. Monoclonal antibodies will be used more widely to treat patients. These may be targeted to reach specific sites, tissues, or organs.
6. Improved methods of delivering medicines should become available.
7. We will develop our knowledge of the chemical structure of targets for new medicines. These are primarily at the active sites or receptors on proteins.
8. We will learn about previously unknown compounds in the body and the use of some of these as therapeutic agents.
9. There will be a greater awareness of circadian and other biological rhythms.
10. Synthetic vaccines that can control more diseases will be developed.

methodologies will be used, and (3) how will the medicines work? The answers to these questions will affect and will be affected by the directions taken by large pharmaceutical companies. For example, it is possible that new oral medicines will be discovered to treat effectively a wide range of presently untreatable or inadequately treated viral diseases. Another possibility is that novel delivery systems will be used to direct anticancer medicines to just those organs affected by a tumor. A third possibility is that genetic experiments will result in the ability to replace defective genes *in utero* or shortly after birth, curing specific genetic-linked diseases. Additional and even more revolutionary approaches to new medicines could be described. What pharmaceutical companies must determine is where to focus their research efforts. A list of some trends in medicine that are likely to

be extremely important in the future is shown in Table 28.2.

The pharmaceutical industry must decide in which therapeutic areas to place resources and which specific types of targets, methods, and approaches should be used. In making these decisions and choosing a direction to pursue, scientific managers may adopt a cautious evolutionary approach or they may take the risk of applying large amounts of resources toward one or two revolutionary approaches. I believe that an evolutionary approach leads to better planning for future medicine discoveries.

NEAR-TERM, INTERMEDIATE-TERM, AND LONG-TERM (i.e., DISTANT) FUTURES

Planning for the near-term, intermediate-term, and long-term future require totally different approaches (Table 28.3). Planning for the near-term future (i.e., up to approximately two years) is characterized by assessing ongoing work (past and present trends) as well as anticipating events that may have an impact in the future. Simply projecting the present trends over the next 24 months is generally sufficient to develop appropriate plans, as long as all factors that may affect the near-term future are considered and their probable influence incorporated in the plans.

The two- to ten-year horizon (i.e., intermediate-term future) for commercial introductions of new medicines is characterized by projects currently in the development pipeline. Most medicines that will be introduced within the next decade are being currently developed in the clinics or are being evaluated in the laboratory as recently discovered compounds of interest. Some new, serendipitous clinical uses of existing medicines are likely to be made as well. The methodologies that will be used to discover new medicines, which in turn, will be marketed after the next decade, are currently known.

The period beyond ten years is defined as the long-term or distant future. Chapter 18 describes one approach to viewing the intermediate-term and long-term

TABLE 28.3. *Major influences to consider when predicting the future*

Future period	Time	Major influences[a]
Near term	0 to 24 months	1. Continuation of past trends and directions 2. Known influences that will have an impact 3. Unknown factors
Intermediate term	2 to 10 years	1. Known influences that will have an impact 2. Megatrends 3. Past trends and directions 4. Unknown factors
Long term (distant)	Beyond 10 years	1. Megatrends 2. Human values 3. Unknown factors 4. Past trends and directions

[a] These are listed in general order of importance.

future that focuses on various environments (e.g., regulatory, social, political, academic, medical and health care, commercial and business, and internal company). The distant future is the focus of this chapter.

THREE APPROACHES TO PREDICTING THE DISTANT FUTURE: SCIENCE FICTION, SIMPLE EXTRAPOLATION, AND ANALYSIS OF MEGATRENDS

In looking at the distant future of medicine and pharmaceuticals, a variety of approaches may be used. The science-fiction approach describes many exciting changes that supposedly will affect everyone's life. This approach is favored by many popular authors and reporters for magazines and newspapers. Authors use their imaginations to create an entire scenario of future events based on something they have heard or observed. In some cases, the validity of the current situation is not adequately established. In other cases, there is little relationship between the future predictions and present realities, or the future predictions are discussed as probable but have only a remote possibility of occurring. In summary, the science fiction approach is characterized by projections of future events that are not logically connected to present realities and/or are not reflective of future likelihoods.

Many marketing research and basic science professionals predict the distant future by making extrapolations from the present. The most popular method for doing this is to describe present trends and then project these trends into the distant future. This is the most widely used model for predicting marketing trends of the future. This approach is limited in that it can mislead, particularly if the projection is made far into the future (i.e., the long term). If one fails to consider human values then one can be easily led astray in making extrapolations, even when using realistic megatrends that are either currently operational or are estimated to be operational in the future.

To predict the distant future most appropriately, it is necessary to identify those specific factors and megatrends that will be important in the distant future. It is necessary to determine how those trends will be influenced by human values and, in turn, how they will influence the various environments in which medicine discoveries are made. These environments are characterized by (1) need for new medicines, (2) scientific knowledge, (3) nature of medical practice, (4) regulations, (5) economic costs of discovery and development, (6) commercial and business, (7) social pressures, (8) availability of suitable staff and investigators, (9) political climate and pressures, (10) marketing practices, and (11) third-party reimbursements. One or more megatrends should

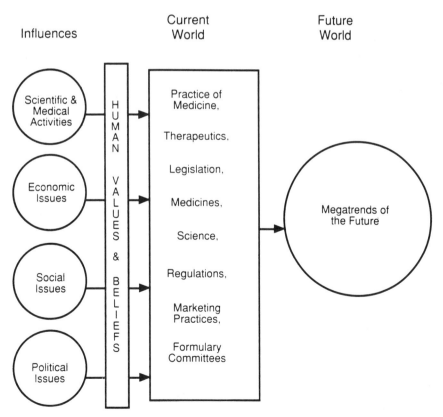

FIG. 28.1. Interactions of various influences and factors that create the megatrends which will influence/affect our future world.

TABLE 28.4. *Steps to follow after distant future megatrends are identified*

1. Evaluate each megatrend.
2. Determine which megatrends are of major importance for the company.
3. Determine which of those can be used by the company to establish a direction, program, or activities.
4. Decide how each megatrend is likely to be affected by human values.
5. Define specific activities to pursue.
6. Determine the resource efforts appropriate for each activity and the time at which resources should be allocated.
7. Determine criteria that will be used to judge whether these activities remain appropriate to pursue.
8. Determine the mechanism to be used to review each activity on a periodic basis.

be identified that deal with how each of these environmental characteristics will be modified over the next ten to 20 years.

New developments and advances in many areas of science will influence (1) which currently untreatable diseases will become treatable with medicines, (2) which currently unknown or unable to be utilized methodologies will be available for the development of medicines, and (3) which scientific targets or mechanisms of action that are currently unknown will yield new medicine discoveries. More and more ethical issues relating to science will be raised in the future. Many of these are expected to be based on recent breakthroughs in medicine and science that have the potential to affect the basis and nature of life itself. A general approach to identifying megatrends is shown in Fig. 28.1 and the steps to follow after megatrends are identified are listed in Table 28.4.

FLAWS IN MAKING PREDICTIONS ABOUT THE DISTANT FUTURE

The two major pitfalls in predicting the distant future involve the failure to use appropriately methods of extrapolation and the failure to consider human values.

Many individuals base their predictions of the future on straight-line extrapolations from present trends. For example, flat trends in the past are often projected to be flat in the future and upward trends are predicted to continue unabated in an upward direction. This process may be suitable for planning the near-term future, but it becomes progressively tenuous when it is used in the intermediate-term future. For the long-term future it is clearly inappropriate, unless other factors that may affect the extrapolation, as well as human values, are also considered.

A typical revolutionary prediction of medical events is quoted below. This prediction was not written in a popular magazine but in a scientific journal. It is extremely unrealistic and reflects extrapolation of what the author

believed was the start of an exponential rate of change into the future. One could also say that it represents a science-fiction approach to predicting the future, one commonly found in reports generated by large medical consulting companies under titles such as "The Next Pharmaceutical Revolution."

> Sometime in the *early part* (emphasis added) of the next century, it is generally felt that we will be relatively free of disease and that new drug development research will focus more on cures and on the correction of deficiencies.... Drugs will be "engineered" rather than "discovered" and therefore the process will be more efficient ... it seems likely that virtually any receptor or enzyme will be able to be characterized (both functionally and structurally) by the year 2000.

Although it might seem that this prediction was made in 1967, it was actually made in 1987 (Unger, 1987). Other unrealistic predictions relate to sales forecasts, such as one that predicted (in 1987) a $60 billion market in biotechnology products by the year 2000.

For every Leonardo da Vinci or Jules Verne who has had some success in predicting the long-term future, there are innumerable prophets whose predictions have proven to be incorrect. Some use faulty logic or a mistaken understanding of science or medicines as the basis for their predictions. Even use of good judgment and sense does not lead to clairvoyance about the future and most predictions will just be wrong. Many of Leonardo da Vinci's ideas did not come to pass for several hundred years. Some potentially simple advances in technology predicted to occur over the next few years may also take decades, if not centuries, to become reality. Cold fusion may be one of those ideas that will take a long period to achieve, and innumerable perpetual motion machines were "invented."

The greatest single scientific truth that humans have learned during the 20th century is the realization of how little humans know. Scientists have continually uncovered more and more levels of ignorance, rather than advancing us toward a state of perfect knowledge. At the close of the 19th century there were numerous people who believed that humans were approaching the state of complete knowledge. In fact, the head of the United States Patent Office, Mr. Charles H. Duell, recommended to President William McKinley in 1899 that the Patent Office be closed because "everything that can be invented has been invented" (Gerry Mossinghoff, personal communication). Fortunately, his suggestion was ignored. Mr. Duell failed to understand the megatrends that were taking place and would shape the future.

Failure to Consider Human Values in Making Predictions

Basic human values have generally changed little over the centuries. Those values influence the choices humans make as they create our future world. Values associated with the structure of the family and a desire to be connected with the past will influence the distant future. For example, some people predict that the family physician will virtually disappear as patients are forced, often for economic reasons, to be treated in highly impersonal systems.

The physician–patient relationship is the cornerstone of medicine. Patients like to be able to return to the same physician—a person in whom they place their trust—and patients want this practice to continue. The high-tech world of specialists, subspecialists, and consultants is often threatening to patients, especially when caring and compassion are replaced by impersonal interactions. In the future, patients will be unwilling to accept totally impersonal care and will insist on a degree of continuity and familiar comfortable relationships with their health care providers. Most patients (rightfully) desire to have their care orchestrated by a single leader and desire the Norman Rockwell romantic image of doctors who know and care about their patients.

Simplistic futuristic views and projections that ignore human values and needs will be almost always wrong, whether in politics or in planning for medicine discoveries. At a time when the world is becoming a "global community," each neighborhood within that community seeks harder to retain its own identification. This apparent contradiction must be understood in terms of both individual and group values. Ethnic groups all over the world have brought back, often after a great struggle, nearly dead languages, extinct folk customs, and various traditions that are part of their culture and heritage. These separatist influences in many countries today are brought back at the same time that the walls between some neighboring groups or countries are breaking down (e.g., European Community). Both aspects may be seen as part of a cycle of unification and separation driven by two sets of potentially conflicting human needs and values.

In conclusion, all scientific managers must make assumptions about the distant future to guide current planning and decision making. Because most specific breakthroughs that will occur in science and medicine cannot be predicted, the best model to guide one's thinking, plans, and actions about the distant future is an evolutionary one. It is important to be both realistic and logical about the future—to build on the past in the discovery of new medicines. This means that the chances of success, in medicine discovery activities, will be enhanced when known methodologies are used and realistic targets are set. At the same time, it is critically important for the pharmaceutical industry to look for the unexpected and to seek breakthroughs and for the pharmaceutical scientist to be prepared to explore each revolutionary idea that does not demand excessive resources or long periods of time to evaluate. The key to successful planning for the distant future is to understand the human values, human thinking, and the megatrends that will influence it.

SECTION IV

Research and Development Organization and Management Issues

29 / Organizing Research and Development

Organizing Research and Development 307
   Determining Whether to Utilize a Centralized
     or Decentralized Research and Development
     Organization 307
   Organizing Research and Development by
     Scientific Discipline 308
   Organizing Research and Development by
     Therapeutic Team....................... 308
   Organizing Research and Development by the
     Matrix Approach......................... 310
   Critical Mass Necessary to Have an
     Independent Research and Development
     Function................................. 311

Organizing Basic Science Departments 313
   Rigid Organizational Structure................ 313
   Totally Open Organizational Structure........ 313
   A Hybrid Approach 313
   Coordinating Committee Approach........... 313
   Basis of Establishing a Research Project or
     Program 315
   How Are Preclinical Departments
     Established?.............................. 315
Organizing Medical Departments 315

The success of a corporate R&D program becomes visible only in the light of its mission and purpose. If the choice is to adopt a generic, loosely market-coupled approach, then organization requires a strong discipline orientation and close attention to the number and excellence of contributions to the technical literature. If the choice is to adopt a targeted, tightly market-coupled approach, then organization needs a project orientation and must link its rewards to ultimate business success. Failure inevitably comes from trying to organize, appraise, and reward according to one approach while expecting results typical of the other. Roland W. Schmitt, *Harvard Business Review* (May–June, 1985, p. 128).

ORGANIZING RESEARCH AND DEVELOPMENT

Multinational pharmaceutical companies are often organized in two parts, focused on the United States and the rest of the world. This occurs regardless of whether the headquarters of the company are in the United States or not. The reasons for this two-part division are numerous and include the large medicine market in the United States and the relative importance of the Food and Drug Administration worldwide.

Most companies approach organizational issues at the research and development level in ways similar to those described for the entire company. The reader is referred to Chapter 10 on organizational issues at the corporate level for this discussion.

Determining Whether to Utilize a Centralized or Decentralized Research and Development Organization

Large multinational companies usually conduct research and develop medicines at two or more sites in different countries. If a company has two or more such groups, their organization and coordination may either be centralized or decentralized. Some advantages and disadvantages of decentralization are described below. Those for centralization at a corporate level are discussed in Chapter 10.

Advantages of a Decentralized Approach

Some advantages of a decentralized approach for conducting research are:

1. Scientists with different educational, scientific, and cultural backgrounds often approach a research problem in different ways. Multiple groups, either together or independently, may be more likely to solve problems and to discover medicines than those from a single site who share a common background. In addition, the managers at one site may tend to have a single approach.
2. A lively exchange of opinions between individuals at

different research centers may be fostered. This tends to generate ideas, support fact finding, and stimulate medicine discovery.

3. Each particular type or area of research may be performed at the site(s) where the best experts and best facilities are located.
4. Local development and support facilities can usually provide more rapid and more appropriate assistance for patenting medicines. Local staff usually understand government regulations better than do staff operating from a foreign country.

Numerous other advantages exist for a decentralized research organization in terms of management and also in training of staff. Advantages include reducing the number of steps of communications required to have decisions made, involving more people in decision making, dispersing power and authority, and training more executives for other positions.

The same type of advantage exists in the development of new medicines. These include the probability of improved negotiations with local registration authorities and the development of dosage forms, dosage strengths, and the use of colors that are most desired.

Disadvantages of a Decentralized Approach

Disadvantages of a decentralized approach include difficulties in (1) planning an overall direction to follow when different philosophies of medicine development exist at each site; (2) coordination of activities at each site; (3) decision making on a single project being developed at multiple sites; (4) development of intergroup rivalries; (5) existence of different standards, policies, and basic approaches; (6) lack of highly trained and competent managers; and (7) greater cost to the company. Conflicts may develop between the headquarters and its subsidiaries because autonomy of local sites tends to increase at the expense of the central group's authority. Autonomy at multiple locations is often valuable and may even be essential for some companies to conduct effectively basic research and discover medicines, but autonomy is much less essential and may be counterproductive for conducting preclinical, clinical, and technical development studies on new compounds and medicines. Moreover, autonomy of multiple sites in medicine development activities may be counterproductive in this era of global medicine development.

Decentralized companies or territories may be run like a series of walled cities, each governed by a ruler who makes all decisions and rarely communicates with the central palace. Another decentralized model is where there is a loose confederation of independent cities that band together when necessary for mutual protection and benefit. The mayors of these cities may be wary of each other but tend to have even less trust of the state's leader.

Organizing Research and Development by Scientific Discipline

The research effort at most companies is more formal and organized today than it has been in past decades. Like most industries, pharmaceutical companies are primarily organized around basic functions such as research, marketing, finance, legal, personnel, and manufacturing. There are two general approaches that pharmaceutical companies have followed in organizing their overall research and development activities. These are to organize by discipline (Fig. 29.1) and by therapeutic teams (Fig. 29.2). In the more common approach, scientific disciplines such as pharmacology, toxicology, medicine, and organic chemistry are established as separate departments (Fig. 29.1). The progress of a compound through the three stages of discovery, development, and marketing involves "passing" the compound along from department to department, but activities also persist for a long period within any one department. Also, multiple departments must work closely together at most stages of a medicine's development. Even when a medicine's application for regulatory approval is submitted to a government agency, the organic chemistry department may be synthesizing additional compounds for patent protection, and the pharmacology department may be learning more about the medicine's mechanism of action. Other departments are also involved in studying the medicine and are equally busy. Individual departments may be grouped into multidepartment groups (e.g., divisions or units) of research, technical development, medical personnel, and support services (Fig. 29.1). Another way of grouping departments is to divide them into medicine discovery and medicine development divisions.

Large departments may be divided into sections that each reflect specific therapeutic areas or on another basis. For example, both pharmacology and medical departments are usually divided into sections specializing in therapeutic areas such as cardiovascular, central nervous system, gastrointestinal, or respiratory therapy. If size warrants, these groups may be further subdivided, generally by specific diseases. For example, a cardiovascular section could be divided into separate groups working on hypertension, angina, and congestive heart failure. Another type of subdivision is based on the type of medicine under study. For example, a cardiovascular section could have separate groups working on calcium channel blockers, beta-receptor antagonists, and angiotensin-converting enzyme inhibitors.

Organizing Research and Development by Therapeutic Team

Another major organizational structure is the therapeutic team. In this approach the entire research and

TRADITIONAL ORGANIZATION OF RESEARCH AND DEVELOPMENT

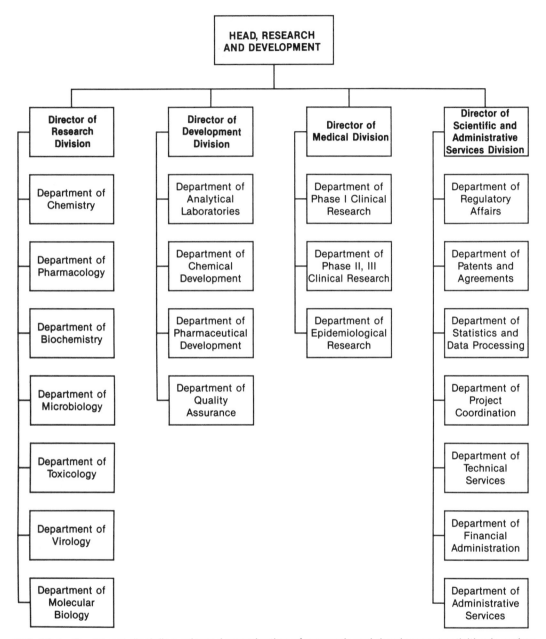

FIG. 29.1. Traditional discipline-oriented organization of research and development activities in a pharmaceutical company.

development unit involving both medicine discovery and development functions is divided into therapeutic areas like cardiovascular, gastrointestinal, or central nervous system (Fig. 29.2). This approach was used by The Upjohn Company for many years. Their experiences over the first five years of this approach have been summarized (Weisblat and Stucki, 1974). In this general model each group contains representatives of all scientific disciplines (e.g., biochemistry and pharmacology) and medicine, while other groups (e.g., patents, regulatory affairs, and toxicology) are centralized and provide general services to all therapeutic groups. The major advantage of this approach is that it brings people together from numerous disciplines and increases their collaboration and hopefully their productivity. People from various disciplines within the larger group (e.g., cardiovascular) can easily be assigned to develop a specific medicine.

Organizing Research and Development by the Matrix Approach

A third approach to the overall organization of research and development involves the matrix concept (Fig. 29.3). Most large research-based companies organized by scientific discipline have incorporated matrix concepts into their organizational structure. Each scientist reports to a superior through the traditional "vertical" hierarchy. Some scientists are also assigned to a project and report in a "horizontal" structure to the project leader or project manager. A strong matrix system requires professionals working on a project to have a formal or semiformal reporting relationship to both a line manager and a project leader or manager. In a weak matrix, dual reporting relationships are more informal. Matrix systems are described more fully in Chapter 32.

THERAPEUTICALLY-BASED ORGANIZATION OF RESEARCH AND DEVELOPMENT

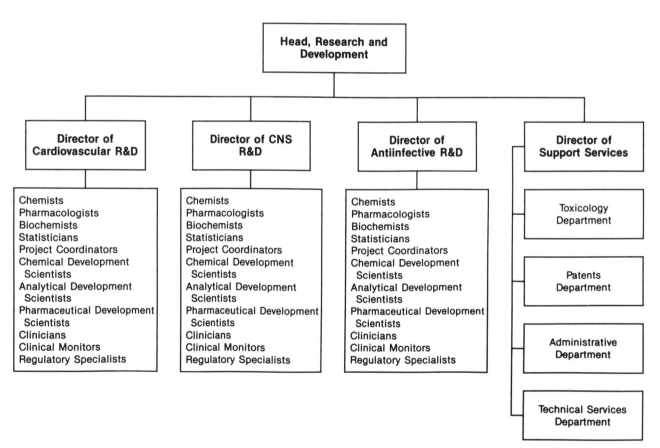

FIG. 29.2. Therapeutically based organization of research and development activities in a pharmaceutical company. CNS, central nervous system; R&D, research and development.

MATRIX ORGANIZATION OF DRUG DEVELOPMENT PROJECTS

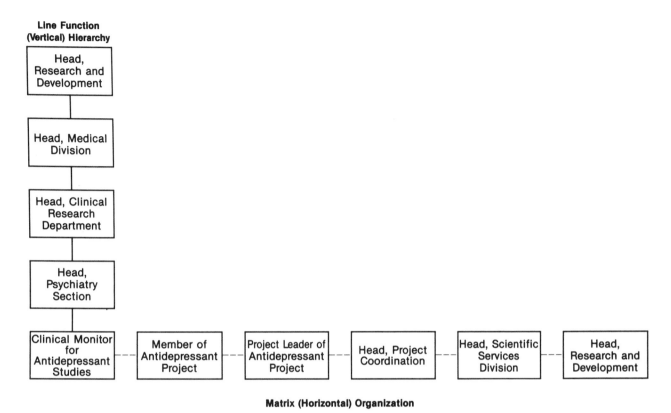

FIG. 29.3. Matrix (horizontal) organization of medicine development project activities in a pharmaceutical company.

Critical Mass Necessary to Have an Independent Research and Development Function

The actual size of the overall research and development function that constitutes a critical mass for medicine discovery and development is a difficult number to derive. This figure depends on many variables. Nonetheless, several senior research and development managers from various pharmaceutical companies have estimated the number to be on the order of 600 to 800 people (Bartholini, 1983). The size of the essential core for either the discovery or development function is even more difficult to estimate because many departments support both efforts. On the other hand, a research and development group can grow much larger before its size per se begins to decrease its efficiency.

It is important to consider this concept on several levels. At the overall research and development level, critical mass refers to having sufficient personnel and skills within a company to handle the important activities necessary to discover and develop a medicine. It does not preclude an occasional need to contract highly special-

ized work to outside contractors because no company would ever desire to have in-house all of the equipment, staff, and facilities necessary to handle every contingency that could arise. That would be a foolish goal, but it is a worthwhile goal to be able to respond rapidly to most or all common situations and problems that arise. A rule of thumb is that commonly required functions should be available in-house if contracting them would decrease performance quality and/or substantially increase the time to complete the task. Some less frequently required functions that are of particular interest to a company should also be present in-house. This might include tests conducted infrequently on one of the company's major products.

Medicine Discovery

At an individual research department or discipline level (e.g., organic chemistry or pharmacology) the concept of critical mass could be defined similarly. In medicine discovery, the term is often used to describe the amount of research effort believed necessary for each research project. If the effort is too small, there is a danger that the approach would be too superficial to have a high likelihood of discovering a medicine or achieving the research goal. This would result in wasting time, energy, and money. If a large number of appropriate resources are applied to a small number of research topics, there will usually not be a question of achieving a critical mass, but of whether the resources could be more efficiently allocated to explore a larger number of topics. Regardless of the quantity of resources placed on any research program, the chances are quite limited for discovering a compound that will reach human studies, because only approximately one or two out of every 1,000 compounds made achieves that goal. Of those that reach human testing, 20% to 40% reach the market at most companies.

Medicine Development

Each company should evaluate whether its development activities (in addition to research activities) have achieved a critical mass. This implies that all important activities needed to develop a medicine may be efficiently conducted in-house, except for a small number that are cost-effective to contract to outside groups. If

there are severe bottlenecks in the medicine development pipeline and resources to correct the bottlenecks are not available, it may indicate that the company has not yet achieved a critical mass. Some individuals have suggested that a research and development budget of between $150 and 200 million per year (1993 levels) is the minimum amount of money necessary for a research-based pharmaceutical company in the United States to obtain and maintain a critical mass in its research and development activities.

Support Services

Critical mass cannot only be viewed as a total number or overall concept. There is also a critical mass that exists within technical development, medical, research, and support services. Appropriate numbers of staff that constitute a critical mass could be judged on many bases, including (1) the number of people in each area per project, (2) the amount of medicine sales per research and development employee, and (3) the number of people in each area at other pharmaceutical companies of a similar size.

Figure 29.4 illustrates one means of conceptualizing the various levels and types of support services provided for medicine discovery and development activities. Sci-

TYPES AND LEVELS OF SUPPORT FOR DRUG DEVELOPMENT ACTIVITIES

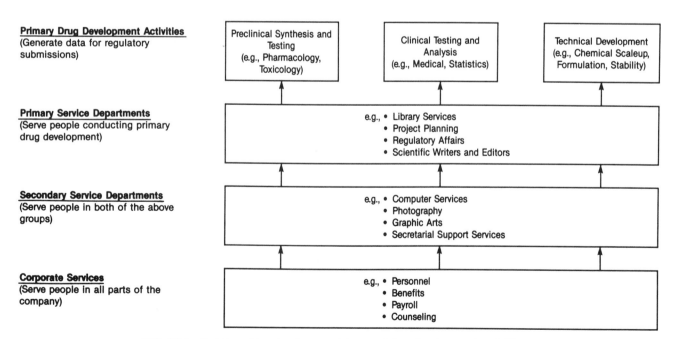

FIG. 29.4. Types and levels of support for medicine development activities.

entific support departments include toxicology, metabolism, patents, regulatory affairs, scientific planning, and library services. Technical support departments include chemical development, analytical development, and pharmaceutical development.

ORGANIZING BASIC SCIENCE DEPARTMENTS

Most newly synthesized compounds are initially intended for evaluation in a single biological system or therapeutic area. The compound may also be tested in numerous additional biological tests or therapeutic areas at the chemist's (or biologist's) suggestion. Assume that three different and unrelated chemical compounds are all made for biological screen 1 by chemist A. Also assume that these three compounds each had activity in other biological test screens for various projects. The ways in which additional follow-up compounds would be made for each project varies substantially between companies. Figure 29.5 illustrates common systems used by pharmaceutical companies to deal with this situation.

Rigid Organizational Structure

Panel A in Fig. 29.5 illustrates a highly rigid organizational structure in which a research chemist is assigned to act as a leader within the chemistry section for each biological program or project. In this situation, if one of chemist A's compounds is found to be active in another biological project, chemist A must turn over all ideas and chemical leads for that project to the appropriate chemist who is the liaison for that project. Taken to an extreme, this could mean that two or more chemists could be making similar (or even identical) compounds, although they would be intended for different biological projects.

Another disadvantage of this system is that chemists would have to become familiar with an extremely wide variety of synthetic chemistry techniques, depending on what chemicals were found to be active in the biological screens and tests for which they had chemical responsibility. This approach could present problems because the expertise of most chemists is limited to selected areas of chemistry. On the other hand, this problem is usually not too serious, because good chemists may convert to a new area in approximately six to 12 months. This structure is being used in some pharmaceutical companies although it is felt to be an inefficient system.

Totally Open Organizational Structure

Panel B in Fig. 29.5 illustrates the opposite system as in panel A. In situation B, a chemist follows up on all biological leads himself or herself. On the positive side, each chemist has the freedom to pursue medicine discovery paths of interest. It is more difficult to control and coordinate this totally open system and to direct resources to those biological projects of greatest interest and priority to the company. Unless the people involved in this system have many chemical leads of interest to work on, a sense of competition and even jealousy may also develop. This situation could occur because all groups of chemists are essentially competing for the attention of the biologists who are testing and screening compounds. Because the biological groups have limited resources to test compounds and have to prioritize their efforts, this open system (i.e., panel B) is likely to create problems. This is because the compounds of some chemists will be tested before those of others, even though the delayed compounds may have a higher priority.

A Hybrid Approach

Panel C in Fig. 29.5 illustrates one of numerous hybrid systems possible. In this system, chemists coordinate their work with other chemists, but limit their interactions to the single biological project (or projects) that they are primarily supporting. This approach readily allows for coordination of all efforts within a single project. Priorities and allocation of resources are easier to establish and control. Multiple chemists may prepare compounds for a single project, especially when the synthetic techniques require different types of chemical expertise. A single chemist is assigned to coordinate the various activities amongst the chemists who are involved with a specific project. This individual, in conjunction with the chemistry section and department heads plus the senior biologists, establishes the priorities within chemistry.

Coordinating Committee Approach

Panel D in Fig. 29.5 illustrates approaches in which each pharmacology project or therapeutic area has a committee to coordinate the various activities within the disciplines involved. This committee identifies or at least approves the compounds to be made and their relative priority for synthesis. The committee decides when to request additional tests (e.g., advanced pharmacology or toxicology) and when to recommend that the compound be studied in humans. If a therapeutic area is organized in this manner, the committee may have authority over a single or many pharmacological projects. The committee may be a small group of a few senior individuals or it may contain a relatively large number (i.e., ten to 15) of members.

ORGANIZATIONAL RELATIONSHIPS FOR CHEMISTS AND BIOLOGISTS TO DISCOVER NEW DRUGS

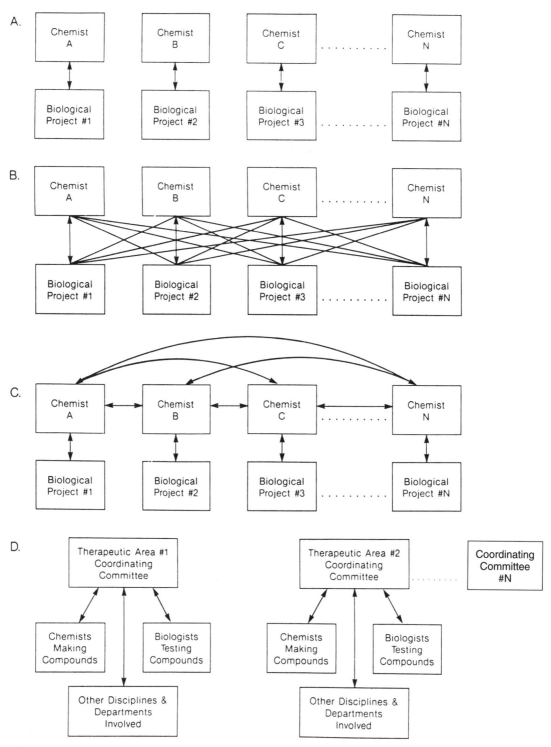

FIG. 29.5. Organizational relationships and interactions between chemists and biologists in medicine discovery activities. Companies usually adopt one of these systems, although hybrid systems are also possible. Interactions are for (1) setting priorities, (2) planning new chemical structures to synthesize, (3) choosing old compounds to study, (4) collaborating on compound synthesis, and (5) other functions. Panels **A–D** are described in the text.

The committee approach may also be grafted to one of the preceding types of organizations (i.e., panels A to C). In one of those situations, the personal interactions illustrated would operate until a chemical "lead" was discovered that met certain criteria. The committee structure would then be used to plan and direct additional work either on that chemical series, or on that specific compound. A committee approach seems worthwhile for larger pharmaceutical companies. It enables a company to have an efficient system while utilizing the ideas of a number of scientists on a specific topic.

Basis of Establishing a Research Project or Program

Within a department, the projects or programs of particular interest may be based on a disease, target, enzyme, physiological function, chemical class of compounds, and/or therapeutic area. The author prefers the therapeutic area approach in most situations. One advantage of using therapeutic areas as a basis for organizing the company's research activities is that it encourages more interaction with groups in other departments studying the same therapeutic area. Whichever model is chosen as the basis for defining research projects or programs, it is generally desirable to be consistent. A company should have a strong rationale if it mixes projects based on different criteria.

How Are Preclinical Departments Established?

Most companies establish preclinical departments and organize their research based on major scientific disciplines (e.g., chemistry, biochemistry, and physiology). Others utilize hybrids of scientific disciplines (e.g., molecular pharmacology, metabolism and kinetics, and molecular biology), and still others use therapeutic areas (e.g., cardiovascular and gastrointestinal), or arbitrary titles usually depending on historical tradition or people around whom a scientific department is constructed (e.g., investigational science, experimental biology, and exploratory research). Departments may also be created around one of the company's successful medicines. Another approach is to organize research according to the function of medicines (e.g., prophylactic or therapeutic). These companies may also have a group primarily assigned to conduct exploratory research.

Size of Individual Departments

The size of individual departments may be an issue. Some companies divide their chemistry department into two or more smaller sized departments, whereas other companies prefer to keep them intact, even if they contain over 200 people. The motivation to divide or remain whole should be based on logic, plus efficiency of medicine development. Nonetheless, decisions are usually based on views and opinions of key personalities within the company that are inadequately critiqued.

ORGANIZING MEDICAL DEPARTMENTS

Many of the same type of organizational questions exist within clinical areas as for basic research departments. A company may be organized with a single medical department where the staff are involved with all clinical trials from Phase I to Phase IV. Alternatively, walls may be erected and different departments established which only plan, initiate, monitor, and analyze clinical trials in one, two, or three clinical phases or in certain therapeutic areas on specified projects. The United States pharmaceutical industry has examples of almost all of the possible permutations of dividing medical departments to work on specific phases of medicine development. Medical departments have been established to conduct only Phase I, II, III, or IV trials, or Phases I and II, II and III, or I, II, and III trials. A rationale of some validity may be described for each of these choices and many pros and cons of each alternative could be presented. One important principle is that the fewest number of walls possible should be established between clinical departments. Methodologies and objectives differ most for Phase I and Phase IV trials. Therefore, any division of a medical department into two or more separate departments should preferably be to divide one or both of those phases from the others.

If a pharmaceutical company assigns medical staff to specific therapeutic areas, this is usually done for Phases II and III, but not for Phases I and IV. Phase I trials are usually conducted in normal volunteers and the question of a medicine's ultimate use is not usually critical to the study design and methodologies used. There are, however, a few exceptions to this principle (e.g., anticancer medicines and antiarrhythmic medicines are originally studied in patients).

30 / Managing Research and Development

Introduction **317**
Levels and Issues of Research Management ... 317
Information Flow 318
The Meaning and Use of Target Dates 319
Balancing Work Effort on Discovery,
Development, and Line-Extension
Activities **319**
Should Medicine Discovery Research
Activities Be Isolated from the Rest of a
Pharmaceutical Company? 320
Preventing a Drought of New Products within
a Company 320
Reviewing Projects 320
Assessing the Reality Level of Plans and
Proposals: How to Spot Unrealistic Plans ... 321
Planning for Meetings 321
Subcategories of Medicine Discovery,
Medicine Development, and
Line-Extensions.......................... 322

Contracting Medicine Development........... 322
Allocating Resources........................ **323**
Methods to Allocate Resources 323
Achieving a Balance Between Discovery,
Development, and Line-Extensions through
Allocation of Funds 325
Allocation of Resources Based on a Medicine's
Commercial Potential 325
Allocation of Resources Based on Therapeutic
Areas 325
Evaluating Whether Resources Are Allocated
as Intended 326
Other Issues................................ **326**
Promotions................................ 326
Planning and Documentation................. 327
What Options Exist When Work on Important
Projects Cannot Progress at Top Speed?..... 328

There is, indeed, a specific fault in our system of science, and in the resultant understanding of the natural world . . . This fault is reductionism, the view that effective understanding of a complex system can be achieved by investigating the properties of its isolated parts. The reductionist methodology, which is so characteristic of much of modern research, is not an effective means of analyzing the vast natural systems that are threatened by degradation. Barry Commoner, American writer. From *The Closing Circle.*

Never make a threat. Reason with people. Don Corleone (the Godfather)—Mario Puzo. From *The Godfather.*

INTRODUCTION

Levels and Issues of Research Management

Various levels of research and development management are illustrated in Fig. 30.1. This figure stresses the functional responsibilities (e.g., discovery and development) rather than specific disciplines. It is intended to show that management principles, beliefs, and philosophies may be (and often are) extrapolated from one level of management to another. Some of the basic issues that frequently arise in the management of research and development are listed in Table 30.1. Some of these issues are discussed in this chapter.

Most research, development, and medical department heads and many individuals within those departments

tend to believe that the company's research and development activities revolve around their own axis. It reminds one of traveling to different countries and noticing world maps that place their own country in the center of the map. Science is a sensitive plant and scientists must often be careful gardeners. Many management questions arise every day, and managers must be careful about how they respond. Although one or two approaches may suggest themselves at once, there are almost always many ways of approaching any question or issue.

In addition to the levels of research management described in Fig. 30.1, there are other levels at which basic decisions are made about research. These decisions include (1) whether a company should do any research to discover novel medicines, (2) which therapeutic areas (e.g., cardiovascular or central nervous system) should

317

EXTRAPOLATING MANAGEMENT INFORMATION AND BELIEFS THROUGH VARIOUS LEVELS OF R&D MANAGEMENT

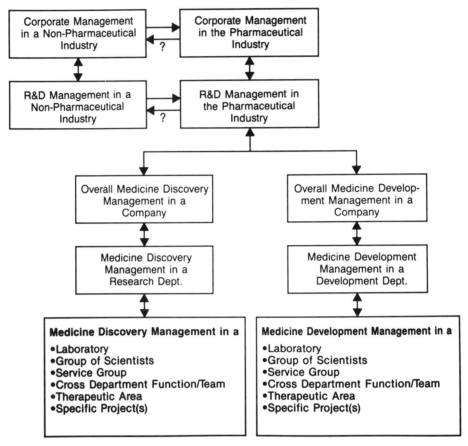

FIG. 30.1. Extrapolating management information and beliefs through various levels of research and development (R&D). *Arrows* represent extrapolations. The question marks (?) from pharmaceutical industry to nonpharmaceutical industry indicate that the extrapolation is usually in the other direction.

be researched, (3) which diseases should be researched, (4) which biological targets should be chosen to define activity, and (5) which methodologies should be used to approach each target? There are also issues of how much effort and resources should be expended on each research project and who should make the decisions on the five questions listed above.

The decision to pursue research in specific therapeutic areas may be made by scientists who are actively conducting and directing the research and/or by senior managers who review and supervise those scientists. Some companies allow scientists more freedom than others in this matter. If a company encourages its scientists to make decisions on which diseases to study and which approaches to use, then the managers of the scientists are probably more concerned with allocation of resources, priority setting, and review of progress, rather than controlling the specific research direction that each scientist is taking.

At most companies, however, the decision of which therapeutic areas to pursue (level 2 above) and often which diseases to research (level 3 above) are made by senior research managers. The decision of how to approach each disease (levels 4 and 5), however, is often left to senior scientists. Managers may not only control the broad therapeutic areas and specific diseases that are researched, but may also control each target established within each of those diseases. The determination of specific methodologies to be used is commonly delegated to scientists at most companies.

Information Flow

It is important for managers to consider the means whereby they receive and disseminate information. This will allow them to determine whether currently used mechanisms should be modified. If so, then means to do

TABLE 30.1. *Basic issues frequently considered in the management of research and development*

1. Should medicne discovery be centralized or decentralized?
2. Should medicine development be centralized or decentralized?
3. Should medicine discovery be conducted entirely internally (i.e., within the company)?
4. How much and which parts of medicine development should be contracted out?
5. How productive is the entire research and development group?
6. Are the activities of medicine discovery, medicine development, and line-extensions in balance?
7. How much money should be spent on research, development, and line-extensions?
8. How may communications and interactions be optimized at all levels within research and development and between all relevant departments?
9. How may communications and interactions be optimized between research and development and marketing (and production)?
10. How may activities be appropriately prioritized and resources allocated?
11. How much authority should be given to the matrix system of project management?
12. How closely should activities be monitored and leaders held accountable for meeting estimated dates for completion of activities?

this may be determined. Each person who reports directly to a manager should be providing information on both a periodic and ad hoc basis. People who have a dotted-line (i.e., informal) reporting responsibility, have special relationships, or are peers of the manager, are other sources of information. If insufficient or inappropriate information is being received, then steps must be considered to rectify this situation.

Delays in the flow of information may occur anywhere along the path, and this is another aspect that may have to be addressed. Senior managers should utilize several different systems to expedite both upward and downward flow of information to themselves. Likewise, careful attention should also be given to methods used to disseminate information to others who are both higher and lower in the company as well as at the same level. It is hoped that readers of this book are not hoarders of information, but want to share it with all relevant people within their company or organization.

The Meaning and Use of Target Dates

Target dates are usually established for achieving major milestones (e.g., New Drug Application [NDA] submissions and product launches) as well as for completing many of the individual activities and tasks that must occur for major milestones to be achieved. Target dates are used differently in different companies and sometimes by individual groups within the same company.

Dates may be used (1) as a specific formal tool to develop work schedules and responsibilities, (2) as an informal guide to plan activities and work, or (3) as a general guide to assist people in establishing priorities. Production groups and some highly technical departments tend to use the formal "specific tool" approach and scientific researchers use the "general guide" approach.

Dates may be estimated on an *ideal* or *theoretical* basis. On this basis, dates indicate when activities could be completed if all resources were available and no conflicting activities were competing for priority. Alternatively, dates may be estimated on a *realistic* basis that includes consideration of all projects being developed. Even using a realistic approach, dates may be chosen that are optimistic, pessimistic, or in between.

Optimistic dates are sometimes used in plans to spur and encourage the people working on a particular project. Although this method may be effective for a few activities, it is usually counterproductive over the life of a project. Most people prefer to gauge their work using target dates that are achievable without a superhuman effort. It is important for all project dates (e.g., time for Investigational New Drug Application [IND] or NDA submission and time of medicine launch) to be established using the same approach and for all medicine projects to use the same approach. Dates are useful guides for most people to use in planning their work, even though the targets established are not always met. Dates for obtaining regulatory approvals on various submissions are particularly difficult to set accurately. They may be expressed with confidence, however, as long as the year of approval is not listed.

BALANCING WORK EFFORT ON DISCOVERY, DEVELOPMENT, AND LINE-EXTENSION ACTIVITIES

The optimal balance between efforts expended on each of these three functions is influenced by the overall health and goals of the company. The pressures on research and development to stress either short-term or long-term horizons depends on the view of stockholders, board of directors, and research and development managers, plus input from marketing. If a company's goals are heavily oriented toward short-term profits or the company is in poor financial health, it will tend to emphasize work on line-extensions. If a company's orientation is toward long-term scientific breakthroughs and novel medicine development, it will often emphasize discovery research. If a balanced concept is stressed, then efforts will be approximately balanced on all three functions.

A long-term company commitment to medicine discovery is necessary to have an efficient, effective, and motivated professional group of scientists who are attempting to discover and are actively developing medicines. As a company grows in size and it markets more novel medicines, the time spent on developing line-extensions and on other activities necessary to support marketing activities generally increases. A pharmaceutical company and its research and development managers need flexibility to adjust and maintain an appropriate balance between these three functions. The process of balancing these functions should be performed at least every two or three years, if not annually or more subtly on an ongoing basis. The medicine discovery function cannot be turned on and off easily like a water tap each time a reassessment is made. Nonetheless, additional funds can almost always be spent on specific research activities of particular interest or on development activities where a bottleneck has occurred.

Should Medicine Discovery Research Activities Be Isolated from the Rest of a Pharmaceutical Company?

When scientists are worried about their jobs and/or the attitudes of company managers, it becomes difficult for most to think creatively. Some people have suggested that it is desirable to remove medicine discovery research from the company environment and to place it in an isolated research institute. This would theoretically allow scientists to concentrate on their research activities. The record of medicine discoveries made in such research institutes of pharmaceutical companies, however, is not impressive, even though these centers often contribute significantly to basic research. If the criteria of success are based on research publications then such groups have been successful.

There is another approach that emphasizes creation of a positive work environment for basic research scientists (see Chapter 27). Scientists are not isolated from other activities and are encouraged to interact with development-oriented scientists and marketing-oriented personnel. Some discovery-oriented scientists also have the opportunity (if desired) at most companies to participate in medicine development activities as members of project teams.

Preventing a Drought of New Products within a Company

There is no magic formula to achieve the goal of having a continual flow of new medicines. All companies are bound to have periods when few, if any, new products are developed. This is an important issue in all companies and a critical concern in some. In fact, much of this book is directed toward this concern. Some of the factors that tend to minimize the chances of this problem (i.e., a drought of new products) occurring are to (1) hire the best staff possible, ensuring that a sufficient number of

highly creative people are present; (2) develop and maintain a positive atmosphere and environment, where people are encouraged to be bold and imaginative; (3) utilize licensing as an important adjunct to supplement in-house medicine discoveries; (4) organize the company and its research departments to encourage flexibility; (5) maintain a critical mass of skills and talents; (6) build and maintain up-to-date equipment and facilities; and (7) maintain high ethical standards.

Within the project portfolio there should be an appropriate mix of short-, mid-, and long-term projects. These groups of projects may be defined in many ways, but the specific definitions per se are not important to this discussion. What is more important is that the projects not only have appropriate medical and commercial value, but also reach the market at a steady rate. Any big gaps in this respect should be addressed through licensing, acquisition, or some other approach. Research programs should also be established to provide an appropriate mix of short-, mid-, and long-term research programs.

Reviewing Projects

There are many groups that review projects in a company. Reviews occur at different levels and for different reasons. A number of important considerations and questions for review groups are presented below.

1. *Purpose of meeting* Are the meetings held to review projects intended as an information-sharing exercise or as a time to discuss issues, set strategies, and/or solve problems? If issues are to be discussed, it may be useful for the reviewers to identify the issues before the project leader or others are invited in to the meeting.
2. *Asking the right questions* In reviewing potential research activities and projects and making decisions, it is important to ask the best questions. The question, "Is this something we can do," may elicit a different answer than if the managers ask "Is this something we should do?"
3. *Reaching decisions* Are decisions reached by consensus, by vote, or by the chair making a ruling? The first method is usually best since unpopular executive decisions often are not enacted or meet great resistance and may adversely affect morale.
4. *Where is the focus directed* Do reviewers focus both on basic objectives of the project and the specific details and issues, or do they sometimes lose sight of the former and thereby allow the project to head in an inappropriate direction away from its goals? Are goals reassessed at appropriate intervals?
5. *Focus on past versus future activities* Do reviews focus solely on the project's past achievements and current status (i.e., a retrospective review) or do they *also* focus on the next steps in the project and on

future activities (i.e., a prospective future-oriented review)? Do reviewers evaluate the overall direction in which the project is moving? Do reviewers confirm (insofar as possible) that several years into the future the market potential for the anticipated medicine will still be adequate to justify the medicine's development?

6. *Allocating priorities* Priorities in the overall portfolio often change, and a project may have to be slowed to allow others to speed up. How does the group handle this? Unless this step is carried out carefully it may be demotivating to a company's staff. If this occurs, a project's momentum may slow or even come to a complete stop.

7. *Sharing of information* Since information is power, how do senior and other managers deal with information? Do they share it openly or guard it carefully and only provide it to others as necessary? Is it easy or difficult for each group to obtain the information it needs to operate effectively?

8. *Preparation for meetings* Do reviewers come to meetings prepared to conduct their reviews? Have they read and digested material sent to them ahead of time or do they spend time being walked through material they should already know?

Assessing the Reality Level of Plans and Proposals: How to Spot Unrealistic Plans

Various types of unrealities either creep into plans or are purposely put there. It is essential for all professionals and all managers to be able to recognize problem zones, to eliminate them where possible, and to question them where not.

The first type of problem is familiar to everyone who understands statistics. That is the problem of using numbers incorrectly, such as describing the effects of a medicine that affects the heart rate or any of hundreds of other parameters by terms such as 5.434% or 5.434 beats per minute. This practice gives the veneer of being highly precise and accurate, but is often misleading and may be deceptive. Two examples of where this occurs in medicine development plans are:

1. Planning to complete a medicine study in 15.33 months.
2. Planning to submit a particular NDA in 5.72 years.

Given the number of years and number of uncertainties in medicine development, the 5.72 years is misleading and the 0.72 should be dropped or the date changed to 6 years. Alternatively, the time to NDA submission may be expressed as a range of five to six years.

Another type of unreality in medicine development plans is where an excessive number of events are described in minute detail. This is highly unrealistic because all development plans are usually modified several times before they are completed. In fact, it is more accurate to say that many medicine development plans are modified several times per year. One example of an unrealistic plan is when a highly detailed clinical plan up to the time of a medicine's marketing is established before the medicine is ever administered to humans. Another example is where a highly developed and detailed plan of all steps from Phase I through NDA submission is formulated at the time when a compound is made a project and the plans for the IND are also being developed.

Unrealistic plans may sometimes be identified by discussing how each of the outcomes would be based on the proposals and recommendations. Unrealistic ideas may be found through contradictions, unrealistic outcomes, or conflicting logic. It is always disheartening when this type of problem is discovered by a retrospective analysis instead of a prospective one.

Planning for Meetings

A calendar of all important company meetings should be established about a year in advance. This provides various advantages to individuals who must attend and assists in organizing which meetings should precede or follow others. Thus, a group or committee that presents their results to another group may schedule their meeting(s) appropriately. An international as well as national calendar may be developed. This may be done at the level of the entire company, a specific function (e.g., marketing or production), a department, and/or a section within a department (see Fig. 8.3).

Quid Pro Quo

A long-term company commitment of resources to research and discover medicines includes the responsibility for an appropriate number of research activities to succeed. This means that the heads of research and research departments, plus section heads of research departments accept accountability for discovering new medicines. Their budgets may be lightly tied to their productivity in extreme cases. This could mean that the amount of increase in a budget from year to year would depend (in part) on the number and quality of compounds that reach development. For example, there could be a minimum budget established, plus an amount based on performance within research, research and development, or within the entire company. If this practice were followed it would be necessary to prevent wide fluctuations in budgets and in head counts. Care would also have to be taken to ensure that productivity was real and that compounds were not advanced primarily to increase the research budget. One means of preventing abuses and establishing a fair system would be to use a moving five-year average in determining the number of compounds advanced for development.

Subcategories of Medicine Discovery, Medicine Development, and Line-Extensions

In addition to balancing medicine development efforts between medicine discovery, medicine development, and line-extension activities, it is necessary to balance efforts *within* each of these three major categories.

Medicine Discovery

Subcategories primarily relate to the number of therapeutic areas and diseases being researched and the depth to which each is pursued (see Chapters 20 and 27 for discussion of this topic).

Medicine Development

Subcategories refer to the number of medicines being developed, the resources applied to each, and the current stage of each project.

Line-Extensions

The subcategories used for medicine development may also be applied to line-extension activities.

Because development costs increase as a medicine progresses through the pipeline, a larger sum of money is generally spent on all of a company's medicines in Phase III than on medicines in Phases I and II. If this is not the case, a serious review of the situation should occur. It may mean that the company has (1) an insufficient number of medicines in Phase III, (2) a surfeit of medicines in Phases I and II, or (3) a serious imbalance in the allocation of resources.

Contracting Medicine Development

Many aspects of medicine development may be contracted to outside groups. For the last ten to 25 years it has been common for research-based pharmaceutical companies to contract a number of their clinical trials to contractors for completion. These contractors either conduct the studies themselves or act as middlemen to place the trials with other investigators. In the last decade there has been a gradual increase in the types of contracting services available and a steady increase in the amount of work that companies place with contractors. The major motivation in using contractors is to save time, which is especially important during periods of peak work load. In other situations (e.g., specialized toxicology studies) a company may be unable to do the work

itself. This subject is discussed in Chapter 58 of *Guide to Clinical Trials* (Spilker, 1991).

Contractors Versus Consultants

Although contractors could be considered to be consultants (and vice versa) a sharp distinction is drawn between these two groups. Consultants provide advice, opinions, evaluations, and recommendations, whereas contractors provide a service that is usually more tangible (e.g., a specific report or study). Consultants are mainly discussed in Chapter 27. Contractors are considered as for-profit businesses and therefore must also be differentiated from academicians, government agencies, and institutions that interact with pharmaceutical companies.

Locating Contractors

Locating contractors is not usually a problem for any pharmaceutical company because most contractors advertise heavily. Each relevant group (e.g., clinical, toxicological, or regulatory) should retain files of available contractors. Evaluations of their past performances, plus references and other related information, should be kept in a readily accessible place and available to appropriate staff. Ex-employees of a company often make excellent contractors for certain purposes (e.g., writing final medical reports) if they are not employed at a competing company and conflict-of-interest issues do not arise.

Services Provided by Contractors

In general, contractors are pleased to tailor their activities to the needs of the companies. Most contractors offer to provide the entire clinical trial process, including preparing a protocol, conducting the trial, editing data, entering it into computers, quality assuring the data, preparing a statistical report, and preparing a medical report. Other contractors specialize in only certain of these processes, such as entering data and preparing statistical reports. Contractors also conduct toxicology and other preclinical studies and prepare regulatory submissions, especially if there is a model for them to work from. Another role they fill is to prepare final medical reports for numerous studies using one company-prepared report as a template or model. A few contractors are willing to develop a company's entire program on a new dosage form or totally develop a new chemical entity all the way to a finished regulatory submission.

Choosing a Contractor

Issues that arise in dealing with contractors include how best to measure the time saved by using their services (before the contract is signed) versus the amount of effort required on the part of the internal staff to help the contractor initiate the project and to monitor their efforts to ensure high quality work. In some cases the efforts necessary to train contractors and to monitor their activities is almost the same as having the company's staff conduct the work themselves. In this situation any time gained by using the contractor would be minimal because company staff would have to fit the training and monitoring activities into their busy schedules. Any contractor that has previously conducted similar work for a specific company would generally require less training and should be able to conduct the work in a timely fashion. Turnover in the contractor's staff is only one of many reasons that could mitigate against this advantage.

Another issue is the importance of requesting references from potential contractors. It is relatively easy for many contractors to put a polished presentation together and give the appearance of being able to meet a company's needs. Carefully checking references of other pharmaceutical companies who have used the contractor provides invaluable information on areas to pay particular attention to and means of ensuring a successful relationship. Most professionals at pharmaceutical companies the author has contacted have been quite willing and open about providing references on consultants, contractors, or investigators. In some situations it would be worthwhile having several contractors bid for the same project. Bids should usually be judged primarily on the basis of their overall quality rather than strictly on price.

ALLOCATING RESOURCES

The most important control over allocation of resources is the initial decision to undertake a research or medicine development project. Another area of control occurs at the time of project review, which occurs on both an ad hoc and periodic basis. Reviews to discuss specifically the allocation of resources may occur at an annual, semiannual, or quarterly meeting. This review is held in addition to various others within departments and divisions (e.g., medical, technical development, and marketing).

Essential questions to pose in considering allocation of resources include (1) what will it take to achieve a specific goal, (2) are resources actually allocated according to the major criteria used, and (3) what are the rate-limiting steps in progressing toward each project?

Methods to Allocate Resources

There are several ways for senior research and development managers to review the allocation of resources on different projects and to reallocate those resources when priorities are revised. For example, in the clinical area,

managers may initially focus on projects, staff, or indications when they conduct this exercise (e.g., Fig. 30.2).

1. Start with a list of all areas where professional staff are currently allocated. Review each project and other areas (e.g., medical services, education and training, and computer services) and decide if the number of MDs, PhDs, and junior-level staff is appropriate for the next six, 12, and 18 months. Other time periods could be used. Identify staffing needs that are anticipated to occur if the project moves forward as expected. Determine the increases and decreases per project at each time point. At the end of the exercise, add up the additions and deletions of head count and determine if the net change is realistic to implement. If not, review the changes to bring them in line with totals that are considered realistic.

2. Start with the total number of MDs, PhDs, and junior-level staff available. Apportion staff to each project and then to specific tasks for the next six

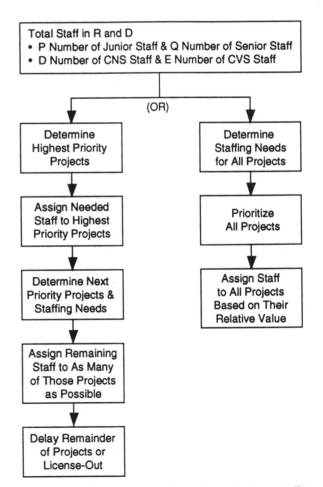

Assigning Personnel to Projects

FIG. 30.2. Different approaches to assigning staff to projects.

ASSIGNMENT OF PROJECTS TO STAFF

Projects	Names of Staff							
	A	B	C	D	E	F	...	N
1 _____	20%	100%	—	—	10%	—		—
2 _____	—	—	20%	60%	—	—		—
3 _____	50%	—	—	—	—	—		—
4 _____	—	—	50%	30%	—	100%		—
5 _____								
6 _____								
...								
N _____								

Percents equal the amount of time that a person devotes to each project.

Fig. 30.3. Assigning staff to projects, showing that a specific person may be assigned to one or more projects.

months, one year, and two years (Figs. 30.3 and 30.4). Any shortfall of staff will require hiring additional staff, cutting some projects, and/or reapportioning staff assigned to different projects. This list may then be compared with how staff are currently allocated. Discrepancies must be discussed and resolved.

3. Start with all of the indications pursued for all proj-ects. This number will be greater than the number of medicines being developed. Then assign a priority rating to each indication and follow-up by conducting the exercise described under point number two above.

4. Allocate available money to each project, therapeutic area, or indication after one of these staff allocations

ASSIGNMENT OF TASKS

Project Tasks	Names of Staff							
	A	B	C	D	E	F	...	N
1 _____	R	I	I	S	—	—		—
2 _____	S	I	I	R	S	—		—
3 _____	I	R	R	—	—	I		—
4 _____								
5 _____								
6 _____								
...								
N _____								

R = Responsible for the task.
S = Provides support for the task.
I = Informed about status of the task.

Fig. 30.4. Assigning tasks to specific staff and indicating their degree and nature of involvement with the task.

is made. This financial allocation is not done in some companies and is a way of life in others. A variation of this exercise is to limit the allocation of funds to money spent for external clinical trials or for all external grants (e.g., including toxicology).

To help achieve a balance in the allocation of funds to different research or development projects under development, one may rank the order of all projects according to the money spent over the last one, three, six, 12, or other number of months. This list of money spent and the name of each research or development project may be reviewed to see if the relative amounts of money spent is in accord with the desires of research management. The same data could also be expressed for each research or development project as (1) a percent of all money spent, (2) the total work effort in terms of months of effort, and/or (3) the percent of total work effort. Any of these analyses could be presented by an individual department, division, or other group.

Achieving a Balance Between Discovery, Development, and Line-Extensions through Allocation of Funds

When a company undergoes a period of rapid growth (or decline) in size, the balance between the three areas of research and development activity may be adversely affected. Either new staff will have to be employed (or cut) or the activities conducted will have to be modified. Research may be initiated in new therapeutic areas. The traditions of a company as well as its current strengths will provide useful bench marks to help decide where new funds should be allocated.

In allocating funds to these three functions (i.e., discovery, development, and line-extensions) money may be sent to the separate divisions responsible for conducting medicine research and development. On the other hand, the entire research and development function may receive a single pot of funds, and the head of the entire group may then allocate money to different groups. If the money allocated to research and development by the company is given as a lump sum then money may be allocated by research and development managers to those departments or projects that create the loudest noise. These are usually departments and activities closest to commercialization of products. They usually emphasize the near-term benefits to the company if funds are allocated to certain development or line-extension activities. If there are no spokesmen for research or means of protecting their resource allocation, then there may be a temptation to cut the research budget or have it grow at a low rate. These actions may appear to be reasonable, but when the total mass of the research effort decreases below a critical level, the negative impact on research productivity will usually be disproportionate and far greater than anticipated.

Allocation of Resources Based on a Medicine's Commercial Potential

Resources in research and development may only partially be allocated based on a medicine's commercial potential, assuming that a company wanted to do this. There are several reasons for this. First, only a limited number of people can work on a medicine at certain stages of its development, regardless of its commercial potential. This occurs because many medicine development activities must be conducted in a sequential order. For example, if the medicine supply is highly limited, little toxicology, clinical, or other trials can proceed until more medicine is available. When a medicine is in Phase II or III there are usually more opportunities to speed its development by adding resources (i.e., money and people). Second, the commercial potential is closely tied to the eventual clinical profile of the medicine. Until this is well known (usually in Phase III), commercial forecasts are usually best guesses and may have to be significantly modified. Commercial estimates sometimes show marked swings and it is generally unwise to crank up or down many research and development activities based on the most recent marketing values. Third, there may be problems with a medicine and only a small number of people will be able to sort through the problem and determine the outcome. Until this is done and a solution reached, most other work may have to be placed on hold, either by the company or in some cases by the Food and Drug Administration or another regulatory authority.

If resources are allocated to a project on the basis of a medicine's commercial potential after the medicine has reached Phase II, it is essential that the methods used to estimate commercial forecasts are comparable for each medicine. For example, if five projects are each estimated to have third-year postmarketing sales of $20 million, it is important to know which (if any) have a much higher potential for sales and which projects have limited potential (e.g., a range of $18 to 22 million). A single number of estimated sales (e.g., $20 million) is usually insufficient information on which to form an opinion of a medicine's commercial potential (see Chapter 35). A single number based on a set of clinical assumptions about a medicine does not indicate (1) the confidence that the marketing forecasters have in the number's accuracy, (2) the variability associated with the number's accuracy, (3) the medicine's potential to become more successful, and (4) how stable or unstable the estimate is likely to be if the medicine's profile becomes slightly modified.

Allocation of Resources Based on Therapeutic Areas

It is often desired in medicine discovery and medicine development activities to focus on and allocate resources to specific therapeutic areas. This approach may be used to emphasize the company's strengths, build up their areas of weakness, or otherwise allocate resources to certain therapeutic areas. Figure 30.5 illustrates one method of how resources applied to areas of strengths and weaknesses may be presented.

If certain therapeutic areas are identified as targets for increased (or decreased) spending over a period of time, it is important to confirm that progress is being made in that direction. Figure 30.6 illustrates one means of tracking whether or not allocations are made in the desired manner over a period of years.

Evaluating Whether Resources Are Allocated as Intended

The most direct means to evaluate whether resources are allocated as intended is to sum up retrospectively the time and effort reports separately for each group of interest (e.g., project, section, department, and division) and to compare their planned and actual work totals. These reports are usually collected as hours or weeks spent on a specific activity and may be converted to a financial total. This information may be plotted or tabulated periodically. In some cases it may be interesting to determine whether a section or department's activities paralleled those of the entire division. In that situation it would be possible to plot the percent of total effort in the entire division on a specific project over time as well as that of the department(s) in question. Other methods of evaluating the allocation of resources are shown in Chapter 35.

It is clear that data of some departments will not mirror the percent allocation of resources of the entire division. This is appropriate because the top priorities of the entire research and development group are only reflected by the time and effort spent in some departments (e.g., medical, statistics, and data processing). Other departments spend a larger proportion of their time and effort on projects that are at an early stage of their development (e.g., pharmaceutical development). Other departments vary in this regard (e.g., patents and regulatory affairs).

OTHER ISSUES

Promotions

There are many ambitious people who desire to advance in research management. In choosing individuals to promote, it is essential to determine who puts the company's interests first in their thinking and actions and who puts themselves first. The motives of all individ-

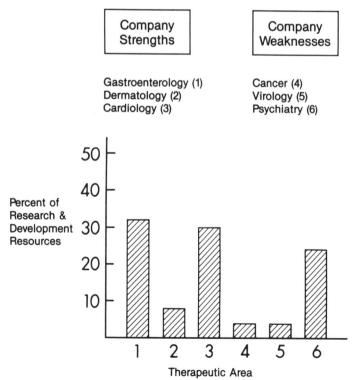

ACTIVE THERAPEUTIC AREAS IN RESEARCH & DEVELOPMENT

Company Strengths

Gastroenterology (1)
Dermatology (2)
Cardiology (3)

Company Weaknesses

Cancer (4)
Virology (5)
Psychiatry (6)

Fig. 30.5. Evaluating how research and development resources are being applied to areas of company strengths and weaknesses. The ordinate could be expressed in terms of money. This figure could illustrate any department or division of research and development.

THERAPEUTIC AREAS TO EMPHASIZE OVER NEXT TEN YEARS

Gastroenterology (1)
Infectious Diseases (2)
Cancer (3)
Dermatology (4)
Pulmonary/Respiratory (5)

ALLOCATION OF RESEARCH AND DEVELOPMENT RESOURCES

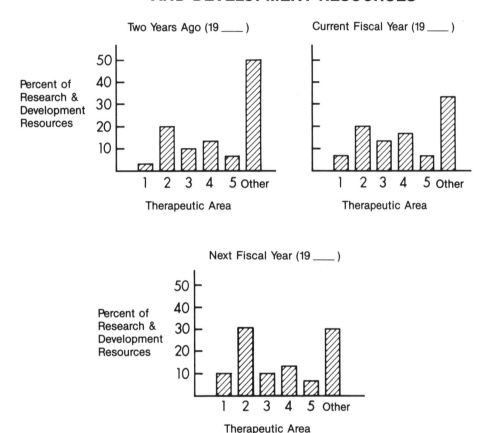

Fig. 30.6. Evaluating how research and development resources are being moved to areas of particular interest. This figure could illustrate just medicine discovery activities, medical activities, all medicine development, or any particular department or group.

uals being considered for promotions are important to evaluate. As T. S. Eliot wrote about motives in *Murder in the Cathedral,* "The greatest treason is to do the right deed for the wrong reason."

Pharmaceutical companies usually desire to make most, if not all, of their important promotions from within their company, which is excellent for morale. People who are promoted, however, sometimes rate higher in loyalty and social skills than in their abilities to help the company succeed. Thomas J. Watson, the retired chief executive of International Business Machines wrote (1987), "I never hesitated to promote someone I didn't like. The comfortable assistant—the nice guy you like to go on fishing trips with—is a great pitfall. Instead I looked for those sharp, scratchy, harsh, almost unpleasant guys who see and tell you about things as they really are. If you can get enough of them around you, and have patience enough to hear them out, there is no limit to where you can go."

Planning and Documentation

Within each company many documents are generated to provide both general and detailed plans for medicine development. Each company has its own types of plans and documents and no single set is *a priori* best. Nonetheless, there are a number of plans that are useful to generate and use.

Strategy documents of various types should be generated (see Chapter 113 in *Guide to Clinical Trials* [Spilker, 1991] and various chapters in this book). Even if they are not widely used, they force the people who prepare them to focus and organize their thoughts on critical issues. Reports to senior managers are also a useful means of keeping managers abreast of current activities, even if the reports are quite general. Various types of schedules dealing with the overall project system, individual medicine projects, and parts of medicine projects are important. Plans of current allocations and future needs for additional staff, facilities, and money are also important to document and review in a systematic way. Representative documents are described in various chapters of this book.

What Options Exist When Work on Important Projects Cannot Progress at Top Speed?

This is a common problem for productive companies and also for those able to license-in important new medicines. Some options include the following:

1. *Place some projects in a slower development mode* This may entail using a priority system. One drawback of this approach is that it may discourage scientists to whom the delayed project has great importance.
2. *License the project to another company* This has the disadvantage that it usually provides little revenue and is not usually worth doing if it is possible to develop the medicine oneself at a slower rate. This approach, however, may be more attractive to a company if it includes a cross-licensing, joint venture, or other business opportunity.
3. *Proceed with all projects a bit more slowly* This view is predicated on the fact that medicines that fail cannot be predicted in advance, and a slight delay in each (or most) may be less damaging to the company's future sales and to employee morale than other alternatives.
4. *Contract out part or all of the development program for some investigational medicines* For discrete smaller projects this may be a viable option. Otherwise, only one or a few aspects (e.g., statistical analyses) may usually be contracted out.

31 / Personnel Issues in Medicine Discovery and Development

Personnel Issues at the Overall Research and
    Development Level **329**
    Roles of Scientists 329
    Metamorphosis of One's Role Within a
        Company 330
    Career Development Opportunities 330
    Who Are the Creative Scientists? 331
    The Core Group of Highly Creative Scientists . 331
    Influence and Control of Scientists 331
Personnel Issues at a Medical Department Level **331**

Training of Physicians 331
Training of Scientists 332
Utilizing Staff Time Efficiently 332
Primary Roles of Physicians in Medicine
    Development 332
Secondary Roles of Physicians in Medicine
    Development 333
Maintaining Clinical Skills 334
Cascade Effect of Hiring a New MD or PhD ... 335

Basic research is very competitive . . . The competition starts at the lab bench. Alfred W. Alberts, Merck & Co., Inc.

If you have bright, highly motivated people who feel responsible for their work, they will discover great things. Dr. Edward M. Scolnick, Merck & Co., Inc.

[A] venture capitalist I know says, somewhat in jest, that the first thing he looks at in a business plan is the financial projection. Frankly, how anyone can figure out what sales and earnings and returns are going to be five years from now is beyond me. The first place I look is the resumes, usually found at the back. To me, they are the essence of any plan. Arthur Rock. From *Harvard Business Review* (November–December, 1987, p. 63).

PERSONNEL ISSUES AT THE OVERALL RESEARCH AND DEVELOPMENT LEVEL

Numerous issues relating to personnel are discussed in Chapter 18 (e.g., consultants, special deployment teams, task forces, and hiring professionals). Although those issues relate to corporate (i.e., general company) issues, they also relate to research and development. Issues in this chapter primarily relate to research and development.

Roles of Scientists

Scientists who discover and develop medicines have many different roles to play in a pharmaceutical company. Some are assigned one of these roles and do not deviate throughout their professional careers. Others are assigned two or more distinct roles (either simulta-

neously or sequentially) or through their own initiative take on additional roles because of apparent needs in their company.

The roles of scientists may be classified as follows:

1. *Generator of new medicine discoveries* This is usually applied to someone in a chemistry department, although some scientists who generate ideas for new medicines work in a biological department (e.g., pharmacology or microbiology) and collaborate closely with chemists to design new compounds.
2. *Evaluator of biological activity* These scientists are by definition in a biological discipline and test compounds for activity. A series of biological tests is designed systematically to progress the evaluation of new compounds over a series of hurdles (i.e., compounds that are active in one test proceed to the next test(s) and so on).
3. *Technical development scientist* Evaluations and im-

provements in several scientific areas come under this heading (e.g., formulation development, stability testing, chemical scaleup, and analytical evaluations).

4. *Project leader or project manager* One or more individuals lead the development team that takes the compound from the laboratory to the clinic and to the market.

5. *Administrator and manager* Some scientists direct the work of other scientists, review progress, and monitor activities associated with medicine development.

Scientists need to have many skills to conduct any one of these activities effectively. These skills, which include those of the entrepreneur, teacher, and diplomat, in turn usually depend on an individual's personality, interests, and abilities. These interpersonal skills may be developed, but they are not readily taught.

Metamorphosis of One's Role Within a Company

Few pharmaceutical companies allow their scientists and other professionals in research and development a great deal of flexibility in defining their roles. People who are unhappy with their roles may request a transfer to a different department, join a different company in a new role, or retrain themselves through education. At those companies that allow some professionals to redefine their roles, people who see an unmet need that they could fill may move slowly in that direction by an amoeba-like growth. Amoebas send out a small part of their cell bodies to explore a new area. If they do not encounter resistance they may move their entire cell in the new direction. A positive aspect of this approach is that the person who is exploring a new area is highly motivated to do a good job and the company will probably benefit from their activities. The negative aspects are that many people may be seeking new areas to work in and creating numerous conflicts throughout the company. If an individual is successful in the new area, he or she may be engaged in activities for which they were not hired and their original job function(s) may be inadequately performed or covered.

Career Development Opportunities

Many scientists perceive their careers as a stepwise building process where each advance made in their professional disciplines (e.g., professional publication or positive contribution to the company) is viewed as helping in their career advancement. Scientists often have overlapping careers within their pharmaceutical companies, as well as within their general discipline of science or

medicine. Outside their companies they may (1) teach courses, (2) present lectures, (3) author manuscripts, (4) conduct research, (5) engage in patient treatment, (6) serve as officers in professional societies, (7) work for a trade association, or (8) help organize and chair meetings and symposia of various types and groups.

It is ironic that the most effective and creative scientists in a pharmaceutical company may only be promoted at most pharmaceutical companies by giving them administrative responsibility and taking them out of the laboratory. This is a major issue because they are often of greatest value to the company working actively in the laboratory. This has always been a difficult personnel issue in pharmaceutical companies among ambitious senior scientists whose professional career growth has outstripped their administrative career growth. In a pyramid type of organization there are usually few positions and even fewer opportunities for promotion available that will satisfy ambitious scientists. Some companies have addressed this issue by creating a system of "half-level" promotions. This approach, however, merely serves to increase the company's bureaucracy and often complicates the career problems and possibly medicine development as well, rather than solving these issues.

Dual Career Track within a Company

To recognize differences between scientific and administrative career paths, many pharmaceutical companies have formally established two separate career tracks. A series of professional ranks is often created, possibly comparable to those of instructor, assistant, associate, and full professor in academic institutions. This approach is usually not completely successful on its own if a promotion merely represents a new title and does not bring with it other forms of recognition or changes in job responsibilities. Promotions should be accompanied by public recognition (e.g., an announcement in a company publication or a notice on the bulletin board) plus tangible benefits (e.g., dinner for the employee plus his or her spouse, a raise, or a bonus). In addition, a dual career track should allow scientists to remain active in the laboratory without taking on additional or undesired administrative functions or being penalized financially.

Another solution to the problem is to promote senior research scientists to be heads of therapeutic areas for medicine research. They are given the responsibility of supervising and directing several scientists in different scientific disciplines under a matrix approach, while at the same time remaining active as creative scientists. This type of matrix approach is superimposed on traditional department line functions. Chapters 10, 29, and 32 discuss the matrix approach further. Panel D in Fig. 29.5 illustrates one type of therapeutic area committee.

Who Are the Creative Scientists?

Creative scientists often develop an individual approach or style in how they develop their ideas and seek to reach their goals. They differ greatly from each other and do not fit a single pattern. They desire certain freedoms to pursue their own ideas, though the paths they follow are often extremely different. General goals should be established by managers for their efforts and activities. A large majority of scientists (as well as others) prefer having a clear goal and direction to follow that is supported by the company's managers and will enhance the company's overall health.

Scientists are motivated by different factors. Some of the factors that influence employees' motivation are listed in Table 13.1. One of the most frequently mentioned factors is freedom. The word freedom, however, has many definitions and applications. These include freedom to (1) choose their research topic, (2) conduct research in their own manner, (3) attend scientific meetings, (4) publish scientific research, and (5) direct a number of laboratories. Other factors that motivate scientists are the same as those affecting all employees. These include the possibility of achieving a high visibility in the company and obtaining a salary commensurate with their talents and in line with the salaries paid at other companies.

The Core Group of Highly Creative Scientists

It has been stated that a pharmaceutical company with 2,000 scientists has most of its best ideas come from approximately 1% of its scientists, or approximately 20 people. Loss of a significant number of those important staff members would have a major impact on any pharmaceutical company. Most of these scientists are well known to other scientists and managers in a company, and their identity can easily be learned by managers in other companies who are interested in obtaining this information. This means that every company is potentially vulnerable to raids on its most outstanding and important scientific staff, much as entire academic departments are sometimes raided by other universities. These creative scientists should be supported fully by the company because they are so important and valuable.

Other scientists should be encouraged to be creative, but no one can be commanded to be innovative. All scientists should be helped to achieve their highest level of creativity. From a management perspective, one means of achieving this goal is by encouraging and rewarding risk in scientific thinking and by not punishing failures. It is usually clear which people are seeking new challenges and which people are trying to avoid them. It is also usually clear which people are always advertising and promoting themselves within a company and which are primarily promoting the company's interests.

It is the author's view that a company is better off with a mediocre medicine (or idea) and great people to develop it, than to have a great medicine (or idea) and mediocre people to develop it. In medicine development (or in life) there is not sufficient time to make every mistake, even once. A company must have managers and staff who can anticipate and avoid as many problems as possible. This emphasizes the importance of hiring the best people a company can identify and attract.

Influence and Control of Scientists

Many enlightened research and development executives adhere to a laxer policy of influencing or controlling employee activities during the medicine discovery period and adhere to a more regimented policy during the medicine development period. This issue is discussed more fully in other chapters. During each of these periods, it is necessary to balance a laissez-faire attitude in which scientists are given little supervision and a regimented approach in which their efforts are tightly controlled. The balances relating to loose versus strict territorial limits and the types of barriers between departments are discussed in Chapter 27.

Control of Science by Nonscientists

There is often a strongly negative influence felt within research and development offices and laboratories when nonscientists with MBA degrees or business backgrounds become managers of research and development. Nonscientists often use an excessive amount of "foreign" jargon and apply "foreign" concepts (from the scientist's perspective) to measure and also to *control* what is going on. These efforts usually create a strongly negative reaction in scientists, similar to the fur rising on a cat's back (i.e., piloerection). It is usually in the area of control of research where the most serious issues and problems arise with nonscientist managers of research.

PERSONNEL ISSUES AT A MEDICAL DEPARTMENT LEVEL

In staffing a medical department there is a need for a wide variety of personnel with different backgrounds and orientations. There is a need for professionals with MDs, PhDs, PharmDs, and other degrees and training.

Training of Physicians

MDs are trained (in medical school hospitals) to make rapid decisions even though the information available on which to make a decision is often incomplete. This occurs frequently in the hospital care of patients and not only in medical emergency situations. Treating patients in private medical practice usually requires that treatment plans are also initiated before all relevant data can be obtained. MDs are taught to develop and use the skills of clinical judgment. This judgment is heavily based on one's prior experience and knowledge of clinical probabilities of outcomes in various situations.

Training of Scientists

PhDs and other scientists are trained quite differently than MDs. As scientists, PhDs are taught to withhold judgment(s) and decisions until they have sufficient information of adequate quality to defend their position solidly. They are taught to approach a problem logically and to solve it systematically, collecting all necessary and appropriate information.

Awareness of these general differences in training of MDs and PhDs enables one to understand better the perspective of a scientist or clinician in both approaching problems and answering questions. It also helps explain why PhD scientists have become important staff members of medical departments at pharmaceutical companies, and why a coterie of traditionally trained MDs is usually insufficient on its own to develop medicines efficiently. Both clinical and scientific perspectives are needed in medical departments. In recent years more MDs have received training in science and can now better appreciate and utilize both the clinical and scientific approaches in dealing with issues of medicine development.

Utilizing Staff Time Efficiently

Most of a MD's time at a pharmaceutical company is not spent on work that requires a MD degree to accomplish. The same is true for PhDs, although probably to a lesser extent. The issue of how companies utilize their MDs' time is answered differently at various pharmaceutical companies. Some companies put their MDs on the "front lines" and have them lead important projects, with or without responsibility for administrative duties that could be delegated.

Some companies assign a PhD to assist each MD, because the PhD is able to provide high-level scientific support. Administrative control of a project is often given to a MD. Companies with a small number of MDs often utilize them as general (or specific) consultants to deal with important medical questions or issues. In this situation, each MD assists non-MD staff on several medicine development projects at the same time. Even using these approaches, most of a MD's activities in the pharmaceutical industry do not require a MD degree to complete

successfully. On the other hand, some companies tend to put experienced PhDs in charge of medical sections and have MDs report to them. Experience has shown that this approach works well when the appropriate staffs are present.

MDs may be assigned to projects or other activities that require all of their time and are extremely challenging and fulfilling. On the other hand, this situation often does not occur, and many physicians may not be utilizing their time in a fully productive manner. One alternative to assigning each physician to a single project is to assign each to two or more different projects. This approach may also be used for clinical research assistants and other staff working in the clinical area. It often provides advantages to both the individual and the company to have them working on multiple projects, especially when there is insufficient work to do on one of those projects at all times.

Primary Roles of Physicians in Medicine Development

Physicians serve many functions in medicine development as follows:

1. Physicians serve as an important internal source for clinical opinions and advice on a wide range of issues, including (1) medical emergencies that arise involving the company's medicines, (2) serious adverse reactions to investigational or marketed medicines, (3) strategies for the marketing of the company's medicines, (4) ethical concerns that arise in various situations, and (5) medicolegal evaluations regarding product liability.
2. Physicians serve as internal experts for various aspects of clinical research, including (1) clinical feasibility of the experimental design, (2) study conduct, (3) clinical interpretation of data, (4) extrapolation of data, and (5) generation of new hypotheses to test.
3. Highly trained and experienced physicians who are both clinicians and scientists have an important role in bridging the gap in understanding that often exists between basic research and therapeutic challenges in medical practice. This role is manifested, in part, through evaluation of the potential need and place for new medicines or medical products. The MDs can comment on anticipated reactions in the medical community to proposed medicines, services, or other products.
4. Physicians function as administrators, whose activities include such responsibilities as project leadership and providing medical input on numerous committees at all levels within an organization. Many pharmaceutical companies have at least one member of their board of directors who is a physician.
5. Physicians represent the company at many meetings outside the company with regulatory authorities,

other government agencies, academicians, professional societies, trade associations, the media, and various other groups.

Many functions of a physician involve interactions with statisticians to help plan studies, analyze the data, and interpret the results. Interactions may be complicated when colleagues in a second, third, or even more countries are involved. Figure 31.1 illustrates a simple example to indicate some possible interactions.

Secondary Roles of Physicians in Medicine Development

Efficiency is believed to be enhanced in medical departments, as in almost all other departments in a pharmaceutical company, when individuals are working in areas where they are most experienced. Because of the need for clinical expertise in many areas of a pharmaceutical company, MDs are often asked to deal with issues that are outside the area of clinical trials. These activities are usually not secondary in importance to the company, but are often secondary in importance to the clinician in relation to his or her primary functions. Secondary functions of physicians in industry include some or all of the following:

1. Analyzing legal cases relating to the company's products, and acting as liaisons with the legal department and its outside attorneys.

2. Reviewing and approving the medical content of advertisements, compendium submissions, and various other documents prepared either inside or outside the medical department.
3. Corresponding with health professionals on medical questions raised by the outside health professional.
4. Holding telephone conversations with health professionals who raise medical questions and/or other problems.
5. Reviewing and approving (or denying) requests from scientists for medicine samples to be used in animal or human studies.
6. Reviewing and approving (or denying) requests from physicians who desire investigational medicines for compassionate plea protocols or use.
7. Corresponding with sales representatives on questions about marketed and/or investigational medicines.
8. Communicating with medical or other representatives of regulatory agencies.
9. Providing a medical review of compounds or medicines being evaluated for potential licensing.
10. Training new staff in the medical department.
11. Preparing annual reports on marketed medicines for the Food and Drug Administration.
12. Hosting guest speakers and other visitors from outside the company.
13. Speaking to various organizations on medical aspects of medicine development.

INTERACTIONS AMONG CLINICIANS & STATISTICIANS AT DIFFERENT SITES OF ONE COMPANY

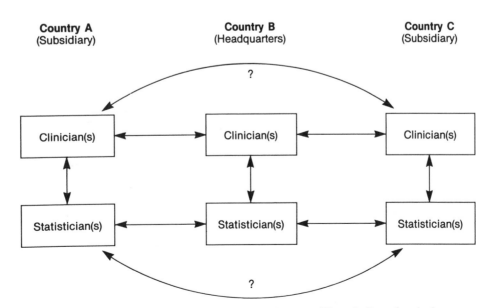

FIG. 31.1. Interactions among clinicians and statisticians at different sites of a single company.

In many larger pharmaceutical companies some or all of these issues are handled by specialized groups, either within or outside the medical area. Although it may improve efficiency to have a separate group of non-MDs handle most of these issues, difficult questions should still be handled by the company's medical experts. Non-MDs who concentrate on these areas often perform these activities as well as or better than trained medical personnel, who often view these requests for assistance as interruptions of their major work.

Maintaining Clinical Skills

Over a period of years, it is natural for physicians in the pharmaceutical industry to become less sensitive and

SUPPORT AND SERVICES REQUIRED
WHEN AN ADDITIONAL MD JOINS THE STAFF

WITHIN THE MEDICAL DEPARTMENT:

Added Administrative Support

*Secretarial Services
*Administrative Services

Added Technical Support

*Monitors
*Technical Assistants

WITHIN THE RESEARCH & DEVELOPMENT DIVISION:

Added Statistical Support

*Planning Studies
*Reviewing Protocols
*Analyzing Data

Added Management Support

*Reviews of Any New Projects
    Assigned to MD

**Any Project Added for MD
To Develop**

*Many Other Departments Affected

Drug Development Laboratories

*Synthesis of Study Drug
*Packaging of Study Drug
*Shipment of Study Drug

Information and Data Processing Support

*Data Editing and Entry into Computers
*Data Tabulations
*Library Services
*Data Documentation, Storage, and Retrieval

Other

*Regulatory Affairs
*Preclinical Sciences

OUTSIDE THE RESEARCH & DEVELOPMENT DIVISION:

Corporate Affairs

*Personnel/Benefits
*Employee Health
*Payroll
*Parking and Local
    Transportation

*Cafeteria
*Printing
*Photography
*Purchasing
*Travel

*Design Graphics
*Engineering
*Training Programs
*Others

Other Groups

*Legal
*Marketing
*Patents

FIG. 31.2. Support and services required when a MD joins the staff of a pharmaceutical company. This illustrates the cascade or pyramid-like effect of hiring a MD to initiate clinical trials.

aware of many medical issues and subtleties faced by practicing physicians with their patients. In fact, clinical skills atrophy over time when they are not actively used. In addition, medical practice changes rapidly in many therapeutic areas. Thus, as the physician in industry becomes more skilled within his or her administrative and research-scientist roles, he or she simultaneously loses those clinical skills that were developed during medical training and practice. Many physicians function less skillfully as clinical researchers and medical consultants over time because they have been away from the trenches and direct hands-on activities with patients. These were the very experiences that originally provided them with the knowledge and experience they needed and used in designing protocols, providing medical advice, and interpreting data.

Companies handle this problem in a variety of ways. One of the most common approaches is to hire numerous physicians and to accept a relatively rapid or frequent turnover of personnel. In this manner, it is always possible to have some recently trained clinicians on hand. Obviously, such an approach has substantial drawbacks and cannot meet all of a company's needs for current information.

A short period of intensive clinical exposure would enable some company physicians to retain and further develop medical acumen and skills. These skills are critical to the optimum functioning of their clinical and advisory roles. This goal could be achieved in several ways, including a one- to three-month ward rotation every number of years. These short sabbatical periods would provide benefits both to the company and the physicians that could not be achieved by attending professional meetings, conferences, and seminars. Another possibility is for the company to encourage its physicians to spend one or even two days per week at a local hospital where their clinical skills could be maintained. These approaches would stimulate the physicians in addition to accomplishing several other goals (see Chapter 61). There are already pharmaceutical companies that follow this practice (e.g., Burroughs Wellcome Co. and Boehringer Ingleheim Corp.). Other companies offer their MDs a half or whole day per week at a local hospital, but some discourage their MDs from fully utilizing this time.

Cascade Effect of Hiring a New MD or PhD

The effect of an additional person hired into a pharmaceutical company differs depending both on the specific department and on the person's position. The general effects of hiring a MD into a medical department are indicated in Fig. 31.2. This illustrates that other departments are affected. The MD who is initiating clinical trials probably requires more additional support throughout the company than any other single person hired into a pharmaceutical company at an entry level. This additional support is in terms of the work generated in other departments. Hiring a single MD would probably not require additional staff to be hired in other departments, although their work load would increase.

A MD who is hired into a medical department will (under most situations) plan and initiate clinical trials. These studies in turn demand additional services and technical support in many areas of the company. A PhD scientist hired into a research department at a comparable level to the MD usually has much less impact on the resources of a company. If a company hires two or more additional MDs at one time, they have to be prepared and willing to deal with the cascade effect seen in other departments that occurs approximately six months to a year later.

32 / Balancing Line Function and Matrix Approaches

Definitions and Background 337
   General Description of a Matrix 337
   Levels within an Organization at Which
      Matrix Groups May Function 338
Key Players in a Matrix System 339
   Overseeing a Matrix System 339
   Project Team Leaders 339
   Project Team Managers 341
   Utilizing Project Managers Versus Project
      Leaders 341
   Project Team Members 341
   Project Coordinators/Planners 342
Initiating New Projects 342
   Initiating Projects in a Multinational
      Pharmaceutical Company 342
   Types of Projects Initiated 342

Number of Projects Initiated 342
Getting a Project Off the Ground and Moving
   Ahead 343
Keys to Project Team Success 343
Project Team Meetings 344
Establishing a Strong Versus Weak Matrix 344
   Characteristics of a Strong Matrix 344
   Characteristics of a Weak Matrix 345
   Problems and Issues of a Weak Matrix 345
   The Matrix Network 345
   Conflict-of-Interest Issues in a Matrix
      Organization 345
   Having Little Turf or Line Authority May Be a
      Source of Strength 347
Golden Rules of Project Management 347

Because change is so rapid it is not uncommon for an individual in midcareer to find that the hierarchy is passing him by. In other words, he has climbed part way up the ladder and feels competent. He stops to rest, but rapid technological change goes on. He intends to catch up, but when he tries he is technologically obsolete. He has become uneducated for his job simply by standing still. Laurence J. Peter. From *The Peter Prescription.*

DEFINITIONS AND BACKGROUND

General Description of a Matrix

The management hierarchy present in almost all companies is referred to as line management. This is the so-called pyramid or vertical system where people report to others above them in a chain of command. There is a second management system referred to as the matrix or horizontal system that is used for medicine development by most medium and large pharmaceutical companies, as well as by some smaller pharmaceutical companies. In this system each new medicine and line-extension of a medicine that is being developed is called a project. The progress of each project is planned, facilitated, and reviewed by an interdisciplinary group of members referred to as the project team. People who perform the work on a medicine, or who are responsible for the work, may be the project team member or may informally report to the team member from their department or discipline. The disciplines represented on most projects include pharmacology, toxicology, technical development areas (e.g., chemical development and pharmaceutical development), statistics, regulatory affairs, project planning, and medicine. At some pharmaceutical companies the project team also includes marketing- and business-oriented members. Each team has a leader who reports (possibly on an informal basis) to an individual who then reports either through line management or directly to the head of research and development.

The matrix system represents a second reporting relationship. At some companies this reporting relationship is formal, and this may lead to conflicts with line managers. A major technique used to avoid these conflicts is to have matrix-reporting relationships loose and informal. Interpersonal skills, diplomacy, tact, and above all, a desire for this system to work are required to have a successful system.

The major aspects of developing medicines using a project-driven matrix management approach may be broken down into various components. Cleland (1984) has proposed nine elements in this philosophy, which are shown in Fig. 32.1.

Levels within an Organization at Which Matrix Groups May Function

The matrix function usually is most visible in a company when it is used to develop new medicines toward an Investigational New Drug Application (IND) and a New Drug Application (NDA). A matrix approach to management also functions at several other levels within a company. At the most general level, the matrix concept may be used to organize an entire company. Chapter 10 describes various organizational aspects of this approach. Figure 10.3 illustrates how this concept can be used to organize a company, and Fig. 29.3 illustrates the use of a matrix approach for organizing a research and development group.

Internationally

At the international level, members from various countries, who are part of a multinational company, work on teams (or committees). Such teams exist and operate at different levels of the company's hierarchy. This topic is discussed further in Chapter 60. These teams may be concerned with international policies, strategies, plans, and/or activities. These groups or teams may focus on one or more of the following functions: establishing, monitoring, reviewing, problem solving, or coordinating. In many ways, the board of directors, which is composed of both staff members and senior line managers from different countries, is a matrix function.

ELEMENTS OF A PROJECT-DRIVEN MATRIX

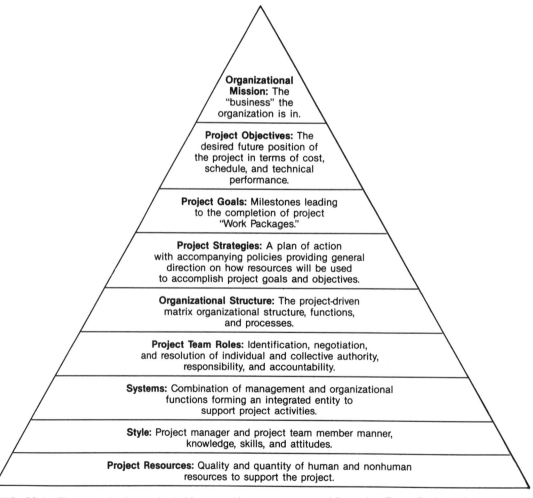

FIG. 32.1. Elements in the project-driven matrix management philosophy. From *Project Management Journal* (Cleland, 1984) with permission of Project Management Institute.

It is the team that operates at the company's highest level.

Nationally

Many types of matrix groups function at the national level. There are numerous areas where people from different disciplines get together outside the traditional hierarchical structure of the company. Most of these groups have other names, such as task forces, and many are used on a temporary basis. All issues and functions described under the international level may also operate at the national company level.

Medicine Development

This level relates to the project groups (i.e., teams) that are planning and carrying out the many activities of medicine development. Project teams may be national and/or international in their make-up. Figure 29.3 illustrates how project teams report in a matrix organization. This is the activity that is usually referred to when one reads about project groups or teams in the pharmaceutical industry.

Research Projects

The matrix approach within research and development may be used to assist medicine discovery as well as medicine development activities. For medicine discovery, an independent team of scientists from different disciplines and/or departments (e.g., chemistry, biochemistry, pharmacology, and microbiology) may work together on a formal or informal basis. This group may focus its efforts and goals on one or more therapeutic areas (e.g., cardiology and gastroenterology), diseases (e.g., angina and sickle cell disease), physiological effects (e.g., to shift the oxygen dissociation curve to the right), biochemical effects (e.g., to stimulate or inhibit a specific enzyme), or pathological effects (e.g., to prevent necrosis from developing in ischemic tissues). This group may have a member who helps the team by (1) coordinating its activities, (2) monitoring its progress, (3) communicating its activities and results to senior management, (4) drawing up plans for advanced testing of active compounds, and (5) helping to facilitate the resolution of disputes or other issues. Various organizational structures used for medicine discovery are shown in Fig. 29.5 and are discussed in Chapter 29. The matrix approach tends to be more informal at the early stages of medicine discovery and more structured at later phases of preclinical research when a specific compound is being evaluated and considered for further development.

KEY PLAYERS IN A MATRIX SYSTEM

Overseeing a Matrix System

At both national and international levels, it is generally valuable to have a small department oversee the matrix system. The functions of this department would include planning, monitoring, troubleshooting, and facilitating solutions to problems. Other major activities could include generating financial records (e.g., tracking project costs), conducting analyses of the project system, and serving as a source to collect and analyze archival information.

At each level where one or more matrix groups may function, there may be an individual who is assigned the role of coordinating activities. This person may or may not be a member of the individual project teams. If no one is assigned this coordinating responsibility, it becomes the function of the groups' leaders and/or line managers. In addition to the person who coordinates activities, any department with a representative on the team may also have a separate individual (or group) that coordinates all activities and all studies conducted within their department.

Most pharmaceutical companies benefit if they have an individual who has few line managerial responsibilities in charge of coordinating and improving the efficiency of international medicine development and project-related activities. This person receives information about activities and problems from all medicine development groups. He or she provides input where needed to keep communications lines operational and ensures that all relevant groups are communicating effectively.

Project Team Leaders

The leader of a project team is usually appointed by one or more senior managers through either a formal or informal mechanism. A project team may have a single leader for its entire life, but often there are two or more leaders, although at different points in the project's life. One common pattern is to have a preclinical scientist lead a project until an IND is filed and clinical trials are initiated. The project is then turned over to a clinician who leads the project until the NDA is approved. After that point a marketing-oriented individual is appointed to lead the project. A separate project team of primarily different members who focus on production and marketing issues may be created at any time, but this is likely to occur during Phase III (Fig. 32.2). The advantage of forming a separate team in production and/or marketing is that it enables each group to function more efficiently because each is primarily concerned with different activi-

LEADERSHIP OF A PROJECT TEAM

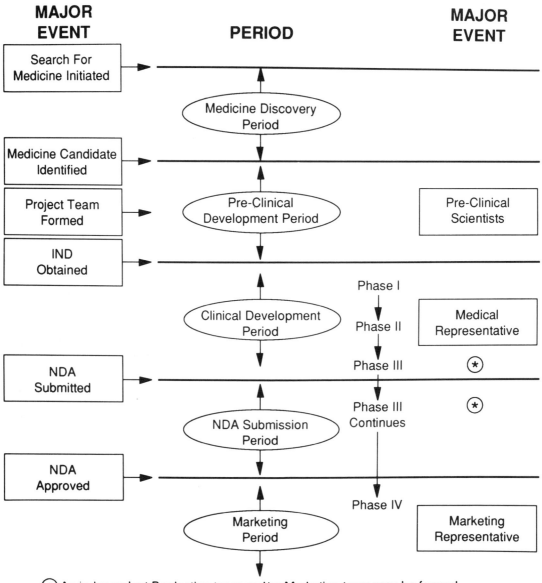

FIG. 32.2. Leadership of a project team as it changes from a preclinical scientist to clinical scientist and to a marketer. IND, Investigational New Drug Application; NDA, New Drug Application.

ties. A few people, especially the project team leaders, should be on both (or all) teams. This helps ensure close coordination of efforts. The same principles apply to a research and development team established in two separate countries where the medicine is being developed (see Chapter 60).

Project leaders are often viewed as project champions. To obtain project leaders who are effective project champions it is important that project leadership be viewed as a privilege and honor rather than a burden or as a reward

for other services or work. If people are merely rewarded for their hard work in their own discipline by being made a project leader, it is more likely that they will not do as effective a job as those people chosen because they are the best candidates. Individuals who are most highly motivated to act as project champions are often chosen as project leaders.

Numerous advantages and disadvantages of this approach exist. See *Guide to Clinical Trials* (Spilker, 1991) for details.

Project Team Managers

A totally different approach to providing project leadership is practiced by those companies that have project managers. These individuals are not primarily scientists or clinicians, but are full-time managers of a small number of projects. Managers are chosen for their administrative ability to move projects ahead rapidly, efficiently, and in the desired direction. Good project managers are independent, aggressive, and objective; pay attention to detail; and have a high level of interpersonal skills. They usually have a scientific or medical background because some scientific training is usually important for their success with new chemical entity projects. People with a PhD or MD are desirable candidates, if they also possess the other characteristics described. Individuals with a business, production, or marketing background could also be suitable candidates for selected types of projects (e.g., over-the-counter medicines, marketed prescription medicines, and Phase III medicines), especially if they have demonstrated the requisite skills and talents. The differences in focus between project managers and line managers on a project are shown in Fig. 32.3.

Utilizing Project Managers Versus Project Leaders

Major advantages of having project managers rather than project leaders are that the managers do not have commitments to line-function managers, and do not have the responsibility of also running a program in their own discipline (e.g., the medicine's entire clinical program). Therefore, they have more time to devote to administrative issues and other matters outside their discipline than do project leaders. Project managers also will tend to be more objective and independent about decisions they make. Managers are also desirable to use when a company has too few project champions or when it is difficult for champions to cross department boundaries to have work accomplished.

It is the author's opinion that most companies will utilize project managers rather than project champions/project leaders in the future. The project managers are professionals whose job is to achieve the project's goals and whose performance is judged by the success of this effort. The project leader is often an "amateur" at leading the project, and his or her line managers (i.e, supervisors) may resent the time spent on directing a project, especially if it interferes with the higher priorities of the manager. It is inefficient for a company continually to train new champions for a long period before they become effective project leaders. Moreover, project leaders focus their energies on achieving their discipline or function goals. It is ironic that many of the best project leaders have insufficient time to devote to running their project because of their almost total commitment to their line-function responsibilities.

Individual Project Plan

FIG. 32.3. Illustrating the different orientation of a line manager and project manager for conducting work on an individual project. Each manager generally has interest in the entire pyramid but focuses his or her attention on the specific portion shown.

Alternative Approaches

Two alternative systems to utilizing a pure project leader or project manager system are:

1. *A transition system* One example of a transition system is when project leaders head projects from their inception through the Phase II go–no go decision point. Once this decision is reached, the project is turned over to a project manager who leads the project administratively until the medicine is marketed. The ex-project leader usually continues to remain active on the project within his or her discipline (e.g., clinical research). This system has the disadvantage that the transition occurs at one of the busiest times in the project's life.

2. *A combination system* An example of a combination system is to have project leaders focus on scientific and policy issues (e.g., strategies and objectives) and an assistant project leader who focuses on administrative issues (e.g., planning, tracking, writing reports, and troubleshooting). Each person who has this role could assist from one to six or so project leaders, depending on the work load within each project.

Project Team Members

It should be clear to the project leader (or manager) why each member of their team was appointed. The reasons could include (1) providing invaluable expertise, (2) providing an opportunity to learn about a new activity or therapeutic area, or (3) being drafted because no one else was interested, available, or willing to serve. Some teams change their membership rather frequently as the project goes through various stages along the medicine development pipeline. If there is any confusion about who is actually on the team, this issue should be rapidly settled by the project leader. This is usually resolved through discussions with project members, department heads, or senior managers. Some companies appoint department heads to serve as members of a project team, but most companies appoint more junior personnel.

Project Coordinators/Planners

An important member of the project team is the person who serves as navigator for the project. Whereas the project leader serves as the captain, each project needs an individual to draw up plans, track progress, and help ensure that the project remains on course. This individual raises a red flag when the project goes astray or runs into problems. This individual usually reports to a separate department of project coordination or project management and has limited authority to facilitate a solution to problems or issues.

The role of project coordinator is not clearly defined at most companies, which has both advantages and disadvantages. The advantages include the ability to be more effective in expediting those services most needed by the project (e.g., tracking the writing and reviewing of various reports, tracking medicine use and need, and following competitors' activities). The disadvantages include the ability of the project leader (1) to exclude this individual from information needed to perform his or her role effectively, (2) to ignore their role and work, and (3) to have another individual in the project leader's discipline carry out much of this work. Solutions for the coordinator often relate to finding those services that the project leader desires and can utilize in running the project. If a project manager is running the project, then a project coordinator may act as an assistant project manager. Another approach to a solution is to strengthen the matrix system so that the responsibilities of the coordinator are more clearly defined.

INITIATING NEW PROJECTS

Initiating Projects in a Multinational Pharmaceutical Company

One of the most basic issues in a project system is whether or not a compound must meet formal criteria prior to elevation to project status. These criteria could be established in terms of scientific profile, medical need, and commercial value. If a multinational company develops medicines at two or more separate sites, it is possible that new projects may be only established or initiated by the central headquarters, or initiation may occur at each of the semi-independent sites developing medicines. If the latter situation prevails, then it must be determined how each site is to react to projects initiated by the other sites. Their reactions could be to do nothing except to follow the new project's progress, to form an independent group that would also develop the medicine, or to develop an international project team. Another approach to establishing new projects is to require joint approval of new projects by all sites where the medicine will be developed.

Types of Projects Initiated

Some companies believe in one type of medicine project, i.e., all investigational medicines are intended to be marketed unless work is terminated by toxicity, by lack of efficacy, or for another reason. Other companies or even a different site within the same company may believe that some projects should be established to test a theory, even though it is known that the compound being tested will not become a marketed medicine. The author believes that this second type of project should not be initiated by pharmaceutical companies, except if considered extremely important, and then only on a limited basis.

Number of Projects Initiated

How should a company react if a very large number of compounds simultaneously come through internal discovery activity and are proposed for development and eventual marketing? The first principle is that everything possible should be done to make the staff who are proposing the new compounds for project status feel that their accomplishments are greatly appreciated and will lead to success for the company. At the same time, it is important to stress that the company's resources are stretched and cannot presently pay adequate attention to each. The scientists should be encouraged to learn more about their compound in toxicology, metabolism, and other areas of preclinical science before it is made a project. While this may cause a delay in the progress of the project, it increases the amount of data to be collected before a compound is made into a project.

Another generally less desirable approach is to fill the project system to overflowing in the expectation that a number of projects will drop out and allow the best projects to continue. While this assumption is valid, the danger is that this approach to creating a project portfolio will slow development of the highest priority projects. A counterargument is to assign the new project a low priority. However, this usually sanctions the project for a longer life than if higher standards are used, and the compound continues competing to achieve those standards.

Some people might propose licensing the compound to another group, but this is rarely a worthwhile strategy at the early stage described. Even if the company has other similar medicines in development it is uncertain which will ultimately be the best and the most successful. In addition, the royalties received are relatively small compared to the financial return if the company developed the medicine itself.

Getting a Project Off the Ground and Moving Ahead

Some of the many issues that must be dealt with in starting a new project and maintaining the momentum of existing ones include:

1. *Authority* Where is it and how will it be used? How much is the direct authority of those involved and how much is indirectly derived by personal or reporting connections to those who have direct authority? Also, are there people who exert authority although there is no evidence that they have a right to do so, i.e., that authority was delegated to them from more senior managers? If a project team is composed of department heads or more senior managers, this will not be an issue, whereas if junior people are members it may represent a major problem.
2. *Communication* What are the processes and mechanisms to be used in communicating both to higher and lower levels in the company? Are they operating efficiently? How could they be improved?
3. *Decision making* Who makes decisions at each level in the company and how are they made? Are issues raised for debate as a "front" after the real decision has been made? For example, does the medical representative ask for views about conducting a certain study at a project meeting after the protocol has been written and the investigator chosen?
4. *Review* How are activities reviewed by managers at various levels in the company? How does the project group review its activities?
5. *Priorities* How are priorities established and by whom? Are they in harmony at different levels of the company and between different departments at the same level?
6. *Resources* How are resources allocated? How are conflicts handled? Conflict-of-interest issues are discussed separately in this chapter.
7. *Commitment* What is the real commitment by senior managers to the project? Where does the project fit on the scale ranging from "no interest" to "vital for the company's survival."
8. *Team assessment* Are members assessed by how well

they represent their function as a sort of ambassador, or by how well they push the project ahead within their discipline and meet their responsibilities? Are project members and leaders only assessed by line managers or is there an additional assessment through the project system, i.e., by an appropriate manager of the matrix system?

Each project tends to develop its own style and rhythm after it has been operating for a period of time. This style is influenced by individuals on the team, the importance and nature of the medicine being developed, and many other factors. There is often a striking difference between the project leader and line managers in how they view a particular project. Senior research and development managers must view the entire project portfolio and assign a priority and resources to each. Priorities may be given in an informal understanding or using a formal system. Many projects often receive a lower priority and fewer resources than the project group and project leader believe appropriate. This same discrepancy sometimes occurs at the corporate level, where the board of directors and/or chief executive officer may not view the project portfolio, or a selected project, with the same degree of enthusiasm or caution as senior research and development managers. If this occurs, the reasons should be evaluated.

Valuable opportunities for the company could be lost if corporate executives are not provided sufficient information and appropriate education to understand relevant scientific and clinical information. On the other hand, it is also important for senior research and development managers to understand fully the overall corporate perspective. These topics are discussed in more detail in *Guide to Clinical Trials* (Spilker, 1991).

Keys to Project Team Success

The project team is the central concept underlying the matrix system. The team depends on cooperation for success, as does the entire matrix concept. Without cooperation within the team and within the company, the matrix system tends to break down. One or two senior managers who place their own power base and personal considerations above the company's interests can severely damage or even destroy a matrix. This is especially true for a weak matrix.

Successful project teams have the appropriate people on them in terms of experience, skills, and authority. It is also desirable, although not essential, that members work within close physical proximity. The team's overall performance depends on several factors that relate to the team.

1. *Roles and relationships* Each person on a team should understand his or her role in having the proj-

ect progress and achieve its goals. Their relationships with other project team members should be clear as well as their relationship with the department they represent.

2. *Goals* The goals of a project team should be clearly defined and communicated, both to its members and to others. It is usually preferable, although not mandatory, for the team to propose their goals and to request the endorsement of senior management.

   Alternatively, goals may be established by more senior managers. Even in that situation, the team itself would establish many of the more detailed goals that would be required to achieve the major ones. For example, if the major criteria for the medicine to achieve in a certain disease state are established by senior managers, the components of those criteria and the appropriate paths to reach those goals may be established by the project team.

3. *Processes* Processes refer to the mechanisms utilized to achieve a team's goals. They include the plans, schedules, and procedures that a team uses. Although the general approach may be dictated by a company, it is still possible for a team to utilize creativity and imagination in how they achieve their goals. A suitable motto for many teams would be "whatever it takes," i.e., they will do whatever it takes to achieve their goals. This may involve putting in longer hours, working weekends, brainstorming to find a creative solution to a difficult problem, or reaching a compromise solution with the team working on the same project at a different company site.

4. *Relationship with the company* The team must operate in the context of the company's environment. To work effectively it must work in harmony and not at cross purposes with the company's structure, culture, and lines of authority and power.

Project Team Meetings

Team meetings are held periodically at some companies and on an ad hoc basis at others. The author favors the latter approach, although a minimum number of meetings may be required each year. A more pertinent issue is whether project meetings are held for the purpose of (1) information exchange, (2) problem solving, or (3) strategic planning. In the former approach, each relevant person usually presents a brief or full report of the project's status in his or her department. This is generally an inefficient use of people's time and there are other ways (e.g., reports) to fulfill this need. It is better to use people's time discussing and debating either problems or project strategies, plans, tactics, and goals. This latter approach helps to build consensus. Nonetheless, it is vital that the discussion is directed by the project leader and is not allowed to wander aimlessly. The project

TABLE 32.1. *Sample project meeting agenda*

Issue	Initials of presenter	Time allotted (minutes)
Technical issues		
Progress on new formulation		
Pharmaceutical report	AB	10
Toxicology report	BC	15
Marketing report	CD	10
Clinical issues		
Update on indication I	DE	5
Update on indication II	EF	10
Safety issues	DE	15
Data management report	FG	5
Regulatory issues		
Bioequivalence issue	GH	10
Other issues	HI	10
Project coordination		
NDA plans	IJ	10

leader should usually establish alternatives and determine the pros and cons ahead of time. He or she may have already chosen the "best" approach and may have lobbied several members prior to the meeting. A sample project meeting agenda is shown in Table 32.1.

Brief action items or points should be used as minutes, along with a list of who is responsible for each. These could be reviewed at the end of the meeting and then sent with copies of relevant overhead projections, or other material, as project minutes. It is well known that traditional project minutes are filed and rarely read or referred to by most project members.

ESTABLISHING A STRONG VERSUS WEAK MATRIX

The terms "strong" and "weak" refer to the relative importance and power of line managers and project managers. In a strong matrix the balance of power favors the project manager and in a weak matrix it favors the line manager.

Characteristics of a Strong Matrix

There is a continuum from strong to weak matrices. A strong matrix is usually characterized by (1) a formal dual reporting relationship, (2) authority of project leaders to control resources and make decisions on resource allocation, (3) assigning budgets to each project where the funds are controlled by individual project leaders, and (4) having project leaders reviewed by the head of the matrix system. Target dates are more meaningful to use as goals in a strong rather than in a weak matrix. A strong matrix requires more documentation of activities and more time spent on administrative matters. More emphasis is placed on costs and accountability for costs. People are also held accountable for slippage in time as well as cost overruns.

Advantages of a strong matrix are that it (1) gives a clear organization and direction to the project, (2) avoids ambiguity for project members, (3) allows for judging progress more clearly against a plan, and (4) minimizes the chance of people going off on tangents.

Characteristics of a Weak Matrix

A weak matrix is characterized by almost none of the above characteristics, except that an informal dual reporting relationship exists. The head of the matrix system has no real authority in a weak matrix. Relationships in a matrix between project leaders and (1) project members, (2) project coordinators, and (3) the head of the matrix are weak and almost totally controlled by line managers.

Advantages of a weak matrix are that it (1) is highly flexible, (2) avoids problems of dual reporting relationships, (3) works well if everyone cooperates, and (4) allows people to operate in their most effective manner and utilizes their internal drive.

Problems and Issues of a Weak Matrix

A major disadvantage of a weak matrix is that individual project leaders cannot easily obtain resources. In addition, they have little or no authority when they negotiate for additional resources with line managers. If a project leader also has a position of line authority, this issue is less important, but for those project leaders who do not have the "requisite" line authority it may become an even greater issue (see conflict-of-interest section below).

Another issue in a weak matrix is that project leaders feel less need to inform the head of the matrix system about their problems or to solicit help in addressing them. As a result, less information about problems may filter up through the organization. This may lead to various other problems because an important responsibility of a matrix group is to supply information, as well as to help a project move forward. It is easier for project leaders and project members to hide or suppress information if the matrix system is weak. This suppression is usually intended to be "temporary, of course," until the problem is resolved within their department, but the problem may become worse and a crisis situation may occur. Thus, project leaders may take their project in an unapproved direction (purposely or inadvertently) and not inform relevant people.

One way of determining if a matrix is too weak for a company is to ask if senior managers are promptly informed about problems or if they are often surprised. Are senior managers informed about problems by line managers who hear the news directly from the project leader? Does the project leader also inform the head of the matrix system?

There are many possible approaches to consider in addressing the issue of a weak matrix. One is to have the central matrix group continually track the progress of all projects and periodically report on any significant delays or problems. Another possibility is for the project leader or project manager periodically to report any and all delays in the project's timetable plus any significant issues to senior managers.

The Matrix Network

Project coordination staff within research and development may be the only matrix staff in a company and would interact directly with all company project teams and all project team representatives. Alternatively, the company may have project coordinators in one or more areas (Fig. 32.4). The most obvious areas for a company to have coordinators are where other project teams have been formed (e.g., production, marketing, and over-the-counter medications).

The coordinator's function outside the central group could be fulfilled by a single individual who interacts with all project team staff in his or her area. Alternatively, the central coordinator in the outside ring of Fig. 32.4 could interact with other coordinators within the discipline or function (Fig. 32.5). Another possibility is that some or all of these disciplines could have multiple coordinators, each responsible for a group of projects. Each of these disciplines based on coordinators would interact with appropriate project coordination staff (Fig. 32.6). Figures 32.5 and 32.6 show two models of interactions for project coordinators and technical development coordinators, but many variations are possible.

Conflict-of-Interest Issues in a Matrix Organization

The matrix system has a number of inherent characteristics that sometimes lead to conflict-of-interest situations. One of those situations involves section heads who are also project leaders or managers. Conflicts of interest result from the desire of some managers to assign a disproportionate number of available personnel to their own project and fewer head count to other projects in their section. This bias exists when assignment of personnel would not be considered appropriate by an independent reviewer. This bias can generally be easily justified by the section head with numerous rationalizations. If a department head is also a project leader, the temptation to move his or her own project rapidly ahead at the expense of other projects will generally be strong. It may be difficult for senior managers to perceive how the biases of section or department heads have affected the

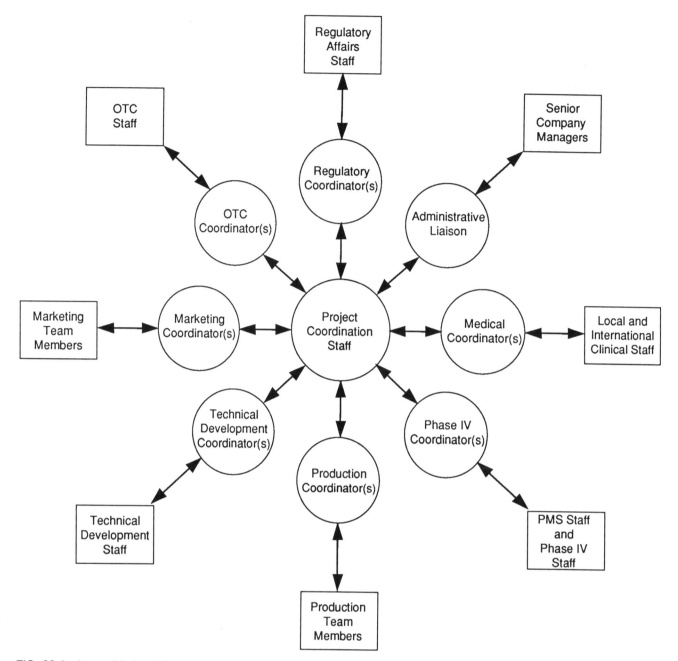

FIG. 32.4. A possible basis for establishing project coordinators within selected functions or disciplines to interact with the central project coordination function—usually within research and development. Models describing relationships between the central and a peripheral group are shown in the next two figures.

allocation of resources among projects because of the many rationalizations and justifications that may be raised.

Another conflict-of-interest issue derives from the fact that a matrix gains its strength at the expense of line managers. There is an inverse relationship between the authority and power of line managers and matrix managers. This means that line managers must agree to give up some of their "turf" when a matrix system is either established or strengthened. This places an obvious conflict-of-interest issue out in the open. If line managers agree to strengthen the matrix system, it is clear that they will lose at least some of their power and influence. Thus, they usually present reasons why the matrix should remain unchanged or even be weakened. It takes an extraordinary line manger to recommend strengthening the matrix system. This person is usually one who places the company's interests above his or her own territoriality. Usually that individual is a secure, self-confident person whose main motive is not personal "empire-building," but rather productive corporate building.

Project Coordination Staff

Technical Development Coordinators

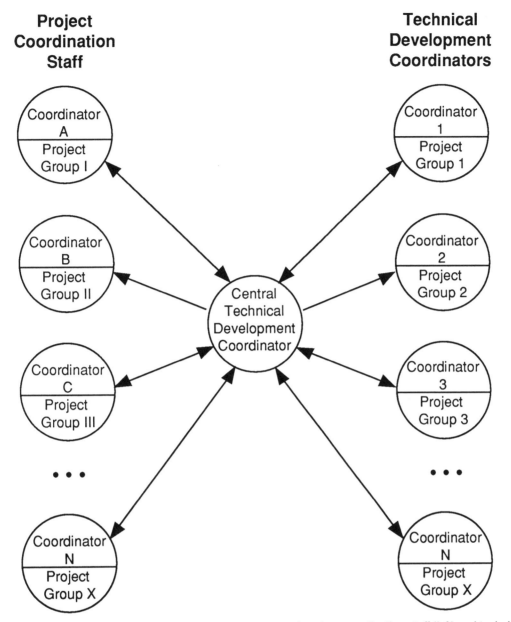

FIG. 32.5. A model for the interaction between the central project coordination staff (*left*) and technical development coordinators (*right*).

Having Little Turf or Line Authority May Be a Source of Strength

Managers in an organization are almost invariably concerned about retaining and expanding their power. Because many people believe that a good defense is a strong offense, there is usually a great deal of maneuvering, posturing, and infighting within any large company in an attempt to secure one's power base and to gain additional power. In a weak matrix system there is little power along the horizontal axis so that matrix managers do not have to be as concerned as line managers about protecting their turf. These managers may therefore

spend more of their energies identifying problems and also finding solutions to them.

GOLDEN RULES OF PROJECT MANAGEMENT

A number of golden rules are presented below and other golden rules of planning are presented in the full chapters on golden rules in this book and in *Guide to Clinical Trials* (Spilker, 1991).

1. Have representatives of major sites create a single international plan for each compound and medicine at the start of its development. If agreement between

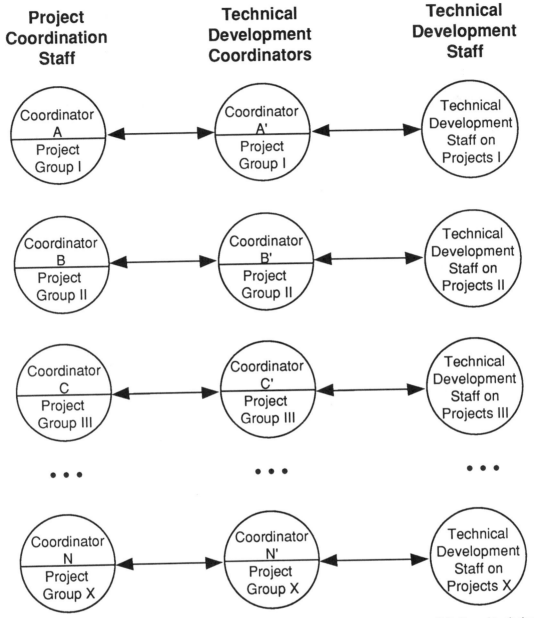

FIG. 32.6. A model for the interaction between the central project coordination staff (*left*) and technical development coordinators (*right*).

sites on a single plan is unobtainable, then individual plans may be required for each site participating in the medicine's development. In that circumstance coordinate plans as well as possible. Local (i.e., individual country) plans are also required.

2. Attempt to create as detailed routes for the medicine's development as possible. This usually means a single overall plan, one for each major group (research and development, marketing, and production), and one for each major division or department (e.g., toxicology, medical, regulatory affairs, and market research). If a road map outlining the routes to the major point of the trip (marketing) is impossible, then create the route through Phase I or

II and complete it when possible. If a road map is not possible in a few unusual cases then create a navigational chart for the team to use in steering the project.

3. All plans must have flexibility but not excess slack. They must be designed and endorsed so that they are taken seriously.

4. Provide realistic dates with some degree of stretch and ensure that they are so before accepting a project leader's assertion that a certain event will be completed on X date. The dates he or she may give could be too conservative or too ambitious. Each person setting dates for a department should operate using the same principles. Dates that are realistic

often change because new data make the project of higher (or lower) priority. Also, events often arise that create delays though no one could have foreseen the problem or prevented it.

5. Use the project plan frequently to assess whether any problems are appearing. If so, develop a plan to address those issues or problems.

6. Use a plan as a guide and not as the "Bible." Working smart is far more important than working hard. Ensure people are not trying to hide information or data that will affect the plan.

7. Create an annual calendar of important meetings and events to use in developing a planning cycle. Events include the milestones of the budget cycle. Meetings include major board of directors' strategic meetings, international planning meetings, and any others of importance to the planning cycle. These dates can be arranged in a logical cycle that may force some to be rearranged one time on the annual calendar of activities.

8. Secrecy about plans should be strongly discouraged within the project team. It demotivates staff and there is little, if any, information or strategies on a project that is legitimately confidential from project team members.

9. List all major assumptions under Gantt charts or on a separate page. This allows others to understand better or question aspects of the plan.

10. Ensure that all managers agree with the plans being used by the project team. A summary of the progress made should be compared to the plans and presented to appropriate managers on a periodic basis.

11. Development plans should reflect regulatory authority needs rather than formal requirements, although these two categories are often the same.

12. Specific people must be held accountable for meeting their dates with high-quality outputs. Poorly written reports submitted on time will create many problems and greater delays at a later date than if addressed earlier.

13. Consider placing large dry-mounted schedules in appropriate places. Use colors to denote different categories of activities. Consider a thermometer-style drawing that is filled in as certain activities are in the process of being completed (e.g., patient recruitment in a major trial).

33 / Choosing the Number of Medicines to Develop

Identifying Types and Numbers of Projects to
   Develop................................. **351**
   Introduction.............................. 351
   Research Projects and Full-Scale Development
      Projects.............................. 352
   Should the Focus of This Activity Be on
      Medicines, Indications, or Other Factors?... 352
Approaches to Determining the Number of
   Medicines to Develop Simultaneously....... **352**
   Developing a Mathematical Model to Predict
      the Appropriate Number of Projects to
      Develop............................... 352
   Keeping the Pipeline Full.................... 352
   Allocating Many Resources to Few Medicines
      Versus Allocating Few Resources to Many
      Medicines............................. 353
To Trim or to Add—Is That the Question?...... **353**

Project Costs 353
Are the Chances of Commercial Success
   Increased by Trimming or Adding Projects?. 353
Focusing Activities on an Appropriate Number
   of Projects 353
Special Cases................................. **354**
How Many Orphan Medicines Can a
   Company Afford to Develop?.............. 354
Sexy Medicines with Pedestrian Effects........ 354
An Appropriate Answer to the Question Posed by
   the Chapter's Title **354**
Reasons Why It Is Better to Place Many
   Projects in a Portfolio 354
How to Ensure that Only the Best Medicines
   Remain in the Portfolio 354
Do Increased Resources Always Speed a
   Medicine's Development? 355

We thought that if we didn't grab the business, someone else would, and that we would never have this kind of opportunity again. We always thought of an order lost as a disaster. So we decided to push the company as rapidly as the market would permit. Thomas J. Watson, Jr. Former chief executive of International Business Machines. From *Fortune* (August 31, 1987).

IDENTIFYING TYPES AND NUMBERS OF PROJECTS TO DEVELOP

Introduction

The major reason to consider this topic is that pharmaceutical companies want to improve their ability to discover and develop medicines that will keep the company viable. Every company experiences fruitful periods where increased numbers of new products are introduced and dry periods when fewer new products are developed and marketed. If a critical number of viable projects are able to be kept in the medicine development pipeline (i.e., in basic research, preclinical development, and clinical systems), it will help increase the number of fruitful years and minimize the number of dry years. Another method to achieve this goal in addition to in-house medicine discovery is through licensing-in worthwhile medicines that meet the company's needs.

The number of medicines or projects a company undertakes at any one time depends on many factors that must be periodically reassessed. The number of projects that a specific department within a company may undertake simultaneously must also be periodically reassessed. Nonetheless, each department must balance its capabilities (e.g., number of staff, amount of budget, equipment, and facilities) with current and future requirements of actual and potential projects. This balance may usually be assessed and controlled more precisely in a single department than in the entire company. This situation is somewhat analogous to the budgets of the United States and the individual states. Almost all states (analogous to individual departments) must have a balanced budget each year and therefore know which activities are possible to carry out. On the other hand, the federal government (analogous to the company) has the ability to spend money and go into debt to take on activities that are of interest to them. Thus, an entire company may borrow money to carry out affairs of interest, whereas individual departments are limited by their budgets and usually have a fixed amount of resources to apportion.

Research Projects and Full-Scale Development Projects

The appropriate number of projects to keep in the pipeline depends on whether preclinical research projects or full-scale clinical development projects are being discussed. The number of preclinical medicine discovery projects may be further broken down into active projects involving exploratory nonfocused studies in broad therapeutic areas and research projects on highly targeted diseases. Research projects may or may not be required to have a chemical lead before they qualify as an official research project.

Once a commitment is made to take a compound to humans for clinical testing, it may be considered as a full-scale development project. Some companies divide this group of full-scale development projects into two categories, those which will be taken to market (if possible) and those which will only be evaluated in humans to address a specific question.

Should the Focus of This Activity Be on Medicines, Indications, or Other Factors?

Although projects on individual medicines are described as the lowest common denominator between pharmaceutical companies, each project may also be described in terms of the medicine's individual indications, dosage forms, routes of administration, and dosing regimens being studied. An equal or greater amount of work may be expended on studying a minor route of administration for one medicine as the entire effort spent on another medicine project. Also, a single indication of a major project may require far more resources than all the indications of several other projects. Although the rest of this chapter discusses projects, it is necessary and important also to consider and evaluate within each project the resources allocated for each indication, dosage form, and route of administration currently under study or planned.

APPROACHES TO DETERMINING THE NUMBER OF MEDICINES TO DEVELOP SIMULTANEOUSLY

There are two totally different ways to approach this question. The first is to evaluate previous company experience, then to add in new factors that are relevant, and also to consider future goals. The additional factors include (1) consideration of projected growth or diminu-

tion of staff and other resources, (2) knowledge of activities that are competing for resources within the company, (3) outside competition, and (4) future medical need for the medicines being developed.

The second method is to develop a theoretical mathematical model. This method requires the developer to make a number of assumptions, and is described below in more detail.

Developing a Mathematical Model to Predict the Appropriate Number of Projects to Develop

One approach to determining the number of medicines to develop simultaneously involves a theoretical approach. This is perhaps best accomplished through mathematical modeling. Mathematical modeling of the appropriate number of projects for a company to develop requires consideration of the company's goal (e.g., a new medicine generating $20 million or more is desired every five years). Estimates may also be required of any number of additional parameters that the company wishes to identify and control. These parameters include (1) the rate at which projects will be successful, (2) the average number of projects to be initiated each year, (3) the average length of time and costs (resources) required to achieve a successful project, (4) the length of time required to terminate an unsuccessful project, and (5) the total costs to be spent on unsuccessful projects. Instead of using a single estimated average for any of these parameters, it is possible to use two or more different averages, or a range of values (assuming a normal distribution). These estimates should be derived from past company experience, present trends, and future goals. When the past, present, and future estimates for a parameter differ greatly it would be desirable to derive the model using each set of values, or to use the two extreme values.

When this type of mathematical simulation is run, wide fluctuations are observed in most of the outputs. Because of uncertainties of assumptions used in the model and variations in numbers used, the appropriate number of projects to develop simultaneously turns out to be a relatively wide range.

Keeping the Pipeline Full

Any company's portfolio of investigational medicines may be improved in quality by adding better projects in terms of medical and commercial value. An issue discussed later is when should less attractive projects be trimmed from the portfolio. An important issue for a research and development-based company is to determine how many clinical development projects and how many research projects with chemical leads are required to keep the medicine development pipeline full. No one can answer this question with certainty at any one company because many factors determine whether compounds and medicines will be successful. Moreover, only some of these factors are able to be controlled. One means of attempting to keep the pipeline full is to determine mathematically the steady-state number of projects necessary to achieve one's goals, as previously described. It is then the responsibility of senior managers to ensure that this number of projects is present. A more practical means is to evaluate the contents of the company's portfolio to determine whether the pipeline is full. This may be done by investigating the activities of all departments involved in medicine discovery, development, and sales.

Many managers believe that each component part of research and development should be operating at or near maximal capacity in a highly efficient and productive manner. By keeping the overall research and development system (as well as individual departments) taxed beyond their capacity to handle the current work load, it will be more likely that the system is being used efficiently. The drawback to this approach is that it ensures that every department is busily working, but does not ensure that they are working on the most important projects, on the most important activities within those projects, or in an efficient manner.

Allocating Many Resources to Few Medicines Versus Allocating Few Resources to Many Medicines

There has been a controversy for many years within the pharmaceutical industry about how to proceed most rapidly toward a New Drug Application (NDA). Some people advocate concentrating all of a company's available resources on a few projects, hoping to expedite their progress. Other people advocate distributing available resources among several or many projects and therefore trying to move a greater number of potential medicines toward the market and increasing the chances of commercial success.

The specific path chosen by each particular company has depended on several factors, including the following:

1. The philosophy of the individual(s) in charge. The views of that person or persons usually affect the entire research and development organization more than any other factor.
2. The historical experience and culture of the particular organization.
3. The quality of the specific projects that are available at a given moment within the company.

Specific methods used to allocate resources are discussed in Chapter 30.

TO TRIM OR TO ADD—IS THAT THE QUESTION?

Project Costs

The most expensive projects are those that (1) are nearing NDA submission (i.e., are in Phase III of development), (2) have had their NDA submitted, or (3) have had their NDA approved and new indications or dosage forms are being studied. Most major new medicines that successfully reach the market continue to require large sums of money to support research and development activities for several additional years. As a result, the most expensive projects are usually the most promising and advanced ones. The converse is also true, in that the youngest projects are usually the cheapest ones. Expensive lifetime toxicology studies and expensive Phase III clinical trials are almost always begun after the medicine's activity has been clearly demonstrated.

Are the Chances of Commercial Success Increased by Trimming or Adding Projects?

No one has ever devised a satisfactory formula to predict which investigational projects will be commercially successful. Thus, it must be concluded that no minor project can ever be dropped from a company's portfolio with full assurance that it might not someday have become a "major" corporate asset. Cutting the number of projects to a select few will primarily affect projects in the early phases of development that will not cost significant sums of money, except in future years, should those projects prove promising and merit further development.

No medicine can ever be totally written off as always remaining a minor player and having no chance to grow in medical importance or to become highly profitable. Some medicines launched with little fanfare or for orphan indications have later been found to possess significant activity in diseases with large markets and have made significant contributions toward corporate wealth. It must, however, be said that this course of events is uncommon.

Focusing Activities on an Appropriate Number of Projects

At some point a company may have too many projects in its portfolio. This situation can threaten efficient medicine development if scientists do not concentrate enough of their energies on an appropriate number of the most promising projects. These individuals may work randomly on different medicines, or try and push too many research and development projects ahead simultaneously. Perhaps the most extreme situation would occur if there were so many projects that there was only a single clinical trial being conducted on most projects at any one time and no trials on others. Although this is an unlikely scenario, there are many enthusiastic scientists and clinicians at most companies who eagerly seek and/ or accept all new challenges for developing new indications, new dosage forms, and new medicines. These enthusiasts sometimes lose their ability to focus attention on accomplishing critical project activities and sticking to their commitments. This is a real problem, regardless of the underlying psychological reason why they jump from project to project, or from indication to indication within a project, or from study to study within an indication. These people are always looking for new challenges to take up, rather than finishing tasks they have started.

The opposite extreme is also counterproductive. This is exemplified by individuals who tenaciously adhere to a previously accepted development plan when everyone else is convinced about the need to move on to a new study, new indication, or new project.

SPECIAL CASES

How Many Orphan Medicines Can a Company Afford to Develop?

Numerous answers have been given to this question that vary from specific responses (e.g., none, one, or three) to functional replies (e.g., only those with commercial potential, only those with medical potential, or only those with commercial and medical potential). The correct response primarily depends on the company's financial condition. Companies in a financial crisis can ill afford any funds going toward nonprofitable ventures. The traditions of the company and outlook of the most senior executives will clearly influence a company's perception of this issue.

The most important characteristic of orphan medicines from a medicine development perspective is that they are a heterogeneous and not homogeneous group of medicines. Their widely differing characteristics and potential for profit have been described as well as their pros and cons from an industry perspective (Spilker, 1985, 1986, 1990a).

Sexy Medicines with Pedestrian Effects

Everyone at a pharmaceutical company gets excited when a novel medicine is discovered and is found to be active in treating a disease that had previously been either untreatable or inadequately treated. If the medicine has a totally new chemical structure and mechanism of

action, then the excitement it generates is much greater, both within the company and the medical community.

Situations also arise when a medicine has an exciting new chemical structure and mechanism of action, but the clinical usefulness does not offer any significant advantages over currently available therapy. Medicines of this nature may be characterized as sexy medicines with pedestrian effects. They usually have little chance of being incorporated into most physicians' armamentaria. Some companies may still choose to develop this type of medicine and to promote it heavily. These companies largely predicate their decision on the appeal that the novel chemical structure and mechanism of action will have for some physicians. This decision may represent wishful thinking by company executives and must be carefully evaluated. Marketing research can be asked to assess how well the medicine will eventually do in the real world of clinical medicine.

AN APPROPRIATE ANSWER TO THE QUESTION POSED BY THE CHAPTER'S TITLE

Reasons Why It Is Better to Place Many Projects in a Portfolio

There is no doubt that, if a company only had a few projects with positive potential, then it would of necessity concentrate its efforts on a small number of projects. It is clearly a moot point to discuss the number of projects that should be in a portfolio when a company has little choice because of limited research results and limited licensing opportunities. Nonetheless, in an era where it is recognized that an average medicine requires eight to 12 years to reach the market, a policy that places all efforts in a concentrated way on a few "big players" is generally imprudent. That approach would be virtually a guarantee for ensuring long dry spells of new medicines in the future. Moreover, the long and complex path a medicine follows to reach the market makes it unlikely that several projects in different stages of development will compete for the same resources. Concentrating corporate resources on the few potentially best compounds and medicines increases the corporation's risk if those medicines should fail. Including more projects in the company's portfolio is generally viewed as a more prudent and conservative approach.

How to Ensure that Only the Best Medicines Remain in the Portfolio

The major method of ensuring that only the best medicines remain in the company's portfolio is to terminate promptly those that do not meet the minimum criteria for continued development (see Chapter 34). If a company has either too many projects in its portfolio or must obtain resources from some projects to assign to others, it is possible for the marketing group to raise the minimal standards that some or all projects must meet to remain in the portfolio. This exercise will undoubtedly cause some projects to be terminated, thus freeing resources for use on other projects. It is important to evaluate whether those terminated projects would be candidates for licensing out to other companies.

Do Increased Resources Always Speed a Medicine's Development?

An important consideration in deciding whether or not to place more funds and resources in certain projects relates to whether the increased funds would significantly increase the rate at which the medicine could progress toward a NDA. There is no doubt that for some projects a large increase in personnel and money would have a significant effect on the rate at which the project would proceed. This is especially true if the work can be contracted to outside groups for assistance, or if the additional staff could be dedicated to a rate-limiting step, such as writing final medical reports.

Developing a medicine is primarily a sequential activity, and there are only a limited number of things that can be done during Phases I and II to increase the speed of most medicine development activities. One important step is to ensure that the quality of all work performed meets acceptable standards. Another is to have a clear clinical path established that does not meander or deal with less relevant issues. In a typical Phase I medicine

evaluation, a single-dose trial is followed by a multiple-dose trial where volunteers receive doses for a specified time up to approximately one month. In Phase II, pilot efficacy trials are conducted double blind and then a major well-controlled efficacy trial is conducted. If the personnel and other resources put on a project prior to Phase III are excessive, it may mean that (1) a variety of ancillary trials are conducted that are not required for a NDA submission; (2) other therapeutic indications are pursued, often too early in a medicine's life for maximal efficiency and benefit; and/or (3) some trials (e.g., metabolism or toxicology) are being done earlier than necessary in a project's life, and may not speed the overall process. In addition, Phase III-type trials may be initiated before Phase II trials have clearly demonstrated medicine activity. If the medicine is later found to be toxic, insufficiently active, or is terminated for another reason, then many trials and efforts will have been "wasted." Of course, if the medicine turns out to be active, then some time will have been saved. The trick is clearly knowing (i.e., guessing) at an early stage of development which medicines will reach the market and determining which steps will result in saving the most time.

A whole web of inefficiencies and unnecessary problems often develops in a project that has too many activities going on simultaneously. A sound approach has always been to emphasize, insofar as possible, an efficient, streamlined approach toward the company's goals, applying resources where they have the greatest benefit. Ironically, additional resources would often have the most value or effect if put on those projects that are being slowed due to a low priority and are the most likely candidates to be trimmed from an overfilled portfolio.

34 / Criteria for Developing Medicines

The Need for Criteria for Evaluating Medicine
    Discovery and Development 357
Relationship of the Terms: Criteria,
    Characteristics, and Standards.............. 358
The Transition from the Discovery Period to the
    Development Period....................... 358
Ideal Criteria 358
Realistic Criteria 359
Minimally Acceptable Criteria 360
    Time Frame for Developing Minimally
        Acceptable Criteria....................... 360
    Subminimally Acceptable Criteria 360
Desirable Versus Essential Characteristics 360

Who Establishes the Specific Scientific/Medical
    Characteristics? 361
Establishing Quantitative (or Semi-Quantitative)
    Standard for a Medicine's Performance
    During its Development 361
    Orphan Medicines........................... 362
    Technical Development Characteristics 363
Examples of the Three Types of Criteria 363
Other Uses for Minimally Acceptable Criteria... 363
Can a Company Mix Different Types of
    Criteria? 364
Conclusions..................................... 364

No house should ever be on *any hill or on anything. It should be* of *the hill, belonging to it, so hill and house could live together each the happier for the other.* Frank Lloyd Wright. From *An Autobiography* (1932).

Excessive delegation is abrogation. Dr. Alan Eggleston. The Wellcome Foundation.

THE NEED FOR CRITERIA FOR EVALUATING MEDICINE DISCOVERY AND DEVELOPMENT

Many of the problems faced by pharmaceutical companies indicate that there is a need for a set of criteria to guide the medicine development process. A few typical problems are:

1. Determining how good a new compound must be to justify spending large sums of money on its further development.
2. Difficulty knowing when an investigational medicine should be terminated—when its profile no longer justifies pursuing the medicine's development, or when the marketplace is changing and physicians are no longer using the type of medicine being developed.
3. Difficulty assessing whether development of a new medicine should be continued when certain safety and efficacy characteristics are less than expected, though other characteristics are better than expected.

Two major processes are described in this chapter. The first provides a means to recognize whether research has led to a new medicine or only an interesting compound that is one step toward the potential medicine.

The second process provides a means to determine when a medicine's development should be terminated.

Three sets of scientific/medical criteria can be used to judge the discovery and development of new medicines: *ideal, realistic,* and *minimally acceptable.* It is proposed that, for evaluating both the discovery and the development of medicines, the set of minimally acceptable criteria is preferable.

Another way of looking at the three sets of criteria is through the metaphor of a high jump. (This metaphor is discussed in more detail in Chapter 3.) The high jump's bar is set at a height that is based on the criteria that the newly discovered compound or medicine must achieve or surpass. Separate high jump bars exist for a medicine's safety and efficacy. A compound or medicine must achieve the criteria set to be viable from the points of view of medical value, commercial value, and public relations image value. For example, if the high jump bar for safety is set so high using ideal criteria that only a perfect compound could exceed the criteria, then these criteria do not indicate how high is enough for a very good and acceptable (but not perfect) compound to jump.

This chapter focuses almost entirely on the category of

scientific/medical characteristics, although the same three sets of criteria may be applied to the category of commercial characteristics used by marketing groups to judge a new medicine. Some companies refer to commercial criteria as hurdle rates (i.e., the anticipated commercial return needed to justify the medicine's development).

RELATIONSHIP OF THE TERMS: CRITERIA, CHARACTERISTICS, AND STANDARDS

The relationships among the terms "criteria," "characteristics," and "standards" must be clear if the approach described in this chapter is used to expedite a compound's discovery or development. The major relationships are shown in Table 34.1. The three sets of criteria (i.e., ideal, realistic, and minimally acceptable) would each have the same listing of scientific/medical characteristics, although this list would change as a compound moved through the development pipeline. Each characteristic has one or more associated standards for the medicine to achieve. It is generally preferable if these standards are quantified, although this is not always possible. Actual examples of characteristics and standards are provided in Table 34.5, although that table presents a simple example. A more complex example would include more characteristics and would indicate linkages among characteristics for any one set of criteria (e.g., if characteristic number 3 is not achieved, then numbers 2, 4, and 5 must be).

THE TRANSITION FROM THE DISCOVERY PERIOD TO THE DEVELOPMENT PERIOD

The preclinical discovery period during which scientists search for a new medicine begins with the evaluation of organic or inorganic substances in biological test systems; a chemist prepares or obtains materials for the biological scientist to test. The materials may be natural or synthetic compounds, mixtures, extracts, distillates, or biotechnologically derived substances. The discovery period is completed when the biologist (e.g., pharmacologist or virologist) or group of biologists state that a particular compound or material meets certain criteria of activity and safety and should be developed further as a medicine. At that point, the compound enters the development period, even though it will usually be a number of years before the compound is actually tested in humans. Many additional preclinical studies must be done to characterize further both the safety and efficacy profiles of the substance before clinical testing may be initiated. Although the separation of the discovery and development processes is generally clear as a concept, these processes usually overlap in time. There is a period of time until a single agent can be firmly identified as the candidate compound for further development. In some situations, a number of compounds are chosen for initial progression with the expectation that only one will ever reach the market.

Scientists, marketing staff, and senior managers use various criteria to help make important decisions about the discovery and development of medicines. Companies may create formal or informal criteria to determine when a compound completes the discovery period and enters the development period. After a compound of interest is identified in the discovery period and progresses through preclinical and clinical development, it is possible to use the same criteria to judge the medicine, or new, specific criteria may be adopted. Three distinct sets of criteria are described below.

IDEAL CRITERIA

The ideal criteria for all characteristics that a company hopes a medicine will possess can be used as criteria by which a new compound is defined as a meaningful dis-

TABLE 34.1. *Relationship of criteria, characteristics, and standards*

I. Ideal set of criteria
    List important scientific/medical characteristics[a] for the
        compound/medicine
	Standards to achieve for each characteristic[b]
	A. Qualitative
	B. Quantitative

II. Realistic set of criteria
    List of important scientific/medical characteristics for the
        compound/medicine (Same characteristics are listed
        as in I above)
	Standards to achieve for each characteristic
	A. Qualitative (may be the same or different
	    than in I above)
	B. Quantitative (may be the same or
	    different than in I above)

III. Minimally acceptable set of criteria
    List of important scientific/medical characteristics for the
        compound/medicine (Same characteristics are listed
        as in I above)
	Standards to achieve for each characteristic
	A. Qualitative (may be the same or different
	    than in II above)
	B. Quantitative (may be the same or
	    different than in II above)

[a] Separate or overlapping lists of marketing, production, and other characteristics may be identified and listed with scientific/medical criteria or they may be listed separately. Examples of selected scientific/medical characteristics are listed in Table 34.4.

[b] Examples of standards to achieve for each characteristic are shown in Table 34.5.

TABLE 34.2. *Advantages and disadvantages of using the ideal set of criteria for medicine discovery*

Advantages
1. These aid in identifying one's goals (i.e., ideal criteria establish a beacon or guide to follow).
2. They facilitate the comparison of activities obtained with tested compounds with ultimate goals. This enables scientists and managers to judge progress and trends and to assess how close the compounds are to the ideal.

Disadvantages
1. Although ideal criteria are useful for developing new animal models, they are less useful for judging medicine discoveries and the preclinical development processes (e.g., after the potential medicine is identified).
2. Since the perfect medicine is never obtained, it is difficult to know how close to the ideal a compound must be to commit resources and develop it into a medicine.
3. Business decisions are not helped and are only hampered with ideal criteria because it can always be argued either that the compound is close enough or that it is not close enough to the ideal goal.

covery. Ideal criteria are often useful as goals. It is possible to describe the ideal criteria of any medicine for any disease. It is also useful to compare new compounds with standard medicines to judge how much closer the new compound approaches the ideal. Any compound can be judged by how close it is to a number of ideal criteria. The advantages and disadvantages of using ideal criteria are summarized in Table 34.2.

This approach, however, does not facilitate business decisions. Ideal criteria do not reveal whether or not a specific compound is good enough to be successful commercially. Ideal criteria, per se, do not facilitate the decision of whether a compound being tested should be continued or terminated because these criteria do not indicate how close the characteristics of a compound must be to those of an ideal medicine in order to say that the compound represents a meaningful discovery that is worthy of pursuit. How close is close enough when the activity is getting closer to the ideal? Ideal criteria do not allow one to decide how close to the ideal a new compound must come to be considered suitable for further development. It is always possible for someone to claim that the criteria are not achieved by any compound. Some examples of ideal criteria for establishing a clinical model of antipruritic activity have been published (Spilker et al., 1984). Ideal criteria may be used when creating new animal models or for judging them. For example, most compounds evaluated in a series of animal models would consider time to onset of activity, magnitude of activity, duration of activity, tolerance, selectivity, solubility, mechanism of action, interactions, plus other relevant characteristics. Ideal criteria are rarely considered during a medicine's clinical development because it is apparent that no medicine is ideal.

REALISTIC CRITERIA

Most pharmaceutical companies understand that it is impossible to achieve an ideal medicine in a specific therapeutic area. As a result, many companies develop realistic criteria. These are standards that the managers and scientists believe the medicine can achieve, and in many cases should achieve to be commercially viable. Realistic criteria are more helpful than ideal criteria for making scientific and commercial decisions about advancing a compound. As a result, many companies establish a realistic target or create a realistic set of criteria to use in judging medicines. Managers often tell their scientists to come up with a new compound that possesses realistic activities. With this approach, companies are better able to make scientific and commercial decisions. Essentially, they must determine which established criteria (established by already marketed medicines) their product must beat to be successful.

Realistic criteria are developed to help predict if the compound will be successful, but these criteria can easily be manipulated when the medicine's progress is being reviewed and evaluated by senior managers. This manipulation may occur at any level within a company, but the criteria are most susceptible to manipulation by senior managers. These criteria may be manipulated to either terminate or expedite work on a project, depending on the managers' preconceived biases (many managers have their own favorite projects). Political games can be played using realistic criteria, particularly if the vested interests of certain managers are associated (or believed to be associated) with the medicine's success or demise. Because realistic criteria appear to make sense, they are like a siren luring companies into troubled waters. Any results obtained on a medicine may be rationalized and justified when realistic criteria are used to evaluate that medicine's progress. As a consequence, a project may be pushed forward and given excessive resources and/or priority. Even in the face of bad news, one often hears statements such as, "If you do only one or two more studies

TABLE 34.3. *Advantages and disadvantages of using the realistic set of criteria for medicine discovery*

Advantages
1. Useful for comparing activities obtained with new compounds to those of other medicines
2. Enables better scientific and commercial decisions to be made than when idealistic criteria are used
3. May be used for development processes as well as for discovery processes of a new medicine
4. Makes inherent sense to marketing
5. May be more easily reviewed and adjusted to current marketing and scientific beliefs than are ideal criteria

Disadvantages
1. May be easily manipulated by people who want either to start, advance, or terminate a project
2. Are not useful management tools for reaching decisions on project termination

or trials, the compound's data will look better." Another manager could use the same data and the same realistic criteria to claim that it is fruitless to progress with the medicine, thereby "killing" the project. Realistic criteria for medicine development are frequently endorsed and manipulated by whoever has the power to make decisions. It is apparent from discussions with managers at many pharmaceutical firms that many, if not most, companies use realistic criteria in creating their medicine development plans. The advantages and disadvantages of this approach are summarized in Table 34.3.

MINIMALLY ACCEPTABLE CRITERIA

Minimally acceptable criteria are the least acceptable standards that a medicine must achieve, i.e., the real hurdles that a new medicine must surpass to progress with its development. These are described in terms of specific (1) clinical hurdles, (2) technical hurdles, (3) marketing hurdles, and in some cases, (4) regulatory hurdles. Minimally acceptable criteria should be established through collaboration of both marketing and research personnel. These criteria should be reviewed periodically, and revised, if necessary, as the medicine progresses through the discovery and development pipeline.

The set of minimally acceptable criteria is the best set of criteria to use for both the discovery and development periods. With this approach, junior and senior managers, scientists, and marketing personnel can state, based on objective criteria, whether further studies are justified and whether development of the compound (or medicine) should be terminated. These criteria tend to prevent (or at least to decrease) the games that different people are able to play to advance or to hold back new medicine discoveries. Minimally acceptable criteria also help review committees terminate clinical trials and a medicine's development before large sums of money and years of valuable effort are wasted.

Market research data are sometimes used to define and to refine the minimally acceptable criteria. The minimally acceptable criteria for an investigational medicine may have to be markedly revised if a major new medicine is introduced or clinical practices change in treating patients with the same disease.

Time Frame for Developing Minimally Acceptable Criteria

The most important characteristics by which to evaluate a medicine should be established at the outset of a project. In addition, the quantitative (or qualitative) standards that will be used as minimally acceptable criteria to progress the medicine's development should also be established at the outset of a project. A major problem could develop if the company's marketing, scientific, and clinical experts attempt to establish minimally ac-

ceptable criteria after clinical trials are completed and data are available. These criteria directly affect whether the project is advanced or terminated, and the judgment of involved individuals can be significantly altered by the outcome of clinical trials. The problem is particularly severe if the characteristics to be used have not been chosen, and therefore, the criteria that *must* be met to proceed with development are not established.

It is also true that, after clinical trials are completed, marketers, scientists, or clinicians may feel pressures to reach one conclusion or another. These pressures increase the possibility that the professional will bend the criteria (even subconsciously) to suit these influences. If the standards for evaluating the characteristics are determined before the data are collected, a more objective set of minimally acceptable criteria will be established that can be impartially applied.

Subminimally Acceptable Criteria

Individuals in any group helping to establish criteria may propose some criteria that are below minimally acceptable standards. The most likely causes of this problem are methodological or judgment errors resulting from ignorance or naiveté, or from a failure to conduct the appropriate market research. It is also possible that the "hurdles" the medicine must pass (i.e., criteria) were proposed at inappropriately low levels because of the individual's strong personal desire to pursue the project, almost regardless of the data obtained. A consensus should be reached within medical and marketing groups that all of the minimally acceptable criteria are appropriate and acceptable. These groups should also agree on which criteria are most important for making the decision to market the medicine. Failure to achieve any one of those hurdles will facilitate the decision to terminate the medicine's development.

DESIRABLE VERSUS ESSENTIAL CHARACTERISTICS

After choosing between these three sets of prospective criteria for use in medicine evaluation, it is necessary to identify and quantify the individual characteristics that will make up the chosen type of criteria. A number of specific characteristics that could be used are listed in Table 34.4. Specific financial and regulatory characteristics are not listed or discussed in this chapter but could be created for a medicine's development. In viewing each of the specific characteristics it is important to determine which ones are musts and which ones are shoulds, i.e., the characteristics must be described in terms of their relative importance. The latter category of characteristics (i.e., the shoulds) are those that are desirable, but not essential, for a compound or medicine to meet. In some circumstances a range of values rather than a single value

TABLE 34.4. *Selected scientific/medical characteristics that could be used to establish specific standards*[a]

1. Time to onset of effect
2. Duration of action and biological half-life
3. Tolerance
4. Cumulative effects
5. Reversibility of toxicity
6. Therapeutic ratio
7. Presence of active metabolites and degree of metabolism
8. Stability at room temperature
9. Solubility
10. Type, incidence, and severity of adverse effects
11. Magnitude of effect
12. Patient preference
13. Amount of absorption
14. Potency in clinical models A, B, and C
15. Activity in models M, N, and O
16. Safety profile for specific organ systems
17. Interactions with specific medicines
18. Ability to induce hepatic microsomal enzymes

[a] Any of these could be considered either solely for a specific compound (medicine) or as a comparison with a standard medicine. The standards for these characteristics may be described in general or highly specific quantitative terms.

may be used in describing a specific characteristic. Also, combinations of certain specific characteristics should be assembled that would be used either to progress or terminate a medicine. There is often a "seesaw effect" or trade-off for a medicine where a greater degree of one characteristic offsets a lack or failing of another. These considerations should be established at as early a stage as possible, although not all possible combinations of characteristics are possible to describe in advance, nor should they be described.

The distinction between musts and shoulds depends on the specific medicine and characteristic being considered. For example, the most important characteristic for a new over-the-counter line-extension could relate to its dissolution rate, or to masking its odor. An ideal, realistic, or minimally acceptable criterion would be assessed for this characteristic. For other projects, the dissolution rate or masking a tablet's odor would be relatively minor, albeit desirable, characteristics.

If a new medical indication of interest is identified during the discovery or development period, the relevant characteristics for the medicine may be entirely (or partially) established retrospectively, instead of prospectively, as described in this chapter.

WHO ESTABLISHES THE SPECIFIC SCIENTIFIC/MEDICAL CHARACTERISTICS?

The answer to this question is far from obvious and can become quite complex. The simplest answer is that discussions among the marketing and medical professionals on the project team should be the basis for establishing most, if not all, of the medical criteria used to

evaluate a new medicine. This approach should be followed, even in a company that considers itself to be driven by its research and development group. In some (or many) cases, the medical personnel use their judgment about marketing statements when establishing criteria. For example, a company physician may believe that a new medicine must (or should) have certain characteristics to be useful and valuable in therapeutics. The hunches and beliefs of that physician may be affirmed or challenged by a marketing group that conducts research into physician and patient needs and reactions to the medicine's expected profile. In other words, most specific medical criteria are actually the same as marketing concepts based on medical needs. For example, the minimally acceptable medical characteristics in Table 34.4 are all marketing characteristics as well. This means that unless the medicine meets these criteria, doctors will not use it and the company cannot sell it. It could also be argued that setting specific characteristics is the responsibility solely of marketing (or of medical) groups.

Criteria may be determined by supervising managers or by individual scientists or clinicians. However, a bottom-up process is usually preferable. This means that individual scientists or clinicians on the project team propose the specific minimally acceptable criteria after discussions with experts in numerous areas, including marketing. These criteria are assessed by relevant committees. Eventually a senior level manager or committee may be asked to conduct a final review and to approve the criteria (Fig. 34.1). Except for criteria focusing on early-stage medicine discovery, it is essential that the criteria be created with significant marketing input. Nonetheless, these criteria should not be imposed on scientists by marketing groups, although a marketing orientation to developing specific characteristics is also used by scientists when they decide the degree of activity and safety a new compound requires in order to be considered a candidate medicine (i.e., to state that a new medicine is discovered). Scientists usually decide on the criteria to be used for each characteristic based on their readings and discussions with numerous people including physicians, marketers, and other scientists.

ESTABLISHING QUANTITATIVE (OR SEMI-QUANTITATIVE) STANDARDS FOR A MEDICINE'S PERFORMANCE DURING ITS DEVELOPMENT

Compounds that have achieved the quantitative standards established for each important characteristic assessed during the discovery period for a specific target disease or activity (e.g., enzyme inhibition), in terms of efficacy and safety parameters, are advanced into the development period. Even if clear measurable standards for each important characteristic have not been established during the preclinical discovery period, it is im-

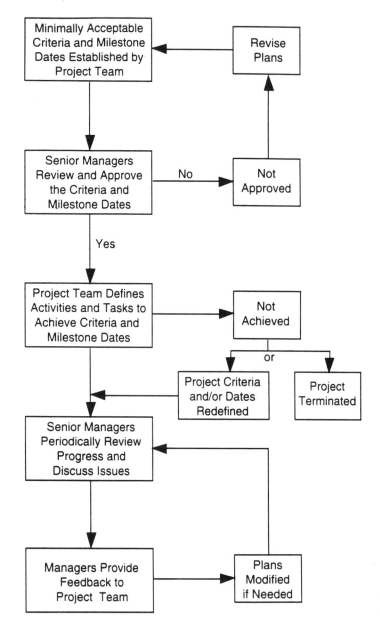

FIG. 34.1. General process of establishing, monitoring, and reviewing criteria and dates (i.e., deadlines) for project milestones.

portant to establish and write down the quantitative standards for each important characteristic assessed during a medicine's development. The primary purpose of having written standards for each relevant characteristic is so that everyone associated with the medicine's development can agree on the criteria to be used for judging when development should be accelerated or terminated. Understanding the minimally acceptable criteria to be used facilitates effective communication about each investigational medicine.

Standards established at an early stage of development should include medical, technical, and commercial considerations. If the medicine falls below or otherwise fails to meet these standards, then its termination should be considered.

Orphan Medicines

A company may choose to develop one or more orphan medicines where there is little hope of ever repaying the development costs. Appropriate criteria should be established for orphan medicines, just as for all other medicines in development. Thus, the company's senior management could agree to accept lower minimally acceptable commercial criteria (i.e., hurdle rates) for some medicines. A project's termination is facilitated when the medicine's characteristics demonstrate that even minimally acceptable criteria cannot be achieved.

An important new medicine with great medical value for a select group of patients may have limited commercial benefits to a company, but this type of medicine often provides numerous other benefits and values to a company's marketing group. These benefits may be enhanced company image and reputation, or improved access to physicians by sales representatives. The company's overall reaction to any type of medicine primarily depends on its original expectations. These expectations are, in part, related to the type of criteria established for evaluating the medicine's development.

Technical Development Characteristics

Technical development characteristics include: masking of any unpleasant odor, stability of the formulation that would yield a shelf life of three years, capsule size no larger than 2–0, and a formulation that does not contain dyes banned in specific countries.

EXAMPLES OF THE THREE TYPES OF CRITERIA

Examples of the three sets of criteria to evaluate a hypothetical antiepileptic medicine are given in Table 34.5. Although the example concerns the clinical development process, the same (or slightly modified) characteristics could be used in the discovery process and in the preclinical development process. The realistic and minimally acceptable values (or the ideal and realistic) for some criteria in Table 34.4 may be exactly the same; these values may differ for some other criteria. This latter point is noted in the values for duration of action. In terms of adverse effects, the realistic criterion might state "few," and the minimally acceptable criterion would state that the medicine is no worse than the major competitor (medicine X). This type of comparison creates the possibility of problems if the profiles of adverse effects associated with the two medicines are quite different and one must compare unlike groups of potential

problems. Quantification of each characteristic is desirable or even mandatory.

Some pharmaceutical companies establish realistic criteria by creating a hypothetical label (i.e., package insert) for a medicine. The value of this approach, however, should be seriously questioned. Those companies usually spend significant time and effort creating and updating a set of criteria that do not help them reach any business decisions. It is unnecessary to write down and identify each detail of a medicine's actual labeling until the regulatory dossier is nearing the end of its review. It would be better, as discussed earlier, to agree on even a few minimally acceptable criteria.

If five to 15 minimally acceptable criteria were established, they would not necessarily be listed in the order of importance. Using minimally acceptable criteria is not a simple issue of stating that a certain number of criteria exist, and then stopping the medicine's development if one of the criteria is not met. It may be stated, however, that, if specific combinations of the criteria are not achieved, then development of the medicine should be terminated. Minimally acceptable criteria are stated in terms of safety or efficacy and may be phrased in comparison with a standard medicine. The simplest way of expressing this concept is that its safety has to be at least as good as that of the major competing medicine. It is preferable also to identify and apply minimally acceptable criteria for each specific aspect of safety that is important. Criteria also may be expressed without reference to other medicines (Table 34.5).

OTHER USES FOR MINIMALLY ACCEPTABLE CRITERIA

In addition to their use in judging whether a compound (1) represents a new medicine discovery or (2) should be continued in its clinical development, minimally acceptable criteria can be used as follows.

TABLE 34.5. *Examples of ideal, realistic, and minimally acceptable criteria for a hypothetical antiepileptic medicine during its clinical development*

Medicine characteristics	Standards to be achieved		
	Using ideal criteria	Using realistic criteria	Using minimally acceptable criteria
Activity[a]	100% decrease	50% decrease	25% decrease
Frequency	Once a day	Once a day	Twice a day
Onset of action	30 to 45 minutes	One hour	One hour
Duration of action	Eight hours	Five hours	Three hours
Adverse reactions	None	Few serious	No worse than medicine X[b]
Interactions	None	None	No worse than medicine X[b]

[a] Activity is defined in terms of the number of seizures. Improvement for any medicine is described in the specific terms in which it is measured (e.g., overall clinical improvement judged by the investigator at the end of a clinical trial or change of a specific disease parameter measured objectively).

[b] These must be more clearly and specifically identified and quantified (if possible) in the text or in another table (e.g., no interaction with medicines Y or Z at their usually given doses).

1. To create new or improved animal models in which to test compounds for biological activity and, possibly, toxicity.
2. To elevate a compound from the stage of early preclinical development to a formal development stage that includes a commitment to human Phase I testing.
3. To develop commercially oriented criteria that focus on the question of whether to market a new medicine.

A company's decision to market a medicine depends on both the medical/scientific criteria and the commercial criteria that the company creates. Some commercial criteria are dependent on the medical/scientific profile of the medicine, while others (e.g., changes in medical practice, new formulary practices, and new competitive medicines) may change independently of the medical/scientific set.

CAN A COMPANY MIX DIFFERENT TYPES OF CRITERIA?

The answer to this question is yes. For example, some medicines may use realistic criteria in their development and other medicines may use minimally acceptable criteria in their development. Alternatively, a company could use minimally acceptable criteria for judging discovery activities and realistic criteria for judging development projects. The major caveat is that both managers and professionals should understand which types of criteria are applied to each situation. The wisdom of using a mix of different types of criteria, however, is a different issue. The author believes that the most efficient and productive criteria are those that are minimally acceptable. It is counterproductive to mix ideal criteria that will not be achieved with either or both of the other types of criteria.

It is important that the major criteria used to judge an individual project's development not be mixed among two of the three sets. This could occur because of naiveté, illogical thinking, failure to develop specific criteria clearly, or for other reasons. If that were to happen, then the usefulness of any of the criteria would be negatively affected.

CONCLUSIONS

The best set of criteria for evaluating both medicine discovery and development activities is that which presents minimally acceptable criteria. When specific criteria are identified they may be used to decide whether to continue or terminate development of a compound or medicine. When these criteria are written down, openly discussed, and approved, the decision to continue or terminate development is facilitated. This process diminishes game playing by those who wish to proceed with a nonviable project or to terminate a viable one. When criteria are developed and discussed by scientists, clinicians, and marketers, communication is facilitated and a sense of overall teamwork is fostered. When these criteria are utilized by a pharmaceutical company, they tend to improve its efficiency and productivity in both medicine discovery and development activities.

35 / Evaluating a Portfolio of Investigational Medicine Projects

Objectives and Perspectives of a Portfolio
Analysis **365**
What Does Portfolio Analysis Mean? 365
What Are the Purposes of a Portfolio
Analysis?................................. 366
Lowest Common Denominator.............. 366
Levels of Projects......................... 366
Portfolio Gaps............................. 366
Perspectives of Various Groups Conducting a
Portfolio Analysis 367
Reviewing a Multinational Company's Overall
Portfolio and Those of Individual Sites 368
Developing a Portfolio **368**
Determining an Ideal Portfolio.............. 368
Determining a Realistic Portfolio 368
Analyzing the Value of a Portfolio.............. **369**
Comparison of Scientific Versus Medical
Value 369
Judging the Scientific Value of a New
Medicine.................................. 369
Rating the Medical Value of a New Medicine .. 369
What Is the Therapeutic Utility of a New
Medicine?................................. 370
Forecasting the Commercial Value of a New
Medicine.................................. 370

Analyzing a Project Portfolio in Five Steps **371**
Steps to Follow............................. 371
Projects to Include in a Portfolio (Step One)... 371
Measuring Individual Projects in a Portfolio
(Step Two)................................ 371
Measuring Groups of Projects in a Portfolio
(Step Three).............................. 376
Interpretations of a Portfolio Analysis (Step
Four) 395
Utilizing a Portfolio Analysis to Modify a
Company (Step Five)....................... 396
Other Portfolio Issues **396**
Financial Analyses.......................... 396
What Does High Priority Mean? 396
Pruning the Portfolio 397
Mathematical Models of a Portfolio........... 397
Defining Therapeutic Areas.................. 398
Estimating Future Staff Needs 398
Should New Medicines Be Developed Only if
Their Forecast Achieves at Least a Minimal
Value?.................................... 398
A Potential "Danger" of Creating a Portfolio
Analysis.................................. 398
Other Pitfalls Regarding a Portfolio Analysis .. 399

Trying to assess basic research by its practicality is like trying to judge Mozart by how much money the Salzburg Festival brings in each year. Konrad Lorenz, Austrian naturalist.

OBJECTIVES AND PERSPECTIVES OF A PORTFOLIO ANALYSIS

What Does Portfolio Analysis Mean?

The term "portfolio analysis" is used to describe an examination of a group of compounds and/or medicines using medical, scientific, commercial, financial, and/or other parameters. Medicines that are evaluated may be (1) investigational, (2) marketed, (3) a combination, or (4) may focus on any subset of those groups (e.g., the ten most important projects in terms of commercial value or effort). The analysis of any parameter may vary from a subjective appraisal to a precise quantitative evaluation using standard financial or other methods.

A portfolio analysis may be conducted as a special

one-time exercise or as part of an annual or other periodic review. If the analysis is conducted as a special one-time exercise, there is a greater likelihood that it will be performed (in whole or in part) by outside consultants rather than by internal company staff.

The analysis may be limited to assessing medical and commercial values, or it may include other aspects as well. Although there is substantial information to be obtained from analyzing the previous year or half-year, the most important information usually comes from comparing results with those obtained on several past occasions. This allows trends to be identified and may raise issues that should be addressed. An analysis will have value if (1) the information used is valid, (2) the information used is current, (3) appropriate methods are used to conduct the analysis, and (4) a sufficient effort is expended on the exercise.

What Are the Purposes of a Portfolio Analysis?

The purpose(s) of the portfolio analysis must be defined in advance of the exercise. A portfolio analysis may be used to provide characteristics of the therapeutic areas and even the businesses the company is in. A company may thus evaluate whether the therapeutic areas being researched and targeted with new projects match those that they wish to pursue. The analysis may also be used to demonstrate whether the company is actively engaged in businesses that provide long-term growth opportunities. Another purpose may be to identify potential gaps in the portfolio over various periods of time when new products are not expected.

A portfolio analysis may also be used to decide which projects should be retained and which should be pruned. If the analysis is not limited to looking at each project as an overall entity, but examines each of the indications, dosage forms, and routes of administration separately, then it is possible to evaluate which of those aspects should be retained and which should be pruned. Projects may be pruned or temporarily allotted minimal resources to reallocate finite resources to higher priority projects.

Pruning projects from a portfolio does not necessarily mean that the projects clipped are to be terminated. Another possibility is that pruned projects may be licensed-out or used as trading material (*quid pro quo*) for cross-licensing with another company. If medicine discovery becomes less fruitful for a company, it will have a much stronger motivation to increase licensing-out of its pruned projects or even pruned dosage forms. An intermediate step is to diminish resources allocated to a project so that it barely remains alive or progresses at a minimal pace.

Lowest Common Denominator

The principle focus of thinking about a portfolio is in terms of the individual project. It is, nonetheless, insufficient to focus solely on projects as the lowest common denominator in analyzing a portfolio. Each indication, dosage form, route of administration, and dosing regimen studied should be evaluated independently in terms of its medical and commercial importance. Resources applied to their development should be appropriate, both in terms of quantity and also in terms of timing. For example, it may be appropriate to ask if development of some indications of a medicine should be delayed. Each of several indications pursued in a large project may utilize the same quantity of resources allocated to the sum of five (or even more) small projects. Only through a thorough analysis of a project's individual parts can the value of the overall project be adequately ascertained.

When discussing secondary indications of a medicine, it is relevant to consider whether they are spin-offs and closely related to the primary indication or whether they are in different therapeutic areas. An indication that was originally secondary in importance may become the primary one for a medicine in medical and/or commercial terms. As the number of indications being evaluated increases, it is essential to determine whether a fixed quantity of resources is being divided into smaller pieces or whether there is an incremental growth in resources. The answer to this question should have a significant impact on the strategy developed for each project.

Levels of Projects

In conceptualizing the portfolio exercise it is useful to think in terms of levels of projects. This is shown in Fig. 35.1. as four levels: (1) individual projects, (2) projects in a disease area, (3) projects in a therapeutic area, and (4) all projects. The various issues, questions, and problems associated with the portfolio can then be associated with the appropriate project level. For example, when individual data are being collected and reviewed for a single project within a given therapeutic area in the portfolio, it usually is premature to question whether the entire therapeutic area should be eliminated (or resourced at a greater level). The four levels of conceptualizing projects also provide a basis on which to organize the first steps of the portfolio analysis.

Portfolio Gaps

Numerous types of gaps may exist in a portfolio. For these to be adequately addressed they must first be identified by type (see below). Each of these gaps is based on the company not achieving its goals. Goals must be iden-

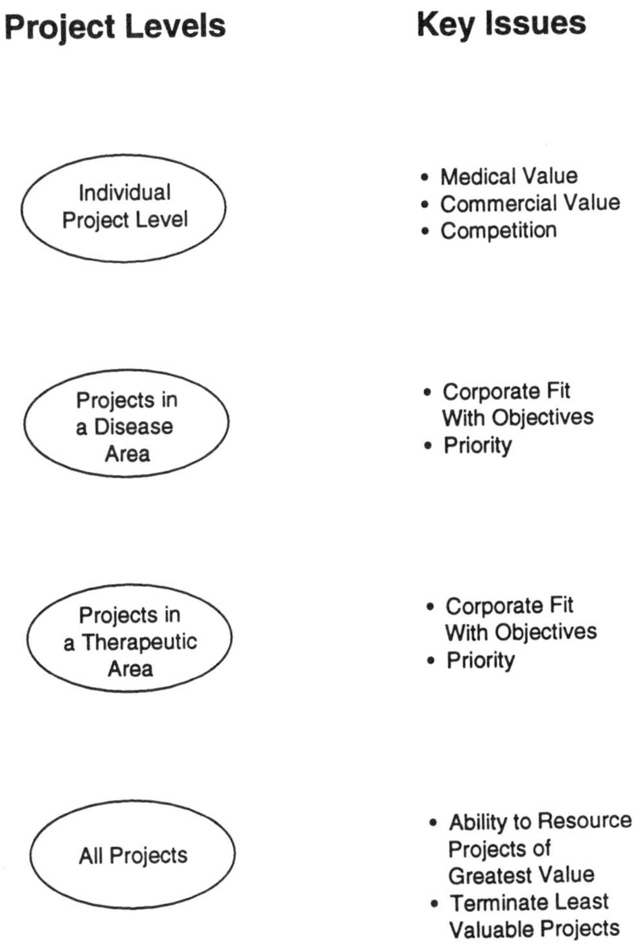

Project Levels	Key Issues

Project Levels

Individual
Project Level

Projects in
a Disease
Area

Projects in
a Therapeutic
Area

All Projects

Key Issues

- Medical Value
- Commercial Value
- Competition

- Corporate Fit
  With Objectives
- Priority

- Corporate Fit
  With Objectives
- Priority

- Ability to Resource
  Projects of
  Greatest Value
- Terminate Least
  Valuable Projects

FIG. 35.1. Illustrates the four levels of viewing projects in a portfolio analysis and the key issues associated with each level.

tified prior to determining that a gap is actually present or is projected to occur sometime in the future.

1. *Gaps in research activities* Inadequate medicine discovery activities are being conducted in therapeutic areas of importance to the company. Alternatively, research may be ongoing in areas of interest, but research goals may not be met.

2. *Gaps in discovering novel compounds of importance* An inadequate number of important chemical leads have emerged from research that have entered the medicine development system (i.e., project system). The company is not meeting its medicine discovery goals.

3. *Gaps in developing compounds of importance* Inadequate or no projects are active in the medicine development pipeline in certain therapeutic areas. Alternatively, no projects are active in specific phases of development, or other medicine development goals (e.g., number of projects in the system) are not being met.

4. *Gaps in submitting New Drug Applications (NDA)* Research and development is not meeting its goals of submitting X number of NDAs per year of new chemical entities (NCEs) and Y number of supplemental NDAs for line-extensions.

5. *Gaps in financial forecasts* Products to be marketed plus current products are not expected to meet the company's financial goals.

6. *Gaps in licensing activities* Goals set for licensing activities to fill any of the above-noted gaps are not being met.

7. *Gaps in marketed medicines* Various types of gaps may exist in specific therapeutic or disease areas.

Portfolio gaps resulting from lack of new products could also be viewed in terms of potential financial shortfalls over a specific number of future years. If short-term gaps are identified (i.e., within a four- or five-year period), an attempt may be made to fill them through (1) acquisition of new products, (2) acquisition of another company, (3) corporate merger, (4) licensing-in of marketed and/or investigational medicines, or (5) rapid development of line-extensions. Long-term gaps (i.e., greater than an eight- to ten-year period) could be addressed through changes in basic research, proactive licensing, joint ventures, or acquisition of other companies.

Perspectives of Various Groups Conducting a Portfolio Analysis

The group conducting a portfolio evaluation may be based in research, marketing, finance, or another section of a company. Their approach, methodologies, and orientation will undoubtedly be affected by their training and the purposes of the review. Any of these groups could conduct the entire portfolio exercise without soliciting help from other groups. This means that the medical value may be assessed by marketing personnel and the financial value by research personnel, but this approach would generally yield data that would be less believable to most reviewers and corporate officers than if the analyses are conducted by those who are most expert in that field. If asking help from other groups creates a problem (e.g., too much time required), then a nonpartisan person or group may be chosen to conduct and direct the entire exercise. This may require the services of an outside consultant who has the requisite capability and credibility. Another alternative is to have internal staff generate the report, and to have either staff at a separate company site or a consulting group audit and review the results.

An important part of the perspective used in approaching portfolio analysis includes consideration of

(1) which pharmaceutical businesses (e.g., prescription, over-the-counter medicines, generics, and biotechnology) will be considered; (2) the scope of projects, medicines, and/or research compounds to be considered; (3) which geographical area is being considered (e.g., single country, single development site, single company, or worldwide operations); and (4) who is making the decisions at each level. Separate portfolio analyses could be conducted on marketed medicines, investigational medicines, and research compounds. Other types of portfolios are described in the next section.

Reviewing a Multinational Company's Overall Portfolio and Those of Individual Sites

Multinational pharmaceutical companies often conduct research and develop medicines in two or more countries simultaneously. Each of the major sites for these activities may have relative autonomy and independence, although their efforts are coordinated to some degree with the other sites. In this situation, the portfolio of one country's projects will undoubtedly overlap with that of other sites. In addition to the portfolios of the individual sites, the portfolio of the company as a whole should be analyzed. Comparisons may be made between these site-specific portfolios as well as comparing portfolios with industry averages. Managing directors within each country where a company's medicines are sold may also conduct portfolio analyses.

Even if portfolios of two separate sites developing medicines for the same company contained the exact same projects, the commercial value of each portfolio could be completely different. Imagine that one site was developing medicines for the American market and the other site was developing the same medicines for the rest of the world. The commercial value of medicines being developed to treat tropical diseases would clearly differ between the two sites. The value of medicines for many other diseases would also differ markedly between sites because of other factors. These factors include (1) the status of existing and projected competition, (2) the way that medicine is practiced in different countries (e.g., whether certain types of medicines are or are not commonly used), (3) the size of the pharmaceutical market(s), (4) the ability of each site to sell the medicine, and (5) numerous other factors.

DEVELOPING A PORTFOLIO

Determining an Ideal Portfolio

There may be occasions in reviewing the company portfolio, evaluating the portfolio of another company, or planning in which direction to develop a company's portfolio when it is important to consider what the ideal medicine portfolio would look like.

The ideal portfolio for one pharmaceutical company would differ from that of another company, depending on the businesses they are in, their mission, and traditions. Although some characteristics would be identical (e.g., the importance of long patent life of investigational medicines), most will vary to a small or large degree from company to company. A portfolio of prescription medicines under development may be viewed as consisting of three separate types of investigational medicines: (1) innovative medicines, (2)"me-too" medicines (NCEs), and (3) line-extensions. The ideal portfolio, according to the director of research, may differ from that defined by the director of marketing or the director of production. There is therefore no single concept of an ideal portfolio, except possibly in the most general terms.

Determining a Realistic Portfolio

Factors that must be considered in choosing new compounds or medicines to include in a portfolio are:

1. *Patent life remaining at the time of a medicine's launch* This estimated period should be adequate to recoup development costs and to make a profit. Exceptions may be included if agreed to by relevant managers.
2. *Regulations* Regulations that must be followed to have medicines developed and approved must be attainable.
3. *Time to develop and market medicines* This time should be near the lower end of the average range, insofar as possible. Medicines vary greatly in this regard, so that a more reasonable goal might be to have a mix of short-, mid-, and long-term projects.
4. *Costs to develop and market medicines* Projected costs should be reasonable, unless the anticipated return on investment justifies larger development costs. Spending huge sums to develop an orphan medicine is rarely realistic.
5. *Social attitudes about medicines* These should be positive or neutral. If problems are anticipated, then an educational campaign or another approach should be considered. If this is not feasible or would not be cost effective, then the medicine's development plan should be reassessed.
6. *Clinical feasibility* Medicines should be possible to study in terms of patient availability and clinical parameters to measure. It may be possible or even necessary to utilize new efficacy parameters to evaluate a medicine, but the credibility of such parameters to the Food and Drug Administration and prescribing physicians must be assessed.
7. *Medical value* This should be high, although it can-

not be accurately established for most investigational medicines until after a number of patients have been studied.

8. *Commercial value* The portfolio's overall value should be appropriate from the perspective of meeting the company's financial goals. Financial goals should allow room for a limited number of less commercially attractive medicines to be included in the portfolio when they contribute high medical value and have a high likelihood of being marketed.

9. *Probability of achieving marketing* This should be high for most medicines in the portfolio. Long shots from a medical efficacy or safety perspective should generally have high commercial value if a decision is made to develop the medicine.

10. *Legal considerations* There should not be significant legal issues (e.g., probability of product liability suits) or social issues (e.g., potential for medicine abuse) for most, if not all, medicine portfolios. Oral contraceptives are a group of medicines where numerous social issues have been raised (e.g., use in underdeveloped countries and religious sanctions), as well as a major issue on the changed benefit-to-risk ratio over the last 25 years.

11. *Competitive value* Two aspects of competitive value should be considered. *First,* medicines in the portfolio should offer a real advantage over existing medicine therapy. This advantage may be in terms of an improved benefit-to-risk ratio or another advantage such as improved absorption, quality of life, convenience, compliance, or acceptability to patients. If the medicine will compete with one of the company's own products, competition may enhance sales or lead to severe cannibalization of the marketed medicine's sales. *Second,* the number of competitors present in the therapeutic areas where medicines are being developed should be determined and their potential impact assessed. Assessments should be in terms of expected time to market, as well as important advantages and disadvantages of the competitor's medicines in comparison with the company's medicine.

ANALYZING THE VALUE OF A PORTFOLIO

Comparison of Scientific Versus Medical Value

There is an overlap between the parameters used to assess the scientific and medical value of a portfolio. *Medical value* refers to the actual need for the new medicine in medical practice and includes consideration of the direct benefits it will provide to patients and the indirect benefits it will provide to health care providers. *Scientific value* relates to the interest in a new medicine from an academic and research perspective. This includes consideration of the medicine's scientific novelty and mechanism of action. Medicines with high scientific and low medical value are described in Chapter 33 as "sexy medicines." Few new medicines have high medical and low scientific interest because the mechanism of how an important new medicine works would usually be of great interest to academic scientists. Nonetheless, one possible example of a medicine that has high medical and low scientific value was the discovery that mannitol was an important new treatment for brain edema through its production of an osmotic diuresis. The mechanism of this effect was believed to be known, and there was relatively little scientific interest generated by this important medical discovery. "Me-too" medicines are in a different category because they have little scientific and little medical value but may achieve significant commercial success (see Introduction).

Judging the Scientific Value of a New Medicine

The scientific value of individual medicines may best be gauged on a relative scale from low to high. Determining where a medicine fits on this scale is usually straightforward and noncontroversial. As a medicine's medical value changes, there is often, but not always, a concomitant change in its scientific value. The scientific value is based to a large degree on the scientific novelty of a medicine's mechanism of action and the chemical novelty of its structure. Medicines that are unique in the way they act have a high scientific value, but unless they have desirable clinical properties, their medical value may be low. A medicine that is found to be toxic and is withdrawn from the market (i.e., loses its medical value) may retain its scientific value and interest if it is the only known medicine to stimulate or inhibit a receptor of interest, or has another property of interest.

Medicines with high scientific value may be marketed in part on that basis. Marketing claims may state that medicine X is the first of a new type of medicine to treat disease D, that medicine X is the only commercially available medicine to inhibit the Y receptor, or that medicine X is the first medicine to stimulate enzyme Z. Whether the latter two claims are accompanied by desirable clinical effects or remain merely pharmacological activities must be assessed by the physicians who read these or related claims.

Rating the Medical Value of a New Medicine

The medical value in terms of the benefit to patients and the practice of medicine may be most easily described for each project in the portfolio according to one or more simple scales. Examples of such scales include the following.

1. The medicine has high, moderate, or low medical value (based on a subjective assessment, questionnaire, or other method). This assessment is made with a three-point scale.
2. The medicine has extremely high, high, moderate, adequate, little, or no medical value. This is a six-point scale.
3. The benefits of the medicine are expected to reach: over ten million patients/year, over a million patients/year, over ten thousand patients/year, or another number of patients/year. These numbers may be estimated by marketing groups using input from research and development about the medicine's characteristics.
4. The medicine is viewed as providing life-saving therapy, relief of a debilitating disease, high or moderate relief of a chronic disease, or high or moderate relief of an acute disease.
5. The percent of all patients with the target disease who are expected to use the medicine is: 75% to 100%, 50% to 75%, 25% to 50%, or 0% to 25%.
6. The overall medical benefits of the medicine may be rated by a group using an arbitrary scale of one to 100.
7. The ability of the medicine to displace current therapy for a disease.
8. The likelihood of physicians prescribing the medicine for their patients.

Almost all of these scales assess a medicine's medical value relative to existing medicine and nonmedicine therapy. Only Scale 4 can be rated independently of existing therapy.

Another method of determining the medical value of a medicine is to compare the therapeutic ratio of a medicine with those of existing medicines. The therapeutic ratio equals the dose that causes adverse reactions divided by the dose that causes a beneficial effect. The larger the number is, the safer the medicine is. This approach would only be practical for medicines that have completed Phase II. Prior to that point it would be impossible to assess a medicine's therapeutic ratio. The therapeutic ratio of some medicines entering Phase III studies is still difficult (or impossible) to determine accurately.

What Is the Therapeutic Utility of a New Medicine?

The therapeutic utility of a new medicine depends on the perspective of the group that is asking the question as follows.

1. *To a pharmaceutical company* How do perceived medical benefits compare with perceived commercial benefits? Do benefits sufficiently outweigh risks so that the medicine will be able to be marketed?
2. *To a regulatory agency* Can the benefits of a new medicine be demonstrated in an adequate population of patients? The benefits and risks are considered on a level of the entire society, i.e., for all patients who may use the medicine.
3. *To a physician* How will the physician's ability to treat patients be affected? The answer is usually phrased in general terms.
4. *To an individual patient* Will the treatment diminish the intensity of symptoms, improve chances for a longer life, and/or provide a better quality of life than was available with prior therapy? The risks and benefits are considered strictly for the single patient affected. The direct effects of a medicine on a patient may lead to indirect effects on others (e.g., family, friends, and business associates).

Forecasting the Commercial Value of a New Medicine

There is no doubt that the commercial value is usually the most important parameter at pharmaceutical companies for judging individual projects, as well as the overall portfolio. The commercial value of a particular investigational medicine project (or the overall portfolio) may be expressed in many ways but is always based to some degree on numerous unknown factors. It may be expressed as a forecast of:

1. Third-year (or other) sales of the medicine after it is marketed.
2. Total sales for first three (or other) years on the market discounted to its present value.
3. The estimated range of sales for third-year (or other) sales.
4. The net profit after taxes for the first five (or other) years on the market.
5. The number of years to pay off the research and development costs from the stream of net earnings after taxes.
6. The third-year (or other) sales times the probability of success. This is a risk-adjusted forecast.

The above forecast may be based on the medicine's achieving an optimistic profile, expected profile, or minimally acceptable profile. Alternatively, multiple forecasts may be given for each medicine.

It is essential that all project forecasts in a portfolio be made using the same approach for all projects. This can usually be best accomplished by a single person or group that evaluates all projects. Any of the above forecasts may be compared with opportunity costs of using the money invested in research and development in other ways.

New product forecasting is an inexact science that is subject to many changes in the market as well as changes in a medicine's profile. Most of these changes cannot be accurately defined or predicted early in an investigational medicine's development. In some situations, the number of patients to be treated after the medicine is marketed is extremely difficult to estimate and any forecast may be highly inaccurate. This situation may occur when a new medicine is to be used for an as yet untreatable disease. Each year that most medicines are on the market it generally becomes easier to forecast their sales with greater accuracy.

There is usually pressure for marketing groups to provide a forecast early in a project's life. Providing a range of numbers based on a medicine's attaining either the ideal or minimally acceptable profile is desirable. This range allows others to determine whether the minimally acceptable profile would affect the expected sales (based on the projected profile) by up to 10% or by tenfold. A range also allows others to understand the degree of variability and confidence placed in the numbers provided by those who developed them. If marketing reports estimate third-year sales of $40 million for the *expected* medicine profile, it is uncertain whether their calculations are ±10% or ±100%. Even if a range is provided as a forecast using the expected medicine profile, it is uncertain how the minimally acceptable medicine profile would affect the forecast. Marketing forecasters must be cautious about clinicians who provide them with overly positive attributes about the medicine and glorify the compound's profile.

ANALYZING A PROJECT PORTFOLIO IN FIVE STEPS

Steps to Follow

The first step in evaluating a portfolio of investigational and/or marketed medicines is to determine which projects should be considered as part of the portfolio. The second step in evaluating a portfolio is to evaluate each project in terms of its individual characteristics. The third step is to evaluate the overall balance and composition of the portfolio using the methods desired. The fourth step is to interpret the results. This interpretation is based on changes, trends, progress toward goals, and various comparisons. The last step is to use the results to modify the company, or business area.

Projects to Include in a Portfolio (Step One)

Categories of the portfolio include (1) marketed medicines, (2) investigational medicines, (3) medicines that are both marketed and investigational, (4) investigational medicines that have passed their go–no go decision point and are definitely going to be developed, and (5) research compounds. Other categories could also be defined.

The current phase of development or status may be illustrated for each project in the portfolio in several ways. A common method is to use a horizontal bar for each project listed along the left margin (ordinate) to show whether it is currently pre-Investigational New Drug Application (IND), or in Phase I, Phase II, Phase III (pre-NDA submission), Phase III (post-NDA submission), or is marketed. Another method is to have years along the abscissa (X axis) and to show dates of regulatory submission and approval for each project. Many alternative categorizations may be used, depending on the make-up of the medicines in the portfolio.

The total number of projects or medicines in the portfolio can be easily illustrated on a year-by-year basis with a line graph or histogram. This type of graph may also show the number of projects terminated per year. The number of projects initiated may be (1) expressed as a number per year, (2) compared with a standard goal, or (3) described on a moving multiyear average (Fig. 35.2A). A graph of all projects may be shown (Fig. 35.3).

Measuring Individual Projects in a Portfolio (Step Two)

Some of the parameters that may be applied to the measurement of individual projects are described below. Not all of these are usually used in an analysis.

1. *Probability of submitting an NDA, Product License Application, or other regulatory submission* Minimal criteria for which a regulatory application will be submitted should be established for each medicine. Based on these criteria, a probability may then be established for submitting each project in the portfolio. This probability provides a useful single means for estimating the likelihood of marketing each medicine. The major disadvantage of this measure is that with few exceptions, it is directly related to a medicine's phase of development, i.e., medicines in Phase I usually have a low probability of being marketed, those in Phase II have a higher probability, and those in Phase III have the highest probability. The probability may be assessed as quartiles (i.e., 0% to 25%, 25% to 50%, 50% to 75%, and 75% to 100%), deciles (i.e., in tenths), or even on a scale from one to 100. The 100-point scale is clearly too detailed because small differences would not be meaningful. If a medicine's profile becomes tarnished, it is worthwhile establishing at what point a regulatory submission would not be submitted.

2. *Probability of achieving clinical goals* This probability is assessed in terms of safety, efficacy, and other

NUMBER OF PROJECTS INITIATED

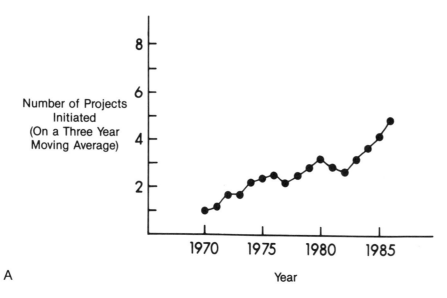

A

HEAD COUNT APPLIED TO A PROJECT

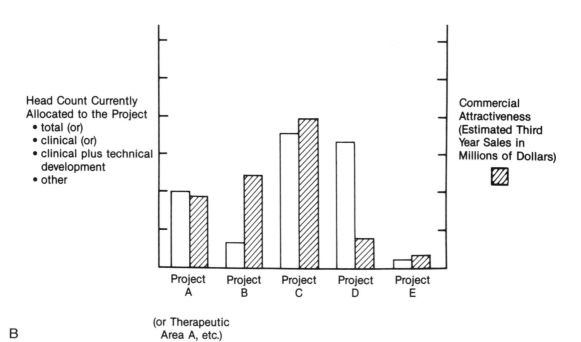

B

FIG. 35.2. A. Number of new projects initiated per year. This graph could be a histogram, or could only illustrate the actual number per year instead of a moving average. The term ''three-year moving average'' means that the value(s) of the year in question plus those of the previous two years are averaged. **B.** Head count currently applied to a project and its commercial attractiveness. This type of graph could also be used to illustrate specific therapeutic areas.

TRACK RECORD ON NCE PROJECTS

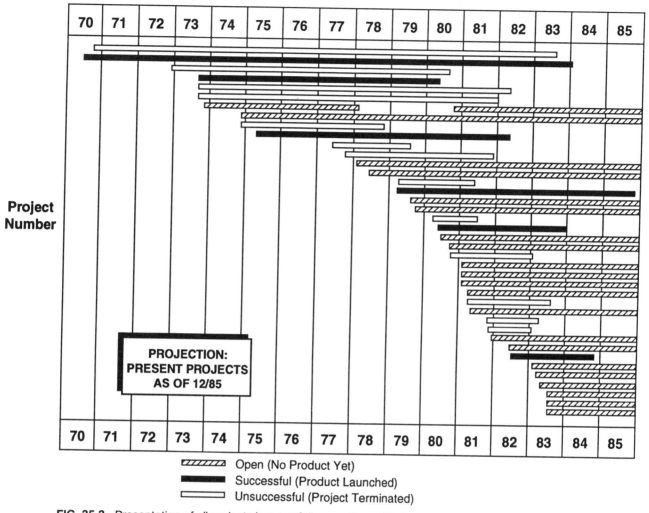

FIG. 35.3. Presentation of all projects in a portfolio over time with the outcome of each project shown. The projects are listed by number and name on the ordinate. Many variations of this table are possible. For example, the definition of success could be said to NDA submission.

important targets (e.g., pharmacokinetics or quality of life). This point and that listed under point three below are subsets of point one and may be expressed numerically in any of the ways discussed under point one.

3. *Probability of achieving technical goals* This probability relates to issues of formulation, chemical scaleup, stability on storage, and numerous other considerations mentioned in Chapter 46. The goals are usually expressed as the minimally acceptable standards that allow continuation of a medicine project. The rating of the technical attractiveness of a project may be based on answering one of several questions. What is the probability of:

a. Getting the product to the market?

b. Supporting existing business?

c. Getting to Phase III (i.e., passing the go–no go decision point at the end of Phase II)?

d. Getting to Phase II (i.e., passing Phase I)?

4. *Number of staff* Is the number of staff working on each project sufficient? This question may be assessed in purely subjective or objective terms. An objective assessment is shown in Fig. 35.2B, where a balance is sought between staff allocated and potential value of the medicine. Several other scales that could be used are also indicated in Fig. 35.2B, such as the percent of total staff or the percent of anticipated sales to come from current investigational medicines. The percent of staff could refer to all development staff, total staff working on projects, senior staff, medical staff, or any other defined group. Cumulative scientist or clinician years of effort expended could be plotted for each project, for high versus low priority projects, or for projected versus actual values.

Another aspect of staffing could be graphed as the number of people needed per project versus the number available per project. The best means of graphing this comparison might be as two vertical bar histograms per project plotted alongside each other. This approach would enable a rapid comparison to be made for each project.

5. *Market attractiveness (i.e., value) of the project* Each project should be commercially attractive to the company, or else there should be some other compelling reason to develop the medicine (e.g., an orphan medicine may enhance the company's prestige and also enable patients to be helped who previously had no effective treatment). Various scales may be used to measure market value. These include (1) third-year (or other) sales forecast, (2) total of first three years' forecasted sales discounted to present value, or (3) broad ranges of third-year sales. An example of the ranges could be (a) up to $5 million, (b) $5 to 25 million, (c) $25 to 50 million, and (d) above $50 million per year. The percent of current projects in each range may be determined.

Many marketers prefer a single point of value to a range of values. Their reasoning is that a single number minimizes the confusion that may occur in determining where in the range the project actually lies. The profit of a medicine may also be measured in numerous ways as follows: (1) specific amounts of money, (2) profits of a medicine in the third year (or fifth year) after marketing, (3) the number of years until the project begins to make a profit, and (4) the total profits on a medicine.

Commercial attractiveness may be rated based on the medicine achieving its minimally acceptable profile for each specific indication, or overall. It may also be rated based on the medicine achieving the desired (or realistic or ideal) profile for each specific indication, or overall.

The first measure is much more useful in making decisions about the medicine (e.g., should we market the medicine if it only achieves the minimally acceptable profile? If the answer is no, then the minimally acceptable criteria must be increased until the answer is yes). Caveats may be used to rate commercial attractiveness (e.g., this is the commercial value if the medicine is approved by 1995, and the value decreases by X percent or Y amount of money if approval occurs two years later).

6. *Medical attractiveness (i.e., value) of the project* Each project is evaluated as to its medical importance. This can be described using several systems that are discussed elsewhere in this book.

7. *Political pressures influencing the project* This comes from pressures either within or outside the company and they may be positive or negative pressures. The strength of pressures are extremely high for certain types of medicines (e.g., abortion-inducing medicine).

8. *Money spent on each project* What is the rate of spending and how does it compare to previous projections? How much money still has to be expended? The percent of the total spent may be followed and tracked in many ways (Figs. 35.4 and

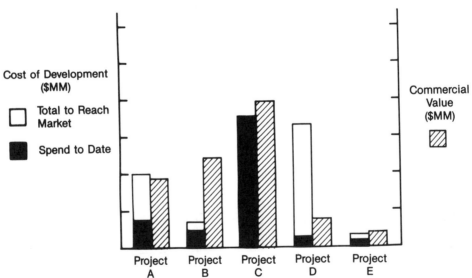

COST OF DEVELOPMENT VERSUS COMMERCIAL VALUE

FIG. 35.4. Cost of development (i.e., research and development) and commercial value of individual projects. The commercial value is the net present value or the net profit stream before or after taxes. This type of graph could also be used to illustrate specific therapeutic areas. Other research and development parameters could be illustrated, e.g., the medical utility of each medicine and time to get to a NDA.

THERMOMETER MODEL OF PROJECT SPEND

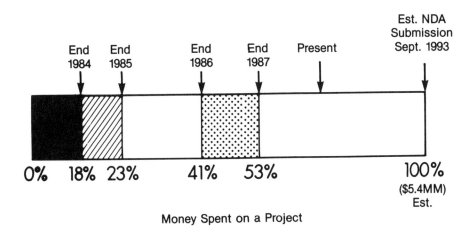

FIG. 35.5. "Thermometer" model used to illustrate the proportion of money already spent on a project. NDA, New Drug Application.

35.5, for examples). Numerous additional means of tracking and presenting expenditures are shown and described in Chapter 53.

9. *Competition* What is the status of competitive products that might have an impact on each project? In how much of a competitive race is each project? What is the level of competition in terms of the quality of their products and the intensity of activities in the field? Will resources allocated by a company to a medicine's development be sufficient to meet or beat the competition? If not, what options and strategies are available?

10. *Project fit* Does each project fit the company's culture, long-term plans, and strategy for medicine development? These should be easy questions to answer for most projects. Projects that lie outside the company's comfort zone may present problems that could be addressed in such ways as cross-licensing, comarketing, or using other alternatives.

11. *Uniqueness of the concept or risk* There are two types of risk that may be measured for each medicine in a portfolio. The first type relates to the probability that the medicine will reach the market. This is primarily related to its phase of development and is covered under points 1, 2, and 3 above. The second type relates to the uniqueness of the concept and whether the medicine represents an untried or unproven theory or a known concept. For example, a new cephalosporin antibiotic represents a low-risk

medicine, whereas a new enzyme inhibitor designed to treat a disease where no treatment is available represents a high-risk project. A company that has a great deal of basic research underway in disease areas where high-risk projects exist usually decreases its overall risk. The risk in high-risk projects also diminishes after clinical efficacy and safety are established. Therefore, this type of risk is also related to the phase of a medicine's development. Resource-related data that may be collected on projects are listed in Table 35.1.

TABLE 35.1. *Possible data to determine for projects in a portfolio[a]*

1. Days of work per month, quarter, or year
2. Number of full-time equivalents
3. Calculate the percent of all projects for number 1 or 2 above
4. Internal costs on each project
5. External and total costs on each project
6. Calculate the percent of all projects for numbers 4 and 5 above
7. Determine the totals for all projects together in categories 1, 2, 4, and 5
8. Break down each of the above seven categories by division, department, and section
9. Break down all of the above by quarters for two (or more) years and plot the results

[a] Projections for the next six quarters or two years can be made and illustrated in separate tables or graphs.

**Measuring Groups of Projects
in a Portfolio (Step Three)**

The third step in analyzing a portfolio is to evaluate the entire group of projects in the portfolio, or possibly only a specific subset of projects. The groups of projects could be those in a specific therapeutic area or those targeted for a single disease or in a specific category (e.g., over-the-counter medicines). The methods used either illustrate each project separately in a scattergram, table, or other format, or combine all values into a cumulative or overall figure.

Allocation of Resources

A histogram, table, scattergram, grid, or other visual depictions may be made to illustrate the amount (or percent) of resources (e.g., head count or money) allocated to each project. Using the histogram format shown in Fig. 35.6 it would be simple to determine if any projects were out of balance as to the number of staff working on it. This assumes, of course, that the allocation of staff is

to be based on a project's commercial value. Other values or an index could be created as a basis for staff allocation. An apparent imbalance might be acceptable to a company and certainly does not mean that staff should definitely be reassigned. A similar histogram could be constructed for the cost of a project and its commercial value illustrating both the amount already spent and the amount forecasted either to complete planned activities or to get the medicine onto the market. Another histogram could illustrate the current phase of development of each investigational compound and medicine in the portfolio.

Figure 35.7 illustrates how resources are actually used on some or all projects. This type of graph can also be used to illustrate planned allocation of resources. The specific way in which resources are measured (e.g., total dollar allocation, months of effort, number of head count, external grants, and percent of total effort) will have some impact on how the data appear. The parameter chosen to plot as a measure of resource allocation or resources used is often important in influencing the type of conclusion reached. The projects may be listed in the order of expenses incurred over the preceding X number of months, the percent of effort, or the chronological

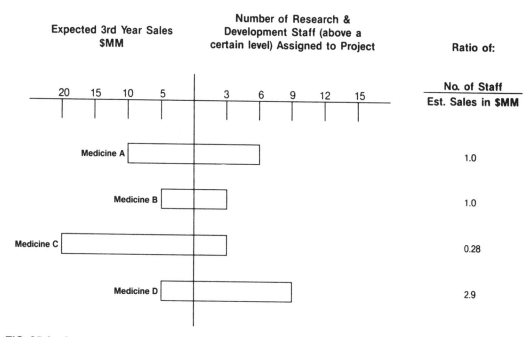

FIG. 35.6. Comparison of staff allocated to a project and expected sales of that project. Changes from a previous year could be shown as a hatched bar. The number of staff could be the current resource allocated or the total number of person years to complete a project. Each medicine could be illustrated with multiple bars to show different indications or dosage forms. Effort expended to date could be shown with a dotted bar.

AVERAGES FOR ALL DEVELOPMENT PROJECTS

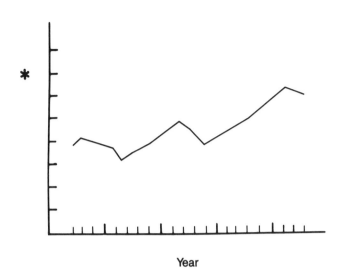

Year

* 1. Average cost of a month of work effort per project (constant dollars).
2. Average effort in scientist months per project.
3. Average cost per project (constant dollars).
4. Average total head count per project.

FIG. 35.7. Average cost of work effort on a project. The ordinate may also be average effort, average cost in constant dollars, or average total head count per project.

TOTAL HEADCOUNT PER PROJECT

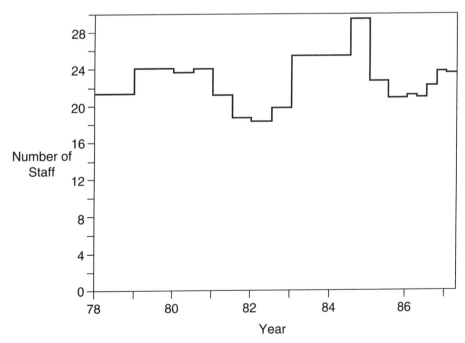

FIG. 35.8. Illustration of total head count across all projects. This type of graph can be used to illustrate many different aspects of the overall project system (e.g., money spent per month, number of people months spent per month, and external costs per month).

PORTFOLIO OF INVESTIGATIONAL MEDICINES
(i.e. Projects)

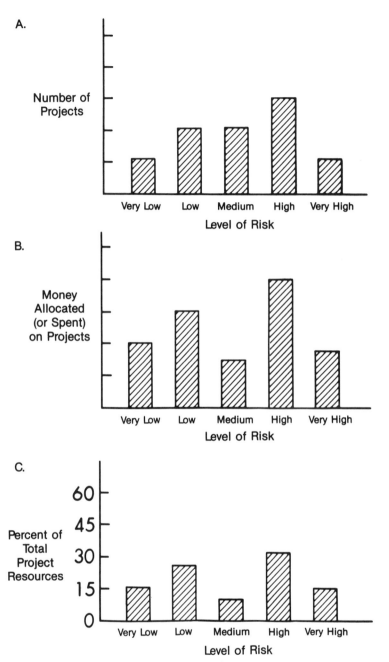

FIG. 35.9. Illustrating a portfolio of new medicines on the basis of risk. The five categories of risk would have to be defined prior to creating this figure. The risk might be defined in terms of the probability of success. Changes from year to year could be illustrated.

formation of the project. The projects may be grouped by therapeutic area or by priority (if one is assigned) and the expenses or another parameter relating to resources can be graphed along the ordinate. Each project could be represented by a bar, or dot on the abscissa. The plots of actual versus projected allocations of resources may also be prepared. The averages for all projects may be shown (Fig. 35.8).

Figure 35.9 illustrates the allocation of resources according to the level of a project's risk. The risk is usually defined in terms of the probability of marketing a medicine. This, in turn, relates primarily to the medicine's phase of development, but also includes consideration of patent status, licensing issues (if any), and the likelihood for early-phase projects to demonstrate efficacy and safety. The total resources required to bring one large project to market are much less in many areas (e.g., toxicology, regulatory affairs, and data processing) than to bring many small projects to market.

Commercial Parameters

Commercial parameters (e.g., expected third-year sales) are generally used to analyze the overall portfolio.

Examples of other commercial and financial parameters include: (1) the return on the investment, (2) the expected sales over the first two or three years, (3) the expected contribution to profit, and (4) the amount of money saved per year through the use of the medicine.

The ratio of commercial value to (1) head count, (2) total cost of development, or (3) another parameter may be determined for each project. These ratios may be plotted for a project from year to year to illustrate trends. A scattergram of these ratios at any one point in time would illustrate any projects that are outliers. Outliers may be acceptable and may not require any adjustments, but the method would flag them for attention. A combined ratio for all projects could be determined and compared with the ratios from previous years.

The commercial value is shown in Figs. 35.6 and 35.10 to 35.14 and the competitive position is shown in Fig. 35.15 to 35.16.

Medical Parameters

The relative medical value could be expressed as the (1) number of patients to be treated, (2) the percent of total patients to be treated, (3) the number of surgeries

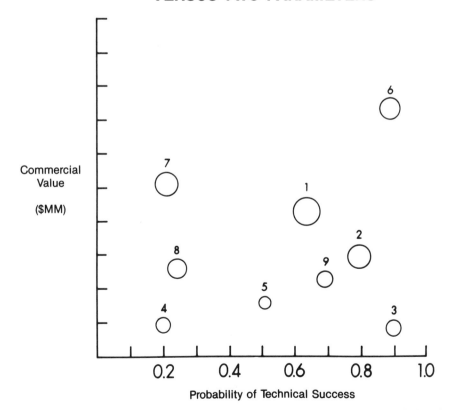

PROBABILITY OF TECHNICAL SUCCESS VERSUS TWO PARAMETERS

Commercial Value

($MM)

Probability of Technical Success

FIG. 35.10. The probability of technical success versus the commercial value of individual projects. The size of each circle is used to indicate a third parameter. This third parameter may be the cost of the project to develop, the medical need for the particular medicine, or any other parameter of interest. The numbers refer to a particular project which would be identified on a separate list.

PROBABILITY OF TECHNICAL SUCCESS
VERSUS COMMERCIAL VALUE

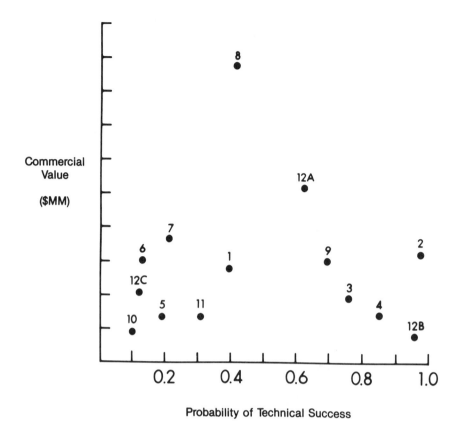

FIG. 35.11. The probability of technical success versus the commercial value of individual projects. Each dot represents a different project, except for 12, where each letter represents a different indication studied for the same project. A separate key must be provided to identify the projects. Technical success and commercial value may be defined in several ways. The probability of submitting a Product License Application or NDA could be used as the abscissa.

CHANGE IN PORTFOLIO OF PROJECTS
OVER TIME

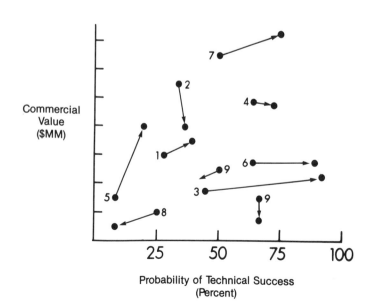

FIG. 35.12. Illustrating a change in a project portfolio over a period of time (e.g., year).

380

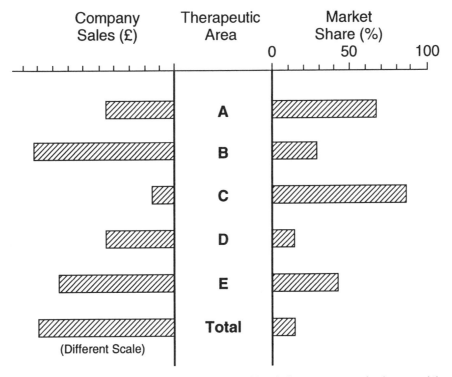

FIG. 35.13. A comparison of the relative market share with relative company sales in several therapeutic areas. Disease areas could also be illustrated to evaluate whether the company's major sales come from markets they dominate or not.

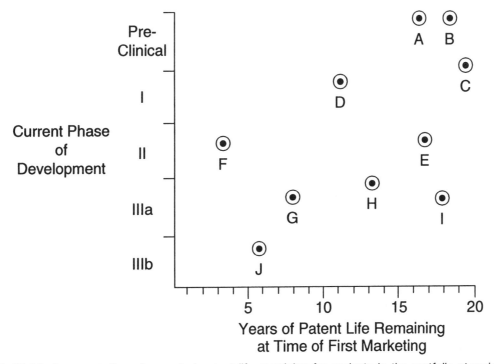

FIG. 35.14. A presentation of expected patent life remaining for projects in the portfolio at various stages of development.

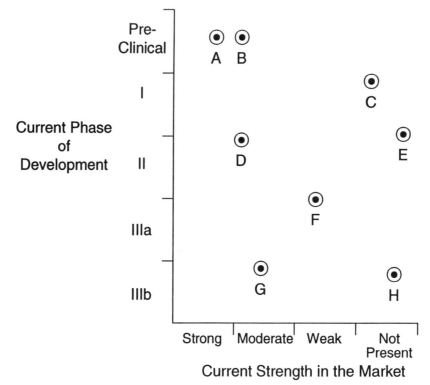

FIG. 35.15. A presentation of projects at different stages of development and what their strength is expected to be in the market.

PORTFOLIO OF INVESTIGATIONAL MEDICINE PROJECTS

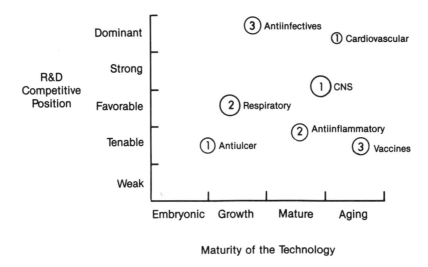

Size of circle is proportional to degree of effort.
The numbers inside the circles indicate the number of drugs under development

FIG. 35.16. Illustrating a portfolio of new medicines on the basis of the technology's maturity. The size of the circle is proportional to the degree of effort. The numbers inside the circles indicate the number of medicines under development. Although this figure illustrates therapeutic areas, the same format could be used to illustrate individual medicine projects. CNS, central nervous system; R&D, research and development.

avoided, (4) the number of hospital days avoided, or (5) using various other parameters.

Regulatory and Project Management Parameters

Many regulatory parameters should be followed for groups of projects in terms of their current status, as well as in terms of trends over the past several years and future projections. Examples of this include:

1. The number of regulatory submissions per year or per some other time period (Fig. 35.17).
2. The time from regulatory submission to approval for the company's NDAs (Fig. 35.18).
3. The number of IND submissions per year (Fig. 35.19).
4. The time from project formation to first filing of an IND (Fig. 35.20).
5. The number of regulatory staff assigned to high priority projects (Fig. 35.21).

6. The number of IND, NDA, or abbreviated NDA submissions made per quarter and projected over the next several quarters (Fig. 35.22).
7. The movement over time of projected dates for regulatory submissions and market launch (Fig. 35.23).

Financial Methods to Analyze a Portfolio

1. Determine the total value of the portfolio. This concept could be illustrated as a graph depicting several years' values, preferably with money expressed in constant amounts. This graph would clearly show how the overall portfolio's value is changing.

Although sophisticated cash flow analyses may be conducted as part of the portfolio analysis, this is often too sophisticated by the group analyzing the portfolio. Other factors, such as strategic objectives and corporate fit, may have greater significance in deciding the fate of various projects. If it is desired to con-

ACTUAL AND PROJECTED NUMBERS
OF REGULATORY SUBMISSIONS

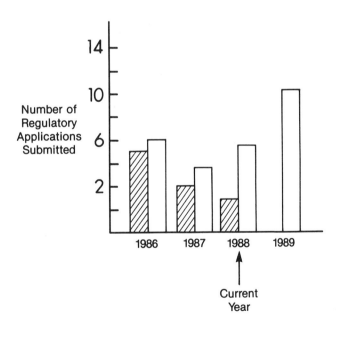

FIG. 35.17. Illustrating the number of regulatory submissions made per year. This plot may be made for specific types of submissions and may be made on a semiannual or other basis. The precise category (categories) of submissions to be tracked must be defined.

TIME FROM REGULATORY SUBMISSION TO APPROVAL

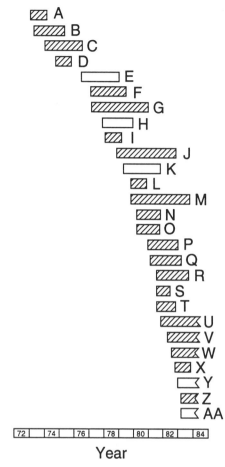

Year

FIG. 35.18. Illustrating the time taken for a large number of projects (i.e., **A** to **AA**) to be approved after submission. A broken side on the bar indicates that approval has not yet been received. The *open* and *hatched rectangles* can be used to show two types of projects (e.g., prescription and over the counter).

duct a cash flow analysis some of the following evaluations may be made.

   a. The present value of each project can be assessed using tools that are briefly mentioned in the following descriptions.

   b. The net present value is the current value of a project net of any costs.

   c. The internal rate of return is the effective compound interest rate received on investments in the project.

   d. The payback is the number of years until the company recoups all of its expenses on the project medicine.

2. The return on investment (ROI) may be graphed as a percent versus the probability of exceeding ROI (Fig. 35.24). Although it is important to set high financial goals for a company, the higher they are set in terms of ROI, the less likely it is that they will be achieved.

3. Investigate how the overall portfolio's value changes from year to year. This may be simply illustrated or it may be shown how results meet or exceed certain financial criteria or goals (e.g., amount of sales generated from new products or yearly increase in sales targeted). Figures 35.25 to 35.27 illustrate the sales and profits generated from new products.

4. Evaluate the ratio of net income after taxes for a marketed medicine over a one- to five-year period since it was marketed to the total research and development costs for that medicine. This ratio can be constructed for all medicines of a company, for medicines grouped into major therapeutic areas, or for medicines grouped by line-extensions and research-based new chemical entities. This ratio will give an idea about the medicine's value.

5. It is also possible to evaluate the profits on a medicine since its initial marketing. In addition to determining the total value for a medicine since it was marketed these evaluations can be determined for each year of the medicine's marketing, for every two to three years, or on a moving two- to five-year average.

6. The cost of research necessary to generate each IND, project, and/or NDA may be calculated in constant dollars. This number may be calculated for separate two- or three-year blocks or by using a moving average (see Fig. 35.28 upper graph for an example).

7. The average number of dollars spent per project per year and/or the average number of staff hours or months expended per project per year or on medicine discovery are also useful indicators to track (Fig. 35.28 lower graph).

Visual Grids or Scattergrams of Various Types

Selected grids or scattergrams are shown in Figs. 35.10 to 35.12. The axes of the figure generated could include almost any two of the following:

1. The total time required to develop each product (in years), or the time needed to develop each medicine, starting at the present.

2. The projected commercial sales for each medicine over a period of X years. X usually equals from two to five years.

3. The projected profits for each medicine over a period of X years. X usually equals from two to five years.

4. The staff needed to develop each product in terms of the total years of effort. This maybe calculated separately for junior and senior staff. Other breakdowns of expressing staff requirements could be used.

5. The total financial cost to develop each product.

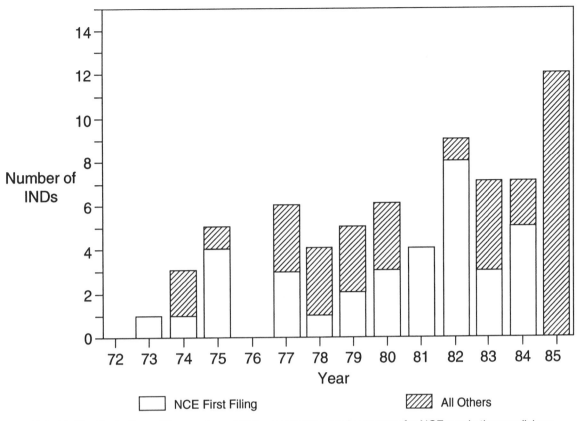

FIG. 35.19. Illustration of the number of IND submissions made per year for NCEs and other medicines.

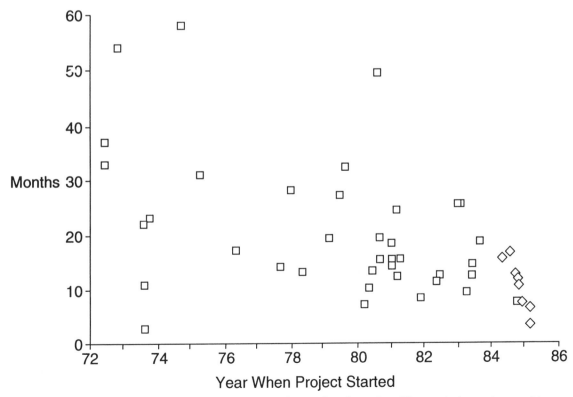

FIG. 35.20. Presenting the time for filing an IND after project formation. The symbols can be used to illustrate different types of projects.

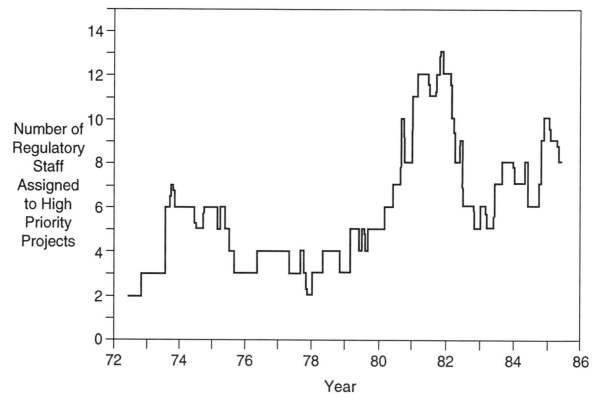

FIG. 35.21. The number of regulatory staff assigned to high-priority projects over the period between 1972 and 1985. The number and nature of high-priority projects should be known to help interpret this graph. Many variations on this graph are possible.

This may be broken down as internal costs and external grants.

6. The cost of additional capital equipment and facilities required to manufacture each product.
7. The current resources allocated to each project in terms of money, staff, or both. The changing amount of this cost, or effort, for each project over a period of several years could be shown to demonstrate (1) how the total has changed, (2) how the percent of the total expended on that project has changed, or (3) how accurate were the forecasts that were made.
8. The medical value of each investigational and/or marketed medicine.
9. The probability of achieving the minimum criteria on each investigational compound or medicine to obtain a marketed product.
10. The probability of submitting a regulatory dossier on each medicine. This parameter could be illustrated separately for each indication and dosage form being studied.
11. The intensity of competition in relevant disease areas. The quality of a competitor's medicines could be illustrated as well as their status.
12. A comparison of investigational compounds or medicines with other companies' investigational medicines, in terms of regulatory approval, medical value, commercial value, or another parameter.
13. The anticipated date of filing the initial (or any) regulatory application.

Three-dimensional graphs could be plotted with three of the above axes. The grids may consist of discrete points (e.g., one point per project or one point per indication being pursued). It is also possible to divide most axes into three or more ranges (e.g., high, medium, and low; Fig. 35.29).

It is important to identify the major assumptions made in compiling any of these grids. This should prevent, or at least minimize, misunderstandings about what the data represent and how they should be interpreted. A few examples of assumptions that could be identified include:

1. The market value is based on 19XX dollars and reflects the actual (or potential) market size in 19XX.
2. The projected project costs do not include research expenses spent to identify the compound or development expenses on earlier lead compounds.
3. The competitor's projects are (are not) considered in this analysis.

Scales such as market attractiveness may be presented in terms of a score (e.g., one to 100 or high, medium,

DATE OF PROJECTIONS

IND, NDA, ANDA SUBMISSIONS

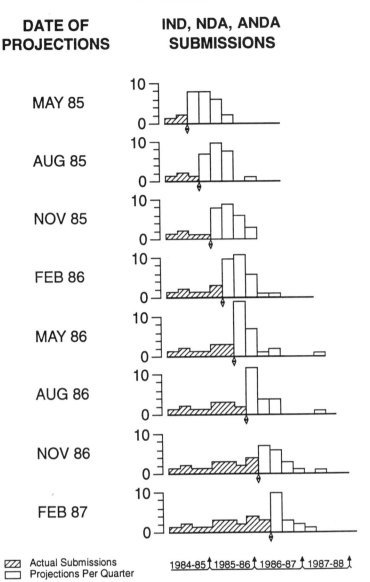

MAY 85

AUG 85

NOV 85

FEB 86

MAY 86

AUG 86

NOV 86

FEB 87

▨ Actual Submissions
▢ Projections Per Quarter

1984-85 ↑ 1985-86 ↑ 1986-87 ↑ 1987-88 ↑

FIG. 35.22. Illustration of a series of projections and actual results of regulatory submissions made over a few years. This is a two-year rolling forecast. NDAs, INDs, and major product supplements may be illustrated on separate charts.

low) or as money. If a score is used it may be quantitative where each factor is identified and a weight is assigned. It is important to identify the person or group that is completing these scales. If both marketing and research and development personnel are involved it would be interesting to compare their views. This topic could be the basis of a fruitful discussion.

An interesting alternative would be to weight all relevant parameters and to create a single score for each medicine in the portfolio. Although this approach would simplify the assessment, medicines are too complex to be reduced to a single figure, especially if research or business decisions will be based on that score.

Other grids may be used to illustrate an overall portfolio. These vary from simple ones (Fig. 35.30) to much more sophisticated ones (Figs. 35.31 to 35.33). Each of these grids have different goals and are clearly more suitable for illustrating certain types of data. For example,

the grids shown in Fig. 35.31 to 35.33 are usually used to illustrate businesses a company is engaged in, rather than illustrating a collection of medicines. Each project or medicine on a grid may be rank ordered by its position along either axis, or as a combination of the two axes. Variations on each of these approaches are possible, such as by assigning different weights to each axis. Figures 35.31 and 35.32 could illustrate therapeutic areas of marketed medicines where each pie shape would be the market share of the separate market.

The grid in Fig. 35.33 may be used to assist a company that desires to allocate resources to businesses on the basis of their overall importance to the company. The grid may also be used to evaluate whether a company has businesses that are appropriately positioned. Related diagrams of the same businesses may be made where each square illustrates current, planned, or forecasted (1) sales, (2) profits, (3) business locations, (4) characteristics

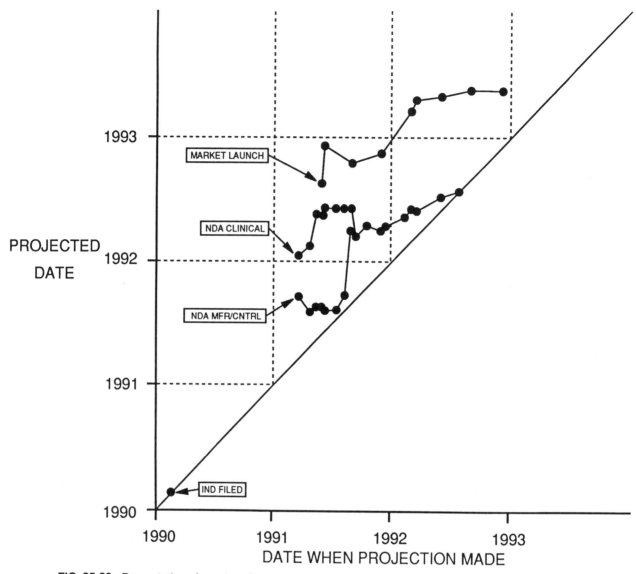

FIG. 35.23. Presentation of a series of projected dates for three separate activities and how those dates changed over time.

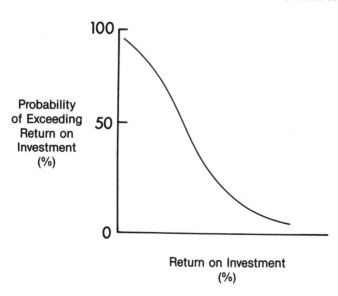

RETURN ON INVESTMENT (ROI) VERSUS PROBABILITY OF EXCEEDING ROI

FIG. 35.24. Return on investment in a portfolio versus the probability of exceeding the return on investment.

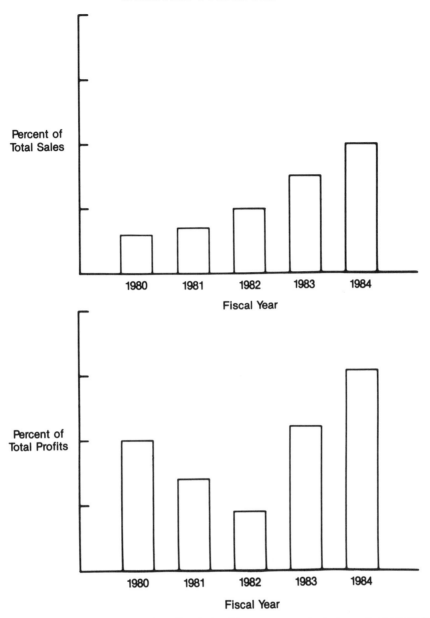

PERCENT OF SALES AND PROFITS DERIVED FROM NEW PRODUCTS

FIG. 35.25. Percent of total sales and profits derived from new products in each of several years. The term "new" is usually defined as three, four, or five years from the time of product launch. Products may be defined as a new dosage form (e.g., capsule, ointment, or solution) or only as the first dosage form launched. If multiple countries are considered then additional assumptions must be made. Future projections may also be illustrated on the figure.

SALES AND PROFITS FROM NEW MEDICINES

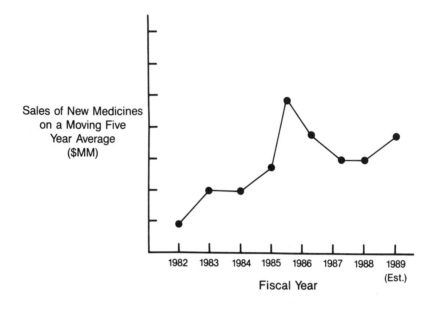

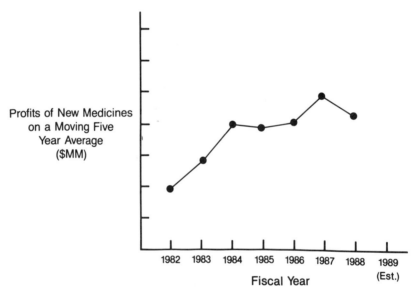

FIG. 35.26. Sales and profits of new medicines per year. The values may be calculated on a per year or moving three- to five-year average.

PERCENT OF SALES AND PROFITS FROM NEW MEDICINES

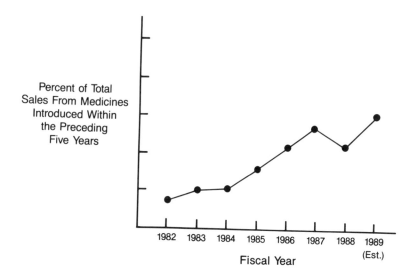

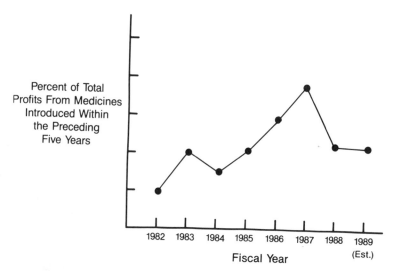

FIG. 35.27. Percent of a company's total sales and profits derived from new products. The values may be calculated per year or on a moving three- to five-year average. Both actual and projected data (i.e., past and future years) may be shown. "New" products must be clearly defined.

RESEARCH COSTS

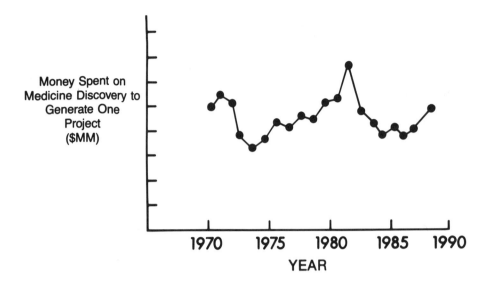

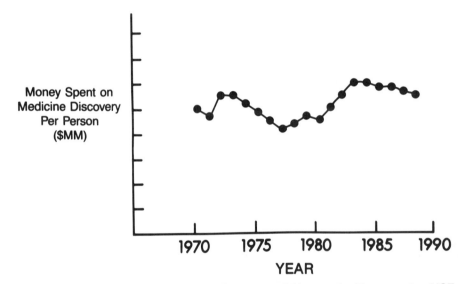

FIG. 35.28. Research expenditures on medicine discovery activities required to generate a NCE project. A three- to five-year moving average may be used.

MARKET SIZE VERSUS MEDICAL NEED

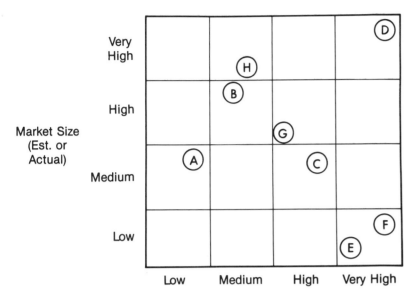

Level of Medical Need for a New Medicine

(A) to (H) may represent therapeutic areas or specific diseases.

FIG. 35.29. Grid of market size versus level of medical need. The size of the overall market in dollars, pounds, marks, or other currency will dictate what the labels along the ordinate mean.

GROWTH/SHARE MATRIX

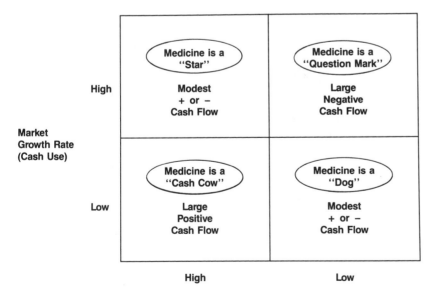

FIG. 35.30. Growth share matrix illustrating four basic types of medicines or businesses.

PRODUCT/MARKET EVOLUTION MATRIX

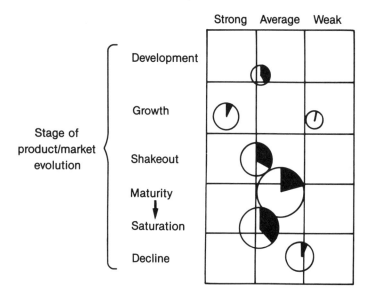

FIG. 35.31. Product market evolution matrix. From Hofer and Schendel (1978) with permission of West Publishing Co. The area of the circle is related to the size of the market. A pie section shows the proportion of that market controlled by the company.

GENERAL ELECTRIC'S NINE-CELL PLANNING GRID

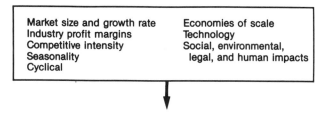

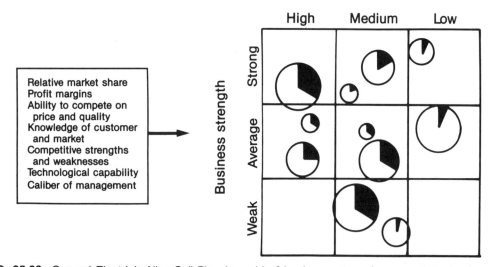

FIG. 35.32. General Electric's Nine-Cell Planning grid of business strength versus industry (product market) attractiveness. From Hofer and Schendel (1978) with permission of West Publishing Co. The area of the circle is related to the size of the market. A pie section shows the proportion of market controlled (i.e., market share).

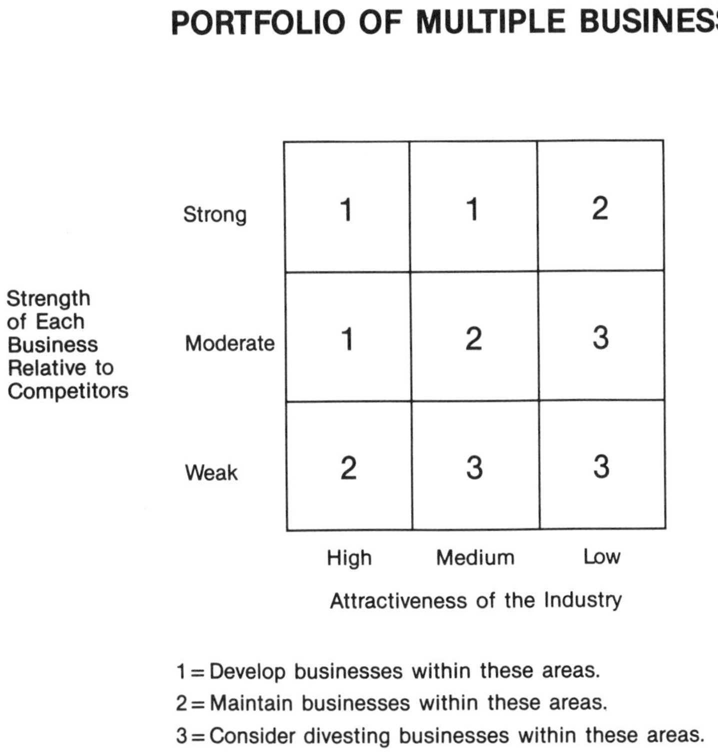

PORTFOLIO OF MULTIPLE BUSINESSES

FIG. 35.33. Company position versus industry attractiveness figure. Work effort on a project. The ordinate may also be the average effort, average cost in constant dollars, or average total head count per project.

of the labor force, or (5) other characteristics of each business.

Interpretations of a Portfolio Analysis (Step Four)

After all of the analyses are conducted and the tables and figures completed, the data must be interpreted. These interpretations will enable important decisions to be reached at different managerial levels relating to budgets, resource allocations, and other issues. If the managers who are interpreting the results lack the expertise to understand the meaning of the data (e.g., the probability of a compound becoming a success), they might allocate an excessive (or inadequate) amount of resources toward developing a particular medicine. Selected questions to consider in interpreting a portfolio analysis are listed in Table 35.2.

Percent of Projects that Are Successful

The above discussion has considered the situation where all investigational projects will be successful and the products will be marketed. However, this is clearly not the case. Industry-wide averages show that only about one in seven medicines tested in humans is ever marketed. For some companies this ratio is either higher or lower. *The value of this ratio per se does not indicate that a company is either more or less productive than the industry as a whole.* This is because different companies define projects differently, are more or less conservative

about elevating compounds into project status, and may easily manipulate this ratio if they wish to do so. The portfolio analysis may be based on the assumption that only one project in seven, five, or any other number will be successful. This number is derived by a historical review of what has transpired within that company.

The overall value of any medicine is an evolving con-

TABLE 35.2. *Selected questions to consider in interpreting a portfolio analysis*

1. Is the company working on the right number of projects?
2. Is the company working on the right specific projects?
3. Are we terminating projects promptly enough?
4. How many projects can we fund adequately?
5. Are there too many projects in the portfolio?
6. Are there too many low-priority projects in the portfolio?
7. Is the net present value of the portfolio adequate?
8. How many additional people in each major area do we need to do everything at maximal speed?
9. How much larger must the research and development budget be to progress all high-priority projects at maximal speed?
10. What additional sales can we expect if we increase the budget by X?
11. Is the company getting medicines to market at an appropriate speed?
12. Is there appropriate medical, commercial, and image value for each of the projects?
13. What are the highest priority projects?
14. Which projects should be terminated?
15. Which disease areas should be terminated?
16. Are the minimally acceptable criteria for each project too high, too low, or correct?

cept that develops during the years that the medicine is studied. This value relies heavily on the interpretation of the medicine's profile in relation to both its desired clinical profile and its minimally acceptable profile. Knowledge of a medicine's commercial potential also must be factored in to determine a medicine's true value.

Once the portfolio analysis is complete, it may be compared with:

1. Similar data obtained in previous years.
2. Other semiautonomous research and development groups within the same company (e.g., two separate sites of research and medicine development).
3. Available data on the industry's performance. These data may be obtained from trade associations, publications, or other sources.

Data may then be compared with previously established goals to identify whether these goals were achieved. Trends in the data may be evaluated, especially if goals were not met, and in the final step mentioned below, plans of how to maintain, improve, or reverse the trends may be proposed.

Utilizing a Portfolio Analysis to Modify a Company (Step Five)

After the portfolio analysis is completed and the data are interpreted, it remains a sterile exercise unless it influences future decision making. This may be in the context of issues that arise independent of the portfolio analysis, or attention may be directed toward using the interpretation to modify the company in a specific way. Senior managers must question the person or group presenting the portfolio analysis to learn the following:

1. How much money will the portfolio deliver and over what time frame?
2. How can the company best reallocate its resources to improve the future revenue stream in terms of both certainty and speed?
3. What specific recommendations can the group make who has evaluated the portfolio?
4. Are the highest priority projects receiving the fullest attention and resources needed?

The answers to these questions will enable senior managers to decide (1) if the company is moving in the best (i.e., right) direction, (2) if the portfolio is satisfactory to meet the company's minimal and desired financial goals, and (3) if the system appears to be operating appropriately and efficiently. Senior managers may revise their strategy(ies) in many ways. For example, they may decide:

1. To reallocate resources to emphasize certain therapeutic areas or projects.

2. That certain projects do not fit their portfolio and license them to other companies.
3. That the company is spread too thinly across many therapeutic areas.
4. That certain gaps in the portfolio must be addressed by any of several techniques.
5. To terminate certain projects that fail to meet minimally acceptable criteria.
6. To increase (or decrease) the number of staff in one or more areas.
7. To increase (or decrease) the risk level of their projects.

OTHER PORTFOLIO ISSUES

Financial Analyses

To conduct portfolio analysis on a strict financial basis as is done in numerous industries requires sophisticated cost-accounting systems. For each project such systems consider the (1) investment required, (2) degree of risk, and (3) return on the investment desired. It is not realistic to utilize this sophisticated financial system in a number of companies because the degree of accuracy required for the calculations is not possible to attain.

What Does High Priority Mean?

While everyone in a company may agree that two (or more) specific projects are high priority, the exact meaning of that term often differs. One group (or person) may believe that everything on that medicine must be done before anything on other projects when there are questions of how to allocate resources. Another group (or person) may state that, in addition to the above, all resources needed must be allocated to the project even at the expense of other projects. A third group may believe that in addition to the above a sense of urgency must prevail to ensure it is developed as rapidly as possible.

A related issue is on what basis a project is named of high (or highest priority). Apart from the obvious commercial criteria, there are political pressures, medical criteria, and other criteria that may be applied.

One aspect of the issue relates to the criteria used to select high-priority projects. If it is simply the result of a discussion among 20 or so senior managers, then there is a possibility that almost every project will be designated as a high-priority project. It is better to decide, prior to identifying which specific projects are high priority, the precise number of projects or the precise percent of the overall portfolio to receive that designation.

One caveat is that insufficient information about a medicine's characteristics is generally available on early-stage projects. As a result, it is impossible to compare adequately early- and late-stage projects (i.e., those in preclinical and Phase I evaluations versus those in Phases II and III). One implication of assigning priorities to all projects is that the importance of early-phase projects often changes radically and frequently over the course of time, and to designate some early-phase projects as less than high priority could demotivate the staff working on them.

Another point in favor of not designating early-phase projects according to the same priority system as late-stage projects is that the resources being expended on the early-stage projects are usually much smaller than those on later-stage projects, and it would not generally help the company significantly to reallocate resources from an early-stage to a late-stage high-priority project. In addition, the chances of success (i.e., reaching the market) are relatively low for preclinical compounds, and designating them as high priority could create anticipation of great profits in the minds of the board of directors or stock analysts who learn about them.

For all of these reasons, it is not useful to refer to early-stage projects as being in the high-priority category. Nonetheless, there should be a means of identifying which of the early-stage compounds or medicines should not be slowed down in their development. An intra-early-stage project distinction should be made to publicize this difference. Table 35.3 lists aspects to identify for each project.

Pruning the Portfolio

The first step in pruning the portfolio is to establish whether the goal is to smooth some bumps, shave off projects that do not fit, eliminate nonproductive projects, identify licensing-out candidates, or make drastic cuts. With the exception of the last choice (i.e., to make drastic cuts) the best solution may be to focus on what the true problem is rather than reaching an artificial solution.

The underlying problem in developing a portfolio may be the need to:

1. Add resources in one or more areas.
2. Increase productivity by identifying and improving areas of inefficiency.
3. Improve the management of existing resources.
4. Make the minimally acceptable criteria more appropriate for certain projects.
5. Redistribute the existing resources.

If a portfolio has an excessive number of small projects that need to be reduced in number, there are several ways to do this. Research in an entire disease or therapeutic area may be eliminated. This approach has appeal to many people because it focuses the company on fewer areas and achieves a seemingly clean scalpel-like cut of certain projects. However, if the projects to be cut include one or more that are of great interest or if there is a large research effort in that area, then this approach is generally unwise and will also demoralize many staff.

To achieve the goal of having the best projects of greatest commercial and medical value in the portfolio, a second approach is preferable to the one mentioned above. The desired method is to increase the standards of the minimally acceptable criteria. These standards can be titrated upward so that the least desirable projects of the lowest priority group start to fail the challenge of meeting higher standards. The portfolio's quality becomes progressively higher in terms of its medical and commercial value. This approach is often worth conducting until further cuts would free staff and focus the company's future on too few projects.

Mathematical Models of a Portfolio

A model may be created using all available company data to estimate what the ultimate return is or should be for each dollar spent on research (or research and development). This model may provide a basis for estimating the minimal research budget required to maintain an adequate number of projects in the development pipeline. This approach would also provide data to justify maintaining or changing the amount of money spent on research.

A mathematical model may be created in either a forward or backward manner. In the forward approach, current budget allocations are used and future outcomes

---

TABLE 35.3. *Aspects to identify for each project relating to its priority[a]*

1. Priority number, code (e.g., A and B), or category (e.g., highest)
2. Project name
3. Commercial rationale for its development
4. Rationale for priority
   Positive aspects
   Negative aspects
5. Estimated launch date
6. Estimated third-year sales
7. Importance to the company
8. Resources required for development (e.g., full-time staff and money)
9. Resources available for development (e.g., full-time staff and money) plus any shortfall
10. Departments affected by the shortfall

[a] Individual tables may be created listing all projects for any of these ten categories or subcategories (e.g., highest priority projects).

are predicted, usually based on a best-case prediction. This model is evaluated over a number of years to assess its accuracy and to fine-tune (i.e., improve) the model. In the backward approach, one or more goals are identified that were achieved. Working backward from those goals, data are then derived to calculate the quantity of resources that were required to achieve the target. In either the forward or backward case, it does not follow that the next project will be discovered with X dollars and Y years of effort, but over a ten- to 30-year period with average productivity (based on retrospective data), it may be possible to obtain an approximate indication of these numbers and make reasonable predictions.

If the amount of money spent on research that generated a new project (or new marketed medicine) were calculated, this value could be tracked on a moving three-year (or five-year) basis. This trend would be one indication of whether productivity in research was changing. This analysis would require that constant dollars were used.

Defining Therapeutic Areas

Therapeutic areas have been classically defined primarily on the basis of body systems. These include cardiovascular, respiratory, gastrointestinal, genitourinary, dermatology, and central nervous system. Therapeutic areas also overlap with broad disease groups, such as bacterial diseases, viral diseases, and oncology. A newer way that is being used by some professionals to categorize projects into major areas includes immunologicals, intensive care medicines, geriatric medicines, biological modifiers, and biotechnology products. Each company has to determine the best classification of its products.

Some individuals view therapeutic areas as merely an arbitrary means of dividing a portfolio of investigational and marketed medicines into convenient categories for analysis. Others believe that therapeutic areas provide the basis of a business-driven franchise that looks at linkages between the medicines in an area and marketing activities focused on specialists and market segments.

Estimating Future Staff Needs

There are numerous methods used to project staff needs for future work. They may be simple or complex, and no one method is best in all companies. These are:

1. Extrapolate from precious experience using one's best guess.
2. As above, but request more staff than truly believed necessary because one expects to get one-half or one-third of one's request.

3. Calculate future work load and analyze resource allocations. Then, based on previous experience, estimate staff needs.
4. Conduct an analysis as above but factor in numerous considerations of possible project terminations, priorities of projects, and other influences on the department's work load that are similar to past experiences.

Method two is least desirable, and method four is best.

Should New Medicines Be Developed Only if Their Forecast Achieves at Least a Minimal Value?

Some companies reportedly have a magic cutoff number for what dollar value constitutes a minimally acceptable third-year sales forecast. If a medicine's forecast does not achieve this figure, then its development is terminated or at least significantly slowed. This is a narrow-minded approach for several reasons. First, it is a medicine's profit and not its sales that should be important to a company. Development costs may be low for some medicines (e.g., orphan medicines). Second, some medicines may not initially appear to be commercially attractive because the right questions have not been asked (e.g., the patient population may be greater than perceived or the medicine may have desirable benefits in terms of compliance or quality of life that were not appreciated). Third, a commercially unattractive medicine at the time it is initially evaluated may become more valuable over time. Fourth, there may be other reasons to develop and market a medicine (e.g., company image, entrance into a new therapeutic field, high medical value, filling out a franchise or product line, or keeping a competitor out of an area).

A Potential "Danger" of Creating a Portfolio Analysis

When enormously complex projects are reduced to a few numbers, it becomes relatively easy for some senior managers to look at the "bottom line" or another number and say that a specific project should be cut or de-emphasized. The appropriate time for seriously questioning whether a specific project should be established is when the project is initiated. That is also the time to establish the minimally acceptable standards each project must meet for its development to continue. At some companies the head of research and development has the final say about this point, whereas at others it is the chairman of the board and board of directors.

Other Pitfalls Regarding a Portfolio Analysis

Other pitfalls to avoid in developing and analyzing project portfolios include (1) unnecessary complexity, (2) flashy presentations, (3) analyses that focus solely on"where we're at," and do not adequately address, "where we're going" and "how are we to get there," and (4) one-shot exercises that fail to establish an ongoing process of portfolio analysis, review, and evaluation.

Additional information on pharmaceutical prognostications are found in an article by Balthasar et al. (1978).

In conclusion, aspects of the portfolio analysis may be used to modify many areas of a company as well as to evaluate the productivity of research and development (see Chapter 36) and to plan the commercial development of new medicines (see Chapter 47).

36 / Productivity, Innovation, and Project Success

Definition and Description of Productivity and Innovation	**401**
Introduction	401
Definition and Description of Productivity	402
Definition and Description of Innovation	402
Productivity and Innovation Versus Value	403
General Methods to Measure Productivity	**403**
Levels at Which Productivity Is Measured	403
Establishing a System to Evaluate Productivity	403
Making "Snapshot" Evaluations at a Single Point in Time Versus Developing Trends Over a Period of Time	404
Who Will Conduct This Evaluation?	404
Specific Parameters to Measure Productivity	**404**
What Components of Research and Development May Be Assessed to Measure Productivity?	404
Parameters to Measure Overall Research and Development Productivity	404
Parameters to Measure Various Aspects of Research and Development Productivity	406
Commercial Parameters	407
Medical Parameters	407
Precautions	408
Measuring Productivity in a Subsidiary	408
Parameters to Avoid in Measuring Productivity	**408**
What Comparison Data Are Available?	**409**
Improving Productivity	**409**
General Principles	409
Factors Influencing How Rapidly a Project Moves through the Medicine Development System	410
Identifying Company Problems That Affect Productivity	411
Measuring the Success Rate of a Company's Projects	**411**
Definitions Used in Determining the Rate of Success of a Company's Portfolio	411
Methods Used to Calculate the Success Rate of Compounds	412
Methods Used to Calculate the Success Rate of a Company's New Medicines	413
Reasons Why Research and Development Groups Often Fail to Achieve Complete Success	416

Science when well digested is nothing but good sense and reason. Stanislaus, King of Poland. From *Maxims.*

Measures of productivity are like statistics on accidents: they tell you all about the number of accidents in the home, on the road, and at the work place, but they do not tell you how to reduce the frequency of accidents. W. Edwards Deming. From *Quality, Productivity, and Competitive Position.*

DEFINITION AND DESCRIPTION OF PRODUCTIVITY AND INNOVATION

Introduction

Virtually every organization and group, regardless of their functions and goals, desires to improve their productivity and number of innovations. For research-based pharmaceutical companies, the productivity of their research and development function is vital for corporate prosperity and, often, for its survival. Measuring and tracking a company's productivity and innovations enable senior managers to assess whether the funds they commit to research and development are well spent and are ensuring the future success (and even existence) of their company. It is also relevant for senior research and development managers to measure, analyze, and report on the productivity and innovativeness of the groups they manage when justifications are required to support their annual budget requests or to defend the effectiveness of research and development. Evaluations of a group's productivity or innovativeness may also be used as a means to identify problem areas and as a guide to improve the effectiveness of medicine discovery and development activities.

Productivity and innovation are commonly used terms in the pharmaceutical industry that everyone understands, or do they? Dictionary definitions of these concepts cannot be directly applied to medicines or the pharmaceutical industry without making numerous assumptions and decisions about what factors to consider and how they should be applied. One of the reasons for this situation is that both words (productivity and innovation) have several definitions with various shades of meaning. As a result, both terms are defined operationally in this chapter, and other definitions could be proposed. Unfortunately, most discussions of productivity and innovations in the scientific and medical literature do not clearly specify the precise definitions used.

Definition and Description of Productivity

Chambers 20th Century Dictionary (Cambridge University Press, Cambridge, UK, 1983) defines productivity as "the rate or efficiency of work, esp(ecially) in industrial production." *Webster's New International Dictionary of the English Language* (2nd edition, Merriam-Webster Inc., Springfield, MA, 1953) includes the phrase "yielding or furnishing results, profits, or benefits." These definitions indicate that productivity is a rate or ratio. It is usually viewed as an output divided by some type of input.

In the manufacturing area the most traditional definition of productivity is output per labor hour. In marketing, finance, and other disciplines, definitions generally emphasize how well the company earns money and is able to accomplish the same or an increased number of tasks with fewer people, less time, and/or less money. The most important aspect of productivity in research and development is the number of commercially viable new medicines that were discovered, developed, and marketed. This number may be expressed per dollar spent on research and development or by another parameter (e.g., per 1,000 people-years of work). A productive company will be able to demonstrate this quality through the number of new medicines it "produces."

The productivity of research and development is evaluated in many different disciplines and areas (e.g., the number of patients who complete a given trial per month or number of key strokes of data entered per hour by a data entry operator). The term *productivity* includes consideration of the efficiency of an activity or operation, whereas the term *innovation* does not.

Definition and Description of Innovation

The definition of innovation in numerous dictionaries is (1) something new or different and (2) introduction of

new things or methods. Although there may be many innovations relating to the process of medicine development (e.g., an improved method of conducting any one of thousands of activities), in this chapter the term is restricted to the discovery and development of new medicines.

The process of innovation was described as having four separate functions or components (Scherer, 1970). These functions may be modified to fit the medicine industry.

1. *Invention* Conceptualization of a new medicine, at least in a rudimentary form, plus the demonstration that the compound or medicine possesses either biological or clinical activity of interest.
2. *Investment* This involves the risking of funds and commitment of resources for a compound or medicine's development.
3. *Entrepreneurship* Management's decision to pursue a compound or medicine's development and the commitment to efforts required for efficiently organizing and carrying out the development.
4. *Development* This involves the lengthy and complex steps required to bring an investigational compound to market. If a medicine is already marketed, then new development activities may be necessary to attain regulatory approval for the newly discovered activity.

This description indicates that innovation involves much more than just medicine discovery. The primary quantitative measure of innovation, however, is the number of new medicines or medicine forms (e.g., dosage forms or creative packaging) developed. This number is often expressed on a per-year basis. It is unclear whether a medicine must be marketed for a company to count it as an innovation. A medicine that is sold in country A and is rejected by regulatory authorities in country B would usually be considered as an innovation in country A, but not in country B. A different end point than medicine marketing should be used to define an interesting compound as an innovation. A logical end point would be to use the time a compound becomes a medicine. This has been defined as the moment when the first human is given a compound in a clinical trial. On the other hand, it is also possible to define a chemical compound as an innovation at the time that a company's management has made the commitment to invest money and to pursue the medicine's development (i.e., the step of entrepreneurship). This is usually the time when a compound is elevated to project status. Whichever of these three time points is chosen as a criterion of defining a new chemical entity (NCE) as an innovation (i.e., commitment to development, first human exposure, or initiation of marketing), that criterion should be consistently applied. Other time points are possible to define.

Although the preceding discussion was written as if each medicine represents a single innovation, there are several reasons why this is not always true.

1. There may be innovations in different therapeutic indications for a single medicine, in which new and important uses are discovered. These discoveries may occur almost anywhere along the medicine discovery and development pipeline, from preclinical studies to the testing of clinical theories to serendipitous events. A major innovation has little or no precedent in the medicines used for that indication, and represents an improvement in therapy.
2. Innovations may occur in marketing and production, in addition to research and development. Novel manufacturing processes may allow a medicine to be produced that otherwise would be impossible or would be too expensive to be competitive in the market.
3. Medicine is practiced differently around the world and some medicines used, even in industrialized counties, vary greatly. A number of well-known and highly used medicines in one country may be little known and little used just across the country's border. Thus, an innovation in one country will not always be considered as an innovation in all countries.
4. Numerous creative ideas contribute to the development of virtually all medicines. These "innovative" ideas are not innovations in the sense that the overall medicine is a single innovation. Nonetheless, some creative ideas leading to advances in a medicine's development (e.g., discovering a new route of chemical synthesis) could be defined and considered as innovations.

Productivity and Innovation Versus Value

Many definitions and descriptions of productivity and innovation do not consider the value of the medicines developed. Value may be measured and/or judged in both commercial and in medical terms. Numerous aspects of these values, as well as scientific value, are described in Chapter 35 and the Introduction. A company may wish to judge its research and development group, not solely by the number of medicines under development and how well they are being developed, but also by their value. Methods and parameters that include both commercial and medical value should be considered.

A research and development group may work hard and efficiently in developing medicines, but through no fault of its own, most or all of their important investigational medicine projects may have to be terminated. This could occur for many reasons, such as toxicity in animals, adverse reactions in humans, or lack of sufficient efficacy in human patients. A research and development group in this situation might still be rated as highly

productive and innovative, depending on the specific definitions used. It is also possible that the number of their innovations would be zero, and their productivity would also be zero, if the definitions used required a medicine to be marketed.

Medicines may have a high medical value but low commercial value and never repay their development and marketing costs. It may be debated as to whether these medicines contribute to a company's productivity. On the one hand, they clearly do because of all the benefits that patients will receive, but on the other hand, a company that is highly productive but only markets this type of medicine will eventually go out of business.

GENERAL METHODS TO MEASURE PRODUCTIVITY

Levels at Which Productivity Is Measured

It is usually important to measure productivity at multiple levels, including that of an individual scientist, a group of scientists, an individual research department, a project team, all research departments, all development departments, all research and development personnel, an entire company site, or an entire multinational company. Some methods that are appropriate for one level are not suitable for others.

The productivity of individual scientists is usually measured as part of their annual performance review. This chapter is concerned with judging the productivity of the entire medicine research or medicine development effort, not that of the individuals who plan, conduct, and supervise this effort.

Establishing a System to Evaluate Productivity

One approach to evaluating productivity is to divide the evaluation into the following questions:

1. What is to be assessed?
2. What general tools and techniques are available to evaluate productivity?
3. What are the pros and cons of each method for the specific tasks intended?
4. Which tools and techniques are best to use and which parameters are best to measure?
5. How many parameters should be measured and is it worth combining the results into an overall index?
6. Will greater precision in measurement make any difference in actions taken to improve productivity?
7. What comparison data are available?
8. How will these evaluations be conducted?
9. Who will conduct this evaluation and interpret the results?
10. Who will review and approve the results?
11. How will the results be applied to the company (e.g., to improve productivity)?

A number of additional questions and issues should be considered before setting up the exercise as follows.

1. Are there preconceived end points or results that the evaluation is supposed to demonstrate or attain? If so, are these results hidden or clearly stated? Are there mechanisms to prevent this type of bias from influencing the evaluation?
2. Does the staff in charge of the evaluation have vested interests in having the outcome fit a predetermined pattern? How may these vested interests be controlled so that they do not bias the outcomes?
3. To what depth will the measure(s) be used to evaluate productivity, i.e., is a superficial or an in-depth analysis being conducted?
4. Is this activity a one-time analysis or is it intended to become a periodic (i.e., ongoing) activity?

Making "Snapshot" Evaluations at a Single Point in Time Versus Developing Trends Over a Period of Time

Comparing the effectiveness or productivity of a research and development function with similar groups in other companies often compares activities and situations at a single point in time. This is analogous to evaluating a photograph of the research and development function at a specific moment in time. It is also important to judge changes over a period of years to determine whether a company's performance is improving, deteriorating, or remaining constant. Evaluating changes over time could be viewed as analogous to studying a movie version of research and development or whatever function is being assessed.

Who Will Conduct This Evaluation?

There are basically three answers to this question. The analysis may be conducted primarily (or solely) by (1) internal company staff, (2) external consultants, or (3) by a joint effort of both. There are a number of consulting groups with experience in reviewing all or part of a pharmaceutical company's research and development organization. External consultants will require significant assistance in time and effort from the company's staff, even when the consultants perform all of the analyses and evaluations themselves.

In the situation where both company staff and outside consultants are involved in performing the analyses, several scenarios may be followed. The first is where members of the evaluation group are chosen from both the company and consultants to work as a unified team, perhaps being instructed in the general approach to follow by the consultants. Another possible scenario is for the consultants to adopt a more passive role and serve as facilitators helping guide the company staff and keeping them on track as they gather information and conduct the analyses in-house. The opposite situation, in which company personnel serve as facilitators for the consultants, is possible but unlikely to occur.

SPECIFIC PARAMETERS TO MEASURE PRODUCTIVITY

What Components of Research and Development May Be Assessed to Measure Productivity?

A company may evaluate the productivity of a highly specific part of their research and development division or they may wish to conduct a sweeping evaluation of the entire research and development function. In either case, each of the components that is to be assessed must be identified. If a highly specific part of research and development is to be evaluated, it may consist of a single component. If the entire division is to be assessed, it may be desirable to choose some global measures or to examine separate components. Data on any parameter obtained at different times may be plotted to evaluate trends.

Parameters to Measure Overall Research and Development Productivity

Research and development productivity may be globally measured using parameters such as (1) the number of Investigational New Drug Applications (INDs) filed, (2) the number of projects started, (3) the commercial value of projects started, (4) the number of New Drug Applications (NDAs) filed, (5) the number of NDAs approved, (6) the speed of NDA approval compared with other companies, and (7) how closely the total group met their annual goals in terms of the first six parameters listed. The first six parameters may be expressed on a per-year basis and the trends may be analyzed over time. In addition, these parameters may be evaluated on a per-research and development-person basis (per year) to make the comparison a bit more fair from year to year because the company's total research and development effort is likely to change from year to year in the number of people employed and the money spent. Only professional staff above a certain level could be considered. A three-year (or other) moving average could be used to smooth out differences further that often occur from year to year. The money spent per person per year on the three major functions of research and development groups (medicine discovery, medicine development, and market-oriented activities, including line-extensions) could be determined separately or together. See Chapters 35 and 53 for examples of figures that illustrate research and development expenditures.

A number of other objective parameters that may be used to measure productivity are listed in Table 36.1. A

TABLE 36.1. *Parameters for measuring productivity of research and development activities[a,b]*

A. Regulatory parameters
    1. Number of new products reaching the market in X years
    2. Number of new regulatory submissions for NCEs[c] in the United States and/or several specific countries
    3. Number of countries approving specific medicines
    4. Speed of regulatory approval
B. Commercial parameters
    1. Amount of sales and/or profits generated from products that reached the market within the last three years[d]
    2. Percent of sales and/or profits generated from products that reached the market within the last three years[d]
    3. Number and value of medicines licensed-in within the three years[d]
    4. Number and value of medicines licensed-out within the last three years and how the company benefits
    5. Potential commercial value of all investigational medicines (e.g., total of estimated third year sales times the probability of marketing the medicine)[e]
    6. Potential commercial value of projects established within the last year
    7. Number and value of line-extensions currently being developed
    8. Average cost to complete each stage of development[f] (e.g., preclinical, Phase I, Phase II, Phase III)
    9. Average research cost to discover an NCE that reaches project status
    10. Ratio of new medicine sales over X years divided by research and development expenditures over that same period
C. Research and development parameters
    1. Medical value of all projects with investigational medicines
    2. Medical value of projects established within the last year
    3. Number of new projects established within the last year
    4. Number of compounds reaching human trials within the last year
    5. Rapidity with which unsuccessful projects have been terminated within the last three years (i.e., the number of months from project formation to termination)
    6. Degree of congruence between projected goals and actual accomplishments
D. Personnel parameters
    1. Number of senior staff who left the company within the previous three years
    2. Evidence of positive staff morale
    3. Number of publications by staff
    4. Image of the research and development departments
    5. Number of staff with academic appointments

[a] Effectiveness or productivity would be assessed by comparing the value of a parameter with those obtained for an equal preceding period or with values obtained in previous years. Trends would be of particular importance. If the parameters had not been previously measured, then a new analysis of older data may be conducted. All of these values could be presented in tabular or graphical form. Two or more of these parameters could also be combined.

[b] Not all of these parameters are considered worthwhile measures of productivity. The use of some would depend on the specific situation.

[c] NCE, new chemical entity.

[d] A different number of years could be used.

[e] These numbers may be reduced by multiplying by the percent of compounds or medicines put in the project system that historically reached the market (i.e., success rate).

[f] Financial comparisons should be made using dollars of comparable value to correct for inflation. Other corrections may also be used, but must be clearly defined.

variety of grids or scattergrams could be produced to illustrate the status of investigational medicine projects. Grids from two or more years could easily be compared to determine whether the movement of projects was in a desirable direction and was adequate in amount (see Fig. 35.12).

A highly gross and imperfect measure of productivity would be the number of months taken by a regulatory authority to approve NDAs or Product License Applications (PLAs, Fig. 36.1). The number of months taken for a medicine or the average number of months for all medicines approved in a given year or group of years could be compared with the company's previous performance. These values could also be compared with those of the pharmaceutical industry. Numerous caveats are re-

quired for this comparison because the time taken by a regulatory authority to approve medicines depends on many factors. These include the type of medicine, the medical need for the medicine, and the specific reviewers involved. This measure would be related to a company's productivity if there is a correlation between the quality of the data submitted and the speed of regulatory approval. The author believes that this correlation is relatively high for initial NDA applications. This measure is less indicative of productivity when evaluating supplemental NDAs.

Another criterion of overall productivity would be degree and quality of the liaison between research and development and other functional areas in a company. Feedback from other groups that frequently interact

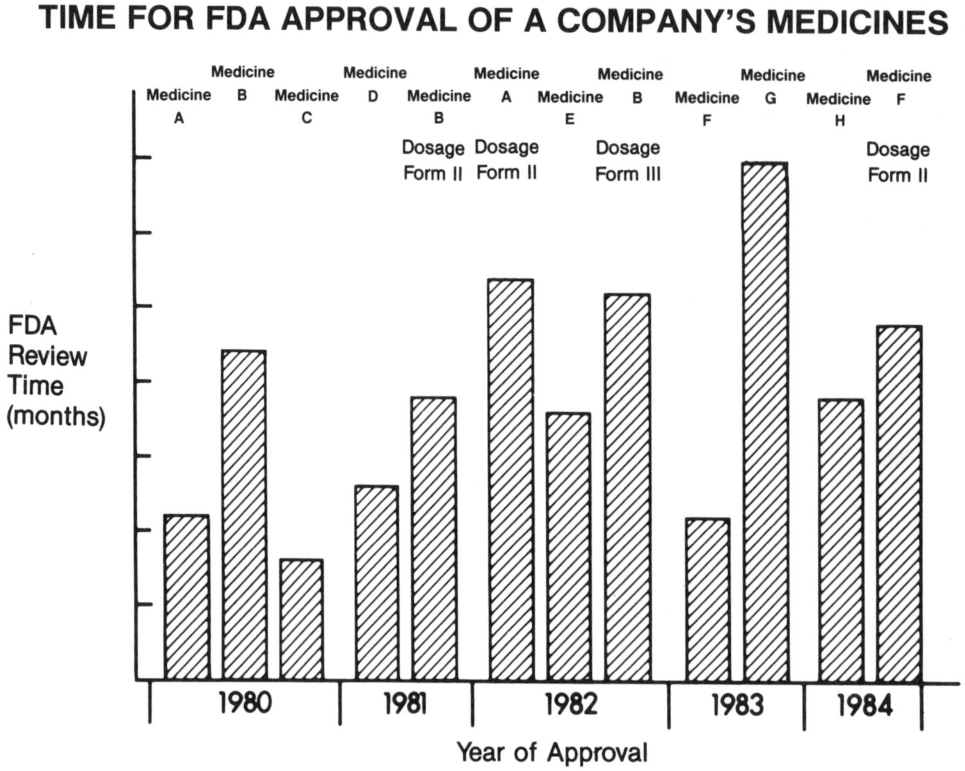

TIME FOR FDA APPROVAL OF A COMPANY'S MEDICINES

FIG. 36.1. Tracking the time required for regulatory review and approval of new medicines. A similar graph could track regulatory supplements.

with research and development (e.g., marketing and production) would be important to judge how well the liaison was being accomplished. It would be ideal to measure both the number and value of good ideas and good decisions made as an assessment of productivity. Unfortunately, this cannot be accurately done.

Parameters to Measure Various Aspects of Research and Development Productivity

In addition to evaluating the productivity of the overall research and development function described above, it may be relevant to measure the productivity of its component parts. Various parts (e.g., medicine discovery, medical group, and technical development) or departments may be evaluated with some or all of the following parameters. Numerous caveats will be necessary in using each of these measures.

1. The number of therapeutic areas or disease areas being researched.
2. The specific choices of therapeutic areas being ex-

plored for new medicine discoveries in terms of medical need and commercial value.
3. The number of compounds and medicines or NCEs in the project system.
4. The speed and efficiency with which medicines are moving through the medicine development pipeline. Evaluate the number of months from project formation to IND submission, the duration of Phase I, Phase II, Phase III, and total development time to NDA submission.
5. The time from IND filing to NDA submission. This may be evaluated on a moving three-year average and compared to the company's previous performance as well as the industry average.
6. The percent of regulatory submissions (e.g., NDAs and PLAs) that are in each category of therapeutic importance (e.g., 1A, 1B, and 1C; priority or regular).
7. The relative portion of total research and development resources hypothetically allocated to each project versus that portion actually used by each project.
8. The relative portion of resources spent on (1) medi-

cine discovery, (2) medicine development, (3) product support, and (4) other activities compared to previous years and to an ideal industry-wide or company standard.

9. The relative commercial and medical value of projects under development compared with previous years.
10. The status of activities on licensing-in medicines.
11. If the licensing function is based within research and development, then the status of licensing-out or cross-licensing activities may be assessed.
12. The quality of currently used systems may be evaluated for (1) coordinating efforts among different medicine development sites, (2) choosing compounds for development as medicines, (3) obtaining new technologies, (4) communicating results, (5) avoiding unnecessary duplication of efforts, and (6) making decisions in a rapid yet effective way.
13. The organization of research and development activities may be assessed in terms of effectiveness.

Within any company, the appropriate responses to these and many other related issues change over time. In addition, there is rarely just a simple answer or approach that is adequate for any issue, and different sites of a single company often address these issues independently. Also, many individuals have differing opinions on each of these issues. Therefore, pharmaceutical companies are almost constantly reassessing their responses, even when it appears that a consensus was reached only a short time before. When a new president is appointed or a new director of research and development takes charge, one of their first steps is often to reexamine one or more of these issues. The ways that they choose to approach the examination are discussed below.

Choosing the Best Methods to Assess Productivity

Both hard and soft measures may be used to assess the productivity of research and development. The most important single measure from a company's perspective is the commercial value of all new marketed products developed over the last X years. The value of X should probably be based on a moving multiyear average, usually three, four, or five. This technique avoids the ups and downs that often occur from year to year. In addition, limiting the number of years to five is important because it does not extend the focus so far back in time that the sales of newer products contribute relatively little to this category because of the presence of some financially important "old timers."

The parameter of commercial value may be used for both marketed and investigational medicines. A research and development group may be judged to be productive if its portfolio of investigational medicines and line-extensions are commercially valuable. To assess their value it is often desirable to consider medicines in a

number of separate categories. Investigational medicines that were developed in-house may be evaluated separately from medicines that were licensed in. Line-extensions may be evaluated separately from NCEs. The portfolio as a whole may be analyzed and judged in many different ways (see Chapter 35 on portfolio analysis).

Commercial Parameters

The approximate value of each investigational medicine may be estimated by multiplying the probability of marketing the medicine by the total forecasted sales for a given period. The probability of each investigational medicine's being marketed at some point is estimated by the people who are most knowledgeable about that probability, i.e., usually senior managers in research and development. The total forecasted sales for the first three (or other number) years of marketing are estimated by the appropriate staff in marketing. This is based on many factors in addition to the medicine's profile, including the (1) current market size, (2) projected market trends, (3) ability of available methods to treat the disease, (4) severity of disease symptoms, and (5) nature of the population to be treated (e.g., children or debilitated patients).

Values for each investigational medicine are calculated to provide an estimate of the total projects' portfolio value. This number may be easily graphed on an annual basis to illustrate how the overall portfolio's value is changing in commercial terms. If a company's productivity and progress is strictly measured in commercial terms, then this value, and its comparison with values from previous years, is particularly important.

Medical Parameters

The above method does not consider the portfolio's medical value. Each investigational (or marketed) medicine may be evaluated on a crude or sophisticated scale to judge its medical value. A qualitative four- or five-point scale (e.g., little = 1, moderate = 2, strong = 3, and exceptional medical value = 4) is usually adequate to express the medical value of most medicines, especially investigational medicines. This is because the clinical profile of investigational medicines is incomplete. The numbers corresponding to medical values for each medicine in the portfolio may be added to obtain a total score. The average medical value score per medicine may also be determined. The values obtained with either of these methods could be plotted on a year-to-year basis. The trend of these analyses would indicate how the portfolio's medical value is changing over time. This trend would also relate to a company's productivity in research and development in some situations.

Precautions

The approach described in the above two sections is oriented toward a global commercial and medical view of the portfolio. This approach is insufficient on its own, however, to present the status of research and development. Moreover, the results may be misleading. From a commercial perspective, one major new medicine may skew the picture of the portfolio in a highly positive manner and tend to mask the fact that few other commercially attractive medicines are in the development pipeline. That fact should generally act to stimulate more licensing activity to be conducted to fill potential future therapeutic and financial gaps. If the major medicine in the pipeline falters (e.g., new adverse reactions arise or the efficacy is not as good as anticipated) or stronger competition arises from other companies, then the entire company may be vulnerable and its future could be placed in jeopardy.

Measuring Productivity in a Subsidiary

A subsidiary that is helping to develop and register medicines can be judged in terms of the relevant parameters listed below.

1. The number of INDs submitted to the regulatory authority.
2. The number of NDAs submitted to the regulatory authority.
3. The number of NCE projects initiated.
4. The quality of publications.
5. The recruitment of patients into clinical trials in terms of percent achieved versus the plan.
6. The contribution of patients as a percent of the company's overall total.

The first three parameters must be judged relative to what was planned or expected because the headquarters may not have requested the subsidiary involvement. The last three parameters are sometimes more closely associated with the subsidiary's productivity. Each of these (or other measures) may be assessed either informally or formally.

PARAMETERS TO AVOID IN MEASURING PRODUCTIVITY

There are a number of parameters that should generally *not* be used to measure the productivity of research and development. This is primarily because they relate to *output* and not *productivity*. The former is merely a tabulation of effort and activity that may bear no relation to productivity. These parameters include:

1. *The number of chemicals synthesized* The amount of work required to synthesize new chemicals varies enormously from compound to compound. The difficulty of synthesizing each chemical varies from those prepared using well-established and straightforward synthetic steps to those requiring creativity, long hours, and repeated attempts, with low yields. The importance of each new chemical made varies greatly. Some are made to complete a series for patent protection, others to evaluate a structure–activity relationship, some are from new series, and some are believed to represent a major therapeutic advance. Merely evaluating the numbers of new chemicals synthesized would generally be a highly misleading measure of productivity. If this parameter was to be used in a pharmaceutical company, then at least some chemists would probably generate larger numbers of less important chemicals in order to demonstrate their high degree of productivity. The company's true productivity would suffer as a result.

2. *The number of compounds screened for a specific or general biological activity* This parameter is inappropriate for analogous reasons to those described above for the chemistry department. Screening is usually carried out in biological departments.

3. *The number of patents filed or obtained* The number of patents filed or obtained on new chemicals would also superficially appear to be a reliable indicator of productivity. Unfortunately, this parameter could also easily be manipulated by chemists or others who might attempt to patent more compounds than would be prudent from the company's perspective. Given the high costs of obtaining and renewing patents plus the large amount of work involved in filing patents in many countries, using this approach to measure productivity could be an expensive mistake.

4. *The number of clinical medicine trials conducted* Many clinical trials are conducted for product support, to replicate prior studies, to increase statistical validity, or to increase the patient population treated as part of Phase III or postmarketing surveillance. All are legitimate practices but are poor indicators of productivity in research and development. The size of a trial varies greatly and there is often little correlation between a trial's size and its relative importance to a company.

5. *The number of patients evaluated in medicine trials* Parameters number four and five may be easily manipulated if desired, and are not inherently useful as measures of productivity. While some trials are able to process relatively large numbers of patients through a clinic, others evaluate few patients in great detail. If determining the total number of patients studied was strongly desired as a parameter, then it should be modified to measure the total number of patient days (or weeks or months) of treatment and to improve its reliability. The drawback of even this particular modification of the parameter is that a few

long-term trials of many patients, where little effort was expended, would strongly influence the results. One way of preventing this would be to divide the trials into categories based on the length of patient treatment (e.g., less than one week, between one week and a month, between one and six months, and over six months).

6. *The number of publications authored by staff* Although the connection between the number of publications authored by company staff and the research and development productivity seems farfetched, some people and publications have proposed this parameter (and each of those above) as appropriate tests of productivity.

WHAT COMPARISON DATA ARE AVAILABLE?

Each pharmaceutical company would like to compare the results and conclusions of its own internal analyses with those of other companies. This is rarely possible for several reasons, only one of which is company secrecy. The large number of variables used to conduct any comprehensive evaluation in a company illustrates that data from another company would probably have been obtained using different assumptions and methods. Publicly available data about other pharmaceutical companies are not usually adequately detailed and reliable enough to base important judgments on them. Most data from other companies would therefore have limited usefulness for direct comparison. Differences do not only include the assumptions and methodologies used but also definitions of terms (e.g., project or success) and specific questions asked. These could all differ markedly between companies. In addition, it is generally believed that most companies are not internally consistent in their definitions of these terms from year to year or from department to department.

In terms of medicine discovery, it would be useful to compare the productivity of in-house discovery efforts and that of other companies. The value of licensed-in medicines to a company may also be assessed in comparison with in-house medicines. This issue may be evaluated through several approaches. One is to determine separately the return on investment for medicines discovered by in-house research and medicines that were obtained as a result of licensing activities. Another is to focus on how well each of these groups of medicines achieves the goals established for that function. For example, if medicines are licensed-in to fill certain financial gaps or to utilize available staff time in most development departments, then the success of the medicine in meeting those goals must be assessed.

Pharmaceutical Trade Associations

One alternative is to compare the values of a company with the industry average. This latter type of information is collected by the Pharmaceutical Manufacturers Association in the United States and by numerous other pharmaceutical trade associations around the world from their member companies. The advantage of this type of comparison is that the trade association usually collects and processes the data in the same way for each company and is consistent over a period of years. This consistency means that differences in definitions used by different companies tend to become less important. On the other hand, there could be inconsistencies in trade association data from year to year if (1) different companies are included in the data base, (2) the questions posed to the companies are modified or changed, or (3) companies answer questions somewhat differently each year because the company's respondents use different assumptions, interpretations, or definitions.

A pharmaceutical trade organization is in a good position to collect data in a uniform format from many research-based companies. The associations would then circulate industry-wide results so that each company could compare itself with the industry mean (or range). In fact, this is being done at present (e.g., *PMA Statistical Fact Book*), and the amount of industry-wide data available from trade associations appears to be increasing. This is generally a satisfactory source of comparison data, if the data address questions of interest.

Other Sources of Industry Data

Other useful sources of industry data include the Food and Drug Administration, other regulatory agencies, the World Health Organization, pharmaceutical industry financial analysts, Scrip, and organizations like the Centre for Medicines Research in the United Kingdom (Woodmansterne Road, Carshalton, Surrey, England SM5 4DS) and the Center for the Study of Medicine Development in the United States (Tufts University, 136 Harrison Avenue, Boston, MA 02111). The activities of the Center in Boston have been described (Anonymous, 1987b). Various sources of marketing data are also useful places to obtain such information. The single most appropriate and useful source of data for comparison purposes is that of the company itself. Older records, data, and reports provide material that may be analyzed and used for comparative purposes (see Chapter 7, Institutional Memory).

IMPROVING PRODUCTIVITY

General Principles

The most important principle to improve productivity is the necessity to pay attention to both the details and the big picture in developing medicines. It is necessary to be concerned with all aspects of medicine development and to maintain an objective view. There have been many techniques and tools proposed to help improve productivity. Some of these are only applicable for one or a few levels at which productivity may be assessed (see earlier discussion in this chapter). The tools often change as technology changes and must be continually reassessed.

A major means to improve productivity is to adhere to simple principles, such as honesty and openness, and to create a desire for people to want to be productive. People usually desire to understand what activities they are supposed to perform in a company and how their work assists the company. It is useful to assume (at least initially) that all of the staff are highly motivated, want to conduct their work in an efficient manner, and desire to have positive relationships with their co-workers. Most workers are better able to adjust their own work to achieve the company's objectives rather than for a manager to direct them closely. All good managers learn how much independence each of their subordinates can handle.

The productivity in production and elsewhere in a company increases as the quality improves because less reworking is necessary. Less reworking reduces the waste in employee time, equipment time, and materials. Deming (1982) proposed 14 points to increase the productivity in production areas. Many of these points (Table 36.2) are also applicable to research and development. His book elaborates on these points. He states that quality is everyone's job, but the effort to improve quality is led by management. Many of the chapters in this book contain principles that (if followed) will lead to improved productivity. It is the responsibility of senior managers to implement these points. A number of considerations are listed in Table 36.3.

Numerous personnel issues that are intended to improve productivity are discussed in Chapter 13.

Factors Influencing How Rapidly a Project Moves through the Medicine Development System

The following are major factors that influence the speed of a project's movement.

1. *The priority of a project in the organization* Although this point is obvious, there is sometimes a distinction between a stated priority and an actual priority.
2. *The resources applied* Increasing the resources placed on a project does not necessarily increase the speed with which a project moves. Nonetheless, there is a direct relationship during much of a project's life between the number of staff and the amount of money spent with the rate of progress. Whether the change and movement that occurs is in the desired direction and represents progress is another issue.
3. *A sound development plan* The development plan

TABLE 36.2. *Points designed to increase productivity and quality[a]*

1. Create constancy of purpose toward improvement of product and service, with the aim to become competitive and to stay in business, and to provide jobs
2. Adopt the new philosophy. We are in a new economic age. We can no longer live with commonly accepted levels of delays, mistakes, defective materials, and defective workmanship
3. Cease dependence on mass inspection to achieve quality. Require, instead, statistical evidence that quality is built in, to eliminate need for inspection on a mass basis
4. End the practice of awarding business on the basis of price tag. Instead, depend on meaningful measures of quality, along with price. Eliminate suppliers that can not qualify with statistical evidence of quality
5. Find problems. It is management's job to work continually on the system (design, incoming materials, composition of material, maintenance, improvement of machine, training, supervision, retraining)
6. Institute modern methods of training on the job
7. Institute modern methods of supervision of production workers. The responsibility of foremen must be changed from sheer numbers to quality. Improvement of quality will automatically improve productivity. Management must prepare to take immediate action on reports from foremen concerning barriers such as inherited defects, machines not maintained, poor tools, fuzzy operational definitions
8. Drive out fear so that everyone may work effectively for the company
9. Break down barriers between departments. People in research, design, sales, and production must work as a team to foresee problems of production that may be encountered with the product or service
10. Eliminate numerical goals, posters, and slogans for the work force, asking for new levels of productivity without providing methods
11. a. Eliminate work standards that prescribe numerical quotas. Substitute leadership
    b. Eliminate management by objective. Eliminate management by numbers and numerical goals. Substitute leadership
12. a. Remove barriers that rob the hourly worker of his or her right to pride of workmanship
    b. Remove barriers that rob people in management and in engineering of their right to pride of workmanship
13. Institute a vigorous program of education and retraining
14. Create a structure in top management that will push every day on the above 13 points. Put everybody in the company to work to accomplish the transformation

[a] From *Quality, Productivity, and Competitive Position* by Deming (1982) with permission of MIT and C. Edwards Deming. A few modifications of these points were made based on changes by Dr. Deming in his book *Out of the Crisis*, also published by MIT.

refers to individual preclinical, clinical, technical development, marketing, and production plans that are all coordinated on a national and international basis. Without a carefully crafted and detailed blueprint of a project's strategy and direction, it is easy for various people to direct the project in new or multiple direc-

TABLE 36.3. *Considerations of how to improve productivity in pharmaceutical research and development*

1. Improve management by identifying problems and addressing them
2. Redistribute resources within or between groups
3. Add new resources
4. Cut the weakest part of the portfolio
5. Slow the low-priority work
6. Increase minimum standards
7. License-in (or out) more medicines
8. Co-develop more products
9. Assign more work to the most productive staff

tions. Some of these directions may be conflicting, raise problems, or at the least decrease efficiency.

4. *Monitoring of progress* It is critical to keep a company's stethoscope on the pulse of its projects. This is accomplished with an appropriate number of plans and schedules that are followed. These plans and schedules allow a company to measure the *progress* of a project and not merely the *activities* conducted. Any group within a company may be extremely busy and highly motivated, but if the group is pursuing tangents or is "spinning its wheels" and not moving forward, the project is not benefitting. In fact, many tangents are actually counterproductive to the medicine's development (e.g., resources may be drained from the major activity or new problems may be created).

5. *The effectiveness of management* Managerial effectiveness is required to make decisions with appropriate input and speed. Managerial effectiveness in keeping a project on track and avoiding most tangents is also essential to move it rapidly toward its goals. Management may demand that a medicine be developed faster than the staff believe is possible. Novel approaches to development (e.g., greater risk, collecting less data per patient and per trial, or raising standards) may enable the company to achieve its goal.

Identifying Company Problems That Affect Productivity

In dealing with issues relating to company problems, it is critical to identify whether the problem is one of structure and organization or one of personalities independent of the structures. Some people blame the organizational structures and systems used when the real problem involves the attitudes and styles of some people. Another issue is whether the organizational structure itself is the problem or if it is the way it is functioning and is being utilized. Sometimes, altering the way people are working may be sufficient to elicit a desired change, without the need to modify the company's organizational structure.

MEASURING THE SUCCESS RATE OF A COMPANY'S PROJECTS

A research and development group's rate of success may be defined in several ways. A common definition of success refers to the percent of initiated projects that become useful medicines. The precise definitions and assumptions used in characterizing projects greatly influence the rate of success that is calculated. The types of analyses performed also may skew the results in one direction or another.

Definitions Used in Determining the Rate of Success of a Company's Portfolio

Number of Projects and Compounds

Each single compound developed as a medicine is only counted as one success or one failure. The terms "success" and "failure" are mutually exclusive. Each compound or medicine is considered separately, even if more than one compound was designated as being in the same project.

Successful Medicine

This is a medicine where at least one formulation has been approved by a regulatory authority for marketing. Alternative definitions are possible, such as including medicines where at least one NDA has been *submitted* for approval. The project associated with a successful medicine may either be terminated or kept active.

Unsuccessful Compound or Medicine

This is a compound or medicine where no formulation or indication studied has resulted in the approval of a regulatory application. Also, work on the compound or medicine has been terminated or suspended.

Investigational Compound or Medicine

This is a compound or medicine that is currently being evaluated preclinically and/or clinically. This may include marketed medicines that are being tested (1) in new indications, (2) with new dosage forms, or (3) using new routes of administration. The decision of whether marketed medicines may also be considered as investigational medicines depends on whether the categories of successful medicine, unsuccessful compound, and investigational compound are defined to be mutually exclusive. If they are not, some compounds or medicines could fit into two or even all three of the categories.

TABLE 36.4. *Analyses used to calculate success rates of compounds developed as medicines*

Analysis	Type of success rate[a]	Type of compounds	Number of projects in the analysis
A	Cumulative	NCE[b]	All[c]
B	Cumulative	NCE	Completed[d]
C	Cumulative	All	All
D	Cumulative	All	Completed
E	Individual phase	NCE	All
F	Individual phase	NCE	Completed
G	Individual phase	All	All
H	Individual phase	All	Completed

[a] See Fig. 36.2 for an illustration of these two concepts.
[b] NCE, New Chemical Entity.
[c] All projects includes currently active projects.
[d] Completed projects were completed either successfully or unsuccessfully.

Stage of Development at the Time of Termination

Multiple formulations and indications have been (or are being) pursued for some compounds and medicines. The highest stage achieved by any formulation for any indication is considered to be the stage of development at the time of project termination.

Methods Used to Calculate the Success Rate of Compounds

Calculating the success or failure rates of compounds entered in a project system appears to be a straightforward matter until a number of additional questions are considered:

CUMULATIVE PHASE SUCCESS RATE

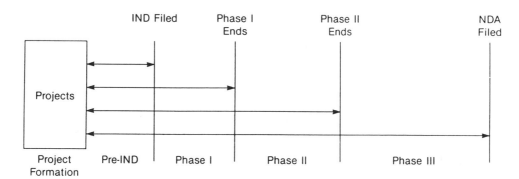

INDIVIDUAL PHASE SUCCESS RATE

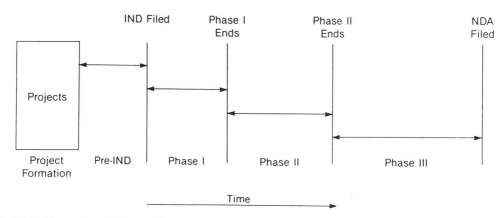

FIG. 36.2. Illustration of the cumulative phase success rate for compounds reaching a milestone and individual phase success rate for compounds entering each specific phase of development. IND, Investigational New Drug Application; NDA, New Drug Application.

1. Should all compounds be included in the analysis or just the NCEs?
2. Should the group of compounds considered in the analysis include currently active projects or only those already judged as successful or unsuccessful?
3. Should success (or failure) be evaluated separately for each stage of development (e.g., preclinical and Phases I, II, and III), i.e., independent of other stages, or should rates of success be determined cumulatively from the onset of designating an investigational compound as a project?

If each of the possible analyses using these three questions is conducted, there will be eight separate analyses. Table 36.4 enumerates these analyses. A graphic depiction of question 3 is shown in Fig. 36.2. Because the success and failure rates are complementary and together equal 100% for all analyses except A and C, only the success rate will be discussed. The success rates of compounds and medicines shown in Fig. 36.2 are listed in Table 36.5.

Analyses A to D ask the following question. Of all the projects formed, how many were successful at filing an IND, completing Phase I, Phase II, or filing a NDA?

In analyses A and C, the cumulative success rate for any specific milestone is illustrated in Fig. 36.3. This shows the number of active projects at each stage. The percentages shown in this figure are based on the total number of compounds entering the project system minus the cumulative number of active compounds.

In analyses B and D, the cumulative success rate for any specific milestone is calculated by using as the denominator the total number of compounds entering project status in the set of terminated or successful projects. The numerator equals this total minus the cumulative

number of failed compounds. Therefore, if 50 compounds had entered the system and five were terminated before IND filing, seven were terminated in Phase I, four were terminated at Phase II, and the remainder have gone past Phase II, then the cumulative success rate through

$$\text{Phase II} = \frac{50 - 5 - 7 - 4}{50} = \frac{34}{50} = 68 \text{ percent.}$$

The cumulative failure rate equals the complement of this number, or 32%.

Analyses E to H ask the following question. Of all the projects entering a specific stage of development (e.g., Phase I or Phase III), how many successfully completed that stage?

The individual stage success rate equals the number of compounds that completed that stage successfully, divided by the number that entered, minus the number now in that stage. From the illustration above, 38 compounds have entered Phase II, three are now in that stage, and four were terminated in that stage. The remainder (31) were successful. Thus, the individual Phase II success rate is:

$$\text{Phase II} = \frac{38 - 4 - 3}{38 - 3} = \frac{31}{35} = 89 \text{ percent.}$$

The individual failure rate of that stage of development equals the complement of this number, or 11%. The success rates are summarized in Table 36.4.

There are published success rates of one in five (20%) to one in ten projects (10%) in the pharmaceutical industry as being successful. Success is defined as a medicine that is marketed. The considerations discussed in this chapter, plus the various definitions and characteristics of projects at different companies, make success rates unwise to compare across companies. Within a single company these rates may be compared, but most companies would be more pleased with a low rate that produces an occasional blockbuster medicine, as opposed to a high rate of successful "me-toos" that are commercial failures. Obviously, there is a large middle ground between these two extremes.

Methods Used to Calculate the Success Rate of a Company's New Medicines

Many methods may be used to calculate the success rate of a company's new medicines. Commercial parameters are discussed in Chapters 35, 36, 47, and 53. Medical parameters are primarily discussed in Chapters 35 and 36. Regulatory and project management parameters are briefly discussed below and in Chapter 35.

A comparison of the time to United States filing of a regulatory submission may be made for multiple companies (Fig. 36.4). Acute medicines must be evaluated sepa-

TABLE 36.5. *Calculating the success rates for compounds and medicines shown in Fig. 36.2[a]*

Phase	Cumulative success rate[b]	Individual phase success rate[c]
Pre-IND[d]	$\frac{79}{95} = 83\%$	$\frac{79}{95} = 83\%$
Phase I	$\frac{59}{90} = 66\%$	$\frac{59}{74} = 80\%$
Phase II	$\frac{27}{72} = 38\%$	$\frac{27}{41} = 66\%$
Phase III	$\frac{15}{64} = 23\%$	$\frac{15}{19} = 79\%$

[a] The failure rate is equal to 100 percent minus the success rate.
[b] Active projects in that phase and previous phases are excluded from the analysis.
[c] Active projects in that phase are excluded from the analysis.
[d] IND, Investigational New Drug Application.

CUMULATIVE SUCCESS RATE

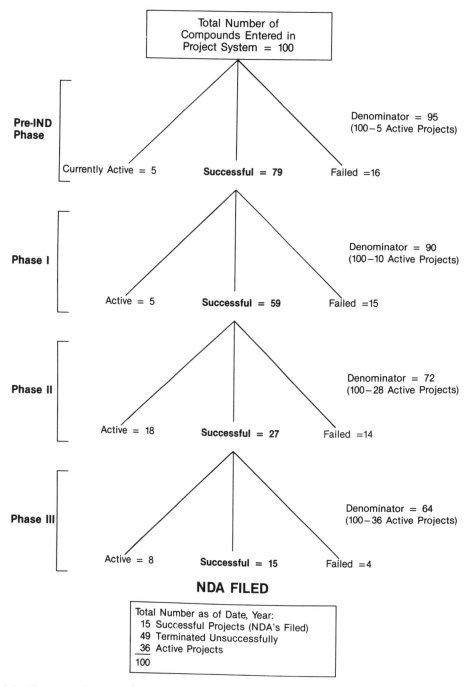

FIG. 36.3. Example of determining the success of projects based on the individual phase success rate. IND, Investigational New Drug Application; NDA, New Drug Application.

PHARMACEUTICAL FIRMS' PERFORMANCE — DEVELOPMENT LEAD TIME
(Patent to U.S. NDA Filing, 1973 – 1991)

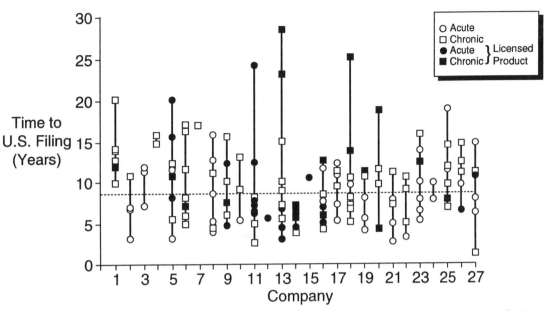

FIG. 36.4. Time taken for 27 companies to file specific NDAs from the time of patent filing. Similar graphs could illustrate IND to NDA filing, patent filing to first European launch, or NDA filing to approval. The dotted line represents the overall average value.

PROJECT A

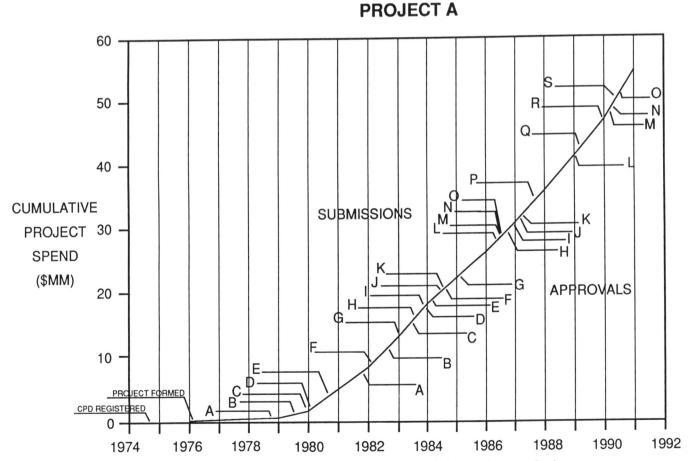

FIG. 36.5. Illustration of a large project with many regulatory submissions and approvals shown on a time versus cumulative spend on the project.

rately from chronic ones, and licensed products may also be viewed separately. Similar figures may be prepared for the (1) time for regulatory approval, (2) time from project formation to IND submission, and (3) number of NCE INDs submitted per year.

Multiple submissions and approvals on a single medicine may be documented in various ways to illustrate relative success. Two approaches are shown in Figs. 36.5 and 36.6.

Reasons Why Research and Development Groups Often Fail to Achieve Complete Success

The heading of this section uses the term *complete success* because it is often difficult to state that a group has had no success. The pertinent question is whether their success could have been substantially greater through their own efforts, given the same opportunities. The major aspects affecting success are considered to depend on research and development management and in some situations on senior corporate management. A few convenient categories of reasons are (1) capabilities, (2) organization, (3) portfolio, (4) attitudes, and (5) atmosphere.

Capabilities

Capabilities include consideration of the strength of all important departments. Are department heads and senior executives capable and competent managers? Is there a critical mass present in each department in terms of equipment and personal expertise? Are there weak links? Are some departments perennial bottlenecks or trouble spots?

Organization

Does the company's organization facilitate communication between people at the same level as well as up (and down) the hierarchy? Does the organization facilitate the transfer of a medicine from department to department? Is there an excessive number of administrative levels in the company? Do people complain about the amount of paper work? Are barriers being raised between groups or do existing walls hinder communication and productivity?

Portfolio

Is the portfolio being built and maintained in a systematic or in a haphazard way? What types of projects are going into the portfolio? Is the portfolio analyzed on a periodic basis and is it analyzed appropriately? What is done as a result of the analysis?

Attitudes

Is there a positive attitude throughout the company toward medicine development? Are people anxious to promote a medicine's development or do they raise objections, pursue tangents, or digress into unnecessarily

CUMULATIVE SALES AND LAUNCHES

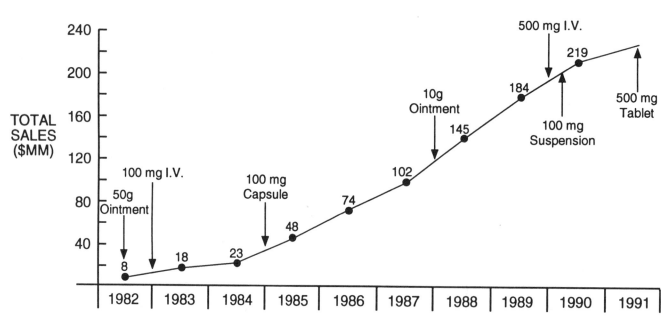

FIG. 36.6. Cumulative sales of a single product over time with superimposed time of introduction of various dosage forms and dosage strengths of that product.

detailed or extraneous points and experiments? Are there conflicts between preclinical and clinical personnel, or do they and other groups cooperate appropriately?

Atmosphere

What is the work environment like? Is there a positive environment? Do people receive recognition for important accomplishments? Are senior managers trying to improve the work environment?

The above are a few of the considerations and factors that are necessary to achieve a successful and productive research and development group. Other factors relate to the emotional and financial support of company management and a relative independence of the research and development function from manipulation and control by senior company managers.

SECTION V

The Medical-Marketing Interface

37 / Corporate Issues Regarding the Medical– Marketing Interface

Introduction to Medical–Marketing Interactions **421**
    The Marriage Between Medical and Marketing
        Groups 421
    External Versus Internal Company
        Interactions 423
Corporate Personality.......................... 423
Are the Decisions of Marketing or Research and
    Development Driving the Company? 423
Selected Medical–Marketing Issues 424
    Integrating New Personnel Into a Company... 424
    Holding New Marketing Personnel to
        Agreements Made by Their Predecessors.... 425

    Holding New Medical Personnel to
        Agreements Made by Their Predecessors.... 425
    Establishing Contracts Between Marketing and
        Clinical Groups 425
    Deciding if Marketing May Contract With
        Technical Development or Production
        Groups Outside the Company 426
    Should Aggressive Marketing Practices Be
        Encouraged? 426

To found a great empire for the sole purpose of raising up a people of customers, may at first sight appear a project fit only for a nation of shopkeepers. It is, however, a project altogether unfit for a nation of shopkeepers; but extremely fit for a nation whose government is influenced by shopkeepers. Adam Smith.

The world of medical and marketing professionals must be viewed primarily at the various levels within each of their hierarchies and also consider how the two functions interact. This chapter attempts to set those two functions in a larger perspective, that of the entire corporation. A number of corporate issues that influence medical and marketing are discussed.

INTRODUCTION TO MEDICAL–MARKETING INTERACTIONS

There is a notorious chasm between medical and marketing staff in some pharmaceutical companies, while the staff at other companies appear to coexist or even to interact on a fairly productive basis. What is the basis for the differences and what can those companies and individuals do to improve the quality and often the amount of their interactions? It is assumed that improved interactions lead to increased productivity in developing and marketing both investigational and marketed medicines.

Individuals can do many things to help in this regard in their own interactions as well as in catalyzing their company to improve relationships between the two groups. One of the major prerequisites to achieve an optimal state of interactions is to understand the other person's and group's perspective and have at least a general knowledge of their activities and goals.

Most professionals have limited time to learn about the nature of the field of other professionals with whom they interact. While this section cannot provide that information, it seeks to provide an orientation to many of the issues and activities that relate to the medical–marketing interface.

The Marriage Between Medical and Marketing Groups

There was a song in the 1950s called "Two Different Worlds." That title characterizes the feelings of many people within clinical development and marketing about their two disciplines. Each group understands itself and its approaches, but does not adequately understand or trust the other. In some cases, a feeling of hostility develops between the two groups. Regardless of the current relationship between the two groups within a company, the relationship should be viewed as a marriage.

In the best marriages, the partners work together in relative harmony. However, marriages fall along a spectrum, and at the other extreme, a great deal of strife exists. A separation may result if each communicates coldly, is not honest with the other, acts alone without consulting the other, or maintains their distance from the other. The secret of good relations between medical and marketing groups is to emulate the characteristics of a successful marriage: open, honest, frequent, and complete communication and an active desire to make the

marriage work. This can only exist when there is trust between the partners. It is best if the partners are also friends and not solely partners in a professional relationship. Unfortunately, the partners sometimes stay together solely because of their children (i.e., the medicines being developed and sold), and each partner would like a divorce. Although the activities within marketing and medical are generally well defined, many members of each group incorrectly believe that their activities can be conducted with minimal assistance from the other group. Although the above analogy casts the medical and marketing groups as two individuals, each group is made up of many people who must interact in complex ways and with company staff from other disciplines as well. The principles guiding the relationship between medical

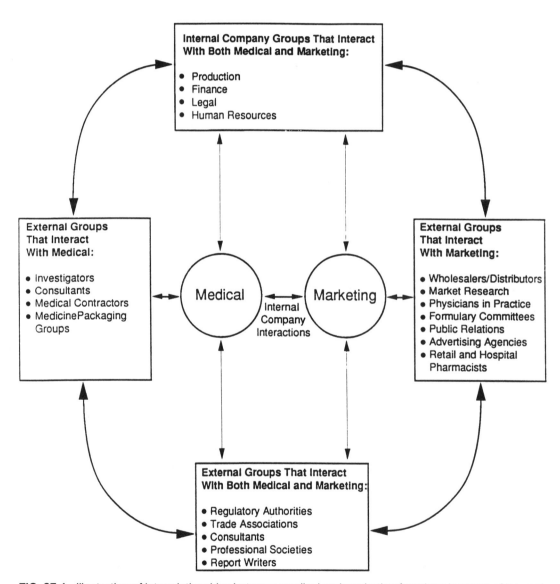

FIG. 37.1. Illustration of interrelationships between medical and marketing functions in terms of internal and external company groups that interact with each other. Additional groups could be listed in each box.

and marketing disciplines also apply to two individuals from these groups who are working on the same product/project team.

External Versus Internal Company Interactions

Medical and marketing employees interact with a wide variety of individuals and organizations that are external to the company. Thus, consideration of the interface between medical and marketing units must include external company interactions as well as internal ones. The marketing and medical staff interact with many of the same external groups, and even those that are different often have professional connections and relationships that close the circle (i.e., establish a connection among the groups). Thus, consideration of many external company interactions must also be included when discussing the medical–marketing interface within the pharmaceutical industry (Fig 37.1).

CORPORATE PERSONALITY

Any professional with pharmaceutical company experience who spends even a few days at another company and talks with a number of staff can discern certain aspects of the other company's personality (e.g., the attitudes of the staff and the style of management). It often takes longer to develop a feel about their traditions (e.g., specific activities and company history) unless one is taken to special events or places (e.g., a company museum). The personality of a company may be manifest in such mundane aspects as:

1. Who parks where? Are reserved parking places respected?
2. Who eats where? Do senior managers eat separately from professional staff?
3. Do professional staff eat separately from workers?
4. What level of security is present at the outside gate (if one exists) and at the building?
5. How friendly are the staff one encounters who do not know you personally?
6. Do professionals seem generally happy with their jobs?
7. Do professionals seem generally happy to be working for the company?
8. Does the company appear to be particularly concerned about corporate secrecy?
9. What is the general atmosphere within and between different groups?

These aspects of a corporate personality, as well as many others that could be described, are often apparent to outsiders fairly quickly. Of course the more interactions an appraisal is based on, the more likely it is to be accurate and complete. The corporate personality also is determined by which internal group has the greatest influence on the major decisions and directions of the company. Although any major group (e.g., production, finance, or marketing) could, in theory, fulfill this role, in practice it is more likely to be marketing or research and development than it is to be legal, production, or finance. This issue is discussed in the next section.

ARE THE DECISIONS OF MARKETING OR RESEARCH AND DEVELOPMENT DRIVING THE COMPANY?

Most pharmaceutical companies' decisions are dominated by the thinking of senior managers in either marketing or research and development. Those people or that person influences corporate decision making and corporate direction more than their colleague(s) in the other fields. It is rare to hear of any pharmaceutical company where both marketing and research and development are viewed as equal partners. The trend during the last 20 or so years in the industry has clearly moved toward increased domination by marketing interests. During the 1990s, this effect will be increasingly apparent as research-based companies act on the knowledge that they must discover new medicines of commercial value in order to survive (Fig. 37.2). Production was a more important influence prior to 1945, and during the 1950s, 1960s, and 1970s, in many companies research and development became a more significant driving force.

Research and development personnel often resent this swing of the pendulum to commercial values and believe that too many of their activities are governed by purely commercial decisions made by marketing staff. Instead, these people would prefer that decisions be based on commercial decisions interpreted by research and development staff or based on commercial values influenced by medical values. A more enlightened view is that both marketing and research and development are influenced by business realities and pressures. These business pressures drive the other groups to interact and cooperate to a greater degree. Figure 37.3 illustrates four models of interactions (relationships) between the medical and marketing function. These models are not mutually exclusive. Parts of each group could follow one model while another part follows a different one. Integrated groups could be applied to projects or to other aspects of the two functions. Model A characterizes, unfortunately, the situation in many companies today, where marketing is dominant.

Although it may sound like an ideal state, the author believes and expects that there will be a greater partnership in the future (i.e., model C of Fig. 37.3) where decision making will be shared between research and development and marketing. Decisions made by one group without discussions with and agreement by the other

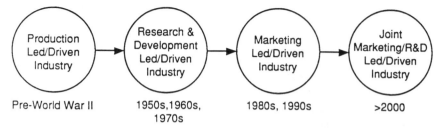

FIG. 37.2. Schematic to show the predominant forces influencing the pharmaceutical industry and its decision making during the 20th century. A prediction (or hope) for the 21st century is also shown.

group should not be acceptable to a company. Joint decision making should be the norm, and neither group should be viewed as dictating policy to the other.

SELECTED MEDICAL–MARKETING ISSUES

A series of questions and topics are discussed that relate to medical and marketing issues. Many other issues are discussed in the other chapters of this section.

Integrating New Personnel Into a Company

There is a basic difference in how medical and marketing professionals are integrated into a pharmaceutical company. Medical professionals, primarily physicians but also those with a doctoral degree in science, can only work as clinical scientists in a small number of industries (e.g., medical devices). These people become closely identified with and in a sense become part of a com-

Models of Marketing–Medical Relationships

A. Dominant–Subservient

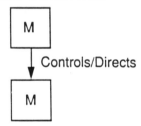

B. Separate But Equal

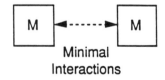

C. Strongly Linked Partners

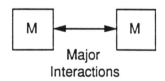

D. Integrated Groups

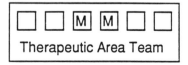

FIG. 37.3. Four models of medical–marketing relationships. The two "Ms" in each model represent medical and marketing functions.

pany's soul. This is because of the physicians' traditional role in patient care and their responsibility for developing new medicines on which their company's survival depends and because physicians as a group usually play more of a role in ethical issues than do others within the company.

Marketing professionals, on the other hand, are trained to work in almost any industry and there are always marketing people entering a pharmaceutical company from dissimilar industries. Although the roles of many marketers are similar across most industries, the dynamics of the pharmaceutical industry are extremely different than those of most other industries in terms of (1) the long period needed to develop a medicine after it is discovered, (2) the great extent to which the industry is regulated by the government, and (3) the enormous uncertainty about a compound's ability to reach and remain on the market. Thus, marketing people who join a pharmaceutical company must be educated about the characteristics of the industry and in a sense must be molded to fit their new environment.

Holding New Marketing Personnel to Agreements Made by Their Predecessors

This question is a critical one that often arises in the pharmaceutical industry. Professionals in any discipline believe that they should have the ability to utilize their knowledge, experience, and judgment to create the strategies and plans they are hired to develop and implement. While this concept is appropriate in many cases, the plans agreed to by various marketing managers cannot be overturned every time a new professional joins a marketing group or is transferred to a new position. This is particularly true if senior corporate managers have reviewed and endorsed a marketing plan.

In some companies, marketing personnel turn over rapidly. New product managers often desire to impart their personal views on the plans affecting their products. This is natural and appropriate at the outset of a project or at an important decision point or milestone. At other times, however, changes in marketing strategy may create major problems and repercussions within the organization. Such decisions include choice of dosage form, strength, and color; strengths to launch; and quantities of each strength to be manufactured. Another reason it is important for new marketing staff to adhere to decisions made by their predecessors (assuming that the data on which the decisions were made are unchanged) is that marketing personnel appropriately do not want to make firm decisions on many important questions until the last possible moment. They understand that many markets change (or are liable to change) in important ways that would affect their decisions. When marketing professionals are pressured by other groups (e.g., medi-

cal, technical development, and production) or by senior marketers into making decisions at an early stage, the marketing people sometimes feel compelled to modify their views at a later date. This often creates strong tensions because technical development, production, and medical groups require long lead times to accomplish their work. They require marketing commitments on which to initiate and orient their activities.

Holding New Medical Personnel to Agreements Made by Their Predecessors

Medical professionals who join an existing medical group desire (in most situations) to review and appropriately modify the clinical development plan that they must follow. This is usually less of a problem than the comparable situation described above for marketing professionals because medical plans must address agreed-on medical indications, and these are generally not easily changed. Also, less impact on marketing or on other nonmedical groups usually occurs by changes in a medical plan than by changes in the marketing plan. One major exception is when medical groups embark on a tangent that wastes resources and delays the time to marketing of the medicine for its primary indication.

Marketing and medical professionals who are not committed to executing their own plans and agreements should not be allowed to modify those plans, unless reasons for requesting a change are compelling. If plans that are generally viewed as adequate are unnecessarily or inappropriately changed in a major way, consideration should be given to having the professional who made the change transferred or removed from his or her position. This suggests that a process should be in place to ensure that senior medical and marketing management review all major proposed changes to plans.

Establishing Contracts Between Marketing and Clinical Groups

Some companies approach the issue of whether (and how) to codify agreements between marketing and medical groups by insisting that formal arrangements be expressed in the form of a contract. This approach is advantageous when the details of the agreements are clearly specified, including the identification of the person or group that has the responsibility for each event and the dates when the activities will be completed. One potential disadvantage of a formal agreement is that it can create barriers between the groups instead of creating a feeling of teamwork. The consequence may be the development of a "we" and "they" attitude that tends to separate the groups into two sets of people with different goals and interests.

The potential benefit of using contracts depends to a

large degree on the environment and traditions of the company or companies involved. If the company's environment and atmosphere are highly formal, then this approach might be an appropriate one, whereas in an informal atmosphere, such an approach would likely be counterproductive to maintaining positive working relationships.

If deemed appropriate, a contract could focus on one or more specific marketing studies that medical groups will conduct, or it could focus on the characteristics of each specific dosage form being developed (e.g., size, shape, color, dosage strength, formulation, imprinting, engraving, and packaging). Whereas marketing groups often want to withhold their decision on some or all of these specifications as long as possible, technical development (e.g., stability testing and formulation development) and medical groups require numerous decisions to be made relatively early in a medicine's development. This issue is particularly important for biotechnology products because clinical trials must be conducted with the final product. In addition, stability tests on the product for a New Drug Application may only begin once these decisions are made.

If "final decisions" by marketing staff are changed for reasons considered by research and development to be unimportant, then strong feelings of anger may develop within research and development and a serious morale problem can occur. This type of problem should be prevented by managers who are sensitive to these issues and by a system that requires final decisions to be made at the appropriate time.

Deciding if Marketing May Contract With Technical Development or Production Groups Outside the Company

Some companies allow the marketing function groups to contract for certain services either within or outside the company, while other companies force their marketing staff to utilize the company's own resources (if at all possible) regardless of cost and scheduling. The groups outside marketing that are most often considered in this regard are technical development (e.g., formulation development, scaleup development, and assay development) and production. In theory, many other types of medicine development activities could also be contracted outside the company (e.g., clinical trials or packaging development). Not included here are activities within the marketing function that may or may not be contracted to groups outside the company (e.g., market research, advertising, and public relations).

If a marketing group is allowed to contract work outside a company that the company's own technical development departments could perform, the decision to do so is likely to be based on or influenced by price. This usually places a sophisticated research-based company's technical group at an unfair disadvantage because of its large overhead, which often is not present for the group bidding on a contract. Moreover, there are so many games involved in supplying bids that the outside company's bid may be falsely low. They may count on having cost overruns or raising the bid after winning and signing the contract.

Another major motivator for marketing groups to go outside a company is to save time. This issue may be discussed among senior managers, but many cases will occur where more time will be required to do the work in-house.

Whatever the reason and basis for the marketing group's decision to go outside the company for work that the company could perform in-house, this process may initiate or continue a cyclical situation. The company's technical group is likely to be adversely affected in terms of both decreased morale and decreased work load if the marketing group contracts out work that the internal staff wish to do. This could lead to a decreased desire and/or ability by the technical staff to satisfy the marketing group on other development projects at a later date. This spiraling trend would encourage marketing managers to sign even more contracts with outside groups instead of having the work done in-house.

While the above scenario may seem somewhat extreme, it is the author's view that this potential problem is a very realistic possibility and should be avoided. The best way to do so is to have a company policy that outside contracts cannot be signed by marketing if internal groups are able, willing, and technically capable of doing the work. If the internal group does not have either the time or resources available to meet the specifications of the work, then an informal agreement should be reached by senior managers that allows the marketing people to contract with groups outside the company. If the marketing group has strong feelings about the desirability of using an outside contractor and the internal staff in the department affected are not in agreement, then a means of appealing this decision should be reached as part of the company's standard operating policies. If it is agreed that the work should be contracted out, then the in-house technical group should be involved in the contracting process. This will minimize (or avoid) the "we-they" feelings.

Should Aggressive Marketing Practices Be Encouraged?

The degree to which a company's marketing group pursues an aggressive marketing policy is really a corporate issue and one that the most senior managers (i.e., board of directors) must endorse. An aggressive company may be identified based on the practices its sales representatives follow, how closely its promotional practices adhere to the package insert and guidelines of regulatory authorities, and the nature of the marketing studies conducted. Two other indications of aggressive corporate behavior are how a company conducts its licensing activities and the ethical standards it follows. Most marketing personnel (as well as many others) believe that it is possible to be both aggressive and ethical.

Medical staff as well as the marketing staff are watchdogs of the ethical standards used in promotion. Medical staff believe they have this role because improper claims are usually based on clinical data they collect, and improper marketing claims or practices may lead to appropriate patients being treated inappropriately or to inappropriate patients being treated. Ethical standards on certain issues vary widely between cultures and even within a single culture. This means that many legitimate disagreements may arise as to whether certain marketing claims or practices are or are not ethical. Some of these ethical issues or problems have to be settled by the most senior managers in a company.

38 / Organizational and Staffing Issues Regarding the Medical–Marketing Interface

How Are Marketing Groups Organized? **429**
   Line Function System 429
   Matrix Function System: Strategic Business
     Units 429
   Physical Locations of Marketing and Medical
     Groups 430
How Are Medical Groups Organized?........... **431**
Where Should Various Groups and Functions Be
   Placed Within the Company's
   Organization? **431**
   Licensing, Pharmacoeconomics, Health
     Policy, and Quality of Life Activities........ 431
Staffing Issues **434**
   How May Medical Groups Best Support
     Marketing Needs?......................... 434

Transfer of Staff Within and Across Functions   434
Visits of Staff From One Function to Another   435
Should Medical Personnel Work in Marketing
   and Vice Versa?........................... 435
Professionals With Formal Training in Both
   Disciplines 435
Should Technical Development Departments
   Dedicate Some of Their Staff to Marketing
   Activities?................................. 435
Organizational Links Between Medical and
   Marketing Groups **435**
   Building Formal Bridges Between Medical and
     Marketing.................................. 435
   Building Informal Bridges Between Medical
     and Marketing 437

Pareto's Law (the 20/80 rule) =
20% of events yield 80% of results
20% of your customers produce 80% of sales
20% of donors contribute 80% of gifts
20% of your inventory produces 80% of volume

HOW ARE MARKETING GROUPS ORGANIZED?

Within a pharmaceutical company, a marketing group is usually organized into either a discipline-oriented line function system or a matrix function system. The latter consists of strategic business units, each of which acts as an independent entity containing groups and individuals to conduct all necessary activities.

Line Function System

Most line function systems keep individuals in each marketing service group (e.g., advertising, research,

health economics, and new product development) together; from here they provide help to the major groups (Fig. 38.1). The major advantage of the line function approach, which keeps professionals in similar disciplines together, is the achievement of greater esprit de corps and greater synergy in ideas and performance. A critical mass is sought and, hopefully, achieved in most marketing areas to progress medicines efficiently.

Matrix Function System: Strategic Business Units

The approach to organizing the matrix system in marketing is similar to that used for organizing the project

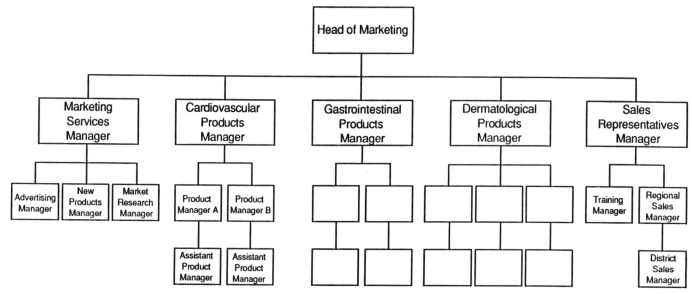

FIG. 38.1. Organizational chart for the marketing function based on line management structure and focusing on therapeutic area products.

system in research and development (Spilker, 1991). This means that various service groups (e.g., market research or advertising) usually are divided amongst the major groups to create interdisciplinary "business" units (Figs 38.2 and 38.3), though sometimes they are not (Fig. 38.4). Each of these business units may act independently with its own general manager and even with its own sales staff. Business units may be established for (1) over-the-counter medicines, (2) large retail and wholesale accounts, (3) hospitals, or (4) prescription medicines, or business units may be established for individual therapeutic areas if the company is large enough. A number of marketing services partly shown in the figures are more completely listed in Table 38.1.

Two specific problems that can arise when strategic business units are used are briefly mentioned. First, many of the company's products are sold by two or more of the strategic business units. This usually means that each has its own forecast to meet. If it is difficult to track sales achieved for a particular medicine for each strategic business unit, an approximate percentage of sales can be determined. If two or more units are competing for sales that could be achieved in a hospital versus a national account, or in physicians' offices, counterproductive competition within the company may become established.

Second, since there is no single person identified as the overall product manager within the company for most products, some type of unity of purpose is required. This may be achieved by having periodic meetings of all relevant personnel to review the product's status, the success of its current strategy, and plans to chart the products' future course. Without this type of meeting or other communication to yoke together various groups, it is possi-

ble, and even likely, that at least some groups will move in different directions or will assign the products' activities a different priority than that given by other senior managers.

Physical Locations of Marketing and Medical Groups

The issue of where medical and marketing groups should be located in relation to one another rarely arises as a major consideration in pharmaceutical companies. Medical and marketing groups are placed in separate areas of the same building, in separate buildings on the same site, in separate locations within the same city, or in separate cities. Nonetheless, if the concept of a team approach to medicine development is truly considered important, it makes sense to consider placing at least some medical and marketing representatives in relatively close proximity or even in the same area. Some companies have placed all members of a therapeutic area team (e.g., rheumatology or cardiovascular) together. These individuals work to develop all medicines in that therapeutic area. Medicines are each established as separate projects, just the same as for other organizational approaches. To create the best environment for this approach to be successful, it makes most sense for the medical personnel to be responsible for carrying out all phases of clinical development (i.e., Phases I to IV). If one medical group handles only one or two phases of development and a separate medical group handles the others, numerous problems could arise in terms of interactions with marketing professionals.

The approach of integrating medical and marketing personnel sacrifices some of the benefits that marketing

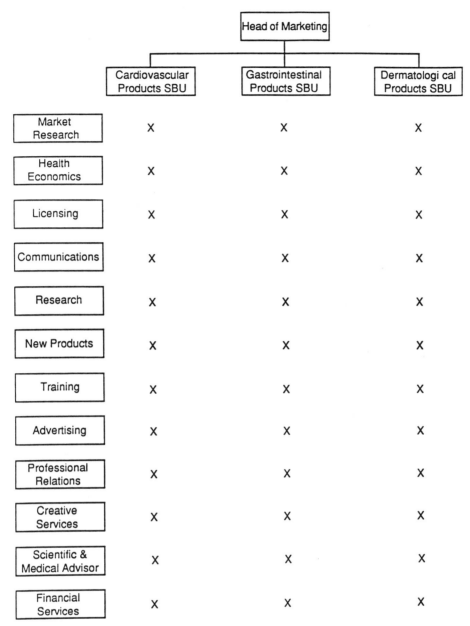

FIG. 38.2. Organizational chart for the marketing function based on a matrix management structure of separate business units (SBU).

(and medical) professionals gain by being in close proximity and interacting frequently with their colleagues in related medical or marketing fields. Trade-offs must be considered when deciding whether greatest efficiencies and benefits are achieved through a closer working relationship and physical proximity of medical and marketing groups or through interactions within their own area. Other disciplines could also be closely brought together with marketing and medical, such as various research (e.g., pharmacology, chemistry, and biochemistry) and development (e.g., metabolism, chemical scaleup, analytical development, and formulation) groups. This would involve consideration of appropriate laboratory locations.

HOW ARE MEDICAL GROUPS ORGANIZED?

A discussion comparable to the above for marketing is given and schematics are shown and described in more detail in Chapter 29.

WHERE SHOULD VARIOUS GROUPS AND FUNCTIONS BE PLACED WITHIN THE COMPANY'S ORGANIZATION?

Licensing, Pharmacoeconomics, Health Policy, and Quality of Life Activities

Every case is unique and should be determined independently without application of rigid rules. Each of the

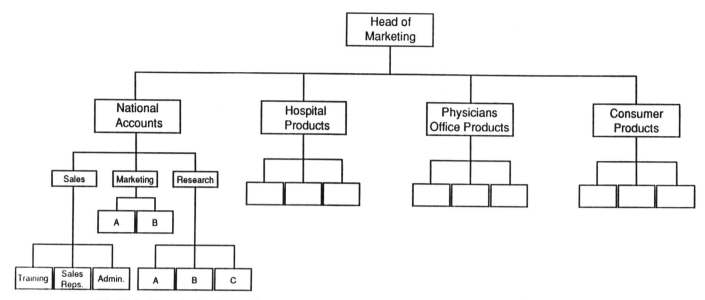

FIG. 38.3. Organizational chart for the marketing function based on a line management structure focusing on the customer's facilities, type of customer (i.e., national accounts) and type of product (i.e., hospital products or consumer products). Many variations of this chart could be drawn.

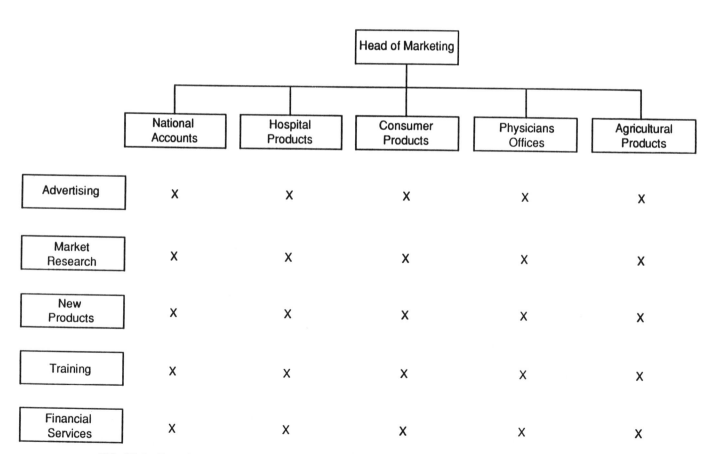

FIG. 38.4. Organizational chart for the marketing function based on a matrix management structure.

TABLE 38.1. *Marketing services that are often provided within a marketing division*[a]

1. Advertising standards
2. Market research
3. Creative services[b]
4. Advertising production
5. Meetings and conventions
6. Professional relations
7. Speakers' bureau
8. Financial services
9. Licensing
10. Strategic planning
11. Forecasting systems
12. Pricing
13. New products
14. Communications
15. Training
16. Competitive awareness

[a] The exact services provided by each of these groups would vary from company to company.

[b] This group would include developing suggestions for generic and brand names.

above groups could be organizationally located in several different areas of the same company. Moreover, the optimal arrangement could change over the years depending on various factors, such as changes in pressures on the company, the nature of the investigational or marketed medicine portfolio, or the personalities and strengths of the senior managers. This section describes those factors that should be evaluated in determining where to place a specific function. A suggestion is then made about the most commonly acceptable group in which specifically to place each of the four functions listed in this section's heading.

The major factors that influence the decision of where to place various functions in a company, particularly new functions, are:

1. *Traditions of the company* A strong group within a company usually offers more status to a new function placed under its aegis. If the leaders of the overall group and new group have similar views about the new function, this placement offers certain advantages. A weaker group could be the best place for a new function if its fit would be widely viewed as making the most sense and also strengthening the weaker group.

2. *Current organization of the company* The company may have similar groups placed in a certain organizational area; sometimes it is logical to place the new group there as well. Duplicating a function and placing it in a different area usually fosters competition. At the very least, it is counterproductive and sets up a negative hurdle for many people to overcome in attempting to expedite a medicine's development. Although duplicating functions in various areas is often

initially viewed as improving efficiency, it eventually causes diminished efficiency.

3. *Ability to have a senior-level protagonist within the company* A senior manager of one function may be much more interested in having the new function placed under his or her direction than are other managers. This highly motivated individual could assist the new group to accomplish more of their goals (and to set higher goals) than if the new group is placed under several layers of management in the function of someone with less interest in having the group thrive.

4. *Ability to get things done* This relates to the current organizational structure. Some parts of an organization can expedite work more efficiently than others. This may be because of the personalities of the staff working there, the management of the group, or the lack of encumbrances that are present in other areas. The manager of a new function is likely to prefer to report to the manager of a group that has demonstrated an ability to get things done and who is willing to delegate authority to the manager of the new group.

5. *Interest of the people within the company* Logic may dictate that a specific organizational group should supervise a new group or function. Nonetheless, there may be little interest in placing the people in the logical group and strong interest in another organizational approach. The new group's success is often more likely to be attained if it is managed by a more strategic than logical choice.

The author's general recommendation, for which exceptions certainly exist, is to place each of the groups as follows within the organization.

Licensing This function should generally be placed outside of both research and development and marketing, although it will interact with both functions on a frequent basis. This group should likewise not be placed under the direction of legal, financial, or any other specific discipline managers. It should report directly to the company's chief executive officer, or possibly to one of his or her major staff members. This enables the group to attain the most senior manager's attention when required and prevents it from being viewed as primarily a function of any specific group.

Pharmacoeconomics This activity should generally be situated under a public policy or health policy group if one exists within the company; otherwise, it may be placed within the marketing function. The major goals of pharmacoeconomic studies are to help (1) place newly marketed medicines on formularies, (2) justify the price when it is being established by regulatory authorities, (3) obtain reimbursement by third-party payers, and (4) promote a medicine both before and after it is officially launched. These are primarily marketing functions, and whether the actual studies are performed by economists, physicians, others, or all, the discipline of pharmacoeconomics is much closer to marketing than to medical. It is reasonable to place this group as part of a medical department controlled by marketing, if one exists.

Health policy The usual choice for a company generally is not between placing this function within the marketing group or the medical group, but between placing it within a corporate affairs type of structure or a marketing group. Alternatively, this activity may be granted more independent status. The best choice between these three approaches (or others) within a company depends more on the nature of the particular company than do the choices for placing the licensing or other groups discussed. An alternative approach to those discussed is to decentralize this role so that each relevant discipline (e.g., marketing or corporate affairs) has their own "expert" or small group for health policy issues. A central committee of experts from each area of the company could also be formed to coordinate activities and plan an overall strategy to meet the company's interest.

Quality of life Strong arguments may be made for placing this group within a medical or within a marketing group. If this group is primarily oriented toward economic issues, then a market placement makes more sense. If the group is medically oriented and focuses on patients' feelings of improvement and abilities to carry out essential physical, psychological, and social activities, then a medical organization is preferable. An independent placement is not desirable because, without a strong champion, the effective functioning of this group could readily be compromised.

Pharmacopolitics A central coordinating function for the wide panoply of pharmacopolitical activities is desirable. This role should report directly to the chief executive officer. This is discussed more in Chapters 6 and 58.

STAFFING ISSUES

How May Medical Groups Best Support Marketing Needs?

Medical groups that support marketing functions can be under the management of marketing or medical departments. A number of advantages can be presented to support either structure, and there are numerous companies that are organized each way. Marketing naturally prefers to have control of such supporting groups so it can influence priorities, timetables, and even protocol design. However, numerous interviews with physicians working under marketing control convince me that they often feel like second-rate citizens compared with the

physicians who develop investigational medicines. As a result, there is often a morale problem in those medical departments that are controlled by marketing managers. If such a problem can be resolved (or does not exist), then there should be no significant objections to this organizational arrangement. In fact, this arrangement often helps to lessen some of the tension that can be created when marketing groups seek medical resources. Sometimes this organizational issue is settled on the basis of who the company wants to please, i.e., the marketing interests or the physicians who are working in this department. Of course, for companies with a medical staff of under 100 or so, it generally is most efficient for a single medical group to plan and implement all clinical trials.

Transfer of Staff Within and Across Functions

Companies train their staff in many ways to enhance their effectiveness. Gaining experience in other marketing functions on a temporary basis will often improve a marketer's overall effectiveness in his or her original function as well as improve his or her understanding of related areas. Moreover, cross-training helps prepare professionals for more senior level positions, particularly those in which managers supervise multiple functions. Thus, a temporary assignment of employees from one function (e.g., within marketing), to another function (e.g., within medicine) is sometimes used within pharmaceutical companies. The duration of a temporary assignment is usually specified in advance.

For such a program to succeed, careful preparation is needed both by the company and by the professionals involved. A number of general principles are listed.

1. *Identify objectives as clearly as possible and inform those involved.* It is not adequate to inform employees about their temporary transfer to a new function without providing a clear description of what the company hopes to achieve. If the objective is not clear in the minds of the managers proposing the program, then those managers should spend sufficient time clarifying their thoughts and objectives before implementing the plan. Merely describing what will occur to employees could lead to a counterproductive situation, particularly if the person or people mistakenly perceive they have been chosen for a rapid promotion.

2. *Determine how the company will benefit.* Clearly, the individuals chosen for temporary cross-assignment benefit from the program through personal education and new experiences, but if there is no clear benefit to the company, then the program should be compared with others that may offer the company more advantages. For example, if some current systems were modified or standard operating procedures rewritten so that some professionals could perform their jobs

more efficiently or with less friction with other staff, it would create a positive change. These types of improvements should always be sought because the company and its environment are always in a state of flux and no system remains "best" forever.

3. *Provide enough time for the participants to prepare.* At least a month is needed for most professionals to accept this concept, complete their current outstanding tasks, turn their work load and responsibilities over to others, and prepare themselves to accept a new role.

Visits of Staff From One Function to Another

It is not always possible to exchange staff between functions. Even when this is done only a few people are generally involved. At the other extreme (time-wise), a lecture or two is insufficient to achieve more than a superficial understanding of another function. An in-between option is to have visits of groups of scientists, clinicians, or marketers in the other functions' facilities for one day up to two weeks. During that time they would be exposed to a planned series of activities, talks, workshops, or demonstrations. The size of the group (two to 30) would have to be carefully considered as well as the entire content and formats that would justify this major effort in education.

Should Medical Personnel Work in Marketing and Vice Versa?

While few physicians have the skills, temperament, or interest to work full-time in marketing, even for three to six months, there are other medical staff who would be valuable assistants in a marketing group. Some marketing departments are primarily staffed by personnel from medical and/or scientific departments. In these departments, it would make total sense to rotate medical personnel through the marketing group. Pharmacists are trained both in science and commercial practices and should be considered for this cross-functional training.

On the other hand, it is unreasonable to expect marketing personnel to move into medical positions, except in special cases. One of those areas is for marketers to help provide information to physicians and health care providers.

Physicians and clinical staff may work in a medical group under marketing control doing the same work they would do in a department supervised by medical professionals, but within a different organizational structure. Whether or not this is considered a good idea varies from individual to individual within each company.

Having the right people (i.e., those who are competent, experienced, open-minded, and willing to work hard) is an essential part of creating successful results. Of course, this is true in virtually all areas of a pharmaceutical company.

Professionals With Formal Training in Both Disciplines

Many physicians or scientists may become knowledgeable and proficient in marketing. Such individuals, if talented, gain credibility and become respected in their new discipline. Few marketers, however, are able to join and contribute fully to traditional medical or scientific disciplines because of their training—certainly not because of their ability. Nonetheless, they might join service groups within research and development (e.g., medicine information, scientific documentation, project coordination, and regulatory affairs) and gain respectability and credibility.

Another approach to bridging the gap between the two groups is to support a new "breed" of professional who would be trained in both areas. At present, a likely prospect would be a pharmacist with an advanced pharmacy degree who had additional business training and a MBA. This person would be in a good position to provide cross-discipline expertise and to contribute to marketing while indicating research and development concerns/issues.

Should Technical Development Dedicate Some of Their Staff to Marketing Activities?

Some pharmaceutical companies dedicate staff in their technical development departments to marketing activities (e.g., creating new formulations). There is no way to say that this practice is correct or incorrect all the time. Moreover, the best approach for a company at any one time may be inappropriate a year or two later. Having managers who seek to cooperate and solve problems is more important than the exact procedures they use. Groups that work well together and have good will usually solve problems appropriately, regardless of their organizational structure. The opposite is also true.

ORGANIZATIONAL LINKS BETWEEN MEDICAL AND MARKETING GROUPS

Building Formal Bridges Between Medical and Marketing

The relationships between medical and marketing staff should not be allowed to develop solely on their own. Such a scenario would lead to an unpredictable and probably frequent change of relationships, depending on the degree of teamwork, the nature of personalities, and other factors. Instead, there should be a formal series of contacts between medical and marketing staff. These contacts or bridges usually start at the top (i.e., at the board of directors) in terms of setting the tone and nature of the developing relationships. A strong relationship at the top of a management's hierarchy facilitates bridge building, effective communications, and efficient working relationships at all levels of the company. The opposite, unfortunately, is also true.

Excellent relationships between medical and marketing personnel at any one level of a company are insufficient to sustain adequate communications and relationships between these two hierarchies. Strong professional bonds must be created at *all* levels. The forging of these links is facilitated if there is respect for the professionalism of the other group. If one group generally feels that the level of competence is lower in the other group, true bridge building is difficult if not impossible. The chief executive officer and the board of directors must address such a problem; they could remove or transfer a few individuals who are obstacles to the relationships they consider essential, or they could address the problem in less direct ways. Selected areas and activities at which both formal and informal relationships are developed are shown in Fig. 38.5.

Types of bridges that can be built between the medical and marketing groups are for each to involve the other group on various standing committees, ad hoc committees, task forces, and other formal groups. Representatives from the other group should be asked to attend major meetings, retreats, and conferences; if appropriate, they should be invited to participate actively. All project groups, whether based in research and development, marketing, or production, should have representatives of the other functions. In all other areas where formal relationships can be established between separate functions they should be considered. An important exception is when there is nothing for one group to contribute and they do not want to be present. Those situations should be readily identifiable.

Forming bridges between two functions at different subsidiaries (i.e., the marketing group at one site with the medical group at the other) or between the headquarters and one of its subsidiaries may create problems and should be carefully considered and discussed before proceeding. The best plan is to involve all parties (i.e., marketing and medical groups from both sites concerned) to

Interfaces Between Medical and Marketing Groups

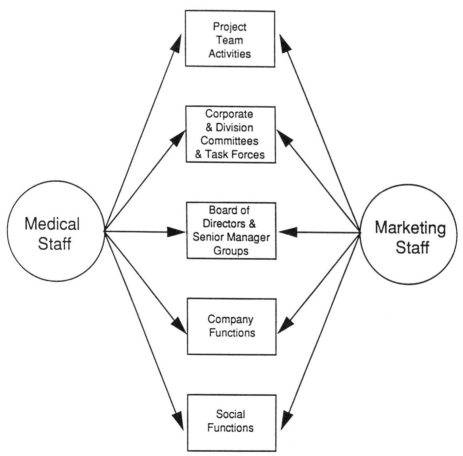

FIG. 38.5. Selected areas and activities at which medical and marketing staff interact on a formal and informal basis.

investigate possible organizational methods of achieving the company's and the group's objectives.

Building Informal Bridges Between Medical and Marketing

Informal bridge building primarily relates to developing personal relationships between individuals from each group who work together. These bridges may be facilitated by (1) having more people work together; (2) physically locating groups closer together, rather than in separate buildings or in separate cities; (3) having some people rotate through the other group; and (4) establishing special social, professional, or other events (e.g., dinners or sports events) where both groups are brought together. In addition, through the formal bridge-building procedures, many informal bridges will be forged. The one pitfall to avoid is creating artificial situations and environments that are contrived for this purpose and are viewed by the staff in a negative way.

39 / Medical and Marketing Needs, Wants, Possibilities, and Problems in Developing New Medicines

Defining Needs and Wants..................... **439**
Comparing Marketing's Needs and Wants With
  Those of Medical **440**
Comparing Marketing Priorities and Resources
  With Those of Medical.................... **440**
  Priority Setting 440
  Resource Allocation 441
  Consequences of Imbalances in Resource
    Availability Within One Group But Not the
    Other 441
  Communicating Marketing Priorities 441
Marketing Information That Is Important for
  Scientific and Medical Decisions............ **441**
  How Does Marketing Information Enhance
    the Medical Value of a Product?............ 441
  How Does Marketing Data Help Make
    Scientific and Medical Decisions?.......... 443

Why Is It Essential for Medical Groups to Use
  Marketing Data? 444
What Marketing Data Are Needed to Evaluate
  a Medical Project?......................... 444
Will a Specific Clinical Trial Truly Provide the
  Data That Marketing Needs? 444
Problems Between Medical and Marketing
  Groups.................................... **445**
  Medical Staff Give Marketing Studies a Low
    Priority 445
  Staff Turnover............................. 446
  Distrust of the Other Group's Motives 446
  Medical Staff Are Not Interested in Developing
    "Me-Too" Medicines of Commercial
    Importance to the Company................ 446
  Personnel Issues 446
  Conclusion................................. 446

Market competition is the only form of organization which can afford a large measure of freedom to the individual. Frank Hyneman Knight. From *Freedom and Reform* (1947).

Every individual necessarily labors to render the annual revenue of the society as great as he can. He generally indeed neither intends to promote the public interest, nor knows how much he is promoting it. . . . He intends only his own gain, and he is in this, as in many other cases, led by an invisible hand to promote an end which was no part of his intention. . . . By pursuing his own interest he frequently promotes that of the society more effectually than when he really intends to promote it. I have never known much good done by those who affected to trade for the public good. Adam Smith.

This chapter seeks to differentiate between the necessary standards a new medicine must achieve in order for the company to determine that it will launch the medicine on the market, and those standards that are desired in order for the medicine to be medically or commercially successful. These differences are described as needs and wants.

DEFINING NEEDS AND WANTS

Marketing needs and wants are described in terms of a medicine's technical and clinical profile. This combined profile consists of a number of the medicine's characteristics, which are described in the package insert, and is used as the basis for the medicine's positioning and pro-

TABLE 39.1. *Selected examples of standards used to define minimally acceptable or desirable criteria for a medicine*

1. Onset of a clinically significant effect must occur within one hour.
2. The duration of action must be at least six hours.
3. The medicine must be cost effective when compared with the market leader.
4. The incidence of serious adverse reactions must be less than 3%.
5. The magnitude of change for the primary (well-established) clinical parameter of efficacy must be at least 30% in at least 50% of patients receiving the medicine.
6. Medicine must be able to support an acceptable dosing regimen (e.g., ten times/day would not be acceptable).

motion. In positioning and promoting a medicine, all marketers desire a profile (i.e., a series of medical and nonmedical characteristics) as close to that of the ideal medicine as possible. Because this goal is virtually never achieved, it is important to establish at the outset of a medicine's development the profile of clinical and other characteristics that represent *marketing needs* (i.e., the minimally accepted profile of characteristics that must be achieved to keep the project alive). The profile that represents *marketing wants* (i.e., the desirable profile) should also be discussed and identified. The individual characteristics of both the minimally acceptable and desirable profiles should be described and quantified to the degree possible at the initiation of a project (Spilker, 1991). Both sets of characteristics should be written on paper and periodically reviewed and modified throughout the project's life.

Just as a set of marketing needs and wants may be listed for each medicine, medical departments have a set of needs and wants for the same medicine. A set of preclinical needs and wants exists also; these are the standards against which the compound was measured before the decision was reached to test that compound in humans as a potential medicine. Also, the formulation, toxicology, assay, and other preclinical groups have a series of needs and wants. In all three cases, *needs* are defined by a set of minimally acceptable criteria or standards for a number of characteristics, and *wants* are defined by a set of desirable criteria for the same and possibly additional characteristics. In many cases, the individual standards for evaluating characteristics may be quantified or semiquantified. A few examples of these standards are listed in Table 39.1.

COMPARING MARKETING'S NEEDS AND WANTS WITH THOSE OF MEDICAL

In viewing the marketing and medical needs for a specific project (i.e., investigational medicine) there should be no quantitative differences for the standards of any characteristic that appears in each list (e.g., duration of action). It is both desirable and practical to establish a

single list that combines both marketing and medical *needs.* The same observations generally hold for marketing and medical *wants.* Even if there are large differences between medical and marketing wants, these should not influence the medicine's development because that progression is based on the medicine achieving the minimally acceptable profile.

The marketing needs for a specific medicine often differ. If these differences are acceptable to medical groups, then establishing a different list of criteria and standards for the same characteristics is acceptable. This could occur, for example, if marketing could accept a twice-a-day dosing regimen in one country but required a once-a-day dosing regimen to compete successfully on the market in another country. In some situations, marketing groups might be willing to accept a lower standard than that acceptable to medical groups. For example, a relatively high incidence of serious adverse reactions could occur with one of the company's medicines compared to other medicines of the same class. This might make the medicine marginally acceptable to some less developed countries and might lead marketing groups to suggest marketing the medicine only in those countries. Medical groups might object strongly to this proposal on the basis that it would not be acceptable to market the medicine anywhere. This issue should be resolved within the company as soon as possible, or else it could become an unanticipated major dilemma during the medicine's development.

In the process of addressing the needs of marketing and medical groups, the following questions typically are considered.

1. What indications should each new medicine be developed for?
2. In what order should these indications be pursued? Which indications should be developed simultaneously and which sequentially? How should the timing be arranged?
3. What dosage forms and routes of administration should be developed?
4. In what order should these dosage forms and routes of administration be developed?
5. What comparison medicines, placebos, or treatments should be used in clinical trials? Can the same ones be used in all countries?
6. What patient populations, disease subtypes, disease severity, and other relevant characteristics should be chosen to study and in which order?

COMPARING MARKETING PRIORITIES AND RESOURCES WITH THOSE OF MEDICAL

Priority Setting

Pharmaceutical companies are often better able to synchronize marketing and medical needs than they can synchronize the priorities of the two groups. Often the two will differ in the perception of a need to establish formal priorities; medical groups usually see less of a need.

One of the reasons for this difference is that medical groups know that early and midstage projects change their relative priority when the medicine's safety or efficacy is less than anticipated, or when one medicine's priority changes, putting it ahead (or behind) another medicine. While all staff should know whether the priority of a medicine is *relatively* high or low, a much more precise description of priority is not necessary as it is not helpful in implementing work allocations in most departments. This topic is discussed in more detail by Spilker (1991).

Resource Allocation

Even when the relative priorities of investigational medicine projects are purportedly the same within the medical and marketing groups, the resources allocated within a group may not be in balance. Resource imbalance may be manifested in a number of ways.

1. A relative imbalance of resources allocated by the medical (or marketing) group may exist when the entire portfolio of projects and products is considered. Some lower priority projects may, for example, be receiving a relative excess amount of resources compared to other medicines in the portfolio.
2. An absolute shortage of resources may be allocated to a project by only medical (or by only marketing) groups, even though the relative apportionment of resources within the portfolio is correct.
3. A relative imbalance of resources may exist within some of the medical groups but not within others. For example, there may be an insufficient number of data processors and statisticians to handle the data generated, or there may be an insufficient number of monitors available to handle the number of trials planned and initiated by other medical groups.
4. An absolute shortage of resources may exist within some medical (or marketing) groups, but not within others.
5. A relative imbalance may exist in the types of resources available within the medical (or marketing) groups. For example, there may be sufficient head count, but insufficient funds (or vice versa). Other types of resources where imbalances could occur would include equipment.

The relative and absolute imbalances listed above were all examples *within* a medical or within a marketing group (Fig. 39.1). An entire additional series of problems could be listed for relative imbalances *between* medical and marketing groups. Furthermore, the type (i.e., appropriateness) and experience of staff could raise an additional series of imbalances.

Consequences of Imbalances in Resource Availability within One Group But Not the Other

The major consequences of imbalances in resource availability within medical but not within marketing (or vice versa) are that:

1. Work will be delayed within that group (i.e., either medical or marketing), but not within the other. This imbalance presumably occurs either because only one group has sufficient resources or because the priority assigned differs between the two groups. If this latter issue is a problem, then discussions should be held by managers to resolve this.
2. Work will be delayed within both groups because of the impact of activities conducted by one group on the other one.
3. Work will not be delayed within either group because that group is (1) not on the critical path to delay the overall project, (2) able to hire temporary staff to do the work, or (3) able to work late and on weekends to prevent delays.

Communicating Marketing Priorities

One means of communicating marketing priorities to medical and other groups (e.g., production) is to create a list that is periodically updated. Separate lists could be created for (1) marketed prescription products, (2) marketed over-the-counter products, (3) investigational prescription products, (d) investigational (i.e., under development) over-the-counter line extensions, and (5) proposed projects for over-the-counter products. Possible category headings for the information to be included in such tables are shown in Table 39.2. These tables should be periodically updated (e.g., every three to six months), sent to senior medical staff, and discussed informally, or formally, if necessary. Medical commitments should be received to conduct at least the most important studies required to achieve the highest marketing priorities.

MARKETING INFORMATION THAT IS IMPORTANT FOR SCIENTIFIC AND MEDICAL DECISIONS

How Does Marketing Information Enhance the Medical Value of a Product?

Few people would be surprised to hear a discussion of how marketing activities enhance the commercial value of a product, but it may seem strange to state that marketing information enhances the medical value of a product. Yet there are many examples where marketing information and decisions have clearly enhanced a product's medical value, for example:

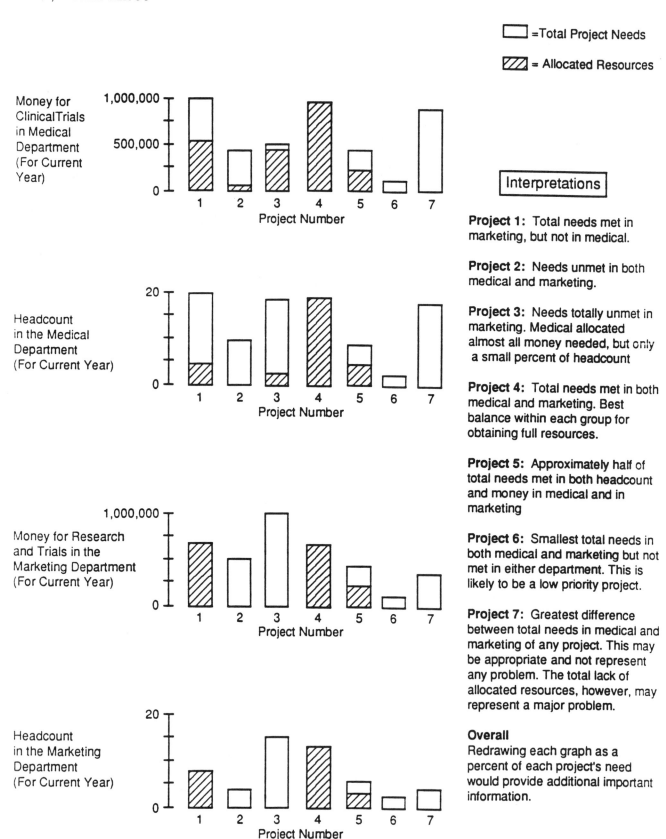

FIG. 39.1. A hypothetical comparison of project needs versus allocated resources in terms of both money and head count in medical and marketing departments. Representative interpretations are presented.

TABLE 39.2. *Headings to consider for tables presenting marketing priorities*

1. Project name
2. Project code
3. Indication
4. Product manager
5. Project leader
6. Person to contact
7. Next milestone
8. Target date to reach next milestone
9. Launch date
10. Third-year sales
11. Priority code
12. Priority status
13. Current status
14. Current activities
15. Assignment of responsibilities

1. Marketing groups may target a medicine for use by a more broad (or narrow) patient population than originally conceptualized by the medical group. As a result, the medicine may eventually be used more widely, or at least more appropriately, by those patients who benefit most.
2. Marketing personnel may create a new means of packaging a medicine that enables it to be used more easily and correctly. For example, a cumbersome preparation that required a solvent, heavy shaking, and then adding a diluent before being taken up through a hypodermic needle into a syringe could be replaced by either a similar system that is organized more clearly, facilitating its use, or alternatively, it could be replaced by a single vial formulation that greatly simplifies the dilution process and provides a savings in time. This latter approach would also decrease the probability of errors occurring in the medicine's preparation.
3. If the marketing group recommended developing a sustained-release form of a medicine for once-a-day use rather than using an instant-release form four times every day, patient compliance might be enhanced. This, in turn, would enhance the medicine's medical value.
4. Marketing groups could simplify instructions for intravenous infusions of medicines that would make their preparation simpler and less error prone.

Table 39.3 summarizes marketing data often required by medical groups, and Table 39.4 shows a means of tracking project data.

How Does Marketing Data Help Make Scientific and Medical Decisions?

The following brief examples illustrate how marketing data can contribute to the making of scientific and medical decisions in a pharmaceutical company.

TABLE 39.3. *Marketing data required by medical groups*

1. Size of the projected therapeutic and/or disease market in money and possibly in units
2. Market trends in that area over the previous several years
3. Future projections for changes in the market
4. Factors that are expected to influence the market in the future
5. New competitive medicines under development, their phase of development, and reported characteristics (i.e., advantages and disadvantages compared to market leaders and the company's medicine)
6. Types of niche markets that could be successful both medically and commercially
7. Important medical and other characteristics (e.g., cost or convenience) that would make a new medicine commercially successful
8. Minimal criteria that the company's medicine must achieve to enter the market successfully[a]
9. Timing at which various development stages (i.e., milestones) must be achieved to maximize the chances of success in the market
10. Dosage forms, dosage strengths, colors desired, plus comments on the formulation (e.g., is a preservative possible and if so, which one(s)?)

[a] See Chapter 34 for a detailed discussion about this topic.

Issue: A new investigational medicine that has never been tested in humans could be developed in either of two different therapeutic areas. The company's physicians believe that the medicine will have approximately equal clinical usefulness in both indications. For which therapeutic area should the medicine be developed first?

Approach: Marketing data should be collected on (1) the size of each therapeutic market, (2) the satisfaction of physicians with currently available products in each market, and (3) the perceived deficiencies of these products. Research and development personnel may be able to determine if the compound/medicine is likely to have properties that will meet those desired for improvement in either (or both) of the therapeutic areas.

TABLE 39.4. *Selected headings for a form to track the progress of projects*

1. Project name
2. Activity code
3. Department code
4. Function
5. Activity
6. Start date: estimated
7. Start date: actual
8. Finish date: estimated
9. Finish date: actual
10. Number of days to complete activity
11. Contact person

Issue: A new investigational medicine could be developed in several dosage forms and input is requested from marketing to help choose which one(s) to develop and in which order they should be developed.

Approach: Marketing data on the popularity of various dosage forms in treating patients with that disease should help settle this question, although good data are not always available. The correct marketing response is likely also to depend on the specific countries for which the medicine is being developed.

Why Is It Essential for Medical Groups to Use Marketing Data?

The answer seems totally obvious at first ("to make the right decisions"), but a number of additional points should be considered.

1. Most medical decisions are not black or white but involve consideration of many conditions, caveats, and alternatives. The quality of medical decisions is enhanced when the perspectives and data of marketing as well as other groups are included in the considerations. It is therefore essential that all major groups that depend on each other for the company's success also involve the others in providing input and also in ratifying the approach taken to achieve optimal success. This may sound like a cliché, but the practice of this principle is far from optimal in most pharmaceutical companies.

2. The issue of teamwork is also important. It takes enormous effort within a pharmaceutical organization to create a smooth working development team, but it takes only a small amount of dissension and lack of trust to disrupt it seriously. Involving marketing personnel in appropriate medical discussions is essential if this teamwork is to be successful.

What Marketing Data Are Needed to Evaluate a Medical Project?

Although the exact type of marketing data required for each situation differs, there are basic types that are generally useful in evaluating medical projects. These types of data are listed in Table 39.3. Not all of the data needed are required at the outset of the project, and not all are needed on all projects. Nonetheless, the data that are needed should be obtained as early as possible in the life of the project. Marketing data are generally followed over time to evaluate trends and important changes that occur throughout the life of the project. Major changes may (and often do) occur in the relative medical and commercial value of a project before it is finally launched. A new medicine that appears to be a major

medical breakthrough at the start of a project may become a "me-too" medicine by the time it reaches the market. The opposite phenomenon also occurs. During the 1980s, a number of investigational medicines that were in Phase IIIb or IV (e.g., Merital and Zimeldine) had to be terminated or withdrawn from the market because of toxicity. This created unexpected opportunities for other medicines (e.g., antidepressants and antiepileptics).

Will a Specific Clinical Trial Truly Provide the Data That Marketing Needs?

An alternative form of this question considers whether the protocol design and objective should be modified. For example, if common medical practice does not mirror the approach followed in the clinical trials, it may be important to redesign the trial or add an additional trial to the development plan. This is a critical issue to consider, not only for marketing-oriented trials, but also for pivotal Phase II trials. A series of trials may be identified that will provide sufficient data to address the clinical development plan, but these data must meet marketing needs as well. Therefore it is important for marketers to review the clinical plan. Marketing groups can be appraised of clinical trial status through tables summarizing the information listed in Table 39.5.

Marketing staff must determine whether publications of clinical trials to be used in a medicine's promotion several years hence will be helped by having the world's authorities participate as investigators. If primary care physicians are investigators of a trial, it is possible that they will be viewed by the target physicians as providing more appropriate data. The publication may also have more impact promotionally and in influencing clinical practice if it is presented in a specialty journal rather than in a generalist's journal. The answer to this issue is often of critical importance and should not be left to chance.

TABLE 39.5. *Selected headings to use for a table summarizing medical trials for a marketing group(s)*

1. Medical department
2. Project
3. Study name
4. Study number
5. Priority code within each (medical/marketing) group
6. Desired completion date by marketing
7. Estimated completion date by medical
8. External costs
9. Internal costs
10. Total costs
11. Comments
12. Perceived potential problems

PROBLEMS BETWEEN MEDICAL AND MARKETING GROUPS

Most problems arise because of failure to understand the perspective and thinking of the other group. This occurs not only because many stereotypes, clichés, and misunderstandings exist, but also because of different training, orientation, and goals within each group. Some of these differences are schematically illustrated in Fig. 39.2. Each of the spectra shows general differences between the groups. This figure too is a stereotype and many exceptions exist to each of the points shown. When the concepts underlying these spectra are well understood, tolerance for the other person's or group's views may be engendered, even if one does not agree with them. A few specific examples of problem situations are described.

Medical Staff Give Marketing Studies a Low Priority

Assume that a research and development–based pharmaceutical company at a steady-state period in its own development has a balanced distribution of resources and priorities among all of its disciplines and functions. This means that the discovery, development, and market-enhancement functions of research and development are all operating in a relative balance. To achieve such a balance, the marketing studies that occur late in a medicine's development (i.e., Phase III) and during the market-enhancement period (i.e, Phase IV) must receive appropriate resources and priorities.

If medical staff have little interest in designing and implementing these studies and fail to provide adequate services to marketing groups, then the marketing managers feel obligated to discuss this problem with senior medical or research and development staff. Some of the solutions to this issue are to (1) form a medical group within the marketing hierarchy that has as its primary function the planning and conduct of marketing studies, or (2) form a medical group within the medical hierarchy that is dedicated to marketing studies. Another possible solution is for senior marketing and medical staff to meet periodically (e.g., every four or six months) to review necessary studies and their relative priorities. The

A. Usual Time Frame for Development Plans

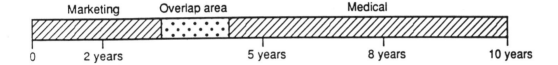

B. Tolerance for Uncertainty

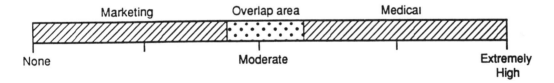

C. Education and Training

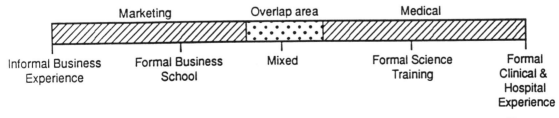

FIG. 39.2. A comparison of medical and marketing training and orientation along three spectra. Numerous exceptions exist to these generalizations.

author favors the latter approach, particularly when combined with the second one described above. Not only does this approach enable marketing staff to communicate their needs as a single voice to medical staff, but it prevents personal friendships or forceful personalities from having inappropriate influence to have clinical studies designed and conducted that are of minor importance to the company's objectives.

Staff Turnover

The rate of staff turnover at each level of employee (e.g., clerical, junior staff, senior staff, and managers) should be evaluated on an annual basis. Trends in the data that are increasing or rates that are above the industry average should be investigated. Such trends may have a direct bearing on productivity within the group as well as in the quality of interactions with other groups. Consider the situation where one group's turnover is extremely high and the other is extremely low. At the time when a member of the group with a low turnover becomes familiar with his or her counterpart in the other group and has developed a positive working relationship, the counterpart often seems to leave. This requires starting all over, attempting to build a relationship, and educating the new worker.

Distrust of the Other Group's Motives

If medical (or marketing) personnel believe that the ethical standards of the marketing (or medical) personnel or professionals within their area are inappropriate, then serious company problems may arise. These issues must be dealt with promptly or they may adversely affect mutual respect, relationships, the cooperation of staff, and the productivity of the entire organization. A variation of this issue is when the marketing group utilizes methods of promotion that medical people believe are undesirable. While these methods are not *unethical,* it may be useful to discuss their *propriety* in an appropriate forum.

Medical Staff Are Not Interested in Developing "Me-Too" Medicines of Commercial Importance to the Company

Medical staff do not usually refuse to develop a "me-too" medicine, but they may apply little enthusiasm and create delays in such a project. Delays may or may not be created purposefully, but they do cause problems because there is, invariably, a need for speed in development of a "me-too" medicine.

Personnel Issues

There are various approaches to facilitating communication between medical and marketing groups. Four approaches are (1) to place physicians in "pure" marketing roles, (2) to exchange personnel for a three- to six-month period to broaden their perspectives, (3) to rotate personnel through a variety of positions in the other groups, and (4) to conduct a formal or informal course or series of seminars.

Conclusion

Given the synergies and differences between medical and marketing needs and wants, the question is how to blend the two to maximize their efficiency and productivity in developing and selling medicines. The answer has to be in stressing two functions—understanding and communication. These are both fostered by a series of educational seminars, panel discussions, minicourses, and other education/training vehicles. Understanding and communication also are fostered when staff see that the most senior managers of these areas are setting good examples and are instructing their staffs to do the same. Third, both groups should work together on as many committees and projects as deemed worthwhile.

40 / Joint Medical and Marketing Activities

Interactions Between Marketing and Medical
  Groups. 447
  Informal Interactions Between Marketing and
    Medical Groups. 447
  Formal Interactions Between Marketing and
    Medical Groups. 448
  Achieving a Spirit of Partnership that
    Facilitates Productive Relationships 448
  Joint Planning Activities Between Medical and
    Marketing Groups. 448
  Developing a Single, Clear Marketing Message 449
  Converting a Prescription Medicine to Over-
    the-Counter Status 449
  Moral Obligation to Develop a New Medicine
    Versus the Marketing Opportunity It Offers . 449
Collaborative Approaches to Various Activities . . 450
  Licensing Activities. 450
  Portfolio Analysis 450
  Market Research 450
  Interpreting Market Research 451
  Educating Sales Representatives. 451
  Providing Information to Health Professionals 451

Review of Marketing Information by Medical
  Staff and Vice Versa 452
  Marketing Data that Influence Medical
    Decisions 452
  Commercial Decisions Made by Marketing
    Versus Commercial Decisions Made by
    Research and Development. 452
  Review of Proposed Advertisements by
    Medical Staff. 453
  Review of Proposed Package Inserts by
    Marketing Staff 454
  Providing Marketing Forecasts for Early-Stage
    Investigational Medicines. 455
  Marketing Input into Medical Strategies. 455
  Enhancing the Quality and Acceptance of
    Marketing Input to Medical Groups 455
Visually Characterizing a Market 456
  Illustrating the Importance of Specific Factors
    Desired in a New Medicine. 456
  Illustrating the Targeting of Specific Factors for
    Marketing a New Medicine with Clinical
    Spectra. 458

Fundamentally, there are only two ways of coordinating the economic activities of millions. One is central direction involving the use of coercion—the technique of the army and of the modern totalitarian state. The other is voluntary cooperation of individuals—the technique of the marketplace. Milton Friedman.

Some people say that cats are sneaky, evil, and cruel. True, and they have many other fine qualities as well. Missy Dizick.

A great deal of this book deals with strategic issues, and medical or marketing strategies often benefit by input from the other group. This chapter differs because it discusses various areas where the development of the plans and strategies of a new medicine is viewed as a joint activity. Many medical activities benefit from joint planning and coordination with marketing, and the opposite is also true. Just like the statement above on cats, each group is often seen as full of surprises for the other.

INTERACTIONS BETWEEN MARKETING AND MEDICAL GROUPS

Informal Interactions Between Marketing and Medical Groups

There is a wide spectrum of informal professional interactions that occur between marketing and medical people within a company or between internal staff and external people. These interactions include spontaneous meetings and discussions, ad hoc meetings, preplanned brainstorming sessions, information presentations, or advice-seeking meetings. Requests for an informal reviews of plans, promotions, protocols, or reports are also considered informal interactions.

Formal Interactions Between Marketing and Medical Groups

Common types of formal interactions are considered under the following four broad headings.

1. *Reviews without sign-off* Requests are often made from marketing to medical for reviews of specific information. This type of request is also made from medical to marketing groups. Reviews may be requested of ideas, documents, plans, protocols, reports, or other types of information. The output may be either verbal or written. These may be discussed at small and/or large joint meetings.
2. *Reviews with sign-off* The activities described above may require a written sign-off to ensure that the other group is in agreement. The traditions and formality of the company determine the degree to which this is necessary. The standard operating procedures should indicate whether special forms, a memorandum, or a note on the document constitutes a sign-off.
3. *Requests for activities to be performed* This usually involves marketing requesting medical groups to conduct one or more clinical trials. Other marketing requests for medical activities include conducting scientific symposia, preparing articles for publication, and staffing scientific exhibits at a medical convention. Medical may request marketing to participate in specific medical meetings (e.g., to present a marketing perspective), to provide marketing advice or data at any of many meetings, or to provide advice on protocols. Medical personnel who are astute about marketing issues may request market research to be conducted.
4. *Committees* Representatives of both groups may be asked to serve on any of several types of committees within the company. These include:
   a. Marketing (or medical) committees, to which one or more members of the other group are invited as members or as observers in a more informal capacity.
   b. Committees of a nonmedical and nonmarketing group (e.g., finance) on which both medical and marketing representatives sit.
   c. Corporate committees (e.g., board of directors) on which both medical and marketing representatives sit.

Achieving a Spirit of Partnership that Facilitates Productive Relationships

Positive relationships between marketing and medical groups are most likely to occur when there are positive relationships among the most senior managers. Their feelings about the other group are unintentionally communicated (as well as intentionally) and rapidly spread throughout their own group. A desire for a true partnership is an important prerequisite to a positive relationship between groups. It is extraordinarily difficult to have a productive relationship when one or both people do not want the relationship to succeed, or do not care if a successful relationship is created.

Companies with organizations and management systems that facilitate these relationships have a better chance at creating productive ones. No single organization or management style is best or is required for success, but the desire for success is necessary. It is sometimes a moving experience to see two people communicate effectively even though each speaks a different language and may not even understand much of what the other is saying. Whereas two people who share the same culture, language, and even training often cannot agree or communicate effectively, despite attempts to do so. Such failure is often the result of unconscious (or conscious) desires not to communicate and agree.

Joint Planning Activities Between Medical and Marketing Groups

Joint planning activities should be (1) nonrigid, (2) initially broad in concept, and (3) sensitive to the need for modifications based on regulatory change or changes in medical practice (e.g., new medicines introduced). The broad concepts listed below involve medical and marketing groups and are intended as guides to help create meaningful plans with the least number of problems.

1. Identify the time frame and priority of marketing studies to be conducted by medical groups.
2. Review the contents of medical protocols that are written for marketing-oriented studies or that contain aspects of particular interest to marketing.
3. Choose appropriate indications to develop a new (or older) medicine.
4. Review a new medicine's development plan.
5. Identify areas where both groups have major interests (e.g., pharmacoeconomics and quality-of-life studies).
6. Consider all areas where the other group is involved and their input would be useful. Have them critique and evaluate the content or meet with them to secure their buy-in to the plan that is developed.

Developing a Single, Clear Marketing Message

It is extremely important to create a single clear marketing message for every medicine. Multiple messages, particularly for a new medicine, tend to be confusing to physicians and others. Moreover, the messages are not remembered and can be counterproductive in that physicians will not prescribe a medicine whose use and benefits are vague, complex, or confusing. Although it is the responsibility of marketing personnel to develop this message, it is desirable for the medical group to play a major role in its creation, and in its review.

To develop this central message, marketing people traditionally ask medical staff such questions as:

1. What features of this medicine are most unique?
2. Why would a physician choose this medicine over other therapies to treat their patients?
3. What role would this medicine be expected to have in the treatment of disease X?
4. What types of patients would you treat with this medicine, in terms of disease type, severity, and other characteristics?
5. If everything went as well as you hope in the clinical trials, what important benefits would this medicine offer?
6. If everything went as you expected in the clinical trials, what important benefits would this medicine offer?
7. What advantages does this medicine have over other treatments (both on the market and known to be in development) for the same disease?

While the answers to each of these questions could be almost identical, subtle differences might be elicited that would help the marketer develop a single marketing message. This concept should initially be discussed within the medical group. If the group is not in favor of the proposed message, the basis of their objections must be determined—e.g., accuracy, ethics, or other reasons. It might be possible for medical to suggest a revised message that would be acceptable to marketing. Alternatively, marketing might decide to field test their message among an external group of physicians. At this stage it is quite possible that marketing would have a number of messages they would want to compare. Market research could evaluate a number of messages with physicians who would be expected to be prescribers of that medicine.

Converting a Prescription Medicine to Over-the-Counter Status

In several countries medicines are sold in three categories—prescription, pharmacy status, and general sales.

"Over-the-counter" refers to the latter category and "pharmacy" status refers to restricted sales controlled by the pharmacist.

A company that desires to take a prescription medicine to over-the-counter or pharmacy status must develop a comprehensive strategy to accomplish this goal. This strategy should consider the following.

1. Collection and summary of efficacy data in humans.
2. Collection and summary of safety data in humans.
3. Collection and summary of safety data in animals.
4. Preparation of a scientific review of the rationale to take the medicine over the counter.
5. Presentation of the above to experts and opinion leaders in the field, and a request for their assessments and recommendations. This meeting should also seek their buy-in to the over-the-counter concept.

After the latter meeting, the strategy should be reviewed by the company and revised as necessary. A meeting with regulatory authorities is desirable if it can be arranged. Further meetings with important groups affected by the proposed change (e.g., pharmacists) may be necessary or important to conduct.

Specific points to consider are whether it is desirable to (1) use a lower dosage strength for over-the-counter use than for prescription use, (2) withdraw the prescription medicine when the over-the-counter use is approved, (3) prepare a patient package insert, and (4) use the same message in all countries about the over-the-counter and prescription medicines. The regulatory package of information should contain postmarketing surveillance studies that provide convincing safety data as well as efficacy data. All spontaneous adverse reaction reports received by the company should be assessed and compared to the data received in the clinical trials. Finally, a benefit-to-risk analysis should be conducted to assess the impact that placing the medicine on over-the-counter status would have on patients with the disease. This should consider the ability of patients to diagnose when to treat themselves adequately and to take appropriate doses.

Moral Obligation to Develop a New Medicine Versus the Marketing Opportunity It Offers

One difficulty with using the particular scale of moral obligation is that the moral obligation for one person (or company) who is judging a compound could be the exact opposite of another person's moral obligation. For example, an abortifacient that is safer and more effective than previous therapy could be viewed either as a major medical advance or as a major sin. A new medicine that falls on the line of equivalence in Fig. 40.1 has relatively the same strength for both the extent of moral obligation to develop and the marketing opportunity. The further a

Marketing Opportunity to Develop a New Medicine

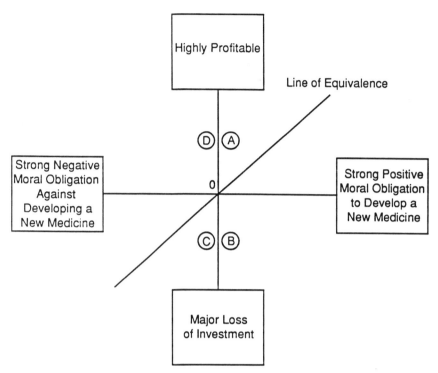

FIG. 40.1. A method to illustrate marketing opportunity to develop a new medicine in terms of moral obligation versus the potential (or likelihood) of profit.

medicine is located from the line, the greater the potential for dissension and problems in a company. Some companies might choose not to develop a new medicine of great profit if the moral obligation and reactions were strongly negative.

Negative moral reasons against developing a medicine could include that the medicine has less safety or efficacy than existing therapy or that the purpose of the medicine is considered immoral (e.g., an abortifacient).

COLLABORATIVE APPROACHES TO VARIOUS ACTIVITIES

Licensing Activities

Most medical and marketing activities in evaluating licensing opportunities are conducted independently. At some stage during the process, a group including both medical and marketing representatives should meet to review and critique the evaluations. They could also plan appropriate next steps and decide which questions and issues should be addressed. The final decision to agree to negotiated terms on a licensing opportunity generally involves a more senior group of representatives. Details of

evaluating licensing activities and negotiating points to consider are described in Chapter 48.

Portfolio Analysis

The group that conducts this exercise for the company should include both medical and marketing representatives from the outset. It is also customary in some companies for the marketing (and/or medical) groups to conduct their own internal review of the portfolio. This exercise should be conducted on a periodic basis, usually once a year. A specific system is usually developed at each company to conduct this exercise. Specific details of procedures to follow and the analyses to use are not presented here, but they are discussed in Chapter 35.

Market Research

In most pharmaceutical companies, market research is the exclusive province of a group located within the larger marketing function. This is appropriate from an organizational view, but from a procedural view, market research should be conducted in collaboration with scientists and/or medical personnel within the company.

While this may sound like heresy to many marketing and medical professionals, this approach is one of the most effective means of improving the standards used in market research. Improved market research will, in turn, improve the validity and value of the data and results obtained. Finally, the decisions that are based on the market research data obtained will be of improved quality.

Most medium and large pharmaceutical companies have marketers who design some or all of the research they sponsor. These studies are often then conducted by outside groups. Some companies use external vendors (i.e., contractors) to design and conduct all of their market research.

The primary involvement that appropriate medical professionals within the company should have is in the design phase of the market research. This involvement may vary from review and sign-off of the protocol to be used for market research to direct involvement at meetings specifically called to design the research. Innumerable variations will occur, even within a single company, but there are major reasons why there should be medical involvement. First, the quality of the research and subsequent decisions is likely to be enhanced by medical input. Second, there will be a greater chance that the research will include questions and issues of interest to medical professionals, and third, the likelihood of medical acceptance and buy-in of the results is greater because of the involvement of medical professionals in the process. Medical personnel may also attend focus groups or other market research studies, in addition to participating in the design of the research protocol.

Medical input should not be limited to people who are clinically trained, but should also include statisticians and, if appropriate, psychologists. It is desirable to have a multidisciplinary team of scientists, along with several marketing functions, on the team that designs market research. This will help ensure that the research conducted achieves the standards required for valid results.

The history of market research is replete with faulty instruments that have been poorly applied to address a question. No matter how intelligent the people are who base their decisions on such data, their decisions are bound to be distorted, inappropriate, or wrong in many cases if the basis of their decision is flawed. The standards used for much of market research are so poor in part because such research has not been subjected to government regulation as have other areas of research (e.g., toxicology, clinical research, and pharmacokinetics). Recent years have witnessed the development of more objective and more quantitative methods that market research vendors attempt to promote. However, their goals are to provide services their clients want, and they will be reluctant to promote more expensive studies strongly that yield more valid data if their clients do not want that.

The ways to include scientists in the market research design process include adding scientists and medical personnel to the marketing research group or asking them to serve as research and development representatives on marketing teams or marketing research committees that deal with planning market research.

Interpreting Market Research

In addition to using medical input in the design and conduct of market research, it is generally useful to have medical staff interpret the results of such research. Even if an outside vendor or consultant has prepared a report on the market research conducted, the relevant medical and scientific group(s) should review the report and discuss its interpretation. This provides additional assurance to the company that the interpretation has not (1) overlooked important factors, (2) included biased or confounding factors that question or invalidate results, and (3) ignored other interpretations. An additional advantage is that the medical personnel will be more committed to the results and their consequences, provided that they are medically correct and ethical. Taking a devil's-advocate perspective is often valuable in evaluating interpretations.

On the other hand, medical input is not needed with many market research projects. The desirability of involving medical groups must be determined by marketing staff.

Educating Sales Representatives

The education of sales representatives is usually planned by company experts in education and people from the marketing function. Medical representatives are often asked to lecture in specific courses and on specific topics. It is desirable for the course organizers to identify the best teachers/lecturers within medical groups and to assign them specific topics. Medical staff should view this as a service they provide for the marketing group. Some companies prefer not to involve their regular medical department in this responsibility. In reality, this activity is meaningful to some clinical staff and is tedious or even odious to others. A detailed curriculum should be prepared so that the scope and depth of information represented is not left to the whim of the teachers.

Providing Information to Health Professionals

A separate group that provides medical information on request to health professionals exists within each major company. This group is usually placed within the medical or marketing function. There is little reason to prefer one approach strongly over the other in theory. In practice, if the group is staffed by pharmacists and others with a scientific background, they would probably prefer their organizational association to be within a medical function. Answers to the most commonly asked questions should be prepared and stored in computers to facilitate replies by telephone, facsimile, and letter.

REVIEW OF MARKETING INFORMATION BY MEDICAL STAFF AND VICE VERSA

Marketing Data that Influence Medical Decisions

Any or all marketing data can be important to making medical decisions. The following are a few specific cases where marketing data often are sought and used to make medical decisions.

1. Should a new compound be taken into the clinic for evaluation? The marketing criteria to consider for a new project are summarized in Table 40.1. A very different approach to a medicine's profile is illustrated in Fig. 40.2.
2. Should a new compound be developed if two (or more) competitors are almost certain to reach the market first? The certainty of competitors reaching and remaining on the market is never 100%. One or more advantages for the company's medicine should be sought.
3. Can a medical niche be found for an investigational medicine to justify entry into an already crowded market? Sometimes the presence of a key clinical advantage is unknown when a new medicine begins development. Astute professionals seek to identify potential advantages that will create a niche. Novel

dosage forms or means of delivering the medicine may be considered.

4. Can a nonmedical niche be found for an investigational medicine to justify entry into an already crowded market?

Nonmedical advantages include (1) decreased cost; (2) increased convenience for pharmacists or nurses in storage (e.g., first nonrefrigerated product), preparation (e.g., easier to prepare the parenteral dose), or use; and (3) increased convenience for patients in terms of smaller tablets, improved packaging, or less frequent dosing (the last could be considered a medical advantage as well).

Commercial Decisions Made by Marketing Versus Commercial Decisions Made by Research and Development

Different experts often reach different interpretations of the same data whether or not they are trained in the same field. Nonetheless, strong tensions sometimes develop between medical and marketing groups about differences in interpretations and decisions when the same data are evaluated. Situations where interpretations are based on different sets of data are not discussed here because these primarily raise the issue of sharing and communicating data more completely.

A few examples are described in which each group reaches different conclusions using the same data.

1. Research workers are studying muscle metabolism because they believe that they may be able to unlock information that would lead to a commercially valuable medicine to treat inadequately treated muscle diseases. Marketing colleagues believe the tests are too theoretical for researchers to pursue because they are not targeted closely enough to a specific disease.
2. Research workers uncover an enzyme inhibitor with potential use in treating one of a few commercially important diseases, but they have little evidence of specific biological activity in their preclinical tests. They believe it is important to test the compound in humans, but marketing believes the approach is too speculative and is not in favor of developing the compound.
3. Clinical staff uncover some adverse reactions in clinical trials of an investigational medicine that could point to a valuable commercial market to explore. Marketing staff believe this serendipitous result is potentially interesting to test at a later time, but that it currently represents a tangent that will delay progress on the major indication being pursued at this point. The same scenario could be described with the roles of medical and marketing staff reversed.
4. Clinical staff wish to test a new chemical entity in an inadequately treated medical disease, believing that

---

TABLE 40.1. *Marketing criteria to consider for a new project*[a]

1. Current market size
2. Potential market size in X years
3. Numbers of patients
4. Current sales of all marketed medicines
5. Projected sales of the current proposed medicine (e.g., three years after launch)
6. Current competition on the market and degree of patient satisfaction with therapy
7. Current new medicines under development
8. Patterns of prescriptions
9. Minimally acceptable criteria required to develop the medicine
10. Advantages and disadvantages of the current proposed medicine
11. Critical factors required for success (e.g., launch before medicine X)
12. Ability to market the product effectively

[a] These topics may be evaluated for one or for multiple countries, depending on the interest and need for the information.

Medical-Marketing Profiles of a New Medicine

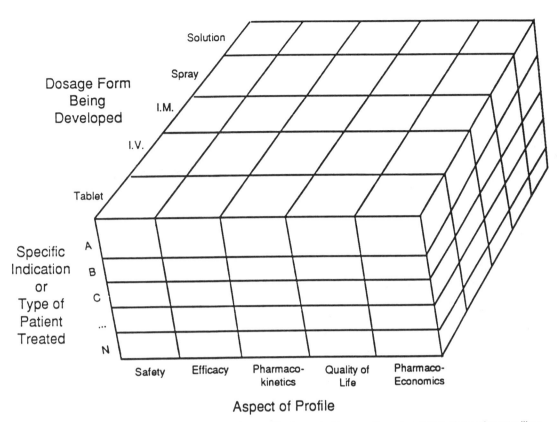

FIG. 40.2. One means of conceptualizing the medical–marketing profile using three dimensions to illustrate dosage form, indication, and the aspect of the profile.

an active medicine will do well financially. Marketing examines the market, does not envision the same commercial potential, and urges development in another indication.

5. The same scenario as above could readily occur in which the choice must be made to develop one of two or more different dosage forms.

6. Clinical marketing studies are designed to a less rigorous standard than are Phase I to Phase II clinical trials. The medical group may believe that marketing will be better able to promote and sell a new medicine if the marketing study uses a better designed and controlled clinical trial. Marketing staff may seek to use the type of protocol usually followed for marketing studies and not see any commercial benefit in following higher standards.

7. If an old medicine is found active in a new indication, the marketing group may wish to see a regulatory submission made so that the indication can be promoted. The research and development managers may be lukewarm to this concept because the standards for manufacturing and controls have markedly increased in the interim and the older regulatory pack-

age may not meet current standards. There also is a possibility that the regulatory authority will open up manufacturing and controls issues and request or even require more work to be done. A regulatory authority could also change important parts of the package insert for a medicine, which would adversely affect the sales of its current indications on existing markets.

The relative importance of marketing input on influencing research and development activities is summarized in Table 40.2.

Review of Proposed Advertisements by Medical Staff

All advertisements on a company's products should be reviewed and formally approved by medical staff before they are used. This review is necessary because the company physician(s) can assess the promotional material to evaluate (1) how physicians will read and interpret the statements, (2) whether statements made are true, (3) whether statements made are ethically defensible, (4) whether any statement distorts the facts, and (5) whether

TABLE 40.2. *Relative importance of marketing input in research and development activities*

Research and development activities	Relative importance of marketing input[a]
Discovery of new medicines	+ or ++
Selection of compounds to enter the project system	++ or +++
Establishment of minimally acceptable criteria to advance the medicine	+++ or ++++
Choice of indication to pursue	+++ or ++++
Choice of dosage form(s) to develop	++++
Choice of route of administration to pursue	++++
Choice of dosage strength, shape, and color of oral dosage form	++++
Decision to conduct quality-of-life trials and their design	++ to ++++
Decision to conduct pharmacoeconomic trials and their design	+++ or ++++
Regulatory strategy for submission of dossiers worldwide	++ or +++
Marketing study designs and details	+++ or ++++
Decision to conduct trials to expand claims	++++

[a] + = extremely minor input, ++ = modest input, +++ = strong input, ++++ = critical and essential input.

all statements are covered by the officially approved labeling of the medicine.

A medical reviewer who makes suggestions for changes in the copy, photographs, or drawings in an advertisement should not sign-off (i.e., formally approve) the advertisement until the requested changes are made. It is possible that other reviewers will alter the advertisement further and old problems may not be resolved, or alternatively, new problems may be introduced. While the reviewer of advertisements could, in theory, be someone with a nonmedical degree, physicians have important knowledge and experiences that nonphysicians do not. Thus, in almost all cases a physician should be involved in the review and sign-off of advertisements. Nonphysicians also can make valid ethical judgments about advertisements whether the people are in marketing or in other departments. The distinction between physicians and nonphysicians lies in the specific medical knowledge and experience that physicians have, and not their expertise in making ethical decisions.

The degree to which advertising and other promotional copy is critiqued by medical reviewers varies enormously among companies and sometimes within the same company. Unless a company establishes guidelines for this type of review, it is certain that many major issues will arise. The ground rules should specify both the approach that should be taken in conducting the review and the process to follow if differences of opinion cannot be easily resolved.

A number of different perspectives could be taken by a medical reviewer who is reviewing a proposed advertisement. This person could ask himself or herself the following questions.

1. Would the regulatory authority definitely (or almost so) allow this advertisement to be used?
2. Would the regulatory authority possibly allow this advertisement to be used?
3. Do I as a physician believe anything in this advertisement is unethical, inappropriate, or distorted?

4. Is it likely that physicians in the community or nation would find anything in this advertisement that is unethical, inappropriate, or distorted?
5. Is the advertisement in poor taste (e.g., does it exploit a minority group) or might it be considered offensive by some (e.g., showing a partially naked woman)?
6. Does the advertisement present a balanced, honest, and complete representation of the topic discussed?
7. Are there vague comments that may be interpreted in two or more ways?

Issues raised by a medical reviewer should be discussed and resolved by the marketing staff. If this approach does not resolve the problems, then other procedures must be used. Generally, differences should be settled using a a stepwise approach.

1. The medical and marketing professionals should meet to discuss their perspectives about the issue(s) and then attempt to resolve differences.
2. A designated arbiter could meet with the primary medical and marketing staff involved and attempt to facilitate a solution.
3. A meeting or discussion among the supervisors of the professionals could be held to resolve differences. This meeting might or might not include the primary protagonists but usually should.
4. An appeal to a more senior individual or committee to make a final decision could occur.

Review of Proposed Package Inserts by Marketing Staff

Regulatory authorities usually discuss details of a package insert with medical and regulatory staff of a company to finalize the details. Apparently small changes, such as substituting "a" for "the" (or vice versa), may have a major influence on the exact promotional campaigns that may eventually be mounted or that may be possible to mount. For this reason it is important that experienced marketing staff review the final wording in the proposed package insert as it is developed and modified. Review should occur at meetings to prepare for labeling negotiations. The process of obtaining maximum benefit from each word and term in the label is known as "wordsmithing." Each company should identify who the best wordsmiths are inside or outside their company (e.g, at advertising agencies or consultants). Multiple versions of a label may be assessed in advance of the final labeling negotiations to determine the ability of each to enable the company to promote the medicine most effectively.

Providing Marketing Forecasts for Early-Stage Investigational Medicines

Having a single number forecast is attractive to many people, but highly unrealistic for many reasons. Providing a range of values makes more sense, particularly if the forecast concerns the second, third, or fifth year of sales (or profits) after initial marketing. These ranges may be given as either predetermined ranges (e.g., $0 to 25 million, $25 to 50 million, $50 to 100 million, and above $100 million) or as ranges created individually for each medicine. This approach is inappropriate once a medicine reaches Phase III or is on the market. Marketed medicines should have single-figure forecasts for the next year(s). An easily used variation on this approach is for marketing groups to provide a single forecast with confidence limits (e.g., ±20%) that illustrates how sure they are of the value. This essentially provides the range of values forecasted that was described above. The forecasts provided for any medicine at any stage of development are more meaningful if they are given for each major indication.

In the early stages of a medicine's development, it is usually unclear what the final clinical characteristics—its clinical profile—will be. This profile has an enormous influence on the eventual sales of the medicine and creates the dilemma of what profile to base the forecast on. One approach to this problem is to base the forecast on the most likely profile to be obtained. The disadvantage of this approach is that no one can accurately state at an early stage of development how likely it is that the medicine will obtain a certain clinical profile. A better approach is to base the marketing profile on the minimally acceptable profile; sales information is obtained on the worst possible clinical profile that would still justify marketing and would presumably enable marketing to be successful. An even more desirable approach in some cases is to create a series of two to four separate market forecasts. Each could be based on a different, but clearly defined, clinical profile. For example, forecasts could be based on the medicine's (1) minimally acceptable profile, (2) realistic profile, or (3) desired profile. After a certain period of time, the actual clinical profile emerges and replaces the first two. The reason it does not

replace the third is that additional studies may often be planned to improve the claims that may be made about a medicine. These studies could be designed to remove a warning or precaution in the package insert (i.e., labeling).

It is desirable to write the characteristics of the product and all the underlying assumptions on paper so that the medical and marketing groups may get together and reach agreement. Market forecasts should be based on a product profile that has been jointly reviewed by medical and marketing staff. Marketing and medical staffs should agree on the following.

1. Which of the potential profiles should be used to create forecasts.
2. How the forecasts will be created.
3. How the forecasts will be reviewed and revised.
4. How to describe the actual profile as it begins to emerge in Phase I and takes more definitive shape throughout development.

Number 2 is generally solely a marketing activity.

Marketing Input into Medical Strategies

No medical strategy or development plan should be constructed without careful evaluation of all relevant marketing considerations. A relevant question is whether the marketing input should be entirely provided by medical groups, marketing groups, or by a combination of both. The answer for each company will differ, based primarily on the degree to which they are marketing driven or medical driven. The traditions and environment within the company also influence this point.

If the interaction occurs only at one or possibly two time points, the nature of the interaction is likely to be compromised. A preferable approach is to have periodically scheduled meetings where these interactions take place. They could occur on a fixed time basis (e.g., annually) or at predetermined milestones (e.g., the end of Phases I, IIa, IIb, IIIa, and IIIb). Clearly, the attitudes of the people involved and their willingness to listen to "outsiders" is going to meet with resistance. Neither group wants to be told by the other "how it will be" and this approach is going to be met with resistance. Neither groups wants to be controlled by the other, but both are usually willing to listen to advice, pointers, and suggestions. Either group that attempts to educate the others with the proper spirit is far more likely to achieve their goals. Standoffs or confrontations may have to be dealt with by senior managers within each discipline.

Enhancing the Quality and Acceptance of Marketing Input to Medical Groups

The acceptance of marketing input to medical groups' decision making can be enhanced if the marketing staff accept the following principles.

1. A willingness to join the development team for an investigational medicine as equal partners with those in research and development.
2. An openness to new ideas and concepts.
3. A willingness to have medical professionals review marketing questions, issues, and concerns raised.
4. A desire to educate medical staff about marketing viewpoints on issues with which the medical staff may be uncomfortable. Many problems or issues cease to exist when explained and placed in their proper context by experts in that discipline.
5. A commitment to provide factual, clearly understood, and useful information in a timely manner. This approach enhances the credibility of the market-

ing group and increases the likelihood that the information will be used. The same information provided a month after it is needed may be ignored and constitute a totally wasted effort. Even worse, it may be counterproductive to building harmonious relationships.

VISUALLY CHARACTERIZING A MARKET

Illustrating the Importance of Specific Factors Desired in a New Medicine

Various illustrations can be developed by medical or marketing groups that both can use to communicate

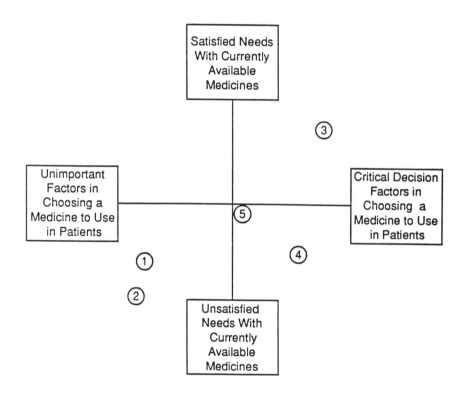

Spectra of Physician Needs and Decision Factors Used in Choosing Medicines for Patients

Key to Identifying the Factors Illustrated

1 = Likelihood of causing adverse reaction A
2 = Need for individual dose titration
3 = Control of disease symptoms
4 = Frequency of daily dosing
5 = Interactions with other medicines

FIG. 40.3. A method to illustrate the spectra of physicians' needs and the importance of different factors in choosing a medicine to use in their patients. Unsatisfied needs with currently available medicines (or treatments) may be limited to or may include investigational medicines that are potential competitors.

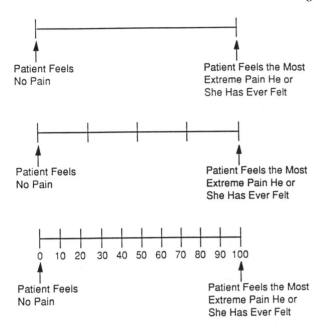

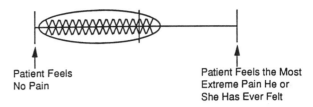

FIG. 40.5. A *hatched area* superimposed on a one-dimensional spectrum to illustrate the segment of a market being targeted with a new medicine.

FIG. 40.4. Three examples of one-dimensional spectra shown as visual analogue scales for pain. The two anchors are identical on each extreme but the interior scales differ on the lower two and do not exist for the top one.

their views better on a particular topic of a medicine's development. A few of these are described below and others are shown in *Presentation of Clinical Data* (Spilker and Schoenfelder, 1990).

The factors that are desired in a new medicine can be illustrated on a graph (Fig. 40.3). This graph may be used by preclinical scientists to help them decide which characteristics to include in the minimally acceptable criteria they establish for advancing compounds through the process of discovery. The discovery of a new medicine is almost never an all-or-none process (i.e, is this compound going to be a successful new medicine or not?),

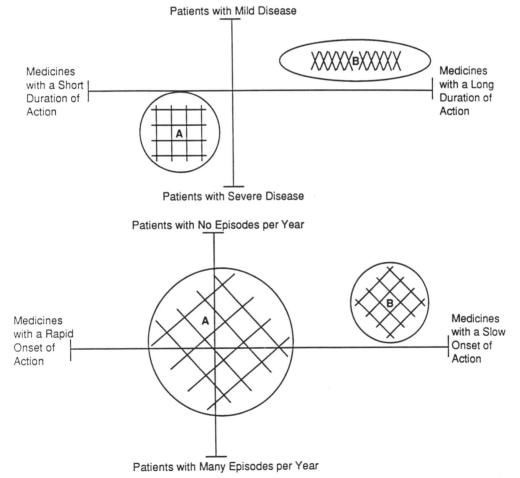

FIG. 40.6. Two examples of two-dimensional spectra to illustrate different characteristics. The letters in the *hatched areas* would be described in the text or figure legend.

but it is a matter of whether the efficacy and safety profiles achieved are likely to be improved by further molecular modifications, and whether the time and costs of synthesizing the new compounds would be worth the wait.

While there is literally no limit to the number of factors that could be illustrated in the graph of Fig. 40.3, practical considerations usually limit this to about 15.

Illustrating the Targeting of Specific Factors for Marketing a New Medicine With Clinical Spectra

A new medicine's target market can be illustrated using spectra of various clinical features. These spectra differ markedly from the graph shown in Fig. 40.3. The same type of spectra may be used to illustrate market segments for medicines currently being marketed.

Single Spectrum

Any clinical spectrum may be indicated as a straight line where descriptive anchors are placed at or near the extremes. Additional descriptive anchors in numbers, words, or any appropriate symbols may be used. A few examples of chronic pain spectra are illustrated in Fig. 40.4. The market area that a medicine has, or will be targeted for, can be superimposed on any of these spectra. For example, the hatched area in Fig. 40.5 illustrates the intended market segment for a mild analgesic.

Double Spectra (Two-Dimensional)

Although the marketing target(s) for a single medicine could be described or illustrated with a series of individual one-dimensional spectra, it is often desirable to use two spectra that cross or are somehow connected to illustrate the true market segment more clearly for a new medicine. Figure 40.6 illustrates two examples of double spectra (i.e., two-dimensional). The upper views the spectra of disease severity and duration of action. The resulting figure presents a different concept than the lower spectra that presents the onset of action and the number of episodes per year. Any two clinical spectra may, in theory, be combined. The two-dimensional visualization presented in Fig. 40.6 shows the combination of patient experience/symptoms with a part of a medicine's clinical profile.

Triple Spectra (Three-Dimensional)

A third axis could be drawn on the two-dimensional graph described above to create a three-dimensional graph. This approach would unnecessarily complicate the illustration and is not recommended for most cases. Using multiple examples of single and double spectra would provide a more effective and more readily understood presentation.

SECTION VI

Technical and Functional Issues and Activities

41 / Information Technology

Types of Information in a Pharmaceutical
    Company................................... **461**
    Raw Data 461
    Published Literature 462
    In-House Company Documents 462
    Media References to the Company's Products. 462
    Competitive Intelligence..................... 462
    Institutional Memory........................ 462
Flow of Information.......................... **462**
    Obtaining Information 462
    Confirming the Accuracy of Information...... 463
    Organizing and Categorizing Information 463
    Processing and Indexing Information 463
    Storing Information 463
    Retrieving Information 463
    Analyzing Information 464
    Interpreting Information..................... 464
    Communicating Information 464
Offering Information to In-House Professionals . **464**
    Philosophical Approaches Toward Indexing
       Information................................ 464
    Disseminating Published Information........ 465
Essential Questions and Procedures **465**
    Are You Trying to Find a Computer Solution
       to a Management Problem? 465
Selected Uses of Computer Systems............. **465**

Contribution of Computer Systems to Various
    Research and Development Functions 465
    International Clinical Trial Tracking System .. 466
    Electronic Publishing 466
Roles of Information Managers **468**
    Identifying and Achieving Goals 468
    Steps to Become More Proactive.............. 468
    Potential Pitfalls to Avoid.................... 469
Storing Documents: Which, Where, How Long,
    How Many, and How Coded?............... **470**
    Which Documents to Store? 470
    Where Should Documents Be Stored?......... 470
    How Long Should Documents Be Stored?..... 470
    How Many Copies Should Be Kept and in
       What Form? 470
    How Do Documents Get to a Central
       Repository? 470
    Coding Documents for Storage and Retrieval.. 472
    Principles to Decrease the Quantity of
       Materials Stored........................... 473
    Access to Information 473
Financial Issues **473**
Golden Rules for Information Technology **473**
Information Management Challenges............ **474**
    Future Technologies......................... 474

The very first principle of Systems-design is a negative one: Do It Without A System If You Can . . .
    Systems are seductive. They promise to do a hard job faster, better, and more easily than you could do it by yourself. But if you set up a system, you are likely to find your time and effort now being consumed in the care and feeding of the system itself.
    New problems are created by its very presence. Once set up, it won't go away, it grows and encroaches. It begins to do strange and wonderful things. Breaks down in ways you never thought possible. It kicks back, gets in the way, and opposes its own proper function. Your own perspective becomes distorted by being in the system. You become anxious and push on it to make it work. John Gall. From *Systemantics.*

TYPES OF INFORMATION IN A PHARMACEUTICAL COMPANY

Pharmaceutical companies are extremely information-intensive enterprises. A large quantity of information is obtained from external sources and is also generated internally throughout discovery, development, manufacturing, and marketing periods. Information is systematically recorded for easy retrieval to support each product's survival, from its conception through its life in the market.

While information exists in every aspect of a company this chapter focuses on medicine development activities. The information generally falls into the following categories.

Raw Data

Enormous quantities of raw data from preclinical, clinical, technical, marketing, and financial groups are continually processed, analyzed, and illustrated in tables and figures. Analyses and reports enable appropriate decisions to be reached on important issues. Many of these data and the reports produced from them form the backbone of regulatory submissions. Nonetheless, a large volume of raw data generated is of little importance to a company and means should be in place to ensure that the least amount of effort and attention are spent in their generation and in their evaluation.

Published Literature

Scientific or technical books and journals housed in company libraries meet most basic information needs of employees. Access to the published literature and various data bases is facilitated by many computerized on-line bibliographic and other data bases.

Literature on company products receives special attention. Articles from the worldwide biomedical literature are gathered, analyzed, indexed, and entered into in-house, on-line computer data bases to make information rapidly available. These data bases are also used to provide data for periodic reports on company products to regulatory agencies.

In-House Company Documents

These include a wide variety of meeting minutes, reports, analyses, regulatory submissions, archives supporting Good Manufacturing Practice and Good Laboratory Practice procedures, litigation records, and other material. These are usually kept in one or more repositories, and many documents are recorded in machine-readable form. Important materials are often also indexed and key terms are identified for computer searches. To condense data and to avoid storing large quantities of old data and reports, microfiche and microfilm may be used. Optical storage facilities on laser disks are used by an increasing number of companies. Supporting software is needed for most of these uses.

Information on Chemicals Synthesized

Records may contain a great deal of information beyond the chemical structure and its physical properties, such as amounts synthesized in each batch, amounts remaining from each batch, physical locations where the material resides, and specific chemical and biological test results obtained with the material. The topic of computer modeling of new compounds is discussed in Chapter 20. Data about chemicals used as raw materials often may be purchased on magnetic tape from manufacturers or may be obtained on line.

Media References to the Company's Products

This can be organized by product and will contain newspaper, news magazine, and other media references. This file may be started when a compound is first tested in humans, passes an efficacy go–no go decision point, or is marketed. Clipping services may be used, not only for hard copy text, but to provide written verbatim texts of radio and even television reports.

Competitive Intelligence

Relevant information may be collected on the competitors' activities, status of competitive medicines, size and nature of relevant markets, trends in those markets, plus any other useful information. It is easy to collect huge amounts of data on competitors' medicines. The challenge for any company is to keep this file limited to the true essentials and to update the material periodically so that it remains current. This is usually too expensive or too arduous a task to perform on any but the most important products of the competitors. Rather than use this approach at all, most companies run searches on external data bases as the need arises. Addressing selected questions and focusing on specific topics are two methods that may be used to accomplish a company's goals.

Institutional Memory

See Chapter 7 for a description and discussion of this topic.

FLOW OF INFORMATION

Figure 41.1. illustrates general ways of visualizing the flow of information. Many variations of this flow exist depending on the type and uses of information involved. This figure is a simplified theoretical approach illustrating the steps involved. The initial step of identifying the information needed is not shown. The real situation is usually much more complex, primarily owing to numerous feedback loops and cycles that occur among different stages in this scheme. Computer and other systems may be targeted to deal with particular stages of the flow.

A few of the many types of considerations and aspects associated with each stage are described.

Obtaining Information

Information comes from scientific, clinical, and other experiments; sales data; production information; and many other sources both within and external to the company. Data arrive electronically, verbally, and/or in hard copy.

INFORMATION FLOW

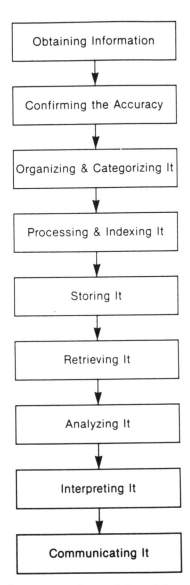

FIG. 41.1. Prototype pattern of how information usually flows from the time it is obtained. These steps occur after the specific information needed is identified and a plan is developed and implemented to collect the information. Numerous variations exist on the order of steps followed in specific situations.

Confirming the Accuracy of Information

This may involve editing data via various means. Computer programs may be able to check the accuracy of some scientific data, raising "flags" when data are outside preset limits or have internal inconsistencies. The topic of artificial intelligence is becoming more important each year and has numerous applications to confirming the accuracy of information and to medicine de-

velopment. This is discussed in Chapter 43, Data Management and Statistics. Despite efforts to modernize, most pharmaceutical companies still use a substantial amount of manual labor in reviewing and checking data, particularly clinical data.

Organizing and Categorizing Information

Information must be categorized and organized by knowledgeable people prior to being processed and indexed. A variety of systems may be used to classify the information. The two major types are a classification based on the contents of the information itself that is to be categorized, and the other is a classification based on the needs and interests of the group for whom the information has been collected.

Processing and Indexing Information

Processing information involves putting it into a computer, photographing it on microfiche or microfilm, and indexing it for eventual retrieval. The data must be processed so that the company retains the ability to combine and/or analyze it efficiently at the present time or at a later date.

Storing Information

Information may be stored as hard copy, electronically in a computer, on microfilm, on microfiche, and/or on optical disks. Each of these methods has particular features that make it desirable for use in active files, archival files, or files that have both functions. Specific systems and equipment are usually purchased based on factors listed in Table 43.3. This table does not list various general criteria such as servicing, number of units sold, availability, reliability of the equipment, and so on. Companies usually have a backup system for protection, or at the minimum they store important information in at least two geographically separate places.

Retrieving Information

It is essential to separate the topics of information storage and retrieval because the procedures used for each can be quite different. Different types of access to data exist (e.g., physical access and logical access). These types of access and other related topics are discussed by Blair (1984). Information is usually indexed with key terms to make it easier to retrieve. The same report would tend to be indexed differently by different people. Thus, a variety of indexing terms usually needs to be searched to obtain a broad coverage of topics. As a result, nonexperts are usually unable to identify all reports on complex questions and skilled information scientists are necessary to retrieve relatively complete outputs or listings.

A critical issue about retrieval sometimes concerns the people who have access to stored information. A common question is whether the person who is requesting data or a report has a *desire* or a *need* to know the information.

Analyzing Information

This may be done by many techniques varying from casual observation to formal statistical analyses. Analysis often means selecting, combining, or organizing the information into tables or figures so that it may subsequently be interpreted.

Interpreting Information

The meaning of the information is gleaned using the analyses as the basis of the interpretation. After the interpretation is made, it may be extrapolated to other situations.

Information Transfer/Exchange

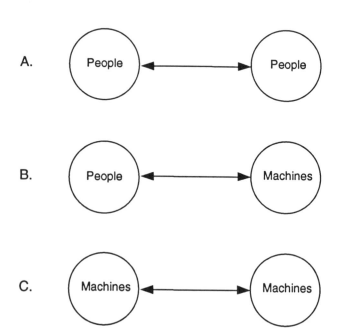

FIG. 41.2. The relative amount of information transfer is increasingly occurring between people and machines (panel **B**) and also between machines (panel **C**).

Communicating Information

Information must be effectively communicated to achieve its appropriate and full impact. If all of the above steps are conducted, but the results are either not communicated or are not communicated well, then most of the value in the above exercise (i.e., steps 1 to 8 in Fig. 41.1) may be lost. The transfer of information may be between people or machines (Fig. 41.2).

OFFERING INFORMATION TO IN-HOUSE PROFESSIONALS

For information from central data bases or other centralized sources to be used by professionals, a number of steps must be followed. First, the various uses and limitations of information must be known by potential users. Second, the groups of potential (and actual) users must be identified. Third, information about available resources must be disseminated. The process of informing staff may be done by providing an easy-to-understand menu of the types of information available and typical uses of the information plus services provided by those who have or control access to the information. One useful method of informing staff about potentially useful services and information available may be to illustrate which types of information would be helpful at each stage of drug discovery, development, manufacturing, and marketing. One of the essential principles for many information services to follow is that providing a few valuable and useful references or documents to assist users in reaching a decision or solving a problem is preferable to burying the requester under a large data dump. This approach may be considered as a "value-added service." Large quantities of unimportant information dishearten the recipient and may be counterproductive to the goals of the data search.

Philosophical Approaches Toward Indexing Information

Two quite different approaches may be followed in indexing articles for later identification and retrieval. One approach puts significant effort into indexing articles in detail prior to any request for their contents. Then, when a search of the data base is run, only the most relevant articles will be identified and the requester has less bulk to deal with. Another approach is to index articles more superficially to save time for the indexing staff. The potential problem that arises using this approach is that when a request is made a large amount of material may be identified and must be sorted through to find the most relevant documents.

The choice of a preferred approach depends, at least in part, on the salaries and levels of the people who have to index the material and those who must winnow down the output. Available funds are also important.

Disseminating Published Information

How may a company efficiently deal with the enormous amount of published data, some of which is critically important? Some companies categorize all data into different classes. For example, one system uses three categories with the following definitions. Priority-1 reports have a direct and immediate impact on marketing or medical strategies. Priority-2 reports would add to product knowledge, and Priority-3 reports would be the least important and serve as supporting knowledge. The priority of any report or piece of information is not static, but may change drastically and suddenly in unanticipated ways (e.g., an old regulatory letter may acquire new importance based on more recent information or a response to a recent question).

ESSENTIAL QUESTIONS AND PROCEDURES

The most critical question in this world of overwhelming quantities of information is, "Do you have the best information and is it presented in the most useful and optimal way?" The quality of the information obtained and used is more critical than ever because the decisions made that are based on the information may lead to company successes or failures. Information is needed to discover new medicines in the laboratory, to assess one's competitors accurately, and to make correct board room decisions. Physicians state that the main reason they see sales representatives is to obtain information. Clearly, information is the central basis for operations of a pharmaceutical company.

Are You Trying to Find a Computer Solution to a Management Problem?

Many managers consciously or subconsciously avoid dealing with a management problem by describing it as a systems problem. They state that, if the technical information flow could be improved, the specific issue could be addressed. They may be correct that a specific problem could be improved somewhat by creating or improving a system, but if this occurs they will have achieved the right result for the wrong reason. More likely, adding to or modifying the system will not influence the problem significantly, or the situation may deteriorate further. New managers in an area may recognize that a management problem exists. Systems should never be instituted to solve what are known to be management problems.

SELECTED USES OF COMPUTER SYSTEMS

Some of the most important issues to address in developing a data base management system are listed in Table 41.1, and issues that concern computer validation are listed in Table 41.2. The life cycle of a system is shown in Fig. 41.3. A number of other issues are discussed below.

Contribution of Computer Systems to Various Research and Development Functions

While computer systems are able to facilitate several functions within research and development, they are essential for a number of others. Those functions where sophisticated computer systems are required include:

1. Molecular modeling to assist in medicine discovery research.
2. Pharmacokinetics activities, particular simulations, and modeling require computer systems that handle large amounts of data.
3. Clinical data collection, editing, storage, tabulation, and statistical analyses require sophisticated systems.
4. Project management and development plans require many programs to create the plans and charts needed.
5. Regulatory computer-assisted new medicine submissions are becoming more and more computer dependent.
6. Communications, particularly between distant sites, are facilitated by various systems such as electronic mail.

TABLE 41.1. *Issues to address in developing a data base management system*

1. What are the deficiencies and problems of the current system?
2. How much time, effort, and money will it take to correct those deficiencies and problems versus building (or buying) a new system?
3. Are an appropriate number of support staff available or budgeted for the new system?
4. What is the compatibility of each alternative proposal for a modified or new system with other systems within the company?
5. How well can each alternative be integrated with different types of systems?
6. Would microcomputers be networked or stand alone?
7. What size data bases are needed?
8. How does access to the data base (i.e., security) compare among systems?
9. Will centralized or distributed data bases be needed?
10. Are data bases needed that are internal or external?
11. What type of search language is needed?
12. Should the system be relational or hierarchical?
13. Should the input, update, and searches be on line or batch?
14. Should there be variable or fixed fields?

TABLE 41.2. *Issues in validating computer systems*

1. All documentation must match the program.
2. All system procedures must be followed and adherence enforced.
3. New program procedures should be verified by independent staff.
4. Passwords should be periodically changed.
5. The source code must be verified.
6. Steps must be taken to prevent access to the data base by unauthorized personnel.
7. A log of irregular events must be kept and the contents periodically reviewed by appropriate staff.
8. The system must be rechecked after every significant modification.
9. Vendors who work on the system should be carefully screened.
10. Plans for disasters should be made and adequate steps taken in advance to minimize the impact of any crisis.

Each of the above, as well as many other functions that utilize computer systems, can be evaluated in terms of whether the overall contribution of the system is ranked as low, medium, or high. The priority of each discipline or area involved can also be graded into low, medium, or high categories, thus creating a 3 × 3 grid. A third parameter to evaluate is the systems adequacy. This can be graded as adequate for the short-term, adequate for the long-term, or inadequate.

International Clinical Trial Tracking System

Many companies have a computer-based system to track and to access information about protocols and investigators for all clinical trials. This system provides online access for all of the company's sites, allowing them to follow progress on patient entry on all trials. The system also is used to send adverse experience reports to the central data base to assist regulatory personnel in preparing periodic reports required by regulatory authorities.

Electronic Publishing

Electronic publishing involves the use of computer systems to create documents more rapidly and efficiently. It thus facilitates both document and information management. It is suitable as a means of creating many regulatory documents (e.g., Investigational New Drug Applications, New Drug Applications [NDAs], and annual reports) and research documents (e.g., research reports and project proposals), in addition to memoranda. A schematic is shown in Fig. 41.4.

Electronic publishing is important to companies because creating NDAs (1) takes too long, (2) is of variable quality (both within and between NDAs), and (3) contains documents of different consistency. Modifying a NDA for other regulatory authorities or creating revisions also suffers the same problem.

Life Cycle of a System

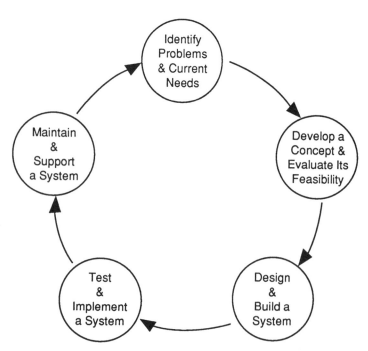

FIG. 41.3. Showing the cyclical nature of computer systems.

Electronic Publishing

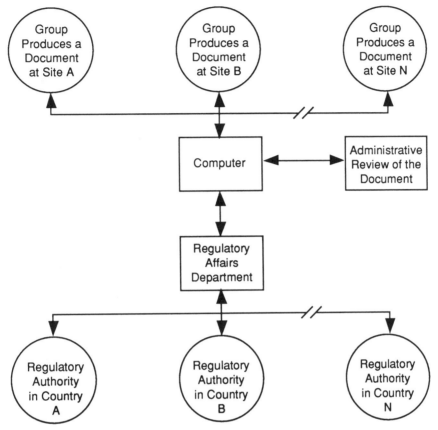

FIG. 41.4. Example of how electronic publishing facilitates submission of documents to regulatory authorities by using a computer to help in regulatory dossier preparation.

In a research report the use of electronic publishing allows the authors to integrate chemical structures, tables of data, graphs, text, and scanned images (e.g., photographs). Before electronic publishing was available it was necessary to cut and paste various items onto pages or to assemble separate pages from multiple sources.

Besides improving records management and decreasing the need for paper storage, electronic publishing creates faster and more effective integration of the various text elements mentioned above, often enhances the appearance of documents, improves the ability to revise documents, and tends to enforce standardization of formats. On-line access to completed or partially completed documents and electronic distribution and review of documents are other advantages.

If the electronic publishing is strictly an effort to get improved documents generated more rapidly, the system created will be simpler than if the system is also designed as a fully interactive entity. The former approach solely to improve document creation has fewer technological requirements, is production oriented, and thus can be established more rapidly than the more complex system.

The information system uses more complex optical and electronic technologies and requires a search-and-query capability to allow people to find what they want and print it. This system would service more users than would one limited to publishing documents. A system requires a search-and-query capability to find whatever you put into regulatory submissions or other complex documents.

The next logical steps to discuss involve document assembly and the methods to develop systems by batch-mode processing versus interactive approaches. The technologies are evolving in this area and most companies are custom designing their systems, often using multiple vendors. Different companies require individually tailored approaches to address the same question. Thus, these issues are not discussed further.

ROLES OF INFORMATION MANAGERS

Identifying and Achieving Goals

The major challenge for information managers in the 1990s is to become more proactive. This will be more widely practiced as people recognize that information is an essential aspect of gaining competitive advantages in all areas of a company. Information is used to evaluate and solve business problems and develop all types of strategies. It will take significant time and effort for information managers to achieve the goal of providing new information proactively that has not been specifically requested. A newsletter can facilitate this process by describing assigned tasks and how they were successfully achieved and advertising services that currently can be provided. An open house for company staff that is held in the information area may be useful. Plan carefully for this event by preparing signs, exhibits, and speakers.

Possibly the most important point is to have personal discussions and small group meetings, using predeveloped approaches and strategies to influence important decision makers within the company.

The overall goal of information managers should be to understand the goals and needs of the users of their information, and to fulfill them. This will enhance the value of information provided to users. This goal may be approached through many of the activities described above. If one is successful in achieving earlier goals in Fig. 41.5 then one may begin to approach the ultimate goal of seeking wisdom.

Steps to Become More Proactive

A description of the basic steps to follow to become more proactive is given below.

1. Do not merely archive data in a passive manner. Experienced staff are needed to read and evaluate important documents and articles to find information of value. These people should extract the full value of information from all sources by considering as many possible uses of the data as possible. There are many hundreds of data bases to consider, and it is necessary to make informed choices. The staff can best fulfill this role when they know the needs of the user.

2. Meet with decision makers at many levels within the organization, and seek to learn what types of information each requires. Also determine the major questions that each of these people ask.

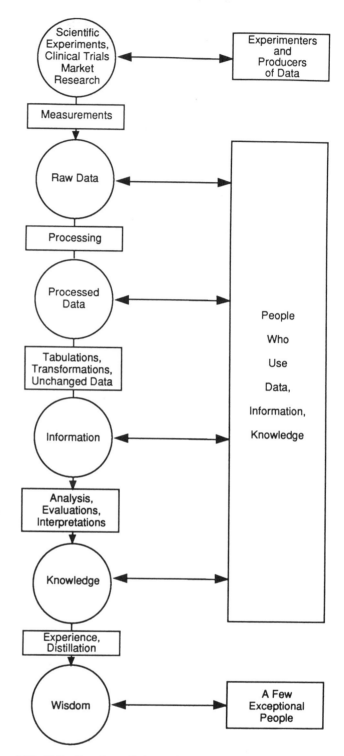

FIG. 41.5. Creation of information and data, plus its progressive enhancement and use by various groups.

3. Look for methods to help scientists and clinicians speed medicine development. These methods could be determined by brainstorming sessions with relevant people.

4. Demonstrate to the relevant people in the organiza-

tion that the information specialist plays an important role in medicine discovery, development, and marketing and provides vital information for making many important decisions. Demonstrate that important decisions and activities rely on using and/or providing information (Fig. 41.6).

5. Focus on the quality of the questions asked. It has often been said that asking the right question is exceptionally important. A proactive information manager will try to have input in formulating the questions posed.

6. Identify the questions that people ask and seek to improve the questions. Insofar as possible, teach the staff to formulate better questions.

7. Increase the accuracy of information communicated within the organization. It may take time and effort to position oneself where increasing accuracy becomes a possibility, but if it is a goal, then opportunities may arise when this objective can be put into operation.

8. Increase the accuracy of information communicated between the company and various external groups.

9. Hire creative people to work within the information group. Have them analyze data bases to answer specific (and general) questions of importance. Enable them to spend at least a half-day per week on special information projects.

Potential Pitfalls to Avoid

1. Be careful about turf issues (i.e., stepping into other people's areas of responsibility). An appropriate attitude and sensitivity regarding turf issues is essential if one is to succeed at the above goals.

2. Consider the users of information that is collected or generated. Users should be contacted prior to collecting information to ensure their interest. It is useless to create information or answer questions if the users are not interested or have changed the question.

3. Focus on *inter*disciplinary or interdepartmental questions in implementing and conducting the proactive roles described above. *Intra*departmental information needs are best discussed and provided with only the degree of creativity desired by those who will receive the information. Nonetheless, creative people in information management can often enlighten those who receive the information in a way that is viewed positively.

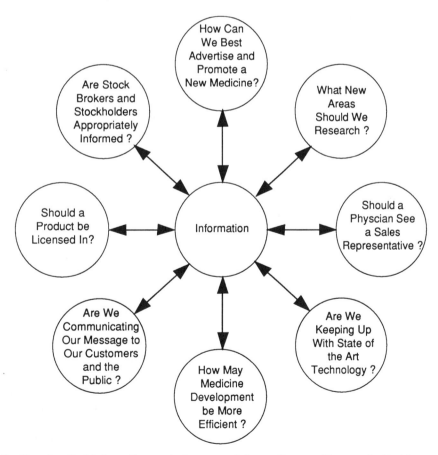

FIG. 41.6. Showing that information underlies essential questions and issues decided in a medicine's discovery, development, and marketing.

4. Discuss each step of the process with the client or user, unless they have "commissioned" you to do more.

The information discussed can be provided to any group (e.g., marketing, production, and research and development).

STORING DOCUMENTS: WHICH, WHERE, HOW MANY, AND HOW CODED?

Which Documents to Store?

A company should store documents that potentially or actually have value or importance. The general guideline is, when in doubt—store. Almost all formal reports and official documents (e.g., communications with regulatory authorities and legal documents) must be stored. Minutes of meetings are also valuable records.

Where Should Documents Be Stored?

Most people who generate documents maintain a copy in their own files. In addition, the person or group receiving a copy often maintains a copy, but that person or group cannot be relied on to retain the document, except if it is in an office or in a group that is generally known to maintain and store documents (e.g., regulatory affairs or legal department). A third category of places where documents are stored is a group designated as the official repository for documents.

How Long Should Documents Be Stored?

A company should have a policy on this issue or it will find that some documents are stored only as long as the individual with a copy stays at the company, while other individuals dispose of their documents sooner than the company desires. The number of years to maintain documents depends on the type of document. Routine correspondence differs from company minutes of important meetings in terms of the length of storage required. Regulatory authorities mandate certain periods of storage for documents that support a NDA, and the trade associations also may have guidelines. Documents related to an ongoing legal case cannot be disposed of until the case is totally settled.

A standard operating procedure should be devised to describe the company policy in this matter and also the procedures for disposal. Senior managers who have documents that may not be in the company's central repository may wish to send their documents to this site for review as their primary method of document destruction. This practice ensures that at least one copy of important documents are maintained in the central records.

A company director of this central repository may view his or her collection as a historical resource or archive of the company's institutional memory that could be used for future research. If this possibility is considered in addition to the usual archiving function, then it will undoubtedly influence the type and quantity of articles maintained.

How Many Copies Should Be Kept and in What Form?

The number of copies of any document stored should decrease over time until the only copy is the one in the company archives or permanent regulatory storage. The company's procedures for document distribution and destruction should ensure that this occurs.

The paper, electronic, film, or optical form that documents are kept in (i.e., hard copy, microfilm, microfiche, or laser disk) depends on numerous factors that change over time. These factors include company policies, regulations, technology, culture, and personal preferences of relevant managers. Thus, there are few overall golden rules. These include:

1. Maintain a backup copy for extremely important documents.
2. Keep the backup copy in a separate physical location.
3. Maintain adequate security at each physical facility where documents are stored.
4. Maintain adequate security for access to the documents (e.g., use multiple levels of confidentiality or use different key words to access different computer files and change them frequently).

How Do Documents Get to a Central Repository?

The easiest method for a central company repository to obtain a copy of all the documents it needs is for someone to issue a memorandum to all people who generate (or potentially may generate) documents and inform them of this practice. Whether this approach will be effective depends on several factors.

1. The person issuing the request. If it is the head of the repository or someone within that group, it is less likely that the request will be complied with fully. If a more senior person issues it there should be better compliance, unless the person is too senior. A request from the company's president or chairman of the board about a relatively minor issue is likely to be ignored by many people.
2. The level of the request. The memorandum requesting cooperation may state that one *should* or may state that one *must* comply with the request.

3. Company culture. Some companies have an institutional culture in which such a request is more likely to be followed.

Regardless of the approach to this issue, any memorandum will achieve limited success. Other methods can also be used to inform staff about the company's policy on documents. These include notices on bulletin boards, announcements at meetings, and numerous other techniques. None of these approaches is likely to be totally satisfactory to the managers of the central repository. If success is not great, then the central repository will be unable to provide all the information to answer requests that are received from the company staff.

The answer to this problem, which is illustrated by model 1 of Fig. 41.7, is to utilize another approach (models 2 or 3). The central repository should decide that they need a system that does not depend on the voluntary cooperation of many people within the organization, but occurs as a matter of policy and simple procedure. The best way to achieve this is by agreeing that it is the responsibility of the central repository managers to devise a

A. Push Method to Obtain Documents/Reports

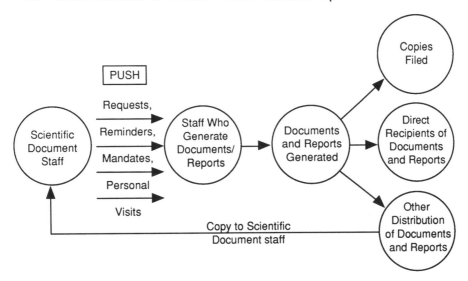

B. Pull Method to Obtain Documents/Reports

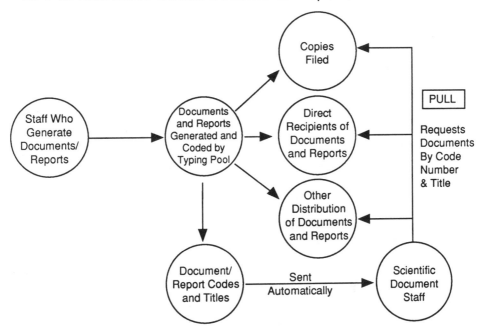

FIG. 41.7. Three models by which documents arrive at a central repository or archive. These models are discussed in the text.

C. Flow Method to Obtain Documents/Reports

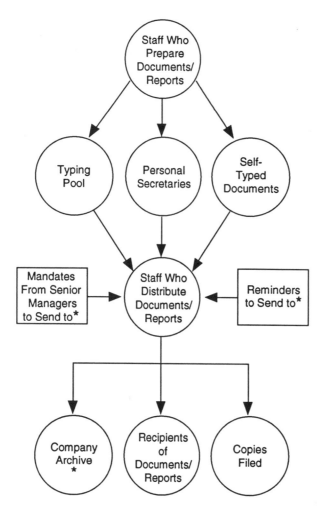

FIG. 41.7 *Continued.*

system whereby they "pull" all documents from various sources by their own activities (e.g., reviewing titles of all documents generated and requesting copies of those that are of interest). An ideal model would be if all documents "flowed" from typing pools to the central repository for their review. Methods would have to be developed to capture all documents generated by individuals who bypassed the typing pool. For example, printing "cc: Central Repository" on all memorandum paper could help in this regard if the staff who distribute documents are informed about the policy and the importance of adhering to it. The pull or flow models require the support of senior managers to operate effectively.

Coding Documents for Storage and Retrieval

Using a code for documents is essential in most cases to facilitate storage, retrieval, and the ability to characterize contents. Codes may be simply key terms used to index the contents and nature (e.g., minutes, NDA docu-

ment, and department report). This approach is useful because the title may be totally uninformative or absent and a number or letter code may be insufficient to capture the contents. The index terms should be assigned by the central document repository staff utilizing standard procedures and vocabulary control. This uniformity in indexing is important to retrieve all relevant documents when addressing a question.

Documents may also be assigned codes by staff who create the document, or by staff who type it. These codes could indicate the year, the group creating the document, the physical site or country of origin, and possibly other information as well. These codes must be simple and provide a number and letter code to expedite storage and retrieval. A code that indicates the level of confidentiality of the document itself is particularly important. This assists the central repository staff in knowing whether the copy must be handled by special staff and locked in a special secured file. A large variety of codes can be used to characterize various types of security for the document and to control who has access to it. It is clearly desirable for all sites of a multinational company to use the same codes. If this is not done, then obtaining specific documents from foreign or other national sites will be made more difficult.

Principles to Decrease the Quantity of Materials Stored

Whatever system is established must inspire confidence that the existing materials are sufficient to meet company needs and can be rapidly accessed. A few basic principles help ensure that a company does not store more materials than it needs.

1. Eliminate the need for departmental files by having documents filed by individuals in a central repository. It is also possible that a department file could replace individual files, but this approach is more difficult to achieve because most people like to keep their own documents, even if their file system is haphazard or is not well maintained.
2. Establish and annually review the policies for document destruction.
3. Establish a maximum file capacity for individuals. This ruling forces individuals to purge their files when the cabinets become full in order to store newer documents.
4. Establish department guidelines for how long certain specific documents should be kept by people in the department or in the department's library.
5. Transfer documents to various electronic forms. Destroy all but one copy (or all copies) of hard-copy documents.

Overall, a company should determine if certain documents or classes of materials have to be created at all. Not creating documents is an effective way to decrease the quantity stored.

Access to Information

In-house staff should be able to access data in a central repository from their own computers, or alternatively, they should be able to scan the titles of reports and documents maintained. A third possibility for accessing data is communicating with repository staff who obtain the data for them.

Access to information is a constant issue within a company. The confidential nature of internal data dictates different levels of access to various data bases. One means of achieving this goal is to have different passwords for a single data base that control access to each part of the data base.

Other issues include: (1) who owns what data, especially if it resides in a central source; (2) who maintains the data; (3) in what format should the data be kept; and (4) how detailed should summary data be made. Access

to a data base may be compromised if it becomes so large that it is unwieldy. This may arise if different data bases are merged and the thesaurus becomes quite large. Caution must be used before merging data bases that serve different purposes (e.g., basic research and clinical).

FINANCIAL ISSUES

In evaluating who is benefiting from a system as well as who is paying for the system, there are a number of financial issues to evaluate. It is often important to determine the money spent as cash and as a percent of the total on (1) staff, (2) hardware, (3) software, (4) network equipment, and (5) outside services.

Each major group (e.g., marketing, production, and research and development) should be evaluated separately in terms of the most appropriate categories, as above, or using other items such as (1) computer equipment, (2) programming, (3) automation, (4) end-user support for personal computers, (5) network, (6) training, and (7) outside services.

Some of these categories may be allocated to individual parts of the company, whereas others are not. After the money spent on each group is determined, it is useful to assess which systems support each of the company's business functions and then to evaluate the adequacy of this support. The overall potential contribution that a system can make to each function also must be determined. The answers to these questions allow one to evaluate the high priority areas for information systems to be applied to business functions. This priority ranking is always changing as systems are developed to meet pressing needs or as changes in business create new needs or require existing systems to be modified.

GOLDEN RULES FOR INFORMATION TECHNOLOGY

1. Being the first to use a major new technology usually requires more time, effort, and money because of the many unanticipated glitches in the system.
2. Dividing the acquisition and implementation of major new systems into several distinct phases is usually worthwhile. These phases (or stages) include (1) planning, (2) feasibility analyses, (3) testing, (4) installation of a prototype, (5) review, and (6) full-scale implementation.
3. Ensure that the benefits of a major new computer system are nearly 100% certain to occur and not merely likely to occur.
4. Determine if the savings claimed are merely possible, are likely, or are nearly 100% certain to occur. Evaluate whether anticipated savings will be made in the amount of work that has to be done or in terms of the work or money saved.

5. Expensive systems should provide a competitive edge and not merely do better what is done adequately today (e.g., hiring staff more appropriately or counting various financial measures), unless the improvement will save substantial resources.

6. A company's systems for the same function must be able to communicate internationally. Ideally, the same hardware will be used, but if not, ancillary methods and software must ensure rapid, accurate, and easy-to-operate international systems of communication.

7. The company's policies and needs should determine the systems created and used and not the other way around.

8. Seek to place the company's investment in information technology in those areas that best address its needs.

9. Do not make rapid decisions on major switches to new information technology systems. This is an area where delays often allow a newer generation of equipment to be marketed, needs to be better assessed, or bugs in new systems to be worked out. A well-functioning system should be retained even if it does not represent the most technologically advanced system.

10. Critique all proposals on information technology as rigorously as possible. Identify all costs, savings, and benefits, as well as the likely life cycle of the system. Evaluate how important these are to the company.

11. Senior management should understand the overall processes involved in the creation cycle (i.e., creating the data and parts of the document), the publishing cycle (i.e., creating the overall document), and the document management cycle (i.e., indexing, distributing, and accessing the documents). This understanding will facilitate purchasing decisions as well as coordinating activities among countries.

INFORMATION MANAGEMENT CHALLENGES

The role of information services within the pharmaceutical industry has changed radically over the past several decades. During the 1950s and 1960s, the roles of most professionals in this area could best be described as passive. They archived data and literature that were received. They stored data and shared it with those who requested it and with others who they felt should be informed.

During the 1970s and 1980s, the role of information services changed; as a result of enabling technologies, information services became reactive. In this reactive model, information was increasingly abstracted and referenced on computers and eventually placed *in toto* into computers. Coordinating functions became more evident as the number of services provided to users greatly increased and networks between computer systems were developed. Some of these services included interlibrary loans, literature services, and editorial assistance.

During the 1990s, state-of-the-art activities may be described as using a proactive model. Some information management professionals are creating new information through analyses and evaluations of existing data; they integrate data from various sources and contribute to medicine development in a more direct and participative way.

Future Technologies

The pace of technological change has been so rapid over the last two decades that it encourages the belief that future changes in this field will also be as rapid. This is probably true. However, before investing in the "next technological revolution," one must remember that many false starts are taken and dead ends are explored before the overall field advances.

The major technologies likely to be important include greater use of lasers, voice-recognition systems, artificial intelligence, and telecommunications. People are likely to use more information in their homes and in their cars (e.g., using note pad and pen computers with voice-activated instructions). It is hoped that the improved technology will lead to decreased development time for bringing important new medicines to the market.

42 / Providing Product Information

Introduction 475
The Information Group's Organizational
    Location 476
Types of Questions Received 476
Responding to Questions 477
    Preparing a Written Response 479
Relationship with Internal Company Information
    Groups.................................. 481

Quality Assurance of Communication with
    External Health Professionals 481
Research Opportunities 482
Personnel.................................... 484
    Size of Information Staff.................... 484
Issues to Consider 484

GUIDELINES FOR BUREAUCRATS
1. When in charge, ponder.
2. When in trouble, delegate.
3. When in doubt, mumble. James H. Boren

INTRODUCTION

Virtually all pharmaceutical companies with marketed products have a person or group designated to provide information about their products to health professionals. This group may or may not have additional responsibilities (e.g., providing medicine samples, responding to requests for compassionate plea medicines, or providing information on investigational medicines) to outside health professionals. In some companies the same group also provides information on products to company staff and is also involved in advertising review and literature support activities. This chapter does not discuss the many "drug information centers" based outside the pharmaceutical industry in hospitals, schools of pharmacy, or other institutions (e.g., local, state, and national government centers for poison control, smoking, or health). While most of these centers provide information to health care professionals, a few provide information to patients and the public as well. This chapter focuses entirely on the role of providing information to health professionals outside the company.

The product information group generally acts in a reactive manner rather than a proactive one to achieve its goals (Table 42.1), although there are noteworthy exceptions. (For example, preparing responses to anticipated questions prior to launching a new medicine. With good planning 75% of responses can be anticipated.) In-quiries come from a range of sources, from health professionals to sales representatives or employees within the company. The various functions that this group often fulfills are listed in Table 42.2. Proactive dissemination of product information (e.g., dear doctor letters) to health professionals is usually done by marketing groups. Other names for the product information group include professional communications, medical information, and medical and scientific information.

Specific details of individual company product information services have been presented in several symposia and journals (e.g., Anonymous, 1990a). Because company-specific computer hardware and software used to carry out this function vary widely and change continually, those aspects are not discussed here. Various computer systems used by many companies are described by Worthen et al. (1985).

TABLE 42.1. *Standard goals of medicine information groups*

To provide health care professionals with information that is:
1. Accurate, balanced, and correct as to opinions and data
2. Factually detailed and succinct so that the information is useful
3. Professionally reviewed and sound in any interpretation(s) made or expressed[a]
4. Rapid in its turnaround

[a] Some regulatory authorities may prefer that interpretation of data not be done.

TABLE 42.2. *Types of functions that may be assigned to a product information group[a]*

1. Respond to external requests for information[b]
2. Respond to internal requests for information
3. Prepare information for annual regulatory reports of investigational and marketed medicines
4. Update investigator brochures used in clinical trials
5. Prepare package labeling draft documents
6. Coordinate changes to the package label
7. Help train medical staff, marketing staff, and sales representatives
8. Coordinate adverse reactions reports with responsible groups
9. Coordinate information issues with other information services within the multinational company
10. Handle product complaints
11. Prepare updates to compendia
12. Prepare updates to brochures issued by trade associations
13. Coordinate with public relations groups within the company

[a] Some of these functions are conducted entirely within the company (e.g., Numbers 2, 9, and 13), but most involve external interactions.

[b] This is the only function that is assumed to be always assigned to the information group described in this chapter.

THE INFORMATION GROUP'S ORGANIZATIONAL LOCATION

There are numerous areas within a pharmaceutical company that would provide an appropriate "home" for the group that interacts with external health professionals to answer questions and provide information. These include:

1. the marketing professional services area;
2. the postmarketing surveillance group;
3. the technical information group that provides information to professionals within the organization;
4. a Phase IV medical services group;
5. corporate services; and
6. numerous other areas (e.g., medical, safety surveillance, regulatory affairs, legal).

Of these possibilities, the two generally favored by the author are Groups 3 and 4, although any of these choices could be optimal in a specific company.

Members of research and development departments often assume that, if a group within marketing responds to an information request from a health professional, the reply will be biased, whereas they would provide a scientifically based response. This view cannot be accepted, particularly because well-trained scientists could work within a marketing information group to provide such services (or, conversely, marketers could work with research and development to provide the information). To prevent a marketing orientation in replies to external questions most companies do not place the product information group under marketing control.

TYPES OF QUESTIONS RECEIVED

Questions are received by the information group directly from physicians and other health professionals via telephone, letter, or facsimile or are submitted to the group by the company's sales representatives. The most common areas questioned are listed in Table 42.3. The company may distribute postage-paid cards at scientific exhibits, at conferences, or by mail to elicit questions, but the company must be prepared to address conscientiously large numbers of such cards (if they are signed by physicians). Telephone calls received at the company are initially screened and then routed by company operators (Fig. 42.1) unless there is a toll-free telephone number that rings directly in the product information group. For this to occur the number must be appropriately disseminated (e.g., in the front of the *Physicians' Desk Reference* [PDR]). If company operators are used to route telephone calls, then they should receive adequate training to do this correctly.

Most questions received from health professionals about a company's products deal with off-label use of medicines because most questions on labeled uses are answered by the label or by conventional sources of information. Probably no source external to the company has as much information on off-label use of a company's medicine as the product information group. Most health professionals would think of contacting a sponsor first if the question was clearly identified as an off-label one. The information group often seeks input from others within the company to help prepare answers (Fig. 42.2) so that it can provide information to a wide spectrum of external groups (Fig. 42.3). Note that Fig. 42.3 also illustrates a company's indirect relationship with patients: companies seldom provide product information to patients directly, but they often provide information requested by consumer organizations. Most companies refer patients to their physicians because of the learned intermediary concept that is an important part of a legal defense. Some companies are willing to provide patients with readily available product information in the public domain. There is a trend at several companies toward providing more information directly to patients.

TABLE 42.3. *Representative areas in which questions are asked by health professionals[a]*

1. Unapproved indications
2. Adverse experiences
3. Clinical use
4. Interactions
5. Compatibility
6. Dosages
7. Stability
8. Pharmacology
9. Chemistry
10. Market availability

[a] These are listed in the approximate order of the frequency of request from most to least.

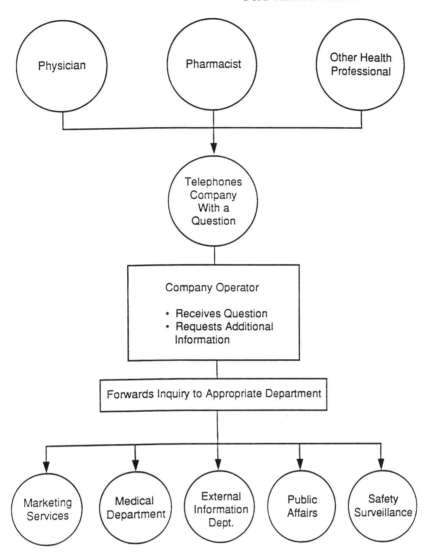

FIG. 42.1. Flow of questions from health professionals into a pharmaceutical company and routing to various departments for a response.

If the question received directly from a health professional is unclear or inappropriate, it may be relevant for the company's sales representatives to act as an intermediary. A sales representative also may act as the conduit for questions even though the response is sent directly to the health professional who raised the question. (Often the company will send a copy of the response to the sales representative involved and even to sales representatives in the local area who were not involved in the transmittal of the questions. On the other hand, this practice is avoided by some groups who believe that the sales representative may use the information as promotional material.) If the unclear or inappropriate question was received via a sales representative, then the company's information group would probably contact the professional directly.

Some companies require that health professionals seeking information on unapproved uses of a medicine submit their questions in writing. This procedure is de-signed to help protect the company against accusations that it is promoting the use of the medicine for unapproved uses. Moreover, in providing information on unapproved uses, the company often reminds the health professional that the medicine is not approved for the indication and may mention the basis on which the medicine could be used in that indication. Care must be exercised to avoid promoting the medicine for the unapproved indication. This could be achieved by stating that the company has no recommendations regarding its use for the purpose discussed.

RESPONDING TO QUESTIONS

A company should respond to all questions received. If a question relates to a generic version of the company's medicine, it is still generally relevant for the company to address it. If the question concerns another brand of the

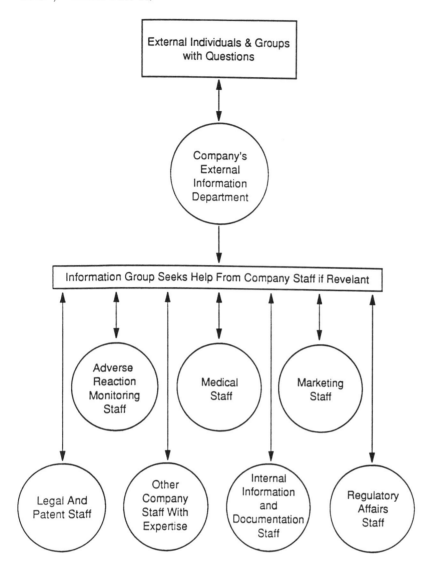

FIG. 42.2. Processing a question by a company's external information department when additional help from the company's staff is needed.

same medicine, the company must either refer the caller to the other company or answer the question and send a copy of the response to the other company. The latter approach is generally preferable because it helps build good will.

Figure 42.4 illustrates the work flow of preparing a written response to an inquiry. Numerous variations on these procedures exist at different companies and also within a company for uncommon requests. A library of product-related reprints can be maintained within the physical area of the medicine information group that accepts and answers the questions. This would facilitate the group's interactions with health professionals. Copyright issues must be considered if the company intends to provide free copies of articles to external callers.

The most critical issues for a company to consider are (1) the quality (i.e., accuracy, balance, and usefulness) of the response, (2) the speed of the response (i.e., efficiency of the system), and (3) the cost of the response. Hermann and Wanke (1987) compared the costs of three methods to obtain a response and found that the textbook search

combined with a verbal answer was much cheaper than conducting a literature search and providing a written answer. It makes sense for a busy medical information group at an academic institution to limit their search to the least expensive method, particularly if resources are a major issue, but this is not so true for a pharmaceutical company. Answers to many questions cannot be found in textbooks, and companies often require a written record (for legal reasons) of what was communicated to the health professional. The categories of information that a company provides are listed in Table 42.4.

A more sophisticated approach is to perform almost all literature searches on a product once and then to follow up by collecting, categorizing, indexing, and storing the reprints as hard copy or preferably as an image (Filenet). Periodic literature searches are required to keep the information current. Standardized letters on the most frequently asked questions should be prepared and reviewed prior to responding to specific questions. These letters can be stored in a computer and sent rapidly at a probably lower cost to answer most questions, although

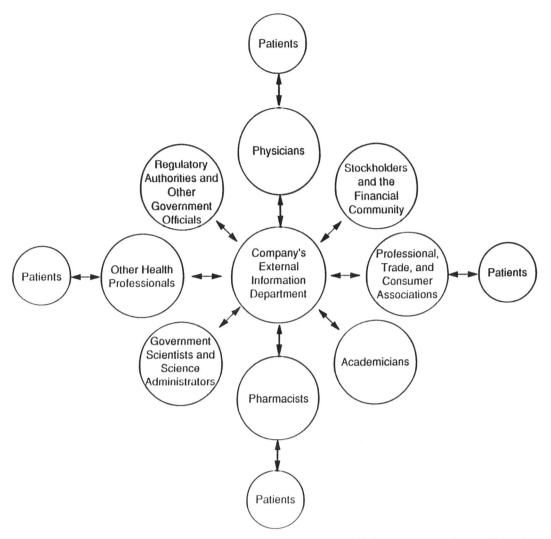

FIG. 42.3. Possible groups that interact with a company's external information department. The external groups may interact primarily, or solely, with other company groups than the external information department.

the initial start-up costs may be relatively high. Well-researched standard letters tend to be expensive to create and update, whereas customized letters may contain less scholarship and time. Standard letters are an important means, however, of decreasing the time it takes a company to respond. The answer to which approach is more expensive for a particular question depends on how often the standard letter is used and the amount of time spent on its creation and that of all custom letters that would be created to address the same question. A variety of formats that can be used to present information are listed in Table 42.5.

Preparing a Written Response

A unique case study of presenting product information on the first medicine to have a treatment-IND (Retrovir) was described by Kirk et al. (1989). They used a contract group to help process the large number of requests for information. A company that uses a contractor must ensure that they monitor the contractor's performance because the company is responsible for what the contractor does.

Although many (if not most) health professionals want an immediate telephone answer to their telephoned question, it often takes time for a company professional to prepare a thoughtful response. A standardized letter is generally more useful than a verbal answer, and it is often easier to supply. This is because a written record is more permanent, it documents what is said, and it provides more information than can be given over the telephone. Moreover, a letter bypasses the problem created when a health professional is unavailable or difficult to reach. Letters also eliminate the possibility of follow-up questions being raised on the telephone that are not critical but would require additional time to answer. Some (or most) companies do not discourage these follow-up questions.

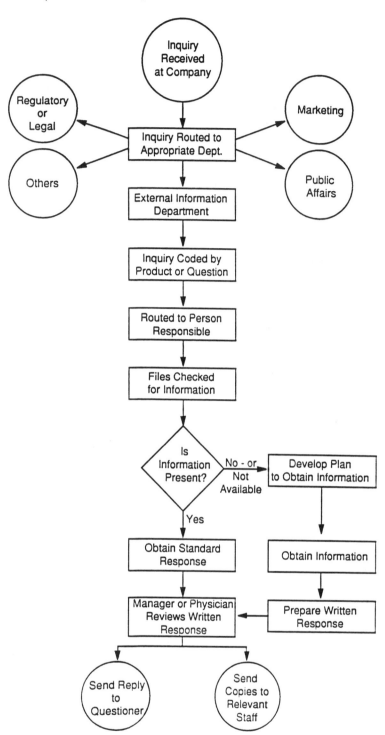

FIG. 42.4. Processing a question by a company's external information department when the answer can be determined within the department.

TABLE 42.4. *Categories of information provided to health professionals by a company*

1. Information on the proper ways of using a specific medicine within its labeled uses
2. Information available to the company on unlabeled uses of its medicines
3. Information on research being conducted on a marketed medicine
4. Information on the disease treated by the company's products
5. Information on topics tangential to the above that the company chooses to address (e.g., about other diseases, about other treatments)

Because many questions on any one product tend to be repetitive, an average-sized company may have about 500 or more standard letters prepared that address about 80% to 90% of the questions received. Many of the other 10% to 20% will require at least some research, often including a literature search, and will necessitate a custom letter to the person who contacted the company. If the written response will take a week or more to leave the company, it is often politically appropriate and wise to send a standard letter informing the professional that research is being conducted to help answer his or her question and that a more complete reply will be sent within one to two weeks. It may be helpful to provide a brief summary at the front of a letter when its length is more than two pages. In addition to storing the standard letters on a computer, digitized signature capability may be useful.

Appropriately worded disclaimers must be developed and included in the letters, particularly for off-label uses. It may be desirable to include disclaimers at both the start and end of a letter.

The decision to prepare a new standard letter is usually made after observing that a custom letter on the same topic has been requested more than just a few times. The number of requests needed to trigger the preparation of a new standard letter may be fixed (e.g., three to ten), but this approach depends on the company. All new standard letters should be carefully scrutinized, not only within the group in charge of information but also by other groups within a company that could be affected

TABLE 42.5. *Formats of information provided*

1. Letters
2. Reprints
3. Bibliographies
4. Videotapes[a]
5. Brochures for health professionals
6. Brochures for patients
7. Audiocassettes[a]
8. Books
9. Package inserts
10. Prerecorded messages

[a] These are probably the least common methods used.

by any letter (e.g., legal, medical, regulatory) or by specific letters with a particular focus. The author knows of a situation where this was not done and major problems arose because the letter's author speculated on how the company's product could theoretically cause certain adverse effects. The letter may or may not list references. References are sometimes listed at the bottom of a letter and are sometimes sent with the letter. Relevant copyright issues regarding reprints must be considered. An 800 (toll-free) telephone number may be listed for recipients to call if they want to receive an actual copy of one or more reprints referenced in the letter.

A policy should be established as to the grammatical nature of standard letters in terms of voice (i.e., active versus passive), tense (i.e., present versus past), person (i.e., second or third), style, and other characteristics.

If the company wishes to disseminate specific data on a product to health professionals, it could provide postcards (at meetings) that could be used to request more information on specific (or general) questions that are frequently asked about that product(s). The Food and Drug Administration (FDA) is reviewing this and related practices in the United States and may alter the degree of freedom that pharmaceutical companies currently have to conduct this and other related activities.

RELATIONSHIP WITH INTERNAL COMPANY INFORMATION GROUPS

The relationship of a product information group (that interacts with external health professionals) with the company's own internal information group (i.e., those who provide information to the company's staff) depends on the organization of the company. The externally oriented group usually does not have responsibility for internal information services, which makes sense given the vastly different orientation and goals of the two groups. Nonetheless, close collaboration and good working relationships are essential to achieve mutual benefits. If internal competition and stress are not a problem between groups, then the organization has achieved a significant goal. A periodic meeting of all company groups concerned with providing information services would be a useful way to help ensure that they were communicating appropriately and identifying areas of contention or potential problems that need to be addressed.

QUALITY ASSURANCE OF COMMUNICATION WITH EXTERNAL HEALTH PROFESSIONALS

One product information group in a midsized pharmaceutical company reportedly handles 90% of their telephone inquiries within minutes. When a quick response like this is not possible, callers can be told that the information they seek is currently unavailable but that the

TABLE 42.6. *Table heading for a form to evaluate the progress of the information staff in responding to questions from health professionals outside the company*

Inquiries per month	Professional staff		Support staff		Number			Turnaround time (working days)	
	Number	Staff/10,000 inquiries	Number	Staff/10,000 inquiries	Telephone calls	Standard letters	Custom letters	Standard forms	Custom letters

company will get back to them promptly, usually within 24 hours. In some cases a literature search will be conducted and a written reply drafted and sent within a few days. Companies should establish guidelines for time of reply and track their results to see if they are meeting their goals.

While it is not mandatory at present to have another group audit the performance of an external information group, the information group should periodically have its own performance assessed. This could be done by the following.

1. Discussions could be held at weekly or biweekly meetings to review issues of efficiency, difficult inquiries, problems, or other matters.
2. A series of prepared questions could be sent to a sample of health professionals who requested information. These people would be asked questions about the group's performance. This could be done on a periodic basis (e.g., one to four times a year).
3. Another group within or outside the organization could be requested to conduct an audit of the group's performance.
4. The performance of the group's productivity could be evaluated (e.g., Table 42.6).
5. Complaints received or solicited could be evaluated (e.g., Table 42.7).
6. A survey of end-users could be conducted.

TABLE 42.7. *Representative complaints from outside health professionals about pharmaceutical company information departments*

1. Being transferred by operators from person to person to person
2. Being informed that the information is proprietary to the company
3. Merely having the package insert repeated
4. Being given a reply that is too general and does not address the question
5. Being given out-of-date or inaccurate information
6. Refusing to admit that the company does not know
7. The *Physicians' Desk Reference* (PDR) does not always indicate whether a company will accept a collect telephone call, whether a toll-free (800) telephone number is available for inquiries, and what telephone number should be used for emergency telephone calls outside normal opening hours[a]

[a] This responsibility is also shared by the publishers of the PDR.

A series of 19 activities conducted by an information center at a teaching hospital is presented by Park and Benderev (1985) along with procedures that could be used to conduct a quality assurance check of each activity. The authors also present methods for monitoring ten separate information service functions, explain how to identify the person to conduct the monitoring, and suggest a recommended frequency of the evaluation. Each of the major characteristics of an information group (Table 42.8) may be assessed. Repchinsky et al. (1988) describe a quality assurance audit for a regional and hospital medicine information service. Many, but not all, companies are focusing on quality assurance activities. The primary reason that these activities are not being examined by the entire pharmaceutical industry is that there are no regulatory requirements to do so. In addition, the quality of service provided to health professionals is far better than in the past—even ten years ago. The Upjohn Company sends postcards to health professionals to evaluate the quality of their medical and drug information service. A copy of their postcard is illustrated in Fig. 42.5.

RESEARCH OPPORTUNITIES

Sales representatives who provide physicians with useful information tend to have the opportunity to spend more time with physicians detailing medicines. This is an important consideration at a time when it is becom-

TABLE 42.8. *Characteristics of a state-of-the-art medicine information group*

1. Provides a 24-hour-a-day, 7-day-a-week telephone answering service[a]. Answering machines are listened to hourly, and information staff are contacted when required
2. Rapidly refers emergency and other questions to appropriate staff
3. Has sophisticated operational system in place to achieve its goals[b]
4. Has quality assurance procedures in place
5. Maintains liaisons with all relevant groups both within and external to the company
6. Is sensitive to the regulatory and legal restraints on providing information to health professionals and sends package inserts for all products discussed in its replies

[a] A professional answering service is usually used when the company's offices are closed.
[b] See Table 42.1.

MEDICAL & DRUG INFORMATION
QUALITY ASSURANCE SURVEY

94-1666 1/92

QUALITY ✓

Dear Inquirer,

You need the best possible service from us when you have a question about Upjohn prescription products. **Please** take a minute **to evaluate our response to your written inquiry/telephone call** regarding

This mailing included: Written Response   Literature Search   Articles

1. **Did the response answer your question?** *(Check one)*

    ☐ Completely   ☐ Partially   ☐ Not at all

2. **How would you rate specific aspects of our response?**
    (Check one response per statement)   A=Agree   D=Disagree   N/A=Not Applicable

    The response arrived within a reasonable amount   ☐ A   ☐ D   ☐ N/A
    of time

    The response is clearly and logically presented   ☐ A   ☐ D   ☐ N/A

    The response appears to be balanced   ☐ A   ☐ D   ☐ N/A

    The conclusion or recommendation is appropriate   ☐ A   ☐ D   ☐ N/A

3. **Did/will you apply the information to patient care?** *(Check one)*

    ☐ Yes   ☐ No   ☐ Not Applicable

4. **What response format is MOST USEFUL to you?** *(**CHECK ONLY ONE**)*

    ☐ Written Response   ☐ Telephone Response

    ☐ Computerized Literature Search   ☐ Articles

    ☐ Other *(specify):* _____

5. **Profession** *(Check one)*

    ☐ Physician   ☐ Pharmacist   ☐ Nurse   ☐ Dentist

    ☐ Other: _____

6. **Comments/suggestions** *(If you prefer to discuss our response with us, please provide your name and telephone number or call us collect, 616-329-8244):*

    _____

    _____

    _____

FIG. 42.5. Illustration of the message side of a folded postcard sent to health professionals by the Upjohn Co. to request an evaluation of their medical and drug information service. Reprinted with permission of the Medical and Drug Information Department of the Upjohn Co.

ing increasingly difficult for sales representatives to visit with physicians. A major source of product information used by sales representatives for physicians is the information group discussed in this chapter. To test this hypothesis, an investigator could randomly assign a sufficient-sized group of sales representatives to detail a control group of physicians. These representatives would be instructed not to use the company's information group or, alternatively, the representatives would receive no special instructions about the information group. The experimental group of representatives would be strongly encouraged to use the services of the company's information group. After a sufficient period, the output (i.e., sales in the area) and the attitudes of both groups of representatives would be evaluated and compared.

Another research project could involve asking the information staff to discern important trends in uses of their company's products. These trends would be based, at least in part, on the questions received by the group. The information staff should provide this information to both marketing and medical managers for evaluation. They also should be able to identify needs for clinical studies to provide often-requested and important information, such as clarifications of ambiguities in the package insert or pharmacokinetic information.

PERSONNEL

Previous experience of full-time professional staff may be in medical, sales, marketing, or a hospital-based information service. A company may find that it is relatively easy to hire temporary staff to provide information to health professionals. Nonetheless, that approach creates several problems. The temporaries will be unlikely to know the workings of the company, they will require repeated and often more extensive training than others, and, as dependency on them increases, they will become a cadre of "permanent temporaries." This often raises morale problems and tensions between permanent staff and long-term temporaries over company benefits and other issues.

While many companies hire pharmacists for this department, some companies have hired physicians. These latter companies report that external physicians like to speak with company physicians, although few external physicians insist on this. Moreover, the additional costs in salaries and benefits are claimed to be made up by improved relationships with the company's customers.

Size of Information Staff

There is a balance between an information group that is too lean in number or experience to meet the company's workload and a group consisting of so many individuals that it is wasteful of company resources. A relatively small-sized group not only has a more difficult time completing its assignments, but also is usually less creative and experiences more stress and burnout in trying to handle the workload. The attitude of management toward this group has a lot to do with the staff's reaction to their heavy workload. On the positive side, a small but efficient group generally has an excellent *esprit de corps*, at least initially, and can solve crises fairly well.

ISSUES TO CONSIDER

Some people believe that providing more information to physicians than what is in the package label increases the company's liability. It is also conceivable that the more information a company provides to physicians and other health professionals the better the medicines will be used; furthermore, it is possible that fewer legal suits will result that involve the company.

Company employees must be sensitive to the issue of whether they are harassing their callers with persistent requests for official reports of adverse experiences. For example, imagine that a doctor calls the company asking a question about a patient's adverse experience. The company responds with the information and asks that the physician complete an adverse experience report that the company will submit to the government's regulatory authority. Then the company sends the physician the appropriate form to fill in. If the physician does not return the form within a predetermined time, the company sends him or her another form. Eventually the physician may become upset and view this practice as a form of harassment. He or she may decide not to contact any pharmaceutical company with questions in the future. On the other hand, companies have an obligation to collect adverse experience information, particularly if the caller mentions a patient's specific experience. If no patient is mentioned it is not clear whether the company representative should ask if a patient was involved. If the adverse experience was serious there is more reason to ask this question and, depending on the answer, to follow up. This overall issue is a major problem for information groups dealing with physicians.

A final issue is that all information groups have a surge of requests after the company launches a new medicine. The company must be prepared to deal with this increased workload.

Some companies treat the issues discussed in this chapter much more seriously than do others. It is the author's view that these issues deserve the utmost care and attention of all companies because providing product information is one of the major places where direct communication occurs between the company and its customers. Providing accurate and appropriate information is a means of demonstrating in practice what many groups claim to be their primary concern but fail to deliver when they are actually called on to do so.

43 / Data Management and Statistics

Data Management 485
  The Universe of Data Management 485
  General Issues in Data Management 486
  Specific Data Management Issues 487
  Integrated Systems: Small, Big, and Giant 488
  Levels of Integration Between Data Bases 488
  Developing an Integrated System 489
  Problem Areas and Issues in Developing an
    Integrated System 489

Statistical Considerations 490
  Roles of Statistics and Statisticians in Medicine
    Development 490
  Broad Issues Involving Statistics and
    Statisticians 490
  Examples of Poorly Applied Statistics 491

We are an intelligent species and the use of our intelligence quite properly gives us pleasure. In this respect the brain is like a muscle. When it is in use we feel very good. Understanding is joyous. Carl Sagan, *Broca's Brain*

When something can be expressed in a numerical way, it is an aid to more precise and accurate thinking. Richard Ascher

DATA MANAGEMENT

The Universe of Data Management

Data management is a general phrase that has many meanings within a pharmaceutical company. A number of years ago fewer areas were concerned with data management than today, and issues were much less complex. Large quantities of data are generated by all functions of a company. Data must be processed, combined, interpreted, and used in ways that are clear, efficient, and designed to achieve one's goals. The term *data management* refers to the processes whereby some or all of these steps are handled, monitored, and controlled. This section describes major areas in research and development where large amounts of data are generated.

Research

Medicine discovery activities utilize computers to an increasingly greater degree to generate, store, and analyze data. This category includes many preclinical activities in chemistry, pharmacology, and other biological sciences. Results obtained on each of a company's compounds should be stored and made readily available to scientists. Molecular modeling is an area requiring sophisticated data handling.

Toxicology

The flow of toxicological information and data into formal reports suitable for registration dossiers is becoming more automated. In many individual studies a large number of animals are involved, a large number of parameters are measured in each animal, and evaluations are made at numerous scheduled time points. This means that efficient systems must be developed and utilized to handle an enormous quantity of data. Good Laboratory Practice (GLP) regulations require high standards of data management in addition to high standards of animal care and treatment.

Clinical Trials

The huge amount of data generated in even a single clinical trial requires sophisticated data management systems. Data management involves many aspects including data collection, data transmittal to the sponsor (this is done by remote entry methods in some trials), data editing, data entry into computers, data verification, data analysis by statisticians, and data interpretation. For large scale multicenter trials, special groups and monitors at both a central site and the individual trial sites are often required in addition to the sponsor's staff.

Regulatory Affairs

Compiling regulatory dossiers involves numerous data management techniques. These include collating and completing reports, numbering pages, transferring data to another medium (e.g., microfilm, microfiche), and submitting different subsets of data to numerous regulatory agencies around the world in a variety of different formats and languages.

Technical Development

Numerous aspects of technical development generate large amounts of data (e.g., stability tests conducted under various conditions, with samples obtained and analyzed at numerous time points). Capsules can now be weighed individually and their quality assured. Complex clinical trial medicine labels and bottles may be prepared and the bottles filled with capsules or tablets using sophisticated systems requiring computer-assisted data management. Chapter 46, Technical Development, describes other examples of technical development where large amounts of data are generated.

Data and Information Storage

Keeping up with all of the company's reports, minutes, and other documents is a major effort requiring a variety of systems to keep these records in order. Documents must be indexed for retrieval and other uses. Published literature on the company's medicines and other topics of interest must also be systematically analyzed and referenced for easy retrieval.

Postmarketing Surveillance

Reports on adverse reactions to marketed medicines reach companies from many sources, as described in Chapter 45, Clinical Trials. The quality and relevance of those data vary to an incredible degree. The data must nonetheless be dealt with rapidly and accurately because of their importance, as well as regulatory requirements.

Quality Assurance Procedures

Quality assurance (QA) procedures are used in many areas of a company in relation to medicine development, including toxicology and medicine manufacture. The large volumes of data generated require automated computer-assisted systems to help in this effort.

General Issues in Data Management

Although each functional area of a company has particular issues with regard to data management that are unique to their function, many issues are common to several areas. General issues, plus a few more specific ones, are mentioned.

The most important point about data management is that it must be a planned process where a great deal of forethought has gone into the creation of systems, flow of information, checks and balances, and other aspects of the plans that are implemented. Rushing any part of this process may easily cause complex problems to develop that can take years and significant effort and money to unravel. This process cannot be allowed to develop on its own in a topsy-turvy manner. Many data management issues involve reassessing an area where the company has fallen behind the state of the art or believes it can handle data in a better way. New systems must be evaluated, chosen, and then implemented.

Few areas of data management are not intimately connected with computers and computer uses. The use of computers in data management is undergoing rapid change because advances in both hardware and software have had a dramatic effect on the roles that computers can play in data management (Tables 43.1 and 43.2). Because of this ongoing change, most general issues relating to computer hardware or software are not discussed here, nor are the myriad of more technical computer issues.

Choosing Systems and Equipment and Establishing Policies for Their Use

How may companies best determine the amount of money, time, and staff effort to devote to data management? The rapid changes in computer software and hardware make decisions about purchasing equipment more difficult. Lease arrangements have become more

TABLE 43.1. *Selected medicine development areas that may be automated*

1. Accounting and budgeting at a company or smaller level of organization
2. Statistical analyses
3. Data acquisition from laboratory instruments
4. Production procedures
5. Data processing of clinical and other areas
6. Investigational medicine inventory control
7. Personnel deployment
8. Project planning
9. Remote data entry of laboratory data
10. Evaluations of investigators
11. Clinical data storage, maintenance, retrieval, and analysis
12. Same as Item 11 above for toxicology, metabolism, pharmacology, chemical stability, or other types of data
13. Registry of compounds made and test results
14. Quality assurance results of samples tested
15. Published reports of interest
16. Adverse reactions from various sources (e.g., company, other sites, regulatory agencies)

TABLE 43.2. *Selected clinical areas of medicine development that may be automated[a,b]*

1. Protocols (e.g., per medicine, per department, per key elements of trial design)
2. Data collection form library
3. Contracts with investigators
4. Payments to investigators
5. Patient enrollment information
6. Adverse reactions[c]
7. Laboratory data
8. Patient visit data
9. Medicine inventory control (e.g., supplies on hand, where supplies went, where supplies are located in a warehouse)
10. Clinical trial materials (e.g., orders, status of orders)
11. Cross-trial tabulations
12. Labeling of containers for medicine trials
13. Information on investigators
14. Information on trial centers (e.g., reliability, performance)
15. Time allocation of staff spent on various medicine projects

[a] Certain areas may be automatically flagged (i.e., brought to the users' attention) when data exceed certain limits or meet certain criteria (e.g., serious adverse reactions, laboratory values that exceed a prespecified number).
[b] Some of these functions may be integrated into a network as described in the text.
[c] These may be integrated from various sources (e.g., investigational trials, marketed studies, foreign sites).

attractive in many situations. Many of the primary factors used to select systems and equipment to store data are listed in Table 43.3. Other functions of equipment require different considerations.

After an elaborate system is installed, what should a company do about encouraging employees to use that system? Should the company make the system mandatory (i.e., modify their standard operating procedures so that everyone must adhere to and use the new computer approach)? If the company makes the system optional, then few people will use it in some cases. This could mean that a great deal of effort and money may have been "wasted." Clearly, the answer to this problem is to evaluate the needs of the potential users ahead of time and to give priority to those systems that are most important to the company, rather than of particular interest to a small number of protagonists. This often turns out to be difficult to identify accurately in practice. Choices often have to be made between competing systems, with different characteristics, or between a well-known system and a newer one that could be far superior but would require a great deal of effort in installation, maintenance, and/or reeducation of staff.

Should a Company Be Among the First to Use a New System?

A common problem arises for a company when a vendor is attempting to sell a new system that has all the features desired by the company, but the vendor has not

sold any of the units or has sold only a few. A conservative view suggests that a company should generally not be one of the very first clients to purchase and operate a new system. It is virtually certain that the system will have many bugs and will require much more time and effort to become operational than anticipated. In some cases, highly touted systems never become operational. Another problem about being among the first companies to purchase a system is that the system's concept may not be feasible in practice, or in the pharmaceutical industry, because of a large input required in time and effort compared to a relatively small gain or output or because of other factors.

On the other hand, there is a strong temptation within many people and companies to be first to get new systems. This is to get ahead of or to gain on their competition. Another motivation is that most computer or technically oriented people like to have the newest gadgets available. These urges and requests must be controlled because there is a certain probability that the company's progress may actually be slowed in one or more areas by a new system that has many bugs. On the other hand, it is not advisable to be the last company to purchase a new system, because by that time it will be fully operational and helping other companies to develop medicines.

Specific Data Management Issues

More specific data management issues currently being explored within the pharmaceutical industry include the following.

1. Validation techniques for the many steps in the handling and use of data. How to validate vendor-supplied validation systems?
2. Tracking movement of data from process to process. It is important to establish an audit trail to be able to track data movement at a later date.
3. Minimizing or avoiding poor quality data submitted to regulatory authorities.

TABLE 43.3. *Primary factors used to select systems and equipment to store information[a]*

1. Time to store information
2. Ease of storing information
3. Time to access information
4. Ease of access to information
5. Degree of control of the system or equipment
6. Cost of hardware
7. Cost of maintenance
8. Degree of security
9. Erasability of disks or tapes
10. Capacity for storage
11. Flexibility for different uses
12. Ability to integrate with other systems

[a] Many general criteria relevant to purchasing any equipment (e.g., reputation of manufacturer and vendor, service guarantees, availability) are not included in this table.

4. Copying data efficiently and rapidly using high technology (e.g., microfiche, microfilm).

5. Numbering data and pages rapidly and correctly in a regulatory submission.

6. Remote data entry from investigator's sites to a company or to central laboratories. All clinical data or a small subset (e.g., laboratory data) may be handled in this manner.

7. Planning and tracking multiple project activities on a worldwide basis.

8. Developing and utilizing adverse reaction dictionaries for clinical data.

9. Submitting periodic reports on time to the Food and Drug Administration (FDA) and other regulatory agencies.

10. Collecting only relevant data in a trial. Any trial that collects too much data is in jeopardy of compromising the trial's value to the company. Careful consideration must be made of each parameter measured and the amount of data obtained on each parameter. This includes questioning the total length of data collection forms and the amount of data to be collected.

11. Planning production activities in many different geographical areas.

12. Developing artificial intelligence systems. This primarily involves expert systems that try to capture the decision-making ability of an expert within a specific domain of knowledge. It is attempted for areas where algorithms are not appropriate. Some potential uses include (1) molecular modeling, (2) interpreting biological screen data, (3) statistical design analysis and interpretation, (4) automating quality assurance procedures, (5) scheduling production activities, (6) developing marketing plans, (7) controlling complex manufacturing procedures, and (8) predicting medicine interactions.

Integrated Systems: Small, Big, and Giant

Other terms for small, big, and giant networks are local area systems, integrated systems across departments or functions, and company-wide integrated systems.

Many scientists and managers have established data bases of various sizes. It was realized many years ago that there were many advantages to be gained by linking some of the data bases with networks (i.e., programs and hardware), so that cross–data base communication and cross-tabulations are possible. Links among data bases are referred to as network systems. Networks enable new questions to be addressed and additional problems to be solved and, in general, improve communications. All of the data bases that are linked together by a network constitute an integrated system. Another term used is *umbrella system*. Small integrated systems have been available for a long period.

The trend toward putting more data bases within the same integrated system has been rapidly increasing.

Many large integrated systems cover function-wide data and may be accessed from multiple computer systems using multiple types of data management. The linkage between desktop personal computers and large mainframes, plus networks among various users, has been expanding. The linkage among various information data bases at a department level has also been increasing. Companies that are unable to communicate among their various sites efficiently are behind the state of the art. It is important to integrate both the various pieces of hardware and also the various software packages. If only the former is integrated, then the system will not usually be treated as an integrated tool by the users.

Although the trend toward developing large integrated systems is progressing rapidly, there is presently no overall giant system that can cover and link all of the research and development data bases. This type of integrated system would enable a professional to tap and use any data at his or her level of clearance. This futuristic possibility may not be a completely desirable goal because of possible problems of misuse, security, and difficulties if the system is not operating properly. The largest data base possible within a company would involve information from most, if not all, divisions. This too may not be feasible because of security, practicality, and the limited number of people who should have access to all information.

Nonresearch and Development Integrated Systems

In addition to research and development data bases, other functions are developing the means of linking some of their data bases in areas where they share interests. These functions include finance, marketing, and production. Examples of uses include better production planning, marketing forecasts, financial reporting of results, and so on. Uses of large data bases that are maintained outside a company are discussed in Chapter 45, Clinical Trials, under postmarketing surveillance. Such data bases include those tracking individual patients, medicines being used, hospital admissions, diagnoses, and other information. Questions on a company's medicines may be posed to these data bases.

Levels of Integration Between Data Bases

There are several levels at which systems or people are integrated.

1. Physical connection of hardware—Machines from different manufacturers and also from a single manufacturer must be connected or networked if they are to be integrated or operate as part of a single system.

2. Compatibility of software—Even after the equipment operates as a single system, the software used must be made compatible.

3. Data structure—Compatibility bridges—This is the most important level of integration. It requires that the data being handled by the system are compatible, so that pieces may be combined.

4. Translation bridges—This relates to making different applications work together in a single system. It is hard to maintain bridges (linkages) between in-house software and commercial software. Many pharmaceutical companies seek commercial vendors to provide this software. Each company requires different bridges for their systems.

5. Application system—A system may be designed to unify many data bases. This is the most overall view of what is developed. Another way of viewing issues of integration is as two types: integrating people to work together and integrating technology to perform as desired. The five levels presented all relate to the technology aspects but require the people developing, using, and maintaining the system to be integrated (i.e., work together).

Developing an Integrated System

Probably the most important principle is to keep the system simple and make it work. An important corollary of this principle is that it should be developed from the outset by technically oriented people working closely with those who will be using the system. It is also imperative that the concept of the system be supported, if not championed, by one or more senior executives with enough clout to ensure that the work is completed. After the system has proved its worth, it may be expanded to take on other functions or it may be joined to another network.

It is, ironically, those companies that did little or nothing to develop data bases in the past that have an advantage today. They do not have many established pieces (data bases) that have to be integrated into a system. This allows them an opportunity to develop a more ideal system than those companies that made large financial investments in developing systems and data bases that are less readily connected by networks and integrated into a total system.

The first step in getting started to develop an integrated system is to ensure that the people who will be using the system are working cooperatively with the technical people who will set it up. The person who will use the system often must be willing to do his or her work in a different manner after the system is established. This may require a major selling effort by computer-oriented professionals who make recommendations about the type of integrated system to develop. At the same time it is essential for the user to ensure that the right issues are being addressed by the technical staff. This is where the commitment from relevant senior managers is important.

Without adequate attention to these steps it is possible for computer people to design and build integrated systems that no one really wants. Whether computer staff develop a new system quietly (i.e., without prior knowledge of the eventual users) or not, the end result is the same—the system will not be used.

The plan proposed must be critiqued to see if it is cost-effective (i.e., if the effort is worth the expected outcomes) or, using a more slang expression—is the juice worth the squeeze? Benefits must be judged in terms of timeliness, accuracy, and comprehensiveness of information obtained.

Problem Areas and Issues in Developing an Integrated System

1. A large amount of software and hardware is present in a company that is too valuable to discard and too difficult to integrate into an efficient system.

2. The justification for establishing a new system is usually based on cost savings. These estimates are difficult to establish and involve many assumptions, which may be challenged.

3. Numerous vendors of computers must be dealt with, especially across different disciplines (e.g., production, marketing) and among different countries.

4. Few reliable vendors of application software exist. This often forces companies to write their own.

5. Different sites of the same company often have different beliefs about what are the most important issues and how to address them.

6. There is a balance between developing adequate security for an integrated system and still retaining user-friendly systems.

7. Technical personnel to develop and maintain the systems may be centralized, peripheralized into individual functions (e.g., marketing, production), or used in some combination (e.g., distribute maintenance personnel to peripheral functions but centralize systems development).

Other Issues about Integrated Systems

Many data management issues have little to do with either hardware or software. The same type of data at two sites, in different departments at one site, or from study to study at one site may be collected in different formats and at different depths or expressed differently. The perfect computer system cannot readily combine data that have such differences. This problem may be readily addressed in some cases by senior managers making decisions about company policy (e.g., regarding forms to be used to collect clinical data). But, if the end-users differ either in their philosophy or in their uses of the data, there may be greater difficulties resolving this issue. For example, preclinical animal test results may be desired by some users in a format indicating merely that data are positive (+) or negative (−), but others will desire exact data (e.g., doses used, results in detail).

There is usually a great reluctance to establish data bases when they are initially suggested. This is because the owners of the separate files have a vested interest in systems they have developed and territory they try to protect. On the other hand, this reaction is appropriate in many situations. Ownership of a data base usually means responsibility and commitment to its appropriate use.

When a new integrated system is being established a great deal of education may be necessary for the staff who will eventually use it. It usually takes time to get all relevant people to accept the need for and the characteristics of a new system. Many technical issues must be determined and agreed to, including (1) system requirements, (2) data base design, (3) record structure, (4) material to be included, (5) who will set up the system, (6) formats for printing outputs, (7) the thesaurus to be used, and (8) who will maintain the system.

Other related questions include the following. (1) How user-friendly will the system be? (2) May the information be transferred (i.e., downloaded) from a central mainframe computer to a user's individual terminal for manipulation? (3) If the answer to Question 2 is yes, may manipulated data now be uploaded back into the central computer with or without an audit trail? (4) How many people outside the core group who establish and maintain the system will have access to it? (5) Should information stored be solely what is needed or should it contain information that would be nice to know?

The future in this area promises to be even more exciting and challenging. A skeptical attitude, however, will serve companies well; that attitude will force them to focus their approach and to utilize their resources most effectively. This will enable them to take best advantage of data management technologies and to learn from other people's experiences and mistakes. Utilizing integrated software from outside the company is usually desirable, even when internal resources are available to develop a unique software program.

STATISTICAL CONSIDERATIONS

Someone once said that there are "liars, damned liars, and statisticians." This has been attributed to Benjamin Disraeli and Winston Churchill, as well as Will Rogers (and possibly others). Whatever its source, it conjures up the image of a statistician being able to make the numbers say whatever you want them to say. Another similar comment relates to the joke about three people who were asked the sum of two plus two. The first was a banker and he answered "four." An accountant was second, and he gave the same response. But, when a statistician was asked the sum of two plus two, he took the questioner aside before responding, "What do you want it to equal?"

Roles of Statistics and Statisticians in Medicine Development

Before describing some of the many issues concerned with statistics, it is useful to broadly define the universe of statistics in medicine discovery and development. In the preclinical area, scientists utilize statistical principles and methods in the design, execution, and analysis of their experiments. The statistics department may be asked to become involved in individual experiments where sophisticated analyses or concepts are required. Statisticians may also act as consultants to departments that need advice or assistance with data analyses, data automation, or another function.

The largest role of statistics in the pharmaceutical industry in terms of assignment of personnel is in the clinical area. Regardless of whether statisticians are organizationally part of a clinical group, there are close interactions between them. These focus primarily on clinical trials in the areas of trial design, protocol development, data analysis, and statistical report writing. Statisticians are often asked to analyze special problems or issues and to accompany clinicians or scientists to regulatory meetings.

A third area where statistics has intimate involvement is in the quality assurance area of production. A number of the roles played by statisticians in quality assurance are described in Chapter 50, Production Issues.

Broad Issues Involving Statistics and Statisticians

A few representative issues are indicated to provide a flavor of the many types of issues that are encountered.

1. Is it required for statisticians to review all clinical protocols *prior* to their implementation? Over the last 30 years, the pendulum has swung from an almost total "no" to an almost complete "yes." There are still pharmaceutical companies, particularly outside the United States, where this practice is not required.

2. How much interaction and discussion is there between the clinician and statistician about how to analyze the data collected? Is the decision on which groups and subgroups to compare reached by mutual agreement, or does one group have total authority in this matter?

3. Are statisticians integral members of each project team? This is an accepted and standard practice at most pharmaceutical companies.

4. Are statisticians involved in any research activities seeking new or improved methods of analysis, or are they methodically turning out cloned reports on medicine trials?

5. How may company statisticians convince regulatory authorities about the appropriateness of utilizing a specific approach in a specific situation? Even nationally respected statisticians in academia have been unable, at least on some occasions, to change the minds of nonstatisticians at regulatory agencies who insist on having companies use the "FDA approach" to data analysis.

A problem faced by pharmaceutical companies in dealing with regulatory agencies is that some regulators who are untrained in statistics unilaterally decide on statistical issues, even though prominent academic and pharmaceutical industry statisticians strongly disagree with their approach. Moreover, some regulators have arbitrarily created new statistical rules that have been enforced as FDA policy. On the other hand, a major issue often arises between two (or more) valid approaches to a set of data from a statistical perspective. Too often, individual statisticians claim that their analyses are the "best" way to handle the data. Nonetheless there are often multiple ways of analyzing data and pros and cons to each.

Some statisticians believe that *all* data obtained in a trial must be analyzed because, no matter whether patients should have been treated, met protocol requirements, or never even received the medicine, there was an intention to treat. A more clinically oriented approach is to analyze data of patients that make clinical sense and delete data of other patients from the analyses. The author believes that all relevant statistical analyses should be conducted and some or all presented to regulatory agencies. The analysis that the company believes to be most relevant should be noted and its appropriateness defended and supported. This may save time if a single analysis is presented and a regulatory agency then asks a company to conduct others.

Another issue relates to two development sites of a company each wishing to analyze data from a single clinical trial using different statistical tests. Unless agreement is reached on a joint position, the company may be placed in a difficult position if different interpretations of the trial are reached.

One of the greatest difficulties in clinical trials regarding statistics is the large number of biases that may enter a trial and affect the results. Bad statistics lead to incorrect conclusions about cause-and-effect relationships (e.g., did the medicine cause the adverse reaction?) and to a flawed understanding of the relationship being studied.

Examples of Poorly Applied Statistics

The newspapers are full of statistical distortions every day. For example, one study claimed that older automobile drivers are safer than younger adults. But that study was based on the number of accidents per year. Because older people drive less, they have fewer accidents. But, if the comparison was based on the number of accidents per mile driven, then older drivers were the second-to-worst category of all drivers.

Another problem that is frequently noted occurs in advertising. Numbers and data are often twisted beyond recognition. A long history of distorted use of statistics in marketing claims is so pervasive that it has helped create generations of skeptical people and has destroyed a great deal of trust both between physicians and pharmaceutical companies and between pharmaceutical companies and regulatory agencies.

Two commonly reported situations where more information is required to understand a situation are presented below.

1. As a holiday weekend approaches and commences, we are given results in the media of the precise number of people killed locally, statewide, and nationally. The assumption is made that it is more dangerous to drive on holiday weekends. A careful review of traffic accident data illustrates that approximately one-third more deaths occur on holiday weekends compared to an average weekend. But there are at least one-third more cars on the road during holiday weekends, so that the probability of any car having an accident resulting in death is no greater than on other weekends. In fact, the probability may be somewhat lower because of increased driver awareness and the visible presence of more police officers on the highway.

2. Women are often reported to earn less than men for comparable work, but there are many factors involved in how people accept positions and are paid. One situation experienced by many couples where both are highly paid professionals is when the husband looks all over the country to select the best job possible to advance his career. Then his wife looks for a job in the specific area chosen by the husband. In most situations she will earn less money than if the area of her search was not as restricted. The point is not to challenge the initial claim, which is probably true, but to illustrate some of the factors that complicate its interpretation.

44 / Toxicology Issues

Introduction 493
Types of Medicine Toxicity 493
   Types of Long-Term Studies................. 494
   Studying Higher Versus Lower Dosages in
      Toxicological Studies...................... 494
Planning a Toxicology Program 494
   Core Studies.............................. 494
   Specialized Studies 494
   Timing of Toxicology Studies................ 494
   Are All Toxicological Studies Conducted
      According to One Standard?............... 495
   Cost of Toxicology Studies................... 495
Issues in Study Design 495
   Representative Factors...................... 495
   Reasons Why Multiples of the Anticipated

Peak Human Dose Are Used in Toxicology
      Studies.................................... 496
Dose-Response Relationships................. 496
Studies of Biologicals and Biotechnology
      Products 496
Regulatory Issues.............................. 497
   Regulatory Guidelines....................... 497
   Regulatory Requirements in Different
      Countries for Toxicology Testing 497
   Regulatory Requirements in Different
      Countries for Mutagenicity Testing 497
Mutagenicity Issues 498
   Categorization of Mutagenicity Tests......... 498
   Selected Issues Involving Mutagenicity Tests .. 498

It has been stated that animal toxicology has as much predictive value in terms of a compound's potential toxicological profile in man as the ritual hepatoscopy practiced by the Babylonians using sacrificial goats in their attempts to foretell the future. This practice is referred to in the Old Testament in Ezekiel Ch. 21. It was also practiced in the Roman era during the siege of Jerusalem in 70 AD and was documented by Josephus. Before dismissing this ancient practice as having no predictive value, it might be well to note that the goats' livers on both occasions accurately predicted the fall of Jerusalem. It would be even more foolish to dismiss the predictive value of animal toxicology studies so lightly. John P. Griffin, English physician. From *Predictive Value of Animal Toxicity Studies in Long-term Animal Studies: Their Predictive Value for Man.*

All substances are poisonous, there is none which is not a poison; the right dose differentiates a poison from a remedy. Attributed to Paracelsus, 16th century.

INTRODUCTION

Newspapers are often replete with stories about the latest chemical or environmental pollutant or medicine that is found to be toxic. The news is blasted forth in the media and sales of the medicine plummet; sometimes the company's stock falls as well. Although some of the news stories are justified, others distort a complex relationship by representing it in black and white terms. For example, are vitamin A and selenium toxic? This question may seem silly, but arctic explorers sometimes developed serious vitamin A toxicity from eating too much whale blubber or other local foods. Also, reports that selenium was carcinogenic at high concentrations led to its being purged from some people's diets. As a result, it has been claimed that "many human deaths have occurred from selenium deficiency" (Berry, 1986). At low doses, selenium is an important nutrient. It is therefore incorrect to

state that humans should avoid all chemicals that may cause cancer at high doses.

Toxicology studies can never demonstrate that a medicine is safe. They can only define the toxicity of the medicine under the specific conditions of the study. Toxicity is a characteristic of all substances, when studied in sufficient doses. Some studies show that a medicine is not toxic under the conditions tested. New human or animal data may be uncovered at any time before or after a medicine is marketed that demonstrate a medicine to be more or less safe (at least under the conditions studied) than previous toxicology studies indicated.

TYPES OF MEDICINE TOXICITY

One classification of medicine toxicity considers two major types. The first are those toxicities that result from an extension of the pharmacological activity that is related to the medicine's therapeutic effect. This may be viewed as a continuation of the dose-response relationship beyond the peak beneficial effect. The other major type of toxicity is unrelated to a medicine's beneficial effects and may either be predictable to occur in patients (e.g., gout caused by thiazide diuretics) or unpredictable (e.g., hyperplasia of the gums caused by phenytoin, retroperitoneal fibrosis caused by methysergide).

Types of Long-Term Studies

To evaluate chronic medicine toxicity, investigators conduct three major types of long-term animal studies. The first is chronic testing to evaluate gross (i.e., large) and microscopic changes in the body, plus behavioral changes. The second type is carcinogenicity studies that last for the natural life-span of rats and mice (approximately two years). The third type is reproduction studies that include three subtypes: fertility, teratology, and perinatal evaluations. It is often useful to retain some animals from chronic toxicology studies when the exposure phase is finished. These animals are used for evaluating the reversibility of specific adverse effects. This information enables the potential significance of positive toxicity findings to be better assessed.

Studying Higher Versus Lower Dosages in Toxicological Studies

There are numerous well-known reasons why high doses of a chemical or medicine may produce entirely different effects than those produced by a lower dose. For example, at high doses the body may be unable to metabolize a medicine that is handled in a therapeutically useful and safe way when lower doses are given. Toxic metabolites may be produced at exaggerated dose levels that are not formed at therapeutically useful dose levels. Alternatively, the body may be unable to eliminate large doses of a medicine and the medicine may build up (i.e., accumulate) to levels that cause toxicity in safety tests but would be unlikely to occur in humans taking recommended doses. There may also be marked differences in effects noted in different species with high doses of a medicine.

PLANNING A TOXICOLOGY PROGRAM

Core Studies

A core number of toxicology studies are usually conducted with few if any modifications. For most medicines it is essential to perform subchronic tests (e.g., 30, 60, or 90 days of exposure) in two species. The information obtained is used as a starting point to plan further studies. Core studies contain both short-term and long-term studies.

The specific studies conducted for a medicine depend on its eventual route of administration to patients, the duration of patient exposure, and previous clinical and toxicological information on related compounds or medicines, plus regulatory requirements and requests. Depending on these factors, a number of additional studies are usually added to the core group of studies to be conducted. Beyond this group of studies are a large number of potential studies that could be considered. Some companies are more conservative than others in their approach to toxicology and usually go beyond what would be considered to be a minimum number of studies by most regulatory agencies.

Specialized Studies

In addition to long-term toxicology studies and the appropriate battery of short-term studies, a number of specialized studies often must be conducted. The nature of these studies depends on the nature of a medicine (i.e., its therapeutic use, its chemical class, and specific clinical and pharmacological characteristics of its profile). These studies could involve additional species of particular interest or special strains of animals with certain genetic characteristics. Also, specific routes of administration, new parameters, or various formulations of the medicine could be evaluated. For example, if analyses for impurities in a medicine undergoing stability tests demonstrate that 15% of a specific breakdown product is formed, it may be useful to conduct toxicology studies on that breakdown compound, either as part of the parent medicine mix or when tested independently. In addition, the biological activity of breakdown products should be measured. If breakdown products are either isomers of the parent medicine or biologically similar to the parent medicine, then it may be possible to obtain regulatory approval for a shelf life that would permit this degree of degradation in the final medicine product.

Timing of Toxicology Studies

There is one major "Catch-22" situation that often arises in determining the appropriate timing for conducting toxicology studies. This relates to the general desire to wait for the efficacy of a new medicine to be established in Phase II trials before initiating the long-term toxicology studies (i.e., one-year studies and lifetime carcinogenicity bioassays, each done in two separate species). These studies not only are extremely expensive to conduct (approximately a half million dollars for each rodent bioassay used to assess carcinogenic potential), but also consume large quantities of investigational medicine. The medicine may not yet have been synthesized in sufficient amounts to allow such testing to occur at an earlier stage, and there may be various problems associated with obtaining sufficient medicine. Nonetheless, if the go–no go point in Phase II is used as the time to initiate long-term toxicology studies, the clinical trials on some medicines could be completed and ready to submit to a regulatory agency before toxicology reports are ready. It is undesirable for toxicology reports to be a rate-limiting step in submitting a regulatory application.

In practice, there are generally ways to provide for adequate time to complete the toxicology program necessary for a regulatory submission before all clinical reports are finished. One way of dealing with the Catch-22 situation with long-term studies is to make every effort with computers, scheduling, and other techniques to reduce the lag, commonly six months to one year or more, between completion of long-term dosing and availability of the final report. If a problem of timing seems to be likely, then long-term toxicology studies can be initiated earlier in the development program, with the understanding that the money to pay for these studies would possibly be wasted if the medicine had to be terminated. The term *possibly* is used because, if the medicine's toxicology profile demonstrated the absence or presence of specific findings, it could provide important information to help plan the future development of the entire chemical series.

Some research and development managers desire to start many toxicology studies on all new investigational compounds as soon as the medicine supply is available. This makes sense if there are few medicines undergoing development at the company and the company is in the fortunate position of having abundant resources. Most pharmaceutical companies are clearly not in this position. But, if a company is effectively prioritizing the development of its investigational medicines and if it is concerned about not wasting dollars and resources, then it is generally wise to delay the start of long-term toxicology studies until after some Phase II trials are completed. These studies should clearly demonstrate efficacy, confirm that the safety profile is adequate, demonstrate acceptable pharmacokinetics, and provide an overall indication that a regulatory submission (e.g., Product License Application [PLA], New Drug Application [NDA]) will probably be prepared for the medicine.

Are All Toxicological Studies Conducted According to One Standard?

There is great variation in the quality of contract toxicological laboratories that conduct studies for the pharmaceutical industry. A pharmaceutical company that bargain shops looking for the cheapest place to conduct a toxicology study is usually foolish. There is no faster way to kill a promising medicine unnecessarily or to delay its

progress than by raising toxicological questions that must be addressed. Clinical programs are often put "on hold" by the Food and Drug Administration (FDA), by other regulatory authorities, and/or by the company itself when toxicological issues arise.

Quality studies are essential and corners should not be cut. In situations where specialized toxicology studies are required, there may only be a few laboratories qualified to do the work. These groups may be unable to schedule a company's work as soon as desired. This presents a potentially serious dilemma. It is usually better to wait for the best group, provided that the development program is not unacceptably delayed. When delays are unacceptable and the study must be contracted to another group, the contracted study must be monitored intensely.

Cost of Toxicology Studies

Pharmaceutical company executives are aware that toxicology studies are often extremely expensive. There are a few occasions when these studies are the single greatest expense in developing a new medicine. This situation could arise either if questions arose that required numerous additional studies or if the costs of clinical trials and technical development were rather modest. For example, if a new medicine was being developed for a rare disease, the clinical trials might rely heavily on a few case studies, whereas the toxicology "package" of studies could be quite extensive and expensive. Although orphan medicines are usually approved with abbreviated efficacy data compared to a medicine intended to treat a large patient population, the amount of safety data required for approval may not be commensurately reduced by the FDA. Although toxicology studies are expensive, they usually account for a relatively minor portion (approximately 11%) of the total medicine development cost (see Chapter 23, Golden Rules of Medicine Development).

ISSUES IN STUDY DESIGN

Representative Factors

Many factors relating to the medicine substance, animals, and the intended clinical use of a medicine must be considered when designing toxicology studies. These will not be enumerated or described in detail because they are adequately discussed in the toxicology literature. A few general factors, however, will be mentioned to provide a flavor of issues encountered. Diet is an important consideration because it can affect tumor incidence and the animal's longevity; therefore, it must be carefully controlled. The specific strain of rat or mouse used also has an influence on tumor incidence and the duration of carcinogenicity bioassays (i.e., some strains live longer than others). Choosing a species to study is sometimes difficult when it is known that animals metabolize a medicine differently than do humans or have unique toxicities not observed in humans. In addition, not all animal species exhibit toxicities that may be specifically sought to evaluate (e.g., rats do not vomit). The more one delves into the field of toxicology, the more variables one observes that may affect a study's outcome and interpretation.

Three dose levels of a compound are often chosen to give to animals. The low dose is expected to be a no-effect dose and is set at least five times the expected or known therapeutic dose (if possible). The high dose is chosen to identify toxic effects but is not set so high as to jeopardize completion of a study. An intermediate dose is usually set at the mean of the high and low dose. The amount of a dose received by animals depends in part on whether it is physically given to the animals (e.g., by injection, by placing it in their stomachs) or placed in their food (e.g., once a day for a specific period, provided *ad lib.*).

Reasons Why Multiples of the Anticipated Peak Human Dose Are Used in Toxicology Studies

The major reason why large multiples of the anticipated peak human dose are studied is to determine what might be the worst possible scenario of the medicine's toxicity. That belief, based largely on empirical observations, is that, if 100 times the peak human dose does not produce unacceptable toxicity in laboratory animals, the dose given for therapy in clinical practice should be safe. A second reason for using large multiples of the anticipated peak human dose is to avoid using large numbers of animals. For example, if a toxic event actually occurs in 5% of all animals (or humans), it is necessary to study 60 animals in order to be 95% certain that you will observe a single case in the sample you are studying or 100 animals to be 99% certain that you will observe one case. It is assumed, primarily on a statistical basis, that the use of higher doses will help identify potentially important toxicity using smaller numbers of animals. This assumption may (or may not) be valid. Dose-response relationships are therefore vital to the process of safety assessment.

Dose-Response Relationships

The dose-response pattern often provides more useful information than that gathered by preclinical testing at excessive dose levels. Various toxic dose levels may be determined to provide a profile of a medicine's safety in animals.

1. *No-observed-effect dose*—no effects of any type noted
2. *No-observed-adverse effect dose*—effects noted but judged minimal and unlikely to cause significant toxicity in patients
3. *Adverse-effect dose*—moderate toxicity observed
4. *Frank-effect dose*—severe toxicity noted

These four levels of dose-response relationships in toxicological studies provide a comparison with doses shown or projected to be used and safe in humans.

There is no magic formula that states a medicine must not produce toxicity in laboratory animals at X times the dose needed for therapy if the medicine is to be clinically useful. The same principle applies to the human situation. The ratio of the toxic dose to the therapeutic dose (i.e., the therapeutic ratio) should be as high as possible. The magnitude of this number clearly depends on the particular disease and situation. Serious adverse events in humans are often acceptable with a new anticancer medicine but would be totally unacceptable for diseases where relatively safe medicines already exist or for diseases characterized by low morbidity.

Studies of Biologicals and Biotechnology Products

As a compound's structure progressively departs from a natural chemical found in humans, the initial toxicological requirements of regulatory agencies increase. This means that a company planning a toxicology program for a natural substance it is developing may shift the bulk of the work to a later time. This usually occurs *after* the medicine's efficacy and safety have been identified. This is important because medicine supply is usually a major issue early in a biotechnology-derived medicine's development. This does *not* mean that natural sequence proteins or other biologicals are necessarily safe for use in humans or do not require extensive toxicological tests.

Biotechnology products are evaluated in both short-term dose studies for up to a few days and in longer-term dose studies for up to four weeks. In addition to more traditional aspects of toxicity, animals are examined for antibodies, effects on the immune system, and local tolerance. Most natural products can be given in either physiological or pharmacological dosages. *Physiological doses* are relatively low doses given to replace absent or low levels of that substance in patients (i.e., to bring patients' own levels to normal). Adrenal steroids, thyroid hormone, insulin, and human growth factor are examples of hormones that may be replaced by physiological doses in patients who are deficient. *Pharmacological doses* are usually multiples of physiological doses given to patients to elicit an effect. These relatively high doses may cause marked toxicity. Examples of natural products used in this way include interferon, tissue plasminogen activator, and heparin.

REGULATORY ISSUES

Regulatory Guidelines

Guidelines for conducting toxicological studies on most new medicines are relatively straightforward (Table 126.12 in Spilker, 1991). Those guidelines, however, are both directly and indirectly controlled and influenced by regulatory agencies around the world. As a result, the guidelines established for choosing the basic experimental design, as well as the numbers, species, sex, age, and feeding conditions of animals to be studied, are not always the same for each country. The doses of medicines to be studied are usually based on dose-ranging studies. These are pilot studies of short duration used to evaluate toxicological effects at several prespecified dose levels. Definitive toxicological studies of many kinds utilize the information obtained in dose-ranging studies.

Methods and parameters used are also indicated and described in the protocol. Specific measurements and evaluations conducted on live animals are generally well established, as are the methods of necropsy and obtaining both gross and microscopic tissue samples. Measurement of medicine levels in blood is an important part of toxicological testing because this information is often useful in extrapolating results of preclinical tests to humans.

Interpretation of results obtained in preclinical toxicological tests requires extensive experience if the testing is to be used to maximum advantage in the medicine development process. Disagreements are inevitable when lesions or other adverse events do not fit accepted clear and unambiguous criteria. Pathologists often reach different diagnoses of the lesions they "read" in microscopic slides. There may also be great differences of opinion among toxicologists who interpret the significance of findings reported in any specific test. Even when two or more toxicologists agree about the diagnosis of a lesion or the nature of another adverse event, there are often great differences in how they assess the potential significance of the data for humans.

Regulatory Requirements in Different Countries for Toxicology Testing

Differences between countries are sometimes based on political or social rather than scientific considerations. Unfortunate experiences with a medicine or class of medicines can be the source of some of these differences. For most countries except Japan there are relatively minor differences between toxicology requirements. Japanese requirements are identified more precisely and are itemized in greater detail than in other countries. In some situations a study or two may have to be redone or added by a sponsor to provide additional information required for a Japanese regulatory submission.

Differences in toxicology requirements among countries include (1) the number of studies to be done as part of a regulatory submission, (2) the type of studies to be done, (3) the design of each study (e.g., duration of treatment, manner of feeding animals, parameters to be measured), and (4) the rate at which studies must be conducted during the medicine development process. For example, if a study to evaluate a medicine in humans for three months is to be conducted as part of a Phase II clinical plan, the regulatory requirement for a specified duration of already completed toxicology studies to support the safety of the human study varies between countries.

Decisions of regulatory agencies in requesting or recommending (but not requiring) toxicology studies are often questioned by pharmaceutical companies on the basis of scientific rationale. Nonetheless, most companies comply with all regulatory requests for studies from those agencies that are considered less flexible. Some regulatory requests appear to be based not on science but on either a desire to complete a checklist or obscure reasons.

The development and testing of enantiomers as opposed to racemic mixtures is currently more of an issue in several European countries than in the United States.

Companies are now evaluating plasma levels in all or almost all of the relevant toxicology studies, whereas this was seldom done during the 1980s. Communications between toxicology professionals and those in metabolism groups is extremely important to plan, conduct and interpret results of studies most effectively. The subject of plasma level evaluation in toxicology studies has generally not been a contentious regulatory issue as companies understand the benefits for them and usually are pleased to measure these plasma levels.

Regulatory Requirements in Different Countries for Mutagenicity Testing

One of the current issues in toxicology concerns different regulatory requirements and guidelines for mutagenicity testing. Mutagenicity tests are short-term tests that are thought useful by some people to predict the carcinogenic potential of compounds. These tests are hotly debated as to their relevance for predicting a medicine's carcinogenic potential (Clive, 1987). The major problem is that a high rate of false-positive results is obtained with some of the most widely used *in vitro* tests. This means that, although a medicine may be found to be a mutagen in one or more tests, it may later be found not to cause cancer in laboratory animals. Tests to evaluate cancer in animals involve dosing animals for approximately two years and are considered a more reliable indicator than mutagenicity tests as to a medicine's potential to cause a cancer in humans.

One of the major reasons for requiring mutagenicity tests at an early stage of a medicine's development is to better protect normal volunteers and patients exposed to the medicine. Because carcinogenic studies are often not initiated until after a medicine's efficacy is demonstrated, demonstrating that a medicine is inactive in mutagenicity tests is believed by some to reduce the likelihood that patients in clinical trials are being given a carcinogenic medicine. Some patients might receive long-term treatment with a mutagenic medicine if this property is not evaluated at an early stage of medicine development. On the other hand, the significance of this point is often unknown and, because the false-positive rate for demonstrating mutagenicity is relatively high, a more likely consequence is that potentially useful medicines are dropped unnecessarily.

One of the counterarguments for conducting long-term (i.e., two-year) carcinogenicity studies focuses on the fact that most medicine-induced cancers are observed rather early in the course of lifetime carcinogenicity bioassays, usually within the first 6 or 12 months. Some people believe that a shorter period of medicine testing than two years could be used to assess medicine safety in animals (Walker and Dayan, 1986).

The FDA does not *require* that any mutagenicity tests be conducted to have a new medicine approved. It may, however, either *request* or *recommend* that certain specific mutagenicity tests or a general battery of such tests be performed. Because of the requirements for mutagenicity testing outside the United States, most American-based pharmaceutical companies routinely conduct such tests, and almost all medicines approved by the FDA have data from some of these tests.

The European Economic Community (EEC) does *require* a battery of mutagenicity tests to be performed. They have established various categories of tests and allow each company to choose the specific tests it desires to conduct from each of the separate categories. Requirements in Japan are even more extensive. Their attitude appears to be a desire to identify the dose that causes mutagenic effects and to describe these effects, rather than to test medicines in such tests at reasonable multiples of the actual human dose. Thus, their emphasis appears to be on characterizing a medicine's toxicity rather than testing for its safety. This difference is important to consider when observing how different regulatory agencies interpret safety data.

MUTAGENICITY ISSUES

Categorization of Mutagenicity Tests

One categorization of mutagenicity tests includes evaluations of the following three situations.

1. *Point mutations* (i.e., single gene mutations that are undetectable microscopically). These are usually eval-

uated in bacteria. This is most frequently evaluated using the well-known Ames test.
2. *Chromosomal breakage in vitro.*
3. *Chromosomal breakdown in whole animals.*

The assumption is made that, if a medicine causes chromosomal breakage, then future generations of cells may be abnormal. A major issue is how extensive chromosome repair is in humans and what role it can play in reversing chromosomal damage. Unfortunately, little information is currently known about chromosomal repair.

Selected Issues Involving Mutagenicity Tests

Each compound must be tested separately in mutagenicity tests because two compounds with similar chemical structures may yield entirely different results. Chemicals with similar structures may have opposite potencies as mutagens and carcinogens. This makes it difficult to extrapolate mutagenicity data to humans. Even if a medicine is positive in both mutagenicity and carcinogenicity tests, it may not be concluded that the same mechanism is involved.

Assume that a new metabolite is discovered in human studies late in a medicine's development and that the metabolite is present in relatively large amounts. If large amounts of this metabolite were present in the animal species evaluated, then its toxicological profile would be known. If this metabolite was not present in the animal species evaluated for the long-term toxicological effects of the parent medicine, its toxicological profile would not be established and a difficult situation could arise. One question is whether new mutagenicity tests must be performed. The new compound may have to be tested in several mutagenicity tests to register the parent medicine in EEC countries, whereas these tests might not be required in the United States.

Given the possibility of a false-positive response in mutagenicity tests, would it be worthwhile at this relatively late date for a company to conduct these tests? Would it be preferable to conduct the more predictive (and much longer) carcinogenicity studies instead? The risks of a false-positive result would be to (1) give strong ammunition to any competitors, (2) delay launch of the medicine, and (3) put an albatross, perhaps permanently, around the medicine's neck. Of course, some regulators might not require mutagenicity testing of all metabolites formed, especially if small amounts of the compound were present in animals that were part of the carcinogenicity studies or if the company committed itself to conduct new carcinogenicity studies on the metabolite. Many options exist in this scenario, and input must be received from many functions of a company before a decision is reached.

45 / Clinical Trials

Principles and Approaches of Clinical Trials..... **500**
  Types of Clinical Trials........................ 500
  Levels of Clinical Trials....................... 500
  Categories of Clinical Indications 500
  Choosing the Indications to Pursue 500
  How Is a Clinical Question Posed in a Trial? .. 502
  How Many Questions May Be Asked in a
    Single Clinical Trial? 502
  Posing Questions About Adverse Reactions ... 503
  How Are Appropriate Clinical Trials Chosen?. 503
  Other Principles Concerning Clinical Trials ... 505
  Bringing a Patient into a State of Clinical
    Balance: Attempting to Titrate Doses
    During Clinical Trials 508
Medicine Safety **509**
  What Does the Term *Safety* Mean for a New
    or Old Medicine?.......................... 509
  How Rapidly Should a New Medicine Be
    Taken to Humans for Testing? 509
  Sources of Information on Medicine Safety ... 509
  How May One Determine Whether a Specific
    Medicine Caused a Specific Adverse
    Reaction?................................. 510
  Evaluation of Medicine Safety by Regulatory
    Agencies 510
  The Period Between Regulatory Submission
    and Approval 511
Clinical Significance and Statistical Significance **511**
  Situations Where Statistically Significant
    Results Are Not Clinically Significant....... 511

  Situations Where Clinically Significant Results
    Are Not Statistically Significant............ 511
Postmarketing Clinical Studies.................. **511**
  Objectives of Postmarketing Surveillance...... 512
  Methods of Postmarketing Surveillance 512
  Assessing Whether Reported Rates of an
    Adverse Reaction Reflect the True
    Incidence 513
  Regulatory Requirements for Postmarketing
    Surveillance.............................. 513
  Regulatory Requirements for Adverse
    Reaction Reporting 515
  When Should Newly Observed Adverse
    Reactions Be Put in a Medicine's Labeling?. 515
  After Regulatory Approval, Why Does the
    Number of Clinical Trials Usually Stay the
    Same or Even Increase? 515
  Reactions of Pharmaceutical Companies to
    Postmarketing Surveillance Needs 516
  Coordination Between Different Sites
    Conducting Phase IV Trials 516
  Specific Issues of Collecting and Processing
    Adverse Reaction Data.................... 516
  Benefits of Postmarketing Surveillance 517
Quality-of-Life Trials and Issues **517**
  Uses of Quality-of-Life Data 518
  Measures Used to Evaluate Quality of Life 518
  Different Perspectives on Quality of Life 519

The history of medicine has never been a particularly attractive subject in medical education, and one reason for this is that it is so unrelievedly deplorable a story. For century after century, all the way into the remote millennia of its origins, medicine got along by sheer guesswork and the crudest sort of empiricism. It is hard to conceive of a less scientific enterprise among human endeavors. Virtually anything that could be thought up for the treatment of disease was tried out at one time or another, and, once tried, lasted decades or even centuries before being given up. It was, in retrospect, the most frivolous and irresponsible kind of human experimentation, based on nothing but trial and error, and usually resulting in precisely that sequence. Bleeding, purging, cupping, the administration of infusions of every known plant, solutions of every known metal, every conceivable diet including total fasting, most of these based on the weirdest imagines about the cause of disease, concocted out of nothing but thin air—this was the heritage of medicine up until a little over a century ago. Dr. Lewis Thomas. American physician and essayist. From *The Medusa and the Snail.*

PRINCIPLES AND APPROACHES OF CLINICAL TRIALS

Types of Clinical Trials

Although numerous classifications have been proposed about how to categorize clinical trials, they are generally similar. *Safety* trials are discussed in this chapter, and in fact all clinical trials contain some safety considerations, even if safety per se is not an objective of the trial. The other major category is *efficacy,* which usually is evaluated during Phases II and III. Other categories of clinical trials include *pharmacokinetics* (absorption, distribution, metabolism, and excretion), *pharmacoeconomics, compliance,* and *quality of life.*

Levels of Clinical Trials

Different sets or levels of clinical trials exist. Five discrete levels of clinical trials are shown in Fig. 45.1. A number of sublevels of each of these levels are also indicated. These levels and sublevels may be used to understand the types of clinical trials. Any particular clinical trial will be a part of multiple levels and may be viewed from different perspectives. This is especially important to consider when data from different trials are compared and possibly combined.

This book cannot go into detail about the design and conduct of a single clinical trial, the interpretation of data resulting from clinical trials, or the planning and management of multiple clinical trials. Readers who desire this information are referred to the *Guide to Clinical Trials* (Spilker, 1991). That book focuses on Level 1 of Fig. 45.1, although numerous examples are given from all levels. Many books are written about methods, data, or medicine treatment at Levels 3 and 4. There are few references of practical information on clinical methods at Level 2 (see Spilker, 1991 for an example). This chapter presents general concepts and principles relating to clinical trials for individuals who seek an overview of this field.

Categories of Clinical Indications

Virtually all medicines are evaluated for activity in more than one indication (i.e., disease or medical problem). For any medicine this usually occurs sequentially for some diseases and simultaneously for others, although a company may decide to test numerous indications for a medicine either sequentially or simultaneously. In planning the clinical development for a medicine it is important to develop a strategy of how the medicine's activity (i.e., efficacy) will be determined in terms of timing of trials and order of regulatory submissions. This is done for each indication of interest. This strategy is a critically important decision in terms of how a medicine is to be developed. This decision is usually made before the medicine has been studied in humans, even though it may be revised at later times. To assist in this effort, the possible indications to test may be divided or categorized into several groups. One such categorization is listed below.

1. Indications already included in the labeling of a comparable marketed medicine
2. Indications that have been submitted to a regulatory agency, for either a marketed or investigational medicine
3. Indications that are currently being evaluated where efficacy is established and there is a firm intention to submit a regulatory application
4. Indications being evaluated for an investigational medicine where efficacy has not yet been well established, for which a regulatory application is planned to be submitted if safety, efficacy, and other data are acceptable
5. Indications that will be evaluated in pilot trials when time and resources permit
6. Potential indications that may be evaluated in the future
7. Indications for which regulatory approval will not be sought, but where clinical publications are desired.

This same type of categorization could be devised for various routes of administration and/or dosage forms of a medicine.

After the categorization is complete, it is possible to prioritize the order in which each specific indication will be pursued and to begin to allocate resources appropriately to pursue this effort. The overall plan may be only to choose one indication, one route of administration, and one dosage form and not to deviate from the first human exposure until the New Drug Application (NDA) is filed. This has been referred to as a laser approach (Spilker, 1991). Few medicines follow such a highly targeted path. Most medicines either initially start out with multiple indications being pursued or start out with a single indication and gradually accumulate more indications over time. Different visual models of these (and other) approaches are shown in Fig. 17.4.

Choosing the Indications to Pursue

Different groups of people within a pharmaceutical company often have different perspectives and opinions on this issue. Scientists usually approach the question mainly from a scientific value point of view. Marketing personnel emphasize commercial aspects. Clinicians consider patient need and the therapeutic utility of a potential new medicine. All three views may be in concert, but disagreements and disputes sometimes arise. For example, both marketers and scientists may be enthusiastic

LEVELS OF CLINICAL TRIALS

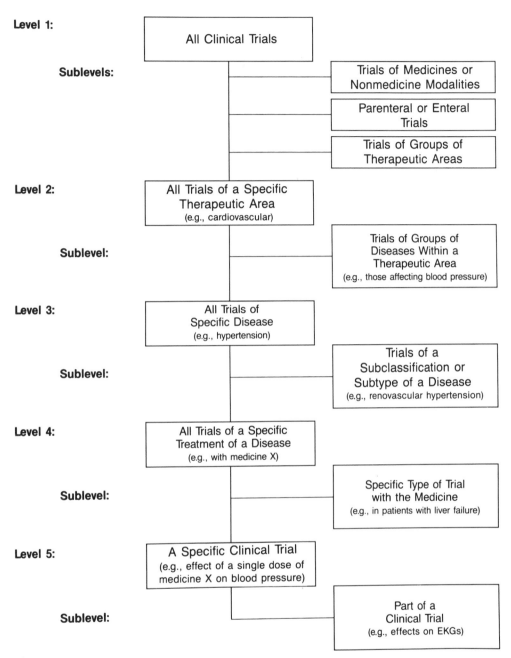

FIG. 45.1. Levels and sublevels of clinical trials.

about pursuing a new medicine to treat chicken pox in children. But the pharmaceutical company's clinicians probably realize that practicing physicians are unlikely to prescribe a new medicine for most children with mild cases of chicken pox because (1) the disease is self-limiting, (2) the risk-to-benefit ratio for using the medicine in children does not mandate that the disease must be treated, (3) the disease often is either not diagnosed or misdiagnosed in children, and (4) it would be necessary to prove that children treated with the medicine prophylactically developed long-term immunity that was at least the same as that obtained after the disease. This is necessary because chicken pox is often a much more serious disease when it occurs initially in adulthood.

At some companies the indications that are pursued are primarily selected by senior research and development managers, while at other companies medical personnel have this responsibility. It is important to develop each new medicine according to a broad plan that is appropriately reviewed and accepted. Some clinical staff may spend a significant amount of time planning unauthorized trials or evaluating entire indications that lie outside the approved plan. This is usually done in the hope that they will be able to eventually convince relevant managers that the indication of interest to them is worthwhile to develop or should be evaluated at an earlier point in the medicine's development. This practice should be strongly discouraged because it destroys the resource allocation system and encourages individuals to go in their own direction.

Another approach is to develop a list of factors affecting the choice of indication and assign either numerical scores to each or at least qualitatively evaluate (e.g., little importance, great importance) each factor. Those with the highest scores would be chosen for development.

How Is a Clinical Question Posed in a Trial?

The way in which a clinical question is specifically worded in the protocol (detailed outline of the clinical trial) greatly influences the design of the trial that will be conducted to answer the question. The question posed is called the trial's *objective* and is the major purpose for conducting the trial. For example, when developing a new antihypertensive medicine, many different questions are asked at various stages of the medicine's development. Initial questions in Phase I relate to a medicine's safety, but in Phase II questions of efficacy become more important. To illustrate this point, I list two of the questions that could be the major objective of a trial and relate to efficacy, along with a few comments on an appropriate trial design chosen.

1. *What doses of the medicine cause a lowering of blood pressure by 8 to 15 mm Hg for one month?* A trial testing several doses of the medicine would be conducted in patients treated for a month after they had been screened, enrolled in the trial, had other medicines removed, gone through a baseline period, and then had the medicine's dose gradually raised to a stable level. One or more control groups could be included. Patients in a control group would usually receive a placebo or a different active medicine.

2. *Is the blood pressure–lowering effect of the medicine the same for patients who are treated twice a day as for those who receive the same total dose divided into four individual doses per day?* A trial would be conducted comparing effects of two similar groups of patients given the two different dosage regimens. It is possible that, at the end of a specific period of time, each patient would be switched to alternate treatment. If the trial was to be double-blind, then each patient would take medicine four times a day, but those on the twice-a-day regimen would take the active medicine twice a day and a placebo

twice a day. This would either require a special packaging of the medicine (e.g., blister pack where each day's dose is labeled) or the use of two different bottles of medicines. The blister pack method is easier for patients to use and would most likely enhance their compliance. A different trial design using a separate group of patients for each regimen could also be used.

During Phase III and IV trials more sophisticated questions could be posed. For example, how many years of antihypertensive treatment are required to prolong life for one year? Do patients who receive antihypertensive medicine treatment live longer than patients who do not take medicine therapy? These examples help illustrate that the trial design chosen depends on the question asked and that it is necessary to phrase a trial's objectives as precisely as possible.

How Many Questions May Be Asked in a Single Clinical Trial?

There is a strong temptation when designing a clinical trial to ask too many questions. Because it is possible to design a trial that asks numerous questions, many people from fields outside of medicine (e.g., science, marketing) believe that it is better to conduct a single large trial to answer many questions, rather than conducting a series of trials (which may or may not be smaller in size) but only ask one question each. This desire is like the siren luring Ulysses. It is an alluring prospect but will probably lead to serious problems and could lead to a medicine's destruction on the rocky shore. Others may see this issue as deciding whether to gamble the medicine's future on a large, risky trial that will save development time if it works, rather than being more conservative and conducting several smaller trials that will require more time to complete. It is often necessary to conduct several small trials, and this is usually a more sound approach to medicine development.

When a number of factors are varied in a single trial, the specific reason for a particular clinical outcome is often unclear. For example, assume that two important factors are changed in a trial of an active medicine. Also assume that the new clinical results do not demonstrate that the medicine worked. Then, it is usually uncertain as to which of the two factors was responsible for the failure to demonstrate medicine activity. As an illustration, if an investigational medicine was shown to be effective when a 500-mg dose was given four times a day, it might be important to learn if a 300-mg dose would be active and also if dosing patients twice a day would be effective. A trial that evaluated a 300-mg dose given twice a day could be designed and conducted. If the medicine was inactive, however, it would not be known whether the loss of activity was because the dose was lowered from 500 to 300 mg or because the frequency of dosing was lowered from four to two times a day (or both). This simple example illustrates how critical it is to design clinical trials that do not attempt to accomplish too many objectives.

The example given is similar to a situation that occurs thousands of times every day when patients visit their physicians. Assume that a patient is taking a medicine that is not working effectively or is causing adverse reactions. The physician may alter several parameters at once and hope that the patient's situation will improve. These parameters could include adding a new medicine, stopping the main medicine, changing the dose of the main medicine, changing the dose of a concomitant medicine that may be interacting with the main medicine, changing the patient's diet or level of physical activity, and so forth. If the patient improves, it is usually unclear which specific change or combination was responsible. If the patient does not improve, it is still possible that only making a single change would have led to improvement. Further, if an unexpected outcome occurs, then it will be totally unclear as to which factor(s) are responsible. On the other hand, it is usually extremely difficult for a physician (unlike a scientist) to change only one parameter at a time. Patients are often unwilling to return each week as the physician slowly evaluates many possibilities over a period of months, although this situation does occur when an allergist seeks to identify an offending allergen. A balance between these extremes must be sought.

Posing Questions About Adverse Reactions

Within medical departments, important questions often relate to the objectives of a clinical trial. The way a trial is eventually designed, conducted, and analyzed relates to that question. If the most appropriate question to ask is not posed, then the best data and answers are usually not achieved. A brief example will illustrate this point. The phrasing of each of the following nine questions about a medicine's adverse reactions would influence the trial design chosen to answer that question.

1. What types of adverse reactions does Medicine X cause?
2. Did Medicine X cause Adverse Reaction Y in Patient Z?
3. Does Medicine X cause Adverse Reaction Y in patients with Type Z disease?
4. What types of adverse reactions does Medicine X cause in Patient Population A?
5. Does the route of administration affect the adverse reactions caused by Medicine X?
6. Does the dosage form of Medicine X affect the type (or number) of adverse reactions it causes?
7. Does Medicine X cause more adverse reactions than does Medicine C?
8. Does Medicine X cause more serious adverse reactions than does Medicine C?
9. Does Medicine X cause more serious adverse reactions of Type H than does Medicine C?

Many other variations on this theme could be listed. It is apparent that the trial designs needed to address these questions would focus primarily on the types of patients chosen, the types of treatment given, and/or the types of adverse reactions expected to be observed.

How Are Appropriate Clinical Trials Chosen?

A few basic approaches primarily determine the types of clinical trials conducted and designs used. These include the following approaches for new medicines.

1. Determine the type of labeling desired. This includes identifying the specific indications to be targeted. This points the project in a certain direction in terms of the type of evidence and clinical trials needed to obtain the required data.
2. Determine how many indications, dosage forms, and routes of administration are desired in the first group of regulatory submissions. Evaluate the total amount of suitable resources available and the priority of the medicine compared with others in the company's portfolio to determine the amount of resources to be allocated to its development.
3. Determine the types and amount of data needed to get a medicine approved. This includes consideration of the patient population(s) to be studied. Then work backward to determine each of the clinical trials needed. Certain assumptions are usually made, such as the necessity in most instances to conduct two well-controlled trials for each indication desired.

Each of these three approaches is logical and allows a clinical plan to be developed that proceeds from one's current position to the goal (i.e., regulatory approval). Not all companies pursue this type of systematic and logical medicine development. Some companies initially sponsor academic-type clinical trials (e.g., mechanism of action) or focus on pharmacokinetic trials at an early stage. Others approach trial designs in a random manner or follow another pattern (see Figs. 45.2 and 3.6). The number of medicines "developed" in this inappropriate manner is diminishing. When a choice of trial designs or approaches to medicine development exists, it is usually preferable to conduct a few large trials rather than many small ones. This does not mean that many questions should be posed in each trial, but it does mean that an adequate number of patients should be enrolled to achieve sufficient power to detect an effect if one is present. Some people, however, seem to have a talent for asking clinical questions that lead them to pursue tangents, and only belatedly (or never) can they achieve

SELECTED APPROACHES TO CLINICAL MEDICINE DEVELOPMENT

A. Focused Approach

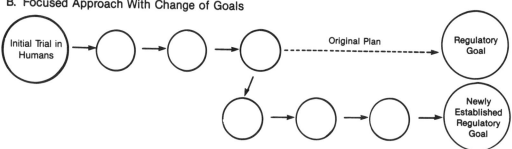

B. Focused Approach With Change of Goals

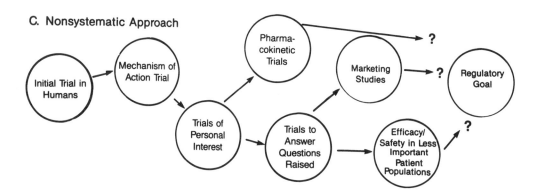

C. Nonsystematic Approach

D. Nonfocused, Broad-Front Approach

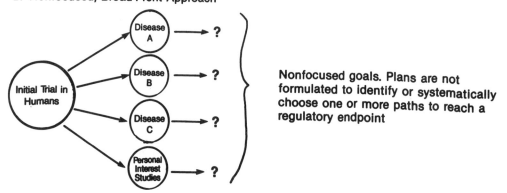

FIG. 45.2. Selected approaches to clinical medicine development. Goals are defined in terms of indications, formulations, populations, and other factors.

TABLE 45.1. *Selected means to increase the rate of clinical medicine development*

1. Increase the number of patients in each trial
2. Increase the number of sites conducting each trial
3. Increase the number of trials conducted simultaneously
4. Reduce the bottlenecks and rate-limiting steps that are slowing the medicine's progress
5. Initiate trials evaluating additional indications
6. Reduce all periods of administrative delays as much as possible (e.g., period between protocol completion and submission to the Ethics Committee/IRB,[a] period between Ethics Committee/IRB completion, shipment of medicine, and initiation of the trial)

[a] IRB, Institutional Review Board.

their goals. Methods that may be used to speed a clinical program are listed in Table 45.1.

A series of clinical trials may be necessary to evaluate the best way to give a medicine (e.g., once or three times per day), the best dose of a medicine to give, and the specific type of patients who will respond best (e.g., those with mild versus severe forms of the disease, those with or without certain complications, those with specific subtypes of the disease). With some medicines it is also necessary to determine if the therapeutic effect is related to the peak blood level of the medicine, the total dose given, the duration of treatment, or some other factor. If patients included in an early clinical trial evaluating one of these (or other) questions are not appropriate, problems may arise that will literally terminate a medicine's development. Thus, caution must be used in choosing how rapidly to permit a medicine to be developed. At the same time, a medicine's development must not be delayed unnecessarily.

Medicines that have numerous indications and dosage forms under development simultaneously have them in various stages at one time. One means of illustrating the status of various activities is shown in Fig. 45.3.

Other Principles Concerning Clinical Trials

1. Humans clearly exhibit great variability in their responses to medicines, and, unfortunately (in some ways), clinical trials cannot be controlled as well as animal trials. Many important factors cannot be adequately controlled in most trials. This is especially true in outpatient trials where the patients' diets, exercise regimens, and amounts of stress vary and their compliance with the protocol cannot be assured.

2. Pilot efficacy trials conducted early in Phase II have a high likelihood of yielding positive data if they are not well controlled. This may lead a company to believe that an inactive or only marginally active medicine is much better than it really is. This in turn could easily lead a company on a wild goose chase costing substantial money and wasting time and effort of valuable staff who

are not available for more productive work. The best method to avoid this problem is to design well-controlled pilot trials, although enrolling only a small number of patients in each. *One of the most important clinical principles is that good data in a few patients are far better than mediocre or poor data in many patients.* Although this sounds rational and makes good business and good medical sense, it is apparent that many companies do not adhere to this principle.

3. Patients with chronic relapsing or cyclic diseases often enter clinical trials when their disease is at its worst. These patients tend to improve, regardless of whether or not they have been treated with medicines. The statistical name for this phenomenon is regression toward the mean. This is only one of many pitfalls to avoid (or control for) in designing clinical trials. The most common means of controlling this factor is to have a placebo group or no-treatment group of patients. This phenomenon would not apply to patients with a chronic progressive disease (e.g., metastatic cancer).

4. All clinical trials should clearly and fully state the purpose(s) or objective(s) in the protocol. The protocol describes the objective(s) of the trial and the means whereby the objective(s) are to be addressed and hopefully answered. Even the interpretation of clinical data is related to how the objectives were stated and the trial designed.

5. It is unacceptable to change the clinical endpoint on which the success of a trial is based after a trial is complete. It is also unacceptable to change endpoints during a trial, especially if the change is based on results of an interim analysis. Many analyses are sometimes conducted looking for a positive result that was not originally part of a trial's objectives. This is called *data dredging.* An analysis of a new measurement or parameter may be made after the trial, however, to form a hypothesis that may be tested in a subsequent trial.

6. Pharmaceutical companies usually spend a great deal of time and energy polishing clinical protocols to the point where they are internally consistent and sparkle like a gem. Unfortunately, in almost all situations, the quality of clinical trials is far from perfect in the way in which they are conducted because of difficulties in controlling human behavior and clinical exigencies that arise. It is rare when a trial totally follows the protocol, although pharmacokinetic trials often approach or may achieve this ideal. There is, therefore, a point of diminishing returns for a company in the amount of time and effort that should be spent fine-tuning the niceties of each protocol's details, when the details are not able to be (or could be but are not) followed in practice. On the other hand, multiple reviews of clinical protocols are necessary to eliminate flaws that might destroy the value of a trial. Also, if all relevant measures are not included in a protocol it could become necessary to repeat the entire trial at a later date. This could relate to as simple a point

FLOW OF A MEDICINE'S DOSAGE FORMS FOR VARIOUS INDICATIONS THROUGH THE MEDICINE DEVELOPMENT PIPELINE

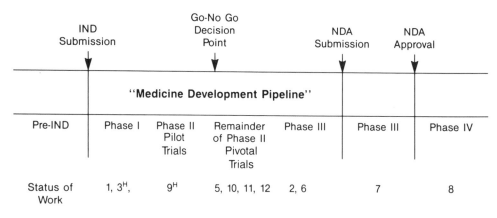

	Pre-IND	Phase I	Phase II Pilot Trials	Remainder of Phase II Pivotal Trials	Phase III	Phase III	Phase IV
Status of Work		1, 3^H,	9^H	5, 10, 11, 12	2, 6	7	8

H = On Hold

CURRENT STATUS OF ACTIVITIES

Indications Being Studied (A to E)

Dosage Form Being Studied		A	B	C	D	E
	Oral	1^a		2		3
	Solution	4	5	6		
	Transdermal Patch				7	
	Cream				8	9
	Depot	10	11			12

^{a} The numbers refer to the diagram above.

FIG. 45.3. Planning and tracking the indications and dosage forms studied. The go-no go decision point refers primarily to efficacy. Safety is an ongoing consideration. The *numbers* to the right of "Status of Work" refer to the exact indication and dosage forms being studied, as shown in the chart below. The numbers are placed under the stage they are at the pipeline. *IND,* Investigational New Drug Application; *NDA,* New Drug Application. Trial designs change from phase to phase (Spilker, 1987a).

as measuring a specific blood test to evaluate renal function at the start and end of a trial.

7. More and more protocols at pharmaceutical companies are written by nonphysicians. These people usually lack clinical experience and do not understand what is reasonable to request of a patient in different clinical situations. For example, they often request far too many blood draws and too frequent requests for information from the patient. Although nonphysicians may be well-trained clinical scientists, their scientific expertise should be complemented by the clinical expertise of a physician. Their protocols should therefore be carefully reviewed by experienced physicians.

8. A company may place a great amount of resources on clinical trials, to speed its development program. As a result, the company may outstrip its ability to (1) produce the medicine, (2) complete toxicological trials, (3) complete technical development work, or (4) solve other medicine development problems. This means that an overall coordinated effort is necessary to complete all work in a timely manner. Rushing to complete one part of a development program may be wasteful and nonproductive if other areas are being delayed or are progressing at a much slower pace.

9. All clinical trials that last more than a week or two require a great deal of effort to maintain staff enthusiasm and morale at sites where the trials are being conducted. It has been said that investigators are like radioisotopes because their interest decays with time. Also, unlike fine wines, most medicine trials do not improve with age.

PATIENT RECRUITMENT AND PARTICIPATION IN A CLINICAL TRIAL

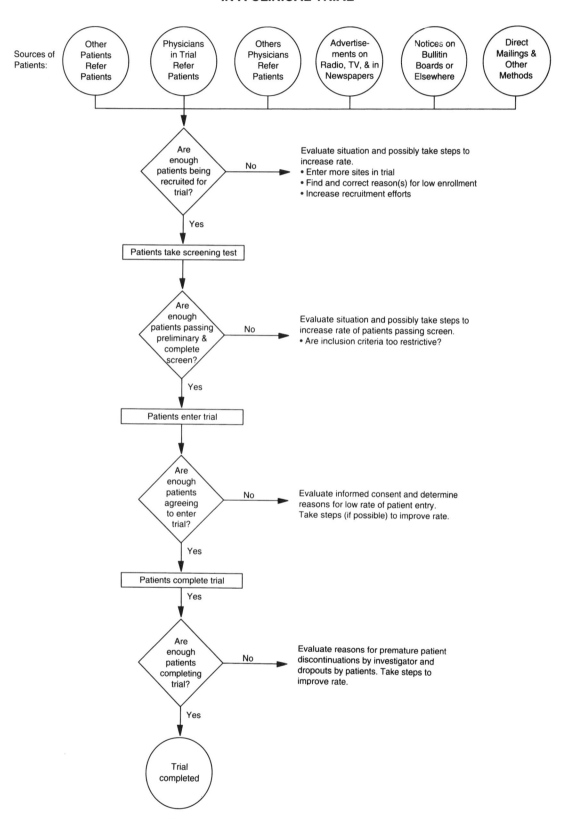

FIG. 45.4. Patient participation in clinical trials.

Therefore, careful thought and attention must be given to this aspect of clinical trials, which is described in more detail in the *Guide to Clinical Trials* (Spilker, 1991).

10. Recruitment of patients is a major issue in almost all clinical trials. The steps usually involved in patient recruitment and participation are shown in Fig. 45.4. Investigators almost always promise that more patients will enter their trial than they are able to actually enroll. This is so well known that it has led to the phenomenon called *Lasagna's Law* (Fig. 45.5), named after Dr. Louis Lasagna, Dean of Tufts University Medical School. For details see Spilker and Cramer (1992).

11. Important clinical trials to conduct from a scientific or medical perspective are sometimes not important trials to conduct from a medicine development perspective. If a company's objective is to market a new medicine as rapidly as possible, then the former group of academically oriented trials are usually an undesirable diversion to this goal, especially during Phases I and II. In addition, these academically oriented trials may raise questions or problems that must be addressed if the trials are inappropriately designed, conducted, or analyzed. Even if the questions or issues raised are legitimate, they

are often inappropriate to address at an early stage of a medicine's development. On the other hand, those trials are often extremely important to conduct during Phase III, after a medicine's efficacy has been established and it is known that the medicine will be marketed.

Bringing a Patient into a State of Clinical Balance: Attempting to Titrate Doses During Clinical Trials

A patient's physical (or emotional) condition is sometimes analogous to a pendulum. Patients usually visit a physician when something has gone too far out of balance. The physician wants to improve a patient's symptom(s) or reduce a risk factor. For example, if a patient has diarrhea, it is necessary to tighten his stools and to decrease the frequency of bowel movements. If a patient's blood sugar is high, then it must be lowered. Too much of an appropriate medicine in such patients, however, often causes too great an effect (i.e., constipation in the former patient or low blood sugar in the latter patient). Therefore, physicians often increase a medicine's dose relatively slowly (i.e., the dose is titrated upward

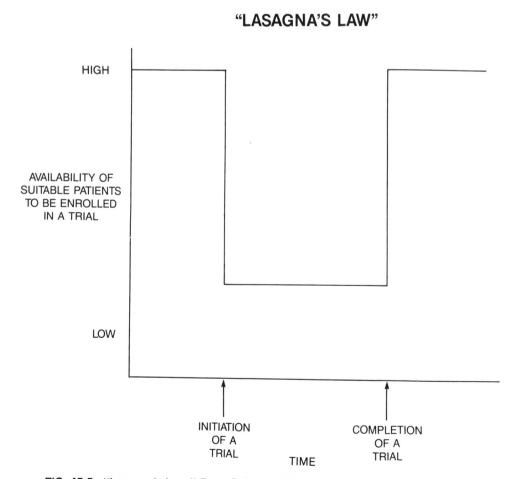

"LASAGNA'S LAW"

FIG. 45.5. "Lasagna's Law." From Spilker (1991) with permission of Raven Press.

until the desired effect is obtained). If adverse reactions occur, then the dose is often titrated downward in the hope that the adverse reaction will disappear while the clinical benefit remains.

These same principles apply when many patients are treated during clinical trials. Although it is possible to evaluate the effects of a fixed dose in patients, it often makes more sense to titrate a dose to a given clinical endpoint (e.g., absence of pain), biochemical endpoint (e.g., decrease in cholesterol in the blood by 15%), or another type of endpoint (e.g., pharmacological, pathological).

MEDICINE SAFETY

What Does the Term *Safety* Mean for a New or Old Medicine?

Safety is a relative concept that involves a great deal of judgment. It is relative in that some medicines are safer than others and there is a gradient from medicines that are generally considered safe to those that are generally considered unsafe (i.e., toxic). Safety is a relative concept in another way as well. Over a period of time, more and more information is collected and understood about a particular medicine, and therefore a greater proportion of the safety profile is understood. Before a medicine is tested in humans, little is known with certainty about its safety in humans, although some reasonable guesses can generally be based on animal experiments. After a medicine has been marketed for many years, most of the important information about its safety is known. But for every medicine there is always a chance that unknown toxicities will emerge and alter the benefit-to-risk ratio of using the medicine.

Safety is also a relative concept in a third way. A medicine that is intended to treat a life-threatening disease for which no adequate therapy is available (e.g., acquired immune deficiency syndrome [AIDS] in 1985) may be relatively toxic and still be acceptable. The extent of toxicity acceptable would relate to the benefit-to-risk ratio.

Complete safety information is never known on any medicine for several reasons. First, new adverse reactions may always emerge that are currently unknown. This is expected for adverse reactions that may result from interactions with future medicines or from changes in the natural history of the disease being treated. Second, some toxicities take many years to develop (e.g., thyroid cancer in people who received radiation of their neck 20 to 30 years before). Third, toxicities may not directly occur in patients exposed to a medicine but may affect a later generation (e.g., vaginal precancerous and cancerous lesions occurred in young women born to mothers who used diethylstilbestrol 20 or so years before). Fourth, the absence of an adverse reaction after a

medicine is used in many patients may be because the adverse reaction occurs rarely and has not been detected or it may indicate that the medicine does not cause that adverse reaction. It is also possible that the medicine causes the adverse reaction but, because the problem is relatively common anyway, there is no way to detect the additional cases caused by the medicine. For example, if a medicine caused lung cancer in 1 out of 1,000 patients, it would be almost impossible to detect this problem in humans in most situations. The reassuring answer is that toxicology trials would be used to detect this problem and have a reasonably good chance of observing it.

How Rapidly Should a New Medicine Be Taken to Humans for Testing?

Table 27.4 presents reasons to move new compounds into humans rapidly and Table 27.3 presents reasons to move more slowly. Counterarguments are also given. The correct response to arguments presented in these two tables is that each situation is different and no single approach is always correct. For companies that have a relatively large number of existing medicines under development, higher overall standards should be applied before adopting new compounds for eventual human testing. For a company that has few potentially exciting medicines under development and has underutilized resources, relatively lower standards should be applied. On the other hand, a company that has promising medicines under development should not raise its standards even higher for newer candidates. These compounds require relatively little effort or money for their early development. They may replace other medicines which fall by the wayside or may even be licensed to another company under certain conditions. The number of medicines to test simultaneously is discussed in Chapter 33, Choosing the Number of Medicines to Develop.

Sources of Information on Medicine Safety

Information on medicine safety comes from human trials, patient experience, and toxicological trials conducted in animals. From the medical perspective, animal data provide information of *potential* safety problems for humans, whereas data from humans, even though they are often imperfect, usually provide *actual* evidence of safety problems. To improve understanding of medicine risks, one must use both actual and potential sources of data. Thus, a medicine's safety profile is based on both human and animal data. The extrapolation of animal data to humans is described in Chapter 25, Extrapolating Animal Safety Data to Humans.

It is unfortunate and often tragic when patients overdose themselves intentionally. Nonetheless, a great deal of valuable information about a medicine's safety profile is often obtained in this way. Information is obtained about (1) manifestations of a medicine's toxicity, (2) methods for its diagnosis, and (3) techniques for patient treatment. This information is also sometimes obtained through unintentional overdose of patients. For example, if a patient has an unsuspected genetic deficiency and cannot metabolize a medicine, the medicine levels may build up and cause toxicity. Also, a patient may misunderstand directions and take too much of a medicine, the physician may prescribe too high a dose, or an interaction may occur with another medicine that leads to medicine accumulation and a toxic event.

After all the safety data on a medicine are obtained and analyzed, the risk to a human patient taking the medicine must be estimated. This risk may be clear; if not, further trials and discussions are usually warranted.

How May One Determine Whether a Specific Medicine Caused a Specific Adverse Reaction?

Innumerable problems and complexities are associated with establishing the connection between a medicine and an adverse reaction that the medicine may have caused. Sometimes it is not even easy to identify what is the adverse reaction (Fig. 45.6). All unwanted responses resulting from a medicine are defined as adverse reactions, even if they occur in a sort of chain reaction where one leads to another (e.g., orthostatic hypotension may lead to fainting on standing). Medical problems resulting from nonmedicine events are not considered adverse reactions, even if indirectly caused by the medicine. This means that neck pain experienced after an automobile accident is not an adverse reaction, although the accident may have resulted in part from a medicine-induced sedation.

Factors that may complicate the association of a medicine with a particular adverse reaction include (1) the natural progression and changes of the patient's disease, (2) other medicines the patient is taking, and (3) other diseases the patient has. Once these issues are sorted out, then there are a whole host of additional factors relating to the patient or medicine which may have played a major role in affecting the occurrence or severity of the adverse reaction. A few of these include the patient's age, sex, and genetic makeup as well as the medicine's dose, formulation, and age.

Even after all of these issues are completely sorted out (which rarely happens), there is often little assurance that the medicine actually caused the adverse reaction. Additional evidence that favors the association is obtained from answers to two specific questions: (1) if the medicine was stopped, did the adverse reaction improve? and (2) if the medicine was subsequently restarted, did the adverse reaction reappear? This latter technique is called rechallenge, and data from such trials usually provide the best information that a specific medicine caused a specific adverse reaction. Nonetheless, it is often impractical and in many situations it is unethical to consider conducting a rechallenge. Discussions with the patient, physician, and the Ethics Committee or IRB are required before a rechallenge is attempted.

Some companies use algorithms to answer the question of whether a specific medicine caused an adverse reaction. Many have been proposed, but they are not considered reliable by most people. Readers interested in more information on this topic should refer to *Monitoring for Drug Safety* (Inman, 1986) and *Guide to Clinical Trials* (Spilker, 1991).

Evaluation of Medicine Safety by Regulatory Agencies

There are no standard acceptable guidelines for regulatory agencies to use in evaluating a new medicine's safety. It has been proposed that evidence of safety (and efficacy as well) could be assessed by a group of independent clinical pharmacologists and other specialists. Their judgment would serve as the basis for the government's evaluation.

IDENTIFYING THE ADVERSE REACTION

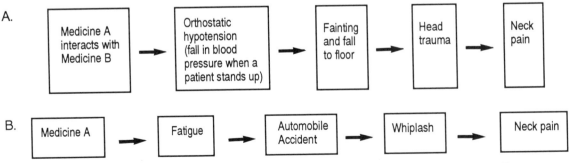

FIG. 45.6. Identifying the adverse reaction. The *arrow* means "causes" or "leads to."

To some degree this is presently being done by the Food and Drug Administration (FDA) when they convene their Advisory Committees. On the other hand, these panels function strictly in an advisory capacity and the FDA has no mandate to accept their conclusions. Because the FDA is carefully scrutinized by many governmental and nongovernmental groups, they have become overly cautious in most instances and consider worst-case possibilities to a greater degree than is generally deemed appropriate by many outside scientists and clinicians.

The Period Between Regulatory Submission and Approval

Phase III clinical trials continue after an NDA or Product License Application (PLA) is submitted to regulatory authorities. For applications that take several years to review, the period between submittal and approval may generate as much or even more data than had been generated prior to submittal. Because of the additional medicine exposures, the frequency of adverse reactions can usually be better predicted toward the end of this period. Additional patient populations and indications are often also evaluated during this period.

For some medicines this period is the time to establish a compassionate plea protocol. This protocol is intended for patients who do not qualify to enter a clinical trial, who live too far from a trial site, or who otherwise are not able to be placed in a trial. Epidemiological methods may be used to establish a well-designed protocol during this period. The experience with the Phase III compassionate treatment Investigational New Drug Application (IND) for Retrovir (zidovudine) conducted by the Burroughs Wellcome Co. demonstrated that good science and data collection can be achieved in this type of trial. There is no reason why ad hoc distribution schemes without systematic data collection should be used for lifesaving (or other) medicines given on a compassionate basis in Phases II and III.

CLINICAL SIGNIFICANCE AND STATISTICAL SIGNIFICANCE

Data in clinical trials are usually analyzed by statisticians who determine the probability that two treatments (e.g., medicine and placebo) are different. This is the statistical significance of the data. This does not indicate whether the data are also important from a clinical perspective. To determine this, someone who is qualified to make this medical judgment must interpret the data and their statistical analyses. There are situations where data are statistically significant but are not clinically significant (important), and vice versa. Both types of situations are described below.

Situations Where Statistically Significant Results Are Not Clinically Significant

There are innumerable examples of this situation, and they undoubtedly occur in most clinical trials. Examples include obvious situations, such as (1) increases or decreases of three or four beats per minute in mean heart rate in one or more groups of patients or (2) increases or decreases of one and a half breaths per minute in mean respiration frequency in one or more groups of patients.

In various other safety or efficacy parameters, small changes that are not clinically significant are often found to be statistically significant. One reason for this is that many comparisons are usually made and some are statistically significant because of chance alone.

Less obvious examples of this effect include situations where a safety or efficacy parameter's change was unexpected and a group of experts is in agreement that the changes observed are not clinically significant. Numerous examples occur in most trials. Another situation is when it is uncertain as to whether or not the statistically significant change is clinically meaningful. Sometimes it requires additional data from new trials to finally resolve this issue. At other times this issue is never resolved and dangles like a loose thread in the medical literature.

Situations Where Clinically Significant Results Are Not Statistically Significant

One such situation would be in treating an otherwise untreatable disease. In this situation, a clinical result that approached but did not achieve statistical significance could be immensely important clinically.

In many clinical trials where clinically significant data are not statistically significant, better ways to conduct a new trial become apparent. It is also possible that the statistical standards established to define medicine activity were too stringent and that results were significant clinically. Important differences in the second trial's design may be in the (1) choice of parameters, (2) ways and times that parameters are measured, (3) duration of treatment, (4) dose of the medicine, (5) type of patients enrolled, and so forth.

POSTMARKETING CLINICAL STUDIES

Phase IV is the period when a medicine is marketed. Many types of clinical trials occur during Phase IV, including proactive, carefully planned active experimental trials to determine the nature or characteristics of actual medicine use and passive observational surveillance trials. The term *surveillance* implies a sentinel-like watch on medical practice to learn what is happening with a medicine. In informal surveillance trials the world of medical practice is carefully monitored, as with a stethoscope, to learn what is occurring.

Objectives of Postmarketing Surveillance

The primary objectives of postmarketing surveillance are to better evaluate the risk-benefit relationship that must be considered each time a decision is reached to use a medicine as therapy and to protect the public health against unexpected consequences of medicine exposure. More specifically, this is done to (1) gain a better understanding of these events both medically and scientifically to enable patients to be more effectively treated, (2) prevent individual patients from being treated incorrectly, (3) adhere to regulatory requirements, and (4) protect the company from liability in numerous situations. An underlying principle of these trials is that the more a company knows about its own medicines the better it is for the company and for the patient. These objectives are achieved largely by identifying and evaluating the type and frequency of a medicine's adverse reactions.

Postmarketing studies are also conducted to evaluate patient populations that were not specifically studied in premarketing studies (e.g., children, pregnant women) and to evaluate the effects of a medicine on large scale, long-term morbidity and mortality. The company therefore wants to understand the answers to several questions.

1. *Why is the medicine used?* This refers to the indications for which the medicine is used, in terms of disease severity, symptoms, and signs. What is the basis for choosing the medicine in actual practice?

2. *How is the medicine used?* This refers to dosing schedules, duration of treatment, concomitant treatment, and related issues.

3. *In which patients is the medicine used?* What are the demographic characteristics of the patient population in which the medicine is used? Do they have concurrent diseases, or are they using concomitant medicines?

4. *What are the results of the medicine's use?* Companies look at the number of adverse medical events in patients receiving their medicines (and possibly other medicines as a control) to evaluate whether there is an excess number associated with the medicine. It is also possible that unexpected clinical benefits may be observed.

5. *Are the adverse reactions reported really a result of the medicine?* Companies should be able to counter any unjustified associations of their medicines with adverse reactions. They should also understand or be able to determine the true incidence of their medicine's adverse reactions when reports come to their attention via the literature, regulatory agencies, internally received information, or other sources.

Methods of Postmarketing Surveillance

The specific pharmacoepidemiological methods used for any medicine in Phase IV depend on the type of data desired and the most rigorous and cost-effective means of obtaining those data. This means that the approach must be custom designed for each particular medicine and situation. Methods used to conduct postmarketing surveillance include the following.

1. Collecting and analyzing reports of adverse reactions reported spontaneously to the company from all countries where the medicine is sold. These reports come from physicians, pharmaceutical company sales representatives, some national regulatory agencies, subsidiary company offices, and even patients. This group of voluntary reports includes the "1639 Forms" sent by physicians in the United States to the FDA and the "Yellow Card Scheme" sent to the Committee on Safety of Medicines (CSM) in the United Kingdom.

2. Following case reports, formal trials, and other published information reported in the medical literature.

3. Questioning physicians in a local or national area on either an ad hoc or systematic basis about a specific adverse reaction. The United Kingdom is undertaking an important experiment in this context, called Prescription Event Monitoring. This is an example of systematic surveillance.

4. Collecting general information ad hoc from participating hospitals and physicians about a relatively large number of patients treated with a newly available medicine. These data may be collected in a prospective or retrospective manner. No matter how elegant these trials may have been, they are extremely expensive and have generally had a modest return of worthwhile information. This approach is being gradually replaced by use of the automated multipurpose data base described in Point 5 below. Nonetheless, this approach could be valuable and even necessary in certain situations where it is impossible to use a data base and it is necessary to find a specific patient group. It is hoped that regulatory agencies will be selective in their requirement for pharmaceutical companies to conduct such trials on newly approved medicines.

5. Utilizing large multipurpose data bases to address a question of interest formulated as a hypothesis. Multipurpose data bases are automated administrative data bases of large health care plans where data already exist from patients who are members of a group. A major advantage of large automated data bases for postmarketing studies is that patients do not have to be enrolled in a Phase IV trial. Patients are studied who are being treated with the test medicine under usual or current conditions. Examples of such

data bases are in health maintenance organizations (HMOs) (e.g., Kaiser-Permanente in Portland, OR; Group Health Cooperative of Puget Sound in Seattle, WA), hospitals (e.g., automated files and records at the Harvard Teaching Hospitals), Medicaid (e.g., in the State of Tennessee), and a provincial health insurance scheme (e.g., Saskatchewan, Canada). These data bases contain demographic information on patients enrolled, names and doses of medicines for prescriptions filled by the health care pharmacies, hospital admissions and discharge diagnoses, medical problems, and other data. The data bases may be searched to determine whether patients taking a specific medicine had more hospital admissions (e.g., for a myocardial infarction or other problem) than did patients with the same disease who were taking a competitive medicine. These data bases have been used successfully to evaluate hypotheses (Jick et al., 1985) and have raised the entire field of pharmacoepidemiology to a new level of trial design and potential to address important issues.

Record Linkage

Record linkage is an important concept that underlies the use of large multipurpose automated data bases. Record linkage is where two or more record files are linked, usually by computer. This allows questions to be addressed that previously could not be. For example, pharmacy records of outpatients with patient identifier numbers may be linked with the hospital inpatient experience of the same patients with a diagnosis code. These records may also be linked with the inpatient medicines prescribed during hospitalization. Many trials may only be conducted with computers that search these data bases looking for specific linkages. For example, the outpatient medicine history may be checked for all patients who had an admitting (or discharge) diagnosis of X. Alternatively, all patients receiving a new medicine may be tracked to identify their next hospitalization.

Assessing Whether Reported Rates of an Adverse Reaction Reflect the True Incidence

Figure 45.7 illustrates that reported rates of all adverse reactions from a single medicine or even the rate of a single adverse reaction from one medicine vary throughout a medicine's life. The reasons are generally quite straightforward. Rare adverse reactions (i.e., those that occur less than once in 10,000 patients) can hardly ever be discerned during premarketing studies, where usually a total of only 1,000 to 3,000 patients are exposed to a new medicine. After marketing, most medicines are used by many thousands of patients and rare adverse reactions are observed more often. Eventually, those adverse

reactions are associated with the medicine and are reported in the medical literature. At this point, many physicians are alerted about the adverse reaction. Shortly thereafter it becomes overdiagnosed and widely reported by zealous or naive physicians. Some physicians are anxious to publish reports while others may not be experienced in making an accurate diagnosis of the adverse reaction. In addition, the same diagnosis may refer to different conditions in different countries or may be referred to by different terms. After a period of time there is often less interest in the medical community about reporting each case of a moderate or serious adverse reaction that is perceived as well known and documented. As a result, the number of reports received by the company and by regulatory authorities represent an underreporting of some or all adverse reactions for a particular medicine.

Commonly occurring adverse reactions are observed during premarketing studies. In general, the more common the adverse reaction, the closer the reported incidence is to the true incidence (Fig. 45.7A). After marketing there is usually less incentive for physicians to spontaneously report common adverse reactions or those that are well known (e.g., Fig. 45.7D). Figure 45.7C illustrates a flurry of attention to an adverse reaction after marketing that eventually is reported less often. The premarketing period in panel C could have virtually no reporting of the adverse reaction. It must be noted that the *true* incidence of an adverse reaction is not always characterized by a constant rate but may vary greatly, further complicating reporting patterns. Many variations on the themes in Fig. 45.7 occur (e.g., some adverse reactions of a medicine may be underreported, while others are overreported).

Regulatory Requirements for Postmarketing Surveillance

Until recently, pharmaceutical companies did not systematically seek to collect postmarketing information. They used the information received spontaneously to adjust a product's labeling (i.e., package insert). This was primarily done by indicating serious adverse reactions that had been reported. Now, several national regulatory agencies are requiring postmarketing surveillance studies as a condition for approving a medicine for marketing. In many situations this is a reasonable request.

Data from Phase I to III trials cannot be generalized to all uses a medicine will be tried in after marketing, including how the medicine relates to different populations (e.g., pregnant women, children) and different conditions of use. One issue arises if a company has already begun a large postmarketing study for Country A and now Countries B, C, and D also want postmarketing stud-

TYPES OF REPORTING PATTERNS OF ADVERSE REACTIONS

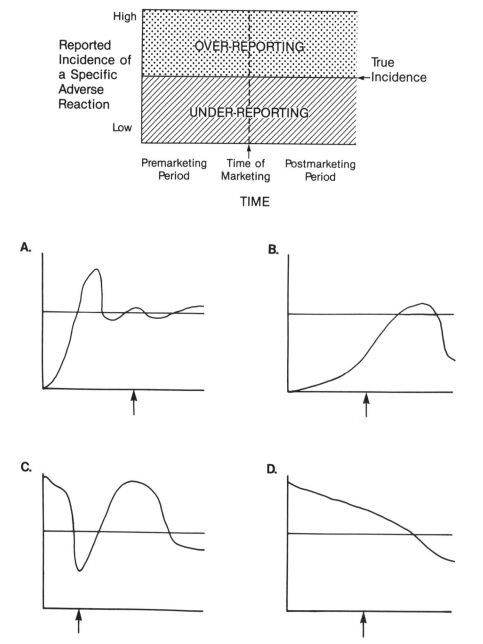

FIG. 45.7. Hypothetical types of reporting patterns of adverse reactions over time. Innumerable variations of these and other patterns are possible.

ies conducted. This exercise could become an unreasonable condition forced on companies who want to have their medicine approved.

There are several precedents by regulatory agencies of forcing companies to conduct trials that may not have been necessary. For instance, assume that a company has conducted all required pharmacology, toxicology, and clinical trials necessary to have a new medicine approved in an industrialized country with high regulatory standards. The company now wishes to register the medicine in several other countries but learns that Country B requires that the pharmacology must be repeated within that country, Country C requires that most toxicology and some clinical trials must be repeated, and so on. Although there may occasionally be a rationale for some of the repetition (e.g., to confirm that Japanese patients who weigh less will react the same to a fixed dose of a medicine as heavier Westerners), most of these requirements are forced on a company to help the economy of the other country and to feed their national pride. Some people have raised the same issue about the FDA's reaction to data for medicines developed elsewhere.

Regulatory Requirements for Adverse Reaction Reporting

While exact requirements differ among countries, there is a clear trend for regulatory agencies to mandate receipt of a growing amount of information. In addition to requiring postmarketing studies, many countries are also requiring reports on the numbers, trends, and even details of all serious adverse reactions reported to the company from all over the world.

Some regulatory authorities want reports of all serious and unexpected adverse reactions, whereas others want reports on all serious adverse reactions, whether unexpected or not. Imagine the complexity when each country requires different information on different official forms at different periods of time with different analyses of the data. All multinational pharmaceutical companies are wrestling with these requirements, which also may change from year to year. A major advance made by CIOMS (CIOMS Working Group, 1990) is helping to standardize forms and reporting practices.

When Should Newly Observed Adverse Reactions Be Put in a Medicine's Labeling?

There are no simple answers to this issue, only a large number of further issues to consider. The only guide is that each situation must be evaluated independently. Although it might superficially appear that a single universal package insert or medicine labeling for each medicine would be desirable to better standardize the medicine's use, this does not really make sense. For example, different doses may be recommended in different countries. This may occur for any of many reasons (e.g., the medicine may be approved to treat different diseases). In addition, different dosage forms (e.g., oral, intravenous) may be marketed in different countries, physicians may use the medicine differently (e.g., by itself in one country and elsewhere in combination with other medicines), and so on. The more years a medicine is on the market, the greater is the tendency for more adverse reactions to have been reported and therefore to be listed in a medicine's labeling.

After Regulatory Approval, Why Does the Number of Clinical Trials Usually Stay the Same or Even Increase?

This question is sometimes raised by senior corporate managers, especially those not experienced in clinical medicine development. The number of trials on a newly approved medicine sometimes decreases, but those situations seem to be the exception. Numerous types of trials are conducted after medicine approval, some of which are unlikely, undesirable, or even unable to be conducted prior to medicine approval. These trials include the following.

1. *Clinical trials.* A new medicine is often compared with its competitors to evaluate differences and detect possible advantages of the new medicine. The new medicine may be evaluated in special populations to determine their responses in terms of efficacy, safety, or another aspect (e.g., quality of life, pharmacokinetics). Trials may be conducted to obtain data that can be used to request (1) new indications; (2) improved medicine labeling in terms of additional populations in which the medicine may be used (e.g., children, elderly, pregnant women); (3) removal or downgrading of a warning, precaution, or contraindication in the medicine's labeling; or (4) any other change desired in the labeling. Some trials may be carried out to obtain promotional data (e.g., trials that will hopefully show superiority over the competitor's products) even though no changes in the medicine's labeling are requested. These trials may have a different motivational driving force behind them, but they may be well-designed and important clinical trials. Cynics may claim that some of these are solely driven by commercial desires to obtain a publication. Optimists may claim that if the data are publishable they probably add to our body of scientific and clinical knowledge, irrespective of motivation.

2. *Line-extensions.* Developing and studying line-extensions may be considered either as marketing studies or as a separate category. Each line-extension requires a different amount of work and number of clinical trials. Line-extensions include new (1) dosage forms (i.e., solutions, creams, capsules), (2) package sizes (e.g., number of tablets in a bottle), (3) packaging (e.g., blister pack), (4) dosage strengths (e.g., more or fewer milligrams per tablet), (5) flavorings, (6) combinations with other medicines, (7) new excipients (e.g., preservatives), or (8) other modifications.

3. *New indications.* Many medicines that are originally approved by a regulatory authority for one or a small number of indications are often evaluated in other diseases or conditions. Regulatory applications that are approved for new indications are usually a valuable source of additional revenue.

4. *Mechanism-of-action trials.* Preclinical studies that attempt to delineate a medicine's mechanisms of action are often conducted prior to a medicine's approval and marketing. Depending on the interest in the medicine, academicians and others may continue these trials long after a medicine is approved. Clinical mechanism-of-action trials generally tend to be de-emphasized by phar-

maceutical companies during a medicine's early clinical development. Such trials are often sponsored by the company as well as by academicians during Phase III or after a medicine is marketed.

5. *Postmarketing surveillance studies.* The importance of postmarketing surveillance studies is rapidly increasing throughout the world. These trials have various designs and objectives but are generally intended to improve understanding about a medicine's safety in large patient populations. These trials are described in more detail elsewhere in this section.

Reactions of Pharmaceutical Companies to Postmarketing Surveillance Needs

A few years ago, some forward-looking pharmaceutical companies hired epidemiologists to address the Phase IV questions that arose in regard to their products. Now, most companies are assembling relatively large departments to deal with these issues. Companies that have major research and development activities being conducted in two or more sites have additional issues brought about by having to link and coordinate their activities. Each site should be sharing its Phase IV clinical data on both an ad hoc basis for important adverse reactions and a periodic basis for complete sharing of data. These data are used both for reports to regulatory authorities and for internal company information and analyses.

Some companies have established a single worldwide data base of Phase IV data from spontaneous signaling systems, but there are problems with adopting this approach. For instance, the data from many countries are usually so poor and fragmented that they are hard to combine with better quality data from some industrialized countries. Some reports of adverse reactions are third- or fourth-hand accounts with little detail, while other reports are carefully detailed by treating physicians. Also, a single medicine is usually marketed in different formulations and combinations and may be prescribed in different dosages around the world. As a result of these and other issues, some companies do not want to create a single worldwide data base of adverse reactions. But these companies usually coordinate all relevant activities among their different sites and share all relevant information on adverse reactions, although the data are not put into a single data base.

Coordination Between Different Sites Conducting Phase IV Trials

Coordination between two or more different sites of a company in different countries has a number of components. The first is that computer systems used must either be identical or compatible. It makes no sense for a company to have incompatible systems, yet there are at least several companies where this has occurred! Second, the systems used to gather, process, analyze, and report data should be compatible. There will definitely be differences in how these steps are conducted in different countries, but there must be easily adapted methods to provide for needs of other important countries. Third, the coordination and cooperation of staff (and management) between countries must be harmonious. Whatever steps are necessary must be taken to ensure that these goals are achieved. Without compatible computer systems, a company will be unable to deal effectively with the myriad of issues that always arise during Phase IV.

Specific Issues of Collecting and Processing Adverse Reaction Data

A small selection of issues that arise in regard to collecting and processing adverse reaction data is briefly described.

1. A great deal of data collected either are "bits and pieces" (e.g., grossly incomplete reports) or are obviously full of inaccuracies and may be considered as "junk" data. How are "junk" data handled from around the world, especially when there is no means to go to a specific physician or other reliable source for additional information? Are data of very different quality being combined?

2. How are data of differing qualities handled within a single country for multiple medicines?

3. Reporting rates and procedures differ among nations and over time. To what extent may adverse reaction data from different nations or from different periods be pooled?

4. How can one differentiate between adverse reactions resulting from an overdosage of the medicine versus those occurring with normal usage? Also, is it important to differentiate between intentional and unintentional medicine overdose?

5. Because the rate of an adverse reaction's occurrence is more important than merely the number of occurrences (i.e., the numerator of a fraction), what characteristics should be placed in the numerator of the fraction used to determine the rate and what should be used as the denominator (e.g., the number of patients treated)? Many different criteria may be used to define the specific categories of patients, medicines, and adverse reactions used as numerators or denominators.

6. Given the enormous bias in collecting adverse reaction data in spontaneous systems, under what circumstances is a comparison of rates justified among different medicines or even for a single medicine over time?

7. Should adverse reactions that occur in patients using a medicine for unlabeled (i.e., unapproved) indica-

tions be considered separately from indications that are approved and recommended? What about adverse reactions that occur in patients who should not have used a medicine because of contraindications? Is it appropriate and fair to express a rate of a certain adverse reaction occurring in all patients, when a significant number should not have received the medicine? Is it appropriate and fair not to include them?

8. There is almost always some uncertainty about whether a medicine caused a specific adverse reaction. How should this issue be handled? No matter what is decided, there will always be many loose ends because important questions will not always be able to be answered if the patient, or even the treating physician in many cases, has to be contacted.

9. How should adverse reaction reports be handled when it appears that the adverse reaction was due to a concomitant medicine or to a concurrent disease?

10. Who should decide which reports must be submitted to which regulatory authorities? Should this be the local medical director where the adverse reaction occurred, someone at the central headquarters, or someone in the country requiring the report? On which basis is this decision made? How are serious adverse reactions differentiated from nonserious ones? What about situations when the severity cannot be established? How much effort should be expended to obtain new information? Are important adverse reactions being rapidly and appropriately communicated between sites of a pharmaceutical company?

11. Does the company or the physician reporting the adverse reaction determine whether the adverse reaction was attributable to the medicine? On what basis does the person decide, as there are many systems available for reaching a decision? Should a company use only a single method?

12. If a situation similar to that in Fig. 45.6 occurs, what would be considered to be the adverse reaction? In most cases, all of the symptoms would be adverse reactions, even though physicians may only see the final outcome, which includes the symptom(s) reported.

Many other issues relating to adverse reactions are discussed in Chapter 80 of *Guide to Clinical Trials* (Spilker, 1991).

Benefits of Postmarketing Surveillance

One of the questions akin to that asked by the small boy in "The Emperor's New Clothes" is to ask what is the benefit of the various approaches to postmarketing surveillance studies? Does the information from new techniques have greater value than the older sentinel system of having alert physicians publish case reports? This is the method that was used to alert the medical community to problems associated with the use of the beta-

receptor antagonist practolol after approximately five years on the market in the United Kingdom. The oral form of this medicine was then removed from the market. The intravenous form is still available but only for emergency use.

The answer to the basic question posed is that large automated multipurpose data bases have already demonstrated enormous value in being able to confirm and to clarify reports of serious adverse reactions as well as less serious ones identified through pharmacoepidemiological sentinel systems. These sentinel systems include published case reports and spontaneous reports made to regulatory authorities or pharmaceutical companies. The information obtained provides a sound basis for modifying a medicine's labeling. Postmarketing surveillance studies conducted to test an hypothesis also have great value. However, one point learned over the last 15 years is that conducting large and expensive postmarketing surveillance studies without a specific question in mind is generally unproductive and wasteful of resources.

We are now in a better position to recognize problems with new medicines at an earlier stage and thereby to save patients from having adverse reactions. In addition, we are now able through large data bases to evaluate hypotheses which provide assurance in some cases that a medicine should *not* be removed from the market. Because these data bases exist for other reasons, the cost to test hypotheses is not prohibitive and answers may often be obtained within a short period.

Although pharmacoepidemiological studies are primarily used to assess adverse reactions, they may also be useful for assessing the prevention of disease (e.g., stroke, heart attacks, fractures due to osteoporosis), as well as identifying the benefits of treatment.

QUALITY-OF-LIFE TRIALS AND ISSUES

Pharmaceutical companies have been interested in quality-of-life issues for well over a century. Every attempt to reduce adverse reactions of one medicine by developing a medicine with fewer or less severe adverse reactions is an attempt to improve the quality of life for patients taking the medicine. Quality-of-life measures can demonstrate an increased benefit-to-risk ratio and thus make the medicine more acceptable to the medical community. This may occur as a result of improving benefits, reducing risk, or both. Sometimes the benefits of a medicine on quality of life are not adequately evaluated or assessed from a patient's perspective. Thus, the full information is not always available to the company's marketing representatives, who help educate physicians about the medicine's benefits.

Quality of life relates to a quantification of human values relating to patients who have a chronic disease. It is a relative concept that differs from society to society and also differs within a society at different times. The patient is in a particular setting in which he or she influences decisions about initiating, continuing, modifying, or stopping a particular therapy. Measuring the quality of life from a patient's perspective includes consideration of five major areas: (1) economics, (2) psychological well-being, (3) social interactions, (4) physical abilities, and (5) physical state. Economics includes the ability of patients to work and support themselves as they previously were doing. Measures could include days spent at work and days spent in the hospital. Psychological factors, on the part of patients and often their families, are intimately involved in how treatment results are assessed. The same is true for a patient's physical and mental abilities. Physical abilities refers to capabilities and is a more dynamic measure than the baseline status of a patient's physical state. Examples of physical abilities include the ability to dress oneself and the ability to get into and out of a chair or car.

Uses of Quality-of-Life Data

It is becoming increasingly important to evaluate improvement in a patient's quality of life while receiving a new medicine and to compare this evaluation with the quality of life of patients receiving another medicine or placebo treatment or another treatment modality (e.g., surgery, radiation, biofeedback). This comparison may be made in clinical trials where quality-of-life issues are the primary objective, or a few quality-of-life measures may be included in clinical trials primarily oriented toward evaluating a medicine's safety or efficacy.

There are instances where patient perception of quality of life has had a significant influence on medical treatment (e.g., the trend away from radical mastectomy to limited surgery for breast cancer). The measures chosen to evaluate quality of life should focus on those characteristics that patients most strongly desire. But many new medicines are unable to elicit an adequate improvement in these parameters. A central issue is whether the medicine improves relevant parameters sufficiently to convince hospital or HMO formulary committees that the new medicine is worth putting on the formulary and on the pharmacy shelves, either in place of or in addition to currently stocked medicines.

It is clearly a difficult decision to choose or reject a medicine for a formulary when the medicine has both advantages and disadvantages in comparison with medicines currently on the formulary. Comparisons between unlike measures abound (e.g., Medicine A provides somewhat greater efficacy but also increases the risk of minor adverse reactions; Medicine C makes patients feel better more of the time compared with existing therapy

but increases the risks of a specific serious adverse reaction from 1 in 100,000 to 1 in 10,000 cases). If one medicine must replace another on the formulary, then the decision becomes much more difficult.

Another difficult decision is when a new medicine offers minor benefits over existing therapy but costs more than current therapy. Whether the additional benefits justify the added costs is often a difficult issue to resolve. This issue must be carefully evaluated before a new medicine is officially priced by the company. A number of considerations for a formulary committee to weigh in judging new medicines are listed in Table 45.2.

Measures Used to Evaluate Quality of Life

Measures of quality of life are multifactorial and may be combined into a single index score of well-being, or they may be used separately as a battery of assessments. The difficulty in the latter case is that some may be positive and others negative, or many will vary in their degree of change. Unless one has established a hierarchy of different tests, this may lead to a quagmire when the data are interpreted. Many methods used to measure quality of life have not been adequately validated by careful trial. Therefore, claims made about "proven benefits" may later turn out to be incorrect or strongly challenged.

Measures vary from standard validated questionnaires and evaluations using objective and/or subjective parameters to general questions prepared informally as an interview or questionnaire in a clinical trial. These latter unvalidated tests or scales may be insensitive to changes brought about by medicines, and responses to the questions may not be reproducible. Future evaluations in this

TABLE 45.2. *Considerations for a formulary committee to weigh in evaluating a new medicine[a]*

1. Efficacy
2. Adverse reaction profile
3. Number of follow-up visits required to monitor patients
4. Number and cost of laboratory tests to monitor patients
5. Duration and cost of hospitalization required
6. All direct costs associated with the medicine (e.g., diagnostic procedures, medical consultations, additional physician visits, preparation costs, pharmacy costs, monitoring costs)
7. All indirect costs associated with the medicine (e.g., time required to be away from work or home, family costs)
8. Quality of life issues (e.g., impact of the medicine on the patient's ability to function socially, physically, psychologically, and economically)
9. Convenience of use and other nonefficacy or safety issues (e.g., compliance)

[a] These are usually considered both for the medicine alone and also in comparison with standard medical therapy (i.e., nonmedicine and medicine).

field will undoubtedly lead to greater validation and systematic approaches than exist at present. It is anticipated that both objective and subjective measures will be found essential to use. It is necessary to agree on the different attributes and relative importance of each test ahead of time. In some situations a single overall index relating to quality of life is highly desirable. Until the last decade, the patient's quality of life was generally assessed in clinical trials, if at all, through the filter of the physician.

Many existing quality-of-life scales may be applied to patients with any disease. In addition, disease-specific scales are available. Neither category should be viewed as preferable, and there are proponents of using general scales even when disease-specific scales are available. This is usually based on a greater degree of validation of the scale.

When it is uncertain as to which type(s) of tests to use in measuring quality of life in a specific clinical trial, it is usually appropriate to use a battery of tests that measures each of the major aspects of quality of life. This may be done using both standard assessments that are applicable to many diseases and also trial-specific measures designed for that particular disease. Caution must be used to choose tests that have been validated. There is a great temptation in this field for people to make up their own test and not to appreciate the importance of validating their test.

Different Perspectives on Quality of Life

From a *health planner's* perspective, the quality-of-life issue is usually one of obtaining the greatest benefits with limited financial resources. The government, HMO, or other planner wants to spend the limited money and resources available where it will achieve the greatest return on the group's investment. The health planner has a predominantly economic perspective. The perspective on this issue from a *psychologist's* point of view is to maximize the social functioning of the individual patient. *Clinicians* focus primarily on a patient's medical health and physical abilities. *Patients* focus primarily on their feelings and any disabilities they may have had. If they are being treated to minimize a risk factor they will focus on the perceived benefits versus the inconvenience, cost, adverse reactions, and risk of the treatment. *Pharmaceutical companies* want to obtain data to show benefits of their medicines over the competitors for marketing advantages and also to help get their medicine listed on hospital, HMO, and other formularies.

Although there is some overlap between these assessments and the quality of life that would be assessed for a specific patient using each perspective, there are also significant differences. One of the most important differences is that health planners are usually oriented to effects that are measured in a patient population rather than to effects in a single patient.

46 / Issues of Technical Development

Introduction **521**
    General Activities of Technical Development
    During Periods of Medicine Discovery,
    Development, and Marketing.............. 522
    Priorities for Technical Development
    Departments............................. 522
Chemical Issues **523**
    Issues Relating to Scaleup of the Chemical
    Synthesis................................. 524
    Process Development........................ 524
    Development of Optically Pure Medicines 525
Pharmaceutical Issues **526**
    Formulation—Creating Medicines from
    Chemicals................................. 526
    Stability and Shelf Life 527
    Dissolution Studies......................... 528
    Medicine Compatibility...................... 528
    Determining the Number of Formulations,
    Dosage Forms, and Dosage Strengths to
    Develop.................................. 528
    When Should the Final Formulation Be
    Developed? 529
    Making Final Dosage Forms................. 530
    Increasing the Duration of a Medicine's
    Action 530
Resource Issues.............................. **531**

New Technologies............................ 531
Planning the Work Effort..................... 531
Sourcing the Medicine........................ 531
Allocating Medicine Supply................... 532
The Changing Cost of Making a Medicine
    During Its Development.................... 532
Analytical Issues.............................. **533**
    Medicine Purity 533
    Degradation Products........................ 533
    Medicine Analysis and Bioassays.............. 534
Liaison Issues **534**
    Interactions of Technical Departments with
    Production............................... 534
    Interactions of Technical Departments with
    Marketing................................ 535
"Catch-22" Situations in Technical Development **535**
    Increasing the Medicine Supply 536
    Allocating a Small Medicine Supply........... 536
    Apportioning Work Effort 536
    Padding Medicine Requests.................. 536
Conclusion..................................... **537**
    Setting Priorities............................ 537

I never varied from the managerial rule that the worst possible thing we could do would be to lie dead in the water with any problem. Solve it, solve it quickly, solve it right or wrong. If you solved it wrong, it would come back and slap you in the face and then you could solve it right. Lying dead in the water and doing nothing is a comfortable alternative because it is without immediate risk, but it is an absolutely fatal way to manage a business. Thomas Watson, Jr., former chief executive of IBM. *Fortune* (August 31, 1987).

INTRODUCTION

Many people in technical development do not accept Watson's view in relation to their problems. They attempt to logically and systematically solve problems correctly and appropriately, even if their approach takes more time than attempting a quick fix. This more delib-

erate approach is generally appropriate in the pharmaceutical industry.

This chapter identifies and briefly describes a small selection of the many issues and problems that occur during a medicine's technical development. Most of these could be (or are) the subject of an entire chapter or book. This chapter provides the reader with a flavor of the types of problems that frequently arise in the technical development of medicines. This category includes scaling up the synthesis of a medicine substance (i.e., the active ingredient) from milligrams to tons, formulating the medicine substance into a medicine product (i.e., the finished medicine tablet, capsule, or other dosage form) with up to approximately 30 different ingredients, and developing analyses for the medicine substance and medicine product. Although Good Manufacturing Practices (GMPs) are not specifically discussed in this chapter, they affect almost all stages of a medicine's path through technical development. One of the major issues faced by technical development managers is identifying at what point the GMPs begin to influence technical activities in a medicine's development.

General Activities of Technical Development During Periods of Medicine Discovery, Development, and Marketing

Technical development departments play a minor role in medicine discovery, although they may carry out some activities to facilitate this effort. Activities focus on providing large amounts of relatively few compounds for preclinical evaluation (e.g., toxicology) or involve preparation of radioactive compounds for specialized studies (e.g., metabolism). Other activities during the discovery period include limited efforts to address specific or general questions in areas such as formulation, stability, or assay development. Finally, patent activities may be handled within the technical development division. Table 46.1 summarizes these activities.

During the medicine development period, most types of activities associated with technical development are conducted. Many of these are described in this chapter and include (1) scaling up the chemical synthesis of medicine, (2) developing a suitable process for chemical scaleup, (3) developing a medicine formulation, (4) developing the process for formulating the medicine, (5) supplying compound and the dosage forms (e.g., tablet, capsule, solution) required for clinical and other trials, (6) developing methods to analyze the medicine in biological samples (e.g., blood, urine), and (7) transferring the process to production for large scale manufacture.

TABLE 46.1. *Activities of technical development departments during the medicine discovery period[a]*

1. Synthesize larger quantities of selected compounds for research evaluations and for toxicological testing
2. Submit patents on all inventions and conduct work to protect them
3. Conduct limited formulation development
4. Synthesize radioactive compounds

[a] This period ends when a candidate compound is chosen for development.

TABLE 46.2. *Selected roles of technical development departments during Phases I to III[a]*

1. Interact with all other groups within the company (e.g., licensing, patenting, legal, marketing, medical)
2. Produce and supply compound or medicine for preclinical studies (e.g., toxicology, metabolism) and for clinical trials
3. Scale up the laboratory synthesis[b]
4. Develop a synthetic process that is safe, economically feasible, efficient, and rapid and that produces minimal waste
5. Develop procedures to eliminate waste products of chemical synthesis
6. Develop a formulation for the compound and a process to make it
7. Develop analytical methods to assay the active compound, impurities, and degradation products
8. Transfer the analytical methods to quality assurance staff along with their validation
9. Transfer the synthesis to production staff and facilities
10. Transfer the formulation and process development to production along with its validation
11. Prepare reports needed in regulatory submissions
12. Answer questions raised by regulatory authorities
13. Troubleshoot any problems within production

[a] Although most of these functions are conducted for research and development, they are also done for marketing or production groups.
[b] The average chemical substance and final formulated product are scaled up one million fold by time the medicine is launched.

Other major activities depend on the organization of the particular company (e.g., obtaining medicine names, patenting compounds, developing waste-handling methods). Almost all activities require regulatory submissions that describe the work in detail. Regulatory submissions are also required for various compendia (e.g., *United States Pharmacopeia*). See Table 46.2.

The greatest amount of technical development work occurs after a medicine is marketed. This primarily relates to both the large quality assurance efforts during manufacturing (see Chapter 50, Production Issues) and other support activities to solve problems and keep production on schedule (Table 46.3). Technical development is also an essential part of creating new medicine formulations and line-extensions during the marketing period.

Priorities for Technical Development Departments

The major internal company customers of technical development services are (1) production, (2) project team, (3) marketing, (4) clinical research, (5) preclinical research activities, (6) licensing, (7) contract manufacturing, (8) foreign subsidiaries, and (9) international partners.

Each of these groups may view technical development departments as primarily existing for their assistance.

TABLE 46.3. *Activities of technical development departments after a medicine is marketed*

1. Assist production staff as needed to solve problems
2. Develop improved procedures for synthesis, analysis, formulation, or quality assurance
3. Conduct quality assurance on the manufacturing operations and environmental issues within production
4. Develop new formulations, dosage strengths, and dosage forms for clinical testing and eventually for marketing
5. Respond to regulatory questions received
6. Prepare regulatory reports to meet regulatory requirements
7. Prepare regulatory reports to request modifications of existing procedures

However, the major priorities of technical development staff are (1) to develop a viable process for the production of medicine substance and formulated product, (2) to support production (primarily postlaunch), and (3) to provide quality assurance on all processes according to GMP. This is done by troubleshooting problems that develop, providing assistance in certain areas of manufacturing (e.g., extremely small scale or complex processes), and conducting quality assurance of production's activities.

CHEMICAL ISSUES

Primary Functions

There is a twofold mission of the chemical development group inside a pharmaceutical company. Their first function is to develop a process to manufacture the compound, initially for clinical trials and at a later stage for the manufacturing group. There is a series of necessary steps to scale a synthesis from laboratory quantity to production quantity, and each of these may require significant time and resources to complete. The process developed should be safe, reproducible, cost-effective, and environmentally sound.

The second function is to provide chemical compound (i.e., medicine substance) of appropriate purity and quality for both clinical and preclinical studies. Synthesis for preclinical studies is primarily for toxicology tests.

Basic Dilemma

These two functions of a chemical development group create a basic dilemma. If a chemical group spends most of its time and resources improving the process of synthesizing the active compound or working on scaleup methods, they may not be providing adequate supplies of the medicine for clinical and toxicological testing. When they spend most of their efforts developing a process, the compound may be terminated and all of the process development and scaleup will have been for naught. If the group eschews the process development and instead devotes itself to providing compound, the needs for more and more compound (Table 46.4) will outstrip the group's ability to provide it on schedule. The group may not have researched the scaleup adequately so that they cannot simply convert to a larger scale synthesis. Thus, the chemical group risks being the rate-limiting factor in the medicine's development.

The best solution to this dilemma is to spend most of the group's efforts on providing compound early in the project's life and to spend more time on process development as the compound enters Phase III. Of course, the strategy chosen must depend to some degree on regulatory pressures. Regulatory authorities are tending to request more process development and validation of the process at an earlier stage of development.

Color

In addition to issues of finding universally acceptable dyes that meet requirements of marketing, other color issues may arise. One issue concerns whether the formulated medicine without dyes possesses a color and, if so, whether it will show through the hard gelatin capsule used in most Phase I trials. Colored powders are visually apparent in capsules, even when put in opaque capsules. If placebo is white then the difference in color inside the capsule would be apparent and this could be an important issue to address. Also, different strengths of an active medicine could have different intensities of color. To solve the issue of differing colors of capsules in a clinical trial the manufacturer may add a coloring agent to both the active and the placebo powders before they are placed in colored capsules. Colors in other dosage forms (e.g., tablets, suspensions) are usually less of an issue.

TABLE 46.4. *Typical scale factors for chemical syntheses*

Stage	Amount needed	Factor
Research stage	1–5 g	1
Preliminary development	50–500 g	10–100
Intermediate development	5–50 kg	1,000–10,000
Late-phase development	500–1,000 kg	100,000–200,000
Production	5–50 metric tons	1,000,000 to 10,000,000

Content Uniformity

When an active compound is mixed with a relatively small quantity of excipients, there is usually excellent uniformity of the powder for filling into capsules or pressing into tablets. However, if a highly active medicine with a few milligrams to be put in each pill is mixed with hundreds of milligrams of excipients, a major issue of obtaining an equally dispersed mixture may arise. The problem is how to assure equal dispersion of only a few milligrams of the active compound throughout the much larger mixture of excipients. One solution to this issue is to micronize the active medicine powder because that yields an improved dispersion.

Issues Relating to Scaleup of the Chemical Synthesis

One goal of chemical development is to minimize the number of separate chemical steps required in a medicine's synthesis. Advantages of fewer chemical reactions are both practical and economical. This goal may be addressed by (1) exploring alternative synthetic routes early in the development process, (2) purchasing raw materials that are closer to the final synthetic step or that allow the chemists to reach the final step more easily, or (3) contracting the manufacture of dangerous, toxic, or highly specialized steps to other companies.

It is rarely possible to go directly from a laboratory scale of synthesizing milligrams or grams to a manufacturing scale where hundreds of kilograms or even metric tons of a chemical may be required (Table 46.4). Scaleup often requires chemists and chemical engineers who were not involved in the original laboratory syntheses. Large glassware containers are used to make greater amounts of a medicine. Still larger nonglassware reactors are used at the pilot plant scale. This is a stage between laboratory scale and manufacturing scale. Monitoring and testing systems must be developed to evaluate the performance and ruggedness of the various chemical stages. This must be done during the chemical operations and after each step in the synthesis to assure that quality, purity, and yield are maintained. One objective of this process is to fully automate these operations. The number of separate scaleup stages a medicine goes through should be minimized.

The number of separate scaleup stages necessary in a pilot plant depends on the medicine and problems encountered. One of the many reasons why problems arise is that numerous aspects of scaleup cannot be directly extrapolated from one size chemical vessel to a larger size. For example, (1) the temperature gradients may vary more in a larger vessel, (2) there are mechanical differences in stirring (e.g., sheer forces), (3) a loss of visual observation occurs because the metal reactors used are opaque, (4) the changing surface-to-volume ratio that occurs is critical to heat transfer, and (5) the mechanical handling operations generally take longer on a larger scale. All of these factors may contribute to the variable performance of the process. These factors and others can markedly affect the chemical reaction and results obtained. The general quantities used for various functions are summarized in Table 46.5.

Process Development

The chemical development staff must balance priorities and available resources to successfully complete process development and provide project support work. Chemical development specialists modify or develop new synthetic routes for ultimate use in production. Their goal may be to improve bulk medicine yields or purity, decrease costs, or eliminate manufacturing hazards and toxic by-products. At the same time, an adequate supply of medicine substance must be generated to continue the various development activities (e.g., toxicology, clinical trials) on the project. Resource issues typically involve shortages in (1) personnel assigned to the work, (2) available starting materials, (3) available equipment, or (4) time to explore fully new chemical technologies. This is sometimes the central dilemma in a compound's development.

Safety of the Process

Safety is a critically important factor to consider in improving the process of synthesis and scaleup. Some of

TABLE 46.5. *Typical quantities of a compound required by various groups for conducting development activities*

1. Pharmacology	50–500 g
2. Toxicology	
90-day trial	2–8 kg
Lifetime trials	50–150 kg
3. Pharmaceutical development of a solid dosage form	
Preformulation and stability	50–500 g
Formulation development	5–10 kg
Final formulation development	100–200 kg
4. Clinical trials	3 kg–3 metric tons

the primary factors to consider in this regard are listed below.

- Temperature changes occur more slowly in large scale reactions.
- Thermodynamics must ascertain whether the reaction is safe and will not run away.
- Increasing the temperature of a reaction by 10° may double its rate of reaction. This may cause unwanted by-products, reduce yield, influence product uniformity, and affect equipment functioning.
- Heat must be removed rapidly at the right time.

Reproducibility of the Process

The underlying principle in scaleup is that a reaction at one size vessel may behave differently at a larger scale. A six-inch-diameter stirrer in a small flask has its tip moving at 4.5 feet per second. The propeller-driven agitator in a 200-gallon reactor with a diameter of 30 inches has its tip moving at 13 feet per second. The tip could beat the crystals of the reaction into small particles and change the product's uniformity, yield, purity, and consistency.

Cost-Effectiveness of the Process

The cost of synthesizing a compound is based on (1) materials cost, (2) labor costs, (3) overhead costs, and (4) yield. Overhead refers in part to the specific equipment used and how long it is used, as well as to other plant operations.

Some routes of synthesis are more cost-effective than others. The major factors include the costs of starting materials, number of steps involved, batch processing parameters, and cost of environmental cleanup. If starting materials are impure or unavailable it may be necessary to synthesize them or to find other suppliers.

Environmental Cleanup of the Process

Waste materials are recycled if possible and cost-effective. More regulations are being passed that require companies to control emissions of reactors, evaluate all waste streams, and perform environmental assessments. Incinerators sometimes have scrubbers in them to clear materials burned. If possible, expensive and volatile solvents are recovered. Table 46.6 lists the sections of an environmental impact analysis that must be included in a New Drug Application (NDA). Costs for environmental cleanup are rising rapidly.

Synopsis of the Process

Modern chemical reactors are like giant thermos containers (i.e., metal containers [usually stainless steel]

TABLE 46.6. *Requirements of an environmental assessment in the United States[a]*

1. Date
2. Name of applicant
3. Address
4. Description on the proposed action
   Summary of appropriate portions of the application
   Locations where the product is to be made
   Locations where the products will be used and disposed of
   Types of environments at and adjacent to the above locations
5. Description of the chemical substances involved
6. Introduction of substances into the environment
7. Fate of emitted substances in the environment
8. Environmental effects of released substances
9. Use of resources and energy
10. Mitigation measures
11. Alternatives to the proposed action
12. List of preparers
13. Certification
14. References
15. Appendices

[a] The regulation is detailed in 21 Code of Federal Regulations Part 25.31a. This table lists the sections required. The Pharmaceutical Manufacturers Association has prepared a guide for the pharmaceutical industry for compliance with these regulations.

around a glass-lined interior). Fluids flow between these two layers to heat or cool the contents. Heat is generally applied with steam and cooling by refrigerated glycol or running water.

After a chemical reaction is complete, it is often necessary to separate two immiscible layers where the less dense phase is on top of another. In a glass flask it is easy to see the two layers and to separate them, whereas that is impossible in a stainless steel reactor. This problem is solved by removing the lower (i.e., heavier) fluid through a small glass opening through a spout until the other colored fluid is observed at the interface. If the two fluids are both uncolored or the same color, then a nonreactive dye could be added to facilitate the separation.

The product is then isolated from solution with a solvent remover. The solvent can be evaporated away to crystallize the product from solution or dried to yield a crystalline product. The solid material is then isolated by filtration, centrifugation, or recrystallization and then washed a number of times and dried. A vacuum oven may be used with material on drying trays, or a tumble dryer may be used.

Development of Optically Pure Medicines

The issues and debate surrounding chirality (i.e., molecules with one or more asymmetric centers) and the development of optically pure medicines have become more intense in recent years. Companies have developed optically pure medicines (i.e., single enantiomers) in the past when it was clear to them that racemates (i.e., a compound with an equal proportion of enantiomers) were less safe or effective. New biotechnologies have made the isolation and scaleup of optically pure enantiomers more practical. Some companies have exploited these technologies by patenting isomers of well-known medicines that were not patented by the originator.

The Food and Drug Administration (FDA) issued a "Policy Statement for the Development of New Stereoisomeric Drugs" in mid-1992 (referenced in the *Federal Register,* Vol. 57, No. 102, Wednesday, May 27, 1992, page 22249). The document discusses three categories of compounds: (1) those where both enantiomers have similar desirable actions (e.g., ibuprofen), (2) those where one enantiomer is active and the other is inactive (e.g., propranolol), and (3) those where the enantiomers have different activities (e.g., sotalol). The policy statement advocates clinical evaluation of both enantiomers even if only one is chosen to be developed or if the racemate is developed. The major point is that a company must examine the issue scientifically during the early development period and reach a rational conclusion before Phase II trials are completed.

This policy is reasonable in that it does not consider all clinical medicines as a single group and also because it encourages development choices of enantiomers to be based on good science and logic. It rejects the claims of some scientists that all new medicines should be single enantiomers.

A single enantiomer should be developed if it is easy to synthesize and if it has different clinical activities than the racemate. Other reasons to develop a single enantiomer are ease of development to obtain absorption, metabolism, excretion, or physiological advantages. Racemates should be developed if there is a rapid interconversion of enantiomers, if individual enantiomers are difficult to synthesize, or if the separate enantiomers have similar activity and safety profiles.

PHARMACEUTICAL ISSUES

The major functions conducted by a pharmaceutical development department are listed in Table 46.7.

Formulation—Creating Medicines from Chemicals

Master Formula

There is a big difference between an active ingredient (medicine substance) and a medicine product. Most chemicals are a single pure compound or possibly a mixture of different compounds, whereas medicines contain added materials called *excipients.* These materials are combined according to a precise formula, and each in-

TABLE 46.7. *Activities conducted by a pharmaceutical development department*

1. Develop the master formula for the medicine
2. Design the type, strength, and appearance of the dosage form along with marketing and medical input
3. Evaluate stability of the active compound, formulated material, and final dosage forms
4. Help ensure availability of material for clinical trials and other studies
5. Prepare reports for regulatory submissions
6. Determine physicochemical properties of the active compound and formulated medicine
7. Work closely with the chemical and analytical development groups
8. Work closely with all other members of the project team responsible for overseeing the medicine's development

gredient in that formula has a specific function. Some people refer to the medicine formula as a recipe, but this is somewhat misleading as it implies a certain degree of imprecision. Medicine formulas specify ingredients to four significant figures, and all changes in the formula for both marketed and Investigational New Drug Application (IND) medicines must be approved both by the company's strict internal standards and by the FDA.

Agents that should be added to the final medicine formula must be determined. Choosing the most nearly optimal list and proportion of ingredients that together make up a medicine often takes substantial time and effort. What are the implications of adding each of these substances? Excipients must not react with the medicine substance or affect its absorption into the body. Controlled release formulations are one exception where excipients are specifically chosen to delay the medicine's absorption.

Marketing Impact

Most of these issues are handled by pharmaceutical development experts, but sometimes other groups must become involved. For example, a dye color may be banned by one or more regulatory agencies. A decision must be made by marketing experts as to whether to choose a less desirable dye that would be universally acceptable or whether to develop multiple formulations, each with their own dyes that could be sold in specific countries. There may be strong marketing preferences for different tablet or capsule colors in certain countries. This issue is discussed in Chapter 93 of *Guide to Clinical Trials* (Spilker, 1991).

In addition to a medicine's color, its size, shape, odor, and taste are usually important considerations from a marketing perspective. Small capsule or tablet size may be difficult to achieve if the amount of each dose is large. Unique tablet shapes enhance product identification but may cause problems in production. Masking the taste of bitter medicines is often difficult.

Preservatives

It is important to prevent bacterial growth in solutions, suspensions, gels, creams, and other dosage forms intended for oral or topical use. Solid dosage forms do not generally have a problem with bacterial growth owing to their low moisture content. The selection of a suitable bacterial preservative is sometimes difficult because of varying regulations in different countries. Only preservative agents and other excipients that do not interact with the medicine are used. In addition, the excipients must be shown not to interact chemically with each other. Excipients are chosen based on the ease of working with the compound in production as well as on scientific considerations.

Parenteral Medicines

Parenteral medicines plus most ophthalmic and otic products must be sterile. Parenteral products should also be free of pyrogens (i.e., substances that increase body temperature). The pH (measure of acidity or alkalinity) of parenterals, ophthalmics, and otics is also a consideration and may raise challenging technical issues. For example, to achieve chemical stability and solubility a certain pH may be required, but this pH may not be close to the body's pH, and therefore the medicine would cause marked irritation. Another formulation issue of parenteral medicines involves the degree of solubility of the medicine in solution. Solvents besides water or saline are often required to enable a sufficient quantity of medicine to dissolve in solution. These solvents have their own biological, chemical, and physical characteristics that must be considered.

Stability and Shelf Life

The shelf life of a medicine is the time period during which the medicine has been shown to remain stable and is therefore acceptable for clinical use. As established in regulatory documents this means that its potency is known to stay within specifications over a defined period of time. A typical medicine might have to be within 10% of its labeled strength. To evaluate stability for the medicine, a company conducts studies under various storage conditions on both the active ingredient alone and on the pharmaceutical preparation (i.e., medicine product). These studies are important to determine if the compound decomposes (1) at a rate that would lead to an unacceptably short shelf life, (2) to a toxic by-product, or (3) to a by-product that has synergistic or antagonistic effects on the medicine itself.

Chemical stability of all medicines must be tested under various conditions of light, moisture, and temperature for as long a period as is desired for the expiration date. This may be as long as five years for prescription medicines and is even longer for some over-the-counter (OTC) medicines. If the dating is "too short" (usually less than 18 months), then many companies will decide not to market the medicine in its present form. In addition, obtaining regulatory approval to market the medicine will usually be more difficult. Alternative formulations that achieve a longer expiration date will probably be sought if they are acceptable from a marketing perspective. Each formulation being developed must undergo a separate series of stability tests. Longer dates may be achieved with modified packaging that protects moisture-sensitive or light-sensitive medicines. Light-sensitive medicines need protective (e.g., amber color) containers, although amber ampules are not customarily used in many European countries. Another method to lengthen dates is to modify recommended storage (e.g., to go from room temperature to 5°C).

Physical stability issues include whether there is absorption of a medicine by the cap liner inside the container or binding of an active compound to an excipient. If liquid medicines become absorbed to the cap liner or walls of a container, a different material will be selected for the cap liner (e.g., Teflon, rubber) or container (e.g., glass, one of many types of plastics). Stability tests have to be done at each site where a medicine is made or packaged because of differences in excipients and packaging.

Accelerated Stability Tests

Some stability studies subject a medicine substance or medicine product to experimental conditions that help predict how much decomposition would occur over a longer time period under more common or usual conditions of temperature, humidity, and light. This is referred to as an accelerated stability study. Regulatory authorities in the United States and some other countries (e.g., Japan) are moving away from allowing a medicine's shelf life to be based on such accelerated tests. The FDA now demands "real" time tests, which means that 24 months of satisfactory stability testing will allow a medicine to have 24 months of shelf life. Even though accelerated tests for new chemical entities (NCEs) were previously accepted by the FDA, they were always accepted only on a temporary basis until real time tests were completed successfully. The FDA is currently accepting accelerated stability data for minor changes in existing products or for well-characterized products already on the market. Accelerated tests use extreme conditions of temperature, humidity, and/or light.

When Does the Dating of Shelf Life Begin?

Another issue regarding shelf life that sometimes arises is identifying the date when shelf life begins. Is this the day when bulk chemical synthesis is completed, the day the medicine formulation is complete, or the day the formulation is packaged? There may be reasons why any one of these or other dates would be preferable and would also be logical to use for a specific medicine. No single approach is followed for all medicines. Differences in establishing shelf life exist between countries that require worst case data and others that use mean data. Some countries also may adjust shelf life on a batch-by-batch basis if results are borderline.

Dissolution Studies

Dissolution tests measure the rate of solubility of a medicine under various conditions of agitation rate, pH, and additional factors. Dissolution studies are conducted because of the assumption that medicines which do not adequately dissolve cannot be well absorbed into the body, and medicines that are not absorbed usually cannot lead to the desired clinical effect. Dissolution tests are a widely used measure of batch-to-batch variability for newly made medicines and thus function as a quality assurance test. Conditions used to study a medicine's dissolution involve many factors (e.g., amount of medicine, solvent, type of capsule, protective coatings, intensity of stirring, temperature) and may vary enormously in different types of dissolution tests.

Changes in dissolution rates of a known compound or medicine may reflect either physical or chemical effects. Physical changes could relate to polymorphic (i.e., crystal structure) changes in the medicine substance. Chemical changes could result from interactions with the excipient that cause the tablet to disintegrate. Alternatively, decomposition products of the medicine could waterproof the tablet and delay its dissolution.

The correlation of data in humans with rate of dissolution studies *in vitro* depends primarily on the type of apparatus used and its operating conditions. Types of equipment vary in major respects, including both type and intensity of agitation used, plus more than half a dozen more technical attributes. Over 100 varieties of equipment have been proposed (Barr, 1972). Figure 46.1 illustrates a few types of apparatus used for dissolution studies. The major issue is that different methods yield different results, some methods are not suitable for certain medicines, and new methods require extensive review from manufacturers, the FDA, and the *United States Pharmacopeia* (USP) convention.

A company proposes the type of dissolution studies on a new medicine to a regulatory agency. The methods proposed may or may not be accepted as suitable. Because variations in equipment and conditions influence results, numerous issues may arise that must be discussed and resolved.

Medicine Compatibility

A medicine may react with proteins or other chemicals when it enters the blood. Medicines may also interact with substances in other body fluids or with other solutions being put into the body. It is therefore necessary to confirm that a medicine is compatible with and stable in blood and other body fluids. These tests are conducted prior to clinical trials.

Medicines that are given intravenously must be compatible with the solvents that are used to either dissolve or dilute the medicine. It must be determined which solvents and which physiological solutions (e.g., saline, sugar and water) may be used with the medicine. These tests are routinely conducted. Major issues may arise when incompatibilities are found.

Determining the Number of Formulations, Dosage Forms, and Dosage Strengths to Develop

There are a large number of potential dosage forms that may be requested for development (e.g., creams, ointments, gels, whips, suppositories, sprays, aerosols, solutions, suspension, powders, lotions, tablets, capsules). The need for each dosage form requested must be carefully assessed.

How does a pharmaceutical company decide how many formulations, dosage forms, and dosage strengths (e.g., 50, 100, 250, and 500 mg) of a single medicine to develop and market worldwide? Also, which dosage forms should be developed, and in which order? This is a major international issue for most medicines. Local marketing requirements can readily be demonstrated for specific dosage forms (e.g., national preferences for or against certain dosage forms). These often lead to a proliferation of dosage forms being developed, even when the central headquarters desires to minimize this proliferation.

The company may decide on a central policy and approach for each medicine and then require local subsidiaries to request an exception. Another approach is to allow each country to decide which tablet and/or capsule size, shape, color, strength, printing, coating, and formulation would be best for their territory and to contract with the parent company or other companies to have it made. The author favors the former approach of having some central control to minimize the proliferation of different forms of the same medicine and to reduce the consumption of valuable technical development resources. A bioequivalence study between two (or more) dosage forms or between two formulations of a medicine is usually necessary when the final formulation or dosage form of the medicine to be sold is not the same as the formulation used in at least one major clinical trial.

APPARATUS USED FOR DISSOLUTION STUDIES

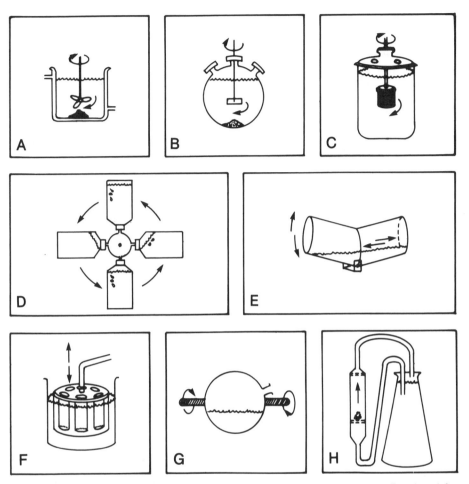

FIG. 46.1. Selected types of apparatus used to evaluate medicine dissolution. Reprinted from Barr (1972) with permission of S. Karger.

When Should the Final Formulation Be Developed?

This important question is debated for almost every new medicine developed. To develop the final formulation it is necessary to have (1) a sufficient amount of the active ingredient; (2) knowledge of its potency, stability, and bioavailability as determined in clinical trials; (3) the color and dosage form desired by marketing; (4) the physical size and shape of each dosage form desired by marketing (and tested by medical groups); (5) validated analytical assays; (6) developed quality assurance procedures; and (7) anything that marketing wants to print or engrave on the tablet (or print on a capsule).

Medical groups want the final formulation at the start of pivotal trials, even though they are able to conduct most Phase III trials without the final formulation. One important exception is for biotechnology medicines, where the final formulation must be used for pivotal trials.

Production groups are generally willing to have the final formulation provided to them at the last minute if the manufacturing steps are identical and the requisite number of production-scale batches can be made under appropriate conditions. Marketing groups also are content to have a final formulation close to launch. Thus, the major reason for developing the final formulation earlier in development relates to conducting clinical trials and expediting the medicine's development.

The ideal time to start a final formulation is when the active ingredient in a medicine is available in its final synthetic process completed on a production scale. In reality it is impractical to wait until process development is complete and it is necessary to begin work at an earlier time. This work generally begins when dictated by strategic considerations and the compound and staff to do the work are available. Formulation development usually overlaps process development of the medicine substance.

Making Final Dosage Forms

The final dosage formulation must be processed through manufacturing equipment without encountering problems and be able to be compressed into tablets, filled into capsules, or made into another dosage form. The physical form of a medicine may raise major issues, for example, if the medicine is fluffy (i.e., low bulk density) and not compressible into a tablet, if the material occurs in several crystal forms (i.e., polymorphism) which cannot be adequately controlled from batch to batch, or if the active ingredient is not uniformly mixed with its excipients.

At what point during a medicine's development does a company switch from the slow and cumbersome method of hand-filling capsules for clinical trials to filling capsules by machine? A machine-fillable method must be developed that utilizes powders of suitable bulk density, particle size, and content uniformity that can be encapsulated without adversely affecting machine performance. Also, there must be a sufficient amount of medicine available to develop this method and allow wastage resulting from the use of mechanized equipment. This amount of extra medicine may not be acceptable (or available to allocate) early in a medicine's development.

Particle shape and size, bulk density, and polymorphic form are affected by the synthetic methods used to make the medicine substance. These properties have profound effects on the medicine product and may affect (1) uniformity (consistency within a batch), (2) reproducibility (consistency from batch to batch), (3) dissolution rate, (4) chemical stability, and (5) processing and production feasibility. These properties often change as the chemical synthesis method is changed. This means that formulation development is conducted on medicine substances with properties that may be different from those of the final commercial product. The formulation developed must be robust to allow for such changes in properties. A synopsis of common issues faced in creating pharmaceutical formulations is presented in Table 46.8.

The mixing of an active medicine substance plus its excipients may raise numerous issues. The major issue is whether nonuniform mixing occurs in some or all situations. For example, mixing may be uniform and appropriate for capsules but not for tablets. Unattractive spots may show on the surface of tablets that were not present in capsules. The search for an attractive medicine product that meets all necessary physical, chemical, and biological characteristics may require great efforts to succeed.

Increasing the Duration of a Medicine's Action

When should a novel medicine delivery system (e.g., transdermal patch, depot injection) or sustained action

TABLE 46.8. *Selected issues in the development of a medicine formulation*

A. Appearance
  1. Size
  2. Shape
  3. Color
  4. Odor
  5. Taste
B. Physical characteristics
  1. Sterility—for parenterals, ophthalmics, otics
  2. Pyrogens—for parenterals
  3. pH—for parenterals, ophthalmics, otics
  4. Hardness or friability—for tablets[a]
C. Availability of medicine at its site of action
  1. Solid dosage forms—dissolution used as a quality assurance test
  2. Transdermal patches—medicine diffusion studies
D. Stability and shelf life
  1. Medicine substance (i.e., the biologically active chemical[s])
  2. Medicine product (i.e., the formulated medicine with excipients)
  3. Compatibility of parenteral products with the solvents used to dissolve or dilute the medicine
E. Production feasibility[b]
  1. Uniformity—consistency within a batch
  2. Reproducibility—consistency from batch to batch
  3. Practical considerations (e.g., equipment availability, ability to scale up process from hand-filled to machine-filled capsules, time and efforts required to prepare the dosage forms and dosage strengths requested or required, safety precautions required when handling or working with the unformulated compound and formulated medicine)
F. Interaction of various disciplines
  1. Marketing defines product characteristics
  2. Medical determines the number of dosage strengths to develop
  3. Project manager helps plan work effort and allocates medicine supply
  4. Chemical development refines and scales up the synthetic method. During these stages the properties of the medicine substance may change
  5. Analytical development evaluates the purity of the medicine. When problems arise (e.g., low amounts reported in assays) it is not always clear if the problem results from the formulation (e.g., poor degradation, poor content uniformity) or from the analytical method used
  6. Production groups must be able to manufacture the medicine and often require assistance during the transition from medicine manufacture in a pilot plant to a full production plant

[a] This is a measure of a tablet's ability to withstand subsequent packaging and film-coating processes.
[b] Critical parameters must be defined and controlled.

dosage form be developed to prolong the activity of a medicine? This approach must be considered in situations where the duration of a medicine's clinical effect is insufficient. The determination of a desirable duration of action is largely assessed in terms of technical feasibility, competitive medicines that are available, and perceived benefits for the patient.

This problem, like most others in technical development, can be approached in many different ways. Most extended release dosage forms have been developed in an empirical trial and error manner. Several formulations are made and tested *in vitro* and eventually in animals to determine which have the desired characteristics. Technical modifications to a pharmaceutical preparation may be made in terms of (1) excipients, (2) physical form, (3) the addition of a retarding agent to slow a medicine's dissolution, (4) the coating of a medicine with a different substance to delay its absorption, or (5) other techniques such as using a concomitant medicine that slows metabolism of the main medicine and thus prolongs its clinical effect. One objective might be to decrease the rate of a medicine's elimination from the body by giving another medicine that decreases elimination of the major medicine. This effect would maintain therapeutic blood (and possibly tissue) levels of the medicine, thereby possibly prolonging its effect.

Another physiological objective could be to increase the duration of a medicine's clinical effect by enhancing the medicine's ability to bind with its receptor. This might be accomplished by inhibiting the system that normally inactivates the medicine. For example, the enzyme monoamine oxidase (MAO) inactivates medicines known as catecholamines. By giving a patient an inhibitor of monoamine oxidase, the action of catecholamines and other medicines metabolized by MAO can be extended for a longer period.

RESOURCE ISSUES

New Technologies

How may new technologies that are believed to improve medicine manufacturing and quality control processes be best evaluated? Also, how may new state-of-the-art technologies be incorporated into an existing program of medicine development and production? A recent example involves the use of robotics (Table 46.9) and other forms of process automation (e.g., autoanalyzers), which are gradually assuming a larger role in technical development. These specific technical issues are not discussed or described in detail.

Each company wrestles with these and related issues

TABLE 46.9. *Selected uses of laboratory robotics*

1. Nuclear magnetic resonance (NMR) sample preparation and spectral determination
2. High-pressure liquid chromatography (HPLC) tablet sample preparations for analysis
3. Radioimmune assays (RIAs) of clinical samples
4. Bacterial endotoxin assays
5. Tests conducted on sterile cell cultures
6. Filling capsules for clinical trial material

TABLE 46.10. *Selected responsibilities of a person (or group) who plans and coordinates activities among technical development departments[a]*

1. Serve as a member of each of the relevant project teams (e.g., marketing, production, research and development) for each medicine
2. Periodically meet with representatives of all relevant technical development departments (who may or may not be project team members) to review status and issues on all projects
3. Ensure that all regulatory requirements are met through the quality and type of work conducted
4. Evaluate the allocation of technical development resources to projects and the need for resources
5. Present current updates to relevant management groups
6. Ensure technical development review and sign-off on all reports
7. Coordinate technical development responses to regulatory authority questions
8. Participate in other activities as requested

[a] See also Figs. 32.5 and 32.6.

on a continual basis. Small teams or task forces are often assembled to evaluate newer technologies, run pilot programs, and make recommendations. There are no general answers to these issues and each new technology must be evaluated on its own merit for each particular company.

Planning the Work Effort

Can technical efforts expended on product line-extensions of existing medicines be balanced with time spent on investigational medicines (new chemical entities)? Also, can technical issues and problems that markedly delay a medicine's development be anticipated? Efficient planning requires consideration of department work schedules, backlogs, and priorities. It is often advisable to place project activities in each department's queue as soon as possible. This action may not prevent a project's request from being bumped out of the queue at a later date, but it increases the probability that the work will be done in a timely manner. Most technical departments prefer to work on project activities after it is known that the medicine has an acceptable efficacy and safety profile in patients. On the other hand, this situation is not always possible and a great deal of technical work is often conducted at an early stage of medicine development. Having a single person coordinate activities among all the various technical development departments can be a valuable means of improving efficiency. The responsibilities of this person are listed in Table 46.10.

Sourcing the Medicine

Companies must decide where every investigational and marketed medicine will be manufactured. This may appear to be a straightforward issue, but often it is not. Multinational companies usually have two or more major sites where medicines are manufactured, and it is usually preferable to choose to make the medicine at one of these sites at an early stage in a medicine's development. The decision as to where to make a medicine will be based on availability of personnel and suitable equipment as well as labor issues, tax issues, ability to export the medicine, level of hazard involved, and other factors. Other options besides choosing one of a company's plants to make the medicine include (1) having a contract facility manufacture the medicine, (2) having one facility manufacture a number of intermediate compounds and then sending the intermediate to another plant to complete the operation, (3) building a new facility, (4) having two (or more) plants make the medicine, (5) making some dosage forms at one site and others at a different site, and (6) manufacturing a medicine in bulk at one site and compressing it into tablets or filling it into ampules or vials at another site. Many additional variations exist. Numerous considerations will influence the decisions reached, which may also change during the investigational period, as work loads change and requirements become more firmly established (see Fig 24.2).

Allocating Medicine Supply

There are few major issues in the allocation of medicine supply when a medicine is easily synthesized and a sufficient amount is available. This situation allows medicine development activities to move forward at a maximal pace. In the more typical situation, however, medicine supply is limited, especially during early stages of development. In some cases, medicine availability may be the rate-limiting step that is controlling progress of medicine development. This situation requires careful allocation of the available medicine to those activities that will move the project forward as rapidly as possible. At the same time, solutions to supply additional medicine must be aggressively sought. This may include the development of new synthetic routes.

Medicine supplies can be in great demand. Early in its life, supplies of a compound may be required to develop formulations, to develop an assay method, to conduct stability tests, to synthesize related compounds, to prepare additional salts, and/or to make analytical reference materials. Later, stronger demands on available medicine are often made for large-scale clinical and toxicological studies, developing new dosage forms, and even preparing prelaunch stock.

If medicine requests are not prioritized and coordinated, medicine supply may be consumed by less important needs and not allocated to work that is critical to the success of medicine development. This dilemma may be solved by assessing short- and long-term medicine re-

quirements, based on the medicine development plan. Most critical activities are planned and medicine supply is scheduled according to the time projected for preparation, assay, and formulation. Interesting questions arise when (1) the medicine development plan demands more medicine than can be reasonably supplied, (2) starting materials are not present and their availability is uncertain, or (3) process development work encounters unexpected problems. For example, if the most critical group involved in a medicine's development requires approximately 500 g of medicine and only 100 g are available, but future syntheses of 500 g are *scheduled* to occur in 6 (or 12) months, should the 100 g be given to another group for their work? It is readily apparent how complex medicine allocation issues can become.

Many additional factors can make medicine allocation issues even more complex. For example, the dilemma of whether or not to delay clinical trials so that development of a medicine's final synthesis can proceed (for its eventual production) is usually settled in favor of maintaining the schedule of clinical activities. It would make little or no sense to perfect a medicine's synthesis if the next clinical trial showed that the medicine was too toxic or lacked sufficient efficacy to be developed further.

Related examples are: should a clinical trial be started with capsules if a tablet formulation is scheduled to be ready in four months? Should a large Phase II well-controlled clinical trial be initiated with available capsules if capsules with the medicine's final formulation are scheduled to be available in three to six months? Will a new formulation be ready on time for a pivotal study (generally the most well-controlled study) that is needed to support a Japanese submission?

The Changing Cost of Making a Medicine During Its Development

Many medicines are extremely expensive to make during the early stages of their development. Almost all medicines become less expensive to make as the development process continues. This results from a decreased cost of raw goods as larger quantities are purchased, better suppliers are found, or a company manufactures the raw materials themselves. As chemical development continues, more efficient and less expensive routes of synthesis may be found, and increased yields (i.e., percentage of active compound obtained from starting materials) may occur.

No matter how expensive (within reason) a medicine may be in its early stages, its manufacturing costs may decrease by orders of magnitude. Difficulties abound at an early stage of a medicine's life in estimating the ultimate cost to manufacture a compound as a marketed medicine. Marketing demand, and thus the number of kilograms or metric tons needed, cannot be estimated until the clinical profile is known with reasonable certainty. This profile is rarely known prior to completion of Phase II trials and sometimes not until later. The doses required to treat patients are likewise not known with a reasonable degree of certainty until later in Phase II. As a result, it is difficult to estimate the production cost of a day's or week's supply of medicine for a patient. Thus, it is important not to terminate a medicine's development because it appears to be too expensive to make. Solutions to this dilemma may often be found.

ANALYTICAL ISSUES

Medicine Purity

Is the medicine's purity adequate? This is really a case-by-case decision based on the nature of impurities present. Are they toxic? Are they present in the same amount each time a medicine is made? Most marketed medicines are well over 90% pure. The related substances present include process impurities (i.e., generated during manufacture of the medicine substance) and/or degradation (i.e., breakdown) products. The quality and purity of most medicines increase during the course of development. The quality of a medicine is a measure of numerous factors including reproducibility of the physical state in repeated batches in terms of particle size, crystal structure, color, density, and other characteristics. The ability of the medicine to be processed is another measure of its quality. The analytical development department evaluates these questions (Table 46.11).

Although it is desirable to have a medicine's active ingredients and excipients as pure as possible, the effort, time, and cost to maximize purity can become prohibitive after the point of diminishing returns is reached. Moreover, almost all synthetic medicines that are less than 100% pure are not toxic in any way to humans

because of the trace impurities that are present. These impurities are often inactive breakdown products of the active ingredient. The identity of impurities usually occurs during Phase II or III. Limits are established for the allowable amounts of impurities that may be present. A reasonable level is to identify all impurities present at 0.5% at the Clinical Trial Exemption/Investigational New Drug Application (CTX/IND) stage and to chemically identify those present at 0.1% at the NDA stage. The regulations of different countries vary on this issue.

Purity may be improved by obtaining more pure starting materials. The reliability of suppliers to provide consistent material must be determined and assured. Reliability is usually assessed in terms of meeting dates and providing ordered amounts. The ability of suppliers to scale up their supply at desired purity levels and at a reasonable cost is also an important issue.

The most pure batch of a medicine substance is carefully prepared and analyzed at great effort to obtain the reference material with which all batches of production material are compared. This is the "gold standard," and samples of this material are given to the FDA when the NDA is submitted. The purity of a medicine used in clinical trials and for toxicology studies should be of comparable purity to the medicine that is ultimately marketed. If toxicological studies are done with a more pure form of the medicine than that marketed, it could raise questions about the toxicity of impurities in the marketed medicine.

This raises the issue of whether a small scale synthesis or even an early scaled-up synthesis can be further scaled-up and still produce medicine with the same purity, quality, and stability profiles. If clinical and toxicological studies are conducted on a certain purity medicine, but the manufacturing process changes or produces variable quality medicine, a major issue arises about whether to repeat clinical trials. Some countries such as Japan have far more stringent requirements relating to this issue than do most countries.

TABLE 46.11. *Selected functions of the analytical development department*

1. Develop analytical methods to test and monitor the purity and quality of active compounds, excipients, and dosage forms, plus raw materials and intermediates used in the synthesis
2. Automate the methods developed
3. Validate the methods developed to meet regulatory authority standards
4. Document the methods developed
5. Transfer analytical methods to the quality assurance group at the appropriate time during development
6. Use the analytical methods developed to analyze samples from multiple batches made and from all stability study samples at the appropriate time
7. Document the results of analytical studies for regulatory authorities

---

Degradation Products

Breakdown products that develop from handling or storing a medicine are identified chemically and are then synthesized if it is important to evaluate them further. Other breakdown products may be isolated biochemically as an alternative to chemical synthesis. Obtaining a sample of major breakdown products is important because each breakdown product has its own spectrum of activities in terms of both efficacy and toxicity, and these must be understood to ensure that a medicine's quality, purity, and efficacy are unchanged. Therefore, breakdown products are evaluated in many of the same biological tests used to study the parent medicine.

Breakdown products of a medicine that are formed by

metabolism in animals and humans are also identified chemically and then synthesized. Although breakdown products identified in animals may not be formed in humans, they are important in understanding a medicine's metabolic action. Each species metabolizes medicines in somewhat different ways, and there is no single best animal species in which to obtain data that can be extrapolated to humans.

Medicine Analysis and Bioassays

Identifying and quantifying the amount of a medicine present in various biological fluids (e.g., plasma, urine) and in solutions prepared for assay are extremely important. Many different techniques are used to assay medicines. Finding the most sensitive and reproducible method often takes a great deal of time and effort, and the method selected must be balanced with the needs and limitations of the production environment. Some of the most difficult issues involve (1) quantifying extremely small amounts of a medicine and degradation products, (2) detecting a chemical compound in a complex mixture of excipients, (3) assaying complex biological compounds such as proteins, (4) validating new assay technologies, or (5) setting purity specifications. Bioassays (i.e., assays that use a living system [animals, tissues, microorganisms] to assay activity) involve many complex issues.

When the same validated assay procedure is performed on the same sample at two (or more) sites of a company, the analysis at each site must give the same result. The degree to which this occurs is a ruggedness test of the assay method. Assays may be developed independently at two or more sites or even in two different departments at the same site (e.g., analytical development and biochemistry), but this is usually an unnecessary duplication of effort and should be avoided. If multiple procedures are used to assay medicine levels, different results may occur and lead to many new issues. To cross-validate assay systems it is usual for the sites to exchange both standard operating procedures for conducting the assay and actual samples. If results differ between sites, scientists often visit the other site(s) and attempt to resolve the discrepancies.

Bioassays of Biologicals

Biologicals include genetically engineered medicines, medicines obtained from natural sources, and other types listed in Chapter 24 (Biotechnology) that are not chemically synthesized. Numerous additional problems are likely to arise in the development of biological products. In part, these problems relate to the fact that biological products are usually much more chemically complex and exhibit more batch-to-batch variability than most synthesized chemicals. Impurities may include particles of bacteria or yeast, DNA, host cell antigens, viruses, and endotoxins in addition to typical contaminants (e.g., degradation products) seen with synthetic chemicals. Because the activity of biological agents can vary from batch to batch, which affects medicine performance, their concentration or strength must be assayed. Assays to evaluate biological activity tend to develop "bugs" and do not always give reproducible results. This problem may also occur with assays used to evaluate synthetic chemicals but is usually less common.

Existence of an assay is a prerequisite for developing a biological product. If an assay is unavailable, there is no means to determine the amount of a product present or to develop the product as a medicine. There is sometimes an issue of whether the amount of medicine should be quantitatively determined in terms of bioassay units of product or milligrams of protein present. An international reference standard, if available, must be used if bioassay units are necessary to quantitate the medicine. Variations in manufacturing procedures will probably make a true international reference standard an impossible objective to achieve for most medicines. In the case of bioassay units it becomes difficult to know whether (1) the material assayed is completely pure, (2) the methods used to assay the product are perfectly reproducible, (3) the product will remain stable over time, and (4) the different manufacturing processes used by companies are actually producing the same material. If no international reference standard exists, as occurs for some proteins, then each company working with the product will report results using their own assays. Consequently, there may be little agreement between data obtained by different companies, and each medicine will need to be evaluated on its own merit.

LIAISON ISSUES

Technical development departments must interact closely with research, medical, production, and marketing departments in the development of new medicines.

Interactions of Technical Departments with Production

Technical development departments are responsible for developing and transferring manufacturing processes for new medicines to production staff. These are usually medicines that development chemists and pharmacists have been producing in a pilot plant stage, prior to the final scaleup to manufacturing scale. Analytical scientists assist in the testing of intermediate and final products and transfer the necessary analytical method to quality assurance. To avoid potential conflicts of interest, quality assurance personnel do not report to managers in a production group.

An issue that often arises in pharmaceutical companies is the desire of production groups to acquire their own technical development staff. Different companies reach different solutions concerning this issue, often depending on logistical considerations (e.g., site location) and how cost-effective the duplication of this effort is viewed. Technical development departments in research and development that assign a low priority to production requests can expect a stronger demand from production managers for technical personnel based in production or for more work to be contracted to outside groups. Normally, support and service to chemical and pharmaceutical production receives the highest priority within technical departments.

Two of the questions process development scientists and chemical engineers frequently raise are (1) How can yield of an active compound be increased? and (2) How can the manufacturing process of a medicine be improved to make the product more efficiently at higher purity?

Each of these questions is directed to technical development and, to the degree that they are able to help, their assistance is valued. If they are too busy to help, however, then it creates pressures within production to seek their own dedicated staff to address these questions. This raises sensitive issues that senior managers must usually resolve.

Interactions of Technical Departments with Marketing

Interactions between technical departments and marketing groups are mainly concerned with developing investigational medicines and product line-extensions of prescription and/or OTC medicines. Line-extensions include new formulations, dosage strengths, dosage forms, and packages but not new active ingredients. Technical development work on product line-extensions generally covers the same range of activities that are performed on new investigational medicines, except that issues relating to the chemical manufacture of medicine substance are unnecessary.

The issue of allocation of research and development support services to marketing arises when each division reports to different managers in the organization. This is because marketing managers are unable to prioritize research and development work. Some marketing personnel express interest in having a small technical development group under their (i.e., marketing) control. This request often derives from inadequate technical department responses (from a marketing perspective) to marketing requests for services. It makes little sense, however, for a marketing group to establish its own small technical development group. Such a group would not have the expertise of the larger technical departments

within research and development. In addition, duplication of scarce scientists, specialists, and expensive equipment is inefficient. The service that marketing would receive from a small group under their control might be more rapid, but it probably would not adequately address many facets of product development because sophisticated personnel in many technical areas would not be present.

The appropriate response to this issue is for the two groups to meet and determine how to improve the technical development department's services to marketing. The service provided to marketing may be judged inadequate or poor on an overall basis because each marketing professional deals independently with technical staff. In practice, good service may be provided (1) to those who scream loudest, (2) to those who have the best personal relationships, (3) to those with the highest priority projects, and/or (4) by those with the lightest work load. In this system there is no *systematic* approach for marketing to use when interacting with research and development departments.

It would be preferable for marketing groups to present periodically a unified list of priorities and a marketing strategy to technical development and senior research and development managers for review and discussion. The managers would establish (1) those activities that could be conducted in-house within the time frame established by marketing, (2) those activities that could be contracted to outside groups, and (3) those activities that would have to be delayed. This last group of activities could be discussed by the group in more detail if desired. This type of meeting could be held at appropriate intervals (e.g., once, twice, or four times a year) and on an ad hoc basis. To advance line-extension projects along at a maximal rate and to coordinate activities between technical development, marketing, and production, it would be desirable to have a full-time professional manager assigned to one or more projects. The number of projects assigned to each manager would depend on the amount of time required to administer each project. This individual would ensure timely progression of his or her project(s) through the system. This collaborative effort would prevent unnecessary technical work on line-extensions that did not have the agreement of all relevant managers as to its appropriateness, priority, and timing.

"CATCH-22" SITUATIONS IN TECHNICAL DEVELOPMENT

Many "Catch-22" type (i.e., circular, paradoxical, or no-win) situations involving technical development can be described. A number of these situations are mentioned by Spilker (1991). A few others are mentioned to illustrate types of problems that often arise.

Increasing the Medicine Supply

Assume that the raw materials needed to synthesize a potentially important investigational medicine are made by only one or two companies in the world. Also assume that the pharmaceutical company does not have the resources to make the starting material itself. The chemical companies are able to supply only small amounts of raw materials and do not want to increase their capacity unless a customer (i.e., pharmaceutical company) contractually agrees to a long-term commitment to buy substantial quantities of the raw material. Obviously, the pharmaceutical company does not want to give this type of commitment until the medicine is known to be safe and effective and has a reasonable chance of reaching the market.

Many medium and even large pharmaceutical companies cannot justify spending large amounts of money for a medicine that may have only a small chance of being safe and effective. As a result, insufficient medicine is available for the development program. During the period of slow progress on the medicine's development, the patent clock ticks away, potential sales in future years are lost, and opportunity costs mount. After clinical efficacy is demonstrated, the company willingly makes additional commitments for medicine supplies. There is no easy answer to the dilemma of how to increase medicine supplies early in a project's life when raw materials are scarce. Companies with greater resources are more likely than companies with limited resources to assume a financial risk at an early stage of a medicine's development.

Allocating a Small Medicine Supply

A substantial amount of a medicine substance or key raw material is required to conduct research, develop new formulations, explore better means of making a medicine, develop a production process, or support other technical activities. When the bulk medicine is in short supply and that supply is needed to conduct clinical trials, there is a dilemma of how to allocate and use the precious supply. Allocating medicines to clinical trials is often advantageous even at the expense of slowing technical development, especially when the medicine is needed for important studies. There is no easy answer to this dilemma except that each situation must be carefully evaluated. This problem is extremely common because several groups often compete for available supplies of a medicine early in its development, and the problem becomes more intense when a medicine is targeted for rapid development.

Apportioning Work Effort

The appropriate amount of technical development work that should be initiated prior to the company's reaching a firm go-no go decision on whether to proceed with a medicine's development to an NDA is often difficult to identify clearly. If a company invests its technical development resources on too many projects that later fail, it will create a highly inefficient system of medicine development and may compromise the development of medicines that eventually reach the market. On the other hand, waiting for a firm "go" decision on a medicine, which occurs somewhere in late Phase II, before investing resources on technical development is impossible. Some technical departments have a rough rule that 80% of their work is performed after the go-no go point has been passed. Other departments, however, cannot operate under this rule, especially when technical success influences the go-no go decision. There are also special considerations (e.g., commercial importance, degree of certainty that a specific compound will reach the NDA stage, medical benefits) that may accelerate or delay the amount of technical work required on a specific medicine.

Padding Medicine Requests

When clinical, toxicological, and other staff prepare their estimates of medicine requirement for the chemical development laboratories to synthesize, it is natural for those requesting a medicine to pad (i.e., round up) their requirements. This makes sense because many unknown problems may occur that may require more medicine to complete their activities. How much additional medicine should they request? If their need is for 100 mg or even 100 g and 40 or more kilograms are being made, they could pad their request by up to 100% and it would probably make no difference. If a group requires 40 kg and the synthetic amount to be prepared will be just tailored for that one group, then how much should they pad their request? If they add more than 15% or so then their request may affect pilot plant schedules and potentially interfere with the synthetic development of other medicines, besides being wasteful of the company's resources.

In clinical trials there are several areas where padding often exists: (1) extra tablets per bottle in case patients cannot return to the clinic for a few days past their scheduled appointment, (2) a few additional bottles for each patient to allow for breakage or additional time on the medicine, (3) bottles of medicine for additional patients (10% to 50% overage is often used) beyond those required by the protocol, to allow for dropouts to be replaced or for additional patients, and (4) additional tablets prepared that are not bottled for a particular trial.

This situation is complicated for the chemists who synthesize medicines by other forms of padding: (1) requests for a medicine to be made for studies that are tentatively planned but are not certain or (2) requests for a medicine sooner in time than really needed because the staff wants to have a medicine available to use when they are ready and believe that the best way to ensure this is to place an early request.

These issues should be controlled by an astute project leader and staff from the chemical development group that receives requests. Any suspicious requests and all large requests should be reviewed with appropriate staff. Anyone who abuses company guidelines in regard to these padding issues will eventually be viewed as the boy who cried "wolf."

CONCLUSION

Setting Priorities

It is known that a major responsibility for technical development departments is to provide service to production to ensure that the company products are pro-duced on schedule. A request to assist production may cause major (or minor) delays in progressing on investigational medicine products. The balance can be difficult if technical development is asked to help work on a minor marketed product that would save production about 50,000 dollars or pounds per year but would delay work on an investigational medicine that is expected to earn one million dollars or pounds per week.

It often seems inevitable to technical development scientists that, after years of heroic effort spent on solving difficult technical issues, a company toxicologist or clinician announces that a serious safety or efficacy problem has arisen and recommends that the medicine's development be terminated. Another way of expressing this point is that if chemical development can make it, analytical development can analyze it, and pharmaceutical development can formulate it, then technical staff say that a medicine is bound to die in the clinic. Let's hope not.

47 / Marketing Issues

Introduction **540**	Identifying the Customer 550
General Considerations About New Products . 540	Creating a Medicine's Profile 551
Market Cycle—Birth, Life, and Death of a	**Naming a Medicine** **551**
Medicine **540**	**Pricing, Costs, and Economics** **553**
Birth and Life of a Medicine 540	Using Price as a Strategic Tool 553
Why Do Marketed Medicines Die? 540	Costs of a Disease: Direct, Indirect, and
Why Do Investigational Medicines Die? 541	Intangible 553
Identifying the Need for a New Medicine **542**	Cost-Effectiveness Claims 554
How Many Medicines Constitute 50% of a	Standardization of Economic Comparisons ... 554
Company's Sales? 542	**Introducing a Medicine** **554**
How Many Medicines Make a Profit for Their	**Promoting a Medicine** **555**
Company? 544	Advertising Issues 555
Research and Development—Marketing	Direct-to-Consumer Advertising of
Interface 545	Prescription Medicines 555
The Relative Importance of Marketing Versus	Assessing Medicine Claims 556
Research and Development in Influencing	Professional Over-the-Counter Medicines 557
Medicine Development 545	**Distributing and Selling a Medicine** **558**
Providing Input to Research and Development	Medicine Distribution 558
During Medicine Development **545**	Accuracy of Market Predictions of New
Periodic Management Meetings Between	Product Sales 558
Marketing and Research and Development . 545	Where Does a Company Focus Its Activities
Medical Groups Controlled by Marketing 546	on the Physician-Patient-Pharmacist Chain? 559
Conducting Marketing Research **547**	Promoting Medicines to Physicians in
Methods and Types of Studies 547	Primary, Secondary, and Tertiary Care
Depth of Market Research 547	Practices 561
Sources of Marketing Data Obtained from	**Protecting a Medicine** **561**
Outside Groups 547	Effect of Marketing Decisions in Other
Determining Marketing Strategy **548**	Countries 561
Providing Information to Consumers **548**	Protecting Medicines from Tampering and
Providing Patients with Information about	Counterfeiting 561
Medicines 548	**Expanding a Medicine's Market** **561**
Deciding Where to Sell a Medicine **549**	Increasing Market Share 561
In Which Country Should a New Medicine Be	Conversion of Prescription Medicines to Over-
Registered First? 549	the-Counter Status 564
Who Decides in Which Countries a New	Sales of a Medicine for Unapproved Uses and
Medicine Should Be Registered? 549	Obtaining Regulatory Approval for Those
Positioning a Medicine **550**	Uses 565

All who drink of this remedy recover in a short time, except those whom it does not help, who all die. Therefore it is obvious that it fails only in incurable cases. Galen, 2nd Century A.D.

In recent times, modern science has developed to give mankind, for the first time in the history of the human race, a way of securing a more abundant life which does not simply consist in taking away from someone else. Karl Taylor Compton (1887 to 1954), American atomic physicist. From an address to the American Philosophical Society, 1938.

INTRODUCTION

This chapter briefly presents a number of issues faced by marketing personnel in developing new medicines. It does not systematically detail the processes followed by marketing groups to assist in developing new medicines. Interactions that take place between marketing and medical departments are described in Chapter 129 of *Guide to Clinical Trials* (Spilker, 1991) and in Section V of this book.

General Considerations About New Products

New products are introduced for numerous reasons, but the most widely discussed is to increase company sales in existing as well as new markets. New products are also introduced to provide a means of protecting, if not actually expanding, a company's current share of a particular market. For example, a company may develop and market a new product that merely substitutes for one of their older medicines. This often made sense approximately 20 to 30 years ago when an older medicine came off patent or was losing market share because of adverse publicity or problems that the newer medicine did not have. Substitution strategies were successful with various classes of medicines, including antibiotics, analgesics, and antianxiety agents. In today's market, especially with generic competition and high costs of medicine development, it is essential to have a demonstrable added value for new medicines to be successful.

New products that are quite similar to existing products sometimes do extremely well on the market. This is especially true when claims are made for a new medicine that differentiate it from existing medicines or expand the potential uses for which it can be sold. Another basis

on which new medicines sometimes do extremely well relates to the aggressiveness or the particular approach used by sales representatives who contact and detail physicians. Several parameters considered by marketing when a new product or project is being discussed are listed in Table 47.1. This list is presented to provide a flavor of marketing considerations about new products.

MARKET CYCLE—BIRTH, LIFE, AND DEATH OF A MEDICINE

Birth and Life of a Medicine

Market cycle refers to the life cycle of a product. If the date of a medicine's initial marketing is defined as the moment of its birth, then medicines go through many of the growth and maturing phases and steps experienced by humans. The product eventually reaches old age and is gradually (or rapidly) replaced by newer medicines, by generic equivalents, or by newer medical practices (e.g., nonmedicine approaches to patient treatment). Eventually, most medicines die and are withdrawn from the market. Marketing-related activities that occur during the market cycle are listed in Table 47.2. Most of this chapter discusses the processes of birth and life in more detail. A medicine's death is described below.

Why Do Marketed Medicines Die?

Medicines, like people, may die suddenly and unexpectedly (e.g., from newly observed or reported serious toxicity in animals or patients), or they may have a long, lingering "illness" before death occurs. Another analogy with human experience is that the death of some products is totally unexpected and/or extremely painful to the company parents (in terms of lost sales or possible damage to their reputation). The death of other medicines may leave a bitter aftermath in terms of legal wrangles in courts. Finally, many medicines die quietly and peacefully in old age with few patients, physicians, or even company officials to mourn their passing. The comments in this section refer to the death of a generic-named medicine and not to a brand name medicine whose sales are being eroded by generic competition.

Few studies have examined the detailed factors of why medicines die and are removed from the market. The most common reason is that their sales and profits have fallen to the point where there is little or no business reason to keep them on the market. If there are no compelling medical reasons to keep such medicines available, then they are usually withdrawn from sale.

Sales usually decline for several reasons. These reasons may primarily involve marketing (e.g., poor or inadequate marketing practices by the company, better or more aggressive marketing practices by competitors) or

TABLE 47.1. *Assessment of new products by marketing*

1. Sales estimates (third year)
2. Market potential in terms of number of patients
3. Patentability and/or exclusivity (e.g., orphan medicines)
4. Market trend for the therapeutic area or disease area
5. Development time necessary before an NDA[a] on the medicine may be filed
6. Promotional effort required in cost and its projected effectiveness
7. Breadth of medicine use by medical specialists or generalists
8. Existing market versus need to create one
9. Competition in terms of number of companies and medicines, plus how well they are satisfying current and anticipated demand
10. Effect on other company products (e.g., effect on sales, degree of fit)
11. Pricing situation in terms of stability and competition
12. Ability of sales force to promote the medicine (e.g., number of staff, training required)

[a] NDA, New Drug Application.

TABLE 47.2. *General types of marketing-related activities in the medicine industry*

A. Advertising and promotion
  1. Corporate advertising
  2. Product advertising
  3. Advertising agency policy decisions
  4. Media selection or purchase
  5. Sales promotion
  6. Product publicity
  7. Merchandising
  8. Packaging
B. Sales and distribution
  1. Sales to major accounts
  2. Sales to other selected classes of customers
  3. Sales to all other customers
  4. Export sales
  5. Other foreign marketing operations
  6. Distributor or dealer relations
  7. Physical distribution of products
  8. Sales training
  9. Customer service
  10. Product service
C. Business research and analysis
  1. Research on current and future markets
  2. Research on competitors
  3. Advertising research
  4. Environmental scanning and analysis
  5. Economic research and analysis
  6. Sales analysis
  7. Sales forecasting
  8. Marketing information systems
D. Products and planning (excluding R and D)[a]
  1. Preparation of marketing plans
  2. Product pricing
  3. Market development
  4. Product line extensions
  5. New products related to existing lines
  6. New products not related to existing lines

[a] R and D, research and development.

TABLE 47.3. *Reasons for termination of medicine projects by Hoechst-Roussel Pharmaceuticals Inc. between 1972 and 1978[a]*

Reason	Preclinical	Clinical	Total
Synthesis problem	4	0	4
Patent problem	1	1	2
Instability	4	0	4
Toxicological finding	12	2	14
Efficacy less than expected	16	16	32
Adverse reactions	5	3	8
Price problems	1	0	1
Better competitors	3	1	4
Total	46	23	69

[a] From Seidl (1983) with permission of Raven Press.

medical aspects of the medicine. Medical reasons often relate to the benefit-to-risk ratio of the medicine and how it has changed over the years or how it has changed in comparison with other medicines and treatments. Factors may also relate to competitor's medicines. The overall factors affecting the duration of a medicine's life may be internal to the medicine (e.g., adverse reactions or other toxicity), external (e.g., newer medicines), or a combination of both.

Why Do Investigational Medicines Die?

Few studies have been conducted to determine the reasons why investigational medicines are terminated before reaching the market. Seidl reported (1983) the reasons why Hoechst-Roussel Pharmaceuticals Inc. discontinued 69 investigational compounds between 1972 and 1978 (Table 47.3). Twice the number were discontinued for preclinical than for clinical reasons. Prentis and Walker (1986) presented data on 197 compounds evaluated in humans for the first time by seven United Kingdom companies between 1964 and 1980. Table 47.4 lists the fate of the 137 that died. The remainder were marketed or were still under investigation at the time of their paper's publication. There are several reasons why these sets of data from Germany and the United Kingdom are not totally comparable and therefore cannot be compared (e.g., different years and countries were evaluated, one study evaluated a single company whereas the other study evaluated seven). Nonetheless, it is interesting that 16 of the 23 compounds that were terminated in the clinic were terminated by Hoechst-Roussel Pharmaceuticals Inc. for in-

TABLE 47.4. *Reasons for termination of new chemical entities under development by seven United Kingdom-owned companies between 1964 and 1980[a]*

Reason	All NCEs[b] studied[c]	NCEs except anti-infectives
1. Problems with human pharmacokinetics	67 (49%)	6 (9%)
2. Lack of proven efficacy	31 (23%)	29 (41%)
3. Adverse reactions in humans	15 (11%)	13 (19%)
4. Toxicity in animals	12 (9%)	10 (14%)
5. Miscellaneous	12 (9%)	12 (17%)
Total terminated	137	70

[a] This table was modified from a figure presented by Prentis and Walker (1986) with permission of the Pharmaceutical Society of Great Britain.
[b] NCE, new chemical entity.
[c] This category was composed of 67 anti-infective medicines, and the data were presented both including and excluding this group of medicines.

sufficient efficacy (70%), three of 23 were terminated because of adverse reactions (13%), and two of 23 (9%) were terminated because of toxicity observed in animals. The comparable data of new chemical entities (NCEs) from the United Kingdom, excluding anti-infectives, were, respectively, 41%, 19%, and 14%.

IDENTIFYING THE NEED FOR A NEW MEDICINE

All research-based pharmaceutical companies perceive new medicines as their lifeblood. Just how true this perception is may be noted from the following discus-sion, which indicates the dependence of most pharmaceutical companies on a small number of medicines for most of their sales.

How Many Medicines Constitute 50% of a Company's Sales?

Some companies make 50% or more of their sales from a wide variety of medicines. But these companies are exceptions. Most medium and large size pharmaceutical companies make at least half their sales from a small number of medicines. Table 47.5 was assembled from Intercontinental Medical Statistics (Ambler, PA)

TABLE 47.5. *Top medicines in sales of leading manufacturing companies in the United States in 1985[a]*

Company	Product name	Sales in millions ($)	Percentage of total (%)	Cumulative percentage (%)
Merck Sharp & Dohme	Total	1,319	100.0	
	Aldomet/Aldoril/Aldoclor	229	17.4	17.4
	Mefoxin	221	16.8	34.1
	Clinoril	135	10.25	44.3
	Timoptic	120	9.1	43.5
	Indocin	103	7.8	61.3
Smith Kline & French Laboratories	Total	1,013	100.0	
	Tagamet	482	47.6	47.6
	Dyazide	262	25.9	73.5
	Ancef	97	9.6	83.1
Eli Lilly and Company	Total	932	100.0	
	Insulin (all)	216	23.2	23.2
	Darvon (all)	143	15.4	38.6
	Ceclor	132	14.2	52.7
	Mandol	89	9.6	62.3
The Upjohn Company	Total	737	100.0	
	Xanax	147	20.0	20.0
	Motrin	108	14.7	34.7
	Cleocin (all)	102	13.9	48.6
	Halcion	56	7.6	56.2
Pfizer Laboratories Division	Total	669	100.0	
	Feldene	240	35.9	35.9
	Procardia	180	26.9	62.8
	Minipress/Minizide	111	16.6	79.4
Roche Laboratories	Total	648	100.0	
	Valium/Valrelease	299	46.2	46.2
	Bactrim	50	7.8	54.0
	Dalmane	48	7.5	61.5
Wyeth Laboratories	Total	600	100.0	
	Birth control pills	186	31.0	31.0
	Ativan	124	20.6	51.6
Parke-Davis	Total	550	100.0	
	Dilantin (all)	82	14.9	14.9
	Procan	51	9.3	24.1
	Meclomen	33	6.0	30.1
	Benadryl (all)	32	5.9	36.0
	Erythromycin	29	5.2	41.2
	Anusol	27	5.0	46.2
	Lopid	25	4.5	50.7
Ayerst Laboratories	Total	534	100.0	
	Inderal/Inderide	366	61.6	61.6
	Premarin	97	18.2	79.7
E. R. Squibb & Sons Inc.	Total	521	100.0	
	Corgard/Corzide	113	21.7	21.7
	Capoten	112	21.5	43.2
	Prolixin (all)	36	6.9	50.1
	Velosef	29	5.6	55.7

TABLE 47.5. *Continued.*

Company	Product name	Sales in millions ($)	Percentage of total (%)	Cumulative percentage (%)
Burroughs Wellcome Co.	Total	454	100.0	
	Zovirax	58	12.8	12.8
	Lanoxin/caps	51	11.1	23.9
	Septra	48	10.6	34.6
	Actifed	41	9.1	43.7
	Sudafed	38	8.3	52.0
Schering Corporation	Total	451	100.0	
	Proventil	55	12.1	12.1
	Lotrimin/sone	34	7.5	19.6
	Diprolene/sone	26	5.8	25.4
	Afrin	26	5.7	31.1
	Drixoral	29	6.5	37.6
	Garamycin	21	4.6	42.3
	Valisone	21	4.6	46.8
	Chlor-Trimeton	19	4.2	51.0
Syntex Laboratories, Inc.	Total	436	100.0	
	Naprosyn/Anaprox	285	65.3	65.3
	Norinyl (all)	56	12.9	78.2
	Lidex	38	8.8	87.0
Glaxo Inc.	Total	428	100.0	
	Zantac	303	70.7	70.7
	Ventolin	47	11.0	81.7
	Fortaz	17	4.0	85.8
Dista Products Company	Total	402	100.0	
	Keflex	238	59.1	59.1
	Nebcin	75	18.6	77.8
	Nalfon	49	12.1	89.9
Stuart Pharmaceuticals	Total	392	100.0	
	Tenormin/Tenoretic	231	59.0	59.0
	Mylanta	49	12.6	71.6
	Nolvadex	49	12.5	84.1
Bristol Laboratories	Total	368	100.0	
	Platinol	63	17.2	17.2
	Amikin	32	8.6	25.8
	Polycillin	26	7.1	32.9
	Naldecon	24	6.4	39.4
	Mutamycin	23	6.3	45.7
	Cytoxan	23	6.3	52.0
Ortho Pharmaceutical Corporation	Total	364	100.0	
	Ortho-Novum (all)	257	70.6	70.6
	Monistat (all)	69	19.0	89.5
	Modicon (all)	11	3.1	92.7
Lederle Laboratories	Total	359	100.0	
	Pipracil	64	17.7	17.7
	Minocin	56	15.6	33.3
	Maxzide	29	8.0	41.2
	Methotrexate	24	6.6	47.8
	Diamox	19	5.2	53.0
Abbott Laboratories	Total	350	100.0	
	Tranxene	93	26.7	26.7
	E.E.S.	46	13.2	39.9
	K-Lor/K-Tab	34	9.7	49.6
Sandoz Pharmaceuticals Corporation	Total	327	100.0	
	Fiorinal	50	15.2	15.2
	Mellaril	36	11.0	26.3
	Restoril	35	10.7	37.0
	Parlodel	34	10.5	47.5
	Sandimmune	33	10.0	57.5
Ciba Pharmaceutical Company	Total	327	100.0	
	Transderm-Nitro	122	37.4	36.4
	Ritalin	25	7.7	45.1
	Apresoline	23	6.9	52.0

(Continued)

TABLE 47.5. *Top medicines in sales of leading manufacturing companies in the United States in 1985*[a]

Company	Product name	Sales in millions ($)	Percentage of total (%)	Cumulative percentage (%)
Geigy Pharmaceuticals	Total	310	100.0	
	Lopressor	163	52.6	52.6
	Tegretol	60	19.4	71.9
	Brethine	30	9.6	81.5
Private label	Total	307	100.0	
	Small volume generics			
Marion Laboratories, Inc.	Total	293	100.0	
	Cardizem	133	45.4	45.4
	Carafate	39	13.2	58.6
	Os-Cal	30	10.2	68.8
Boehringer Ingelheim Pharmaceuticals, Inc.	Total	281	100.0	
	Catapres	92	32.9	32.9
	Persantine	91	32.5	65.4
	Alupent	52	18.4	83.8
Searle Pharmaceuticals Inc.	Total	276	100.0	
	Calan	49	17.9	17.9
	Norpace	48	17.5	35.4
	Aldactazide/Aldactone	39	14.1	49.5
	Nitrodisc	24	8.6	58.1
Hoechst-Roussel Pharmaceuticals Inc.	Total	266	100.0	
	Lasix	79	29.5	29.5
	Claforan	78	29.2	58.7
	DiaBeta	21	8.0	66.7
Merrell Dow Pharmaceuticals Inc.	Total	365	100.0	
	Nicorette	45	16.8	16.8
	Seldane	30	11.3	28.1
	Norpramin	25	9.6	37.7
	Tenuate	15	5.8	43.5
	Cepacol	14	5.5	48.9
	Novahistine	14	5.2	54.2
McNeil Consumer Products Co.	Total	255	100.0	
	Tylenol	228	89.3	89.3
	CoTylenol	14	5.3	94.7
	Sine-Aid	6	2.3	97.0
Roerig	Total	255	100.0	
	Cefobid	81	31.7	31.7
	Sinequan	39	15.5	47.2
	Navane	35	13.7	60.9
McNeil Pharmaceutical	Total	250	100.0	
	Haldol	86	35.1	35.1
	Tylenol w/Codeine	64	26.1	61.2
	Tolectin	50	20.4	81.7

[a] Sales above 250 million dollars. Data obtained from Intercontinental Medical Statistics (IMS) America, Ambler, PA. Some of these medicines are manufactured by subsidiary corporations.

(IMS) data of 1985 total sales in United States pharmacies and hospitals. The sales included generally represent between 75% and 100% of a company's total sales. These data do not include sales of medicines to government agencies, supermarkets, or other sources. Of the 31 companies listed in this table, the number with 50% or more of their sales coming from one to four medicines are as listed in Table 47.6.

The fact that this table contains out-of-date data is immaterial to its main point and the reason why it is included in this volume. The fact that most companies depend on an extremely small number of medicines (e.g., one to three) for at least half of their sales is as true today as it was in 1985.

Although the numbers of companies are fairly evenly distributed across Table 47.6, it illustrates that 16 of the largest 31 pharmaceutical companies made at least half their sales from only one or two medicines and that 22 of this group of 31 companies made at least half their sales from one to three products.

How Many Medicines Make a Profit for Their Company?

Most medicines launched by a company never make a profit for the company and actually never repay development costs. Of all medicines introduced on the market,

TABLE 47.6. *Number of medicines constituting 50 percent of a company's sales*

	Number of companies
One medicine accounts for 50 percent or more of company sales	8
Two medicines account for 50 percent or more of company sales	8
Three medicines account for 50 percent or more of company sales	6
Four medicines account for 50 percent or more of company sales	2
Total	24
More than four medicines account for 50 percent of company sales	7
Total	31

there is general agreement that only approximately one-fourth to one-third ever repay their cost of development and break even (Virts and Weston, 1980; Grabowski and Vernon, 1982; Drews, 1985; Joglekar and Paterson, 1986). On the other hand, the evidence for this conclusion is not hard, and the true proportion of those that break even or make a profit may be somewhat greater.

Research and Development—Marketing Interface

To be highly productive and successful, it is critically important for companies to have a positive relationship between research and development and marketing. Some research and development personnel do not understand that the commercial success of a medicine depends on timely registration and medicine differentiation. Others may not believe that marketing personnel are selling the company's products effectively. In these situations relationships are likely to become strained and marketing input will not be sought and incorporated in research and development thinking.

On the other hand, marketing personnel may not (1) understand the complexity of clinical research and technical development, (2) believe that the company's research is adequately focused or concentrated in the most commercially attractive therapeutic areas, or (3) believe that appropriate priorities or allocation of resources are being used. In either situation, relationships will become strained and the two groups will probably not work smoothly together developing new medicines and line-extensions. If marketing personnel provide a sales forecast on an investigational medicine that research and development managers consider too low, it may initiate a conflict between the two groups. Discussions of each group's assumptions and methods will usually resolve this issue and achieve joint support of most plans and actions.

The fate of medically attractive medicines with little commercial value differs depending on the company involved. The factors that determine a medicine's fate relate to (1) the company's tradition, (2) the company's current portfolio of projects, (3) how well the medicine fits the corporate comfort zone, (4) the power of the medicines' protagonists (and antagonists, if any), and (5) whether there may be alternative reasons to develop the medicine. The cooperation of research and development and marketing groups may be severely tested when an investigational medicine has a high medical and low commercial value and the project draws resources (or would draw resources) away from projects that the marketing group believes have greater commercial value and are of high or medium medical value.

The Relative Importance of Marketing Versus Research and Development in Influencing Medicine Development

Balancing the influence of research and development and marketing forces in developing medicines and driving the corporate business is a major challenge at most companies. One group or the other is usually more influential in decisions made about medicine development. One factor that affects which group becomes more influential depends on whether the company traditionally defines success solely in financial terms or whether the equation for success also includes the medical value of new medicines. Another factor relates to whether the company is publicly or privately owned. If the risk to a company's survival or well-being develops, different factors and forces will become dominant (i.e., commercial considerations must dominate).

PROVIDING INPUT TO RESEARCH AND DEVELOPMENT DURING MEDICINE DEVELOPMENT

Marketing groups often review disease or therapeutic areas that either are currently being explored by research and development or where new development projects are being considered. Marketing factors included in the evaluation are (1) description of the market, (2) actual trends, (3) potential trends, (4) patient prevalence, (5) current sales data, (6) projected sales data, (7) leading marketed products, (8) prescribing patterns, (9) competitive pressures, (10) competitive products, and (11) market trends.

Periodic Management Meetings Between Marketing and Research and Development

Marketing and research and development managers interact on many levels from the board of directors down through the company to the trench levels and on many specialized committees. In addition to these and other formal (and informal) interactions, there should be a periodic meeting to review the priorities of research and development activities conducted for the marketing group. This meeting would review ongoing work and plans for the coming year and perhaps discuss long-term future requests for assistance. Advantages of this meeting are that:

1. Marketing would assemble a list of all the clinical trials and other activities that research and development is conducting and is requested to conduct for marketing. These would be prioritized from a single marketing perspective, thus avoiding many separate marketers telling many people in research and development that their particular trials are most important to conduct.

2. Research and development can review, at a single time, all of the marketing requests for assistance and each of their priorities. Research and development can

therefore comment at an early stage if particular trials pose significant problems, should be handled in a different manner, or will require more time to complete.

3. Agreement on the appropriate financing for each of the activities may be achieved prior to a commitment to proceed.

4. Most importantly, marketing would be assured that its top priorities were being addressed and would not "fall through the cracks." Marketing could make alternative plans (e.g., contract work to an outside group) if the research and development departments were unable to conduct specific trials of particular interest to marketing.

Medical Groups Controlled by Marketing

Marketing may desire to control their own medicine development function to "more effectively" expand the range of indications on marketed medicines, develop

MANAGING MEDICAL ACTIVITIES
TO SUPPORT OTC MEDICINES

A.

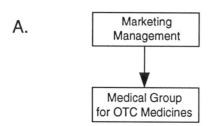

- It is difficult to attract top medical staff to this type of organization.
- This approach may become demotivating to medical staff.

B.

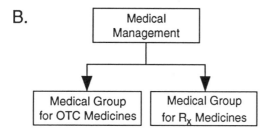

- Physicians should be encouraged to circulate through both groups.

C.

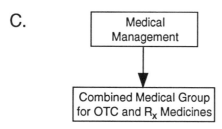

- OTC studies are often given low priority.
- Marketing groups find it more difficult to influence priorities and resource allocations.

FIG. 47.1. Three models of how medical groups can be organized to conduct marketing studies.

new dosage forms, and conduct studies for promotional purposes. This ability could entail developing both medical and technical development expertise (e.g., pharmaceutical development, analytical development) and groups. Although a number of pharmaceutical companies have medical groups controlled by marketing, this approach is often extremely controversial. A number of possible approaches are shown in Fig. 47.1. The control of a technical development group by marketing is described briefly in Chapter 46, Technical Development.

CONDUCTING MARKETING RESEARCH

Methods and Types of Studies

Marketing research departments conduct various types of studies, interviews, and literature evaluations relating to investigational and marketed medicines. These include (1) general market evaluations on a medicine, disease, therapeutic area, or other category, (2) tests on products (e.g., flavor tests, name recognition tests), (3) pricing studies, (4) environmental studies (e.g., surveys, field trips), (5) tests on packaging, and (6) tests on the value of potential commercial claims.

The methods used in marketing research are basically the same as the scientific methods used in sound research and development. First, the problem or issue is defined; next, a hypothesis is developed; and then a study is designed to test the hypothesis. The study is conducted and data are then analyzed and interpreted. Finally, recommendations are made and the results are reported in a verbal and/or written presentation.

Another source of marketing data is to conduct telephone or direct physician interviews to better understand their reactions to new and old medicines. These interviews may primarily be oriented toward understanding the need for new medicines, problems of older medicines, or acceptability and desirability of medicines currently under development. Characteristics of an actual or hypothetical medicine may be tested with physicians to determine their reactions to its advantages and how often they might prescribe it.

It is sometimes desirable to enlist the help of an outside organization to conduct a market research study. This may be a result of limitations in expertise, contacts, time, facilities, or another factor within the marketing research group. If an outside group is to be utilized, it is necessary to develop criteria to be used in choosing the most appropriate one.

Depth of Market Research

Market research, like research in any other area, may be superficial or comprehensive, may ask highly imaginative and specific questions, or may plod methodically through a general or traditional approach. Each company wants to obtain reliable information in a cost-effective manner, but some are financially able to place more resources in their marketing research efforts than others. Also, some companies are more interested in using these data to make decisions.

There are proponents of a no-frills approach to marketing research (Saltzman, 1985). Saltzman makes the important point that the level of time and expenditure applied to a marketing question should be titrated according to the relative importance of the decision(s) that will be made. One of the keys to reducing costs of market research is to attempt to locate the information needed in secondary sources that are already available. These sources include published literature and computer data bases. Another method is to interview a few selected industry experts and opinion leaders rather than to conduct a broad survey of many individuals. Of course, some companies prefer to place more weight on opinions of physicians who would be the ones to prescribe a product than on experts who may not be correct in their opinions. No matter which or how many of these (or other) types of groups are approached, it is critical to ask the correct questions, phrased in the correct way, and with proper background information.

Questionnaires used in written surveys, in interviews, or on the telephone must be evaluated and validated before they are used. It is extremely easy to introduce substantial bias into the questions asked. A marketing group that desires a certain outcome of their survey may easily bias the questionnaire, even unintentionally. The danger, of course, is that a company may make wrong business decisions based on incorrect marketing data. Marketing researchers are usually aware of this pitfall and take appropriate steps to avoid it.

Sources of Marketing Data Obtained from Outside Groups

Companies with adequate financial resources usually obtain some of their market data from IMS in Ambler, PA. Intercontinental Medical Statistics provides actual quantitative data in dollars sold, units of medicine, numbers of tablets dispensed, number of prescriptions written, and numerous other categories of information. These data enable companies to track the size and trends of the market in both pharmacies and hospitals for medicines of their competitors as well as to compare those results with their own. Medicines sold in supermarkets and a number of other locations (e.g., beauty aid shops) are not included. Some of the data available include the following.

1. *Pharmacy and hospital audits*—These supply market trends, effects of promotional practices, impact of

new product introductions, influence of seasonality, and other information.

2. *National disease and therapeutic index*—These supply usage patterns of medicine use in office-based practices.

3. *National prescription audit*—This measures both medicines prescribed by physicians and medicines dispensed by pharmacists. This gives information on pricing, dosages, packaging, promotion, prescription volume, market share, trends, and characteristics.

Intercontinental Medical Statistics also conducts a national audit of journal advertising, detailing to physicians, and mailings to physicians. Numerous other related marketing services are available from IMS. Various other sources of marketing data gathered by independent companies (e.g., Pharmaceutical Data Services, Scrip, deHaen, stockbrokers), trade associations, and government agencies also exist.

DETERMINING MARKETING STRATEGY

There is no magic list of factors that constitute a marketing strategy because many types of strategies must be developed before and during a medicine's life. The broad areas that are usually considered as part of a marketing strategy are the major headings in the rest of this chapter, plus others that are not discussed or are not discussed in detail, such as medicine distribution, financial credit, and medicine packaging. Thus, most of this chapter discusses marketing strategies. References to books that provide details and discussions of marketing strategies are listed in the back of this book (e.g., Smith, 1991).

PROVIDING INFORMATION TO CONSUMERS

Providing Patients with Information About Medicines

It is apparent that many patients want to know more about the medicines they take, but companies are hesitant to provide information directly to patients. This is gradually changing and some companies are starting to advertise about their new prescription medicines in magazines, in newspapers, and on television. It is anticipated that these and other patient-related issues will become much more important to pharmaceutical companies in future years.

Currently, pharmaceutical companies rely on physicians, pharmacists, nurses, and other health professionals to provide patients with information about prescription medicines. This is correct and pharmaceutical companies have spent a great deal of effort and money on educating these and other groups. Another means of providing information is via patient package inserts.

Patient Package Inserts

Patient package inserts are information sheets on a medicine written for patients and provided to them by a nurse or physician with each prescription or by a pharmacist when the prescription is filled. The use of these sheets for prescription medicines is controversial in countries where it is not mandated by law and there are strong defenders of multiple opinions.

Although most patients want to be guided by their physicians in medicine use (and not by a package insert), the author believes that patients have a right to a certain amount of information about any prescription medicine they are advised to take by a physician. If the patient chooses not to read a package insert then that is their concern. If a physician chooses to provide additional information, then that is his or her professional prerogative. But the use of patient package inserts would guarantee that each patient would have ready access to the same standard or minimum amount of information about the medicine prescribed. It may also be argued that package inserts are an ethical requirement that accompanies the sale of a medicine.

If a package insert is being developed for a medicine, it is important to understand the range of patients' attitudes as to potential adverse reactions they may experience from the medicine. These range from mild to severe adverse reactions that are reversible. It used to be considered that death was the worst adverse reaction imaginable. But it is clear from patient interviews and the literature that there are several physical and/or mental states that are considered to be worse than death. For example, if patients believe that the risk of a stroke is worse than the risk of a fatal reaction from using a medicine, then this is important information in determining how the patient package insert should be written. Numerous social, legal, political, ethical, and regulatory issues must be solved before patient package inserts are widely used.

The Association of the British Pharmaceutical Industry has endorsed the concept of patient package inserts (Anonymous, 1987a). They have also issued a series of recommendations that identify each of the elements they believe should be included in the leaflet as well as suggestions for their preparation and dissemination.

Other Vehicles for Companies to Reach Patients

It is possible to provide information about medicines to patients based on the ways in which they obtain medicine information. Thus, a different strategy could be developed to try to reach patients who learn about medicines from doctors, friends, news media, magazines, or other sources. This could be done for both nonprescription and prescription medicines.

Patient Participation in Medicine Therapy

Some medicines require patients to participate more in their treatment than to just swallow a few tablets each day. The requirements for effective medicine use may affect a patient's lifestyle, such as modifying diet, physical activity (e.g., driving), or personal habits (e.g., smoking or drinking). Examples of such medicines include those that help patients stop smoking, reduce their eating, change the types of foods they eat, and decrease cardiac pain. Special marketing aids to instruct and assist patients and/or physicians are useful approaches to improving patient compliance and benefits. Careful preparation of information about these aids will greatly assist patient (and physician) education and compliance.

How Much Information Should Physicians Give Patients?

When physicians communicate information about adverse reactions to patients, they must decide how much information to provide and also what type of information. Some details can impart fear, and the patient may not ingest their prescribed medicine. On the other hand, physicians who say too little to patients do not adequately inform them about potential risks. The correct balance is to provide each patient with enough of an understanding of both benefits and risks to enable the patient to make an informed decision about whether to continue taking the medicine. This is a difficult goal to achieve.

DECIDING WHERE TO SELL A MEDICINE

In Which Country Should a New Medicine Be Registered First?

The most obvious answer is to initially market the medicine in that country with the largest market. For most therapeutic areas and diseases, that country is the United States. But most medicines are not initially registered in the United States. Why? The answer primarily relates to the relatively higher standards used by the Food and Drug Administration (FDA) for medicine approval and the longer period of regulatory review compared with most other countries. There are numerous reasons why the FDA takes longer than other countries to approve medicines. The FDA usually has a higher "comfort level" that must be achieved by sound data on a new medicine. It is generally true that the FDA will more rapidly approve a medicine that is already being marketed in another country or countries, although they usually believe that some well-controlled data should be generated within the United States. Preferably, the medicine would be marketed in one or more highly developed countries whose standards of approving medicines are also high and where some postmarketing data have been obtained.

If the company does not immediately attempt to market the medicine in the country with the largest market, then should it try to market the medicine in the country where it could reach the market fastest? This sounds reasonable, except that those countries where new medicines can generally be marketed most rapidly are countries that would only sell small amounts of the medicine. Therefore, those countries could not provide sufficient postmarketing data of high quality to help expedite medicine registration significantly in larger markets.

The actual approaches used by multinational companies to target countries for early registration vary, depending on their headquarters, site(s) of medicine development, nature of the medicine, and anticipated markets. In general, each medicine is viewed individually and a strategy is developed to market the medicine in as many different countries in as short a time as possible. The particular country in which it is first marketed is often of little consequence to a multinational company because numerous registration submissions are made at approximately the same time. The factors of market size, speed of approval, accumulation of safety, and possibly efficacy data in a short period are prime considerations in the strategy developed. A company that addresses medicine registration in a primarily sequential manner loses a large amount of potential sales in multiple countries.

Although these points should appear obvious, there is an enormous difference in the speed and efficiency with which different large multinational companies bring their medicines to market in many countries.

Who Decides in Which Countries a New Medicine Should Be Registered?

There are two extreme positions in addressing this question. Those multinational companies that are organizationally centralized usually make this decision at their headquarters, in conjunction with input from regional managers and local directors within each country. Those companies that are decentralized usually make this decision at a local level. What may be a more important issue is whether promotional studies conducted in one country may have a positive or negative effect on medicine sales in another country. For example, if patients in an intensive care unit (ICU) are found to respond to a medicine in Country A, this use may become widely used in Country B. If a higher dose of the medicine is listed in the labeling in Country B, it may lead to serious adverse reactions, resulting in negative publicity for the medicine in that country. This raises the question of whether a central group should approve local promotional studies, especially if the studies do not adhere to a centrally approved data sheet on a particular medicine or are evaluating a nonapproved use.

POSITIONING A MEDICINE

In determining how the company wants the medicine to be perceived by physicians, patients, and others (e.g., pharmacists, formulary committees), it is essential for marketing personnel to identify an appropriate niche in the market. Although that niche is usually based on broad issues such as safety or efficacy, it may also be based on more narrow or specialized aspects such as medicine costs, compliance, packaging, or quality of life.

The group(s) of patients to be targeted must also be identified. A medicine may be aimed at all patients with the disease or only to those with a specific disease subtype or characteristic. The medicine could also be targeted to older patients, younger patients, those with kidney impairment, or any other specific group(s).

Identifying the Customer

Many business articles and books preach to the international business communities that focusing on the customer is essential to improve a company's profitability and market share. Nowhere has this point been more dramatically demonstrated than in the American automobile market. For many years, large domestic automobile companies virtually ignored the public's strong desire to have a small car that worked as well as larger cars. This unwillingness to provide small cars of high quality allowed Japanese and German manufacturers to enter and steadily enlarge their share of the American automobile market.

This general concept is also true for the pharmaceutical industry. It is natural in the current environment of increased cost containment efforts and increased competition that greater interest is focused on a pharmaceutical company's customers. Many companies are trying not only to identify their customers better, but also to develop specific strategies to target their promotion and selling to each. Companies that try too strenuously to protect out-of-date medicine characteristics such as packaging, unpleasant tastes, large size capsules, and dosage forms eventually have their market encroached upon by more imaginative companies that provide medicines in a way the public wants. This point is particularly true for over-the-counter (OTC) medicines.

Companies that are customer-oriented attempt to determine the services that their customers desire and to provide those services. Companies that are less customer-oriented tend to interact with their clients

based on the medicines they have for sale, stressing their perceived advantages. It is often shortsighted to view medicines merely as things to sell rather than as means to satisfy customer needs.

Who Are the Customers of the Pharmaceutical Industry?

Ten to 20 years ago the physician was considered to be the customer of prescription medicines. The physician's customer in turn was the patient. Physicians were reached by pharmaceutical companies primarily through advertising in medical journals and by visits from sales representatives. Secondary customers of pharmaceutical companies were retail pharmacists, although they were primarily customers for over-the-counter (OTC) medicines. Other customer groups were viewed as having lesser importance because a company's activities were focused on causing a prescription for their product to be written.

Today, customers for pharmaceutical companies include the traditional ones described, but also include purchasing agents for health maintenance organizations (HMOs) and preferred provider organizations (PPOs), hospital formulary committees, distributors, wholesalers, large retail chains, pharmacists, government agencies, nursing homes, ambulatory care clinics, and patients themselves. Patients are no longer considered as a single entity, but are thought of as members of groups, such as the elderly or youth.

Identifying Customer Needs

Customer needs are usually identified by marketing research (Table 47.7). This research may be conducted in several ways. The most limited way is to do the work entirely from literature sources and staff meetings. A preferable approach is to go directly to the customers, interviewing them and soliciting their input. Medicines

---

TABLE 47.7. *Selected methods used to assess customer needs and satisfaction[a]*

1. Toll-free telephone numbers used to obtain comments and complaints as well as to answer questions
2. Focus group meetings on existing or potential products
3. Questionnaire surveys via telephone or mail
4. Customer education materials
5. Employee training in customer relations
6. Interviewing customers in pharmacies
7. Enclosing comment cards in medicine packages

[a] A report by the American Management Association edited by Bohl (1987), from which this table is modified (with permission), identified the first three points as the most effective. Whereas the final customer is clearly the public for over-the-counter medicines, customers are primarily physicians for prescription medicines. A further discussion of identifying customers is given in the text.

should be market tested to determine which groups of customers perceive the product in the best light and have the most interest in it. The reasons for their interest as well as lack of interest should provide clues for additional marketing efforts.

Creating a Medicine's Profile

At an early state of a medicine's development, marketing estimates of sales may be based on the medicine profile that is minimally acceptable to market the medicine. Alternatively, the average profile that is likely to be obtained or the most optimistic or optimal medicine profile may be used. Examples of these types of profile are presented below. Each type of profile could be expressed in terms of various parameters.

Frequency of Dosing

A minimally acceptable profile might be to take the medicine four times per day. The optimal profile might be to take the medicine once a day.

Level of Efficacy

A minimally acceptable profile might be to demonstrate that the medicine is equally active as Medicine X, whereas the optimal profile would be to demonstrate medicine activity significantly greater than that of Medicine X.

Level of Safety

A minimally acceptable profile might state that warnings are needed for patients with hepatic or renal compromise. The optimal profile might demonstrate fewer serious adverse reactions in patients with compromised hepatic or renal function than with existing medicines.

Quality of Life

A minimally acceptable profile would not lead to any restrictions in the labeling apart from a statement similar to the following: "Gastrointestinal distress and malaise may persist for up to 10 days but rarely persist for a longer period." The optimal profile might demonstrate that the medicine was tolerated better by patients than was Medicine X, Y, or Z and that the compliance observed was better than with those medicines. Quality-of-life issues are discussed further in Chapter 45, Clinical Trials.

NAMING A MEDICINE

Almost all medicines have four types of names: chemical, company, generic, and trademark. It is generally believed that good trademarks (i.e., brand names) help to sell a medicine and that bad names often hurt sales. But what is a good name? The answer depends on several factors and on which type of medicine and name is being referred to. Some medicines also have trivial names. Chemical and company names are neither good nor bad per se. Qualities of generic names and trademarks that are considered positive by companies are described in those sections below.

Chemical Names

A chemical name unambiguously identifies the molecular structure of the medicine substance (active ingredient) in the medicine product. Although chemists may draw the medicine's molecular structure based on the name alone, a single chemical structure may usually be identified in more than one way. Chemical names are rarely, if ever, used by physicians, patients, or even most pharmaceutical company employees. The names are used primarily by chemists, patent officers, and information specialists.

Company Names

Companies assign internal registration or code numbers to all chemicals they synthesize or otherwise prepare (e.g., extract, isolate). These numbers are a form of trivial names and are assigned for ease of communication both within the company and with external groups until a generic name is formally assigned. There is no need for most chemicals made to receive other names. Marketed and investigational medicines from other companies are also often assigned a code number. Most code numbers have one to three letters that usually identify the company followed by a series of numbers that usually are assigned in a sequential order. Some companies include the year of original synthesis in this code.

Generic Names

The main criterion in selecting a generic name is that it should be derived in part from previously named structural analogues, from the chemical name, or from the intended therapeutic use. Obviously, the name must not duplicate or closely approximate existing trademarks, generic names, or common names. Generic names are not allowed to imply excessive benefits or unproven usages of the medicine substance. It usually takes approximately eight months to two years to complete this process. One reason for the long time required is because it is necessary to examine the name in other countries as to various sensitivities (e.g., names may have an undesirable meaning or connotation in another language). There are certain conventions about names and phonetic requirements that are generally followed, such as ending barbiturate names in "al" (e.g., Seconal, barbital, pentobarbital) and ending many alcohol names in "ol." Conventions sometimes change over time, especially when certain syllables and syllabic combinations become overworked, and it is necessary to avoid similar sounding names. The International Nonproprietary Name Committee (under the World Health Organization [WHO]), United States Adopted Name Council (USAN), and other adopting agencies set patterns and then try to follow them. Each reserves the right to make its own decisions. Companies usually prefer that generic names for medicine substances are difficult to pronounce and remember, so that both patients and physicians will better remember the company's more euphonic trademark.

Generic names are formally adopted for all marketed medicines and many investigational medicines. In the United States the USAN conducts this process. The USAN is a private agency sponsored by the American Medical Association, the United States Pharmacopeial Convention, the American Pharmaceutical Association, and the FDA. The USAN has a mandate from the FDA to conduct its work. The five-member USAN Council works with the company, the International Nonproprietary Name Committee, and various other international agencies to select a single name for the medicine substance that will be internationally acceptable.

The USAN generally wants companies to wait until efficacy is shown before a sponsor applies for a generic name. This policy is designed to decrease a large number of applications and also their issuing names that will never be used for a marketed medicine.

Trademarks

Trademarks are names assigned by a company after determining that other companies or groups are not using that name or one extremely close to it with which it could be confused. A major issue may arise if the generic name or trademark is not approved when the medicine is discussed in public. This situation occurred with the names Retrovir and zidovudine (trademark and generic name, respectively). Because of the medicine's ultrarapid development only the trivial names AZT and azidothymidine were available for public disclosure after news of early successes were released. After product launch, the old names continued to be used by both the lay press and health care professionals.

The trademark is used in a company's advertising, in promotional campaigns, and extensively by the health care industry to differentiate between products. The name may be purposely chosen to be high tech and slick sounding or scientific and stodgy sounding, depending on how the medicine is to be promoted and advertised. Pharmaceutical companies spend a great deal of time, effort, and money to derive the most appropriate trademark possible. Computer programs are often used by companies to generate candidate trademarks. There is a general trend and desire toward finding a trademark that may be used internationally in most, if not all countries. This enhances name recognition and facilitates use of a single distribution channel. Even a single company used to have multiple trademarks for one medicine sold in many countries. This was partly a result of the difficulty in finding a single name that may be used worldwide. Also, local marketing people have their own views on desirable names, and in some companies may control the local trademark chosen. Some generic versions of a brand name medicine also have their own trademarks, which adds confusion to this area. Several letters of the alphabet have been so frequently used as first letters of trademarks that many companies have elected in recent years to choose names starting with less commonly used letters to improve recall. Generic names and trademarks are derived by any of numerous approaches ranging from simple brainstorming sessions within the company to hiring outside companies that specialize in inventing names. Table 47.8 lists a number of criteria that have been used to select trade names.

Trivial Names

Some medicines acquire a common name or nickname during the course of medicine development. This name is usually used for convenience but is often difficult to eradicate, once formal names are approved. One example is zidovudine (Retrovir), which has the trivial name of azidothymidine or AZT. This name (AZT) was widely used in the press because of the medicine's great amount of publicity, rapid development, and lack of an approved generic name.

Over-the-Counter Names

In the OTC market, names for similar (or even identical) products such as antacids vary from scientific sounding names (e.g., Gelusil, Mylanta, Amphojel) to more commercial sounding names (e.g., Tums, Rolaids) to old-fashioned, familiar sounding names which have acquired folksy overtones (e.g., Alka-Seltzer, Bromo Seltzer). This issue is discussed further under "Promoting a Medicine," later in this chapter.

TABLE 47.8. *Potential methods to select trademarks*[a]

Selection criterion	Example of criterion	Trademark
Direct relation to generic name	Tetracycline	Tetracyin
Indiction of therapeutic action	A diuretic	Diuril
Sales message or appeal	Ultimate tranquilizer	Ultran
Running theme use of same prefix (e.g., from company name)	A. H. Robins company	Robitussin Robinul
Literary significance		Soma
Reflect chemical structure	Novrad	Darvon (spelled backward)
Route of administration	Oral administration	Chymoral
Dosage schedule	B.i.d. every 12 hours	Combid
Source of raw material	Pregnant mares' urine	Premarin
Not related or related obscurely[b]	Miltown, New Jersey	Miltown

[a] From Smith (1975), with permission of Lea & Febiger. See also Smith (1991).
[b] The example given is actually related in that it is the name of the town near where the medicine was developed.

PRICING, COSTS, AND ECONOMICS

Pricing a medicine is usually considered the most important factor in a marketing strategy. Nonetheless, pharmaceutical companies are unable to establish a price for a medicine on their own in many countries. This is because regulations or guidelines involve government agencies in the price-setting process. This subject is discussed in more detail in Chapter 63, Interactions and Relationships with Government Agencies.

Using Price as a Strategic Tool

One reason why physicians choose one medicine rather than another when they are approximately equal in medical value is because of a difference in their cost. To gain market share it is necessary either to attract new customers or to increase a medicine's use by existing customers. Attracting new customers may be achieved by many promotional techniques or by lowering the price. Although lowering prices below cost may keep potential competitors (i.e., generic manufacturers) out of the market, this is called predatory pricing and is illegal. If the goal is to price a totally novel medicine for the first time, a price must be chosen that is consistent with the medical value of the medicine in the consumer's view. To increase medicine purchases by current customers (e.g., large retail stores, groups of hospitals) it may be important to offer volume discounts and special prices to a select group of customers. New customers may be attracted by special prices on a product line or selected products that are being promoted. It is important for a company to offer the same special price on volume purchases to all customers in a group(s) (e.g., distributors).

The previous discussion is based on the assumption that a pharmaceutical company establishes the price it is to charge for its own medicine. This situation occurs in few countries. Even in countries where this occurs, various systems and mechanisms influence or control the price asked. The regulatory authority plays a major role in setting prices in most countries. They may establish a price (1) before (or after) the medicine is approved for marketing, (2) totally on their own or in conjunction with information presented by the company, or (3) in a rapid period or in a drawn-out process. The pattern differs greatly around the world. Tucker (1984, p. 130) presents numerous difficulties that confront regulatory agencies in establishing fair prices for medicines.

Costs of a Disease: Direct, Indirect, and Intangible

Cost of medical treatment for any specific disease may be determined by methods ranging from a rough guesstimate to highly sophisticated techniques. The overall costs of a patient's treatment include considerations of direct costs, indirect costs, and intangible costs. *Direct costs* of treatment include such costs as the cost of physician's services, hospitalizations (if required), and prescriptions. *Indirect costs* are financial expenses not directly attributed to treatment. They include transportation to and from the place of medical treatment, meals bought at the treatment site, and lost income because of time taken for treatment. *Intangible costs* include discomfort and pain from the disease, plus any embarrassment resulting from the disease or treatment. Although these costs are described for patients, many indirect and intangible costs are also borne by the patient's family, friends, and others who interact with the patient. In addition, there are numerous costs from society's point of view. These costs are not described in this chapter and are primarily in the province of health planners and government officials.

Direct costs are the most easily measured cost. Nonetheless, a study to compare direct costs of two treatments may be conducted in several different ways, and different types of cost comparisons may be made. Calculating

TABLE 47.9. *Costs of three medicines of the same type (e.g., beta receptor antagonists) expressed in three ways[a]*

	Medicine A	Medicine B	Medicine C
Cost per pill	$1.00[b]	$1.50	$2.00
Cost per dose	2 tablets make up one dose and costs $2.00	1 tablet costs $1.50	1 tablet costs $2.00
Cost per day	Medicine taken twice a day and costs $4.00	Medicine taken three times a day and costs $4.50	Medicine taken once a day and costs $2.00

[a] Other ways to express the costs of the medicine include cost per course of treatment, monitoring costs, cost of professional visits and services, and costs of hospitalization. Alternative or additional ways to express costs relate to costs saved or a comparison of costs with other treatments for the same problem.
[b] The least expensive medicine for each description is underlined. This illustrates that each medicine could be described as the least expensive, depending on how the data are expressed.

and comparing indirect and intangible costs for two or more treatments is much more complex, and no single agreed-on method is available.

Cost-Effectiveness Claims

Most companies desire to demonstrate that their products are cost-effective in comparison with those of the competition. What exactly does this mean? Cost-effectiveness analyses involve comparisons between two (or more) medicines within the same therapeutic category or between a medicine and the currently available nonmedicine treatment. If no treatments are available, then medicine costs will be compared to the prevailing therapeutic approach and its costs.

For cost comparisons, it is important to compare medicine regimens that yield equal effects. Many factors enter the determination of medicine efficacy so that finding equivalent medicine regimens is not always easy. Moreover, efficacy may be expressed in many different ways. Also there are many types of costs involved and many ways of expressing those costs.

Standardization of Economic Comparisons

When the cost effectiveness of two medicines is compared, each may claim to be superior based on totally different criteria. Issues of comparing apples and oranges abound. For example, assume that Medicine A decreases an average patient's hospital stay from ten days to one day but that it increases the risk of moderate adverse reactions and a fatal reaction compared with the equally effective Medicine B. How should the costs and risk be assessed and compared? The *cost-to-benefit ratio* is better for Medicine A compared with no treatment and is the same as for Medicine B. The *cost-to-risk ratio* is worse for Medicine A than for Medicine B. Also, the *risk-to-benefit ratio* may be worse than originally hoped. If the latter ratio has changed sufficiently to alter the clinical significance of the medicine relative to existing

therapy (Medicine B), then the medicine's future should be reassessed. If alternative treatment is not available, then the medicine should probably be approved by HMOs and other formulary committees for stocking in the hospital. If an existing treatment is available, then a formulary committee may request data on a clinical comparison between Medicines A and B before Medicine A is approved for stocking.

It is easy to understand how several competitors with similar medicines for a single disease may each claim that their medicine is more cost-effective than their competitor's medicine. For example, the claims of one company may focus on the wider range of disease subtypes treated and a reduced need for pharmacies to stock several different medicines that each treat only a single subtype. Another company may claim better cost effectiveness based on superior efficacy and reduced duration of hospitalization. A third competitor could claim decreased cost of the medicine per week of treatment compared with other medicines that yield the same effect. A fourth competitor whose medicine's efficacy and cost are the same as others could still claim cost effectiveness based on an improved quality of life or improved patient compliance. An example is shown in Table 47.9.

INTRODUCING A MEDICINE

The real launch date of a medicine is no longer a specific day shortly after it is officially approved for marketing. That day used to be the time that the trumpets blared out the announcement of the new arrival. Now, the effective launch date may occur several years ahead of market approval. Many activities are conducted to sensitize physicians to the medicine's existence and relevance for their practice. This is done via publications, symposia, and various other events and speeches by thought leaders and industry personnel.

The initial marketing of a medicine is an important moment in a medicine's life. If the medicine is promoted too aggressively and too widely, then it will be prescribed to many inappropriate patients and possibly at inappropriate doses. This will probably lead to a large number of adverse reactions, which could be "fatal" to the medicine (e.g., benoxaprofen). A more cautious introduction of a new medicine is usually a wiser approach than a heavy advertising blitz, although that approach may be acceptable in some situations.

Dr. Grahame-Smith (1987) describes 13 parameters of a typical new medicine at the time of its introduction. He scores the understanding of each parameter by a sponsor or developer of the medicine on an analogue scale of 1 to 10 and gives high scores (7 or 8) for basic pharmacology, preclinical safety testing, and clinical safety. Low scores (2 or 3) are given to risk, overall benefit, medicine-disease interaction, method of use, and types of patients who will benefit most or least from the medicine.

Some of the issues associated with launching a medicine are described in Chapter 129 of Spilker (1991). Other issues are described in Chapter 68 of this book (Interactions and Relationships with the Media), regarding press conferences, press releases, and other types of public relations activities on a medicine.

PROMOTING A MEDICINE

One means of differentiating between marketing and promotion activities in positioning a medicine is to consider marketing activities as an attempt to determine people's needs and then to design products that meet those needs. Promotion activities, on the other hand, attempt to change people to meet the attributes of the product.

Advertising Issues

Advertising is considered to be a subset of promotion. Promotional activities also include public relations' efforts and the provision of product-related information to physicians (e.g., using books, journals, newsletters, brochures). This information does not always mention the medicine directly and may be only indirectly related to the product. Even indirect promotion, however, helps educate readers about a specific disease or therapeutic area affected by the medicine. Scientific exhibits at conventions usually contain product advertising but also may include or even concentrate on nonproduct approaches to diagnosis, treatment, or prevention of the particular disease associated with the medicine of interest. Television advertisements about the disease (rather than the medicine used to treat it) are another type of indirect promotion. As a result of this advertising, it is hoped that patients with the disease will visit their doctor to inquire about the advertised treatment.

One of the central issues in medicine advertising is to determine and evaluate the payback in sales and profits on a specific product (or product line) for each dollar spent advertising that product (or product line). If spending a dollar on advertising a medicine does not generate at least a dollar return in sales, then the only reason to advertise the medicine is as a "loss leader" to bring a certain product to the attention of a given audience.

For most products, more than a dollar must be returned in sales for each dollar spent on advertising. As this ratio falls, it eventually reaches a point where it becomes uneconomical to continue advertising a specific product. Either a less expensive medium or a new approach to advertising the medicine must be found. A new approach might be to focus better on the content of the promotional message or to direct the same message to a more selective audience (e.g., to dermatologists rather than to family practice and other physicians who treat skin diseases). In either case, the effectiveness of the medicine's advertising must be increased.

Direct-to-Consumer Advertising of Prescription Medicines

Advertisements in magazines, in newspapers, on television, and on radio that inform the public about a specific disease have become more common in the 1980s. The ads say, in essence, "Now there is something that can help you control or treat this disease. See your doctor for more information." Physicians and sometimes patients understand which medicine is referred to, even though the medicine's name is usually not specifically mentioned. Recent newspaper advertisements for a prescription antihistamine have changed this "no-name" approach and stated the medicine's name.

Some of the advantages for a company to advertise a prescription medicine directly to consumers are that

1. it helps patients distinguish when professional input is needed in their care from areas where self-care is appropriate,
2. it informs the public about new products that are available,
3. it provides an update about alternative medical treatments, and
4. it indirectly encourages physicians to use a company's medicines.

Television advertisements are most effective when there is only a single marketed medicine to which the advertisement could be referring. The message will be acted on differently by the audience when there are multiple products that could be referred to in the advertisements.

Future advertisements to the public are likely to increase in number if regulations do not prevent their growth. This might occur if consumer or health care professional groups strongly object to the practice. Some advertisements will also provide more sophisticated information because a growing number of people desire to know more about the medicines they take. These people also desire to have a greater role in their medical care. Information on patented medicine delivery systems, which increase patient compliance or provide other benefits, may also increase in the future. The FDA, Federal Trade Commission (FTC), and even the public do not have a single clear perception or opinion about this issue, and the eventual outcome of this type of advertising is uncertain.

Assessing Medicine Claims

After listening to hyped claims for new medicines made by some company personnel, it is easy to conclude that medicines that have not been tested in patients always seem to have better profiles than medicines that have been tested. Medicines tested in only a few patients also often appear to be better than after they are tested in a larger number. Another way of stating this principle is that medicines usually start their life in a pristine or virginal state but acquire warts and blemishes as they move toward the market. Unlike fine wines, most medicines do not improve with age, except in the eye of the medicine's promoter.

A small number of reported claims of medicine superiority are listed below. The claims are assumed to be true, according to one or more of the possible interpretations given.

1. *Medicine A is ten times as potent as Medicine B*—This claim literally means that one-tenth a given amount of Medicine A causes the same response as ten times the equivalent amount of Medicine B (Fig. 47.2). This usually means that a tablet or capsule of Medicine A has one-tenth the number of milligrams of a tablet of Medicine B and the rest of the medicine is made up of various excipients. If the two medicines have the same efficacy and safety profile, then the medicine that is more potent usually has no clinical advantage. There would be an advantage for the more potent medicine if a smaller capsule size could be used that was more acceptable to patients. For a few intravenous medicines where large quantities have to be given (e.g., the diuretic, ethacrynic acid), the development of a more potent medicine has practical advantages.

2. *Nine out of ten doctors recommend the ingredient in Medicine A*—This may be a true statement, but it is not saying that the doctors have recommended Medicine A per se. If there are several medicine products containing the same active ingredient, there may be important reasons to prefer a different medicine than A for some patients (e.g., different salt, different dosage form, different excipients). The claim may not indicate how these ten doctors were chosen, and their selection may not have been totally random.

3. *Medicine A cured 90% of all patients within X days*—This may be a true statement, but the disease treated may be self-limiting within X days. Therefore, most patients would have improved without receiving any treatment. This applies to minor colds and other minor ailments. Alternatively, the course of the disease may have been shortened from 20 days to 19 days (on average), which could be statistically significant but would not be clinically important. It would be necessary to examine the data and study design(s) to evaluate the clinical relevance of this statement.

4. *Medicine A causes improvement in 90% of all patients with Disease X*—But what happens when the medicine is stopped? Do problems recur? Is there actually a rebound effect (i.e., return or exacerbation of the original symptoms)? Is there a withdrawal phenomenon? How does the medicine compare with others in these regards? Numerous related questions could also be posed.

5. *Medicine A has the following three activities. It does X, Y, and Z*—But are any of these activities related to how the medicine works clinically? Do these activities explain the medicine's beneficial effects in patients? It is also possible that these activities were observed only in animal studies, were observed only at toxic doses, or were observed only in a small number of patients.

6. *Medicine A is as good as the most powerful medicine available to treat Disease X*—But can one treat Disease X with more mild medicines? How good are any medicines in treating this disease? How do physicians usually treat patients with this disease? What adverse reactions occur with Medicine A versus others used to treat patients with Disease X?

7. *The competitor's Medicine B was not as active as Medicine A in patients when each was tested at equal doses*—But if higher doses of the competitor's medicine were given, would it have been more active and equally safe? Equal doses of two medicines in terms of number of milligrams may not be relevant to compare unless it is known that the two medicines are equally effective or at least have comparable efficacy.

8. *Medicine A has fewer side effects than the competitor's medicine*—But were the two medicines compared (1) at comparable equi-effective doses, (2) in the same study, and (3) in an identical patient population? Also, was a comparison of a single entity and a combination medicine made? This would be an especially unfair comparison if the side effect profile on one medicine was affected by the second medicine in the combination product.

9. *Four out of five hospitals use Medicine A more than Medicine B*—Hospitals usually choose one medicine over another generally similar medicine of the same type because of price. The medicine manufacturer may have supplied the medicine at a lower price particularly to obtain hospital use. Were all hospitals in the sample in one geographical area, possibly the one where the com-

Potency

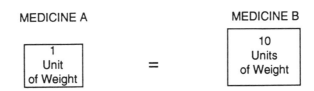

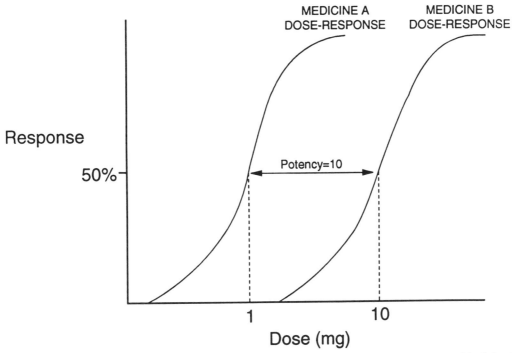

FIG. 47.2. Illustration of the concept of potency where Medicine A is ten times as potent as Medicine B.

pany promoted its medicine heavily? How many hospitals were in the sample? Was it 5, 10, or 410? Many additional factors could also have influenced this statement.

The issue of possible medical questions asked and interpretations drawn is complex. From the advertiser's perspective, a major issue is what type and how much information should be provided to medical readers. An appropriate approach to this issue is to provide the information that a reasonable physician would want to know. The quantity and quality of this information can easily be determined in most situations by discussing the issue with physicians, either inside or outside the company. From a physician's perspective, many marketing claims unfortunately remind one of the title of Shakespeare's

play—*Much Ado About Nothing*. It is the task and goal of marketing personnel to avoid this problem and to explain claims in ways that meet the physician's needs and answer the most frequently posed questions.

Professional Over-the-Counter Medicines

There appears to be a new group of OTC medicines that are promoted and perceived differently than older established ones. These are sometimes referred to as professional OTCs. Their characteristics, as compared with traditional OTCs, are listed in Table 47.10. It is clear from this table that professional OTCs share many characteristics with prescription medicines. They usually come from prescription medicine manufacturers, are

TABLE 47.10. *Profile of traditional and professional types of over-the-counter medicines*

Professional OTC[a] medicines	Traditional OTC medicines
Rationally based	Emotionally based
Sophisticated upper income orientation	Middle-America lower income orientation
Advertising intensive	Advertising insensitive to a degree
Contemporary state-of-the-art image	Folklore based, used by one's parents

[a] OTC, over-the-counter.

packaged and promoted in a more high-tech and professional manner, and are named more like prescription medicines than are heavily advertised popular medicines like Tums, Rolaids, or Alka-Seltzer.

Marketing data demonstrate that the total market share of professional type OTCs is growing at the expense of traditional OTCs. Some of the reasons for this include (1) increased sophistication of consumers; (2) increased self-medication by consumers, partly as an alternative to expensive physician visits; and (3) availability of new OTC medicines that are perceived as more effective and usually safer than older traditional OTCs. Whatever approach a company takes toward characterizing and advertising each OTC medicine, it is probably most essential to be consistent to avoid confusing consumers.

Most OTC medicines cannot be placed entirely in just the professional or traditional group. OTC medicines vary along the spectrum between these extremes. A number of examples of antacid medicines that fit the general category of popular, heavily advertised, traditional OTCs are Tums, Pepto-Bismol, Rolaids, Alka-Seltzer, and Bromo-Seltzer. More professional OTCs are Gelusil, Maalox, Riopan, Mylanta, and Gaviscon. Differences exist within each of these two groups as to how scientific or folksy the medicine is presented.

DISTRIBUTING AND SELLING A MEDICINE

Medicine Distribution

Companies distribute their medicines in a wide variety of ways that include some or all of the following:

1. direct to retail stores, such as (1) pharmacy chains, (2) supermarket chains, (3) mass merchandisers, (4) individual pharmacies or supermarkets, and (5) other outlets;
2. to hospital chains and individual hospitals;
3. through wholesalers to the above retail stores;
4. through mail-order organizations to the public; and
5. to underdeveloped countries and other groups via specific charities. This last channel is used with guarantees by the charity that the medicines donated will not reenter the markets of developed countries.

Accuracy of Market Predictions of New Product Sales

Pharmaceutical companies attempt to forecast future sales on every medicine they sell. Forecasts are made for the next fiscal year, as well as for two or three years in the future. These figures are the critical numbers that production groups use to determine how much of each product to manufacture. If the forecast for any product is much lower than customer demand, it results in back orders and customer dissatisfaction. Forecasts that are much greater than sales result in a high inventory of unsold medicine, in addition to tying up manufacturing equipment that could possibly have been used to make other medicines. Either of these situations may create significant additional problems for a company. Some of the factors that may lead to inaccurate market forecasts are listed in Table 47.11.

It is common at some companies to hear disparaging comments within research and development departments about the relative inaccuracy of many marketing predictions. These comments are generally unfair because marketing estimates often have to be made long before the clinical profile of a medicine is established. In addition, marketing estimates are often made before the target population size or makeup is known, especially for novel therapeutic agents. The extent of nonlabeled medicine use for a new medicine is also uncertain.

Moreover, the methods used to predict a medicine's sales are not precise, especially for a new medicine. This is even more pronounced for the initial medicine marketed for a new indication. Forecasts are based on discussions with physicians about why they prescribe certain medicines, the problems they see with those medicines, attributes of a new medicine that would make them change to a new medicine (or at least try a new medicine), and other factors. Physicians who are interviewed, however, may not be representative of the total population of physicians or may not follow through on their own pronouncements.

Other factors that go into marketing forecasts include the quality of clinical data and opinions of scientific (and nonscientific) people, both within and outside the phar-

TABLE 47.11. *Factors that may lead to an inaccurate marketing forecast*

1. OTC competition increases substantially, causing sales of marketed products to fall.
2. Prescription medicines face increased competition.
3. New products fare poorly and do not reach forecasted sales.
4. Marketing costs rise more than anticipated.
5. National and international economies do poorly.
6. Regulatory delays are longer than anticipated.
7. Sales representatives did not promote the medicine sufficiently, accurately, or appropriately.
8. Marketing forecaster was inexperienced.

maceutical company. Part of the inexactitude of marketing estimates therefore relates to uncertainty within research and development as to identifying the precise indications and populations the medicine will work on, how well it will perform, and the characteristics of its safety profile.

Where Does a Company Focus Its Activities on the Physician-Patient-Pharmacist Chain?

After a new prescription medicine is approved for marketing and launch, it has the *potential* to help patients with one or more diseases. Before patients may be helped there are many activities that must occur. Activities involved in the medicine's production, quality assurance, packaging, shipping to wholesalers, and distribution to pharmacies will not be discussed. Activities at the other

end of the spectrum (i.e., relating to the patient, pharmacist, and physician) are briefly reviewed.

Figure 47.3 illustrates the usual chain of events that leads to a physician prescribing a medicine for patients and for patients obtaining and following medical treatment. Pharmaceutical companies have traditionally attempted to influence two of the three parts of this relationship (i.e., they have provided the physician with information and education hoping that a prescription for their medicine will be written). Companies encourage the pharmacist to stock their medicine and encourage them to dispense their medicine when generic equivalents are also available. With generic medicines taking a greater share of the overall market, the relationship between company and pharmacy is becoming more important for all manufacturers. The threat of therapeutic substitution (i.e., having a pharmacist dispense a different medicine than the one prescribed but one which is theo-

INTERACTIONS OF PHYSICIANS, PHARMACISTS, PATIENTS, AND PHARMACEUTICAL COMPANIES

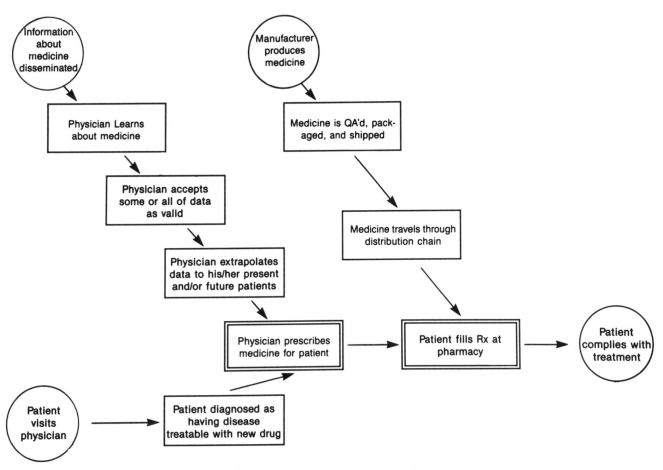

FIG. 47.3. Interactions of physicians, pharmacists, patients, and pharmaceutical companies. *QA,* quality assured.

STEPS A PATIENT FOLLOWS IN INITIAL TREATMENT WITH MEDICINES

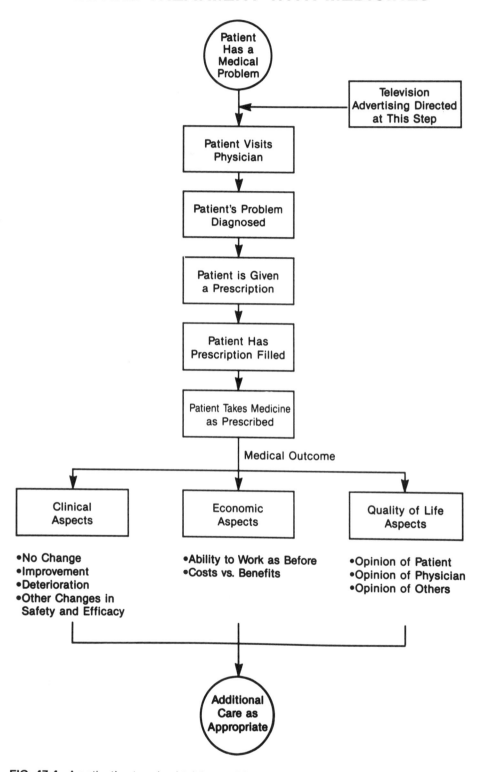

FIG. 47.4. A patient's steps in obtaining and following medical treatment with medicines.

retically equivalent to the medicine prescribed) will exponentially increase the importance of this relationship.

Companies did not approach patients to influence prescription medicine use until recently. Contact via direct newspaper, television, and magazine advertising is becoming more common and is discussed elsewhere in this chapter. Steps followed by patients in obtaining and following medical treatment are shown in Fig. 47.4.

Promoting Medicines to Physicians in Primary, Secondary, and Tertiary Care Practices

Academicians in tertiary care hospitals (i.e., referral centers) and primary care practitioners treat most diseases in generally similar or identical manners. For a few diseases the differences in treatment (or diagnosis) are great. This usually relates to (1) the use of sophisticated equipment that is often not readily available to primary care physicians or (2) situations where clinical practices espoused by physicians in teaching hospitals are not adhered to or followed by private physicians in the community. The reasons for this latter gap are many and may have a major influence on a company's medicine sales (either positively or negatively, depending on the particular situation). Companies are therefore forced to promote some medicines differently to various groups of physicians. This distinction is also observed in how physicians in different specialties use the same medicine. These differences may relate to the types of patients treated, the usual dose range used, or other factors. It is often important for a marketing department to help educate physicians in private practice about medical practices in tertiary care academic centers. This education not only can help increase sales of a particular medicine, but also will disseminate current state-of-the-art opinions about a given therapy.

PROTECTING A MEDICINE

Effect of Marketing Decisions in Other Countries

Marketing decisions made in one country are having a continually greater effect on marketing issues and decisions made in other countries. There is a current trend toward more uniform pricing of a single product in multiple countries. The European Economic Community (EEC) and World Health Organization are looking at and comparing prices set in different countries in an attempt to achieve greater uniformity across national boundaries. Because most countries have agencies that control prices charged for medicines, this is also being done at the national level.

Protecting Medicines from Tampering and Counterfeiting

In recent years several well-publicized cases of medicine tampering have led to unfortunate deaths of innocent victims. Some of these cases have had a drastic effect on a company's sales and on sales of the entire pharmaceutical industry. The industry's response has been swift, responsible, and positive. Some companies have totally given up manufacturing medicines in capsule form in favor of using more tamper-resistant dosage forms such as caplets and tablets and have increased their use of blister and bubble packs. Other firms have begun placing gelatin bands as a sealing device around each capsule joint. No totally tamper-resistant method is available to protect medicines. Present techniques, however, including shrink seals on containers, seals on cartons, and many other methods, provide a major advance in assuring patients about the integrity and safety of marketed medicines.

Another problem that is sometimes encountered by successful medicines is that of counterfeiting. Capsules without printing and tablets without imprinting may be counterfeited most easily. Therefore, the printing or imprinting on a capsule or tablet of a company's name, logo, or a medicine name provides some protection against counterfeiting. Caution must be used when determining the exact name, symbol, code number, or other information to be printed on the capsules. If too much material is printed on a capsule, patients may perceive that they are ingesting an excessive amount of ink and become upset instead of reassured. Tablets are harder to manufacture than capsules and thus they add additional protection for a company against fraudulent manufacturing, especially if a unique tablet shape is used. Coloring or film coating of tablets are other processes that help in this regard.

These processes do much more than merely make counterfeiting more difficult. Each of these steps helps create brand recognition and, it is hoped, brand loyalty. Patients offered generic versions of their branded medicines sometimes insist on sticking with the "small round orange ones" because of the patient's experience and knowledge that they work.

EXPANDING A MEDICINE'S MARKET

Increasing Market Share

Defining Market and Market Share

The term *market* is a measure of the actual or potential commercial value of a medicine or group of medicines. A market may refer to (1) a specific medicine in which multiple companies are competing with generic and/or brand medicines (e.g., the market for propranolol), (2) a group of medicines of one type (e.g., the market for beta-receptor antagonists), (3) a specific disease (e.g., the market for medicines that treat hypertension), (4) a specific therapeutic area (e.g., the market for medicines used in cardiology), or (5) all medicines in all markets. When two or more medicines are sold in a market they each have a certain share of that market. The most common measure used to define market share is percentage of the total market, which is usually based on sales in terms of money. Other measures of a market include the (1) number of new prescriptions, (2) number of new plus refilled prescriptions, (3) number of units of medicine sold, and (4) number of tablets and capsules dispensed. Each of these four measures may also be expressed as a percentage of the total market.

The Stable Market

Most therapeutic area markets remain relatively flat from year to year in terms of constant money (i.e., adjusted for inflation). Figure 47.5 illustrates this situation. The effects of inflation may give monetary data the appearance of slow or rapid growth. The number of units sold or prescriptions written is less influenced by inflation. In this type of a relatively flat market, new products must compete with existing medicines for market share and sales. When a new medicine is introduced into the market, the total market size may remain unchanged and the market share of competing products is redistributed. Figure 47.5 illustrates this situation.

The Expanding Market

Another possible situation is shown in Fig. 47.6. This illustrates that the introduction of newer antiarthritis medicines expanded the total market over the period shown (1976 to 1981). In this type of expanding market, new products do not need to take major sales volume or dollars away from existing products to achieve significant sales.

Some possible reasons for the phenomenon of an expanding market are discussed below.

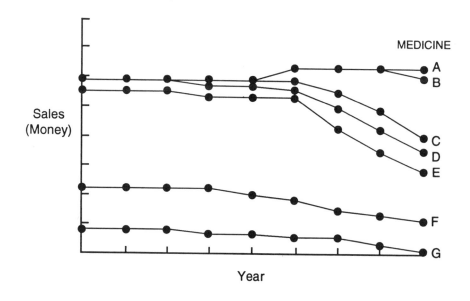

A. Newest entry without sufficient time to establish a pattern.

B. Most recent entry to garner a major and growing share of the market.

C. An entry that gained a small and unchanging market share.

D. A long-term entry whose market share has remained relatively stable.

E. The major medicine in terms of market share that also was the major loser of market share.

F. The second largest selling medicine and has not lost much market share.

G. The oldest medicine on the market where erosion over the last few years has led to its losing out to its competitors.

FIG. 47.5. Market share for seven medicines over a period of years illustrating a stable total market size. New introductions divide the existing market as described in the figure.

SALES OF ANTIARTHRITICS

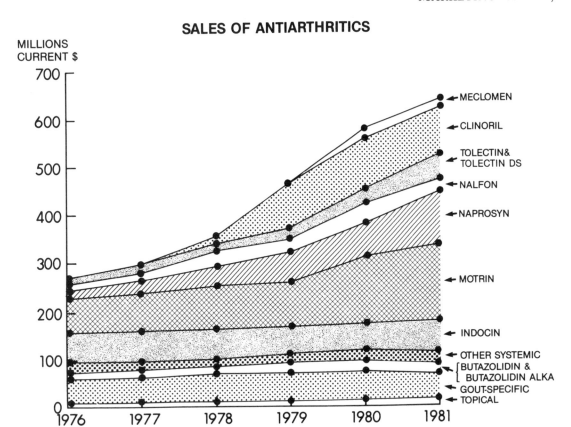

FIG. 47.6. Market share for antiarthritic medicines over 1976 to 1981, illustrating an expanding market.

1. There is a larger patient population from year to year. This may occur for many reasons. For example, the disease that the medicine treats may be spreading (e.g., the acquired immune deficiency syndrome [AIDS] patient population is growing).

2. Patients are using the medicines to treat other medical problems. For example, the nonsteroidal anti-inflammatory medicines introduced for arthritis were used to treat pain resulting from other causes.

3. The patient population is not growing, but more patients are being diagnosed as having the disease. There may have been a public health awareness campaign aimed at physicians or patients because of long-term underdiagnosis or because of the availability of new diagnostic methods. For example, the number of patients treated with antihypertensive medicines increased during the 1960s and 1970s because previously undiagnosed patients were being diagnosed and treated.

4. Some patients who are unable to tolerate existing medicine therapy are able to tolerate newly marketed medicines. This occurred with nonsteroidal anti-inflammatory medicines.

5. Some patients who did not benefit from previous medicines are benefiting from newer ones.

When the size of a particular market is noted to change, it is important to determine if this occurred because (1) there are more (or fewer) products on the market, (2) there are more or fewer units of the products being sold, or (3) the prices are changing. It is important to track these parameters (as well as those listed above) when trying to understand the reasons underlying changes in a market. Other analyses that may be conducted are to compare commercial trends of (1) older medicines versus more recently introduced medicines, (2) more expensive medicines versus the least expensive medicines, or (3) any two other categories. This type of analysis helps a company better understand what is influencing the market changes observed.

Approaches to Increase Market Share

Basic approaches to increase market share may focus on any or all of the following means of positioning and promoting the medicine: developing a new or improved (1) product formulation, package, or line-extension; (2) sales approach and pricing strategy; or (3) promotional approach. Some of the specific approaches used by pharmaceutical companies to increase the market share for their products include product-related approaches, sales approaches and pricing strategies, and promotional approaches.

Product-Related Approaches

1. Develop more line-extensions in terms of dosage forms or routes of administration. These must be chosen

to minimize cannibalization of a company's own products. The timing of the product's launch must be chosen to minimize the return of products from pharmacies.

2. Change the medicine's packaging to achieve an advantage over the competition. Some OTC medicine packages are similar to detergent boxes and almost jump off the pharmacy shelf with bright colors and striking patterns. Others are designed to be more quiet and "professional."

Sales Approaches and Pricing Strategies

1. Increase the amount of activities and time spent by marketing representatives detailing (i.e., promoting) the product of interest.

2. Develop a specialized sales force to handle the product, either specifically or along with a small number of other medicines. This specialized sales force could be targeted to a specific type of physician (e.g., psychiatrists) or to a specific type of institution (e.g., hospitals).

3. Utilize a new distribution system for some or all of a company's medicines.

4. Give medicine samples to physicians and hospitals to familiarize them with the medicine and its uses.

5. Identify the reasons for a medicine's poor sales performance (e.g., Table 47.12) and then address each of the possible points.

6. Decrease medicine price, either as a short-term promotion to pharmacies and others or as a long-term strategy.

Promotional Approaches

1. Increase advertising in quantity, change the advertising's message, or upgrade (or downgrade) the advertising's quality.

TABLE 47.12. *Possible reasons used to explain poor sales performance*

A. Medicine related
  1. New adverse reactions reported
  2. Efficacy was perceived to be less than anticipated
  3. Difficulties encountered in manufacturing the medicine
  4. Other problems encountered with the medicine itself
B. Market related
  1. Prices set at too high a level
  2. Estimate of potential patient numbers too high
  3. Competitors more firmly established in the marketplace than was anticipated
  4. Advertising and promotion campaigns unable to position the medicine as planned
  5. Other competing medicines introduced
  6. Medicine backordered for a prolonged period
  7. Misdirected distribution, sales, and/or promotion efforts
  8. Difficulties encountered in distributing the medicine
C. Other reasons
  1. Medical practice shifted in an important aspect
  2. Problems related to the company's image emerged

2. Develop more public relations activities for the product (see Chapter 68, Interactions and Relationships with the Media).

3. Develop data to better differentiate the medicine from its competitors. This may be in terms of cost benefits, quality of life, or other characteristics.

4. Target advertisements and other promotions more closely to those specialists who have the highest use of that class or type of medicine. A company could, for example, decrease their advertisements for ophthalmic anti-infectives placed in general medical journals and increase their advertisements in journals specifically oriented to and read by ophthalmologists.

5. Increase the number of exhibits at medical meetings. Emphasize presentations of posters and talks by company and noncompany personnel.

6. Develop and distribute (or only distribute) medical literature, texts, or other material that is educational and only indirectly promotes a product or does not promote the product at all. The distribution of authoritative medical information on a disease treated by the medicine is valuable from the company's perspective, even if the medicine's name is not mentioned.

7. Sponsor clinical trials that would be of interest to physicians and could be promoted by sales representatives. Other publications of clinical trials may stimulate sales for both new uses as well as the medicine's original use(s), even if sales representatives may not distribute reprints or promote the uses.

8. Change the name of a product to reflect the image that the company wants to project. Is the image of the product better achieved with Foot Guard or Tinactin? Icy Hot or Myoflex? Gas-X or Mylicon? Daycare or Comtrex?

Conversion of Prescription Medicines to Over-the-Counter Status

The migration of medicine brands from prescription to OTC status has been accentuated over the last decade. The reasons for this primarily reflect the fact that medicine sales are greater when they are off-prescription. One reason is that patients are able to choose the specific medicine brand they want to buy, and the pharmacist is generally not in a position to have the patient switch to a generic brand. There are no established regulatory or other criteria for switching from prescription to OTC status in the United States, although the FDA usually requires at least three years of marketing experience and documentation of at least 5,000 cases. Nonetheless, every case is unique and must be evaluated by the sponsor as well as the FDA on its own. FDA approval is necessary to make this conversion to OTC status. Conversion in Europe varies among countries.

A number of reports have claimed that the public saves a large amount of money when prescription medicines are sold OTC (Vickery, 1985). This money appears to primarily relate to a decreased number of physician visits. For example, MIT economist Peter Timmon estimated that the availability of hydrocortisone OTC saved Americans over a billion dollars between 1980 and 1982 (Vickery, 1985). These are strong arguments in favor of the prescription-to-OTC conversion of relevant medicines in this era of medical cost containment.

Sales of a Medicine for Unapproved Uses and Obtaining Regulatory Approval for Those Uses

Medicines are used to treat patients with one of two types of diseases or indications: indications that are approved and indications that are not approved by regulatory authorities. This latter group of indications are often referred to as unlabeled indications. The amount of a medicine's use that is for unlabeled indications varies from medicine to medicine and also varies for any one medicine during the course of its marketing life. Physicians often experiment on their own and use medicines for unapproved indications. Alternatively, some new uses for medicines are discovered through serendipity (see Table 20.2).

Companies must decide whether to seek regulatory approval for unlabeled indications of a new medicine. One aspect of this decision relates to whether the medicine works in some or all patients with the disease. Another aspect is whether the medicine effect is as strong as clinicians think necessary before they would incorporate the medicine into their own practice. A meta-analysis is a sound basis to evaluate whether there is sufficient clinical evidence to approve medicines for currently unlabeled uses. It is hoped that this concept will be endorsed by regulatory authorities.

48 / Licensing Issues

Overall Concepts **567**
  Traditional Views 567
  Benefits in Licensing-Out 568
  Goals and Purposes of Licensing 568
What One Licenses **568**
Types of Licenses **569**
Creating a Licensing Strategy **569**
  Examples of Simple Licensing Strategies 569
  Identifying the Focus 570
  Identifying Major Types of Gaps 570
  Elements of a Licensing Strategy 571
  Roles of Orphan Medicines in a Licensing
    Strategy 571
Creating a Proactive Approach to Licensing-in
    Compounds and Medicines **571**
The Business of Licensing: Organizational and
    Methodological Issues **572**
  Where Does Licensing Fit Best in a Company's
    Organization? 572
  Obtaining Information and Data on New
    Opportunities 573
  Should a Licensing Group Coordinate or
    Conduct the Opportunity Reviews? 573

Processing Licensing Opportunities 573
Criteria for Screening Licensing Opportunities 575
Sources of Licensing Opportunities 575
Facilitating the Signing of a Licensing
    Agreement 576
Financial Issues in Licensing **576**
  Assigning Value to Potential and Actual Deals 576
  Types of Payments 577
  Approaches to Balancing Financial Risk 577
Legal Issues **578**
  Negotiation Phase 578
  Preparing the Contract 578
  Cross-Licensing and Choosing the Quid Pro
    Quo 580
  Obligations by Each Partner 580
Regulatory Issues **581**
Problems, Principles, and Predictions **582**
  Potential Problems and Issues 582
  Golden Rules of Licensing 583
  Predictions for the Future 583

A few bad reasons for doing something neutralize all the good reasons for doing it. F. M. Cornford

OVERALL CONCEPTS

Traditional Views

The traditional view of licensing that was prevalent throughout the 1960s and 1970s has been extensively modified in recent years. During those years, the traditional view of the licensing of a medicine to another company (i.e., licensing-out) was held by major companies that wanted to prune their portfolio and obtain whatever value possible from the removed pieces. In other words, some large companies in the United States and elsewhere wanted to flog the dregs of their portfolio to gain some financial return for the money they had spent on medicines they now wanted to stop developing. Companies were not generally taken in by this ruse and few were successful in gaining money from their discards. During this same period other companies, particularly in Japan, had other more positive views of licensing-out.

These companies understood that some of their medicines had substantial value and could increase their sales in countries where their medicines were not being marketed or were marketed only weakly. They therefore sought or agreed to license valuable medicines to partners that were strong in countries where their own presence was small or nonexistent. Licensing was generally a one-way agreement in these situations. Company A (i.e., the licensor) licensed their medicine to company B (i.e., the licensee) in one or more countries where company A either did not have sales representatives, development, and/or regulatory capabilities; or, had only limited capabilities.

In major pharmaceutical companies the traditional motivation behind licensing-in new medicines was the hope of finding rare gems lying about on a generally bleak landscape. Some companies searched obscure places in Eastern Europe and Japan, combing the landscape in search of a gem that they could acquire for almost no money or royalties. A number of well-publicized successes began to interest other companies in proactively utilizing this approach. Whereas research and development-based companies have as their motto "Research and Development," the pure licensing-based companies have as their motto "Search and Development."

During the late 1970s and early 1980s, companies that had valuable medicines to license-out began to place a greater importance on them and demand greater value in exchange. A more modern view (after the mid-1980s) is that companies want to enhance their portfolio by strategic trades and deals. It is now more common for parties in a license arrangement to seek a win-win situation rather than attempt to trick or outsmart each other.

Benefits in Licensing-Out

Some strategic benefits that currently exist for a company to consider when licensing out a product of value are briefly described. A company may

1. Earn more money for a medicine than it otherwise would, particularly if the product will be marketed in a country where that company is not operating.
2. Inexpensively explore the possibility of establishing a new subsidiary by determining how well one or more of their products sell in the particular country.
3. Expose itself to fewer risks than if it attempts to market a medicine with its small sales force, or a larger sales force that does not contact the type of physician who would prescribe the new product.
4. Enter a new market more easily and more rapidly than attempting to build both a subsidiary and a sales force.
5. Receive a medicine or other product/technology in return that is extremely valuable and meets strategic goals.
6. Retain the right to enter the new market at a later date after it has developed the capability of selling and promoting the medicine effectively (e.g., Boots licensing ibuprofen to Upjohn and later also selling it themselves).
7. Obtain expertise in clinical, development, regulatory, and other areas through collaboration with an experienced partner.

Most companies prepare a full brochure of information on the products or other types of opportunities (e.g., technologies) they wish to license out. A prototype table of contents for such a brochure is shown in Table 48.1.

Goals and Purposes of Licensing

The overall goal of licensing is to add value to a company either by licensing-in or -out the rights to an idea,

TABLE 48.1. *Prototype table of contents for a licensing-out proposal*

1. Summary (one to three pages)
2. Scientific rationale
3. Background information
4. Overall development plan and strategy
5. Preclinical efficacy data, status, and issues
6. Toxicological data, status, and issues
7. Clinical data, status, and issues
8. Marketing history of the compound and disease area
9. Marketing forecasts
10. Technical development status and issues
11. Production status and issues
12. Patent status and issues
13. Overall major issues and plans to address each of them
14. References
15. Appendices[a]

[a] Includes specific documents referred to in the text. The length of the proposal cannot be specified because both long and abbreviated versions could be prepared for the same opportunity.

compound, medicine, or technology. Medicines may be licensed-in (or out) at any stage of development. "This ranges from licensing a general concept or idea for a new medicine where specific molecules may not have been designed, to licensing a compound that is in an early, middle, or late, preclinical stage. A medicine could be licensed that is in any stage of clinical investigation or have achieved regulatory approval and be marketed in one or more countries."

Licensing-in compounds or medicines may be viewed in terms of achieving corporate goals through either building a new franchise, protecting a current franchise, or expanding an existing franchise. Apart from enhancing a company's portfolio or marketing position in the short term, a reasonable licensing approach for a company may be based on filling in certain gaps over a five- to ten-year (or even longer) period. These gaps are defined in the section on strategies.

To add value to a particular therapeutic line of products, a company may attempt to increase the number of different products by licensing-in new ones. A more traditional approach to increasing value of a specific line of medicines is to focus on expanding the number of line-extensions (e.g., new dosage strengths, dosage forms, and packaging). Often, both approaches are followed simultaneously.

WHAT ONE LICENSES

Most licenses involve one of three things—patents, knowledge, or trademarks. License for a patent is usually the best type of license to get because it offers the greatest protection to the licensee. A license of secret knowledge or "know-how" is less secure to the licensee because others may independently discover the information, may find alternate approaches so that the information becomes less valuable, or may examine the item or process and identify the nature of the knowledge. Because the value of licensing knowledge generally lasts for a shorter time than a patent, less royalties are usually given for it than for a patent-protected license.

The third type of license is for a registered trademark (e.g., brand name). This is usually more valuable for over-the-counter than for prescription medicines. Nonetheless, a licensor may require the licensee of a prescription medicine to license the trademark and to pay a royalty for it.

Part of the package that may be licensed along with the patent, know-how, or trademark could be technical assistance needed for the transfer of the technology. This could include training of staff in manufacturing methods, marketing approaches, quality control, and improvements as they are developed.

TYPES OF LICENSES

The types of rights granted in the license may be exclusive or nonexclusive. Exclusive rights means that only the licensee has rights to the patent, knowledge, or trademark for one or more dosage forms in one or more countries. It is common to license-out all dosage forms of a medicine for all countries, although specific limitations on either dosage form or country are possible.

Nonexclusive rights means that the licensor may license the medicine to as many licensees as they desire. A sole license means that the licensor also retains rights to market the medicine, but only licenses one other group.

Almost any arrangement that can be conceived may be proposed between two or more groups. A few of the more common types of agreements are briefly presented.

1. One company licenses a medicine to another for worldwide development and marketing.

2. One company licenses a medicine to another for development and marketing in only one country or in selected countries. The original company may participate in the medicine's development or may only retain marketing rights in selected countries after the other company has developed the medicine.

3. One company initiates medicine development and the second may begin their participation at any of several stages (e.g., Phase I, Phase II, marketing). Royalty fees for the license become progressively higher if the second company waits for a later stage before beginning their participation.

4. There may be money paid as part of the original agreement or money may be paid according to any agreed-on schedule (e.g., at end of Phase II, on NDA submission, at time of marketing).

5. A company may develop a medicine but license it to another for comarketing in one or more specific countries. The advantage for the developer is to achieve a better depth and breadth of market penetration.

Factors that are covered in an agreement include (1) identification of what is being transferred (e.g., patents, dosage forms, manufacturing process, marketing services, technical knowledge), (2) the payments that are to be made, (3) the countries involved, (4) the nature of the licensee's participation, (5) how the property transferred is to be used, (6) time requirements (e.g., for completing various stages of medicine development), (7) duration of the agreement, (8) any penalties, and (9) conditions under which the contract may be renegotiated or voided.

CREATING A LICENSING STRATEGY

Examples of Simple Licensing Strategies

The most simple licensing strategy is to license medicines or technologies that are going to earn the greatest profit for the company. Some companies utilize this strategy by reacting to all proposals that are presented to it from outside sources (e.g., other companies, academic investigators, institutions). Although this general strategy has been effective and successful for some companies, in this increasingly competitive world, this approach is too simple to be an effective modus operandi and a more systematic and proactive approach is usually preferred by large pharmaceutical companies.

A more specific strategy may be developed by utilizing portfolio analysis methods to identify various types of gaps in the portfolio that could be closed with a licensed medicine or product. In addition to (or instead of) gaps, a company may focus their strategy on creating a strong defensive position around their therapeutic areas or medicines of greatest commercial value. Once the characteristics of desired products or types of opportunities are completed in terms of therapeutic area, stage of development, and potential market size, it enables the person or persons seeking licensing opportunities to have a general "feel" as to what types of products would be most desirable and have the best fit with the company. It is undesirable, however, to develop a highly specific strategy that is too restrictive and becomes almost impossible to achieve. An example of this would be to seek to license an antihypertensive medicine currently in Phase II that acts via a specific mechanism and has a specific commercial potential in its third year of marketing.

On the other hand, seeking to proactively license actual medicines under development by other companies is a realistic strategy to pursue.

Some companies adopt the attitude that any product licensed in must be able to be developed and sold using their existing resources and facilities. Companies at the other end of the spectrum believe that if a license has great value for the company, it is essential to find sufficient resources to develop it appropriately, even if they have to borrow money.

It is clear from the discussions below on focus, gaps, and elements that a company may develop extremely complex and detailed strategies in addition, or instead of the rather simple ones described above.

Identifying the Focus

Each company must decide whether to be proactive, reactive, or both in terms of licensing strategy. Another aspect of a licensing strategy is focus: a company must decide to focus efforts on enhancing the company's strengths, or developing new areas, or to pursue a combination approach. Companies usually receive many unsolicited offers for potential licensing in their areas of strength because those are the areas for which the company is most well known (e.g., Burroughs Wellcome Co. receives numerous antiviral offers). The licensor recognizes that a substantial knowledge base and extensive development and marketing experiences have been acquired by the potential licensee, which can be applied to new compounds or medicines.

Identifying Major Types of Gaps

Nine gaps are described.

Research Gaps

A gap may exist in an important research area for potentially important medicines or technologies. A new compound requiring some additional work could fill this gap. Other types of research goals that could be met by licensing include licensing-in a new technology to help develop novel compounds or to improve existing ones, or to obtain a series of compounds to test.

Financial Gaps

A financial gap could be a financial shortfall in terms of projected sales (or profits) for marketed and investigational medicines (in the future) compared to the company's goals. These gaps must be closely examined for each of the caveats and assumptions underlying the financial gaps; subtle assumptions may have major influences on the outcomes that are projected (e.g., are some or all of the projects in the portfolio counted on for future revenues, and if some, which ones or what percentage of the total portfolio and how are these numbers derived?).

Risk Gaps

Risk gaps for a company are defined in terms of projects currently in the portfolio. A company may want additional projects in its portfolio that have a higher (or lower) risk than the present ones. Some companies limit the number of high risk projects in their portfolio, whereas others are more concerned about limiting the proportion of resources devoted to high risk projects.

Therapeutic Area Gaps

Therapeutic area gaps are gaps in the list of medicines currently in development within each therapeutic or disease area. Goals may be expressed either in terms of overall number (or value) of medicines from a specific area, and/or according to each phase of development.

Strategic Gaps

Strategic gaps are approaches that are desired to have (e.g., biotechnology) but for which the company does not wish to build up an infrastructure. A license of know-how may bring such expertise into the company.

Phase of Development Gaps

Phase of development gaps refer to the numbers of early-, mid-, and late-stage compounds. The phases may either be evaluated in terms of the overall number (or value) of medicines in each phase or may be subdivided by specific therapeutic areas.

Marketed Product Gaps

Gaps may exist in the number or the value of already marketed over-the-counter or prescription medicines in a specific therapeutic or disease area.

Resource Gaps

A company with insufficient resources to develop adequately a new medicine may license it to another company that has more resources. Another possibility for a company with a resource gap is to try and fill it through financial borrowing or codevelopment with another company.

Production Capacity Gaps

A company with insufficient ability to produce its own medicines usually contracts the manufacture to another company rather than licensing their medicine out. The creation of new facilities or expansion of existing plants is also explored.

Elements of a Licensing Strategy

1. Stage of development—The earlier in development the compound is, the less expensive it will generally be to acquire, but the more uncertain its future will be. Licensing compounds at a later stage of development is more expensive, but there is greater assurance that the medicine works as hoped.

2. Commercial potential—Marketing groups must examine the projected market for the new product at the time that it is estimated to be introduced. A certain amount of profit may be required as a minimum incentive to proceed with licensing negotiations.

3. Research and development staff to develop the medicine—Appropriate expertise and resources must be available to place on the medicine's development. In some situations some or all of these activities may be contracted to others.

4. Corporate comfort zone—The product must fall within the company's desires and abilities to have the medicine produced and marketed. Parts of these and related activities may be contracted out, but the product should be one that fits the portfolio of marketed products or is a product that is desired to be marketed. Abilities of sales representatives to handle the product must be considered.

5. Production capabilities—The company must be able to make the medicine themselves or to contract it to another company.

6. Therapeutic category of the licensed medicine or product—This parameter varies in importance from little to critical depending on the precise situation.

7. Business terms and arrangements—The company may be required to utilize a cross-licensing agreement to acquire the product. Various aspects of the agreement may be determined at an early stage of negotiation (e.g., will up-front money be required, will the license be worldwide, does the other company wish to comarket the medicine, is the patent life acceptable?). Cross-licensing agreements are becoming increasingly popular and even demanded by some companies with valuable medicines to license.

8. Risk—This term includes aspects of several of the other elements, plus additional ones. The risks to a company in licensing a medicine may be determined in terms of the medicine's (1) potential to create liability suits, (2) probability that it will not work as hoped, (3) probability that the medicine will not possess adequate safety, (4) projected cost to take the medicine to the go-no go Phase II decision point, or to New Drug Application (NDA) submission, (5) probability that it will not be

marketed in time to obtain a minimally accepted profit, (6) potential for a complex or unclear patent situation, or (7) having formulation or other problems of technical development of manufacture that may not be able to be completely solved.

The most highly developed licensing strategy is only one aspect in obtaining valuable opportunities. Some of the crucial factors responsible for one company obtaining licensing rights to a specific medicine of great value instead of another company include timing, personal contacts and relationships, reputation of being a (the) major company in that area, and serendipity.

Roles of Orphan Medicines in a Licensing Strategy

It might seem strange or even incongruous to discuss orphan medicines and licensing-in strategy in the same paragraph, but there are several important connections. For example, a company may wish to expand its franchise in a particular disease or therapeutic area, and an orphan medicine could be used as a means of both enhancing the company's image and broadening its franchise. Another purpose that would be served by licensing-in an orphan medicine in an area where the company is strong would be to keep competitors out of the specific disease area. An orphan medicine may therefore be used to gain a competitive edge in terms of image and publicity, even if the medicine is not a major commercial success.

Finally, an important orphan medicine may be used as a means of gaining access to physicians through sales representatives. Sales representatives are finding it increasingly difficult to approach many physicians. A new and important orphan medicine can facilitate entry into physician's offices, whereby representatives can then promote more commercially important medicines. This approach can involve promoting an orphan medicine in one of the company's established therapeutic areas or in one that the company hopes to enter in the relatively near future. One major company licensed-in an orphan medicine for use in a therapeutic area the company was planning to enter. This promoted familiarity with the therapeutic area among both medical and marketing staffs. Problems in approaches and procedures could be worked out, and staff could prepare for a more determined and efficient effort once the more important medicine they were expecting reached that stage of development.

CREATING A PROACTIVE APPROACH TO LICENSING-IN COMPOUNDS AND MEDICINES

Creating a proactive approach to licensing-in compounds involves six steps.

1. Step One—Identify the therapeutic areas of interest and also the specific diseases of interest within each therapeutic area. Specific technologies of interest may also be identified.

2. Step Two—Identify the stage of development that an opportunity must be in to be of interest (e.g., preclinical, Phase I, Phase II). This may be specific to one therapeutic area only or may apply to all areas. Clarify on a disease-by-disease basis if necessary. There is often some overlap between this step and the following one.

3. Step Three—Identify the minimally acceptable scientific and medical properties that a compound or medicine must possess to be of interest in each disease area. This overlaps with step two because a compound of interest may be defined as one that is in Phase II or III and possesses certain properties, or one that is in a preclinical stage but has a different set of specific properties that make it extremely attractive for licensing.

4. Step Four—Identify all of the specific medicines either marketed or known to be under active development from the literature, word of mouth, or other sources that meet the established criteria for each disease of interest. Because not all medicines that actually meet the criteria will be known, several should be included on the list that just possibly (or probably) meet the criteria.

5. Step Five—Consider which of these medicines to pursue. Make appointments with companies or institutions to discuss the possibility of their licensing-out the compound/medicine. It may be necessary to offer an exchange (i.e., cross-licensing) or to offer some other inducement for the other group to be willing to have even a low-risk informal discussion.

6. Step Six—Either before or after visiting the owner of the medicine of interest, decide what products or other inducements can be offered in exchange. The compounds or medicines offered may be limited to certain countries, to certain dosage forms, or both. In addition, the identity of the specific medicine to exchange can be made known at a later time, even after the original medicine is licensed (as long as the details are specified in the contract). Nonetheless, the proactive company should have thought through its licensing stance with respect to cross-licensing.

To increase the probabilities of successfully licensing-in medicines or technologies using a proactive approach it is important to:

1. Follow the patent literature closely because one may sometimes identify potential licensing opportunities of interest at an early stage of development.

2. Talk to consultants who are aware of pharmaceutical or biotechnology industry activities and have many personal contacts. Provide important consultants (under confidentiality agreements) with the characteristics of the medicines you are seeking to license.

3. Follow the literature on new medicines (e.g, Pharmaprojects, SCRIP, Drug News and Perspectives).

4. Initiate a dialogue with important investigators in the therapeutic field(s) in which one is particularly interested in finding a new medicine. Choose those investigators who are most likely to learn about new medicines at an early stage of development.

5. Visit other pharmaceutical companies to build personal relationships and networks, but to be selective in this approach. This can be a black hole that absorbs all of the time and travel dollars that one wishes to spend without accomplishing anything of substance.

6. Utilize personal contacts of the company's scientific staff. These people may inform your staff of important opportunities at scientific meetings or elsewhere.

7. Consider licensing-in and licensing-out simultaneously. Do not conceptually separate these two activities because trades or various types of agreements are often possible or even necessary. Such exchanges may not have been conceived of during the initial discussions or even well into the negotiations.

8. Most large pharmaceutical companies should only consider licensing-in preclinical compounds that are extremely novel and have great promise based on the preclinical data generated. The number of hurdles for preclinical compounds to jump is extremely large. Preclinical compounds should be licensed, whenever possible, on a worldwide basis. Licensing-in ideas for compounds that have not yet been synthesized and tested is rarely advisable.

THE BUSINESS OF LICENSING: ORGANIZATIONAL AND METHODOLOGICAL ISSUES

Where Does Licensing Fit Best in a Company's Organization?

The major options concern where to place the licensing group: under marketing, finance, research and development, or corporate planning. A licensing group also could report to a very high senior corporate officer as an independent group. Pros and cons exist for each approach; the choice will depend to a large degree on the traditions of the company and the people involved. Licensing also may be placed in a more broadly defined business development function. The term business development is used to include not only licensing activities, but also efforts directed toward mergers, acquisitions, and divestitures. In most cases, an independent licensing group reporting to the chief executive officer or a staff assistant makes the most sense.

Pharmaceutical companies have developed a large variety of internal staff groups to deal with licensing. Different individuals may be in charge of licensing opportunities in different business areas (e.g., animal products, over-the-counter medicines [OTCs], diagnostics, ethical human medicines, contract manufacturing) of a company. Alternatively, two or even all of these areas may be assigned to a single person. Regardless of the number of licensing groups, a central coordinator is needed if licensing activities are being conducted in multiple businesses. If a coordinator is not used then separate licensing people from one company may independently visit another company and unwittingly create confusion and even negative reactions. Each independent business or research and development (R and D) site in a company may develop its own strategy that may not work well together, unless coordinated.

The size of a group working on licensing opportunities varies from one or a few full-time people up to large organizations of over 100 people. In the latter case, there are people to analyze (1) the research and technical development aspects of what has been accomplished and what remains to be accomplished, (2) marketing aspects and commercial potential, (3) production issues, (4) legal aspects, and (5) financial aspects of the agreement.

Obtaining Information and Data on New Opportunities

The process of licensing may be thought of as having three periods: 1. Review of the opportunity. 2. Negotiation of the contract. 3. Execution of the contract's terms.

The initial step is review of nonconfidential information on a product or technology, usually in the form of a report or letter. This is generally sufficient for an experienced group to judge the interest of the company. The opportunity may be compared to a list of therapeutic areas within the company's comfort zone, or it may be compared to a much more detailed description of desired stage and mechanism for specific diseases. The concept may also be discussed with scientific, medical, or marketing staff to determine if sufficient interest exists to sign a confidentiality agreement. In this legal document the reviewer agrees not to disclose the information contained in confidential reports supplied by the licensor. This agreement protects the licensor from a public disclosure of information that might compromise a patent or provide an important research lead to others. These documents typically contain two to four pages of legal terms and sometimes require significant negotiations before they are agreed to and signed. At that point, the licensor sends the licensing company all available pertinent information on the product.

A company working in the same area as the potential opportunity may choose not to sign the agreement and receive the data. This would prevent the possibility of a future suit arising from claims of using the information.

This generally is most relevant for preclinical scientific studies where both companies are working in exactly the same chemical or biological area.

Should a Licensing Group Coordinate or Conduct the Opportunity Reviews?

Whether a licensing group conducts or only coordinates reviews of potential licensing products and technologies depends on its defined role. The choice is to either provide sufficient professional staff so that the licensing group can conduct its own reviews, or to keep the licensing group relatively small so that its staff coordinates reviews conducted primarily by permanent staff within marketing, research and development, legal, finance, production, and other appropriate departments. Given that the greatest expertise of a company lies in its professional staff, it generally makes more sense for the licensing group to coordinate most reviews rather than to conduct them. It is the author's opinion that when these analyses are conducted by the regular staff that a stronger commitment to the licensed medicine results, although it undoubtedly takes more time for the regular staff to complete necessary evaluations than for a staff dedicated to these activities. Of course, many opportunities initially presented to the licensing group may be easily dismissed or encouraged without any formal reviews. The fate of numerous other opportunities may be settled through a short telephone conversation with the in-house expert in that specific scientific or marketing area.

An alternative is to use a combination approach to reviews of potential licensing opportunities. For example, a company's research and development staff could review preclinical and clinical data and assess staff resources that would be necessary for further development of the product or technology. Experts in the licensing group would review the products' characteristics, assess competitive medicines under development and on the market, estimate sales forecasts for 5 to 15 years, and determine the overall strategic fit of the opportunity with the company's objectives.

Processing Licensing Opportunities

All pharmaceutical companies should have an organized approach to handling opportunities submitted from external groups. Failure to do this would cause major problems in terms of (1) potentially losing the chance to license or acquire an important medicine or technology, (2) spending excessive amounts of staff effort reviewing uninteresting opportunities that should be rapidly screened, and (3) conducting unnecessary high level meetings. Standard steps in processing a typical licensing opportunity are listed in Table 48.2.

TABLE 48.2. *Standard steps in processing a typical licensing opportunity*[a]

1. Initial contact is made by the licensor about a potential license (for a proactive approach the initial contact may be made by the licensee).
2. Nonconfidential material is sent to the company for review.
3. Licensing office logs in the opportunity.[b]
4. Material is sent to an in-house expert for review or is reviewed (screened) by licensing office using established criteria.
5. If interest exists, subsidiary notifies the headquarters about the contact (or vice versa).
6. Confidentiality agreement is signed.[c]
7. Licensor sends company more extensive and confidential information.
8. Material is logged in and sent for review to research, technical development, marketing, production, finance, and legal experts. A sequential review may be done (i.e., only those opportunities passing certain hurdles go to finance and legal experts).
9. If the consensus of reviews is positive, then negotiations may proceed. A request is made by the company to learn the general terms the licensor has in mind.
10. Additional reviews and negotiations continue.
11. Senior management reaches a decision on the proposal.

[a] Numerous additional steps or variations are possible.
[b] Separate logs may be maintained for (1) opportunities actively considered for licensing-in, (2) opportunities actively considered for licensing-out, (3) completed agreements, (4) terminated unsuccessful agreements, and (5) inactive opportunities. A master list cross-indexed by major categories of the licensing log may also be created.
[c] A great deal of variation exists in the amount of detail in standard confidentiality agreements.

Current Status Logs

A formal system should be established to record all opportunities that are received. A separate log should be maintained for identifying the current status of both licensing-in and licensing-out opportunities. Code numbers, with or without letter prefixes as identifiers for each licensing opportunity, should contain four or five digits. Rather than maintain a list of all opportunities that are (1) terminated, (2) undergoing active review or negotiations, (3) inactive, or (4) approved on the same log, it is easy to create four separate logs. A master log also may be established in a computer data base.

Evaluation and Negotiation Logs

A separate system should be established to track the progress of the reviews being undertaken within the company and/or by outside consultants. A separate system should track the progress of negotiations leading to agreements and controls. Examples of appropriate data to track are presented in Table 48.3. As part of this sys-

tem (or as an independent activity), it is useful to create a method to remind one to follow-up on all opportunities being discussed or considered. This method ("tickler file") usually involves marking a calendar for dates on which to check specific questions (e.g., on May 10, call Dr. Y to ask if the review on medicine X is complete). This approach is necessary if the licensing group serves a coordinating function and does not conduct expert reviews (and possibly is not central to some negotiations).

Contract Logs

A third tracking system should be enacted that follows progress on all signed contracts. Numerous milestones may exist that require payments or transmittal of information or data. The person responsible for each activity or report should be noted on the log and reminded in sufficient time to meet his or her deadline. Financial departments will create their own systems to track payments, either into or out of the company.

TABLE 48.3. *Representative types of information to track on licensing opportunities*[a]

1. Identification number (i.e., license code assigned)
2. Date received
3. Name of company or organization that submitted the opportunity
4. Name of the compound, product, or technology submitted
5. Specific disease or therapeutic area intended
6. Brief description of the product or idea
7. Name of primary scientific reviewer within company (if one is designated)
8. Name of other scientific reviewers
9. Name of primary marketing reviewer
10. Name of primary financial reviewer
11. Name of primary legal advisor
12. Date opportunity sent to each reviewer
13. Date report due from each reviewer
14. Brief synopsis of each review[b]
15. Next step(s) to be taken
16. Person within the licensing group coordinating the reviews
17. Person within the licensing group coordinating the negotiations
18. Key technical issues, including research and medical issues
19. Key marketing issues
20. Financial terms requested
21. Financial terms offered
22. Key financial issues
23. Major legal issues
24. Major resource issues
25. Key production issues
26. Key regulatory issues
27. Patient status and issues

[a] This information could be tracked in a variety of ways and using various forms and systems that would differ at each company.
[b] This could be tracked on a separate form using a subset of the headings from this table.

Criteria for Screening Licensing Opportunities

Although it would be desirable to thoroughly review every licensing opportunity, shortages of time and available personnel invariably require that each company establish basic rules and systems for the efficient operation of a licensing group. These approaches should be designed to expedite reviews and enable a company to reach a decision on whether (and how) to follow-up each opportunity as rapidly as possible. These systems are dependent on a company's licensing strategy. For example, if a company's strategy is that (1) no cardiovascular medicines will be licensed and (2) no medicines without human clinical experience will be licensed, then the company has already created two important criteria that will enable rapid screening of many opportunities.

It is often possible to establish a single set of criteria that can be used to both screen and evaluate many opportunities for each disease or therapeutic area. These same criteria may be used for proactive searching and a reactive evaluating approach. This is extremely beneficial in that it enables the efficient processing of many opportunities. For example, certain therapeutic areas may be outside a company's comfort zone and should be identified. Other therapeutic areas may be identified as ones in which the company seeks to license-in only certain types of medicines. These therapeutic/disease areas could be areas the company currently is strong in and wishes to build further, or they can be areas of current weakness that the company wishes to develop. A third group of therapeutic/disease categories that does not fit either of the above two types (unless the company divided all therapeutic areas into two types) often is created. The third set would require individual consideration of each opportunity using more general criteria.

A minimal phase of development for an opportunity also could be defined for each therapeutic category on a disease-by-disease basis. Important caveats should be appended to these criteria so that potentially valuable new treatments are not rejected because of overly rigid criteria. For example, the criteria for cardiovascular medicines might state that at least some human data are required, unless the medicine is believed to work by a novel mechanism of action. Alternatively, some specific mechanisms could be identified as being of particular interest to the company. Table 48.4 illustrates a competitive analysis approach in which specific mechanisms (e.g., D) are identified that are of particular interest for licensing opportunities (because no investigational or marketed medicine currently has that mechanism of action). In this example, mechanisms A, B, and C probably would not be of interest. Identifying one or more mechanisms of action as necessary for a licensed-in medicine in a specific disease area would make the screening of some opportunities quite straightforward. Other factors to consider are listed in Table 48.5.

In a reactive mode (i.e., responding to unsolicited opportunities), one could rapidly screen many opportunities by determining several parameters in advance and then asking the following three questions:

1. Is the disease or therapeutic area one of interest?
2. Is the stage of the medicine's development acceptable? For example, only Phase II or Phase III opportunities might be of interest unless a few specific caveats are met.
3. Does the medicine meet the established standards in terms of its safety? For example, a safety specification may be specifically identified by the company, stating that the medicine must have fewer adverse reactions than a specific market leader or standard medicine. This question would not be pertinent if standard medicines do not exist (e.g., in Alzheimer's disease). Alternatively, the company may specify safety standards in general terms (e.g., the new medicine must be as safe as medicine X). Comparable statements could readily be developed for evaluating efficacy.

These same three questions could also be asked of other companies during a proactive search for new opportunities, or when critiquing published information on new medicines under development.

Sources of Licensing Opportunities

The major sources in which opportunities are sought include:

TABLE 48.4. *Competitive analysis table that compares medicines that work by different mechanisms to treat a single disease[a]*

Investigational medicine	Name of company	Medical/scientific approach to treat the disease				Comments
		A	B	C	D	
Medicine 1		X		X		
Medicine 2			X			
Medicine 3						Mechanism not yet identified
. . .[b]						
Medicine N		X				

[a] The purpose of this table is to categorize the mechanisms of how medicines, currently being investigated, act in a specific disease. Gaps where no medicine is being developed (i.e., D) can be identified.

[b] These dots refer to any number of additional medicines that could be listed.

TABLE 48.5. *Factors for a company that is licensing-in a medicine to consider in evaluating opportunities[a]*

1. Number and type of additional headcount which would be needed to develop the medicine
2. Effect that meeting the milestone requirements would have on ongoing projects
3. Reputation and reliability of the new partner and degree of trust in the proposed partner
4. Identification of important issues or points that are not suitable for negotiation
5. Understanding of the real reason(s) why the other group wishes to enter the agreement
6. Clarification of specific details of the agreement that could have a major influence (e.g., how will the supply price be determined?)

[a] These factors are in addition to those relating to science, medicine, marketing, finance, and production.

1. Universities—Individuals, departments, entire universities, and entrepreneurial groups created or sponsored by universities offer opportunities for licensing. In recent years, many universities have increased efforts toward licensing-out products or technologies. The biggest drawback to these opportunities is that they often are submitted to companies for consideration at an extremely early stage of development.

2. Venture capital groups—These groups usually act as agents for individuals or small companies.

3. Corporations—Many licensing opportunities come from other pharmaceutical companies or other types of companies. Opportunities flow from large to small companies and vice versa, as well as between similar-sized companies. In addition, two or more companies may share expertise and capital to form a joint venture or to cross-license two (or more) products.

4. Individuals—Many individuals create new compounds or technologies with biological activity and the potential to be commercially useful. While companies understand that some individuals have valuable or potentially valuable ideas or compounds, there are a high proportion of naive or unreliable people who submit opportunities to companies. Most of their ideas or compounds are not generally what they are initially claimed to be.

5. Governments—Some governments license medicines they have patented. Applications from interested sponsors are usually sought and then evaluated.

Pharmaceutical companies of medium or large size usually receive and process 500 to 1000 licensing opportunities each year. A book that describes sources in great detail and discusses approaches to use is *Finding and Licensing New Products and Technologies From the USA* (Morehead, 1988). This book is highly practical, although rather elementary.

Facilitating the Signing of a Licensing Agreement

Merely signing a licensing agreement does not ensure the licensee or the licensor that all terms will be met and both partners will be satisfied. Licensing agreements between two partners is like a marriage: both must continually work hard to ensure that the relationship is successful. Each partner must demonstrate an understanding and sensitivity to each other's professional culture and traditions. In addition, there are some specific approaches that can increase the probability of success for the agreement. For instance, a single person in each group must be assigned overall responsibility for the implementation and success of the negotiations. Numerous other factors that should be considered during evaluation and negotiation phases of licensing agreements are listed in Table 48.5 and in the later section on preparing the contract.

FINANCIAL ISSUES IN LICENSING

Assigning Value to Potential and Actual Deals

Given the large number of variables that are involved in structuring a licensing agreement and the large sums of money often involved, it is imperative to have a reasonably accurate assessment of what the deal is worth. This is often a highly inaccurate exercise because many of the most important factors (e.g., clinical characteristics of the medicine) are unknown. Nonetheless, it must be done. Utilizing a few basic principles it is possible to derive a reasonable financial evaluation.

A profit and loss statement should be created for a ten-year or longer period to identify how all investment costs for the licensee, including milestone payments and development costs will be balanced by sales minus cost of goods, promotion costs, and royalties. These values and others that may be relevant can be placed on a spreadsheet. A positive balance should be noted for future earnings to offset the costs of development.

An extremely large number of parameters can be fed into the financial model. These may include (1) inflation rate, (2) tax rate, (3) selling price, (4) units sold, (5) sales forecast, (6) cost of goods, (7) royalty, (8) overhead, (9) rate of return, (10) discount rate, (11) market share, and (12) length of the agreement. On top of these financial and marketing factors there are critical development factors—(1) phase of development, (2) competition intensity, (3) chance of technical success, and (4) alternative treatments.

This model can be used to identify how changes in royalties, milestone payments, and other factors affect the bottom line. It therefore assists the negotiation phase by identifying how much each side can stretch the deal.

Timing of payments is often an important factor. Licensees usually want to delay them to the time when they have greater assurance that the product will in fact earn money.

Types of Payments

Monetary payments are a regular part of most licensing agreements. While royalties based on the amount of sales are perhaps the most frequently discussed payment, several additional types exist. Even terms such as profit and fully burdened costs should be discussed and defined to prevent future misunderstandings.

Option Payments

When a company (X) allows another company (Y) to consider licensing its product, and a period of time (typically 3 to 12 months) is needed for Y to evaluate one or more areas in depth, company Y often pays company X a fee for this option (i.e., exclusive right) period. In most cases the option agreement stipulates whether or not the option may be renewed, and if so, on what terms and conditions. An option agreement usually removes some stress for both parties. The licensor knows the opportunity is being carefully reviewed and is progressing, so that even a negative response is often accompanied by new data that may be extremely important.

Development/Milestone Payments

A company (Y) often pays another company (X) for the right to develop a medicine it has licensed from X. Payments may be scheduled to occur at the time of signing and at fixed time periods (e.g., annually) or at preestablished milestones (e.g., filing of the IND, start of Phase II, submission of NDA, FDA approval). Fees paid typically escalate because the medicine is worth more money as it survives successive development hurdles. Initial payments are sometimes referred to as entry fees or up-front payments and may be nonrefundable or recoverable as an advance on the royalties. If entry fees can be adjusted, the basis for this should be described in the contract. A licensor may request comarketing rights on another medicine of the licensee in lieu of milestone payments.

Royalties on Sales

Royalties may be a fixed percentage (e.g., 4% of sales worldwide) or they may be based on an escalating scale (e.g., 3% of the first ten million dollars of sales, 4% of the second ten million dollars sold, and 5% on all sales above 20 million dollars). Royalty clauses may stipulate that a minimum amount of money will be paid per year after approval of the medicine in the first major country, or the contract may stipulate that royalties begin following approval in any country. Royalties based solely on a patent cease when the patent expires because it is illegal in most countries to demand payment thereafter. Royalties based on a nonpatent license may persist for an indefinite period. Even if they continue, the percentage paid usually decreases after the patent expiration. The contract must describe how royalties are to be paid: (1) from which specific company, (2) from which country (important for a large multinational company), (3) in which currency, and (4) how rates of exchange will be determined.

An old rule about royalties is that paying about 25% of the profits from the licensed product was viewed as a fair royalty. Percentage of profit is not currently used, however, because the calculation of profit is subject to many interpretations and "creative" accounting practices.

Purchase Price

A medicine or an idea for one may be sold outright to another company. This transaction may be discussed at the outset of the negotiations or at a later time after an initial negotiated agreement has been signed. The possible purchase at a later date may be discussed at the outset and details identified in the contract.

Supply Price

If company A licenses a medicine to company B, the former may continue to manufacture the medicine and sell it to company B for a price, known as the supply price. Company B determines the price they can sell the product for in the market (i.e., distribution price) and may tell company A what they are able to pay for the product. Alternatively, company A may make the initial offer to supply at a certain price. If the two companies are far apart on terms, another approach may be considered. For example, company A may sell or license the manufacturing know-how to company B.

Approaches to Balancing Financial Risk

Both sides want to minimize their financial risk. If the licensor wants a large sum of money from the licensee for signing a contract, the licensee may want the money to be applied to future obligations. For example, a large sum(s) may be paid at several stages prior to marketing. The licensor may be pleased to get the money up front, particularly if it is a small company. They are usually willing to trade-off some or all of that money against future royalties. For example, a highly successful medicine (i.e., 100 million dollars in sales in a year) may pay 10% in royalties (i.e., 10 million dollars). If the licensor received two million dollars in up-front money, then they would not be unhappy to have that money applied against royalties. This procedure helps to balance the risks.

Another way that financial risk can be balanced is to stipulate that some of the money is refundable if the medicine is terminated prior to completing Phase II, or prior to achieving another milestone. Other ways to balance the risk, particularly among medium and large companies, are for two companies to share the development costs (e.g., one conducts clinical trials and the other develops the scale-up and manufacturing process). The company that is licensing the medicine may or may not want to manufacture the medicine. In addition, that company may or may not wish to comarket the medicine from the outset or at a later time.

LEGAL ISSUES

Negotiation Phase

There are many issues to consider during the negotiation phase of the licensing process and diligence is required to evaluate them all in detail. Errors are often made in how these issues are decided, but for a company not to consider relevant topics is negligent. Each major area of a company that is involved in the license should identify as many actual and potential issues as possible so that relevant ones may be discussed internally and with the other group. Issues typically occur in research, medical, technical development, regulatory, marketing, legal, financial, production, and quality assurance areas. A range of extremes for several issues is shown in Table 48.6, points to discuss and settle are listed in Table 48.7 (and elsewhere in this article), and some production issues are given in Table 48.8.

The true value of the product should be established during this period. Although it may be difficult, every effort should be made to come up with a value. Each of the costs that will be incurred must be identified and assessed. Issues such as market share, medical value, and the effects of old and new competitive products each must be assessed.

During the negotiations, the two sides may seem to be far apart in terms or not progressing toward a solution. There are several books that provide information on negotiation styles and getting to a "win-win" solution (Fisher and Ury, 1983; Cohen, 1980; Korda, 1987). Before moving from your initial negotiating position you should assess how far apart you truly are from the other group and also how confident you are in the data and values generated by your staff that are the basis for your position.

A market survey or market research may have to be done before the license is signed. This can help with the negotiations, and usually will bring to light information about the competition and the demand for the product. (It also gains one time during which a balanced assessment can be reached.)

Preparing the Contract

General types of agreements made between companies are listed in Table 48.9 and the items covered by a typical agreement are given in Table 48.10. Either the licensee or licensor may create the draft document from which the final contract is eventually created. A duration or limit of the time a contract is in effect is important to specify. All situations are susceptible to change over time, so it is reasonable to have a multiple year limit to the life of a contract, usually based on patent life. Many issues arise that should be discussed and incorporated into the contract. For instance, (1) may the licensee subcontract or enter in joint arrangements with a third company for any or all of the development, marketing, or other aspects of the contract? or (2) may the licensee

TABLE 48.6. *Range of positions on major licensing issues*

Licensing issue	Range of positions	
	Extreme A	Extreme B
Royalties	Fixed	Based on sales or targets established for each dosage form
Equity	None	Significant
Milestone fees	None	Fixed or escalating fees related to technology or development milestones
Up-front (i.e., initial) fees	Yes	No (all fees put into equity)
Manufacturing	Exclusive to one company	Shared
Marketing	Exclusive to one company	Comarketing
Territory	Worldwide rights	Geographically restricted to a single country
What is licensed	Single compound for specifc disease	Multiple compounds for an entire therapeutic area

TABLE 48.7. *Selected points to settle during negotiations and to clarify in contracts*

1. Who owns what? Each specific aspect of what is being licensed or sold must be discussed and identified in the contract.
2. When does each element in the agreement become effective? Are there time points or performance measures to specify?
3. What is the price for each aspect or component? Prices based on two different currencies should specify which currency is to be used and how the exchange rate will be determined.
4. How is the technology to be transferred?
5. Is equity involved? If so, contractual details must be specific.
6. What specific aspects are excluded? It is insufficient to assume that areas not mentioned are not covered.
7. Is any information being withheld that is required for decision making? Although this is not a question that may be asked directly, if answers to issues are vague or change without cause, suspicion may arise.
8. Who will be responsible for the contract after signing? It is generally best if a single person at each group is identified.
9. Are times to reach regulatory submissions based on the first IND and NDA worldwide in any country or in only one or more specified countries?
10. How certain is it that the licensor will get a patent—Is it being contested? By whom and why?
11. Will the agreement prevent the company that licenses-in the medicine from introducing other similar products onto the market?
12. Is the license exclusive (for a specific medical device or technology) or nonexclusive? Is the license for a certain type of product (e.g., 24-hour liquid medicine) granted on a product-by-product basis to several or many licensees?
13. On what basis do you trust the other company? How should this affect the negotiations? What are their references and their reputation? Have they been easy to deal with or not?
14. What separate legal agreements must be signed (e.g., patents, knowledge and know-how, trademarks, supply)?
15. Are the positions of different development sites of a company the same regarding the licensed product? If not, how does this affect the licensing issue? What should be done, if anything, to bring the two (or more) sites into closer harmony?
16. Who else should discuss the issues before the company signs the agreement?
17. What would happen if the other company becomes bankrupt? How would the licensing arrangement be affected and how can a company protect itself?
18. How long a period for an option should be given? Should the option be renewable? How much should be charged and should this money be applicable to royalties or other costs?
19. Should the agreement be divided into two or more separate agreements? Who will supply product? Are there advantages to both partners?
20. Should there be two or even more go/no go decision points identified in the agreement (e.g., decision to sign option and get samples, go to market test, decide to go to market, decide on who will be the supplier)?
21. A company must determine the number of patients and amount of money needed to get the medicine to market. If this number is very different in one country than in another, can terms very different from those the licensor company has with other licensees be justified?
22. If the licensor supplies the medicine, is it at the bulk, formulated, or packaged stage? Will labels be applied? Is there a minimum price to protect the manufacturer?
23. Should specific subgroups for each major potential project to emerge be established?
24. How can negotiations arrive at a decision in the shortest possible time? Would it expedite negotiations to have CEOs from both companies participate?
25. If the contract is in two languages, do they say the same thing? One should confirm this by having the translation back-translated to the original language by a different person and then comparing the two versions.
26. If an option agreement is being signed, what is its duration (and price), is it renewable, and if so, under what terms? How often may it be renewed and what are the price and quantities for supplies to be furnished?
27. In what form will the medicine be supplied (e.g., raw chemical, bulk medicine, capsules, unlabeled containers)?
28. At what time point and under what conditions is technical information supplied?
29. When does the date of expiry begin? Is it after the bulk product is synthesized, formulated, and filled into vials, labeled, or taken out of storage for shipping?
30. What occurs if the manufacturer cannot supply the medicine?
31. What options should be put into the contract?

IND, Investigational New Drug Application; NDA, New Drug Application; CEO, chief executive officer.

sublicense the medicine to a third party? If so, under what conditions?

Many practical details of a licensing agreement are not put in a contract, but should be settled before the final contract(s) are signed. For instance,

1. Who is the primary contact person at each company?
2. What is the connection of the primary contact person to the project and to the company?
3. Who has responsibility for what activities?
4. Who pays for what costs?
5. Who manufactures what?
6. Who owns the NDA/PLA?
7. Who controls what?
8. How may supplies of medicine be ordered? Describe all paperwork, all processes, and all types of medicine (e.g., bulk, finished).
9. How soon after the contract is signed can the medicine be supplied?

TABLE 48.8. *Considerations in evaluating the desirability of manufacturing a licensed-in medicine*

1. Utilization of current and planned capacity with and without the new product
2. Utilization of current and planned staff
3. Availability of any additional staff needed
4. Availability of suitable equipment
5. Ability to adequately handle the waste produced
6. Ability to manufacture the product at the backup site if problems occur at the site in question
7. Ability to conduct necessary regulatory procedures (e.g., preparing reports, ensuring compliance, interacting with the regulatory authorities)
8. Ability to conduct quality assurance on the project
9. Profitability for the company
10. Ease of obtaining supplies
11. Necessity to conduct special steps in the synthesis and preparation of the final product that are hazardous or dangerous
12. If the product is investigational, determination of who will prepare the manufacturing and controls portion of the NDA
13. Interest of the other party in manufacturing the medicine
14. Terms for obtaining manufacturing know-how (e.g., financial terms, when will know-how be furnished)

---

10. In what form will the medicine be supplied? Provide all details of the containers, labels, packages, size, and so forth.
11. What is the status of the stability trials and assays? Which of these will be transferred or done jointly?
12. What issues exist about the Drug Master File?
13. What issues exist about all technical details, preclinical studies, clinical trials, and how will each of these be addressed?
14. What mechanisms for communications are to be established in terms of methods, frequency, people involved, conduits, and those to be copied?
15. If the word "may" is in the contract it is important to identify what it means.

TABLE 48.9. *General types of agreements made*

1. Option agreement to consider the product further.[a] This period could be designed to test market the product, test it in the laboratory, compare it with other products, or conduct other tests. One or more extension periods may be described in the agreement, along with the costs of each extension
2. Outright purchase of the product, product line, or other group of medicines
3. Comarketing arrangement from the outset or a number of years after the contract. This may be renewable by mutual agreement of both parties
4. Copromotion agreement
5. Cross-licensing agreement
6. Joint development of a product owned by one of the partners

---

[a] Fees may be paid on a fixed basis (e.g., annual) or at specific milestones during the licensing agreement.

TABLE 48.10. *Contents of a typical license agreement*

1. Identification of the parties to the agreement, plus addresses and general description of the business
2. General and specific description of what is being licensed
3. Definition of all key terms in the contract
4. Description of all grants made
5. Consideration (i.e., payment) details
6. Transfers of know-how and patents, plus specific terms
7. Transfers of improvements or additional data obtained
8. Records and accounting procedures to be used
9. Trademarks
10. Secrecy
11. Termination
12. Infringement
13. Assignment
14. Warrranty and disclaimer
15. Translations of documents
16. Arbitration
17. Notices
18. Approval of the agreement if necessary
19. Applicable law (e.g., which country and state)
20. Other legal details

Cross-Licensing and Choosing the Quid Pro Quo

More and more pharmaceutical companies want medicines rather than money in exchange for licensing their medicines to another company. This is referred to as cross-licensing. Most companies do not have the item that makes a perfect exchange; instead, a variety of possibilities may be discussed. These include an exchange of

1. A medicine on an exclusive basis for X group of countries.
2. Two medicines on a nonexclusive basis for Y group of countries.
3. Specific formulations for specific countries.
4. Medicines within a specific therapeutic class to be offered within X years. If no offers are made, then a payment of a specific amount of money is due.
5. A medicine plus cash.

Some simple details of various product trades are shown in Table 48.11. Figure 48.1 diagrams one way that a successful trade can be arranged.

Obligations by Each Partner

The control of development of a new compound is usually in the hands of the licensee. The licensor must place controls in the contract or they will have no recourse if the licensee is not assiduous in developing the product. The best way to influence a partner is to put time limits into the contract. If the milestones are not achieved, a penalty must be exacted. This penalty could vary from a small fine to a large fine or even to losing all rights to the product and giving up all data generated in

TABLE 48.11. *Examples of major types of product trades*

Type of trade	Company(ies) involved	Countries included in the agreement	Medicine(s) involved	Dosage forms
1. Complete	A	Worldwide	X	All
	B	Worldwide	Y	All
2. Limited	A	Country I	X	1
	B	Country I (or II)	Y	1
3. Variation I	A	Group I countries	X and Z	1, 2, 3
	B	Group II (or I) countries	Y and future rights on another	1
4. Variation II	A	Worldwide	X	1
	B, C, D	Worldwide for each company	Y	1, 2, 3

the interim. Another possibility is to lose one's exclusive rights. A less severe termination clause is to extend the rights for a specified time (e.g., one or two years) if a due date is not met, at a much higher cost to the licensee. If the licensor has few or no other products, this arrangement may be financially appealing; it implies that the licensee will become more assiduous in their development of the product. The licensee may be willing to pay the higher fees to retain exclusivity to the license.

REGULATORY ISSUES

Regulatory issues should be discussed and resolved prior to signing the agreement. Such issues include identifying the group and terms for

1. Filing regulatory submissions (e.g., IND, NDA)
2. Interacting with some (or all) regulatory authorities
3. Handling adverse experience reporting

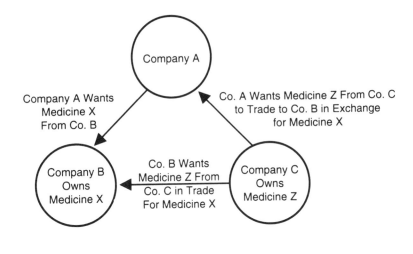

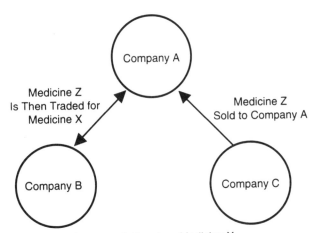

FIG. 48.1. The *upper* diagram describes a complex licensing situation that was successfully solved using the approach in the *lower* panel. The negotiated terms for this exchange and sale were complex.

4. Preparing and submitting periodic and annual reports
5. Preparing and submitting manufacturing and controls documents
6. Preparation and submission of advertising
7. Quality assurance
8. Responding to questions about the product
9. Dealing with labeling issues
10. Ensuring compliance with regulations
11. Assuming liability

PROBLEMS, PRINCIPLES, AND PREDICTIONS

Potential Problems and Issues

1. An agreement that is unlikely to be satisfactorily fulfilled should be identified as soon as possible. If a company considering licensing-in a product has serious doubts about either the priority or the quality of the work that they must do to develop the medicine, it might be preferable not to sign the agreement.

2. Most examples of licensing-out a medicine do not yield significant profits in the pharmaceutical industry. Royalties are generally modest in scale. If there is a choice and no convincing reason to license the medicine, it may be preferable for a company to develop and market the medicine themselves. A few medical contractors are qualified and able to handle the development role for a company that has sufficient money to take this approach. However, careful consideration must be given to the ability of successfully marketing the medicine once it is developed.

3. Complex barter arrangements involving several companies and countries have sometimes provided profitable solutions for each party. Conducting business in Eastern European and poor countries with limited foreign currency often raises questions of whether a barter arrangement should be considered.

4. It is essential for a company to develop a strong sense of trust in its potential partner at the outset of the negotiations because it is otherwise more likely that strains and cracks will develop in the relationship. The concept of a good fit is critical. Part of this comfort derives from an understanding of what your partner is looking for. The licensing discussion may be an introduction or pretext on their part. They may seek a research partner (i.e., a coresearch agreement is desired), a medicine development partner (i.e., a codevelopment agreement is desired), a marketing partner (i.e., a comarketing agreement is desired), a purchaser (i.e., a sales agreement is desired), or a licensor (i.e., a licensing agreement is desired). Confirming that the data support claims made and that the medicine is as advanced as is claimed are important means of building trust. Exaggeration or distortions on the part of the licensor should raise major qualms in the mind of the potential licensee.

5. Patent issues on biological products have mushroomed in recent years. Having a compound patent on a biological product is often not sufficient to be able to manufacture and sell the product. This is because there could be various blocking patents owned by others that relate to the method of production or purification of the product.

6. Taking on a licensing opportunity without assuring that sufficient staff are available to devote to its necessary development activities is a major blunder. This may or may not expose the company to penalties for failing to meet deadlines, but it will certainly delay the project and cause a significant loss of revenue for all parties.

7. A single individual (i.e., a conduit) must also be identified who will facilitate interactions between the two groups after the contract is signed. In most situations this is not the person who is assigned overall responsibility for the negotiations but is an individual concerned with the day-to-day administration and functioning of the agreement. If different groups within the licensor company perceive that adhering to the contract has a different priority, then numerous problems will be created. If all personnel copy the conduit on all correspondence, reports, and memoranda about the project then that individual will be able to identify potential or actual problems of priority and to deal with them effectively. This person should monitor compliance with the contract. Table 48.12 lists several items that are generally monitored to ensure compliance. Implementation and even monitoring major licenses may be best handled with a special team.

Technical information on licensing in general can be found in a book by Robert Goldscheider, *Technology Management: Law/Tactics/Forms* (1988). A more general introduction is given by Morehead (1988).

TABLE 48.12. *Topics to include in forms that are used to track compliance with agreements*[a]

1. Type of agreement (e.g., license, option, research)
2. Name of other party
3. Log number
4. Purpose of agreement
5. Business office details (e.g., project number, cost center number, account code, authorized signatures)
6. Agreement draft, review and approval (e.g., people, dates, departments)
7. Final agreement execution (e.g., people, titles, dates)
8. Terms of agreement listing all payments and dates separately
9. Person responsible for compliance with financial terms and requirements
10. Person responsible for compliance with technical terms and requirements
11. Conditions for termination of the agreement
12. Record of amounts paid, dates, and check numbers

[a] Any of these could be included on separate forms.

Golden Rules of Licensing

The first rule of licensing is that the value of an idea, compound, or medicine equals its intrinsic value times its stage of development to the fifth power. A corollary of this rule is that a mediocre medicine in Phase III is worth far more than a brilliant idea for a new compound that has not yet been synthesized. There may be a few noteworthy exceptions to this rule, but it would be extremely difficult to identify them in advance.

Most medicines tend to start their life in the clinic in a pure state and gradually accumulate warts and blemishes as they pass through the development pipeline. When competition is high in a specific disease area, it is necessary to market a medicine that would be described as a beautiful person, whereas in other disease areas it is possible to market a medicine of only average beauty. There is little doubt that in the early stages of treating an untreatable disease some fairly "ugly" medicines have been promoted to patients. For example, the early anti-AIDS medicines (prior to Retrovir) were extremely toxic and also ineffective.

A second rule of licensing is that people who own a clearly valuable medicine usually license it to their friends or to a company that happens to be in the right place at the right time. A company's reputation for expertise in the therapeutic or disease area often has a major influence in this aspect. Nonetheless, individuals who develop and cultivate large networks of personal contacts and friends often find that they receive more opportunities of value than colleagues with minimal networks.

Other golden rules that relate to licensing activities are mentioned.

1. Create a separate group dedicated to licensing activities, although scientific, marketing and financial analyses and evaluations may be conducted within those functional groups within the company.
2. Create strong links between the licensing group and marketing, strategic planning, legal, financial, and research and development departments.
3. Target specific diseases and approaches of particular interest for proactive licensing activities, as well as for review of unsolicited opportunities. Develop criteria to expedite reviews.

4. Evaluate all opportunities with speed and accuracy, but do not spend more than a reasonable amount of time on any of them.
5. All levels of the organization must agree with all terms in a negotiated contract. Ideally, all senior managers should also agree that the contract should be signed.
6. Carefully consider the commitments in the contract in terms of additional staff needs and resources required.
7. Ensure continuous interaction and communication among participants using agreed-on systems.
8. Seek a worldwide license whenever possible, unless there are specific reasons not to do so.
9. Attempt to obtain a one year option to license a product if the opportunity appears worthwhile (or is at least interesting) but additional data must be obtained (e.g., specific tests conducted) before a decision can be made.

Predictions for the Future

A few predictions of future activities in licensing are:

1. More creative business arrangements will be found to facilitate mutually beneficial negotiations and deals.
2. More acquisitions of biotechnology companies will occur, primarily by larger research-based pharmaceutical companies.
3. More exchanges of commercially valuable medicines will occur ending in mutually beneficial deals. This will help preserve the existence of more companies in an era of steadily increasing regulatory and business pressures.

In some ways, business opportunities with value are similar to children. They are all different and must be treated differently to help them to grow and develop to the best of their abilities. A corporate sponsor is like a prospective parent looking over a large number of children at an orphanage seeking one or more to adopt. The prospective parent (corporation) must closely examine the genetic stock and family history of each. This will increase the probability that the adopted child (medicine) will mature into the type of adult (product) the parent (sponsor) desires and is proud of.

49 / Regulatory Affairs

Functions.................................... 586
   Preparing/Publishing Documents for
      Regulatory Submissions.................... 586
   Interacting With Regulatory Authorities....... 586
   Developing Regulatory Strategies 587
   Interacting With Company Staff 589
Major Organizational Levels At Which
   Regulatory Affairs Professionals Operate ... 589
   Regulatory Authorities....................... 589
   Pharmaceutical Company Level Interactions .. 589
   Interactions at a Larger Organizational Level
      (i.e., Within the Research and Development,
      Marketing, or Other Division in Which It's
      Based) 589
   Regulatory Affairs Department Level
      Interactions 590

Selected Issues Regarding Regulatory Affairs.... 590
   Being Passive Versus Active Regarding the
      Contents of Regulatory Submissions........ 590
   Being Proactive Versus Reactive with
      Regulatory Authorities 591
Organizing A Regulatory Affairs Group 591
   Organizing a Regulatory Affairs Group by
      Function................................... 591
   Organizing a Regulatory Affairs Group by
      Therapeutic Area.......................... 592
   Organizing a Regulatory Affairs Group Using a
      Hybrid Model............................. 593
   Providing Opportunities for Expanding
      Professional Breadth and Depth 593

"There are three kinds of people in all types of organizations—rowboat people, sailboat people, and steamboat people. Rowboat people need to be pushed or shoved along. Sailboat people move when a favorable wind is blowing. Steamboat people move continuously, through calm or storm. They usually are masters of themselves, their surroundings, and their fate." Anonymous

The world of pharmaceutical regulations is changing as rapidly as the world of science, but there is an additional complicating factor in the field of pharmaceutical regulatory affairs: Whereas scientific findings and theories are the same internationally, regulations often differ markedly between countries. Generally, many approaches to a scientific problem are explored in depth before the conclusion is reached that a specific approach is unlikely to lead to new discoveries. New research approaches are then pursued. Each national regulatory authority may focus attention on different disciplines, and use different criteria to evaluate regulatory applications. Approaches to reviewing applications and maintaining public welfare differ even though all authorities have the same intention of maintaining high (or even raising) medical and technical standards and improving the health of their country's population. Fortunately, many regulatory authorities, particularly those in Europe, have been moving closer together both in requirements and in terms of interauthority communication.

The regulatory affairs department within a pharma-ceutical company is unique in several ways. First, the department may be based organizationally in several different areas (e.g., research, clinical research, development, legal, marketing) or it may be organizationally independent of these traditional groups. Second, regulatory affairs personnel are usually the only people within a company who are authorized to speak and interact with regulatory authorities, except at meetings to which other company personnel are invited. Third, because the output of their efforts is so critical to the success (and in some cases the existence) of a company, they are often in the main spotlight of a company. While being in a spotlight can be enjoyable, finding a searchlight or inquisitor's light shining on one is generally unpleasant. The switch from being in the limelight to being under the third degree sometimes occurs very rapidly.

Overall, the regulatory affairs group may be viewed as the critical liaison between the pharmaceutical industry and government regulatory authorities. This chapter presents two approaches for viewing the roles of the regulatory affairs group of a pharmaceutical company by function and by organizational level—and then discusses a number of issues relating to how those roles are carried out.

FUNCTIONS

The various functions of most regulatory affairs groups are summarized in Table 49.1 and several of these are described in more detail below.

Preparing/Publishing Documents for Regulatory Submissions

The format and content of all regulatory submissions must be evaluated to ensure that they comply with all appropriate regulations. Although regulations differ around the world, major steps toward harmonization are occurring. Preparing and submitting regulatory documents to a regulatory authority may be viewed as a publication activity. This activity involves collecting manuscripts and reports, and then copyediting them, paging them, indexing the contents, adding cross-references, copying and binding them, and then distributing the copies (Table 49.2). This is an extremely complex and difficult process to carry out rapidly and efficiently. Documents must be well organized and written in a style that is easy to read and understand. The submission should

TABLE 49.1. *Selected functions of regulatory affairs professionals*

1. Ensure compliance of regulatory submissions with relevant regulations
2. Ensure compliance of relevant activities and reports with GMP, GLP, and GCP[a]
3. Serve as a liaison with one or more regulatory authorities
4. Serve as liaison with the headquarters or subsidiary of the company
5. Serve as a member on project teams and guide the direction of various activities using a regulatory perspective
6. Attend relevant meetings of regulatory authorities that discuss the company's medicines
7. Attend relevant open meetings of the regulatory authorities discussing competitors' medicines
8. Write letters and telephone regulatory authorities as appropriate to ask or answer questions or to present information
9. Follow relevant pharmaceutical news and events through reading professional literature, attending professional meetings, and contacting one's network
10. Help develop and propose a regulatory strategy for the company and for individual medicines
11. Maintain records of all regulatory submissions and provide an information retrieval service for company staff

[a] GMP, Good Manufacturing Practice; GLP, Good Laboratory Practice; GCP, Good Clinical Practice.

TABLE 49.2. *Selected steps in preparing documents for regulatory submission[a]*

1. Collect reports
2. Collect material and write reports
3. Copyedit documents and/or reports
4. Enter material (e.g., reports, data) into computers
5. Add cross-references to all reports
6. Paginate documents according to regulatory requirements
7. Index the contents of all reports and summaries
8. Copy hardcopy submissions
9. Copy electronic submissions
10. Bind and label hardcopy submissions, label electronic copy
11. Ensure that all minor details are correct (e.g., paper size, any color photographs, larger size pages and illustrations clear and correct)
12. Distribute to appropriate company staff, subsidiary staff, and regulatory authority

[a] Not all of these steps will be done for any one submission (e.g., typically, one would do 1 or 2, 8 or 9).

also be easy for reviewers to follow in terms of scientific logic and internal consistency (e.g., always proceed in order of small to large animals in presenting results for toxicology, metabolism, and pharmacokinetic studies). The style of expert reports should adhere to preferences of the regulators. Every page of a New Drug Application (NDA) should have a document page number and an NDA page number, and the application must comply with appropriate formats.

Some of the problems previously encountered in this process (e.g., time required, inconsistencies of various types) resulted from the manual collection of reports, manual page numbering, retyping of reports; inability to merge text and graphics; large quantities of hardcopy to file; manual creation of indexes, references, tables of contents; and inclusion of different types and prints in the report. Electronic publishing is one means of addressing these problems.

Interacting With Regulatory Authorities

The scope of interactions between regulatory affairs professionals and regulatory authorities depends on the country involved, the company, and the type of interaction. Regulatory affairs professionals often act as a liaison between personnel in the company and regulatory authorities. This coordinating role is crucial because it circumvents people in the company independently or semi-independently interacting with regulatory authorities. That approach could lead to major problems if different people say different things to regulatory authorities. Regulatory affairs personnel must also document all interactions. Some of the topics discussed with regulatory authorities are listed in Tables 49.3 and 49.4 and types of documents submitted are listed in Table 49.5.

TABLE 49.3. *Selected topics that are discussed between a regulatory affairs department and regulatory authorities on an investigational medicine's development or dossier*

1. Format, content, and completeness of the dossier to be submitted
2. Date when the application is officially received and is filed
3. Auditing of sites selected by the regulatory authority
4. General design issues of a clinical trial that is planned or has been initiated
5. Specific design issues of a clinical trial that is planned or has been initiated
6. Adverse reactions experienced in a clinical trial
7. Submissions and presentations for an advisory committee or other regulatory meetings
8. The division or group within the regulatory authority that should receive the dossier
9. Meeting with a regulatory authority to discuss (1) the initial request to conduct clinical trials in humans, (2) a particular problem or issue, (3) the end of Phase II status and plans for Phase III development, and (4) the proposed contents of the regulatory submission for marketing authorization
10. Personnal issues concerning one or more clinical investigators who conducted a trial(s)
11. Changes to a protocol
12. Labeling issues
13. Preclinical requirements
14. Chemistry and manufacturing issues
15. Special priority for the review (e.g., treatment-IND,[a] accelerated approval, Subpart E designation)
16. Compliance issues (e.g., questions about monitoring a clinical trial)
17. International issues (e.g., import-export issues, inspection of various facilities)
18. Annual reports

[a] IND, Investigational New Drug Application.

Developing Regulatory Strategies

A simplified approach to creating regulatory strategies is to answer the following questions. The answers to each of these questions may be thought of as points on a spectrum or as discrete choices for each question.

1. Should the regulatory submission contain data for a "lean" or a "fat" development plan? The terms lean and fat refer to the number of studies conducted in each area of development (e.g., toxicology, medical, preclinical), the number of patients or animals in each study, and the amount of data collected on each patient or animal. The answer to this question is ideally based on a risk-to-benefit assessment for any medicine, on special status or need (e.g., an important orphan medicine versus a me-too medicine), as well as on special regulations that may be utilized (e.g., accelerated approval treatment—Investigational New Drug Application [IND]). Because all data available from anywhere in the world must be filed on a new medicine for most regulatory authorities, the choice of a fat versus lean plan must be considered at the outset of a new medicine's development. Nonetheless, a submission may be lean in some areas

TABLE 49.4. *Selected topics that are discussed between a regulatory affairs department and regulatory authorities on marketed medicines*

1. Adverse reactions reported to the company
2. Changes in labeling requested by the company or by the regulatory authority
3. Annual report of activities on each medicine
4. Submissions requesting a new indication, formulation, or change to over-the-counter status
5. Import or export of medicines
6. Definitions of important terms or concepts affecting a medicine
7. Interpretations of law, regulations, guidelines, or monographs affecting a medicine
8. Clarifications of comments made by regulatory authority staff at meetings or in letters sent to the company
9. Advertising issues
10. Other marketing issues
11. Product problems
12. Postmarketing studies
13. Status of a submission

and fat in others. Failure to plan a medicine's development internationally may generate undesired or undesirable data and force a company to adopt a different regulatory strategy than the preferred one.

2. Should one combined regulatory submission for

TABLE 49.5. *Selected types of documents submitted to regulatory authorities*

1. Applications to initiate clinical trials in humans (e.g., IND, CTX)
2. Application for approval to market an investigational medicine (e.g., PLA, NDA) or a marketed medicine for a new use or in a new dosage form
3. Supplements to modify one or more aspects of an approved regulatory submission (e.g., to add a vendor of specific supplies, to change conditions)
4. Amendments to modify one or more aspects of a pending regulatory submission
5. Updates to a pending regulatory submission
6. Annual report of activities on a medicine that has an IND or NDA
7. Adverse reactions report on an investigational or marketed medicine as required by law
8. Protocol that is being initiated, with required information on the investigator(s)
9. Amendments to an ongoing protocol (e.g., new investigator, modifications to inclusion criteria)
10. Compassionate plea submission describing medicine sent to a physician for a specific patient
11. Response to questions received on a regulatory submission
12. Request for a meeting with a regulatory authority group
13. Submission of information or data for consideration by an advisory committee to the regulatory authority
14. Request for a clarification of something received (e.g., letter, telephone call) from the regulatory authority
15. Appeal of a decision made by the regulatory authority
16. Request for marketing exclusivity or another specific item (e.g., orphan medicine)

CTX, Clinical Trial Exemption; PLA, Product License Application; NDA, New Drug Application.

marketing authorization (e.g., NDA) be made on multiple indications, or should multiple submissions be made for the same medicine, each on a single indication? The answer to this question is often a matter of senior research and development managers trying to second-guess the reviewing policy of a specific regulatory authority as well as marketing managers trying to second-guess the reception of the medicine for each indication in the marketplace. Second-guessing the actions of a regulatory authority is seldom possible, despite the most sophisticated reviews of the regulatory affairs staff. A limiting factor is that many companies are unable to codevelop multiple indications simultaneously and submit applications at the same (or nearly the same) time.

3. Should the initial regulatory submission for marketing authorization (e.g., NDA) be made in the country in which (1) the fastest approval is expected, (2) the least amount of data are required, (3) the largest market exists, or (4) the best opportunity exists to obtain postmarketing data? Alternatively, should the submission be delayed until it is submitted to many countries simultaneously? It is desirable to follow the last approach whenever possible, but regulatory applications in Japan usually follow a few years later for practical reasons.

By submitting a similar dossier with the same data to many countries simultaneously one avoids the problem of having to redo expert reports for new dossiers when additional data are obtained. This could create major problems if different interpretations are reached in multiple versions of an expert's report, or in reports written by different experts at different times. Within Europe this is becoming less of an issue because new regulations are likely to mandate that the dossier go to all European members of the Economic Community at one time. In addition, more countries are seeking membership in that organization, which will further simplify the regulatory submission process. For many other countries the question of resolving differences between submissions still exists; but this issue is less relevant in almost all countries that receive submissions several years after the initial ones are submitted.

4. Assuming that a core package of data is assembled, how large should it be? Should it be as small as possible or quite large with many modules that may be used in multiple submissions? A large core package without modules should be avoided. The question of core size should be addressed at the outset of a new medicine's development. Many of the issues surrounding this question are discussed in *Guide to Clinical Trials* (Spilker, 1991).

5. Should an electronic submission be made, and if so what part(s) of the application should be submitted electronically? There is a wide range of possible options for electronic submission, from submitting an optical disk of the reports, which is essentially a hard copy that cannot be manipulated to a submission enabling word-processing capabilities to be achieved, to supplying raw data (plus reports), which enables the regulatory authority to freely explore new analyses. If a Computer-Assisted New Drug Application (CANDA) is to be used, then planning (and, preferably, interaction with the regulatory authority) should begin early in the development process. The decision-making role of the regulatory affairs group in the area of electronic submission varies considerably among companies, but recommendations always should be sought from this group.

6. Should a company proactively interact with a regulatory authority at all stages of the development process, or should it adopt a totally reactive position—only responding to questions from the regulatory authority? It is particularly important to prepare the regulatory authority to view an application on a novel medicine or a request for information in the way intended. Submitting a novel regulatory application without attempting to prepare the mindset of the regulators is likely to lead to delays in processing and review. In the United States there are specified times during a medicine's development when it is appropriate to present and discuss data and plans with the FDA. These occur usually at the end of Phases I and II and at a pre-NDA stage, although meetings at other times (e.g., pre-IND) are possible.

7. Should the company attempt to anticipate all important questions that could be raised about the application and conduct studies to answer them? A balance should be sought between preventing the waste of company resources and attempting to answer the most obvious, likely to be asked questions. No company could ever obtain a sufficient amount of data to preclude relevant and important questions from being raised by regulatory authorities. Data that are merely gathered to address subtle questions about nuances of the application are unlikely to be required prior to the medicine's approval. It is possible to determine the most likely questions to be raised. Collecting data to address these questions is likely to enhance the likelihood of the medicine's approval, even if the data are collected after the application is submitted (but prior to its approval).

8. How should the company respond to questions from regulatory authorities about a regulatory submission? The company may respond anew to each request for information, or it may have established standard operating procedures for responding to regulatory questions. Major letters requesting data and information can be assigned to a task force or to an individual who can prepare a written response or coordinate the work needed to obtain a response.

9. How and when should a company prepare draft labeling for new medicines? At some stage it is necessary to prepare a proposed package label for new investigational medicines. The copy submitted to the FDA in the United States must be fully annotated. This means that each statement in the draft label must be referenced to a

specific item, volume, and page in the NDA or other appropriate place (e.g., Federal Register) that supports the statement.

The contents of the label may be driven by requirements for class labeling or by a particular style that the regulatory authority desires. A committee may be formed about a year prior to the anticipated submission to develop the label. One person may prepare an early draft and after committee review, the draft could be circulated to the company's experts within medical, marketing, legal, regulatory affairs, and other relevant groups for further comment and revision.

Marketing forecasts are based on the medicine's labeling. While tentative sales forecasts are made throughout a medicine's development, the most critical one (i.e., the one that influences the amount of medicine manufactured) is the one completed from a few months to approximately a year before the final approval is expected. If the labeling submitted to a regulatory authority is unrealistic, then the marketing forecast based on that label will be unrealistic as well. This may cause a major problem if the company believes its own fantasy and manufactures an excessive quantity of the medicine. The company may create an excessively high inventory, even if the medicine is approved at the predicted time.

The critical importance of a medicine's labeling may also be demonstrated by the fact that the labeling establishes the bounds within which a medicine may be promoted; the major purpose of an NDA document may be viewed as providing the evidence that supports the labeling. In the event that a critical aspect of proposed labeling is rejected by a regulatory authority, the company should have a fall-back position that can be more strongly defended.

10. When should a company modify its package insert? Some companies are much more reluctant than others to request that regulatory authorities allow modifications to their package inserts (e.g., to include additional adverse experiences). The initial suggestion to consider this possibility may come from legal, medical, regulatory affairs, or marketing personnel, and it often necessitates a meeting in which the company's position on such a proposal can be constructed. The company's decision often depends on whose perspective is considered most influential, i.e., the representative from any of the above areas may be the most important (or persuasive) one in a specific company or on a specific topic.

11. Should the regulatory strategies be designed to achieve regulatory success or to achieve commercial success? The former type of strategy focuses on obtaining approvals most rapidly. The latter type involves attempts to influence decision leaders, planning symposia, developing an approach to publications, and conducting appropriate clinical trials on quality-of-life and pharmacoeconomic endpoints. Ideally, the regulatory strategies chosen will attain both goals.

Interacting With Company Staff

Regulatory affairs staff should be present on all project teams and all relevant committees within the organization. Thus the staff can provide regulatory input, answer questions, and instill relevant regulatory concepts to enhance medicine development. Frequent personal interactions with company staff throughout the organization are required to fulfill the mission of regulatory affairs.

MAJOR ORGANIZATIONAL LEVELS AT WHICH REGULATORY AFFAIRS PROFESSIONALS OPERATE

Regulatory Authorities

Interactions between regulatory affairs groups within a company and national regulatory authorities occur on a daily basis between and across all hierarchical levels (see Fig. 49.1) and on an extremely wide range of subjects. A few of the topics discussed on investigational medicine dossiers (Table 49.3) and general regulatory issues (Table 49.4) are listed. Other interactions between a company and a regulatory authority are presented in other sections of this chapter. The nature and extent of interactions depends both on the country and the specific company's philosophy.

Pharmaceutical Company Level Interactions

Regulatory affairs is one of the most critical areas for senior managers to focus on in charting the future course and prospects for a company. The head of the company's regulatory group, or one of his or her senior managers, regularly reports on progress and problems to all major company groups, including the board of directors. Regulatory affairs groups usually are asked to make predictions about when the company can expect to receive regulatory approval of the company's submissions. Predictions are also requested about questions the various regulatory authorities are likely to raise on a wide variety of topics. A company's course of regulatory action, marketing plans, and manufacturing plans often are significantly influenced by these predictions.

Interactions at a Larger Organizational Level (i.e., Within the Research and Development, Marketing, or Other Division in Which It Is Based)

The regulatory affairs group may play a major or minor role in determining the company's regulatory strategy. Within the larger organizational group (e.g., research and development, marketing, legal), regulatory

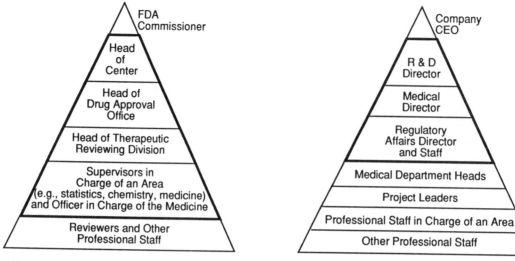

Food & Drug Administration

Pharmaceutical Company

FIG. 49.1. Two schematics of the hierarchies within the U.S. Food and Drug Administration and a pharmaceutical company. The dark line encases those individuals who are the primary contacts that interact and liaise with the other hierarchy.

affairs helps to influence and coordinate administrative activities that have a direct regulatory effect. These include various analyses of the company's performance, in terms of time for regulatory approvals over previous years, and predictions for the near and long-term future. Tables, graphs, and textual material are prepared to illustrate activities, status, or trends of interest to relevant managers. The best outlines, formats, and presentations to use are those that have been well received in the past by the particular group that receives the report. A proactive approach by regulatory affairs professionals to influence each project team will help ensure that the various departments involved in development conduct the correct studies and write reports in the appropriate way to facilitate a smooth and expeditious approval process.

Regulatory Affairs Department Level Interactions

Regulatory affairs acts as the coordinating group that consolidates all reports and data before they are submitted to regulatory authorities. Activities that expedite dossier submission must be handled with the greatest efficiency possible within the organization. In some cases, a number of professional writers who prepare reports are based within the regulatory affairs group. Regulatory activities could be conducted using different types of organizational structure and standard operating procedures (SOPs). The optimal organization and SOPs would depend to some degree on the specific company and its traditions, operations, and management style. Several organizational structures are described later in this chapter.

SELECTED ISSUES REGARDING REGULATORY AFFAIRS

Being Passive Versus Active Regarding the Contents of Regulatory Submissions

Different companies have different attitudes about the value of having regulatory affairs professionals actively involved in determining the content of submissions. At one extreme, the regulatory group is viewed as a service group that merely collects whatever reports other groups prepare and send to it. It in turn submits these reports to the regulatory authorities. This is an extremely narrow, out-of-date, and inefficient model for conceptualizing the roles of regulatory affairs.

The other end of that spectrum is when regulatory affairs personnel determine what data and reports should be in each regulatory dossier and direct the creation of reports. This approach is not recommended because it leads to major conflicts with line managers and project managers, who rightfully have much of this responsibility. A more moderate and realistic approach is to have regulatory personnel serve on project teams where they interact with other professionals to influence design of studies and quality, quantity, type, data, formats, and general style of reports generated. The specific reports to include in each group's contribution may be markedly influenced by regulatory affairs staff.

Whether the regulatory affairs group plays an active or passive role is strongly influenced by the director of the major division to which regulatory affairs reports (e.g., research and development, legal, marketing). This person's personal views and managerial style, as well as that of the director of regulatory affairs, affect the exact placement of regulatory affairs in the organization, and more importantly, the nature of its role and degree of influence. The personalities of these senior managers also influence the background and level of individuals recruited into the regulatory affairs department. Another component of finding the most appropriate balance between passive and active roles for regulatory professionals is in the area of membership on, or presentations to, those committees that review and approve regulatory strategies.

Being Proactive Versus Reactive with Regulatory Authorities

It is generally believed that one can be proactive only with the United States regulatory authority (the FDA). The actual situation is that companies may adopt a proactive posture and seek regulatory guidance on major questions in most countries and there is a trend toward increasing the number of interactions in Europe. This does not mean that it is always, or even occasionally, possible to arrange meetings to discuss the details of a development plan, regulatory strategy, or submission. But a company can generally obtain answers to general questions about plans and strategies in an informal or formal setting. The proactive role taken by the FDA in many instances, and its obvious interest in participating in and guiding medicine development coupled with high standards, means that it is leading and influencing most other regulatory authorities in terms of encouraging interactions.

Within the United States some companies have adopted the approach of minimizing company initiated interactions with the FDA. Those companies prefer to react to FDA requests or questions, apparently believing that that approach achieves the best responses. Other companies position staff in the FDA's hallways seeking to glean information that might help in decision making. This latter approach is sometimes taken to the extreme of having senior company managers finely dissect informal comments made by junior level regulatory authority staff. The company must cautiously interpret comments such as "If you had more data on X it would make the evaluation of your application easier." An important principle is that a company should not allow a regulatory authority to direct development of its medicine in ways that the company strongly disapproves of and believes to be inappropriate.

ORGANIZING A REGULATORY AFFAIRS GROUP

It is possible to organize a regulatory affairs group based on functions, therapeutic area, or using a combination approach. The first two approaches are described below; within each of these organizational approaches several variations exist. For example, staff could be responsible for all medicines in a broad therapeutic area assigned to them. Alternatively, if the company is large enough, the individual projects could be divided among the staff.

Regardless of how the regulatory affairs group is organized it may be situated within legal, research and development, or marketing. In addition, the regulatory affairs group may function independently and report to the company president. Another possibility is to decentralize the function and to have smaller regulatory affairs groups located within several different disciplines. The goal of this last approach would be to provide more responsive service and to improve interactions with the staff who are using the services.

Organizing a Regulatory Affairs Group by Function

Various functions of regulatory affairs are described at the start of this chapter. Regulatory affairs groups that are organized by function may be divided into five separate groups. Each group focuses on one of the areas below in interacting with regulatory authorities, reviewing proposed regulations, and conducting other activities shown in the tables (see Fig. 49.2).

1. Preclinical issues
2. Clinical issues
3. Manufacturing and controls issues. This group is concerned with coordinating, organizing, and progressing the data on a medicine's chemistry, manufacturing, and quality assurance.
4. Preparing documents for inclusion in regulatory submission. This includes many varied functions required to collect, edit, paginate, index, cross-reference, copy, bind, and distribute documents. While these activities could be conducted manually, current practice in most companies involves sophisticated computer systems to track reports and to operate other parts of this system.
5. Regulatory compliance is an auditing function for ensuring that Good Clinical Practice (GCP) and Good Laboratory Practice (GLP) are in compliance. This includes preparing sites in advance of regulatory authority inspection.

Each of the first three categories above generally includes responsibility for questions about the submission and status of investigational as well as marketed medicines. Over-the-counter medicines may be handled separately (i.e., by a different group). Some companies have a separate group that has responsibility for biologics projects.

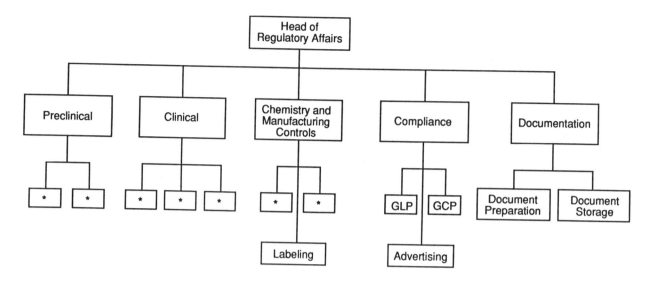

* = Could be organized by therapeutic area

FIG. 49.2. Regulatory affairs organizational chart for a group organized primarily by functional discipline.

Organizing a Regulatory Affairs Group by Therapeutic Area

A company may organize its regulatory affairs group according to therapeutic areas. These companies adopt the philosophy that dedicating a group of regulatory staff to each major therapeutic area enables the staff to learn the needs of the project groups in that area and to serve them better. This is graphically shown in Fig. 49.3. In addition, it facilitates interactions with regulatory authorities that are similarly organized.

There are a few disadvantages to this organizational approach, though means exist to overcome them.

1. A therapeutic group's major projects may suddenly expand resulting in a great increase in workload and placing demands on the dedicated regulatory staff that cannot be met. Temporary staff could be hired to help with some activities.

2. A therapeutic group's workload may decrease freeing up the time of the dedicated regulatory staff; however, they would not be prepared to rapidly turn to other

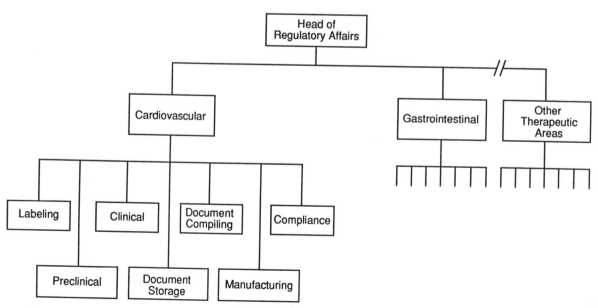

FIG. 49.3. Regulatory affairs organizational chart for a group organized primarily by therapeutic area.

projects outside the therapeutic area. While the staff could be loaned or transferred to another therapeutic area, that approach can lead to other issues (e.g., staff who feel like outsiders, having a senior professional who requires basic training). This can be avoided somewhat by conducting cross-training on an ongoing basis.

3. Not all therapeutic areas require a critical mass of regulatory staff to handle the workload. This can be addressed by combining a number of therapeutic areas into a single category. The categories chosen could be aligned with those used by the major regulatory authority with which the company interacts.

4. Each person in a therapeutic area group is required to become more of a generalist than they would in a function-oriented organization. As a result there would be fewer people within the total group who could be called on for expertise and advice. Several people would have to learn about a technical area previously handled by a single or by a few individuals (e.g., labeling requirements, regulations in specific countries, biotechnology regulations).

Organizing a Regulatory Affairs Group Using a Hybrid Model

The function oriented approach is generally viewed as a preferable organizational structure than the therapeutic area approach. Some regulatory professionals, however, believe the best organization is the hybrid or combination approach, which ideally achieves the best characteristics of both the therapeutic and functional approaches while also facilitating growth of the staff is breadth and depth. Whether a hybrid approach should be chosen would depend on the size of the regulatory staff and numerous other factors.

Providing Opportunities for Expanding Professional Breadth and Depth

A regulatory affairs group may become highly specialized because of the large number of different activities that must be performed. As people learn their roles and becomes more effective, they generally become more and more entrenched in those roles and have less time (and opportunity) to learn other roles. Weekly staff meetings, external courses, and participation in trade associations can address this problem to some extent, but other approaches may help as well. First, people may be rotated for 4 to 12 months to another position at the same level within the department. This may be viewed as an internal sabbatical period or as a professional rotation to learn numerous functions. This procedure not only provides stimulation and satisfaction to those individuals who agree to try new positions, but it provides backup at times when an individual is unavoidably absent.

A variation on the above approach is to have small groups of individuals learn two, three, or even four separate jobs at the same time. In that way they can fill in for each other, if needed, or the staff can rotate their responsibilities on a schedule chosen by their manager. Attending outside courses and professional meetings may facilitate this approach.

A totally different approach is to switch the organization of regulatory affairs from function-oriented jobs to therapeutic or disease area jobs. The first approach probably results in greater improvement or at least maintenance of efficiency, even if people are rotated through several positions over a period of time or simultaneously, as described above. A combination or hybrid organization of both therapeutic and functional approaches probably allows the most movement between groups with the least disruption in activities. This approach can best facilitate the growth of individuals in both breadth and depth.

In conclusion, the best regulatory results are achieved by aiming for the highest scientific standards with the greatest efficiency, and by presenting clear, precise, and well-organized data (and reports) to regulatory authorities. This goal is facilitated by organizing a regulatory affairs group with care, and by devising a company's regulatory strategy on all medicines at the outset of their development.

50 / Production Issues

Production Projects 596
  Types of Projects in Production 596
  Project Team Members 596
  Enhancing Coordination Between Production,
    Research and Development, and Marketing
    Teams Working on the Same Project 596
What Is Produced? 597
  Differences Between Producing Medicines,
    Foods, and Other Materials 597
  When Does Production Become Involved with
    Investigational Medicines? 597
  Balancing Production Effort with a Medicine's
    Value to a Company 597
  Contract Manufacturers 598
How Is It Produced? 598
  Transferring a Manufacturing Process from
    Technical Development to a Production
    Group 598
  Which Equipment Is Used to Produce
    Medicines? 598
Where Is It Produced? 598
  Single Versus Multiple Sourcing 599
  Contracting Manufacture Out 599
When Is It Produced? 599
  Choosing a Date to Manufacture Launch
    Material 599
  The Production Order 599
How Well Is It Produced?—Quality Control and
  Quality Assurance 600
  Roles of Quality Assurance and Quality
  Control 600

Reporting Relationships and the Potential for
    Conflict-of-Interest Issues 601
  Commitment to Total Quality 601
  Sterility Testing 602
  Process Validation in Manufacturing Steps 602
  Sampling of Tablets for Testing 603
  Methods of Sampling 603
  Inspecting Samples Chosen 603
  Cosmetic Issues of the Medicine Product 605
  Improving Medicine Quality with New
    Equipment 605
  Bar Codes 605
How Much Is Produced? 605
  Number of Manufacturing Plants 605
  Level of Service to Customers 605
  Use of Marketing Forecasts 606
  Production Capacity 606
  Just-in-Time Versus Just-in-Case Inventory ... 606
Why Are Production Costs So High? 606
  Waste Minimization and Disposal 608
Challenges for Production 608
  Planning and Scheduling Issues 608
  Issues Between Production and Marketing 609
  Alternatives If Production Cannot Meet
    Product Demands 609
  Competitive Pressures 610
  Medicine Tampering 610
  Deciding on an Appropriate Level of Risk 610
  Vertical Integration 610
  A Summary of Current Challenges for
    Production 611

We can no longer live with commonly accepted levels of mistakes, defects, material not suited to the job, people on the job that do not know what the job is and are afraid to ask, handling damage, failure of management to understand their job, antiquated methods of training on the job, inadequate and ineffective supervision. Acceptance of defective materials, poor workmanship, and inattentive and sullen service as a way of life in America is a roadblock to better quality and productivity. We have learned to live in a world of mistakes and defective products as if they were necessary to life. It is time to adopt a new religion in America. W. Edwards Deming. From *Quality, Productivity, and Competitive Position.*

A number of production issues that are relevant for many pharmaceutical companies are discussed. As with the marketing and finance chapters, the issues covered represent a select sample intended to provide a general overview. Issues are grouped into a few broad categories.

PRODUCTION PROJECTS

Types of Projects in Production

Basic types of projects exist in production groups.

New Product

Project to launch a new medicine. A project team is assembled with representatives from all relevant groups. This team functions analogously to that in research and development, although it clearly has different goals. Product could be for either prescription or over-the-counter (OTC) use.

Transfer Manufacturing

Project to transfer manufacturing from one site to another. This project is quite different than the one above and involves some or all of the activities listed in Table 50.1.

Produce an Intermediate

Project to start the manufacture of an intermediate that previously was made outside the company. This project also involves some or all of the nontransfer items listed in Table 50.1.

Contract Manufacture

Project to manufacture a product for another company. This is done under contract, usually to utilize un-used plant capacity. Another reason to do this is as a quid pro quo for something the other company is doing for yours.

Major Changes in Formulation or Packaging

The amount of work required to make a change in formulation or packaging varies greatly, and often requires a full team to plan, coordinate, and conduct activities.

Expansion of Facilities

Some companies would not consider the expansion of facilities with modifications to equipment used as a project in the same context as those above where a product is manufactured. Nonetheless, focusing attention on an important building change by making it a project helps ensure the involvement and cooperation of all departments affected. Moreover, it places the activity in a system where appropriate reporting and reviews can be conducted.

Introduction of New Technologies

As with the above type of project there is no actual product manufactured. Yet, the same reasons as above can be given to make the introduction of important new technologies a project.

Project Team Members

The individuals on a production project team can be as variable in function and responsibility as those on a research and development project team. Typically, members come from the departments listed in Table 50.2.

Enhancing Coordination Between Production, Research and Development, and Marketing Teams Working on the Same Project

In some cases there are separate project teams for an investigational (or marketed) project within production, research and development, and marketing; and in other cases one or two such teams exist. In any of these situations the relevant marketing, production, or research and development project head should be a member, or at least receive all correspondence of the other two teams. The three leaders may at some stages during the medicine's life find it worthwhile to meet as a small group on a periodic basis. Another possibility is to call a combined meeting of relevant representatives from all three disciplines.

TABLE 50.1. *Selected production activities to support various projects*

1. Transfer or acquire the technology
2. Transfer or obtain (e.g., lease, purchase) the equipment and install or modify utility services as needed
3. Transfer or acquire the contract(s)
4. File appropriate regulatory supplements (e.g., change of manufacturing site or process)
5. Obtain any regulatory approvals required
6. Cooperate with regulatory inspections
7. Validate the manufacturing process
8. Coordinate initial production schedules, export or import licenses, and other documentation needed
9. Establish material specifications
10. Choose vendors
11. Prepare and store stability batches
12. Preapproval inspection of the manufacturing site and validation records

TABLE 50.2. *Production and other groups that are often on a production project team[a]*

1. Operations planning
2. Product engineering systems
3. Package engineering
4. Solid dose formulation division
5. Engineering
6. Quality assurance including microbiological services
7. Industrial engineering
8. Sterile products division
9. Ointments, creams, and liquids formulations
10. Pharmaceutical process technology support
11. Chemical manufacturing division
12. Contract management operations
13. Materials management
14. Small scale production
15. Engineering validation
16. Customer order processing
17. Distribution operations
18. Validation and technical services
19. Purchasing
20. Marketing representatives
21. Technical development representatives
22. Research and development project manager

[a] Not all of these groups will be represented on any one team.

WHAT IS PRODUCED?

Differences Between Producing Medicines, Foods, and Other Materials

The major difference between producing medicines and other materials is that government regulations are more extensive and the standards are higher for producing medicines. Most of the relevant manufacturing regulations are referred to as Good Manufacturing Practice (GMPs) in the United States. Some of the differences between producing foods and medicines are fascinating. For example, most foods that are produced by humans (as opposed to natural foods such as fresh fruits) are not produced aseptically (i.e., under sterile conditions). Nonetheless, most foods are made or prepared in clean conditions. People rarely become ill from food that is nonsterile. The stomach and intestines contain numerous bacteria that are not harmful to us, and some produce vitamins that are even essential for our good health. Injected medicines, however, must be sterile and pure because the injection of nonsterile or nonpure preparations (e.g., with glass or pyrogen contamination) into the bloodstream could create significant medical problems for a patient.

When Does Production Become Involved with Investigational Medicines?

There appears to be a trend at many pharmaceutical companies for production personnel to become involved with investigational medicines at an earlier point in the development process than they did approximately 15 years ago. Traditionally this involvement was sometime during Phase III, but it is now generally during Phase I or II. When a number of formulations are being considered for development, it is important to consider production's ability to manufacture each formulation. There may be significant differences in the investment in equipment required, the degree of risk involved, the amount of hazardous waste products produced, the labor required, or other important factors associated with their production.

Dialogue between production and technical development personnel should be established as early in a project's life as is convenient and practical. A committee structure is often an appropriate mechanism to ensure that relevant questions are both posed and answered satisfactorily. This allows production at an early stage to begin monitoring a project's progress, develop an awareness of potential future events, and consider various options for facilities and equipment that may be used to make the medicine.

Balancing Production Effort with a Medicine's Value to a Company

Is it logical to believe that the effort expended on a medicine's production should relate to the amount of sales a product generates or is expected to generate? This question may be interpreted as either referring to each unit of medicine made or to the total effort for the entire medicine's production. In fact the number of units of a medicine produced often do not correlate well with the medicine's sales. Some medicines have extremely low prices and a high number of units are sold, and the opposite situation also occurs. In addition, small volume products (i.e., when few units are produced) may require a relatively large amount of plant capacity and resources to manufacture them. This places pressure on those resources (i.e., equipment and labor) that are also needed to manufacture other products. Potential solutions to this problem include (1) having small volume products synthesized and packaged by other manufacturers, (2) increasing the number of work shifts, (3) expanding plant capacity, and (4) selling or dropping the product from the company's line.

A new medicine may require equipment and processes at more than one plant for its production. This issue may be addressed in several ways.

1. A new facility may be built to focus primarily or exclusively on the new medicine.
2. An existing facility may be "beefed-up" to handle the medicine.
3. Several existing company manufacturing facilities may each handle certain parts of the manufacturing.

4. Part or all of the manufacturing may be contracted out to other companies.

Contract Manufacturers

All companies that manufacture medicines periodically have to decide about whether to utilize contract manufacturers to make certain medicines. This question becomes particularly important when new techniques or equipment are required to make a new medicine and it is uncertain whether a company desires to bring that technology in-house. A company may have a tradition of manufacturing all of their own products, but it makes little sense to rigidly adhere to this principle when it is economically preferable to have other manufacturers make a new medicine.

HOW IS IT PRODUCED?

Transferring a Manufacturing Process from Technical Development to a Production Group

The sense of urgency with which the manufacturing process is transferred from technical development (i.e., research and development) to production varies greatly from medicine to medicine. If the sense of urgency is high, there may be insufficient time to develop a robust process (i.e., a reliable, reproducible process that is insensitive to minor changes in conditions) where all of the relevant parameters have been optimized.

Some of the issues that determine when a process is ready to be transferred to production include (1) is the process robust, (2) have all of the important manufacturing factors and possibilities been considered and worked out or at least evaluated, and (3) is the batch to batch variation acceptable in terms of the specifications that must be met? It is desirable to increase the medicine's yield to a significant degree before manufacturing begins. Most of the work on this issue is usually completed prior to transferring the process to production.

In most situations when a technical development department turns over a process to production, that process is well defined and has been tested on a full-scale production basis. Personnel from both development and production groups will have tried the manufacturing as an "EX" (experimental) batch using the actual equipment that will eventually be used. During the later stages of technical development's experimentation, they often "borrow" production equipment to test the best method.

Which Equipment Is Used to Produce Medicines?

Medicines may require new or highly specialized equipment for their manufacture. A decision has to be reached about whether to invest in new equipment. The pertinent issue is to determine which criteria to use when deciding about purchasing or leasing new equipment. It is often helpful if a standard approach has been developed that may be applied to a new situation so that a decision may be reached rapidly. The main alternative is to redefine the criteria and procedures to follow each time an important question arises. This would result in unnecessary delays and a great deal of frustration.

Return on investment is the primary criterion used to address the issue of obtaining new equipment. This is determined using cost accounting procedures. The total cost for the purchase of new equipment plus medicine manufacture is determined and contrasted with the total cost either using existing equipment or following another course. If the new equipment will lead to a savings over the current methods, then the time to reach a savings equal to the equipment's purchase and installation price is calculated. This is the payback time. If the payback time issue is not relevant, then other factors must be considered (e.g., competition, time to install the equipment, production downtime) in reaching a decision on whether to purchase the new equipment.

Another aspect relating to new equipment is how should a company optimally utilize automation and remain current with state-of-the-art technologies. These technologies include use of computer-controlled production, robotics, and other equipment. These issues are a continual concern to companies because there are always new procedures and equipment to evaluate and new medicines or line-extensions to manufacture. In addition, the competition between companies in many therapeutic areas and with generic medicines places a high premium on achieving greater cost-efficiencies in production.

WHERE IS IT PRODUCED?

Companies often make most of their medicines in more than one manufacturing plant, or at least they develop contingency plans to make each medicine at multiple plants. Companies must protect themselves against unknown situations that could threaten, decrease, or eliminate a plant's ability to make one or more medicine. One reasonable approach to reduce threats and the dependency of a company on a single plant is to build, lease, or occupy a second backup plant. Alternatively, a second manufacturing source could be approved to manufacture one or more medicines, if necessary. This plant must become licensed by the Food and Drug Administration (FDA) to manufacture medicines of interest to the company and could be a contract manufacturing facility.

Single Versus Multiple Sourcing

When a compound enters the project system it usually must be scaled-up to provide supplies for tests throughout research and development. Where will this compound be made? Some of the possibilities are shown in Fig. 24.2. If a company has only a single site to manufacture all of its medicines and compounds then the answer simply depends on whether they wish to contract the work out or make it themselves.

For most multinational companies with more than a single possible manufacturing site the issue of sourcing must be addressed. Single sourcing of a medicine is a realistic strategy to follow early in a medicine's development, but as the medicine approaches the market this approach is often unrealistic.

Some of the concerns that limit a company's ability to use a single source of a medicine worldwide are:

1. Need for a common formulation. This is another goal that is often abridged because of different regulations and marketing practices in various countries. While many different formulations can theoretically be made in one factory, it is usually unfeasible because of the possibility of higher manufacturing costs, limited capacity, limited human resources, transportation costs, and regulatory considerations.

2. Need for a backup plant exists in case of any problem such as fire, flood, prolonged strike, sabotage, and so forth. A company's income could be seriously affected if any of those situations occurs. For investigational medicines the problems described could greatly delay development.

3. There are differences in production worldwide that limit a company's ability to adhere to using only a single plant.

4. Policies of the company also play a role in influencing this issue.

Although a single standard is desirable for producing a medicine anywhere in the world there are constraints on a company that may make this goal difficult to achieve. In general a single sourcing of medicine during preclinical and early clinical development followed by multiple sourcing is a realistic strategy. A New Drug Application (NDA) submission requires identification of sources and presence of adequate stability data for all sites of manufacture. This may limit the number of sites indicated in an initial NDA.

Contracting Manufacture Out

Small pharmaceutical companies routinely have other companies manufacture under contract some or all of their products for them. In addition, there are various reasons why a large pharmaceutical company might de-

sire to do the same. For example, a company could then focus more attention on research, development, and marketing. For other companies, contract manufacture might free a single-purpose plant for other uses, or prevent the need to build a plant. The environmental waste issues discussed briefly in this book are becoming far more acute for pharmaceutical companies, and the contract manufacture strategy tends to indirectly avoid the time and direct expense a company must spend on such problems.

Another advantage of contracting manufacture for relatively small companies is that the decision to build a plant is likely to occur before the full profile of the medicine is known. At that point in time an accurate forecast of production needs is impossible to make. The chance of error is great whether the forecast is too low and the company eventually cannot meet the demand or the forecast is too high and the huge inventory sits and possibly passes its expiration date. The plant that is built could just as easily be too small or large for the actual needs. Larger companies with numerous medicines on the market and some degree of excess capacity are buffered to a degree from these particular problems.

WHEN IS IT PRODUCED?

Choosing a Date to Manufacture Launch Material

Every company faces a minor or major dilemma when deciding when to manufacture an unapproved medicine for launch. The major influences on choosing a date are (1) the relative certainty of regulatory approval by a target date, (2) the shelf life of the medicine, (3) the cost and difficulty of manufacture, and (4) both current and future capacity and utilization of the company's manufacturing plants. Another critical factor is the risk-taking behavior of the company's board of directors.

A company that chooses early manufacture wants to be ready to market as soon as possible after approval is received. They also want to know that problems will not develop and there will be opportunities to order all raw materials and components needed to make the medicine.

A company that chooses to wait before manufacturing a medicine may be concerned about the (potentially) large inventory costs, the money tied up in the inventory, and the fact that the medicine may have to be destroyed if regulatory approval is delayed and the remaining shelf life is too short to ship the medicine, or it may have already expired.

The Production Order

A production order from marketing is a contract between marketing and production. It specifies a description of the item requested, the amount needed, and the specific date when the product is needed. Any difficulties that production anticipates meeting the request are usually communicated rapidly back to marketing.

The production order usually comes from the product manager and its course through production is usually facilitated by a product coordinator in the matrix management group within production.

The time required for production to prepare a new product for launch depends on the availability of (1) specific equipment needed for manufacture, (2) raw materials, and (3) a safe and reliable process. If substantial equipment needs to be ordered, the lead time for delivery could be 18 to 24 months, but if no equipment is needed and validation of the process is completed, then a shorter period of 3 to 6 months should be sufficient. For line-extensions requiring stability tests a full year is required, and for increased production for special offers or deals a four to six week lead is generally adequate.

The format of the production order could be designed to address each of the above types of requests. This process could also be conducted electronically.

While it takes time to obtain the required approvals in marketing before production initiates action on purchasing or shipping goods, there is a temptation to anticipate their approval and to initiate production orders. This is a temptation that should be avoided by production. This principle is so important that it should be regarded as a golden rule. The only violation of this principle should be with the approval of the most senior production manager.

HOW WELL IS IT PRODUCED?—QUALITY CONTROL AND QUALITY ASSURANCE

The quality of a finished medicine product is not an all-or-none question, but requires conscious decisions by a company as to what quality is to be used as a minimum standard and as a goal. These decisions must consider both compendial (e.g., *United States Pharmacopeia* [USP]) and regulatory requirements. Quality assurance has become a specialty in recent years and the science underlying their activities has become better established. Major functions are listed in Table 50.3.

Roles of Quality Assurance and Quality Control

The quality assurance department is often viewed as a "policeman" in reviewing production activities. This relationship varies enormously, not only between companies, but also within a single company. Quality may be described in terms of (1) purity of raw materials, (2) ability of medicines to meet chemical and physical specifications, (3) consistency of manufactured products from batch to batch, (4) validation of procedures, (5) valida-

TABLE 50.3. *Major quality assurance functions on investigational medicines prior to marketing*

1. Audit vendors and contractors who supply materials or various services
2. Develop and validate microbiological test methods
3. Ensure compliance with all regulatory standards
4. Approve validation requirements for new medicines
5. Ensure correct calibration of laboratory equipment
6. Test and release raw materials, synthesized materials, formulated materials, and packaging components
7. Develop expiration dating guidelines
8. Develop monographs and standards for quality assurance

tion of systems, and other factors. Companies may determine that they want a goal of absolutely no product recalls, even for minor issues. This goal implies that the company's regulatory strategy is to avoid even small issues arising with the FDA. This is, however, an unrealistic standard for even the most conservative pharmaceutical company because of the many ways of interpreting federal regulations and GMPs and the uncertainty of what may happen to medicines in actual use situations. Nonetheless, all companies must determine goals and standards in terms of product quality.

A few decades ago, quality control (QC) was the process used to ensure that medicines met official specifications (Fig. 50.1B). It became apparent, however, that just because a medicine met the final-stage specification requirements did not mean that it also met requirements at each intermediate step. The only tablets or other dosage forms tested that one was certain of were the ones actually tested. If a group of 20 tablets was tested out of a batch of six million made, it did not provide adequate assurance that the entire batch met the standards used. Also, if the final requirements were not met and the product was flawed it was difficult, if not impossible to identify the source and reason for the problem. Therefore, the concept of quality assurance developed as an ongoing evaluation process of most (or all) of the individual steps (Fig. 50.1A). Quality assurance (QA) also means that the methods used to audit the manufacturing processes are validated. Quality assurance depends on interpreting the GMPs plus state-of-the-art practices in industry. Most companies have one set of QA standards for all medicines that pass through a plant, whether produced for a contract, to supply a generic manufacturer, or to provide a brand name product. Many medicines have over 100 separate steps evaluated as part of their QA testing procedures.

Panel A of Fig. 50.1 is the most conservative method of conducting QA and QC operations because each step in the process is quality assured and approved before the next step is initiated. An example could be in manufacture of certain sterile products, where steps such as assays of sterile water, pyrogen tests, material tests for contamination, filling procedures, and final sterilization are each

QUALITY ASSURANCE AND QUALITY CONTROL

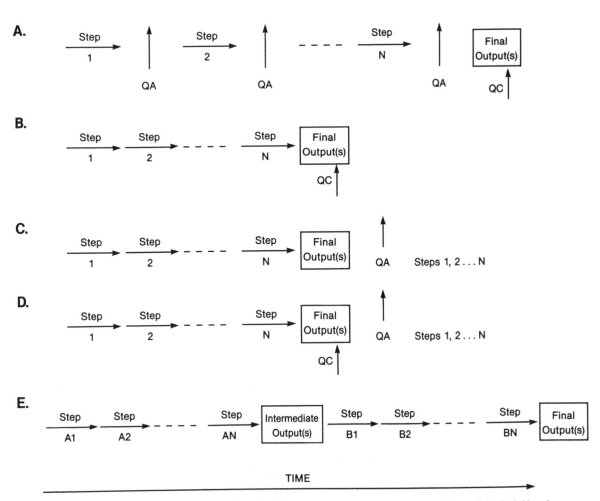

FIG. 50.1. Procedures of quality assurance and quality control. The final output for a clinical trial is when the last patient is completed. The final output for production is when the finished medicine is made (or packaged), and the final output for toxicology is when the final report is written. Panels are discussed in the text.

evaluated. Panels C and D show operations where QA is conducted after the products are made. These approaches would be considered reasonable only for highly reliable products and procedures because, if the product fails the test, then the entire batch must be discarded. A hybrid of panels A plus C or D is also possible. Panel E would be appropriate for chemical syntheses where intermediates en route to the final chemical are evaluated. Many variations exist for conducting QA procedures in panel E including A to D, plus various hybrid-type models.

Reporting Relationships and the Potential for Conflict-of-Interest Issues

Because of the sensitive nature of the work conducted by the quality assurance department and the potential

for conflict-of-interest issues, it is essential that QA managers not report to the head of production. Quality assurance workers might feel pressure to approve a step in a process, whether the pressure was present or not. This pressure would be much stronger if someone in production had the authority to determine the final outcome of a "gray" issue relating to QA. Good Manufacturing Practice regulations require separate reporting through to the senior management level.

Commitment to Total Quality

This concept involves a thorough analysis of all aspects of a task. Positions are often judged in terms of satisfying their customers, even if all of their customers also work in the same or an adjoining group within the company. An agreement is reached between people who supply and those who receive a service or product. This practice is really not new because employees have always been expected to communicate with those who were before and after them in various pipelines and subpipelines of manufacturing processes and activities. This concept is also applicable, of course, to all other areas of a company.

Problems develop when people assume they are doing their job and state that "it's too bad" if the person they supply wants it differently because "this is the way we've always done it."

This concept is another aspect of implementing Edward Deming's approach to improving productivity through commitment to total quality in production.

Sterility Testing

One of the most sensitive issues between quality assurance and production involves the evaluation of products produced in a sterile environment. Eliminating sources of contamination in manufacturing and minimizing environmental contamination in medicine testing are two important goals for all companies that manufacture sterile products. Unfortunately, these goals are usually difficult to achieve. When evaluating a product for sterility, it is extremely easy to introduce environmental contamination. The issue is whether a product that fails a sterility test does so because of manufacturing problems or of contamination introduced by quality assurance personnel during the testing procedure. The issue involves much more than just egos because a great deal of money is usually invested in the suspect medicine batch. If a medicine batch is discarded unnecessarily, a loss of significant effort and money can result.

Until recent years, most sterile products were manufactured under generally clean, but nonsterile, conditions and then were sterilized at the end of their processing, usually by heat. A number of samples were taken for sterility testing and if only one failure was observed, another set of samples was tested. If the second set were all acceptable (i.e., without failures) then it was assumed that the entire batch was sterile and the sterilizing process was effective.

A recent change in the above sterility-testing procedure was brought about by the *United States Pharmacopeia* (USP). The new procedures do not allow a repeat test unless the failure can be shown to be related to a laboratory error. One of the reasons for this change is that some products are not stable enough chemically to be sterilized by heating to a high temperature. At the present time many products are prepared under aseptic conditions over a period of days and are not sterilized at the end of the procedure. As a result of this change, a simple test for sterilization is inadequate. To further ensure sterility, samples are taken of the environment for parts of each day of manufacture. These include samples of (1) air in the room, (2) wall surfaces, (3) whatever settles out of the air onto special culture dishes placed on tables, and (4) finger daubs of the operators in the aseptic areas. In the last test, the operators touch their fingers to an agar plate that is then incubated to check for bacterial contamination.

There are two major issues that have arisen in regard to this change. First, there are no fixed limits or guidelines as to what degree of environmental contamination is sufficient to pass or reject a batch. Thus, the decision about rejection is based on the comfort level felt by individuals who evaluate the data. They typically look for trends or spikes in the data. Each case is separate and it may not be possible to establish clear guidelines. The second issue is that environmental samples are placed in an incubator for three days. Thus, it is three days after contamination occurs that anyone is aware of a problem, whereas with the original system, it was suspected almost immediately and in many cases was remedied by a retest or a resterilization. The consequences to a company in terms of wasted time, resources, and effort are greater in the second situation. These issues have significantly raised the pressures on both production and QA departments to produce medicines in an environment that is as close to microbial-free as possible. The cost of approaching this state is so expensive that all sterile medicines are likely to continue to escalate in price, and if greater steps in this direction are taken, probably for relatively little gain in sterility, costs may increase even faster.

A related issue that may become more important in the future is the environmental conditions under which nonsterile products are produced. One of the specific questions concerns bacterial contamination of tablets, capsules, and liquids. It is clear that the stomach and intestines provide adequate protection for patients in most situations. Any changes in regulations governing this aspect must be carefully evaluated to ensure that the interests of patients are truly served by any regulations proposed.

Process Validation in Manufacturing Steps

A validated procedure is one that is proven to do what it is stated to do. This is an important part of GMPs. Validation lies at the heart of quality control systems. Ongoing evaluations and checks ensure that all equipment is properly calibrated, operating appropriately, all appropriate materials are identified, and all materials are handled correctly at all stages of manufacturing. Validation procedures are conducted with up-to-date monitoring equipment, modern statistical designs, and tests that demonstrate the integrity of the procedures. The validation procedures and data generated from tests and monitoring activities are thoroughly documented.

Validating computer systems used in manufacturing medicines is a major issue in the pharmaceutical industry today. The Computer Systems Validation Committee of the Pharmaceutical Manufacturers Association (PMA, 1986) has issued a report with additional information. Substantial effort continues in this area at numerous organizations (e.g., FDA, Drug Information Association).

Sampling of Tablets for Testing

When companies manufacture tablets it must be determined that the tablets are acceptable for sale. The quality control/assurance group must pass the material (i.e., certify that it meets agreed-on standards). One of the first standards to consider is the potency of the material. The assay methods that evaluate a tablet's potency destroy the tablet in the process of evaluation. Thus, no matter how rapid and inexpensive an assay system is developed, only a sample of an entire medicine lot may tested. Thus, rules must be established as to how many tablets to sample and the basis on which specific tablets will be chosen for testing. Criteria are also established that tablets must meet to pass inspection. For example, the active ingredient in a tablet might be required to be within ±10% of the amount stated on the label of the medicine. This variation might represent true tablet to tablet differences, but there are also variations in the amount measured owing to the assay variability. Major factors affecting assay variability are the skills of the person who is running the test, instrument variability, and week to week (or shift to shift) variability in assay results obtained.

Methods of Sampling

Five specific methods are described. Each has its place in a manufacturing operation, and the choice of one (or more) is usually based on statistical considerations, although practical aspects may influence or override the mathematically preferred method. For example, although it may be desirable to choose random samples of cartons in a warehouse for close inspection it may be impractical to do so and thus another approach must be chosen.

Random Sampling

Samples are chosen at random from the entire lot or group of items. A mathematically derived number of items must be inspected or tested to ensure that the random sample is sufficient for the conclusions to be made.

Two-Stage Sampling

If a lot consists of two or more different types of items then it may be possible to choose some of each type as a first stage. In the second stage, specific samples are chosen from each of the types. This ensures that all types of items made are evaluated.

Stratified Sampling

The entire lot is divided into a number of strata and random sales are taken from each strata. If the entire lot is homogeneous then each strata and the samples chosen should be identical or nearly so.

Cluster Sampling

A cluster representing a certain fraction of the total lot is taken as the sample. This method may be used when each component of the lot is dispersed in equal proportions in all sections.

Selected Sampling

A sample may be chosen from one part of the entire lot. An example would include obtaining the sample at a specific time or only sampling one component of a mixture.

Inspecting Samples Chosen

In pharmaceutical manufacture the inspection process usually destroys the product (e.g., tablet or capsule) chemically or physically and thus differs from testing automobiles or most electronic goods. In the latter case, items are inspected to ensure they operate appropriately and are then packaged and sold. In such cases every item produced may be inspected (i.e., total inspection). Sampling inspection is not only required when the item is destroyed in testing, but when extremely large numbers are produced (e.g., ampules and other containers or when an extremely long length of something (e.g., plastic intravenous tubing) is made and unrolling it would be difficult.

There is a tradeoff between inspecting a larger number of samples more superficially or inspecting a larger number of characteristics on fewer samples. Critical characteristics must be inspected. If the people who manufacture products also self-inspect them, then the number of inspectors needed is fewer. This is generally what is done in Japan and is becoming more routine in the United States. It is impractical for inspectors to examine every item.

Once the standards of a normal inspection are established, if the rate of errors or problems found exceeds a certain number then a tightened inspection (i.e., increased number of inspections) may be done until the rate returns to an established number. The opposite situation of conducting a reduced inspection may also be considered in selected cases. The procedures used in sampling and inspection are described in more detail by Ishikawa (1976).

Acceptance Quality Level

The highest percentage of defective units (e.g., tablets) that is acceptable as a production average is called the *acceptance quality level.* The unacceptable quality level is the percentage of defective units for which there is a low probability that the batch will be acceptable. Different types of sampling plans may be chosen to select random samples for testing. The selection of the method to use depends largely on statistical considerations. Because of the great importance of sampling a manufactured medicine appropriately, expert statisticians are usually involved in the choice of a sampling design. Their goal is to design a method to obtain samples that are representative of the entire batch or lot. Sometimes, interval samples (e.g., every nth tablet) are studied instead of random samples to evaluate the production run.

Disintegration and Dissolution Characteristics

The disintegration and dissolution characteristics of tablets must be tested. In both of these tests, six tablets are tested under identical conditions and must meet standard specifications. If one or two tablets do not meet specifications, the test is repeated on 12 additional tablets using higher acceptance criteria.

Dissolution tests are time consuming and expensive. Figure 46.1 illustrates some of the standard methods used. The USP and other formulary requirements specify which of these specific methods must be used in dissolution testing.

Tablet Weight

Sample tablets must be weighed to confirm that their weight is within a prespecified range. The general standard for uncoated tablets in the USP is "weigh individually 20 whole tablets, and calculate the average weight: the weights of not more than 2 of the tablets differ from the average weight by more than the percentage tested and no tablet differs by more than double that percentage." See Table 50.4 for examples.

TABLE 50.4. *Measurement of tablet weight*

Average weight of tablet (mg)	Acceptable difference in weight (%)
130 or less	10
130 to 324	7.5
More than 324	5

Other Tests

Other tests that must be conducted (when relevant) include tests for metal particles in ophthalmic ointments and for pyrogenicity in biological products. *Pyrogenicity* refers to the ability of the material to raise body temperature in a sensitized animal. Pyrogenicity is a rough measure of the amount of foreign protein in the product and the product's potential to elicit an allergic or anaphylactic reaction in humans. Other tests include microbiological tests to evaluate sterility.

In-Process Testing and Control

The discussion above describes the testing of a medicine after it is manufactured. Although these procedures are currently followed, they are insufficient when performed on six or so tablets to assure the acceptability of lots of up to ten million tablets. In addition, if serious problems occur it would be extremely expensive and potentially disastrous for a company if an entire lot had to be destroyed. The major alternative procedure is to test a medicine at all stages of its manufacture. This is referred to as in-process testing and control.

Some of the relevant issues involved with in-process testing and control are potency and control charts.

Potency

The active compound must be evenly dispersed throughout the dry powder before it is compressed into tablets or filled into gelatin capsules. Also, a precise amount of the powder must be compressed into tablets or filled into the gelatin capsule.

Control Charts

These are graphical depictions of performance data that illustrate how well samples perform on some important measure. They illustrate whether the process is operating within its capability and at an acceptable level. Different types of control charts are used in the pharmaceutical industry. These charts are a valuable tool to use in identifying batch-to-batch trends.

Cosmetic Issues of the Medicine Product

This category includes consideration of the following questions: (1) may any of the dyes or inks used to print a name and/or number on a capsule or tablet be smudged or illegible? (2) may the medicine packaging and/or cartons be used if the color tones are somewhat different from the standard? (3) may the cartons be scuffed or scratched? (4) may the printing be slightly off-center? or (5) may other aspects of the cosmetic appearance of the medicine be less than perfect? If a high standard of cosmetic appearance is used to pass all individual medicine tablets and capsules intended for sale, then the rejection rate after the medicine is manufactured plus the cost of the passed product will both be relatively high.

People who work in a quality assurance department usually express concern about these or other relatively minor cosmetic flaws. Nonetheless, if the medicine itself is in compliance with all regulations, then marketing considerations must dictate what decisions are made about cosmetically flawed products. This is almost always addressed on a case by case basis.

The standards used by a company for judging a medicine's cosmetic appearance may be lowered after a brand name medicine goes off patent because the medicine must now compete in price with those produced by generic manufacturers. Passing medicines with an adequate but not perfect appearance is one means of controlling the cost of manufacturing. Most companies want to establish and maintain uncompromising high quality for new chemical entities while they are protected by patent.

Improving Medicine Quality with New Equipment

New state-of-the-art equipment may sometimes produce medicines with more consistent quality than with older equipment. There might be fewer impurities when new equipment is used to synthesize the active medicine substance. There might be more consistent moisture content of medicine granules if the equipment is used to dry granules prior to compressing them into tablets. Most companies conduct careful analyses to determine the cost-effectiveness of new equipment. Comparing costs from outside contractors is usually also taken into account before a decision is reached on whether to purchase major pieces of new equipment. Product quality is also considered when new production processes are evaluated as a means to cut manufacturing costs. There is a certain point at which the cost savings are not economical because of an unacceptable decline in a medicine's quality. The exact balance or trade-off between quality and cost differs for each medicine and is greatly dependent on the company's attitudes.

Bar Codes

Bar coding is being used more and more extensively in pharmaceutical companies. In production it is used for identifying and tracking raw materials and packaging components that arrive at a company. As these materials become converted into medicines, package labels, and shipping labels, other bar codes are usually generated. The bar code on the individual finished product containers has the specific medicine and specific packaging identified, to enable optical scanners to ring a price on the retail cash register.

The PMA is attempting to have vendors that supply the pharmaceutical industry place two labels on the packages they sell to the industry. One label will identify the vendor and the product item number. A second label will contain a series of about eight separate bar codes to indicate (at a minimum).

1. Unit of measure and quantity
2. Purchase order number of the customer
3. Component code number
4. Vendor's lot number
5. A unique container identifier

Additional information on the label can be negotiated by the vendor and customer (e.g., expiration date, date of manufacture, customer's lot number). Interested people can obtain more information from the PMA.

HOW MUCH IS PRODUCED?

Number of Manufacturing Plants

There are several aspects to this particular topic. The first is the issue of how much of one or multiple medicines *can* be physically produced at a single plant. Another issue, which is usually more difficult to answer, is how much of a medicine *should* be produced at one plant? To address the latter issue, one must consider both the present and future (projected) size of the labor force at a plant plus the amount of manpower that is available or is possible to recruit. Other major criteria relate to (1) total volume of products produced at the plant, (2) available and total plant capacity, and (3) considerations of specific medicines manufactured at the plant. This information is necessary to help determine the appropriate size of a plant. The issue of deciding when and where to build a new manufacturing facility is particularly complex.

Level of Service to Customers

Another issue that affects the amount of medicine produced at a particular plant relates to the type and level of service that is to be provided to customers. This service relates in part to the turnaround time necessary to ship goods. This depends in turn on the amount of the medicine kept in inventory. The types of methods and systems used to track and process both inventory and orders are critical to determine how much a company's inventory may be decreased.

Use of Marketing Forecasts

Marketing forecasts indicating the number of units of each product to be sold are necessary for production planning. These forecasts are issued for the next 12- to 18-month period and also on a long-range basis (e.g., five years). The long-term forecast is prepared using one to three cases: a base case (i.e., most likely scenario), a pessimistic case, and an optimistic case. These allow long-term production planning in terms of equipment and labor utilization. Using pessimistic assumptions or considering "what if . . ." exercises allows senior managers to plan contingency operations more effectively. Some of these assumptions are listed in Table 47.12 as general comments. More specific assumptions along these lines would have to be made in a "real life" situation. Shorter term forecasts are used for master scheduling of products, materials' planning of parts, and capacity planning of time.

Production Capacity

A related issue concerns utilization of a plant's capacity. Most companies attempt to utilize plant capacity at a predetermined optimal level. If the operating level is low, then there will always (or almost always) be an excess of spare capacity. If the operating level is set at an extremely high level, it may threaten the ability to manufacture important new products after regulatory approval or to deal with serious problems that arise. A clear policy and set of goals must be established on this issue. After that is done, plans may be developed to reach that goal.

Adjusting production capacity to appropriately meet demands placed on production is a constant issue for all companies. This balance will fluctuate over time. It may either fluctuate within a narrow range or fluctuate widely, as the demand for products rises and falls. Seasonal cycles of some products are able to be anticipated, but a sudden marked increase or decrease in number of units sold may upset this balance. In practice there is rarely an excess of capacity in all areas of a plant. There will commonly be a small excess in some areas and a greater excess in others.

Companies that have excess plant capacity may perform contract work for other pharmaceutical companies, the government, or other customers. When excess plant capacity still exists, a company will usually scale down their capacity to save money (e.g., a second or third shift may be eliminated) or utilize the capacity through other means. Plant capacity is often increased as older equipment is replaced or supplemented with newer equipment. For example, many new state-of-the-art machines operate much more rapidly than the machines they replace.

If excess plant capacity has been sold by a contract with a customer, and the company has a sudden and unexpected need for new capacity, a severe problem could easily develop. A company must ensure that filling excess capacity with contract work, for example, will not affect its most profitable product lines. If this problem develops, one temporary alternative is to go to outside contractors to produce some products. Outside contractors, however, may be limited in the capacity that they have for sale, since they may be committed to other companies and may not be able to accept additional contracts. In addition, regulatory approval must have been previously obtained to have the contractor produce the company's medicine(s).

Just-in-Time Versus Just-in-Case Inventory

One of the major new production concepts over the last decade is called just in time manufacture. Simply, this means that raw materials and other items needed to manufacture a medicine arrive at a plant just in time to be used. This avoids costs associated with carrying inventory and is a more efficient method of manufacture, assuming that the concept works in practice.

It is apparent that any problems with delivery of materials needed, the quality of materials received, or the production of finished goods will create an almost instant back-order situation. The older concept of maintaining a large inventory just in case orders arrived allowed enough slack in the system to have a reserve of raw materials that would allow a company to be unaffected by small or even possibly moderate problems or increased demand.

The more frequently and efficiently that marketing groups can assess their customer's pulse (i.e., the customer's inventory and ordering patterns) and the more that marketing communicates with production groups, the more effective will be production's response. Production staff should be able to redirect or divert raw medicine rapidly from one dosage form to another or to ship raw materials to another production site to address any problems they might have.

WHY ARE PRODUCTION COSTS SO HIGH?

This is clearly a relative question and does not apply to all companies equally and does not apply to all medicines manufactured by a single company. There are many reasons for high production costs which may include

1. new construction, remodeling, and maintenance of facilities;
2. labor costs;
3. new state-of-the-art equipment;
4. quality assurance and quality control systems implemented to ensure high production standards;
5. packaging of medicines in more technologically sophisticated containers and methods (e.g., blister packs);
6. disposal of waste products according to all local, state, and federal regulations;
7. protection of the public from tampering by utilizing more expensive manufacturing and packaging techniques; and
8. maintenance of inventories at a level that ensures the ability to supply customer's needs rapidly.

Each of these issues has been discussed in numerous articles and books. In this overview only a few points of general interest are briefly described.

Administrative Costs

Administrative costs are often an area where some progress may be made in cost trimming. Some pharmaceutical companies build large staffs to provide services to professional workers. The functions of many of these service personnel may often be combined with those of other workers. Administrative systems may also be simplified or streamlined in many situations.

Location of Manufacturing Facilities

Manufacturing facilities situated in large urban areas usually produce goods at higher costs than do plants situated in rural areas. Several American pharmaceutical companies have taken advantage of reduced taxes in Puerto Rico for several decades. The favorable tax status of Puerto Rico, however, may be removed by Congress at any time.

Plant Size

The size of a plant is another major factor influencing cost of goods produced. Cost advantages are gained with a large-sized production plant, but only up to a certain size. Once a plant exceeds a certain size there are no longer benefits to be gained from further expansion. It is not always apparent to company managers when that size is being approached, although it usually becomes obvious when that point has been passed.

Inventory Size

Inventory issues relate to the entire production pipeline, from raw chemicals and supplies (e.g., bottles, labels) to finished products. Companies must determine the appropriate balance between a sufficiently large inventory of medicines that allow a company to supply its customers rapidly and a small inventory that requires a lower investment of working capital. Are criteria used to establish a policy for one medicine suitable for others, or should different policies be adapted? Companies usually have a single policy regarding inventory for all their prescription medicines and a separate one for over-the-counter (OTC) medicines. The number of inventory turnovers per year is calculated by each company. This number comes from the cost of goods sold per year divided by the average inventory. This number varies between companies for various reasons. First, generic companies usually maintain high inventories because their customers are not likely to back-order medicines, but will turn to another manufacturer or distributor of generic medicines. New products tend to be stocked at high levels if a company is able to make sufficient amounts of the medicine because forecasts may be highly inaccurate. Companies also like to maintain large inventories of lifesaving medicines. Thus, inventory strategies for some medicines often differ within a single company.

One extreme approach is to adopt a flexible system called "just-in-time inventories." In this system, raw materials arrive at a company's plant just in time to produce the number of products that were ordered. No inventories are maintained. Most companies do not use this approach and are more concerned about how they may shift their inventories from finished products to bulk materials (e.g., medicine powder, medicine capsules) that may be rapidly packaged into whatever size unit is most needed.

Other Questions and Issues on Production Costs

What additional means could be used to reduce costs? Are a company's costs comparable to those of others in the industry? Which products, if any, could be made more cheaply by outside contractors? What are the reasons for this? Could the answers be applied to internal costs? If not, then are there plans to contract out the work? If so, are they being implemented and if there is no implementation, why is this so?

These are just a few of the additional questions that may be raised on this topic. Clearly, it is critical for companies to raise and focus attention on the most important questions for their situation. Focusing on less important or even irrelevant questions will dilute their corporate effectiveness and allow their competition to gain or overtake them.

Waste Minimization and Disposal

Over the last decade the emphasis has changed from external disposing of waste to decreasing its production and improving the company's own ability to dispose of it. The capacity of a company to dispose of its own waste has increased through creation of more sophisticated and larger treatment systems (e.g., incinerators). Decreasing waste production results from recycling solvents and other chemicals that were previously considered waste products. Building systems to recycle solvents (e.g., pyridine, toluene, acetone) is often expensive and a company has many solvents that must be considered as potentially recyclable. More efficient or new syntheses and formulation processes may be chosen for the production process primarily because less waste is generated. An apparently more expensive synthesis may be no more expensive than the alternative one when the costs of waste management are factored in.

Companies also spend more efforts monitoring the air above their factories, the gas emissions from the incinerators, ground water runoff, as well as solid waste produced. Incinerators are of various types and commonly burn materials at 2,000°F with close to 100% efficiency. Companies are moving toward incinerating more materials (e.g., out of date medicines, medicines that failed quality assurance tests) that previously would have been buried in landfills.

CHALLENGES FOR PRODUCTION

Many production techniques and tricks-of-the-trade are not published in any journal or book. Nonetheless,

TABLE 50.5. *Selected production issues relating to a physical plant and its equipment*

1. Determine at what rate and in what manner old equipment should be replaced
2. Determine how well each of the facilities and major equipment are operating
3. Determine on what schedule older plants should be closed, modernized, or expanded
4. Determine if automation, robotics, and computer-controlled equipment can be installed in a cost-effective way
5. Determine how much capital is available to purchase additional and replacement equipment
6. Determine if new medicines are being developed that will require new equipment or facilities
7. Determine if it is possible to improve the layout and product flow in the plant
8. Determine how equipment may be modified to reduce set-up time between production runs
9. Determine how to protect plants from the danger of catastrophic events (e.g., sabotage, natural disasters) and protection from other problems originating inside or outside the plant

TABLE 50.6. *Selected production issues relating to the processes conducted*

1. Evaluate if technical support from research and development in terms of expertise and priority are adequate to transfer manufacture of medicine from the pilot plant to full production
2. Determine if technical support from research and development is adequate to support various other issues (e.g., troubleshooting, quality assurance)
3. Determine if demands on production equipment by research and development to manufacture clinical study supplies are greater than anticipated
4. Determine if government regulations are requiring more time and money to meet and validate
5. Evaluate if inventory systems may be improved to increase turnover and decrease current inventory
6. Evaluate if improved systems may be implemented for planning material requirements, aiding manufacturing with computers, streamlining paper flow, and evaluating quality control
7. Evaluate if improved technology may be introduced to improve manufacture of medicine

much of this information is available and many state-of-the-art ideas are freely traded between companies. Production staff members acquire this information at professional meetings and by visiting facilities of other companies. Every company wants to learn how the competition does it. Many ideas are nontransferable because they reflect one-time operations designed to custom fit a specific production line or to solve a specific problem. Current and ongoing challenges for production groups are mentioned in Tables 50.5 to 50.9.

Planning and Scheduling Issues

A few issues faced in planning production runs are: How tightly may the runs be scheduled? How much

TABLE 50.7. *Selected production issues relating to people involved*

1. Determine if higher standards should be used to hire new employees
2. Determine which training programs are most effective
3. Determine which training programs should be added
4. Determine if the number of employees may be reduced through improved processes, new equipment, or other methods
5. Determine how labor disputes may be handled most effectively
6. Determine how threats to production facilities may be handled
7. Determine how the company may deal with a labor pool that is inadequate to provide enough highly competent employees
8. Evaluate team building programs that may be instituted (e.g., quality circles)
9. Determine how employees may be given more responsibility

TABLE 50.8. *Selected production issues relating to products made*

1. Marketing forecasts may either be too high or too low, resulting in unsold inventory or large backorders
2. Suppliers of important raw materials may be unreliable as to delivery dates
3. Suppliers or contractors may not be totally reliable in meeting agreed specifications and quality of raw supplies or finished products
4. A sudden increase in demand for products may exceed the plant's capacity
5. Quality assurance procedures and standards may change, resulting in a greater number of rejected tablets or other dosage forms
6. Less expensive starting or intermediary materials may be possible to use
7. Assembly line procedures may be improved in speed or efficiency
8. Product recall or tampering may have a marked effect on production schedules

slack time is necessary to build into the plan to avoid problems at a later date? How much lead time is necessary when scheduling production runs in different areas of manufacturing? Are these times growing? Are lead times too long? If so, at what point should additional production lines be established?

In terms of medicine development and transferring new medicines into production, two major questions are: One, are investigational medicines integrated into production in an efficient manner? Two, is the project leader in production working closely with project leaders in marketing plus research and development? Project plans and scheduling issues are reviewed by various groups. It is useful to have summaries of production-oriented issues for the review of projects. Maintaining a synopsis of production issues on each project would include tracking points listed in Table 50.9.

Issues Between Production and Marketing

Even in companies where production and marketing groups communicate well, there is an underlying tension between them. This is based on their having diametrically opposite needs in the most critical part of their interaction—ordering medicine. Production groups need to know how much of a medicine they need to make. They ask their marketing colleagues for an estimate. Marketing personnel know that the market share they can capture and the amount of medicine they can sell depends on how effective and safe the medicine is. Effectiveness and safety cannot be known until clinical trials are well into Phase II or even Phase III. Other factors also affect this estimate, such as price of the medicine and the ability to be good salespeople. Therefore, marketing does not want to provide estimates prematurely to production because they may be highly inaccurate. But, these esti-

mates are necessary for production to determine whether they will be able to manufacture the medicine in-house or will have to have it made by outside contractors. A new plant may possibly have to be constructed and dedicated to producing the medicine. Alternatively, new manufacturing equipment to make the new medicine may have to be purchased or sources of raw materials found. If marketing personnel wait until the clinical profile of a new medicine is well established before providing estimates to production of the number of kilograms and units required for launch and Year 1, then production may not have sufficient time to gear-up their operations and iron out "bugs" in their system prior to the product's launch.

One approach to solving this dilemma is to develop a series of alternative plans, each with different assumptions. Then, as each major new piece of information is gathered, the most suitable decision will become more clear. In reality, a medicine's career often changes suddenly by a new finding of toxicity in animals or humans or because of another problem (e.g., another medicine approved for the market, technical problems). Plans often have to be greatly changed, sometimes with little warning, and the most important information for marketing staff to know (i.e., what is in the labeling) is only known shortly prior to a medicine's launch. Fortunately, most medicines that are terminated prior to marketing die before passing the go-no go decision point that is usually reached sometime during late Phase II.

Alternatives If Production Cannot Meet Product Demands

No company wants to be caught in the position of being unable to supply material to customers. One of the worst times for this to occur is when a medicine is initially launched. A poor impression or image can so tarnish a medicine such that its sales might never recover.

In this situation a company has a number of alternatives to consider, and the best choice would vary depend-

TABLE 50.9. *Items to include in a synopsis of production status for individual medicines*

1. Date of report
2. Project name, number, and leader
3. Accomplishments
4. Marketing requests and schedules
5. Meetings with marketing and research and development
6. Critical uncertainties
7. Problems
8. Resource status
9. Quality assurance and validation issues
10. Inventory issues
11. Packaging issues
12. Major action points and time schedules for completion
13. Summary

ing on the nature of the medicine, level of demand, and the speed at which the supply can be increased. No matter which method is chosen it should be one that will not limit future sales. Perhaps the worst alternative is to go on back order. Another undesirable approach would be to purposely attempt to prevent or decrease interest and sales through a plan that restricts ordering by decreasing customer demand. Assuming that the problem is noticed before the marketing plan is publicized, it is possible for a company to limit the distribution until sufficient supplies are available, Distribution could be limited to (1) hospitals only, (2) patients who meet certain clinical criteria, or (3) patients whose physicians call a central telephone number to obtain a supply.

Competitive Pressures

In some disease areas (e.g., hypertension, angina) there is often a great deal of internal company pressure to reduce the cost of branded medicines because of the need to compete in the marketplace. During the period when a company has a patent on a unique medicine, they may concentrate on producing the best product possible and pay less attention to manufacturing costs. If other companies also have medicines in the same therapeutic class that are equivalent, or even better, then there is more incentive for a company to compete on cost.

As soon as its patent expires a medicine becomes subject to generic competition. At this point, producing medicine at minimal cost is always critical. It is important to develop improved manufacturing processes continually during a medicine's life and not wait until these pressures mount. Efforts to improve the manufacturing process are often handled jointly by both technical development and production departments. New technologies, equipment, and ideas must be evaluated to help improve a medicine's manufacturing processes.

Medicine Tampering

The wave of tampering with medicine products in the 1980s has sent a shock down the spine of the American public and others around the world. No longer can all medicine capsules be viewed the same way. The pharmaceutical companies involved and the entire industry handled this massive problem in a completely appropriate and responsible manner. The industry has developed several alternative methods for producing capsules. which has had a marked effect in decreasing (and, we hope, eliminating) this problem. Improvements include (1) taping boxes, (2) putting heat shrink seals on bottle tops, (3) putting a band around the joint of gelatin capsules, (4) sealing capsules by spot welding, (5) using capsules of a different shape that are more difficult to sepa-

rate, (6) using more blister packs, and (7) eliminating capsules altogether.

The concern with capsules has carried over to other dosage forms, where additional security measures (e.g., heat shrink seals, wrapping containers) have been implemented. The methods developed have cost significant sums of money to implement. These costs must ultimately be passed on to the consumer. Marketing aspects of the medicine-tampering issue were discussed in the preceding chapter.

Deciding on an Appropriate Level of Risk

There are always major questions of risk involved in manufacturing new medicines. At one extreme, a company could await FDA approval before ordering the equipment they will need to manufacture a medicine. At the opposite extreme, this equipment could be ordered when a project is initially established, based solely on results in animals. In either case the company is almost always being risk-foolish. Finding the right balance, however, is often difficult and always requires sound judgment.

As a medicine progresses from project initiation to market approval, and as more information becomes known, the risk to a company in purchasing equipment and/or building facilities clearly changes. Educated guesses must be made in terms of how soon the medicine is expected to reach the marketplace and also in terms of what type of medicine labeling the company expects to have. A company that establishes its market forecasts based on one set of assumptions and finds that the approved labeling is much more restrictive will have to greatly reduce their forecast. If the original forecast was used to justify a new building dedicated to manufacturing the medicine or to purchase new expensive equipment for the same purpose, then there may be some extremely embarrassed people around. If the company resisted the urge to make these moves, then the same people will be greatly relieved (although also disappointed at the bad news about labeling). One of the few guidelines for determining when to go ahead with the decision to risk significant capital is to carry out a dialogue among the people involved, allow time for thoughtful judgment, and obtain the most accurate forecasts possible of quantities needed and dates that decisions must be made.

Vertical Integration

Vertical integration refers to a company obtaining control of additional steps in the process of turning raw goods into finished products and having them sold to the final customer.

Each medicine manufacturer purchases supplies and raw materials used in manufacturing, packaging, and shipping their products. Many companies contract these activities for some or all of their products to other companies. There are trends within some companies to bring more of these activities "in-house" to gain control over the processes involved. Other companies are moving in the opposite direction and are attempting to have contractors prepare medicines for them, or to synthesize key intermediates. Two of the factors that influence these trends and a company's decisions are the costs of various approaches and the capacity of a company's current manufacturing plants to perform the necessary operations. Changes in tax and other laws will influence each company's perception of which approach is preferable for each of their products.

Backward Vertical Integration

There are two types of vertical integration, backward and forward. Backward vertical integration means that a company manufactures or controls the supply of starting chemicals they need instead of buying them. If a raw product is mined it might mean that the company purchases a mine. The driving forces behind this move are to save money and to gain control over the availability of supplies.

Forward Vertical Integration

Forward vertical integration means that a company becomes active in the distribution chain of its finished products. This might include operating wholesale or retail sales businesses in those countries where it is legal. Owning retail pharmacies or distribution networks would allow greater control over marketing activities. The primary driving forces behind a decision to move a company in this direction are to earn greater profits and gain better control over marketing of medicines.

Issues of Vertical Integration

Some of the issues that affect decisions about forward vertical integration are whether to sell competitors' products in a distribution network or a retail store. In the former, the answer is usually no. In a retail pharmacy, the answer is yes; otherwise, it would be difficult to attract customers to a pharmacy that only sold medicines of a single company. An issue faced by new entries into these areas is that other retailers and distributors are likely to consider this practice unfair and will react in a strongly negative way to this new type of competition.

Backward vertical integration may require a large investment to achieve the necessary financial return. Gradually adding additional syntheses to a company's repertoire, however, may be a relatively inexpensive and painless way to approach this goal.

A Summary of Current Challenges for Production

Some of the current challenges that production plants must cope with are listed below.

1. Construct and maintain an appropriate number of modern facilities for manufacturing medicines on a worldwide basis.
2. Introduce state-of-the-art techniques and equipment for manufacturing and packaging medicines.
3. Manufacture, package, and ship new products almost immediately after they are approved by the FDA and/or other regulatory agencies.
4. Meet unexpected challenges in a rapid, efficient, and ethical manner (e.g., to develop tamper-resistant packaging).
5. Produce products in a cost-efficient manner.
6. Improve emissions, effluents, and waste products leaving the plant in a socially responsible yet economic manner.
7. Develop contingency plans in case of major catastrophes or emergencies.
8. Sell excess production capacity while retaining the ability to expand production of one's own products if the need arises.
9. Achieve a low rejection rate of finished medicines of high quality.
10. Produce investigational medicines to assist chemical development groups while utilizing resources for manufacturing.
11. Track time and effort of all employees while not spending excessive resources on this activity.
12. Develop a cadre of motivated and dedicated employees.
13. Turn inventory a sufficient number of times per year (based on cost of goods sold).
14. Utilize sophisticated computer inventory systems so that it is no longer necessary to physically segregate materials passed by a quality assurance group from materials that have not yet been passed.
15. Process, ship, and invoice all orders within a preset time period.

A summary of production issues are listed that relate to a physical plant and its equipment (Table 50.5), processes conducted (Table 50.6), people employed (Table 50.7), and products made (Table 50.8).

51 / Patent Issues

What Is a Patent?	613
Patents Versus Trade Secrets	613
What Can Be Patented?	614
Duration of a Patent	614
Procedures for Obtaining a Patent	614
Where and When to File a Patent?	614
Basis of Issuing a Patent	615
Criteria for Awarding Patents	615
Paris Union Convention of 1870	615
First-to-File Versus First-to-Invent	616
Patents Granted Without Data	617
Invention Cascade	617
Protecting a Company's Innovations and Inventions in the 1990s	617
Importance of Having Strong Patent Law for Pharmaceutical Companies	617
Effective Patent Life	617
Types of Patent Extension	617

Orphan Medicines	618
Formulating a Patent Strategy	618
Patents and Licensing	618
Interference	618
Patent Pirates	619
Biotechnology Patents	619
Patents on Animals	619
Deposit Issues	619
"Catch-22" Situations	620
Confidential Information	620
What Information Is Considered Confidential?	620
Sharing Confidential Information	620
Canadian Issues	621
Golden Rules of Patenting and Disclosure	621
The Future of Patent Laws	621

Ingenuity should receive a liberal encouragement. Thomas Jefferson

Congress intended statutory subject matter to include anything under the sun made by man. Chief Justice Warren Burger, majority opinion, Diamond V. Chakrabarty

---

Intellectual property laws seek to protect discoveries of thinking. Areas of the law include not only patents, but also trademarks, designs, trade secrets, and copyrights. These laws encourage people to invest in research and development.

WHAT IS A PATENT?

A patent is a legal right granted by a government. It establishes exclusivity of the use of an intellectual or tangible property by the inventor for a specified period of years. Each country has its own patent laws. The patent describes what is patented through a series of claims that precisely set the limits of the claimed invention. As such, a patent is also a technical document that describes the invention in sufficient detail to permit one "skilled in the art" to perform the invention. The patent also has barter or sale value in business transactions. Patents may be bought, sold, licensed, or assigned to individuals or organizations (e.g., a company, university, hospital). Most, if not all research based companies require staff who are awarded patents to assign them to the company in return

for their salary. In a real sense a patent may be considered to be a contract between the inventor and a government, giving the inventor the right to control the property for a set number of years in return for a full and complete disclosure of the invention.

Patents Versus Trade Secrets

Information on a patent application outside the United States usually becomes public knowledge 18 months after the first filing date of the patent. Sometimes companies find it more valuable to keep information within the company (i.e., a trade secret) rather than to disclose it through a patent. The increased value of trade secrets is that they do not have a predetermined lifetime. Keeping an invention a trade secret only provides protection if no one else independently discovers the information or, in the case that the same discovery is made independently, it is not patented first. In the United States it is possible to contest such a patent on the basis that your company discovered it first (assuming that to be the case), although this argument would fail elsewhere in the world. One exception is when a company suppressed or concealed the invention. The other requirements to keep a trade secret are that no one will deliberately, or even accidentally, leak the secret or mention it in public and that commercial exploitation will not reveal its nature.

Many countries outside the United States have "prior user" rights that allow an earlier inventor to continue practicing an invention later patented by another, although the prior user cannot contest the validity of the patent as they may do in the United States.

WHAT CAN BE PATENTED?

Ideas and concepts are not patentable per se, but the embodiment of an idea or concept in tangible form may be patented. Patents are given for material substances, items, processes, and uses having an industrial application or any other practical utility. (Perpetual motion machines are per se not patentable.) The statutes specifically list "process, machine, manufacture or composition of matter."

For medicines it is possible to patent

1. an active compound or substance itself (i.e., a compound patent);
2. a new medical use of an unpatented or off-patent (i.e., known) medicine or a patented medicine (i.e., a use patent);
3. a pharmaceutical formulation of a compound (i.e., a formulation patent); or
4. a new or improved process to make a medicine (i.e., a process patent).

DURATION OF A PATENT

The normal life of a patent in the United States—17 years after issue—is an arbitrarily derived number determined in the past by the United States Congress. Historically, the period of patent protection has ranged from 14 to 21 years in the United States; currently it is 20 years (from filing) in many European countries. Significant efforts are underway to internationally harmonize patent laws and the expectation is that the term of a U.S. patent will be changed to 20 years from the date of filing.

The "birth" and life of a patent may be viewed as consisting of five stages. These are schematically shown in Fig. 51.1. There is little or no overlap between these stages, although the duration of each stage may be very variable. There is no publication of a U.S. patent application prior to grant of the patent.

PROCEDURES FOR OBTAINING A PATENT

Each country's patent requirements and procedures must be observed. However, the contents of a patent

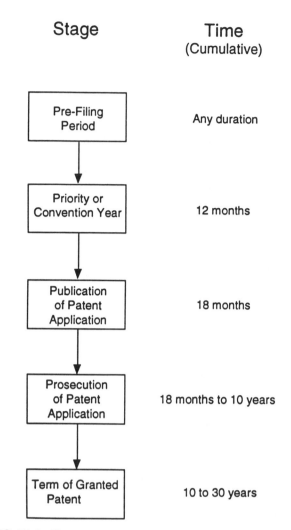

FIG. 51.1. Five stages of a patent. The "publication of patent application" stage is not applicable in the United States. The filing of a patent occurs at 0 months between the pre-filing period and the priority or convention year.

application are similar among most nations; the general categories of contents of a patent application are listed in Table 51.1. The general events and procedures for the patent process are schematically shown in Fig. 51.2, along with approximate times.

Where and When To File A Patent?

Many companies file patent applications first in the United Kingdom or other European countries because that procedure allows them an additional year, referred to as a convention period, in which to file in the United States and elsewhere and still achieve complete protection. The initial patent application in the United Kingdom may be limited in the information it contains, in terms of claims or supporting data and claims. These aspects are included in subsequent applications on the same invention. An alternative strategy to obtain an extra year of patent protection is to file the original patent

TABLE 51.1. *Contents of a patent application*

1. Introductory page
2. Abstract
3. Brief description
4. Drawings
5. Background, including prior art[a]
6. Full description of the invention
7. Examples of how to make the invention
8. Claims detailing the limits of the invention to be patented

[a] Prior art refers to information known before the filing date that relates to the patent application. It includes information presented orally at meetings in addition to printed material.

application in the United States. The first application must contain the claims, but not necessarily the examples. Filing a "continuation-in-part" (c.i.p.) after one year allows one to add material later. The advantage of an early filing in the United States is that it allows you to file as soon as you discover the invention, but to add some of the important materials up to one year later.

A company should do whatever it can within the patent law to extend the life of a patent. The most valuable (i.e., profitable) years of patent life are usually those at the end of the patent period because minimal advertising and promotion are needed to sell what is probably an established medicine. It is usually at that point as well that the financial return on the medicine is maximal.

BASIS OF ISSUING A PATENT

Criteria for Awarding Patents

In each country the exact basis for awarding patents may vary slightly, but the major criteria that must be satisfied are (1) novelty of the invention, (2) nonobvious nature, and (3) utility (i.e., practical application). The "nonobviousness" aspect relates to prior art and is somewhat subjective. In Europe there is a one-year grace period allowed after publication of an invention, by which time the patent application must be filed in the United States. Grace periods do not exist for filing in many other countries.

If the patent application does not meet all requirements, then the patent examiner notifies the applicant. The applicant may respond with answers to the points raised or possibly with more data. There may be several stages of correspondence between the inventor and the Patent Office. Patents usually experience resistance from the Patent Office, and it is typical for the claims to be rejected on the initial review. This initial rejection is often on the basis that (1) the applicant is making claims that are broader than the supporting evidence, (2) the invention is obvious, (3) the invention does not work, or (4) the invention is already known.

Paris Union Convention of 1870

The Paris (1870) agreement permits an inventor who files a patent application in any country that signed the convention to file in any other convention country up to one year later while still keeping the benefits of the earlier filing date. Thus, a single patent application filed, for example, in Japan gives the inventor the right to file in

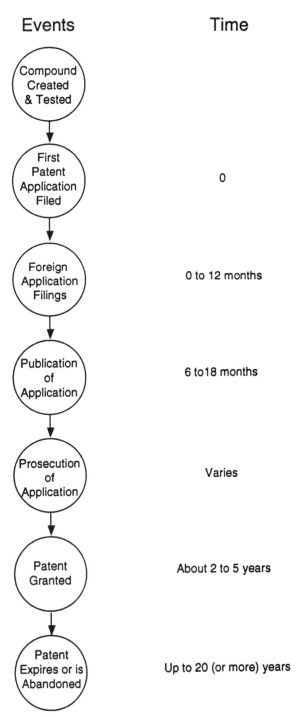

Events	Time
Compound Created & Tested	
First Patent Application Filed	0
Foreign Application Filings	0 to 12 months
Publication of Application	6 to18 months
Prosecution of Application	Varies
Patent Granted	About 2 to 5 years
Patent Expires or is Abandoned	Up to 20 (or more) years

FIG. 51.2. Series of major events in the patenting of a new compound. The middle stage ("publication of an application") is not applicable in the United States.

any or all convention countries within one year. All such filings have an effective filing date that is the same as that of the initial filing in Japan.

First-to-File Versus First-to-Invent

The concepts of first-to-file and first-to-invent are at the heart of many patent problems where more than one person or group claim to have made the invention or discovery. Nearly all countries of the world, except for the United States and the Philippines, vide infra, can be characterized as first-to-file countries. This means that the person or group who files first in a member country's patent office is awarded a patent regardless of who actually invented first. This issue is schematically shown in Fig. 51.3, where two different people could each obtain a patent for the same invention.

The United States and Philippines are the only first-to-invent countries. This means that the patent is awarded in these countries to the inventor who first conceived, diligently reduced to practice in the country and filed a patent application and claimed the invention regardless of whether he or she was first to file. If the United States adopted the first-to-file system, it is certain that the number of patent applications would markedly increase. For example, in Japan there are over 500,000 patent applications each year, far more than in the United States.

Formal proceedings used to determine who has the priority of invention in the United States are known as "interferences." The person considered to be the inventor in the United States is the one who first conceived the invention and is diligent in reducing it to practice, not necessarily the one who filed the patent application first. Laboratory notebooks are important document sources that are often used to demonstrate the dates on which a

Three Independent Scientists
Who Make the Same Discovery

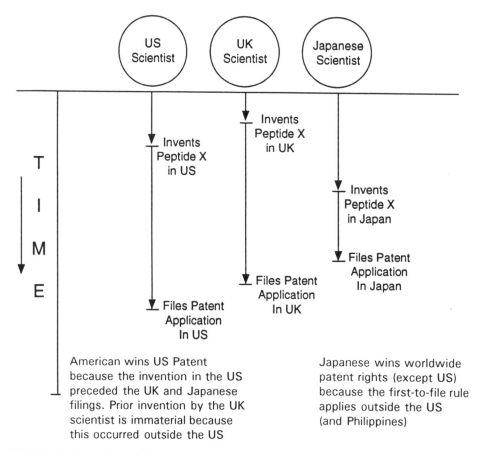

FIG. 51.3. Illustration of how differences between first-to-invent and first-to-file patent systems may lead to different results. The outcome shown in this figure would apply whether the scientists filed first in their home country or elsewhere.

specific compound was conceived, synthesized, and tested. In some situations defining the concept is rather difficult, such as with totally new scientific ideas or discoveries that evolve over a period of time before they become fully appreciated, formulated, and identified.

Patents Granted Without Data

Patent applications are sometimes filed based on a theory or hypothesis, even if no actual data have been obtained. This is called a constructive reduction to practice. If the basic criteria are met and the patent examiner does not require proof—e.g., that the novel compound(s) have the medical uses claimed—a patent may be granted. This is more likely to occur if the compound to be patented is a derivative of a known patented compound with a theoretical advantage. For example, a chiral form of a molecule may be hypothesized to have a theoretical advantage and a patent may be obtained without actually demonstrating an advantage. Another example might be a segment of a known polymer that may be hypothesized to have advantages over the higher molecular weight parent polymer. In most cases, however, the patent examiner will require proof of new and unexpected properties to grant a patent for a variant of a known compound.

It has been stated (primarily in jest) that many basic scientists have switched their approach to conducting research because of the biotechnology revolution. In the years prior to 1975, a scientist would form a hypothesis, design experiments, collect data, and then apply for a patent. Since that time it seems that scientists working in biotechnology first formulate a hypothesis, then apply for a patent, and lastly raise 15 to 20 million dollars in order to conduct the experiments to test the hypothesis.

Invention Cascade

A company seldom files a single patent application in isolation; usually there is a series of applications. Within eighteen months after global filings on invention A, there is publication of the patent application (e.g., the European patent application). If the research on invention A has progressed and a company wishes to file on invention B, the company should file before the publication occurs. If it does not file within this time, then the prior art established by the publication of the patent application on invention A may well make invention B unpatentable. Before the publication of the patent application on invention B, a company may file on invention C, and so forth. This is referred to as an invention cascade.

PROTECTING A COMPANY'S INNOVATIONS AND INVENTIONS IN THE 1990s

Importance of Having Strong Patent Law for Pharmaceutical Companies

Patent protection is essential for the pharmaceutical industry to remain viable and prosperous. Without a period of enforced marketing exclusivity, a less expensive generic version, authorized or not, will be sold by competitors and one's market share will sharply decline. Strong patent protection also helps to minimize piracy of one's medicines. It has been suggested that some pharmaceutical companies lose up to ten percent of their worldwide sales through the piracy of their products. Pirates are primarily based in a few countries that have weak or negligible patent laws for pharmaceutical products (see discussion below).

Effective Patent Life

The traditional method of protecting inventions is to obtain patents. This is still the single most important method by which an inventor obtains protection for his or her compound(s). The "effective patent life" of a new medicine is the amount of time remaining in the patent at the time the medicine is initially marketed. This is almost always less than the total patent life granted because patents almost always are issued during the medicine's development (i.e., before the medicine receives governmental approval for sale). The decline in the length of effective patent life for a new compound has been severe: effective patent life has eroded from 16 to 8 years in the last 20 years (5 years according to some studies). Various legislative acts, though offering some protection, are not applicable to certain specific medicines. The optimal situation is to have a newly issued patent at the time of initial marketing, or even to have the compound patent issued after the medicine is marketed. This is a spectrum and the weakest position is not to have any patent protection or to have solely a process patent.

Types of Patent Extension

The decline in effective patent life has signaled a crisis call to the pharmaceutical industry, particularly in the United States. The industry's response has been energetic lobbying through its major trade association, the Pharmaceutical Manufacturers Association. This lobbying activity contributed to the passage of the 1984 Patent Term Restoration Act by the U.S. Congress. Under this act, newly developed medicines and those in the regulatory queue would receive an additional period of patent protection—minimum of five years exclusivity for newly approved medicines. This helps primarily those compounds that are near to patent expiration by extending the period of exclusivity beyond the life of the patent. This exclusivity is based on preventing an Abbreviated New Drug Application (ANDA) being filed on a newly approved new chemical entity product for five years. It is not an extension of the patent. Patent term extension allows you to recover up to five years of patent life lost while waiting for Food and Drug Administration (FDA) approval.

It is worth noting that another part of the same 1984 act also established the ground-rules under which generic equivalent medicines would receive rapid approval. That event triggered the subsequent explosive growth of the generic medicine industry. This served to hurt primarily those research-based companies who did not have a strong presence in the generic medicine business and whose medicines were (or shortly would be) vulnerable to generic competition.

Orphan Medicines

Another area in which protection for certain medicines may be obtained relates to orphan medicines. Orphan medicines with this designation from the FDA receive a seven-year period of marketing exclusivity from the time that the New Drug Application (NDA) is formally approved. This provision has been debated both within and outside Congress for several years. One debated question is whether this marketing exclusivity should be viewed as a reward for innovation and/or medicine development for a rare disease, or whether the exclusivity should be used as a stimulus to companies to encourage them to develop such medicines.

Formulating a Patent Strategy

The strategy chosen by an individual or a company is based to a large extent on the degree of competitiveness in the specific area. One does not usually want to file a patent too early in a "new area" because that creates prior art and stimulates competitive activity that may prevent the patenting of better compounds at a later time. If the therapeutic or chemical area is a highly competitive one, it may be necessary to file for patent protection much earlier.

The ideal strategy is to progress with development almost all the way into Phase I trials before filing patent applications, although this is rarely possible. It is highly desirable to have filed a patent application prior to initiating clinical trials because information on the invention will be disclosed to a large number of people before the trials can be initiated. Any disclosure of an invention to external people or groups that are associated with clinical trials prior to the filing of a patent application must be preceded by a confidentiality agreement.

Some pharmaceutical companies prefer to file many patent applications relatively early on in the life of a potentially new and important compound. This provides early protection of the compound(s) of interest while the company "fine tunes" the chemical direction it will pursue. This "shotgun," broad approach to obtaining protection tends to be substantially more expensive than the opposite approach of filing a minimal number of patent applications. The financial savings accrued using this latter approach are especially significant when patent filings are made in multiple countries.

Many pharmaceutical companies develop their own particular habits or strategies of dealing with patents. Company strategies must be periodically reevaluated or else they become merely habits. All assumptions and conclusions of the past should be periodically reexamined and challenged when appropriate.

Other companies carefully examine their nonpatented compounds that have shown biological activity and prepare relatively few patent applications to protect their rights to the compounds of particular interest. These companies may either file early to ensure protection or hold back the filing to increase the total life of a patent.

Patents and Licensing

In most cases, a property that is licensed from another group is protected by one or more patents. In some cases important trade secrets or know-how (but no patents) may be involved. Entering into a license contract when patents are not present, but are thought to be, is inexcusable. Entering into a license contract when the patent situation is unclear or contested is generally foolish— that is, one should understand the full limitations of the patent issues and the associated risks. Major disappointments may readily arise if the protection proves to be illusory.

Owning a patent or license is not sufficient insurance that one will be able to practice the invention without infringing on patents owned by others. In fact, someone else may have a blocking patent that prevents you from expressing a gene, synthesizing a compound, producing your medicine, or marketing a product.

Interference

If the United States Patent Office determines that two or more inventors have filed patent applications claiming the same invention, then a formal procedure, referred to as an interference, is initiated. This procedure is used to decide who did what and at what time. It is a legal proceeding that determines ownership of the patent. One issue that often arises in an interference is that a person or group may clearly appear either to have been first to discover something or to have been close to discovering something, when they apparently stopped work on the invention. It is critically important to establish whether or not the individual or group actually stopped work in pursuit of the discovery because any significant time-break in activity can be considered abandonment and the patent may be awarded to the other group.

Patent Pirates

Any country that maintains weak or no patent laws is guilty of allowing people to pirate the ideas and intellectual property of others. Certain countries are worse offenders than others, and currently there are ineffective or nonexistent provisions to protect medical inventions in Argentina, Brazil, and India. Korea and Mexico recently passed improved patent laws. Manufacturers of patented products who do not own a patent or license to manufacture a product are sometimes referred to as patent pirates. Pirates manufacture and sell medicines invented by other companies because the government legislation in their countries is inadequate. They are estimated to cost the pharmaceutical industry about 5 billion U.S. dollars in lost sales per year.

The major reasons these countries do not respect patents are the desires to (1) protect their own industry from foreign competition by allowing national companies to make and sell new medicines, (2) avoid paying royalties they can "ill afford" to patent owners who live in other countries, and (3) help control prices of medicines within their country.

BIOTECHNOLOGY PATENTS

The major case that opened the path for patenting genetically engineered plants and nonhuman animals was Diamond versus Chakrabarty (477US303[1980], 100 S. Ct. 2204 [1980]). The U.S. Supreme Court stated that a live microorganism made by a human is patentable because it is a "manufacture" or "composition of matter." This ruling provided a major stimulus to the biotechnology industry during the 1980s.

Biotechnology patent applications generally are in process for longer time periods than other pharmaceutical patents. This has had major implications within the biotechnology industry (U.S. Congress, Office of Technology Assessment, 1991). The average time before a patent is issued is 36.1 months (date of application to date of issue) versus 21.0 months for all patents. The major reasons cited for this extended review period are

1. the newness of the technology and the need for extremely careful review;
2. the high turnover of patent examiners, resulting in a need to hire and train replacements; and
3. the large number of applications received relative to the size of the staff.

These factors contribute to the higher cost of obtaining a biotechnology patent (usually $8,000 to $15,000 in 1990) relative to that for other types of patents (usually $3,000 to $6,000). A currently debated issue is whether more narrow patents will be awarded in the future, for biotechnology products and for processes.

PATENTS ON ANIMALS

The first United States patent on an animal was awarded to Harvard University in 1988 for mice that were genetically engineered to contain a gene that causes cancer. The trademark of the mouse is Onco Mouse, and it contains the *ras* oncogene in all germ and somatic cells. It is sold commercially to researchers studying cancer and potential treatments. There was a great deal of pressure to issue this patent because of the expected role this animal would play in searching for better treatments for cancer. As of September 1992, no additional animal patents have been issued, although at least 120 animal patent applications are pending (U.S. Congress, Office of Technology Assessment, 1991, page 214).

Most countries now accept the patentability of new microorganisms, but the patentability of transgenic animals is much more questionable. The European patent on Onco Mouse was filed in June 1985 and went through a series of negative decisions and reversals. This case was still unsettled as of August 1991 (U.S. Congress, Office of Technology Assessment, 1991, page 217). Overall, the United States is the most liberal nation in its approach to patenting new plant or animal life forms.

DEPOSIT ISSUES

The United States Patent and Trademark Office started recommending in 1949 that inventors seeking to patent an invention involving microorganisms deposit a sample with their application. Although this is not a legal requirement unless the microorganism is necessary to practice the invention, it is usually done. This practice has spread, and the Budapest Treaty in 1977 created a system with International Depository Authorities. Twenty-three countries had signed the treaty by 1991 and agreed to require a deposit when a claimed invention cannot be reproduced without the deposit. If words suffice to inform people how to recreate the invention, than a deposit is not needed.

Cultures of such deposit are routinely made available in the United States to anyone who requests one and pays a small charge (U.S. Congress, Office of Technology Assessment, 1991). This is tantamount, in some people's view, to giving away the invention, particularly because many microbial cultures are taken all over the world and pirated.

Although the use of a deposited culture is technically a

patent infringement, most countries allow this if the work is limited to research experiments unrelated to the development of a commercial product. Given the close connection between a great deal of research and entrepreneurial companies, this practice appears to be unfair to the inventor. As may be imagined, this issue had led to some extremely complex legal cases.

"CATCH-22" SITUATIONS

The natural tendency of scientists, and even companies, when they have made a major discovery is to apply for a patent to protect their invention. But they know they will have a greater degree of protection and greater chances of success if they can synthesize related compounds or biological products and describe the biological activities of those as well. Such work is pursued while the lead compound progresses through preclinical testing and eventual clinical development. At the same time, chemists are exploring other chemically related areas to better define activities and to better delineate and support the patent coverage. It is ironic that a company's own patents serve as "prior art" (after one year in the United States, and immediately upon publication in most of the world) and may serve to block a company from patenting additional new compounds that are related to those in an earlier patent. Only if the inventor can overcome the rejection by the Patent Office on the basis of obviousness will it be possible to patent the new compounds. The obviousness factor may be challenged if the new compound has unexpectedly high activity, a new activity, or improved physical properties.

An inventor who files a patent application should (at least in theory) consult all the prior art available to ensure that his or her invention is novel. One area that the inventor does not have access to is the backlog of unpublished applications that are being reviewed and are awaiting review. It may be several years in the United States before the inventor learns that his or her invention will be rejected because of another invention that was discovered earlier—even though there was no way the second inventor could have known about it. The irony is compounded by the fact that the inventor must file in many countries, at great expense, to be adequately protected. A further irony is that the larger the backlog of applications grows—and in recent years it has grown markedly in biotechnology—the greater the amount of hidden undiscoverable information becomes (as does the uncertainty of the effect of this information). The issue of undiscoverable information only exists in the United States.

An additional problem can arise from delays in awarding patents to an individual or company: such delays often mean that the 17-year patent period starts at a later time. This delay can be worth many millions of dollars to a few inventors, although delays in obtaining a patent may discourage some investors at the start of a medicine's development. This problem can have a far greater influence on the fate of a start-up company than would the potential for making much more money 17 or so years in the future.

CONFIDENTIAL INFORMATION

What Information Is Considered Confidential?

Any secret information that will give an actual or a potential advantage of any kind to a competitor or potential competitor would be considered confidential. Samples of new compounds that are not patented or are not yet fully evaluated and patented are highly confidential; these could be readily analyzed to identify their structure. There is a spectrum of confidentiality ranging from information that is critically important to the company's future to information of such low confidentiality that its disclosure would not cause the company any problem. Confidentiality is often highly time dependent because what is extremely confidential today usually becomes progressively less so over time. The time period over which confidentiality requirements decreases to zero can be in terms of hours or up to years. Table 51.2 lists several types of company data and information that are confidential.

Sharing Confidential Information

Companies share highly confidential information when they conduct collaborative or contract research or contract manufacture or enter into joint ventures. These activities should occur only after a confidentiality agreement is signed by both parties. Confidential information

TABLE 51.2. *Types of data that are truly confidential*

1. Sales and profit forecasts (e.g., one-year and five-year forecasts)
2. Preclinical targets being used and hypotheses being tested
3. Preclinical animal models that are not described in the literature
4. Preclinical animal models that are being used differently than described in the literature
5. Compound structures and biological results for lead and interesting series being evaluated, whether patented or not
6. Potential or actual problems in preclinical or clinical development that are being actively investigated
7. Strategies for developing medicines (e.g., clinical)
8. Patent strategies for certain series of compounds
9. Details of potential licensed-in medicines
10. Various details of the clinical development program (e.g., endpoints being measured, protocol design, investigators being used)
11. Methods used in manufacture

may be shared with other corporations (often other pharmaceutical companies), as well as with universities, government agencies, and individuals from various groups. A few cautions are mentioned below.

1. Information sent to the government may be subsequently disclosed (e.g., Freedom of Information Act in the United States). However, information sent to the United States Patent Office is not available to the public under the Freedom of Information Act.

2. Do not disclose secrets at professional meetings or seminars by presenting data or by discussing secrets in conversation. This is considered a public disclosure under the patent laws of most countries and can prevent one from obtaining global patent coverage.

3. Contact the legal or patent attorneys in one's company to determine if information may be disclosed.

CANADIAN ISSUES

A 1969 amendment to the Canadian Patent Act introduced compulsory licensing to import chemicals to manufacture medicines. This license meant that generic companies could manufacture patented medicines developed by other pharmaceutical companies. A minimal royalty typically set at 4 percent of the gross sales of the licensee was given to the patent holder. Recent licenses, however, have had higher royalty rates. This mechanism, which was introduced to control medicine prices, was vigorously challenged by the pharmaceutical industry for many years. Because of lost sales, many multinational pharmaceutical companies were reluctant to invest heavily in their Canadian operations.

The Patented Medicine Prices Review Board (PMPRB) that reviews medicine prices, evaluates the prices charged in other countries for new medicines under review. The board also compares the price for a new medicine with Canadian prices for other medicines of the same therapeutic class.

The Canadian Parliament passed a new act in 1987, referred to as Bill C-22, that was a major step toward reestablishing effective patent protection. Bill C-22 tied patent protection (10 years) to increased spending in Canada for research and development. The bill stipulates that the percent of sales spent on research and development must increase from the average of 4.9% (1986) to 8 percent in 1991, 9 percent in 1994, and 10 percent in 1996. This bill has led to much higher spending levels by large multinational companies in Canada, primarily for clinical trials.

GOLDEN RULES OF PATENTING AND DISCLOSURE

A few golden rules of patenting and disclosure are mentioned.

1. Develop a patent strategy at the earliest possible time and periodically review it. Modify it as needed for each new invention.
2. Have patent applications reviewed and critiqued by at least two patent attorneys before they are filed.
3. If doubt exists about whether or not certain information is confidential, treat it as being confidential.
4. Do not publish scientific papers on the invention for up to a year after the original filing because it is still possible to abandon the claim and to refile it, to either start the time clock anew, or to add new material to the application.

THE FUTURE OF PATENT LAWS

The problems discussed in this chapter, and many others are well known to patent examiners, attorneys, managers, and staff around the world. Many people desire more uniform laws, and there are several international forums where discussions are occurring (e.g., World Intellectual Property Organization, General Agreement on Tariffs and Trade). The European Patent Convention has introduced much patent harmonization in Western Europe and talks with the United States are underway, also discussing patent harmonization. It is hoped that the many differences between countries can be lessened over the coming years and that the increasing backlog of patents pending will be reduced.

52 / Legal Activities and Issues

Types of Activities Conducted in a Legal
  Department **623**
  Corporate Activities That Require Legal Input
    or Review................................ 624
  Employee Activities That Require Legal Input
    or Review................................ 625
  Regulatory Activities That Require Legal Input
    or Review................................ 625
  Product Liability Activities That Require Legal
    Input or Review.......................... 626
  Medical Activities That Require Legal Input or
    Review................................... 626
  Patent Law................................. 627
Educational Role of Legal Staff **627**
Organizational Placement of Legal Staff......... **627**
Personnel...................................... **627**
  Internal and External Attorneys.............. 627
  Plaintiffs Who Sue a Company................. 628
  Perspectives in Legal Cases 628
Suits Versus Companies **628**
  Trends in Court Cases........................ 628
Product Liability.............................. **629**
  Failure to Warn—the Major Reason for
    Product Liability 629
  How Pharmaceutical Companies Warn
    Physicians About the Risks Associated with
    a Medicine................................ 629

Strict Liability............................... 630
Negligence 630
Comment k 630
Learned Intermediary Doctrine 630
When a Company Should Add New Warnings
  to Its Package Insert....................... 631
Investigational Versus Marketed Medicines ... 631
Types of Awards.............................. 632
Litigation Arising from Activities of Sales
  Representatives **632**
Preparing Nonlegal Staff for Presentations in
  Courtroom Cases.......................... **633**
  Distinctions Among Medicine, Science, and
    Law...................................... 633
  Choosing Expert Witnesses 633
  Training Physicians and Scientists for a Legal
    Case 633
  Pretrial and Predeposition Preparation........ 634
  Two Approaches to Presenting Expert
    Testimony 634
Good Legal Practices for Nonattorneys to Follow
  in a Company **635**

Life and law must be kept closely in touch, as you can't adjust life to law, you must adjust law to life. The only point in having law is to make life work. Otherwise there will be explosions. Arnold Toynbee

This chapter discusses some of the activities performed by legal departments as well as some of the ways in which other company staff interact with a company's attorneys. Attorneys usually advise on directions that a company or its employees may (or should) take, but attorneys rarely make the actual business decisions as to the specific actions to follow. Nonetheless, because of the high costs and often severe penalties of litigation and regulatory violations, legal advice and recommendations usually carry great weight within a pharmaceutical company.

This chapter is written for nonattorneys, using the plain style of language found elsewhere in this book; it does not attempt to provide legal advice or thorough discussions of legal issues. Anyone interested in legal opinions should seek the advice of an attorney.

TYPES OF ACTIVITIES CONDUCTED IN A LEGAL DEPARTMENT

The major types of legal activities conducted within a pharmaceutical company are described under a number of arbitrarily chosen headings: Corporate Activities, Employee Activities, Regulatory Activities, Product Liability Activities, and Medical Activities. An alternative classification could be based on the groups within the company and external to the legal department that it interacts with (e.g., Finance, Marketing, Medical). Other classifications are also possible, reflecting the proactive or reactive nature of a problem. Whereas most clients approach attorneys in private practice in reaction to a problem, many company attorneys concentrate on problem prevention. Their goal is to avoid problems by having early input to business decisions. In addition to prevention-focused activities, some company attorneys react to problems (e.g., lawsuits, regulatory letters) that arise.

Corporate Activities That Require Legal Input or Review

Contracts

Negotiations of contracts and their subsequent implementation are common activities conducted by groups throughout the company. Implementation of contracts involves monitoring the actions of the company and the other party to ensure that terms are being met on time, and that there are no breaches of the contract. Almost every area of a company is at some time involved with many types of contracts that require legal input (Table 52.1). A few examples include the following.

1. Licensing contracts to license a product from, or to, another company. Highly complex contracts are commonly encountered in this area, in part because a period of several or many years may be covered and many contingencies and terms (e.g., royalties, patent expiration) must be identified and discussed in detail. In addition, some terms of the license agreement may be very complex.

2. Contracts with academic institutions prior to initiating a clinical trial. These contracts vary markedly in complexity and may involve indemnification agreements that will apply if certain unexpected problems arise (e.g., a patient sues the hospital).

3. Production contracts or supply agreements are required before a company is willing to produce a product or bulk chemical for another company, or to have another company prepare a chemical or product.

4. Contracts between pharmaceutical companies and contract research organizations. Yingling (1992) discusses contract negotiations between pharmaceutical companies and contract research organizations, focusing on the United States experience. The article discusses relevant Food and Drug Administration (FDA) regulations and includes a sample contract as well as a list of subjects that should be considered in negotiations.

5. Consulting agreements between individuals, groups, or companies. These generally describe terms agreed to by both parties.

6. Service agreements with vendors to produce a book or videotape, organize a symposium, or provide other services.

TABLE 52.1. *Types of contracts and legal agreements*

1. Commercial license agreements (e.g., patent, know-how, trademark)
2. Long- and short-term financing agreements
3. Purchase of materials, equipment, supplies, and services (e.g., major contracts, purchase orders)
4. Insurance contracts
5. Auto lease contracts
6. Leases of computer equipment
7. Acquisition agreements
8. Advertising contracts
9. Marketing service agreements (e.g., market research contracts)
10. Government contracts for sale of marketed products
11. Company's standard distributor or agency agreements
12. Leases of regional sale offices
13. Options for a license
14. Confidentiality or disclosure agreements
15. Divestiture agreements
16. Agreements relating to employee benefits (e.g., medical insurance contracts, trust agreements)
17. Purchase or lease of real property
18. Construction contracts
19. Leases of office and plant equipment
20. Agreements for contract manufacturing of products by or for the company
21. Leases of laboratory and pilot plant equipment and/or facilities
22. Research grants
23. Agreements with clinical investigators or contract research organizations, including indemnity agreements
24. Consultancy and collaboration agreements
25. Screening agreements (unless licensing of patents or know-how is also involved)
26. Agreements for contract manufacture or purchase of chemicals and other specialty supplies
27. Process development and analytical development agreements
28. Options for a license

While the other group may have a standard form contract, every contract is a negotiated agreement between two or more parties and no company should assume that it cannot negotiate every important point. Originals of all contracts should be stored in the same place. Ideally, the company should appoint someone with the responsibility of ensuring that the company fulfills its duties under the contract. This person is usually outside of the legal department.

The legal review of any document is partly intended to ensure that what is written has a single clear meaning that reflects the intent and desires of the client (e.g., a company). The goal is to minimize the opportunities for opposing attorneys, in any future lawsuit, to present a different meaning in court than what the company intended. Attorneys also consider the public relations and corporate politics of material they review as well as laws of the country, regulatory policies, grammar, and possible litigation.

Other Corporate Activities

Some of the other corporate issues that are handled by a company's attorneys include

1. securities and exchange (e.g., stock) issues,
2. antitrust laws,
3. copyrights and trademarks,
4. corporate by-laws,
5. company resolutions, and
6. charters.

The most important and routinely encountered legal issues involve food and medicine law. That topic is discussed further in other sections of this chapter.

Employee Activities That Require Legal Input or Review

Many employee activities require legal help, review, or input. Attorneys have to deal with many questions about company policies and treatment of employees. These include the need for the company, through its legal staff, to do the following.

1. Adhere to all national, state, and local laws (e.g., Antitrust laws, Equal Employment Opportunity laws in the United States). Attorneys may help develop company policies and practices to ensure that the company meets all laws. The attorneys review these policies and may also monitor relevant company practices to ensure that the company is fulfilling its legal responsibilities.

2. Adhere to fair practices within the company to prevent discrimination based on gender, race, religion, handicap, age, or other factors. The basis of this adherence may be law, company guidelines, or commonly accepted ethical standards. Fair balance must be involved in applying such discrimination guidelines because the nature of a position may require particular attributes (e.g., agility) or particular practices (e.g., the wearing of hair nets) that some people may not possess or may not be willing to accept.

3. Provide employees with programs to help individuals with drug abuse, alcohol abuse, or other related problems find means to avoid these practices. Other employees benefits may also require legal input (e.g., disability leave, child care, health care, pensions).

4. Ensure that dismissed employees are treated fairly and that their rights are upheld during termination procedures. In this situation the attorney primarily represents the company's interest.

5. Be informed of its legal obligations regarding potentially hazardous materials that employees are exposed to. There are right-to-know laws in many countries, so employees may learn about the chemicals they work with or are exposed to. Safety in the workplace (e.g, safety glasses, lighting restrictions) is a broader aspect of this issue.

6. Understand immigration law. This need arises when a company desires to employ people from another country. The new employees may or may not already work for the same company in another country.

Attorneys are often involved in what appears to be a difficult position: protecting the rights of both the employees and the company. What is in the interests of one may not be in the interests of the other. For example, if protecting the rights of one or more employees will cost the company a large amount of money, then the interests of the two groups can be viewed as divergent. But if regulatory or other government groups would enact enormous penalties if something was not done for the employee(s), then the interests of the two groups will be more or less consonant. Nonetheless, the company lawyer does not directly represent the interests of employees because the attorney's client is the company.

Company attorneys do not represent employees in an adversarial proceeding versus the company, nor do company attorneys provide advice on personal matters. Employees are urged to hire their own attorneys in relevant situations. On the other hand, an officer of the company sued (in addition to the company) by an outside group would generally be defended by the company's attorneys.

Laws protecting handicapped employees have led to major changes in the design and construction of various facilities as well as in hiring practices within pharmaceutical companies.

Regulatory Activities That Require Legal Input or Review

Interactions between regulatory authorities and regulatory affairs groups within a company encompass the following activities.

1. Evaluation of legal implications and propriety of statements made in regulatory documents and in some or all correspondence submitted to the government. Issues identified are dealt with according to the standard operating procedures of the individual company. These activities and evaluations may have a profound effect on product liability exposure.

2. Review of advertisements and promotions to ensure that they adhere to company standards and regulatory guidelines. Other professionals (e.g., marketing, medical, regulatory affairs) also review these documents. A formal sign-off procedure usually exists, either through routing documents or at formal team meetings.

3. Compliance with environmental regulations. Environmental laws that apply to pharmaceutical companies have become increasingly important and complex over the last decade. This category includes disposal of hazardous waste and low-level radiation waste. Air, water, and

ground pollution must be minimized or totally prevented. This involves not only a recycling of solvents and other materials, but in some countries also includes a degree of responsibility for vendors and their activities. Both the costs of compliance and the potential fines for noncompliance often constitute large sums of money. The interpretation of these laws is often complex and requires considerable expertise.

4. Development of labeling. The team responsible for development of a product's label should always include an attorney. Typically, attorneys evaluate labeling rather than write it. Labeling should avoid any guarantees, warranties, or vague statements. Attorneys look for omissions in the labeling and are sensitive to whether sentences are written in a positive or negative way. The labeling is the means by which the company satisfies its duty to warn, the failure of which can lead to significant product liability risks.

5. Review of scientific discourse in continuing medical education programs, reprints given out by sales representative, and other professional scientific or clinical programs. Review of symposia will be in terms of policies and codes of (1) the company, (2) regulatory authorities, (3) trade associations, and (4) any other groups (e.g., medical societies) that are involved. The credibility of the speakers, medical value of the program, and any sensitive issues are also evaluated.

6. Attendance at meetings. Attorneys often accompany professional staff to meetings with regulatory authorities. In some companies this is mandatory.

An excellent discussion of regulatory law focusing on the United States is given by Hutt and Merrill (1991).

Product Liability Activities That Require Legal Input or Review

When a pharmaceutical company is sued it must prepare its defense. Some companies appear to be more willing than others to settle certain types of cases (i.e., make payment to a plaintiff) without going to trial rather than risk adverse publicity and the possibility of losing even more money. Other companies have a policy of contesting vigorously every legal case that arises. Even the largest pharmaceutical companies do not have a large enough legal staff to take their cases to court themselves. As a result, companies hire outside legal firms to handle their cases. Outside attorneys work closely with internal company attorneys to help prepare the case. The company attorneys (1) assist with identifying expert witnesses, (2) conduct specific investigations to help the case, (3) assist in identifying and obtaining relevant information, (4) arrange depositions, (5) manage outside attorneys, (6) answer interrogatories, and (7) work with outside attorneys in a large variety of other ways. This topic is discussed in greater detail later in this chapter.

Medical Activities That Require Legal Input or Review

Although attorney involvement in medical activities often focuses on regulatory activities, there are additional situations that involve attorneys (e.g., contracts between a company and institutions). Most medical professionals interact with the company's legal staff at several points during their careers. If involvement with the defense of legal cases will be required of medical staff, this should be made clear during the hiring process. Many physicians enjoy the challenges of being involved with legal issues, either in providing legal analyses, depositions, or courtroom testimony. If there is a choice of medical candidates within a company who are needed to assist attorneys, then those people should be chosen for the legal assignment.

While problems with some investigational medicines initiate legal suits, the majority of legal problems a company encounters involve marketed products. As a result, medical staff in Phase IV groups and in marketing support operations are more likely to become involved in legal cases than are those staff in most other clinical areas.

Contracts For Clinical Trials

Prior to 1984, few contracts were drawn up between medical investigators conducting clinical trials and pharmaceutical companies that sponsored them. The number of such contracts and letters of indemnification has grown rapidly over the last decade. Many of these are required by the investigators' institution and some are required by the pharmaceutical company. At present, no statutes require such contracts to be negotiated and signed.

The advantages to drawing up such contracts are that they

1. clarify the basis and details on which the clinical trial is based (e.g., the sponsor owns the data generated);
2. address more potential issues than does an informal letter of understanding between the two parties;
3. may be used to retain rights for the company to any patents resulting from new uses of the medicine;
4. may be used in a positive manner to build a relationship (as opposed to treating the investigators as if they are the enemy);
5. may clarify publication rights (e.g, right of investigator to publish whatever he or she believes based on the data) and specify the prior review by the company (e.g., to ensure no patent problem could arise) and the allowed time allotted for such review; and
6. may clarify details of responsibilities (e.g., financial) for a clinical trial with two or more sponsors.

A standard contract may be processed expeditiously if it is agreed to by the institution and the company.

Disadvantages of clinical trial contracts are that they

1. may delay the start of a clinical trial, possibly by several months, while details are being discussed;
2. may prevent a clinical trial from ever being initiated;
3. require a significant amount of both legal and medical staff time and effort to complete (the time preparing and negotiating a contract might be better applied elsewhere, depending on what other activities are competing for staff time); and
4. may be used for ulterior purposes. For example, either side may insert items into a contract that they know cannot be met; these are then used as "bargaining chips," to give up in exchange for points they strongly wish to retain. This approach may greatly delay or even stifle progress on negotiating the contract.

Adverse Reactions

Attorneys may check to assure that adverse reactions are reported to regulatory authorities, particularly if they are reported to the company through an irregular route. Any adverse reaction represents a potential product liability lawsuit. The connection between adverse reactions and labeling changes is one that must always be considered.

A company may wish to include many possible adverse reactions in the informed consent that the patient signs. The principal investigator may believe that listing more than a few adverse reactions, even as remote possibilities may discourage patient recruitment or may disagree with the listing for other reasons. If either the investigator or Ethics Committee/Institutional Review Board (IRB) says not to include certain adverse reactions in the informed consent, the sponsor has no legal right to insist on their inclusion.

Attorneys are frequently responsible for working with the medical staff who receive and monitor adverse reactions. Attorneys help ensure that systems are in place and operating for the timely reporting of relevant events to regulatory authorities; they also consider the influence, if any, of such reports on product liability.

Patent Law

Patent law is a crucial issue to every company. Patents are the basis of protection of intellectual property and require highly specialized attorneys. Because of this, the patent group is often separated organizationally from other legal activities within a company. This group also may deal with trademarks, copyrights, trade secrets, confidentiality, and disclosure issues. See Chapter 51, Patent Issues.

EDUCATIONAL ROLE OF LEGAL STAFF

Attorneys should become familiar with the procedures and issues involved in discovering and in developing, producing, and marketing new medicines. They should establish strong networks of relationships inside their company with senior professionals in medical, marketing, regulatory, and other departments. A wise attorney may be able to anticipate problem areas at an early stage and counsel physicians, marketers, and others about what activities to modify to avoid litigation. An attorney can also inform staff about the types of legal cases that are likely to involve the medical staff.

Attorneys may want to provide a few open seminars on various topics of the law each year to help educate interested company employees. These talks may include information on compliance with new laws and regulations, as well as review of regulatory policies. Such sessions could enable junior-level employees to identify whether they might like to become more involved in legal activities.

Attorneys help educate company employees in other ways, for example, through training classes for sales representatives and Good Manufacturing Practices (GMP) training for production personnel. Company staff may attend professional meetings that focus on legal issues (e.g., those sponsored by the Food and Drug Law Institute).

ORGANIZATIONAL PLACEMENT OF LEGAL STAFF

All of a company's attorneys may be centrally based in a single legal department. Alternatively, they may be decentralized and located in marketing (e.g., to review advertising and promotion), licensing (e.g., to prepare and review licensing contracts), human resources (e.g., to review employee rights issues), production (e.g., to prepare and review hazardous waste practices, contract manufacturing), medical (e.g., to prepare and review clinical trial contracts), and so forth. Another approach, termed the hybrid approach, is to use both a centralized and decentralized organization.

Within a legal department the regulatory attorneys may be each assigned separate projects (e.g., medicines) and have all legal responsibilities for those medicines. This would include contracts with medical institutions, licensing activities, regulatory activities, and other issues that arose. In contrast to this general approach, a few companies assign all contracts to specialists and all regulatory issues to regulatory attorneys.

PERSONNEL

Internal and External Attorneys

Companies hire outside attorneys to represent them in legal cases, not only because their litigation staff is limited in size, but also because the local attorneys know local rules better and, if state or provincial law applies, are likely to be more familiar with them.

The nature of the relationship between in-house attorneys and external attorneys depends on the company, its traditions, the nature of the case, and the personalities of the people involved. More recently, cost-control has influenced these relationships; attorneys at the outside firm are monitored to ensure that their time is spent productively on the case. Internal lawyers manage and direct the work of outside lawyers.

Plaintiffs Who Sue a Company

A plaintiff is the person, group, or organization who sues another person, group, or organization, called the defendant. Plaintiffs who sue a pharmaceutical company must prove four things to win their case.

1. There was a duty to the consumer (i.e., patients) existing on the part of the pharmaceutical company.
2. A breach of that duty occurred on the part of the pharmaceutical company. For example, the warning given in the label was inadequate.
3. The breach of duty must be shown to have caused the harm (i.e., the medicine must be shown to be a cause of the problem).
4. There must be harm (i.e., damages) that can be determined or quantified (e.g., loss of earnings, pain and suffering). Punitive damages are sometimes assessed.

Perspectives in Legal Cases

In viewing a legal case it is helpful to be aware of the perspectives of various groups that may participate in a courtroom proceeding.

- Attorneys—represent the interest of their client and go all out to win their case as the company's strong adversary.
- Scientists—would like to see a trial as a scientific roundtable where issues are debated and the jury or judge reach a Solomon-like decision. However, trials are a different type of forum where everyone is bound by strict judicial rules of evidence.
- Marketers—view the proceedings as threats to the sales and commercial value of the product on trial. Implications for their company are often great.
- Jury—have an advantage over the other groups in that they can use hindsight in evaluating the case. The jury can assemble all of the information and clearly isolate, for example, the one factor out of an extremely long list that the company forgot to consider, or considered in a less appropriate way, given the benefit of hindsight. The intensity of hectic activity, pressure, stress, and long hours that the company staff may have experienced before reaching a decision, does not generally

exist for a jury that is forced to listen over many hours to a great deal of detailed testimony. On the other hand, most juries and even judges cannot adequately grasp complex scientific and business issues involved in many legal cases involving a pharmaceutical company.

SUITS VERSUS COMPANIES

Many countries outside the United States are passing laws that make it easier to sue pharmaceutical companies than it was in the past. In the United States such suits have been relatively easy for many years. Now that attorneys can legally advertise for clients in the United States, they are able to find large numbers of patients much more easily. Another recent practice that hurts companies is that attorneys can share or sell documents they obtain from companies and also inform other attorneys about the services of specific expert witnesses. When a major new medical problem arises, attorneys advertise their services within days or weeks and rapidly find hundreds or even thousands of clients. The rise of patient interest and involvement in their perceived rights is creating an increasingly hostile environment in which pharmaceutical companies must constantly defend themselves.

The size of legal claims outside the United States is increasing and numerous other countries are expecting higher financial settlements. The system of attorneys accepting contingency fees does not exist outside the United States. But several countries have adopted a system called "legal aid," by which patients petition the government for money to help them sue a pharmaceutical company. This means that the government, in essence, pays the plaintiff to sue the company. Of course the government must believe that the plaintiff has a reasonable case. But if it does, it can supply whatever funds are required to conduct the suit.

In international cases lawyers are paid by the hour. Therefore, it is in the interests of the plaintiff's attorneys to extend the case for as many hours as possible and not settle with the company. Other advantages for the attorneys are to use the media to keep publicity alive, which also helps them obtain more cases. The incentive is quite different, however, in the United States. In the United States it is often in the plaintiff's interests to settle cases rapidly to get the money and pay the contingency fee to the attorney. The attorney also wants to settle in most cases so that he or she can earn the fee and then handle other cases. The contingency fee leads to a larger number of lawsuits and has been referred to as the "poor man's ticket to the courthouse."

Trends in Court Cases

In the 1980s there was often a "partnership" between pharmaceutical companies and physicians who were sued by plaintiffs. When the plaintiff's attorney questioned the physician it was along the lines of whether he or she warned the patient and how well the warning was given. Physicians are sometimes indemnified by companies if they prescribe a medicine according to the labeling and are sued. Such cases are now "dragging" companies into participating in legal cases even where the company is not directly sued.

It has recently been reported that more plaintiffs' attorneys are now asking the physician if the warning provided by the company was really adequate. Prescribers of medicines who are sued about medicine-related problems may think that they can transfer responsibility for the warning onto the pharmaceutical company who made the medicine. As a result more legal cases are being brought by plaintiffs in cooperation with practicing physicians against a pharmaceutical company than in the past.

The Copper 7 Intrauterine Device was taken off the market worldwide solely because of litigation in the United States. The manufacturer (G.D. Searle) felt that it could not keep the product on the market in other countries because of the increased probability of litigation elsewhere. Bendectin was taken off the market because of litigation, even though every independent group that examined the issues of birth defects found no correlation with use of the medicine (see Spilker, 1991 for references).

Some of the trends that many attorneys representing the industry expect are that

1. litigation will become more frequent as more cases are initiated and pursued to court;
2. the costs to defend products will continually rise; and
3. proportionally more cases will come from plaintiffs outside the United States, particularly dealing with the adequacy of warning when different labels are being used worldwide.

A number of pharmaceutical companies have decided that they need a program to prevent, or at least minimize, the number and nature of lawsuits even before a company launches a new medicine.

Many foreigners sue companies in the United States, where the headquarters is based, because of the ease of deposing people and because of the ease of obtaining documents. Furthermore, juries in the United States are viewed as being extremely generous in awarding damages to plaintiffs. Foreigners who file in the United States can often have United States laws apply as to the amount of damages. Lawyers representing clients in international cases are increasingly demanding a large number of documents from companies in the United States.

PRODUCT LIABILITY

Most cases of product liability affecting pharmaceutical companies involve medicines that actually cause harm to patients. There are three theories about manufacturer responsibility that may be used as a basis for such a case: (1) strict liability, (2) negligence, or (3) breach of an actual or implied warranty. The first two theories are most often used in cases of product liability involving medicines, and are briefly described below. Strict liability holds a manufacturer liable for a defective product regardless of fault. The major focus is on the condition of the product itself. Negligence means that the manufacturer must have failed to follow appropriate standards in the product's development or sale. An important caveat known as Comment k is also discussed. Actual cases where each of these concepts applied are not discussed. It is relevant first to describe how companies warn physicians about the risks associated with medicines and how lawsuits arise.

Failure to Warn—the Major Reason for Product Liability

Medical practitioners are the intermediaries (i.e., learned intermediary concept) between the manufacturer and the patients. Companies have a responsibility to warn the medical profession about dangers that they know are associated with, or that they believe are likely to be associated with the use of their product. This responsibility is primarily met by providing a package insert. Other means of discharging this responsibility are mentioned in the next section.

Package inserts for health professionals must be updated according to current knowledge. The manufacturer cannot be expected to know unknown effects of a medicine, unless they should be obvious based on current knowledge. Package inserts for patients are discussed in Chapter 55, Patient Package Inserts.

How Pharmaceutical Companies Warn Physicians About the Risks Associated with a Medicine

Pharmaceutical companies have numerous formats and means available to warn physicians and other health care professionals about risks associated with their medicines. These include the following:

1. the official package insert approved by regulatory authorities in each country;
2. *Physicians' Desk Reference* (PDR) in the United States or other official compendia of information in other countries;
3. detailing information (e.g., brochures, reprints) and materials (e.g., pads of paper, pens, calendars) that identify the product;
4. "Dear doctor" letters;
5. "Dear pharmacist" letters;
6. "Dear hospital administrator" letters;

7. talks by medical professionals at various meetings and conferences; and
8. articles published in the medical literature.

In legal cases the courts attempt to determine if the company adequately communicated an appropriate message about a medicine's risk to the medical profession. It is therefore important for sales representatives to document what they give to a physician as well as what they say to the physician.

Strict Liability

The principle of strict liability describes the theory that the plaintiff injured by a product (e.g., medicine) does not have to prove the manufacturer was negligent. Strict liability, therefore, does not involve fault or bad intentions on the part of the manufacturer. The plaintiff does have to show that the product was defective and that this defect exposed those who used the product to an unreasonable risk of harm. The defect can be in design, manufacture, or failure to adequately warn the physician (or patient for over-the-counter medicines) about the risks of using the product.

The principle of strict liability came into common usage in the 1960s. Prior to that, the attitude of "let the buyer beware" was more appropriate, and strict liability (where the manufacturer was held liable even though there was not negligence) did not really exist. Two reasons are given for the emergence of strict liability. First, manufacturers are better able financially to cover the cost of any harm caused by their medicines (prices can be increased to cover the costs of any lawsuits, thereby spreading the cost of accidents among all users). Second, it is often difficult for a plaintiff to prove that negligence actually exists on the part of the manufacturer, and it is usually much more expensive to conduct this type of case.

Negligence

A manufacturer that fails to use reasonable care in the design and manufacture of a product, or that fails to give reasonable warnings about a product, is guilty of negligence. This was the only legal basis that any person harmed by a medicine had available to prove liability prior to the early 1960s. Negligence still exists as a cause of action. The underlying principle is straightforward in that any company that makes a product and does not use reasonable care is responsible for any injury caused by the product and must pay for the cost resulting from the injury.

Comment k

Comment k represents an important legal principle used in some product liability cases. It refers to situations when products (e.g., medicines) that are "unavoidably unsafe" also have important benefits. The example used in Comment k is that of the Pasteur treatment of rabies. The product used is known to be toxic and unsafe and cannot be made more safe based on available knowledge at the time. But the product also provides a benefit to victims of bites of rabid or probably rabid animals that outweighs the risks of the product's toxicity. This means that pharmaceutical companies are not strictly liable if one of their medicines is appropriately manufactured and if, the physician who uses the medicine in a patient (or recommends its use by a patient) receives appropriate information about the use of the medicine and appropriate warnings about its toxicity. In essence, Comment k establishes a standard of negligence that can be used to judge the behavior of a pharmaceutical company. Comment k differs from strict liability because it requires that a manufacturer knew (or should have known) about the defect when the product was sold in order for the manufacturer to be guilty of negligence. The duty of the manufacturer to warn the learned intermediary is the critical element raised by Comment k.

Learned Intermediary Doctrine

This doctrine states that a manufacturer of prescription medicines discharges its duty to warn its customers (e.g., patients) if it fully informs the physician (the learned intermediary) through the product's labeling. The physician in turn interacts with and warns the patient. The company's duty, according to this doctrine, is only to provide warnings about a medicine to the physician. It has no obligation to warn the patient directly about prescription medicines.

Over the decades since this doctrine was adopted in the late 1940s, a number of exceptions have arisen where courts in several countries have decided that patients must be directly warned by the company about the risks associated with certain medicines. This modification of the learned intermediary doctrine has been applied to the use of contraceptives and vaccines in the United States and to all prescription medicines requiring patient package inserts in European countries. One of the reasons that the two exceptions to the learned intermediary doctrine were enacted in the United States is that a physician does not always see the patient. For example, a woman who goes to a clinic for oral contraceptives, and school children who are vaccinated in their school, do not usually see a physician.

The future of the learned intermediary doctrine is unclear, and some attorneys predict many more exceptions in the future by various courts. One area of potential compromise may arise if companies overpromote their medicines and the courts believe that physicians are being misled by advertisements. A recent article has made this claim (Wilkes et al., 1992). In such cases the courts may find that companies are liable for certain problems encountered by patients.

When a Company Should Add New Warnings to Its Package Insert

A frequently considered question at pharmaceutical companies is when to revise a package insert (i.e., the official labeling). In some cases it is obvious that the label must be changed, in others it is obvious that it should not be, and in still others the decision is uncertain. This last category is discussed below.

Adverse experience reports received by a company from its own as well as other countries (e.g., yellow cards in the United Kingdom, 1639 forms in the United States) are an important source of information about potentially new adverse reactions. If the experiences of all reports received were included in a medicine's label, most medicines would list hundreds of adverse reactions, and physicians, as well as the public would be overwhelmed with generally useless and confusing information. Even if the incidence of reports was included in the labeling the situation would only be partly remedied. The major problem is that of many thousands of adverse experience reports investigated, an assessment of cause and effect is possible in only a few cases. To assume that the medicine has caused all or even most events would only confuse the evaluation of the medicine's true activity.

The following statement occurs on page 194 of the record of Doe V. Miles Laboratories Inc., Cutter Laboratories Division (927F.2d 187, 4th Circuit 1991): "If pharmaceutical companies were required to warn of every suspected risk that could possibly attend the use of a drug, the consuming public would be so barraged with warnings that it would undermine the effectiveness of these warnings. Hence, we find that the risks then known to be associated with the use of Koyne were not explicit enough to expect Miles to have known or foreseen them in September of 1983. Accordingly, because our finding involves no issue of material fact, we affirm the finding of the district court that no warning was necessary to inform the prospective user of the then-suspected risk attending the use of Koyne."

A regulatory authority may request that a company include an adverse reaction in its labeling. If the company disagrees with the request, it may accede to the request or it may present the reasons why it disagrees. If the company appeals the request by presenting another view, then it should follow up to achieve a resolution of the issue. One should never assume that absence of a response means that the regulatory authority has accepted the company's reasoning. When a company is well-informed of the regulatory authority's attitude and behavior, it may assume tacit agreement. However, this is not as desirable as thoroughly documenting the response. There have been cases where the failure of the company to follow up in this situation was taken as evidence by the plaintiff's attorney of a failure by the company to comply with a regulatory request to change the package insert. While that opinion was unjustified in the particular case, the jury had insufficient evidence to accept the company's assertions and characterization of the regulatory authority's usual behavior.

Once a warning about an adverse reaction is placed in a medicine's label, it is very problematic to remove it because the warning can benefit a plaintiff's attorney if any case arises. On the other hand, a company may agree with a regulatory request to add a warning that might not be justified simply to smooth and expedite a medicine's approval. This is an example of a business versus scientific conflict that sometimes arises.

A company that behaves more conservatively would generally desire to include more warnings in a medicine's official label. Some of the signals that a company would be well advised to include a new adverse reaction in its labeling include (1) a significant report in the medical literature, (2) the competition, who markets a similar medicine, placing the warning in their labeling, or (3) class labeling from another country requiring it. If any of these three events occur, or the regulatory authority requests placement of a warning in the label, the company should evaluate the decision carefully following a standard operating procedure.

Investigational Versus Marketed Medicines

Companies are better protected against legal suits for problems with investigational medicines than they are for problems with marketed medicines for the following reasons. The informed consent used in clinical trials describes the risks of the medicine in substantial detail to patients, and patients acknowledge that they are freely taking an experimental medicine. Another reason is that the number of patients exposed to an investigational medicine is usually in the range of 500 to 5,000, whereas the number of patients exposed to a marketed medicine is often hundreds of thousands (or even more). Also, there are relatively few cases in the legal system on investigational medicines, although this may be because companies are more willing to settle such cases out of court to avoid bad publicity.

On the other hand, with little precedent in the law, any particular judge may utilize a different standard for investigational medicines that in essence penalizes the company for its investigational status. It is difficult to obtain evidence in support or to refute effectively the points in this section.

Readers who want to evaluate cases involving investigational (as opposed to marketed) medicines are referred to three cases in the United States:

1. Basko versus Sterling Drug Inc., 416 F. 2d 417 (2d Cir 1969) (New Jersey);

2. Gaston versus Hunter, 121 Ariz. 33588 P.2d 326 (Ct. App. 1978) (Arizona); and
3. Tracy versus Merrell Dow Pharmaceuticals Inc., 58 Ohio St. 3d 147, 569 N.E. 2d 875, 1991 Ohio LEXIS 697 (1991) (Ohio).

Other related cases that may help to establish precedents are

1. Brown versus Superior Court, 44 Ca. 3d 1049, 245 Cal. Rptr. 412, 751 P. 2 d 470 (1988) (California);
2. Grundberg versus The Upjohn Company, 160 Utah Adv. Rep. 20, 1991 Utah LEXIS 44, 813 P. 2d 89 (May, 1991) (Utah);
3. Toner versus Lederle Laboratories, 112 Idaho 328, 732 P. 2d. 297 (1987); and
4. Castrignano versus E.R. Squibb & Sons Inc., 546 A. 2d 775 (R.I. 1988).

Types of Awards

There are three types of damages (i.e., money) awarded in product liability suits.

1. Compensatory damages. These are financial awards for actual harm caused by the product (e.g., medical expenses, loss of earnings). Economist often calculates this value for each side in a dispute.
2. Pain and suffering. These awards attempt to compensate a person for the pain, suffering, or loss of companionship experienced as a result of the injury. It is difficult to assess a fair value for this category of award.
3. Punitive damages. The underlying concept is that malicious conduct (when present) should be punished and deterred. The actual value assigned is often related to the wealth of the guilty party.

The pharmaceutical industry believes that companies should not be subject to punitive damages if all reasonable care has been used during the development of a medicine and it has been approved by the relevant regulatory authorities. There are no objective guidelines for deciding whether or not a court should impose punitive damages.

LITIGATION ARISING FROM ACTIVITIES OF SALES REPRESENTATIVES

Sometimes lawsuits against a pharmaceutical company arise from activities of their sales representatives. Examples of five such situations are given below.

1. Failure to report postmarketing surveillance results of importance or premarketing adverse reactions in detailing a medicine.

2. Minimizing the seriousness of severe adverse reactions that should be mentioned in detailing.
3. Promoting the medicine for an off-label use (i.e., an unapproved indication).
4. Overpromoting a medicine.
5. Ignoring serious warnings mentioned in the medical literature in the detailing of a medicine.

The most well-known legal case that dealt with the failure to mention serious adverse reactions was with MER-29 (Walden, 1985). One aspect of this quite complex case involved sales representatives who neglected to say that the medicine might be able to cause cataracts even though they were aware of data from animal studies that clearly showed corneal opacities. This was interpreted by the court as a presumption of negligence because sales representatives should have mentioned the potential problems to the physicians they detailed.

Another well-known case involving the failure of sales representatives to warn about adverse reactions reported in the literature concerned the risk of thrombembolic disease in women taking oral contraceptives (642 F.2d 652; CCH Prod. Liab. Rep. p. 8914 March 3, 1981). At the time when this problem developed, there was no warning about it in the label and no warning was given to the physician by the sales representative.

An important principle is that it makes no difference if the pertinent information is available to the physician if it is not included in the promotion. Physicians are so inundated with information that sales representatives must provide all warnings to physicians that are important for them to know. Sales representatives have been declared by certain courts to be the most effective means of conveying information from a company to physicians. Therefore, their actions and words supersede the label.

Two other principles that evolved from cases involving sales representatives are that (1) sales representatives may not advise physicians to ignore warnings present in the package insert and (2) a company may not attempt to water down (i.e., dilute) the effect of a "Dear doctor" letter.

The code of marketing practices accepted by the Pharmaceutical Manufacturers Association in the United States and related codes approved in other countries detail specific promotional activities that are unacceptable. One implication of these codes is that breach of those practices could potentially lead to litigation.

Overall, it should be standard practice at pharmaceutical companies that all written material sent to sales representatives is reviewed by the company's legal staff. Sales representatives also should be educated about the codes of acceptable promotional practices that apply to their country. This information should be periodically reinforced in training sessions and in written communications.

PREPARING NONLEGAL STAFF FOR PRESENTATIONS IN COURTROOM CASES

Distinctions Among Medicine, Science, and Law

Practicing physicians are trained to believe that achieving a positive medical outcome in their patients is the most important part of their work. Scientists believe that the scientific method is the best approach to learning the truth. In law, the process and procedures themselves are extremely important. Attorneys generally believe that if everyone follows the rules and procedures the right outcome will occur (at least in most cases); they therefore view due process as very important. Physicians and scientists may believe that the process itself hampers the attempt to establish the scientific and medical truth. This distinction explains why many physicians and scientists are often frustrated by legal proceedings and are unhappy in court. Moreover, the legal system uses an adversarial approach that may make the physician or scientist feel that he or she is personally on trial. An intensive deposition during the discovery process or an intensive cross-examination in court is not designed to make physicians or scientists feel good about themselves.

Choosing Expert Witnesses

A company that is sued often looks to outside physicians as expert witnesses. This is because their own physicians have an inherent conflict of interest based on being a paid employee of the company (i.e., there is a question of their impartiality, regardless of their true expertise, reputation, or impartiality). Independent consultants, academic physicians, physicians in private practice, and those working for other pharmaceutical companies are all suitable candidates.

The budget for a lawsuit may influence which experts a small or financially limited company chooses. Rates for internationally known and respected experts are usually much greater than for less well-known local scientists and clinicians. Attorneys ask colleagues and others for names of potential experts who have been good witnesses in the past. It is also beneficial to call as expert witness someone who can relate well to people and be personable with the jury. If a case is being tried in a rural area, it is usually important to have a local expert to complement a "big city" expert.

Training Physicians and Scientists for a Legal Case

Scientists or physicians who are inexperienced with legal proceedings and the process of written and oral discovery should never be exposed to their first deposition without adequate preparation. Adequate preparation is usually planned and supervised by the company's attorney and may include watching a videotape of a deposition or a videotape that describes the process. Another means of educating physicians is to have them attend a courtroom trial to observe the process. A conversation with the defense attorney they will work with should be mandatory. It would be a major misjudgment to assume that scientific or medical experts will learn "on-the-job," particularly because they might inadvertently say or do something to jeopardize the company's case.

Some of the specific principles of courtroom conduct that are second nature to most attorneys but that should be communicated to both neophyte and legally experienced expert witnesses include the following.

1. Learn when during the proceedings you may enter the courtroom. Arrange to be told by someone when that time has come.
2. Be quiet (i.e., do not discuss a case) in the restroom or in courtroom hallways.
3. Do not show emotions in the courtroom.
4. Do not talk very much in the courthouse or in public areas where a deposition is to be taken.
5. Learn what you may (or should) take to the witness stand in terms of papers, notes, books.
6. Do not give caveats to every question in front of a jury, unless instructed to do so.
7. Answer most questions in one or a few words, unless there is a specific point the expert wishes to make. This is particularly true for answering questions of the plaintiff's attorney.
8. Speak clearly to the jury and in an appropriate tone, assuming that they are interested in being educated.
9. Do not speak over the head of the jury, but attempt to communicate to them as if one is addressing patients, or nonprofessional friends.
10. Explain terms that may not be familiar to the jury, and keep jargon to an absolute minimum.
11. Answer only the question asked by an attorney and do not anticipate the following one. For example, the answer to the question "Do you know the color of the chair?" is "Yes" not "Red." Likewise the answer to the question "Do you have an opinion about X?" is "Yes," and not "I believe that. . . ."
12. Learn the differences in definitions of relevant terms that are used differently in law and medicine. For example, authoritative means that everything included in the document is 100% accurate and true—when the word is used, legally; but, when it is used in a medical context, "authoritative" means that the person who made the statement or wrote the material is recognized as an expert and that many or most people would accept the comments. Causality means a strong cause and effect relationship exists when the term is used legally, but the term only means that there is a certain probability of the event occurring when the term is used medically.

13. Learn how to deal with a harsh attorney who belittles the expert. The guiding principle is to be polite and not to allow the attorney to make one upset.

14. Request as much data as you need to prepare your case. If certain essential data are not provided, you still should have asked for them.

15. Start to prepare for a deposition or trial a few weeks ahead of time. Suggest exhibits to the attorney that could be prepared to help you explain your points to a jury or judge.

16. Sit erect on a chair with both feet on the floor when you are being videotaped during a deposition or during courtroom testimony.

17. Dress appropriately (i.e., conservatively).

18. Learn how to address the judge (i.e., your honor) as well as when one may address the judge directly.

19. Do not be impatient with procedures, questions, or delays. It may encourage the plaintiff's attorney to drag out the proceedings even more. Impatience makes a bad impression on a jury and may affect one's credibility.

Pretrial and Predeposition Preparation

Scientists and physicians should make sure that the company's attorney will help them to be well-prepared for a deposition or trial. The expert should not accept secondary preparation, nor allow themselves to be "mistreated." Some attorneys prepare loose-leaf study books for witnesses to help in their preparation.

Discuss with your attorney, or with the attorney with whom you are working, what approach or strategy they wish to take in regard to your testimony. It is acceptable (before a trial) for the attorney to inform you about the general types of questions he or she will ask. It is also possible to learn the actual questions and to review one's answers with one's attorney. An important point for professionals who become involved in legal issues is that any impatience and anxiety to complete the proceedings and to stop "playing legal games" is not shared by the attorneys and may get their side into trouble.

The attorney may also indicate the types of questions that are likely to be raised on cross-examination by the opposing attorney. Appropriate responses may be discussed and certainly the demeanor to be used in responding is invariably discussed. The preceding section on general principles describes several of the important lessons to be learned ahead of time.

The other side's attorney(s) must be thought of as an adversary dedicated to discrediting your testimony and even your character. Whether that attorney appears to be a "nice" person or a "nasty" one, one must never relax in responding to a question. Admit the obvious, be straightforward, and avoid caveats, if possible. State if a question cannot be answered with a yes or no response.

Two Approaches to Presenting Expert Testimony

Experts must present their testimony using language that the jury and judge will understand. A number of principles of how to present testimony are given above, and two approaches or strategies to organize the testimony are mentioned below. The approach to use in a particular case may be decided upon by the attorney or physician (scientist) alone or through a joint discussion.

Major Opinion(s) Model

If there is a large amount of information—including particularly complex material—in a legal case, it may be best to identify the one, two, or three most important and crucial points to convey and to limit one's testimony to those issues. In this approach the expert states that after examining all of the information, he or she had one to three major opinions. These opinions are then stated. After stating the opinions succinctly, subsequent testimony would focus on the issues regarding each opinion in turn. The defense attorney would systematically explore each opinion using the same series of questions if possible. One series could include the following questions for each major opinion.

- Please explain what your first statement means.
- What are the reasons for your opinion?
- What is the evidence that supports each of these reasons?

After all opinions are explored then every major statement would be repeated and a conclusion made.

Progressive Unfolding Model

This model is like an archery target where the crux of the issue (i.e., the bull's eye) is first described. The information that is most directly relevant to addressing that point is described, followed by a description and discussion of progressively less relevant issues. This archery target concept must be kept in mind as one progresses through the testimony and answers cross-examination because the other attorney is likely to try to confuse the pattern described by the expert.

The expert leads the jury (or judge[s]) stepwise through the material following a logical and (it is hoped) common sense approach. A series of exhibits should be utilized if possible to assist in this process. Exhibits are usually large, easy-to-read poster boards set on an easel for the jury and judge to study as the expert moves over from the witness stand (if allowed by the court) to point out pertinent aspects.

GOOD LEGAL PRACTICES FOR NONATTORNEYS TO FOLLOW IN A COMPANY

From a purely legal perspective a company is better off if it does not sell any medicines; then the company's liability risk would be zero. Attorneys strive to decrease and minimize the risk to a company. Some guiding principles that, if followed by all company staff, can help minimize the risk of litigation, follow.

1. Do not write memoranda or other documents with imperative, inflammatory, or emotional statements. Take the necessary time to cool one's temper before putting one's thoughts on paper. Statements that "come from the heart" somehow look different when analyzed with the brain, particularly if this is done in court. Moreover, the parties involved may have left the company, but have left a paper trail unfairly documenting possible or actual issues and problems.

2. Documents should be perused before they are entered into the company archives/records to ensure that appropriate principles are being upheld. Eliminate documents from the company's records after a few years according to the company's records retention policy. A commonly heard statement from attorneys is to save as few written records as possible, and primarily just those of high quality.

3. Many industry documents are not subject to limited record retention schedules and must be saved for long periods. These include data collection forms, clinical trial protocols, and all documents submitted or that may be submitted to a regulatory authority. Regulations and company practice govern the duration of their retention.

4. Institute procedures within the company to settle disputes in a fair way and in an appropriate forum. Preventing interpersonal and even professional-based disputes from disrupting a company is important.

5. Be as accurate and systematic as possible and institute careful reviews of company policies. Increased regulatory attention to promotions that are unacceptable can cause the company significant harm if unacceptable practices prevail.

Adherence to basic legal principles spread by brochures, memoranda, and seminars in a company, plus appropriate standard operating procedures, will help prevent legal suits and ensure that the company is best able to defend itself against those that do arise. The myriad of other legal activities should also be discussed with appropriate employees.

53 / Financial Issues

Corporate Issues............................... **637**
  Comparing the Financial Status of Companies 637
  Financial Parameters That May Be Used as a
    Company's Goal 637
  Joining Financial Policies to Corporate
    Objectives................................. 638
  Degree of Acceptable Financial Risk 638
  Financial Forecasts 638
  Sources of Financing 639
  Purposes of Budgets 640
  Allocation of Resources...................... 640
  Psychological Aspects of Spending Money on
    Questionable Projects 641
  Transfer Pricing 641
  Cost-Effectiveness Data 642
  Differences in Accounting Principles Between
    Functions of a Company 642
Research and Development Budget **642**
  Essential Questions to Address............... 642
  Organizing the Research and Development
    Budget................................... 642
  Accountability for the Research and
    Development Budget...................... 642

  Determining the Size of the Research and
    Development Budget...................... 643
  Justifying the Size of the Research and
    Development Budget...................... 644
  Allocating Research and Development Funds 644
  Tax Implications of the Research and
    Development Budget...................... 645
  Clinical Trial Budgets....................... 645
Research and Development Expenditures **645**
  Definitions of Categories Used to Track
    Expenditures.............................. 645
  Accounting for Research and Development
    Expenditures.............................. 645
  Presenting Data on Research and
    Development Expenditures................. 647
  Interpreting Data on Research and
    Development Expenditures................. 651
  Forecasting Future Research and Development
    Expenditures.............................. 651
  Financial Analyses of Projects 653

We demand that big business give the people a square deal; in return we must insist that when any one engaged in big business honestly endeavors to do right he shall himself be given a square deal. President Theodore Roosevelt. From *Autobiography.*

CORPORATE ISSUES

This chapter does not present or discuss detailed financial aspects of running a company, how to improve a company's financial performance, or detailed analyses of financial issues. Rather this chapter identifies some of the important financial issues a company faces. This chapter is written for the neophyte in financial matters who is interested in an overall view of financial issues within a pharmaceutical company.

Comparing the Financial Status of Companies

All pharmaceutical companies frequently compare their financial status with other companies and with aggregated values. The most common parameter measured is in terms of sales. But sales can be total company sales or only those of pharmaceutical products. If pharmaceutical products are compared, one issue is whether over-the-counter medicines (OTCs) should be included. Then, it becomes apparent that a company with higher profits for a given level of sales may be considered as doing better.

The fact is that there are many important parameters to use that are much more informative than sales (Table 53.1), and many of these are used by most companies. Some are focused on as of particular importance for creating and/or achieving company goals.

Financial Parameters That May Be Used as a Company's Goal

Although it is not essential for a company to establish and use specific financial goals, such goals facilitate an

TABLE 53.1. *Selected categories to use in comparing the financial status of pharmaceutical companies*

1. Pharmaceutical sales
2. Pharmaceutical sales as a percentage of total sales
3. Budget allocated to research and development
4. Budget of research and development as a percentage of pharmaceutical sales
5. Total sales
6. Growth rate of sales over three years (or another time period)
7. Total research and development budget as a percentage of total sales
8. Net income
9. Growth rate of net income over three years (or another time period)
10. Total assets
11. Pretax income as a percentage of total sales
12. Return on equity
13. Number of employees
14. Sales per employee
15. Sales per square foot
16. Net income per employee
17. Inventory turnover[a]
18. Current assets divided by current liabilities (i.e., current ratio)[b]
19. Long-term debt, other notes, and loans divided by shareholders' equity (i.e., debt-to-equity ratio)[c]
20. End-of-fiscal year common stock price divided by the earnings per share for that fiscal year (i.e., price-to-earnings ratio)[d]
21. Units produced per payroll dollar

[a] This parameter is a measure of operational efficiency.
[b] This parameter is a measure of short-term solvency.
[c] This parameter is a measure of credit worthiness.
[d] This parameter is a measure of value for shareholders.

evaluation of each time period and also serve as a motivator of staff. A company may use any specific measure or series of measures for this purpose. A few common measures are

1. percentage of growth in sales per year,
2. percentage of return on sales per year,
3. percentage of return on net assets,
4. percentage of growth in earnings per share, and
5. pretax profits.

Once a measure to use is chosen, it is necessary to set a specific quantitative goal. This may be done as

1. a minimum percentage of increase per year,
2. an ideal percentage of increase hoped for per year,
3. a range from the minimum to the ideal,
4. a realistic target goal from within the range, or
5. a target that tracks the industry average.

The above assessments are all intracompany. It is also important to compare the company to others in the industry. This can be done using any of the five measures above or others that are chosen. Some of the most important goals used are pretax profit per employee, sales per employee, and research and development spending as a percentage of sales. Others are shown in Table 53.1.

Joining Financial Policies to Corporate Objectives

A company's corporate objectives and goals include financial objectives and goals. These may be used to help ensure that the company's detailed financial policies and procedures are directed toward meeting these goals. If they are not, then it would be essential to redirect the financial policies and procedures or to establish new ones. Progress toward financial goals must be monitored and reviewed. Procedures to conduct various financial activities must be developed that are in concert with policies.

Accounting practices should be changed whenever necessary to better reflect company practice within the limits of generally accepted accounting principles. Accounting procedures should be viewed as to their true purpose of helping to record and communicate business transactions. They are most useful in doing this when they are closely tied to actual business practice, and are expressed in easily understood terms. The "numbers" are an aid in decision making, and should be used as a tool and not as an oracle or as an end in themselves.

Degree of Acceptable Financial Risk

The degree of financial risk that is acceptable to a company is a policy issue decided by the chief executive officer or the company's board of directors. The risk deemed acceptable varies widely between companies and within a company at different periods. Companies determine acceptable risk based on numerous factors including (1) stability of the core business(es), (2) current rates of return on the company's investments, (3) financial and other corporate goals, (4) degree of solvency, (5) degree of operating leverage (relationship of fixed to variable costs), (6) personalities of the senior managers, (7) preferences of certain important outside groups (e.g., bankers, shareholders), and (8) opportunities available. The answer to this question of acceptable risk influences many other business decisions made by a company and reflects itself in the company's reputation in the business community as relatively risk-oriented or risk-averse. Financial risk issues are even more complex within multinational companies, especially during periods of rapidly fluctuating currency exchange rates.

Financial Forecasts

How far into the future should a company attempt to extend its financial forecast and plans? The horizon in some businesses (e.g., dress designers) is short and even a single year may be too long. In others, a 20-year cycle is necessary (e.g., forest products, because of the life cycle of trees that are harvested). For medicines, a three- to seven-year time period is reasonable, given that the usual length of time required to bring a new medicine to market may be up to 14 years. The major parameters used to develop a financial forecast are sales forecasts, promotional expenses, capital items, head count, and noncapitalized expenses (e.g., clinical trial costs, grants to investigators). These categories are also accounted for at the end of each year. At that time the previous year's forecast is compared with the actual expenses incurred. In addition, most companies compare spending and sales against budget on a monthly basis. Finally, all personnel, capital, and noncapital items from all company functions may be folded together to give an overall expense and capital investment picture of the short-term budget and the long-term forecast.

Early discussion of potential or likely financial problems to be faced during the prospective three- to ten-year period is important. This discussion would allow senior managers to take preventive steps to avoid problems and also to determine how tightly to control head count and other expenditures.

An ideal financial model considers all relevant inputs and gives the most senior managers as accurate a projection as possible of the company's performance usually over the next 3 to 10 years. The inputs into the financial model include those parameters listed in Table 53.3. Different outputs may be obtained from using this model (e.g., net present value, internal rate of return). The

model may be used to evaluate different pricing strategies (see Chapter 59, Costs and Pricing). Figure 53.1 shows how future sales can be projected using either current products or new expected products (both adjusted for likely terminations). If a company has a goal or objective, then that information may be illustrated for comparison as well as the expected mean industry growth.

Sources of Financing

There are three usual approaches to financing a company's activities. These are to use internal, external, or a combination of financial sources. The overall degree to which each is used depends on many factors that are well-known to financial professionals. Actual choices, however, are often based on personal decisions of the chief executive officer, or are politically influenced by the board of directors and/or key outsiders. Carefully developed criteria are sometimes used to establish the basis for reaching a decision. Even if this logical approach is followed it will be necessary to adjust the criteria used to meet each specific situation. This is because conditions relating to criteria change, and there are specific situations for which certain criteria may not be ap-

PROJECTION TO 1996
SALES GROWTH INDEX

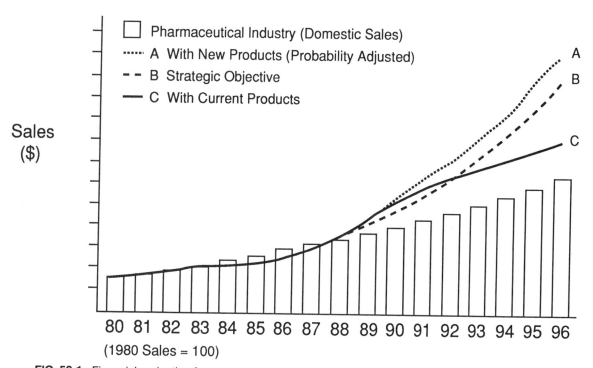

FIG. 53.1. Financial projection for a company over a number of years, with different assumptions shown in the figure. The *bars* represent the industry average.

propriate. The question of whether to finance multiple businesses of a company separately or collectively generally depends on the company's objectives, as well as on the overall organization of those businesses.

Purposes of Budgets

Budgets are considered an essential device in almost every company, and they serve several functions.

1. *Coordination.* Budgets coordinate the activities of each group within a company or organization. They prevent a single group from conducting a much larger (or smaller) number or range of activities than desired.

2. *Communication.* Budgets communicate to managers (in a top-down manner) their spending limits, both minimal and maximal, and communicate among groups within a company about which groups will be doing more (or fewer) activities. This helps others (e.g., service groups) plan their future activities. Budgets also communicate the needs of line managers to senior management in a bottom-up manner.

3. *Benchmarks.* Budgets provide one means to measure performance. Status on monthly progress can be shown easily in tables or figures.

4. *Accountability.* Managers who greatly exceed their budgets without acceptable reasons are usually held accountable for their actions.

5. *Management Tool.* Managers who review performance versus budget find budgets useful to question what happened and why it did. This is an effective means of learning and guiding future plans and actions, as well as identifying problems for current management action.

Allocation of Resources

Corporate resources are allocated to various activities in a complex manner that differs greatly from company to company and from time to time within any company. Decision makers who allocate capital and other resources to capital equipment and facilities, acquisitions, spending on core businesses, and dividends to stockholders are the most senior managers of a company.

A closely related issue is that of forecasting the availability of future resources, especially capital resources. Standard financial techniques used to determine these numbers are available in financial textbooks. Monitoring previous forecasts within the company will indicate the degree of accuracy of methods used and ways in which methods were used. Ongoing monitoring of past resource allocations and utilizations as shown in Fig. 53.2 is another integral part of being able to forecast future needs for resources. Ongoing monitoring is usually conducted within the overall corporation as well as within each subsidiary company business or division. It is also possible to conduct this activity at a department or even section level.

Senior company managers must decide how much risk they are willing to take when they approve the re-

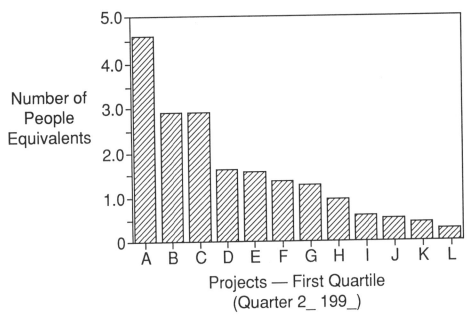

CLINICAL STATISTICS PROJECT EFFORTS

FIG. 53.2. Illustrating the staff assigned to a select group of projects (i.e., first quartile) for a specific period. Similar graphs may illustrate other time periods, other portions of the portfolio, or other departments.

search and development budget. Regardless of a company's current financial performance, rationales are readily available and are used to justify spending more, less, or the same amount of money on research and development in the future. This is discussed later in this chapter. The amount of risk that the top research and development managers want to take and their plans for the money included in the budget request should be explainable to the company's top nonscientists. Nonscientists should never accept comments along the lines of "This is too technical to explain to this group," or "The scientific reasons are too complex to simplify." Senior managers were hopefully chosen for their superior intelligence and their ability to understand principles. These nonscientists may request or hire other scientists to evaluate any detailed scientific hypotheses, concepts, or rationales. This could be handled either by contacting noncompany board members who are scientists or by approaching independent consultants.

Senior company managers should also assure themselves that there is an appropriate balance between resources allocated to medicine discovery, medicine development, and market support. Without an appropriate balance (which will likely change over the years) for the entire company, it is easy for a company to stray in the wrong direction. This is a major pitfall to avoid.

Psychological Aspects of Spending Money on Questionable Projects

One particular issue will be addressed. This is the question of deciding whether to spend additional money on a project about which serious questions have arisen after a moderate or large amount of money has already been spent. This important issue appears to arise quite often at all levels of decision making. Arkes and Blumer (1985) investigated this phenomenon, and they reported that there is definitely a greater tendency to continue work and spend money on a highly questionable endeavor after some money and effort has been expended and invested. More importantly, they observed that the chances of success of the undertaking are inflated by those who have incurred the sunk cost as opposed to those who have not.

Projects and other activities develop momentum once they are initiated and after a period of time take on a life of their own. It therefore takes more courage for managers to question and stop a project after it is initiated than before it is begun. There is also a strong theoretical basis to the fact that people are often willing to "throw good money after bad." This is why one frequently reads statements such as "To terminate a project in which $1.1 billion has been invested represents an unconscionable mishandling of taxpayers' dollars" (Senator Denton, November 4, 1981, quoted by Arkes and Blumer, 1985).

Some research and development directors require virtually 100% certainty that a project has no potential to succeed before they are willing to terminate it. This means that they will be investing money when the chance is over 90% that success will not be achieved. Other directors are willing to terminate a project at an earlier stage and place resources on other projects with a higher likelihood of success. The difference in behavior between two such directors could be viewed as one company moving ahead in a series of competitive races with one or more albatrosses around their neck. If one assumes that each company began each race with approximately equal resources (which is rarely true) then the one who sheds albatrosses, or does not acquire any, has a better chance of winning an important race against their competitors.

Transfer Pricing

Different businesses, divisions, or departments within a company often provide services for other parts of the company or to other business units. In addition to services, chemicals, medicines, or intermediate products may be "sold" within the company or overall business entity. The value to set for these services or goals (transfer price) and the manner of handling these transactions varies widely between companies, and also between different business groups within the same company.

Labor charges for employees in one business doing work for another business may be sold at cost. This cost usually includes an amount for overhead. The amount one business or function charges another may be based on (1) actual hours of time spent, (2) standard costs for products, (3) an average number of hours per year, (4) a percentage of one group's budget for negotiated services, or (5) a contractual basis that deals with each request for services as a separate contract to be negotiated. Tax considerations are often a critical factor in choosing which method(s) to use.

A major issue that arises in transfer pricing relates to the amount of money charged and how this figure is derived. There are many implications relating to these decisions. One concerns the amount of duty paid to customs for importation of a medicine. The greater the declared value, the greater (generally) is the customs duty, and vice versa. But, if the declared value is set at a low figure, then the amount the company may eventually be allowed to charge for the medicine in many countries will also be affected. In some situations it is possible to set a relatively low value for an investigational medicine and to raise it at a later date, after the medicine has been approved for marketing. Tax paid on a higher profit will be higher, so that tax rate differentials need to be considered.

Medicine supplies are transferred from one part of a company to another, as (1) finished goods ready for sale, (2) bulk medicine needing packaging, (3) raw medicine needing packaging, (4) raw medicine needing formulation, or (5) as a chemical that may or may not require additional synthetic steps. Major issues relating to medicine transfer charges involve customs, taxes, import and export valuations, and duties. When a medicine is manufactured at one site and shipped to another country for sale, the subsidiary country receiving the medicine pays the manufacturing company. This payment is usually done by adjusting the current account ("the books") between the two companies.

Cost-Effectiveness Data

Future large-scale purchasers of medicines at health maintenance organizations (HMOs), preferred provider organizations (PPOs), and hospital chains will demand to see more cost-analysis data before they are willing to put a newly approved medicine on their formulary. Cost-benefit and cost-effectiveness analyses are not discussed in this section. A brief review is included in Chapter 42 of *Guide to Clinical Trials* (Spilker, 1991). The calculation of costs involved in conducting medical trials and in developing an entire medicine from start to finish are described in Chapter 130 of *Guide to Clinical Trials* (Spilker, 1991).

Differences in Accounting Principles Between Functions of a Company

Combining financial statements from multiple subsidiaries into a consolidated single company statement is a complex endeavor with multiple accounting issues. Different countries handle many accounting issues using different systems and definitions that make consolidation of various figures extremely difficult. The way that is usually taken to get out of this dilemma is to utilize a number of assumptions and conventions, and to follow them consistently. By adhering to the same approaches each year, one year's set of numbers may be compared with others.

RESEARCH AND DEVELOPMENT BUDGET

Essential Questions to Address

The major financial question in research and development for most companies is how much money is the company willing to invest to generate new medicines. Concomitantly, another issue is how the funds will be spent (i.e., on internally generated medicines, licensed medicines, or purchased medicines). Most other consid-

erations about what can be afforded flow from decisions reached on these two questions.

Although most of this section concerns a research and development budget as a whole, there are various other budgets that could be and are often prepared. These include business area budgets (e.g., diagnostics, over-the-counter medicines [OTCs], pesticides), therapeutic area budgets, and individual project budgets. Some companies have many groups within a research and development group that are primarily service in function (e.g., computer services, photography, library, engineering, information services). This may complicate comparisons made between companies.

Organizing the Research and Development Budget

The research and development budget may be organized by individual department functions, or by products (i.e., projects), or a mixture of both. If the department approach is used, each department may be subdivided by projects they are working on and/or by their functions.

The amount of detail and effort to put into a budget must be carefully evaluated. Too much time, energy, and paperwork devoted to completing budgets may not be productive. Part of the reason for this is that many factors and activities will change before the budget year is completed. Projects will be added and dropped or new responsibilities may totally reshape how the allocated money is being spent. In viewing the appropriate amount of time to spend preparing a budget, it must be decided "if the juice is worth the squeeze."

The law of diminishing returns is very steep in this area, in terms of the effort expended and increased accuracy or benefits obtained. It takes moderate effort to develop a reasonable plan and often a great deal of effort to make it fairly accurate. Additional accuracy usually requires a disproportionate amount of time and money and even then may not achieve the goal because of the reasons stated above. It is virtually impossible to create totally accurate plans (or budgets). The only thing one knows for certain about a plan is that it is wrong. It is desirable to assess in hindsight in what ways it was wrong, and by how much. This may help the planning process improve its accuracy in future cycles.

Accountability for the Research and Development Budget

On a retrospective basis, senior managers within research and development (or at the corporate level) may ask for a synopsis of progress achieved with money spent over the last "X" years. This accountability for moneys allocated to research and development may be handled in several different ways. Ultimately, the issue boils down to one of trust. Either the most senior managers trust their subordinate managers and delegate them responsibilities and resources or they do not. If not, confrontational and uneasy situations are likely to occur within management, and the morale of the organization may become adversely affected. Tension created by management uneasiness over financial matters may filter down to staff and affect or even disrupt scientific creativity and productivity.

Determining the Size of the Research and Development Budget

The question of how much money is necessary or advisable to spend on research and development certainly could be dealt with in several long chapters, if not a book. The most appropriate answer for a research-based company depends on numerous factors, many of which change from year to year. Most importantly, science requires a long-term company commitment to maintain an appropriate spending level to keep scientists both productive and happy. Spending levels that do not achieve this result can have devastating effects on a company's morale and productivity that may be extremely difficult to repair in the short term. Scientists, as others, understand that there are sometimes compelling reasons to cut their budget (e.g., for the company's health), but they

expect cuts to be applied fairly and appropriately throughout the organization. One means of visualizing the budget is in terms of progressively smaller sections of a pie as one moves to smaller groups within an organization. This is shown in Fig. 53.3.

The amount of research and development's budget relates to considerations of the past, present, and future nature of a company's internal environment as well as to the external environment that affects the company. Approaches to determining the size of a budget for research and development may focus in a major or minor way on one or more of the following.

1. Identifying an appropriate percentage of sales to allocate to research and development. Some companies follow this approach in part because it allows them to easily calculate the size of the budget and track changes and trends.

2. Identifying a percentage of profits. This parameter is more reflective than percentage of sales of a company's financial health. On the other hand, profits are often highly volatile and do not provide as stable a base as sales.

3. Comparing a company with its major competitors. The research and development budget of comparably sized companies of the same general type (e.g., research-based) and productivity are used to help determine an approximate range of spending needed to support research and development activities.

GENERATING A BUDGET

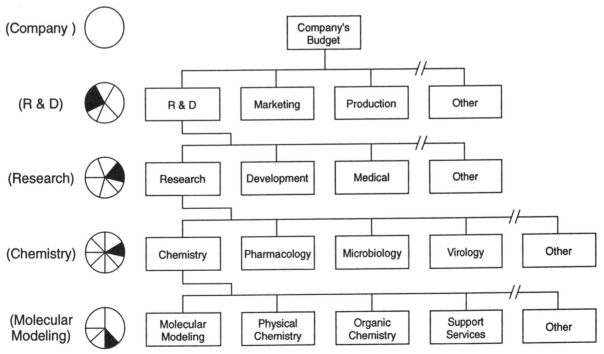

FIG. 53.3. Illustrating the hierarchical levels in a company at which actual budgets exist, from the overall company to individual sections within a department. Successively smaller slices of the "financial pie" illustrate this concept for the groups shown.

4. Developing mathematical models to extrapolate past research and development expenditures required for maintaining an acceptable level of productivity into the future. This approach requires a large amount of data to develop a valid model, depends on many assumptions regarding the nature of future productivity, and may not be more accurate or appropriate than using either of the above methods.

5. Taking the current budget and increasing it by a percentage that accounts for inflation and what is considered to be appropriate growth. This is the method apparently used by United States presidents in calculating certain parts of the nation's budget.

6. Identifying all major activities to be conducted over the coming year and adding the costs together to derive a total. This approach has the disadvantage that activities planned and those conducted often differ.

Justifying the Size of the Research and Development Budget

The author's opinion is that each of the approaches described above can be used to justify any given amount of money considered necessary to spend on research and development. The question is whether a company picks a number and works backward to justify it, or works forward to identify what an appropriate number should be.

If a company is doing well financially, then a strong case could be made for any of the following possibilities: (1) maintain research and development (R and D) spending at the present level to keep the company prospering, (2) increase R and D spending to further fuel the company's development and growth and exploit the productivity of R and D, or (3) decrease R and D to use some of the money "saved" to fund other ventures.

If a company is doing poorly financially, then arguments could also be made to (1) maintain R and D spending at the same level because the company cannot afford more funds and it is important not to cut back on the budget at a time when a successful medicine is desperately needed; (2) increase R and D spending because, if a new significant medicine is discovered, it will provide the company with the greatest potential economic benefit; or (3) decrease R and D spending, possibly by cutting out research in those areas least likely to be productive, and thus increase the chance of continuing in those areas with the greatest likelihood of success.

These brief comments indicate only a few of the many arguments that may be used to support any position on how to determine and justify the research and development budget, regardless of the financial position of the company. The exact reasoning chosen may be utilized before the budget is selected, to help determine its most appropriate size. Alternatively, this exercise may be un-

dertaken after a draft or final budget is established, as a means of justifying the size of the budget chosen. Licensing-based companies that solely develop medicines discovered by others or are generic manufacturers with little research or development costs have somewhat different considerations. There is usually a greater degree of certainty that their planned activities on medicine development will be actually conducted.

Allocating Research and Development Funds

There is a common misconception that pharmaceutical companies have broad flexibility to use the many millions in their research and development budget much as a gambler uses poker chips. In this metaphor the company places more or fewer chips (i.e., resources) on one project or another. That scenario would generally be liked by senior managers if it were true. It would allow them to move resources easily to have one or more projects move rapidly ahead. The facts, however, are that fixed costs plus management and administrative costs take up a substantial portion of the research and development budget dollars. Even after all fixed costs are allocated, there are many types of technical support services that must be financed before the relatively few discretionary dollars may be placed on the hot leads or exciting projects. Furthermore, even applying large resources of money and professional staff on a project cannot always move important projects ahead more rapidly. There may be rate-limiting steps that take time to complete before further work may be conducted. In addition, almost any type of preclinical, clinical, regulatory, or technical problem may arise that delays progress.

Fixed costs in a budget include salaries of permanent employees, their fringe benefits, rent on space, lease payments on equipment, utilities, taxes, depreciation, and any allocated costs passed on from the overall corporation (e.g., computer services, other company costs). Administrative costs include the many services provided by nonresearch and development groups including: personnel, payroll, finance, employee benefits, graphics, purchasing, engineering, maintenance, counseling, and training. Technical support services that are usually placed within research and development include: animal maintenance, library and information services, regulatory affairs, data processing, statistical services, project planning and tracking, computer services, analytical laboratories, and formulation laboratories. All of these costs must be allocated regardless of the specific work they perform.

The remaining funds that are available to pay for emphasizing one project versus another are rather limited when expressed as a percentage of the total research and development budget. If a company reemphasizes or reallocates their efforts on projects, it would be desirable to confirm that desired changes have in fact been appropriately initiated and followed. This may be done by evaluating time and effort reporting forms that track actual time spent by scientists and other personnel.

Tax Implications of the Research and Development Budget

A tax credit is granted to a company for moneys spent on research and development in the United States and most other countries. In the United States some companies may obtain a small additional percentage tax credit for money spent on clinical trials of officially approved orphan medicines. This is described in the Orphan Drug Act of 1983. This tax credit applies from the time that the orphan application is approved until the time that the New Drug Application (NDA) is approved. Part of the research and development budget may therefore be viewed as being "paid" by taxes saved because of various tax deductions the company takes.

One question that arises is whether money used to fund research and development should come from company profits, borrowed funds, or stock sold to generate cash. Research-based companies usually use company profits, whereas start-up companies often fund research and development from proceeds of stock sales and borrowed money.

Clinical Trial Budgets

The budget may be prepared if the head counts are known beforehand for the next fiscal year. It is important to jointly plan clinical grants and head counts to obtain the necessary balance. Budgets for trials paid for by marketing may be a special case, particularly if they are conducted within medical. To shift money earlier in time (for budgetary reasons) it is often possible to initiate trials earlier or to pay investigators or external contract groups earlier (see below). Another approach is to purchase materials to make investigational medicines earlier, although there are limits to how much time may elapse after the end of a fiscal year by which the medicine must be used to consider the expense in the earlier year. This period is approximately three to four months.

Justifying additional or expensive projects or activities may be approached by presenting (1) the current budget, (2) the proposed new budget, (3) the percentage and actual money spent to date, and (4) the reasons for the increases. Any such requests should be presented in terms that are important and relevant for the company. The importance of remaining within budget limits varies among companies. The benefits of the proposed additional activities (costs) should be indicated to provide a basis for decision making.

Early Payments

According to good accounting practices, expenses are to be recognized in the fiscal period in which the indebtedness arises (i.e., the time when the work is done, in part or in full). The time when the payment is made is mostly irrelevant. Exceptions are made for up-front payments to initiate a trial. Simply paying an investigator early might create a prepayment that would not be recognized as an expense until the work it covered was done. The work should therefore start earlier or proceed more rapidly if the intention exists to pay the investigator earlier, rather than merely making payments earlier.

RESEARCH AND DEVELOPMENT EXPENDITURES

Definitions of Categories Used to Track Expenditures

Actual expenditures for a medicine's development vary depending on many factors, not the least of which are the various definitions used of categories to track those expenditures. Some of these issues are discussed in Chapter 130 of *Guide to Clinical Trials* (Spilker, 1991). Actual development costs vary greatly from medicine to medicine, year to year, and company to company, depending on whether the definitions used are uniform or change, in addition to actual changes.

Two published reports of the percentage of research and development money spent on various functions of medicine development are illustrated in Fig. 53.4. The percentage figures shown are based on averages of many medicines. These data are expressed in generally similar categories, although there are some differences between them. Despite any caveats about definitions, there is quite close agreement between the two sets of data. One interpretation of these data is that money to be allocated for medicine development may be planned for various functions or categories with some degree of accuracy. Each medicine will have a different profile of expenditures from these average figures, but overall expenditures at most research-based companies probably resemble this composite picture.

Accounting for Research and Development Expenditures

If a company desires research and development to account for money spent, then this may be done in a number of ways. Efforts and progress reported by research and development may be described in general terms or to any level of detail required. Data indicating where money was spent may be organized and expressed in terms of one or more of the following categories.

RESEARCH AND DEVELOPMENT EXPENDITURES

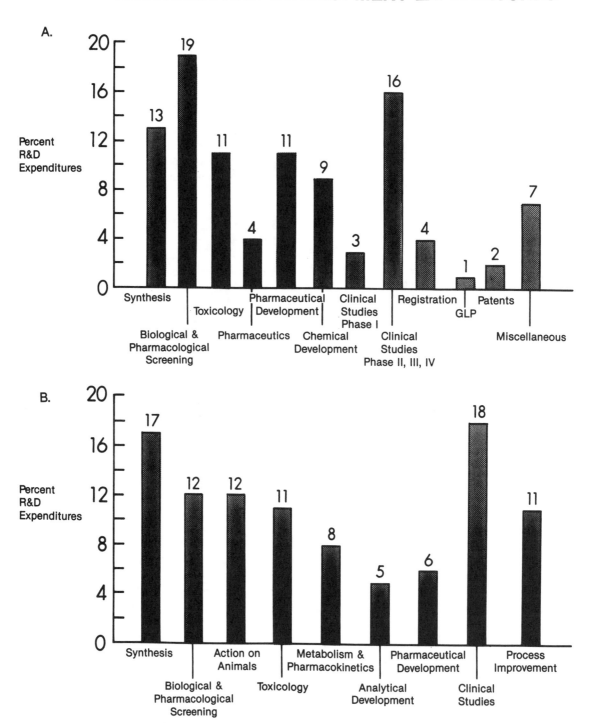

FIG. 53.4. Research and development expenditures by function. Panel **A** reprinted from Prentis and Walker (1985) with permission of *The Pharmaceutical Journal.* Panel **B** reprinted from Seidl (1983), with permission of Raven Press. *R&D,* research and development; *GLP,* Good Laboratory Practices.

TABLE 53.2. *Research and development expenditures by function in West Germany and the United States*

	Percent of total costs	
	West Germany[a]	United States[b]
1. Synthesis of chemicals and isolation of natural products	17	11
2. Pharmacological screening	12	18
3. Secondary testing	12	—
4. Toxicology	11	9
5. a. Metabolism and pharmacokinetics	8	—
b. Bioavailability studies	—	3
6. Analytical development	5	—
7. Pharmaceutical development	6	10
8. Process development for manufacturing and quality control	11	10
9. Human clinical trials	18	24
10. Other	—	15
	100	100

[a] From Seidl (1983) with permission of Raven Press. This breakdown is based on data from seven major West German pharmaceutical companies for 1980. The four types of expenditures in a research budget were for personnel (65 percent), material (20 percent), capital (8 percent), and a reserve of 7 percent.

[b] From Table 20 of *PMA Annual Survey Report 1980–1983*, with permission.

1. Research projects, development projects, and product support activities. This refers to medicine discovery, medicine development, and market support functions.

2. Research division, development division, medical division, and scientific support division. Administrative expenses may be identified separately or folded into each of the four divisions.

3. General and specific activities that require the largest resource commitment and expenditures.

4. Activities which involve marketed products or products close to the market.

5. Specific therapeutic areas.

6. Functions of medicine development (Table 53.2).

7. Business areas the company is involved in (e.g., agricultural products, veterinary medicines, human prescription medicines, human OTC medicines).

The parameters that may be evaluated for each product included in a financial analysis model are listed in Table 53.3.

Presenting Data on Research and Development Expenditures

There are innumerable ways to present data on research and development expenditures for a specific company. A few are shown in Figs. 53.5 and 53.6. In addition to presenting these data according to the functions of research and development (Fig. 53.6), similar graphs could be presented to illustrate expenditures according to therapeutic classes of medicines studied (e.g., cardiovascular, anti-infective, anticancer, gastrointestinal) or medicines in different stages of development (e.g., preclinical, Phases I through IV). Although these figures illustrate changes from year to year, it is also possible to explore a single year's expenditures for departments, business units, or groups within a specific department. Data may also be presented on an annual basis as five year growth rates or percentage of sales. When comparing distant periods, data should be adjusted for inflation. Figure 53.7 illustrates another approach to presenting expenditures on projects in research, development, or both. This type of graph may also be used to present sales or profit of marketed medicines according to therapeutic area.

TABLE 53.3. *Parameters evaluated for each product included in a financial analysis model[a]*

1. Sales forecast in units and money in constant dollars or another currency
2. Anticipated increases in prices
3. Promotional expenses
4. Amount of sales lost to other company products (i.e., cannibalization)
5. Probability of launch for investigational projects only
6. Total costs to bring investigational projects to market
7. Capital costs needed to produce the product
8. Cost of goods sold
9. Distribution costs
10. Market research costs
11. All other marketing costs
12. Royalties and licensing fees
13. Import duties
14. Transfer prices
15. Working capital (e.g., inventories, receivables, payables)
16. Administrative costs
17. Other costs

[a] Not all of these will be applicable for each project. Applicable parameters must be assessed for each year (e.g., 1 to 20) into the future for which a model will be used to forecast, together with historical data. In addition to data on each product and potential project, many external factors must be entered (e.g., tax rates, interest rates, inflation).

OVERALL R&D EXPENDITURES

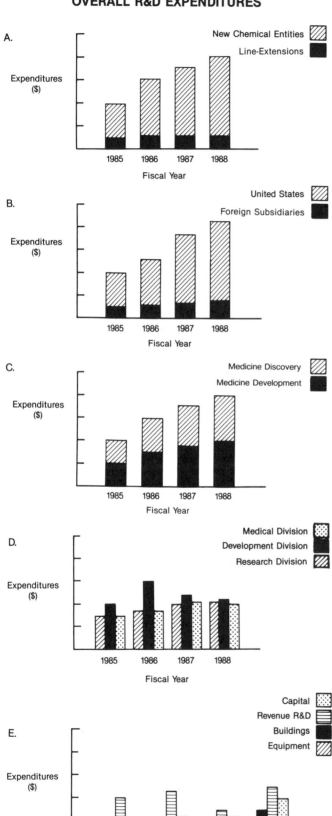

FIG. 53.5. Selected methods of illustrating overall expenditures within research and development (*R&D*). Similar graphs could be prepared to illustrate production or marketing expenditures.

R&D EXPENDITURE BY FUNCTION

A.

(e.g., Toxicology)

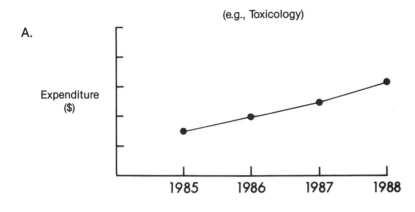

B.

(e.g., Toxicology)

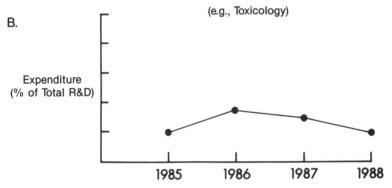

C.

(e.g., Toxicology)

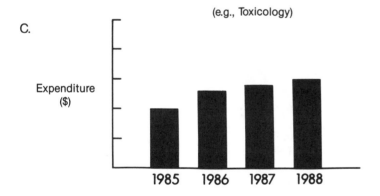

FIG. 53.6. Selected methods of illustrating expenditures within research and development (*R&D*) according to function. Each function could be presented separately as in Panels **A** to **D** or combined as in Panels **E** and **F**. Most panels could also be presented as percentage of the total amount spent in addition to exact sums of money. These types of graphs may also be used to illustrate expenditures based on therapeutic area of medicines studied, phase of development, specific department or division involved, country involved, or with another parameter. Similar graphs could be prepared by marketing or production groups.

D.

(e.g., Toxicology)

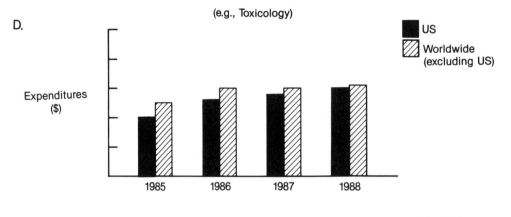

E.

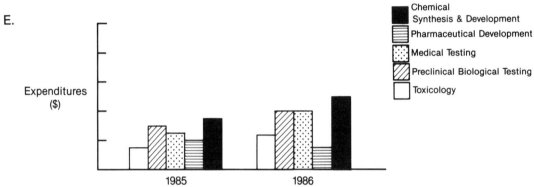

F.

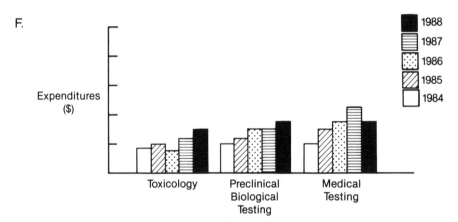

FIG. 53.6. *Continued.*

RESEARCH EXPENDITURES

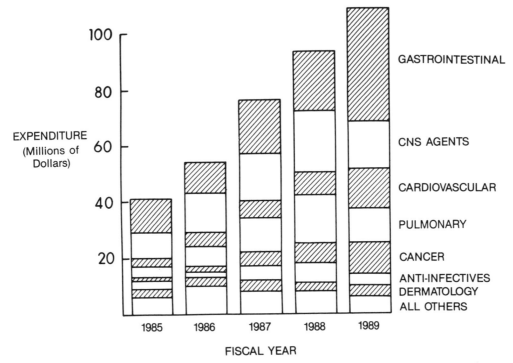

FIG. 53.7. Illustrating expenditures in various therapeutic areas over a period of years. This approach could illustrate development projects, research projects, or both. *CNS*, central nervous system.

Expenditures may be tracked during a period and illustrated by comparing projected with actual costs (Fig. 53.8). This approach may be used in many different ways in most areas of a pharmaceutical company. For example, sales are often tracked by comparing forecasted and actual monthly sales.

Interpreting Data on Research and Development Expenditures

Caution must be used in interpreting these graphs for numerous reasons. A few examples are given.

1. A decrease expressed in percentage from one year to the next may in actuality represent an increase in money spent (i.e., a smaller percent of a larger pool).
2. Definitions of categories may change from year to year or between countries whose data are combined.
3. A specific reason may readily explain an otherwise unexpected change in any numerical figure.
4. Money spent may not have been discounted to express all numbers in constant units of currency (e.g., dollars, marks, pounds).
5. Data may have been collected differently from year to year, or from country to country.

6. Money spent may not have been adjusted to account for inflation.

Forecasting Future Research and Development Expenditures

A simple means of approximating expenditures on research and development activities is to break them down into component parts. These parts are medicine discovery projects, development projects, technical support services, and so on. Each of these broad categories may be divided into various components such as internal time and effort, external grants to investigators (e.g., for medical and toxicological contracts), and equipment.

Each of the components may be forecasted separately on a level that can be dealt with comfortably, and necessary components combined. A graph of each component's previous levels of spending over a few years will establish trends. Next, one or more people must be enlisted who know to what degree work on each particular project will probably change (increase, decrease, or stay the same) over the next year or two. This enables an extrapolation of the expenditure curve to be made into the future. The better each component is understood, the more accurate is the forecast that will be reached.

PROJECTED VERSUS ACTUAL EXPENDITURES

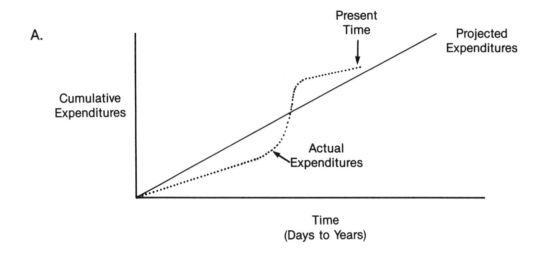

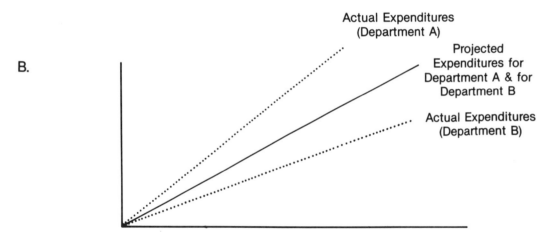

FIG. 53.8. Graphing projected versus actual expenditures over a period of time (e.g., days, weeks, months, years). Panel **A** illustrates a complex pattern that is presently close to its target. Panel **B** illustrates under- and overspending for two different departments. This type of graph may also be used to track actual sales versus sales forecasts in marketing or actual production versus production forecasts.

Financial Analyses of Projects

Both retrospective and prospective data on projects are collected and used at pharmaceutical companies (Table 53.3). Retrospective data focuses on a tracking of money and time spent on a particular project. This may be done in either a superficial or detailed manner. There is, however, a point of diminishing returns involved in this exercise. The time spent collecting data becomes steadily greater as more data are required, but the quality of the data may not necessarily be more accurate or helpful in interpreting results. Moreover, the staff's resistance usually increases as more data are requested. Most companies require forms with this information be completed every one to three months, although the same company may use shorter (or longer) time intervals as well, depending on the function being surveyed and the use that will be made of the resulting data.

Prospective forecasts of expenditures on a project may be made based on retrospective data plus knowledge of future activities that must be conducted. Forecasts may focus on costs to reach any of several time points (i.e., milestones) in a project's life. These include the go–no go decision point, time of NDA submission, or time of initial marketing. Forecasts may be broken down to department, division, or other level, in addition to providing an overall amount. Although many if not most companies make these forecasts, not all actually go to the step of creating budgets for individual projects to use in reaching their goals.

Major Corporate Issues and Challenges

54 / Animal Testing and Animal Welfare

The Central Issue............................ **657**
  Primary Uses of Animals in Research........ 658
Responsibilities of Institutions Conducting
    Animal Studies........................... 659
  Oversight Committee........................ 659
  Guidelines 659
  Animal Care and Use Committee............ 659
  Training..................................... 660
  Protocols for Experiments Using Animals..... 660
Ethical Use of Animals in Pharmaceutical
    Research.................................. 660

Refinement of Technique..................... 660
Reducing the Number of Animals Used....... 660
Kinds of Animals Used...................... 661
Alternatives to Animals...................... 661
Principles of Animal Use in Scientific Research 661
Political Issues 662
  Politics of Animal Testing 662
  A Possible Role for Consumer Advocates 662

The public will choose to believe a simple lie rather than a complex truth. Alexis De Tocqueville

Everyone "knows" what animals are, but the word animal may be defined in several ways. The United States Public Health Service defines an animal as "any live vertebrate animal." This definition draws a line between vertebrates and invertebrates, which is a useful distinction in most people's minds and serves as a basis to identify the scope of the animal testing issue. Another term used to draw a line between types of animals is sentient (i.e., an animal that can feel; having feelings). One problem with the use of this term is that it is unclear where to draw a distinction between animals that are and are not sentient. The presence of primitive nervous systems that enable simple reflexes to occur do not indicate that the animal can feel.

Figure 54.1 presents visual schematics of three ways of conceptualizing all animal species. The models differ based on whether qualitative distinctions are made between humans and vertebrates and between vertebrates and invertebrates. Virtually all representatives of the pharmaceutical industry and the groups that conduct animal experiments conceptually believe in model 1 or 2, whereas some (or many) animal rights advocates believe in model 3. Model 3 states that all animal species are qualitatively the same, although whether all invertebrates or nonsentient animals are included in the definition varies among those who would state that model 3 is correct. It is one thing to say animals are sentient (i.e., responsive to or aware of sensory stimuli) and another to

say they have rights. Animals can be said to have interests and therefore some level of moral considerability. This level is clearly less than that of humans. The moral rights of humans are based on views expressed by various philosophers, particularly Locke and Kant. Moral consideration of animals is based on their interests. Nonsentient creatures (e.g., plants) have needs, but not interests in the sense of sentient animals.

The most important point from a pharmaceutical company's perspective is that there is a distinction between humans and nonhumans as illustrated in models 1 and 2. This chapter is therefore based on the philosophical belief underlying models 1 or 2.

THE CENTRAL ISSUE

The balance is widely debated about how our society should best protect the environment and its human and animal inhabitants while at the same time utilizing environmental resources to improve the status of people. There is general agreement that animal research has played a pivotal role in discovering new medicines and surgical methods that have saved human lives, lessened human suffering, and advanced scientific knowledge. Part of the price for these advances are animals that are sacrificed. Most of these animals, however, are specifically bred for that purpose.

657

Three Models of Conceptualizing Animal Species

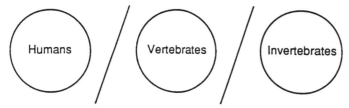

Model 1: Three Types of Animal Species

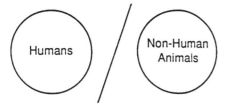

Model 2: Two Types of Animal Species

Model 3: One Type of Animal Species

FIG. 54.1. Three models of conceptualizing the animal world, based on the qualitative distinctions one makes between different species or groups of species. An alternative to model 1 is based on whether nonhuman animals are sentient or not.

Over the last 20 years the debate over animal welfare has intensified. The extreme position of animal abuse exemplified by dog fighting and cock fighting is abhorred by almost all members of our society. The major issue in conducting research in animals that has arisen over the last 20 years involves the less extreme spectrum of whether scientists should have complete freedom to conduct research with animals without any restraint on how they treat animals to those who state that all research involving animals should be stopped. While there are people who adhere to one of these extremes most scientists represent the middle ground. Intense debate and even violence have erupted over where along this spectrum a modern society should stand. What is the correct balance between allowing appropriate research and protecting the welfare of the animals? This issue is sometimes described as identifying the conditions that must be present for animal experiments to be conducted, and ensuring appropriate care of the animals when experiments are conducted.

This chapter does not attempt to explore the background, or details of the social, philosophical, or political issues that have focused on this debate. This chapter has a far simpler goal of attempting to present some of the major issues behind the animal testing controversy from a pharmaceutical company's perspective on procedures that should be followed in assuring that protocols for animal studies are appropriately reviewed, that animals are treated appropriately, and reviewing alternative uses to animals in research.

Primary Uses of Animals in Research

Animals are required in pharmaceutical research to determine if compounds have specific biological activity at pharmacological doses or toxic effects at toxicological doses. Animals are also used to develop new procedures or tests that may assist in improving surgery in humans or for testing certain medical devices that cannot be initially evaluated in humans. Animals are also used for behavioral studies and for a wide range of educational purposes (e.g., teaching medical students).

RESPONSIBILITIES OF INSTITUTIONS CONDUCTING ANIMAL STUDIES

Oversight Committee

Current standards as well as laws in many countries require that an oversight committee be established to review and approve all nonhuman animal protocols before they are initiated. These protocols include all studies conducted in toxicology, pharmacology, and other scientific disciplines (e.g., biochemistry, metabolism, pharmacokinetics, microbiology, virology), where animals are used. This or another committee must also be charged with the responsibility of ensuring appropriate care and housing of all animals in the institution.

Guidelines

In the United States, relevant guidelines are described in the 83-page *Guide for the Care and Use of Laboratory Animals* (U.S. Department of Health and Human Services, NIH Publication 86-23, revised 1985). Federal laws are identified in an appendix to this booklet, which stresses that professional judgment is essential when applying these guidelines. The laws on which these guidelines are based are (1) the 1985 amendments to the Animal Welfare Act (1966) administered by the U.S. Department of Agriculture, and The Health Research Extension Act (1985). The latter act is important for groups funded by the U.S. Public Health Service. These laws mandate a local review (oversight) committee at each institution that uses animals (i.e., the Institutional Animal Care and Use Committee). Such a committee must include a veterinarian experienced in animal care and a person who is unaffiliated with the institution. The functions of this committee are to inspect animal research areas at least twice a year to ensure that relevant guidelines and regulations are being followed, and to review protocols for proposed experiments to ensure humane treatment of animals.

Several European countries also have approved regulations that protect animal welfare and in some cases provide for mandatory licensing of scientists and technicians who operate on or use animals in experiments. A summary of the early experiences with ethical committees for protecting animals in the United Kingdom and Sweden is given by Britt (1983).

Animal Care and Use Committee

Every research institution in the United States that uses animals must have an animal care and use committee. One exception is for institutions that only use species not covered by the Animal Welfare Act (i.e., mice, rats, and birds) and do not receive Public Health Service

funding. In some other countries an Animal Care and Use Committee is also mandated by law, but if not, institutions should establish such committees. This committee may have a different name, but its function is to oversee the care, humane use, and protection of animal welfare at the facility/institution. Existing regulations in some countries influence the makeup of the committee. It must (should) include a scientist who is experienced in animal research, a veterinarian, a "well-respected" member of the community, and others as required (or desired) by custom or law. Depending on the laws of the country involved and interests of the company, the animal care and use committee could be the same as the oversight committee described above.

Functions of the Institutional Animal Care and Use Committee include the following:

1. establishment (or endorsement) of procedures for the facility/institution regarding animal care and use;
2. monitoring of the animal care and use at the institution to ensure that all relevant guidelines and policies are being met;
3. periodic meetings (e.g., one to four times each year) to discuss issues that arise relating to animal care and use, including (1) certification and training of relevant students, staff, and technical personnel; (2) occupational hazards (e.g., animal bites, disease transmission); (3) protective clothing; (4) protection of staff from hazardous biological, chemical, and physical agents; and (5) supervision of hazardous agent and animal projects;
4. periodic meetings to review protocols for conducting scientific experiments submitted by institutional staff;
5. preparation of an annual report on the status of the above points for relevant administrators (in the United States, this would be the United States Department of Agriculture and the Public Health Service, which also inspects animal care facilities); and
6. semiannual program review and facilities inspection.

Each pharmaceutical company conducting research in the United States must have an animal use committee that reviews and approves protocols for scientific experiments involving use of animals (*in vitro* or *in vivo*). Pharmaceutical companies conducting research using animals in other countries should have such committees. The membership of this group can vary in number but three to six people are generally sufficient. Their mandate is to ensure that the methods of animal care, treatment, and handling adhere to principles of the company plus all regulations. This group can also have an oversight responsibility to ensure that animal husbandry and all facilities meet appropriate standards. Individuals who supervise or audit Good Laboratory Practice (GLP) regulations could also report to the committee on a periodic basis to review their activities and findings. These last few functions go beyond conducting protocol review and a company may choose to have these activities reviewed by other groups. The point is that attention should be given to ensuring that a specific group is identified that has responsibility for all functions relating to animal well-being.

Training

In the United Kingdom and some other countries as well, all scientific staff who use animals must be licensed. In all countries, staff lacking adequate prior experience must be trained by the company. One option is to establish a brief training course to review basic animal behavior and techniques for handling and using animals in research. If anesthetics are to be used, then appropriate training on that subject should be included as part of the course.

Protocols for Experiments Using Animals

Protocols for proposed experiments on animals should be prepared in a standard format (Table 54.1). Protocols will vary in length from a single page to many pages. Inclusion of standard information about animal care and housing in an appendix will add substantially to a protocol's length. The major sections listed in Table 54.1 may be modified in many ways, and not all sections are relevant for all protocols. The most important parts are the

1. purpose(s) of the experiment;
2. type and number of animals to be used and their handling;

TABLE 54.1. *Suggested contents of a protocol for experimenting on animals*

1. Basic information
    Title of experiment
    Scientists involved plus their signatures
    Date of protocol
    Other standard information
    Signature of responsible manager (e.g., head of the department)
2. Background of the experiment
3. Justification for conducting it
4. Objective(s) of the study
5. Source, type, number, and other details of animals to be used
6. Discussion of the facilities used to house animals
7. Description of how animals will be cared for and treated
8. Description of the experiment(s) to be performed
9. Standard information not included above (e.g., licensing of scientists to perform the studies, certification of the facility)[a]

---

[a] The specific information in this section will depend on the country and laws involved.

3. description of the procedure(s) to be used in the study for the experiment and for dealing with any anesthesia or pain that may be experienced; and
4. disposition of the animals after the experiment is completed.

It is useful to resubmit the protocols annually or biannually to the animal care and use committee even if there are no changes. Specific regulations may require that the number of animals to be used for each protocol be specified, and that major protocol modifications be approved by the committee.

ETHICAL USE OF ANIMALS IN PHARMACEUTICAL RESEARCH

Scientists may differ slightly in their view of whether alternatives exist to the use of animals in pharmaceutical research. Whether the alternatives are feasible, reasonable, and worthwhile depends on a variety of factors that must be considered for each situation. Overall, the consensus is that few animal experiments could be replaced by nonanimal experiments. However, there are ways to substantially improve the conduct of research using animals (Committee on the Use of Animals in Research, 1991).

Refinement of Technique

All scientists are (or should be) aware of methods that minimize suffering for animals used in research. This is a fundamental principle underlying all research involving animals and must be discussed by the institution's committee that reviews protocols for experiments.

Reducing the Number of Animals Used

Utilizing each animal to the maximal degree possible decreases the total number of animals used. This is often accomplished by having two or more groups use different parts of an animal or use the animal in different ways. For example, after one group completes their experiments they could turn the animal over to another group instead of euthanizing the animal. On the other hand, the Animal Welfare Act generally prohibits more than one surgical procedure on the same animal. Another example would be when multiple groups of scientists arrange to use different parts of the same animal for *in vitro* experiments and thereby decrease the number of animals used.

Careful planning and design of research studies has often decreased the number of animals used. The number of animals to be used in a study is seldom derived arbitrarily. These choices are usually based on personal experience, information in other scientists' published articles, regulatory guidelines, peer review, or on statistical analyses. If statistical analyses have not been used, they should because they may demonstrate that fewer animals are required to statistically demonstrate a certain effect. An example of the use of statistics to plan a trial design is given by Berndtson et al. (1989). In those cases where fewer animals are required, some animal lives may be saved. The opposite situation—more animals are needed to conduct a scientific study—may also result in a net savings in animal lives because the data obtained may be more convincing and definitive than if a smaller number was used. This, in turn would obviate the need for additional experiments to repeat or confirm the results.

Two major changes within the pharmaceutical industry have significantly reduced the number of animals used in toxicology studies. These are to replace LD50 values with much smaller acute experiments designed to quickly establish target organs and doses of the medicine needed to elicit effects. The second change is to delete the requirement for one year toxicology studies in rodents. Careful review of existing data showed that such studies add little to the safety evaluation process. In many medical and other schools, the use of live animals for teaching purposes has been reduced by replacement with single demonstrations, use of videotapes, and other approaches.

Kinds of Animals Used

An important principle that many, if not most, scientists follow is to use the lowest species on the evolutionary tree necessary to generate appropriate data. It is generally believed preferable to use 100 dogs instead of 100 monkeys in a study, or to use 100 rats instead of 100 dogs. While this practice does not reduce the number of animals used it is important to protect "higher" species, particularly simian primates which are in short supply and which may not be required to answer the research question posed. This principle is not accepted by all scientists.

Alternatives to Animals

This approach is frequently advocated by animal rights groups who claim that nonanimal models can replace animals. At this point in time there are extremely few instances when it is possible to use microorganisms, cell cultures, tissue cultures, or computer models in lieu of animals in research. This is one area where research should continue to remain active because replacement of animals is a desirable goal.

In vitro methods will never totally replace *in vivo* methods, but are a useful technique for assessing certain aspects of safety and efficacy from a pharmacological perspective. *In vitro* methods usually include the use of isolated organs and tissues and therefore require use of animals. The use of homogenized cells or tissues in biochemical studies also requires the use of animals. The point is that using *in vitro* methods does not necessarily decrease the number of animals used.

Most types of cells can be maintained for an indefinite number of generations. This permits more research on the use of these cultures as replacements to animals in pharmacological testing. One of the drawbacks of evaluating the effects of compounds on cells is that isolated cells do not communicate with other cells the way that they do when they are part of tissues. Furthermore, isolated tissues do not function as do whole organs, or organ systems, or whole organisms (i.e., the intact animal).

In vitro studies have several additional limitations, including the following.

1. They do not provide information on interactions between different organisms, or interactions within an entire organism.
2. Even if they can detect a hazard of using medicines, they lack both qualitative and quantitative refinement that would allow the finding to be used for risk assessment purposes.
3. They cannot indicate unexpected benefits of using medicines.

It is certain that future discoveries will lead to a decrease in the numbers of animals used in specific areas of scientific research. Improved methods will allow the use of more cell and tissue cultures in the future, but it is highly unlikely that many animals can be replaced by the use of cultured cells in scientific experiments today. An example of a project that might achieve this goal is the creation of a test tube environment for growing the bacterium that causes leprosy. At present it is necessary to use mice or armadillos to culture the bacteria. Even if this is achieved and used to discover potential new therapies for leprosy, the actual development of the leads thus uncovered would require the use of whole animals.

PRINCIPLES OF ANIMAL USE IN SCIENTIFIC RESEARCH

The following is a partial list of important principles underlying animal use.

1. Establishing the quality, safety, and efficacy of new medicines requires tests conducted in animals.
2. Stress should be reduced in animals used in scientific research by whatever means are ethical and appropriate.
3. Dogs and cats should not be obtained by research institutions from any but the most reliable sources for use in research. Stray animals should not be used in research because this practice encourages some people to

TABLE 54.2. *Principles of the humane use of animals[a]*

1. Make the greatest use possible of nonanimal methods
2. Justify the decision to use animals for biomedical research by the potential benefit to human health
3. Use the fewest animals consistent with a successful experiment. A bad experiment is a tragic waste of animals
4. Care for the living animal using the highest ethical standards and humane considerations
5. Provide the best possible care and housing, using state-of-the-art technology
6. Avoid or mitigate animal pain to the fullest extent possible
7. Euthanize as painlessly as possible
8. Foster a considerate, humane, well-trained staff, including caretakers, technicians, and scientists

[a] Reprinted with permission from Rall and Hoffman (1990).

steal animals. This statement is based on anecdotal stories over the course of many years rather than on a systematic study. The lack of information on an animal's genetic background and medical history can be an important disadvantage in some studies.

4. Appropriate standards for the care and housing of animals should be placed into laws and regulations in those countries where the laws are inadequate. Existing standards and laws should be enforced in those countries where adequate laws exist.

5. Animal facilities should be inspected (and certified) periodically by government officials if this is not already being routinely done. Inspectors should arrive unannounced.

A number of additional principles for the humane treatment of animals are presented in Tables 54.2 and 54.3; specific principles guiding the housing of animals are listed in Table 54.4.

TABLE 54.3. *Selected veterinary principles used in animal care*

1. Observe all animals every day, including holidays and weekends.
2. Prevent disease and injury in animals by following acceptable practices.
3. Diagnose and treat appropriately any problem that develops.
4. Follow appropriate standards in all aspects of caring for and experimenting on the animals. This includes environmental factors such as temperature, humidity, ventilation, lighting, and noise, as well as food, water, sanitation, bedding, and waste disposal.
5. Ensure that a qualified veterinarian is called whenever any relevant problem is discovered.
6. Use appropriate methods to identify all animals and to record relevant data for their care as well as for the protocol. These data include surgical history, source of the animal, disposition, strain, name(s) of investigators, and relevant dates.
7. A veterinarian should be associated with every animal facility.

TABLE 54.4. *Selected physical characteristics of animal housing facilities that must be considered in designing and regulating such facilities[a]*

1. Separate functional areas to receive, quarantine, isolate, and house animals
2. Separate functional areas for surgery, intensive care, necropsy, radiography, food preparation, experimental procedures, diagnostic laboratory tests, treatment of animals, and any other special facilities
3. Separate areas for storage and use of any hazardous or radiolabeled materials
4. Receiving and storage areas for supplies and materials
5. Administration offices
6. Lockers, showers, and related areas for staff
7. Place for staff eating, drinking, and relaxing
8. Area for cleaning and sterilizing equipment as well as for storing unused or damaged equipment
9. Area to store waste until it can be removed
10. Security of the facility

[a] Many features of construction require special consideration but are not described here.

POLITICAL ISSUES

Politics of Animal Testing

In some parts of the United States and in other countries, groups of academic, government, and industrial institutions that use animals in research have formed organizations to counterbalance the loud vocal statements of groups criticizing the use of animals in research, and to present a balanced picture to the public. These groups have eschewed the loud rhetoric and categorical statements used by some animal rights activists and groups, and have instead identified benefits to society from the humane use of animals. These groups are attempting to counter many myths and to demonstrate that appropriate care and treatment of all animals used in research is the norm. Activities include brochures, letter writing, posters, displays, educational symposia, visits to facilities by local and other political officials, legislative breakfasts, public speaking engagements, and telephone lines to receive complaints. It is clear that collective efforts must be initiated and maintained whenever and wherever there are unfounded attempts to modify or severely and inappropriately restrict animal research. Additional activities through pharmaceutical trade associations or on the company's own behalf are also extremely important. Discussions of interest on this general topic are given by Tannenbaum (1986), Meier and Stocker (1989), and Vance (1992).

A Possible Role for Consumer Advocates

If a goal is to reduce the number of animals used in medical research, the major approach should be to ensure greater worldwide harmonization of toxicology requirements. Pharmaceutical companies must study many animals in toxicology studies to ensure and to assess the safety of new medicines. If they desire to market the same medicine in another country then some or many of the toxicology studies may have to be repeated, depending on the particular country. The reason for this is that many countries have slightly or broadly differing toxicology requirements and if the studies performed do not meet all of the differing requirements in each country, then the company is forced to redo the tests, at great expense and at a great cost of animal lives.

Active consumer groups could attempt to affect either the relevant regulations in several countries or they could attempt to liberalize the interpretation of these regulations. Before any efforts are expended in this direction, however, it is important to know why these regulations are in place. There are two major reasons. The first is that scientists differ among themselves in many areas about what is important in a specific area. It is not surprising that the toxicologists and other scientists who in-

fluenced the structure of the regulations created somewhat different requirements (e.g., on the numbers of animals to be tested, the number of species, the type of food, and the duration of the study). Many of these differences should be able to be harmonized if representatives from all relevant countries met to reach a consensus position. The second reason is that there is a great deal of chauvinism and economic incentive in at least some countries to have studies repeated. What this means is that companies must often repeat studies within the countries that have special requirements. In the 1990s it is unreasonable to suggest that there is a relevant scientific basis for this policy.

In conclusion, science is beyond any reasonable point of ceasing animal use in scientific experiments. Future discoveries of new medicines to treat many serious and life threatening diseases will require animal use. We should do whatever we can to ensure that the fewest number of animals are used and that they are all treated appropriately and humanely.

55 / Patient Package Inserts

The Rationale for Patient Package Inserts....... **665**
  Patients Desire More Information about Their
    Medicines................................... 665
  Why Patients Have a Right to Receive Written
    Information.............................. 666
Objectives of Providing Patient Package Inserts **666**
Major Issues in Preparing a Meaningful Patient
    Package Insert **666**
  Current Examples of Information Directed to
    Patients.................................. 667
  Who Should Prepare Patient Package Inserts? 667
  Who Should Supply Package Inserts to
    Patients?................................. 667
  Should Patients Have to Ask for
    Information/Inserts? 668

The Argument for "Class Labeling" of Patient
    Package Inserts........................... 668
Potential Problems with Patient Package
    Inserts 668
How Should the Content of a Package Insert
    Differ from Professional Labeling?.......... 669
Research on Patient Package Inserts **669**
  Interview and Testing Procedures............. 670
  Pilot Testing................................. 670
Alternative Systems for Providing Information
    about Medicines to Patients **670**
  Patient-Oriented Brochures................... 671

Consumers have the right to safety, the right to be informed, the right to choose and the right to be heard.
John F. Kennedy

Printed information for patients about a medicine that is included in a package or dispensed simultaneously with a medicine is defined as a patient package insert. This material differs from official package inserts written for health care professionals in that the language is targeted to a different audience. The development of patient package inserts for most or all medicines was discussed in numerous forums within the United States in the late 1970s, but was dropped from consideration because of widespread opposition from both physicians and pharmaceutical companies. During the early 1990s, the momentum for creating and dispensing these documents is growing. In Europe the impetus was supplied by the European Community's decision to require them (i.e., regulations are driving companies to supply patients with information). In the United States pressure from the public is building (i.e., active consumers are driving companies to supply them with more information). The Food and Drug Administration (FDA) is also expected to be influenced by European regulatory changes and to promote the practice of supplying patient package inserts in the United States.

THE RATIONALE FOR PATIENT PACKAGE INSERTS

Customers in all countries receive detailed instructions on how to use each new electronic piece of equipment they purchase, whether it is a simple hair dryer or a sophisticated computer. These instruction manuals are often written in four or more languages and present great detail, even covering what the customer should do in case of problems with simple machines. Yet when patients are given medicines that have a major effect on their health, and which do not yield as consistent and reproducible results as electronic goods, the only information patients usually receive are some verbal comments by an often rushed physician or nurse who may or may not remember to mention important information about the medicines. Even under the best conditions and with a conscientious physician or nurse, patients often find it difficult to remember accurately everything they have been told. Moreover, patients rarely ask all the relevant questions that will occur to them over the next day, week, or month and many relevant questions are unknown to them.

Patients Desire More Information About Their Medicines

Numerous surveys, as well as common sense, indicate that many patients desire much more information than they receive (typically only the physician's recommendation and basic instructions). Thus it seems important to provide written information that interested patients will use, and which those without interest may ignore. Strull et al. (1984) report that there is often a major difference between patients' desire for information and their desire to make medical decisions. Physicians have tended to underestimate the former and overestimate the latter. This supports the view that patients desire far more information than they currently receive. In addition, physicians believe they spend much more time informing patients about their medicines than they truly do (Joossens, 1991). A major means of addressing these problems is to provide patients with package inserts.

Why Patients Have a Right to Receive Written Information

There are a number of important reasons why the information that would be included in a patient package insert is both a patient right and a moral requirement for prescription medicines.

1. Physicians and other health professionals often fail to provide relevant and important information to their patients about medicines. Whether physicians forget to present the information, are too rushed to present the information, or believe the patient should not have the information, the end result is the same—patients who want information do not receive it.

2. Patients have a right to know relevant information about the medicines they are prescribed. Patients also often forget important information they have been told or remember facts incorrectly at a later date. Patients also have a right to consent to treatment in general practice, and patient package inserts are one means of ensuring informed consent, by presenting relevant information about any medicines that may be prescribed.

3. Patients may misinterpret important information at the time they hear it because of stress, denial, fatigue, failure to hear, or lack of understanding of one or more aspects of the information presented. Patients who are receiving information about their medicines often have difficulty hearing it and remembering it accurately because they are often in an environment that they consider unfriendly or have negative associations about—no matter how cheerful and friendly the staff or how gaily painted the walls.

4. Physicians may provide too little or too much information about a medicine for a particular patient. Having a package insert written in language that can be clearly understood by patients ensures that a prespecified minimum amount of data are available for each patient. Physicians often present information to patients using jargon or in complex terminology. Physicians may be unaware of doing this, but patients frequently do not understand or misinterpret the physicians' statements.

5. Physicians almost never truly assess whether their instructions and information are appropriately understood. Sometimes they ask a patient "Do you understand"? This is a totally inadequate means of assessing patient comprehension because patients who do not fully understand what they have heard are often too embarrassed to admit this and would rather avoid this admission. Other patients think they understand what they have heard, but would be unable to repeat what they have heard, and will soon forget the details, or understand something different than what they were told.

6. Patients may be on vacation or on a trip when they have questions about their medicine and they may not have any means of obtaining a rapid answer to an important question.

OBJECTIVES OF PROVIDING PATIENT PACKAGE INSERTS

The assumption underlying this article is that patients have a basic right to be informed about their medicines, and that this requires that they receive more information than is usually provided by physicians. Even if a patient is given a totally perfect and complete explanation about a medicine, he or she is likely to forget or misinterpret some of the specific details heard.

Ethical standards require that information provided must be given honestly, responsibly, and truthfully, and using language that will be understandable by patients. The specific objectives of providing information are to

1. inform patients of benefits and risks associated with the medicines;
2. inform patients how to use the medicine properly (this is not just for "unusual" delivery systems [e.g., nasal insufflation, constant infusion pump] but also for basic issues such as whether to take a medicine before or after meals and how much water to use when taking the medicine);
3. inform patients about possible interactions the medicine may have with other treatments;
4. promote patient compliance through improved understanding about the medicine, including awareness of the consequences of poor compliance;
5. provide information about potential problems or common questions that may arise; and
6. provide information on how to respond to problems that may arise.

MAJOR ISSUES IN PREPARING A MEANINGFUL PATIENT PACKAGE INSERT

Specific issues that must be considered when package inserts are prepared include the determination of the

1. categories of information and specific topics to be discussed;
2. amount of information to be presented on each topic and the total length of the insert;

3. style and tone to be used (e.g., conversational, formal, humorous) in the written document, as well as format of the document and technical details (e.g., size of type);

4. educational (i.e., reading) level of language to be used (e.g., length of sentences, number of syllables, word choice);

5. organization of the document to ensure a logical flow with clear topic headings and sufficient white space between paragraphs;

6. layout and illustration, which should be clear and contain easy-to-read type without many variations in type, with ragged right margins and line drawings that do not interfere with text; and

7. manner that information is to be presented (e.g., should the statements made be explained), particularly for statements that are often misinterpreted (e.g., use as directed, take with meals).

A number of other issues to consider are listed in Table 55.1.

Current Examples of Information Directed to Patients

Public bookstores contain a wide variety of books that discuss both prescription and over-the-counter medicines from a patient's perspective. Many of these are excellent sources of useful information. Many people that desire this information, however, do not have access to such books because they cannot afford them, they have

---

TABLE 55.1. *Selected issues and questions to consider in preparing patient package inserts*

1. Should large type size be used? If so, should it be used for some or for all of the package insert?
2. Should a black box be placed around particularly important information? If so, what information?
3. What should the length of the package insert be and what topics should be identified with headings or subheadings?
4. At what reading level should the vocabulary and sentence structure be targeted?
5. Should a simple introductory synopsis of all information be presented up to one page in length followed by a two- to four-page description of the same information written at a higher reading level?
6. Should some boldface type be used to highlight specific information of particular importance? What tense and person should be used?
7. Should consumer or other groups assist in the creation of package inserts? If so, which groups?
8. To what degree should class labeling be used?
9. Who will write and review patient package inserts?
10. Should all patient package inserts use the same format?
11. Should all patient package inserts use the same level of language?
12. Should patient package inserts be approved by regulatory authorities? If so, how?

---

an "antibook" attitude, they are unaware of their existence, or for other reasons.

Patient package inserts have been prepared in various countries for different groups of medicines (Anonymous, 1990b). Patient package inserts are required in several European countries. In the United States patient package inserts are currently mandated for oral contraceptives (21CFR 310.501), progestational agents (21CFR 310.516), estrogens (21CFR 310.515), isoproterenol inhalation products (21CFR 201.305), and intrauterine devices (21CFR 310.502). A well-written, detailed legal discussion of this subject is presented by Hutt and Merrill (1991). Literature and brochures from various associations, companies, compendia, and other groups are currently serving the purpose of patient package inserts for many medicines. Blattmann (1992) discusses current issues of patient package inserts in Europe.

Who Should Prepare Patient Package Inserts?

It is likely that pharmaceutical companies would prepare drafts of patient package inserts, just as they generally prepare the drafts of professional package inserts. Guidelines for the preparation of these documents (e.g., categories to cover, reading level, degree of completeness) should be issued by national regulatory authorities to standardize the approach. Whether those regulatory authorities would also have to approve each patient package insert will probably vary from country to country. A preferable approach would be for companies to prepare package inserts and submit them to the regulatory authority. If a company did not receive a rejection or a request for change within 30 days, then the document would be deemed "approved." This is similar to the current approach to processing Investigational New Drug Applications (INDs) at the FDA.

Who Should Supply Package Inserts to Patients?

While the answer may appear obvious to many people, there are several candidate groups for this job. The major ones are (1) the physician who writes the prescription, (2) his or her nurse or office staff, or (3) the pharmacist who dispenses the medicine. If pharmacists in a country dispense medicines in original packages (e.g., as in most European countries), then the manufacturers can insert leaflets at the time of packaging. In some countries (e.g., the United States), the pharmacist usually dispenses pills from a large container, or breaks down a prepared package into smaller size containers. In this situation the manufacturer would be unable to provide the inserts and the pharmacist would have to insert a medicine-specific brochure into the container. The European system of dispensing medicines has often been proposed for use in the United States and is considered a desirable system for providing patient package inserts.

Should Patients Have to Ask for Information/Inserts?

Some people believe that patients who are interested in obtaining information on their medicines have the responsibility to ask for that information. These people believe that if patients must request package inserts, they will do so, providing they know the inserts are available. While there is some truth to this assertion, one can also state that patients who are interested in the information may

1. forget to ask the pharmacist or physician for the information;
2. be in too much of a hurry to wait for the information (e.g., there may be a long line);
3. have a friend or relative pick up their prescription who does not ask for it;
4. be unaware of exactly how to request the information; or
5. be embarrassed to ask for the information.

Furthermore, patients who think they are not interested in the information may

1. become interested once they start to read the package insert;
2. be able to use the insert as a reference at a later date;
3. be misinformed about what information the patient package insert contains;
4. have a friend or relative who is interested in the information; or
5. find that their physician does not give them all the information they want after they read the insert.

Overall, providing the same minimal amount of information to all patients assures society that patients have been provided with at least a predetermined quantity of basic information.

The Argument for "Class Labeling" of Patient Package Inserts

Patients are generally switched from one medicine to another when it is medically necessary to improve efficacy and/or decrease the incidence of adverse experiences. As a result, patients often are prescribed a series of similar medicines in a sequential order (e.g., beta-receptor antagonists, diuretics, calcium channel antagonists, antianginals, nonsteroidal anti-inflammatory agents). Patients in this situation who consult information invariably desire that the patient package inserts all be written in a generally similar format. Even having identical text for relevant portions of the patient package insert would be an important advantage for the patient,

and would minimize any confusion that could arise if each manufacturer adopted its own style and approach to create a patient package insert for similar medicines. This confusion could easily have important medical consequences in many situations (e.g., patients become confused by the differences and stop taking the medicine, or overdose, and experience medical sequelae).

Having class labeling that is agreed to by a regulatory authority, manufacturer, and patient group representatives is one means to address this issue. Including patient representatives on the review committee should ensure that the patient's perspective is sufficiently and appropriately addressed. The material in the package insert must make sense to patients and their relevant concerns must be addressed by authors of the insert.

Potential Problems with Patient Package Inserts

There may be situations when a physician believes a patient should not receive a patient package insert. The physician may believe that the package insert could have a harmful influence if the patient reacted emotionally to the information or learned about his or her true diagnosis. Nonetheless, modern ethical views stress that patients have a right to know their diagnosis. Patients who

TABLE 55.2. *Categories of professional labeling in the United States[a]*

1. Boxed or bold letter warnings (if any)
2. Description
3. Clinical pharmacology
4. Indications and usage
5. Contraindications
6. Warnings
7. Precautions
   General
   Information for patients
   Laboratory tests
   Interactions
   Carcinogenesis, mutagenesis, impairment of fertility
   Pregnancy: teratogenic effects
   Nursing mothers
   Pediatric use
8. Adverse reactions
   Reactions for each system may be listed separately
   Adverse laboratory changes may be listed
9. Overdose
10. Dosage and administration (these categories may be presented separately)
11. How supplied
    Containers, strengths, and sizes
    Storage conditions
12. References and any educational materials available

[a] Tables may be used to present such information as adverse reaction incidence, serum levels at different doses, and adjustment of dose based on renal function or body weight. Drawings may be used to present chemical formulae, instructions for use, or other information. Photographs are used in the professional labeling of some products (e.g., Humulin L).

cannot emotionally handle or deal with the knowledge of their diagnosis often block or deny this information. If the package insert was placed into a box containing the medicine, as in Europe, it would be difficult to remove it in cases like the one described, as compared with a system where the pharmacist could be instructed on the prescription not to dispense the insert.

Another potential problem that has been raised about patient package inserts is that they could decrease patient compliance with the medicine because patient fears about possible adverse experiences would be increased. Another claim is that patient package inserts will increase the number of actual adverse experiences that patients experience because of patient suggestibility. There is little doubt that all of these problems are likely to occur in a small number of patients. Nonetheless, the overwhelming international consensus is that the benefits of providing information to patients outweighs the risks. In addition, it may be argued that the additional knowledge about their medicine will provide greater comfort to many patients and will actually stimulate them to increase their compliance.

How Should the Content of a Package Insert Differ from Professional Labeling?

The categories in professional labeling (i.e., package inserts) are listed in Table 55.2; these are based on United States labels but do not differ significantly in most other countries. Note that not every category is necessary or relevant to include in the labeling of every medicine. While some of these categories are relevant to include in a patient package insert, others could be revised. For example, instead of informing patients that a series of specific adverse reactions may be observed, it would be preferable to describe constellations of problems that possibly may arise, such as flu-like problems or swelling of various parts of the body. For relevant types of problems, the patients may be advised to see their physician. Selected categories to consider for a patient package insert are listed in Tables 55.3 and 55.4.

TABLE 55.3. *Selected categories of information that should be considered for inclusion in a patient package insert[a]*

1. Description of what the patient package insert is
2. How and when you should take your medicine
3. Things to remember about your medicine (e.g., take your medicine as directed, keep medicines away from children)
4. What to consider before you take your medicine
5. Potential or likely side effects you may experience
6. Storing your medicine
7. What is contained in the tablet
8. How to obtain additional information about this medicine

[a] See Table 55.4 for a more detailed version.

TABLE 55.4. *Selected categories for inclusion in a patient package insert[a]*

1. What is in the pill?	Answer relates to showing or describing the chemistry and the class of the medicine
2. How does the medicine work?	Answer relates to pharmacology
3. What is the medicine used for?	Answer presents the indication(s) and possibly some limitations (e.g., specific types of diseases where it does not work)
4. How is the medicine given?	Answer describes route of administration and whether it is taken with water, before or after meals
5. How is the medicine supplied?	Answer describes the package and dosage strength
6. Are there reasons not to take the medicine?	Answer describes contraindications in terms such as "Do not take this medicine if" or "Discuss with your doctor before taking this medicine if . . ."
7. What side effects may occur?	Answer describes common adverse experiences
8. What precautions should be used?	Answer describes special patient groups that should not use the medicine as well as possible influences the medicine may have on driving or other activities
9. How should the medicine be stored?	Answer describes conditions for storage and also instructions for discarding the medicine
10. What should be done if an overdose occurs?	Answer describes antidotes that may be useful as well as standard procedures for treating overdoses
11. Are there foods or other medicines that may interact with this medicine?	Answer describes interactions that have been shown to occur and precautions that should be taken
12. How long do I need to take the medicine?	Answer varies for acute and chronic conditions and based on other factors
13. How can one obtain more information?	Answer discusses going to or calling a physician, pharmacist, or hospital

[a] See Table 55.3 for another version.

RESEARCH ON PATIENT PACKAGE INSERTS

Ronald Mann (1991) edited a valuable book that presents information on the status of providing patient information about medicines in many European countries and describes some of the research being conducted in this field. Various studies have been conducted on the various types of inserts that can be prepared (Servizio di Informazione, 1990).

Two major types of studies can be performed to assess the effects of changes in package insert format and con-

TABLE 55.5. *Selected topics that could be discussed in a patient-oriented disease brochure*

1. What is Disease X?
2. Why do you have the disease?
3. What triggers the onset of a disease episode?
4. What are the warning signs of an impending episode?
5. What treatments are available for Disease X?
6. Can Disease X be cured?
7. What are the differences among the different medicines used to treat Disease X?
8. How often should I see my doctor?
9. Why should I take my medicine every day?
10. What is Medicine Y?
11. Should I contact my doctor if the medicine does not work or causes side effects?
12. What should I do in an emergency (e.g., hospital admission, run out of medicine)?

tent. The first type of study involves interviews and tests the effects of changes in a laboratory or in the patients' home environment. The second type of study involves pilot testing of package inserts by substituting them in place of package inserts currently in distribution. These two approaches are described further below.

Interview and Testing Procedures

In this testing procedure, volunteers are asked to read patient package inserts that vary with respect to format and content. Structured interviews and tests elicit information on comprehension and attitudes toward the medicine described and the presentation used. This type of study has low risk with respect to any adverse effects on the volunteers and permits exploration of a wide range of package insert formats and contents. This type of study is a logical predecessor to pilot testing and is desirable to use in the early stages of evaluation.

Pilot Testing

This type of testing procedure involves dispensing patient package inserts that vary in format and content with selected medicines. Patients are asked for their willingness to be interviewed or to complete a questionnaire. Information is collected on reading comprehension, attitude toward the medicine, formats used, and whether or not the medicine was taken as prescribed.

This type of study has a potential for adversely influencing the subjects and therefore should only be conducted after review by an Ethics Committee/Institutional Review Board. It is also desirable to have completed all relevant studies of the patient interview type conducted in a research setting. Behavioral and demographic data may be obtained in these pilot studies to get data on the personalities of the patients. Those data would be important in interpreting the results of the test

and particularly in determining whether the results could be extrapolated to other patient populations.

ALTERNATIVE SYSTEMS FOR PROVIDING INFORMATION ABOUT MEDICINES TO PATIENTS

In addition to (or instead of) a patient package insert in the form of a printed leaflet, patients may receive the same information via a computer printout that is given to them automatically at the time that a medicine is dispensed. This computer printout could be printed out if the person filling the prescription activates a computer system in the pharmacy or store—or somehow initiates the system. Advantages of the pharmacy printout system (rather than a preprinted leaflet) is that the printout could contain the name, address, and telephone number of the pharmacy, as well as the name of a contact person at the pharmacy in case any problems arose. Updating this type of package insert would be a relatively simple matter.

Just as officially approved package inserts are collected into the *Physicians' Desk Reference* (PDR) in the United States, a compilation of patient package inserts could be collected and published. Given the enormous popularity of the PDR among nonphysicians (it is the most widely used book in the New York City public library), it is expected that a comparable annual collection of patient package inserts would also be a highly popular and widely used book. The benefits of this approach would far outweigh any risks.

TABLE 55.6. *Selected topics that could be discussed in a patient-oriented brochure about a specific medicine*

1. How may this booklet be used?
2. What is Medicine Y?
3. How does Medicine Y work against the disease and help me?
4. How safe is Medicine Y and what side effects may be noted?
5. How should the medicine be taken each day?
6. How is the effectiveness of the medicine checked?
7. How long must I take this medicine?
8. What types of benefits may I expect and how long will they last?
9. Are there other medicines that I should not take?
10. What should I do if I forget to take one or two doses?
11. Can I drink alcoholic beverages while I'm taking this medicine?
12. Can I take this medicine if I am pregnant or nursing a child?
13. Are there any food restrictions or interactions, and should I take this medicine before or after meals?
14. Are there interactions with other medicines I should know?
15. What should I do if I have more questions?

Patient-oriented Brochures

Brochures describing a medicine may be prepared for patients by a company. Brochures are often printed in color, have more pages than patient package inserts, and may include information on the disease itself or other topics. Patients should be informed that the brochure is a summary and does not provide full information. Patients should be advised to discuss their particular questions with their physician and to rely on their physician's professional judgment in regard to their specific case. Two sets of categories that could be discussed in a patient-oriented brochure are shown in Tables 55.5 and 55.6. Brochures may be prepared that focus more on the patients' disease than on the particular medicine. These educational brochures would not replace patient package inserts.

Disclaimers or caveats to help interpret the brochure should be directed separately to physicians and patients if a single brochure is prepared for patients. Physicians should be informed that the contents of the brochure do not provide full information about the disease or medicine. Physicians should also be advised to determine how the brochure can be used by patients and what information they could provide as a supplement or as caveats. Thus the information could be individualized for each patient, particularly if the brochures reach patients via their physician. Care should be taken to ensure that disease-oriented brochures are not merely seen as advertising for a particular medicine.

56 / Patent Expiration

The Problem 673
Methods to Address the Problem of Patent
    Expiration 674
    Develop Backup Medicines.................. 674
    Develop Second-Generation Medicines 674
    Modify the Formulation.................... 674
    Create Novel Delivery Systems............. 675
    Develop Specific Chiral Formulations........ 675
    Manufacture Generic Medicines 675
    Develop New Dosage Forms................. 675
    Develop Line-Extensions 675
    Demonstrate Differences Between Brand and
        Generic Products........................ 676
    Switch the Product from Prescription to Over-
        the-Counter Status 676

Lobby to Modify Patent Laws 676
Discover a New Use for the Medicine......... 676
Develop a Rational Combination Medicine ... 676
Develop Patented Generics 677
Secure Raw Materials........................ 677
Increase the Standards of Technical
    Specifications 677
Lower Prices 677
Exchange Exclusivity for Profits............... 677
Create a Generic Company 677
Introduce New Brand Names 677
Choosing Among the Methods 677
    Developing and Implementing the Strategy.... 678

Pricing is a major microeconomic factor at the time of [patent] expiry: the patent holder has the option of joining the fight with a price drop, he can leave it where it is and bank on smaller volume and a good continuing margin, or he can drop it selectively to large volume areas of sale. Steve Kiss—*MM&M*, November 1976

THE PROBLEM

All utility patents expire after a finite period regardless of type (i.e., compound patent, use patent, process patent). After the patent expires any other manufacturer can seek and obtain regulatory approval to make and sell that medicine. In some cases the new manufacturer must conduct bioequivalence tests in humans to assure that the generic version is as bioavailable as the original (i.e., the area under the concentration-time curve is within certain limits). Patent expiration has become progressively more important to pharmaceutical companies over the last two decades. The consequences and severity of the effects of patent expiration vary.

The most serious threat to the owner of an expiring patent, or to the company to which the patent was licensed, is the likely loss of sales to generic medicines. Generics may or may not have brand names, but they are invariably less expensive than the original medicine. The speed at which the erosion of sales and profits occurs has gradually increased in most developed countries over the last 20 years. The three major reasons for this are that (1) many regulatory authorities and legislatures have simplified requirements for obtaining approval to make and sell generic equivalents, (2) cost-containment pressures have led to various incentives for physicians to prescribe and for pharmacists to dispense generic medicines, and (3) patients have been encouraged to request generic equivalents from their physicians and pharmacists. Moreover, the level of competition among companies has increased and led to more companies incorporating generic medicines into their marketed product portfolio. Generic competition has reached the point that almost all commercially valuable medicines have multiple generic competitors as soon as the patent expires, or very shortly thereafter.

The problem of patent expiration leading to decreased sales is compounded because the effective patent life of medicines has shrunk over the last three decades and there is a shorter period of protection during which the company must recoup its costs and make a profit.

Not only are generic competitors able to reach the market more rapidly than in the past, but a number of market forces conspire to increase sales of generic medicines at the expense of the original brand name product. These forces differ from country to country but include

1. government contracts that are awarded to the lowest bidder—these are often major contracts to supply the

national health service, the military, or government hospitals;

2. reduced reimbursement rates by government and other third-party payers after the patent expires;
3. financial bonuses given by third-party payers to pharmacists who dispense generic products; and
4. greater profits afforded pharmacists who dispense generic products even when they are sold at lower than brand name prices.

The evaluation and development of a strategy to protect a profitable medicine after its patent expires should occur soon enough to allow sufficient opportunity to achieve the strategy. This evaluation must occur a number of years prior to patent expiration. Clearly, opportunities will be fewer the later that this evaluation occurs. For most products the appropriate time to consider developing a strategy is approximately three to six (or even more) years in advance of patent expiry. Companies should have a mechanism in place that triggers this evaluation; it could be the responsibility of the patent officer, marketing personnel, or someone in research and development. Developing a strategy should not be left to chance within a research-based company.

METHODS TO ADDRESS THE PROBLEM OF PATENT EXPIRATION

Twenty specific methods are briefly described in this section and are listed in Table 56.1.

Develop Backup Medicines

A backup medicine is a new chemical entity for the indication that is listed for the original marketed medicine. The backup is generally of the same chemical class with a chemical structure that is related to the original compound, although this is not a mandatory requirement. The mechanism of action of a backup medicine is usually the same as that of the original medicine, although this too is not a rigid necessity. It is essential, however, that the backup medicine be patentable. It is desirable to obtain a longer patent life as well as several other advantages over the original medicine. Generally, a backup medicine with a similar chemical structure and only one or two minor advantages over the original medicine is extremely difficult to patent; and even if it is patented, it is difficult to market such a medicine successfully. Common types of advantages sought are: (1) fewer doses per day in order to enhance compliance, (2) smaller size capsules if the original medicine was in a large size capsule to enhance convenience and compliance, (3) any safety improvement, or (4) availability in an important, previously unavailable (in the original) dosage form.

TABLE 56.1. *Approaches to extend the commercial life of a medicine whose patent is expiring*[a]

1. Develop backup medicines
2. Develop second-generation medicines
3. Modify the formulation
4. Create novel delivery systems
5. Develop specific chiral formulations
6. Manufacture generic medicines
7. Develop new dosage forms
8. Develop line extensions
9. Demonstrate differences between brand and generic products
10. Switch the product from prescription to OTC[b] status
11. Lobby to modify patent laws
12. Discover a new use for the medicine
13. Develop a rational combination medicine
14. Develop patented generics
15. Secure raw materials
16. Increase the standards of technical specifications
17. Lower prices
18. Exchange exclusivity for profits
19. Create a generic company
20. Introduce new brand names

[a] Each of these is discussed in the text.
[b] OTC, over-the-counter.

If the backup medicine is needed to replace the original medicine because of toxicity problems in animals or humans, it will be critical to demonstrate a different toxicity profile.

In many companies a second (i.e., backup) medicine is sought even before the original has proven itself to be effective and safe in the investigational period. Chemists, pharmacologists, and other biologists (e.g., microbiologists, virologists) are oriented to seek closely related compounds that have one or more desired advantages over the original even before the original is tested in humans.

Develop Second-Generation Medicines

Whereas a backup medicine is similar to the original marketed one in chemical structure and properties, the chemical structure is usually different than the first medicine. A second- (or third-) generation medicine has important advantages over the initial medicine and overcomes deficiencies inherent in the first medicine. These advantages may be in terms of safety, efficacy, quality of life, or other features. Depending on many factors, a second-generation medicine could be licensed to other companies or developed by another division of the same parent company.

Modify the Formulation

Modifying the formulation of a marketed product may lead to improvements that may be patented. A new formulation could include the development of sustained-release capsules or tablets. If this dosage form modification was patentable and also provided a therapeutic advantage, such as fewer capsules or tablets necessary per day, it would offer the patient benefits in terms of improved compliance. If the new formulation had safety advantages (e.g., a reduced peak plasma level might prevent some adverse events from occurring), then the new formulation would likely lead to a new product that would be able to compete effectively with generic equivalents of the instant-release formulation. Film coating a tablet could offer important clinical advantages if the new product had a better taste than the competitor's product and enhanced compliance. Commercial advantages could be gained over generic competitors from this film-coating process, particularly if it could be patented.

Formulation modifications in manufacturing might lead to new processes that could be patented. A process patent is generally considered weak protection compared to a compound or use patent. Nonetheless, a process patent could act as a deterrent to some manufacturers in selected countries (e.g., in the United States). For instance, if the original synthesis and manufacture is difficult and the potential market size is small, it may not be worth the effort for the generic manufacturer to enter that market.

Certain manufacturing breakthroughs could enable a company to produce one of their off-patent products at much lower cost, even if the process they discovered is not patentable. The discovery could still decrease the price differential between the brand and generic product, and provide less incentive for customers to purchase, or for physicians or pharmacists to recommend, the generic product.

Create Novel Delivery Systems

The number of novel delivery systems and also the number of companies developing these systems appears to be increasing at a rapid rate. Some systems might offer advantages for a medicine, although most of those that combine the medicine with something else, by chemical modification or physical insertion or dissolution, lead to the creation of a "new medicine." This new medicine would have to be developed from the early preclinical stage. While that prospect is not desirable or practical in many cases, it could present a valuable opportunity if the new medicine was patentable and offered one or more important advantages over the original medicine.

The advantage(s) over the "parent" medicine would have to be significant in the opinions of regulators, physicians, formulary committees, and others, not solely in the opinion of a company physician or marketer who believes that it could be important. Evaluating this issue at the outset of the discussion on whether to develop the

new product is important, if the company is to avoid wasting many years of effort and a great deal of money on an activity that is unlikely to be successful.

Develop Specific Chiral Formulations

Many medicines are marketed in a racemic form. Companies are aware of the chiral forms and often make small amounts to test. In some situations a patent may be obtained on one of these forms and would be worthwhile to develop as a new medicine. The decision to proceed in this direction would be quite clear if the chiral form possessed clinical advantages over the original medicine. The advantage most often sought would be an improvement in the safety profile of the medicine. Another advantage of developing a chiral form is that a New Drug Application (NDA) would not require as much clinical, technical, and preclinical data to be generated as was produced for the original medicine.

Manufacture Generic Medicines

Most research-based pharmaceutical companies also manufacture generic versions of some of their medicines. A company may sell generics itself, but also may sell them to other companies for further sale. If the manufacturing process is particularly onerous and difficult, there could be advantages in adopting this approach. Regardless of the strength of senior management opinions about generic manufacture, it is important to prepare a business case to evaluate this issue, to explore all options available, and to reach a decision based on a sound and logical approach. Some research-based companies also manufacture generic versions of their competitors' medicines.

Develop New Dosage Forms

Developing new dosage forms for a medicine can provide important medical advantages for selected patient groups. The degree of protection available for new dosage forms varies enormously and must be assessed on a case-by-case basis. It is also possible that the new dosage form could be developed for a new indication to achieve greater protection from competitors.

Develop Line-Extensions

A company that expands its line-extensions and makes existing products more appropriate for patients should be in a position to compete effectively for prescriptions. Detailing and advertising this information to physicians are effective means of demonstrating benefits of prescribing the brand-name product. Most physicians can recall seeing advertisements that show 20 to 30 dosage forms, dosage strengths, and package sizes of the brand-name product and show (or state) that only a few dosage strengths and dosage forms of the generic competitors exist. Depending on the disease targeted and the need for physicians to tailor therapy to individual patients, this approach can convince physicians to prescribe specific packages or dosage forms of the brand-name medicine.

Demonstrate Differences Between Brand and Generic Products

A frequently heard statement is that a certain brand-name product offers therapeutic benefits not always obtained with the generic "equivalent." The truth of this statement is not easy to prove (or disprove) for any product, but there are well-known cases in the past where this was true (e.g., Lanoxin versus generic digoxin, Bayer aspirin versus some generic aspirins). A sound scientific basis may often be found that accounts for such differences (e.g., variable or larger particle sizes versus consistent particle sizes for the brand-name product). Whatever the scientific reason(s), any differences may be extremely important and should be looked for. But even if some differences are found and publicized, the problem is likely to be corrected and after a short period the generic manufacturers will be competing with equivalent products. If the problem was one of fermentation or some other biological, rather than chemical difference, it is likely that the generic product will have acquired a stigma that will be extremely hard to erase, and both physicians and dispensing pharmacists are more likely to choose the brand-name product for a considerable period of time.

Switch the Product from Prescription to Over-the-Counter Status

If a great deal of safety data have been collected and if the disease and medicine have an appropriate profile, an effective strategy can be to switch the product to OTC status. The many issues and potential problems that should be considered in this area are described in Chapter 57. This approach is not appropriate for many medicines, but if it is, then timing is extremely important. The conversion program should be initiated at an early enough stage so that the switch can be accomplished prior to the patent expiration. Although this is not mandatory, it will increase the likelihood of achieving the maximal promotional value and protection for the product.

Lobby to Modify Patent Laws

Strong patent laws are absolutely vital to the continued health of the research-based pharmaceutical industry. At least one major trade association in the United States has defined its major role as one of lobbying for improved patent laws and preventing any erosion in the protection offered by existing laws. Companies also lobby legislators on patent-related issues. Some companies may decide to lobby for new patent laws or for special laws designed for orphan products, high-technology products, biotechnology products, breakthrough products, or those products that require lengthy development periods. In the United States, the 1984 Patent Term Restoration Act provides up to five years of additional patent life for a new Food and Drug Administration (FDA)-approved patented product. It also provides five years of product exclusivity for a newly approved new chemical entity—independent of patent protection. This law is referred to as the Waxman-Hatch Act.

Discover a New Use for the Medicine

Often after years of marketing a specific medicine, a new use is found for that medicine that can be patented. Even though the company may obtain a use patent, the medicine cannot be protected against generic competition for the original indication. While this makes it appear that the use patent is commercially useless, this is not always so. For example, if a new dosage form is developed for the new indication, then protection would be conferred on the new form. If a new formulation (e.g., sustained-release) could be patented and used for the new (and even for the original) indication, then this would also confer protection. Also, if a new dosage strength was needed to treat the new indication, this also it would contribute to the protection. The best situation would be for two or more of these modifications to occur.

A different strategy may also be used in the same situation, such as not seeking regulatory approval for the new indication, even if appropriate data are available. This approach makes most sense if a follow-up-medicine is being developed for the new indication and the company decides not to market the original medicine for the new use.

Develop a Rational Combination Medicine

Fixed combination medicines are generally frowned on by both regulatory authorities and academic physicians. Nonetheless, certain medically rational combinations are well-accepted, and many of these are liked by general practitioners of medicine and their patients. A medicine whose patent is expiring may be a good candidate for combination development and the resulting combination may be patentable. Although a great deal of clinical and other studies are usually necessary (and will be expensive) to develop the combination, it is quite possible that the combination could preserve a significant portion of the original medicine's market. Even if the combination medicine cannot be patented, there may be other protections that the company could utilize (e.g., Waxman-Hatch Act in the United States, orphan medicine protection) that would make development of the combination commercially valuable.

Develop Patented Generics

A company may have ideas of how to improve the safety, efficacy, or another characteristic of a generic medicine that is currently on the market. It may modify the delivery system or may create one or more optical isomers with better activity or an improved safety profile. It could also use other technologies such as biosensors that could be patented. Any of these advances would provide a company with a long-term franchise that potentially could be exploited commercially.

Secure Raw Materials

A minority of medicines are derived from naturally occurring or extremely difficult to obtain starting materials. In some cases a company may reach an agreement with their supplier to purchase and utilize all available supplies for a considerable time period. Depending on alternative supplies, this approach might make it difficult (if not impossible) for a potential generic competitor to enter the market and to compete with the brand-name product.

A variation on this approach occurs when a company owns a patent for producing a necessary intermediary in the synthesis of a medicine that has gone off-patent. This intermediary, or the rights to it, may be licensed to another company for an advantageous price.

Increase the Standards of Technical Specifications

For medicines that are difficult to manufacture with a high degree of purity, or for which the narrow technical specifications are difficult to achieve, a company could attempt to raise those specifications (i.e., make them narrower). If the increased standards are adopted by national pharmacopoeias, then competitors may be discouraged from entering the market.

Lower Prices

Depending on manufacturing costs and product margins, it may be possible to decrease the price of a medicine. This approach would be most desirable if the price was lowered sufficiently to keep other manufacturers from entering the market.

Exchange Exclusivity for Profits

William Haddad (1992) describes the concept whereby the patent owner allows a generic company to market the patented product for a period of time (e.g., six to twelve months) while the product is still protected by patent. In exchange, the generic company provides a share of their profits to the patent holder for a longer period of time. The advantage of this arrangement for a generic company is to obtain a large market share during the period of their generic exclusivity and to hopefully be able to hold onto that share during subsequent years. Haddad states that "In one case, the net advantage to the brand name company over a three year period was well over US $50 million."

Create a Generic Company

A research-based company could form its own subsidiary company to manufacture generic medicines solely of its own formerly patented products or additionally of other products as well. A variation of this approach is when a research-based company forms a subsidiary company to sell, but not to manufacture, generic medicines.

Introduce New Brand Names

A large pharmaceutical company, particularly one with subsidiaries having different names can introduce new brands of a product prior to or shortly after the patent expiration. In order for this strategy to be successfully used the costs of entry for a new brand must be justified by the forecasted sales and profits minus the canibalization.

CHOOSING AMONG THE METHODS

Some of the initial questions to consider when choosing an approach for protecting a product going off patent are listed below.

1. What are the clinical, commercial, and technical strengths of the product?
2. What are the weaknesses of the product?

3. What areas of opportunity appear most promising?
4. Where are the major threats to the product coming from?

The answers to these questions can provide the basis for idea generation. The better ideas should be evaluated in terms of feasibility, chance of success, cost, use of company personnel and other resources, and legal and regulatory issues.

Developing and Implementing the Strategy

Part of strategy development should be to consider and compare each conceivable method for protecting a profitable medicine. A Gantt chart may be used to illustrate some aspects of the data. This allows each method to be evaluated and compared in terms of practicality and of time required to implement each approach. Knowing the time required enables one to estimate when individual activities should begin and be completed. Thus activities that could be completed prior to patent expiry are identified. Nonetheless, because activities tend to be delayed and require more time to complete than anticipated, it is wise to implement a strategy as far ahead of patent expiry as possible. For every medicine, a unique strategy must be developed. The strategy should include extra time to resolve all issues and complete all activities. Regulatory review is often required and the time allotted for this step can only be estimated in most cases. There are a few legitimate reasons (e.g., insufficient resources) why an early start to implementing the strategy may not be able to be initiated, and may have to be delayed. The speed of pursuing the strategy chosen must be reevaluated during each stage of the process.

Careful planning and monitoring throughout the implementation process is important to maintain the timetable for achieving all milestones. Any deviation from the plan should be addressed just as for any important project of an investigational medicine.

In most situations it is desirable to appoint a single person to lead or manage all activities. However, assigning a single leader for a project may or may not be appropriate, depending on the strategy adopted. Sometimes, a team approach is more likely to lead to achievement of the company's goals. In some situations it may be desirable to have separate managers or leaders responsible for different parts of the strategy (e.g., reducing production costs, converting the product to OTC status, and develop-

ing a backup product). The likelihood of success is enhanced if each part of the strategy is handled similarly to other company projects with the company's traditional systems and procedures.

When major resource constraints are present, the implications should be considered for each of the methods being evaluated; this ensures that each method is evaluated fairly. Decisions about which methods to choose ideally should not be based solely on cost even though the total cost of each method should be determined in advance. If the number of persons available to carry out the plan is more of a limitation than money, then certain aspects of the chosen strategy could be conducted by contractors or consultants.

Every possible method to extend the life of a medicine going off patent should be explored in detail. The pros and cons for a method will vary for each case and a formal evaluation of methods is required. This evaluation should present the pros and cons of each approach and the options for implementing each method. Finally, an overall strategy should be proposed that would include most or even all of the methods to help the particular product retain as much of its present market share as possible.

Note added in proof. Another approach to protect a medicine's sales when the patent is close to expiring is to initiate sales directly to patients. This method is used only for chronically used medicines and can be conducted by having sales representatives inform physicians of an alternate means for their patients to obtain the brand-name medicine, i.e., direct via mail through calling a toll-free telephone number. Some mail-order companies obtain insurance payments for patients in addition to sending medicines by mail. Advantages for patients with this approach are: (1) a system that provides the convenience of having medicines sent directly to them and also handles their insurance, and (2) lower prices than available at retail pharmacies for patients who pay directly. Advantages for companies include: (1) market share is protected, (2) marketing groups have a new message to promote, and (3) sales representatives have a new marketing tool that will encourage more detailing calls.

This method is particularly well suited for the indemnity market where patients and physicians have more discretion to choose specific brand-name medicines.

57 / Switching Prescription Medicines to Over-the-Counter Status

Definitional Issues	679	The Consumer's Perspective	683
Reasons for a Company to Consider Switching a Medicine to OTC Status	680	The Physician's Perspective	683
		Marketing Issues	684
Major Issues to Consider Before Deciding on a Prescription to OTC Switch	680	Regulatory Issues	684
		Regulatory Mechanisms for Approving OTC Medicines	685
Strategic Issues	681	Monographs on Over-the-Counter Medicines	685
Selling Both Forms of a Medicine Versus Selling Only the OTC Form	681	Approval Mechanisms in the United States	685
Dosage Strength	681	Alternative Strategies to Switching	685
Methods of Switching	681		
Steps to Follow in Switching Medicines from Prescription to OTC Status	681		

Quantitative changes suddenly become qualitative changes. From all of Marxism, which I once thought attractive enough, I find only this dictum remaining in the realm of my opinions. Water grows colder and colder and colder, and suddenly it's ice. The day grows darker and darker, and suddenly it's night. Man ages and ages, and suddenly he's dead. Differences in degree lead to differences in kind. John Barth

Discussions of the switch from prescription to over-the-counter (OTC) status generally conclude that all cases are unique and how it is not possible to define a strict set of guidelines. On the other hand, there are a variety of issues that can be identified for consideration and a fairly well agreed upon series of basic principles that should be adhered to, or at least considered, by any sponsor seeking to make this conversion. This chapter presents those issues and principles.

DEFINITIONAL ISSUES

It seems extremely obvious that prescription medicines require a physician's order (i.e., prescription) for patients to receive them, and that over-the-counter medicines (OTCs) are those that may be purchased without a prescription. Nonetheless, there are numerous complicating factors. First, prescription medicines can be bought over the counter in many countries. Second, there is a third category of medicines in some countries, referred to as transition class medicines or third category

medicines. Pharmacists dispense these medicines when they are convinced that the patient or requester has a legitimate need. The concept behind the third category is widely supported by pharmacists and pharmacist organizations in the United States, but is rarely supported by physicians, pharmaceutical companies, or their trade associations. The notion of "learned intermediary" is used to encourage acceptance of this third class of medicines. The learned intermediary is the last professional interface between a medicine and the consumer: the pharmacist for most prescription medicines and the labeling for OTC medicines. Labeling should provide complete educational information telling patients how and when to use the product.

Lastly, some medicines are sold both by prescription and as over-the-counter products in a single country, although the dosage may differ (e.g., in the United States ibuprofen 200-mg tablets are sold OTC, whereas 400-mg tablets are sold only with a prescription).

Another definitional issue applies to the different types of OTC medicines in Europe. Semiethical medicines are sold OTC and are reimbursed by the government (where applicable) as if they were prescription medicines. Registered OTC medicines are sold OTC but are not reimbursed by the government. Mass market medicine products include vitamins and minerals, and non-registered medicines include homeopathic and herbal medicines; both categories are sold widely in Europe. OTC issues in Europe have been recently discussed (Dudley, 1992).

REASONS FOR A COMPANY TO CONSIDER SWITCHING A MEDICINE TO OTC STATUS

The major reason to consider this switch is the certain loss of patent protection on a commercially important medicine, and the eventual generic competition that will rapidly erode sales of that medicine. In another case, a patented medicine that is showing declining sales often can be revived once it is sold OTC. If sales are stable or increasing on a prescription medicine that has no patent protection, the OTC market might still be much larger than the prescription market. Another reason to switch to OTC status is that the medicine might complement existing OTC products or product lines. Table 57.1 lists other potential reasons for making the OTC switch.

There is a theoretical possibility in the United States that a medicine switched to OTC status can be granted a period of marketing exclusivity by the Food and Drug Administration (FDA). This would be based on submitting new information and data that are pertinent to the

TABLE 57.1. *Reasons to consider switching a medicine from prescription to over-the-counter status*

1. More consumers desire to treat their own medical problems, particularly if they do not believe the ailment is severe.
2. Over-the-counter medicines generally have a good reputation and are convenient to obtain.
3. Patients save money caring for themselves by decreasing the number of office visits they must make to physician offices and by purchasing less expensive medicines.
4. The aging population is growing in many societies, and it is this segment of the population that purchases most of the OTC[a] medicines sold.
5. Converting medicines to OTC status is an effective strategy for preventing generics from capturing the entire market after the patent expires.[b]
6. The image of OTC medicines is positive in terms of safety and effectiveness.
7. OTC medicines are a method of increasing sales (and profits) of selected older prescription medicines with declining sales.
8. There is a possibility that a company may obtain marketing exclusivity for a number of years by making the prescription-to-OTC switch.

[a] OTC, over-the-counter.
[b] Other strategies of countering this problem are discussed in Chapter 56, Patent Expiration.

switch that were not presented or relied on for obtaining the prescription indication.

In evaluating the OTC conversion issue, some potentially negative consequences should be considered.

1. Over-the-counter medicines have smaller profit margins compared to patent-protected brand-name prescription medicines.
2. Over-the-counter medicines require large promotional costs, particularly in their early years.
3. Decreased prescription sales are likely to occur if the medicine also remains on the prescription market after conversion to the OTC market.
4. There is a possibility that the OTC application will be turned down by regulatory authorities; if this is considered highly likely, then efforts should progress only to the point where feedback from regulatory authorities may be obtained.

In general, prescription to OTC switching has been less successful in Europe than in the United States. This primarily relates to different reimbursement policies for patient visits to physicians. In the United States patients often save money by purchasing OTC medicines in lieu of paying for an office visit to a physician. This is not common in most European countries because patients do not pay (or only pay a small amount) for visits to personal physicians. Other factors that complicate the European OTC system are country-specific cultures, traditions, and distribution systems for OTC medicines. Furthermore, final EEC guidelines on this matter have not been issued. Experiences with switching large numbers of products in Denmark are discussed by Raith (1992).

MAJOR ISSUES TO CONSIDER BEFORE DECIDING ON A PRESCRIPTION TO OTC SWITCH

A few questions must be addressed prior to reaching a decision to convert a prescription medicine to OTC status.

1. Are patients willing to self-diagnose the problem that the OTC medicine treats? While this may appear to be a strange question, patients in some countries are uncomfortable diagnosing certain diseases. Patient education might be necessary to change this perception.

2. Are patients able to self-diagnose the problem that the OTC medicine treats? While some false positives and false negatives in diagnosis may be allowable, most patients must be able to diagnose the problem fairly accurately before they can treat it. Patients may have to visit physicians for their initial diagnosis and only self-diagnose recurrences. Education could play a role major here too (e.g., drawings of how to use the medicine could be placed on package inserts).

3. Are patients able to easily treat themselves? For example, patients may be willing and able to self-diagnose a problem, but if it requires them to inject themselves most would be unwilling or unable to do so appropriately.

4. What are the consequences for a patient of failing to correctly make a diagnosis (i.e., a false-negative diagnosis) and not seeking medical help? For a headache or minor pain there are usually little sequelae, but for certain problems the disease will progress and the patient's condition may become exacerbated by the delay in receiving appropriate treatment.

5. What are the consequences for a patient of using the treatment when it is not indicated (i.e., a false-positive diagnosis was made)? If the medicine has an appropriate level of safety there should be little or no sequelae from inappropriate treatment.

6. What is the likelihood of the patient taking an accidental overdose and what would the results be? The same question about effects should be considered for a purposeful overdose.

7. What is the likelihood of the patient taking a purposeful overdose (i.e., abuse of the medicine) to obtain a euphoric feeling?

8. For OTC products that require the patient to modify their behavior (e.g., dieting, stopping smoking), how willing would patients be to do this on their own? This question could be addressed in some clinical trials—but the artificial nature of some trials could give misleading results.

STRATEGIC ISSUES

Selling Both Forms of a Medicine Versus Selling Only the OTC Form

It is important to decide whether to retain the prescription form of the medicine after the OTC form is launched, or whether to discontinue the prescription medicine. If the decision is made to discontinue the prescription medicine, this could be done over a period of years and not necessarily immediately or within a few months after the OTC medicine is introduced. Such a plan would enable the marketing group to gauge the value of the prescription market and how well it could be maintained with a certain level of promotion.

Dosage Strength

A second issue is whether to introduce a smaller dosage strength of the medicine for the OTC market. This issue is generally viewed together with the first issue. Companies are more likely to simultaneously market the same medicine by prescription and OTC if a smaller dosage strength is sold OTC. This approach may be necessary if the larger dosage strength has a safety profile that is less "clean" than that of the lower dosage strength. In addition, efficacy at the lower dosage strength would have had to be demonstrated in clinical trials. This would require the conduct of new clinical trials if the original ones did not adequately study the lower dosages.

METHODS OF SWITCHING

Steps to Follow in Switching Medicines from Prescription to OTC Status

While these steps follow a logical order, several will progress simultaneously and others may be initiated earlier or later for different situations. Step 6 will vary greatly in comparison with the others as to the best time for its implementation. These steps may also be viewed as golden rules for converting prescription medicines to OTC status, and should only be initiated after a company analyzes the eight major issues described above and has made a tentative decision to proceed.

1. Conduct preliminary market research to explore the proposed switch. It is important to seek the views of numerous groups of consumers, health professionals, and other affected groups.

2. Develop a proposal that considers scientific, medical, marketing, legal, production, and other issues within the company.

3. Evaluate the proposal to make the switch and prepare a document that discusses advantages, disadvantages, and the likelihood of regulatory, medical, and commercial success. Describe specific scientific, regulatory, medical, and marketing issues and propose strategies to deal with each.

4. Obtain a senior managerial decision to make the switch and to commit sufficient resources to do the job appropriately and within the time schedule proposed. The general time period required to conduct the tests and to file the documents is two to four years, but shorter or longer times are possible. A clear commitment by the most senior managers of a company must be made to support the conversion. It is preferable that this commitment be put in writing.

5. Form a multidisciplinary project team that will coordinate the effort within all of their areas, and appoint a team leader. This team should have representatives from regulatory affairs, marketing, production, medical, legal, and other relevant disciplines. Any of these representatives or another person (e.g., professional administrator) may be appointed as the team's leader. The personality and characteristics of this leader are far more important than his or her discipline. Professionals who have previously worked on the prescription medicine should be involved in some capacity with the prescription-to-OTC

conversion process. This could be either as team members or as advisors to the team.

6. Utilize outside consultants and medical experts who have experience with conducting switches successfully. This should occur at an early stage (i.e., prior to meetings with regulatory authorities) while strategies are being developed and the choice of a candidate for conversion may not be totally fixed. Not only can consultants provide valuable advice here, but they can also help marketing groups design research that will help position the medicine appropriately.

7. Meet (if possible) with all relevant regulatory authorities to discuss the company's plans. The timing of this meeting is critical. If it occurs too early in the process, the company may not have all of its strategy and approaches worked out to convince the regulators of the appropriateness of the conversion. If the meeting is delayed, however, until everything is worked out, the regulators may disagree with the approach and suggest another direction that could add much time and cost to the project. The endorsement of the plan by regulatory authorities is an important goal, but even if that goal is not achieved, it is important that the regulatory group's problems with the strategy (as well as their suggestions) are addressed. This may require a clinical trial or another approach. Seek a champion (if possible) within the regulatory authority who believes in the concept and can serve as an ally.

8. Collect all safety data available on the medicine including experiences in pregnant women, postmarketing surveillance observational studies, adverse reactions reported to the company, and evaluations of large automated multipurpose data bases. Estimate the number of patient exposures in each major country for the prescription medicine and determine the number of units sold. Are there any special toxicities, interactions, or pharmacokinetic issues reported? Discuss each of these fully. A certain number of patient exposures should be identified as the minimal amount of data necessary to justify conversion to OTC status.

9. Conduct state-of-the-art market research to identify the consumer's need for the medicine, other OTC medicines being used, and the number of patients who will benefit; also determine any delays in seeking treatment—does this cause problems? In addition to the marketing people, the entire OTC team should "review" the market research plans prior to their implementation, or at least have an opportunity to provide input to the designs used.

10. Address regulatory authority concerns; and, seek opinions and comments from (1) pharmacists in various organizations, (2) practicing physicians, (3) consumer groups, (4) medical organizations, (5) nurses, and (6) individual consumers in developing and revising a sound strategy and specific plans to make the switch. The strategy should include consideration of the work of all major

groups involved in the conversion. Having the support of consumer groups may be "essential" to achieving the prescription to OTC switch.

11. Conduct any clinical trials that are required. This step may be initiated early in the process. It is important not to wait until regulatory input has been received before this is initiated—unless the regulatory input is received quite early in the process. Identify what conditions could be masked by the medicine, and what would be likely to happen if the medicine did not help patients.

12. Attempt to demonstrate a public health benefit from the switch to OTC status. Use sound scientific and medical arguments to do this. Seek advice if this does not seem possible. This is an important goal to attain.

13. Write package labeling and develop a patient brochure to help educate patients about the disease/condition, the product, and its proper use. A full patient package insert should be considered. Consider creating (1) product literature for physicians and pharmacists to dispense, (2) articles for newspapers and magazines to print, and (3) video computer messages for pharmacists to play in those pharmacies that have the equipment.

14. Ask the regulatory authority to convene a public advisory committee (if relevant) to discuss whether the product is appropriate for conversion to OTC status and to review the evidence supporting the switch. Help the regulatory authorities, if possible, frame the questions for the committee to consider. Prior to the meeting, rehearse consultants and staff. Seek permission to provide the committee with a white paper in advance of the meeting that discusses the issues. This is a public forum in the United States that usually offers more benefits than disadvantages to a sponsor.

15. File a state-of-the-art New Drug Application (NDA) or supplemental NDA that presents the data and arguments clearly and logically. It should not be a surprise to the regulatory authority, but rather should be the culmination of frequent interactions and discussions on the application's content and the approaches used.

16. Develop a public relations and promotional campaign, particularly if it is necessary to prepare the community for a new type of OTC. Prepare an extensive marketing program that seeks buy-in (i.e., support) of the professionals who currently prescribe and use the medicine. Do not skimp on efforts to educate this group and to seek their endorsement. This group includes physicians, nurses, pharmacists, and often others. This should be initiated well in advance of the switch but definitely not until after the company is convinced it will receive approval. This campaign must be in accordance within the law, and never without the explicit or tacit approval of regulators.

17. Contact the regulatory authorities after an appropriate period if there is no response to the application and request that they provide a response. If their response is negative, it will be necessary to conduct new

clinical, technical, or other studies to address their response. Determine what their concerns are. Is there a special population (e.g., elderly, renally impaired, pregnant) where special issues exist? If so, how can they be addressed?

In developing an overall strategy for the conversion, it may become evident that insufficient resources exist within a company to complete the regulatory dossier within the desired time. Alternatively, the sales force needed after approval may not be prepared to detail an OTC medicine. The most appropriate response to either of these problems could be for the company to form a strategic alliance with another company to copromote or comarket the product. Another alternative is to license the medicine's OTC rights to another group, but that approach should only be considered if the company does not have any presence in the local territory (i.e., country) where OTC approval is received.

Every case of switching a medicine is different. Do not become restricted by the lessons obtained from other switches that may not be applicable to your particular case. Have brainstorming sessions to develop new ideas. Focus on the disease more than the medicine in both developing and pursuing a strategy that will be convincing. Adhere to the highest scientific standards possible in the conduct of all trials and work for the OTC submission.

THE CONSUMER'S PERSPECTIVE

A consumer who is choosing among OTC medicines in a store or using a mail-order catalog perceives price as a major factor, even when he or she has a preference for a different product. The effect of price on a person's choices varies greatly among product categories and also among specific brands. This is similar to the situation of consumers choosing among many products (e.g., paper towels or napkins) in a supermarket. They may note that the brand they usually do not buy is on sale and their preferred brand is not. Their thinking is often along the lines that they like Brand X, but Brand Y is less expensive today and if the difference in price is significant they are likely to purchase Brand Y. Brand loyalty may prevail, but its importance is difficult to measure and varies greatly among products. This analogy is also appropriate because most OTC medicines have significant competition and purchasers make comparisons when they shop. Consumers are aware of the benefits that OTCs provide in being able to forgo a physician's visit. Depending on the country involved, this may provide a significant cost savings.

Consumers often have a variety of beliefs about OTC medicines that may or may not be true. False beliefs among the consumer public should be identified by the company. The following are some typical, generally held beliefs about OTC medicines.

1. Over-the-counter medicines contain a lower dose of the medicine than the prescription product.
2. Over-the-counter medicines are safer because the dose is lower.
3. Over-the-counter medicines do not have all the ingredients found in the prescription medicine.
4. Over-the-counter medicines are less expensive than prescription medicines.
5. Over-the-counter medicines that are switched from prescription status are more powerful than other traditionally sold OTCs.
6. Over-the-counter medicines that are switched act more specifically against a disease than do the older, safer, and more familiar OTCs.

It has been estimated that consumers have a 92% satisfaction with OTC products (Vickery, 1985). The widespread use of OTCs attest to their essential role in providing health care to a majority of the population of adults in developed countries.

THE PHYSICIAN'S PERSPECTIVE

Physicians respond to detailing and sampling in the OTC as well as in the prescription medicine area. Companies may have separate detailing forces for OTC and prescription medicines in some countries. Providing relevant information to physicians is essential because a significant percentage of physicians (estimated at 25%) stop using a product once it goes OTC. The reasons for this include (1) decreased ability for physicians to supervise patients using OTC medicines, (2) the patients they see "expect" a prescription, and (3) loss of income results from recommending an OTC medicine if patients decrease their number of visits as a result.

Physicians are generally conservative in the ways they practice medicine, and in some countries the initial reaction of physicians to a new OTC medicine is generally negative. Physicians represent an important source of medical information for patients. Thus they too must be educated about the benefits, if any, in recommending the OTC version of a formerly prescription-only product. Their initial reaction is likely to be that the OTC product will lead to fewer patient visits. If they are employed by a national health service, or a prepaid health organization (e.g., HMO), the switch may not be a problem, but if they are in a fee-for-service group or are self-employed it could represent a major issue—namely, the economic loss incurred when patients can treat themselves with OTC medicines and eliminate a visit to their physician.

A carefully thought through and tested plan to reach physicians should be developed. Anything less than a perfectly conceived and executed plan could cause the medicine major harm as an OTC and the company could suffer commercially. Physician perceptions can be elicited in advance and used to improve the company's approach. Attention must be given to how current and previous switch treatment practices will differ and how the physicians role in patient care will change, if at all.

MARKETING ISSUES

Differences between marketing strategy for prescription medicines and that for OTC medicines are so great that companies usually have two separate marketing groups to deal with these two groups of medicines. The OTC group is more concerned with patient behavior and decision making than is the prescription group. This leads to more market research and evaluation about (1) whether to proceed with an Rx to OTC switch, (2) how to proceed, and (3) which indication to pursue (if there is a choice). For example, some antihistamines were used for allergies, colds, sinus problems, pruritus, and as sleep aids. Each of these is a separate market and would require a different marketing strategy. Thus a company must prioritize these markets in terms of their efforts to convert a medicine to OTC status. If all indications are converted to OTC status, then prioritization of resources must be made in terms of how much money each indication will receive for promotion, as well as staff efforts. The positioning of an OTC product may not be the same as that of its prescription version. For example, diphenhydramine is now sold OTC for primarily allergy use in the United States, whereas a decade ago it was primarily sold as a prescription medicine for other indications.

Marketing focus groups, in-depth interviews, and concept testing are important methods by which a company can discern consumer thinking. The message a company wants to deliver to consumers should be broadly tested to ensure its clarity and acceptance.

In designing a market research program, it is important to focus on combinations of relevant factors about the product and not to evaluate each factor individually. Most people make trade-offs in the process of deciding which product to purchase. Factors such as price, quantity, dosage form, frequency of dosage, and duration of effect may all be varied in several ways in questioning a group of 100 to 200 potential consumers. For example, if consumers do not relate well to price per dose or price per treatment, but instead focus on the total price per package, it may be best to introduce smaller and cheaper packages.

Regulatory Issues

The 1938 Food, Drug and Cosmetic Act requires that a medicine must be sold only by prescription if it is (1)

habit-forming, (2) not safe to use except under supervision (e.g., because of toxicity or parenteral use), or (3) has an NDA. Otherwise, all medicines are potential candidates for OTC status. In practice, few medicines are originally introduced OTC and most usually remain prescription products for many years. The FDA uses five additional criteria to evaluate whether a medicine may safely be used over-the-counter.

1. Margin of safety. This relates not only to whether the medicine is habit-forming or possesses unacceptable toxicity, but also to whether the benefit-to-risk relationship is acceptable. This requires judgment of several types of risk (i.e., the risk to people who turn out not to have the condition the medicine treats, as well as the risk to those who have the condition but do not visit a physician). A number of safety issues are listed in Table 57.2.

2. Effectiveness. The FDA considers effectiveness in terms of (1) Is OTC use anticipated to be similar to the current prescription use? (2) How broad a patient population was included in the clinical trial conducted? and (3) If approval of a lower dose than that currently approved is requested, has effectiveness been adequately demonstrated at that dose? What is the minimally effective dose and has a dose-response relationship been demonstrated? How well are the pharmacodynamics understood?

3. Related issues. Some of the questions that will be raised by the FDA include: (1) Can patients diagnose the condition? (2) Are the symptoms or signs recognizable by patients? (3) Can the condition be treated appropriately by patients? (4) Is it necessary to monitor the patients' medical status with laboratory tests? and (5) Is it necessary for a physician to follow patients on this medicine?

4. Adequate labeling. Can adequate warnings against unsafe use be written? Can adequate directions for proper use be written? Is it certain that patients will understand the label? Does the label indicate the maximum duration of use? It is possible that an OTC could be sold only for recurrences of a problem, but the initial occurrence would require a physician's visit and diagnosis.

5. Additional issues. These depend entirely on the na-

TABLE 57.2. *Safety issues to consider*

1. No serious adverse reactions should occur in patients, particularly the young or elderly.
2. Ensure that the medicine is not habit-forming.
3. Any adverse reactions must be acceptable in nature and allow patients to function.
4. There should be a sound rationale for the medicine.
5. The safety margin (i.e., therapeutic index) must be large.
6. The safety profile must be delineated at the highest recommended dose.
7. Any possible interactions with other medicines should be explored.

ture of the disease, medicine, or personality of the regulatory reviewing officer. Experience in other countries where the medicine is sold OTC would be highly relevant.

There is no checklist or series of guidelines to follow because each case is judged on its own merits. A thorough review of the literature must be made to identify any issues raised. Decisions made by regulatory authorities usually consider opinions of the public, medical professionals, legislators, pharmacists, and multiple groups within the regulatory authority. A basic principle is that benefits must outweigh the risks.

Regulatory Mechanisms for Approving OTC Medicines

Regulatory mechanisms for making the switch from prescription to OTC status vary greatly among countries probably more than they do for prescription medicine approval. For example, a very large number of medicines that are prescription only in most developed countries are sold OTC in Denmark, whereas the sale of any medicine in Greece without a prescription is illegal.

Monographs on Over-the-Counter Medicines

The FDA has been involved since 1972 in an extensive review of the approximate 700 active ingredients in OTC medicines. The purpose has been to ensure that these ingredients are both safe and effective, and that the products are labeled accurately and appropriately. Products were placed in approximately 58 different major therapeutic categories. Advisory review panels reviewed the ingredients used in the OTC products available in specific therapeutic areas for safety and efficacy. They also reviewed claims made for these products and recommended suitable labeling for (1) indications, (2) dosing, and (3) warnings. The panel phase of this project took nearly 10 years to complete.

Based on the reports of the advisory panels, the FDA issues its own findings as a series of tentative final monographs. After a period of public review and comment the FDA then issues a rule in the form of a final monograph. These monographs establish the regulatory standards for marketing nonprescription medicines. An important element of these monographs is that marketing approval is not required if the sponsor follows their recommendations and standards.

Approval Mechanisms in the United States

In the United States there are four mechanisms for converting prescription medicines to OTC status (i.e., switch regulations, NDA filing, OTC Drug Review Monographs, NDA Deviation). Switch regulations were established in 1956 to enable anyone to petition the FDA for an exemption of prescription-only limitations if it is unnecessary to protect the public's health. The FDA Commissioner may also initiate this process on his or her own. An NDA filing of a supplement has been used to convert several medicines to OTC status (e.g., Actifed, Benylin). Any medicine may be marketed OTC after it is published in an OTC final monograph. Anyone can petition the FDA to amend the monograph and add one or more related prescription products. Finally, the NDA Deviation based on regulation 21CFR330.11 allows a new indication for a monographed product. A sponsor submits pertinent data and information to justify its request.

ALTERNATIVE STRATEGIES TO SWITCHING

A few of the alternatives to switching a prescription medicine to OTC status are listed below.

1. Develop a combination medicine for prescription use rather than attempt to convert the medicine to OTC status.
2. Buy an established OTC brand. This is a standard practice and perhaps the easiest way to enter a new OTC area.
3. Create a new prescription brand name and retain the original brand prescription medicine. This can be extremely expensive to do in terms of advertising and promotion if there is already competition in the area. Many companies that have tried this approach have failed.
4. Develop line-extensions for the prescription medicine. This is a common approach used to increase prescription (or OTC) medicine sales.
5. Review OTC monographs and seek novel combinations of ingredients and novel approaches for new OTC medicines that can be marketed more easily than pursuing the prescription-to-OTC conversion. One problem is the large amount of competition in most commercially valuable areas.

Adherence to the principles discussed should improve the chances that an Rx to OTC conversion will be successful.

58 / Interaction with Legislators and the Public

The Problem 687
Past Responses 688
Current and Future Goals 688
Changing the Focus of the Debate 689
   National Value of the Pharmaceutical Industry 689
Creating a New Image 690
   Poor People 691
   Commercial Messages and Advertisements 691
   Other Approaches to Improve Industry's
     Relationship with Legislators and the Public 691

Organizing a Public Health Policy Group within
   a Company 692
Should Company Activities Be Funneled Through
   Their Major Trade Association? 692
How a Company Can Help Achieve Industry
   Goals 693
Educating the Public: Framing the Debate
   Among the Pharmaceutical Industry,
   Legislators, and the Public in Terms of
   Economic Value 694

Lowering the time it takes for drugs to be approved for the market would probably go much farther in reducing drug prices than instituting new regulations to tighten the screws on an innovative industry. "Drug Store Economics," *The Providence Journal-Bulletin,* November 1991

A government that robs Peter to pay Paul can always depend upon the support of Paul. George Bernard Shaw

THE PROBLEM

Increasing United States government regulation of pharmaceuticals, government and nongovernment requirements for placing Food and Drug Administration (FDA)-approved medicines onto formularies before they can be prescribed, and the potential for legislators to control medicine prices are three major threats to the very existence of many research and development–based pharmaceutical companies, not just in the United Sates, but also worldwide.

Companies are now realizing that a radically new approach must be used to educate external groups about the nature of our industry and the pressures that are faced. This chapter presents a focus or theme for dialogue with the public and legislators. The theme is a dual one and is based on discussing the economic value of medicines to patients and to society rather than the economic costs and burden to the company. Second, the economic value of the industry to American society and its well-being should be promoted. The social value of our industry and the costs of research and development should not be major themes to develop and pursue with either Congress or the public at this point in time.

If new medicines are not discovered and successfully marketed, then, within a single patent life cycle (i.e., 17 years in the United States and up to 20 years in Europe), no patented medicines will be sold. In reality, this threat is even more acute because the effective patent life of a newly marketed medicine (i.e., years of patent life remaining at the time the medicine is launched) averages about seven to ten years. Companies would like the clock on patents to begin after a new medicine is marketed, yet they want protection from the time of their first patent filing. Pharmaceutical companies find it increasingly difficult (and expensive) to discover medically important and valuable new medicines. Regulations that facilitate rather than hinder this process would have an enormous effect on the future environment in which new medicine discoveries will occur. Regulatory standards imposed on pharmaceutical companies for achieving market approval are continually rising in all developed countries, so that the efforts and resources required by companies to achieve commercial successes are also increasing.

More and more prescriptions are being written each year for medicines that are placed on formularies. If a company does not have its medicine listed on a formulary, the number of prescriptions possible is diminished. In Canada, each province has its own formulary so that approval by the Health Protection Branch (HPB) in Ottawa and launch by the company does not represent the start of sales, but a prelude to attempts to have the provincial formularies include the medicine on its list. The third issue mentioned is that of price controls. Price controls operate in most developed countries but not within the United States.

Given such important issues, pharmaceutical companies must react appropriately to efforts by Congress and the American public to impose price controls and higher regulatory standards for medicine approval.

PAST RESPONSES

It is apparent that the pharmaceutical industry in the United States has a relatively poor record convincing Congress and the public of the high value and standards of our industry. Simply reviewing the critical comments made at a recent congressional hearing about the need for price controls would convince anyone that the tide of pressures is mounting. Even mainstream consumer activist groups and other public groups are often highly critical of the industry. More and more citizen and professional groups are calling for some type of control on prices. Compared to medicine prices, quality and access to medical care are relatively unimportant topics to the public.

What has the industry done for the last 15 years to counter the widespread impression that it is too profitable, has low ethical standards, and requires more regulation? The answer is that it has often emphasized to the public that the costs incurred in discovering and developing new medicines are "extremely high," that these costs are escalating faster than inflation, and that there are substantial risks involved in research. Studies are often quoted by industry spokespeople and supporters, stating that the average cost of discovering and developing a single new medicine was approximately 54 million dollars in 1976, 87 million dollars in 1982, 125 million dollars in 1987, and 231 million dollars in 1990. Another widely quoted statement is that unless pharmaceutical companies are allowed to charge their requested prices for new medicines, research for medicine discovery will either shrivel or become concentrated within the few mega-sized pharmaceutical companies that can survive the "discover or die" price control pressures on all research-based pharmaceutical companies. These economic statements and approaches have not been effective in convincing Congress or the public that the industry is not merely intent on making as high profits as possible and should be protected from stringent regulations. Moreover, the industry has often presented itself as an offshoot of the priesthood of medicine. This ap-

proach has led to the industry being judged by the same ethical standards that are applied to physicians. This is a standard that cannot be met and is inappropriate because the research-based industry must make sufficient profits to survive and carry out research and development activities.

A little reflection would readily convince almost anyone that the above-described approach was unlikely to achieve its goals. The industry is widely perceived as "crying wolf" about the dangers it faces. The pharmaceutical industry overall is highly profitable when compared with other industries, and individual pharmaceutical companies are highly profitable on the average when compared with companies in other industries. Therefore, why should Congress or the public care how much it costs to develop a new medicine or how risky the endeavor is? Moreover, a total of 231 million dollars to discover and develop an important new medicine may seem like a true bargain to many legislators who are used to discussing extremely large sums of money for projects that often yield little return. The fact that numerous companies have been forced to merge or be acquired over the last 15 years is not unique to the pharmaceutical industry and also does not draw much sympathy from either the public or legislators.

Individuals and groups who must pay for medicines focus on how much medicines cost and often ignore or do not value appropriately the benefits they receive for their money. Moreover, most benefits are taken for granted. These people want to know if they can afford new medicines that are being introduced with high price tags. None of the vocal public or government groups are convinced that the industry has a valid claim to support the relatively high prices they charge for many new medicines. A relatively successful relationship, however, has often been achieved by the industry with formulary committees. These groups often accept expensive new medicines onto their formularies, in part because most of their medicine costs are passed on to third-party payers. Formulary committees at government hospitals are an obvious exception.

CURRENT AND FUTURE GOALS

Before the industry can choose the best approaches and techniques for presenting its message to Congress and the public, it must have a series of goals or objectives it hopes to achieve. The industry should develop a plan to achieve each of the goals that includes both proactive and reactive (i.e., defensive) approaches or methods. Short-term highly specific industry goals are not described in this chapter. Instead, the general, longer term goals of altering public and congressional attitudes and perceptions that represent major threats to the industry are identified.

The following seven goals for the U.S. pharmaceutical industry are all important, although they represent an incomplete list. There is no particular significance to the order of the goals listed.

- To be better understood in the Congress and to have legislators more sympathetic to the needs of the pharmaceutical industry, particularly in terms of pricing.
- To be better understood by the public in terms of (1) the economic value that the industry has for the nation, (2) the life-saving and medical value that medicines have for patients, and (3) the cost-effective value of most medicines in comparison with other treatments or compared with no treatment (for specific diseases).
- To have the potentially fragile nature of the industry and the danger for permanent damage that excessive regulations or price controls are likely to cause understood by as many people as possible.
- To receive some protection against the pressures that threaten the industry's future.
- To change our reputation from that of a greedy, overly profitable industry that makes money off of sick people and sets high prices in disregard of those who must pay to an industry that is in business to make money but provides excellent value to society in terms of money saved on its total health care costs. The industry should also be perceived as one that provides great value to the nation in terms of (1) generating a positive balance of payments, (2) providing many jobs, (3) conducting research at high standards, and (4) producing products of high quality. The message that substantial prices are often required to maintain the state-of-the-art research required to discover yet newer medicines must be communicated more effectively.
- To counter the forces that want to either control or cap medicine prices under the pretext of preventing the industry from making "outrageous profits."
- To have Congress and the public view the occasional cases of ethical misconduct as exceptions to the overall high ethical standards and behavior that generally are observed within the industry.

CHANGING THE FOCUS OF THE DEBATE

One of the major issues underlying these seven goals is the need to change the focus of debate in Congress and in the public arena from the charges and costs of individual medicines to a focus on the true value of individual medicines and whether the bill presented to society for an expensive medicine can be justified in terms of real savings in other areas of the total health care bill. When any group or institution focuses on only one aspect of an extremely large and complex issue, that group tends to

believe that a simple change will bring about the desired result (Fig. 58.1A). Nowhere is this narrow perspective more obvious than in the area of medicine prices. A simplistic approach by any group to the issue of "high prices" ignores the many other pressures and factors that influence and are influenced by the same issue (see Fig. 58.1B and C). It is critical for the industry, Congress, the public, and all other parties interested in the health policy debate to ensure that all relevant elements of the pricing-cost equation are considered.

A recent example where many of the elements of the pricing-cost equation were ignored occurred when Congress attempted to achieve the same price discounts on medicines for Medicaid patients that pharmaceutical companies offered to the Department of Veterans' Affairs (DVA). Legislation passed by Congress was based on the simplistic view that both Medicaid and the DVA were government groups and each was paying different amounts for the same product and that this difference was unfair and should be corrected. Congress failed to consider the reasons that justified the discounts, including the large distribution service fulfilled by the Veterans' Administration (VA) hospitals. These cost savings to the industry that were being passed on to the DVA would not occur under Medicaid. The industry reacted by removing all discounts to the DVA. The strong negative reactions in Congress and by the public to this step may turn out to be a stimulus for Congress to pursue further price control measures. The original pressure for Congress to enact legislation was political in nature and is understandable. But meaningful dialogue with the industry to resolve differences and to understand each other's perspective did not occur. Although the industry can blame Congress, the industry must share responsibility for not ensuring that the necessary dialogue occurred.

One of the reasons for the DVA problem is that Medicaid pays for medicines (and other items) on a line basis, whereas Medicare pays for medicines lumped with other health services using diagnosis-related groups (DRGs). The pharmaceutical part of the Medicare budget is not easily identified, and the industry has not been attacked concerning the medicine costs of Medicare. This raises the possibility that, if Medicaid reimbursement were to use the process that Medicare does, less adverse publicity could be focused on the cost of medicines per se and would rightfully focus on the total costs of the health system for specific diseases and patient groups.

National Value of the Pharmaceutical Industry

Beyond the debate over cost of individual products is the issue of the value of the industry to U.S. national interests. There are few American industries with as strong a positive balance of payments as the pharmaceutical industry. (The pharmaceutical industry in many de-

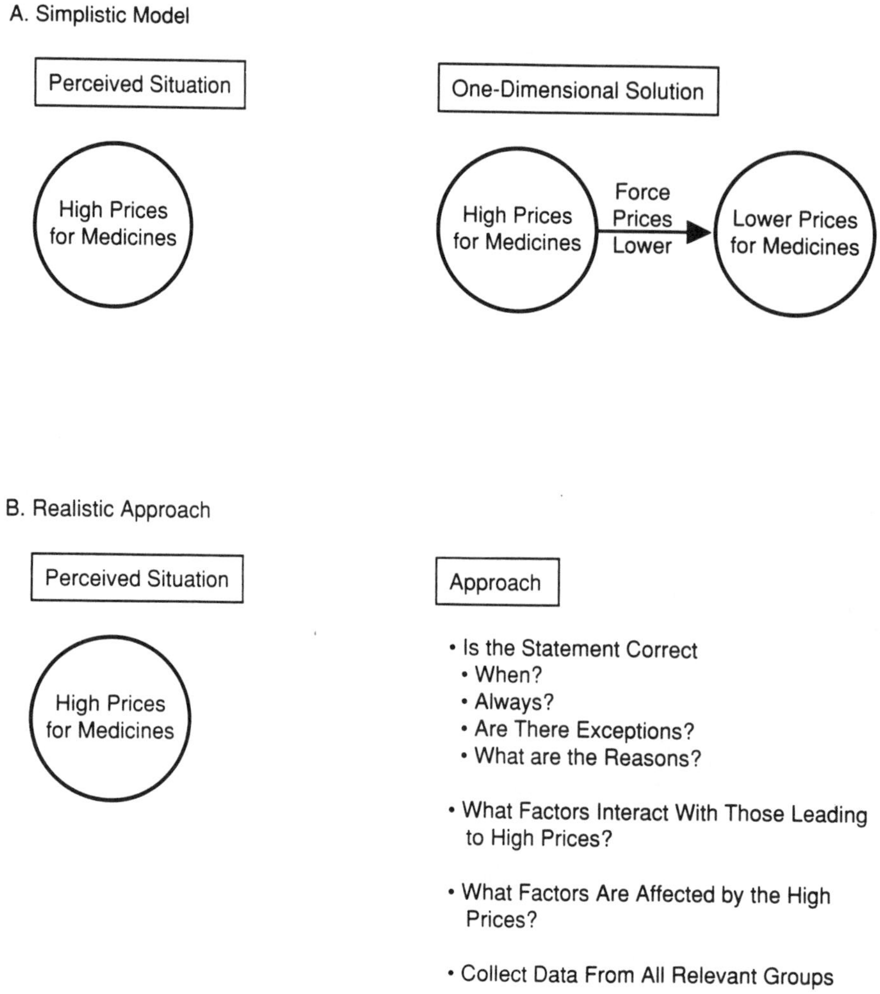

A. Simplistic Model

B. Realistic Approach

FIG. 58.1. Different approaches to viewing prices of medicines. **Panel A** is a simplistic model. **Panel B** presents a realistic series of questions to ask.

veloped countries also has a positive balance of payments.) Instead of having Congress incessantly badger and the FDA excessively regulate the industry, a collaborative relationship should be forged that would meet the needs of both government and industry. Unless a less adversarial relationship is forged, it appears likely that the government will increase its pressure on the U.S. pharmaceutical industry until the industry becomes less viable, as has already happened to the electronics, steel, and other once-strong American industries.

It is incumbent upon the industry to take the lead in forging a new dialogue and a new sense of partnership with the government. The industry must be proactive in working on all major activities that will help secure its own future. The government is unlikely to approach us to improve the overall relationship; therefore, we must approach them and the public. No single approach or simple formula will achieve the goals described above. The best approach will undoubtedly involve a multifaceted, coordinated effort by trade associations, individual companies, external organizations, and individuals from both within and outside the industry.

CREATING A NEW IMAGE

The major need today is to improve the industry's public image. This will require a major proactive approach and should occur in the near future—before an intense national debate on health care takes place (See *Note Added in Proof,* p. 695). Once that debate occurs and the rhetoric heats up, the public will be unwilling to listen to and be convinced by our message and the opportunity for meaningful dialogue with the government will be lost. When price controls are being debated in Congress in front of television cameras, it will be too late for the industry to mount a proactive approach. The industry will be forced into a reactive mode. Any work done now to help form public opinion will be important when health care debates move to the top of the nation's priorities.

Poor People

To achieve a positive image of the industry several approaches are suggested for consideration. The first approach involves a major unified industry-wide initiative for poor Americans who cannot afford medicines. While several individual companies are doing this to a significant degree by providing free medicines, each has a different approach and program and there is no coordination across all companies. A unified program with more publicity would have greater benefits in terms of goodwill toward the industry and improved patient health than the individual company efforts that are currently in place. The advantages of this plan are that (1) it would be highly visible, (2) it is greatly needed, and (3) it is morally a correct and valuable contribution. Disadvantages are that (1) the cost could be extremely high and (2) poor people tend not to make as much noise in Congress as do the middle class and many, if not most Americans, may not be adequately impressed by this approach. Any program considered must be equitable and leaders from the community and other groups must be involved to ensure that the program is effectively implemented.

Commercial Messages and Advertisements

The second approach is to develop a series of simple messages to be presented to the public via advertisements and other means. The commercial messages should portray a positive image of the industry and engender a positive reaction to the industry's goals. Some messages could indicate that people are living longer and acquiring more chronic illnesses, so that funding the discovery of new medicines will be just as important in the future as it was in the past when infectious diseases were rampant. The message should state that, in order to do this, the industry must retain its vitality and be able to fund research. Images could include (1) a mother saying that a certain medicine helped save her baby's life, (2) an elderly patient saying that a specific type of medicine (e.g., antihypertensive) has reduced symptoms and has improved his quality of life, or (3) a narrator commenting about the small amount of antibiotic that probably would have saved the life of many people before 1945 or the new lung surfactant that would have saved the lives of many babies.

These or other simple images and messages would, I hope, be remembered and could be used as positive symbols of our industry and its products. Suitable mottos, expressions, or images should be sought and used in advertisements. The American public must be shown that they should have pride in the medicines discovered within the United States and that even better medicines will probably be discovered here in the future.

Other Approaches To Improve Industry's Relationship with Legislators and the Public

Other components of an overall program to improve the image of the pharmaceutical industry could include one or more of the following.

1. Provide Congress and state legislators with information that focuses on improving the industry's reputation. Attempt to steer the legislative debate to an appropriate context that considers all of the relevant aspects of a topic.

2. Encourage independent groups with important credentials and impeccable reputations (e.g., National Academy of Science, the Institute of Medicine) to become involved in some of the major industry issues. Their involvement could take the form of investigations, evaluations, and analyses that are published and widely disseminated to appropriate recipients and groups.

3. Approach important people who influence public opinion and encourage them to become active in countering specific public misperceptions about the industry. For example, Dr. Louis Lasagna, Director of the Center for the Study of Drug Development, and Dean at Tufts University, has provided a balanced viewpoint on the pharmaceutical industry for many years.

4. Encourage well-respected academicians in relevant fields (e.g., economics, public policy, competitiveness, ethics) to study various aspects of our industry. If their funds come directly from the industry, it would *a priori* undermine the credibility of the studies in many people's opinion. Instead, the money for grants could be given by companies or the industry as a whole to independent groups or societies that would in turn award the funds to successful applicants. While the industry could not interfere with or influence this process, it would be important to carefully frame the scope of the subject to be studied so that biased anti-industry material is less likely to be created.

5. Provide relevant consumer, foundation, medical society, and professional health care groups with suitable brochures or short books about the industry and the process of discovering and developing new medicines (e.g., *Inside the Drug Industry* by Spilker and Cuatrecasas, 1990). The public's knowledge about these important areas is woefully inadequate, and most legislators also do not have an adequate understanding of the processes or issues involved.

6. Existing brochures of the Pharmaceutical Manufacturers Association (PMA) that document the cost-savings nature of medicines must be widely disseminated to all pharmacists and physicians and to many patients and public organizations.

7. Invite Congressmen and their staffers to visit the company's facilities for a tour and orientation to the

discovery, development, marketing, and production functions.

ORGANIZING A PUBLIC HEALTH POLICY GROUP WITHIN A COMPANY

A company may allocate any degree of resource desired to addressing the pharmacopolitical and health policy concerns discussed in this chapter, from establishing an entire department to assigning a part of one person's efforts. The scope of issues that lie within the province of pharmacopolitics is described in Chapter 6. The initial three steps for companies to take are straightforward.

1. Companies should acknowledge the importance of these issues at the appropriate board level and other meetings and reach a consensus among senior managers that the company should become involved.

2. Each company should create an internal group that focuses its efforts on these issues. This group would coordinate the company's activities and integrate them into those of the industry as a whole.

3. Companies should determine how much of a proactive role they wish to take in addressing these issues.

After the company decides on a position for a specific issue they must develop a passive or an active plan to implement their views and achieve their goals.

It is essential to consider whether an independent group within the company is the optimal approach or whether a committee from all relevant disciplines (e.g., legal, marketing, research and development, finance) could accomplish their goals more effectively. The major advantage of establishing a separate department is the full-time focus and attention those people would devote to the major issues. There are two potential disadvantages to this approach. First, there would be enormous pressure on the staff to generate work and activities to fill their time and to utilize the group's resources. This group could commission studies and create reports that might not be read (or used) by relevant managers and the group's efforts would not have any significant effect within the company. The well-known Parkinson's law of staff creating work, filling space, and spending time and money would apply. Second, the health policy group might not have the necessary commitment from some or all senior managers in charge of critical functions within the company. For example, if the health policy department of a major pharmaceutical company had a full-time attorney, economist, marketer, scientist, clinician, and public affairs specialist, these people could easily become isolated from their original departments and disciplines and therefore represent only their own personal views.

A separate health policy group could report to a senior manager within research and development, marketing, finance, or public affairs. Alternatively, it could report directly to the company's president. The organizational location within a company would undoubtedly influence not only the nature of its activities but also the consequences of those activities (i.e., a strong leader of an important company function would be in a better position to implement ideas than the leader of a weaker function).

An alternative organizational approach that would enable a company to be proactive in public health policy issues without forming a special group is for each relevant senior manager to appoint a staff member to join a permanent committee. This committee would meet periodically (or on an ad hoc basis) to discuss important issues, problems, and opportunities and to develop appropriate plans and strategies. A single full-time person focusing on health policy issues could be hired to lead this group. This approach has the advantage of enabling the company to develop an integrated stance on each issue. The members appointed to the committee would have access to their senior line manager to ensure their manager's support for any decisions made and directions taken. The major disadvantage of this approach is that the people appointed to the committee might be amateurs in the field of health policy and not sufficiently knowledgeable about the industry and the complexity of the issues to have formulated cohesive and well-thought-through views. Another disadvantage is that the members' day-to-day responsibilities would have priority over their committee work. These problems could readily lead to a committee that was overly conservative or risky and made poor decisions. The leader of this group must therefore be both knowledgeable and skilled in the entire arena of health policy. It is possible that this person could serve as the company's main lobbyist.

SHOULD COMPANY ACTIVITIES BE FUNNELED THROUGH THEIR MAJOR TRADE ASSOCIATION?

Because the primary problems discussed in this chapter are industry wide rather than specific company problems, it makes most sense for the industry to address these issues in a united way. This can be done either through the major trade association(s) or independently. The major trade association in the United States is the Pharmaceutical Manufacturers Association (PMA). This association currently has a policy for its board of directors that sometimes prevents the PMA's taking prompt and effective action. That policy is that consensus should be achieved on important issues.

It is uncertain whether the PMA will achieve the consensus needed to form and lead the strong proactive approach that the industry needs at this time. If the PMA does not achieve consensus, a second possibility is for a group of concerned companies to discuss these issues and plan a series of activities as an informal consortium to proactively address the issue of improving the legislative and public policy subjects discussed in this chapter. The initial group of companies would, it is hoped, invite most or all other individual companies to join them so that a united front would be created. The threat that price controls in the United States represents is so great to the research and development–based industry that the potential stresses that could be created within the PMA by this approach are probably an insufficient reason to *a priori* abandon this second alternative.

The chief executive officers of some individual companies may not desire to take proactive steps to address this issue as a group. They may react by trying to protect their companies from the consequences of price controls or other unfriendly regulations and legislation. But building higher walls around their walled city is as useless a precaution in 1992 as it was in the late middle ages. The increasing number of enemies gathering outside their walls must be met—not in pitched combat, because the companies will certainly lose those battles—but in going outside the walls and reaching agreements with them that will preserve as much of the company's interests as possible. For those companies that desire to be proactive on their own there are several things that may be done.

HOW A COMPANY CAN HELP ACHIEVE INDUSTRY GOALS

A company that decides to adopt a proactive role in influencing legislators and the public can choose from numerous activities to pursue. Most of these activities are obvious and many are being pursued today. Within any company, it is important to evaluate periodically the effectiveness of each approach used and also the relevant resources to commit to it to ensure its success. Some of the major activities to consider are discussed below.

1. Create a philanthropic group that targets contributions that are supportive of one or more of the goals previously discussed. A clear strategy for giving money should be agreed to and used to increase the effectiveness of gifts. An ad hoc approach to donating money, even if the money is not wasted, cannot achieve the full benefit possible for the company that more targeted contributions would have. Do not focus efforts at the national level as this would require an extremely large amount of money to have even a small effect. The same funds spent at the province, state, or local level have a far greater influence.

2. Adopt an active and broadly based role in the community. Be seen as a good corporate citizen. Activities supporting this approach should be coordinated within each company to address a clear strategy and set of goals. Contribution of money is not sufficient to achieve relevant goals in the community. Encouraging employees to be involved in community activities is usually an important component of this program.

3. Adopt an active role within trade associations. An informal ranking of their importance to the company should be based on the ability of the association to advance company policy and interests. Major companies often have different views as to the value and certainly the effectiveness of specific trade associations, and the companies also have greatly differing views of allowing their staff to participate in association activities.

4. Encourage scientists, clinicians, and other professionals to adopt an active role within various professional societies. It is important to adopt and promulgate a company policy on this issue in order to send a clear message to the staff.

5. Publish scientific and medical articles of importance. Allow the names of relevant company personnel to be included as authors. This helps to motivate one's staff and shows the readers that the industry supports and sponsors first-class clinical research. Various companies have different policies and views on authorship, including a near ban of company staff names appearing on clinical articles, a hands-off approach, or active encouragement.

6. Develop a positive relationship with politicians who represent the geographical areas in which the company has operations, including minor facilities, warehouses, and regional offices. Also target important and influential legislators. Contributions to their campaigns (if appropriate), invitations to important events at the company, private tours of company facilities, and periodic meetings with senior managers are a few worthwhile activities to pursue.

7. Have company representatives present talks about the industry at various types of external meetings, including those at (1) local civic clubs, (2) patient organizations, (3) medical societies, (4) professional societies, (5) activist groups, and (6) other community organizations. Develop a strategy for how this approach can be handled most effectively by the company (and also by the industry) to influence public opinion. Short videos showing patients discussing the benefits they receive from medicines may be used to enhance many talks. Prepare various types of materials for the speakers to use as background preparation and also to partially standardize the presentations.

8. Invite students of all ages and faculty to visit company facilities to participate in planned educational activities conducted by company employees. Develop programs to help educate teachers about the pharmaceutical industry. Do not solely attempt to educate teachers of mathematics and science. Invite relevant groups to tour manufacturing plants or research facilities. Provide each visitor with a special packet of informational materials about the company and the pharmaceutical industry. Have specially trained speakers meet with them to help

them better understand both (1) the processes of medicine discovery and development and (2) the issues faced by the industry.

9. Hire one or more lobbyists to be based in Washington, DC, or to visit Washington, DC, on a frequent basis. Lobbyists should have extensive prior experience (1) as a lobbyist for another organization, (2) as a congressional staff member, or (3) in another capacity relevant for lobbying. The need for professional input (and not amateur dabbling) is essential for every pharmaceutical company.

10. Hire one or more lobbyists to work at the state level. These individuals could be based either at the company's headquarters or "in the field" at important state capitols.

11. Hire a public relations firm to assist in designing important programs of interest that help advance the company's image and meet its goals.

Many other activities can be used to achieve the company's pharmacopolitical goals. Brainstorming sessions should be held within the health policy committee and possibly at other committees to determine those concepts and approaches of most interest to its members and to its company.

EDUCATING THE PUBLIC: FRAMING THE DEBATE AMONG THE PHARMACEUTICAL INDUSTRY, LEGISLATORS, AND THE PUBLIC IN TERMS OF ECONOMIC VALUE

Some (or possibly many) people who have an important influence on the industry's future have strong and entrenched negative views of the pharmaceutical industry's ethical standards and practices. It is inappropriate for the industry to state that those people's views are

wrong and to challenge these views directly. Nor is it appropriate for the industry to say that its own behavior was sometimes incorrect in the past but that the industry has reformed and has become a model corporate citizen. Instead, it is necessary to indicate to critics, using appropriate tone and logic, that the industry was (and is) widely misunderstood and criticized because it was described, evaluated, and judged inappropriately. For example, inappropriate questions that have sometimes been used as the sole basis to judge the industry are: What are the actual company costs per tablet to manufacture a new medicine? and How much profit does the industry make? These are inappropriate because prices of medicines (or any product) in a free market are based on what competitors are charging, the duration of the patent, the costs to conduct research to discover new medicines, costs to pay for many failures, and other concepts illustrated in Figs. 58.1B and 58.2.

The industry must educate the public that the correct framework within which to describe, evaluate, and judge the pharmaceutical industry is in terms of its economic value to society and the medical quality of its products and that the correct framework within which to describe, evaluate, and judge the prices of individual medicines is in terms of the total costs and benefits provided to the entire health care system. One of the numerous models to influence patient attitudes, albeit a highly indirect one, is shown in Fig. 58.3. Evaluation of the pharmaceutical industry's economic value to society should be made using both a macro and a micro approach. With a macro approach, it is appropriate to ask: What is the value of this industry to our nation? Does it contribute economically, socially, politically, and ethically to the continuation and growth of our country? Is the industry overall contributing in a significant way to cost contain-

Realistic Model

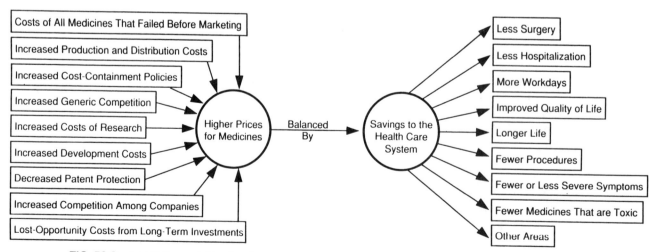

FIG. 58.2. A realistic model to view factors leading to higher prices and the balance achieved by savings in the health care system.

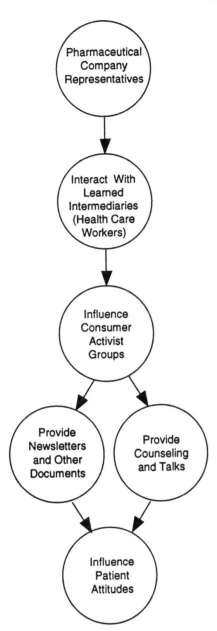

FIG. 58.3. An indirect model of how pharmaceutical companies can attempt to influence patients and the public about the industry's view concerning prices.

ment of health care? In this context, the answer is a resounding "Yes." This is not the place to present the vast amount of evidence that supports this conclusion, but numerous authors have presented evidence that convincingly demonstrates the cost effectiveness of most medicines and vaccines despite the apparently high price of many of them.

At the micro level, the pharmaceutical industry's value to society should be judged by how well or how poorly each of the medicines it discovers, develops, and markets affects patients' quality of life and the overall economics of having each particular medicine available.

Examinations of economics of new medicines, as viewed by the public and legislators, usually focus only on their costs. This is highly biased. It is essential that all costs, benefits, and economic savings in every area of health care resulting from the introduction of the medicine are considered to assess what the correct or fair price of a new medicine should be.

The real value that new medicines offer should not be discussed with legislators and insurers in esoteric economic terms, nor in practical medical terms (e.g., pain lessened, improved quality of life), or even in terms of the number of lives saved. The primary unit used to determine a medicine's value should be money (e.g., dollars). Value would be expressed as the difference between current sums spent to treat patients with a specific disease and future sums that would be spent through use of the medicine. The difference equals money saved each year.

In conclusion, it is proposed that the most appropriate means of improving the industry's relationships with legislators and the public is to adopt a proactive and coordinated approach. The industry should attempt to create a new frame of reference in which the economic value of the industry and its medicines will be discussed and judged in terms of their net benefit to patients and to society.

Note added in proof. Since these comments were written health care has become a higher national priority in the United States and attacks against the industry have occurred on a daily basis.

59 / Costs and Pricing

Introduction **698**
Costs Associated with a Medicine **698**
  Research Costs 698
  Development Costs.......................... 698
  Patent Costs................................. 698
  Manufacturing Costs 699
  Construction or Modification of
    Manufacturing Facilities.................. 699
  Distribution Costs........................... 699
  Marketing Costs............................. 699
  Advertising and Promotion Costs 700
  Education Costs 700
  Licensing and Royalty Costs................. 700
  Legal Costs................................. 700
  Administration Costs........................ 700
  Lost Opportunity Costs...................... 701
  Transfer Costs.............................. 701
Pricing Objectives and Strategies............... **701**
  Cost-Plus Pricing........................... 701
  Competition-Based Pricing 701
  Market Penetration Pricing 702
  Skimming Pricing 702
  Value-Based Pricing 702
Factors Influencing the Price of a New Medicine **702**
  Company Reliance on the Medicine for Its
    Own Survival 702
  Amount and Intensity of Competition 702
  Medical Value of the Therapy 702
  Shelf-Life.................................. 703
  Social Importance of the Medicine........... 703
  Purchase Price for Certain Medicines 703
  Inflation................................... 703
  National Laws, Regulations, and Policies...... 703
  Patent Life Remaining at the Time of Product
    Launch 703

Reduction of Current Medical Costs 703
  Quality of Life............................. 703
  Profits to Support Future Research........... 703
  Dividends to Shareholders 704
  Elasticity of Demand 704
  Corporate Comfort Level 704
  Exchange Rate Fluctuations 705
  Who Purchases Medicines? 705
  Health Care Programs 705
  Life Cycle 705
  Economic Factors in the Society 705
Determining a Fair Price to Charge for a New
  Medicine................................... **705**
  Establishing Prices in Different Countries 706
  Prices for "Me-Too" Medicines............... 706
  Prices for One Medicine Used in Vastly
    Different Amounts for Two Indications 706
Areas in Which a Pricing Strategy Is Required .. **706**
Reevaluating the Price of a Marketed Medicine **707**
Testing a Proposed Price Using Market
  Research................................... **707**
Social Issues Regarding Costs of Medicines **707**
  Should Prices of New Medicines Be Based on
    Manufacturing Costs? 707
  Judging the Price of a New Medicine......... 707
  Using Pharmacoeconomic Methods to Provide
    Data on Financial Savings of Medicines 708
  Medicine Costs as a Percentage of Total Health
    Care Costs 708
  Steps Taken by Proactive Companies That
    Address the Issue of Affordability 708
  When Is It Worthwhile to Develop and Market
    a Similar (Me-Too) Medicine?.............. 708
  Influencing the Community to Accept a New
    Medicine's Price 709

Within Europe there are as many pricing and reimbursement systems as there are countries. A low price in one country is undesirable not only because it reduces sales revenue but also because it may stimulate parallel importation and affect the price allowed in those countries where prices abroad are taken into account when setting local prices. If reimbursement status is not granted, it is unlikely to be worth marketing the product at all since patients will be unwilling to pay the full price. Sue Sullman, *Regulatory Affairs Journal,* April 1992

No country that has practiced cost containment in health care at the expense of its pharmaceutical industry has managed to nurture a pharmaceutical industry that can compete globally. Heinz Redwood, Pharmaceutical Consultant

INTRODUCTION

The literature is remarkably bereft of articles about how pharmaceutical companies price individual medicines. While many people would find it worthwhile to read detailed case studies, the companies have not felt it appropriate to describe these in any detail. This chapter does not present specific case studies either. Rather, it describes the types of actual costs and considerations that go into the pricing of an individual medicine. Theoretical discussions and composite evaluations of the pricing for groups of medicines have been published by economists, but the information in those articles does not really help a company to price the next medicine it markets. Although economists use a variety of formulae to establish a product's price in various industries, this is not often done in the pharmaceutical industry. In an attempt to estimate demand and elasticity (as well as other factors), some groups have used the approach of pricing a product at the point where the curves of marginal revenue and marginal costs intersect. Consideration of relevant factors and adherence to logic is a far better approach to pricing medicines than is adherence to one formula or another.

This chapter, therefore, focuses on individual medicines rather than overall industry behavior and uses a descriptive rather than economic or statistical approach. It describes the concepts involved in establishing prices rather than the concepts underlying the equations that are purportedly used by some companies to derive price.

The industry prices its products to cover its costs, fund new research, return a profit to its investors, and promote health care. The act of pricing a medicine is actually extremely complex and is interdependent with many other aspects of a pharmaceutical company including the involvement of private research facilities, risk capital, and regulatory authorities.

COSTS ASSOCIATED WITH A MEDICINE

While many simplistic accusations levied at pharmaceutical companies state that medicines should be sold for their cost of manufacture plus 5%, 10%, or 15% for profit, this is an extraordinarily naive and incorrect view. This "cost-plus" approach ignores a number of additional costs that virtually always must be considered as well. The general categories of costs associated with discovering, developing, and marketing a medicine are listed in Table 59.1 and are described below.

Research Costs

Although it is theoretically possible for chemists to rationally design the best structure for an organic molecule so that it performs a certain activity at the molecular

TABLE 59.1. *Costs associated with discovering, developing, and selling a medicine[a]*

1. Research costs
2. Development costs
3. Patent costs
4. Manufacturing costs
5. Distribution costs
6. Marketing costs
7. Advertising and promotion costs
8. Education costs
9. Licensing and royalty costs
10. Legal costs
11. Administration costs
12. Lost opportunity costs
13. Transfer costs

[a] Each of these is discussed in the text.

level (e.g., inhibit an enzyme), this does not happen. Chapter 20 (The Medicine Discovery Process) describes the "trial and error" approach used most commonly to discover new medicines. Hundreds of compounds are usually made in a given series of compounds in an attempt to improve on activity and disease toxicity. This process is extremely expensive and must be paid for by the few medicines that are marketed and earn a profit.

Moreover, many thousands of newly synthesized compounds do not turn up any interesting potential medicines or result in compounds that will be developed; most are terminated later during preclinical studies or clinical trials. These activities also have to be paid for by the few medicines that emerge and reach the market.

Development Costs

Of the 5,000 or so chemicals that are synthesized, on average, for each one that reaches the market, about a hundred reach early preclinical development and are evaluated in numerous batteries of tests. Preclinical, clinical, and technical development activities discussed in many chapters of this book are expensive activities to conduct. Costs to develop a specific medicine vary widely from approximately one million dollars (or even less) for obtaining case studies to nearly 100 million dollars. When all costs are included (e.g., opportunity costs) as well as failures and other research, the total averages 231 million 1991 dollars (de Masi et al., 1991).

Patent Costs

Companies typically apply for patents in many countries (average approximately 35). Costs for this activity include patent attorney fees in preparing these applications, filing fees in each country, and also the annual renewal fees to keep the patent application or patent itself alive. These facts raise questions such as, when is it reasonable to allow a patent to lapse after the medicine's progress is terminated? The nature of medicine discovery and development is such that discontinued compounds or medicines are sometimes later found (often within a few years of project termination) to be potentially (or actually) useful in treating a different disease or the original disease in a different way. A particular medicine sometimes is not totally protected by a single patent but by a series of patents. The other patents could be designed to protect chemical analogues of the medicine of interest so that similar "me-too" medicines cannot be easily patented by competitors.

Manufacturing Costs

To most people outside the pharmaceutical industry, production costs are the most obvious costs that influence the price of a medicine. It is this overall cost that is generally discussed in the greatest detail when the public tries to calculate what it believes a medicine's fair price should be. Manufacturing costs include the processes of obtaining raw materials, performing chemical syntheses, mixing the formulation, compressing the mixture into tablets (or producing other dosage forms), conducting quality assurance tests, and conducting many other activities described in Chapter 50 (Production Issues). Costs often also involve purchasing expensive equipment, hiring staff, and building waste treatment facilities.

Manufacturing costs also include solving the difficulties involved in obtaining raw materials, synthesizing the active compound, preparing the formulated medicine, packaging the medicine, storing the medicine, and shipping the medicine. Cerudase is an example of a medicine for which the cost of obtaining the raw materials is very high. This extremely expensive medicine is used to treat patients with Gaucher's disease. It is estimated that a single year's treatment for one patient may cost as much as $150,000 to $300,000 (U.S.). But the medicine is obtained from human placentas, and it reportedly requires 22,000 placentas to provide one year's supply of medicine for a single patient.

Construction or Modification of Manufacturing Facilities

Certain medicines require the building of an entirely new manufacturing plant, which may have to be initiated several years before the medicine is approved for sale. An extreme case is one where a plant is built (or at least begun) before it is known with certainty that the medicine possesses adequate efficacy and safety for the medicine to be marketed. Although it is easy to say that this situation should be avoided, it is not always easy or even possible to do so. For example, for a major breakthrough medicine to be available post approval, the company may have to make a commitment to build the plant at an early stage of the medicine's development. However, if the profile of a medicine is less exciting at the time of its marketing, sales will be less and the need for the new plant may have disappeared. This would be an example of a gamble that did not succeed. Associated costs with the start-up of a new facility include plant validation expenses and meeting good manufacturing practice standards in all areas of production.

Distribution Costs

Large-sized packages (e.g., bottles of solution) cost more to ship than do small packages of medicines. Packages that must be stored in refrigeration are more difficult to handle and cost substantially more to transport (and store) than are those stored at room temperature. Packages stored below freezing have separate problems that must be addressed. Each of these factors influences distribution costs and, ultimately, the prices charged.

Medicines taken out of inventory must be packaged and shipped to sites often in other parts of the world. Costs escalate dramatically when there is an urgency in the medicine's delivery, whether it is on a compassionate plea basis or to fulfill a hospital, pharmacy, or physician's emergency requirement. Other special medicines, such as radioactive medicines, have their own distribution requirements and costs.

Marketing Costs

There is an adage stating that "medicines do not sell themselves." Even breakthrough, life-saving medicines require significant marketing costs for educating physicians about their use and to launch them successfully. Marketing costs cover a multitude of activities that begin during the discovery period, intensify throughout the years of a medicine's development, and usually reach a peak during the prelaunch, launch, and first year or two of a product's actual sales.

Costs to develop line-extensions (e.g., new dosage strengths), new formulations, new indications, and new packaging of an already marketed medicine may be considered as costs incurred during the marketing period. However, many of these costs begin during the development period prior to marketing and often are shared among manufacturing, research and development, and other groups within the company. Other costs include clinical studies to compare the new medicine with established treatments that are sometimes referred to as promotional trials.

Many marketing activities influence how well a new medicine does commercially after it is launched. Most of these factors cost a great deal of money and (e.g., promotion to increase awareness, education), and this money usually comes from sales of the medicine. Merck spent a large amount of money to educate physicians about the benefits and appropriate ways to prescribe Mevacor (lovastatin) and Proscar. Some of the major marketing activities that require significant sums of money to launch a new medicine and to keep it afloat are discussed briefly in the following two sections.

Advertising and Promotion Costs

Although marketing promotion and advertising are only a moderate percentage of the total activities conducted by marketing groups, they represent a significant portion of the total money spent on marketing by pharmaceutical companies. In addition, these two activities receive a great deal of attention by the public, legislators, and regulators. Thus, they are discussed separately.

Practicing physicians and other health professionals usually focus on the content as well as the nature of advertisements and promotional practices. These activities serve an important function in disseminating information about a medicine, and it is legitimate to spend money on them. Advertisements and promotions provide information about new and established medicines and are an effective, albeit expensive, method for getting information to those targeted by the manufacturer. Companies without sales forces are unable to compete in the marketplace with their new medicines and usually join forces with a larger company.

Education Costs

There are numerous constituencies who must be educated before a medicine can do well in the marketplace. These include pharmacists, physicians, nurses, formulary committees, compendial committees, hospital administrators, medical press, professional societies, patient advocacy groups, patient medical groups, and many other groups. If the medicine has anything unusual about it (e.g., patients must inject themselves, patients must use a spinhaler, hospital pharmacists must follow relatively complex procedures to prepare a parenteral medicine), then additional educational activities must be conducted.

Educational costs include developing symposia and journal articles, supplements, lecture series, and other appropriate venues. Even advertisements have educational value. The more novel the medicine the greater the costs for education. There is a fine line between education and promotion, and some activities could fulfill both functions depending on how they are performed. Either function could be served by teaching

- what the new medicine is designed for;
- how it differs from other treatment(s);
- what its disadvantages are;

- how it is used;
- what its advantages are; and
- special issues, including economic considerations.

It is obvious that a company's discussions with patient advocacy groups about these six categories will differ from its discussions and materials directed to physicians or the media. This means that a company must prepare separate educational programs for different audiences, even though some specific elements as well as the overall approach and the theme may be the same for all groups.

Licensing and Royalty Costs

Not all medicines have royalty costs, but a significant number do. Royalty fees usually vary between 3% and 10% of sales. These are paid to the owner of the property from whom the medicine is licensed. While licensing costs usually include consideration of royalty fees, there are often additional costs involved in licensing. These include up-front costs and milestone costs, which are lump sums paid as the medicine achieves specific development milestones (e.g., completes Phase I, files a New Drug Application [NDA]).

Legal Costs

Certain medicines are introduced into therapeutic or disease areas that have a history of significant litigation. Because liability insurance is no longer available to most pharmaceutical companies, companies are forced to be self-insured in the United States. Some companies are putting money aside to defend anticipated legal cases, even before (or shortly after) a new medicine is introduced. The extent to which this is done, if at all, depends on the specific medicine and specific countries in which it is sold. Some types of medicines for which litigation can be anticipated include: anticoagulants, contraceptives, vaccines, and anti-drug-abuse medicines. Nonetheless, a certain number of legal cases can be expected to arise for most widely used medicines. Whether or not there is any merit to these cases, a pharmaceutical company must financially be able to defend itself and to pay often extremely high costs if it is found guilty. The only way that a company receives money to pay for litigation is through sales of its products and related fees (e.g., royalties).

Administration Costs

This category includes all of the costs of the entire company that are not included in the activities listed above. Salary and overhead costs of the entire organization must be considered in establishing the price of a medicine. Companies have groups to conduct the activities described as well as staff in human resources, engineering, public affairs, service groups, and so forth whose salaries and benefits must be considered. Some companies are much more staff heavy than others. Being too lean, however, can be expensive if one has to contract out many activities at high prices.

Other administrative costs include the costs of registering the medicine and adhering to regulations in all areas of a company.

Lost Opportunity Costs

Money invested in medicine discovery and in investigational medicine development is not being invested in any financial instrument (e.g., stocks, bank accounts, bonds) and therefore is not earning interest or dividends. The money also is not placed in real estate, precious metals, or antiques where it might appreciate in value. The loss of income from this money is referred to as lost opportunity costs. Of course, the investment is made in the hope that it will yield future profits, if an important medicine is discovered, developed, and successfully marketed. If the cost of capital is 10% or more, it causes opportunity costs to become large, particularly if development times are long.

Transfer Costs

A company that manufactures a medicine in one country and sells it in others must ship the medicine to those countries. The company site that ships a medicine charges the foreign offices of the same company a price for the medicine. This price is called the transfer price. The countries receiving the medicine establish a price, or are assigned a price by the government, at which to sell the medicine. The selling price often is influenced by the transfer price.

Many factors and methods used to calculate the transfer price influence its value. These factors primarily center on (1) taxes paid to customs for import/export goods, (2) regulatory authority practices in establishing a medicine's price (e.g., it may be related to the stated value on the customs declaration), (3) the need for the company to show a larger profit in one country versus another, (4) the specific countries involved, and (5) whether the product requires additional procedures as part of its manufacture (e.g., purification, filling into vials, labeling) and possibly retransfer back to the original site.

In these circumstances it is important to consider whether pricing decisions should be based on maximizing the transfer price for the headquarters or doing what is best for the balance sheet worldwide. A high transfer price to a subsidiary makes sense if it is a means of getting money out of a country that places severe limitations on this. A high transfer price to a subsidiary usually makes little sense if it prices the medicine above the competition and hurts sales.

The Organization for Economic Cooperation and Development (OECD) has published guidelines (1979) on how transfer prices are to be assessed (Transfer Pricing and Multilateral Enterprises). Most countries have tax laws that are based on these OECD guidelines. The major principle underlying the OECD guidelines is "arm's length prices." This means that the transfer prices that should be established are those that would be charged between two groups that are not related. Transfers include not only the transfer of medicines, but also technology, services, trademarks, and so forth.

The arm's length price may be established by several methods. The comparable uncontrolled price method uses a reference to other comparable transactions. Another method, the resale price method, assesses the price charged an independent group or person for the object. A third method is cost plus a fair mark up for the item. See Pradhan (1983) for a further discussion.

PRICING OBJECTIVES AND STRATEGIES

Most companies orient their pricing objectives toward either profit or sales, although a combination of both also could be used. Profit-related objectives establish a money amount for each product or product line or, alternatively, establish a return on investment number. Sales objectives usually are based on a percentage of growth from year to year, although this objective could be expressed in terms of market share.

Whether a company uses sales or profits as their primary goal depends on the medical value of the product, the amount of competition, years of patent life remaining, and other factors.

Cost-Plus Pricing

Cost-plus pricing usually is used by generic medicine manufacturers who have no research costs and only minimal development costs. It is determined by adding a predetermined profit to the sum of all costs (i.e., fixed and variable) of the product, and dividing by the number of units produced. This approach is not suitable for research-based companies and is rarely used because most costs cannot be allocated to specific products and because the other approaches make more sense.

Competition-Based Pricing

Companies often use the prices of their competitors' products as the basis for establishing their own prices. Depending on a large number of factors, they may set their prices above, below, or equal to those of most of their competitors or to that of a particular competitor's product. Using this method, reactions to the prices chosen for a new product are generally known in advance.

Market Penetration Pricing

Market penetration pricing means that a low price initially is chosen to obtain a larger share of the market. It is recognized that profits will be lower, but this consequence is accepted as a trade-off for achieving a high market share in a rapid manner. This pricing policy reduces the risk of failing to enter the market successfully and places great pressure on present (and future) competitors.

Skimming Pricing

Skimming pricing establishes relatively high prices for a medicine to obtain increased profits on (presumably) lower total sales. New breakthrough medicines are candidates for this strategy, as are novel medicines that are expected to have a limited life cycle because of new competitive products entering the market. It may be necessary to heavily promote such products. In some cases where production is extremely difficult or the starting materials are extremely scarce, a high price may hold down the demand and, thus, pressures to make more product. A high-priced product in a competitive market segments the market and, assuming there is a basis for the price, allows the company to promote the product's higher quality.

Value-Based Pricing

A company may conduct economic studies to determine the value of a new medicine for society. This approach evaluates all the benefits of a medicine and the total money saved. Based on the savings (e.g., hospital stays, physician visits, nursing time), a price is established that still provides a substantial savings to society for purchasing and using the medicine.

FACTORS INFLUENCING THE PRICE OF A NEW MEDICINE

Understanding all of the costs mentioned above as well as the strategies involved in pricing is not sufficient to establish a new medicine's price. First, aggregating all costs at the end of the investigational period does not consider that most of the overall development costs actually are spent after the medicine is initially launched. These expenses are for post-marketing studies and for clinical trials on new indications, dosage forms, routes of

administration, and, in foreign countries, to support regulatory submissions. Second, there are many factors apart from a medicine's cost that influence prices. The following discussion moves beyond the consideration of costs to a focus on other factors that influence the price of a medicine.

While all of the factors described below may influence the price of a new medicine, some will not be relevant to a particular company or to a regulatory authority that establishes the price.

Company Reliance on the Medicine for Its Own Survival

A company may have a marked dependence on a specific product being introduced on the market for its economic well-being. This point does not mean that such a company will necessarily charge a higher price for a medicine if its future is in jeopardy or is questionable—but, it is a strategy that may be considered by a company. The opposite situation, where a wealthy company has little dependence on a new product for its financial well-being, does not mean that the price charged will be relatively low.

Amount and Intensity of Competition

The degree of competition in the therapeutic area and the costs of competitive products are important influences on prices and usually provide a starting point for establishing a price. Most medicines are introduced into therapeutic areas where other treatments (i.e., medicines or nonmedicines) exist. It is important to determine accurately how physicians and patients view the established treatment. For health care professionals to be persuaded to use the new treatment there must be an advantage over older treatments. The extent of that advantage, in terms of safety, efficacy, convenience, quality of life, or other aspects may influence the price that is charged. Another aspect of competition is the ease with which competitors will be able to imitate or improve on the medicine.

The competition in the same class of medicines (i.e., those medicines working by the same mechanism of action) is particularly relevant because the prices of existing medicines that are similar to the new medicine have a major influence on new medicine prices. The price of a new treatment recently approved for AIDS, for example, was set close to that for Retrovir.

Medical Value of the Therapy

Medical novelty and value of the new therapy are important factors in influencing the price that can be charged. How important are the advantages offered? What percentage of patients will use the new therapy?

The greater the medical benefit the greater is the possibility of charging a higher price. If there is no major benefit, then charging a lower price than the competition provides an advantage. The medical value of a new therapy is usually related to the estimated market share forecasted for different points in the future. A medicine that treats 75% of the patients with a disease generally has a higher medical value than one that treats 10% of the same patient pool with the disease.

A new medicine that provides important benefits will rapidly be placed onto most formularies almost independently of its price. But a medicine with less obvious benefits over existing therapy or one that provides benefit to only a small segment of the population, will be more difficult (and expensive) to get onto formularies.

Shelf-Life

The length of shelf-life and the need to replace out-of-date medicines are factors influencing prices. A medicine with an extremely short shelf-life generally will lead to more disposal of unused medicine. This makes the medicine more expensive to the company and thus encourages a higher price.

Social Importance of the Medicine

Some medicines for diseases in the public spotlight (e.g., Alzheimer's disease, AIDS) receive significant media attention. The social importance and public visibility of the medicine could lead to the establishment of either lower or higher prices.

Certain medicines improve quality of life for some patients but do not provide medical benefits (e.g., hair growth for bald men). Other medicines are not essential for most people to use, such as vitamins and minerals. Large buyers can refrain from purchasing such medicines and others can avoid placing them onto formularies.

Purchase Price for Certain Medicines

The purchase price from the licensor or from the site that manufactured the medicine influences the price that can be charged. The transfer price or purchase price of a medicine can be a starting point for establishing a price. In some cases it is possible to negotiate a better transfer price or purchase price with the other site or company.

Inflation

Inflation may be a factor, particularly if the country is in a period of high inflation. Under more usual economic circumstances a company may be able to reestab-lish new prices each year, or to request price changes from a regulatory authority at reasonable intervals. Other financial parameters can also be considered.

National Laws, Regulations, and Policies

Many countries have specific laws, regulations, and policies that affect the ability of companies to charge whatever price they choose for new medicines. A synopsis of the approaches used by several European countries was summarized by Redwood (1992) and is shown in Fig. 59.1. The costs of active medicine controls used in Phase III trials may be used to help the government establish the medicine's price.

Patent Life Remaining at the Time of Product Launch

Cumulative profitability over patent life is an important aspect of recovering initial investment in a new product and achieving an adequate profit. The duration of the patent remaining at the time of launch must be considered. A company will generally want to charge more for a medicine that has five years of patent protection remaining than for one with 12 years remaining. In general, pricing of a medicine changes over its life span.

Reduction of Current Medical Costs

Pharmacoeconomic trials can evaluate the degree to which a new medicine reduces costs in another part of the health care system (e.g., less surgery, fewer hospital days, less time visiting physicians, less nursing care).

Quality of Life

Although the term "quality of life" is often misused, there is an important benefit that most patients achieve with certain therapies that makes one medicine preferable to another or to conventional treatment. There are standardized methods to evaluate the financial value of such benefits (see References).

Profits to Support Future Research

Research-based companies are in the business of reinvesting a large portion of the profits made from their successful medicines. These profits may be earmarked for special projects or activities, but invariably they are required to support the company's future research. Biotechnology companies depend on invested capital to support their research until they are able to develop and market profitable medicines.

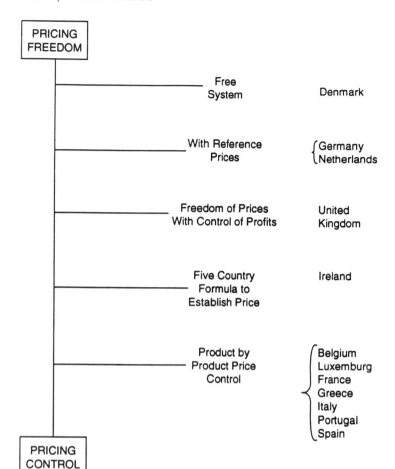

FIG. 59.1. Diagnostic representation of a spectrum of European government policies on pricing pharmaceuticals. Reprinted from Redwood (1992) with permission.

Dividends to Shareholders

It is only possible to attract investors to put their money into risky endeavors or businesses if the potential for reward is present. The greater the risk that investors take the greater the reward they expect. As a result, a company that discovers, develops, and successfully markets a new breakthrough medicine cannot merely charge enough money to pay back their investment in research and development without earning an adequate profit to pay their shareholders a divided for investing in the company. Many of those investors placed their money in the company at a time of substantial risk, possibly before a major discovery occurred. Other investors may have bought stock after the discovery was made but at a time when marketing success was uncertain.

Elasticity of Demand

Some medicines can be sold in whatever quantity is required to satisfy the market, regardless of the price charged (within broad limits). This is what people in the industry call a totally elastic market. Such medicines include important medicines for a presently untreatable disease or problem; examples include many new orphan medicines.

The majority of medicines, however, have a demand curve that illustrates dependence on price—at a low price more units are sold than would be if the price were higher. When the price becomes extremely high there is a precipitous decline in the number of units sold. In an extreme case, only medicines at an extremely low price can be sold, and at that price the company would still lose money.

Corporate Comfort Level

Most companies will not be comfortable charging above a certain price for a medicine. Often the people involved realize that at some level the price will trigger government investigations, negative news items, possible demonstrations (or even calls for a boycott), refusal by formularies to accept the medicine, and ill will among physicians and pharmacist. If the company is aware of this, it can try to gauge at what point a price would trigger the negative public relations that exceed the sales it may receive. Companies attempt to price their medicine below this point in almost all cases, as demonstrated by the relative absence of such major reactions to specific new medicine prices.

At the same time, too low a price can result in insufficient profit to justify marketing and manufacturing efforts. At an even lower price the company would lose money in selling the medicine.

Exchange Rate Fluctuations

While pharmaceutical companies are unable to predict currency fluctuations any better than other companies or individuals, these fluxes are a fact of life that may be considered in setting a price. It is not sufficient merely to compare the economies and future trends of two nations. Companies must learn to evaluate anticipated trends in many countries. This helps explain why the price for a new medicine that is identical in 10 countries on its first (simultaneously launched) day of sale will differ within a week or month. It is impossible to constantly reassess and revise prices on a weekly basis to maintain them at an even level among countries.

Who Purchases Medicines?

The ages and income levels of the patients who will purchase the medicines influence the price that is assigned to that medicine. Will they primarily be children, poor adults, or middle class adults? In recent decades there has been a shift from patients being the primary purchasers of most medicines to third-party payers, including governments, being the primary purchasers. These groups have much greater ability than patients to influence prices and have done so, even when the third-party payer is not a government agency.

Health Care Programs

What will the effects be on the overall costs of health care programs when a new medicine is launched? It is clear that the costs for many apparently expensive medicines will be partially or totally offset by savings in another area of the program. Insurance plans, prepayment health plans, and government health programs should be expected to pay for these medicines. Pharmaceutical companies should attempt to influence legislators to achieve this goal.

Life Cycle

The duration and pattern of the expected life cycle of the new medicine are likely to influence the choice of its price. The shorter the expected life cycle the higher the price the company is likely to charge. Some companies increase the price on a medicine during the last few years

before its patent expires, as a sort of "harvesting" strategy.

Economic Factors in the Society

Many economic, social and environmental factors in the country in which the medicine is being priced influence the price that is ultimately established. These factors begin with national laws and policies regarding compulsory licensing, imports, exports, foreign exchange regulations, and related areas. Government roles in paying for health care and controlling prices of medicines are also important, as is the political climate for viewing medicine prices.

Economic factors include the size of the economy, standard of living, percentage of the gross national product spent on health care and medicines, growth rate and stability of the economy, and trends for medicine prices within the economy.

DETERMINING A FAIR PRICE TO CHARGE FOR A NEW MEDICINE

The specific costs and factors discussed above may be used to determine a price that meets the profit and sales goals of the company for the medicine. A target return on investment is used to help establish price. Both short-term (e.g., one year) and long-term target goals are established for sales and profit.

The pricing strategy for a medicine changes throughout the product's life. Raising prices at some stages of a product's life does not greatly affect the number of units sold. It is usually counterproductive to raise the price after the time when the medicine is forced to compete with generic products. This is because the volume of units sold will decrease to a level where profits are less than the money that can be gained on each unit. This maneuver also generally sets up a chain reaction and eventually shortens the future life of the product.

Among the many relevant factors considered when deriving a medicine's price is the value of that medicine to society. If the medicine replaces costly surgery or decreases the number of days spent in the hospital, then the medicine can be described as having a high value, and this should influence the price. However, if the medicine solely improves a patient's quality of life or prevents later complications of a disease, it is more difficult to include those factors in the computation of a price, even though they are important benefits. The problem with using these factors to compute price is that the benefits are often obtained in the future and those who pay for medicines are usually less willing to pay for future benefits. The fields of pharmacoeconomics and quality of life have developed techniques that may be used in clinical trials to evaluate the relevance and importance of these factors (see Spilker, 1990b, 1991).

The pricing of a medicine often depends on the exact indication that is approved by a regulatory agency. If the FDA approves broad labeling, then the price can be lower (and the converse—restricted labeling—also is true). Thus, pricing is often established much closer to time of approval or even after approval. Other factors that often influence prices are

- the likely window of time that the company has to sell the medicine;
- how much it cost the company to develop the specific medicine; and
- whether or not the company charges a premium price for the medicine. This depends primarily on the medicine's perceived benefits versus those of the competition.

It is usually desirable to price a medicine as close to the time of launch as possible.

Establishing Prices in Different Countries

The above discussion underscores the desirability to establish a scale of prices for a single medicine on a worldwide basis. The expected sales and medical interest in each important country would be considered. Even within a single country, a single price per tablet is not set, nor are single prices set for each package size and unit produced. Rather, a number of prices are established to offer discounts to different types of customer (e.g., retailers, retail chains, wholesalers); typically, such discounts are associated with the volume of purchase. An exception may be made for the military, for example, or for government agencies.

Medicine prices differ between countries for many reasons, including (1) timing of approvals, (2) government decisions, (3) basis for setting the original price, (4) shipping costs, (5) distribution costs, (6) import duties, (7) taxes, (8) product registration costs, (9) transfer prices, and others. Another detailed list of various factors that enter into a medicine's price is given in Tables 6.1 and 6.2 and Figs. 6.2 and 6.3 in Pradhan (1983). A review of pricing policies in various European countries is given by Sullman (1992).

Prices for "Me-Too" Medicines

The pricing policies of various governments exert pressure on companies not to develop and market new chemical entities that the regulatory authorities view as "me-too" medicines. Regulatory authorities also apply pressure on companies not to develop "me-too" medicines by taking longer on average to review such medicines than they generally take to review the first two or three versions of a new type of medicine. This has led to an increased focus within companies on discovering more therapeutically novel medicines. Unfortunately, it is not easy to say "we will only develop exciting scientific discoveries of compounds with novel structures or novel mechanisms of action." Moreover, these scientific breakthroughs often do not lead to improved clinical benefits or to an improved benefit-to-risk ratio over conventional therapy.

Prices for One Medicine Used in Vastly Different Amounts for Two Indications

If a new medicine is being developed for two indications, for which greatly different amounts of the medicine will be used, then a potential pricing problem may develop. For example, one indication could be for an acute problem and the other for a chronic problem, and most of the medicine's use might be in the acute indication. In this situation a premium price for the acute indication would make the price for chronic treatment unrealistic.

This problem is compounded if one indication is approved and the medicine is already priced at a certain level, and a second indication is being studied where a much greater (or smaller) amount of the medicine is required.

To solve these dilemmas one could consider

1. using different packaging for each indication (e.g., prefilled syringes for one indication) that are priced differently;
2. using different formulations and pricing each differently; or
3. giving different trade names to the packages for each indication.

AREAS IN WHICH A PRICING STRATEGY IS REQUIRED

Pharmaceutical companies usually develop a pricing strategy when they are establishing a price for a new medicine. Another occasion when a pricing strategy is desirable is when they are forecasting share volume for a new product. The forecasting of share volume for a new product is critically important because it is the basis of the production order (see Chapter 50, Production Issues). A production order usually becomes more accurate over time, but the original one is based on many educated guesses. The price chosen for a new product clearly affects the number of units sold in almost all markets and thus influences the number of products that have to be manufactured.

In addition to considerations of inflation and general competition, many factors influence how a company modifies its prices on its existing products from year to year. It is optimal if each product manager does not make proposals in a vacuum, but utilizes some basic company principles (i.e., a strategy). A company may attempt to use price in a variety of ways to hold market share or to optimize profits after a medicine goes off patent.

If a company introduces several sizes of a product at its initial launch (e.g., a 25-, 50-, and 100-mg size) it will have developed a strategy of how to price these in relation to each other. If it is currently marketing a 25- and 50-mg strength, the new introduction of the 100-mg strength may or may not be priced in a relative manner. If it is not, the entire line may require a reevaluation. Larger dosage strengths are often priced at a lower cost per milligram.

REEVALUATING THE PRICE OF A MARKETED MEDICINE

In reevaluating the costs and factors that went into the final price for a new medicine, the validity of these data should be assessed periodically, starting at the time when the data are first generated or obtained. What additional factors were important, and which ones were less important than predicted?

Additional factors that are considered when repricing marketed medicines include (1) price changes to other company products, (2) brand loyalty, (3) new competitors on the market, (4) age of the medicine, and (5) trend in the market share captured by the medicine.

TESTING A PROPOSED PRICE USING MARKET RESEARCH

It is undesirable to establish a price for a new medicine by considering numerous factors but without asking for evaluation from physicians, formulary decision makers, and others who can provide sound judgment and important advice. Physicians may be oblivious to a medicine's price, and it may be better to consult formulary committees, pharmacists, or others instead.

In designing a marketing test, it is useful to include one or more reference prices (e.g., prices of the competitive medicines, prices of other nonmedicine standard treatments). It is also important to assess whether the physicians believe the benefits claimed for the new medicine are worth any premium price proposed. Alternatively, one could ask physicians how much money they think the proposed benefits are worth. Several market research methods are used to evaluate the reactions of health professionals, administrators, or patients to prices. A major distinction between methods is whether the test group reacts to a single or multiple prices. Conjoint analysis is used by many firms in this regard.

Conjoint analysis is a market research technique that involves assessing tradeoffs that people make in reaching decisions. For example, a physician who is asked what he or she would like in a new medicine in terms of safety, efficacy, cost, dosing frequency, and packaging usually lists a number of ideal characteristics. This information is of limited usefulness in assessing real medicines. A conjoint analysis would present a number of alternatives and request the physician to make a series of choices (i.e., judgments) that would indicate which characteristics he or she considers more important and how each of them is weighed. A specific example is to present a card with two medicines named A and B (brand names are not used) that says A is 10% more effective than B, A has equal safety with B, A costs 5% more than B, and A is dosed twice-a-day versus once a day for B. The physician then indicates whether medicine A or B is preferred. A series of permutations is then used by presenting other cards and the physician's choices of the preferred treatment analyzed to determine the weightings given each characteristic.

SOCIAL ISSUES REGARDING COSTS OF MEDICINES

Should Prices of New Medicines Be Based on Manufacturing Costs?

Pharmaceutical companies spend, on average, approximately 12% of their worldwide sales on research and development activities, attempting to discover and bring to market new medicines with high medical value. The chances of any one compound synthesized, or even one compound found to be active in animal tests, making it to the market are remarkably small. The risk of investing money to discover a medicine is far greater than that of almost any other industry. The chances of success are small, even for creating a "me-too" medicine that will eventually earn a profit. People do not risk money without a chance of making a profit. Attempts to control prices in the United States, if successful, are likely to decrease the amount of money companies are willing (or able) to spend on discovery oriented research.

Judging the Price of a New Medicine

It is clearly inappropriate to judge medicine cost on the basis of only the single cost of manufacturing. The industry must educate legislators and the public about the fact that money saved in any area of health care by introducing a medicine is an essential component of any discussion of costs. Benefits to patients also should be considered in these discussions, whether the benefits are converted to monetary terms in a cost-benefit analysis, left in terms of the actual clinical improvements in a cost-effectiveness analysis, or converted to a standard unit of life-years saved in a cost-utility analysis. Although some people make the counter-argument that society cannot afford to pay the high prices of many new medicines, the company must demonstrate whether this view only focuses on costs and prices and ignores savings and benefits. As a result of paying apparently high prices for new medicines the entire health care budget is often lowered.

Using Pharmacoeconomic Methods to Provide Data on Financial Savings of Medicines

Several pharmacoeconomic methods currently exist (e.g., cost-benefit, cost-effectiveness, cost-utility, and cost-of-illness analyses) that are well-accepted by health economists and have been well-validated. Each of these methods has different strengths and weaknesses, depending on the way in which they are used (Drummond et al., 1987). One of the major issues being addressed today is how to use these tests because it seems that a test can be found that demonstrates that any medicine saves money if it is used instead of others.

Medicine Costs as a Percentage of Total Health Care Costs

Medicines are responsible for only about 6% to 8% of health care expenditures in the United States. In the remaining part of the health care budget, physicians are responsible for 30%, hospitals 45%, nursing homes 10%, and other areas 7%. Although there are many ways that major savings could be achieved in each of these areas, if the pharmaceutical industry brings them to the attention of legislators: (1) the attempt will be seen as self-serving and as a ruse to deflect the focus away from the industry, (2) medicines are a highly visible target and are more easily controlled than many of the other areas, and (3) legislators will claim they are already dealing with many of the issues in those areas.

Numerous articles state that medicines rose at a much faster rate than the consumer price index (CPI) during the 1980s. This is true, but one major reason is that it rose at a much slower rate than the consumer price index during the 1970s. Other factors include much higher research and development costs in the 1980s and shorter product life cycles because of generic competition. A number of large pharmaceutical companies have already stated that their price increases during the 1990s would, in aggregate, be at or below the consumer price index. These facts should all be presented to legislators, the public, and the media, rather than allow any of these groups to present and discuss only the first fact (price rises during the 1980s) in isolation. Not only are medicines the most cost-effective part of health care, but it is the part that most people take for granted.

Steps Taken by Proactive Companies That Address the Issue of Affordability

Proactive companies in the United States that are concerned about the affordability of their medicines are taking a number of steps to help ensure that patients can receive expensive medicines they require.

1. Patients who can demonstrate need of a medicine and inability to pay for it (as certified by their physician) may qualify for free medicine that many companies offer. The Pharmaceutical Manufacturers Association in the United Sates has a booklet describing this program.

2. Federal, state, and local governments may provide certain medicines to patients at minimal or very low cost.

3. Many people have insurance policies that pay for medicines with small copayments.

4. A number of companies have agreed not to raise prices on their new medicines more than the rate of increase in the consumer price index. While this does not indicate anything about a medicine's original price, it indicates that future increases should be affordable.

5. Pharmacoeconomic studies can be conducted to determine if the medicine actually saves society money in another area of health care. Is a medicine that costs $3,000 per year expensive? The answer has to be "it depends." It depends on who is paying the bill, of course (i.e., you or someone else). But in addition, the answer should depend on whether other health care costs will be saved, and also on the benefits obtained. Everyone should be aware of the huge sums of money that are saved by childhood vaccines and by medicines that prevent myocardial infarctions or treat chronic diseases. Large numbers of infections are effectively cured with antibiotics, antivirals, antiprotozoals, and so forth that otherwise would cost society huge amounts of money to treat.

It is unreasonable for society to say to an industry: We know you have risked hundreds of millions of dollars, pounds, marks, francs, lira, etc., to bring each new medicine to market, and we know it will save our society hundreds of millions in costs we are currently spending to treat these patients today, but we are unwilling to let you make a profit. It must be recognized and accepted that the company will use its profit (in large part) to try and find more new medicines that will save society more millions and treat many more patients who are suffering from untreatable or inadequately treated diseases.

When Is It Worthwhile to Develop and Market a Similar (Me-Too) Medicine?

Although subtle chemical changes may enable a company to patent chemicals that are related to known medi-

TABLE 59.2. *Properties of beta-blockers important in choosing an oral agent for an individual patient or in adusting dosage following substitution[a]*

Property	Acebutolol	Atenolol	Labetalol	Metoprolol	Nadolol	Pindolol	Propranolol	Timolol
Beta selectivity[b]	+	++	0	++	0	0	0	0
ISA[b]	+	0	+?	0	0	++	0	0
Lipid solubility[b]	Moderate	Weak	Weak	Moderate	Weak	Moderate	High	Weak
Elimination half-life (hr)[b]	3–4[d]	6–9	6–8	3–7	14–24	3–4	3–4	4–5
Protein binding (%)[c]	25	<5	~50	12	30	57	93	~10
Major first-pass effect[b,c]	No	No	Yes	No	No	No	Yes	No
Accumulation in renal disease[b,c]	Yes	Yes	No	No	Yes	No	No[e]	No
Liver metabolism important in elimination[b,c]	Yes	No	Yes	Yes	No	Yes	Yes	Yes
Active metabolites[b,c]	Yes	No	No	No	No	No	Yes	No

ISA, intrinsic sympathomimetic activity.
[a] Reprinted from Frishman (1987) with permission.
[b] Important in selecting agent.
[c] Important in determining dosage.
[d] Acebutolol has an active metabolite with an elimination half-life of 8 to 13 hours.
[e] Metabolite accumulates.

cines, it does not mean that the new medicine can be commercially successful. For a me-too medicine to be successful a clinical benefit must be demonstrated that makes a difference to clinicians and encourages them to prescribe the medicine. Although the public (and many physicians) have a simplistic view that similar medicines are only developed to make a profit for a company and have no medical benefits, that view is wrong.

Of all therapeutic areas where similar medicines have been marketed, few (if any) have been said to be more similar than beta-receptor antagonists. Table 59.2 shows important aspects of the clinical profile of all beta-receptor antagonists ("beta-blockers") marketed in the United States. Table 59.3 shows aspects of the clinical profiles of these medicines that differ in important ways. Both of these tables could be used to choose the most appropriate medicine for a particular patient. Many of the issues regarding me-too medicines are discussed in *Guide to Clinical Trials* (Spilker, 1991).

Influencing the Community to Accept a New Medicine's Price

The various communities that a pharmaceutical company interacts with should be considered at an early stage of the pricing process to help avoid controversy over the eventual price charged. These communities include (1) patients, (2) pharmacists, (3) physicians, (4) wholesalers, (5) distributors, (6) formulary committees, (7) insurance payers, (8) legislators, (a) regulatory authorities, and (10) the public. Some of these groups are only

TABLE 59.3. *Selected advantages of the marketed oral beta-blockers[a]*

Advantage	Acebutolol	Atenolol	Labetalol	Metoprolol	Nadolol	Pindolol	Propranolol	Timolol
Preserves renal blood flow			X		X	X		
Once-a-day dosing	X	X		X[b]	X		X[c]	
Reduces post-MI[d] mortality				X			X	X
No change in serum lipid levels			X			X		
Beta 1 selectivity	X	X		X				
Equal effectiveness in blacks and whites			X					
Intrinsic sympathomimetic activity	X					X		
Very low CNS[d] penetration		X			X			X
Vasodilation			X			X		

[a] Reprinted from Frishman (1987) with permission.
[b] Once-a-day for hypertension.
[c] For controlled-release preparation only.
[d] CNS, central nervous system; MI, myocardial infarction.

relevant to consider in certain countries. Strategies should be developed for dealing with each of these groups. For example, one of the most effective methods of influencing patients in a community is to establish a Community Advisory Board of Patients. Such a group would be constituted by the company to improve the environment in that particular community, perhaps through discussion of prices in an open forum. Having outpatient medicines paid for by insurance companies would be a major step toward alleviating the problem of high costs paid directly by patients in those countries where patients must pay costs themselves.

In conclusion, companies take seriously the prices they charge for new and established medicines. The various costs and factors influencing prices should be communicated more clearly to the patients, health care professionals, legislators, and the public. This must be done promptly and effectively to counter increasingly stronger pressure to remove the company's ability to establish the prices of its own products.

60 / International Development

Models of International Cooperation and
 Coordination between Two Medicine
 Development Sites of a Multinational
 Company................................... 711
Planning an International Clinical Program...... 714
In Which Countries Should Clinical Trials Be
 Conducted? 714
Different Methods to Assign Patient Quotas
 among Countries 714
Choosing Project Teams for International
 Medicine Development 714
Reviewing International Development Projects... 717
Pitfalls to Avoid in International Medicine
 Development.............................. 717

Priorities 717
Styles of Development........................ 717
Sociopolitical Issues 717
Product Labeling............................. 717
Compatibility of Systems 718
Terminology 718
Quality of Clinical Trials 718
Choice of Medicines Being Developed 718
Document Preparation 718
Regulatory Submission 718
Duplication of Effort 718
Management Review and Delays.............. 718

A few megacompanies with broad international presence will be supported by a host of small companies that are scientifically and technically highly specialized. It is argued that this scenario will develop at the expense of the national and international companies with only limited representation in the major markets and with only limited access to scientific excellence. Jürgen Drews, [*On International Development*]

The primary question in global medicine development is not whether or *not* a multinational pharmaceutical company should develop medicines internationally, but on what scale should it be done and how it may best be done. Virtually every major multinational company has moved (or is moving) into the era of developing medicines on an international scale. If the company intends to market its medicines worldwide, then it will develop medicines on a global basis. If it wishes to focus on a number of countries or areas, then its medicine development is better described as international. This sharp distinction is not made in this book, unless indicated. Current issues focus mainly on technical details and strategies that enable companies to develop medicines most effectively. Strategies are chosen that reflect the company, its organizational structures, disease areas of interest, and the geographical areas targeted for marketing.

The major goal of global medicine development is to have a medicine reach the market as soon as possible in all targeted countries. Other goals include achieving a financially stronger company, better staff morale, and more efficient medicine development.

MODELS OF INTERNATIONAL COOPERATION AND COORDINATION BETWEEN TWO MEDICINE DEVELOPMENT SITES OF A MULTINATIONAL COMPANY

International cooperation in medicine development between two or more sites may exist on multiple levels. Three models are described. The *first model* is loose cooperation with a sharing of results and information on the status of each site's activities. Nonetheless, each site pursues medicine development in a generally independent manner. The *second model* is when all relevant sites pursue work jointly on medicine development, after a certain point is reached in a medicine's progress. This point may be at the initiation of Phase I or Phase II trials, or after medicine efficacy is demonstrated by one of the sites. This model keeps medicine ownership at the site where work was initiated. The *third model* is when all relevant sites jointly develop a medicine from the time when a project is initiated. This leads to joint ownership of all medicine projects. It may be desirable for a company to initiate work on only those projects that receive

MODEL A

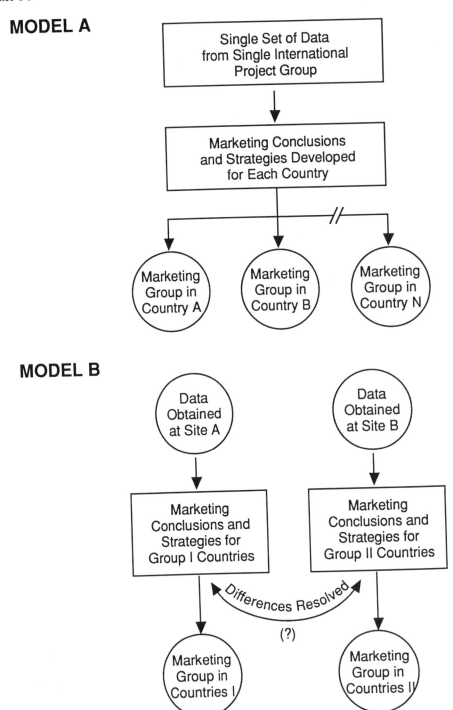

FIG. 60.1. Two models for marketing groups to consider in obtaining the data they need to market their medicines. Various hybrids and variations are possible.

international agreement at the outset. The particular model of medicine development chosen should be the one that is believed to be best able to achieve the company's goals. Two or more models may be used by a single company, the choice depending on the nature of the medicine or its intended markets. Chapter 9 (Models of International Operations) discusses this topic in much greater detail.

A certain number of clinical trials function as the core of most, if not all, regulatory submissions. The requirements for implementing and running the global medicine development system vary greatly from company to company, depending on their experience, goals, traditions, and the number, nature, and location of subsidiaries. Some companies with centralized organizations have relatively complete international medicine development systems and a single clinical plan for international use. A global tracking system is utilized to monitor numbers of patients enrolled at each site and to track whether target dates are being met for each of the milestones (e.g., initiation, completion, report writing) for a clinical trial or for various regulatory activities. Models presented in Figs. 60.1 and 60.2 illustrate that the methods used to obtain data may influence a product's marketing.

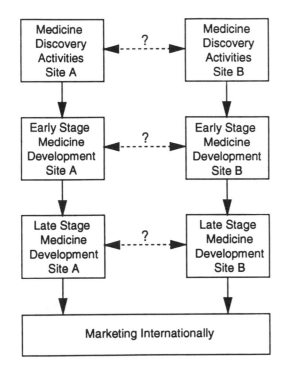

Model A.

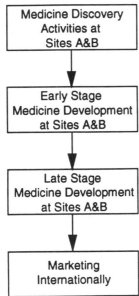

Model B.

FIG. 60.2. Two models of medicine discovery and development that provide data needed by marketing. The *question marks* and *dotted lines* in *Model A* indicate that interactions between the groups shown are possible but not required.

PLANNING AN INTERNATIONAL CLINICAL PROGRAM

Planning an international clinical program for a single medicine requires from several months to a full year from project initiation to ensure that important points are not missed. This period should be taking place while preclinical and technical trials are underway. This clinical plan cannot be rushed, or the resultant program may create problems and questions that may lead the entire medicine's development into serious difficulties.

It is important to review the clinical program with more than a single consultant in each country. These experts in academia, industry, and/or relevant government agencies should be consulted as a feasibility trial. The experts should be asked whether the proposed clinical program is appropriately tailored to the needs and nature of the medical practice of their country and is possible to carry out successfully in the proposed time frame. Situations will arise where a special program must be created within one or more countries that must opt out of the global development scheme. At present, Japan is usually viewed as a country that requires special considerations.

IN WHICH COUNTRIES SHOULD CLINICAL TRIALS BE CONDUCTED?

Although many factors enter this discussion, only a few will be mentioned. It is usually easiest to evaluate initially a medicine in the United States if it is preclinically developed there. Although regulatory requirements to initiate human tests are generally more involved the United States than in other countries, a company usually achieves reliable data and avoids what is often a time-consuming effort in exporting the medicines. Medicines developed in other countries, however, are rarely sent to the United States for their initial testing. Testing new compounds in underdeveloped countries is not usually a good idea because of the (usual) lack of high quality facilities, investigators, and background experience of the staff. Data that result from such studies are usually not reliable. Poor information is much worse than having no information because it can easily send the company on a wild-goose chase trying to answer questions that were raised. This may last several years and cost many millions of dollars, pounds, or marks.

Later in medicine development, foreign locations are often preferable to sites within the United States and are frequently used (1) to complete core trials in countries where data will then be acceptable to their regulatory authorities, (2) to adhere to various countries' regulatory requirements, (3) for promotional trials, (4) to enlist help from local opinion leaders, or for other reasons. In choosing the countries in which to conduct trials, it may be relevant to consider if there is a national death registry to assist in long-term patient follow-up, and also to determine the stability of the patient population.

Local clinical trials are often required or requested by some regulatory authorities, rather than approving a medicine based entirely on foreign data. There are various reasons for this request. For example, most patients in the country may differ from those in whom the trials were conducted in terms of diet, weight, and ethnic factors. Medical practice may differ in the ways that patients are treated. If so, then at least one trial should be conducted under the conditions in which the medicine will be sold. The regulatory authority may not be readily able to audit the investigator's sites if they are in a different country. Finally, there is what may be the major reason in many cases—chauvinism.

DIFFERENT METHODS TO ASSIGN PATIENT QUOTAS AMONG COUNTRIES

One approach to enrolling patients in three (or more) countries (assuming one site per country) is to enter patients as rapidly as possible at all sites until the total quota for the entire trial is achieved. A different approach is to assign a certain quota for each site based on predetermined statistical and practical considerations. In this approach each site continues to enroll patients until they achieve their own specific goal. The potential problem with the latter approach is that one or more sites may complete enrollment much earlier than other sites and not be allowed to enroll additional patients. This could lead to a marked delay in completing the overall trial and in registering the medicine. The best solution is to establish a minimum number of patients for each site (determined by the trial statisticians) to enroll and then to allow sites to enroll a larger number if that is possible for them to do. An upper limit may also be determined for each site.

If the issue is considered prior to initiating a clinical trial then the protocol must be written in a way that allows this approach to be used. For example, if separate sites are assigned different doses or any other differences in treatment or patient characteristics then the trial would become unacceptably unbalanced if one site entered twice their allotted number and another site one-half or fewer their allotted number.

CHOOSING PROJECT TEAMS FOR INTERNATIONAL MEDICINE DEVELOPMENT

Numerous models of project teams for international medicine development may be used (Fig. 60.3). The model chosen should obviously be the one that most suits a company's needs at that time.

MODELS OF PROJECT TEAMS FOR
INTERNATIONAL MEDICINE DEVELOPMENT

A. Centralized (Controlled/Shared) Model

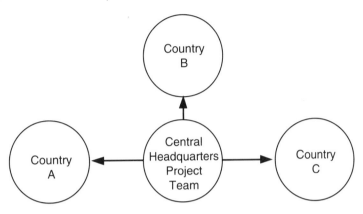

B. Decentralized (Independent) Model

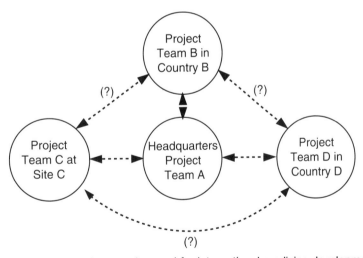

FIG. 60.3. Models of project teams that may be used for international medicine development.

Panel A illustrates the situation where a project team at the central headquarters is the only one in the company. That team directs development worldwide. It may allocate some trials to be conducted in other countries. Company experts from countries A, B, and/or C may participate in discussions, protocol development, or trial implementation and monitoring. One variation of this model is for a member of each country to be on the central project team.

Panel B illustrates where project teams exist at each site where medicine development occurs. The dotted lines between different teams indicates an informal or loose relationship and in the cases with a question mark, relationships may not exist. These teams usually share information and coordinate many of their plans, but each team functions independently.

Panel C is the completely integrated model where an international project team is formed at each site that

C. Network (Integrated) Model

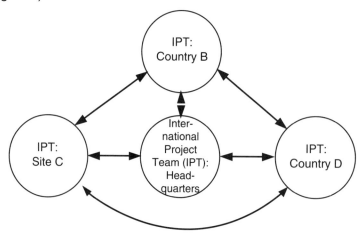

D. Combination Model of Panels B and C

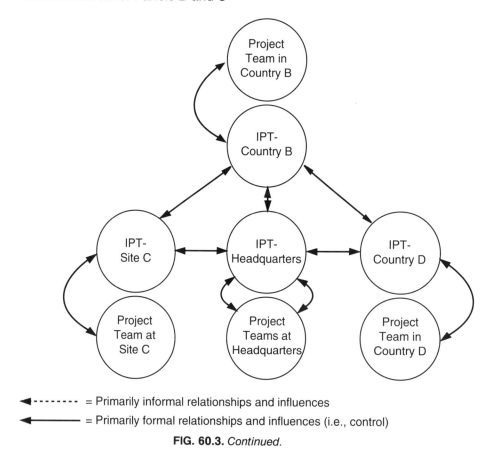

◄- - - - - - - - = Primarily informal relationships and influences

◄─────── = Primarily formal relationships and influences (i.e., control)

FIG. 60.3. *Continued.*

participates in medicine development. There is close co-ordination among all teams. One variation is to have an international project team at the central headquarters and local project teams at the other sites. Each local team may have a representative attend the central head-quarters' team meetings.

Panel D illustrates a combination model of Panels B and C. This shows the distinction between site or coun-try specific teams (often with eight to 20 members) and

international teams (often with two to four members). One variation on this model is to have two major interna-tional teams, one based in the United States and the other based in the European headquarters (for European-based companies). The United States team would have representatives from appropriate disciplines plus the project leader (or project manager) from the European headquarters' team. The European head-quarters' team would have representatives from other countries working on the project (including the United States) in addition to local members.

There may be an international coordinator who leads the international team's effort, but this individual usually has no line authority for work conducted at a foreign subsidiary. Alternatively, two or more project leaders from different sites may share or rotate the role of international team head.

REVIEWING INTERNATIONAL DEVELOPMENT PROJECTS

Progress of each international project team is reviewed by various committees. In addition to the international and/or project teams dedicated to developing a single project, two or more international committees are usually formed to assist global medicine development. One review committee usually deals with general policies, priorities, and overall strategies rather than detailed management issues. They may serve a gatekeeper role for compounds entering the system, share information, enforce the overall adherence to plans, and possible conduct a portfolio analysis. This group generally meets about every two to six months. If the interval between meetings is too short, it takes valuable time away from doing work, whereas too long an interval allows groups to drift apart and for the strategies at different sites to move in different directions. It is essential that development strategies at each site be yoked together.

Another group reviews all international projects for details on their progress and tactics. This committee usually meets more frequently (e.g., every four to eight weeks) and reports to the former committee. International committees that focus on medical activities, technical development, marketing, or other areas may supplement, or even replace the above committees. Both groups may serve as forums for discussions on issues and problems among sites developing medicines. Many variations on these procedures exist within different companies. The topic of global medicine development is discussed in greater detail in *Guide to Clinical Trials* (Spilker, 1991).

PITFALLS TO AVOID IN INTERNATIONAL MEDICINE DEVELOPMENT

Some pitfalls of global medicine development are mentioned above. A few others are briefly discussed.

Priorities

Each research site may have several projects under development in a number of therapeutic areas. Whether there are official priorities or not, each site will have their own priorities for all projects. Unless the central headquarters has absolute authority to dictate priorities to its subsidiaries, it is almost certain that some differences of priorities will occur. If these differences are relatively minor then global development plans on each medicine can be effectively pursued. If, however, there are marked differences in priorities, then even having global development plans for medicines will not be sufficient to achieve a coordinated development effort.

Styles of Development

Different styles in medicine development may lead to great difficulties in reaching agreement on a single clinical plan for global development. One site's research and development director may be highly conservative and prefer to develop a project in small steps, being sure of results before progressing to the next step. Another site's director may want to take large steps between clinical trials by making various assumptions to reach the regulatory submission stage more rapidly. These approaches may clash, or at least be difficult to reconcile. The best approach for each medicine should be considered individually. To create a successful international development program, a number of people must be willing to give up some of their authority and decision making.

Sociopolitical Issues

Numerous social and political issues must be considered during a medicine's development. These include the views of influential opinion leaders in various countries who have a great deal of say about which medicines are used in their country. This situation occurs in the cancer field where many different approaches exist in terms of dose schedules, combinations of medicines, and nonmedicine modalities used. Each approach has strong proponents and new medicines are not necessarily viewed in a totally objective way by all investigators and others.

Product Labeling

Pharmaceutical companies must insist on medicine labeling that is internally consistent across countries. Consistency must be present in such areas of labeling as contraindications, ages of children who may be given the medicine, and maximal dose allowable per day or per course. It is unfortunately impossible to have identical labeling worldwide because of legal and regulatory requirements, plus the fact that a company may pursue different indications for a single medicine in different countries. One goal is to have agreement on exact wording of critically important sentences that are included in labeling worldwide. A system is needed to achieve input from all appropriate groups and people when deriving product labeling. An efficient system is also needed to update and revise product labels on both periodic and ad hoc bases, with appropriate input and reviews. This latter system should indicate guidelines and criteria that may be used to decide whether new data are relevant to incorporate into the label.

Compatibility of Systems

Compatibility of computers between sites is discussed in several places in this book. Many other systems besides computers should also be identical or comparable between sites, including the dictionary used to code adverse medicine reactions. COSTART (Coding Symbols for a Thesaurus of Adverse Reaction Terms) is the most widely used dictionary by pharmaceutical companies in the United States, and the World Health Organization (WHO) dictionary is the one most widely used in European countries. Harmonization is being achieved.

Terminology

Different subsidiaries may not share a common understanding when they use common terms such as "well-controlled clinical trials" or "integration of data bases." This difference is especially likely to occur if one group is very large and the other small, or one group is in Europe and the other is in the United States. Differences in how each group views issues and problems must be sorted out before an attempt is made to derive solutions.

Quality of Clinical Trials

The program of clinical trials conducted on a new medicine must be controlled. If poorly designed or conducted trials are allowed to occur, they may compromise regulatory approval in the United States or other countries. The Food and Drug Administration (FDA) requires information in a New Drug Application (NDA) on all clinical trials conducted with a new medicine. The golden rule in this situation is that it is better to have three well-designed and conducted trials than a mixture of 25 good, average, and poorly designed and conducted trials.

Choice of Medicines Being Developed

Medicines must be developed that local subsidiaries desire to market and sell, or at the minimum, are willing to market and sell. This raises the question of who determines what products each country will register and market. If this is not decided centrally, then it must be established at an early date that medicines being developed are desired by an adequate number of appropriate countries to justify the medicine's development.

Document Preparation

Because each country requires different types of reports and in different formats, it is useful to develop modular-type documents that will simplify assembling a unique Product License Application (PLA) for each national regulatory authority where the medicine's marketing is desired.

Regulatory Submission

PLAs should be submitted to different regulatory authorities as closely together in time as possible. This prevents reports from having to be rewritten and rerewritten because the medicine's data base has grown significantly. If this aspect is not carefully planned, then PLA preparation may become an almost continual process of rewriting documents unnecessarily. Different regulations as well as different company priorities (Table 60.1) must be considered.

Duplication of Effort

Duplication of effort internationally not only slows regulatory submissions, but the increased amount of data slows regulatory review and may raise questions that require additional trials to address. One set of data collection forms should be used.

Management Review and Delays

The management of an international development program is more complex than for a uninational one. There are hundreds of basic problems that may arise and could be discussed. Systems should be enacted and followed to minimize problems in this area.

TABLE 60.1. *Selected causes of differences in technical regulations and general practices among countries*

A. Regulatory authority rules
  1. Limits on impurities allowed
  2. Acceptable sterilization methods
  3. Amount of overages acceptable in dosage forms
  4. Acceptance of different pharmacopeial rules (e.g., United States Pharmacopeia versus British Pharmacopeia)
  5. Ability to ship raw materials or finished products between countries
  6. Isomers permitted to be developed
B. Company practices between countries
  1. Contents of a regulatory submission
  2. Risk-taking nature of a company
  3. Dosage forms desired
  4. Sophistication of quality assurance methods
  5. Differences in methods and equipment used for production
  6. Differences in clinical approaches and dosages used

SECTION VIII

External Interactions and Relationships

61 / Interactions and Relationships with Academic Institutions

Types of Interactions **721**
  Four Types of Alliances...................... 722
  Ideas for New Medicines..................... 722
  Conducting Research in Academic Institutions.. 723
  Conducting Research in a Pharmaceutical
    Company 725
  Interactions That Maintain and Enhance
    Professional Status 725
  Clinical Evaluation of Investigational and
    Marketed Medicines....................... 725
  Sabbatical Periods 725
  Consultations 725
  Philanthropic Activities...................... 725
  Industry-Sponsored Symposia................ 725
  Industry Establishment of a Clinical Unit in an
    Academic Environment 726
  Industry Use of Hospital Data Bases 726
Guidelines for Interactions **726**
Alliances between Companies and Academic
  Institutions................................. **727**

Advantages of Company-Academic Alliances.. 727
Issues to Discuss Prior to Formalizing
  Alliances between Companies and Academic
    Institutions................................. 727
Academic Freedom........................... 727
Confidentiality of Data 728
Intellectual Property Rights.................. 728
General Issues................................ 728
Transferring Discoveries from Academia to
  Industry 728
Other University Concerns 728
Large Scale Relationships...................... **729**
Other Issues.................................. **729**
  Educating Graduate Students about Career
    Opportunities Outside Academia 729
  Contract Services........................... 729
  Patent Issues 729
  Duration of Industry-Academic Relationships 729
  Providing Medicine Samples to Academicians 729

Learning without thought is labor lost; thought without learning is perilous. Confucius, Chinese philosopher. From *Analects* (Book II, Chapter XV).

Shall I tell you the secret of the true scholar? It is this: Every man I meet is my master in some point, and in that I learn of him. Ralph Waldo Emerson, American essayist. From *Letters and Social Aims: Greatness.*

It is demonstrable that many of the obstacles to change which have been attributed to human nature are in fact due to the inertia of institutions and to the voluntary desire of powerful classes to maintain the existing status. John Dewey (1859 to 1952), American philosopher, educator. From *Monthly Review* (March 1950).

TYPES OF INTERACTIONS

Despite the rather pessimistic comments of John Dewey above, both academic and industrial institutions are recognizing the benefits that can be derived from active collaboration. This is generally viewed as a positive trend with potentially important benefits to both. The industrial-academic relationship may be viewed from several perspectives, including that of the government and public sector, in addition to the more obvious per-

spectives of pharmaceutical companies and academic institutions.

There is no doubt that industrial-academic relationships in the United States are increasing both in extent and importance (e.g., Atkinson et al., 1984). One of the major reasons for this change relates to the decrease in unsponsored research funds available per academic scientist. This has led many scientists, departments, and even entire medical schools to pursue opportunities and relationships with the pharmaceutical industry. Pharma-

TABLE 61.1. *Types of interactions between pharmaceutical companies and academic institutions*

A. Academicians' perspective
   1. Consultants from academia assist pharmaceutical companies in many different ways.
   2. Clinical investigators in academic institutions conduct sponsored trials on investigational and marketed medicines.
   3. Academic scientists conduct preclinical trials on compounds furnished by pharmaceutical companies or evaluate ideas suggested by pharmaceutical companies.
   4. Academic chemists synthesize compounds for testing by pharmaceutical companies.
   5. Academic institutions license ideas or compounds developed at the institution to a pharmaceutical company for subsequent development.
   6. Academic scientists present seminars at pharmaceutical companies.
   7. Students work at pharmaceutical companies for specific periods, usually ranging from three months to two years on a fellowship or postdoctoral program.
B. Pharmaceutical company perspective
   1. Industry personnel work on a part-time basis at an academic institution either on a fixed (e.g., one half to two days per week or month) or on an ad hoc basis. Their functions would generally involve teaching, conducting research, providing consulting, counseling, and/or treating patients.
   2. Industry personnel present seminars or act as visiting professors at academic institutions.
   3. Pharmaceutical companies offer philanthropic grants to academicians for research, travel, and/or other purposes.
   4. Pharmaceutical companies support academic conferences, symposia, or other meetings.
   5. Pharmaceutical companies conduct clinical trials at academic institutions.
   6. Pharmaceutical companies offer fellowships, postdoctoral grants, and other professional opportunities for academicians.

from either the academic or the pharmaceutical company's perspective. Few companies utilize all of these approaches, and the nature and degree of interactions vary greatly. Relationships are established between a pharmaceutical company and an academic institution (Table 61.2), between a pharmaceutical company and individual academic scientists, or both. Figure 61.1 illustrates the numerous levels within companies and academic institutions at which interactions occur. An important point of this figure is that interactions may occur across different levels as well as across the same level. Some areas where indirect interactions occur are shown in Fig. 61.2. A number of the possible relationships and interactions are described in the sections below.

Four Types of Alliances

1. Short-term grants targeted to scientific or clinical questions where in-house resources are unavailable or unsuitable to address the question. These grants may or may not be renewable. The terms and funding are strictly negotiated to secure the objective. A scientist may obtain equipment or staff help to assist with conducting the work.

2. Unrestricted grants without any conditions except for the goal of enhancing knowledge. The company may view this grant as providing an entrée into the institution, as a possible future recruitment exercise, or as a public relations exercise to improve the corporate image. These grants are usually limited to a single year, but may have terms for renewing the grant.

3. Licensing relationships are discussed in Chapter 48 (Licensing Issues).

4. Major alliances are discussed further in various chapters in this book.

Ideas for New Medicines

Companies solicit and/or accept ideas from people and groups in academia. A company that establishes products in a new therapeutic area is usually approached by academicians and others with novel ideas. For example, after Burroughs Wellcome Co. introduced some an-

ceutical companies benefit from university expertise, and universities are paid for their time and effort. University scientists and clinicians also benefit scientifically, career wise, and in other ways by working on important projects (Sterman, 1989).

There are many types of interactions between pharmaceutical companies and academic institutions. As indicated in Table 61.1 these interactions may be viewed

TABLE 61.2. *Selected biomedical relationships between universities and medicine companies*

Academic institution (city)	Medicine company	Length of agreement[a] (yr)	Area(s) of agreement
Duke University (Durham)	Du Pont Pharmaceuticals	5	Virology and immunology
Harvard University, Massachusetts General Hospital (Boston)	Hoechst-Roussel Pharmaceuticals Inc.	10	Molecular biology
Washington University (St. Louis)	Monsanto Co.	12	Biomedical areas
University of North Carolina (Chapel Hill)	Glaxo Inc.	5	Numerous

[a] Various options for extensions are included in some agreements.

LEVELS WITHIN MEDICINE INDUSTRY AND ACADEMIA THAT MAY DIRECTLY INTERACT

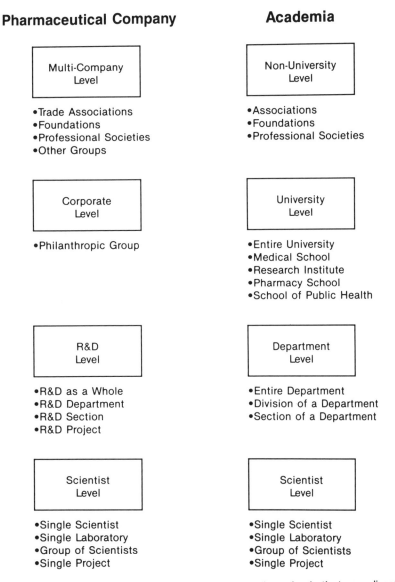

FIG. 61.1. Levels within the pharmaceutical industry and academia that may directly interact.

tiviral medicines, a number of individuals and groups began to approach the company with novel ideas relating to antiviral products. Even when a newly marketed product does not generate large sales revenue it may establish a company's reputation in a therapeutic area that will attract new ideas with greater commercial potential.

Conducting Research in Academic Institutions

The ability of most companies to conduct all relevant research activities "in-house" is often limited by space and resources (both skilled manpower and specialized equipment) rather than financial resources. Collabora-

tion offers the potential for a company to expand its capabilities on a temporary basis to answer specific questions or to probe specific targets. Collaboration with academicians also allows a company to pursue research in areas where (1) it may supplement its strengths, (2) it is weak, or (3) it is not currently active.

Companies sometimes invest or donate large sums of money to help finance an institution, medical department, or scientific group. Benefits desired by the company are usually defined in terms of services and outputs (e.g., compounds, licensing rights) resulting from the institution's scientists. Numerous opportunities exist for valuable collaboration between companies and outside scientists, institutes, and other groups.

SELECTED AREAS WHERE INDIRECT INTERACTIONS OCCUR BETWEEN ACADEMIA AND THE PHARMACEUTICAL INDUSTRY

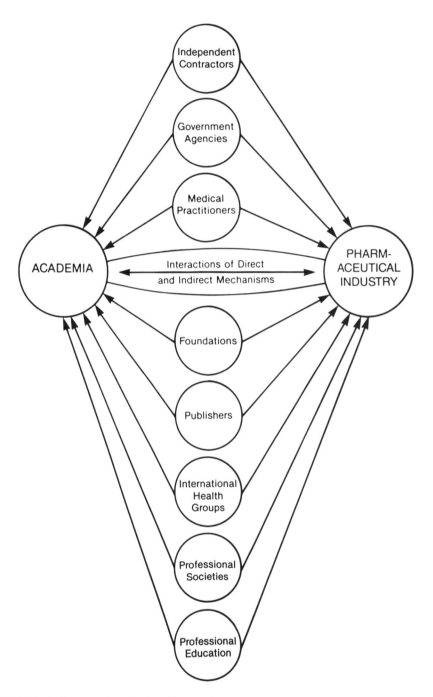

FIG. 61.2. Selected areas where indirect interactions occur between academia and the pharmaceutical industry. *R&D,* research and development.

Several different types of relationships exist for research activities conducted in academic institutions:

1. contract research performed by academicians for a pharmaceutical company,
2. research where a company has the right of first refusal for licensing any outputs with commercial value,
3. research sponsored by a company without the academicians having any special obligations,
4. research conducted by academicians with a medicine supplied by a company,
5. research conducted by pharmaceutical company personnel who also have an academic appointment, and
6. research conducted jointly by academicians and pharmaceutical company personnel.

These relationships, as others in this chapter, may be initiated either by the academic or pharmaceutical institution. If the academic group seeks to contact a pharmaceutical company, they may contact individual scientists, research and development executives, a licensing group, or a new products group in marketing. Industry people may contact comparable people in an academic institution to initiate one of the above relationships.

Conducting Research in a Pharmaceutical Company

Pharmaceutical companies can biologically test compounds synthesized by outside (i.e., academic) scientists, who are given funds to support their work. Companies also conduct research jointly with academicians. This is often the result of an academician approaching the company with a novel idea.

Interactions That Maintain and Enhance Professional Status

Industry scientists are sometimes encouraged to participate *directly* in the activities of academia: in teaching, research, advisory committees, and/or patient care. *Indirectly,* they may participate through various types of collaborations, memberships in medical and scientific organizations, and/or attendance at professional meetings. These activities help keep industry scientists informed about advances in their field, maintain their prestige and credibility within academia, open doors that otherwise might remain closed, and provide valuable stimulation to the individuals who participate. Some of these individuals are recognized for their participation through academic faculty appointments.

Clinical Evaluation of Investigational and Marketed Medicines

Most of the clinical trials that companies sponsor to evaluate medicine safety and efficacy are conducted in academic institutions or at centers associated with an academic institution. Close relationships with investigators, potential investigators, and other academicians are important for the most effective and efficient conduct of these studies.

Sabbatical Periods

The exchange of sabbatical and postdoctoral personnel, plus fellowship programs, represents a mechanism used by some pharmaceutical companies whereby new techniques and skills may be obtained from academic sources. These methods are believed to be a cost-effective means to obtain and provide stimulation to the individuals and laboratories involved. Industry provides these academicians with opportunities to participate in medicine discovery or development in ways that would otherwise be unavailable.

Consultations

Academicians who are recognized experts in a given area are often asked to provide advice to pharmaceutical companies on either a specific or general issue. Some consultants are hired with an annual retainer, whereas others are paid on a per day (or per hour) basis. The exact nature of these relationships are highly variable, even within a single company. Various issues relating to consultants are discussed in Chapter 27, Stimulating Innovation and Increasing Efficiency.

Philanthropic Activities

Many pharmaceutical companies (e.g., Burroughs Wellcome Co., Glaxo Inc., Merck & Co., Inc.) provide unrestricted money to carefully selected academic investigators to pursue their own research in various fields. Moneys are also given to support (1) travel for professional purposes, (2) attendance at meetings, (3) visiting professorships, and (4) other professional activities. A number of philanthropic foundations within the pharmaceutical industry are listed in Chapter 67, Interactions and Relationships with Patients and the Public.

Industry-Sponsored Symposia

Symposia sponsored by pharmaceutical companies are often held in conjunction with medical schools. These may either be part of established clinical or scientific meetings or may be presented as separate stand-alone symposia. The theme is usually centered on a single medicine or disease if one company sponsors the symposium. Many symposia are sponsored by multiple pharmaceutical companies. The information may be published in the medical literature, or printed as a promotional brochure by the company.

Industry Establishment of a Clinical Unit in an Academic Environment

There are several cases in which this has been done. For example, Merck & Co., Inc. established a unit in Thomas Jefferson Hospital in Philadelphia. In some situations the company provides staff to the medicine evaluation unit and expects that unit to evaluate primarily the company's medicines. This was done by The Upjohn Company at their own site. In other cases the only obligation of the unit is to submit a bid on certain protocols and offer the company a specified discount if the company decides to conduct the trial there. This was the original basis of the relationship between Pfizer Inc. and the University of Miami Medical School.

Industry Use of Hospital Data Bases

This occurs primarily in certain health maintenance organizations (HMOs) and other groups such as the Boston Collaborative Drug Surveillance Program. The data base has the ability for making certain linkages of records. For example, records may be linked between patients, medical history of diseases, medicines prescribed, and adverse reactions. It may be used to investigate medicine use and adverse reactions in Phase IV postmarketing surveillance studies.

GUIDELINES FOR INTERACTIONS

More and more individuals and organizations in academia, government, and industry are calling for increased interactions and cooperative efforts between universities and industry (Cuatrecasas, 1984; Bloch, 1986). Successful collaborations usually involve the freedom for academicians to publish the results of their activities. The company must ensure that they have either patented the results of the collaboration or have the right to license any patents obtained. Depending on the specific circumstances, the patent may be shared or assigned to the academicians with licensing rights given to the pharmaceutical company.

Conditions and terms of the relationship should be clearly specified. This includes a detailed account of the amount and nature of inputs to be applied by each partner and the nature and timing of agreed-on outputs. Potential problems should be anticipated and discussed thoroughly. A series of ten guidelines for successful university-industry ties was published relating to industry-sponsored research conducted at universities (Varrin and Kukich, 1985). Interested readers are referred to this article for details on the following guidelines, which were prepared from an academic perspective.

1. Publication rights should be retained by university scientists.

2. Ownership of all patents should be retained by university scientists.

3. Copyright policies should be established for software developed.

4. The use of proprietary information in research should be minimized. Do not require graduate students to sign confidentiality agreements.

5. Research units with faculty and students should be created. Hire full-time researchers to staff such units if necessary.

6. Faculty should not be permitted to consult with sponsors in the sponsored research area. This guideline is intended to prevent conflicts of interest that may arise if a faculty member provides information to a pharmaceutical company as a consultant and is then asked to develop the program through the company's agreement with the university. Patent rights are one example where a major issue could result from this type of situation.

7. An academic faculty member who is an entrepreneur and owns a company should not be permitted to sponsor his or her company's research on campus.

8. International agreements must be viewed with caution.

9. Personnel and equipment should be shared with industry in a mutually agreed-on manner.

10. A model research agreement for potential industrial sponsors should be prepared by each university.

Other types of guidelines relate to the attitudes, expectations, and atmosphere in which an agreement is reached. In general, these are the same guidelines that pertain to any major agreement.

1. The agreement must (or should) represent a true partnership. Each partner must respect the other and not harbor suspicions. Each should be desirous and willing to work to build the relationship in a positive and mutually rewarding manner.

2. The needs and expectations of each partner must be clearly expressed at the outset.

3. A scientific review and appeals committee should be established to confirm that the contract is being met. This group may arbitrate conflicts or other problems. It should be composed of members of each institution involved, plus some independent scientists who are well-respected and are well-known.

4. Each partner must identify the key contacts and representatives. These contacts must ensure that active and full communications occur between relevant people and groups.

A few more guidelines that may be considered include: (1) all manuscripts relating to the project must be sent to the sponsor 30 days before submission for publication, while the company reviews them to ensure that patent protection is not compromised,(2) a guarantee may be given that patent rights will be held within the academic institution, but the company will have exclusive rights to license any patents emanating from the sponsored research, and (3) involvement of younger as well as established scientists will be guaranteed.

Some of the experiences of both academic and industry groups have been published. Lessons learned by the Wisconsin Alumni Research Foundation (WARF) regarding the commercialization of university research were recently presented (Blumenthal et al., 1986). WARF is an independent foundation started in 1925 that administers patents and discoveries of University of Wisconsin faculty. Experiences with academic collaborations from a specific company's perspective (Pfizer Inc.) are described by Price (1985).

ALLIANCES BETWEEN COMPANIES AND ACADEMIC INSTITUTIONS

The primary motivation for a company to seek an alliance with an academic department or an entire institution is to expand the company's internal research capacity, particularly in areas where expertise is lacking. Such an arrangement may enable the company to enter a new therapeutic or scientific area, or to probe an existing area in new ways. This type of alliance, as opposed to those between companies, almost always involves a financial grant.

Advantages of Company-Academic Alliances

The academic institution receives several benefits from a financial grant from a pharmaceutical company. Typically, such a grant is large and represents a long-term provision of funds for the institution's staff. Additional benefits for the academic group include the following.

1. Ability to recruit additional faculty and to expand the scientific base of the institution.

2. Ability to develop a new area of research or to expand an existing area that was not previously attempted because of lack of funds. This additional money may enable the institution to develop a critical mass of staff in one or more scientific areas of particular interest. That, in turn, may be parlayed into important publicity about the growth of the institution and, possibly, additional grants from foundations and government agencies.

3. Possibility of having new or improved facilities paid for by the industrial partner.

Potential benefits for a company entering into an alliance with a competent academic group include the following

1. Increased research capacity in existing scientific areas of importance to the company. This occurs more rapidly than if the growth were solely internal.

2. Development of research capacity in new scientific areas of importance to the company.

3. Increased professional interaction of the company's senior scientists with leading academic scientists who are at the frontiers of research of major importance to the company.

4. Access to existing building(s) and space.

Issues to Discuss Prior to Formalizing Alliances Between Companies and Academic Institutions

Several issues must be discussed and satisfactorily resolved between companies and academic institutions before research agreements may be formally signed. Representative issues are briefly described and other considerations are presented in Tables 5.2 and 5.3.

Academic Freedom

Preserving the freedom of academic scientists is a *sine qua non* of all arrangements between academic institutions and industrial companies. But what exactly is "academic freedom"? This term can be summarized in a few concepts.

- To conduct research in an area of the scientist's choosing
- To conduct research using methods and approaches of the scientist's choosing
- To modify the research program in a manner and direction that the scientist chooses
- To publish papers on topics and in journals that the author(s) chooses and to decide what information and interpretation those papers will contain

Clearly, there are numerous pressures on scientists that influence how they actually pursue each of these activities. These pressures include department requirements, the need to obtain funds to support the research, agreements made with companies or other groups to focus major efforts in one or more specific areas, and continuing the research program initiated by the scientist and for which he or she is most well-known. The subject of academic freedom usually does not lead to problems with a pharmaceutical company that is considering (or is actively) investing large amounts of money in an academic institution, although the potential for such problems is great (e.g., if a well-established scientist suddenly decides to change his or her research area).

Confidentiality of Data

Confidentiality of data is probably the one issue that most commonly leads to difficult relationships between companies and institutions. This has most often become manifested in regard to the research that is conducted by graduate students as part of their thesis or publications. If the research work included evaluation of company compounds, the company may fear that disclosure of the results could be premature and could jeopardize the company's ability to obtain a patent, or alternatively, it might alert competitors to information that the company wanted to keep private for a period. In some cases, this issue is easily avoided by having graduate students work on a carefully designed research program that does not require any company compounds or investigational medicines that the company is not willing to disclose publicly. The golden rule in this area is to consider the issue in advance of providing compounds if graduate students will be involved. If no graduate students are involved, the topic must still be discussed, particularly because the academic scientists must know the company's policy and thoughts in advance of initiating the research.

Intellectual Property Rights

Intellectual property rights to compounds created or discoveries made as a result of the agreement are usually retained by the academic institution, but the company would be given the right of first refusal to license those compounds. In some contracts and agreements, it is possible to describe the broad, or even specific, terms of any future licensing agreements, but in other contracts this possibility is precluded by particular laws or policies. This issue will operate for a considerable period because compounds derived after the agreement has terminated may have resulted from scientific research conducted while the project was still active. Ownership and the rights to license those compounds may have to be separately negotiated before the contract is signed. If this has not been done, then a supplemental agreement should be reached before the period of joint activities is completed.

General Issues

Academic institutions usually wish to retain freedom of choice in the specific topics to be researched as well as the direction to be followed, although the general subject (e.g., inflammation) or disease (e.g., pancreatitis) chosen may be identified in advance and agreed to by both parties. Other requirements for a fruitful relationship are the free exchange of information and collaboration among scientists, control of publications by scientists, and a de-

cision at the outset on which group will take out an Investigational New Drug Application (IND) or other regulatory application to conduct human trials and which will conduct Phase I, II, and III trials. The academic group may be able to conduct Phase I and early Phase II trials within their academic institutions, but this may not be acceptable to the corporate sponsor who may wish to sponsor the trial themselves at another institution.

Transferring Discoveries from Academia to Industry

Many academic scientists have limited expertise in licensing products to other groups. In some cases the problem is not only one of expertise, but also of time available to pursue a generally time-intensive activity. Sometimes it makes sense to hire a person or group who can provide this service; this could be a venture capital group, technology transfer group, patent (or other) attorney, or, most commonly, an office within the academic institution. The subjects of transferring discoveries from academia to industry and licensing are discussed in Chapters 48 and 62.

The company's perspective is that it wishes to influence the direction of some or all research activities covered by the contract. Its most critical need is to ensure that patents on new compounds or technology resulting from the contract are applied for at the appropriate time, whether by the institution or the company. This must occur before any data or ideas are published or disclosed to the public in any way. The other requirement of companies is to have right of first refusal (or exclusive rights) to license patents that are held by the university.

Overall, it must be recognized that success in many alliances is difficult to predict in advance. Some alliances will work smoothly but bear no fruit. Those alliances that will financially benefit both partners are impossible to predict. Nonetheless, a company must judge which relationships are most likely to offer the best opportunities for success.

Other University Concerns

Academic groups generally have other concerns about alliances with pharmaceutical companies, which include the following.

1. To what degree can long-term corporate funding be counted on as a revenue source?
2. Restriction of the faculty's freedom in consulting with other companies and start-up ventures.
3. Whether the agreement will diminish research that would be otherwise pursued (but will not because it does not have commercial interest).
4. How will the occupancy and ownership of buildings funded by the company be determined?

LARGE SCALE RELATIONSHIPS

There have been several well-publicized large scale relationships between major pharmaceutical companies and well-respected universities. These include the specific relationships shown in Table 61.2. Some issues that are discussed about these relationships include the following.

1. Is academic freedom compromised in an unacceptable manner when scientists cannot discuss their research as freely as before?
2. Are the topics being evaluated worthy of research by academic scientists?
3. Are there graduate students who are unable to publish their research findings? If so, how is this issue being addressed?

There are several reasons to challenge the implication that an academic group must make significant compromises in either professional standards or ethics through collaboration with a pharmaceutical company. Each situation must be evaluated on its own because the goals established and agreements reached will differ. A number of issues specifically oriented to relationships in the field of biotechnology are described by Blumenthal et al. (1986).

OTHER ISSUES

A few other aspects and issues of the academic-industrial relationship are briefly described.

Educating Graduate Students About Career Opportunities Outside Academia

Scientific and clinical departments in academic institutions often do not sufficiently educate the students they train about nonacademic careers. This aspect appears to have been overlooked in the education of most graduate students. A more complete education of graduate students would be provided if major types of possible career opportunities were presented. It would also be valuable if opportunities for visits or even extended rotations of two to four months were made available for students to explore their interest in nonacademic areas. These areas include the pharmaceutical industry, government laboratories, government regulatory agencies, publishing activities, professional consulting companies, professional societies, foundations, and private businesses.

Contract Services

Relationships between industry and academia vary widely in the amount of collaboration and interaction required. For example, a company may purchase a service from an academic group. In this situation academicians are hired to conduct work without providing any input into its design or specifications. There are numerous occasions when this strictly contractual relationship may be beneficial to both parties. For example, academic chemists may be asked to synthesize certain molecules or pharmacologists may be asked to test certain compounds for money that the scientists use to pay salaries or otherwise support their research.

Patent Issues

Patent issues between companies and academic groups range from the extremely complex to the straightforward. Most academic scientists work under institutional patent policies that require them to turn any patents over to the university. The university in turn negotiates with pharmaceutical companies to license patent rights.

Duration of Industry-Academic Relationships

The duration of industry-academic relationships vary. Many do not last beyond the time it takes for the work specified in the contract to be completed. In other situations, long-term collaborative relationships seem to offer benefits to both parties (see Table 61.2).

Providing Medicine Samples to Academicians

Companies must determine at what point during a medicine's development it is appropriate to provide small samples of a new investigational medicine to academicians who request them for animal research. If samples are supplied too early in a medicine's development then the company's overall program may be vulnerable to premature publication of unreproduced results, and the company's own scientists may have insufficient opportunity to publish their own results on similar research investigations. If the company waits too long before making medicine samples available, then academic scientists may become annoyed or angry, synthesize the medicine themselves, or lose interest in the company's medicine. There is often a gradual loosening of company policy in supplying outside scientists with medicine samples during Phases II and III. It is in the company's interests to stimulate scientific publications during the late premarketing period. Companies must exercise caution that investigators who are given samples will not attempt to obtain use patents in potentially important areas the company has not yet researched. This should be handled through the agreement between company and academician that is completed prior to supplying the medicine sample.

62 / Technology Transfer from Academia

What Is Transferred? 732
   Patent....................................... 732
   Knowledge.................................. 732
   Concept..................................... 732
How Is It Transferred? 732
How Well Is It Transferred? 732
How Do Academic Scientists Feel About
   Licensing Their Discoveries to
   Pharmaceutical Companies? 732

Which Institutions and Companies Are Actively
   Pursuing Licensing Arrangements? 733
How Are Strategic Alliances Between Academic
   Institutions and Pharmaceutical Companies
   Perceived? 733
Selected Problems That Arise in Transferring
   Discoveries 733
Selected Benefits That Arise from Transferring
   Discoveries 734

Bennett's Classification for Reading Medical Articles

Medical student	*Reads entire article but does not understand what any of it means.*
Intern	*Uses journal as a pillow during nights on call.*
Resident	*Would like to read entire article but eats dinner instead.*
Chief resident	*Skips articles entirely and reads the classifieds.*
Junior attending	*Reads and analyzes entire article in order to pimp medical students.*
Senior attending	*Reads abstracts and quotes the literature liberally.*
Research attending	*Reads entire article, reanalyzes statistics, and looks up all references, usually in lieu of sex.*
Chief of service	*Reads references to see if he was cited anywhere.*
Private attending	*Doesn't buy journals in the first place but keeps an eye open for medical articles that make it into* Time *or* Newsweek.
Emeritus attending	*Reads entire article but does not understand what any of it means.*

Howard Bennett, *JAMA,* Feb. 19, 1992, Vol 267, p. 920

Myths abound over whether academicians or industrial scientists deserve the most credit for discovering new medicines. Some people believe that almost all new medicines originate within academia and others believe that almost none are discovered there. A recent exhaustive study of this issue (Maxwell and Eckhardt, 1990) showed that between 20% and 40% of medicines are discovered in the academic environment. (The percentage varies depending on the criteria used to define a discovery as "originating" in academia—e.g., degree of involvement, the quality of the innovation involved.) This percentage is viewed by most professionals as a major portion of discoveries.

Despite the fact that many medicines originate or are tested within academic institutions, almost all are developed by the pharmaceutical industry. This is because academic institutions lack many essential development functions, personnel, and technologies required to pro-

gress a medicine to the market. In addition, medicine development has not been a designated academic function; such institutions probably would be unwilling to risk the large amounts of money required to turn an interesting compound into a valuable medicine. This chapter describes some aspects of the transfer of medicine discoveries from academia to the pharmaceutical industry in the United States.

Another myth concerning the pharmaceutical industry and academia is that they are two separate worlds that do not collaborate. The truth is that there are many types of collaborations and relationships (see Chapters 48, Licensing Issues, and 61, Interactions and Relationships with Academic Institutions) and the quality of these collaborations is steadily improving in most developed countries. This chapter also describes some of the ways in which these collaborations take place.

WHAT IS TRANSFERRED?

Although the initial response to this question appears straightforward, i.e., the medicine and its patent, the true answer often varies. First, what is licensed are rights to a compound, medicine, technology, or model. A model could be a patent on an isolated and cloned receptor in the brain used to screen compounds for activity. The scientific technology applied to a medicine's discovery, manufacture, or other process may be licensed by a pharmaceutical company from an academic institution. This technology may provide an important competitive advantage for the licensee or it may merely expedite a specific process. Transfer may involve the concepts described below.

Patent

There are various types of patents (e.g., compound, use, process) that are described elsewhere in detail. Patents also have different strengths and abilities to withstand a challenge. This is becoming an enormous issue, particularly in the field of biotechnology where having a strong patent, for example, on the sequence of a protein, may be insufficient protection to produce the protein. Another company may have a patent on the method of manufacture, and another person or group may have a patent on the method of purification. The ability to own a single patent and to make a medicine without infringing on other patents is becoming increasingly difficult in the biotechnology field.

Knowledge

The compound of interest may require a great deal of expertise to develop, test, or otherwise use. This confidential scientific and practical knowledge or "know how" often is transferred to the company. A means of accomplishing this goal is through exchange of scientists; for example, company scientists may visit the academic laboratories and work with the scientists there to acquire a process or to learn relevant information, and vice versa.

Concept

In some cases a pharmaceutical company licenses the concept (or rights to something yet to be discovered) for a particular compound or series of compounds, even though the compounds have never been synthesized. This practice occurs in a different guise when a company forms a strategic alliance with an academic group and the contract stipulates the right of the company to license any compounds of interest discovered as a result of the agreement.

HOW IS IT TRANSFERRED?

More and more academic institutions have created offices for licensing the inventions of their university and its faculty to businesses. These offices have a variety of names but their functions are generally similar. Their value to the entire process is extremely high because their staff understand what steps are involved in the licensing of medicines and understand how to negotiate a reasonable business deal with a company. In the past, scientists often conducted their own negotiations or hired an attorney, and the terms they desired were often unrealistic and resulted in a great deal of time and energy being wasted in negotiations. Some institutions use a brokering/consulting company as their representative in seeking a licensee.

In most instances it is an academic institution's licensing or business group that approaches a pharmaceutical company rather than the other way around. Another common approach is for a scientist who has made a discovery to approach the company independently of their institution. Few companies would consider approaching academic institutions unless the company had a research arrangement with the academic institution or learned of a specific discovery there that interested them. Middle- and large-size companies generally process 500 to 1,000 potential licensing opportunities each year and have extremely limited time to focus on conducting proactive searches, unless a specific medicine is sought.

HOW WELL IS IT TRANSFERRED?

This is a difficult question to answer because there is such a wide range of experiences within every company. In general a few points can be made. Most companies are becoming better at this activity and are directly and indirectly educating the licensing offices within academia about the methods that work best. As a result, the overall level of efficiency of the transfer process is rising, although the range of experiences is extremely broad. Academic offices are becoming much more sophisticated and have alerted the faculty about methods and requirements for appropriately patenting new discoveries. Fewer discoveries are mistakenly revealed publicly prior to patent application than in the past.

HOW DO ACADEMIC SCIENTISTS FEEL ABOUT LICENSING THEIR DISCOVERIES TO PHARMACEUTICAL COMPANIES?

It is important to understand how scientists feel about licensing their discoveries to pharmaceutical companies. Unfortunately there are no broad surveys and no reports to use as a reliable barometer. It is clearly a potentially valuable topic to study. While it is impossible to know how all people react, it is clear that most scientists in the United States are pleased by the development of their discoveries. This is because of the following reasons.

- Useful medicines may be created that will benefit patients and improve people's health. This generally makes the inventor have strongly positive personal feelings.
- The university will benefit in terms of royalties and, possibly, milestone or up-front payments. This financial benefit enhances the overall contribution by scientists to their institution and is viewed positively by the institutions' administrators.
- People have pride in their discoveries and although initially fear losing proper credit for this, are relieved and pleased to learn that industry has no reason to take credit away from them. To the contrary, industry gains by giving scientists full credit for their discoveries.
- Some academicians benefit personally from the development and commercialization of their discoveries. In fact, the rapid growth of the biotechnology industry during the previous two decades was partly the result of academicians leaving their university and establishing a commercial company, or remaining within their university but obtaining company stock in exchange for their discovery. Many other types of business arrangements were also consummated that financially benefitted the academic scientist.

The perspective of an academic institution is presented by Gunsalus (1989).

WHICH INSTITUTIONS AND COMPANIES ARE ACTIVELY PURSUING LICENSING ARRANGEMENTS?

Research and development-based companies used to pay much less attention to licensing than they do now, and the same can be said of academic institutions. Today, it appears that almost all major academic institutions in the United States have organized their licensing activities into a central office to ensure that the institution benefits maximally from the discoveries of its members. Development-based companies (e.g., Marion Laboratories prior to its recent merger) have always been totally dependent on licensing discoveries in from outside their own institution and therefore have always focused on developing close relationships with academic institutions.

Stanford University and the University of California at Berkeley are far ahead of the others in the amount of such activities conducted over the years; these two institutions show great leadership in this area. This arose primarily because of the boom in biotechnology and the transfer of academic discoveries to start-up companies and later to established companies. Both universities have developed and maintain an aggressive program to identify discoveries within their institutions. The technology transfer group meets on a regular basis and alerts scientists to what services their office provides (e.g., help to file for patents). These institutions, as well as others, (e.g., Yale University, Virginia Tech, University of Missouri) provide periodic reports to potential customers listing and describing all available opportunities for license.

Companies understand well that a prolonged period without discovering new medicines of commercial value threatens their very existence. This fact has raised the need for an efficient and effective licensing group within a company to the point of being a necessity and not a luxury. These groups follow both proactive and reactive approaches (Chapter 48, Licensing Issues).

HOW ARE STRATEGIC ALLIANCES BETWEEN ACADEMIC INSTITUTIONS AND PHARMACEUTICAL COMPANIES PERCEIVED?

More and more, pharmaceutical companies believe that it is wise to allocate a small proportion of their money for medicine discovery to research conducted in one or more academic institutions. The usual percentage of the total research discovery budget allocated to these alliances ranges from 5% to 20%. Arrangements vary enormously in magnitude among companies and while the mega-sized agreements received a great deal of press during the last decade, many people believe that these large agreements are not as valuable to a company as having several smaller, well-targeted agreements with several institutions. What a pharmaceutical company does in this area depends primarily on the opinion of the Research Director and/or the Research and Development Director.

SELECTED PROBLEMS THAT ARISE IN TRANSFERRING DISCOVERIES

Each side can describe various types of problems that seem to be more prevalent or bothersome than they would like. From the academic perspective, pharmaceutical companies often do the following.

- Take an extraordinary length of time to review licensing proposals, even short ones.
- Allow the negotiations to get tied up and lost in the company's bureaucracy.
- Do not generally develop and market a licensed-in product as rapidly as the discoverer expects.
- Appear to pay much less for a license than the discoverer believes it is worth.

From the industry perspective, academic institutions and their scientists often do the following.

- Offer licensing opportunities that are at a very early stage of development. In fact, often no development has been conducted (e.g., pharmacological evaluation, metabolic studies, early toxicology studies).
- Have unreasonable expectations about the likelihood of their discovery reaching the market. Because most discoveries are offered for license at an early stage, fewer than 1% have a chance of reaching the market.
- Have unreasonable expectations about the value of their discoveries. They are unreasonable because (1) the chance of the discovery reaching the market is small, (2) a company must risk large amounts of money to develop the medicine, and (3) most marketed medicines do not pay back their cost of development, let alone make a profit.
- Have unreasonable expectations about the speed at which licensing opportunities can be evaluated by a company. Such expectations are based on misperceptions of the speed that is possible (which is determined by the quantity of resources that will have to be applied and the competition for such resources).
- Are unaware of the strong competition among ideas, compounds, and medicines in a company to garner any resources, let alone sufficient resources to progress the discovery rapidly.
- Have not applied for foreign patents and therefore the company cannot obtain strong worldwide patent coverage.

SELECTED BENEFITS THAT ARISE FROM TRANSFERRING DISCOVERIES

Although there are a number of real or potential issues or problems to overcome the number and importance of benefits derived are far greater. A few of these are described below.

From the academic perspective, relationships with pharmaceutical companies often

- provide an insight into how the pharmaceutical industry operates;
- provide a practical vision of the processes involved in medicine discovery and development;
- increase the numbers of collaborators to work with, some of whom have important equipment, skills, or facilities; and
- provide a stimulation that is enjoyable and combined with a broader perspective carries over to improved teaching at the academic institution.

From the company's perspective, relationships with pharmaceutical companies often

- provide consultation opportunities with important academicians;
- provide additional credibility for ongoing research;
- provide stimulation and enjoyment for the scientists involved;
- increase the likelihood of achieving important discoveries; and
- improve the teaching capabilities of the industry scientists to use at their company.

In conclusion, the relationships between academia and pharmaceutical companies for the purpose of licensing discoveries of academicians has greatly improved over the last decade. More activities of a higher caliber are being pursued and the benefits of such activities are positive for both parties.

63 / Interactions and Relationships with Government Agencies

Government Agencies That Interact with the
   Pharmaceutical Industry.................... **735**
   Food and Drug Administration 736
   United States Patent and Trademark Office ... 736
   Department of Agriculture................... 736
   Federal Trade Commission 736
   Environmental Protection Agency 736
   Occupational Safety and Health
      Administration............................. 736
   National Institutes of Health................ 736
   Drug Enforcement Agency................... 736
   United States Post Office.................... 736
Regulatory Issues........................... **737**
   Decision Making on Regulatory Issues by
      Pharmaceutical Company Personnel........ 737
   Regulatory Gossip.......................... 737
   Regulatory Strategies: Comments and Selected
      Examples 737
   Responding to Questions from Regulatory
      Authorities................................ 739
   Computer-Assisted New Drug Applications ... 739
   Are Clinical Trials and Regulatory
      Applications Receiving Due Process? 739
   Regulatory Submissions Made by Subsidiaries 740
Increasing the Speed of Regulatory Approval **740**

Preparing for Meetings with the Food and
   Drug Administration 740
Major Reasons for Delays in Medicine
   Approval Relating to Factors Under a
   Company's Control or Influence........... 741
The Five Cs of Regulatory Applications....... 742
Obtaining Clinical Data in the Country of
   Registration.............................. 742
Major Reasons for Delays in Medicine
   Approval Relating to a Regulatory Agency.. 742
Techniques for Pharmaceutical Companies to
   Speed Approval of Their Regulatory
   Submissions.............................. 743
Proposal to Speed Approval of New Medicine
   Applications 744
Legislatures, Legislation, and Lobbying
Activities **744**
   State Governments 744
   Therapeutic Substitution Laws............... 745
   Lobbying Activities at the State Level 745
   Organizing a Company's Lobbying Activities
      at the State or Province Level.............. 745
   Organizing a Company's Lobbying Activities
      at the Federal (i.e., National) Level 746
   Medicine Tampering 746

There must be a point beyond which, for example, preclinical toxicity or clinical trial requirements become stifling and excessively inhibitory, with a resultant lag in new medicine development. If the only sure way to avoid criticism for having allowed on the market a medicine that later turns out to be unpleasantly toxic is to reject all new medicine applications, it is also the way to ensure that no new effective medicines are delivered to the public. Dr. Louis Lasagna, clinical pharmacologist. From *Psychopharmacology Bulletin* (8: 43, 1972).

GOVERNMENT AGENCIES THAT INTERACT WITH THE PHARMACEUTICAL INDUSTRY

Interactions between pharmaceutical companies and the government occur on multiple levels. The major levels discussed are where either the company as a whole or the research and development part of the company interacts with a government agency. This discussion will be al-most entirely limited to interactions within the United States. Some fundamental differences exist between the types of interactions that occur in other countries. Governments influence pharmaceutical companies through laws and regulations regarding medicine development, marketing, production, plus medicine approval. In addition, regulations influence the physical environment inside the company's facilities. Employees of the company plus patients using the company's medicines are also influenced by many government regulations.

Pharmaceutical companies interact with many federal, state, and local government agencies and offices. The general influence of government on medicine research is described by Stuyt (1983). Some of the most pertinent federal agencies in the United States that affect pharmaceutical companies and a few types of interactions are listed.

Food and Drug Administration

The Food and Drug Administration (FDA) is undoubtedly the single most important government agency interacting with pharmaceutical companies in the United States. The FDA not only must approve all new medicines before marketing, but it also approves all supplemental applications for changes in New Drug Applications (NDAs), monitors prescription medicine advertisements and promotions, and has the authority to remove medicines from the market. It also has broad authority over food substances, cosmetics, medical devices, radiological health materials, and veterinary products.

United States Patent and Trademark Office

The Patent and Trademark Office reviews and approves three types of patents. They are (in decreasing order of commercial value) (1) compound patent (i.e., overall patent), (2) use of a compound for a specific purpose (i.e., "use" patent), and (3) procedural methods of manufacture (i.e., process patent).

Department of Agriculture

The Department of Agriculture (DOA) must approve the importation of biological products into the United States. Products from countries with certain diseases (e.g., hoof and mouth disease) may be quarantined for a period of time.

Federal Trade Commission

The Federal Trade Commission (FTC) monitors and reviews advertisements for over-the-counter medicines and reviews the advertising and promotion practices of a wide variety of consumer products.

Environmental Protection Agency

The Environmental Protection Agency (EPA) monitors materials and the environment involved in manu-

facturing processes and the waste products produced. These must meet certain rigid standards to protect the health and welfare of employees and the public. Both radioactive and nonradioactive wastes are monitored. Radioactive material issues are also dealt with by nuclear regulatory agencies.

Occupational Safety and Health Administration

The Occupational Safety and Health Administration (OSHA) monitors workplace practices for their effects on the safety and health of employees. There is some overlap with the authority of the EPA.

National Institutes of Health

The National Institutes of Health (NIH) frequently interacts with research and development–based companies to collaborate in joint development of medicines (e.g., epilepsy medicines in conjunction with the National Institute of Neurological Diseases and Stroke [White, 1985], anticancer medicines in conjunction with the National Cancer Institute [Schepartz, 1985]). The NIH is primarily concerned in their collaborations with pharmaceutical companies with conducting large (or small) clinical trials. They are not generally concerned with the development of a new medicine.

Drug Enforcement Agency

The Drug Enforcement Agency (DEA) monitors the use of scheduled medicines in production and in research. Scheduled medicines include medicines of potential or actual abuse. DEA tracks all scheduled substances that come into the company (as raw products or medicines to be made into combination products) and also all scheduled medicines that leave the company as finished goods. The DEA occasionally audits the company's records of scheduled medicines and inspects their facilities.

United States Post Office

The United States Post Office (USPO) interacts with pharmaceutical companies on mail-related issues (e.g., may certain medicines be shipped via the mail service). It also interacts with the FDA and numerous other government agencies on medicine issues. The USPO monitors and reviews fraudulent practices that use the mail system for promoting medicines, devices, or substances that affect the public's health and welfare.

Other agencies that interact with pharmaceutical companies include: United States Customs, Department of Treasury, Nuclear Regulatory Commission, Consumer

Products Safety Council, and the Equal Employment Opportunity (EEO) in the Department of Labor. Nongovernmental organizations whose findings and recommendations are accepted by the government include the United States Adopted Names Council (see Chapter 47, Marketing Issues) and the United States Pharmacopeial Convention which is discussed in several chapters.

REGULATORY ISSUES

Decision Making on Regulatory Issues by Pharmaceutical Company Personnel

In some companies the regulatory personnel are able to make professional scientific and medical judgments on issues that arise at regulatory agencies. At others, almost all issues must be referred back to appropriate personnel at the home office for input and decision making except for the most mundane topics. The type of training and regulatory experience of personnel in a company's regulatory group varies widely throughout the pharmaceutical industry. Some heads of regulatory departments are physicians and others are scientists, with or without advanced degrees. A few heads are nonscientists with business, legal, or marketing backgrounds.

There is an enormous level of frustration that is usually experienced by most pharmaceutical companies in trying to have their regulatory applications reviewed promptly. The single most important method to expedite review is to prepare a well-organized application that interprets data fairly, does not attempt to hide any problems, and leads the reviewer in a logical sequence through the application. It is not only useful but almost mandatory to have qualified individuals at a company (who are *not* closely involved with the medicine) read the application for clarity and logic before it is submitted.

Regulatory Gossip

Virtually all companies have groups and individuals who carefully consider and scrutinize every third- or fourth-hand comment from even junior personnel at a regulatory agency and comments made at meetings, in the press, or at advisory committee reviews. The company's managers look for grains of ideas that may help speed regulatory submissions. Comments made in hallways at federal facilities are sometimes raised to the rank of a Delphic Oracle and can influence decisions about company strategies to help move an application along the regulatory path toward approval. It is often difficult for companies to evaluate the validity of "signals" the FDA is sending or whether in fact any signals are being sent. This process is reminiscent of the rites of slaughtering chickens and examining their entrails as a means of predicting the future.

Regulatory Strategies: Comments and Selected Examples

Overall Regulatory Strategies

In the era before 1962 (i.e., the year of passage of the Kefauver-Harris amendments) the FDA responded rapidly to NDAs. It was usually unnecessary during that period for pharmaceutical companies to develop a detailed regulatory strategy. A number of studies were conducted and all materials were written up in a short time and submitted as an NDA. In recent decades, however, it has become increasingly important for companies to develop various strategies to expedite (we hope) progress of their NDA through the agency system and to minimize delays.

Numerous strategies must be developed. The overall strategy is whether or not to have a close or distant relationship during the investigational period. Some companies try to make the FDA a partner in the medicine's development (e.g., Merck & Co., Inc., with lovastatin [Mevacor]; Burroughs Wellcome Co. with zidovudine [Retrovir]). Other companies try to keep a distant relationship with the FDA throughout their negotiations. In addition to this overall strategy, companies develop many other regulatory strategies related to the specific medicine being developed.

Specific Regulatory Strategies on a New Medicine

When actively developing several indications, dosage forms, and routes of administration for a specific medicine, a company must make a number of careful decisions regarding its regulatory strategy. For example, an important decision could be whether to submit a single package of regulatory submissions for related or semirelated indications or to submit a series of individual applications. If the latter approach is adopted, is it better to wait for the initial application to be approved before the second one is submitted or to submit two or more at the same time? The appropriate response to these questions involves the company second-guessing the regulatory agency, often never knowing if they made the best decision.

The regulatory agency may react in many ways to any of these approaches, but the major issue is whether multiple applications on a single medicine will be reviewed simultaneously or sequentially. If it can be determined that the review will be simultaneous (or sequential) then this will affect the company's decision of how to submit the applications.

Early discussions with FDA reviewers may help a company develop the most appropriate strategy, although these discussions may not necessarily lead to the fastest approval of their application. With limited resources and huge backlogs of applications, the FDA develops its response based on work load, complexity of the application, and other departmental priorities. A recent publication (Spivey et al., 1987) has documented what many companies have known for many years: It usually takes the FDA as long or longer to approve a supplemental NDA for a new indication as it does the original NDA.

There are sometimes different mechanisms that may be used to file a regulatory application (e.g., either an NDA or Abbreviated New Drug Application [ANDA]

may be filed, the NDA may be filed with Division A or B at the regulatory agency, the format may follow Guidelines A or B). Many issues arise, and the company's response in a particular situation must be governed by anticipated problems to be encountered with each route and the work load of the different regulatory groups who could receive the application.

Companies desire to minimize their work in preparing detailed and voluminous regulatory dossiers. A typical flow of dossiers between different subsidiaries of the same company is shown in Fig. 63.1.

FLOW OF REGULATORY DOSSIERS BETWEEN COUNTRIES

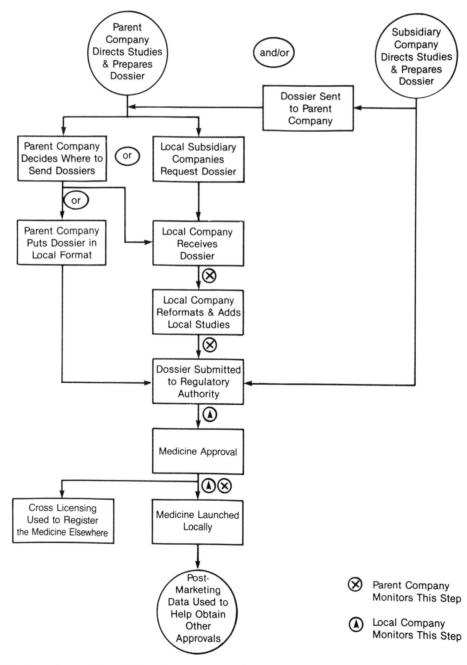

FIG. 63.1. Flow of regulatory dossiers between countries.

Responding to Questions from Regulatory Authorities

When a letter comes from regulatory authorities, the level of a company's response (e.g., letter, reanalysis, new study) must be determined. A team is often assigned the task of completing the company's response. It is possible to respond to a complex or multipart regulatory letter in pieces and not wait until the entire answer is prepared. For example, if a letter contains both chemical and clinical questions, all chemical questions may be answered at one time and all clinical questions may be addressed later. The key point for a company is to be responsive to the FDA's inquiry and prompt in answering.

Computer-Assisted New Drug Applications

The goals of a computer-assisted NDA (CANDA) are to (1) increase the accuracy of information transmission to and within regulatory authorities, (2) increase the efficiency of the regulatory review, (3) shorten the time for a regulatory decision, (4) reduce the amount of paper used, and (5) improve the quality of the regulatory application.

To achieve these goals a CANDA should contain

1. an indexing, filing, and cataloging system of the NDA's contents;
2. a word processing system of the text file to help the regulatory authority prepare its reports (e.g., Summary Basis of Approval); and
3. a data base to query. This is intended to provide the regulatory authority with a high degree of comfort with the quality and accuracy of data presented by the company.

There is no single type of CANDA submission, but a wide range. One extreme is to provide the regulatory authority with a laser disk that merely substitutes (or supplements) for hard copy. At the other extreme, an interactive computer program is given to a regulatory authority so that they may bypass the company and obtain raw data directly from the investigator(s).

Each NDA must be carefully considered as to whether it is a candidate for a CANDA. If so, then the company determines where it should fit along the electronic spectrum. In addition, the sponsor should interact with the regulatory authority (if possible) to ensure that they agree with the company's plans. Kaitin and Walsh (1992) examined the time for CANDAs to be approved by the FDA. They found significant variation between reviewing divisions in comparing the time taken for CANDAs versus non-CANDAs. The overall time for 10 CANDAs approved during 1987 through 1990 was 3.1 years, or 10% longer than for 64 non-CANDAs that were approved. They mentioned that CANDAs permit FDA reviewers to check raw data more easily in the sponsor's data base. They also review some of the pros and cons of this approach. To date, the fear of some people (including this author) that "data dredging" and unwarranted analyses of data would occur has not been reported. If data dredging occurred, it could easily place the company in a highly defensive and untenable position of having to react to regulatory statements regarding analyses the agency performs. Although many, if not most, of these analyses are theoretically possible for an agency to conduct with the hard copy data they currently receive, these analyses are not commonly conducted by most governments today. Rather, the government sends requests to a company to conduct additional analyses. If the company believes a request for additional analyses is unreasonable or inappropriate, they may challenge the request. A company may prepare analyses more easily if they do this prospectively than to respond to an analysis completed by a regulatory agency.

Another issue regarding electronic submissions is that a regulatory agency only has one computer system and pharmaceutical companies have many varieties. Thus, the electronic data of most pharmaceutical companies must be converted to a new format so that they may be compatible with the computers at the regulatory authority. This often takes a great deal of time and effort. Moreover, if electronic data from one company for a single medicine were to be sent to multiple regulatory authorities, it is likely that multiple conversions of the data would have to be made.

Given the FDA's intention of moving ahead rapidly in this direction and their strong commitment to CANDAs, it is important that the outstanding issues be addressed soon, and this is happening.

Are Clinical Trials and Regulatory Applications Receiving Due Process?

Clinical trials were defined as a subtype of clinical studies that deal with evaluations of investigational medicines or are performed with the purpose of being included in a regulatory submission. Clinical studies include all evaluations and research, whether on an investigational or marketed medicine (or device).

The term *clinical trial* raises the question of whether there is an analogy with a legal trial. In a clinical trial it is usually a medicine that is being tried rather than an individual or company. Medicines evaluated in clinical trials that use an inadequate study design are not receiving a fair trial.

When applications for a new medicine at any government regulatory agency are not evaluated according to current scientific and medical standards, but are influenced by various political considerations, then the medicine is not receiving due process. When a government's regulatory agency freely modifies its standards of acceptability for a new medicine application, not in an open forum, but according to the whim of individuals within that agency, then the medicine is again not receiving due process. Even when an agreement on any issue is

TABLE 63.1. *Approaches for a subsidiary that receives a New Drug Application submission from their headquarters*[a]

1. Place a front sheet on the application and submit it unchanged
2. Translate part or all of the application
3. Choose only certain reports and documents to submit
4. Choose only parts of reports or documents to submit (e.g., delete appendices of raw data not usually submitted, tabulations, or data collection forms)
5. Utilize a variation of one of these approaches

[a] Discuss with the central headquarters.

reached with the FDA during a medicine's development, it is not a binding agreement and may be modified by the agency at any time. The practice is sometimes referred to as the company's "trying to hit a moving target."

Many United States pharmaceutical executives yearn for at least certain aspects of the British System for medicine approval. In some situations The Committee on Safety of Medicines (CSM) informs a company by a Section 21 letter that the CSM is thinking of recommending to the licensing authority to grant a license under certain conditions. This letter outlines the deficiencies of the submission and indicates what additional studies, data, analyses, and other work must be done and submitted before the CSM is able to recommend regulatory approval. The company may then direct its activities toward gathering the necessary data. It should be noted that Section 21 letters may also indicate to a company that the CSM is not going to recommend approval of the medicine for reasons that are enumerated.

Regulatory Submissions Made by Subsidiaries

The responsibilities of subsidiaries to prepare or revise regulatory dossiers of the headquarters varies widely. The extent to which they are involved (Table 63.1) usually depends on the model of subsidiaries in place as well as the style of the company's international operations (see Chapter 9, Models of International Operations).

INCREASING THE SPEED OF REGULATORY APPROVAL

The major regulatory issue within the pharmaceutical industry today is how a company may speed up the regulatory evaluation of their applications. A medicine that has an anticipated annual market of 100 million dollars loses by some estimates over a million dollars in potential sales for every four days of its reviewing period. Even small delays become matters of great concern and result in large losses of potential revenue. Under the present system, the FDA can always find reasons to delay an application for years at a time.

On the other hand, too few pharmaceutical company executives put themselves in the position of FDA re-

viewers and try to critique their NDA prior to submission as outside reviewers would view it. Some companies also take extraordinary amounts of time to answer FDA inquiries. This adds to the total review time and is sometimes blamed on the FDA. Merck & Co., Inc. reportedly practiced their presentation on lovastatin for hundreds of hours before going to the FDA's advisory committee for the presentation (Byrne, 1987). That was wise and appropriate. The primary principle that should govern the regulatory submission, review, and approval process is for both a pharmaceutical company and the FDA to use medical and scientific reasonableness.

Preparing for Meetings with the FDA

Asking to meet with the FDA or other regulatory agencies to discuss medicine development issues without a clear understanding of one's position invites problems. The agency may make almost any request, even based on casual spur-of-the-moment comments or considerations. These offhand or even carefully considered comments may directly affect the company's development program for many years. If the company has no previous experience in a specific therapeutic area or with a specific disease, then it is worthwhile and important for them to contact leading academic experts and also potential investigators to create a medicine development plan prior to meeting the FDA. This plan should be tailored both to the specific medicine and to the particular company's requirements.

Thus, an inexperienced company doing research in a specific therapeutic area could rapidly learn the pros and cons of different regulatory approaches from outside consultants and experts prior to requesting meetings with government authorities. The company could invite relevant consultants to these regulatory meetings to provide expertise not available within the company or at the agency. These consultants could help educate the regulators (if necessary) and explain the rationale for the company's suggested development plan. These consultants would also assist the company in responding to questions, criticisms, and other comments from the regulatory authorities. The stature of important and well-respected consultants could be invaluable in helping a company convince regulatory authorities about particular aspects of the proposed or ongoing development plan submitted for a particular medicine.

It is essential that company scientists not embarrass the FDA and especially not draw attention of the United States Congress. It is said by some government "insiders" that the greatest mistake a company could make is to get the FDA and a Congressional subcommittee involved in an individual company's problems. An example involved Viratek Inc. and its studies submitted for a medicine used for treatment of acquired immune deficiency syndrome (AIDS).

Major Reasons for Delays in Medicine Approval Relating to Factors Under a Company's Control or Influence

Some of the reasons for delays in medicine approval relate to those primarily under control of the regulatory authority (see next section) and others are under the control (to a greater or lesser degree) of a pharmaceutical company. A few of the reasons for delays in medicine approval that can be influenced or controlled by a pharmaceutical company are given below. Appropriate attention to each point enhances the probability that the application will be reviewed rapidly.

1. *The submission is a poorly organized document that is not clear to the reviewers*—If the scientific and medical rationale for clinical or other studies are not clear to FDA reviewers or if the material is not presented in a logical order, some reviewers will cease reviewing the submission (and thereby delay the application) rather than immediately asking the sponsor for clarifications. Sponsors must keep in touch with the FDA to follow the status of their applications and to develop an appropriate rapport with the reviewers assigned.

2. *The clinical trials conducted were poorly designed*—Not only should individual clinical trials be well designed, but the overall clinical program should also create a clear picture of what was done and why each trial was conducted.

3. *One or more important clinical trials were not conducted*—If a medicine is eliminated from the body by the kidneys, it is important to evaluate how patients with poor kidney function will handle the medicine. If a medicine will be given in conjunction with another medicine in clinical practice, it is important to determine the extent and nature of any interactions.

4. *Clinical trials were conducted poorly*—This point is self-explanatory.

5. *Data were poorly or inappropriately analyzed*—This point is self-explanatory.

6. *The submission appears to bury or inadequately discuss problems*—Reviewers who detect major deficiencies or problems that they believe are purposely buried in an application may become frustrated and angry and delay progress of the application. Actual or potential problems should be dealt with openly and honestly by the sponsor and the company's perspective presented. Major problems with the medicine should be discussed in pre-NDA meetings so that the FDA's perspective is obtained. This information should help the company present the problem in the most appropriate manner possible.

When medicine-related issues are raised by preclinical, clinical, or technical development scientists, it is important that all three groups should comment on the implications, if any, for the medicine. This also provides the regulatory authority with some assurance that the NDA or Product License Application (PLA) document is a whole and not three separate documents written by people who do not communicate with each other.

7. *Developing a "me-too" product with little clinical benefit above presently available therapy*—The FDA takes a long time (i.e., many years) to review an application for a medicine that they consider of little therapeutic importance.

8. *Submitting additional data to a regulatory authority after an NDA or PLA application is submitted*—Some companies submit additional (unsolicited) data several times to the FDA. This is naturally annoying to any regulatory agency, which is attempting to review the specific set of data that were originally submitted.

9. *Submitting a large amount of "dirty or noisy" data in an application*—The more that these kinds of data are included in the application, the slower will be the review. If the pivotal trials (i.e., generally the most well-controlled clinical trials) are not "clean," then the delays are almost certain to be long ones. One exception would be if only case studies were submitted for certain orphan medicines or medicines for previously untreatable conditions. There is no guarantee, however, that case studies are acceptable on their own, without a controlled trial, to have such a medicine approved. For example, ganciclovir was originally rejected by the FDA's advisory committee because of a lack of controlled trials. Nonetheless, many case reports demonstrated that ganciclovir saved the eyes of many patients with cytomegalovirus infections who could not be treated effectively before this medicine.

10. *Submitting an NDA or PLA prematurely so that the medicine may join the queue for review at the agency*—Regulatory authorities strongly dislike obviously inadequate submissions that are prematurely submitted. A company that utilizes this technique usually does so in the hope of obtaining a shopping list of inadequacies to address. When they receive this list they will presumably have completed the studies in the meantime and can therefore obtain a rapid approval of their medicine. This practice holds up the review, however, of more complete applications. To deal with this issue expeditiously agencies can refuse to file an NDA.

11. *Requesting approval for too many indications*—This approach will delay the entire submission in most instances because the data supporting each indication are judged on their own.

12. *Using inexperienced regulatory personnel*—Company staff who do not follow written and unwritten procedures of dealing with FDA personnel may readily delay the company's applications. For example, labeling conferences vary from "rug-dealing" give and take negotiations to situations where fixed class labels are required to situations where the FDA adopts inflexible positions. The relevant pattern for a particular situation depends on the specific medicine (e.g., are ten other similar medicines available, how strong are the data, how safe is the

medicine?) and the personalities of the negotiators. People who are not aware of, and sensitive to, various situations and subtle personality signs may not achieve the best results possible for their submission.

13. *Delaying responses to regulatory questions*—There is no question but that some delays in approving medicines relate to the time taken by a company in responding to a letter from a regulatory authority. While this time may be appropriate it is also possible that it is excessive.

Some companies believe so strongly in their medicines that they forget that the data must be able to convince others, who review the data with a critical perspective. If the media has praised the medicine prior to submitting an NDA, it often substantiates the opinion of many people in the company about the medicine's value. There is a potential danger that the company may not present the data as well or as convincingly as possible. In assembling each NDA, a company should think of the FDA's "motto" as "In God we trust, from all others we need data."

The Five Cs of Regulatory Applications

The following list of the five Cs is only one of several mnemonics or rules to help guide the approach to preparing regulatory applications.

- Concise Submission—Make the application easy to read and follow.
- Clearly Written—Do not dilate in the text or add excessive materials that do not enhance the value of the submission.
- Correct Information—Ensure the application is carefully reviewed for errors
- Complete Documents—Review the application to make certain that no major omissions are present.
- Consistent Organization—Ensure that the application is logically and consistently organized.

Obtaining Clinical Data in the Country of Registration

There is often a sound medical or scientific rational for the desire of regulatory authorities to have clinical data gathered within their country. This rational could be based on

1. different systems used to diagnose the patients (e.g., ICD-9 versus DSM-IIIR);
2. different diagnoses reached among countries (e.g., hypotension in Germany versus the United Kingdom);
3. different methods of treating patients among countries;

4. different genetic backgrounds of many patients within their country;
5. different cultural approaches to treatment of a specific disease among countries that may be manifested by different types of concomitant medicines used or different types of nonmedicine treatment (e.g., acupuncture); or
6. any other differences that may affect patient responses within that country (e.g., race, diet, age distribution of patients with the disease) compared with the country or countries in which the data were originally collected.

There are also chauvinistic and marketing reasons for collecting data in each local country that must be seriously considered in planning a medicine's international development.

Major Reasons for Delays in Medicine Approval Relating to a Regulatory Agency

Additional Levels of Sign-Off

The major reason for regulatory delays in the United States probably relates to the two additional levels of sign-off for an NDA after it has been fully evaluated and approved by the medical, chemical, pharmacological, statistical, and pharmacokinetic reviewers at the FDA. The first additional level is the director of the division (e.g., Cardio-Renal, Oncology, Surgical Dental, Infectious Disease) in which the NDA was reviewed. This individual must review and approve all applications that have been reviewed and approved by his or her staff. The second level is by the person who supervises all division directors or is delegated by this person to conduct the review. All of these people are under intense public scrutiny and potentially strong political pressures, whether they approve or disapprove a specific medicine. They understand that they may be asked by members of Congress to justify thoroughly their decision in formal meetings. As a result, these regulatory executives appear to demand almost every study or datum that may potentially be required for their defense before they are willing to approve a new medicine.

Another reason why the two additional levels of sign-off is inefficient relates to the work load of reviewers at the agency. Reviewers have a heavy work load. Each division head must review all of the applications in his or her division. This often represents more applications than is reasonable for a single individual to deal with. The person at the next most senior level, who is head of all divisions, is like a final funnel that new chemical entity (NCE) applications from all divisions must pass through. His or her work load is *a priori* unreasonable because of the large number of applications and other responsibilities of their position.

Congressional Review of the Food and Drug Administration

There are certain periods when Congress examines the FDA in intense detail. These times usually relate to examinations of the FDA's effectiveness. Observers of this phenomenon comment that delays on approving new medicines become much longer during these periods. This occurs for several reasons. FDA executives are taken away from their work and have less time to review NDAs. These executives ask FDA reviewers to prepare documents and analyses for their testimony and to help them respond to questions. Thus, the reviewers too have less time to review NDAs. In addition, the FDA executives are less willing to approve (or disapprove) NDAs at a time when the FDA itself, its policies, and actions are being carefully scrutinized by Congress.

Specific Reasons for Regulatory Delay

There are many other reasons for regulatory delays that relate to the regulatory agency. These include the following.

1. Imprecise regulations and guidelines that may be interpreted and thus acted on in many different ways.

2. High turnover rate of personnel who are reviewing applications. This problem relates in part to problems of pay, benefits, working conditions, and political maneuvering.

3. Problems in storage of applications. This relates to limitations in the facilities and also to regulations requiring storage of documents. NDAs have been reportedly stacked on the floor in reviewer's offices, sometimes in the path to the reviewer's desk.

4. Lack of qualified staff to handle the great (and growing) work load. The budget of numerous regulatory authorities for increased resources is insufficient to conduct its assignment appropriately.

5. Bureaucratic "red tape" and regulations. This is self-explanatory.

6. Conservative approach favored by most reviewers. Financial rewards are few for reviewers who approve NDAs. Many fear government action if they appear to have been too lenient in their review, especially if the medicine, once approved, causes a serious adverse reaction to patients.

7. Basic lack of trust in pharmaceutical companies by some regulatory authorities. The adversarial relationship is unfortunate, but few senior regulatory authority managers appear to desire any change.

8. Low priority given NDA applications by most reviewers. They are required to assign a higher priority to assignments from or for Congress. Requests by other government offices or agencies, Investigational New Drug Applications (INDs), and their supervisor's requests also often take precedence. They also must help write new guidelines and deal with postmarketing surveillance issues on approved medicines. It has been stated at public forums that reviewers spend an average of about 30% of their time reviewing NDAs.

Questions raised by the FDA on any NDA are primarily a function of the reviewers' personalities. Some questions will always be raised, so that the FDA may document its diligence if it is ever questioned on the subject. Many NDAs (usually approximately 300) are going through the agency at one time.

Priority of Applications at the FDA

The FDA rates the therapeutic value of new chemical entities. Those with a lower rating are reviewed with a lower priority. There is little that a sponsor can do to increase this rating, apart from a direct appeal to the agency. When an application has a low priority at the FDA it may sit untouched for years before the review process starts. Then, as problems or questions arise, the company must *begin* to address them. If the company knew what the major deficiencies were ahead of time they could begin to address them at an earlier time. But the FDA is unable to do this because of their shortage of reviewers. This is a difficult problem to solve except through using outside reviewers under contract or by hiring more reviewers at the FDA. Some areas of the FDA have more difficulty than others in hiring competent reviewers. Reviewers include pharmacologists, chemists, statisticians, pharmacokineticists, and clinicians. The FDA is addressing this issue and will (we hope) resolve it within a few years.

Techniques for Pharmaceutical Companies to Speed Approval of Their Regulatory Submissions

A few ideas are presented that are generally known and used (when relevant) by pharmaceutical companies. Each situation must clearly be evaluated individually.

Experts from outside the company may review a summary of the regulatory application and write an opinion letter. Their letter should be a critical analysis of the data and not a summary. This might be especially useful for regulatory applications that are weak. For example, if the application primarily uses historical data as controls or utilizes data from compassionate plea trials, experts may express the degree to which the application contains substantial data and evidence that will convince physicians working in the same therapeutic area. The concept of what constitutes substantial evidence has been widely debated over the past few decades (Wardell and Lasagna, 1975). The experts would clearly only comment on the part of the application that they were most familiar with (e.g., clinical interpretation and importance, technical issues, social need).

It is wise to provide a desk copy of the relevant part(s) of the medicine application for the reviewer's personal use. This will also allow the reviewer to mark it up freely. This is advantageous because reviewers are not allowed to mark up the official NDA copy. Some reviewers at the FDA like to have personal interactions with company representatives to discuss the NDA, but others discourage such interactions. In situations where interactions are either acceptable or desired by the regulatory agency, it is critical to determine whether there should be a single person at the company who will act as the contact person. It is often desirable for one person to be appointed to fill this role. The person chosen should have a good rapport with the reviewer and be at the appropriate decision-making level within the company. Some companies prefer to deal with the FDA through legal and marketing representatives, whereas others prefer to have clinicians and scientists primarily involved.

Submitting clinical data on a new medicine given at different doses is extremely important. If dose-response data are not submitted in an NDA there should be a good reason. There should also be an adequate number of patients who have received a medicine prior to NDA submission. This aspect may be phrased in numerous ways. Some companies have reported that there are data on 3,000 patients in their NDA. But when the data are reviewed it may be shown that 1,000 patients received placebo, 500 received an active medicine used as a control, and only 1,500 patients received the trial medicine. Of this latter number, a certain number were normal volunteers and a larger number received subtherapeutic doses and yet others did not receive a full course of therapy. Therefore, it is essential that an adequate number of patients receive adequate doses of a new medicine before the regulatory dossier is submitted.

A few other recommendations that may help to speed approval of a regulatory submission are: (1) hire ex-FDA employees as consultants, (2) do not go to Advisory Committee meetings with an arrogant attitude, (3) discuss the company's regulatory approach with the FDA at the earliest practical opportunity, (4) discuss issues with all relevant areas of the FDA (e.g., if the medicine is a biological product, then discuss issues with both the offices of medicine research and biologics research), (5) do not change the formulation used in a major way during a later stage of clinical trials (if possible), (6) use only one name (generic) for a medicine throughout the application, and (7) prepare reviewer-friendly types of documents that lead the reviewer step by step through the logic and the data in the application. When responding to questions from regulatory authorities, ensure that you know what the reviewer is actually looking for in response to their question.

A principle believed by some companies is that taking an extra 6 to 12 months to assemble a first-class NDA will save regulatory review time and yield a more rapid approval overall. The counterargument is that submitting a less-than-ideal dossier to a regulatory agency allows a company to get into a queue for having its application reviewed and its deficiencies outlined.

Proposal to Speed Approval of New Medicine Applications

One possible answer to the overall problem of expeditiously reviewing NDAs is to change the current system. A reasonable system would be for the FDA to appoint an independent group of experts in the therapeutic field where the medicine is intended to work. This group would review the preclincial and clinical data of one (or multiple) NDA and in conjunction with other reviews of manufacturing data, arrive at a binding decision on the medicine's approval. If the medicine is not approved, then each of the reasons should be stated. A list of additional studies and/or data required for approval should also be given. Once that additional work is completed by the company (or other sponsor) the regulatory application (e.g., NDA) should be approved, unless of course the data suggested that the application should be turned down or significant new problems were uncovered. A similar system is operating, apparently well, in Canada, France, and Japan.

This system would avoid most of the major problems that exist with the current system. These problems are well known and will not be enumerated again. Many details of this type of system would have to be worked out prior to proposing any change through legislation. Whether this or another basic model (e.g., having advisory committees make binding decisions) is used to improve the review and approval of new medicines, it is hoped that a more efficient and rapid system will be implemented that will benefit patients, the public, and the pharmaceutical industry. An important component of an improved system is to have an effective appeal system that does not penalize those who use it.

LEGISLATURES, LEGISLATION, AND LOBBYING ACTIVITIES

State Governments

There has been an increasing involvement between individual pharmaceutical companies, as well as the Pharmaceutical Manufacturers Association (PMA), with state governments during the last decade. Many people attribute this to greater decentralization of government, promoted by the Executive Branch of government. There has been a great deal of cooperation between individual companies in this area with almost none of the competition noted between the marketing groups of many companies. Selected issues are briefly described to illustrate some of the major types of issues faced.

Therapeutic Substitution Laws

A recent issue that is perceived as a threat by research-based pharmaceutical companies and the medical profession, are the proposed therapeutic substitution laws. These laws would allow pharmacists to fill a patient's prescription with a different medicine than the one prescribed, but one which the pharmacist judged to be therapeutically equivalent. Pharmacists claim that they are in a good position to make these decisions.

This practice has greater potential to affect pharmaceutical company sales than even the generic substitution laws, which allow pharmacists to substitute a generic version of the *same* medicine. If therapeutic substitution bills become law, physicians who want a patient to take a specific medicine will not know whether the patient was given the prescribed medicine or another that was judged by the pharmacist (i.e., a nonphysician) to be therapeutically equivalent. The medical implications of this potential change are far reaching for several reasons. First are the obvious implications for patient care. In addition, doctors will be losing part of their decision making to pharmacists or committees that decide on acceptable medicines. On the other hand, many physicians want the right to dispense the medicines they prescribe. Pharmacists see this issue not only as an infringement of their turf and a threat to their livelihood, but also as a conflict of interest for physicians. Both issues are highly complex and raise many questions.

Several states are considering legislation on therapeutic substitution, which is more recently being called *therapeutic alternatives* or *therapeutic interchange.* The pharmaceutical companies have been swift to respond. The PMA has formed a task force in all states that can be rapidly mobilized to develop an organized approach when proposals are dealt with by legislative committees. This task force includes members of a number of research-based pharmaceutical companies and uses the PMA as an umbrella organization. The task force plans their approach to include both direct and indirect lobbying efforts as described below.

Lobbying Activities at the State Level

In terms of direct lobbying, PMA assigns their members to visit different key legislators and their aides. In some situations the legislative aides are more impor-

tant to lobby than are the legislators they support because the aide is often responsible for developing policy. Direct lobbying is also conducted at various social events. This allows the lobbyist and legislator to meet in a more informal setting than in the state capitol and also provides an occasion to develop a better understanding of each other's position and character. The relationship that develops usually improves the quality of subsequent interactions when the lobbyist meets the legislator at the capitol building in a more formal environment. Spouses and aides of the legislators may also be invited to this type of social event. This aspect of lobbying is conducted to a different degree by various companies, depending on their budgets for this type of activity and their interest in direct lobbying activities.

In a few states it is often necessary for a pharmaceutical company to hire specific people to manage their efforts in influencing a bill. This person may be a friend of a powerful legislator who is "suggested" for the role. In other situations it is necessary to "juice the machine" (e.g., contribute to a legislator's political action committee [PAC]) to gain access to a key political leader and/or their aides. This practice is becoming more widespread on the federal level, where certain key Congressmen hold breakfast meetings for their major contributors (i.e., lobbyists) who wish to have an "audience" for discussions and to advise the Congressmen about their views.

Indirect lobbying efforts are conducted by company lobbyists going to consumer pressure groups (e.g., Medicaid recipients, American Association of Retired Persons), medical societies (e.g., state medical associations, American Medical Association), and disease-oriented groups (e.g., American Cancer Society, Arthritis Foundation) and encouraging them to become involved in lobbying efforts. Activities that these groups are encouraged to conduct include (1) organizing a letter-writing campaign, (2) actively supporting or criticizing certain legislation, (3) visiting the legislators (possibly by the busload), (4) holding public demonstrations, and (5) testifying in front of legislative committees.

Initiating a grass roots campaign is often the most effective means for a pharmaceutical company to influence legislation. Companies usually want the public to limit their activities to writing letters or participating in other carefully controlled activities. Companies do not want the public to initiate many different activities. Such activities are often disruptive and counterproductive to the specific goals of a company, which is usually either passage or blockage of specific legislation.

Organizing a Company's Lobbying Activities at the State or Province Level

Companies organize their state lobbying efforts by either centralizing or decentralizing their group of lobbyists and support personnel. The advantages of centralizing this function include a greater ease of discussing issues as a group and also having access to all corporate amenities and staff support. Advantages of decentralization include being closer to the action at the state capitol. But if the company's staff are based in only a few large cities, then they often have to take time consuming airplane rides or long automobile trips to reach the appropriate state capitol. The size of a company's total staff working at the state level usually ranges from 1 to 15 people and is therefore insufficient to be based in each capital. Decentralization only makes sense when there is a large staff or there is a certain person who the company wants to hire but who insists on remaining in a specific locale.

Most states or provinces do not have any research-based pharmaceutical companies and therefore do not view pharmaceutical companies as important contributors to the tax base. Lobbyists who do not live in the state where they are lobbying on behalf of a pharmaceutical company may have a carpetbagger image that they must dispel. To do this they must build a rapport with the legislators, which is primarily accomplished by serving as a reliable source of information. This is also done by attending fund raisers, inviting the legislator to speak to a health-oriented group or to a company sales meeting, contributing to the legislator's political action committee (PAC), and inviting legislators to tour the company's manufacturing or research facilities. This latter activity will provide most legislators with a different perspective of the pharmaceutical industry than the one popularly portrayed by the media. Other activities are to invite legislators to receptions or to a dinner where they may meet people of particular interest to them. Finally, the company may form an umbrella group within a state that acts as a conglomerate of health interest groups to coordinate activities of mutual interest and also to facilitate better access to legislators.

Most companies who have state legislative lobbyists have established some type of early warning system to pick up information to which the company must respond. This may be done through a network of contacts in each state who monitor what is going on within the state government. These monitors may or may not be asked to help with lobbying activities. The monitors learn about relevant information by (1) reading local newspapers, (2) listening to many people, (3) joining various associations (e.g., medical, pharmacy, health), and (4) becoming active in the legislative groups within these organizations. Information on early signs of legislation is especially important because it is easier to block or modify legislation before it leaves a committee. Once

legislation has been reported to the legislature floor, it is much more difficult to modify or influence.

Organizing a Company's Lobbying Activities at the Federal (i.e., National) Level

Almost all pharmaceutical companies draw a line between state and federal legislative activities. Some companies (e.g., Pfizer Inc., Glaxo Inc.) have their own full-time federal lobbyist who lives in Washington, DC. Other companies have someone based at their corporate headquarters who visits Washington as needed. One difference between state and federal activities is that fund raisers for federal legislators are usually held back at their state rather than at their political office (i.e., in Washington).

The types of bills and activities at the federal level usually differ from those at the state level. Federal activities such as patents, imports, and exports of medicines usually do not affect individual state legislators or lobbyists. In many situations, however, issues are dealt with at both the state and federal levels. When the federal government passes a law there is usually no need for state action. In some situations, however, a state may want to go further in their legislation than the federal law. Pharmaceutical companies may then have to respond to additional legislation at the state level.

Medicine Tampering

A specific example of the different levels of legislation arose a few years ago when capsules of some medicines were tampered with and a number of people were poisoned. Some counties in the United States decided to pass ordinances to help control this problem. Many states also had bills introduced to react to this problem. The federal government became involved and eventually passed a bill. This federal bill removed the need for 50 separate states to each have their own bill. Individual state bills had the potential to require medicine manufacturers to produce and/or package their medicines in 50 (or more) different ways to ensure their safety. The burden for the companies and confusion this would have created is enormous.

Lobbying efforts of pharmaceutical companies on this issue were focused in two directions. First, companies told the states that the federal government was trying to pass a bill and suggested waiting for the federal government to act. Second, the companies worked cooperatively at the federal level to obtain the type of bill that they believed would be in the best interests of the general public and the industry.

64 / Interactions and Relationships Between Pharmaceutical Companies: Competition and Collaboration

Competition Between Pharmaceutical Companies 747
    Types of Competition Between Companies.... 748
    Analyzing the Competition 748
    Sources of Information on Competitors 749
    Types of Information Often Obtained on the
        Competitor's Medicine Development
        Program 749
    Interactions Between Companies at
        Professional Meetings 750
    What Separates Successful Research-Based
        Pharmaceutical Companies from
        Unsuccessful Ones? 750

Collaborations Between Pharmaceutical
    Companies 751
    Types of Collaborations Between
        Pharmaceutical Companies................. 751
    Licensing.................................... 751
    Reasons for a Company to Consider Licensing
        a Medicine to Another Company 751
    Joint Ventures.............................. 751
    Writing and Facilitating Agreements Between
        Companies................................ 752

Successful collaborative negotiation lies in finding out what the other side really wants and showing them a way to get it, while you get what you want. Herb Cohen, American writer. From You Can Negotiate Anything.

COMPETITION BETWEEN PHARMACEUTICAL COMPANIES

Competition is a highly complex concept. Few issues concerning medicine development invoke as much emotional reaction as the thought of competition. But competition is not an all-or-none issue. Competition usually does not exist on the basis of Company A versus Companies B, C, and D. Competition may be conceptualized on the basis that each product or investigational medicine has its own spectrum of competitors. This spectrum ranges from no competition to fierce and intense competition. It is generally desirable, although usually impossible, for a company to have most of its products and investigational medicines in disease or therapeutic areas where there is little or no competition. This allows them to have most or all of the market share. On the other hand, controlling 100% of a small market is generally less attractive to marketing managers than having a small share of a very large market. This is the primary reason why companies are sometimes willing to develop a medicine that they know will be a "me-too" medicine in a major market.

Companies that compete in the marketplace with some of their medicines also collaborate with the same or different pharmaceutical companies in (1) comarketing other medicines, (2) developing investigational medicines, and (3) conducting research. These are fairly common practices and illustrate why a company's competitors are usually considered either on a medicine by medicine basis or on a therapeutic area by therapeutic area basis.

Types of Competition Between Companies

Various types of competition exist between companies. One categorization is based on the three areas of medicine discovery, medicine development, and medicine marketing.

Medicine Discovery

If it is believed that a specific receptor or enzyme should be stimulated or inhibited to develop a useful medicine, many companies will develop biological tests using the specific receptor or enzyme as the target. Each company will then search its catalogue of previously prepared compounds, as well as synthesize new chemicals to accomplish their goal. If a company is lucky, it will be the only one looking for active compounds against a specific target or receptor. But, the chances of this happening are not great. Scientists and information specialists at all major pharmaceutical companies continually scour the scientific literature seeking to identify relevant biological receptors, enzymes, or other markers to use as targets for testing compounds. Of course, there will be companies who are alone in looking at certain targets, but these targets will often be ones that are purposely bypassed by other companies.

A company that develops a new animal model to use as a test to evaluate biological activity of compounds has a potentially important competitive edge. The value of this edge depends on both the value of the test and the quality of compounds evaluated in it.

If a pharmaceutical company wanted to weaken deliberately a competitor, one of the most effective ways is to offer the competitor's most creative scientists or group of scientists better positions at the other company. There are usually a small number of highly creative scientists in any company who supply most of the important conceptual breakthroughs. These people may generally be easily identified.

Medicine Development

It has become apparent in recent decades that there is a great difference among companies with respect to the efficiency in how well they develop medicines. Having large sums of money to spend on medicine development is no guarantee of having and utilizing efficient methods. In fact, many people claim that the largest companies require an additional year or more to develop a medicine compared with the time required by smaller, more efficient companies. The large size per se restricts the ability of large companies to mobilize people effectively. The degree to which this belief is true is unknown and certainly would be difficult to test in a quantitative manner.

Current clinical and nonclinical medicine development standards and state-of-the-art methods are described in the *Guide to Clinical Trials* (Spilker, 1991), but are not yet adhered to by many companies, particularly in Europe, where regulatory standards in most countries are not as rigorous as at the Food and Drug Administration (FDA). It is usually possible for an efficient company to develop a specific medicine more rapidly than another company if they utilize good science and logic and have excellent employees.

Medicine Marketing

Marketing is the area that most people initially think of when competition is discussed. It is the aspect of competition that is most exposed to the public and to all pharmaceutical companies. The first medicine of a new class to reach the market usually retains the largest market share after competitors with an equivalent medicine reach the market. This emphasizes the importance of efficient medicine development and of reaching the market as rapidly as possible. If only a few months elapse after the market launch of a new medicine before the second medicine of the same type is marketed; however, it may be possible for the second company to overcome the market lead of the first medicine. The second company accomplishes this by looking for a positive attribute or angle that differentiates their medicine from the first one on the market. This attribute should be important to physicians and/or patients. Marketing groups are hoping to be winners in terms of gaining the largest market share and do not want to be close. It is generally claimed that being close is only desirable in dancing and pitching horseshoes.

There is a great instability in market share for many therapeutic areas. The therapeutic markets that are most stable have the potential to be disrupted when better medicines are introduced. There are extremely few areas where the "perfect" medicine has been discovered. Of 20 major industries, the pharmaceutical industry was found to have the second highest index of market share instability (Schnee and Caglarcan, 1978; the petroleum industry was ranked first).

Analyzing the Competition

It is usually relevant to identify and analyze the competition on a product by product basis. On the other hand, it is sometimes important to evaluate all of the actual (and/or potential) competitors in a therapeutic area or in a specific market segment. Finally, it may be relevant to analyze a particular company. A pharmaceutical company may wish to examine another pharmaceutical company for various reasons (e.g., possible acquisition or merger, cross-licensing agreements, joint ventures).

In looking at a single company, many analyses may be performed. The specific analyses to perform are dictated by the questions posed. A few typical questions are listed below.

1. What medicines are in the company's product portfolio? Is it aging? What is the medical and commercial quality of their investigational medicines? Does the company look at primarily high- or low-risk therapeutic areas? When will the most important new medicines be marketed? What is the forecasted sales picture?

2. What is the financial status of a company and its individual components?

3. What is the quality of the staff, their turnover, their morale, their level of pay and benefits?

4. What is the status of the facilities and equipment in terms of age, value, and state of the art?

5. What are the major corporate strengths and weaknesses? What are the major strengths and weaknesses of the production, marketing, and research and development groups?

Sources of Information on Competitors

Published material in journals, newspapers, professional newsletters, prospectuses, gossip sheets, government reports, annual reports, and other sources sometimes provide useful information on competitors. Many data bases in *Dialog* or other families of data bases are other sources of information that may be searched. Data obtained are often not analyzed or presented in the format of interest. Also, much of these data are out-of-date, difficult to verify, and often inaccurate. Think of the data and information presented on new medicines being developed by your own company. How accurate are the data published in the press and various other published sources?

When a company desires highly specific information on a competitor's medicine, it may be possible to contact individuals who have the desired knowledge. These individuals may be current employees at the competitor or ex-employees. Multiple sources are used whenever possible. All methods must be carefully considered for their acceptability from an ethical perspective before contacts are initiated.

A reliability factor must be assigned to all information obtained. Even if an information source is "usually reliable" and a systematic approach is used to obtain information, it is essential not to make rapid or important decisions based on hearsay or conjecture. The assumptions of the source and their perspective must be carefully assessed in evaluating the value of their information. If five pieces of information on a specific question

are obtained and have to be integrated, it is important to weigh the information based on its potential influence (i.e., does it relate to the key issue or a tangential question) and also on the likelihood that it is true. This process may be done intuitively, through discussion, or even as a result of carefully assigning a probability assessment or score to the data's legitimacy.

Competition in the medicine world does not only exist between major research-based companies, but increasingly involves generic pharmaceutical companies, small biotechnology companies, and chemical companies that are entering the medicine development arena in a major way (Eastman Kodak, E.I. Du Pont de Nemours & Co., Monsanto Co.).

Types of Information Often Obtained on the Competitor's Medicine Development Program

It is generally surprising how much useful information may be obtained about a competitor's investigational medicines through legitimate means. Such information may be legitimately obtained from a variety of sources, both published and unpublished. Some companies spend much more money and effort than others to obtain this type of competitive information. The usual motivation is not to steal secrets, but to learn as precisely as possible (1) in which area(s) the competitors or potential competitors are working, (2) which medicines are being developed, (3) what advantages and disadvantages the competitors' medicines have, (4) how the competitors' medicines will be perceived, (5) what is the current stage of development of the competitors' medicines, (6) who are the investigators working on the other companies' medicines, (7) what are the competitors' protocols like, (8) how rapidly are the competitors' trials progressing, (9) what are the likely indications the competitors will seek approval for, and (10) other relevant questions. Not all of these questions would apply in any one situation. Companies also hope to learn of mistakes, problems, or positive effects found by their competition, so they may, it is hoped, benefit from that knowledge. Although most of this information does not affect decisions or activities at the company that gathers it, there are cases where the information is extremely helpful in determining how much resource to put on a specific medicine project, in determining the development strategy to adopt, or in making another decision.

All companies protect their chemical ideas as tightly as possible before patent applications are filed. After that point it is usually less critical to protect them as tightly. Chemical ideas are rarely stolen prior to being patented. But, once published or available through patent applications, the information may provide another company with interesting or useful prototypes to follow, develop, and exploit. One difficulty for companies that carefully examine published patents and the chemical literature for ideas to exploit is knowing how to separate the 99% of areas that would not be fruitful from the 1% or less that would be. One problem is that many or most of the best areas to explore for future medicines may already be protected by the company through other patents or may have been researched and found to be of little value. In addition, many promising chemical compounds will turn out on further animal (or human) testing to be more toxic or less effective than originally thought. It is therefore difficult, at best, to know which newly reported compounds are worth exploring.

Interactions Between Companies at Professional Meetings

In areas of basic research, scientific methodology, reports on new medicines, and other technical areas, there is often frequent communication between pharmaceutical company personnel at scientific meetings. There are clear limits that scientists and managers generally follow at such meetings. Areas that should not generally be discussed include information not yet made public on: (1) nonpatented compounds, (2) novel uses of known medicines that have not yet been published, (3) strategies of how medicines are being developed, (4) contents of clinical protocols, (5) names of investigators and consultants, (6) specific areas of research, and (7) areas where a potentially important medicine has been discovered. Avoid making the classic error that the public was warned about in World War II England: "Loose lips sink ships."

There is no doubt that some junior-level employees of a company have given away valuable information or even secrets. Chief executive officers have also been accused of giving away important information. The message is that everyone at professional meetings personally knows information that should not be discussed. Remember, the person told may not use the information, but could pass it on (even innocently) to another who might. Many people rationalize their openness by telling themselves "well, I only told one person." But, if that process continued, there would soon be no one left who did not know the information.

What Separates Successful Research-Based Pharmaceutical Companies from Unsuccessful Ones?

Several factors often play a major role in differentiating successful and unsuccessful companies. In a short time span, good fortune or luck is often extremely important. More controllable aspects that relate to success are having a highly motivated, experienced, intelligent staff who are able to judge the most appropriate compounds to develop as medicines, the most efficient means to develop a medicine, the best time to reallocate resources from a dying medicine, and the most appropriate means of marketing medicines. This is not to overlook the importance of production and many other areas that contribute to a medicine's development and success, but they are rarely responsible for the overall success or failure of a company. Having a highly motivated staff depends on many other factors including those previously mentioned, such as work environment, compensation, responsibilities assigned, and ability to conduct and publish company-related research of personal interest.

An Old Battleground

The incentive is almost gone for pharmaceutical companies to introduce more potent medicines that have no clear therapeutic advantages. This "battle of the milligrams" (e.g., where medicine A is claimed to be 10 times as potent as medicine B) was sometimes a worthwhile area to "wage combat" in the 1950s, but pharmaceutical companies have moved to new fields of competition.

Profits

Increasing competition among medicines frequently means that only the most cost-effective ones in each class will be widely prescribed. "Me-too" medicines may be able to achieve commercial success if they can demonstrate cost savings and equal effectiveness to currently marketed medicines. Cost containment pressures will probably continue and even increase in importance in the future. Although it is possible that the number of marketed medicines which repay their investment will decrease below the one-fourth to one-third that are believed to do so now (Virts and Weston, 1980; Grabowski and Vernon, 1982; Drews, 1985; Joglekar and Paterson, 1986) this is unlikely. It is more likely that pharmaceutical companies will become more selective about the compounds they choose to develop as medicines, so that a higher proportion of investigational medicines will be marketed to repay their investment.

Foreign-Based Companies

Pressures on the United States-based pharmaceutical industry will also come from increased foreign competition within the United States. Additional foreign-based pharmaceutical companies have entered the United States since 1960, and the general trend of a weaker dollar favors this movement. Foreign-based companies have been obtaining a steadily larger share of worldwide medicine sales over the last two decades. The influence that foreign-owned pharmaceutical companies have on

American-owned pharmaceutical companies may become a more important issue in the future.

Mergers and Acquisitions

Pharmaceutical companies that are weak because of large legal liabilities, a drought of new products, or another reason are subject to acquisition by another company. This has been a relatively common phenomenon in the pharmaceutical industry over the last century. A merger of equal partners is usually unworkable. It is generally necessary to have one company dominant. The dominant company usually exerts its view on the subsidiary company and often hopes to be able to improve the efficiency of overall medicine development as well as to make a profit.

COLLABORATIONS BETWEEN PHARMACEUTICAL COMPANIES

Types of Collaborations Between Pharmaceutical Companies

There are numerous situations when two or more pharmaceutical companies form a true partnership or alliance. The nature of some of these relationships (e.g., licensing, joint ventures) are briefly discussed (see Chapter 48, Licensing Issues). Other types of collaborations that are not discussed further include providing a clinical trial medicine and matching placebo to other companies. Some companies are more cooperative than others in this regard, although most companies want to review the clinical protocol before they are willing to give any of their medicine to another company. Companies often work together at professional meetings. Finally, trade associations provide a useful forum for various other types of collaborative activities. These are discussed in Chapter 65, Interactions and Relationships with Trade Associations.

Licensing

Independent pharmaceutical companies often collaborate with each other on projects of mutual interest. This may involve licensing activities whereby one company obtains the rights to develop and eventually market one or more medicines of another company. In some situations, companies will exchange the right to license medicines. This is referred to as cross-licensing. Companies may also license technologies (e.g., medicine delivery systems, patented formulations) from another company. Companies initially sign a confidentiality statement in which they promise not to disclose any confidential information given to them. Under such an agreement companies explore their investigational projects and marketed products that they would be willing (or might be willing) to trade with the other company. Some pharmaceutical companies attempt to acquire most or all of their medicines through licensing. Some of them have the motto "Search and Development" instead of "Research and Development." Licensing activities are described in Chapter 48, Licensing Issues.

Reasons for a Company to Consider Licensing a New Medicine to Another Company

Companies that are not actively selling their medicines in a country can explore the potential for having a successful subsidiary there through licensing a medicine. A company usually incurs less risk if it licenses a medicine to another company than if it establishes or acquires a subsidiary in that country. Without the licensing mechanism many companies would have had great difficulty initially entering a new market. Licensing one medicine in exchange for another (i.e., cross-licensing) often has several advantages and is often preferred. Additional income made by the original company through licensing has sometimes been extremely valuable (e.g., Boots' licensing of ibuprofen to The Upjohn Company in the United States).

A few potential pitfalls of licensing include limited profits, tax issues, and obtaining royalties in a place and form (e.g., cash versus goods) that is most desirable. Complex bartering arrangements are sometimes created among several countries. Other potential problems are assuring that the licensee adheres to quality assurance and to development schedules. Provisions should be made in the contract to allow the original owner to enter a market eventually, if this may be desired. Otherwise, a company may be precluded from doing so.

Joint Ventures

Two or more companies may enter into a formal relationship where they agree to work together in a specified way. The goal may be to discover a medicine, but it is most often to expedite a medicine's development or to enhance medicine sales and profits. The partners may or may not be equal in the relationship they forge. They will probably have different roles in the venture. For example, one may provide capital, another research (or medicine development) expertise, or a marketing sales force. Many variations exist, and a single company may be involved in numerous types of joint ventures.

The primary motivation for embarking on a joint venture is usually to enhance profits or the potential for profits. Nonetheless there are various other reasons that cause pharmaceutical companies to enter joint ventures. These include (1) sharing risk on an expensive and high-risk project, (2) sharing costs on an expensive project, (3) achieving a better entry to a desired market, (4) satisfying a foreign government that requires participation of a local company, and (5) achieving a larger or more knowledgeable group of experts who would have a greater chance of success on a specific project. Many developing countries insist that a foreign company which wishes to manufacture medicines in the developing country must form a joint venture with a local company. The foreign pharmaceutical company may only be allowed to be a minority partner in the joint venture that is formed.

Another type of joint venture is for two companies to serve as backup manufacturing facilities to make specific medicines for the other company in case of marketing need or disaster at a manufacturing plant.

Writing and Facilitating Agreements Between Companies

Written agreements between companies must be clear to prevent the myriad of questions that would otherwise result. There may, however, be a few instances when this is not desired. For example, it is not always necessary to provide another company with all of the thoughts of Company A relating to the agreement because some information could be used by Company B with third parties for other agreements or issues that could hurt Company A. A common principle is to provide information in good faith that meets the terms of the agreement, but not to supply more information than necessary.

"What if" exercises can be conducted internally to ensure that most important issues have been considered in the agreement. These exercises are designed to find answers to questions such as (1) who has responsibility for what? (2) who has to approve publications and how will this be handled? and (3) how will changes in the agreement be implemented and problems resolved? Roger Fisher and William Ury stated in *Getting to Yes* (1983) "The basic problem in a negotiation lies not in conflicting positions, but in the conflict between each side's needs, desires, concerns, and fears."

A key person should be identified in each company to act as a single channel to unify most or all of each company's communications with the other. Depending on the nature of the agreement, multiple communication channels may be established (e.g., via board members, project coordinators).

65 / Interactions and Relationships with Trade Associations

Activities of Trade Associations **753**
   Advantages of Trade Associations
      Representing the Pharmaceutical Industry .. 753
   Roles of Pharmaceutical Trade Associations
      and Their Relationships with Companies ... 754
   Criticisms of Trade Associations by Some
      Industry Personnel 754
Major Trade Associations in the United States .. **754**
   Pharmaceutical Manufacturers Association.... 755
   National Pharmaceutical Council 755

Nonprescription Drug Manufacturers
   Association 755
Drug, Chemical, and Allied Trades Association 755
Generic Pharmaceutical Industry Association 755
Major International Trade Associations **755**
   International Federation of Pharmaceutical
      Manufacturers Associations 755
   European Federation of Pharmaceutical
      Industries' Associations.................... 755

It is interesting to reflect on the defecatory habits of the hippopotamus. The male indicates to other hippopotami the extent of his own territory by defecating all around its perimeter. Outside that ring they can go where they please, but if they come inside it he will fight them to the death. So, too, nations make a ring around their territory: To Elizabeth I, the wars in Holland were beyond the ring but the Armada came inside it. No doubt the United States government wishes it had left Vietnam on the outside of its defecatory ring. And so, too, industrial corporations, consciously or unwittingly, make the same sort of ring around products and sales territories and sections of the market. Antony Jay. From *Management and Machiavelli.*

ACTIVITIES OF TRADE ASSOCIATIONS

Trade associations discussed in this chapter are industry-wide associations. There are approximately six to ten major groups in the United States and many others internationally. An extremely large number of other trade associations represent a specific segment of the industry. Industry-wide associations have companies and not individuals as members. Specific associations and their primary objectives are briefly described at the end of this chapter.

Advantages of Trade Associations Representing the Pharmaceutical Industry

Trade associations are involved in many types of activities, including those listed in Table 65.1. Companies are often not in a position to conduct or act on issues that an association is able to act on. This is sometimes a result of the size of the effort required, and in other situations it is the lack of credibility that might be associated with having specific companies sponsor reports or events.

A major trade association activity involves lobbying. It often makes more sense for companies to unite and lobby via their associations than to lobby as independent companies. Many issues that companies want to lobby for (or against) are not medicine specific, but are germane to the entire industry. For example, at the federal legislative level, medicine issues are usually industry specific (e.g., patent issues, product tampering, medicine sampling, animal rights) and not company specific. At the state level, the same principle generally holds, although company specific issues are more likely to emerge.

Another major function of most industry-wide trade associations relates to education. As with lobbying, many education issues relate to the entire industry. Some of the specific activities on both lobbying and education are discussed in this chapter. Other aspects of lobbying are discussed in Chapter 63, Interactions and Relationships with Government Agencies.

TABLE 65.1. *Selected activities conducted by trade associations*

1. Conduct and assist in lobbying efforts
2. Discuss legal issues
3. Conduct educational courses, seminars, and meetings for health professionals, member companies, and the general public
4. Hold discussion forums on a wide range of pertinent topics of interest to the industry
5. Convene problem-solving groups on a wide range of issues
6. Convene advisory groups to assist companies, association committees, and outside groups
7. Provide scholarships, grants, and awards
8. Maintain data bases on relevant information
9. Disseminate information and provide technical assistance
10. Maintain a speakers' program
11. Publish journals, special documents, and/or other periodicals; prepare position papers
12. Establish ongoing relationships with government bodies, health associations, other trade associations, organizations representing health-related groups, academic community, scientific community, consumer groups, news media, trade media, and numerous other groups

Roles of Pharmaceutical Trade Associations and Their Relationships with Companies

1. Important trade associations of the pharmaceutical industry should be able to collect and present information to politicians that will help them in deliberations on current issues. This information may be in the form of background data, white papers on positions of the industry, or ad hoc information assembled at a politician's request.

2. Associations should endeavor to preempt issues that are developing, but have not yet reached a crisis state. Numerous issues such as the use of animals in pharmaceutical research are in this category. This information should be collected and presented to politicians as a preventive measure to help ward off future problems.

3. There are many industry-wide questions that trade associations can address through collecting and statistically evaluating data. The associations are in a good position to do this because they can gather data from multiple companies in the same format. Data of individual companies are kept private and only averaged or merged data is published or made available to members for their use. These data provide industry trends and a benchmark against which (with appropriate caveats) a company may compare its own data. The *PMA* (Pharmaceutical Manufacturers Association) *Statistical Fact Book* is an example of this type of data.

4. Scientific and nonscientific (e.g., marketing, pro-

duction, public affairs) activities of trade associations are highly variable in nature and value. Associations hold many meetings of various types for their members. These are important because they provide a forum for discussing issues of mutual interest. These meetings also help to educate many people. Associations also play an important role in disseminating information on relevant issues to their members.

5. Educational activities include seminars, courses (e.g., for managers and for clinical monitors) and special meetings, in addition to publications and regularly scheduled meetings.

6. Associations have numerous committees to conduct their business and some are composed of professionals who work for their member companies. Some associations request more assistance than others in this regard.

Insofar as lobbying is concerned, associations have a generally successful record of obtaining the type of regulations they support. This is especially true when the association is able to determine and then present a common front of their members who are concerned about a specific issue. There are some occasions when individual companies have widely divergent views. Associations are then unable to present a unified industry view or to lobby effectively.

Criticisms of Trade Associations by Some Industry Personnel

Trade associations are often held accountable for problems they have no control over. An important issue relates to the difficulty of finding a common denominator between their members on many important issues. Because of this restraint, the actions they are able to take become "watered down." In addition, companies are only willing to share information that will not provide any advantage to their competitors, and sometimes an issue is discussed without all of the necessary (and available) information being presented. Discussions may be lacking in substance. All of these limitations relegate many meetings and activities to those of a debating society and may compromise the effectiveness of the association.

MAJOR TRADE ASSOCIATIONS IN THE UNITED STATES

Five major trade associations in the United States are mentioned below. Many other trade associations deal with specific issues of significant importance to the pharmaceutical industry (e.g., marketing, chemistry). They are not discussed because they do not deal with all or most aspects of the industry.

Pharmaceutical Manufacturers Association

The Pharmaceutical Manufacturers Association (PMA) has 85 member companies, 87 associate member companies, and a staff of 95 (as of 1992). Its headquarters are at 1100 15th Street, NW, Washington, DC 20005. They have their own lobbyists at the national level and help to coordinate activities of individual companies. At the state level, company representatives work under the coordination of PMA staff to pursue industry objectives. This includes monitoring activities at the state level.

National Pharmaceutical Council

The National Pharmaceutical Council (NPC) has 28 member companies and a staff of 14 (as of 1992). Its headquarters are at 1894 Preston White Drive, Reston, VA 22091. It is primarily an information source that does not conduct lobbying activities. Their educational activities are often directed to public awareness and keeping their members informed about various issues.

Nonprescription Drug Manufacturers Association

The Nonprescription Drug Manufacturers Association (NDMA), formerly known as the Proprietary Association (PA) has 75 active member companies, 150 associate member companies, and a staff of 38 (as of 1992). Its headquarters are at 1700 Pennsylvania Avenue, Washington, DC 20006. The NDMA focuses on over-the-counter medicine (OTC) issues. They are active in lobbying at the federal level and also try to coordinate lobbying activities at the state level. They do not have their own lobbyists at the state level but look for allies (as do all associations) to help with lobbying activities. These allies would include consumer groups, other trade associations, professional organizations, representatives of member companies, and various societies and groups.

Drug, Chemical, and Allied Trades Association

The Drug, Chemical, and Allied Trades Association (DCAT) has 473 member companies and a staff of three (as of 1992). Its headquarters are at 42-40 Bell Boulevard, Bayside, NY 11361. It provides several types of forums for members of the various companies and industries to meet and discuss issues of mutual interest. They have a broader base than does the PMA because they include the chemical industry and allied industries (e.g., fragrances, packaging). DCAT also provides college scholarships and publishes a digest and newsletter. DCAT does not get involved in lobbying activities.

Generic Pharmaceutical Industry Association

The Generic Pharmaceutical Industry Association (GPIA) has 25 member companies and a staff of six (as of 1992). Its headquarters are at 200 Madison Avenue, New York, NY 10016. The group represents the interests of companies that make generic pharmaceuticals.

MAJOR INTERNATIONAL TRADE ASSOCIATIONS

International Federation of Pharmaceutical Manufacturers Associations

The International Federation of Pharmaceutical Manufacturers Associations (IFPMA) has 51 member associations and a staff of seven (as of 1992). Its headquarters are at 67 Rue St. Jean, CH-1201 Geneva, Switzerland. Its official languages are English, French, and Spanish. In addition to facilitating communication among the national pharmaceutical trade associations that are its members, the IFPMA has many other functions. For example, it operates the IFPMA Code of Marketing and also works with the World Health Organization to train certain government laboratory personnel in developing countries.

European Federation of Pharmaceutical Industries' Associations

The European Federation of Pharmaceutical Industries' Associations (EFPIA) has 16 members and a staff of 15 (as of 1992). Its headquarters are at 250 Avenue Louise, boite 91, B-1050 Brussels, Belgium. It monitors the development of the pharmaceutical industry in Europe regarding public health issues.

66 / Interactions and Relationships with Health Professionals

Identifying Health Professionals 757
  Groups of Health Professionals 757
Types of Relationships......................... 757
  Relationships with Physicians................ 757
  Relationships with Pharmacists 758
  Types of Correspondence Received from
    Health Professionals...................... 758
  Problems Reported by Health Professionals ... 758
Selected Issues 758

Problems Created for Marketed Medicines by
  Health Professionals....................... 758
Problems Created for Investigational
  Medicines by Health Professionals.......... 758
Improving Relationships Between Health
  Professionals and Pharmaceutical
  Companies 759
  Approaching Health Professionals............ 759

A bad doctor treats symptoms. A good doctor treats ailments. A rare doctor treats patients. Sidney Harris.

But nothing is more estimable than a physician, who having studied nature from his end, knows the properties of the human body, the diseases which assail it, the remedies which will benefit it, exercises his art with caution, and pays equal attention to the rich and the poor. Voltaire. From *A Philosophical Dictionary.*

IDENTIFYING HEALTH PROFESSIONALS

Groups of Health Professionals

There is little doubt that relationships between health professionals and companies represent the lifeblood of the ethical pharmaceutical industry. These professionals are the people who cause the company's medicines to be used. Health professionals are described in a broad context and include the following groups.

Practicing (i.e., patient-treating) health professionals

1. Physicians in an outpatient-based practice
2. Physicians in an inpatient-based practice
3. Practicing pharmacists in a hospital environment
4. Nurses in various settings
5. Specialized groups (e.g., podiatrists, optometrists, osteopaths)

Non-patient-treating health professionals

1. Dispensing pharmacists in retail establishments, hospitals, clinics, or other locations (many of these pharmacists provide medicine and other medical information to patients)

2. Health maintenance organization (HMO), preferred provider organization (PPO), or other health organization formulary committees
3. Medicine information specialists

TYPES OF RELATIONSHIPS

Relationships with Physicians

The most well-known relationship involves the sales representative. Physicians usually judge companies by their sales representatives and advertisements, the two most visible parts of a company to practicing physicians. Other less frequent interactions include contacts at professional meetings, symposia, educational courses, and exhibits. Companies attempt to educate physicians about their medicines, and physicians often seek information about medicines from their manufacturers.

Other relationships include those of sponsor (company) and investigator (physician). This relationship is exceedingly complex with numerous responsibilities on both parts and is briefly described in Chapter 45, Clinical Trials.

757

Relationships with Pharmacists

Pharmacists have a large variety of roles in health care delivery (Table 66.1). As a result a large number of relationships exist, and it is impossible to generalize about them as a homogeneous group. Marketers interact with a different group (in general) of pharmacists than do clinical scientists and physicians within a company.

Types of Correspondence Received from Health Professionals

Companies receive various types of correspondence from physicians and other health professionals. Most fit one of the following four types:

1. adverse reaction report,
2. product complaint,
3. professional inquiry for information, or
4. lack of efficacy report.

Many companies currently are dealing with this correspondence more systematically than they have in the past. A great deal of the communications is assisted by computers. For example, responses to many frequently requested inquiries may be filed in computers. Also, each complaint may be given a number and the type of complaint noted. Details are obtained for medicine name, lot number, reporter's name, clinician's name, hospital's name, and National Drug Code (NDC) number. Trends may be analyzed in terms of the frequency of complaints, types of complaints, and products involved (see Chapter 42, Providing Product Information).

Problems Reported by Health Professionals

Most problems reported to pharmaceutical companies by health professionals fall into one of two catego-

TABLE 66.1. *Selected roles of pharmacists who are external to a pharmaceutical company*

---

1. Retail dispensing for an independent or chain pharmacy
2. Hospital or clinic dispensing
3. Information services
4. Poison control services
5. Patient counseling
6. Total parenteral nutrition services
7. Pharmaceutics
8. Market research
9. Promotions and advertising
10. Hospital consultation services (e.g., product selection)
11. Laboratory services (e.g., therapeutic blood level measures)
12. Teaching
13. Pharmacokinetic trials as principal, co-, or assistant investigator
14. Intensive care unit services
15. Synthesis of novel chemicals

---

ries: patients or medicines. In some cases the problems reported relate to both. Examples of medicine-related problems include reports of discolored or crushed tablets. Once the medicine has been ingested by a patient the problem is usually considered patient-related. The distinction between patient- and medicine-related reports is important because many companies have two separate groups that interact with health professionals on this basis.

Serious adverse reactions reported to a company are investigated when deemed appropriate. This is usually done by telephone unless the importance is so great that on-site evaluation is necessary. Many physician reports directed to a company are not statements that a medicine caused a specific adverse reaction, but are specific questions or inquiries. For example, physicians often seek the company's help to rule in or rule out (1) a diagnosis, or (2) a cause of an adverse reaction. Numerous services are often provided by pharmaceutical companies to physicians and other health professionals to help understand a medicine's effect or lack of effect. For example, blood level determinations of an active medicine and/or its metabolites are measured when relevant. Tissue levels or direct analysis of the medicine itself may be conducted by the company.

SELECTED ISSUES

Problems Created for Marketed Medicines by Health Professionals

The major problem for pharmaceutical companies that is created by health professionals usually relates to improper prescribing or use of a company's products. It is generally irrelevant to a regulatory agency and the public reading a news story about an adverse event whether a medicine was improperly used. The important point to them is the problem for the patient(s) who was affected and the issue it raises for the company.

Problems Created for Investigational Medicines by Health Professionals

Many problems occur for a company in terms of broken promises made by physicians in regard to investigational medicines. These broken promises may relate to any part of initiating or conducting a clinical trial. Many of these issues are described in Table 62.16 of *Guide to Clinical Trials* (Spilker, 1991) under the heading "Games Investigators Play."

Other investigator-related problems include publishing data on the same patient(s) in multiple journals. This may be done to assist their career or for other reasons. It is often extremely difficult to determine whether several articles by one author or one group of authors refer to the same or different patients, unless a formal audit of the data is undertaken. The ability to request an audit is in the province of a limited number of groups (e.g., regulatory authorities, Investigational Review Board), which rarely includes a pharmaceutical company, unless it has sponsored all of the research. Even if multiple publications of the same patients is proven to have occurred, it is not illegal. If the publications point out multiple adverse reactions that overestimate the true incidence, it may cause serious repercussions for the company. This may be in terms of having the Food and Drug Administration (FDA) suspend clinical trials or take other actions (e.g., request trials to investigate the high incidence of the problem). There are few alternatives for a company except to investigate the situation as thoroughly as possible and to discuss the problem with the appropriate regulatory authority. Damage to a medicine's reputation by multiple reports on the same patient(s) may be severe and a reputation can be extremely difficult to rebuild.

IMPROVING RELATIONSHIPS BETWEEN HEALTH PROFESSIONALS AND PHARMACEUTICAL COMPANIES

The establishment and maintenance of high standards is the key for research-based pharmaceutical companies to develop successful relationships with health professionals. These standards are of ethical behavior and professional behavior. Respect for a company and its products is important because in many situations a professional must choose one medicine from many similar ones to use or prescribe.

A company chooses health professionals to act as consultants, to conduct clinical trials, to conduct scientific studies, or to perform other services. It is important for the company to choose individuals who will provide the best overall service to the company. Conflicts of interest may arise when people are evaluated who are personal friends or relatives of those in important positions at the company.

Pharmaceutical companies often have professional groups that give presentations on their own medicines or on medicine development in general. These presentations may be given to local or state medical organizations, community groups that are health oriented, or to students in health-related fields.

Approaching Health Professionals

It is beneficial to understand why physicians prescribe specific medicines when they have numerous options. This knowledge can help a company target its message to the various groups who are and will prescribe and use its medicines. Some of the more common reasons as to why a specific medicine is prescribed are as follows:

1. This is the way I was trained.
2. I am most familiar with this medicine.
3. This is the medicine that the pharmacy stocks.
4. This is the medicine that is best for the patient in my experience.
5. This is the medicine that is cheapest for the patient.
6. This is what my friends and colleagues are recommending.
7. This is what the specialists use to whom I usually refer patients.
8. This is the medicine that a sales representative left, and I thought I would try it.

Marketing research groups spend a great deal of time and money attempting to better understand these reasons and to develop ways in which medicine promotion may be most effective in presenting a medicine to physicians. Studies on how physicians acquire information on prescription medicines and how they view the accuracy of different sources were performed by McCue et al. (1986) and Evans and Beltramini (1986).

67 / Interactions and Relationships with Patients and the Public

Describing the Public **761**
  What Is the Public? 761
Industry's Relationship with Its Publics **761**
  Types of Relationships 761
  Publics at the Local Community Level 762
  Publics at the State Level 762
  Publics at the National Level 763
  Philanthropic Groups Sponsored by
     Pharmaceutical Companies 763
  Company Interactions with the Public:
     Product-Related Services and Information .. 763
  Establishing a Group to Focus on Public Policy 764
  Supporting Outside Activities of Employees ... 764

Public Opinion 764
Why Should the Pharmaceutical Industry
    Present Its Story More Clearly to the Public? 765
Reactions and Responses of Pharmaceutical
    Companies to Consumer Groups 766
Public Interest Groups and Conflicts of
    Interest 766
The Public's Relationship with Industry **766**
  Patient Participation in Medical Treatment ... 766
  Groups of Patients Versus Groups of
    Consumers 767
  Problems or Issues Created by Patients 767

The proverbial wisdom of the populace in the streets, on the roads, and in the markets, instructs the ear of him who studies man more fully than a thousand rules ostentatiously arranged. From *Proverbs, or the Manual of Wisdom,* London 1804.

The public is a bad guesser. De Quincey. From *Essays-Protestantism.*

The views of the multitude are neither bad nor good. Tacitus. From *Annales* (Book VII).

DESCRIBING THE PUBLIC

As the quotes above illustrate, there are many different views about the quality of public opinion. One of the reasons for this is that the public is not a simple, straightforward concept.

What Is the Public?

There are many "publics" from a pharmaceutical company's perspective, and each has its own specific needs and orientations. Each public also has its own perspective and viewpoint about the pharmaceutical industry. Publics include all lay people, all patients who use the company's products, the local community, lay organizations related to medicine or health, and consumer pressure groups. Various other publics could also

be described (e.g., company employees, company retirees). Pharmaceutical companies deal with publics on local, state, and national levels.

INDUSTRY'S RELATIONSHIP WITH ITS PUBLICS

Types of Relationships

There are four major types of relationships of a company with its publics: (1) philanthropic, (2) product-related, (3) symbiotic, and (4) employer. The last category is not discussed in detail in this chapter. Philanthropic activities tend to be strongest at the local level and product-related activities strongest at the national level. Symbiotic or *quid pro quo* types of activities may be strong or weak at any level.

Publics at the Local Community Level

Pharmaceutical companies hire people who live in the local communities. The company pays taxes and interacts in many ways on a daily basis with the community. It is therefore in a company's interests to do whatever is reasonable to maintain good relationships with their community. One aspect of company involvement encompasses philanthropic gifts of money or personal services.

Financial Support for Local Groups

Contributions from the company are most effective when they fit into a well-conceived pattern or plan. Pharmaceutical companies receive many more requests for funds than they are able to honor. Their choices are much easier to make and are more consistent when decisions are made in the context of an overall plan.

The plan may be to divide their contributions according to a formula, allocating a certain percentage of the total to local, state, and federal activities. It could also be based on allocating a certain percentage of the total to specific areas (e.g., medicine related, nonmedicine health related, nonmedicine and nonhealth related). A third means of allocation could be according to various topics of special interest to the company. Other methods or combinations of these are possible. Cutbacks in federal support for various health-related or non-health-related activities sometimes place additional pressures on a company to increase its contributions.

Pharmaceutical companies are often asked to donate money to local organizations, institutions, schools, and other groups. These groups often have nothing to do with health care or health issues but appeal to the company on the basis of being located in the same neighborhood. Companies often feel quite strongly about being a good community citizen and supporting local charities, numerous nonprofit organizations, and many other types of local groups.

Nonfinancial Support for Local Groups

In addition to outright financial contributions, companies may

1. loan their facilities so that other groups can have a meeting or party;
2. print brochures at cost or underwrite the cost of printing materials;
3. allow company staff with expertise to assist organizations that desire advice and consultation;
4. make video programs, which may be unrelated to medicines;
5. allow or even encourage employees to serve on local boards;
6. donate used equipment that ranges from typewriters to scientific equipment to schools or offices;
7. provide speakers to local organizations; or
8. provide various services requested.

In providing these or other nonfinancial gifts, the company may not desire recognition or it may restrict its identity to use of its logo or name. This may be at the end of a presentation or on the back of printed material. Services are often provided because they help to promote the company's name.

Support for Employees and Their Families

Another public that the company interacts with at the community level is the company's own employees. Many companies provide matching grants for employees' contributions to help support schools, hospitals, foundations, public television and radio stations, plus other organizations that meet defined criteria. Scholarships for children of employees are another area of activity.

Other Activities at a Local Level

Product-related activities involve providing information about a company's products to the public and also promoting products. This occurs to a limited degree at the local level.

Publics at the State Level

The state level often overlaps with both the local and national levels in terms of how it is perceived by pharmaceutical companies. One reason is that many local organizations are also active at the state level, and many state organizations are also active at the national level.

Companies generally have both philanthropic activities and company interests that are pursued at the state level. Philanthropic activities include support to many cultural, educational, and other organizations located in different parts of the state, as well as some organizations that are statewide. Company interests are also served by providing product-related information to the public.

Symbiotic relationships include providing assistance to legislators and other groups of people (e.g., businessmen). Assistance for legislators could range from support through a company-sponsored political action committee (PAC) to help in drafting new legislation.

Legislative activities at the state level are described in Chapter 63, Interactions and Relationships with Government Agencies. Companies strongly support establishing personal contacts with legislators and building positive relationships, even without having any specific lobbying purpose. Therefore, company executives other than just lobbyists often develop professional relationships with legislators. One type of such contact is for the company to host groups of legislators at a reception with company managers on a periodic basis. Contacts are usually also pursued with individual legislators.

Publics at the National Level

At the national level, pharmaceutical companies usually provide much less money to humanitarian or philanthropic organizations than they do at local and state levels. Companies tend to tie their contributions more directly to their products at the national level. This is primarily because individual pharmaceutical companies are not large enough financially to reach effectively the general public at the national level. A significant amount of company contributions is made to support scientific and medical societies, businesses, and meetings or symposia.

Companies donate more than just money. For example, most companies donate medicines to charitable agencies that send them to lesser developed countries, with the assurance that these medicines will not be recycled illegally into normal trade routes.

When proposed activities are associated with a company's products, it is more likely that the company will become involved as a sponsor. For example, a company may pay for having a brochure printed on a disease that one of its medicines treats. These brochures would then be distributed in various ways (e.g., public health agencies). A company may help underwrite the cost of a television show dealing with a disease the company's products treat, even though none of the company's products are mentioned by name. Various types of educational materials are produced or purchased that are targeted to professional groups. A few companies produce popular-style publications that they send out to physicians or lay people (such as videotapes), while others concentrate on "throw-away" medical journals. One of the best known (and least often thrown away) of this type is *Ciba Symposia*.

Philanthropic Groups Sponsored by Pharmaceutical Companies

In some situations corporate philanthropy is made via the company and in others via a separate independent foundation. Many companies have established a philanthropic group, either independent of the company's control or under it. These groups may give money in a highly targeted way that enhances the company's product profile. On the other hand, donations may be made to the most qualified people with few stipulations. Two

of the best-known groups that provide such money are the Wellcome Trust in the United Kingdom and the Burroughs Wellcome Fund in the United States. Other philanthropic programs within the pharmaceutical industry include the Abbott Laboratories Fund, Bristol-Myers Fund, Merck Co. Fund, Schering-Plough Foundation, Hoffmann-La Roche Foundation, Pfizer Foundation, Sandoz Foundation, and Lilly Endowment. Many large pharmaceutical companies have philanthropic programs.

Charitable contributions and business-related donations are overlapping areas that companies support. Charitable contributions are best made by a centralized company committee that has representatives of the various functions. They generally have a budget of funds that may be apportioned and may have a number of primary groups or themes (e.g., science education, childhood diseases, specific therapeutic area) they support. There are so many possible directions that they can take in giving donations that the company should proactively decide which themes and strategies they wish to focus on. This enables priorities to be established and should create a more marked influence for the company in their chosen area(s).

Another approach to use in making charitable donations is to identify the major groups to which money is given (e.g., education, civic and community groups, health, the arts) and to agree on what percentage of the budgeted money will be allocated to each category. Based on the allocation, the multiyear commitments are first considered to determine the amount remaining. All outstanding requests for funds may then compete for funds in that area. It would be preferable to do this two to six times each year and to limit funds so that all money is not given out the first month that projects compete. A sense of fairness and reasonableness must be used in establishing policies and conducting this exercise.

Business-related donations are made both by the company and by the individual functions. If the request for money is product related then it would generally be defined as a business donation. Professional societies and health issues are usually considered as business related, unless they meet other specified criteria (e.g., employee volunteering time for a local group).

Company Interactions with the Public: Product-Related Services and Information

Companies generally attempt to avoid providing information about prescription medicines directly to the public. Companies refer patients to their physicians for advice and information when patients call or write letters to the company. A company may, however, provide patients with a general pamphlet about a specific disease. Companies do not usually send a photocopy of a medicine's labeling to consumers. Instead the company may refer patients to the *Physicians' Desk Reference,* which is in local libraries and contains the medicine's labeling. This is the most checked-out book at the New York Public Library, which attests to its popularity as a source of medicine information. McMahon et al. (1987) describes the type and source of information actually presented to patients by health professionals.

Companies have an entirely different attitude about sending information about over-the-counter medicines to patients. Many companies provide information on request, relating both to the disease and to the medicine.

Information on risks associated with taking medicines is presented to the public by government, academic, and pharmaceutical industry groups. The government and pharmaceutical industry usually evaluate a medicine's risk in terms of society or on a broad macro level of how all patients with a disease, or those of a particular population, are affected. The public usually desires the opposite information (i.e., how are they, their families, and friends as individuals affected). Their interest and reaction is usually on this micro-level. This type of information is usually more difficult to determine because it concerns a specific patient who may react in many ways. On the other hand, population data refer to averages of many people and can provide overall probability estimates of various types of outcomes.

Establishing a Group to Focus on Public Policy

Public policy within a pharmaceutical company is directed toward obtaining government regulations and public attitudes and behaviors that are consonant with the industry's goals. When government policies, institutional policies, or public attitudes support (1) therapeutic substitution, (2) restrictive formularies, (3) price controls in areas where they do not exist, (4) controls on profits, or many other policies, the companies must act to counter the pressures to implement such policies. Companies must act collectively through trade associations as well as individually and as groups of companies independent of any trade association.

To achieve the companies' goals they must tell their story to relevant groups. To do this effectively requires that it be done proactively and not reactively. This topic is described in more detail in Chapter 58, Interaction with Legislators and the Public.

Public policy differs from government relations in that it encompasses issues that do not necessarily involve government interactions. Thus, one can think of three separate areas.

1. Pure government activities. These are discussed in Chapter 63, Interactions and Relationships with Government Agencies.
2. Overlapping government and public policy issues. Many public policy issues (e.g., government reim-

bursement of medicines, health insurance, access to care) require involvement of both private and government groups.
3. Pure public policy issues.

Organizing a Public Policy Group

For companies with multiple staff in public policy, it is reasonable to have them organized around key issues for the company. These issues are generally grouped into the following three categories, although various other groupings exist: (1) science and technology; (2) health care delivery; and (3) business and trade policy.

A group establishing policies for a company could consider the following approach (i.e., steps to follow).

1. Identify the overall company objectives and goals.
2. Scan the various environments and identify all issues.
3. Choose those issues to address that are of major interest.
4. Determine how to address each issue (e.g., studies, surveys).
5. Decide whether to contract some of the work to external groups.
6. Start to design protocols and collect data.

Supporting Outside Activities of Employees

Many companies support activities in which their employees volunteer or participate. This may take the form of matching the employee's financial contributions to selected types of charities and institutions, or giving money to help organizations with activities that need support. In this latter case, the company usually establishes specific criteria for the organization (e.g., nonprofit), the purpose of the request (e.g., for a specific activity as opposed to general operation expenses) and for the employee's participation (e.g., the employee must be involved and not one of their family members solely). Many criteria are usually established to help the group who decide how to apportion money (e.g., requests over a certain level must be approved by the chief executive officer). It may be desirable for the company to distinguish between volunteering by employees that primarily benefits others (e.g., tutoring others, serving on a board of directors of a civic group), or that primarily benefits their family (e.g., boy and girl scouts activities, trips for a school band, soccer club). Some companies even provide a limited number of hours for employees to conduct certain types of volunteer work (e.g., giving talks in schools).

Public Opinion

Public opinion must be recognized and respected by the pharmaceutical industry as an important force. This statement is based on the influence the public has on (1) shaping new regulations, (2) affecting medicine-pricing policies, (3) influencing their physician, who is thinking about giving them a prescription medicine, and (4) deciding whether to fill the prescription at the pharmacy and to take the medicine as directed. Companies want the public to view the pharmaceutical industry in a highly positive way. The public held a generally positive view of the industry during the 1950s, when miraculous new medicines seemed to appear with great regularity, almost like magic.

Companies also desire to have the public understand something about the complexities, high risks, and high costs of medicine research and development. This understanding would better enable the public to appreciate the efforts that go into discovering and developing a new medicine and the reasons why its price may appear to be expensive. Another concept that is important to communicate to the public is the risk associated with medicines. All medicines involve some degree of risk to the patient, and potential benefits must be compared with potential risks whenever a medicine is to be taken.

Pharmaceutical companies educate the public via several mechanisms. The major means are to work through their trade associations (e.g., public service announcements, symposia), physicians who treat patients (e.g., brochures and other educational materials, symposia), and directly to patients themselves (e.g., magazine and other advertisements, brochures, patient package inserts). The method of working via their trade associations is discussed in Chapter 65, Interactions and Relationships with Trade Associations. Companies may encourage physicians to inform patients about the medicines that they are prescribing. This includes information on potential risks as well as benefits from taking the medicine. The patient's perceived risks are usually more important than the actual risks because the former are usually what motivates people's behavior.

Spokespeople are needed who represent the pharmaceutical industry and can speak to the public about issues in medicine development. These people must use language that the public can understand. Using jargon or technical terms often serves to alienate people and is counterproductive.

Why Should the Pharmaceutical Industry Present Its Story More Clearly to the Public?

A public that is better informed about the complexity and issues of medicine development should be more sympathetic to the pharmaceutical industry. This could have important results, such as those listed below.

1. More patients would be attentive to their physician's instructions and would be more likely to comply with their medicine regimen.
2. The public would exert a more positive influence on political leaders at all levels of government. This would have both direct and indirect effects on legislation.
3. Patients who have deleterious medical outcomes that are possibly (or probably) medicine related would be less likely to sue pharmaceutical companies.
4. Information on positive aspects of industry would help counter the few negative stories that tend to dominate news reports about medicines and the pharmaceutical industry.

The industry has discovered and marketed many medicines that have revolutionized the practice of medicine. Costs of these medicines have markedly fallen relative to the total cost of the nation's health bill over the last 25 years. Profits have also been relatively high for many pharmaceutical companies compared with other industries, but a large percentage of these profits has been reinvested in research and development to discover and market improved medicines for the future. National and state legislatures and regulations have enormous potential to affect both the incentive and the ability of pharmaceutical companies to invest huge sums in research. The ramifications of all government activities that affect pharmaceutical companies should be carefully considered by the public and by the Congress, to prevent a drought of new medicine discoveries in the United States and to avoid killing the goose that lays golden eggs.

Increased public awareness and knowledge of the pharmaceutical industry can help both the public and the industry. The public will be helped by understanding the difficulties involved in discovering, developing, and marketing medicines in a highly uncertain and tightly regulated market. The pressures on companies to discover or develop new medicines is great because without new medicines, companies will fail to thrive and may be forced into a merger or may be taken over. Thus, public pressure to promote positive changes in regulations will help the industry, as well as indirectly helping the public through the development of new medicines. One specific example concerns the "drug lag" and the effect it has had on health.

Drug Lag

When important medicines are available outside a country, but not inside, many patients may be indirectly hurt. The Food and Drug Administration (FDA) claims that the additional time they take to approve medicines and the additional data they require helps to protect the American public from poorly tested medicines. This is certainly true, but the important question is how much delay results from high standards of science and how much delay results from bureaucracy and other nonscientific issues at the FDA that could be reduced.

The increasing "protection" afforded the American public, however, has come at a price. That price is not just the skyrocketing cost of medicine discovery and development, which has reached up to $231 million or more per new medicine, but the decreased freedom of practicing physicians to choose the medicines they wish to use to treat their patients. This primarily occurs because numerous medicines available in other countries are unavailable in the United States and physicians are therefore denied use of these medicines.

It is unclear whether patients have fared better because of the FDA's reluctance and slow rate of approving medicines over the last 20 years. This is an especially important issue because some people believe that individual physicians are in a better position to make medical judgments about their specific patients than is a government regulatory agency, which makes decisions based on usually large groups of patients. The paternalistic perspective within government agencies usually stresses the FDA's role in protecting the American public.

Reactions and Responses of Pharmaceutical Companies to Consumer Groups

The most important principle for companies to adhere to in relations with consumer groups is to follow high ethical and scientific standards in all aspects of research, medicine development, production, and marketing. Although this might appear to put companies and consumer groups on the same side, that is not always true. First, consumer groups sometimes espouse viewpoints that are not scientifically or medically sound. Second, consumer groups have generally identified pharmaceutical companies as villains and have positioned themselves as adversaries. Nonetheless, it is often useful for companies or trade associations to initiate and participate in open and honest discussions with consumer groups. Telling consumer groups that pharmaceutical companies want to cooperate may lead to numerous advantages for the companies. If the consumer group is more interested in a confrontation than in achieving a positive result, this fact will become obvious and may possibly be used by the companies to their advantage.

Consumer groups are often effective lobbyists. In some situations they are on the same side as a particular company, and the consumer group may be directly or indirectly enlisted as an ally. One particular situation when a company may seek out a consumer group is when the company desires assistance with an new medicine near approval that is more effective and/or safer than existing therapy. This relationship will be particularly fruitful if the company's medicine has advantages over a medicine(s) that a consumer group is protesting. The consumer group may create media pressure focused on the FDA and Congress to approve the new medicine or to remove the old medicine from the market.

Public Interest Groups and Conflicts of Interests

Public interest groups have conflicts of interest just as pharmaceutical companies do. Because the public interest groups like to have media attention, because they attract attention by emphasizing perceived problems, and because they are rarely ever sued and taken to court, they rarely have any compunctions about making any statements they wish. These groups sometimes fall in the trap of reverse quackery (at least in the eyes of pharmaceutical companies). This means they say something good (e.g., a new breakthrough medicine) is bad, rather than saying something bad (e.g., certain patent medicines) is good (i.e., quackery).

Although pharmaceutical companies also have conflicts of interest in the information they present, the liability laws place much greater constraints on them to avoid any distortions in claims or warnings about their products.

THE PUBLIC'S RELATIONSHIP WITH INDUSTRY

The public has a general lack of awareness about the pharmaceutical industry. People use the products of the industry and many groups receive philanthropic help from the industry, but the processes of medicine development and the nature of the regulatory environment in which medicines are developed and marketed are almost totally unknown.

Patient Participation in Medical Treatment

For many years little or no interest was paid to patients' views about the medicines they took. With increasing standards of developing medicines, especially after the 1962 Kefauver-Harris Amendments, patients' views have been solicited to a greater degree. Patients' views were originally assessed through the filter of physicians' opinions (i.e., physicians were asked to interpret how patients felt about the medicines they were taking and to describe the beneficial effects of those medicines). During the last decade there has been a gradual change in approach, and now patients are asked directly how they feel about their treatment and how it has affected their disease. Patients are therefore in a better position to have an influence on the type(s) of medical treatment they receive.

One example of patients affecting medical practice concerns the type of surgery used for breast cancer. The views of female patients about their therapy has had a marked influence on the types of surgery performed. The proportion of women who undergo radical mastectomy has fallen and those undergoing simple mastectomy has increased over the last 20 years. This has not occurred because the simpler operation yields better results. It has occurred because the results are not worse for many types of breast cancer and also because more women are now requesting or insisting on the simple mastectomy.

Groups of Patients Versus Groups of Consumers

There is a clear difference between patient associations and consumer groups. Patient associations are usually oriented around a single disease (e.g., cystic fibrosis, muscular dystrophy) or a single therapeutic area (e.g., cardiovascular disease, pulmonary disease). Membership is often composed of patients, family members, friends, and others who are attempting to raise funds that may be used for research, lobbying efforts, education, and sometimes direct help for patients.

Consumer groups tend to be composed of action-oriented individuals who believe that they should improve what they view as a general medical problem. Examples of problems include (1) adverse reactions, (2) medicines that they believe should be removed from the market, or (3) alleged improprieties or ethical misconduct of specific companies. Consumer groups tend to use black-and-white terms in their denunciations of pharmaceutical companies (or the industry) and in their recommendations for corrective action.

Problems or Issues Created by Patients

Companies are often forced to respond to medical pressures brought about by inappropriate uses of their medicines. When medicines are used inappropriately by patients (or by physicians) major problems may be created for the pharmaceutical company. New adverse reactions may be elicited that cause the medicine to be withdrawn from the market, despite the fact that the medicine had been used inappropriately. One classic example of this concerns the use of the analgesic medicine phenacetin. Phenacetin was often combined with aspirin and caffeine in a combination tablet called APC (i.e., the initials of the three medicines, aspirin, phenacetin, and caffeine). This medicine was used to relieve mild pain and only for relatively short periods. Many patients abused this product and took it in larger quantities than recommended by manufacturers or physicians. The medicine was often taken every day, sometimes for many years. This is how the problem of analgesic nephropathy was created. The problem was traced to the presence of phenacetin, often used in combination with aspirin and caffeine. Although cases of analgesic nephropathy were not documented in patients who took the medicine as directed, the medicine was subsequently withdrawn from the market. This was unfortunate for the many patients who used the medicine as directed.

68 / Interactions and Relationships with the Media

Industry's Relationships with the Media......... **769**
Company Policies 769
Interactions Between Pharmaceutical
Companies and the Media................. 770
Reasons for Confrontations Between
Companies and the Media................. 770
Comments on the Validity of Sensational
News on Medicines 771
Public Relations for Medicines.................. **771**
Role of Public Relations in a Pharmaceutical
Company 771
Public Relations of Medicine Products........ 771

Press Releases and Conferences 771
Media Events................................. 772
Special Events and Public Service or Education
Programs 773
Media Tours 773
Media Events Targeted to Health Professionals 773
Public Relations for Over-the-Counter and
Prescription Medicines 774
Public Relations for the Pharmaceutical Industry **774**
Improving the Industry's Image with the
Public..................................... 774

The great advantage of a strong and clear signal from the top is that even quiet junior managers, when they are tuned into it, can make good independent decisions without worrying. They can answer telephone queries, even press queries, sensibly and decisively rather than timidly and evasively, because they know what the business is about. Antony Jay. From *Management and Machiavelli.*

INDUSTRY'S RELATIONSHIPS WITH THE MEDIA

Medical news is one of the fastest growing areas in lay media coverage. The news media are more likely to write about a health or high-tech medical problem than ever before. Reporters often visit government agencies (e.g., Food and Drug Administration [FDA], Public Health Service) and the Congress in search of stories. They also read medical publications, attend medical meetings, monitor activities of local medicine and health care industries, and monitor hospitals and other medically oriented institutions.

Company Policies

Each company has its own policy for dealing with the media. There are, however, a few basic principles to which many adhere.

1. Provide information that is guided by the product's labeling.

2. Restrict comments on other company's medicines.
3. Encourage employee spokespeople not to talk to reporters "off the record" because nothing is really "off the record."
4. Do not comment on questions that are not proper for a company response.
5. Refer detailed medical or marketing questions to the appropriate people.

Although companies do not like to be on the defensive, that is exactly what happens in many cases. Interestingly, the FDA also often finds itself in the same position (as pharmaceutical companies) with the media. For example, if a new medicine is claimed by academic scientists to be great, the media often criticize the FDA and the pharmaceutical company by asking why the medicine is not already on the market. The FDA is often accused of delays and the company of dragging its feet. When a marketed medicine, however, has serious adverse reactions uncovered, the media often asks why the medicine was allowed on the market and states that it should be removed. The FDA is often accused of slackness and the company painted in even a more unfavorable way.

Interactions Between Pharmaceutical Companies and the Media

Types of Media

The approach a pharmaceutical company takes with the media is generally the same for radio, television, and printed forms, although some modifications are usually made for each. Working with television is much more time consuming than working with the other media because of the setup time (in a studio or on-site) and frequent run-throughs that are necessary to get a segment to be correct. Radio interviews can be technically much simpler, especially if they are conducted by telephone. In some situations they are conducted at a studio or at a company. On the other hand, radio tends to be stressful because interviews are often live. In deciding whether or not to accept an invitation to participate in a television or radio interview, a company considers the quality of the show, the likely consequences of participating, and the availability of suitable spokespeople.

Deciding to Interact

A company often asks itself the question—is it worth our time to respond to the media? Who else will be there? How will the company appear if it does or does not participate? The forum must be considered appropriate for the company to be able to present a rational approach, and adequate time must be allotted to the company.

When the Media Contacts a Pharmaceutical Company

When the media calls a company with a reasonable question about one of their medicines, most companies attempt to find and provide an accurate answer that lies within the limits of their proprietary information. Companies may not be willing to talk to the media about issues that lie outside a medicine's labeling. Labeling is considered the Bible from which companies do not stray. Only when a company discusses information presented at a scientific meeting may they be willing to discuss other-than-labeled indications. This is because company scientists are communicating on a scientific level with other scientists and the medical media. Companies often do not even provide reprints of published articles if they relate to indications that are outside a medicine's labeling.

The amount and nature of information presented by company representatives often depends on the question posed by the reporter. If reporters ask, "What is your company doing in the field of biotechnology?" (or Disease X), they will usually get an equally general reply. This type of question usually represents a fishing expedition by a reporter who has not done much homework. A better question is for a reporter to ask, "What is the status of your compound number AB3456?" But even more specific questions are better for reporters to pose, such as "We understand that your compound Number AB3456 is causing the following side effect. Can you comment?"

Reasons for Confrontations Between Companies and the Media

Many news services, newspapers, and reporters read the medical literature on a continual basis and attend scientific conferences. They are quick to pick up stories that they consider newsworthy. Not only do reporters scan well-known periodicals the moment they are available, but they often proactively seek news stories of potential interest. These activities are neither good nor bad per se for pharmaceutical companies because a story may be positive, negative, or neutral. Most stories are rarely neutral, even when they are straight news. Therein lies the issue. Even though the media are charged with the devil's advocate role, many reporters prematurely glorify or condemn a new medicine or an old one. This is often a result of two reasons. First, they are in a rush to print the latest medical news about medicines and, second, they do not adequately understand the processes of medicine development or medicine approval. Companies often respond with a more balanced perspective, but their response is often viewed by the public as a defensive gesture, promulgated solely to protect their product. As a result, many people give the company's side little credibility.

The media often react with skepticism about many verbal reports or press releases from pharmaceutical companies. Many media people do not call companies because they do not expect to be told the truth. Judging from newspaper and magazine articles, the industry's credibility is often low. This usually occurs because the company is expected to present only its perspective, which is assumed to be unbalanced. The media's perception is strongly reinforced if different company people tell reporters different stories.

Some stories about medicines seem to acquire a life of their own, and, no matter how many denials and evidence to the contrary, if the story has public appeal—it lives on and on. One minor example concerns the chemical source of thymidine, which is used to make zidovudine (Retrovir). Herring sperm are a natural source of thymidine and were originally used for making Retrovir. But Burroughs Wellcome Co. began using synthetic thymidine almost from the start of the Retrovir project and not thymidine derived from herring sperm. Even after the company informed the media that herring sperm were no longer the source used for thymidine, the number of articles describing herring sperm as the starting material for Retrovir have been numerous.

Comments on the Validity of Sensational News on Medicines

It almost always seems that the more sensational a news story, the more likely it is that the story is wrong. Reemtsma and Maloney (1974) developed a theory that "the unreliability of instant medical news is so reliable that large profits may be made by betting against the value of medical breakthroughs reported in the lay press." They applied this principle to short sales on the major stock exchanges, advocating Poor's Law (as in Standard and Poor): "Buy on bad news and sell on good." The reasoning behind this is that the insiders have already bought the stock on the good news and forced the price up. As other investors begin to buy stock it will start to fall because the insiders will be selling their stock. These authors present numerous examples of how their principle has worked, plus one occasion when it did not. To prevent mistakes, they recommend attending the press conferences given in association with major announcements so that the value of the breakthrough may be assessed. Most news stories about medicines, however, do not influence the company's stock prices. Moreover, numerous pharmaceutical companies are not publicly owned (i.e., do not have publicly owned stock).

PUBLIC RELATIONS FOR MEDICINES

Public relations to support the marketing of specific medicine products is designed to educate and help the audience think about a product or an issue that may have received little prior thought. Public relations is service oriented, and it is successful because it serves the interests of the listener, reader, or viewer. The information is generally useful because it affects the health of the audience.

Role of Public Relations in a Pharmaceutical Company

The greatest advantage of public relations is the educational orientation. Pharmaceutical companies may work entirely through outside public relations agencies and not have anyone in a company doing this type of work. This approach is rapidly disappearing, at least among medium and large companies, although each company still maintains contacts with some outside firms.

Many companies have their own public relations group or department that works with marketing departments to structure public relations' programs and activities to ensure product awareness. Marketing groups are a major customer of public relations groups and usually work closely with them. Public relations provides an important avenue in the marketing communications effort.

When an important new medicine undergoing investigation is of interest to the public and the media, public relations may work closely with medical and research departments to help manage the flow of information reaching the press.

Public Relations of Medicine Products

This relatively new field has grown rapidly in recent years and has become widely used in the pharmaceutical industry. Public relations techniques are communication tools that complement or supplement traditional methods of marketing communications to physicians for educating an audience about prescription medicines.

Public relations is not advertising per se. It involves providing information to reporters and others in the hope and expectation that it will help shape media coverage. A company decides on the advertisements, detailing plan, and educational tools that make up its marketing plan. Marketing managers must then determine what role public relations can play to better reach the public, physicians, nurses, and other health professionals.

Traditional methods of marketing communications to physicians are primarily (1) detailing to physicians by sales representatives, (2) placing advertisements in medical journals, and (3) developing educational tools through meetings, lectures, and exhibits.

The marketing group in a pharmaceutical company must identify (1) the audience targeted for public relations, (2) the message that they wish to deliver to this audience, (3) alternative means of delivering the message, and (4) the problems with currently used methods. Techniques used in a medicine's public relations effort might include

1. press releases and press conferences,
2. media events targeted to the public,
3. special events and public service or education programs,
4. media tours, and
5. media events targeted to health professionals.

Each of these topics is discussed below.

Press Releases and Conferences

Companies often elect to hold press conferences at the time of a medicine's launch, particularly when the medicine represents a major medical advance. The press conference helps simplify the information and enables the news to be efficiently disseminated. Some companies also react to important news stories about their medicines with a press release. Press releases are also used on a routine basis to provide news angles for ongoing coverage of a company's products.

Press Conferences

A press conference is in essence a mechanism that permits the company to hold many interviews simultaneously. Most press conferences held by the pharmaceutical companies in the United States are held either in New York or Washington, DC, because the major networks and media are based there. A smaller number are held in Washington. These cities are chosen because smaller media sources are not always able to attend a press conference held in other cities or a relatively out-of-the-way place. Pharmaceutical companies not located near New York or Washington often send their representatives there for the conference. Press conferences must have effective speakers who are able to communicate technical information clearly and in language that is understandable. They must also be able to field questions effectively.

Press Materials

In preparing for a press conference a company prepares press materials. These materials usually include some or all of the following types of information in a packet that is handed out to reporters. The objective of the packet of information is to provide complete and balanced information on a given topic to assist reporters in preparing their articles or reports. This material is not intended to be promotional. In addition, advertisements are not usually included.

1. *Basic news release*—This may contain (1) the name of the medicine, (2) how it is to be taken, (3) when it is to be marketed, (4) its common side effects, and (5) a summary of the clinical data.

2. *Background on the disease that the medicine treats*—This material may be prepared by a company, government, academic, or other group.

3. *Fact sheet*—This is a list of questions and answers that relate to the major items in the news release and about the medicine.

4. *Glossary*—Key terms, phrases, and words are defined simply.

5. *Product photograph*—A black-and-white glossy photograph of the medicine or bottle and other photographs of interest are provided.

6. *Chemical structure*—A diagram of the medicine's chemical structure may be enclosed.

7. *Package insert*—This is usually enclosed.

8. *Important reprints*—Published information about the medicine that is covered by the approved labeling is usually included.

9. *Synopses of the reprints*—This might be helpful, especially if the reprints are difficult for the lay reader to understand.

10. *Information about the company*—This would provide an appropriate means to identify the company's approach, mission, tradition, values, or other factors.

11. *Unique aspects about the product*—Many new medicines have unique characteristics that could be featured. Examples would include a large postmarketing surveillance program or an elaborate medicine distribution system.

12. *Information about experts*—Noncompany speakers at a press conference are identified as to their name, affiliation, training, field of specialty, and any other useful information.

Other Uses of a Press Kit and Its Materials

Sometimes one or more pieces of this packet are used for other purposes. For example, the fact sheet may be adapted for use with various groups or individuals. Also, the company may hand out some of the same materials at major scientific meetings. Consumers who contact a company may request disease education booklets or corporate background information. Direct-to-consumer provision of information on specific prescription medicines is, of course, usually inappropriate for a company to provide. Patient education materials of this nature are usually better directed from manufacturers to physicians.

Media Events

Media events intended to help reporters update the public are of various types, and the following are discussed:

1. editorial briefings or press conferences,
2. video news releases,
3. satellite interviews,
4. audio conferences, and
5. special events and programs.

Editorial Briefings

These are conducted for magazines and newspapers to provide updates on important topics. The most up-to-date information available is presented by a panel of experts so that an audience of specific reporters can utilize the data. The panel typically consists of both company and independent researchers. Each of the typically three to five panelists speaks from slides for about five to ten minutes each. This is usually followed by questions and answers. The session is often held in association with a medical conference or can stand alone.

Video News Releases

Just as news releases are developed in written form for reporters, a video format can be used to meet the special needs of television. Television stations often accept a video tape from a company, providing it offers solid newsworthy information in an acceptable format and has high production quality. This video is often appreciated by reporters because it provides footage that may otherwise be difficult or costly for a television station to obtain. It can include interviews with prominent national authorities. It may be used at a station's discretion, in part or in its entirety. Stations may choose to insert part of the piece or to hold it for use at a later date.

Satellite Interviews

Satellite interviewing is a relatively new technique that makes nationally known experts available to television news stations around the country to speak on subjects of considerable news value in a cost- and time-efficient manner. Each station reserves a slot of time on a specified day during which they interview the expert for approximately 10 to 15 minutes on a topic of great interest. In the space of a few hours, successive interviews can be scheduled to several stations who have the requisite technical capabilities. Companies do not charge television stations for this professional service. This method takes significant time to arrange and is usually able to accommodate only a limited number of stations since scheduling more than 10 to 20 stations would make most experts unduly fatigued. One variation of this approach would be for a satellite meeting to be beamed directly into newsrooms around the country and for them to use some of the material presented.

Audio Conferences

Many important newspapers cannot arrange to attend all relevant news conferences held in New York or Washington. The newspaper may be strongly interested, however, in getting its own story. A pharmaceutical company may provide a panel of experts by telephone conference call. This method can be tied to a video or other type of conference or media event, if it is not tied to a press conference. Or it can stand alone. Audio conferences, like press conferences, are held because the company has a major story and is trying to manage the information so that everyone who desires access to it can get the news at the same time.

Special Events and Public Service or Education Programs

There is almost no limit to other events or programs that may be produced to provide public service or public education benefits. One example would be a film that could be shown to high schools. Media activity could be built around some of these programs to gain appropriate interest, participation, or visibility. Other events could include health fairs, charity benefits, seminars, symposia, school education programs, and film premiers. Appearances of various experts or celebrities at special events could be arranged to help ensure the event's success.

Media Tours

Specific local markets or areas of the country may sometimes be targeted for communications activity because of their risk for a given disease or for other reasons. To provide consumer information, companies may identify a local medical expert or help make a national expert available locally to talk with television, radio, and newspaper reporters in that city. This activity is often called a media tour because more than one interview is conducted.

Media tours are designed to provide consumer education on a health topic. Companies usually build a schedule of interviews with the media around a specific theme or news topic. For example, experts on acquired immune deficiency syndrome (AIDS) or other sexually transmitted diseases are currently in demand because the topic is in the news. Some topics come up periodically because of the seasonality of the problem (e.g., head lice), and so any promotional efforts of new medicines to treat lice must be tied to the appropriate time of year. The same principle applies to seasonal allergies, colds, and other medical problems that occur periodically with a higher incidence.

Experts who are on a media tour usually want to communicate a specific point to their audience. This educational effort is designed to enlighten the consumer about a health problem or issue. An example could be where the expert discusses a disease and the information that people should understand about it. People are told that, if they have the disease, they may wish to visit their physician for a checkup or to discuss whether medicine therapy would be appropriate. An address may be given for consumers to write for a free brochure about the disease.

Media Events Targeted to Health Professionals

Media events targeted to health professionals include

1. press releases to medical journals and newspapers,
2. programs targeted via health channels on television or radio stations,

3. lecture tours of noted national experts, and
4. coverage of important symposia or other meetings.

These events are self-explanatory or have already been described. A special report titled "Creating Media Synergy" discusses combining media presentations (Koberstein, 1991).

Public Relations for Over-the-Counter and Prescription Medicines

Companies have more flexibility in communicating about over-the-counter (OTC) medicines than they do with prescription medicines. Programs may be sponsored by a consumer product company, and the connection of the brand to the program is usually obvious. Sports programs are a good example. A connection of a product to the Olympics or another major sporting event may be desired. This type of advertising and exclusive sponsoring rights may often be purchased. For OTC consumer products such as pain relievers, cold remedies, or first-aid treatments, consumer education events and other techniques may also be used to help provide brand-specific information.

For prescription medicines there is educational value associated with public relations programs. The program may initially discuss the disease and include some discussion of treatment options. But the company is constrained by the labeling in how much they can say about a medicine. In fact, medicine names are often not mentioned in a video or other presentation.

PUBLIC RELATIONS FOR THE PHARMACEUTICAL INDUSTRY

Improving the Industry's Image with the Public

The media has done an outstanding job of medical reporting in certain areas such as the tampering of Tylenol and other capsules and the ways in which McNeil Pharmaceutical and other pharmaceutical companies responded. Earlier, the media brought information on hypertension issues of diagnosis and treatment to the public in a responsible manner. One area, however, that usually is poorly presented to the public relates to news stories about new medicine development. Pharmaceutical companies or the FDA is often portrayed as either dragging its feet on an important new medicine or of rushing it to the market with disregard for patients' welfare.

The primary reason for this situation appears to be a lack of understanding of how medicine discovery, development, and approval actually take place. This may be noted in the superficial approach and distortions present in many news stories. Another reason for the lack of balance and understanding in many news reports relates

to the fact that pharmaceutical companies are restricted in what they can tell the press. This restriction is based on protecting proprietary information and withholding certain aspects of a medicine's labeling that may not yet be approved. As a result, some reporters may feel that the company is suppressing information. When an individual or a group makes charges against a company or the entire pharmaceutical industry, any response is made from a defensive position. Some people, including reporters, may be unwilling or unable to eliminate their bias against an accused party when judging the company's response.

There is a vitally important need for the story of medicine discovery and medicine development to be presented to the public. Because pharmaceutical companies are both too small individually and also have different points they would want to emphasize, it is probably best for companies to work together via a trade association or to cooperate with a government agency to tell their story to the public.

There are many paths that may be followed to achieve this goal. These paths include television, radio, publications, and public speakers. Television programs of a documentary nature could be made on medicine development. Wouldn't it be exciting to have a situation drama (comedy?) each week illustrating the trials and tribulations of a research and development director trying to steer a medicine through the maze of activities needed to bring it to market? It is easy to imagine many exciting episodes in this type of program.

Publications could be prepared by individual scientists, companies, or by professional associations. These articles might be designed to fit in with each other and with the television and other stories. They could be directed to the public via various magazines as well as through columns inserted in newspapers, newsletters, and other printed matter. One book that attempts to present the industry's story using simple language is *Inside the Drug Industry* (Spilker and Cuatrecasas, 1990).

Speakers' bureaus may be organized on a state, community, or national level through professional associations as well as individual companies. A trade association or an outside group hired by a trade association could organize these speaking engagements. The speakers could talk about one of a short list of topics of relevance to the public. These talks could be held at professional society meetings, civic group meetings, schools, universities, and many other locations.

The various chapters in this book have attempted to provide an overview of the major issues faced in medicine discovery and development. The incredible complexity of this process virtually ensures that all investigational medicines will face some or many issues not discussed in this book. It is the uncertainty and primarily the challenge of uncovering these issues and solving them successfully that make new medicine discovery and development such an exciting and rewarding career.

Selected Books About Medicine Development or of Particular Interest to the Pharmaceutical Industry*

CATEGORIES PRESENTED:

General.. 775
Future... 775
Medicine Discovery and Innovation.............. 775
Clinical Trial Planning, Design, Management,
    Conduct, Analysis, and Evaluation.......... 775
Biotechnology 776
Pharmacoepidemiology 776
Production....................................... 776
Law 776
Orphan Medicines................................ 776

Regulations..................................... 776
Ethics 776
Marketing, Economics, and Politics 776
History.. 777
Business, Competition, and Strategies 777
Combination Medicines 777
Adverse Reactions 777
Benefits and Risks 777
Personnel Issues Relating to Scientists 777
Toxicology 777
Project Management............................. 777
Licensing and Negotiations...................... 777

GENERAL

Decision Making in Drug Research, edited by F. Gross. Raven Press, New York 1983.

Drug Development, 2nd ed., edited by C.E. Hamner. CRC Press Inc., Boca Raton, FL 1990.

Tragedies from Drug Therapy: For Health Professionals. R.B. Stewart. Charles C Thomas Publisher, Springfield, IL 1985.

The Pharmaceutical Industry: Economics, Performance, and Government Regulation. E. Caglarcan, et al. John Wiley & Sons Inc., New York 1978.

The Pharmaceutical Industry. S.N. Wiggins. Center for Education and Research in Free Enterprise, Texas A&M University, College Station, TX 1985.

Drug Development: From Laboratory to Clinic. W. Sneader. John Wiley & Sons, Chichester, UK 1986.

The Development of a Medicine. R. B. Smith. Stockton Press, New York. 1985.

Inside the Drug Industry. B. Spilker and P. Cuatrecasas. Prous Science, Barcelona 1990.

FUTURE

Pharmaceuticals in the Year 2000: The Changing Context for Drug R&D, edited by C. Bezold. Institute for Alternative Futures, Alexandria, VA 1983.

The Future of the Multinational Pharmaceutical Industry to 1990. B.G. James. Associated Business Programmes, London, UK 1977.

The Second Pharmacological Revolution, edited by N. Wells. Office of Health Economics, London, UK 1983.

The Bristol-Myers Report: Medicine in the Next Century. H. Taylor and G. Voivodas. Louis Harris and Associates Study 861018, New York 1987.

The World Health Market: The Future of the Pharmaceutical Industry. D. Tucker. Facts On File Inc., New York 1984.

MEDICINE DISCOVERY AND INNOVATION

Creating the Right Environment for Drug Discovery, edited by S. Walker. Quay Publishing, Lancaster, UK 1991.

Drug Discovery Technologies. C.R. Clark and W.H. Moos. John Wiley & Sons, New York 1990.

Drug Discovery and Development. M. Williams and J.B. Malick. Humana Press, Clifton, NJ 1987.

Drug Discovery: The Evolution of Modern Medicines. W. Sneader. John Wiley & Sons Inc., New York. 1985.

Innovation in the Pharmaceutical Industry. D. Schwartzman. Johns Hopkins University Press, Baltimore, MD 1976.

Retrospectroscope: Insights Into Medical Discovery. J.H. Comroe Jr., Von Gehr Press, Menlo Park, CA 1977.

Priorities in Research: Proceedings of the Fourth Boehringer Ingelheim Symposium held at Kronberg, Taunus, May 1982, edited by Sir J. Kendrew and J.H. Shelley. Excerpta Medica, Amsterdam 1983.

CLINICAL TRIAL PLANNING, DESIGN, MANAGEMENT, CONDUCT, ANALYSIS, AND EVALUATION

(Several books are heavily oriented toward statistics)

Guide to Clinical Studies and Developing Protocols. B. Spilker. Raven Press, New York. 1984.

---

*Many books could fit multiple categories.

Note: See *Principles of Pharmaceutical Marketing* by M. C. Smith (pp. 514, 515) for a list of additional references from the 1960s and 1970s.

Guide to Clinical Interpretation of Data. B. Spilker. Raven Press, New York. 1986.

Guide to Planning and Managing Multiple Clinical Studies. B. Spilker. Raven Press, New York 1987.

Presentation of Clinical Data. B. Spilker and J. Schoenfelder. Raven Press, New York 1990.

Data Collection Forms in Clinical Trials. B. Spilker and J. Schoenfelder. Raven Press, New York 1991.

Guide to Clinical Trials. B. Spilker. Raven Press, New York 1991.

Patient Compliance in Medical Practice and Clinical Trials, edited by J. Cramer and B. Spilker. Raven Press, New York 1991.

Patient Recruitment in Clinical Trials. B. Spilker and J. Cramer. Raven Press, New York 1992.

The Clinical Research Process in the Pharmaceutical Industry, edited by G. M. Matoren. Marcel Dekker Inc., New York 1984.

Clinical Trials: A Practical Approach. S. J. Pocock. John Wiley & Sons Inc., New York 1983.

Methodology of Clinical Drug Trials. A. Spriet and P. Simon. Karger, Basel 1985.

Issues in Research With Human Subjects: A Symposium, March 20-21, 1978. National Institutes of Health, Bethesda, MD. NIH Pub. No. 80-1858, Bethesda, MD 1980.

Clinical Trials, edited by F. N. Johnson and S. Johnson. Blackwell Scientific Publishers. Oxford, UK 1977.

Clinical Trials. D. Schwartz, R. Flamant, and J. Lellouch. Academic Press Inc., New York 1980.

Concepts and Strategies in New Drug Development, edited by P.U. Nwangwu. Praeger Publishers, New York 1983.

Fundamentals of Clinical Trials. L.M. Friedman, C.D. Furburg, D.L. De Mets, and J. Wright. PSG Publishing Co., Boston 1981.

Principles and Practice of Clinical Trials: Based on symposium organized by the Associated Medical Advisers in the Pharmaceutical Industry, edited by E.L. Harris and J. D. Fitzgerald. Livingstone, Edinburgh 1970.

Clinical Trials: Design, Conduct, and Analysis. C.L. Meinert. Oxford University Press Inc., New York 1986.

BIOTECHNOLOGY

Biotechnology in a Global Economy. U.S. Congress, Office of Technology Assessment, OTA-BA-494 (Washington, DC: U.S. Government Printing Office, October 1991).

Biotechnology Guide USA: Companies, Data and Analysis, 2nd ed., M. D. Dibner. Stockton Press, New York 1991.

PHARMACOEPIDEMIOLOGY

Pharmacoepidemiology: An Introduction, 2nd ed., edited by A.G. Hartzema, M.S. Porta and H.H. Tilson. Harvey Whitney Books Company, Cinncinati, Ohio 1991.

Clinical Epidemiology-the essentials. R.H. Fletcher, S.W. Fletcher, and E.H. Wahner. Williams & Wilkins, Baltimore, MD 1982.

PRODUCTION

Guide to Quality Control. Ishikawa, K. Asian Productivity Organization, Tokyo, Japan 1976.

Understanding Statistical Process Control. 2nd ed., D.J. Wheeler and D.S. Chambers. SPC Press, Knoxville, TN 1992.

Quality, Productivity, and Competitive Position. W. E. Deming. Center for Advanced Engineering Study, MIT, Cambridge, MA 1982.

LAW

Food and Drug Law: Cases and Materials. 2nd ed., P.B. Hutt and R.A. Merrill. The Foundation Press, Inc., Westbury, NY 1991.

ORPHAN MEDICINES

Orphan Drugs: Medical Versus Market Value. C. H. Asbury. Lexington Books, Lexington, MA 1985.

Drug Development, Regulatory Assessment, and Postmarketing Surveillance, edited by W.M. Wardell and G. Velo. Plenum Publishing Corp., New York 1981.

Orphan Diseases and Orphan Drugs, edited by I.H. Scheinberg and J.M. Walshe. Manchester University Press, Manchester, UK 1986.

Orphan Drugs, edited by F.E. Karch. Marcel Dekker Inc., New York 1982.

Cooperative Approaches to Research and Development of Orphan Drugs, edited by M. H. van Woert and E. Chung. Alan R. Liss, New York 1985.

REGULATIONS

New Drug Development: A Regulatory Overview. M. Mathieu. Parexel International Corp., Waltham, MA 1990.

Getting Your Drug Approved: FDA's Own Guidelines, 2nd ed., Washington Business Information, Inc., Arlington, VA 1990.

Regulation and Drug Development. W.M. Wardell and L. Lasagna. American Enterprise Institute for Public Policy Research. Washington. 1975.

Drug Development, Regulatory Assessment, and Postmarketing Surveillance, edited by W. M. Wardell and G. Velo. Plenum Publishing Corp., New York 1981.

Federal Register. Source of specific United States regulations. Supt. of Documents, Washington.

Taking Your Medicine: Drug Regulation in the United States. P. Temin. Harvard University Press, Cambridge, MA 1980.

New Drug Approval Process: Clinical and Regulatory Management, edited by R.A. Guarino. Marcel Dekker Inc., New York 1987.

ETHICS

Ethics and Regulation of Clinical Research (2nd ed). R.J. Levine. Urban & Schwarzenberg Inc., Baltimore, MD 1986.

Case Studies in Medical Ethics. R.M. Veatch. Harvard University Press, Cambridge, MA 1977.

The Handbook of Medical Ethics . British Medical Association, London, UK 1984.

Ethical Principles in the Conduct of Research With Human Participants. American Psychological Association, Washington 1982.

Biomedical Research: Collaboration and Conflict of Interest. R. J. Porter and T. E. Malone. The Johns Hopkins University Press, Baltimore 1992.

MARKETING, ECONOMICS, AND POLITICS

Pharmaceutical Marketing: Strategies and Cases. Mickey C. Smith. Pharmaceutical Products Press, New York 1991.

The Dartnell Marketing Manager's Handbook. Norman F. Guess. Edited by Steuart Henderson Britt. Dartnell, Chicago 1983.

Drug Development and Marketing: A Conference, edited by R.B. Helms. American Enterprise Institute for Public Policy Research, Washington. 1975.

Profits, Politics, and Drugs. W.D. Reekie and M.H. Weber. Holmes & Meier Publishers Inc., New York. 1979.

International Pharmaceutical Marketing. S.B. Pradhan. Quorum Books, Westport, CT 1983.

Principles of Pharmaceutical Marketing, 3rd ed., M. C. Smith. Lea & Febiger, Philadelphia 1983.

A Competitive Assessment of the U.S. Pharmaceutical Industry. Industry Analysis Division, United States Department of Commerce, International Trade Administration, Washington 1985.

Economics of the Pharmaceutical Industry. P.L. Kahn, E.J. Yang, J. W. Egan, H.N. Higinbotham, and J.F. Weston. Praeger Publishers, New York 1982.

Methods for the Economic Evaluation of Health Care Programmes. M. F. Drummond, G. L. Stoddart, G. W. Torrance. Oxford University Press, Oxford 1987.

Patient Information in Medicine, edited by R. D. Mann. Parthenon Publishing Group, Park Ridge, NJ 1991.

Drugs and Health: Economic Issues and Policy Objectives, edited by R.B. Helms. American Enterprise Institute for Public Policy Research, Washington 1981.

Pharmaceuticals Among the Sunrise Industries, edited by N. Wells. St. Martin's Press Inc., New York 1985.

HISTORY

American Self-Dosage Medicines: An Historical Perspective. J.H. Young. Coronado Press Inc., Lawrence, KA 1974.

Herbs to Hormones: The Evolution of Drugs and Chemicals That Revolutionized Medicine. C.L. Huisking. The Pequot Press, Essex, CT 1968.

The Medical Messiahs: A Social History of Health Quackery in Twentieth Century America. J.H. Young. Princeton University Press, Princeton, NJ 1967.

History of Pharmacy and Pharmaceutical Industry. P. Boussel, H. Bonnemain, and F.J. Bové. Asklepios Press, Paris 1983.

Pharmaceutical Company Histories, vol.I, edited by G.L. Nelson. Woodbine Publishers., Bismark, ND 1983.

Chronicles of Drug Discovery, vols. 1 and 2, edited by J.S. Bindra and D. Lednicer. John Wiley & Sons Inc., New York, 1981 and 1982.

BUSINESS, COMPETITION, AND STRATEGIES

(Some references are not specific to the pharmaceutical industry)

Competition in the Pharmaceutical Industry: The Declining Profitability of Drug Innovation. M. Statman. American Enterprise Institute for Public Policy Research, Washington 1983.

Competitive Strategy: Techniques for Analyzing Industries and Competitors. M.E. Porter. Free Press, New York 1980.

Competitive Advantage: Creating and Sustaining Superior Performance. M. E. Porter. Free Press, New York 1985.

Strategy Traps: And How to Avoid Them. R.A. Stringer, Jr. with J. Uchenick. Lexington Books, Lexington, MA 1986.

Competition and Marketing Strategies in the Pharmaceutical Industry. Slatter, S. St. P. Croom Helm, London, UK 1977.

Handbook of Business Strategy, edited by W.D. Guth. Warren, Gorham & Lamont Inc., New York 1985.

COMBINATION MEDICINES

Combination Drugs: Their Use and Regulation, edited by L. Lasagna. Stratton International Medical Book Co., New York 1975.

Fixed Drug Combinations—Rationale and Limitations, edited by K.C. Mezey. Royal Society of Medicine, London, and Grune & Stratton Inc., Orlando, FL 1980.

ADVERSE REACTIONS

The Detection of New Adverse Drug Reactions, 2nd ed., M.D.B. Stephens. Stockton Press, New York 1988.

Monitoring for Drug Safety, 2nd ed., edited by W.H.W. Inman. MTP Press, Lancaster, UK 1985.

Detection and Prevention of Adverse Drug Reactions: Symposium, Oct. 1983, edited by H. Bostrom and N. Ljungstedt. Almqvist and Wiksell International, Stockholm 1984.

BENEFITS AND RISKS

The Life/Death Ratio: Benefits and Risks in Modern Medicines. W.S. Ross. Reader's Digest General Books, New York 1977.

Risk-Benefit Analysis in Drug Research, edited by J.F. Cavalla. MTP Press Ltd, Lancaster, UK 1981.

PERSONNEL ISSUES RELATING TO SCIENTISTS

Scientists in Organizations: Productive Climates for Research and Development, revised ed. D.C. Pelz and F.M. Andrews. Institute for Social Research, University of Michigan, Ann Arbor, MI 1976.

TOXICOLOGY

Safety Evaluation of Drugs and Chemicals, edited by W.E. Lloyd. Hemisphere Publishing Corp., New York 1986.

Long-Term Animal Studies: Their Predictive Value for Man, edited by S.R. Walker and A.D. Dayan. MTP Press, Lancaster, UK 1986.

The Safety of Medicines: Evaluation and Prediction. P.I. Folb. Springer-Verlag New York Inc., New York 1980.

Safety Testing of New Drugs: Laboratory Predictions and Clinical Performance, edited by D.R. Laurence, A.E.M. McLean, and M. Weatherall Academic Press, London 1984.

Animal Toxicity Studies: Their Relevance for Man, edited by C. E. Lumley and S. R. Walker. Quay Publishing, Lancaster, UK 1990.

PROJECT MANAGEMENT

Project Management Handbook, edited by D.I. Cleland and W.R. King. Van Nostrand Reinhold Co. Inc., New York 1983.

Project Management: Combining Technical and Behavioral Approaches for Effective Implementation. R J. Graham. Van Nostrand Reinhold Co. Inc., New York 1985.

LICENSING AND NEGOTIATIONS

Licensing—A Strategy for Profits. E. P. White. KEW Licensing Press, Chapel Hill, NC 1990.

You Can Negotiate Anything. H. Cohen. Lyle Stuart, Inc., Secaucus, NJ 1980.

Getting to Yes: Negotiating Agreement Without Giving In. R. Fisher and W. Ury. Penguin Books, New York 1983.

Technology Management: Law/Tactics/Forms. P. Goldscheider. Clark Boardman, New York 1988.

Finding and Licensing New Products and Technology from the U.S.A. J. W. Morehead. Technology Search International, Elk Grove Village, IL 1988.

References

AHC Task Force on Science Policy (1990): *Conflicts of Interest in Academic Health Centers: Policy Paper #1.* Association of Academic Health Centers, Washington, DC.

Anonymous (1987a): Information for patients about medicines. *Lancet,* II:1077–1078.

Anonymous (1987b): US center for study of drug development 10th anniversary. *Marketletter of IMS International,* 14(11):26–27.

Anonymous (1990a): *Am. J. Hosp. Pharmacy,* 47:1989–2001.

Anonymous (1990b): EC PIL problems still loom large. *SCRIP Magazine,* 1575(Dec. 14):8.

Anonymous (1991): Worldwide pharma alliances analyzed. *SCRIP Magazine,* 1590 (Feb. 13):13.

Arkes, H. R., and Blumer, C. (1985): The psychology of sunk cost. *Organ. Behav. Hum. Decis. Proc.,* 35:124–140.

Atkinson, A. J., Jr., Becker, R. E., Galletti, P. M., Jefferis, J. E., and Wroblewski, R. (1984): University and pharmaceutical industry cooperation: The need to plan for the future. *Clin. Pharmacol. Ther.,* 35:431–437.

Balandrin, M. F., Klocke, J. A., Wurtele, E. S., and Bollinger, W. H. (1985): Natural plant chemicals: Sources of industrial and medicinal materials. *Science,* 228:1154–1160.

Balthasar, H. U., Boschi, R. A. A., and Menke, M. M. (1978): Calling the shots in R & D. *Harvard Bus. Rev.,* 56(3):151–160.

Barr, W. H. (1972): The use of physical and animal models to assess bioavailability. *Pharmacology,* 8:55–101.

Bartholini, G. (1983): Organization of industrial drug research. In: *Decision Making in Drug Research,* edited by F. Gross. Raven Press, New York. pp. 123–146.

Bennis, W., and Nanus, B. (1985): *Leaders: The Strategies for Taking Charge.* Harper & Row Publishers Inc., New York.

Berndtson, W. E., Neefus, C., Foote, R. H., and Amann, R. P. (1989): Optimal replication for histometric analysis of testicular function in rats or rabbits. *Fundam. Appl. Toxicol.,* 12:291–302.

Berry, C. L. (1986): Unprovable verities. [Editorial] *Hum. Toxicol.,* 5:159–160.

Bezold, C. (editor) (1983): *Pharmaceuticals in the Year 2000: The Changing Context for Drug R & D.* Institute for Alternative Futures, Alexandria, VA.

Blair, D. C. (1984): The management of information: Basic distinctions. *Sloan Management Review,* 26(1):13–23.

Blattman, P. (1992): Patient product information (PPI)—Elements for a rational approach. *Drug Info. J.,* 26:271–278.

Bloch, E. (1986): Basic research and economic health: The coming challenge. *Science,* 232:595–599.

Blumenthal, D., Epstein, S., and Maxwell, J. (1986): Commercializing university research: Lessons from the experience of the Wisconsin Alumni Research Foundation. *N. Engl. J. Med.,* 314:1621–1626.

Blumenthal, D., Gluck, M., Louis, K. S., Stoto, M. A., and Wise, D. (1986): University-industry research relationships in biotechnology: Implications for the university. *Science,* 232:1361–1366.

Bohl, D. L. (editor) (1987): *Close to the Customer: An American Management Association Research Report on Consumer Affairs.* American Management Association, New York.

Bolton, R., and Bolton, D. G. (1984): *Social Style/Management Style: Developing Productive Work Relationships.* American Management Association, New York.

Britt, D. P. (1983): The potential role of local ethical committees in the moderation of experiments on animals in Britain. *Int. J. Stud. Animal Prob.,* 4:290–294.

Byrne, J. A. (1987): The miracle company: Excellence in the lab and executive suite makes Merck a powerhouse. *Business Week,* October 19:84–90.

Cantekin, E. I., McGuire, T. W., and Potter, R. L. (1990): Biomedical information, peer review, and conflict of interest as they influence public health. *JAMA,* 263:1427–1430.

CIOMS Working Group (1990): *International Reporting of Adverse Drug Reactions: Final Report of CIOMS Working Group.* CIOMS, Geneva.

Clarke, A. J., Clark, B., Eason, C. T., and Parke, D. V. (1985): An assessment of a toxicological incident in a drug development program and its implications. *Regul. Toxicol. Pharmacol.,* 5:109–119.

Cleland, D. I. (1984): Pyramiding project management productivity. *Proj. Manag. J.,* 15(June):88–95.

Clive, D. (1987): Genetic toxicology: From theory to practice. *J. Clin. Res. Drug Dev.,* 1:11–41.

Cloutier, G., Spilker, B., Lai, A., and Cato, A. (1983): Methods for the assessment of drugs in partial epilepsy. International Epilepsy Meeting, Washington, DC.

Cohen, H. (1980): *You Can Negotiate Anything.* Lyle Stuart Inc., Secaucus, NJ.

Committee on the Use of Animals in Research (1991): *Science, Medicine, and Animals.* National Academy Press, Washington, DC.

Computer Systems Validation Committee of the Pharmaceutical Manufacturers Association (1986): Validation concepts for computer systems used in the manufacture of drug products. *Pharm. Technol.,* 10:24, 26–27, 30, 32, 34.

Comroe, J. H., Jr., and Dripps, R. D. (1976): Scientific basis for the support of biomedical science. *Science,* 192:105–111.

Council on Ethical and Judicial Affairs (1992): Conflicts of interest: Physician ownership of medical facilities. *JAMA,* 267:2366–2369.

Council on Scientific Affairs and Council on Ethical and Judicial Affairs (1990): Conflicts of interest in medical center/industry research relationships. *JAMA,* 263:2790–2793.

Cuatrecasas, P. (1984): Contemporary drug development—dilemmas. *Regul. Toxicol. Pharmacol.,* 4:1–12.

Cuatrecasas, P. (1992): Industry-university alliances in biomedical research. *J. Clin. Pharmacol.,* 32:100–106.

de Bono, E. (1967): *The Use of Lateral Thinking.* Pelican Books, Harmondsworth, England.

DeForest, P., Frankel, M. S., Poindexter, J. S., and Weil, V. (editors) (1988): *Biotechnology: Professional Issues and Social Concerns.* American Association for the Advancement of Science, Publication 88-23, Washington, DC.

Deming, W. E. (1982): *Quality, Productivity, and Competitive Position.* Center for Advanced Engineering Study, MIT, Cambridge, MA.

Dibner, M. D. (1990): The impact of biotechnology on the pharmaceutical industry. In: *Drug Development* (2nd ed.), edited by C. E. Hammer. CRC Press Inc., Boca Raton, FL. pp. 241–254.

Dibner, M. D. (1991): *Biotechnology Guide USA: Companies, Data, and Analysis.* (2nd ed.) Stockton Press, New York.

DiMasi, J. A., Hansen, R. W., Grabowski, H. G., and Lasagna, L. (1991): Cost of innovation in the pharmaceutical industry. *J Health Economics,* 10:107–142.

Drews, J. (1985): Judging pharmaceutical research and development from a financial point of view. *Swiss Pharma.,* 7:21–23.

Drummond, M. F., Stoddart, G. L., and Torrance, G. W. (1987): *Methods for the Economic Evaluation of Health Care Programmes.* Oxford University Press, Oxford.

Dudley, J. (1992): The OTC option in Europe. *SCRIP Magazine,* June:25–27.

Duncan, W. A., and Parsons, M. E. (1980): Reminiscences of the development of cimetidine. *Gastroenterology,* 78:620–625.

Evans, K. R., Beltramini, R. F. (1986): Physician acquisition of prescription drug information. *J. Health C. Market.,* 6(4):15–25.

779

Falahee, K. J., Rose, C. S., Seifried, H. E., and Sawhney, D. (1983): Alternatives in toxicity testing. In: *Product Safety Evaluation.* Vol. 1, edited by A. M. Goldberg. Liebert, New York. pp. 139–162.

Faust, R. E. (1984a): Envisioning the future of R & D, Part I. *Pharm. Exec.,* 4(9):68–70, 72, 74.

Faust, R. E. (1984b): Envisioning the future of R & D, Part II. *Pharm. Exec.,* 4(10):52–53, 56, 58, 61.

Fisher, R., and Ury, W. (1983): *Getting to Yes: Negotiating Agreement Without Giving In.* Penguin Books, New York.

Fletcher, A. P. (1978): Drug safety tests and subsequent clinical experience. *J. Roy. Soc. Med.,* 71:693–696.

Fraumeni, J. F., Jr., and Miller, R. W. (1972): Drug-induced cancer. *JNCI,* 48:1267–1270.

Frishman, W. H. (1987): Clinical differences between beta-adrenergic blocking agents: Implications for therapeutic substitution. *Am. Heart J.,* 113:1190–1198.

Futterman, D. H. (1985): What organizational issues determine corporate success? In: *Handbook of Business Strategy: 1985/1986 Yearbook,* edited by W. D. Guth. Warren, Gorham & Lamont Inc., New York. pp. 28-1-28-14.

Geneen, H. (1984): *Leadership: Managing.* Doubleday Publishing Co., New York. pp. 125–146.

Gluck, M. E., Blumenthal, D., and Stoto, M. A. (1987): University-industry relationships in the life sciences: Implications for students and post-doctoral fellows. *Res. Policy,* 16:327–336.

Goldscheider, R. (1988): *Technology Management: Law/Tactics/Forms.* Clark Boardman, New York.

Goldsmith, J. C. (1986): The U.S. health care system in the year 2000. *JAMA,* 256:3371–3375.

Gottfried, R. S. (1983): *The Black Death: Natural and Human Disaster in Medieval Europe.* Macmillan, London. pp. 158–159.

Grabowski, H., and Vernon, J. (1982): A sensitivity analysis of expected profitability of pharmaceutical research and development. *Managerial and Decision Economics,* 3:36–40.

Grahame-Smith, D. G. (1987): Scores on analog scale for understanding typical new drug at registration (Fig. 1). In: *Innovation and Acceleration in Clinical Drug Development,* edited by L. Lasagna and A. G. Bearn. Raven Press, New York. p. 152.

Grahame-Smith, D. G., and Aronson, J. K. (1984): *The Oxford Textbook of Clinical Pharmacology and Drug Therapy.* Oxford University Press, Oxford.

Gray, D. H. (1986): Uses and misuses of strategic planning. *Harvard Bus. Rev.,* 64(1):89–97.

Griffin, J. P. (1986): Predictive value of animal toxicity studies. In: *Long-Term Animal Studies: Their Predictive Value for Man,* edited by S. R. Walker and A. D. Dayan. MTP Press, Lancaster, UK. pp. 107–116.

Griggs, W. H, and Manring, S. L. (1986): Increasing the effectiveness of technical professionals. *Management Rev.,* 75(5):62–64.

Gunsalus, C.K. (1989): Considerations in licensing spin-off technology. *Soc. Res. Admin. J.,* Summer:13–25.

Guth, W. D. (editor) (1985): *Handbook of Business Strategy: 1985/1986 Yearbook.* Warren, Gorham & Lamont Inc., New York.

Haddad, W. (1992): Testing times for the US generic industry. *SCRIP Magazine,* May:26–29.

Hayes, R. H. (1985): Strategic planning—forward in reverse? *Harvard Bus. Rev.,* 63(6):111–119.

Healy, B., Campeau, L., Gray, R., Herd, A., Hoogwerf, B., et al. (1989): Conflict-of-interest guidelines for a multicenter clinical trial of treatment after coronary-artery bypass-graft surgery. *New Engl. J. Med.,* 320:949–951.

Hermann, F. F., and Wanke, L. A. (1987): Analysis and control of costs associated with answering drug information requests. *Drug Info. J.,* 21:209–216.

Herzberg, F. (1987): One more time: How do you motivate employees? *Harvard Bus. Rev.,* 65(5):109–120.

Heywood, R. (1981): Target organ toxicity. *Toxicol. Lett.,* 8:349–358.

Heywood, R. (1984): Prediction of adverse drug reactions from animal safety studies. In: *Detection and Prevention of Adverse Drug Reactions* (Skandia International Symposia), edited by H. Bostrom and N. Ljungstedt. Almqvist and Wiksell International, Stockholm. pp. 173–189.

Heywood, R. (1990): Clinical toxicity—could it have been predicted? Post-marketing experience. In: *Animal Toxicity Studies: Their Relevance for Man,* edited by C. E. Lumley and S. R. Walker. Quay Publishing, Lancaster, UK. pp. 57–67.

Hofer, C. W., and Schendel, D. (1978): *Strategy Formulation: Analytical Concepts.* West Publishing Co., St. Paul, MN.

Human Resources and Intergovernmental Relations Subcommittee of the Committee on Government Operations House of Representatives (1989a): *Is science for sale? Conflicts of interest vs. the public interest (Hearings, June 13, 1989).* US Government Printing Office, Washington, DC.

Human Resources and Intergovernmental Relations Subcommittee of the Committee on Government Operations House of Representatives (1989b): *Federal response to misconduct in science: Are conflicts of interest hazardous to our health? (Hearing, September 29, 1988).* US Government Printing Office, Washington, DC.

Humble, J. (1980): Time management: Separating the myths and the realities. *Management Rev.,* 69(10):25–28, 49–53.

Hurst, D. K. (1984): Of boxes, bubbles, and effective management. *Harvard Bus. Rev.,* 62(3):78–88.

Hutt, P. B., and Merrill, R. A. (1991): *Food and Drug Law: Cases and Materials.* (2nd ed.) The Foundation Press, Westbury, NY.

Inman, W. H. W. (editor) (1986): *Monitoring for Drug Safety.* MTP Press, Lancaster, UK.

Institute of Medicine Committee on Potential Conflicts of Interest in Patient Outcomes Research Teams (1991): *Patient Outcomes Research Teams: Managing Conflict of Interest.* National Academy Press, Washington, DC.

Ishikawa, K. (1976): *Guide to Quality Control.* Asian Productivity Organization, Tokyo, Japan.

Jick, H., Feld, A. D., and Perera, D. R. (1985): Certain nonsteroidal antiinflammatory drugs and hospitalization for upper gastrointestinal bleeding. *Pharmacotherapy,* 5:280–284.

Joglekar, P., and Paterson, M. L. (1986): A closer look at the returns and risks of pharmaceutical R & D. *J. Health Econ.,* 5:153–177.

Johnsson, G., Ablad, B., and Hansson, E. (1984): Prediction of adverse drug reactions in clinical practice from animal experiments and Phase I–III studies. In: *Detection and Prevention of Adverse Drug Reactions* (Skandia International Symposia), edited by H. Bostrom and N. Ljungstedt. Almqvist and Wiksell International, Stockholm. pp. 190–199.

Joossens, L. (1991): The patient information package insert and aspects of consumer protection. In: *Patient Information in Medicine,* edited by R. D. Mann. The Parthenon Pub. Group, Park Ridge, NJ. pp. 119–129.

Kahn, P. L., Yang, E. J., Egan, J. W., Higinbotham, H. N., and Weston, J. F. (1982): *Economics of the Pharmaceutical Industry.* Praeger Publishers, New York.

Kaitin, K. I., and Walsh, H. L. (1992): Are initiatives to speed the new drug approval process working? *Drug Info. J.,* 26:341–349.

Keidel, R. W., and Umen, M. J. (1984): Winning plays in the R&D game. *Pharm. Exec.,* 4(2):42–44.

Kirk, L. E., Collins, G. E., Joseph, M. C., and Katz, D. (1989): Retrovir® (zidovudine): A unique drug information challenge. *Drug Info. J.,* 23:257–266.

Koberstein, W. (1991): Creating media synergy. Special Report. *Pharm. Exec.,* 11(6):36–64.

Korda, M. (1987): *Power! How to Get It, How to Use It.* Ballantine Books, New York.

Kubinyi, H. (1990): Quantitative structure-activity relationships (QSAR) and molecular modelling in cancer research. *J. Cancer Res. Clin. Oncol.,* 116:529–537.

Laurence, D. R., McLean, A. E. M., and Weatherall, M. (editors) (1984): *Safety Testing of New Drugs: Laboratory Predictions and Clinical Performance.* Academic Press, London.

Lefton, R. E., Buzzotta, V. R., and Sherberg, M. (1980): *Improving Productivity Through People Skills: Dimensional Management Strategies.* Ballinger Publishing Co., Cambridge, MA.

Litchfield, J. T., Jr. (1961): Forecasting drug effects in man from studies in laboratory animals. *JAMA,* 177:34–38.

Litchfield, J. T., Jr. (1962): Evaluation of the safety of new drugs by means of tests in animals. *Clin. Pharmacol. Ther.,* 3:665–672.

Louis, K. S., Blumenthal, D., Gluck, M. E., and Stoto, M. A. (1989): Entrepreneurs in academe: An exploration of behaviors among life scientists. *Admin. Sci. Q.,* 34:110–131.

Lumley, C. E., and Walker, S. R. (editors) (1990): *Animal Toxicity Studies: Their Relevance for Man.* Quay Publishing, Lancaster, UK.

Mann, R. D. (editor) (1991): *Patient Information in Medicine.* Parthenon Publishing Group, Park Ridge, NJ.

Martin, W. B. (March 4, 1985): Are you a manager or a leader? *Industry Week*, 224(5):93–97.

Maxwell, R. A., and Eckhardt, S. B. (1990): *Drug Discovery: A Casebook and Analysis.* Humana Press, Clifton, NJ.

McCue, J. D., Hansen, C. J., and Gal, P. (1986): Physicians' opinions of the accuracy, accessibility, and frequency of use of ten sources of new drug information. *South. Med. J., 79*:441–443.

McMahon, T., Clark, C. M., and Bailie, G. R. (1987): Who provides patients with drug information? *Br. Med. J., 294*:355–356.

Meier, J., and Stocker, K. (1989): On the significance of animal experiments in toxicology. *Toxicon, 27*:91–104.

Meyer, N. D., and Boone, M. E. (1987): *The Information Edge.* McGraw-Hill Inc., New York.

Michael, M., III, Boyce, W. T., and Wilcox, A. J. (1984): *Biomedical Bestiary: An Epidemiologic Guide to Flaws and Fallacies in the Medical Literature.* Little, Brown & Co. Inc., Boston.

Millstein, L. G. (1987): Drug product labeling. In: *New Drug Approval Process: Clinical and Regulatory Management.* Edited by R. A. Guarino. Marcel Dekker Inc., New York. pp. 327–361.

Morehead, J. W. (1988): *Finding and Licensing New Products and Technology from the U.S.A.* Technology Search International, Elk Grove Village, IL.

Nestor, J. O. (1975): Results of the failure to perform adequate preclinical studies before administering new drugs to humans. *S. Afr. Med. J., 49*:287–290.

Park, B. A., and Benderev, K. P. (1985): Quality assurance program for a drug information center. *Am. J. Hosp. Pharm., 42*:2180–2184.

Payer L. (1988): *Medicine and culture: Varieties of treatment in the United States, England, West Germany, and France.* Holt and Co., New York.

Pelz, D. C., and Andrews, F. M. (1976): *Scientists in Organizations: Productive Climates for Research and Development.* Institute for Social Research, University of Michigan, Ann Arbor, MI.

Peters, T. J. (1983a): The mythology of innovation, or a skunkworks tale. Part I. *Stanford Mag.,* Summer:12–21.

Peters, T. J. (1983b): The mythology of innovation, or a skunkworks tale. Part II. *Stanford Mag.,* Fall:10–19.

Pletscher, A. (1983): Drug therapy: Progress and risk. In: *Decision Making in Drug Research,* edited by F. Gross. Raven Press, New York. pp. 25–31.

Porter, M. E. (1980): *Competitive Strategy: Techniques for Analyzing Industries and Competitors.* Free Press, New York.

Porter, M. E. (1985): *Competitive Advantage: Creating and Sustaining Superior Performance.* Free Press, New York.

Porter, R. J., and Malone, T. E. (1992): *Biomedical Research: Collaboration and Conflict of Interest.* The Johns Hopkins University Press, Baltimore.

Pradhan, S. B. (1983): *International Pharmaceutical Marketing.* Quorum Books, Westport, CT.

Prentis, R. A., and Walker, S. R. (1985): Pharmaceutical research and development expenditure in the UK. *Pharm. J., 235*:676–678.

Prentis, R. A., and Walker, S. R. (1986): Trends in the development of new medicines by UK-owned pharmaceutical companies (1964–1980). *Br. J. Clin. Pharmacol., 21*:437–443.

Price, F. D. (1985): Industry and academia in collaboration: The Pfizer experience. *Circulation,* 72(suppl. 1):I13–I17.

Raith, H. H. (1992): Denmark—the aftermath of the PDM to OTC switch. *SCRIP Magazine,* March:20–22.

Rall, D. P., and Hoffman, K. S. (1990): Biomedical research, chemical toxicology, and animal use. *The Pharmacologist, 32*:75–79.

Redwood, H. (1992): Disharmony over EC pricing and reimbursement. *SCRIP Magazine,* May:20–22.

Reemtsma, K., and Maloney, J. V., Jr. (1974): The economics of instant medical news. *N. Engl. J. Med., 290*:439–442.

Rennie, D., Flanagin, A., and Glass, R. M. (1991): Conflicts of interest in the publication of science. *JAMA, 266*:266–267.

Repchinsky, C., Godbout, L., and Tierney, M. (1988): A quality assurance audit for a regional and a hospital drug information service. *Can. J. Hosp. Pharm., 41*:267–269.

Rodwin, M. A. (1989): Physicians' conflicts of interest: The limitations of disclosure. *N. Engl. J. Med., 321*:1405–1408.

Saltzman, E. C. (1985): The no-frills alternative in market research. *Pharm. Exec., 5*(1):58–61.

Schein, P. S., Davis, R. D., Carter, S., Newman, J., and Schein, D. R., et al. (1970): The evaluation of anticancer drugs in dogs and monkeys for the prediction of qualitative toxicities in man. *Clin. Pharmacol. Ther., 11*:3–40.

Schepartz, S. A. (1985): The National Cancer Institute's drug development program. In: *Cooperative Approaches to Research and Development of Orphan Drugs,* edited by M. H. van Woert and E. Chung. Alan R. Liss Inc., New York. pp. 73–82.

Scherer, F. M. (1970): *Industrial Market Structure and Economic Performance.* Rand McNally & Co., Chicago.

Schnee, J. E., and Caglarcan, E. (1978): Economic structure and performance of the ethical pharmaceutical industry. In: *The Pharmaceutical Industry: Economics, Performance, and Government Regulation,* edited by E. Caglarcan, W. J. Campbell, G. D. Harrell, J. E. Schnee, D. A. Siskind, and R. F. Smith. John Wiley & Sons Inc., New York. pp. 23–40.

Schwartzman, D. (1976): *Innovation in the Pharmaceutical Industry.* Johns Hopkins University Press, Baltimore, MD.

Seidl, G. (1983): Cost of drug research. In: *Decision Making in Drug Research,* edited by F. Gross. Raven Press, New York. pp. 189–194.

Servizio di Informazione e di Eucazione Sanitaria, Farmoire Communali Italiane (1990): What information for the patient? Large scale pilot study on experimental package inserts giving information on prescribed and over the counter drugs. *Br. Med. J., 301*:1261–1265.

Shays, E. M., and de Chambeau, F. (1984): Harnessing entrepreneurial energy within the corporation. *Management Rev., 73*(9):17–20.

Sheffield, L. J., and Batagol, R. (1985): The creation of therapeutic orphans—or, what have we learnt from the Debendox fiasco? *Med. J. Aust., 143*:143–147.

Shimm, D. S., and Spece, R. G., Jr. (1991): Industry reimbursement for entering patients into clinical trials: Legal and ethical issues. *Ann. Intern. Med., 115*:148–151.

Shrivastava, P., and Guth, W. D. (1985): The culture-strategy grid. In: *Handbook of Business Strategy: 1985/1986 Yearbook,* edited by S. D. Guth. Warren, Gorham & Lamont Inc., Boston. pp. 2-1–2-19.

Smith, M. C. (1975): *Principles of Pharmaceutical Marketing.* (2nd ed.) Lea & Febiger, Philadelphia.

Smith, M. C. (1991): *Pharmaceutical Marketing: Strategy and Cases.* Haworth Press, New York.

Society of Toxicology Pathologists (1986): Society of Toxicological Pathologists' position paper on blinded slide reading. *Toxicol. Pathol., 14*:493–494.

Spilker, B. (1985): Development of orphan drugs. *Trends Pharmacol. Sci., 6*:185–188.

Spilker, B. (1986): The development of orphan drugs: An industry perspective. In: *Orphan Diseases and Orphan Drugs,* edited by I. H. Scheinberg and J. M. Walshe. Manchester University Press, Manchester, UK. pp. 119–134.

Spilker, B. (1987a): Clinical development of drugs that affect the CNS. In: *Psychopharmacology, The Third Generation of Progress: The Emergence of Molecular Biology and Biological Psychiatry,* edited by H. Y. Meltzer. Raven Press, New York.

Spilker, B. (1987b): Clinical evaluation of topical antipruritics and antihistamines. *Models Dermatol., 3*:55–61.

Spilker, B. (1987c): *Guide to Planning and Managing Multiple Clinical Studies.* Raven Press, New York.

Spilker, B. (1990a): Orphan drugs. In: *Comprehensive Medicinal Chemistry,* edited by C. Hansch. Volume 1, Pergamon Press, Oxford, UK. pp. 667–674.

Spilker, B. (1990b): *Quality of Life Assessments in Clinical Trials.* Raven Press, New York.

Spilker, B. (1991): *Guide to Clinical Trials.* Raven Press, New York.

Spilker, B. and Cramer, JA. (1992): *Patient Recruitment in Clinical Trials.* Raven Press, New York.

Spilker, B., and Cuatrecasas, P. (1990): *Inside the Drug Industry.* Prous Science, Barcelona.

Spilker, B., and Schoenfelder, J. (1990): *Presentation of Clinical Data.* Raven Press, NY.

Spilker, B., Wilkins, R. D., and Perkins, J. G. (1984): A novel double-blind method to evaluate topically applied antipruritic drugs. *Curr. Ther. Res.*, 35:593–605.

Spivey, R. N., Lasagna, L., and Trimble, A. G. (1987): New indications for already-approved drugs: Time trends for the new drug application review phase. *Clin. Pharmacol. Ther.*, 41:368–370.

Steiner, R. P. (editor) (1986): *Folk Medicine: The Art and the Science.* American Chemical Society, Washington.

Sterman, A. B. (1989): The changing academic research scene—new opportunities for academic-industry cooperation. *Clin. Res. Practices, Drug Reg. Affairs*, 7(1):51–59.

Stevenson, H. H., and Gumpert, D. E. (1985): The heart of entrepreneurship. *Harvard Bus. Rev.*, 63(2):85–94.

Stringer, R. A., Jr., and Uchenick, J. (1986): *Strategy Traps and How to Avoid Them.* Lexington Books, Lexington, MA.

Strull, W. M., Lo, B., and Charles, G. (1984): Do patients want to participate in medical decision making? *JAMA*, 252:2990–2994.

Stuyt, L. B. J. (1983): Political and governmental influences on decision making in drug research. In: *Decision Making in Drug Research*, edited by F. Gross. Raven Press, New York. pp. 99–107.

Sullman, S. (1992): Regulatory affairs-marketing interface. *Reg. Affair. J.*, 3:269–273.

Tannenbaum, J. (1986): Animal rights: Some guideposts for the veterinarian. *JAVMA*, 188:1258–1263.

Taylor, H., and Voivodas, G. (1987): *The Bristol-Myers Report: Medicine in the Next Century.* Louis Harris and Associates, Inc. [Study 861018], New York.

Thiede, T., Chievitz, E., and Christensen, B. C. (1964): Chlornaphazine as a bladder carcinogen. *Acta Med. Scand.*, 175:721–725.

Tsurumi, Y. (1982): American management has missed the point: The point is management itself. In: *Quality, Productivity, and Competitive Position*, edited by W. E. Deming. Center for Advanced Engineering Study, MIT, Cambridge, MA. pp. 84–86.

Tucker, D. (1984): *The World Health Market: The Future of the Pharmaceutical Industry.* Facts on File Publications, New York.

Unger, S. H. (1987): Computer-aided drug design in the year 2000. *Drug Info. J.*, 21:267–275.

U.S. Congress Office of Technology Assessment (1991): *Biotechnology in a Global Economy.* OTA-BA-494. US Government Printing Office, Washington, DC.

U.S. Department of Health and Human Services, National Institutes of Health (1985): *Guide for the Care and Use of Laboratory Animals.* NIH Publication No. 86-23. Superintendent of Documents, Washington, DC.

U.S. International Trade Commission (1991): *Global competitiveness of U.S. advanced-technology manufacturing industries: Pharmaceuticals.* USITC Publication 2437, Washington, DC. p. vii.

Vance, R. P. (1992): An introduction to the philosophical presupposi-

tions of the animal liberation/rights movement. *JAMA,* 268:1715–1719.

Varrin, R. D., and Kukich, D. S. (1985): Guidelines for industry-sponsored research at universities. *Science,* 227:385–388.

Vickery, D. M. (1985): A medical perspective. *Drug Info. J.,* 19:155–158.

Virts, J. R., and Weston, J. F. (1980): Returns to research and development in the US pharmaceutical industry. *Managerial Decision Economics,* 1:103–111.

Waddell, W. C. (1986): *The Outline of Strategy.* Planning Forum, Oxford, OH.

Walden, A. (1985): The publicly held corporation and the insurability of punitive damages. *Fordham Law Review,* 53(6):1383–1408.

Walker, S. R., and Dayan, A. D. (editors) (1986): *Long-Term Animal Studies: Their Predictive Value for Man.* MTP Press, Lancaster, UK.

Wang, P-H., Hui, M. B. V., Nandy, P., Banerjee, S., Gao, H., et al. (1991): Quantitative structure-activity relationship (QSAR) analysis of the cytotoxicities of aminohydroxyguanidine derivatives and their antiviral activities *in vitro. Pharm. Res.,* 8:1006–1012.

Wardell, W. M., and Lasagna, L. (1975): *Regulation and Drug Development.* American Enterprise Institute for Public Policy Research, Washington, DC.

Watson, T. J., Jr. (1987): The greatest capitalist in history. *Fortune,* 116(Aug. 31):24–35.

Weatherall, D. (1991): Tomorrow's biotechnology. *Br. Med. J.,* 303:1282–1283.

Weintraub, M., and Northington, F. K. (1986): Drugs that wouldn't die. *JAMA,* 255:2327–2328.

Weisblat, D. I., and Stucki, J. C. (1974): Goal-oriented organization at Upjohn. *Res. Manag.,* January:34–37.

Wells, N. (editor) (1983): *The Second Pharmacological Revolution.* Office of Health Economics, London.

White, B. G. (1985): The antiepileptic drug development program: An example of government-industry collaboration. In: *Cooperative Approaches to Research and Development of Orphan Drugs*, edited by M. H. van Woert and E. Chung. Alan R. Liss Inc., New York. pp. 83–93.

Wilkes, M. S., Doblin, B. H., and Shapiro, M. F. (1992): Pharmaceutical advertisements in leading medical journals: Experts' assessments. *Ann. Int. Med.,* 116:912–919.

Worthen, D. B., Burns, J. M., and Rowles, B. (1985): From the drug information centers: Programme integration to support drug information and dissemination. *J. Clin. Hosp. Pharm.,* 10:389–395.

Yingling, G. L. (1992): The impact of regulatory issues in contract negotiations. *Drug Info. J.,* 26:155–158.

Zinder, N. D., and Winn, J. (1984): A partial summary of university-industry relationships in the United States. *Recomb. DNA Tech. Bull.,* 7(1):8–19.

First Author Index

AHC Task Force, '90; 162
Anonymous, '90a; 475
Anonymous, '90b; 667
Anonymous, '87a; 548
Anonymous, '87b; 409
Anonymous, '91; 53
Arkes, '85; 641
Atkinson, '84; 721
Balandrin, '85; 210
Balthasar, '78; 399
Barr, '72; 528, 529
Bartholini, '83; 217, 311
Bennis, '85; 112
Berndtson, '89; 661
Berry, '86; 493
Bezold, '83; 189
Blair, '84; 463
Blattmann, '92; 667
Bloch, '86; 726
Blumenthal, '86; 727, 729
Bohl, '87; 550
Bolton, '84; 112
Britt, '83; 659
Byrne, '87; 296, 740
Cantekin, '90; 164
CIOMS, '90; 515
Clarke, '85; 269
Cleland, '84; 338
Clive, '87; 497
Cloutier, '83; 282
Cohen, '80; 578
Committee on the Use of Animals in Re-
    search, '91; 660
Computer Systems Validation Committee,
    '86; 603
Comroe, '76; 217
Council on Ethical and Judicial Affairs, '92;
    164
Council on Scientific Affairs and Council on
    Ethical and Judicial Affairs, '90; 162
Cuatrecasas, '92; 162
Cuatrecasas, '84; 726
DeBono, '67; 229, 298
DeForest, '88; 161
Deming, '82; 410
Dibner, '90; 263
Dibner, '91; 259
DiMasi, '91; 698
Drews, '85; 545, 750
Drummond, '87; 708
Dudley, '92; 680
Duncan, '80; 227
Evans, '86; 759
Falahee, '83; 269
Faust, '84a,b; 188
Fisher, '83; 578
Fletcher, '78; 269
Fraumeni, '72; 270–271

Frishman, '87; 709
Futterman, '85; 99–100, 102
Geneen, '84; 112
Gluck, '87; 161
Goldscheider, '88; 582
Goldsmith, '86; 193
Gottfried, '83; 277
Grabowski, '82; 545, 750
Grahame-Smith, '84; 275, 276
Grahame-Smith, '87; 555
Gray, '86; 126
Griffin, '86; 271
Griggs, '86; 145, 291
Gunsalus, '89; 733
Guth, '85; 126
Haddad, '92; 677
Haffner, 262
Hayes, '85; 126
Healy, '89; 160
Hermann, '87; 478
Herzberg, '87; 145
Heywood, '81; 269
Heywood, '84; 269, 270
Heywood, '90; 269, 271, 272
Hofer, '78; 394
Human Resources and Intergovernmental
    Relations, '89a,b; 164
Humble, '80; 119
Hurst, '84; 112
Hutt, '91; 626, 667
Inman, '86; 510
IOM Committee on Conflicts of Interest, '91;
    162
Ishikawa, '76; 604
Jick, '85; 513
Joglekar, '86; 545, 750
Johnsson, '84; 269
Joossens, '91; 666
Kahn, '82; 179, 208
Kaitin, '92; 739
Keidel, '84; 115
Kirk, '89; 479
Koberstein, '91; 774
Korda, '87; 181, 578
Kubinyi, '90; 229
Laurence, '84; 269
Lefton, '80; 111
Litchfield, '61; 269
Litchfield, '62; 269
Louis, '89; 161–162
Lumley, '90; 269
Mann, '91; 669
Martin, '85; 110, 112
Maxwell, '90; 731
McCue, '86; 759
McMahon, '87; 764
Meier, '89; 662
Meyer, '87; 293

Michael, '84; 108
Millstein, '87; 250
Morehead, '88; 576, 582
Mossinghoff, xxxi; 302
Nestor, '75; 271
Park, '85, 482
Payer, '88; 194, 201
Pelz, '76; 144
Peters, '83a,b; 290
Pletscher, '83; 222
Porter, '80, '85; 126 for both
Porter, '92; 162
Pradhan, '83; 701, 706
Prentis, '85; 646
Prentis, '86; 541
Price, '85; 727
Raith, '92; 680
Rall, '90; 662
Redwood, '92; 703, 704
Reemtsma, '74; 771
Rennie, '91; 162
Repchinsky, '88; 482
Rodwin, '89; 164
Saltzman, '85; 547
Schein, '70; 229, 269
Schepartz, '85; 736
Scherer, '70; 402
Schnee, '78; 18, 748
Schwartzman, '76; 208
Seidl, '83; 541, 646, 647
Servizio di Informazione, '90; 669
Shays, '84; 112
Sheffield, '85; 271, 298
Shimm, '91; 164
Shrivastava, '85; 17
Smith, '75; 553
Smith, '91; 548, 553
Society of Toxicology Pathologists, '86; 269
Spilker, '84; 359
Spilker, '85; 354
Spilker, '86; 354
Spilker, '87a; 506
Spilker, '87b; 281
Spilker, '90a; 354
Spilker, '90b; 706
Spilker, '91; 3, 20, 40, 108, 122, 182, 195,
    235, 245, 252, 267, 268, 293, 340, 343,
    347, 430, 441, 497, 500, 510, 517, 526,
    535, 540, 555, 588, 629, 642, 645, 706,
    709, 717, 748, 758
Spilker, '92; 508
Spilker and Cuatrecasas, '90; 691, 774
Spilker and Schoenfelder, '90; 457
Spivey, '87; 738
Steiner, '86; 210
Sterman, '89; 722
Stevenson, '85; 112
Stringer, '86; 123, 126

Strull, '84; 665–666
Stuyt, '83; 736
Sullman, '92; 706
Tannenbaum, '86; 662
Taylor, '87; 188
Thiede, '64; 270–271
Tsurumi, '82; 112
Tucker, '84; 553
Unger, '87; 188, 302
US Congress Office of Technology Assessment, '91; 49, 257, 263, 619

US Dept. HHS, '85; 659
US-ITC, '91; 8
Vance, '92; 662
Varrin, '85; 726
Vickery, '85; 565, 683
Virts, '80; 545, 750
Waddell, '86; 126
Walden, '85; 832
Walker, '86; 498
Wang, '91; 229
Wardell, '75; 743

Watson, '87; 327
Weatherall, '91; 257, 262
Weintraub, '86; 298
Weisblat, '74; 29, 310
Wells, '83; 188, 189
White, '85; 736
Wilkes, '92; 630
Worthen, '85; 475
Yingling, '92; 624
Zinder, '84; 285

Subject Index

A

Abbott Laboratories
  promotion, 54
  sales by product/value, 543
Academia, technology transfer from
  benefits of, 733, 734
  concepts as, 732
  examples of, 733
  licensing as, 732, 733, 734
  myths of, 731
  patents, 732
  problems in, 733–734
  success of process, 732
Academic freedom, 52
Academicians
  attitude to pharmaceutical companies,
    732–733
  as consultants, 725
  medicine promotion to, 561
  medicine samples to, 729
  as researchers in pharmaceutical company,
    725
  sabbatical periods at company, 725
  as senior managers, 139–140
  view of pharmaceutical industry, 10
Academic institutions, see also Company-ac-
    ademic alliances
  company alliances, 51–53, 721–729
  competition for funds/grants, 192–193
  government support of, 192–193
  industry established clinical units in, 726
  industry-sponsored symposia at, 725–726
  pharmaceutical industry support of,
    192–193, 721
  scientific freedom in, 205
  as source & medicine discovery, 217,
    722–723
Acquisitions, corporate, see also Mergers
  agreements in, 56–57
  definition of, 47
  financial evaluations in, 56
Adverse reactions
  in animal safety testing, 268–269
  in animals vs. humans, 269
  in clinical trials, 503
  collecting data, 516
  extrapolating data on, 280–281
  identifying, 510
  labeling information on, 250, 513, 515
  legal aspects, 627
  of major medicines, 270
  marketing and, 440
  medicine safety and, 510
  posing questions in, 503
  in postmarketing studies, 512, 513, 514
  predictabilty of, 269–270
  quality-of-life and, 517–519
  regulatory reporting, 515
  true incidence of, 513, 514
Advertising

costs of, 700
  issues in, 555
  of prescription medicines, 555–556
  review by medical staff, 453–454
  television use in, 555
Africa, 210, 277
Aging population
  medicines for, 192
Alliances, see also Strategic alliances, Com-
    pany-academic alliances of biotech-
    nology and pharmaceutical compa-
    nies, 263
Allocation of resources, see Resource
    allocation
American versus English, 4
American Home Products
  licensing, 53
Analytical development
  of biologicals, 534
  of biossays, 534
  degradation products identification,
    533–534
  functions of, 531
  impurity characterization, 533
  purity of product and, 533
Analytical methods
  costs of, 45
  quality of, 44–45
Animal models
  batteries of, development of, 232–233
  establishing new, 281
  evaluating compounds in, 232–233
  extrapolation of results in, 220
  of human disease, 220
  intraspecies effects, 270, 271
  in medicine discovery, 236
  patents on, 619
  purposes of, 231
  quality standards in, 43
  types of, 231
  validating new models, 231–232
Animals
  definitions of, 657, 658
  humans, distinctions, 657, 658
Animal safety data, extrapolating
  adverse reactions and, 268, 269–270
  benefit-to-risk balance in, 271
  between species, 267–268
  effects on losing useful medicines, 268,
    270–271
  false-negatives, 270
  false-positives, 269
  to humans, 268–269, 270–272, 280–281
  principles for, 271–272
  reliability of, 269–270
  species effects, 270
Animal testing
  alternatives, 661
  animal care committees and, 659–660
  animal use committees, 659–660

ethical issues in, 660–661, 662
  guidelines for, 659
  housing issues in, 662
  justification, 657–658
  kinds of animals in, 661
  laws/regulations on, 659
  licensing of personnel, 182, 659, 660
  minimize suffering in, 660, 661
  politics of, 662–663
  principles of, 661–662
  protocols of animal use, 660
  reducing numbers of animals used,
    660–661, 662
Antiepileptic drug
  characteristics of ideal, 282
Antipruritics, topical
  ideal clinical evaluation method for, 281
Association of the British Pharmaceutical
    Industry, 548
Astra
  Merck joint venture, 105
Audits, See also GCP, GMP
  clinical, 158, 293
  of research/development, 293
  of standards, 45
Australia, 67
Ayerst
  sales by product/value, 542

B

Backup medicines
  advantages of, 674
  description of, 674
BASF
  licensing, 53
Basic research
  in academic institutions, 217
  applied research differences, 216–317
  organization of, 313–315
  types of, 217
Bayer
  licensing, 53
Benefit-to-risk-ratio
  data evaluation, 281–281
  informing patients, 765
  medicine costs and, 554
  medicine development and, 20, 168
  medicine safety and, 271, 281–282, 509
  in OTC medicines, 449, 684
  overall concept, 281–282
  package inserts, 669
  postmarketing appraisal, 587
  in toxicity studies, 271
Beta receptor antagonists
  brand advantages, 709
  clinical profile of, 709
  cost, 554
  ICI Holdings development, 228–229
  as "me-too" medicines, 709
  structure-activity studies, 228–229

Biological levels, 218
Biotechnology
 antigenic issues, 266
 categories of medicines from, 258
 cells as factories, 259–261, 265
 company characteristics, 258, 259, 264
 company types, 258
 definitions, 257
 derived medicines, 219–220
 development history, 257–258
 ethical uses, 262, 265
 future developments in, 262
 gene splicing in, 259, 260, 261
 international competition, 263
 manufacturing issues, 264–265
 medicine delivery issues in, 262
 medicine discovery and, 219–220, 257,
  258, 264
 methodologies used in, 259–261
 patent issues in, 262–263, 619
 pharmaceutical companies and, 263–264
 plant use in, 261
 preparation techniques, 220
 products/processes in, 258
 rational, 261
 recombinant DNA process, 260, 261
 regulatory concerns, 266
 scale up costs, 265–266
 technical issues in, 264
 techniques used in, 261
 trends in, 261–262
Biotechnology products
 patenting of, 619
 toxicity testing, 496
Board of directors
 facilitating communication, 435–436
 knowledge required, 81, 112
 members, 112
 organizational issues, 86
Boehringer Ingleheim Corp.
 physicians clinical exposure in, 335
 sales by product/value, 544
Boots Pharmaceuticals, 751
 licensing, 53
Boston Collaborative Drug Surveillance Program, 726
Brainstorming
 focusing, 292
 stimulating innovation, 292
Breakdown products, see Degradation
  products
Bristol Laboratories
 sales by product/value, 543
Budgets, see also Resource allocation
 purposes of, 640
Burroughs Welcome Co.
 academicians ideas for, 722–723
 entrepreneurship in, 112
 licensing offers to, 570
 6MP, improving activity of, 209
 physicians clinical exposure in, 335
 promotion, 54
 research in, 112, 209
 Phase III trials in, 511
 philanthropic activities of, 725
 regulatory strategies of, 737
 sales by product/value, 543
Business focus, 73–76, 122

C
Calendars, 77, 79–80
Canada, 513, 621, 688, 744
Carcinogenicity studies, see also Toxicology
 extrapolating to humans, 271
 long-term, 494, 497
Career opportunities, 729, 330
"Catch-22" situation, 494–495,
  535–537, 620
Cells
 knowledge about, 274–275
Center for the Study of Medicine Development, 409
Centre for Medicines Research, 409
Cerudase, production costs, 699
Charitable contributions, see Philanthropic
  groups
Chief executive officer, CEO
 characteristics of wise, 139
 in crisis management, 168, 169, 170
 in developing company strategies, 122
 in health care issues, 693
 in licensing negotiations, 579
China, 210
Ciba Pharmaceutical Co.
 sales by product/value, 543
Clinical development, see also Preclinical
  studies
 control of, 247–248
 leadership in, 246
 marketing and, 246–247
 medical department activities in, 248
 regulatory affairs department in, 249
 technical development department in, 249
 testing for other disease effects, 248–249
 time for, 246–247
 toxicology and, 247
 transition from preclinical, 246–247
Clinical goals
 in portfolio analysis, 371, 373
 probability of achieving, 371, 373
Clinical indications
 categories of, 500
 choosing for clinical trial, 500–502
 in medicine development, 500
Clinically significant
 statistical significance and, 511
Clinical studies (see Clinical trials)
Clinical studies, Phase IV (see also Postmarketing studies)
 staffing for, 152
Clinical Trial Exemption, 533
Clinical trials
 adverse reactions and, 503
 allocating medicine for, 535
 audits of, 293
 budgets for, 645
 clinical indications and, 500–502
 computer tracking of, 466
 conflicts of interest and, 164
 contracting of, 322–323
 country of registration and, 742
 data management, 485–486, 487
 defined, 739
 dosage form in, 503, 506
 due process and, 739–740
 facilitating, 505
 for international development, 714, 718

GCP guidelines for, 293
 ideal criteria for, 281
 in academic institutions, 725
 in medicine development pipe-line, 24–25,
  244
 issues in, 505–508
 labeling in, 503
 Lasagna's law in, 508
 legal issues, 626–627
 levels of, 26, 500, 501
 numbers of questions asked in, 502–503
 patient quotas by country, 714
 patients in, 164, 505–508
 phases of, 244
 planning and tracking, 505, 506
 posing questions in, 502
 priority of, 150
 protocols for, 505–506
 quality of, 718
 resources for, 150–151, 152
 staffing for, 149–152
 stages in, 24–25, 150–151
 standards for, 41, 42
 statistics in, 490–491
 time required for, 26
 titrating dosage in, 508–509
 trial site numbers, 149–150
 trial design, 503–505
 types, 500
Clinical trials, postmarketing see Postmarketing clinical trials
Clinicians, see Physicians
Collaboration
 with academic institutions, 41, 721–729
 financial evaluation for, 56
 partner choice for, 56
Collaboration, between companies, see also
  Alliances, Licensing
 agreements, 752
 competition and, 747
 joint ventures, 751–752
 licensing, 751
 types, 751
Comarketing
 advantage/disadvantages, 53
 defined, 53
 examples of, 53
Combination medicine, 676
Commercial value
 forecasting, 370–371
 image value and, 2
 of a medicine, 1, 2, 369
 in portfolio analysis, 370–371, 379, 380,
  381
 probability of success and, 379
 as productivity measure of R&D, 405,
  407, 408
Committee on Safety of Medicines, 512, 740
Common sense, 2–3
Communication, see also Information
 audience for, 136–137
 between scientists, 295
 of committee conclusions, 132–133
 of company strategies, 125, 183
 direction of flow, 133
 emotion in, 136
 four parts of, 127
 improving, 109, 135–138, 294, 295

individuals dialogue pointers, 135
learning to listen, 127
liaison between departments, 147–148, 294
of marketing priorities, 441, 446
methods for, 135–136
nonscientist to scientist, 108
policy on, 130–131
revolution in, 195
role of physicians in, 333
scientist to nonscientist, 132
signs of problems in, 133–135
speakers organization, 137–138
styles, 132
techniques to influence this, 109
types of problems in, 134–135
written, 132
written vs. spoken, 136–137
Communication barriers
assessing, 131
bureaucratic separation of, 131
cultural separation, 128
hierarchical separation, 129–130
models illustrating problems, 130, 131,
133, 134, 135, 136
person's hidden agenda, 127–128, 446
poor listening skills, 128
professional training, 128, 422, 445
Companies, *see below and* Multinational
companies, Pharmaceutical
companies
Company-academic alliances
academic freedom and, 42, 727
academic institution benefits in, 51, 721,
723, 733
advantages of, 727, 733, 734
for clinical evaluation, 725
company benefits in, 51, 723
confidentiality of data in, 52, 728
conflicts of interest, 160–162
contract services and, 729
duration of, 729
examples of, 722, 733
graduate students and, 729
guidelines for, 726–727
indirect interaction and, 722, 724
intellectual property rights, 52, 728
issues in, 52–53, 727, 728, 729
levels of interaction, 722, 723, 729
medicine discovery, 217
medicine development, 731
patent issues and, 53, 729
perception of, 733
rationale for, 721–722
research, 723–725
scale of, 729
secrecy and, 732
transferring discoveries, 52–53, 728,
731–734
types of alliances, 722, 725
university concerns, 53, 728
Company environment, *see also* Institutional
memory
atmosphere, 417
culture, 117, 173–174
employee support services, 118
in future, 188–189
milieu, 287
mutual respect/trust, 117

politics, 215
positive culture, 117–118
positive goals, 117
Company major changes
agreement on change, 120
approach to, 120
evaluation of changes, 121–122
schematic of steps in, 121
Compatability of medicines, 528
Competition, between companies
analysis of, 748–749
assessing, in project portfolio, 375, 379, 382
biotechnology, 263
collaboration and, 747
concept of, 747
foreign-based, 750–751
in marketing, 748
in medicine development, 17, 18, 19, 748,
749–750
in medicine discovery, 748
maturity of technology and, 382
mergers and, 751
obtaining information, 462
professional meetings, information and,
750
profits and, 750
R&D and, 189
in research-based companies, 750
sources of information on, 462, 749
success/failure and, 750
Computer assisted New Drug Application
(CANDA), 588, 739
Computer services
artificial intelligence systems, 488
centralized/decentralized, 103
data management and, 485, 490
developing a data base, 465
integrated systems of, 488–490
for product information, 475, 478
Computers
clinical trial tracking by, 466
data base development, 465
electronic publishing and, 466–468
life cycle of, 466
R&D uses, 465
validation issues, 466
Confidentiality of data, 52, 620–621
Conflict of interest
academic, 726
actual, 155
avoiding, 154–155, 164–165
between company and
external groups, 160
external service provider, 158–160
government agencies, 156
patient in clinical trial, 164
university, 160–161
categorization of, 154
consultation and, 162–163
defined, 153–155
disclosure form, 163
examples of, 153–155, 156, 157–164
factors creating, 155–156
financial gain and, 155–156
government response to, 164
journal publications and, 162
misconduct/fraud and, 160

models of influences on individuals, 157,
158, 159
perceived, 155
physician referral and, 164
potential, 155
in production, 601
in professional opinion, 164
public interest groups, 766
relatives/friends and, 164
resolving, 157
schematic of potential sources of, 155
sources of information on, 161–162
spectrum of, 154
types of conflicts, 156–157
university policies on, 160–162
within company, 157–158
Consultants
approach of, 286
conflicts of interest and, 154, 155, 158,
162–163
contracting and, 322
in crisis management, 169–170
golden rules for, 255
hiring cautions, 285–286
in licensing, 572
to management, 285
in personnel issues, 141
in R&D evaluation, 240, 295
types, 285
Consumer Groups
attitudes, 80
industry response to, 766
pharmacopolitical issues of, 62–63
view of the pharmaceutical industry, 10–11
in toxicology issues, 662
Contracting/Contractors
choosing, 322–323
conflicts of interest and, 158–159
consultants and, 322
legal activities in, 624
locating, 322
in marketing/clinical departments,
425–426
medicine development, 322–323
motivation for, 322, 328
product information service, 479
references for, 323
types of, 624
understaffing and, 140, 141
Copromotion
advantages of, 54
coordination in, 55
defined, 54
examples of, 54
ideal partner for, 54, 55
indications for, 54
issues in, 55
sources of partner for, 55
worldwide, 56
Core team, *see* Medicine discovery
Corporate financial issues
accounting procedures, 642
comparing financial status of companies,
637, 638
corporate objectives and, 638
cost-effectiveness data, 642
financial projections and, 638–639
questionable projects and, 641

Corporate financial issues (contd.)
resource allocation, 641–642
sales and, 637, 638
sources of financing, 639–640
transfer pricing, 641–642
Corporate management, see also
Management
approaches to, 115–120
bias and, 108
boards of directors and, 112
characteristics of, 112, 113
communications in, 108–109
creating an ideal environment, 117–118
defining company objectives, 122
developing strategies, 122–125
dividing R&D between sites, 109
entrepreneurship in, 112
establishing priorities, 125
evaluating medical claims, 108–109
fads/fashions in, 118
functions of, 116
individual responsibilities and, 116
knowledge required, 81
leadership evaluation in, 110–111, 112
liaison between divisions, 147–148
long-range planning, 125–126
in making major company changes,
120–122
medical-marketing interface, 421–427
personnel requirements for, 119
quality of, 115–116
R&D strategies, 119–120
strategic planning, 125
of subsidiaries, 116–117
who's in charge, 118–119
Corporate organization
business-matrix model, 99, 100
business oriented-function model for, 99
centralization/decentralization in, 103
company size and, 104–106
developmental patterns of, 100, 102
distribution of service organzations in,
103–104
factors influencing, 99–100
function oriented model for, 96, 97
hierarchical vs. flow management in,
101–102
issues in organizing, 96, 101–104
matrix model for, 98–99
of multinational companies, 102–103
perspectives on, 95–96
product oriented model, 97–98
schematics of models for, 97, 98, 99, 100,
101, 102
subsidiaries and, 102
CO-START, 718
Cost
analysis, 374–375
concerns regarding, 42
of health care, 42
Cost-benefit analysis, 554, 707
Cost-risk ratio, 554
Costs
administrative, 700–701
advertising/promoting, 700
changing, 532–533
containment, 195

of distribution, 699
of education, 700
legal, 700
licensing, 700
lost opportunity, 701
of manufacturing facilities, 699
marketing, 699–700
of medical treatment, 553–554
of medicine development, 18,
374–375, 532–533, 698
of patents, 698–699
of research, 698
transfer costs, 701
Counterfeiting, 561
Courses, see Education
Creativity
core group of, 331
cultivating, 202–203, 239–240
identification of, 331
recognition of, 205
in scientists, 205, 229, 237, 277, 278, 291,
331
stimulating, 291, 331
Crisis
causes of, 167
in corporate crisis, 167, 168
examples of crises, 168
external groups in, 169
implication of, 170, 171
international strategy for, 172
prevention, 170–171
product crises, 167, 168
ripple effect, 171
types of crises, 167–168
Crisis management
consult experts, 169–170
focused approach in, 168–169
message in, 168–169
news media in, 169–170
proactive response in, 170–172
spokesperson in, 169
task force formation, 168
Criteria, see also Standards and Medicine
development, criteria for
for developing a medicine, 246,
357–364, 396–397
in priority setting, 396–397
Critical mass
in academia, 727
defined, 142
personnel needs for, 48, 142
research and development, 311–313
Customers, see also Patients, Physicians
HMO's as, 550
identifying, 550
identifying needs of, 550–551
of prescription medicines, 559–561

D

Data bases
hospital, 726
integration, 488–489
management system, 465
Data, evaluation, interpretation
commercial, by marketing, 452–453
commercial, by R&D, 452–453
data extrapolation and, 279–280
expectations and, 278

ideal medicine and, 281, 282
reaching conclusions, 279
risk benefits of medicine and, 281–282
traps, pitfalls in thinking and, 278–279
unexpected results, 278
Data extrapolation, see also Animal safety
data extrapolation
animal to animal, 280
of animal safety, 267–272, 280
animals to humans, 268–269, 280–281
human to human, 281
interpretation and, 279–280
purposes of, 280
types of extraplolation, 267–268
Data management
choosing systems, 486–487
data bases and, 512–513
defined, 485
integrated system use in, 488–490
issues in, 486, 487–490
new system problems, 487
policies regarding, 487–488
in postmarketing studies, 512–513
record linkage and, 513
research areas for, 485–486
Deadlines, 77, 179, 319
Degradation products
standards for, 44
Department of Health (UK), 201
Department of Veteran's Affairs, DVA
medicine pricing-cost equation for, 689
Developing new medicines, medical and
marketing in,
communication in, 446
enhancing medical value, 441–443
factors for consideration, 440
marketing needs/wants, 439–440
medical needs/wants, 440
minimal standards for new, 440
morality issues in 449–450
priority setting, 440–441
problems between departments, 445–446
profile of new medicine, 439–440
resource allocation, 441, 442
targeting a market, 458
tracking progress, 443
Development, see Medicine development
Diazepam
metabolites, 221
new medicines derived from, 221
Digoxin therapy
actions of, 276
Discovery, see Medicine discovery
Disease
culture of country and, 201, 277
evolution of, 275–276
factors influencing outbreak, 276–277
natural history of, 277
rare, 202
syphilis as, 277
tuberculosis as, 277
Dissolution studies
apparatus for, 528, 529
factors in, 528
Dista Products Co.
sales by product/value, 543
Distribution
costs of, 699

Documents
   access to, 473
   central depository for, 470–471
   coding for retrieval, 472–473
   for international development, 718
   methods for obtaining, 470–472
   storage form of, 470
   stored how-long, 470
   system for decreasing storage, 473
   which to store, 470
Dosage form
   in clinical trials, 503, 506
   determining, 528
   planning/tracking, 506
Dose-response relationships, 255, 496
Drug, see also Medicine
Drug, Chemical, and Allied Trades Associa-
       tion, DCAT, 755
Drug, defined, 273
Drug lag
   FDA position on, 765, 766
   reasons for, 765–766
Duplication of efforts
   unecessary, 117, 236
   worthwhile, 117, 236
Dupont, 190, 749
   Merck joint venture, 104–105
   Research relationship, 722
Duration of medicine action
   increasing, 530–531
   objectives in, 530–531

E
Eastman Kodak, 190, 749
Education
   cost of, 700
   in crisis, 171
   of employees, 143–144
   of health care professionals, 700
   in industry-academic alliances, 729, 732
   by legal department, 627, 633–634
   of outside groups, 67
   of physicians, 331–332
   of public, 693–695
   of sales representatives, 451
   of scientists, 332
   of senior executives, 170
Efficacy, see also Medical value
   defined, 295
   determining in clinical trials, 505
   establishing, 368–369
   in OTC medicines, 449
   pilot trials of, 505
   terminating medicine for lack of, 541–542
   weak evidence for, 250
Efficiency, increasing see also Productivity
   analysis paralysis and, 296
   communication and, 295
   effectiveness and, 295
   methods for, 294
   of R&D, 294–298
Electronic publishing
   applications/advantages for, 466–468
   as interactive information system, 467–468
   regulatory submissions by, 466–467
Eli Lilly and Co.
   sales of lead products, 542, 763
Emperors' New Clothes Syndrome, 180, 517
Employees, see also Personnel

   attitudes of, 146
   burnout, 141
   characteristics, good, 142–143
   company support of, 762, 764
   critical mass of, 142
   development courses for, 143–144
   difficult, 146–147
   increasing/decreasing numbers of,
       105–106
   judgement, 184
   legal activities of, 625
   morale, 92
   motivating, 144–145
   orientation, 143
   outside activities of, 764
   productivity of, 145–146
   support services for, 118
   training of, 143–144
   working environment for, 117–118
Entrepreneurship
   characteristics in, 112
   in scientists, 112
Environmental impact
   EPA and, 736
   legal issues in, 625–626
   NDA requirements for, 44
   waste minimization and, 608
Environmental Protection Agency, EPA
   functions of, 736
Ethical Issues, see also Conflicts-of-interest
   in animal testing, 660–661, 662
   in biotechnology industry, 266
   in genetic engineering, 262
   in safety testing, 268
Ethics Committee, see Institutional Review
       Board
European Economic Community, EEC
   GCP guidelines of, 293
   mutaganicity testing required by, 498
   patent issues, 262
   patient package inserts and, 665, 667
   pricing strategies in, 561
   standards for new medicine and, 67, 191
European Federation of Pharmaceutical In-
       dustries' Association, 755
Experts, see also Consultants, 119
Expert report, 158
Extrapolation, see Data extrapolation

F
Facts, 274
False positive results, 269
False negative results, 270
Fat development, 182–185, 246, 587
Financial evaluation
   for acquisitions/mergers, 56
Financial issues, see also Corporate financial
       issues, R&D budget/expenditures
   budgets, purpose of, 640
   forecasts and, 639, 640
Folk remedies, 210
   in licensing agreements, 576–578
   modeling of, 576–577, 639
   net income, change in time, 384
   profits, 384, 389, 390, 391
   in project portfolio analysis, 383–384, 388,
       389, 390, 391, 392
   risk as, 577–578, 638
   ROI and, 384, 388

   sales/profits, 389, 390, 391
   sources of, 639
   value change in time, 384, 389, 390
Environmental Impact Analyses, 44
Food, Drug, and Cosmetic Act, 1938
   influence on medicine development, 22–25
   pharmacopolitics and, 60
   reason for passage, 196
   requirements for prescriptions, 684
Food and Drug Administration, FDA
   advisory committees, 744
   approval delays, 741–742
   biotechnology and, 258
   company relations with, 174, 590–591
   drug lag and, 765–766
   formulation approval, 526
   functions of, 736
   as information source, 409
   medicine development time filing, 24, 245
   medicine safety evaluation, 511
   mission, 192
   new medicine and, 769–770
   Office of Orphan Products Development,
       262
   OTC medicines and, 684, 685
   as partner in development, 737
   policy on optical purity, 526
   restrictions on physicians, 24
   preparing for meeting with, 740
   priority of applications and, 743
   time for approval as productivity measure,
       405, 406
   time for filing with, 588
   United Kingdom relations and, 182
Formularies
   prescriptions and, 687–688
Formulary Committees, 63, 215, 518
Formulation
   choosing, 526
   dosage form and, 528–529
   final, 529
   issues in, 530
   number of, 528
France, 201, 744
Fraud
   in science, 161, 201
Freedom of Information Act, 621
Functional organization, see Organizational
       models
Future trends in pharmaceutical industry
   academic environment and, 192–193
   areas of research in, 189–190
   definitional issues, 300
   difficulties in predicting, 188
   environment for, 189
   evolution in, 189
   factors influencing, 195–196
   health care changes and, 193–195
   medicine tampering and, 191
   methods to study the, 300
   OTC medicines and, 191
   population aging and, 192
   predicting, 301–303
   pressure on R&D, 190
   recombinant DNA and, 188
   regulation, public pressure for, 192
   regulatory environment and,
       190–191, 192

Future trends in pharmaceutical industry (*contd.*)
    revolution in, 188–189
    social/political environment, 191–192
    time frame of, 188

G

Geigy Pharmaceuticals
    sales by product/value, 544
Gene splicing, 259, 260, 261
General Electric
    planning grid of business strength, 394
Generic medicines
    company susceptibility to, 175, 176
    demonstrating differences in, 676
    developing potential, 677
    government contracts and, 673–674
    HMO's and, 193
    manufacturing, 675
    patent expiration and, 673–674, 675
    trade association for, 755
Generic Pharmaceutical Manufacturers Association, 755
Genetic engineering
    see Biotechnology
Genetic therapy, principals of, 261–262
Germany, 201, 647, 742
Glaxo, Inc.
    lobbying, 746
    philanthropic activities of, 725
    promotion, 54
    ranitidine development, 228
    research relationship, 722
    research, organization, 96
    sales by product/value, 543
    staff, 96
Golden rules
    agreements between companies, 752
    clinical trials, 718
    company policies, 769
    confidentiality of data, 728
    conflicts of interest, 164
    consultants, 255
    decreasing amount of materials stored, 473
    extrapolation of data, 271–272
    focus areas, 76
    implementation, 256
    information technology, 473–474
    legal, 635
    licensing, 583
    manufacturing, 600
    medicine development, 251–256
    medicine discovery, 235–241
    patents, 621
    plans, 252–254
    portfolio, 254
    project management, 347
    R and D director, 76
    regulatory submissions, 255
    retaining documents, 470
    staffing, 149–152, 254
    strategies, 252–254
    success factors, 76, 81
    systems, 252–254
    values, 254–255
    versus standards, 40

Good Clinical Practice, GCP
    for clinical trials, xxix, 293
    compliance with, 586, 591, 592
    of EEC, 293
    standards, 42
Good Manufacturing Practice, GMP
    compliance with, 586
    quality assurance and, 600, 602
Government agencies, *see also* specific agency
    Department of Veterans Affairs, 689
    Drug Enforcement Agency, 736
    EPA as, 736
    Federal Trade Commission, 556, 736
    interaction with industry, 735–737
    National Institutes of Health, 266
    Office of Orphan Products Development, 262
    OSHA as, 736
    Patent and Trademark office, 735
    pharmaceutical industry interaction, 735–736
    United States Post Office, 736–737
Government executives
    as senior company managers, 139–140

H

Headcount, *see* Employees, Personnel
Health care
    cost containment and, 193, 195
    in Europe, 194
    evolution of, 193
    factors influencing future, 194–195
    future environment of, 193–195
    generics and, 194
    HMO's and, 193
    OTC and, 194
    physician oversupply and, 194
    PPO's and, 193
    in United States, 193–194
Health maintenance organizations, HMO's
    health care environment and, 193
    industry medicine studies and, 726
    pharmaceutical industry trends and, 190
Health policy
    organizational issues, 434, 692, 764
    today, 193
Health professionals
    categories of, 757
    correspondance with, 758
    improving relations with, 759
    industry interaction with, 757–759
    investigational medicine problems, 758–759
    media events targeted to, 773–774
    medical-marketing education, 451–452
    problems reported by, 758
    product information and, 476–481
    questions regarding products, 476–477
Hierarchies, in pharmaceutical companies, *see also* Line, Matrix management
Histamine receptor antagonists
    new medicine discoveries, 227–228
    structure-activity studies of, 227–228
Hoechst-Roussel Pharmaceuticals, Inc.
    investigational medicine termination, 541
    research relationship, 722
    sales by product/value, 544
Human testing

    advancing compound to, 296
    animal data extrapolation, 268–272
    patient recruitment, 507, 508
    preliminary testing before, 235
    timing of, 509
    titrating patients in, 508–509
    variability of, 505
Hype, internal, in medicine development
    description of, 179–180
    in medicine development, 179–180
    minimizing importance of, 180
    reasons for, 180

I

ICI Holdings
    licensing, 53
    tiotidine development, 228
Image
    of company, 75–76
    value of a medicine, 2
Impurities
    standards for, 44
Individualists
    negative/positive influences of, 115
Industry, *see* Company.
Information, *see also* Communication
    access to, 464, 468–469
    accuracy of, 463, 469
    analysis, 464
    brochures and, 763
    communicating, 468
    competitive intelligence as, 462, 749–750
    dissemination of, 109
    flow, 462–464
    flow in R&D, 318–319
    indexing of, 464–465
    in-house offering of, 464–465
    for patients, 549, 763–764
    product related, 476–481, 763–764
    obtaining, 70, 462
    organizing, 463
    prioritizing, 465
    quality of, 465
    questions on products and, 476–477
    reducing gossip/rumors, 109
    retrieval, 463–464
    reliability of, 749
    storing, 463, 470
    sources of, 477
    types, 461–462
Information services
    creation, 468
    documents and, 470–473
    functions of, 249, 468–469
    goals of, 468
    information manager in, 468–470
    interactive computer system in, 467–468
    management challenges, 474
    potential pitfalls, 469–470
    product information groups as, 475–481
    toll-free telephone use, 481, 482
Information technology
    computer systems, 465–468
    electronic publishing, 466–468
    financial issues, 473
    future development, 474
    golden rules of, 473–474

Innovation
cultivation of, 202–203, 331
defined/described, 402–403
economics and, 200–201
factors inhibiting, 202–203
licensing strategy for, 76
matrix of factors influencing, 199–200
measure of, 402
medicine discovery and, 284
myths about, 290–291
need of, 67
patents and, 200–201
process of, 402
value of, 403
Innovation, stimulating
brainstorming, 292
communication and, 294
consultants and, 285–286
creativity and, 291, 292
departmental walls and, 294
environment and, 284–285, 287–288, 291
golden rules for, 239–240
intellectual interaction and, 292
management and, 284, 285, 287, 292–294
nonproductive tangents minimizing, 288–290
operating procedures for, 292–294
personnel issues, 284–285
retreats and, 293, 292
targeting, 291
task force in, 286–287
Institutional Culture, see Company Environment, Institutional Memory
Institutional Memory
components of, 69–70
creation/promotion of, 71
defined, 69
lessons, 70
tangible items of, 70–71
uses of, 70
value of, 70, 71
Institutional Review Boards, IRBs
clinical audits and, 293
for profit, 160
function, xxix
Insurance companies, see Third Party Payers
Intercontinental Medical Statistics (IMS), 544, 547
Integrated data systems
developing, 489
issues in, 489–490
levels of, 488–489
Intellectual property rights, see Licensing
Interferon
commercial development of 26–27
International Federation of Pharmaceutical Manufacturers Associations, 755
International medicine-development, see also Multinational companies
choice of medicine for, 718
clinical programs for, 714, 718
clinical trials for, 714
discovery/development model for, 713
goals of, 711
marketing models for, 711–712, 713
medicine development styles in, 717
plan, 253
priorities in, 717

product labeling, 717–718
project team, models for, 714–717
reviewing projects, 717
sociopolitical issues, 717
International operations
centralized/decentralized, 88–90
organization, choice of, 92–93
organizational changes in, 91
organizational models for, 88–90, 91
organizational schematics, 85, 88, 90
organizational structure, 85, 86
productivity, measures of, 91–92
research in, 87, 93
scope of, 93
staff morale, 92
as subsidiary, 85, 86–88, 89, 90–91
Interpretations, 273–282, 464, 651
Inventory
issues in, 607, 611
just-in-time concept in, 607
Investigational medicine projects, portfolio analysis, steps in (see also Portfolio analysis)
bar graph use in, 371, 372, 373
clinical goals probability of achieving, 371, 373
commercial parameters in, 379, 380, 381
competitive position and, 379, 382, 386
cost of development, 374–375
danger of creating, 398
evaluating balance of projects, step three, 376–395
evaluating each project, step two, 371–376
financial analysis of, 383–384, 388, 389, 390, 391, 392, 396
focus of, 366
INDs filed, 383, 385
interpretation, step four, 395–396
market attractiveness and, 374, 386
marketing forecasts for, 455
market share and, 381
market strength and, 382
mathematical models of, 397–398
maturity of technology and, 382
medical parameters in, 379, 382
modification of company on basis of, 396
NCEs in, 367, 373, 385
NDA filings, 383, 384, 387
pitfalls of, 399
priming and, 397
priorities in, 396–397
problems for created by health professionals, 758–759
product liability for, 631–632
project uniqueness and, 375
quality assurance in, 600
regulatory issues, 383, 384, 385, 386, 387, 388
regulatory staff assigned, 383, 386
research costs and, 392
resource allocation, 376–379, 396
return on investment, 384, 388
risk assessment, 375, 378
sales/profits, 389, 395
staffing, 372, 373–374, 376, 398
success rate of projects, 395
technical goals, probability of achieving, 373, 379, 380

termination reasons, 541–542
therapeutic areas and, 398
track record, presentation of, 373
using results, step five, 396
visual grids for presentation, 384–387, 395
Investigational New-Drug application, IND
clinical audits and, 293
cost of generating, 384
filing time for, 26, 245, 385
matrix organization for, 338, 339–340
numbers filed, 385
preparation of, 587
in project portfolio analysis, 383, 385, 387

J
Japan, 43, 133, 194, 527, 567, 616, 744
Johnson and Johnson
Merck alliance, 105
Joint ventures
advantages of, 50
comarketing, 53–56
factors to consider in, 50
factors for evaluation, 51, 57
marketing in, 51
in medicine development, 178–1798
motivation for, 59, 751–752
production in, 51
research/development, 50–51

K
Kefauver-Harris amendments, 1962
to Food, Drug and Cosmetic Act of 1938
influence on medicine development, 22–25
pharmacopolitics and, 60, 196, 766

L
Labeling
adding adverse reactions, 515
class, 250, 668
conference, 741
creating, 589
for international market, 717–718
market forecasts and, 589
for new medicines, 588–589
for new OTCs, 684
regulatory filings, 588–589
standard for, 250
uniformity in, 250
Lasagna's law
recruitment of patients for trials and, 508
Laws
defined, 37
implementation of, 37
regulations/guidelines relations, 36, 38
Lead compound, 20, 235
Leadership
attributes of, 110
group relationship and, 112, 114
managers, contrasted, 113
scale for evaluating, 110–111, 112
Lean development, 182–185, 246, 587
Lederle Laboratories
legal case, 632
sales by product/value, 543

Legal cases
    claims in, 628
    comment k and, 630
    company suits, 628–629
    court trends in, 628–629
    international, 628–631
    investigational medicines, 631–632
    learned intermediate doctrine in, 630–631
    negligence and, 630
    package insert warnings, 631
    perspectives in, 628
    plaintiffs in, 628
    product liability, 629–632
    strict liability in, 630
Legal considerations, *see also* Patents
    contract preparation, 578–580
    in licensing, 578
    in medicine development, 364
    in negotiation phase, 578, 579
Legal department
    internal vs. external attorneys, 627–628
    organizational placement, 627
Legal department activities
    adverse reactions, 627
    business decisions and, 623
    choosing expert witnesses, 633
    clinical trials, 626–627
    contracts, 578–580, 624, 626–627
    costs of, 700
    document review, 624, 625
    educational, 627
    employee activities, 625
    employee vs. company, 625
    environmental regulations, 625–626
    expert witness preparation, 633–634
    licensing, 578–582, 624
    medical activities, 626
    patents, 613–621, 627
    preparation for court cases, 633–634
    pretrial depositions, 634
    problem prevention, 624
    product liability, 626
    regulatory affairs, 625–626
    in sales representative activities, 632
    service agreements, 624
    presenting expert testimony, 634–635
Legislators
    company image and, 73
    education of, 694–695
    goals, 62
    pharmaceutical industries images with, 9, 10, 687–695
    pharmacopolitical issues of, 62
    of state governments, 744–745
    view of pharmaceutical industry, 11
Lessons, 70–71, 264, 297
Library services, *see also* Information services
    activities on marketed medicines, 249
    centralized/decentralized, 103
Licensing
    in academic alliances, 722, 732, 734
    agreement, contents of, 569
    based on company gaps, 570–571
    benefits of, 568, 571
    Canadian issues, 621
    company position on, 178
    confidentiality of, 751
    conflict of interest, 157
    consultants use in, 572
    costs of, 700
    creating opportunities for, 572
    criteria, 239
    cross-licensing, 580, 751
    in early-stage of development, 239
    establishing probability of, 371
    exchange of, 751
    financial issues in, 576–578
    future trends in, 583
    goals/purposes, 568
    golden rules of, 583
    intellectual property rights, 52
    issues in, 578, 582
    legal issues in, 578–582, 624
    management of, 572–573
    manufacturing, 580
    as marketing method, 567
    as medical/marketing activity, 450
    negotiations, questions in, 579
    of new medicines, 178
    organizational placement of, 433, 572–573
    of orphan medicines, 571
    of patents, 618
    policy, 254
    portfolio analysis in, 569
    potential problems in, 582
    of preclinical compounds, 572
    proactive approach to, 569, 570, 571–572
    processing opportunities, 573–574
    product trades as, 580, 581
    purchase price/payments, 577
    reasons to, 328
    regulatory issues in, 581–582
    risks in, 571, 577–578
    royalties in, 577, 578
    screening criteria, 575, 576
    sources of opportunities to, 572, 573, 575–576
    strategies, 569–571
    tracking system for, 574, 582
    traditional views of, 567–568
    types of, 568–569, 580
Line management
    advantages of, 429
    description, 337
    in international operations, 86
    matrix management and, 337–338, 339
    of medical-marketing interface, 429, 430, 432
Lobbying
    at federal level, 746
    medicine tampering efforts, 746
    organizing for, 745–746
    by PMA, 744–745
    state governments, 744–746
    by trade associations, 753
Long-range planning, *see* Planning

M

Management, *see also* Corporate management
    attitudes in medicine development, 174–175
    in crisis management, 168–170
    difficult decisions by, 297–298
    hierarchical vs. flat, 101–102
    hype, 80
    of international operations, 85–94
    philosophical differences in, 174–175
    of R&D, 317–328
    stimulating innovation, 284, 285, 287, 292–294
    of subsidiaries, 90–91
Management, issues
    judging, balance in, 78, 80
    priorities, differences in, 80
    questions to answer, 78
Management, keys for success
    business, focused, 73–74, 76
    company image, 75–76
    company presentation, 75
    goals/plans, 75
    golden rules for, 81
    market focus, 75
    message, focused, 74
    negative spiral in, 81
    organization structure and, 74
    proactive approach, 170–172
    project balance and, 74–75
    research, focused, 76
    risk-taking and, 74
    standards and, 74
    strategies, focus of, 74, 76
Management models/styles
    four-dimensional model, 111–112
    hard/soft style, 112
    Japanese approach, 112
    social style, 112
    spectrum of, 111
Managers
    academicians as, 139–140
    asking right questions, 115
    characteristics of, 112, 113, 119, 140
    communication skills of, 132, 169–170, 183
    government officials as, 139, 140
    information flow to, 119
    leaders, contrasted, 113
    motivating, 144–145
    as observers/experts/managers, 119
    productivity of, 145
    time management by, 119
Manufacturing, *see also* Production
    biotechnology, 264–265
    construction costs, 699
    contract, 596, 598, 599
    costs of, 699
    just-in-time concept, 606
    quality standards in, 42–43
    sourcing, 599
    vertical integration of, 610–611
Marion Laboratories, 733
    sales by product/value, 544
Market
    evolution of, 394
    expanding, 562–563
    size as medical need, 393
    targeting, 458
    visually characterizing, 456–458
Market cycle
    death of product, 540–542
    life of product, 540, 556
    reasons for terminating product, 540–541
Marketing

activities of, 541, 699
assessment of new products for, 540
attractiveness of market and, 374
as characteristic of company, 175
clinical department contracts, 425–426
competition in, 748
costs of, 699–700
commercial decisions by, 452–453
as consumer information source, 548
country, choosing, 549–550
creating a medicine profile, 551
criteria for new-product, 452
distribution and, 558
expanding a market, 561–565
forecasts, 371, 455, 558–559
future environment for, 189
generic substitution and, 175, 176
growth share matrix, 393
identifying need and, 542–545
inflated estimates, 180, 558–559
input to medical strategies, 455–456
input to R&D, 212, 453, 454
introducing new medicine, 554–555
in joint ventures, 51
launch date, 554
liaison between departments,
    144–148, 447–458
in licensing appraisal, 571
medical departments and, 248, 546–547
medical/scientific decisions and, 212,
    443–444, 545–547
medical value enhancement, 441–443
medicine development and, 20, 21, 23,
    31–32, 175–176, 245,
    246–250, 374, 545–547
message, 449
naming a medicine, 551–552, 564
of new products, 540
personnel integration in, 424–425
physical location, 430–431
physician, pharmacist, patient chain in
    559–561
position, 175–176
positioning a medicine, 550–551
pricing/costs and, 553–554, 564
priorities of, 441, 443
production and, 31–32, 128, 246, 609
of professional OTC medicines, 557–558
profit and, 389, 390, 391, 544–545
promoting a medicine and, 555–558
R&D interface, 423–424, 545–547
review of packaging inserts, 454–455
research, 450–451, 547–548
sales and, 542–544, 564
services provided by, 433
strategy, 548
technical development liaison, 535
Marketing, organization
    charts of, 430, 431, 432
    functional group placement in, 431–434
    line management, 429, 430, 432
    matrix management, 429–430, 431, 432
    medical support and, 434–435
    in multinational companies, 711–712
    staff turnover, 446
Market research
    data sources, 547–548
    depth of, 547

in establishing criteria for development,
    360
interpreting, 451
as joint medical/marketing effort, 450–451
methods, 547
testing a proposed price, 707
Market share
    defining, 561–562
    increasing, 561–562, 563–565
    in project analysis, 379, 381
    sales and, 564
    stability, 562
Master plan, 245
Mathematical models
    of portfolios, 397–398
    of research budgets, 397–398
Matrix organizational approach
    conflicts-of-interest in, 345–346
    conflicts with line system, 357
    description of, 337
    in developing medicines, 338, 339
    for IND applications, 338, 339–340
    in international operations, 86
    initiating new projects in, 342–344
    in innovation, 199–200
    leadership in, 339–341, 346
    to medical-marketing interface, 429–430,
        431, 432
    for NDA application, 338, 339–340
    network in, 345, 346, 347, 348
    overseeing, 339, 346
    project-driven, 338
    project managers in, 341, 346
    project team leaders for, 339–340, 341
    in research programs, 217, 239
    in R&D, 310–311, 339
    strong vs. weak matrix, 344–347
    team meetings, 344
McNeil Pharmaceuticals, 774
    promotion, 54
    sales by product/value, 544
Media, see News media
Medical departments
    activities on marketed medicines, 248
    advertising, review by, 453–454
    clinical/scientific perspectives in, 332
    commercial decisions by, 452–453
    contracts with marketing, 425–426
    marketing control, 546–547
    marketing data use, 444, 452
    new medicine marketing as, 248, 439–446
    organization of, 315
    personnel issues in, 331–332
    physicians role in, 332–334, 335
    problems with marketing, 445–446
    relations with marketing, 435–437
    staff support of marketing, 434–435
    staff utilization in, 332
Medical-marketing interface
    aggressiveness of, 426–427
    bridging, of, 435–437
    characterizing in a market, 456–457
    communication and, 422
    company policy on decision making,
        423–424
    as corporate issue, 421–427
    corporate personality and, 423
    educational differences and, 445

external vs. internal, 422, 423
holding to previous agreements, 425
improving interaction, 421, 545–546
integrating new personnel and, 424–425
interrelationship of functions, 421–423
issues in, 424–427
models of relationships, 423, 424
R&D influence, 423, 424, 545
relationship in, 435–437
schematic of, 436
Medical-marketing interface, organization
    charts for marketing, 430, 431, 432
    line function system, 429, 430, 432
    matrix function system, 429–430, 431, 432
    for OTC medicines, 546, 547
    physical location of, 430–431
    staffing issues in, 434–435
Medical-marketing, joint activities
    committees for, 448
    converting prescription medicines to OTC,
        449
    facilitating productivity, 448
    formal interactions in, 448
    health professional information, 451–452
    informal interactions in, 447–448
    licensing as, 450
    marketing, message of, 449
    marketing forecasts, 455
    marketing research, 450–451
    medical functions, 248
    morality in medicine development,
        449–450
    package inserts, 454–455
    planning, 448
    reviewing marketing data, 452, 545–546
    sales representatives education, 451
Medical Research Council, 202
Medical value, see also Medicine value
    expression of, 379, 383
    marketing enhancement of, 441–443
    as productivity measure of R & D, 405,
        407, 408
    in project analysis, 379, 383
Medication, see also various Medicine cate-
        gories below
    commercial value, 1, 2
    development, common sense in, 2–3
    image value, 2
    medical value, 1, 2
    scientific value, 1–2
Medicine, see also New medicines
Medicine development; see also Developing
        new medicines; Medicine
        discovery/development; Interna-
        tional Medicine development
    allocating resources for, 323–326
    approaches for, 2–3, 15, 17, 177–180
    attitudes on, 174–175, 181
    attrition rate in, 20–21
    benefit-to-risk ratio in, 20
    "candidate" compounds and, 20
    clinical studies, stages in, 24
    common sense in, 2–3
        communication in, 183–184
        company culture and, 173–174, 181
        company marketing position and,
            175–177
        company organization and, 103–104

Medicine development (contd.)
  competition and, 17, 18, 19, 748
  contracting of, 322–323
  cost of, 18, 374–375, 688
  critical mass for, 312
  data management in, 486
  environment for, 188–189
  facilitating, 240–241
  factors influency speed/quality of, 33
  false beliefs and, 184
  FDA and, 24
  financial risk in, 17
  flow chart for, 24–25
  in future, 188–189
  of high risk projects, 178
  hype in, 179–180
  increasing productivity, 410–411
  interfaces in, 31–32
  joint ventures in, 178–179
  "lead" compounds in, 20
  licensing of, 569
  major changes in 35 years, 32–33
  management of, 318, 322
  marketing and, 20, 21, 23, 31–32
  matrix management of, 338, 339
  medical value perspectives, 19
  medicine functions and, 16
  metaphors for,
    connect-the-dots, 28–29
    high jump, 29–30
    horse race, 26–27
    maze, 28
    ocean liner, 27–28
    pipeline, 25–30
    poker game, 27
  milestones in, 178, 179
  minimizing tangents in, 288–290
  of multiple related compounds, 181–182
  myths about, 290–291
  nature of, 243
  NDA submission in, 24, 26
  new product flow in, 320
  "not invented here" syndrome and, 181
  open discussions on, 180–181
  perspectives on, outside of the industry,
    18, 19–20
  pharmaceutical industry perspective on,
    18–19
  phases of, 26, 182–183
  pipeline concept of, 21, 23, 25–26
  plans, 321
  process of, 20–22
  "project" compound and, 20
  rapid changes in market and, 17
  recording company's history of, 297
  regulations, 17, 22–24
  research and, 15
  resource allocation in, 32, 177–178
  reviews, 320
  risk and, 18
  "seat-of-the-pants" approach, 23, 28
  stages of, 20–22
  standards in, 29–31, 181, 185, 243
  statistics in, 490–491
  subpipelines in, 24
  support services for, 312–313
  target dates in, 178, 179
  termination of, 296

  time required for, 3, 17, 20, 26, 32
  toxicology and, 24, 25
  of unmarketable medicines, 181
  values in, 1–2
  visual models of, approaches to, 177
Medicine development, choosing numbers of
    projects
  approaches to, 352–353
  companies goal and, 352
  keeping pipeline full, 352–353
  mathematical modeling in, 352
  only the best, 354–355
  project costs and, 353
  project types and, 352
  resource allocation and, 353, 355
  special cases in, 354
  trim or add, 353–354
Medicine development, criteria for
  advantages/disadvantages of each, 359
  best, 360, 364
  business decisions and, 359
  clinical indications, 500–502
  competitive value, 369
  examples of, 363
  ideal criteria, 358–359
  medicine characteristics and,
    358–359, 360–361
  medicine discovery and, 358
  minimally acceptable, 360, 363–364
  minipulation of criteria, 359
  mixed criteria for, 364
  orphan medicines, 362–363
  process for, 361, 362
  quantitating, 361–362
  realistic criteria, 358, 359–360, 353,
    368–369
  responsibility for establishing, 361
  standards to achieve, 358, 361
  technical basis, 363
  time frame for developing, 360
  transition from discovery, 358
  types of criteria, 357–358
  typical problems in absence of, 357
Medicine development, golden rules, see also
    Golden rules
  a balanced high risk/low risk project, 254
  a balanced planning/conducting effort in,
    252, 253
  formulate a plan, 252–254
  implementing, 256
  medicine discovery and, 235
  of project management, 347–349
  proper attitudes in, 254–255
  reevaluate frequently, 254
  regulatory submissions, 255
  staffing for, 254
  team approach, 253
Medicine development process
  adverse reactions and, 250
  clinical development and, 249, 249
  clinical trials and, 502–505
  company strategy in, 243–245
  criteria for development, 243, 245
  criteria for performance, 246
  efficacy questions in, 250
  FDA filing, 245
  full-scale or research, 352
  labeling and, 250

  marketing and, 20, 21, 31–32,
    175–176, 245, 246–250, 253,
    545–547
  master plan for, 245–246, 252–254
  phases of, 245, 246, 355
  preclinical activities, 245, 246
  regulatory submission, 245, 255
  resources and, 243
  scope of, 246
  sequential nature of, 355
  stages of, 244, 352
  target dates in, 245, 254
  time required for, 354
Medicine discovery
  commitment to, 319–320
  competition in, 748
  defined, 211, 235
  empirical approach in, 204
  management of, 318
  as rational process, 229
  serendipity in, 204, 210, 211, 218, 219,
    229, 236
  spectrum of methods in, 203–204
  stages of, 244
  transition to development, 358
  when, 211
  by whom, 210–211
Medicine discovery, choosing therapeutic
    areas
  ability to evaluate compound, 211, 215
  animal model availability and, 236
  approach to, 213–214, 236–237
  company politics and, 215
  company policy and, 216–217
  core group, 237, 285, 331
  criteria for, 214–215, 218, 236, 246, 358
  decisions in, 318
  initiating research, 216
  marketing input, 212
  market size and, 214
  number of areas for, 213–214
  personnel making decision, 212
  research program for, 217–218
  resources competition for, 215, 216, 325
  sunset rule, 239
  therapeutic area defined, 212
  unmet therapeutic need and, 214
Medicine discovery/development, environ-
    ment for
  academic institutions and, 192–193
  commercial/business, 189–190
  competition in, 189
  creating, 237, 320
  critical mass for, 311–312
  fads/fashion in, 196
  in future, 188, 196
  health care and, 193–195
  internal company, 189
  international, 190–191
  regulatory, 189, 190–191
  revolution in, 188–189
  scientific breakthrough and, 196
  social/political, 191–192
Medicine discovery/development, personnel
    issues
  career opportunities and, 330
  defining scientists role in, 329–330
  identifying creative scientists, 331

in medical departments, 331–332
supervision of scientists, 331
Medicine discovery, factors in
core team for, 285
creativity, 205, 229, 237, 277
culture of country and, 201
at department level, 202
economics and, 200–201
freedom, 205
individual scientist and, 202–205
innovation and, 199–200, 202, 284, 402–403
at institutional level, 202
matrix schematic, 200
myths about, 290–291
at national level, 200–202
pricing of medicine and, 201
rare diseases and, 202
regulatory policy, 201
scientific state of art, 201–202
social policies, 201
Medicine discovery, future of
factors influencing, 301
human values and, 302–303
identifying trends, 302
intermediate-term, 300
long-term, 300–303
major influences on, 300
near term, 300
predicability of, 299–300, 301–302
trends in, 300
Medicine discovery, golden rules
advancing medicine development, 240, 241
allocating resources, 238–239
attitudes for, 237–238
balance in high/low risk project, 236
choosing disease, 236
choosing therapeutic area, 236
create a research environment, 237
create a research plan, 236–237
licensing policy and, 237
medicine development and, 235
reviewing research and, 238–239
solicit ideas, 237
standards and, 237
stimulate innovation, 239–240
Medicine discovery, methods
animal disease models, 220, 231–233
biotechnology derived, 219–220, 257–258, 264
combinations of, 221
criteria for performance, 218
diazepan example, 221
empirical approach, 230–231
hypothetical, 220
mechanism of action as, 218, 220, 221–222
metabolic aspects and, 220–221
new chemical compound and, 218
random screening, 218–219
rational approach, 219, 229
receptor targeting, 220, 227–228
serendipity, 218, 219
structure activity modification, 221
successful molecular manipulation, 222
trial-and-error approach, 219
Medicine discovery, process of

advancing compounds to development, 240–241
adverse reactions and, 208–209
choosing number of compounds, 215
examples of, 207, 209, 211
improving on activity, 209
initiating activity on, 216
levels of research in, 212–213
6MP activity improvements as, 209
pharmacological studies in, 235
schematic of discovery process, 208
serendipity, 204, 210, 211
sources of ideas, 208, 209
sources of new medicines and, 208–209
Medicines, see also Drugs
assessing claims for, 556–557
clinical indications for, 500–501
costs/profits, 18
counterfeiting, 561
criteria for ideal, 281, 282
discovery process, 20, 23, 25–26
distribution, 558
"engineered", 188
"facts" about, 274
functions of, 16
in future, 188–189
levels of activity, 274, 275, 276
perspectives on, 18–20
promedicines and, 274
risk-benefits of, 281–282
schematic of types, 12–13
sources of new, 178–179
unapproved use, 565
in year 2020, 188
withdrawal from market, 298
Medicines, business sources of new, 178–179
Medicine safety, see also Adverse reactions
adverse reactions and, 510
benefit-to-risk ratio in, 509
information sources, 509–510
meaning of, 509
regulatory agency evaluation, 510–511
Medicine, sources of
animals/humans, 209
medicines used in animals, 210
natural plants, 210
old medicines, new use, 209, 210, 211
Medicine tampering, see Product tampering, Tampering
Medicine, value of
commercial, 1, 2, 369
indication for medicine and, 706
in portfolio analysis, 369–371
pricing and, 702–703, 706
rating of, 369–370
scientific value and, 369
therapeutic value and, 370
Megatrends, 67, 101, 301
6-Mercaptopurine, 6MP improving activity of, 209
Merck and Co.
academic alliances of, 726
Astra alliance, 105
avoiding conflict of interest, 154–155
Dupont joint venture, 104–105
education costs, 699–700
FDA presentation, 740
Johnson and Johnson alliance, 105

licensing, 53
lovastatin development, 296
philanthropic activities of, 725
regulatory strategies, 737
sales by product/value, 542
Mergers, corporate, see also Acquisitions
agreements for, 56–57
alliances and, 49, 751
alternatives to, 49
concepts promoting, 47–48
definition of, 47
evaluating company for, 49
factors encouraging, 47–49
formation of a separate company in, 49
goals in, 48
joint ventures and, 50–51
patents and, 57
reasons for, 47–49
strategic alliances and, 49
Merrell Dow Pharmaceuticals Inc
legal case, 632
sales by product/value, 544
"Me-too" medicines
beta-blockers as, 709
desirability of developing, 215, 236, 708–709
marketing, 446, 707
medical disinterest in, 446
pricing of, 706
regulatory review, 741
Metaphors, 22, 25–33, 191, 202, 291, 330, 342, 357, 422, 502, 540, 556, 567, 583, 644, 693, 765
Milestones, 179, 254
Minimally acceptable criteria, see Standards in medicine development
Models of organizations, see Corporate organization
Molecular modeling, see Structure-activity studies
Monsanto, 722, 749
Morale, 92
Morality issues
in new medicine development, 246, 449–450
Motivation
of employees, 144–145
factors in, 238, 331
of scientists, 144, 237–238, 331
Multinational companies, see also Pharmaceutical companies, Companies
categories of, 7–8
centralization of, 103
clinical trials in, 714, 178
choosing countries for, 102
compatibility of systems in, 718
cooperation/coordination of sites of, 711–713
corporate organization of, 102–103, 307
discovery/development models, 713
duplication of effort in, 718
intercompany differences, 297
managers culture/goals and, 89–90, 718
marketing models for, 711–712, 713
matrix organization in, 338–339
organization of, 307
ownership of, 8
portfolio review, 368

Multinational companies (contd.)
  project management in, 342
  regulatory submissions, 718
  research organization of, 307
  subsidiaries of, 89, 102
  troubleshooter in, 297
  worldwide marketing, 711
Mutagenicity testing
  carcinogenicity and, 497–498
  categorization of, 498
  extrapolation to humans, 271
  international differences in, 498
  in vitro tests of, 497

N

Naming a medicine
  for OTC market, 552
  trademarks and, 552, 553
  types of names, 551–552
National Institute of Drug Abuse, 156, 163
National Institutes of Health, NIH
  conflicts of interest, perceived, 156
  pharmaceutical industry interaction, 156,
    736
  research studies, 202
  sponsored trials, 41
National Pharmaceutical Council, NPC, 755
New chemical entities, NCEs
  INDs and, 385
  as measure of success rate, 412, 413
  NDAs and, 367
  in project portfolio analysis, 373
  reasons for terminating, 541
  regulatory delays for, 742
  research costs of, 392
New Drug Application (NDA)
  abbreviated form, 738
  computer assisted, 739
  conservative approach to, 174
  cost of research to file, 384
  electronic filing for, 466–467, 588
  filing mechanisms, 738–739
  filing for OTC medicine, 1685
  matrix organization for, 338, 339–340
  as measure of success, 412, 414, 415
  medicine development and, 24, 26, 244
  minimal criteria for submission, 371
  NCEs and, 367
  preparation, 586, 587
  in project portfolio-analysis, 383, 384, 387
  reasons for delays in, 742
  schematic of approaches to, 177
  speeding approval for, 744
New medicines, *see also* NCEs
  advertising, 555
  assessing claims for, 556–557
  cost effectiveness of, 554
  counterfeiting of, 561
  identifying need for, 542–545
  introducing, 554–555
  labeling of, 588–589
  predicting sales of, 558–559
  pricing strategies, 553–554, 561
  promotion of, 555–558
  regulatory strategies for, 737–738
News media
  audio conferences, 773

confrontation with, 770–771
company policies on, 769–770
copies of media reports, 462
in crisis management, 169–170, 172
editorial briefings, 772–773
events targeted to health professionals,
  773–774
industry response to contact, 770
industries relations with, 769
interaction with, 770
press materials for, 772
press releases/conferences, 771–772
pharmacpolitical issues and, 63–64
public perception of pharmaceutical industry, 63–64
relations with, 172
satellite interviews, 773
tours for, 773
training executives to deal with, 170
types of, 770
video releases, 773
Nonprescription Drug Manufacturers Association, NDMA, 755
Norway, 67
Not invented here syndrome
  ingredients of, 181
  new medicine development and, 181

O

Observers, 119
Occupational Safety and Health Administration, OSHA
  functions of, 736
Office of Orphan Product Development
  (FDA), 262
Operations of a company, *see* International
  operations
Organization, corporate, *see* Corporate
  organization
Organization for Economic Cooperation and
  Development, OECD
  transfer cost guidelines, 701
Orphan Drug Act, 17, 202, 645
Orphan medicines
  criteria for development, 362–363
  licensing strategies for, 571
  marketing exclusibility of, 618
  number to develop, 354
  safety data, 495
  standards, 246, 362–363
Ortho Pharmaceutical Co.
  sales product/value, 543
Over-the-counter OTC, medicines
  active ingredients in, 685
  benefit-to-risk analysis of, 449
  company purchase of rights to, 178
  consumer benefit of, 565, 683
  definitional issues, 679–680
  FDA approval for, 564
  future environment for, 191
  health care in future and, 194
  marketing, 449, 546–547, 557–558,
    682–683, 684
  medical activities supporting, 546–547
  Merck-Johnson & Johnson sales alliance,
    105
  naming of, 552

pharmaceutical company growth, 104
physicians perspectives on, 683–684
professional use, 557–558
review of claims for, 685
spectrum of types, 558
stability/shelf life, 527
Over-the-counter medicines, switching prescription medicines to
  alternatives to, 685
  approval mechanisms, 685
  distribution, 558
  dosage strength and, 681
  exclusive marketing of, 680
  factors in decision, 680–681
  international differences, 680, 685
  market research for, 682
  medical-marketing in, 449
  methods for, 618–683
  negative consequences of, 680
  packaging, 564, 682
  on patent expiration, 676
  patient savings in, 565, 680
  rational for, 564–565, 680
  regulatory aspects of, 564, 682–683,
    684–685
  public relations for, 774
  safety issues in, 684
  strategic issues in, 681, 683
  timing of, 676

P

Package inserts
  categories of, 668–669
  contents, 191
  legal aspects of, 629, 631
  marketing review of, 454–455, 548
  postmarketing modifications, 513, 515
  product information services and, 484
  product liability and, 629
  regulatory requirements, 589
  research on, 669–670
  warnings in, 631
  wording of, 454–455
Package inserts, for patients
  alternatives to, 548–549, 670
  British endorsement of, 548
  brochures and, 671
  compilation/publication of, 670
  contents of, 667, 670
  description of, 548
  EEC requirement for, 665
  format for, 668
  issues in, 666–667
  objectives in, 666
  patients reactions to, 548, 665–666
  patients request for, 668
  patients rights and, 666
  pilot testing of, 670
  preparation, 667
  problems of, 668–669
  research on, 669–670
  who supplies, 667–668
Parenteral medicines
  formulation, 527
Parke-Davis
  Bendectin marketing, 298
  sales by product/value, 542

Patent expiration
    extensions on, 617–618
    in European countries, 614
    generic medicines and, 673–674
    modifying laws on, 676
    problems of, 673–674
    in U.S., 614, 617
Patent expiration, addressing problem
    chiral formulations, 675
    develop backup medicines, 674
    develop combination medicine, 676–677
    develop second-generation medicines, 674
    extend commercial life, 674
    licensing raw materials, 677
    line-extension development, 675–676
    lower price, 677
    manufacture generics, 675, 677
    modify formulation, 674–675
    new brand names, 677
    new dosage forms, 675
    new uses, 676
    novel delivery systems, 675
    strategy for, 677–678
    switch to OTC medicine, 676, 678
Patents
    in academic/industry alliances, 53, 726,
      728, 729, 732
    on animals, 619
    on biotechnology, 262–263, 619
    Canadian issues, 621
    catch-22 issues, 620
    confidential information and, 620–621
    costs of, 698–699
    criteria for awarding, 615
    data required for, 617
    deposit issues, 619–620
    description of, 613, 615
    duration of, 614, 617
    effective life of, 687
    extension of, 617–618, 676
    filing vs. inventing, 616–617
    future of, 621
    golden rules for, 621
    innovation and, 200–201
    interference procedures for, 618–619
    international differences in, 614, 615, 616,
      619, 621
    laws governing, 200–201
    licensing and, 618
    marketing to, 559–561
    as measure of productivity, 408–409
    Paris Union agreement on, 615–616
    pirates, 619
    prior user rights and, 614
    procedures for obtaining, 614–615
    in project analysis, 368, 381
    requirements for, 614
    reviewing life of, 368, 381
    steps in medical treatment, 560, 561
    strategies for, 237, 618, 621
    time to acquire, 615
    trade secrets and, 613–614
Patient package inserts, see Package inserts
Patients versus Consumers, 767
Personnel issues, see also Employees
    career development opportunities, 330
    company culture and, 174
    compensation levels, 141–142, 144

    critical mass of, 142
    employee burnout and, 140, 141, 144
    hiring best staff, 142–143
    hiring scientists/physicians, 335
    hiring senior managers, 139–140
    institutional memory and, 69–70, 71
    integration of new, 424–425
    in international operations, 91–92
    job security and, 145
    liaison between departments, 147–148
    in manufacturing, 608
    morale of, 92, 144–146, 183
    motivating, 144–145, 326–327
    over/understaffing and, 140–141
    pharmacopolitical education of,
      65–66, 139
    productivity, 145–146, 402–404, 405
    promotions, 326–327, 330
    in R&D, 329–335
    recruiting, 71
    resolving problems, 146–147
    rewarding, 205
    scientists as administrators, 81, 330
    staffing, 140–141, 149–152, 323–324
    stimulating innovation in, 284–285
    transfer of staff, 434–435
    underutilized/unproductive, 140
Pfizer Inc.
    academic relationship, 726, 727
    lobbying, 746
    sales by product/value, 542
Pharmaceutical companies, see also Multi-
    national companies, and Company
    academic alliances, 51–53
    attributes of, 17–18
    biotechnology companies and, 263–264
    business for, 122, 124
    as champion of industry goals, 693–694
    competition between, 189
    conflicts of interest in, 153–165
    crisis in, 167
    decreasing employee numbers in, 105–106
    decreasing number of, 190
    developing SOPs in, 106
    environment of, 189
    image of, 75–76
    increasing employee numbers, 105
    international operations, 85–94, 173
    major changes in, in 35 years, 32–33, 64
    new medicine development, 15–16
    objectives, defining of, 122
    organizational structure, 85–86,
      95–106, 432
    personality of, 423
    pharmacopolitical issues of, 62–65
    pharmacopolitical response to, 65–66
    profitability, 17, 18
    public image of, 63–65
    research-based, 15, 190
    resources available to, 32
    sales data, 542–544
    scientists in, 81
    size
      benefits of smaller, 105
      definitions in, 104
      factors decreasing size, 105
      factors increasing size, 104
      is larger better?, 104–105

      optimal size of, 104
    benefits of being small, 105
    defined, 104
    factors in, 104–105
    optimal size, 104
Pharmacuetical companies, differences in
    communications in, 183
    company culture, 173–174
    employees, 174
    FDA relations, 174
    in Phase I trials, 181–182
    management philosophy, 174, 175,
      423–424
    master development plans, 182–183
    medicine development, 174–185, 423
    NDA and, 174
    philosophy, 181–185
    problem situations, 183–185
    R&D philosophy, 174
Pharmaceutical companies, multinational,
    see Multinational pharmaceutical
    companies
Pharmaceutical development
    activities of, 526
    dissolution studies, 528, 529
    of dosage forms, 528, 530
    formulation, 526, 528, 529
    increasing duration of action, 530–531
    marketing impact and, 526
    medicine compatability and, 528
    preservatives and, 527
    product preservatives and, 527
    stability/shelf life and, 527–528
Pharmaceutical industry
    academicians view of, 10
    altering public/government attitudes,
      688–689
    categories of companies in, 7–8
    changing image of, 687–695
    commercial message use, 691
    congressional relations, 689
    consumer groups view of, 10–11
    defined, 7–8, 13
    education of public, 687, 694–695
    financial support of academic institutes,
      192–193
    future changes in, 188–189
    governmental regulation of, 687
    image of, 9–11, 63–65
    improving legislators view of, 691–692
    legislators views of, 11, 694
    managers of, 11, 16–17
    medicine pricing and, 688, 689, 690
    multinational companies and, 7–8
    non-company organizations and, 8–9,
      692–693
    past public response of, 688
    pharmacopolitical issues of, 63–65
    physicians view of, 10
    programs for poor, 691
    public view of, 11, 688
    regulators view of, 9, 10
    revolution in, 188–189
    social pressure on, 9, 10, 687–688
    trade association relations, 8, 10
    trade association use, 692–693
    uniqueness of, 3, 16–17
    value to society, 687, 689–690

Pharmaceutical Manufacturers Association, PMA
   as data source, 409, 754
   description of, 755
   as industry spokesman, 692–693
   lobbying national government, 617
   lobbying state government, 744–745
   patent law revision and, 200–201
   in production issues, 605
Pharmacists
   company relations, 758
   marketing to, 559–561
   pharmacopolitical issues of, 62
Pharmacoeconomics
   organizational placement of, 433–434
   studies, 708
Pharmacological testing
   choosing disease, 236
   choosing therapeutic area, 236–237
   in medicine development period, 235
   for lead compound, 235
Pharmacopolitics
   animal testing as, 662–663
   company organization of, 65, 434
   company recognition of, 65
   company/external interactions in, 59–61
   dealing with an issue, 66
   definitions in, 59, 60
   employee education of, 65–66, 67–68
   environment of, 191–192
   future trends in, 67–68
   government and, 59–60, 61, 687–695
   internal groups in, 60
   issues in, 62–63
   macro/micro levels of, 59–60
   medical profession and, 59, 60, 61, 67
   news media and, 63–65
   of pharmaceutical industry, 63–65
   pressures on companies consulting in, 162
   price controls and, 195
   public and, 59, 60, 61, 62–65, 67, 192
   schematic of, 61
   third-party payers and, 60
   trade associations and, 65
Phase I studies/trials
   adverse reactions in, 182
   company philosophy in, 181–182
   dosage in, 182
   in medicine development, 244
   of multiple related compounds, 181–182
   posing clinical questions in, 502
   termination of, 182
   in United Kingdom, 182
Phase II studies/trials
   chronic toxicity testing in, 495
   efficacy determination in, 505
   prohibitive costs of, 182
Phase III studies/trials
   clinical trials, 502, 511, 513
   evaluating for, 373
   filings in, 23
   model, 98–99
   patent life remaining in, 385
   schematic, 98
   as success measure, 412, 413
Phase IV studies
   definition, xxx

postmarketing surveillance in, 511–513
   staffing, 152
Phase I to IV trials, 52, 315, 322, 325, 355, 412–414
Philanthropic activities, 693, 725, 762–763
Philippines, 616
Physicians' Desk Reference, PDR
   physician warnings in, 629
   as product information source, 476, 482
Physicians, see also Clinicians
   as expert witnesses, 633
   choice of medications, factors in, 456, 457
   company relations, 757
   conflicts of interest, 164
   education of, 331–332
   good legal practices for, 635
   healthcare in future, 194, 303
   hiring of, 335
   legal training for, 633–634, 635
   maintaining clinical skills of, 334–335
   marketing to, 559–561
   in medical departments, 332–334
   OTC medicine perspectives, 683–684
   oversupply of, 194
   patient information, 666
   pharmaceutical company image and, 75
   pharmaceutical issues of, 62, 65
   primary/secondary functions of, 332–334
   product warnings to, 629–630
   referral by, 164
   roles, 332
   view of pharmaceutical industry, 10
Pilot trials, 250
Pipeline concept of development, 23–26, 352, 602
Plants
   genetic engineering of, 261
   as sources of new medicines, 210
Political factors, see also Pharmacopolitics
   in medicine development, 180–181, 191–192, 196, 662
Portfolio analysis, see also Investigational medicine projects, portfolio analysis
   commercial value in, 370–371
   described, 365
   developing, 368–369
   focus of, 74, 75, 366
   gaps in, 366–367, 569, 570–571
   ideal portfolio and, 368
   in licensing strategy, 569
   mathematical models in, 397–398
   medical/scientific value in, 369–370
   of multinational companies, parameters for, 365–366
   perspectives in, 367–368
   pruning, 397
   purpose, 366
   realistic portfolio and, 368–369
   team to conduct, 450
Post hoc issues, 279
Postmarketing, clinical studies; see also Phase IV studies
   adverse reaction analysis in, 512, 513, 515
   coordinator between sites, 516
   data bases for, 512–513
   future trends in, 191
   international requirements, 190, 513–515

mechanism-of-action trials, 515–516
   new trials in, 515–516
   quality of data, 486
   record linkage in, 513
   regulatory requirements, 190–191, 513–515
   surveillance benefits, 517
   surveillance methods, 512–513
   surveillance objectives, 512
Potency of medicines, 557
Preclinical departments
   organization of, 315
Preclinical studies
   establishing basis for development, 358
   loss of useful medicines in, 268, 270–271
   of toxicity, 267–272
   transition to clinical trials, 246–247
Preferred provider organizations, PPOs
   as customer, 550
   healthcare environment and, 193
   pharmaceutical industry trends and, 190
Prescription medicine converted to OTC status, see 564–565, 676, 679–685
Press, see News media
Price of medicines, factors in
   affordability and, 708
   community acceptance, 709–710
   competition, 702
   corporate comfort level, 704–705
   dividends to shareholders, 704
   effect on current treatment, 703
   elasticity of demand, 704
   exchange rates, 705
   fair price, determining, 705–706
   government pricing controls, 704
   indications two different, 706
   inflation, 703, 707
   international differences, 703, 704, 706
   licensing costs, 703
   life cycle of, 705
   manufacturing costs, 707–708
   market dependence, 702
   medical value/novelty, 702–703
   for "me-too" medicines, 706
   patent life remaining, 703
   R&D costs/support, 703
   reevaluation of, 707
   regulations, 703
   share volume, 706
   shelf-life, 703
   social importance, 703
   social issues in, 707–710
Pricing
   as competitive tool, 57
   government regulations and, 18
   medicine discovery and, 201
   research and, 18
Pricing strategies
   competition-based, 57, 701–702
   considerations in, 698, 706–707
   cost-plus, 701
   for transfer pricing, 553–554
   in EEC, 561
   market penetration, 702
   marketing and, 553–554, 707
   share volume/and, 706
   skimming, 702

treatment costs and, 553
value-based, 702
Priorities, 80, 125, 396, 440–441, 522, 537, 717
Proactive/Reactive, see Management
Product information groups
  auditing performance of, 482, 483
  complaints and, 482
  computer system, 475, 478
  disclaimers and, 481
  formats used, 481
  functions, 476
  goals, 475
  health professionals and, 451–452, 476–482
  information sources of, 476–477
  marketing as, 548
  organizational location, 476
  processing questions, 478–480
  questions received by, 476–477
  quick response by, 481–482
  as research opportunities source, 482, 484
  responding to questions, 477–481
  sales representatives and, 477
  soliciting questions, 476
  staffing, 484
  standard letter use, 481
  unapproved use of medicines and, 476, 477
  written responses, 479–480
Product license application, PLA, xxx
Production, see also Technical development, Manufacturing
  capacity, 606
  challenges for, 608–611
  chemical issues in, 523–526
  contracting of, 598, 599
  coordination of, 596
  costs/medicine value and, 597, 699
  equipment for, 598, 608
  facilities for, 597, 598, 601
  FDA licensing of, 598
  of investigational medicines, 597
  inventory size and, 607
  in joint ventures, 51
  launch date for, 599, 600
  marketing and, 31–32, 609
  medicine development and, 31–32
  multiple sites for, 599, 605
  orders for, 599–600
  personnel issues, 608
  project team members, 596, 597
  project types, 596
  quality assurance and, 601
  scale-up of, 598
  site for, 531–532, 598–599, 607, 608
  standards, 44, 597
  support activities of, 596
  technical development and, 523, 531–532, 534–535
  vertical integration in, 610–611
  waste minimization in, 608
Production issues, see also Manufacturing
  competitive pressures and, 610
  cost control, 606–608
  customer service, 605–606
  inability to meet product demands, 609–610

just-in-time manufacturing, 606
marketing department and, 31–32, 128, 246, 609
planning and scheduling, 608–609
production goals, 605–606
product tampering, 610
quality assurance and, 600–605
risks and, 610
Productivity
  best measure of, 407
  commercial measures of, 405, 407, 408
  company problems affecting, 411
  comparison measure of, 409
  defined, 402
  effectiveness and, 405
  evaluation systems, 403–404
  improving, 145–146, 409–411
  in international operations, 91–92
  management issues, 4–11
  measures to avoid, 408–409
  measuring, 91–92, 403–408
  medical value measures of, 405, 407, 408
  motivating factors, 144
  of R&D, 403–411
  personnel parameters of, 405
  regulatory measures of, 404, 405–406, 407
  of subsidiary, 408
  time for FDA approval as measure, 405, 406
  value of tracking, 401–402
  who evaluates, 404
Product liability
  awards in, 632
  comment k in, 530
  failure to warn, 629
  for investigational medicine, 631–632
  learned intermediate doctrine in, 630–631
  manufacturer's responsibility, 629
  media reporting, 774
  negligence and, 630
  package insert warnings, 631
  sales representatives activities and, 632
  warnings to physicians and, 629–630
Product License Application, PLA
  compassionate treatment and, 511
  Phase III clinical trials and, 511
Product tampering
  crisis management, 168–172
  examples of, 167, 168
  future developments in, 191
  legislation, 746
  preventing, 561, 610
  preventing a crisis in, 170–171
Product trades
  examples of, 481
  licensing, 580, 581
Professional societies organizations
  as pharmaceutical industry part, 8
Professional status, 725
Profitability issues
  for "me-too" medicines, 706, 708–709
  in new medicine marketing, 449–450
Profits, see also Commercial value
  basis for assessing, 17
  competition and, 18
  development costs and, 18
  in exchange for exclusivity, 677

instability of, 18
to measure, 374
in medicine pricing, 704–705
products planning, 544–545
regulations and, 18
research costs and, 18, 703
sales and, 389, 390, 391, 544–545
societal issues, 750
Project compound, 20
Project management
  coordinators, 342
  delays, 328
  getting it moving, 343
  golden rules of, 347–349
  identifying types/numbers of, 351–352
  in multinational companies, 342
  keys for success, 343–344
  line function approach, 337–338
  matrix approach to, 337–347
  numbers of, 342–343, 351–352
  team leaders, 341
  tracking progress, 443
  transfer of projects, 246–248
Project management laws, 199
Projects, see also Matrix
  initiating, 342
  levels of, 366, 367
  measuring success rate, 511–417
  meetings, 344
  models for international development, 714–717
  models of numbers needed, 352
  number, 342, 372
  portfolio analysis of, 366
  pruning of, 366, 397
  strong vs weak, 344
  types of projects, 342, 351–352
Promedicine, 274
Promotional activities
  to academicians, 561
  advertising as, 555–556
  costs of, 700
  of prescription medicines, 555–556
Promotions of staff, 326–327
Public policy, see Health policy
Public relations
  at community level, 762
  brochures and, 763
  drug lag and, 765–766
  for employees/families of, 762, 764
  for medicines, 771–773
  at national level, 763
  for OTC medicines, 774
  improving industry image, 774
  institutional memory and, 70, 72
  media and, 769
  of pharmaceutical industry, 687–695
  philanthropic support, 763
  presenting a "better story," 765
  public described, 761
  public opinion and, 764–765
  response to consumer groups, 766
  at state level, 762–763
  types of relations, 761–762
Public/patients
  attitudes, 67, 80
  clinical trials and, 164

Public/patients (*contd.*)
  conflicts of interest and, 160, 164
  marketing to, 559–561
  marketing OTC medicine to, 683
  package inserts for, 548, 665–671
  participation in treatment choices,
    766–767
  pharmaceutical industry image and,
    687–695
  pharmaceutical industry interactions, 75,
    761–767
  pharmacopolitical issues of, 62
  problems created by, 757
  product related services for, 763–764
  view of pharmaceutical industry, 11
Published literature, 462, 693
Pure Food and Drug Act, 196
Purity of medicine
  improving, 533
  nature of impurities, 533

Q

Quality, *see also* Value
  of management, 115
  in manufacturing, 42–43
  of medicines, 42
  standards for, 42–43
Quality assurance/control, *see also* GCP,
    GLP, GMP
  bar codes and, 605
  control charts in, 604
  cosmetic issues, 605
  definitions, xxx
  functions, 42, 600–601
  inspection criteria, 603–604
  for investigational medicines, 600
  new equipment and, 605
  organization of, 601
  overview, 293
  product stability and, 602
  sampling procedures in, 603
  standards for, 600–601, 604
  sterility testing and, 602
  validation and, 602–603
Quality-of-life, 705
  marketing issues, 551
  organizational placement, 434
Quality-of-life trials
  concept of, 517–518
  data applications, 518
  measures of, 518–519
  perspectives on, 519
Quid Pro Quo, 301, 366, 580, 761

R

Recruitment
  of employees, 71
Regulations
  definition, 36, 37
  establishment of, 37
  implementation of, 37
  interpretation of, 44
  laws, guidelines, relations, 37
  standards for, 36, 38, 39, 40, 44
Regulators, *see also* Specific agency

adversarial role of, 10
  pharmacopolitical issues of, 62
  recent changes in, 33
  view of pharmaceutical industry, 9, 10
Regulatory affairs department
  activities in marketing, 249
  document preparation, 586
  electronic submissions by, 466–467, 588
  FDA filings, 588, 591
  functions, 586–589
  GCP compliance and, 586, 591, 592
  interaction with regulators, 586–587,
    589–590
  labeling and, 588–589
  organization of, 589–590, 591–593
  OTC medicines and, 591
  package inserts and, 589
  portfolio analyses, 383–388
  proactive/reactive attitude of, 590–591
  professional growth in, 593
  regulatory approval delays and, 741–742
  strategy development, 587–589, 737
  types of documents prepared, 587, 718
  uniqueness of, 585
Regulatory agencies, *see also* Specific agencies
  adverse reaction reporting, 515
  application rules, 742
  company image and, 75
  conflict of interest and, 156
  electronic publishing for, 466–467
  future environment of, 189, 190–191, 194
  international standards and, 190–191, 585
  legal department and, 625–626
  in licensing agreements, 581–582
  medicine discovery and, 201
  medicine safety evaluation, 510–511
  perspectives on new medicines, 19
  pharmacopolitics and, 59–60
  in postmarketing studies, 190–191,
    513–515
  reasons for delays by, 743
  speeding approval by, 743–744
  standards and, 41, 191
  technical regulations, 718
  in toxicology issues, 497–498
Regulatory cascade
  description of, 35–36
  examples of, 36
Regulatory issues
  in biotechnology, 262–263, 265–266
  changes internationally, 67
  in converting prescription medicines to
    OTC, 564, 682–683, 685, 685
  delays in approval, 741–742
  new medicine strategies, 737–738
  pharmaceutical company personnel deci-
    sions, 737
  in portfolio analysis of projects, 371, 383,
    384, 385, 386, 387, 388
  regulatory dossiers, flow of, 738
  regulatory gossip and, 737
  regulatory strategies, 737, 739
  responding to questions, 739
  subsidiaries, submissions by, 740
  time for approval, 384
  in toxicology, 497
Recombinant DNA, *see also* Biotechnology

engineering, 259–260, 261
  processes in, 260
Research, *see also* Basic research
  in academic-company alliances, 51–53
  allocating resources for, 238–239, 323–326
  auditing, 293
  basic/applied, 216–217, 229–230, 325
  in biotechnology, 263
  choice of country for, 102
  division between sites, 109
  duplication in, 117
  in international operation, 87, 93
  in joint ventures, 50–51
  liaison with, 147–148
  mergers and, 48, 57
  minimizing risk in, 119–120
  minimizing tangents in, 288–290
  predicting future and, 299–303
  programs, 217–218, 315
  rate of return on, 18
  reviewing, 238–239
  spectrum of, in pharmaceutical compa-
    nies, 229–230
  in subsidiaries, 87
  targeted, 229–230, 291
  terminating programs, 296–297
Research and Development, R&D
  allocating resources for, 238, 323–326
  commercial data, interpretation, 452–453
  communication in, 295
  company culture and, 174
  competitive environment of, 189
  costs, 698
  critical mass for, 311–313
  data management in, 485
  costs of, 698
  functions of, 235
  in future, 189–190
  improving productivity, 409–411
  increasing efficiency of, 294–298
  marketing and, 247, 423–424,
    443–444, 453, 454, 545–547
  measuring success of, 411–417
  pressure on, 190, 353
  productivity of, 402, 403–411
  resources for, 312
  reviewing, 238–239
  reasons for less successful, 416–417
  scientists role in, 329–330
  staffing, 323–324
Research and development budget
  accountability for, 642–643
  in allocation of resources, 640–641, 644,
    645
  balance in, 641
  clinical trials and, 645
  comparison with competitors, 643
  early payments and, 645
  essential questions in, 642
  generating, 643–644
  justifying, 644
  models for, 644
  organization of, 642
  as percentage of total budget, 638
  questionable projects and, 641
  tax considerations, 645
Research/development (R&D) director
  characteristics of successful, 76–77

establishing realistic deadlines/target dates, 77–78
identification of objectives, 78
schedules for projects, examples of, 77, 79, 80
success, negative spiral of, 81
target dates use, 319
Research and development expenditures
accounting for, 645, 647
analysis of, 653
categorization of, 645, 646
data presentation, 647, 648, 650
evaluation parameters, 647
forecasting future, 651–653
by function, 646, 647, 649
interpreting, 651
projected/actual expenditure, 651, 652
by research area, 648, 650
by therapeutic area, 651
tracking of, 645, 651, 653
U.S./Germany comparison, 647
Research and development, Managing
allocating resources, 323–326
balance in efforts, achieving, 319–320, 322
contracting, 322–323, 328
decisions in, 320
focusing, 320–321
information flow and, 318–319
issues in, 317–318, 319
levels of, 317–318
meetings, planning for, 321
new product flow and, 320, 353
personnel issues, 329–335
planning/documentation, 327–328
promotions and, 326–327
priorities and, 321
resource commitment, 321–322
reviewing projects, 320–321
target dates use, 319
when progress slows, 328
unrealistic plans, 321
Research and development, organization of
areas of strength/weakness, 326, 327
of basic science departments, 313–315
communication and, 328
coordinating committee approach, 313, 314, 315
critical mass in, 311–313, 315
decentralized approach advantages, 307–308
decentralized approach, disadvantages, 308
efficiency and, 294–295
matrix approach, 310–311
medical departments in, 315
preclinical departments in, 315
rigid, 313, 314
by scientific discipline, 308, 309
support services, 312–313
tables of, 309, 310, 311, 312, 314
therapeutically based, 308, 310
totally open, 313, 314
Resources, 32
Resource allocation, see also Budgets
achieving balance in, 325, 376, 441, 442
based on areas of strength/weakness, 326
based on commercial potential, 325
based on therapeutic area, 325–326
consequences of imbalances in, 441

as corporate financial issue, 641–642
data presentation, 376–379
in developing new medicine, 33, 441, 442
forecasting future resources, 640
illustrating, 376
in managing R&D, 321–322, 323–326 640–641
in medicine development, 353, 376–379
methods, 323–325
monitoring of, 640
prioritizing projects, 323, 324, 325–326
in project analysis, 376–379
risk and, 378, 379, 641–642
staff requirements, 323–324, 376, 377
Retreats, 239, 292
Retrovir
Phase III trials, 511
pricing, 702
regulatory strategies for, 737
Return on investment, ROI
in project portfolio analysis, 384, 388
Risk
benefits of medicine, 281–282
knowledge of, 282
magnitude of, 282
of medicines, 67
in medicine development, 254, 375, 378
minimizing in R&D, 119–120
resource allocation and, 378, 379
Roche Laboratories
employee lay offs in, 105
promotion, 54
sales by product/value, 542
Roerig
sales by product/value, 544

S
Sabbatical periods, 725
Safety testing, see also Animal safety, Toxicology
definition, 509
medicine development and, 235
metabolic studies in, 272
plasma medicine levels and, 271–272
principles of, 271–272
termination of, 296
time for, 235
Sales
by company, product, value, 542–544
in copromotion, 54
costs of, 700
data, 542–544
of future medicines, 194
as indicator in financial analysis, 637, 638
legal activities in, 632
market share and, 564
as measure of success, 416
of new product, for casting for, 371
predicting, 558–559
profits and, 389, 390, 391, 544–545
project portfolio analysis and, 389, 390, 391
representatives activities, 632
representatives education, 248, 451
Sales representatives
activities, 632
as product information source, 477, 482–483

education, 248, 451
legal issues, 632
Sampling of medicines
methods, 603
for quality assurance, 603
for studies, 729
Sandoz
sales by product/value, 543
Sankyo Co., Ltd.
toxicology testing, 296
Schering Corp.
sales by product/value, 543
Scientific value
of medications, 1–2
Scientists
accountability of, 291
careers, 330
conflicts of interest of, 161–164
creativity, 205, 229, 237, 277, 284–285, 291, 331
cultivating innovation in, 202–203, 239–240
education of, 332
environment of, 202, 203, 239–240, 284–285
feedback to, 295
fraud and, 151
freedom for, 205, 331
goals for, 331
hiring of, 335
as individualists, 115
journal article publications, 162
in legal proceedings, 633–634, 635
logic of, 277–278
managerial control/reward of, 81
motivating, 144, 237–238, 331
nonscientist communication, 108
as observers, 277–278
pet ideas of, 240, 291
presentation of their work, 239–240
reaching a conclusion, 279
recognizing creativity in, 205
research ideas, adoption of, 215
retreats for, 239, 292
roles in R&D, 329–330
Screening, see Medicine discovery
Searle Pharmaceuticals
licensing, 53
sales by product/value, 544
Sense of urgency, 78, 240
Serendipity, 204, 211, 218–219, 229, 236
Service companies, 9
Shelf life, 527–528, 703
Smith Kline & French Laboratories, SK&F
cimetidine development, 227–228
histamine receptor antagonist development, 227–228
sales by product/value, 542
Social issues
fraud in science and, 201
for creative environment, 201
in international medicine development, 717
medicine costs/health care costs, 708
in medicine pricing, 703, 707–710
Social pressure
health care trends and, 193–195, 703
regulation and, 196

Squibb
  legal case, 632
  promotion, 54
  sales by product/value, 542
Stability of medicines
  accelerated tests, 527
  of OTC products, 527
  product dating and, 527–528
  standards for, 44
  tests of, 527
Staff, *see* Employees, Personnel
Staffing levels
  changes over time in, 150–151
  for clinical trials, 149–152
  company resources and, 150–151, 152
  employee burnout and, 141
  evaluating staff ratios, 149–150
  fluctuating needs, 141
  estimating for future, 398
  golden rules of, 149–152
  over/understaffing and, 140–141
  in project analysis, 372, 373–374, 376, 377
  quality vs. numbers, 151
  for R&D, 311–313
  staff transfers and, 434–435
Standard Operating Procedures, SOP
  developing, 106
  factors influencing modification, 43
  relations to standards, 38, 39, 43
  research and development, 292
Standards in medicine development, *see also*
      Regulations
  academic influences on, 41–42
  achievement of, 41–42
  for analytical methods, 44–45
  in animal studies, 43
  auditing of, 45
  basis for modifying, 43
  in clinical trials, 41, 52, 74
  company goals and, 39, 74
  controversy about, 39–40
  costs of, 39
  creation of, 36, 37
  for degradation of product, 44
  defined, 37
  establishment of, 42
  ethical, 36, 38, 39, 40, 201
  GCP as, 42
  golden rules and, 40
  high, 185
  implementation of, 37
  for impurities, 44
  industry influences on, 41
  influences on, 41–42
  in international operations, 89
  law guideline relationship, 37
  in medicine development, 243
  in medicine discovery, 237
  minimal acceptable, 41, 236, 254, 360,
      363–364, 374, 398
  professional, 38, 201
  of quality, 42
  reasons for, 36
  regulatory, 36, 38, 39, 40
  relationship between types of, 40–41
  schematic of metaphors for, 38
  SOPs in, 38, 39, 43
  state-of-the-art, 38, 39, 40

technical, 38, 39, 44
  types of, 36, 38
Statistical considerations
  in clinical protocol development, 490
  clinical significance and, 511
  in manufacturing, 603
  in medicine development, 490–491
  poorly applied, 321, 491
  regulatory data and, 491
Statisticians, 333
Sterility testing
  quality assurance and, 602
  USP procedure for, 602
Sterling Drug
  legal case, 631
Strategic alliances
  defined, 49
  examples of, 104–105
  as merger alternative, 49
Strategic planning, *see* Planning
Strategies, corporate
  assessing, 126
  CEOs duties, 122
  choosing strategies, 74, 124–125
  companies objectives and, 122
  communicating discussions, 125
  determining, 122–123
  implementing, 125
  long-range planning, 125–126
  procedures in, 126
  schematic of model for, 123
Strategies, R and D, 252–254
Structure-activity studies
  of antitumor agents, 223
  backup candidates in, 226–227
  of beta receptor antagonists, 229
  biological activity and, 224–226
  choosing compounds for, 223
  in designing better medicines, 228–229
  example of, 223
  in medicine discovery, 221–228
  questions to ask in, 226
  SK&F histamine receptor studies, 227–228
  techniques in, 222
Stuart Pharmaceuticals
  sales by product/value, 543
Subsidiaries
  corporate organization of, 102
  defined, 86
  functions, 87
  international operations, 85, 86–88, 89,
      90–91, 102–103, 117
  major/minor, 87–88
  management of, 90–91, 116–117
  managers of, 88
  measuring productivity of, 408
  multinational companies, 89
  regulatory submissions by, 740
  types of, 8, 87
Success factors, *see* Golden rules
Success rate, measuring *see also* Productivity
  cumulative sales/launches and, 416
  definitions by project, 411–412
  of individual phases, 412–413
  methods for, 412, 416
  NCEs as, 412, 413
  NDAs as, 412, 414, 415
  of new medicine, 413–416

quantitating, 413
  reasons for failure, 416–417
Support services
  for medicine development, 312–313
  types/levels of, 312
Sweden, 659
Symposia, 725
Syntex
  sales by product/value, 543

T

Tampering, *see* Product Tampering
Tangents, 240, 253, 288–290
Target dates, *see* Deadlines
Task forces
  activities of, 286–287
  pitfalls/problems of, 286–287
  in stimulating innovation, 287
Tax considerations
  in R&D budget, 645
Technical development, *see also* Pharma-
      ceutical development
  absorption, 264
  allocating supply, 532, 536–537
  analytical development and, 531, 533–534
  "catch-22" in, 535–537
  changing costs in, 532–533
  characteristics, 363
  clinical issues in, 523–526
  contaminants, 264
  data generated, 486
  dissolution, 528
  environmental compliance, 525
  liaison issues, 534–535
  marketing and, 535
  optically pure isomers, 525
  pharmaceutical issues, 526–531
  priorities of, 522–523, 537
  preservatives, 527
  process development, 523–525
  production and, 523, 531–532, 534–535
  product characteristics and, 523–525
  purity of product and, 525–526
  pyrogenicity, 604
  resource issues in, 531–533
  roles of, 523, 523
  scaleup, 265–266, 524–525
  stability, 527
  synthesis, 524
Technical support department
  activities in marketing, 249
Technology transfer
  from academia, 731–734
  within company, 247
Terminating medicine projects
  reasons for, 541–542
  stage of, 541
Terminating research programs, 296
Terminology, xxix–xxx, 37, 93,
      294–295, 300, 561–562
Therapeutic substitution, 745
Therapeutic utility
  estimating, 370
Therapeutics
  levels of understanding, 274–275
Third-party payers

investigational treatment payments for, 67
pharmacopolitical goals/isues, 63
pharmacopolitics and, 60, 67
Time
    for FDA review, 26
    industries perspective, 4
    in medicine development, 3, 17, 20, 26, 32
    regulatory agencies perspective, 4
Toxicity
    carcinogenicity and, 494, 495–496
    chronic, 494
    diet and, 495
    dose-response relationships in, 496
    mechanisms of, 272
    medicine safety and, 509–510
    predictability of, 269, 271–272
    reproductive studies, 494
    strain of animal and, 495
    subchronic, 494
    types of, 493–494
Toxicokinetics, 270
Toxicology, *see also* Animal safety, Safety
        testing
    animal data, extrapolation, 267–272
    of biotechnology products, 496
    case studies in, 494
    cost of, 495
    data management, 485
    dose levels in, 496
    international differences, 497
    loss of medicines in, 268, 270–271
    medicine availability and, 495
    in medicine development, 24, 25, 235,
        237, 247
    mutagenicity testing, 497–498
    predicting human, 269
    reducing number of animals used, 661
    regulatory guidelines, 497–498
    specialized studies in, 494
    standards of, 495
    study design, 495–496
    timing of, 494–495
Trade associations
    activities of, 8, 676, 753, 754

criticism of, 754
defined, 8
international, 755
listing of major, 755
pharmacopolitical issues and, 65, 692
priorities of, 80–81
relations with companies, 693, 754
as representatives of industry, 753–754
Trade marks
    methods for selecting, 552, 553
    value of, 552
Trade secrets
    confidential information and, 620–621
    patents and, 613–614, 620
Training, *see* Education
Transfer costs
    costs of, 641–642, 701
    nature of, 641–642
    OECD guidelines for, 701
Troubleshooter, 297

U

United Kingdom
    CSM, 740
    dose-range trials in, 182
    individual rights, 133
    medical care, 201
    package inserts, 548
    Phase I trials regulations, 182
    prescription event monitoring, 512
    pricing, 57
    protecting animals, 659
United States Pharmacopeia, USP
    sterility testing procedures, 602
United States Pharmacopeial Convention,
        737
University, *see also* Academic institutions
    industry, conflicts of interest, 160–162
Upjohn Company
    clinical unit, 726
    licensing, 53, 751
    legal case, 632
    product information evaluation, 482, 483

R&D organization in, 29, 310
    sales by product/value, 542
USAN, 552, 737
U.S. Government agencies, *see* Government
        agencies
U.S. International Trade Commission
    definition of a U.S. pharmaceutical com-
        pany, 8
U.S. Patent Office, 618

V

Validation of methods, 44, 264–265
Validation of systems, 466, 602
Value, *see* Medicine value of, Commercial
        value
    concept of, 610
    issues in, 611
    of the pharmaceutical industry, 689
    types, 1–2, 611
Vendors
    golden rules for, 255
Vertical integration, 610–611
Viratek, 740
Visual models of development, 177, 288, 297
Visual models of markets, 456–458

W

What if exercises, 292, 606, 752
Withdrawing a drug from market, 298
World Health Organization, WHO
    creator of ethical standards, 39
    essential medicine lists, 62
    health definition, 35
    as information source, 409
    names of medicines, 552
    price evaluations, 561
Wyeth
    sales by product/value, 542

Y

Yellow cards, 512, 631